1998
POET'S
MARKET

1,800 PLACES TO PUBLISH
YOUR POETRY

EDITED BY

CHANTELLE BENTLEY

ASSISTED BY

TARA A. HORTON

WRITER'S DIGEST BOOKS
CINCINNATI, OHIO

The cover illustration is a detail of a painting by Berge Missakian. Missakian is a Canadian artist from Montreal. He has studied art at the American University of Beruit; Cornell University, Ithaca, NY; and Concordia University, Montreal, Canada. Illusion, imagination and fantasy appear in his paintings and set as elements which unify his compositions with explosively brilliant shapes of color. Missakian, who is listed in several books on art, including *Who's Who in American Art* (22nd edition), exhibits internationally. He celebrates passion over passivity, movement over inertia and joy over melancholic outlook. His internet URL is http://www.generation.net.studiom1

Still Life No. 22
24″ × 30″
acrylic on canvas

If you are a poetry publisher and would like to be considered for a listing in the next edition of *Poet's Market*, send a SASE (or SAE and IRC) with your request for a questionnaire to *Poet's Market*—QR, 1507 Dana Ave., Cincinnati OH 45207. Questionnaires received after March 13, 1998, will be held for the 2000 edition.

Supervising Editor: Barbara Kuroff.
Assistant Managing Editor: Cindy Laufenberg.

International Standard Serial Number
0883-5470
International Standard Book Number
0-89879-796-9

Attention Booksellers: This is an annual directory of F&W Publications. Return deadline for this edition is December 31, 1998.

Contents

The Markets

From the Editor

The reasons people write poetry are as endless as the number of poets who write it. For me, the necessity of a creative outlet to maintain my civility is one reason to write poems. Another might be to gain a better understanding of the world, or to connect with others through shared experiences. Some poets might not logically understand why they create poetry; they simply know they must.

Regardless of the reasons, poetry does exist and with each year its presence in society increases. In fact, according to the May 15, 1997, edition of the *Wall Street Journal*, poetry has even appeared in the fiscal papers of Barnes & Noble, Inc. The 1996 annual report for the megabookstore indicates its poetry sales grew 40 percent from a year earlier. Great news for the more than 1,100 volumes of poetry produced, but what does it mean for poets still struggling for that first sale?

The correlation for poets is that with increased interest comes increased publishing opportunities and more exposure through readings and other poetry-related events. For this edition, it means over 400 new listings and 600 plus pages of information—the largest *Poet's Market* ever.

Along with an increase in pages, the *1998 Poet's Market* also contains a few new elements. First, the Glossary of Poetic Forms and Styles helps you understand the specific poetry forms and styles sought by editors. Second, the Websites of Interest to Poets guides you to websites with information on both craft and potential markets. Moreover, this edition gives you an inside look at the Internet in Trends in the Field: Internet Opportunities for Poets.

The third new element is a set of icons that eases your search for Canadian and overseas listings. A maple leaf (✹) before a listing indicates Canadian markets, an asterisk (*) overseas markets and, regardless of a listing's locale, a bullet (●) indicates unique information giving you additional insight into the markets' preferences.

We also invite you to look at our own poetry preferences with the announcement of the winners of the *1998 Poet's Market* Poetry Contest. You can learn about the winners and read their winning poems on pages 473-476. And, on page 2, you will find the rules for our 1999 contest. In fact, this year's theme allows you to tell us why you write poetry.

To learn more about why some successful poets write, read our interviews with poets Michael Glaser, Taylor Graham, Susan Yuzna and Aleda Shirley. Also, read the interview with David Starkey who tells how he teaches poets to successfully market their work.

And that is what we do with each edition of *Poet's Market*—provide you with information about opportunities for poets and help you make the most of those opportunities. With today's increased interest in poetry, there's more information for you to consider while searching for the perfect market. *Poet's Market* can help you narrow the field and get your poems published.

Whether you write for your sanity or to connect with others does not matter. What matters is that you keep writing and reading poetry. Then become a part of poetry's resurgence—join a writing group, attend a conference, participate in a reading, submit your work. A whole world of poetry is there for you to explore. Enjoy the journey!

Chantelle Bentley
poetsmarket@fwpubs.com

A CALL FOR ENTRIES

To see *your* work in the next edition of *Poet's Market*, simply write a great poem(s) about why you write poetry—and enter your work in our poetry contest. The best three poems will be published in the *1999 Poet's Market*. And the three winners will receive a free copy of our annual directory and a cash prize of $150, $100 or $75, respectively. Read the following rules for details.

1. All poems must be original, unpublished, and not under consideration by any other publisher or in any other contest.

2. *Poet's Market* retains first publication rights to the three winning poems, which will be published in the 1999 edition (to be released in September 1998). All other rights will be returned. Note: *Poet's Market* does not claim *any* rights to any other work.

3. Each poem must relate to the topic: why you write poetry. Poems may be in any form, rhymed or unrhymed, but no poem can exceed 32 lines in length.

4. You may enter as many poems as you like, but each poem counts as one entry and must be accompanied by a $3 handling fee. (Make checks or money orders payable to Writer's Digest Books.)

5. Poems must be clearly typed (single-spaced with double-spacing between stanzas) on one side of 8½ × 11 or 8¼ × 11¾ (A4) white paper.

6. You must submit two copies of each entry. On one copy, include your name, address and telephone number in the upper left corner. The second copy must only contain the poem. Entries will be separated on arrival to allow for blind judging.

7. All entries must be postmarked by midnight, January 31, 1998. **Note that manuscripts cannot be acknowledged or returned**. Every entry will be read and judged by the staff of *Poet's Market*. In the event of a tie, an outside judge will be consulted.

8. Every entry will be read and judged by the staff of *Poet's Market*. In the event of a tie, an outside judge will be consulted.

9. Winning poets will be notified by phone on or before March 13, 1998. To receive the names of the winning poets (after March 27, 1998), you must enclose a self-addressed, stamped envelope (or self-addressed envelope and International Reply Coupon) with your entry.

10. The three winning poets will receive $150, $100 or $75, respectively, and a copy of the *1999 Poet's Market*.

11. Employees of F&W Publications, Inc. and their immediate family members are not eligible.

12. *Poet's Market* reserves the right to forego publication of any winning entry. In such cases, first rights will be returned.

Note: Failure to comply with these guidelines will result in disqualification.

Send entries to: *1999 Poet's Market* Poetry Contest
                                    1507 Dana Ave.
                                    Cincinnati, OH 45207

Deadline: January 31, 1998

How to Sell Your Poetry Using *Poet's Market*

To reap the benefits of *Poet's Market*, you need to know how to use it. After all, this directory not only provides listings of poetry publishers, but it is also designed to help you determine which ones are the best markets for your work.

The first step, however, is to examine your poetry. Do you write poetry that makes a political statement? poetry about wildlife? religious symbols? other poets? Do you write sonnets? prose poems? about a certain area? in a language other than English?

Maybe you don't write any specific type of poetry. Maybe the answer depends on which one of your works we're talking about. No matter. If you've put craft into your poems, you'll find places to publish them.

START WITH THE INDEXES

All Publishers of Poetry listings are coded as to the category of poetry they are seeking. Publishers that desire poetry within certain realms—on certain subjects, in certain forms, or by certain people—can be quickly identified by a **IV** and terms denoting the specialization(s). For example, *Dreams and Nightmares* is coded **IV-Science fiction/fantasy** because it seeks material related to those genres.

Once you've defined your own poetry, you don't need to comb each page for compatible listings. Turn to the Subject Index (where you will find all publishers with **IV** codes divided according to their specializations) and scan the boldface headings to locate the specialization that matches your work. If you write haiku, for instance, check under **Form/Style**. If you're an older adult who writes about the woods near your home, check under both **Senior Citizen** and **Nature/Rural/Ecology** and write down the names of publishers that sound interesting.

Publishers may classify themselves as **Regional** in the Subject Index, but checking the Geographical Index is also helpful. There you'll discover the publishers located in your state or country. While some don't consider themselves "regional" in terms of the poetry they accept, they are often more open to writers from their own areas.

Also useful, particularly if you're trying to publish a small collection of poems, is the Chapbook Publishers Index, which lists publishers who consider chapbook manuscripts (typically 20 to 25 pages of poetry connected by a theme). You'll find more information about both chapbook and book publishing in Charting Your Path to Poetry Publication, on page 11.

Finally, if you've heard about a particular publisher, but can't seem to find its listing, check the General Index. All imprints and publications located at the same address are grouped together. The General Index lists *all* titles in the book, however, and includes cross-references where necessary.

CHECK MARKET CODES

Once you have a list of possible markets for your work—because of specialization or location or an interest in chapbooks—look up each listing and check the market category code(s) following the title to discover how open it is to submissions.

Besides a **IV** code, a publisher can also have **I**, **II**, **III** or **V**. Those with **I** are open to beginners' submissions, so if you're just starting out, try sending to them. Publishers with **II** codes are general markets which expect you to be familiar with literary journals and magazines. Those coded **III** are limited as to the number of submissions they accept, so your chances of publishing with them are limited too. Finally, those with **V** are not accepting unsolicited manuscripts. Although you may have picked such a publisher out of the Geographical Index, you can't submit your poetry to it at this time. That's okay. Cross it off your list and move on to the next one.

When you discover publishers with more than one code, read their listings to determine if they're still possible markets for your work. For instance, a publisher may be **I, IV-Religious**, which means it either wants religious material as well as poetry from beginners or religious material only, including poetry from beginners. To learn more about market category codes, see the Publishers of Poetry introduction.

Also, as you read the listings based on the indexes, others will attract your eye. Don't feel limited by those on your list. Many publications don't want to be noted for a specialization and are open to ALL types of work.

READ CAREFULLY

When you've refined your list of possible markets by checking market categories, study each listing *carefully*. You will be able to narrow your search further by investigating the publications' specific needs, advice, formats and payment. All this is included in the listings in a certain order, allowing you to easily locate specific material.

Quickly scanning the listings you will notice two features: some listings have icons and all listings have boldface. Listings new to this edition are indicated with a ‡, Canadian listings have a ✦, and international markets are designated with a *. To help find something quickly within the listings themselves, certain information is set off in **boldface**. The following paragraphs will tell you what will consistently appear in bold.

After any icons and the name and address of the publication, you'll find the year it was founded. Older publishers have more stability, and sometimes more prestige. However, newer publishers, especially those new to this edition, are often more receptive to submissions. Next is the contact name(s), to whom you should specifically send your poems. This contact is always subject to change. We recommend obtaining a sample copy and verifying the contact on the masthead, or calling the publishers' offices to verify the contact person.

The publication's frequency of appearance follows along with its general description, purpose and contents. Pay attention to this latter information. For example, *Hellas* accepts any kind of poetry but especially welcomes poems in meter. In their listing, they say, "We prize elegance and formality in verse, but specifically encourage poetry of the utmost boldness and innovation, so long as it is not willfully obscurantist; . . ." The needs, in boldface, follow stating what the editors want and don't want. Often this is a direct quote and can give you extra insight into the editors' preferences.

In some listings, following this basic information, we've added our own editorial comment, set off by a bullet (●). This allows us to pass on additional inside information we've learned about the listing. Included here are tips about the market's biases, focus and any unusual aspects. For example, here is the editorial comment for *Blind Man's Rainbow*:

●This is a poetry and art zine; rough but containing some interesting work.

Next is a list of poets the market has published. In addition, listings will often include sample poetry lines. These will indicate what level of writing an editor is seeking and provide insight into editorial tastes. You'll also find the physical description of the publication including the number of pages, size, modes of printing, binding, cover, and whether it includes art, graphics and ads. Carefully reading the description of a publication's format will help you visualize how your poetry will appear in its pages.

When available, the listings indicate how many poems they receive a year, and their approximate acceptance rate. The listing will then detail the press run, number of subscribers (including how many are libraries), shelf sales and to whom it is distributed free. Prices for a single copy, subscription and sample copy are given. The price for the sample copy is in boldface for easy location, and if guidelines are included with the sample, this is indicated. (Obtaining sample copies, often available from your local library or bookstore, is the best way to determine whether your poetry is right for a publication.) For example:

They receive about 300 poems a year, use approximately 15%. Press run is 650 for 500 subscribers of which 10 are libraries, 100 shelf sales. Single copy: $4.50; subscription: $15. **Sample (including guidelines) postpaid: $3.50**.

The succeeding information, submission requirements, may be the most important in the listing and is therefore in boldface. We suggest you follow the requirements for submission carefully. Inappropriate submissions will not only leave a bad impression of your work, but they can also affect a publisher's willingness to accept unsolicited manuscripts from others. You will notice some markets have told us they accept disk or e-mail submissions. Although some listings have included e-mail and fax numbers, it is always best to get permission before submitting to a publisher by fax or e-mail.

Here is how submission information for a magazine might look:

Submit up to 5 poems at a time. Charges reading fee of $1/poem. No previously published poems; simultaneous submissions OK. Cover letter required with brief biographical information. E-mail submissions OK. Reads submissions September through June only.

Next is information about their selection process: time between acceptance and publication; if poems are circulated to an editorial board (in boldface); and whether they comment on rejections (in boldface). If they publish theme issues, this is also included (in boldface). The listing will tell you how to obtain guidelines, whether by sending a SASE or requesting via e-mail, website or fax. If they do have theme issues we will tell you whether the guidelines include the upcoming themes; also, if available, the upcoming themes are given here in the listing.

How soon they report on submissions, whether they send prepublication galleys, what they pay and what rights they buy or acquire are indicated in bold. If the magazine accepts reviews of books or writes their own, and if poets may send books for review consideration, this is included. This information may appear as:

Reports in 6 weeks. Always sends prepublication galleys. Pays 2 copies. Acquires first North American serial rights. Reviews books of poetry in 200 words, multi-book format. Open to unsolicited reviews. Poets may also send books for review consideration.

If the listing offers other venues of publishing, like books or chapbooks, this information will follow the specifics for the magazine. Like the magazines, the book/chapbook needs, requirements, formats and pay will be detailed.

Listings end with news on any contests they sponsor and any contests or awards they or the poetry they publish has won. The market's listing closes with a very important feature: advice. This is perhaps the best way to meet and evaluate editors without actually corresponding with them. Their comments can reveal their editorial biases as well as quirks in their personalities. For example, an editor's advice may read: "Don't even think about submitting poems about your dog," or "Send me that dusty poem that's been at the back of your junk drawer, I will most likely find a place for it in my magazine!"

If you haven't already done so, read Charting Your Path to Poetry Publication. It offers a step-by-step approach to every aspect of the submission process. Many publishers offer guidelines for a self-addressed, stamped envelope (SASE). Send for them. The goal, after all, is to increase—not decrease—your chances of acceptance.

OTHER RESOURCES

As you develop your craft, take advantage of the various resources for poets. For support services and feedback from others, for example, join one of the groups listed in Organizations Useful to Poets. If you're searching for a place to get away and write, check Writing Colonies. Or, if you're seeking instruction and marketing tips, attend one of the events in Conferences and Workshops or consult one of the magazines listed in Publications Useful to Poets.

If you wish to write for greeting card companies, *Writer's Market* (Writer's Digest Books) has a whole section dedicated to these companies complete with contact names, addresses, phone numbers, needs and submission requirements. For poets who are also lyricists, *Songwriter's Market* (Writer's Digest Books) offers pages and pages of opportunities in this field. Both books are available through your library or bookstore, or can be ordered directly from the publisher.

Finally, if you don't recognize a symbol or an abbreviation being used, refer to the Key to Symbols on page 20 or the Glossary of Listing Terms on page 559. If the publisher is looking for a specific style or form of which you are not familiar, the Glossary of Poetic Forms and Styles is on page 558. And, for easy reference, you will find a list of U.S. and Canadian Postal Codes below.

U.S. and Canadian Postal Codes

United States					
AL	Alabama	MI	Michigan	VT	Vermont
AK	Alaska	MN	Minnesota	VI	Virgin Islands
AZ	Arizona	MS	Mississippi	VA	Virginia
AR	Arkansas	MO	Missouri	WA	Washington
CA	California	MT	Montana	WV	West Virginia
CO	Colorado	NE	Nebraska	WI	Wisconsin
CT	Connecticut	NV	Nevada	WY	Wyoming
DE	Delaware	NH	New Hampshire		
DC	District of Columbia	NJ	New Jersey	**Canada**	
FL	Florida	NM	New Mexico	AB	Alberta
GA	Georgia	NY	New York	BC	British Columbia
GU	Guam	NC	North Carolina	LB	Labrador
HI	Hawaii	ND	North Dakota	MB	Manitoba
ID	Idaho	OH	Ohio	NB	New Brunswick
IL	Illinois	OK	Oklahoma	NF	Newfoundland
IN	Indiana	OR	Oregon	NT	Northwest Territories
IA	Iowa	PA	Pennsylvania	NS	Nova Scotia
KS	Kansas	PR	Puerto Rico	ON	Ontario
KY	Kentucky	RI	Rhode Island	PEI	Prince Edward Island
LA	Louisiana	SC	South Carolina	PQ	Quebec
ME	Maine	SD	South Dakota	SK	Saskatchewan
MD	Maryland	TN	Tennessee	YT	Yukon
MA	Massachusetts	TX	Texas		
		UT	Utah		

Trends in the Field: Internet Opportunities for Poets

BY CHANTELLE BENTLEY

My first suggestion, in regard to the Internet, is to have a good book of poetry to read while you surf, or is it wade, through its many sites. And that is not a reproach of the system. The truth is, depending on the speed of your computer's modem, a lot of time is spent waiting for the Net to locate websites, connect to them, and upload the documents and graphics. In fact, during one trip onto the Internet while researching this article, I was able to read through a printed article and pay my monthly bills in between reviewing various electronic publications.

But all the information and connections available on the Internet are what make it such a valuable resource despite the traffic (people utilizing the Net) impeding quick access. Just one query for the word "poetry" on any of the search engines provides a list of more than 10,000 related sites. And all those sites are linked to other sites so you can spend all day weaving in and out, completely losing yourself in an electronic haze.

Having "come around" to the wonderful world of the Internet rather recently—it's amazing how scary a plastic box with a TV screen and telephone hookup can be—my initial experiences with the Web and all its properties were viewed with the eyes of a print-bound skeptic. And while I will never relinquish the desire to hold a book in my hands and turn it page by page while sitting in my favorite chair, I must admit the information provided by the Internet tempts me as well as any library or bookstore can.

GET CONNECTED

But what if you don't currently have access to the Internet? How do you determine if it's worth the time and money? Well, if you already own a computer with a modem, you can sample the various Internet providers through trial memberships to their services. Most providers offer one-month introductory memberships with, typically, ten hours online free of charge. Then you must pay a monthly fee for a specified number of online hours with additional hours charged at a lesser hourly rate. Also, check local advertisements or the telephone directory to find local Internet providers. Local providers offer direct access to the Internet for a flat monthly fee— the telephone company is a good example and the fee is added right to your phone bill.

Another way to sample the Net is to visit your local library. Many libraries maintain computers with Internet access within their facilities for library patrons. For those poets not yet possessing a computer, this is a particularly good way to access the Internet. The only problem with using the library's computer is time and availability. The limited number of computers with Internet access compared to the number of users often results in long waits for a computer and short amounts of time in which to utilize the service.

If you have a good friend with a computer and Internet access, you may want to investigate trading computer time for some other service you can provide, such as proofreading manuscripts, babysitting or even a free dinner. In fact, if you know someone who is willing to share their computer maybe you can split Internet service costs. But regardless of the method you choose for getting to know the Net, the most important step is to get online and see what's there.

FIND WHAT YOU SEEK

Once you have access to the Internet, you will need to become familiar with the various methods for searching/wading through the information. My favorite search engine is Yahoo! (http://www.yahoo.com), a subject-oriented directory with connections to more than 100,000 different sites. When searching for a keyword, Yahoo! looks through every category, title or comment in its database to find listings that match the key. Then the results are presented in an alphabetized list of categories ranging from art and humanities to government to regional to society and culture. Clicking on these categories brings up the end-sites within the categories matching the keyword.

A larger but less organized search engine is Alta Vista (Yahoo! is actually powered by Alta Vista). Alta Vista has access to 31 million pages found on 627,000 servers and four million articles from 14,000 Usenet news groups. In fact, a recent search for the word "poetry" in Alta Vista yielded 400,000 matches. The only problem with Alta Vista is the sites are presented individually and not methodically arranged. Therefore you must search through pages and pages of sites matching the keyword to find those of interest to you.

Becoming proficient at searching on the Internet is just a matter of learning about the various search engines and their search options. A number of introductory guides to the Internet and books on Internet researching have been published which may help you refine your skills. These books also provide lists of useful websites you might not find on your own. Some even guide you through establishing your own website. Look for these titles at your local library or bookstore or order directly through the publishers: *The Little Web Book*, by Alfred & Emily Glossbrenner (Peachpit Press, 1996); *Zen and the Art of the Internet*, by Brendan Kehoe (Prentice Hall, 1996); *The Internet Research Guide*, by Timothy K. Maloy (Allworth Press, 1996); and *Researching on the Internet*, by Robin Rowland & Dave Kinnaman (Prima Publishing, 1995). For a guide to the Internet actually on the Internet, see The Electronic Frontier Foundation's website at http://www.eff.org/.

ONLINE RESOURCES FOR POETS

As you weave your way through the wires, you may discover the Internet offers poets not only alternative places to read and publish poetry but also alternative resources, such as online writing workshops, sites offering online critiques, access to poetry and writing organizations and electronic bookstores. One resource of particular value to poets seeking publication are electronic directories. These directories contain lists of journals and zines published or providing information on the Internet or Web.

These electronic directories are updated frequently and provide direct links to the listed publications. Some also act as search engines by providing a list of keywords from which you can search for journals on a particular topic. Literary organizations and authors' home pages may also be contained on these lists. In fact, U.S. poet laureate Robert Pinsky's online journal *Slate* (actually, he's the poetry editor, not the publisher) can be found within these e-directories—for a shortcut go to http://www.slate.com.

The publishers of these directories are always on the lookout for new listings. So, if your favorite e-zine is not contained in their directory, you can e-mail the information to be included with the next update. (See Websites of Interest to Poets on page 556 for the website addresses of some e-directories and other electronic resources related to poetry.)

PUBLISH VIA THE NET

Now that you've found your way onto the electronic information superhighway, ruined your eyesight during all-night sessions of web browsing and, finally, narrowed the thousands of e-zines to those which suit your style and interests, the next decision is whether or not to submit your poems for electronic publication. Deciding to send your poems flying over the billions of electrons known as the Internet can be difficult since, for most people, the Internet remains a somewhat unknown and volatile entity.

When comparing the submitting and publishing process in electronic publications to that in print publications, you'll find the risks do not change all that much—in some areas, in fact, they improve in the electronic arena.

First, let's consider quality. Many a complaint has been heard from poets unhappy with the quality of a print publication in which their work appears. And, unfortunately, many of these poets were unable to purchase copies of these journals before submitting, so they had no concept of the journal's format until after receiving their contributor's copies. This problem is alleviated when submitting to electronic publications. Unless the editor drastically changes her e-zine's format from the time you view the website to the time your work is published, what you see is what you get. And though not all e-publications are infused with gorgeous graphics, most are very eye-catching. Even the more plain e-journals are not the source of embarrassment for poets that some of the lesser-quality print journals can be.

A second consideration is acceptance rate. Typically, a poet's work has a greater chance of being accepted for electronic publication. Electronic journals accept approximately five poems for every one poem accepted by print journals. Electronic editors are not prohibited by page count or printing costs. However, as more poets become acquainted with the Internet, these editors may find their submission numbers soaring over their print counterparts, once again translating into difficulty getting published for poets. Until that occurs, however, poets can enjoy the ease of publishing on the Internet and the worldwide audience it provides.

Not only does the Internet provide poets with an international audience, it also provides them with a world's worth of advice. Publishing work on the Net allows for readers' critiques to reach you with the push of a button. This instantaneous global commentary can help prepare emerging poets for the more exacting and critical world of printed publications. For those poets already established in the print medium, e-publication gives a wider exposure to their work and may boost the sales of printed collections.

TAKE E-SUBMISSIONS SERIOUSLY

Poets need to be mindful of proper submission policies when submitting to e-publications. Electronic editors require the same professionalism as print editors—the medium does not change the personalities. And regardless of the publication method, reading a journal's guidelines prior to submission is always a good idea. For advice specific to Internet submissions, read the article "Submitting on the Internet" located at website http://www.writerswrite.com/submts.htm.

For those using the Internet not as an alternative publishing venue but as a resource aiding publication in printed journals, many paper journals are also beginning to publish online versions. And though most print journals' online versions only contain the contents page and a few sample poems, they do provide potential contributors with a taste of the type of work sought. Print journals may also publish their submission guidelines on the Internet or accept information requests, queries or submissions via e-mail. Before submitting via the Internet, always check with the publisher in regard to their electronic submission policies.

Also, as most electronic editors are more open to previously published work, the Internet extends publishing possibilities for those with work already included in a print medium. However, poets should keep in mind that the reverse is rarely true and that e-zines will acquire first North American serial rights if the work has not been previously published.

PROTECT COPYRIGHTS ONLINE

Most issues, in regard to rights, are the same when publishing on the Internet as they are when publishing through standard print methods. Even though lawmakers are still working through the details of electronic copyright issues, intellectual property right laws protect your work from the time it is preserved in a tangible form, whether that form be electronic or paper.

Though the ease of copying work online may hamper some poets' enthusiasm for the electronic medium, the fact is plagiarism can occur in any medium. Until electronic copyright issues are defined, the best advice is: if it doesn't feel right, don't do it. Only publish in a medium if you feel comfortable with all its advantages *and* disadvantages.

BE ADVISED

But you needn't only consider my opinions when determining whether or not to utilize the Internet. This year the editors and publishers listed in *Poet's Market* were asked to share their views about the Internet and the opportunities it offers them and poets in general. As the comments below indicate, some see mostly benefits for poets publishing work on the Internet while others see only problems. Read all views, then decide what best suits you and your work.

"The original mission of *The Peking Duck* was primarily one of providing a free, non-profit, literary newsletter to as many readers as possible. To this end, the Internet is like a dream come true. Not only is it far cheaper to publish electronically, but online access allows our potential readership to grow from a few hundred people to millions worldwide. In this way we all benefit. . . . Will there be negatives associated with a multimedia approach to poetry? Of course, but I believe the advantages far outweigh the disadvantages. Moreover, it is important those of us committed to quality literature and the small independent press movement stake our claim in this exciting new medium."

—Edward Cossett, *The Peking Duck*

"The Internet is nothing other than a different medium for data exchange. It may allow wider access/more readers for a particular poet or poem, but it has no effect on the writing of a good poem—the creative process, the value of the work, or the impact the poem has on the reader."   —D. Clement, *Fauquier Poetry Journal*

"The opportunities offered by the Internet to an editor/publisher are extraordinary. Foremost are the low cost and maintenance of an existing website. Secondly, one has the ability to make changes to a website/e-zine on-the-fly. An editor can add poetry, delete poetry or change a website/e-zine even while visitors are perusing the site's contents. Thirdly, the exposure the website receives is universal rather than the provincial exposure that usually encompasses a magazine's distribution area. In short, the Internet offers a wide and diversified set of tools for managing, collaborating and manipulating your material. A diversification that also extends itself to your contributors, subscribers and visitors from around the globe."   —William Rothwell, *The Poet's Attic Quarterly*

"It's an advantage to see the emergence of various forms of poetry on the Internet. The disadvantages seem to be the prevalent placement of purely poor poetry."

—Jeffrey Hillard, *Cincinnati Poetry Review*

"Overall, the Internet can be a very exciting place for poets, publishers, and lovers of literature. We're just beginning to see the potential of the Internet and I'm fairly sure the online poetry world will continue to thrive and grow. As a poet, the Net offers true global exposure of your material and access to easy electronic submissions. For the publisher, it offers a low-cost alternative to traditional print publications, and exposure to audiences beyond the geographical boundaries. Finally, for the readers, the Internet, and specifically the World Wide Web, offers a wealth of free material never before available."

—Erik Jensen, *Black Cross Magazine*

"Like the TV, I think the Internet may discourage reading. I would rather have my poems on the bookshelf in my library where my grandchildren can read them."

—Denver Stull, *Parnassus Literary Journal*

Charting Your Path to Poetry Publication

Though the importance of poetry exists within its creation, publication brings the art full circle and provides the poet with a sense of completion. Placing your work before an audience validates the effort and time spent on the writing and silences, for a while anyway, the internal and external critics telling you to "give up."

The daunting task in publishing your work is wading through volumes of information on the subject. And, if you are like me, finding the time to write is challenging enough. However, knowing the ins and outs of the field is important, just as not knowing them may affect your chances of being published.

In the following paragraphs I have tried to lay out the essentials you need to know to get your work, first, into the hands of editors and then, essentially, into the pages of their journals and books. This information covers the most-asked questions about submitting poetry for those just beginning to submit their poems and provides updates for poets more experienced with the submission process.

Question 1: How do I locate editors and publishers who might be interested in my work?

The first step toward finding an editor or publisher to publish your poetry is to determine where your work fits in the market. For example, does your work focus on a particular theme or topic? Do you write in a certain form or style? Does your poetry have a regional or ethnic flair? Any distinguishing aspects you can assign to your work will help you narrow your focus and locate potential markets. And, sharing common ground with the editors and publishers to whom you submit gives you a leg up on the competition. (To locate markets with shared interests, see the Subject Index at the back of this book.)

After you have selected some publications specializing in your areas of interest, read several sample issues to determine whether your poetry is appropriate for their pages. You may even want to try submitting work to the publications to which you subscribe or purchase frequently from the newsstand. After all, you are already familiar with their contents and you probably have a lot in common with their readers.

Another way to locate markets that may be open to your poetry is to determine which journals and presses have published the work of some of your favorite contemporary poets. Chances are your poetry and the work of poets you most admire share some essential aspects of craft, tone or topic. And, perhaps, the editors of those journals will be attracted to the same aspects in your work.

An important thought to keep in mind as you submit your poems is to start small. Very few true "overnight successes" exist in this business or in any other business. Many poets spend years publishing work in small local or regional journals before they ever make it into the nationally-known publications.

And the same goes with presses. The two-person small press operation that published the collection of the poet you heard read at the bookstore on the corner last week is just as serious and dedicated to the craft of poetry as those publishers in New York with staffs of interns wading through the piles of poetry manuscripts received each day. Even in the publishing world, less is often more.

A point worth adding is that new markets are established all the time. To keep up with new literary journals and small presses, read such publications as **Poets & Writers Magazine** or **Writer's Digest**, both regularly contain information about new markets. On a more local level, check the notices posted on the bulletin board at your library or nearest bookstore. Also, surf the Web. Many electronic directories exist that list electronic and print publications seeking submissions. These e-directories may also provide direct links to those publications. (For more information on electronic publications, see Trends in the Field: Internet Opportunities for Poets on pages 7-10.)

Question 2: What is the proper manuscript format for my submission?

This is where the details can make or break you. For the most part, a standard format exists for poetry manuscript submissions, and most editors' preferences comply with this format. However, there are those who throw a monkey wrench in the works and deviate from the norm. For those editors, we have tried to state their submission preferences within their listings. For all others, the following bulleted list will provide you with the information you need to present a professional manuscript. If you have any doubts, however, send a self-addressed, stamped envelope (SASE) to the journal or press you're interested in and request their writer's guidelines. A self-addressed envelope (SAE) and International Reply Coupons (IRCs) are required to receive information from publishers outside your own country.

• Send only three to five poems at one time, positioning your best poems on top. As most editors don't have time to read past the first few poems, sending more than five is a waste of time and resources. However, sending any less than three doesn't provide the editor with a large enough sample of your work. (When submitting a poetry collection to a book publisher, it is best to request guidelines, since press requirements vary from a query letter with a few sample poems to the entire manuscript.)

• Type or print one poem to a page, single-spaced with double spacing between stanzas. (The only exception here may be for haiku.) Leave at least a one-inch margin on all sides of the page. Avoid handwriting your work.

• Use white, $8\frac{1}{2} \times 11$ bond paper, preferably 16 or 20 lb. weight. The paper should be heavy enough to withstand handling by several people.

• Include your name, address and telephone number in the upper left or right corner. The title of your poem should appear in all caps or initial caps about six lines underneath your address, centered or flush left. The poem should begin one line beneath the title.

• For book manuscripts, use a separate cover sheet for your name, address and telephone number. Center your book title and byline about halfway down the page. Then include your last name and page number in the top left margin of the first and each subsequent manuscript page.

• If your poem carries over to a second sheet, list your name in the top left margin. Underneath your name include a key word from the poem's title, the page number and information on whether the lines at the top are a continuation of the same stanza or the start of a new one (e.g., continue stanza or begin new stanza).

• Proofread carefully. Even the shortest poem can contain typos that elude the eye of the poet all too familiar with the lines in front of her. Also, an occasional white-out is okay, but retype (or correct and reprint) poems with numerous typos.

• Fold manuscript, five pages and under, neatly into thirds (do not fold poems individually) and mail in a business-size (#10, $4\frac{1}{8} \times 9\frac{1}{2}$) envelope. For a manuscript over five pages, fold in half and mail in a 6×9 envelope. Larger manuscripts will look best mailed flat in 9×12 or 10×13 envelopes.

• To ensure a response, you must enclose a SASE (or SAE and IRCs). You can use either a #9 (4×9) reply envelope or a #10 business-size envelope (fold into thirds if you are also using a

#10 envelope to mail your manuscript). To have your manuscript returned, the best method is to enclose a SASE the same size as the mailing envelope with the same amount of postage. Another option is to send a disposable manuscript. However, you must notify the editor the manuscript is disposable and the SASE you've provided is for reply only. NOTE: One IRC is needed for one ounce by surface mail or each half-ounce by airmail. And, three pages of poetry, a cover letter and a SASE can usually be mailed for one first-class stamp.

• When sending electronic (disk or modem) submissions, *contact the editor first for specific instructions and follow the directions carefully.* Always include a printed copy with any disk submission. *Fax or e-mail your submissions only with prior approval of the editor or publisher.*

Question 3: Should I copyright my poems before submitting?

As "original works of authorship" fixed in a tangible form (but *not* the ideas from which they are created) are protected under copyright laws the only thing you need to do to copyright your work is to put it on paper. In fact, the copyright of the poems you create today will be protected for your lifetime plus 50 years. And, you can, if you wish, put the copyright symbol (©) on your poetry, followed by the year of creation and your name.

Yet, copyright notices are typically considered unnecessary as most editors know you own the copyright to your work, and few, if any, will steal your ideas. For some, copyright notices signal the work of amateurs who are distrustful of editors and publishers. In fact, your time would be better spent writing or preparing your poems for submission rather than worrying about them being stolen.

While the decision to use the copyright symbol is yours, it is important to note that most magazines are copyrighted and book publishers will usually register copyrights in your name. In addition, those inclined to "borrow" your ideas will do so whether or not the copyright notice is attached. If you wish to register your copyright, however, you need only complete a form and then send the form, a copy of the work in question and a check for $20 to the Register of Copyrights, Library of Congress, Washington DC 20559. If paying $20 to register each of your poems is not feasible, you can register a group of poems with one form under one title for one $20 fee.

You can obtain more information about copyright from the Copyright Office, Library of Congress, Washington DC 20559. For answers to specific questions (but not legal advice), call the Copyright Public Information Office at (202)707-3000 weekdays between 8:30 a.m. and 5:00 p.m. (EST). Copyright forms can also be ordered at that same number or downloaded from the Library of Congress website at http://lcweb.loc.gov/copyright. The website also includes information on filling out the forms, general copyright information and links to other websites related to copyright issues.

Question 4: What rights do I have to my work once I allow someone to publish it?

The answer to this question depends on what rights the publisher acquires from submitting poets. The Copyright Law states you are primarily offering one-time rights to your work—that is, the editor or publisher may only publish your poem once—unless you and the publisher agree otherwise (in writing). If an editor requests something different, such as the right to also later publish the work in a retrospective anthology, and you are open to such an agreement, make sure the agreement is documented.

Following is a list of various rights. Be sure you know exactly what rights you are selling before you agree to the sale. For more information on rights, including electronic rights, refer to the second edition of *The Writer's Essential Desk Reference*, published by Writer's Digest Books, or the revised edition of *The Writer's Legal Guide*, published by Allworth Press.

• **First Rights (a.k.a. First Serial Rights)**—This means the poet offers a journal or magazine the right to publish the poem for the first time in any periodical. All other rights to the material remain with the author. It's important to note that first North American serial rights means the editor will be the first to publish your work in a U.S. or Canadian periodical. Your work can still be submitted to editors outside North America, or those open to reprint rights.

• **One-time Rights**—A periodical licensing one-time rights to a work (also known as simultaneous rights) buys the *nonexclusive* rights to publish the work once. That is, there is nothing to stop the poet from selling the work to other publications at the same time. Simultaneous sales would typically be to periodicals without overlapping audiences.

• **Second Serial (Reprint) Rights**—Editors and publishers seeking reprint rights are open to submissions of previously published work—provided you tell them when and where the work was previously published so they can properly credit the periodical in which your work first appeared. You'll notice many poetry collections list such "credits," often on the copyright page. In essence, they've acquired reprint rights.

• **All Rights**—Some publishers require poets to relinquish all rights, which means you cannot submit that particular work for publication anywhere else—not even as part of your own collection—unless you negotiate to get reprint rights returned to you. A few publications, such as *Highlights for Children*, request all rights but are noteworthy publications that typically pay poets in cash as well as copies. Other publishers seeking all rights may not be as generous, or as reputable. Ask the editor whether he is willing to buy first rights instead of all rights before you agree to the arrangement, or you can simply refuse payment and withdraw your work. Also, some editors will reassign rights to a writer after a given time, such as one year.

Since the issue of rights is so important, almost all editors and publishers will specifically state (in their directory listing or guidelines) what rights they typically acquire. And once your work is accepted for publication, a number of editors and publishers will ask you to sign an agreement which not only tells you what rights are being requested, but also asks you to certify that the poetry is your own.

Question 5: Should I include a cover letter with my submission?

Though the issue of cover letters is far less serious in nature than selling rights, poets still must determine the appropriateness of including cover letters with their submissions. Some experts in the field say cover letters are unnecessary and may even impede the publication process. And a few editors agree a cover letter has never caused them to accept or reject a manuscript. Recently, however, many editors have begun indicating a desire for cover letters in their market listings and submission guidelines.

Overall, a cover letter allows you to personally present yourself—and your work—to specific editors. To do so graciously, you'll not only want to list the titles of the poems you are submitting, but you'll also want to demonstrate some familiarity with the publication in question, or comment on a poem you enjoyed reading. Editors, of course, like to know their contributors are among their readers. Include a few (no more than five) of your most recent publishing credits as well.

But what if you haven't published a poem yet? Then note that. Some editors are particularly interested in new writers and have special sections for beginners' work. If you are uncomfortable stating you have no prior credits, however, don't mention publication credits at all in your cover letter or, simply, don't include a cover letter. The professional manuscript you submit will make it appear as if you have published poems before.

Before you compose your cover letter, though, check to see if the editor has requested biographical information for the magazine's contributors page. If so, add a few lines about your job or hobbies, particularly if either relates to the enclosed poem. Above all, refrain from praising your work. Let your poems speak for themselves. And, no matter how much information is requested, keep your cover letter to one page.

Finally, address your letter to the person listed as poetry editor (or the editor if the publication is small). Most of the publications in this directory have a particular individual to whom you should direct your submissions. If no one is listed, however, check the publication's guidelines or the masthead of a recent copy. If you are still unable to locate a specific name, simply address

SAMPLE COVER LETTER

Sarah Wetzel
55 Lexington Dr.
Bloomdale DE 19899
(987)654-3210

May 1, 1998

Teresa Erhart
Aurora's Sunglasses
P.O. Box 8963
Falls Creek OR 97914

Dear Ms. Erhart:

Enclosed are three of my poems for your consideration: "Jocular Cadence," "Level Playing Ground" and "Fragmented."

I have found your journal to be a wonderful showcase for attainable poetry with a humorous twist. My writers group closes each meeting by reading one of the poems from your publication. It gives us inspiration and a fresh, positive attitude to begin the month.

In addition to being the secretary of the group, I am also the humor columnist for its newsletter. My poems have appeared in *Life and Rhymes*, *Tea Roses* and *High Density*.

Aurora's Sunglasses is the publication I turn to for poetry that is insightful and educational, as well as fun. It would be an honor to have my poetry appear in its pages.

Sincerely,

Sarah Wetzel

Sarah Wetzel

your letter to "Poetry Editor." Of course, use an acceptable business-style format and make sure your letter is free of misspellings and grammatical errors. (For an example, refer to the Sample Cover Letter on page 15.)

Question 6: Is it necessary to keep track of my submissions?

Not only is it important to keep a record of which poems you have submitted, it is also important to keep copies of those poems. In fact, you may want to keep the original typewritten or computer-printed version of your work and submit good, clean photocopies to editors and publishers. After all, you never know when your poetry will end up lost in the mail or somewhere in the heap of other submissions at a publisher's office. If you submit the one-and-only copy of your work and it gets lost in the process, you're simply out of luck.

To track which poems you have submitted and where and when you submitted them, you can record such information on 3×5 cards arranged alphabetically (by poem title) in a storage container. Or you can use sheets of paper arranged in file folders in which you can also keep the original copy of each poem. (This year, for you to copy and use, we have included a Submission Tracker form. See page 19.) Or you can create a database on your personal computer. In any case, list the title of each poem, the name of the magazine to which it was submitted, and the date your work was mailed. Also note the date of each editor's reply, the outcome of your efforts, and any comments that may prove useful when you're next submitting to that market (such as changes in editors, reading periods or frequency of publication).

Question 7: How long should I expect to wait for a reply to my submission?

By keeping detailed records of when and where you are submitting your work—and the date of the editor's reply—you are also tracking response times. Most editors and publishers indicate (in their market listings and submission guidelines) approximately how long you must wait before you can expect to receive a reply. If an editor does not specify when you will receive a report, it is generally expected to be within three months. Many times, however, the approximate date (or three-month benchmark) will come and go without a word from the editor or publisher.

What should you do when you haven't heard from an editor within the specified time period? Wait another month, then send a note inquiring about the status of your submission. Note the titles of your poems and the date sent. Ask when the editor anticipates making a decision. And enclose a SASE or self-addressed, stamped postcard for the editor's response. If you still do not hear from the market, send a postcard withdrawing your poems from consideration. Then submit your work elsewhere.

By all means, do *not* call editors with questions about submissions. Phone calls are only likely to irritate those who must divide their time between publishing a small press magazine and maintaining a full-time job and family obligations. And you stand little chance of accomplishing your goal anyway as many editors simply cannot supply such answers over the phone. Why risk having your poems completely dropped from consideration?

Question 8: Is it okay to submit previously published poems or to submit work to more than one magazine at the same time?

When you submit your poetry to magazine editors and publishers, they not only assume the work is original (that it is yours and nobody else's), but they also assume the work has not been previously published and is not being simultaneously submitted. Nothing is wrong with sending an editor a poem that has already been published. Some editors, however, are simply not open to such submissions. They want to be the first to publish new work—not the second. These editors are looking to acquire first rights to your poetry—not reprint rights. So before you send any previously published material, check market listings or submission guidelines to see if the editor or publisher in question is willing to consider your work. If so, note (in your cover letter) where the particular poem(s) first appeared.

In regard to simultaneous submissions, poets in recent years have begun sending the same package of poems to several editors at the same time due to the months it takes many editors and publishers to reply to submitted work. And most who engage in this practice believe that a batch of three to five poems submitted to two or more editors has a better chance of resulting in acceptance. However, if you submit your work simultaneously and an editor accepts one of your poems, you must contact the other editor(s) immediately and withdraw your work from consideration. This is likely to annoy (or even anger) the other editor(s) still in the process of making a decision. And future submissions to these markets may no longer be welcome.

To lessen the risk involved with this practice, you need to tell editors up front (in your cover letter) that you are simultaneously submitting your work. This is not only a way of forewarning them, but it may also prompt an editor to make a more timely decision. However, if you're going to tell editors that you're simultaneously submitting your material, make sure they are actually open to such submissions. If not, it is unlikely they will even consider your work. Again, check market listings or submission guidelines for specific information.

Yet, the question remains. Should you simultaneously submit your work? Some editors take the position that simultaneous submissions are the biggest reason for growing slush piles and reporting times. Why rush the process? You certainly don't take shortcuts in writing your poems. Why take shortcuts in submitting? After all, if you're just beginning or are still perfecting your craft, you're likely to quickly collect rejections. That can be discouraging. And if you're already regularly publishing, you're more likely to garner two acceptances at once—which puts you back at the point of having to contact editors and withdraw your work. Of course, you must finally decide what is best for you and your work.

Question 9: After I've had a number of poems published in magazines, what is my next step?

Once you have gathered a fair number of publication credits in literary or small press magazines, you may want to start thinking about book publication. Book publishers, by the way, expect some of the poems in your manuscript to be previously published. And, knowing the difficulty poets face in placing a collection, they are more accepting of the practice of simultaneous submissions. Often, publishing a chapbook is a good middle step between publishing in magazines and publishing a full-length book collection.

A chapbook is a small volume of 20 to 25 pages (or less). As such a volume is less expensive to produce than a full-length book collection (which may range from 48 to 80 pages), a chapbook is a safe way for a publisher to take a chance on a lesser-known poet. Most chapbooks are saddle-stapled with card covers. Some are photocopied publications. Others contain professionally printed pages. While chapbooks are seldom noted by reviewers or carried by bookstores, they are good items to sell after readings or through the mail. You'll discover that, in addition to some book publishers, a number of magazine publishers also publish chapbooks (for a complete list, refer to the Chapbook Publishers Index on page 560).

Whether you're planning to submit your work to either chapbook or book publishers you should always examine sample copies of their previously published collections. This is not only the best way to familiarize yourself with the press's offerings, but also a good way to determine the quality of the product.

Question 10: Once I've found a publisher for my collection, what type of publishing contract should I expect to receive?

Various publishing arrangements exist and greatly depend on the publisher with which you are dealing. Some, in fact, are more beneficial than others. Consider the following options carefully:
• **Standard publishing**—In a standard publishing contract, the publisher usually agrees to assume all production and promotion costs for your book. You receive a 10% royalty on the retail (or sometimes wholesale) price, though with some small presses you are paid a percentage

of the press run instead. Such publishers only release a small number of poetry volumes each year.

• **Cooperative publishing**—This arrangement is exactly that: cooperative. Although the details of such contracts vary, they require some type of investment of either time or money on your part. Some require involvement in marketing. Others specify money for production costs. In any case, know what you're signing. While cooperative publishing is respected in the literary and small press world (and many such publishers can bring your work the attention it deserves), some vanity presses try to label themselves as "cooperative." True cooperative publishing, however, shares both the risks and the profits.

• **Self-publishing**—This option may be most appealing if your primary goal is to publish a small collection of your work to give to family and friends. It is also a good choice for those who prefer complete control over the creative process. In this scenario, you work hand-in-hand with a local printer and invent a name for your "press." Most importantly, you pay all the costs but own all the books and net all the proceeds from any sales (which you must generate). For details, read *The Complete Guide to Self-Publishing* by Tom and Marilyn Ross (Writer's Digest Books). Also, read the article Trends in the Field on page 7 to discover the Internet publishing opportunities available to poets.

• **Vanity/subsidy presses**—This is probably the least desirable option. Companies in this category usually advertise for manuscripts, lavishly praise your work, and ask for fees far in excess of costs (compare their figures to those of a local printer for a book of similar size, format and binding). These companies also make a habit of collectively advertising their books; that is, your work will simply receive a line along with 20 or so other books in an ad placed in the general media rather than a specific market. Worse yet, sometimes you own all copies of your book and sometimes you don't.

It's important to note that some anthology publications fall under "vanity/subsidy" publishing because you must pay a tidy sum to purchase the volume containing your work. If you have concerns about a particular publisher call the Poets & Writers Information Center at (212)226-3586. Calls are welcome weekdays from 11 a.m. to 3 p.m. (EST).

Submission Tracker

Poem Title	Publication/ Contest	Editor/Contact	Date Sent	Date Returned	Date Accepted	Date Published	Pay Received	Comments

KEY TO SYMBOLS AND ABBREVIATIONS

‡—new listing
♣—Canadian listing
*—overseas listing
●—Comment offering additional market information from the editors of *Poet's Market*.
ms—manuscript; **mss**—manuscripts
b&w—black & white (photo or illustration)
p&h—postage & handling
SASE—self-addressed, stamped envelope
SAE—self-addressed envelope
IRC—International Reply Coupon (IRCs should be sent with SAEs for replies from countries outside your own)

IMPORTANT MARKET LISTING INFORMATION

● Listings are based on questionnaires and verified copy. They are not advertisements *nor* are markets necessarily endorsed by the editors of this book.

● Information in the listings comes directly from the publishers and is as accurate as possible, but publications and editors come and go, and poetry needs fluctuate between the publication date of this directory and the time you use it.

● If you are a poetry publisher and would like to be considered for a listing in the next edition, send a SASE (or SAE and IRC) with your request for a questionnaire to *Poet's Market*—QR, 1507 Dana Ave., Cincinnati OH 45207. Questionnaires received after March 13, 1998, will be held for the 2000 edition.

● *Poet's Market reserves the right to exclude any listing that does not meet its requirements.*

COMPLAINT PROCEDURE

If you feel you have not been treated fairly by a listing in *Poet's Market*, we advise you to take the following steps:

• First try to contact the listing. Sometimes one phone call or a letter can quickly clear up the matter.

• Document all your correspondence with the listing. When you write to us with a complaint, provide the details of your submission, the date of your first contact with the listing and the nature of your subsequent correspondence.

• We will enter your letter into our files and attempt to contact the listing.

• The number and severity of complaints will be considered in our decision whether or not to delete the listing from the next edition.

The Markets

Publishers of Poetry

Containing everything from stapled newsletters published by individuals in kitchen-corner offices to perfect-bound, paperback collections produced in large suites by paid staffs, this section of *Poet's Market* provides a comprehensive look at those publishers listed within its more than 400 pages. All the activities a publisher may conduct—whether it's publishing a quarterly journal, sponsoring a contest, or offering writing workshops—are represented within one listing to give you an overview of the publisher's operations. And for those few listings operating activities at different addresses, we've cross-referenced the listings so you still may be aware of all of a publisher's involvements.

Evaluating these publishers to determine which is right for you and your work is not an easy job—and, because our tastes and interests may differ, not something we can do for you. However, learning all you can about publishers and their operations is a huge step on the road toward publication. Therefore, within the following listings, we provide you with as much information as we can glean from editors and publishers—specialized interests, contact names, submission requirements, payment policies, awards received, etc.

We also believe letting editors speak for themselves is an excellent way for you to get an inside look at how a particular editor thinks/works. So, at the end of most listings, there are quotes from editors and publishers on their publishing philosophies, what types of poetry particularly interest them, any pet peeves or recurring problems they have in regard to submissions, or advice they have for poets about the poetry field or submitting in general. You can learn much about publishers by what they choose to include in these brief statements. But, for even more insight into what makes publishers tick, read the editorial introductions included in most publications. Many editors use these first few pages of their journals to let readers know why they do what they do and exactly what kind of work they want.

Along that same line, the editors of *Poet's Market* have added comments to various listings throughout this section. Set off by bullets (●), these comments provide information we think is particularly noteworthy or important information that might not normally be included in a listing.

LOCATE YOUR PERFECT MARKETS

The best way to approach this rather large section of information depends on what you are seeking. If you do not have a specific publisher in mind, dive right in and start reading through the listings. This will give you a good idea of what publishing opportunities are available and what types of markets exist.

However, if you are looking for a particular market, do not begin with this section but in the General Index. Let's say, for example, you've recently written a poem your preschooler just loves and you think a likely market for the poem might be *Turtle*. You won't find *Turtle* in this section alphabetized under *T*, however. The editors requested the listing be under the name of the publisher of the magazine, Benjamin Franklin Literary and Medical Society, Inc., and that's where you will find it. You might not have discovered that without looking in the General Index, where *Turtle* is cross-referenced to the Benjamin Franklin Literary and Medical Society, Inc.

The General Index also contains the names of publishers from the 1997 edition who are not included in this edition and, if known, the reasons for their absence. It also provides a way to find publishers who have changed names: though you will find a publication listed in this section under its new name, you will find the previous name with the appropriate cross-reference in the General Index.

The Publishers of Poetry section contains 1,800 poetry publishing markets, includes 11 "Insider" interviews with editors and poets, and showcases the covers of 12 diverse publications. Also worthy of mention are the more than 400 new markets included in this edition—especially considering that new listings are often more receptive to submissions.

DISCOVER NEW LISTINGS

To locate this year's new listings, look for the double daggers (‡) preceding the listing titles. (You can locate new listings quickly by looking for the double daggers preceding entries in the indexes.) As in years past, some new listings are publications that were in earlier editions of *Poet's Market* but not the previous one. We're happy to welcome back, for example, *Bird Watcher's Digest*, Confluence Press, *Iris: A Journal About Women*, *New Virginia Review*, *Spinning Jenny*, Stride Publications (from Devon, England) and *Verandah* (from Australia).

Other listings new to this edition are actually "new," that is, they are magazines or presses that began publishing in the last few years. These include *First Class*, *Journal of African Travel-Writing*, *Salt Hill Journal*, *Texas Young Writers' Newsletter* and *Wordplay*. Also new to this edition are Gaff Press and Red Moon Press, chapbook publishers, and Urthona Press which publishes three paperbacks per year with one selected through a competition.

We would also like to welcome some of the new listings from outside the United States, including *Ars Poetica* and Mock Frog Publishing, both based in Australia; *Comme Ça et Autrement*, published in France; *Musk Gland Sally* and *Raw NerVZ Haiku*, both Canadian publications; and *Presence* and Sixties Press, from the United Kingdom.

To quickly find those markets located outside the United States, look for the two new icons we have added to this edition of *Poet's Market*. A maple leaf symbol (❧) appears before the titles of all listings from Canada and an asterisk (*) appears before all overseas listings.

REFINE YOUR SEARCH FOR LOCAL AND SPECIALIZED MARKETS

One of the best ways for most poets to become a part of the literary scene is to start in their home territory. Therefore the Geographical Index, located in the back of this book, will quickly lead you to publishers with whom you have a lot in common because of either the state, region or country in which you currently live or from which you originate.

And to help poets with ties outside the United States more easily locate potential markets, we have further defined the countries represented in our directory. Noting an increase in listings from Australia, France and Japan, we have moved these markets from the Other Countries category and, now, list them separately under their own subheads.

For those who write specialized poetry—pertaining to a particular group or subject or poetry written in a particular form—refer to the Subject Index. This index lists publishers according to their specialties. For instance, under the heading Women/Feminism you will find a list of publishers who seek poetry written by women or focusing on issues of interest to women. Under the heading Form/Style you'll find publishers who want haiku as well as those who seek sonnets or experimental work.

The Subject Index has also been refined to aid in your publication search. The category Sports has been expanded to encompass listings that focus on more recreational activities. Therefore, under the new category Sports/Recreation you will find such listings as *The Climbing Art* and *Juggler's World* (formerly listed under Specialized), as well as the listings *Spitball* and *Aethlon: The Journal of Sport Literature*. While these may seem like minor changes, every refinement we make in *Poet's Market* helps ease your search for the right markets for your poetry.

DEFINE YOUR STYLE

Besides locating the publications whose interests match yours, you need to be sure your understanding of the subject matter and the editor's are the same. So, to help you be right on target with your submissions, we have added to this edition the Glossary of Poetic Forms and Styles. This glossary defines the specific poetic forms and styles publishers are seeking. We have concentrated on providing definitions for those forms appearing most frequently in the Subject Index under the subhead Forms/Styles. However, we have also provided definitions for many other forms not listed in the Subject Index, especially the less-known forms. For a more comprehensive list of terms, see *The Poetry Dictionary* by John Drury (Story Press, 1995).

For any terms and abbreviations in the listings with which you are not familiar, see the Glossary of Listing Terms which follows the Glossary of Poetic Forms and Styles at the back of this book.

KEEP AN EYE ON THE DETAILS

Once you have selected the markets you feel match your interests and style, you must pay attention to submission details if you want your poetry to be given serious consideration. While a number of practices are considered standard, more and more editors are opting for variations. Thus, each year we ask editors and publishers to not only update the general information within their listings (such as reporting times and payment policies) but also to clarify specific submission details. (For a more detailed discussion on preparing submissions, see *Poet's Guide: How to Publish and Perform Your Work* by Michael J. Bugeja [Story Line Press, 1995].)

For example, it is important to know if, and when, editors publish theme issues. While some editors develop all their issues around themes, others only publish one or two theme issues a year (or even every few years). Of course, whenever an editor is reading for a theme issue, that's the type of work he or she wants to receive. If you send unrelated work, even if the editor does not normally publish theme-based material, your work will not be considered.

Once again we specifically asked editors to supply details about their upcoming themes and related deadlines. Though a number of editors were able to provide this information for 1998, many had not yet finalized their plans when we contacted them. To be sure your submission will be welcome, send a self-addressed, stamped envelope (SASE) to receive up-to-date information about themes, deadlines, and other submissions guidelines.

Editors also advertise upcoming themes and deadlines in the pages of such periodicals as *Writer's Digest* and *Poets & Writers Magazine*. Checking these publications frequently will keep you current on submission needs.

SNAIL MAIL VERSUS E-MAIL

As you read the listings in this section—and we encourage you to review them all—you will notice an increasing amount of fax numbers and e-mail addresses. Be careful when contacting editors by these means. While some actually encourage electronic submissions, most still prefer manuscripts be sent via regular mail with SASEs for reply or the return of your work. Many editors simply supply fax numbers and e-mail addresses to facilitate requests for guidelines or other information.

Determining the best method for submitting your work is tricky but critical, especially since submitting material in an undesired manner may jeopardize your chances of receiving a response or even being read. Within the listings themselves, we have noted preferences for and against electronic submissions. If a listing includes a fax number or e-mail address but does not state their submission preference, or requires a reading fee, the best method is to contact the publisher before submitting your poems to verify if an e-mail or fax submission is acceptable.

To further eliminate some of the guess work, this year a list of those markets open to e-mail submissions appears at the end of our new Websites of Interest to Poets section at the back of this book.

DON'T FORGET THE REPLY ENVELOPE

For those listings not connected to the electronic world or for those requiring submissions be sent through the post, a reply envelope is, with few exceptions, an absolute necessity. Many publishers run their operations on shoe-string budgets and cannot afford to reply to every submission, query or request for information received. Including a SASE or SAE (self-addressed envelope) and IRCs (International Reply Coupons, for replies from countries outside your own) with all correspondence provides an easy way for overworked and underpaid editors to contact you.

And remember, if you want your manuscript returned you must provide a SASE (or SAE with IRCs) large enough to contain your work and with sufficient postage. If it takes three stamps to mail material, it will take three stamps for the material to be returned—unless you are sending a disposable manuscript. But if you do not want your poems returned to you (that is, the manuscript can be discarded), the editor needs to be told the SASE is only for his or her response.

It's not surprising that editors, frustrated with receiving more and more manuscripts without SASEs, are creating policies in regard to such submissions. Many choose to include disclaimers stating that submissions without SASEs will not be acknowledged. However, some editors are not so kind; they discard submissions without SASEs before the material is even read. Other editors may require a minimal reading fee to cover postage costs. To get past this stickiest of spots in the poet/editor relationship, make a habit of sending a SASE (or SAE and IRCs) with all correspondence. Also, to make sure you are following other expected submission procedures, read (or reread) Charting Your Path to Poetry Publication, on page 11.

AWARDS AND HONORS

As another way of helping you evaluate publishers, we have also included information about awards and honors that have been bestowed on editors and publishers or their magazines and books. For instance, we continue to note which publications have had poetry selected for inclusion in recent volumes of *The Best American Poetry*, an annual anthology highlighting the best poetry published in periodicals during the previous year. (You will find this information near the end of listings.)

Once again, thanks to David Lehman, who edits *The Best American Poetry* series, and his assistant Maggie Nelson, we were able to obtain an advance list of those publications with work included in the 1997 volume, guest edited by James Tate. As a different guest editor compiles the anthology every year, knowing which publications have work included, especially in a number of recent volumes, can provide insight into the type and quality of material used.

In addition, *The Best American Poetry* (published by Scribner, 1230 Avenue of the Americas, New York NY 10020) can help you develop a sense for trends in the field. The 1997 volume, by the way, is published at the same time as this edition of *Poet's Market*. So, when you are ready to read the poetry that has been selected from the publications listed here, check your nearest library or bookstore.

UNDERSTAND MARKET CATEGORY CODES

Finally, all listings in this section include one or more Roman numerals in their headings. These "codes," selected by editors and publishers, can help you determine the most appropriate markets for your poetry. (For details see How to Sell Your Poetry Using *Poet's Market* on page 3.) The market category codes and their explanations are as follows:

 I. **Publishers very open to beginners' submissions.** They publish much of the material received and frequently respond with criticism and suggestions. For consideration, some may require fees, purchase of the publication or membership in an organization, but they are not, so far as we can determine, exploitative of poets.

 II. **The general market to which most poets familiar with literary journals and magazines should submit.** Typically they accept 10% or less of poems received and usually reject others without comment. They pay at least one copy. A poet developing a list of publication credits will find many of these to be respected names in the literary world.

III. Limited markets, typically overstocked. This code is often used by many prestigious magazines and publishers to discourage widespread submissions from poets who have not published elsewhere—although many do on occasion publish relatively new or little-known poets.

IV. Specialized publications encourage contributors from a specific geographical area, age-group, gender, sexual orientation or ethnic background or accept poems in specific forms or on specific themes. In most **IV** listings we also state the specialty (e.g., **IV-Animals**). Often a listing emphasizes more than one subject area; these listings are marked with two codes. To quickly locate such markets, refer to the Subject Index which lists publishers according to their specialties.

V. Listings which do not accept unsolicited manuscripts. You cannot submit to these without specific permission to do so. If, for some reason, the press or magazine seems especially appropriate for you, query with a SASE. But, in general, these folks prefer to locate poets themselves. Sometimes they are temporarily overstocked; other times they have projects lined up for years.

We have included these listings because it is important to know not only where to send your poetry but also where NOT to send it. In addition, many are interesting publishers, and this book is widely used as a reference by librarians, researchers, publishers, suppliers and others who need to have as complete a listing of poetry publishers as possible.

‡A SMALL GARLIC PRESS (ASGP) (III); AGNIESZKA'S DOWRY (AGD) (II), 5445 Sheridan #3003, Chicago IL 60640, e-mail sanrensi@teleport.com, website http://www.enteract.com/~marek/asgp/, founded 1995, editor Marek Lugowski. *Agnieszka's Dowry (AgD)*, is "a magazine of arts and letters published both in print and as a permanent Internet installation of surprising graphics, good words, and a navigation in an interesting space, all conducive to fast and comfortable reading. *ASGP* wants material with detail, imagery, narrative, **crafted language, devices. Have something interesting to say—and say it well. No restrictions on form or type.** We use contextual and juxtapositional tie-ins with other material in making choices, so visiting the online *AgD* is assumed to be part of any submission." The print version of *AgD* is 36-60 pgs., 5½ × 8½, "printed digital-direct," saddle-stapled with color cardstock cover, includes artwork. Single copy: $3. **Make checks payable to A Small Garlic Press. Submit 5-10 poems at a time. E-mail submissions preferred—ASCII only. Previously published poems ("Please include information about where work was previously published and status of publishing rights.") and simultaneous submissions ("Please inform us if work is accepted elsewhere.") OK. Seldom comments on rejections. Guidelines can be obtained via website. Reports in 1-3 months. Pays 1 copy. Acquires one-time rights.** A Small Garlic Press (ASGP) publishes **5-6 chapbooks of** poetry/year. Chapbooks authors are often invited from the authors published in *AgD*. **Query with a sample of 5-10 poems. "See our webpage for policies and submission guidelines. The press catalog and page of links to other markets and resources for poetry are all maintained online at our website."**

*A.L.I. (THE AVON LITERARY INTELLIGENCER) (II), 20 Byron Place, Clifton, Bristol BS8 1JT England, e-mail dsr@maths.bath.ac.uk, founded 1991, editor Daniel Richardson. *A.L.I.* is a quarterly literary newsletter which publishes poetry, fables, fiction, reviews, true stories and news of meetings, courses and performances in the Bristol, Bath and Somerset area. **They want "idealistic, eclectic work; writing in which it is possible to hear the voice of the writer. Nothing unsurprising."** They have recently published poetry by Jim McNeill, Rose Flint and Joyce Walker. As a sample the editor selected these lines from "Aubade" by Len Jenkinson:

> We were going to Barlow's for nails,
> bright morning comes down to me over the years.
> Blue sky, orange chimney pots and birds,
> a seagull from the dump crying round
> across to the blue pearl town woken to its haze of sound.

A.L.I. is 12 pgs. (actually six 11⅝ × 16½ sheets of white paper folded in half), photocopied and unbound. They receive about 200 poems a year, accept approximately 20%. Press run is 150 for 100 subscribers, 20 shelf sales. Single copy: $1.50; subscription: £3 UK or $10 US. **Sample postpaid: $5. Make checks payable to *Avon Literary Intelligencer.* "Payment is also accepted in the equivalent value of unused postage stamps."** Submit

4 poems at a time. No previously published poems or simultaneous submissions. Cover letter preferred. E-mail submissions OK only from subscribers. Seldom comments on rejections. Reports in about 3 months. Sometimes sends prepublication galleys. Pays 1 copy. Reviews books of poetry when time allows. Open to unsolicited reviews. Poets may also send books for review consideration.

ABBEY; ABBEY CHEAPOCHAPBOOKS (II), 5360 Fallriver Row Court, Columbia MD 21044, e-mail greisman@aol.com, founded 1970, editor David Greisman. **They want "poetry that does for the mind what that first sip of Molson Ale does for the palate. No pornography or politics."** They have published poetry and artwork by Richard Peabody, Vera Bergstrom, D.E. Steward, Carol Hamilton, Harry Calhoun, Wayne Hogan and Cheryl Townsend. *Abbey*, a quarterly, aims "to be a journal but to do it so informally that one wonders about my intent." It is 20-26 pgs., magazine-sized, photocopied. They publish about 150 of 1,000 poems received/ year. Press run is 200. Subscription: $2. **Sample postpaid: 50¢. Send SASE for guidelines. Reports in 1 month. Pays 1-2 copies.** *Abbey Cheapochapbooks* come out 1-2 times a year averaging 10-15 pgs. **For chapbook consideration query with 4-6 samples, bio and list of publications. Reports in 2 months. Pays 25-50 copies.** The editor says he is "definitely seeing poetry from two schools—the nit'n'grit school and the textured/reflective school. I much prefer the latter."

*ABIKO QUARTERLY WITH JAMES JOYCE FW STUDIES (II, IV-Translations), 8-1-8 Namiki, Abiko-shi, Chiba-ken 270-11 Japan, phone/fax 011-81-471-84-7904, founded 1988, founding editor/poetry editor Laurel Sicks, is a literary-style annual journal **"heavily influenced by James Joyce's** *Finnegan's Wake*. **We publish all kinds, with an emphasis on poetry written with passion. We include originals and translations. However, we no longer consider unsolicited poetry and fiction. All of our new work comes from our annual international poetry and fiction contest. See** *Writer's Digest, Poets & Writers* **and** *AWP Chronicle* **for details." Contest runs from September 1 to December 31 and is judged by a well-known poet.** They have recently published poetry by Alice Friman, Carrie Ivenson, Kenji Miyazawa, Jon Silkin, Cid Corman, Finn Fordham, Robin Davidson and Edith Shiffert. It is about 800 pgs., 7×10, desktop-published with Macintosh laser printer and perfect-bound with coated paper cover. Press run is 500 for 150 subscribers of which 10 are libraries, 100 shelf sales. **Sample postpaid: $35.** Open to unsolicited reviews. Poets may also send books for review consideration. The editor says, "Poets are in a hurry to publish. Poets, educate yourselves! Read contemporary poetry. In fact, read all poetry! Work at your craft before you attempt to publish. Please remember **U.S. postage does not work** in Japan with SAEs! Send 2 International Reply coupons."

ABOVE THE BRIDGE MAGAZINE; THIRD STONE PUBLISHING (I, IV-Regional), P.O. Box 416, Marquette MI 49855, phone (906)228-2964, e-mail classen@mail.portup.com, website http://www.portup.com/ above, founded 1985, poetry editor Sean MacManus. *Above the Bridge* is a quarterly magazine designed to reflect life and living in Michigan's Upper Peninsula. **"All poetry must relate to life in the Upper Peninsula of Michigan. There is rugged, magnificent country here. Material should reflect that."** The editor says the magazine is 60 pgs., 8½×11, and includes line art and graphics. They receive about 200 poems a year, accept approximately 10%. Press run is 2,500 for 1,000 subscribers of which 50 are libraries. Single copy: $3.50; subscription: $13. **Sample postpaid: $4. Submit 2-3 poems at a time. Previously published poems and simultaneous submissions OK. Cover letter preferred. Often comments on rejections. Send SASE for guidelines. Reports in 4 months. Pays $5 and 2 copies. Acquires one-time rights.** Staff reviews books of poetry only if author or topic is related to Michigan's Upper Peninsula. Send related books for review consideration.

ABRAXAS MAGAZINE (V); GHOST PONY PRESS (III), P.O. Box 260113, Madison WI 53726-0113, website http://www.geocities.com/Paris/4614, *Abraxas* founded 1968, Ghost Pony Press in 1980, by editor/ publisher Ingrid Swanberg, who says "Ghost Pony Press is a small press publisher of poetry books; *Abraxas* is a literary journal publishing contemporary poetry, criticism and translations. *Do not confuse these separate presses!*" *Abraxas* **no longer considers unsolicited material, except as announced as projects arise.** The editor is interested in poetry that is **"contemporary lyric, concrete, experimental." Does not want to see "political posing; academic regurgitations."** They have published poetry by William Stafford, Ivan Argüelles, Denise Levertov, César Vallejo and Andrea Moorhead. As a sample the editor selected these lines from "the silence of lascaux" by próspero saíz:

> in the silence of lascaux a wavering light is fading
> outside the cave the bones of slaughter linger still
> traces of mass killings beneath the cliffs of stone
> yet far from the equine ossuary stubby ponies tumble
> in the vanishing lines of the sacred terror of the horse . . .

The magazine is up to 80 pgs. (160 pgs., double issues), 6×9, flat-spined (saddle-stitched with smaller issues), litho offset, with original art on its matte card cover, using "unusual graphics in text, original art and collages, concrete poetry, exchange ads only, letters from contributors, essays." It appears "irregularly, 4- to 9-month intervals or longer." Press run is 600 for 300 subscribers of which 150 are libraries. Subscription: $16/4 issues, $20/4 issues Canada, Mexico and overseas. **Sample postpaid: $4 ($6 double issues).** *Abraxas* **will announce submission guidelines as projects arise. Pays 1 copy plus 40% discount on additional copies. To submit to Ghost Pony Press, inquire with SASE plus 5-10 poems and cover letter. Previously published material OK for book publication by Ghost Pony Press. Editor sometimes comments briefly on rejections. Reports on queries in 1-3 months, mss in 3 months or longer** "We currently have a considerable backlog of mss." **Payment varies per project. Send SASE for catalog to buy samples.** They have published three books of poetry by próspero saíz including *the bird of nothing & other poems*; 168 pgs., 7×10, sewn and wrapped binding, paperback available for $20 (signed and numbered edition is $35).

‡✿ABRAXIS PUBLICATIONS; ABRAXIS (I); LAUS DEOS (I, IV-Religious), P.O. Box 746, Chester-ville, Ontario K0C 1H0 Canada, founded 1994, editor Heather O'Neil. *Abraxis* is "a general poetry magazine catering to the novice poet. It appears any time we have 20 or more poems—usually bimonthly, sometimes monthly." **They want "any kind, any style, 80 lines maximum. We would like to see more traditional rhyming poetry with a beat. No horror poems, abusive or profane language."** They have recently published poetry by Robert Hogg, R.L. Cook, Russell Sheldon and Gayle Baillargeon. As a sample the editor selected these lines from "With the Barkers and the Coloured Balloons" by Russell Sheldon:

> She sees her life reflected
> In the fun house mirror.
> The warped, elongated
> Veneer of existence,
> Scattered to the night in
> Images of patternless regret.
> The midway demands much.

Laus Deos, first published in April 1996, is a quarterly Christian magazine containing poetry, essays, prayers, commentary and bible study. Both *Abraxis* and *Laus Deos* are usually 6-8 pgs. (bond paper) printed on both sides, 8½×11, side-stapled with illustrated paper cover, graphics, no ads. For *Abraxis*, they receive about 500, accept about 180-200. Press run is 125 for 27 subscribers, 50 are shelf sales, with 25 distributed free to local hospitals, doctors and dentists offices. Subscription: $30/6 issues, $35 foreign. **Sample postpaid: $5. Make checks payable to Heather O'Neil** ("I prefer money orders."). **Send $5 with each batch of poems. In return we guarantee publication of at least one poem." Submit up to 8 poems at a time. Previously published poems and simultaneous submissions OK. Cover letter preferred. "We will accept submissions on 3.5 disk that is IBM and WordPerfect 6.1 compatible."** Time between acceptance and publication is 3 months maxi-mum. **Often comments on rejections. Publishes a Christmas issue. Send SASE (or SAE and IRC) for guidelines. Reports in 1 month. Pays 1-2 copies.**

ACM (ANOTHER CHICAGO MAGAZINE) (II); LEFT FIELD PRESS, 3709 N. Kenmore, Chicago IL 60613, founded 1977, poetry editor Barry Silesky. *ACM* is a literary biannual, with **emphasis on quality, experimental, politically aware** prose, fiction, poetry, reviews, cross-genre work and essays. **No religious verse.** They have published prose and poetry by Albert Goldbarth, Michael McClure, Jack Anderson, Jerome Sala, Nance VanWinkel, Nadja Tesich, Wanda Coleman, Charles Simic and Diane Wakoski. As a sample the editor selected these lines by Dean Shavit:

> Just the facts. Forgotten on purpose.
> This is our land. Yes, you said, "ours."
> A gang of teenagers, too young for the army, too stupid for respect.

Silesky says *ACM* is 220 pgs., digest-sized, offset with b&w art and ads. Editors appreciate traditional to experi-mental verse with an emphasis on message, especially poems with strong voices articulating social or political concerns. Circulation is 2,000 for 500 subscribers of which 100 are libraries. Subscription: $16/year. **Sample postpaid: $8. Submit 3-4 typed poems at a time. No previously published poems; simultaneous submissions OK. Reports in 2-3 months, has 3- to 6-month backlog. Sometimes sends prepublication galleys. Pays $5/ page,** "if funds permit," **and 1 copy. Buys first serial rights.** Reviews books of poetry in 250-800 words. Open to unsolicited reviews. Poets may also send books for review consideration. Work published in *ACM* has been included in *The Best American Poetry* (1992, 1994, 1995, 1996 and 1997) and *Pushcart Prize* anthologies. The editor says, "Buy a copy—subscribe and support your own work."

THE ACORN; EL DORADO WRITERS' GUILD (II, IV-Regional), P.O. Box 1266, El Dorado CA 95623-1266, phone (916)621-1833, fax (916)621-3939, e-mail jalapep@spider.lloyd.com, founded 1993, poetry consul-

---

MARKET CONDITIONS are constantly changing! If you're still using this book and it is 1999 or later, buy the newest edition of *Poet's Market* at your favorite bookstore or order directly from Writer's Digest Books.

tant Hatch Graham, is a quarterly journal of the Western Sierra, published by the El Dorado Writers' Guild, a nonprofit literary organization. It includes "fiction and nonfiction, history and reminiscence, story and legend, and poetry." **They want poetry "up to 30 lines long, though we prefer shorter. Focus must be on western slope Sierra Nevada. No erotica, pornography or religious poetry."** They have recently published poetry by Nancy Cherry and Edward C. Lynskey. As a sample the poetry consultant selected this poem, "Summer's Dead Geranium" by Joyce Odam:

> *The plant is in need of water.*
> *It gasps in the sun-hot window*
> *and curls its leaves in the feverish air.*
>
> *If she, in her chair, rocking and staring*
> *should hear a dry, green moaning,*
> *would she think of water?*

The poetry consultant says *the ACORN* is 44 pgs., 5½×8½, offset-printed and saddle-stapled with light card cover. They receive about 400 poems a year, use approximately 15%. Press run is 200 for 110 subscribers. Subscription: $12. **Sample postpaid: $3. Submit 3-5 poems, neatly typed or printed, at a time. Previously published poems OK; however, no simultaneous submissions. Cover letter with short (75-word) bio and publication credits preferred. "Our issues favor topical items suitable for the season." Deadlines are February 1, May 1, August 1 and November 1.** Time between acceptance and publication is 1 month. **"Poetry consultant screens, then five editors score the poems for content, form and suitability." Graphics editor selects to fit space available." Often comments on rejections. Reports within 1 month after deadline. Pays 2 copies.** Sponsors annual contest. First prize $100, second prize $50, third prize $25. Entry fee: $7/3 poems, 40 lines maximum/poem. Deadline: January 15. All winning entries are published in the contest edition of *the ACORN*. Send SASE for complete rules. The editor says, "If your poetry is about nature, be accurate with the species' names, colors, etc. If you describe a landscape, be sure it fits our region. Metered rhyming verse had better be precise. (We have an editor with an internal metronome!) Slant rhyme and free verse are welcome. Avoid trite phrases."

ACORN WHISTLE (II), 907 Brewster Ave., Beloit WI 53511, founded 1994, first issue published in spring 1995, editor Fred Burwell, appears twice yearly. "We seek writing that moves both heart and mind. **We seek accessible poetry: narrative, lyrical, prose poem. No length requirements. We are not interested in experimental, religious, erotic or New Age work.** We also publish fiction, memoir and personal essay." They have recently published poetry by Mary Legato Brownell, Wendy Taylor Carlisle, Daniel Smith and Ann Struthers. As a sample the editor selected these lines from "Tonight I Come Home" by Joanne Mokosh Riley:

> *Tonight I come home to April and this farm*
> *With its years of apple trees*
> *Whose lichen arms with woolen moss*
> *Now hold wind-frost and blossoms.*
> *Light rain drifts from an almost cloudless sky*
> *And through the white-webbed branches*
> *I find a new moon,*
> *Sharp and open and trying to heal.*

The editor says *AW* is 90 pgs., 8½×11, staple-bound, using b&w photos and art, no ads. Press run is 500. Subscription: $10. **Sample postpaid: $5. No previously published poems; simultaneous submissions OK. Often comments on rejections. Send SASE for guidelines. Reports in 3 months. Pays 2 copies. Acquires first North American serial rights.** The editor says, "We publish no reviews, although we plan to mention publications by our past authors. We wish more writers would focus on material that matters to them, rather than trying to impress an audience of editors and teachers. We seek accessible writing for an audience that reads for pleasure and edification. We encourage a friendly, working relationship between editors and writers."

‡ACROPOLIS BOOKS, INC.; I-LEVEL; AWAKENING; FLASHLIGHT (II, IV-Spirituality), 747 Sheridan Ave., Suite 1A, Lakewood CO 80214-2551, phone (303)231-9923, fax (303)235-0492, e-mail acropolisb ooks@worldnet.att.net, website http://www.acropolisbooks.com, founded 1958, vice president/operations Constance J. Wilson. "It is the aim of Acropolis to publish books that demonstrate the highest level of consciousness— mysticism." They publish 3 paperbacks and 3 hardbacks/year. **They want "poetry that reflects one's inner relationship; that expresses a oneness with the universe, and presents the aspects of the mystical journey. No personal narrative or political verse."** As a sample they selected these lines from "Eternitie" by Robert Herrick:

> *O yeares! and Age! Farewell;*
> *Behold I go,*
> *Where I do know*
> *Infinite to dwell.*
>
> *And these mine eyes shall see*
> *All times, how they*

> *Are lost i' th' Sea*
> *Of vast Eternitie.*

> *Where never Moone shall sway*
> *The Starres; but she,*
> *And Night, shall be*
> *Drown'd in one endlesse Day.*

Usual book format varies upon each ms. **"No queries—please send a cover letter with as many poems as possible that apply to our type of publishing program."** No previously published poems; simultaneous submissions OK. **Cover letter required including "information about the author's background, past work published (if any)."** Time between acceptance and publication is 1 year. **Poems are circulated to an editorial board. "Submissions are read by staff of four, and then the decision is made by committee." Always comments on rejections. Replies to mss in 2 months. Pays 20 author's copies, but is negotiable. Obtain sample books through bookstores.** They say, "We are expanding into poetry and look forward to finding poets whose work reflects a bridge to spiritual awareness. We are eager to publish both children's and adult poetry. If you feel you have a title that includes spiritual principles of living in a non-religious context, you may have the kind of book we're looking for. All submissions will be given consideration, should they include these principles."

*ACUMEN MAGAZINE; EMBER PRESS; THE LONG POEM GROUP NEWSLETTER (I, II), 6 The Mount, Higher Furzeham, Brixham, South Devon TQ5 8QY England, phone (01803)851098, press founded 1971, *Acumen* founded 1984, *The Long Poem Group Newsletter* founded 1995, poetry editor Patricia Oxley, is a "small press publisher of a general literary magazine with emphasis on good poetry." **They want "well-crafted, high quality, imaginative poems showing a sense of form. No experimental verse of an obscene type."** They have published poetry by Elizabeth Jennings, William Oxley, Gavin Ewart, D.J. Enright, Peter Porter, Kathleen Raine and R.S. Thomas. As a sample the editor selected this poem, "Northbound Train," by Ken Smith:

> *Birds rising. These flecks*
> *white on the brown ploughland*
> *flakes of fine snow, they are birds,*
> *they are gulls suddenly flying.*

Acumen appears 3 times a year (in January, May and September) and is 100 pgs., A5, perfect-bound. "We aim to publish 120 poems out of 12,000 received." Press run is 650 for 400 subscribers of which 20 are libraries. **Sample copy: $15. Submit 5-6 poems at a time. No previously published poems; simultaneous submissions OK, if not to UK magazines. Reports in 1 month. Pays "by negotiation" and 1 copy.** Staff reviews books of poetry in up to 300 words, single format or 600 words, multi-book. Send books for review consideration to Glyn Pursglove, 25 St. Albans Rd., Brynmill, Swansea, West Glamorgan SA2 0BD Wales. Also publishes *The Long Poem Group Newsletter* featuring short articles about long poems and reviews of books of long poems. Free for large SASE (or SAE with IRC). Patricia Oxley advises, "Read *Acumen* carefully to see what kind of poetry we publish. Also read widely in many poetry magazines, and don't forget the poets of the past—they can still teach us a great deal."

ADASTRA PRESS (V), 101 Strong St., Easthampton MA 01027-2536, founded 1980 by Gary Metras, who says, "I publish poetry because I love poetry. I produce the books on antique equipment using antique methods because I own the equipment and because it's cheaper—I don't pay myself a salary—it's a hobby—it's **a love affair with poetry and printing of fine editions." However, due to a large backlog, he will not be reading mss in 1998.** All his books and chapbooks are **limited editions, handset, letterpress,** printed with handsewn signatures. Poets published include W.D. Ehrhart, Jim Daniels, Cortney Davis and Miriam Sagan. As a sample the editor selected these lines from "How To Burn" by Christopher Locke:

> *Beyond the breath*
> *Fogged windows, city blocks*
> *Lurch head first towards*
> *The tar papered walls of evening.*

1-4 chapbooks are brought out each year. **Author is paid in copies, usually 10% of the print run. He is not reading mss in 1998. "If you want to see a typical handcrafted Adastra chapbook, send $5 and I'll mail a current title.** If you'd like a fuller look at what, how and why I do what I do, send a check for $12 ($10 plus $2 p&h) and I'll mail a copy of *The Adastra Reader: Being the Collected Chapbooks in Facsimile with Author Notes, Bibliography and Comments on Hand Bookmaking,* published in 1987. This is a 247-page anthology covering Adastra publishing from 1979-1986."

ADRIFT (II, IV-Ethnic), 46 E. First St., #3D, New York NY 10003, founded 1980, editor Thomas McGonigle, who says, **"The orientation of the magazine is Irish, Irish-American. I expect the reader-writer knows and goes beyond Yeats, Kavanagh, Joyce, O'Brien." The literary magazine is open to all kinds of submissions, but does not want to see "junk."** They have published poetry by James Liddy, Thomas McCarthy, Francis Stuart and Gilbert Sorrentino. *Adrift* appears twice a year and is 32 pgs., magazine-sized, offset on heavy stock, saddle-stapled with matte card cover. Circulation is 1,000 with 200 subscriptions, 50 of which are libraries. Single copy: $4; subscription: $8. **Sample postpaid: $5. Make checks payable to T. McGonigle. Simultaneous submissions OK. Magazine pays, rate varies; contributors receive 1 copy.** Reviews books of poetry. Open to unsolicited reviews. Poets may also send books for review consideration.

ADVOCATE, PKA's PUBLICATION (I), 301A Rolling Hills Park, Prattsville NY 12468, phone (518)299-3103, founded 1987, editor Remington Wright, is a bimonthly advertiser-supported tabloid, 12,000 copies distributed free, **using "original, previously unpublished works,** such as feature stories, essays, 'think' pieces, letters to the editor, profiles, humor, fiction, poetry, puzzles, cartoons or line drawings." **They want "nearly any kind of poetry, any length, but not religious or pornographic. Poetry ought to speak to people and not be so oblique as to have meaning only to the poet. If I had to be there to understand the poem, don't send it."** They accept approximately 25% of poems received. **Sample postpaid: $4. No previously published poems or simultaneous submissions.** Time between acceptance and publication is an average of 4-6 months. **Editor "occasionally" comments on rejections. Reports in 6-8 weeks. Pays 2 copies. Acquires first rights only.** Offers occasional contests. The editor says, "All submissions and correspondence must be accompanied by a self-addressed, stamped envelope with sufficient postage."

AEGINA PRESS, INC.; UNIVERSITY EDITIONS (I, II), 1905 Madison Ave., Spring Valley, Huntington WV 25704-2136, phone (304)429-7204, fax (304)429-7234, founded 1983, publisher Ira Herman, is **primarily subsidy,** strongly committed to publishing new or established poets. Publishes subsidy titles under the University Editions imprint. They have also published non-subsidized poetry as well. **Authors of books accepted on a non-subsidized basis receive a 15% royalty.** "We try to provide a way for talented poets to have their collections published, which otherwise might go unpublished because of commercial, bottom-line considerations. We will publish quality poetry that the large publishers will not handle because it is not commercially viable. We believe it is unfair that a poet has to have a 'name' or a following in order to have a book of poems accepted by a publisher. Poetry is the purest form of literary art, and it should be made available to those who appreciate it." They have recently published *Where Have the Wild Geese Gone?* by Miriam Elle; *45 Beads on a Frazzled String* by G.B. Fox; *Echoes of the Muse* by June Philomena; and *The Liquid in Love* by Allison Eir Jenks. As a sample the editor selected these lines from "Imprints" in *Bliss* by Freda Freeman:

> *A sense of timeless continuity—*
> *The ebb and flow*
> *of waves and whelks and walking breathing beings,*
> *Sharing the one unity*
> *of transitory impressions on the land.*

"**Most poetry books we accept are subsidized by the author.** In return, the author receives all sales proceeds from the book, and any unsold copies left from the print run belong to the author. Minimum print run is 500 copies. We can do larger runs as well. Our marketing program includes submission to distributors, agents and other publishers." **Mss should be typed and no shorter than 40 pages. There is no upper length limit. For a query, submit 3 or more poems. Simultaneous submissions OK. Reports in 1 month for full mss, 7-10 days for queries. Always sends prepublication galleys.** They publish perfect-bound (flat-spined) paperbacks and hardcovers with glossy covers. **Sample paperback books are available for $6 each plus $1.50 p&h; hardcover samples are $15.95 each plus $2.50 p&h.**

AERIAL (V), P.O. Box 25642, Washington DC 20007, phone (202)244-6258, founded 1984, editor Rod Smith, is an occasional publication. Issue #8 (published in May 1995) was the Barrett Watten issue (available for $15). They have published work by Jackson MacLow, Melanie Neilson, Steve Benson, Phyllis Rosenzweig and Charles Bernstein. A special issue is in the works, on Bruce Andrews, therefore **they're not looking for new work at this time.** The magazine is 200-300 pgs., 6×9, offset. Circulation is 1,000. **Sample postpaid: $7.50.** Also publishes critical/political/philosophical writing.

AETHLON: THE JOURNAL OF SPORT LITERATURE (IV-Sports/recreation), Dept. PM, English Dept., East Tennessee State University, Box 70270, Johnson City TN 37614-0270, phone (423)439-4339, fax (423)461-7193, e-mail sla@etsu.estu-tn.edu, founded 1983, general editor Don Johnson, Dean, Arts & Sciences, ETSU. **Submit poems to poetry editor Robert W. Hamblin, Professor of English, Southeast Missouri State University, Cape Girardeau MO 63701.** *Aethlon* publishes a variety of sport-related literature, including scholarly articles, fiction, poetry and reviews; 6-10 poems/issue; two issues annually, fall and spring. **Subject matter must be sports-related; no restrictions regarding form, length, style or purpose. They do not want to see** "doggerel, cliché-ridden or oversentimental" poems. Poets published include Neal Bowers, Joseph Duemer, Robert Fink, Jan Mordenski, H.R. Stonebeck and Don Welch. The magazine is 200 pgs., digest-sized, offset printed, flat-spined, with illustrations and some ads. Circulation is 1,000 for 750 subscribers of which 250 are libraries. Subscription is included with membership ($40) in the Sport Literature Association. **Sample postpaid: $15. "Only typed mss with SASE considered." No simultaneous submissions. E-mail submissions OK. Submissions are reported on in 6-8 weeks and the backlog time is 6-12 months. Contributors receive 5 offprints and a copy of the issue in which their poem appears.**

AFRICA WORLD PRESS (V, IV-Ethnic), P.O. Box 1892, Trenton NJ 08607, phone (609)844-9583, fax (609)844-0198, e-mail africawpress@nyo.com, founded 1983, contact Pamela Sims, president/publisher Kassahun Checole, publishes **poetry books by Africans, African-Americans, Caribbean and Latin Americans**. They have published *Under A Soprano Sky* by Sonia Sanchez, *From the Pyramid to the Projects* by Askia Muhammad Toure and *The Time: Poems and Photographs* by Esther Iverem. However, they are currently not accepting poetry submissions. Send SASE for catalog.

AFRICAN AMERICAN REVIEW (IV-Ethnic), Dept. of English, Indiana State University, Terre Haute IN 47809, phone (812)237-2968, founded 1967, managing editor Connie LeComte, poetry editors Sterling Plumpp, Thadious M. Davis, Pinkie Gordon Lane and E. Ethelbert Miller, is a "magazine primarily devoted to the analysis of African American literature, **although one issue per year focuses on poetry by African Americans." No specifications as to form, length, style, subject matter or purpose.** They have published poems by Amiri Baraka, Gwendolyn Brooks, Dudley Randall and Owen Dodson. *AAR* is 6×9, 200 pgs. with photo on the cover. They receive about 500 submissions/year, use 50. Individual subscriptions: $24 US, $31 foreign. **Sample postpaid: $10. Submit maximum of 6 poems to editor Joe Weixlmann. The editors sometimes comment on rejections. Publishes theme issues. Send SASE for guidelines. Reports in 3-4 months. Always sends prepublication galleys. Pays in copies.** The *African American Review* received a Special Merit Award for Editorial Content from the 1995 American Literary Magazine Awards.

AFRICAN VOICES (I, II, IV-Ethnic), 270 W. 96th St., New York NY 10025, phone/fax (212)865-2982, founded 1992, contact poetry editor, is a quarterly "art and literary magazine that **highlights the work of people of color. We publish ethnic literature and poetry on any subject. We do not wish to limit the reader or author."** They have published poetry by Reg E. Gaines, Maya Angelou, Tony Medina and Louis Reyes Rivera. They receive about 100 submissions a year, accept approximately 30%. Press run is 20,000 for 5,000 subscribers of which 30 are libraries, 40% shelf sales. Single copy: $2; subscription: $15. **Sample postpaid: $3. Previously published poems and simultaneous submissions OK. Cover letter and SASE required. Seldom comments on rejections. Send SASE for guidelines. Reports in 6-8 weeks. Pays 5 copies. Acquires first or one-time rights.** Reviews books of poetry in 500-1,000 words. Open to unsolicited reviews. Poets may also send books for review consideration, attn. Layding Kaliba. Sponsors periodic poetry contests. Send SASE for details. The editor says, "We strongly encourage new writers/poets to send in their work and not give up if their work is not accepted the first time. Accepted contributors are encouraged to subscribe."

AFRO-HISPANIC REVIEW (IV-Ethnic), Romance Languages, #143 Arts & Sciences, University of Missouri, Columbia MO 65211, founded 1982, editors Marvin A. Lewis and Edward J. Mullen, appears twice a year, in the fall and spring, using some **poetry related to Afro-Hispanic life and issues.** They have published poetry by Cristina Rodriguez Cabral, Luz Argentina Chiriboga and Lemuel Johnson. **Sample copy: $7.50. Submit 2 poems at a time. "Prefer clean copy with accents." Reports in 6 weeks. Pays 5 copies.** Reviews books of poetry in "about 500 words."

✦**AFTERTHOUGHTS (II, IV-Social issues)**, Pacific Centre North, 1100 Commissioners Rd. E., P.O. Box 41038, London, Ontario N5Z 4Z7 Canada, founded 1994, editor Andreas Gripp, is an "independent periodical of poetic thought and observation," published 2 or 4 times a year (or as funds permit). **The editor is looking for "poems dealing with life experience, personal relationships, episodes of irony, emotional conflict, animal rights, veganism, environmental protection, racial harmony, naturalistic inspiration, and anything else that will touch the very core of the reader's heart. All forms of poetry welcome—quality and originality are the only criteria."** They have recently published poetry by Nancy Berg, Paul Truttman, C.K. Tower, Lyn Lifshin, Nicole Orr and C. David Hay. As a sample the editor selected the poem "Paving" by Lee Moore:

> *Lives can be longer than roads paved.*
> *Constant lane entrances on this bend*
> *hold fragmented secrets,*
> *beyond abstract and obvious,*
> *which can complete the circle,*
> *patch up the mistakes during a second lap.*

Afterthoughts is 60-72 pgs., digest-sized, offset printed and perfect-bound with quality cover stock and b&w illustrations and photos throughout. Press run is 300-400 for 75 subscribers including 15 libraries. Subscription: $12 US, $15 CAN for 4 issues. **Sample postpaid: $5. Make cheques or money orders payable to *Afterthoughts*. Previously published poems and simultaneous submissions OK. "Please include an International Reply Coupon or $1 US with your SAE if you are submitting from the U.S. or overseas. U.S. stamps can't be used in return mail from Canada, and due to high postage costs, we are unable to reply to submissions lacking IRC or $1 US. SASE required for *Canadian* writers." Cover letter with brief bio preferred. Reports in 4-6 weeks. Pays 1 copy. "We reserve the right to reprint accepted poetry in future issues. Other than that, all rights revert back to the poet after publication."** They also publish 1- to 3-page essays dealing with veganism and social concerns similar to the periodical's poetic themes. The editor says, "I'd prefer to hear from poets sincerely interested in our magazine, as opposed to those merely concerned with adding another title to their list of publishing credits."

AGNI (II), Boston University, 236 Bay State Rd., Boston MA 02215, phone (617)353-5389, e-mail agni@acs.bu. edu, website http://www.cais.net/aesir/fiction/AGNI, founded 1972, editors Askold Melnyczuk and Valerie Duff.

AGNI is a biannual journal of poetry, fiction and essays "by both emerging and established writers. **We publish quite a bit of poetry in forms as well as 'language' poetry, but we don't begin to try and place parameters on the 'kind of work' that** *AGNI* **selects."** Editors seem to select readable, intelligent poetry—mostly lyric free verse (with some narrative and dramatic, too)—that somehow communicates tension or risk. They have published poetry by Derek Walcott, Thom Gunn, Maxine Scates, Rosanna Warren, Chinua Achebe and Ha Jin. *AGNI* is typeset, offset-printed and perfect-bound with about 40 poems featured in each issue. Circulation is 1,500 by subscription, mail order and bookstore sales. Subscription: $18. **Sample: $7. Submit 3 poems at a time. "No fancy fonts, gimmicks or preformatted reply cards. No work accepted via e-mail. Brief, sincere cover letters."** No previously published poems; simultaneous submissions OK. Reads submissions October 1 **through April 30 only. Mss received at other times will be returned unread. Reports in 2-5 months. Pays $10/page, $150 maximum, plus 2 copies and one-year subscription. Buys first serial rights.** *AGNI* also publishes Take Three, an annual series of work by three young poets in conjunction with Graywolf Press. Poets are chosen by *AGNI*'s editorial board. Work published in *AGNI* has been included in *The Best American Poetry* (1992, 1993, 1994, 1995 and 1997) and *Pushcart Prize* anthologies.

AG-PILOT INTERNATIONAL MAGAZINE (IV-Specialized), P.O. Box 1607, Mt. Vernon WA 98273, phone (360)336-9737, publisher Tom Wood, "is intended to be a fun-to-read, technical, as well as humorous and serious publication for the ag pilot and operator. Interested in **agricultural aviation (crop dusting) and aerial fire suppression (air tanker pilots) related poetry ONLY—something that rhymes and has a cadence."** As a sample we selected these lines from "Freedom" by Jack B. Harvey:

> So now I dress in faded jeans
> And beat up cowboy boots.
> My flying's done on veg'tables,
> The row crops, and the fruits.
>
> My wife now drives the flaggin' truck
> And marks off all my fields.
> She tells me all about the crops
> And talks about the yields.

It appears monthly, 64-96 pgs., 8½ × 10⅞, saddle-stapled, circulation 7,200. **Buys 1 poem/issue. Pays about $35.** Also publishes a Spanish-language version of *Ag-Pilot* titled *Volando*. For more information, contact managing editor Iris Carias at the above address.

THE AGUILAR EXPRESSION (I, II, IV-Social issues); EROS ERRANT (I, II), 1329 Gilmore Ave., Donora PA 15033, phone (412)379-8019, founded 1986, editor/publisher Xavier F. Aguilar. *Aguilar Expression* appears 2 times/year, and is **"open to all types of poetry, 24-line limit, including erotica that is well written. We insist that all writers send a SASE for writer's guidelines before submitting."** They have recently published poetry by Martin Kich and Gail Ghai. As a sample the editor selected these lines from "The Water Truck" by Donna Taylor Burgess:

> But pockets are as empty
> As the taps
> In a government day
> And water has never been free.

AE is 6-12 pgs., photocopied on 8½ × 11 sheets and corner stapled. They receive about 20-30 poems a month, use approximately 5-10 poems. Circulation is 200. **Sample postpaid: $6. Submit up to 3 poems at a time. "Send copies; mss will not be returned." Cover letter, including writing background, and SASE for contact purposes, required with submissions. Reports in 2 months. Pays 1 copy.** Open to unsolicited reviews. *Eros Errant* appears 2 times/year (June and December) and publishes poetry, fiction and b&w line art. They want poems with adult themes. The format of *EE* is similar to *AE*. Subscription: $5/year. **Sample postpaid: $3. Submit up to 5 poems at a time, 20-line limit/poem. No simultaneous submissions; previously published poems OK. Pays 1 copy. Acquires one-time rights. "We are also seeking poetry manuscripts as we wish to publish 1 or 2 chapbooks in 1998-1999. Send SASE for details."** The editor says, "In publishing poetry, I try to exhibit the unique reality that we too often take for granted and acquaint as mediocre. We encourage poetics that deal with *now*, which our readers can relate to. We are particularly interested in poetry dealing with social issues."

AHSAHTA PRESS; COLD-DRILL; COLD-DRILL BOOKS; POETRY IN PUBLIC PLACES (IV-Regional), English Dept., Boise State University, Boise ID 83725, phone (208)385-1999, e-mail ttrusky@quartz.idbsu.edu, website http://www.idbsu.edu/english, editor Tom Trusky. Ahsahta Press is a project to publish **contemporary poetry of the American West**. But, the editor says **"Don't send paens to the pommel, Jesus in the sagebrush, haiku about the Eiffel Tower, 'nice' or 'sweet' poems."** The work should **"draw on the cultures, history, ecologies of the American West."** They publish collections (45 pgs.) of individual poets in handsome flat-spined paperbacks with plain matte covers, with an appreciative introduction, at most 3/year. Occasionally they bring out an anthology of their authors on cassette. And they have published *Women Poets of the West*, an anthology (94 pgs.) with an introduction by Ann Stanford, and also *The Ahsahta Anthology* (277 pgs.). They have published poetry by Susan Deal, Leo Romero, David Baker, Linda Bierds, Philip St. Clair and Gretel

Ehrlich. As a sample here are lines from Wyn Cooper's "Fun," in the collection *The Country of Here Below* (set to music, it is Sheryl Crow's Grammy-winning "All I Wanna Do"):

> *"All I want is to have a little fun*
> *Before I die," says the man next to me*
> *Out of nowhere, apropos of nothing. He says*
> *His name is William but I'm sure he's Bill*
> *Or Billy, Mac or Buddy: he's plain ugly to me,*
> *And I wonder if he's ever had fun in his life.*

Submit only during their January 1 through March 31 reading period—a sample of 15 of your poems with SASE. Multiple and simultaneous submissions OK. They will report in about 2 months. If your sample is approved, a complete book ms is requested. If it is accepted, **you get 25 copies of the 1st and 2nd printings and a 25% royalty commencing with the 3rd. They seldom comment on the samples, frequently on the** mss. See their press samples and titles at their website and order a few books, if you don't find them in your library. "Old advice but true: Read what we publish before submitting. **75% of the submissions we receive should never have been sent to us. Save stamps, spirit and sweat."** *cold-drill* publishes **"primarily Boise State University students, faculty and staff, but will consider writings by Idahoans—or 'furriners.' "** They do some of the most creative publishing in this country today, and it is worth buying a **sample of *cold-drill* for $9** just to see what they're up to. This annual "has been selected as top undergraduate literary magazine in the U.S. by such important acronyms as CSPA, CCLM and UCDA." It comes in a box stuffed with various pamphlets, postcards, posters, a newspaper, even 3-D comics with glasses to read them by. **No restrictions on types of poetry.** Circulation is 400, including 100 subscribers, of which 20 are libraries. **"We read material throughout the year, notifying only those whose work we've accepted December 15 through January 1. Manuscripts should be photocopies with author's name and address on separate sheet. Simultaneous submissions OK. Payment: 1 copy."** They also publish two 24-page chapbooks and one 75-page flat-spined paperback/year. **Query about book publication.** "We want to publish a literary magazine that is exciting to read. We want more readers than just our contributors and their mothers. Our format and our content have allowed us to achieve those goals, so far." Poetry in Public Places is a series of 8 monthly posters/year "presenting the poets in Boise State University's creative students series and poets in BSU's Ahsahta Press poetry series." The posters are on coated stock. These, like all publications emanating from BSU, are elegantly done, with striking art.

AIM MAGAZINE (IV-Social issues, ethnic), 7308 S. Eberhart Ave., Chicago IL 60619, phone (312)874-6184, founded 1974, poetry editor Henry Blakely, is a quarterly, **"dedicated to racial harmony and peace." They use 3-4 poems ("poetry with social significance mainly"—average 32 lines) in each issue.** They have published poetry by J. Douglas Studer, Wayne Dowdy and Maria DeGuzman. *Aim* is magazine-sized with glossy cover, circulation 10,000. They receive about 30 submissions a year, use half. They have 3,000 subscribers of which 15 are libraries. Subscription: $10. **Sample postpaid: $4. Simultaneous submissions OK. Reports in 3-6 weeks. Pays $3/poem. You will not receive an acceptance slip: "We simply send payment and magazine copy."** The editor's advice: "Read the work of published poets."

‡*AKROS PUBLICATIONS; ZED₂O MAGAZINE (II), 33 Lady Nairn Ave., Kirkcaldy, Fife KY1 2AW Scotland, United Kingdom, founded 1965, contact Duncan Glen. *ZED₂O* is an annual poetry and the arts magazine containing a "variety of special topics in each issue." **They are open to all forms and length of poetry.** The editor says *ZED₂O* is 48 pgs., 210×130mm. They accept approximately 10% of work received. Press run is 500. Single copy: £2. **Make checks payable to Duncan Glen. Does not accept checks in US funds. Submit 6 poems at a time. No previously published poems or simultaneous submissions. Cover letter preferred.** "Submit hard copy initially; disks welcomed after acceptance if compatible with IBM—high density. We get many submissions from USA and UK without SASE or SAE and IRCs." Time between acceptance and publication is 9 months. **Always comments on rejections** "very briefly." **Publishes theme issues. Guidelines included inside magazine. Reports monthly. Sometimes sends prepublication galleys. No payment. Acquires first United Kingdom publication rights. Akros Publications is a poetry press**—"often publishing Scottish **poems."** The publish 1 paperback and **6 chapbooks/year.** Chapbooks (also called pamphlets in the U.K.) are 20 pgs., 210×130mm, offset litho printed. **Replies to queries in 2 months maximum, to mss "quickly." Pays 10% royalties and/or 6 author's copies (out of a press run of 500). "No royalties given if chapbooks are by new poets." Send SAE and IRCs for catalog.**

ALABAMA LITERARY REVIEW (II), English Dept., Troy State University, Troy AL 36082, phone (334)670-3286, fax (334)670-3519, poetry editor Ed Hicks, a biannual, **wants contemporary poetry that is "imagistic—** *but in motion."* **Will look at anything, but does not want to see "lyrics sent as poetry. We want serious craft."** They have published poetry by David Musgrove, R.T. Smith, Ed Peaco, Joanne M. Riley, Martha Payne,

---

† **THE DOUBLE DAGGER** before a listing indicates that the listing is new in this edition. New markets are often the most receptive to submissions.

Edward Byrne and Katherine McCanless. The beautifully printed 100-page, 7×10 magazine, matte cover with art, b&w art and some colored pages inside, receives 300 submissions/year, uses 30, has a 2-month backlog. **Sample postpaid: $5. Submit 2-5 poems at a time. "SASE with appropriate postage is paramount."** Simultaneous submissions OK. **Reads submissions September 1 through July 31 only. Sometimes comments on rejections. Reports in 2-3 months. Sometimes sends prepublication galleys. Pays copies, sometimes honorarium. Acquires first rights.** Open to unsolicited reviews. Poets may also send books for review consideration.

ALASKA QUARTERLY REVIEW (II), College of Arts and Sciences, University of Alaska Anchorage, 3211 Providence Dr., Anchorage AK 99508, phone/fax (907)786-6916, founded 1981, executive editor Ronald Spatz. "A journal devoted to contemporary literary art. **We publish both traditional and experimental fiction, poetry, literary nonfiction and short plays."** They have recently published poetry by Kim Addonizio, Tom Lux, Pattiann Rogers, John Balaban and Dorianne Laux. Editors seem to welcome all styles and forms of poetry with the most emphasis perhaps on voice and content that displays "risk," or intriguing ideas or situations. They publish two double-issues a year, **each using between 25-50 pgs. of poetry.** They receive up to 3,000 submissions a year, accept 40-60. They have a circulation of 1,500 for 450 subscribers of which 32 are libraries. Subscription: $8. **Sample postpaid: $5. Manuscripts are not read from May 15 through August 15. They take up to 4 months to report, sometimes longer during peak periods in late winter. Pay depends on funding. Acquires first North American serial rights.** Poetry published in *AQR* has been selected for inclusion in *The Best American Poetry 1996* and a *Pushcart Prize* anthology. Recent guest poetry editors have included Stuart Dybek, Jane Hirshfield, Stuart Dischell and Maxine Kumin.

ALBATROSS; THE ANABIOSIS PRESS (II, IV-Nature), P.O. Box 7787, North Port FL 34287-0787, phone (941)426-7019, founded 1985, editors Richard Smyth and Richard Brobst. *Albatross* appears: "as soon as we have accepted enough quality poems to publish an issue. **We consider the albatross to be a metaphor for an environment that must survive. This is not to say that we publish only environmental or nature poetry, but that we are biased toward such subject matters. We publish mostly free verse, 200 lines/poem maximum, and we prefer a narrative style, but again, this is not necessary. We do not want trite rhyming poetry which doesn't convey a deeply felt experience in a mature expression with words."** They have published poetry by Simon Perchik, Lyn Lifshin, Ann Newell, William Virgil Davis and Errol Miller. As a sample the editors selected these lines by Michael McMahon:

> a one bulb noon in the manger
> of childhood
> birth blood steaming
> on the straw as the black mare
> exhaled pain and angels

The magazine is 28-36 pgs., $5\frac{1}{2} \times 8\frac{1}{2}$, laser typeset with linen cover, some b&w drawings, and sometimes, in addition to the poetry, has an interview with a poet in each issue. Circulation is 300 for 75 subscribers of which 10 are libraries. Many complimentary copies are sent out to bookstores, poets and libraries. Subscription: $5/2 issues. **Sample postpaid: $3. Submit 3-5 poems at a time. "Poems should be typed single-spaced, with name and address in left corner and length in lines in right corner." No simultaneous submissions. Cover letter not required; "We do, however, need bio notes if published." Send SASE for guidelines. Reports in 4-6 months, has 6- to 12-month backlog. Pays 1 copy. Acquires all rights. Returns rights provided that "previous publication in** *Albatross* **is mentioned in all subsequent reprintings."** Also holds a chapbook contest. **Submit 20-24 pgs. of poetry, any theme, any style. Deadline is May 31 of each year. Include name, address and phone number on the title page. Charges $7 reading fee (check payable to** *Albatross***). Winner receives $100 and 25 copies of his/her published chapbook. All entering receive a free copy of the winning chapbook.** "The Anabiosis Press is a nonprofit, tax-exempt organization. Membership fee is $20/year." The editors say, "We expect a poet to read as much contemporary poetry as possible."

ALICEJAMESBOOKS; BEATRICE HAWLEY AWARD (IV-Regional, women, ethnic), University of Maine at Farmington, 98 Main St., Farmington ME 04938, phone/fax (207)778-7071, founded 1973, is "an author's collective which only publishes **poetry. Authors are primarily from the New England Area. We strongly encourage submissions by poets of color."** They publish flat-spined paperbacks of high quality, both in production and contents, no children's poetry. Their books have won numerous awards and been very respectably reviewed. "Each poet becomes a working member of the co-op with a two-year work commitment." That is, you have to live close enough to **attend meetings and participate in the editorial and publishing process.** They publish about 4 books, 72 pgs., each year in editions of 1,000, paperbacks—no hardbacks. **Query first, but no need for samples: simply ask for dates of reading period, which is in early fall and winter. May contact by phone or fax for submission guidelines only. Send 2 copies of the ms. Simultaneous submissions OK, but "we would like to know when a manuscript is being submitted elsewhere." Reports in 2-3 months. Pays authors 100 paperback copies.** Offers Beatrice Hawley Award for poets who cannot meet the work requirement due to geographical restraints. Their book *The Moon Reflected Fire*, by Doug Anderson, won the Kate Tufts Discovery Award for 1995.

ALIVE NOW (IV-Spirituality, themes); POCKETS (IV-Religious, children, themes); DEVO'ZINE (IV-Religious, youth, themes); WEAVINGS; THE UPPER ROOM (V), 1908 Grand Ave., P.O. Box 189, Nashville TN 37202, phone (615)340-7200. This publishing company brings out about 30 books a year and 5 magazines: *The Upper Room, Alive Now, Pockets, Devo'Zine* and *Weavings*. Of these, three use unsolicited poetry. *Pockets, Devotional Magazine for Children*, which comes out 11 times/year, circulation 90,000, is for children 6-12, "offers stories, activities, prayers, poems—all **geared to giving children a better understanding of themselves as children of God. Some of the material is not overtly religious but deals with situations, special seasons and holidays, and ecological concerns from a Christian perspective.**" It uses 3-4 pgs. of poetry/issue. **Sample free with 7½×10½ SAE and 4 first-class stamps. Ordinarily 24-line limit on poetry. Send SASE for themes and guidelines. Pays $25-50.** The second magazine which uses poetry is *Alive Now*, editor George Graham, a bimonthly, circulation 75,000, for a general Christian audience interested in reflection and meditation. **They buy 30 poems a year, avant-garde and free verse. Submit 5 poems, 10-45 lines. Send SASE for themes and guidelines. Pays $10-25.** The third magazine that uses poetry is *Devo'Zine: Just for Teens*, a bimonthly devotional magazine for youth ages 12-18, offers meditations, scripture, prayers, poems, stories, songs and feature articles to **"aid youth in their prayer life, introduce them to spiritual disciplines, help them shape their concept of God, and encourage them in the life of discipleship."** Ordinarily 20-line limit on poetry. Send SASE for theme and guidelines. Pays $20. *The Upper Room* **magazine does not accept poetry.**

ALLEGHENY REVIEW (I, IV-Undergraduate students), Dept. PM, Box 32, Allegheny College, Meadville PA 16335, phone (814)332-6533, e-mail review@alleg.edu, website http://www.alleg.edu/Student/Organizations/AllegReviews, founded 1983. "Each year *Allegheny Review* compiles and publishes a review of the nation's best **undergraduate literature.** It is entirely composed of and by college undergraduates and is nationally distributed both as a review and as a classroom text, particularly suited to creative writing courses." In the Fall of 1995, they added a section of essays on poetry and literature. (Submit 10-15 typed pgs., double-spaced.) "We will print **poetry of appreciable literary merit on any topic, submitted by college undergraduates. No limitations except excessive length (2-3 pgs.)** as we wish to represent as many authors as possible, although exceptions are made in areas of great quality and interest." They have published poetry by Eric Sanborn, Cheryl Connor, Rick Alley and Kristi Coulter. The *Review* appears in a 6×9, flat-spined, professionally-printed format, b&w photo on glossy card cover. Single copy: $5. **Sample: $4 and 11×18 SASE. Submit 3-5 poems, typed. Submissions should be accompanied by a letter "telling the college poet is attending, year of graduation, any background, goals and philosophies the author feels are pertinent to the work submitted." Reports 1-2 months following deadline. Poem judged best in the collection earns $50-75 honorarium.** "Ezra Pound gave the best advice: 'Make it new.' We're seeing far too much imitation; there's already been a Sylvia Plath, a Galway Kinnell. Don't be afraid to try new things. Be innovative. Also, traditional forms are coming 'back in style,' or so we hear. Experiment with them; write a villanelle, a sestina or a sonnet. And when you submit, please take enough pride in your work to do so professionally. Handwritten or poorly typed and proofed submissions definitely convey an impression—a negative one.'"

ALMS HOUSE PRESS; THE ALMS HOUSE JOURNAL (I), P.O. Box 217, Pearl River NY 10965-0217, fax (914)735-5628, founded 1985, poetry editors Lorraine De Gennaro and Alana Sherman, publishes the biannual *Alms House Journal* and 3-4 chapbooks/perfect-bound books per year. **"We have no preferences with regard to style as long as the poetry is high caliber. We like to see previous publication in the small press, but we are open to new writers. We look for variety and excellence and are open to experimental forms as well as traditional forms. Any topics as long as the poems are not whiny or too depressing, pornographic or religious."** They have recently published chapbooks by Stephen R. Roberts. As a sample the editors selected these lines of poetry:

> *Always before they strained*
> *deeply in two directions*
> *to break soil, stone, horizon.*
> *Smoke now rises softly*
> *higher than any branch or limb*
> *Coils to shape the clouds*

For *AHJ*, **submit 3-5 poems at a time with $5 reading fee. For chapbooks, submit 16- to 24-page ms with $15 reading fee; for longer collections, submit up to 50 pages with $25 reading fee. All mss must be typed with 1 poem/page. No previously published poems or simultaneous submissions. Reads submissions September 1 through February 28 only. Send SASE for guidelines or request via fax. Reports in 2-3 months. Press pays $25 plus 10 copies and 7% of all sales over first 100 books.** They sponsor a poetry reading series and offer a critical and editorial service for $50. The editors say, "We treat every poem, every manuscript and every author with respect. We believe poetry should be well presented."

ALOHA, THE MAGAZINE OF HAWAII AND THE PACIFIC (IV-Regional), P.O. Box 3260, Honolulu HI 96801, phone (808)593-1191, fax (808)593-1327, editorial director Cheryl Chee Tsutsumi, is a bimonthly (every 2 months) "consumer magazine with a Hawaii and Pacific focus. **Not interested in lengthy poetry. Poems should be limited to 100 words or less. Subject matter should be focused on Hawaii.**" *Aloha* is 64 pgs., magazine-sized, flat-spined, elegantly printed on glossy stock with many full-color pages, glossy card cover in color. They publish 6 of the more than 50 poems received/year. Circulation is 95,000. **Sample: $2.95 plus $2.62 p&h. Ms should be typed, double-spaced, with name, address and phone number included.** Poems are matched to color photos, so it is "difficult to say" how long it will be between acceptance and publication. **Send SASE for guidelines. Reports within 2 months. Pays $30 plus 1 copy (and up to 10 at a discount rate).**

ALPHA BEAT SOUP; ALPHA BEAT PRESS (I, IV-Form/style), 31 Waterloo St., New Hope PA 18938-1210, phone (215)862-0299, founded 1987, poetry editor David Christy, appears irregularly **emulating the Beat literary tradition.** *Alpha Beat Soup* is "an international poetry and arts journal featuring Beat, 'post-Beat independent' and modern writing." Christy says **25% of each issue is devoted to little known or previously unpublished poets.** They have recently published works by Pradip Choudhuri, elliott, Joe Rochette, Steve Richmond and A.D. Winans. As a sample the editor selected these lines by Joe Verrilli:

> it's always the sensitive one
> the vulnerable soul
> sought out by the vultures
> of this society.

ABS is 50-75 pgs., $7 \times 8\frac{1}{2}$, photocopied from IBM laser printer, card cover offset, graphics included. They use 50% of the poetry received. Press run is 600 for 400 subscribers of which 11 are libraries. Single copy: $8; subscription: $15. **Sample postpaid: $10. Submit 3-6 poems at a time. Simultaneous submissions and previously published poems OK. Cover letter, including "an introduction to the poet's work," required. Editor comments on rejections "only on request." Sometimes sends prepublication galleys. Pays 1 copy.** Reviews books of poetry in approximately 700 words, multi-book format. Open to unsolicited reviews. Poets may also send books for review consideration. **Alpha Beat Press publishes chapbooks and supplements as well as a monthly broadside series featuring unknown poets. They offer cooperative publishing of chapbooks, "as a way to fund our press and also showcase the unknown poet." Write for details.** Also see the listings for *Bouillabaisse* and *Cokefish*.

AMARANTH (II), P.O. Box 184, Trumbull CT 06611, phone (203)452-9652, founded 1995, editors Becky Rodia and Christopher Sanzeni, is a biannual poetry journal. **The editors would like to see "formal and free verse with clear, concrete imagery; a good sense of sound and rhythm; and attention to line and stanza breaks. Though any subject matter or form is welcome, we especially enjoy prose poems and 'personal' poems. However, we don't have the space to print anything over 70 lines. Please refrain from sending us poems without punctuation and poems which employ the lowercase 'i.' "** They have recently published poetry by Charles H. Webb, Gary Young and Walt McDonald. As a sample the editors selected these lines from "Two Housewives" by Gray Jacobik:

> Sitting across from each other afternoons,
> out babies corralled nearby, we intensified
> one another's misery. A strewn cornucopia
> of toys. Coffee or tea, cookies, and through
> half-curtained windows, as if to expose
> any hidden life, road glare whitened the walls.

Amaranth is 36-40 pgs., $5\frac{1}{2} \times 8\frac{1}{2}$, professionally printed and saddle-stapled with glossy card cover with full-color artwork. They receive about 1,000 poems a year, accept approximately 5%. Press run is 1,000. Subscription: $10. **Sample (including guidelines) postpaid: $6. Submit 3-5 poems at a time, name and address on each. No previously published poems; simultaneous submissions OK, "but please notify us immediately if the work is accepted elsewhere." Cover letter preferred. Often comments on rejections. Send SASE for guidelines. Reports in 3 months, longer if under serious consideration. Sometimes sends prepublication galleys. Pays 2 copies, additional copies available at a discount. Rights revert to authors upon publication.** The editors review chapbooks and books in under 1,000 words, single format. Poets may send books for review consideration. They also plan to run occasional contests. Watch the trade publications for announcements. They add, " 'Amaranth' means 'flower which never fades' and we look for poems that are beautiful, but timeless, hardy, universal and human. We expect our contributors to be well-read in contemporary poetry and to be familiar with the literary publications available these days."

♣AMBER; MARSH & MAPLE (I, II), 40 Rose St., #404, Dartmouth, Nova Scotia B3A 2T6 Canada, phone (902)461-4934, founded 1967, editor Hazel F. Goddard, appears 4 times/year (in January, April, July and October). "*Amber* and its one-page supplement, *Marsh & Maple*, promote and distribute current work. *Amber* is nonprofit, entirely subscription-supported." **They want "free verse, half page, regular line lengths (not over 56 characters preferred), also haiku and occasional sonnet. Any subject, but must be in good taste, *not vulgar.* Original, bright content. No religious verse. Prefer poems to be seasonal, if on nature."** They have published poetry by John D. Engle, Jr., Diana K. Rubin and Tony Cosier. *Amber* is 28 pgs., digest-sized, photocopied on colored paper and saddle-stapled with paper cover. They receive about 500 poems a year, use roughly 70%. Press run is 100 for 90 subscribers of which 3 are libraries. Single copy: $2.50; subscription: $10. **Sample postpaid: $1. Submit 2 poems at a time. Every sheet should bear the poet's name. Previously published poems OK; no simultaneous submissions.** Time between acceptance and publication is 1-6 months. **Seldom comments on**

rejections. **Publishes theme issues. Send SASE (or SAE and IRC) for upcoming themes.** "First acceptance paid for with 1 free copy; continuing submissions expected to be covered by a subscription." The editor says, "I receive many books of poets' poems. If up to an average standard I select from them for publication in my magazine. Most poems are from well-crafted poets, a few new writers. Need not be professional but *must* be good work. When space allows, I list contests poets may like to enter, comment on books poets send and devote centrefold to personal chatting, poets' successes, etc."

*AMBIT (III), 17 Priory Gardens, Highgate, London N6 5QY England, phone 0181-340-3566, editor Martin Bax; poetry editors Edwin Brock, Carol Ann Duffy and Henry Graham; prose editors J.G. Ballard and Geoff Nicholson; and art editor Mike Foreman. *Ambit* is a 96-page quarterly of **avant-garde, contemporary and experimental work.** Subscription: £22 individuals, £33 institutions (UK); £24 ($48) individuals, £35 ($70) institutions (overseas). **Sample: £6. Submit 6 poems at a time, typed double-spaced. No previously published poems or simultaneous submissions. Pay is** "variable plus 2 free copies." Staff reviews books of poetry. Send books for review consideration, attn. Review Editor.

AMELIA; CICADA; SPSM&H; THE AMELIA AWARDS (II, IV-Form), 329 "E" St., Bakersfield CA 93304 or P.O. Box 2385, Bakersfield CA 93303, phone (805)323-4064. *Amelia*, founded 1983, poetry editor Frederick A. Raborg, Jr., is a quarterly magazine that publishes chapbooks as well. Central to its operations is a series of contests, most with entry fees, spaced evenly throughout the year, awarding more than $3,500 annually, but they publish many poets who have not entered the contests as well. Among poets published are Pattiann Rogers, Stuart Friebert, John Millett, David Ray, Larry Rubin, Charles Bukowski, Maxine Kumin, Charles Edward Eaton and Shuntaro Tanikawa. They are **"receptive to all forms to 100 lines. We do not want to see the patently-religious or overtly-political. Erotica is fine; pornography, no."** The digest-sized, flat-spined magazine is offset on high-quality paper and sometimes features an original four-color cover; its circulation is about 1,556, with 612 subscribers, of which 28 are libraries. Subscription: $25/year. **Sample postpaid: $8.95. Submit 3-5 poems at a time. No simultaneous submissions except for entries to the annual Amelia Chapbook Award. Reports in 2-12 weeks, the latter if under serious consideration. Pays $2-25/poem plus 2 copies. "Almost always I try to comment."** The editor says, "*Amelia* is not afraid of strong themes, but we do look for professional, polished work even in handwritten submissions. Poets should have something to say about matters other than the moon. We like to see strong **traditional pieces as well as the contemporary and experimental. And neatness** *does* **count."** Fred Raborg has done more than most other editors to ensure a wide range of styles and forms, from traditional European to Asian, from lyric to narrative. Typically he is swamped with submissions and so response times can exceed stated parameters. *Amelia* continues to place in outside surveys as a top market, because of editorial openness. Brief reviews are also featured. As for Raborg's other publications, *Cicada* is a quarterly magazine that publishes **haiku, senryu and other Japanese forms**, plus essays on the form—techniques and history—as well as fiction which in some way incorporates haiku or Japanese poetry in its plot, and reviews of books pertaining to Japan and its poetry or collections of haiku. Among poets published are Roger Ishii, H.F. Noyes, Knute Skinner, Katherine Machan Aal, Ryah Tumarkin Goodman and Ryokufu Ishizaki. They are **receptive to experimental forms as well as the traditional. "Try to avoid still-life as haiku; strive for the** *whole* **of an emotion, whether minuscule or panoramic. Erotica is fine; the Japanese are great lovers of the erotic."** The magazine is offset on high-quality paper. Circulation is 600, with 432 subscribers of which 26 are libraries. Subscription: $14/year. **Sample postpaid: $4.95. Submit 3-10 haiku or poems. No simultaneous submissions. Reports in 2 weeks. No payment, except three "best of issue" poets each receive $10 on publication plus copy. "I try to make some comment on returned poems always."** *SPSM&H* is a quarterly magazine that publishes **only sonnets, sonnet sequences**, essays on the form—both technique and history—as well as romantic or Gothic fiction which, in some way, incorporates the form, and reviews of sonnet collections or collections containing a substantial number of sonnets. They are **"receptive to experimental forms as well as the traditional, and appreciate wit when very good."** Among poets published are Margaret Ryan, Harold Witt, Sharon E. Martin, Rhina P. Espaillat and Robert Wolfkill. Perhaps it may help to know the editor's favorite Shakespearean sonnet is #29, and he feels John Updike clarified the limits of experimentation with the form in his "Love Sonnet" from *Midpoint*. The magazine is offset on high-quality paper. Circulation is 600, for 432 subscribers and 26 libraries. Subscription: $14/year. **Sample postpaid: $4.95. Submit 3-5 poems at a time. No simultaneous submissions. Reports in 2 weeks. No payment, except two "best of issue" poets each receive $14 on publication plus copy. "I always try to comment on returns."** The following annual contests have various entry fees: The Amelia Awards (six prizes of $200, $100, $50 plus three honorable mentions of $10 each); The Anna B. Janzen Prize for Romantic Poetry ($100, annual deadline January 2); The Bernice Jennings Traditional Poetry Award ($100, annual deadline January 2); The Georgie Starbuck Galbraith Light/Humorous Verse Prizes (six awards of $100, $50, $25 plus three honorable mentions of $5 each, annual deadline March 1); The Charles William Duke Longpoem Award ($100, annual deadline April 1); The Lucille Sandberg Haiku Awards (six awards of $100, $50, $25 plus three honorable mentions of $5 each, annual deadline April 1); The Grace Hines Narrative Poetry Award ($100, annual deadline May 1); The Amelia Chapbook Award ($250, book publication and 50 copies, annual deadline July 1); The Johanna B. Bourgoyne Poetry Prizes (six awards of $100, $50, $25, plus three honorable mentions of $5 each); The Douglas Manning Smith Epic/Heroic Poetry Prize ($100, annual deadline August 1); The Hildegarde Janzen Prize for Oriental Forms of Poetry (six awards of $50, $30, $20 and three honorable mentions of $5 each, annual deadline September 1); The Eugene Smith Prize for

Sonnets (six awards of $140, $50, $25 and three honorable mentions of $5 each); The A&C Limerick Prizes (six awards of $50, $30, $20 and three honorable mentions of $5 each); The Montegue Wade Lyric Poetry Prize ($100, annual deadline November 1).

AMERICA; FOLEY POETRY CONTEST (II), 106 W. 56th St., New York NY 10019, phone (212)581-4640, founded 1909, poetry editor Patrick Samway, S.J., is a weekly journal of opinion published by the Jesuits of North America. They primarily publish articles on religious, social, political and cultural themes. **They are "looking for imaginative poetry of all kinds. We have no restrictions on form or subject matter, though we prefer to receive poems of 35 lines or less."** They have recently published poetry by Howard Nemerov, Fred Chappell, William Heyen and John Frederick Nims. *America* is 36 pgs., magazine-sized, professionally printed on thin stock with thin paper cover. Circulation is 35,000. Subscription: $38. **Sample postpaid: $1.75. Send SASE for excellent guidelines. Reports in 2 weeks. Pays $1.40/line plus 2 copies.** The annual Foley Poetry Contest offers a prize of $500, usually in late winter. Send SASE for rules. "Poems for the Foley Contest should be submitted between January and April. Poems submitted for the Foley Contest between July and December will normally be returned unread." The editor says, "*America* is committed to publishing quality poetry as it has done for the past 87 years. We encourage beginning and established poets to submit their poems to us."

AMERICAN ATHEIST PRESS; GUSTAV BROUKAL PRESS; AMERICAN ATHEIST (IV-Specialized), P.O. Box 140195, Austin TX 78714-0195, phone (512)458-1244, founded 1958, editor Frank Zindler, publishes the biannual magazine with 40,000 circulation, *American Atheist*, and under various imprints some dozen books a year reflecting "concerns of atheists, such as separation of state and church, civil liberties and atheist news." **Poetry is used primarily in the poetry section of the magazine. It must have "a particular slant to atheism, dealing with subjects such as the atheist lifestyle. Anticlerical poems and puns are more than liable to be rejected. Any form or style is acceptable. Preferred length is under 40 lines."** They have published poetry by Julia Rhodes Pozonzycki, Allan Case and Thomas A. Easton. The magazine-sized format is professionally printed, with art and photos, glossy, color cover. They receive over 20-30 poetry submissions/week, use about 12/year. Of their 17,000 subscriptions, 1,000 are libraries. Single copy: $2.95; subscription: $25. **Sample free. Submit 6-8 poems at a time, typed and double-spaced. Simultaneous submissions OK. Seasonal poems should be submitted 4 months in advance. Guidelines and upcoming themes available for SASE, but a label is preferred to an envelope. Reports within 3-4 months. Pays "first-timers" 10 copies or 6-month subscription or $12 credit voucher for AAP products. Thereafter, $15/poem plus 10 copies. Buys one-time rights. Sometimes comments on rejected mss.** Reviews related books of poetry in 500-1,000 words. They do not normally publish poetry in book form but will consider it.

THE AMERICAN COWBOY POET MAGAZINE (I, IV-Cowboy), Dept. PM, P.O. Box 326, Eagle ID 83616, phone (208)888-9838, fax (208)887-0082, e-mail acpm@cyberhighway.net, founded 1988 as *The American Cowboy Poet Newspaper*, magazine format in January 1991, publisher Rudy Gonzales, editor Rose Fitzgerald. *ACPM* is a quarterly "about real cowboys" using **"authentic cowboy poetry. Must be clean—entertaining. Submissions should avoid 'like topics.' We will not publish any more poems about Old Blackie dying, this old hat, if this pair of boots could talk, etc. We do not publish free verse poetry. Only traditional cowboy poetry with rhyme and meter."** They also publish articles, including a "Featured Poet," stories of cowboy poetry gatherings, and news of coming events. Subscription: $12/year US, $15 Canada, $20 Overseas. **Sample postpaid: $3.50. Cover letter required with submissions. Send SASE for guidelines or request via e-mail. Editor always comments on rejections.** Staff reviews related books and tapes of poetry. Send books and cowboy music tapes for review consideration.

AMERICAN INDIAN STUDIES CENTER; AMERICAN INDIAN CULTURE AND RESEARCH JOURNAL (IV-Ethnic/nationality), 3220 Campbell Hall, Box 951548, UCLA, Los Angeles CA 90095-1548, phone (310)825-7315, fax (310)206-7060, e-mail aisc@UCLA.edu, website http://www.sscnet.UCLA.edu/Indian/, founded 1975. The *American Indian Culture and Research Journal* is a quarterly which publishes new research and literature about American Indians. **All work must have Native American content.** The editor says the journal is 300 pgs., 5×9, perfect-bound. They receive about 20-50 poems a year, accept approximately 10-15. Press run is 1,200 for 1,000 subscribers of which 400 are libraries, 10 shelf sales. Subscription: $25 individual, $35 institution. **Sample: $7.50. Make checks payable to Regents of the University of California. Submit 5-6 poems at a time. No previously published poems or simultaneous submissions. Cover letter preferred.** Time between acceptance and publication is 6 months. **Poems are circulated to an editorial board. Often comments on rejections. Publishes theme issues. Reports in 2 months. Always sends prepublication galleys. Pays 1 copy.** The American Indian Studies Center also publishes 1-2 paperback books of poetry in their Native American Literature Series. They have published *The Light on the Tent Wall: A Bridging* by Mary TallMountain and *Old Shirts & New Skins* by Sherman Alexie. **Pays author's copies and offers 40% discount on additional copies.** Send SASE for a complete list of the center's publications.

AMERICAN LITERARY REVIEW (II), University of North Texas, P.O. Box 311307, Denton TX 76203-1307, phone (940)565-4670, editor Barbara Rodman, poetry editor Bruce Bond, is a biannual publishing **all**

forms and modes of poetry. "We are especially interested in originality, substance, imaginative power and lyric intensity." They have recently published poetry by Christopher Howell, David Citino, Laura Kasischke, Lee Upton, William Stafford and Pattiann Rogers. **Sample postpaid: $8. Submit up to 5 poems at a time. Reports in 2 months. Pays copies.**

‡**AMERICAN POETRY MONTHLY (I, II)**, P.O. Box 187, Sapulpa OK 74067, founded 1997 (first issue appeared in May), editor David L. Moore, "publishes quality poetry that moves or enlightens the reader. At *American Poetry*, we hope to reach an entirely new audience with the written word, while not alienating dedicated and long-time poetry readers. We wish to publish poems for people—not necessarily professors—while still maintaining the highest standards for the poetry that appears in the magazine. We hope to publish every poet who is worthy of appearing in print." **They want all styles, subject matter and lengths. No "blatantly religious or spiteful poetry; poetry without depth or substance."** They have recently published poetry by John M. Bennett, Ana Christy and Justin Martino. The editor says *APM* is 28 pgs., digest-sized, professionally printed and saddle-stapled with card cover, some art and ads. Press run is 100, 75 shelf sales. Subscription: $22. **Sample postpaid: $2. Make checks payable to David L. Moore. Submit 5 poems at a time. No previously published poems; simultaneous submissions OK. Cover letter preferred including bio and credits.** Time between acceptance and publication is 2-6 months. **Often comments on rejections. Send SASE for guidelines. Reports in 2-4 weeks. Pays 1 copy.** "We reserve space for poets to advertise their chapbooks, collections, and broadsides at affordable rates. We also publish a special issue each year, in which only the works of subscribers who did not appear the previous year in *APM* will be eligible for publication."

AMERICAN POETRY REVIEW (III), Dept. PM, 1721 Walnut St., Philadelphia PA 19103, phone (215)496-0439, fax (215)569-0808, founded 1972, is probably the **most widely circulated (18,000 copies bimonthly) and best-known periodical devoted to poetry in the world**. Poetry editors are Stephen Berg, David Bonanno and Arthur Vogelsang, and they have **published most of the leading poets writing in English and many translations**. The poets include Gerald Stern, Brenda Hillman, John Ashbery, Norman Dubie, Marvin Bell, Galway Kinnell, James Dickey, Lucille Clifton and Tess Gallagher. *APR* is a newsprint tabloid with 13,000 subscriptions, of which 1,000 are libraries. They receive about 8,000 submissions a year, accept approximately 200. This popular publication contains mostly free verse (some leaning to the avant-garde) with flashes of brilliance in every issue. Editors seem to put an emphasis on language and voice. Because *APR* is a tabloid, it can feature long poems (or ones with long line lengths) in an attractive format. Translations are also welcome. In all, this is a difficult market to crack because of the volume of submissions. **Sample postpaid: $3.50. No simultaneous submissions. Reports in 3 months, has 1- to 3-year backlog. Always sends prepublication galleys. Pays $2/line.** The magazine is also a major resource for opinion, reviews, theory, news and ads pertaining to poetry. Each year the editors award the Jerome J. Shestack Prizes of $1,000, $500 and $250 for the best poems, in their judgment, published in *APR*. Poetry published here has also been included in the 1992, 1993, 1994, 1995 and 1997 volumes of *The Best American Poetry*.

THE AMERICAN SCHOLAR (III), 1811 Q St. NW, Washington DC 20009, phone (202)265-3808, founded 1932, associate editor Sandra Costich, is an academic quarterly which **uses about 5 poems/issue. "We would like to see poetry that develops an image, a thought or event, without the use of a single cliché or contrived archaism. The most hackneyed subject matter is self-conscious love; the most tired verse is iambic pentameter with rhyming endings. The usual length of our poems is 30 lines. Up to 4 poems may be submitted at one time;** *no more* **for a careful reading."** They have published poetry by Robert Pack, Alan Shapiro and Gregory Djanikian. What little poetry is used in this high-prestige magazine is accomplished, intelligent and open (in terms of style and form). Study before submitting (**sample: $6.95, guidelines available for SASE**). **Reports in 2 months. Always sends prepublication galleys. Pays $50/poem. Buys first rights only.**

‡**AMERICAN TANKA (IV-Form/style)**, P.O. Box 49046, Austin TX 78765, e-mail amtanka@usa.net, website http://www.erols.com/mjus/amtanka, founded 1996, contact editor, appears twice a year (Spring and Fall) and is devoted to single **English-language tanka. They want "concise and vivid language, good crafting, and echo of the original Japanese form." They do not want anything that is not tanka.** *American Tanka* is 65-85 pgs., 8½×5½, perfect-bound with glossy cover, b&w original drawings, no ads. Single copy: $10; subscription: $20. **Sample postpaid: $8. Submit 5 poems at a time. No previously published poems or simultaneous submissions. Electronic submissions OK. Submission deadlines: August 15 for Fall, February 15 for Spring.** Time between acceptance and publication is 1-2 months. **Send SASE for guidelines. Reports in 4-6 weeks. Pays 1 copy. Acquires first North American serial rights.** "The tanka form is rapidly growing in popularity in the West because of its emotional accessibility and because it is an exquisite way to capture a moment in one's life."

AMERICAN TOLKIEN SOCIETY; MINAS TIRITH EVENING-STAR; W.W. PUBLICATIONS (IV-Specialized, themes), P.O. Box 373, Highland MI 48357-0373, phone/fax (813)585-0985, founded 1967, editor Philip W. Helms. There are special poetry issues. Membership in the ATS is open to all, regardless of country of residence, and entitles one to receive the quarterly journal. Dues are $10 per annum to addresses in US, $12.50 in Canada and $15 elsewhere. Their journal and chapbooks use **poetry of fantasy about Middle-**

AMERICAN TANKA

$8.00

Issue 1 • Fall 1996

"In *American Tanka*, each poem speaks of one particular moment in that poet's life," says Laura Maffei, editor and founder of the biannual Texas-based publication. "The simple layout and original b&w drawings allow the reader to focus upon the single tanka and the moment it expresses." The white origami crane, which appears on the premier issue's cover, is the journal's logo and also an "easily-recognizable symbol of Japanese culture and aesthetics." Says Maffei, "I chose this gouache painting because of its beautiful simplicity. Also, this cover pays tribute to the fact that the tanka is a Japanese poetry form written continuously in Japan for over 1,300 years." *American Tanka* is committed to the growth of English-language tanka and to continued recognition of the Japanese nature of the form. Cover painting by Michelle Egan.

Earth and Tolkien. They have published poetry by Thomas M. Egan, Anne Etkin, Nancy Pope and Martha Benedict. *Minas Tirith Evening-Star* is magazine-sized, offset from typescript with cartoon-like b&w graphics. Press run is 400 for 350 subscribers of which 10% are libraries. Single copy: $3.50; subscription: $10. **Sample postpaid: $1.50. Make checks payable to American Tolkien Society. No simultaneous submissions; previously published poems "maybe." Cover letter preferred. "We do not return phone calls unless collect."** Editor sometimes comments on rejections. Publishes theme issues occasionally. Send SASE for guidelines. **Reports in 2 weeks. Sometimes sends prepublication galleys. Pays contributor's copies.** Reviews related books of poetry; length depends on the volume, "a sentence to several pages." Open to unsolicited reviews. Poets may also send books to Paul Ritz, Reviews, P.O. Box 901, Clearwater FL 34617 for review consideration. Under imprint of W.W. Publications they publish collections of poetry 50-100 pgs. **For book or chapbook consideration, submit sample poems. Publishes 2 chapbooks/year.** They sometimes sponsor contests.

THE AMERICAN VOICE (II), 332 W. Broadway, Louisville KY 40202, phone (502)562-0045, founded 1985, editor Frederick Smock, is a literary quarterly publishing North and South American writers. They prefer **free verse, avant-garde, in areas such as ethnic/nationality, gay/lesbian, translation, women/feminism and literary.** They have published poetry by Olga Broumas, Odysseus Elytis, Cheryl Clarke, Marge Piercy and Ernesto Cardenal. *TAV* is 140 pgs. of high-quality stock, elegantly printed and flat-spined with matte card cover. Editors seem to prefer lyric free verse, much of it accessible, by well-known and new writers. Circulation is 2,000 for 1,000 subscribers of which 100 are libraries. Subscription: $15/year. **Sample postpaid: $7. No simultaneous submissions. Cover letter requested. Occasionally comments on rejections. Reports in 6 weeks, has a 3-month backlog. Pays $100/poem and 2 copies. (They pay $50 to translator of a poem.)** Open to unsolicited reviews. Poets may also send books for review consideration. *The American Voice* has received an *Utne Reader* Alternative Press Award and has had work included in *The Best American Poetry* (1995 and 1996 volumes) and *Pushcart Prize* anthologies.

AMERICAN WRITING: A MAGAZINE; NIERIKA EDITIONS (IV-Form/style), 4343 Manayunk Ave., Philadelphia PA 19128, founded 1990, editor Alexandra Grilikhes, appears twice a year using **poetry that is "experimental and the voice of the loner, writing that takes risks with form, interested in the powers of intuition and states of being. No cerebral, academic poetry. Poets often try to make an experience 'literary' through language, instead of going back to the original experience and finding the original images. That is what we are interested in: the voice that speaks those images."** They have published poetry by Ivan Argüelles, Antler, Eleanor Wilner, Diane Glancy and Margaret Holley. *AW* is 88 pgs., digest-sized, professionally

 THE MAPLE LEAF symbol before a listing indicates a Canadian publisher, magazine, conference, contest or organization.

printed and flat-spined with matte card cover. Press run is 1,000 for 350 subscribers. Subscription: $10. **Sample postpaid: $6. Submit 8 poems at a time. No previously published poems; simultaneous submissions OK. Guidelines on subscription form. Reports anywhere from 6 weeks to 6 months. Pays 2 copies/accepted submission group.** Since *American Writing* began in 1990, 20 of the authors they have published won national awards after publication in the magazine. The editor says, "Many magazines print the work of the same authors (the big names) who often publish 'lesser' works that way. *AW* is interested in the work itself, its particular strength, energy and voice, not necessarily in the 'status' of the authors. We like to know *something* about the authors, however. We recommend reading a sample issue before just blindly submitting work."

✤**THE AMETHYST REVIEW (I, II)**, 23 Riverside Ave., Truro, Nova Scotia B2N 4G2 Canada, phone (902)895-1345, e-mail amethyst@atcon.com, website http://www.amethyst@atcon.com, founded 1992, editors Penny Ferguson and Lenora Steele, is a biannual publication of poetry, prose and black ink art. **They want "quality, contemporary poetry to 200 lines. No bad rhyme and meter."** They have published poetry by Joe Blades and Liliane Welch. As a sample the editors selected these lines from "Shade Garden of Your Bones" by Shawna Lemay:

> *For me, it was not the rape itself*
> *which leaves its trace on the body*
> *the way espresso stains white linen*
> *and on the heart which is soft and spongy and forgets*
> *for me, it was not even the seven months trial,*
> *but the sibille*

TAR is 84 pgs., about $7 \times 8\frac{1}{2}$, perfect-bound with colored recycled paper cover and b&w art on the cover and inside. They receive 500-600 poems a year, accept approximately 10%. Press run is 150 for 100 subscribers of which 5 are libraries, 25 shelf sales. Single copy: $6 Canadian; subscription: $12 Canadian, $14 US. **Sample (including guidelines) postpaid: $4 US or Canadian. Submit 5 poems at a time. No previously published poems or simultaneous submissions. Cover letter preferred. No e-mail submissions; inquiries via e-mail OK. Always comments on rejections. Send SASE (or SAE and IRC) for guidelines. Reports in 6 months maximum, "usually in 1-2 months." Pays 1 copy. Acquires first North American serial rights.** Occasionally reviews books of poetry published by contributors only. They also sponsor an annual contest with a theme which changes each year. The contest fee is the cost of (and includes) a subscription. First prize is $50 Canadian. Send SASE (or SAE and IRC) for details. The editors add, "Therapy is not always good poetry. The craft must be the important focus."

THE AMHERST REVIEW (II), Box 1811, Amherst College, P.O. Box 5000, Amherst MA 01002-5000, is an annual literary magazine seeking quality submissions in fiction, poetry, nonfiction and photography/artwork. **"All kinds of poetry welcome."** The editor says the review is 50 pgs., 5×8, soft cover with photography, art and graphics. They receive 300-500 poems a year, accept around 10. Most copies are distributed free to Amherst students. **Sample postpaid: $6. No previously published poems; simultaneous submissions OK. Reads submissions from September to February only. Magazine staff makes democratic decision. Seldom comments on rejections. Send SASE for guidelines. Reports in late March. Pays 1 copy.**

THE AMICUS JOURNAL (IV-Nature/rural/ecology), 40 W. 20th St., New York NY 10011, phone (212)727-4412, fax (212)727-1773, e-mail amicus@nrdc.org, website http://www.nrdc.org/eamicus/home.html, poetry editor Brian Swann, is the quarterly journal of the Natural Resources Defense Council. *Amicus* **publishes about 15 poems a year and asks that submitted poetry be "rooted in nature" and no more than one ms page in length.** They have published poetry by some of the best-known poets in the country, including Mary Oliver, Gary Snyder, Denise Levertov, Reg Saner, John Haines and Wendell Berry. As a sample the editors selected these lines from "Into the Light" by Pattiann Rogers:

> *There may be some places the sun*
> *never reaches—into the stamen*
> *of a prairie primrose bud burned*
> *and withered before blooming,*
> *or into the eyes of a fetal*
> *lamb killed before born. I suppose . . .*

The Amicus Journal is 56 pgs., about $7\frac{1}{2} \times 10\frac{1}{2}$, finely-printed, saddle-stapled, on high quality paper with glossy cover, using art, photography and cartoons. Circulation is 250,000. **Sample copies: $4. "All submissions must be accompanied by a cover note (with notable prior publications) and self-addressed, stamped envelope. We prefer to receive submissions by mail, no fax or e-mail. However, poets can request information by e-mail." Pays $50/poem plus a year's subscription.** They also publish *e-Amicus*, an online magazine.

ANACONDA PRESS; FUEL (II), P.O. Box 477699, Chicago IL 60647, e-mail alowry@tezcat.com, website http://www.tezcat.com/~alowry/, editor-in-chief Andy Lowry. Currently publishes *fuel*, "a wiry, highly energized mini-magazine using lots of cool poetry, art and fiction." Also publishes **3-4 poetry chapbooks/year. "We're looking for daring, eccentric works. No academia allowed!"** As a sample the editor selected these lines from "A Child, Dead in Chicago" by Arthur Powers:

INSIDER REPORT

Editor seeks poetry balanced between nature and humanity

According to Brian Swann, poetry editor of *The Amicus Journal* since 1980, nature isn't a natural concept. "We keep using 'nature.' It's not a very good word. It sounds as if it's something separate. I don't see how nature can be grasped, be conceived of apart from the human world. We cannot grasp it, of course. The mystery will always be there."

Swann says he doesn't publish much typical "nature poetry" in *The Amicus Journal*—even though the magazine is an environmental advocacy journal published by the National Resources Defense Council.

Brian Swann

Alongside poems, the journal publishes news, opinions and features about environmental affairs, especially on policies that affect the environment worldwide. The NRDC has a membership of more than 300,000, and *TAJ* is widely read. Poetry is a popular feature in the magazine.

Given this, it isn't surprising Swann looks for poetry reflecting a more sophisticated viewpoint about the environment, particularly humanity's relationship to the natural world. And, he doesn't care for "nature scenes" or poems that present nature simply as a refuge from human culture. In short, he doesn't want any clichéd nature poetry. "I get a lot of 'nature poetry,' which is not what I'm looking for. I'm looking for poetry that's rooted in nature, but not separate from the human."

Although, Swann says, poetry rooted in the natural world can encompass a wide range of subjects—perhaps everything, if it's viewed properly. "I try to focus on what I think of as the larger scene. We have all sorts of poetry. I probably wouldn't publish personal confessions or poems about child molestation, but who knows? It depends on how the subject is treated."

Historically, the best nature poetry recognizes the interdependence of human culture and the natural world. William Wordsworth, for instance, was a poet whose work "responded to the totality of the cultural and political scene," not just depicting scenes of landscape, says Swann.

Because of the journal's particular taste, however, the competition to have a poem published there is tough. Out of thousands of submissions per year, Swann publishes three or four poems in each issue of the quarterly journal. But he says he's very open to work by unknown poets as well as established writers. For example, a recent issue featured Mary Oliver, Philip Booth and Pattiann Rogers—all prominent American poets—and Coral Hull, an Australian writer with little following in the United States.

"I don't just go for big names," says Swann. "Half of the people are pretty well known, half are not so well known. I'm always open to new poets. I don't pay much attention to who writes the poems. I just look from my limited perspective at what I think are really

INSIDER REPORT, *Swann*

interesting poems. The ones that make it to publication are quite extraordinary."

In fact, one type of poetry Swann says he'd like to see more of is poetry translated from other languages into English. Another is political poetry.

In regard to his own work, Swann has published eight books of poetry and numerous volumes of poetry and translations. "Hunting Season," printed below, is a characteristic example of Swann's poetry. The poem is full of sounds and objects to convey the intensity of a particular time of year.

"Hunting Season"

I try to track the note that
seems to come from me up here
& nowhere else
reflecting its bright light outward
knocking bits off itself like stars
that join the wind among
dead leaves under maple saplings
by the stone walls where I follow
as the wind from the mountain-
gap gets among them turning
to snow falling
over silent nests left wedged
in pine & juniper no wind
could uproot here at the edges of things
where wild apple rose &
hawthorn form equivalents
to thoughts whose flowers
are somewhere deep & dark
being shaped by endurance &
whose roots shine black among rocks
resisting
holding their breath

A striking aspect of "Hunting Season" is the way it blends strong images of the physical world with an equally strong sense of poetic rhythm. Iambic beats move in and out of the lines. And while Swann says that wasn't deliberate, he isn't surprised. "I think there's a point when iambic pentameter and speech rhythms almost come together. English seems to fall into something approximating iambic pentameter. When I was a kid, I turned all of **The Canterbury Tales** into contemporary English. Even if it wasn't natural, by the time I was finished it was close to innate."

The images drawn from the physical world in "Hunting Season" are typical of Swann's work. "Native cultures tend to use things to think with. I like to think of things. Physical objects, to me, are like ideas. I don't know what a physical object is until it speaks or I've let it speak."

Swann has a strong interest in native cultures, specifically the different Native American cultures and literatures. And, as he points out, traditional Native Americans don't see the kind of oppositions between humans and the natural world most Westerners do. "When I discovered Native American writing two decades ago, I was struck by how unusual the material is, how different the stories and songs are."

Though Swann was born in England—he is now an American citizen—it is not as surprising as some might think that he would take an interest in Native Americans. "A lot of Americans know less about Native American reality than foreigners," he says.

A fundamental principle that informs all of Swann's work—as editor, critic and poet— is the need for balance and harmony between humanity and the larger world. "I'm kind of obsessed with the idea of psychic health, of psychic pollution. If you don't pollute, you won't get pollution back."

The impossibility of fully understanding the natural world doesn't prevent Swann from trying to understand its various dimensions through poetry, however. "I think the world is how we see it, how we react to it. It doesn't mean there's no there there—there certainly is. But we create those words, and (maybe unfortunately) when we use those words we create the thing we think we're referring to. It's a great responsibility."
—*Kevin Walzer*

> *In twenty countries hundreds of men*
> *stop for a moment, look at the walls*
> *around them, and a great machine stumbles*
> *for an instant to a halt.*
> *By telex at night the messages come in,*
> *tapping sympathy into a dark, empty room.*

fuel is 44 pgs., digest-sized, offset, saddle-stapled with b&w art on card cover, art and ads inside. **Sample postpaid: $3. Submit up to 6 poems at a time. E-mail submissions OK. "Previously published poems are OK if not too terribly recent. Simultaneous submissions are frowned upon. We appreciate cover letters." Send SASE for guidelines or request via e-mail. Sometimes sends prepublication galleys. Pays 2 copies if published in 'zine. Chapbook payment is negotiable. Rights revert to authors.**

ANALECTA (IV-Students), Dept. PM, Liberal Arts Council, FAC 17, University of Texas, Austin TX 78712, phone (512)471-6563, founded 1974, contact Marc Faletti and Jason Hayter, is an annual of literary works and art by **college/university students and graduate students chosen in an annual contest. No restrictions on type; limited to 5 poems/submission. Submissions cannot be returned.** "Our purpose is to provide a forum for excellent student writing. **Works must be previously unpublished.**" It is a 150-page magazine, glossy plates for interior artwork in b&w, 7×10, flat-spined, soft cover. They receive about 800 submissions a year, accept approximately 40. Press run is 800 for 700 subscribers, 100 shelf sales. **Sample postpaid: $7.50. Entries must be typed; name should appear on cover sheet only. Send SASE for guidelines. Deadline is in mid-October. Prizes in each category. Pays 2 copies and $100 for each prize.**

ANAMNESIS PRESS; ANAMNESIS CHAPBOOK CONTEST (II), 50 Austin Ave., Suite 121, Hayward CA 94544, phone/fax (510)265-1214, e-mail kdaniels@ix.netcom.com, website http://ourworld.compuserve.com/homepages/Anamnesis, founded 1990, publisher Keith Allen Daniels, primarily publishes chapbooks selected through its annual contest, though occasionally publishes a larger volume "to preserve poetry that might otherwise be forgotten. **We wish to see poems of intellectual and emotional depth that give full rein to the imagination, whether free verse or formalist. Please don't send us trite, sappy, maudlin or 'inspirational' poetry."** They have published poetry by Joe Haldeman, James Blish, David R. Bunch and Steven Utley. Chapbooks are 25-40 pgs., photo offset and saddle-stapled with 2-color covers. **For the Anamnesis Chapbook Contest, submit 20-30 pgs. of poetry with a cover letter and $15 entry fee between January 1 and March 15 only. Previously published poems (if author provides acknowledgments) and simultaneous submissions OK. "Poets can request guidelines via fax and e-mail, but we do not accept poetry submissions via e-mail or fax." Winners are selected in June. Prize (Anamnesis Award): $750, an award certificate, publication and 20 copies.** The publisher adds, "We encourage poets to purchase a sample chapbook for $5 before submitting, to get a feel for what we're looking for. We use free verse and well done formal poetry."

‡*ANARCHIST ANGEL—YOUTH POETRY MAGAZINE (I), 5 Aylesford Close, Sedgley, West Midlands DY3 3QB England, phone/fax (01902)663315, founded 1994, editor Ms. Elizabeth Berry, is a quarterly "promoting the work of young poets." **They want "all poetry by young writers from 8-25 years of age. There are no restrictions on style, form, length, etc."** As a sample the editor selected these lines from "Laundromatarama" (poet unidentified):

> Inside
> aphrodites renew their virginities in a sea of suds
> grapple with interlocking legs and smalls
> linen lined bodies joined at the waist
> combinations gathered & flushed with the juices of the limb bound by
> the joys of co-operation.

The editor says *AA* is 50-90 pgs., typeset and printed, with illustrated astrolux cover, artwork throughout to illustrate poetry. They receive about 2,000 poems a year; accept approximately 20-25%. Press run is 300 for 270 subscribers of which 10 are libraries, 10 shelf sales. Single copy: £1.50; subscription: £6.50. **Sample postpaid: £2.50. Does not accept checks or money orders in US funds. Submit 2-6 poems, typed with name and address on each individual sheet. Previously published poems and simultaneous submissions OK. Cover letter preferred.** Time between acceptance and publication is 1-3 months. **"All poems are reviewed on a weekly basis. Copyright forms are issued to poets accepted for publication."** Often comments on rejections. Send SASE (or SAE and IRC) for guidelines. Pays 1 copy. "We review books and other magazines sent to us." Open to unsolicited reviews. Poets may also send books for review consideration. They also provide information on poetry competitions. The editor says, "We welcome all poetry from young writers and are very keen to develop and establish a readership within the USA."

‡*ANGEL EXHAUST (III), Flat 6, Avon Court, London N12 8HR United Kingdom, founded 1977, contact Andrew Duncan, appears twice a year and publishes poetry and prose about poetry (95% British). **They want "anything which staves off boredom and desperation even for a moment—poems about engineering, poems about shopping. No poems full of objects, psychotherapy, hypochondria, body parts. No conservative or religious poetry."** They have recently published poetry by Denise Riley, Allen Fisher, Roy Fisher and Maggie O'Sullivan. As a sample the editor selected the poem "Twist" by Helen Macdonald:

> ah, how the hay smokes
> into papaverous skies
> as we address the heights of the C20th
> in a poplin shirt, all declamatory and tired
> with a suit that seals to rest these soft
> & perfect metals.

The editor says *AE* is 120 pgs., 6×9 with laminate cover and photos. They receive poems from about 100 poets a year, accept approximately 20%. Press run is 300 for 20 subscribers of which 3 are libraries. Subscription: $14. **Sample postpaid: $10. Submit 10 poems at a time. Previously published poems and simultaneous submissions OK. Cover letter preferred.** Time between acceptance and publication is 6-12 months. **Seldom comments on rejections. Publishes theme issues. Always sends prepublication galleys. Pays 1 copy.** Reviews books of poetry in up to 6,000 words, single book format. Open to unsolicited reviews. Send books for review consideration. "Poets should have an adequate theory of social agency."

ANGELFLESH; ANGELFLESH PRESS (I), P.O. Box 141123, Grand Rapids MI 49514, founded 1994, editor Jim Buchanan. *Angelflesh* appears 3 times/year ("plus extras") and publishes "today's best cutting-edge fiction, poetry and art." **They want poetry that is "strong, real and gutsy, with vivid images, emotional and spiritual train wrecks. No taboos, no 'Hallmark' verse."** They have recently published poetry by Albert Huffstickler and Michael Estabrook. As a sample the editor selected these lines from an untitled poem by Catfish McDaris:

> only the dead die young
> (everyone's good when dead)
>
> now i just wanna be
> a catfish in the Pecos
> or perhaps Painte Sage
> in a Ghost Dance shirt
> with a new plan for Mt. Rushmore.

The editor says *Angelflesh* is 40-50 pgs., various sizes, photocopied and saddle-stitched. They receive about 1,000 poems a year, accept 10-15%. Press run is up to 500. Subscription: $10. **Sample postpaid: $4. Submit 3-5 poems at a time. Previously published poems and simultaneous submissions OK. Cover letter preferred.** Time between acceptance and publication is 2-6 months. **Seldom comments on rejections. Send SASE for guidelines. Reports in around 1 month. Pays 1 copy.** Under Angelflesh Press the editor also publishes 1-2 perfect-bound paperback and **2-4 chapbooks/year.** Chapbooks are usually 20-30 pgs., 5½×8, photocopied and saddle-stitched with some artwork. **Query first. Replies to queries in 1 month, mss (if invited) in 2-4 weeks. Pay negotiable. For a sample chapbook, send $4 or send a SASE for further details about their chapbook series.**

ANHINGA PRESS; ANHINGA PRIZE (II), P.O. Box 10595, Tallahassee FL 32302-0595, phone/fax (904)442-6323, founded 1972, poetry editors Rick Campbell and Van Brock, publishes **"books and anthologies of poetry. We also offer the Anhinga Prize for poetry—$2,000 and publication—for a book-length manuscript each year. We want to see contemporary poetry which respects language. We're inclined toward poetry that is not obscure, that can be understood by any literate audience."** They have recently published *Hello Stranger* by Robert Dana; *Easter Vigil*, by Ann Neelon (the 1995 Anhinga Prize Winner); and *Isle of Flowers: Poems by Florida Individual Artists Fellows* edited by Donna J. Long. **Considers simultaneous submissions.** Send SASE for rules (submissions accepted January 1 to March 15) of the Anhinga Prize for poetry, which requires a $20 entry fee. The contest has been judged by such distinguished poets as William Stafford, Louis Simpson, Henry Taylor, Hayden Carruth, Marvin Bell, Donald Hall and Joy Harjo.

✿**ANJOU (V)**, P.O. Box 322 Station P., Toronto, Ontario M5S 2S8 Canada, founded 1980, edited by Richard Lush and Roger Greenwald, publishes broadsides of poetry. **"We do not wish to receive submissions because we publish only by solicitation."**

‡**ANTHOLOGY; INKWELL PRESS (I, II)**, P.O. Box 4411, Mesa AZ 85211-4411, phone (602)461-8200, e-mail anthology@juno.com, website http://elwood.pionet.net/~wberger, executive editor Sharon Skinner, publisher Bob Nelson. *Anthology* appears every 2 months and intends to be "the best poetry, prose and art magazine." **They want "poetry with clear conceit. Evocative as opposed to provocative. We do not dictate form or style but creative uses are always enjoyed. Graphic horror and pornography are not encouraged."** They have recently published poetry by Paula Ashley and Carol Michalski. As a sample the editor selected these lines from "Daughter" by Staci Leigh Haynes, winner of the 1996 *Anthology* Poetry Contest:

> *The birds will speak in whispers*
> *fold their wings to the fabric*
> *of storm that sings in their hollow*
> *bones, their mica-bright eyes.*

Anthology is 28-32 pgs., 8½×11, printed on coated glossy paper, saddle-stitched with two-color cover, b&w drawings and clip art inside. Press run is 1,000 for 100 subscribers of which 2 are libraries, with 50-75 distributed free to local coffeehouses, beauty parlors, doctors' offices, etc. Single copy: $3.95; subscription: $17 (6 issues). **Submit 5 poems at a time. Previously published and simultaneous submissions OK. "Please try not to send handwritten work."** Time between acceptance and publication is 2-4 months. **Send SASE for guidelines or obtain via e-mail or website. Reports in 4-6 weeks. Pays 1 copy. Acquires one-time rights.** Sponsors annual contest with cash and other prizes for both poetry and short stories. Entry fee of $1 per poem required. "Send what you write, not what you think an editor wants to hear. And always remember that a rejection is seldom personal, it is just one step closer to a yes."

ANTHOLOGY OF MAGAZINE VERSE & YEARBOOK OF AMERICAN POETRY (III, IV-Anthology), % Monitor Book Company, P.O. Box 9078, Palm Springs CA 92263, phone (760)323-2270, founded 1910, editor-in-chief Alan F. Pater. The annual *Anthology* is a selection of the **best poems published in American and Canadian magazines during the year and is also a basic reference work for poets.** Alan F. Pater says, "We want poetry that is 'readable' and in any poetic form; we also want translations. **All material must first have appeared in magazines."** They have published poetry by Margaret Atwood, Stanley Kunitz, Robert Penn Warren, Richard Wilbur, Maxine Kumin, John Ashbery and John Updike. Indeed, the anthology is a good annual guide to the best poets actively publishing in any given year. 90% of selections are made by the editor directly from magazines, but poets may **submit up to 3 poems per year that have appeared in very recent magazines and journals. Each poem must be identified with the name and date (or issue number) of the magazine in which it originally appeared.** "Phone calls from poets are welcomed."

‡**THE ANTHOLOGY OF NEW ENGLAND WRITERS; ROBERT PENN WARREN POETRY AWARDS (IV-Form); VERMONT POETS ASSOCIATION**, P.O. Box 483, Windsor VT 05089, phone (802)674-2315, fax (802)674-6635, founded 1989, editor Frank Anthony, assistant editor Susan Anthony, appears annually. **They want "unpublished, original, free verse poetry only; 10-30 line limit."**
 • All poems published in this annual are winners of their contest.
They have recently published poetry by Richard Eberhart, Rosanna Warren, David Kirby and Vivian Shipley. *The Anthology of New England Writers* is 44 pgs., 5½×8½, professionally printed and saddle-stitched with colored card cover, b&w illustrations. Press run is 400. Single copy: $3.95. **Sample postpaid: $3. Make checks payable to New England Writers. Submit 3-9 poems at a time with $5 reading fee for each 3 poems. Include 3×5 card with name, address and titles of poems. No previously published poems or simultaneous submissions. Reads submissions September through June 15 (post mark). Send SASE for guidelines. Reports 6 weeks after June 15 deadline. Sometimes sends prepublication galleys. Pays 1 copy. All rights revert to author upon publication.** Sponsors an annual free verse contest with The Robert Penn Warren Poetry Awards. Awards $200 for first, $100 for second and $50 for third. They also award 10 Honorable Mentions, 10 Commendables and 10 Editor's Choice. Winners announced at the New England Writers Conference in July. All submissions are automatically entered in contest. The Vermont Poets Association was founded in 1986 "to encourage the practice and precision and ingenuity in the practice of writing and speaking, whatever the form and style."

Currently has 400 members. Offerings available for poets include extensive writing information, critiques, consultation, and advice on markets. Members or nationally known writers give readings that are open to the public. Sponsors open-mike readings. Meetings are held several times a year. Membership dues: $9, $6 senior citizens and students. Send SASE for additional information.

ANTIETAM REVIEW (IV-Regional), Washington County Arts Council, 7 W. Franklin St., Hagerstown MD 21740-4804, phone/fax (301)791-3132, founded 1982, poetry editor Crystal Brown, appears annually and looks for **"well-crafted literary quality poems. We discourage inspirational verse, haiku, doggerel." Uses poets (natives or residents) from the states of Maryland, Pennsylvania, Virginia, West Virginia, Delaware and District of Columbia. Needs 20 poems/issue, up to 30 lines each.** They have published poetry by Eleanor Ross Taylor, William Aiken and Barbara F. Lefcowitz. As a sample the editor selected these lines from "Salmon People" by Barbara Hurd:

> *Sometimes*
> *I try not to mind*
> *our aging*
>
> *imagine pewter bodies*
> *spawned-out*
> *beyond hunger and loss*
>
> *in the same quiet pool*
> *where we started,*
> *adrift and decomposing*
>
> *in the sureness of home.*

AR is 54 pgs., 8½×11, saddle-stapled, glossy paper with glossy card cover and b&w photos throughout. Press run is 1,000. **Sample postpaid: $3.15 back issue, $5.25 current. Submit 5 typed poems at a time. "We prefer a cover letter stating other publications, although we encourage new and emerging writers. We do not accept previously published poems and reluctantly take simultaneous submissions." Do not submit mss from February through August. "We read from September 1 through February 1 annually." Send SASE for guidelines. Sends prepublication galleys, if requested. Pays $20/poem, depending on funding, plus 2 copies. Buys first North American serial rights.** The editors seem open to all styles of poetry, free and formal, as long as the author is from the designated region. Overall, a good read; but poems have to compete with prose. Ones used, however, are featured in attractive boxes on the page. Sponsors a contest for natives or residents of DC, DE, MD, PA, VA and WV. Send SASE for details. Work published in *Antietam Review* has been included in a *Pushcart Prize* anthology.

♣THE ANTIGONISH REVIEW (II), St. Francis Xavier University, P.O. Box 5000, Antigonish, Nova Scotia B2G 2W5 Canada, phone (902)867-3962, fax (902)867-2448, e-mail tar@stfx.ca, founded 1970, editor George Sanderson, poetry editor Peter Sanger. This high-quality quarterly "tries to produce the kind of literary and visual mosaic that the modern sensibility requires or would respond to." They want poetry **not over "80 lines, i.e., 2 pgs.; subject matter can be anything, the style is traditional, modern or post-modern limited by typographic resources. Purpose is not an issue." No "erotica, scatalogical verse, excessive propaganda toward a certain subject."** They have published poetry by Andy Wainwright, W.J. Keith, Michael Hulse, Jean McNeil, M. Travis Lane and Douglas Lochhead. *TAR* is 150 pgs., 6×9, flat-spined with glossy card cover, offset printing, using "in-house graphics and cover art, no ads." They accept about 10% of some 2,500 submissions/year. Press run is 850 for 700 subscribers. Subscription: $20. **Sample postpaid: $3. Submit 5-10 poems at a time. No simultaneous submissions or previously published poems. Include SASE or SAE and IRCs if outside Canada. Editor** "sometimes" comments on rejections. **Pays 2 copies.**

THE ANTIOCH REVIEW (III), P.O. Box 148, Yellow Springs OH 45387, phone (937)767-6389, founded 1941, poetry editor Judith Hall, "is an independent quarterly of critical and creative thought . . . **For well over 50 years, creative authors, poets and thinkers have found a friendly reception . . . regardless of formal reputation**. We get far more poetry than we can possibly accept, and the competition is keen. Here, where form and content are so inseparable and reaction is so personal, it is difficult to state requirements or limitations. Studying recent issues of *The Review* should be helpful. **No 'light' or inspirational verse."** They have published poetry by Ralph Angel, Jorie Graham, Jacqueline Osherow and Mark Strand. They receive about 3,000 submissions/year, publish 20 pages of poetry in each issue, and have about a 6-month backlog. Circulation is 5,000, of which 70% is through bookstores and newsstands. Large percentage of subscribers are libraries. Subscription: $35. **Sample: $6. Submit 3-6 poems at a time. No previously published poems. Reads submissions September 1 through May 1 only. Send SASE for guidelines. Reports in 6-8 weeks. Pays $10/published page plus 2 copies.** Reviews books of poetry in 300 words, single format. This is a beautiful journal featuring some of the best poems being written by new and well-known writers. *AR* received a First Place Award for Editorial Content from the 1995 American Literary Magazine Awards. Work published in this review has also been included in *The Best American Poetry 1995* and *Pushcart Prize* anthologies.

ANTIPODES (IV-Regional), 8 Big Island, Warwick NY 10990, e-mail pakane@vassar.edu, founded 1987, poetry editor Paul Kane, is a biannual of Australian poetry and fiction and criticism and reviews of Australian writing. They want **work from Australian poets only. No restrictions as to form, length, subject matter or style.** They have published poetry by A.D. Hope, Judith Wright and John Tranter. The editor says *Antipodes* is 180 pgs., 8½×11, perfect-bound, with graphics, ads and photos. They receive about 500 submissions a year, accept approximately 10%. Press run is 500 for 200 subscribers. Subscription: $20. **Sample postpaid: $17. Submit 3-5 poems at a time. No previously published poems or simultaneous submissions. Cover letter with bio note required. The editor says they "prefer submission of photocopies which do not have to be returned." Seldom comments on rejections. Reports in 2 months. Pays $20/poem plus 1 copy. Acquires first North American serial rights.** Staff reviews books of poetry in 500-1,500 words. Send books for review consideration.

APALACHEE QUARTERLY; APALACHEE PRESS (II, IV-Themes), P.O. Box 10469, Tallahassee FL 32302, founded 1971, editors Barbara Hamby, Bruce Boehrer, Beth Meekins, Pat McEnulty, Rikki Clark and Kim MacQueen. They have published poetry by David Kirby, Peter Meinke, Alfred Corn and Virgil Suarez. *Apalachee Quarterly* is 160 pgs., 6×9, professionally printed and perfect-bound with card cover. There are 55-95 pgs. of poetry in each issue. "Every year we do an issue on a special topic. Past issues include Dental, Revenge, Cocktail Party and Noir issues." Circulation is 700 for 350 subscribers of which 75 are libraries. Subscription: $15. **Sample postpaid: $5. Submit clear copies of up to 5 poems, name and address on each. Simultaneous submissions OK.** "We don't read during the summer (June 1 through August 31)." **Sometimes comments on rejections. Send SASE for guidelines. Pays 2 copies.** Staff reviews books of poetry. Send books for review consideration.

APHRODITE GONE BERSERK: A JOURNAL OF EROTIC ART (IV-Erotica), 233 Guyon Ave., Staten Island NY 10306, founded 1995 (first issue published early 1996), editor C. Esposito, is a semiannual journal of erotic art, including poetry, fiction, memoirs and photography. **They want "poetry that deals with the erotic or sexuality in any form and from any orientation or perspective."** The editor says *AGB* is 48 pgs., 5½×8½. They expect to receive about 200 submissions a year and accept approximately 10%. Press run is 1,500. Single copy: $7; subscription: $12. **Previously published poems and simultaneous submissions OK.** Time between acceptance and publication is 6-12 months. **Send SASE for guidelines. Reports in 1 month. Pays 1 copy. Acquires one-time rights.** "We accept books, chapbooks, magazines and videos that deal with the erotic and sexuality for possible review in *AGB*." Also open to unsolicited reviews. The editor says, "Especially when writing erotic poetry, stay away from the cliché and write honestly."

‡*APOSTROPHE (II), 41 Canute Rd., Faversham, Kent ME138SH England, founded 1991, contact editor, published biannually, features "new poetry and poetry in translation, intended to delight, entertain, amuse and provoke." **They want "both rhymed and free verse, shorter poems preferred, no more than 40 lines, the editor is looking for wit and humor; well-crafted poems." They do not want "pornographic, sentimental or self-pitying poetry."** They have recently published poetry by Edmund Harwood, Gerald England and Colin Nixon. As a sample the editor selected these lines from "Domestic Help" by Steve Powell:

> *With silver bells and oyster shells,*
> *She amuses herself,*
> *While I try to remain invisible,*
> *And separate from this jumble*
> *I scrub the stone floors,*
> *With my mind elsewhere.*

Apostrophe is 36 pgs., A5, photocopied, saddle-stapled with medium card cover, b&w line drawings and ads. They receive about 500 poems a year, accept approximately 15%. Press run is 100 for 30 subscribers of which 4 are libraries. Single copy: 7 IRCs (£2.50); subscription: 14 IRCs (£5.50). **Sample copy: 5 IRCs. Make checks payable to Mr. Pillows' Press (U.S. checks not accepted.) Submit 6 poems at a time. No previously published poems; simultaneous submissions OK. Cover letter required.** "Make sure originals are not sent, as poems submitted from outside the UK cannot be returned." **Does not read submissions in August or December 16 to January 1.** Time between acceptance and publication is 4-6 weeks. **Seldom comments on rejections. Send SASE (or SAE and IRC) for guidelines. Reports in 1 month. Pays 1 copy.** Reviews books of poetry. Open to unsolicited reviews. The editor says, "Don't try to be too literary or clever. Simple themes are often the best. Treat your poems like jewels, cut and polish them continually. Length is no indicator of quality. Try and

---

✱   **AN ASTERISK** before a listing indicates an overseas publisher, magazine, contest, conference or organization.

find an unusual or different perspective. Contributors come from the U.S., Canada, Cuba, new Zealand, France, Austria and other countries in addition to the U.K."

APPALACHIA; THE APPALACHIA POETRY PRIZE (II, IV-Nature), 5 Joy St., Boston MA 02108, phone (617)523-0636, founded 1876, poetry editor Parkman Howe, editor-in-chief Sandy Stott, is a "semiannual journal of mountaineering and conservation which describes activities outdoors and asks questions of an ecological nature." **They want poetry relating to the outdoors and nature—specifically weather, mountains, rivers, lakes, woods and animals. "No conquerors' odes."** They have published poetry by Bruce Ducker, Warren Woessner, Lucille Day, Mary Oliver and Thomas Reiter. The editor says *Appalachia* is 160 pgs., 6×9, professionally printed with color cover, using photos, graphics and a few ads. They receive about 200 poems a year, use 10-15. Press run is 10,000. Subscription: $10/year. **Sample postpaid: $5. Submit up to 6 poems at a time. "We favor shorter poems—maximum of 36 lines usually." No previously published poems or simultaneous submissions. Cover letter required.** Time between acceptance and publication is 1 year. **Seldom comments on rejections. Send SASE for guidelines. Reports in 4-6 weeks. Pays 1 copy. Acquires first rights.** Staff reviews "some" books of poetry in 200-400 words, usually single format. Offers an annual award, The Appalachia Poetry Prize, given since 1972. The editor says, "Our readership is very well versed in the outdoors—mountains, rivers, lakes, animals. We look for poetry that helps readers see the natural world in fresh ways. No generalized accounts of the great outdoors."

APPALACHIAN HERITAGE (IV-Regional), Hutchins Library, Berea College, Berea KY 40404, phone (606)986-9341 ext. 5260, fax (606)986-9494, e-mail sidney_farr@berea.edu, founded 1973, editor Sidney Saylor Farr, a literary quarterly with Southern Appalachian emphasis. The journal publishes several poems in each issue, and the editor wants to see **"poems about people, places, the human condition, social issues, etc., with Southern Appalachian settings. No style restrictions but poems should have a maximum of 14 lines, prefer 8-10 lines." She does not want "blood and gore, hell-fire and damnation, or biased poetry about race or religion."** She has published poetry by Jim Wayne Miller, James Still, George Ella Lyon and Robert Morgan. The flat-spined magazine is 6×9, professionally printed on white stock with b&w line drawings and photos, glossy white card cover with 4-color illustration. Issues we have scanned tended toward lyric free verse, emphasizing nature or situations set in nature, but the editor says they will use good poems of any subject and form. **Sample copy: $6. Submit 2-4 poems at a time, typed one to a page. No previously published poems; simultaneous submissions OK. Requires cover letter giving information about previous publications where poets have appeared. Electronic submissions OK. Publishes theme issues occasionally. Send SASE for upcoming themes or request via fax or e-mail. Reports in 2-4 weeks. Sometimes sends prepublication galleys. Pays 3 copies. Acquires first rights.** Reviews books of poetry. Open to unsolicited reviews. Poets may also send books for review consideration. The Denny C. Plattner Awards go to the authors of the best poetry, article or essay, or short fiction published in the four issues released within the preceding year. The award amount in each category is $200.

APROPOS (I, IV-Subscribers), Ashley Manor, 450 Buttermilk Rd., Easton PA 18042, founded 1989, editor Ashley C. Anders, **publishes all poetry submitted by subscribers except that judged by the editor to be pornographic or in poor taste. Maximum length 40 lines—50 characters/line.** $25 for 6-issue subscription plus free entry to 2 special contests. As a sample the editor selected her own "With Pen in Hand":

> *With pen in hand I can confess*
> *my innermost unhappiness,*
> *or wonder in the things I see—*
> *a newborn bird; a lovely tree.*
>
> *This gift that God has given me*
> *Allows my feelings to be free.*
> *With pen in hand I always say*
> *whatever's on my mind each day.*

It is 90 pgs., digest-sized, plastic ring bound, with heavy stock cover, desktop-published. **Sample postpaid: $3. Submit 1 poem at a time. Editor prefers to receive sample of poetry prior to acceptance of subscription. No simultaneous submissions; previously published poems OK. Send SASE for guidelines. All poems are judged by subscribers.** Prizes for regular issues are $50, $25, $10 and $5. Prizes for special contests are $25, $10 and $5.

*AQUARIUS (II), Flat 10, Room A, 116 Sutherland Ave., Maida-Vale, London W9 England, poetry editor Eddie Linden, is a literary biannual publishing quality poetry. Issue 19/20, guest edited by Hilary Davies, contains poetry, fictional prose, essays, interviews and reviews. Another issue on the English poet Roy Fuller and contained prose and poetry. **"Please note the magazine will not accept work unless writers have bought the magazine and studied the style/form of the work published."** Single copy: $10; subscription: $50 (US). **Payment is by arrangement.**

‡ARACHNE, INC. (I, IV-Rural), 2363 Page Rd., Kennedy NY 14747-9717, founded 1980, senior editor Susan L. Leach, focuses on the work of "America's finest rural poets" and publishes **2 chapbooks/year (500**

press run). They want "any style, as long as its theme is rural in nature. No purient subjects." They have recently published poetry by Wallace Whatley. Chapbooks are usually 30 pgs., staple-bound, #10 cover, no graphics. **Submit 7 poems at a time. No previously published poems or simultaneous submissions. Cover letter preferred. "Please include a SASE for return and correspondence." Reads submissions January and June only.** Time between acceptance and publication is 3 months. **Poems are circulated to an editorial board. "Poems selected initially by membership, presented to board for final decision." Seldom comments on rejections. Replies to queries and mss within 3 months.** The editor says, "We will not consider any material of a sexually questionable nature. We remain a conservative press."

ARARAT (IV-Ethnic), Dept. PM, A.G.B.U., 31 W. 52nd St., New York NY 10019, phone (212)765-8260, editor-in-chief Leo Hamalian, is a quarterly magazine **emphasizing Armenian life and culture for Americans of Armenian descent and Armenian immigrants. They use about 6 poems/issue and want any verse that is Armenian in theme. They do not want to see traditional, sentimental love poetry.** Circulation is 2,400. Subscription: $24 ($32 foreign). **Sample copy: $7 plus 4 first-class stamps. Previously published submissions OK. Submit seasonal/holiday material at least 3 months in advance.** Time between acceptance and publication is 1 year. **Reports in 6 weeks. Pays $10. Buys first North American serial rights and second (reprint) rights to material originally published elsewhere.**

♣**ARC: CANADA'S NATIONAL POETRY MAGAZINE (II)**, P.O. Box 7368, Ottawa, Ontario K1L 8E4 Canada, founded 1978, co-editors Rita Donovan and John Barton, is a biannual of poetry, poetry-related articles, interviews and book reviews. **"Our tastes are eclectic. Our focus is Canadian, but we also publish writers from elsewhere."** They have published poetry by Anne Szumigalski, Heather Spears, Robert Priest and Erin Mouré. *Arc* is 80-96 pgs., perfect-bound, with laminated 2-color cover, artwork and ads. They receive about 500 submissions a year, accept 40-50 poems. Press run is 750 for 350 subscribers. Single copy: $7.50 Canadian/Canada, $8.50 Canadian/US, $10 Canadian/overseas; subscription (4 issues): $20 Canadian/Canada, $25 Canadian/US, $28 Canadian/overseas. **Cost of sample varies. No previously published poems or simultaneous submissions. Cover letter required. Submit 5-8 poems, single spaced, with name and address on each page. Send SASE (or SAE and IRC) for guidelines and upcoming themes. Reports in 3-6 months. Pays $25 Canadian/page plus 2 copies. Buys first North American serial rights.** The Confederation Poets Prize is an annual award of $100 for the best poem published in *Arc* that year. *Arc* also sponsors a "Poem of the Year Contest." Awards first prize of $1,000, second prize of $750 and third prize of $500.

*ARC PUBLICATIONS (III), Nanholme Mill, Shaw Wood Rd., Todmorden, Lancashire OL14 6DA United Kingdom, phone (01706)812338, founded 1969, partners Tony Ward, Angela Jarman and Rosemary Jones, publishes 8 paperback books of poetry a year. **They want "literary, literate, contemporary poetry. No religious or children's verse. We specialize not only in contemporary poetry of the U.K. but also in poetry written in English from across the world."** They have recently published books of poetry by Jacqueline Brown, Dinah Hawken (New Zealand), John Kinsella (Australia) and Rose Ausländer (Germany). Their books are 64-100 pgs., 5½×8½, offset litho and perfect-bound with card covers in 2-3 colors. **Query first with 10 sample poems and a cover letter with brief bio and publication credits. "No submissions replied to if there is no IRC." Previously published poems and simultaneous submissions OK. Mss are read by at least 2 editors before possible acceptance. Seldom comments on rejections. Replies to queries in up to 4 months. Pays 7-10% royalties and 6 author's copies (out of a press run of 600). Send SASE (or SAE and IRCs) for current list to order samples.** They say, "Poets should have a body of work already published in magazines and journals, and should be acquainted with our list of books, before submitting."

‡***THE ARGOTIST; ARGOTIST PROMOTIONS (II)**, 221 Chestnut House, Mulberry Court, Mulberry St., Liverpool L7 7EZ United Kingdom, e-mail radged@liv.ac.uk, founded 1995, editor Nick Watson, is "a deeply dilettante review." The biannual features literary and arts criticism and contains a poetry portfolio section. **They want "crafted, formally innovative poems; linguistically astute and provocative work. 50 lines maximum/poem. No descriptive-realist 'chopped up prose.' "** As a sample the editor selected these lines from "Girlington Version (for Margaret)" by Robert Galeta:

> *A beautiful thought*
> *which brings you back to earth*
> *Whilst you must get up early*
> *to talk to God, warming your hands*
> *at the cow's nostrils first*

The editor says *The Argotist* is 48 pgs., 210×265mm, saddle-stitched, 600 dpi graphics, industry-related ads. They receive about 1,000 poems a year, accept approximately 5%. Press run is 1,000 for 50 subscribers of which 10 are libraries, 750 shelf sales. Single copy: £1.50. **Submit 6 poems at a time. No previously published poems; simultaneous submissions OK, "but we must be informed if submitted work published elsewhere whilst held." E-mail submissions welcome. Mss returned only if SAE enclosed. Reads submissions April through June and October through December.** Time between acceptance and publication is 1-2 months. **Publishes theme issues. Request guidelines via e-mail. Reports in June and December only. Pays 1 copy.** Reviews books or chapbooks of poetry in 500-1,000 words. Open to unsolicited reviews. Poets may also send books for review consideration. Argotist Promotions organizes poetry readings. Send SASE or (SAE and IRC) for details.

ARJUNA LIBRARY PRESS; JOURNAL OF REGIONAL CRITICISM (V), 1025 Garner St. D, Space 18, Colorado Springs CO 80905-1774, library founded 1963, press founded 1979, editor Count Prof. Joseph A. Uphoff, Jr. "The Arjuna Library Press is avant-garde, designed to endure the transient quarters and marginal funding of the literary phenomenon (as a tradition) while presenting a context for the development of current mathematical ideas in regard to theories of art, literature and performance; photocopy printing allows for very limited editions and irregular format. Quality is maintained as an artistic materialist practice." He publishes **"surrealist prose poetry, visual poetry, dreamlike, short and long works; not obscene, profane (will criticize but not publish), unpolished work."** He has recently published work by Mike Owens and Keith Gabriel Hendricks. As a sample the editor selected these lines from "Unraked Yard" by Genevieve Stephens:

> *Most beautiful/The texture/Of gold gold gold,*
> *And thicker/Is the carpet*
> *As each day grows old./And here and there*
> *In raised design/Leaves of scarlet/Intertwine.*

JRC is published on loose photocopied pages of collage, writing and criticism, appearing frequently in a varied format. Press run: 1 copy each. Reviews books of poetry "occasionally." Open to unsolicited reviews. Poets may also send books for review consideration. "Upon request will treat material as submitted for reprint, one-time rights." Arjuna Library Press publishes **6-12 chapbooks/year, averaging 50 pgs. Sample: $2.50. However, he is currently overstocked and is not accepting submissions for the journal or the press.** The editor says, "Poets should be aware that literature has become a vast labyrinth in which the vision of the creative mind may be solitary. One can no longer depend upon an audience to entertain the storyteller. The writer may be left lonely in the presence of the creation which should, therefore, be entertainment in its own right if not for an audience then at least for the holder of the copyright."

THE ARK (V), 115 Montebello Rd., Jamaica Plain MA 02130-2907, phone (617)522-1929, founded 1970 (as BLEB), poetry editor Geoffrey Gardner, publishes books of poetry. **"We are unable to take on new projects at this time."** They have published poetry by David Budbill, John Haines, Joseph Bruchac, Elsa Gidlow, W.S. Merwin, Eliot Weinberger, Kathy Acker, George Woodcock, Kathleen Raine, Marge Piercy and Linda Hogan.

THE UNIVERSITY OF ARKANSAS PRESS (V); ARKANSAS POETRY AWARD (I, II), 201 Ozark, Fayetteville AR 72701-1201, phone (501)575-3246, fax (501)575-6044, e-mail uaprinfo@cavern.uark.edu, website http://www.uark.edu/campus-resources/uaprinfo/public.html/, founded 1980, acquisitions editor Kevin Brock, publishes flat-spined paperbacks and hardback collections of individual poets. Miller Williams, director of the press, says, **"We are not interested in poetry that is obscure or private or self-consciously erudite."** They have published poetry by Joe Survant, Sam Hazo, Enid Shomer and John Ciardi. Their books are usually digest-sized, flat-spined, elegantly printed on eggshell stock with matte 2-color card cover. **Query with 5-10 sample poems. Replies to queries in 2 weeks, to mss (if invited) in 2-4 weeks. No replies without SASE. Always sends prepublication galleys. Offers 10% royalty contract plus 10 author's copies. Send SASE for catalog to buy samples.** First-book mss are not considered except as submissions for the Arkansas Poetry Award. The Arkansas Poetry Award competition is open to any original ms by a living American poet whose work has not been previously published or accepted for publication in book form. Chapbooks, self-published books, and books produced with the author's subsidy are not considered previously published books. No translations. Submit 50-80 pgs., not more than one poem/page, counting title page in page count. An acknowledgments page listing poems previously published should accompany ms. Author's name should appear on the title page only. $15 reading fee. Postmark deadline: May 1. Publication the following spring.

ARNAZELLA (II, IV-Regional), Bellevue Community College, 3000 Landerholm Circle SE, Bellevue WA 98007-6484, phone (206)603-4032, e-mail arnazella@prostar.com, established 1979, advisor Woody West, is a literary annual, published in spring, using **well-crafted poetry, no "jingles or greeting card" poetry**. They have published poetry by William Stafford, Judith Skillman and Colleen McElroy. The editor describes this student publication (which uses work from off campus) as 75 pgs., 6×8, offset, using photos and drawings. **They are currently accepting submissions only from poets in Washington, Oregon, Idaho, Alaska and British Columbia.** Of 150-200 poems received/year they use about 30. Press run is 500 for 3 subscriptions, one of which is a library. **Sample postpaid: $5. Submit up to 3 poems. Deadline is usually at the end of December. Send SASE for guidelines. Reports in 1-4 months. Pays 1 copy.**

‡*ARS POETICA (II), P.O. Box 455, Bairnsdale, Victoria 3875 Australia, founded 1995, contact the editors, appears 3 times/year in December, April and August and "promotes the work of established, newer, urban and rural poets with an emphasis on diversity in style and subject matter." They have recently published poetry by Lizz Murphy, chao, Mal Morgan, Ouyang Yu and Les Wicks. As a sample the editors selected these lines from "After Rain" by Christopher Parry:

> *snail-hordes crunch on concrete*
> *Marie Curie dead from exposure*

> *handbones frail under sudden sun*
> *sad clouds are breaking up*
> *mandrake—shrieks torn from the damp earth*

ars poetica is 64 pgs., A5, laser-printed and perfect-bound with glossy card cover containing 4-color artwork. They receive 600-800 poems a year, accept approximately 20%. Press run is 500 for 100 subscribers of which 20 are libraries. Single copy: $7 Australia, $9 overseas; subscription: $20 Australia, $30 overseas. **Sample (including guidelines) postpaid: $5 Australia, $7 overseas. Submit up to 5 poems at a time. No previously published poems; simultaneous submissions OK. Cover letter required. "Poems should be typed on one side of A4 paper, double spaced; name and address on every page. Brief bio desired but not required for Notes on Contributors section."** Time between acceptance and publication is 6-8 weeks. **Seldom comments on rejections. Reports in 6-8 weeks. Pays 1 copy.** The editors say, "To date, *ars poetica* has published poets from all states in Australia and seeks overseas subscriptions and submissions."

❦**ARSENAL PULP PRESS (V)**, 103-1014 Homer St., Vancouver, British Columbia V6B 2W9 Canada, founded 1980, publishes 1 paperback book of poetry/year. They only publish the work of Canadian poets and are **currently not accepting any unsolicited mss.**

ARSHILE; 96 TEARS PRESS (II), P.O. Box 3749, Los Angeles CA 90078-3749, e-mail arshile@earthlink.net, founded 1993, editor Mark Salerno. *Arshile* is a biannual "Magazine of the Arts," including poetry, fiction, drama, essays, reviews and interviews. **They want poetry "that shows evidence of formal innovation."** They have published poetry by Notley, Myles, Moriarty, Ashbery, Koch, Guest, Baraka, Malanga and Towle. As a sample the editor selected these lines from "Who's There" by William Bronk:

> *We need to separate ourselves from ourselves*
> *to be ourselves. All that pain and power:*
> *that isn't us. All that busyness,*
> *the alienation and hate, those love affairs.*

The editor says *Arshile* is 5½×8½, professionally printed and perfect-bound with 4-color cover and b&w art and ads inside. They receive about 1,000 poems a year, accept less than 10%. Press run is 1,500 for 200 subscribers of which 50% are libraries. Subscription: $18 for 2 issues. **Sample postpaid: $10. Submit 5-7 poems at a time. No previously published poems or simultaneous submissions. Reports in 3 months. Pays 2 copies. Rights revert to authors/artists.** 96 Tears Press "brings out small books (64 pgs.) of new writing by new and established authors." **Query first with sample poems. Replies to queries in 1-3 months.** Poetry published in *Arshile* has also been included in *The Best American Poetry 1997*.

ART TIMES: A LITERARY JOURNAL AND RESOURCE FOR ALL THE ARTS (II), P.O. Box 730, Mount Marion NY 12456-0730, phone (914)246-6944, poetry editor Cheryl A. Rice, is a monthly tabloid newspaper devoted to the arts. *Art Times* focuses on cultural and creative articles and essays, but also publishes some poetry and fiction. The editor wants to see **"poetry that strives to express genuine observation in unique language; poems no longer than 20 lines each."** As a sample she selected these lines from "Satin" by Paul Camacho:

> *an encounter with a noticed article,*
> *the satin of a bias smile,*
> *which causes the novice to speak*
> *of no experience save his own:*
> *what is beauty, but articulate bone?*

Art Times is 16-24 pgs., newsprint, with reproductions of artwork, some photos, advertisement-supported. They receive 300-500 poems/month, use only 40-50/year. Circulation is 16,000, of which 5,000 are by request and subscriptions; most distribution is free through galleries, theatres, etc. Subscription: $15/year. **Sample: $1 postage cost. Submit 4-5 typed poems at a time. "Simultaneous submissions discouraged." They have an 18-month backlog. Send SASE for guidelines. Reports in 6 months. Pays 6 copies plus 1-year subscription.**

ARTFUL DODGE (II, IV-Translations), Dept. of English, College of Wooster, Wooster OH 44691, founded 1979, poetry editor Daniel Bourne, is an annual literary magazine that "takes a strong interest in poets who are continually testing what they can get away with successfully in regard to subject, perspective, language, etc., but who also show mastery of current American poetic techniques—its varied textures and its achievement in the illumination of the particular. What all this boils down to is that we require high craftsmanship as well as a vision that goes beyond *one's own* storm windows, grandmothers or sexual fantasies—to paraphrase Hayden Carruth. **Poems can be on any subject, of any length, from any perspective, in any voice, but we don't want anything that does not connect with both the human and the aesthetic. Thus, we don't want cute, rococo surrealism, someone's warmed-up, left-over notion of an avant-garde that existed 10-100 years ago, or any last bastions of rhymed verse in the civilized world.** On the other hand, we are interested in poems that utilize stylistic persuasions both old and new to good effect. We are not afraid of poems which try to deal with large social, political, historical, and even philosophical questions—especially if the poem emerges from one's own life experience and is not the result of armchair pontificating. We often offer encouragement to writers whose work we find promising, but *Artful Dodge* **is more a journal for the already emerging writer than for the beginner**

looking for an easy place to publish. **We also have a sustained commitment to translation, especially from Polish and other East European literatures,** and we feel the interchange between the American and foreign works on our pages is of great interest to our readers. We also feature interviews with outstanding literary figures. As a sample the editor selected these lines from "Houdini" by Joel Brouwer:

> *. . . Look at these arms,*
> *the exhausted rubber muscle. This*
> *is God's work: to trick you*
> *into magic not through illusion nor divinity,*
> *but by beating my scant and bleeding hands*
> *against the darkness—and worse*
> *and more important: to never be fooled myself.*

The digest-sized, perfect-bound format is professionally printed, glossy cover, with art, ads. There are about 60-80 pgs. of poetry in each issue. They receive at least 2,000 poems/year, use 60. Press run is 1,000 for 100 subscribers of which 30 are libraries. **Sample: $5 for recent issues, $3 for others. "No simultaneous submissions. Please limit submissions to 6 poems. Long poems may be of any length, but send only one at a time. We encourage translations, but we ask as well for original text and statement from translator that he/she has copyright clearance and permission of author." Reports in up to 6 months. Pays 2 copies, plus, currently, $5/ page honorarium because of grants from Ohio Arts Council.** Open to unsolicited reviews; "query first." Poets may also send books for review consideration; however, "there is no guarantee we can review them!"

ARTISAN, A JOURNAL OF CRAFT (I, II), P.O. Box 157, Wilmette IL 60091, e-mail artisanjnl@aol.com, website http://members.aol.com/artisanjhe, founded 1995, editor Joan Daugherty, is a quarterly publication based on the idea that "anyone who strives to express themselves with skill is an artist and artists of all kinds can learn from each other. **We want poetry that is vital, fresh and true to life; evocative. Nothing trite, vague or pornographic."** As a sample the editor selected these lines from "Miami Beach" by Karen Mittelman:

> *an island breathes huge*
> *against the arms of ocean,*
> *and every fish in the*
> *dark waters,*
> *swollen with moonlight,*
> *breathes back.*

artisan is 32-36 pgs. (including cover), 8½ × 11, saddle-stitched with card stock cover, minimal graphics and ads. They receive about 450 poems a year, use approximately 10%. Press run is 300 for 50 subscribers, 100 distributed free to coffeehouses and local libraries. Subscription: $12. **Sample postpaid: $3.50. Make checks payable to artisan, ink. Submit 3-5 poems at a time. No previously published poems; simultaneous submissions OK. Cover letter preferred, however "if you send a cover letter, make it personal. We don't need to see any writing credentials; poems should stand on their own merit."** Time between acceptance and publication is 3-9 months. **Often comments on rejections. Send SASE for guidelines. Reports in 2-9 months. Pays 2 copies. Acquires first rights.** *artisan* sponsors an annual contest that rotates between poetry and short fiction. First prize is $200, second is $100. Prize winners and works meriting honorable mention are published in the summer issue. Entry fee varies. Send SASE for guidelines.

ARTS END BOOKS; NOSTOC MAGAZINE (V), P.O. Box 162, Newton MA 02168, founded 1978, poetry editor Marshall Brooks. **"We publish good contemporary writing. Our interests are broad and so are our tastes.** Their publications are distinguished by excellent presswork and art in a variety of formats: postcard series, posters, pamphlets, flat-spined paperbacks and hardbacks. **They will not be reading unsolicited mss until 1999.** The magazine appears irregularly in print runs of 300-500, about 30 pgs. of poetry in each, 100 subscriptions of which half are libraries. **Sample postpaid: $4.** Reviews books of poetry "on occasion, length varies."

‡**ARTWORD QUARTERLY; ARTWORD (II)**, 5273 Portland Ave., White Bear Lake MN 55110-2411, phone (612)426-7059, *ArtWord Quarterly* founded 1995, ArtWord founded 1994, editor/publisher Carol Robertshaw. *ArtWord Quarterly* is interested in "voices that are rich in life experiences. The best poetry, in our opinion, gives readers an epiphanic encounter with the familiar. **We will consider any form, subject matter or style, but we are partial to poems that are image filled, metaphorical, and written with precision and depth. No false appendages, no useless joints, all parts in service to the whole. Please no self-absorbed, pornographic, lovelorn or suicide poems."** They have recently published poetry by Rosemary Hildebrandt, Wayne Hogan, Joe Paddock, Dennis Saleh and Patricia Terry. As a sample the editor selected these lines from "basilica bell tower" by Paul Anderson:

> *up there*
> *on haunches cool and tight*
> *griffins pod*
> *preen behind each other's bat-like ears*
> *leathery wings*
> *nuzzle the bell with wet noses*
> *press toad-like fingers to the cast breast*

> the clapper
> like the foot of someone stepping into a cave
> is invisible

AQ is 40 pgs., 5½×8½, offset and saddle-stapled, with 2-color glossy card cover. They receive about 1,000 poems a year, accept approximately 10%. Press run is 150-200 for 50 subscribers, 25 shelf sales. Subscription: $15. **Sample postpaid: $4. Submit 3-5 poems at a time. No previously published poems or simultaneous submissions. Cover letter preferred. "Name and address should appear on each page. No more than one poem per page, single-spaced, not to exceed 30 lines. Include brief bio, plus publication credits and SASE." Submission deadlines are March 1, June 1, September 1 and December 1.** Time between acceptance and publication is 1 month or less. **Seldom comments on rejections. Send SASE for guidelines. Reports in 1-3 months. Pays 1 copy. All rights revert to author upon publication.** ArtWord provides literary services including creative and technical writing, critiques, book designing, typesetting, editing and and consulting on most aspects of self-publishing—all on a contractual basis. Call or write for information. "We hope to begin publishing chapbooks, anthologies and full-length collections in the near future, but do not do so at this time."

ASCENT (II), Dept. of English, Concordia College, Moorhead MN 56562, e-mail olsen@gloria.cord.edu, founded 1975, editor W. Scott Olsen, appears 3 times/year, using **poetry that is "eclectic, shorter rather than longer."** They have published poetry by Thomas Reiter, Michael Bugeja and Kathleen Lynch. As a sample the editor selected these lines from "Flat Country" by Mark Vinz:

> Give me a landscape where the sky is huge
> with scudding, booming clouds—no walls of trees
> obscuring hovering hawks, except along
> the riverbanks where cottonwood and willow
> watch meandering currents, ox-bowed in
> their own stubborn time.

The editor describes *Ascent* as 64 pgs., 6×9, perfect-bound, professionally printed with matte card cover. They receive about 750 poems a year, accept approximately 5%. Press run is 900 for 250 subscribers of which 90 are libraries. Subscription: $9/year. **Sample postpaid: $4. Submit 3-6 poems at a time. Always sends prepublication galleys. Pays 2 copies.** This continues as one of the "best buys" in the literary world for its low price, openness to all forms and styles, and relatively quick and encouraging response times. The editor says, "Poems are rejected or accepted from 2-8 weeks, usually closer to 2 weeks. Acceptances are usually published within the year." Poetry published here has also been included in *The Best American Poetry 1994*.

‡SHERMAN ASHER PUBLISHING (II), P.O. Box 2853, Santa Fe NM 87504, phone (505)984-2686, fax (505)820-2744, e-mail 71277.2057@compuserve.com, founded 1994, contact Judith Rafaela or Nancy Fay. "We are dedicated to changing the world one book at a time, committed to the power of truth and the craft of language expressed by publishing fine poetry. We specialize in anthologies." They publish 3-5 paperbacks/year. **"Please see our current books as an example of what we look for in poetry. We enjoy well-crafted form. No rhymed doggerel, cowboy poetry or stiff academic work."** They have recently published poetry by Marge Piercy, Galway Kinnell, Naomi Shihab Nye and Judyth Hill. **Submit 5 poems at a time. Previously published poems and simultaneous submissions OK. Cover letter preferred. "We specialize in anthologies and do not accept manuscripts for books. Also, we read submissions only during calls for submissions for our anthologies. Write for list."** Time between acceptance and publication is 3-6 months. **Poems are circulated to an editorial board. "Selection depends on the content/idea of the anthology and how well the poems fit together." Seldom comments on rejections. Replies to queries in 6-8 weeks. Pays author's copies.** Inquire for catalog or buy through local bookstores. "We do not take unsolicited manuscripts—only individual poems during our calls for submissions for our anthologies. Writers can check *Poets & Writers* magazine and other related magazines for these dates, or write us for a list."

THE ASHLAND POETRY PRESS (V, IV-Anthologies, themes), Ashland University, Ashland OH 44805-3702, founded 1969, editor Robert McGovern, publishes anthologies on specific themes and occasional collections. He has published the collection *American Lit* (a sonnet sequence) by Harold Witt; the anthology *Scarecrow Poetry: The Muse in Post-Middle Age*; *War and Lechery: The Poem* by William Sylvester; and *Little Apocalypse* by Wendy Battin, winner of the 1997 Richard Snyder Memorial Poetry Award. **"Watch publications such as**

ALWAYS include a self-addressed, stamped envelope (SASE) when sending a ms or query to a publisher within your own country. When sending material to other countries, include a self-addressed envelope and International Reply Coupons (IRCs), available for purchase at many post offices.

Poets & Writers for calls for mss, but don't submit otherwise. We do not read unsolicited mss; anthology readings take quite a bit of time." Considers simultaneous submissions. On collections, poet gets 10% royalty; anthologies, poets are paid stipulated price when sufficient copies are sold. Write for catalog.

ASIAN PACIFIC AMERICAN JOURNAL; ASIAN AMERICAN WRITERS' WORKSHOP (I, II, IV-Ethnic/nationality, anthology), 37 St. Mark's Place, #B, New York NY 10003, phone (212)228-6718, fax (212)228-7718, e-mail aaww@panix.com, website http://www.panix.com/~aaww, founded 1992. The *APA Journal* is a biannual published by the AAWW, a not-for-profit organization. It is **"dedicated to the best of contemporary Asian-American writing."** They have recently published poetry by Arthur Sze, Mei-Mei and Berssenbrugge and Sesshu Foster. *APA Journal* is 140-190 pgs., digest-sized, typeset and perfect-bound with 2-color cover and ads. They receive submissions from about 150 poets/year, accept about 30%. Press run is 1,500 for 400 subscribers of which 50 are libraries, 800 shelf sales. Single copy: $10; subscription/membership: $35; institutional membership: $50. **Sample postpaid: $12. Submit 4-6 poems at a time. No previously published poems or simultaneous submissions. Cover letter with phone and fax numbers and 1- to 4-sentence biographical statement required. Submissions on 3.5 Macintosh disk (or IBM, if necessary) plus hard copy requested. Deadlines are usually May 15 and January 15 for October 1 and April 1 issues, respectively.** "We will work with authors who are promising." Send SASE for guidelines. **Reports in 3-4 months. Pays 2 copies. Acquires one-time rights.** In 1996 they also published *Contours of the Heart*, a South Asian American anthology and *Flippin*, a Filipino American anthology. The AAWW offers creative writing workshops, a newsletter, a bookselling service, readings and fellowships to young Asian-American writers. Write for details.

‡ASSPANTS (I), 1009½ Castro St., San Francisco CA 94114, e-mail asspants@sirius.com, founded 1996, editors Chad Lange and Michael Barnett, is a "quarterly literary art journal dedicated to publishing, literature and artwork of quality. **We are open to all kinds of poetry. Our quarterly episodes tend to be somewhat dark, but exceptions are made for quality. We prefer innovative and intelligent poems."** They have recently published poetry by Christina Brown, Bob Langdon and Elli Cariveau. As a sample the editor selected these lines from "For A Friend" by Andrew Demacăk:

> *Outside*
> *the window, pools*
> *gather, circle*
> *upon circle. Tonight, even*
> *the rain*
> *can't say enough*

asspants is 60-70 pgs., 8½×8½, printed in various fonts and paper, tape-bound with 4-color card cover, b&w artwork, graphics and photography throughout. They receive about 500 poems a year, accept approximately 10%. Press run is 300 for 40 subscribers, 260 shelf sales. Single copy: $4; subscription: $16. **Sample postpaid: $5. Make checks payable to Chad Lange or Michael Barnett. Submit 5 poems at a time. Previously published poems and simultaneous submissions OK. Cover letter preferred. E-mail submissions OK.** Time between acceptance and publication is 1-6 months. **Poems are circulated to an editorial board. "We have two editors, both of whom read and discuss all submissions." Often comments on rejections. Send SASE for guidelines. Reports in 4-6 weeks. Pays 1 copy. All rights revert to author upon publication.** The editors say, "We strongly encourage reading a sample copy of *asspants* before submitting your work."

ATHENA INCOGNITO MAGAZINE (I), 1442 Judah St., San Francisco CA 94122, founded 1980, editor Ronn Rosen, is an annual of experimental writing and other arts. **They want poetry that is "experimental, surrealist, Dada, etc., 3 pgs. max. No greeting card verse, overly religious poetry or epics."** They have published poetry by Collette Robbins and Jamie Erfurdt. The editor says the magazine is usually 20-30 photocopied pgs. They receive about 50 poems a year, use approximately 15%. Press run is 200 for 50 subscribers of which 2 are libraries, 50 shelf sales. **"All people submitting poetry *must* buy a sample copy—$5.50 postpaid." Previously published poems and simultaneous submissions OK. "Name and address required on all pages. SASE also required." Often comments on rejections. Reports in 1-2 months. Pays 1 copy.** The editor says, "Be well read in world poetry, surrealism and Dada, and get inspired."

ATLANTA REVIEW; POETRY 1998 (II), P.O. Box 8248, Atlanta GA 30306, founded 1994, editor Daniel Veach, is a semiannual primarily devoted to poetry, but also featuring fiction, interviews, essays and fine art. **They want "quality poetry of genuine human appeal."** They have recently published poetry by Seamus Heaney, Derek Walcott, Maxine Kumin, Rachel Hadas, Charles Simic and Naomi Shihab Nye. As a sample the editor selected these lines from "Widow's Quilt" by R.T. Smith:

> *She listens to the rafters, ache*
> *of cradlewood in the attic, night's*
> *owling and antler, crabapple*
> *flowering too early. Deadwood,*
> *well rust, potatoes moonwhite*
> *in the white basin.*

AR is 112 pgs., 6×9, professionally printed on acid-free paper and flat-spined with glossy color cover and b&w

artwork. They receive about 10,000 poems a year, use about 1%. Press run is 6,000 for 500 subscribers of which 20 are libraries, 5,000 shelf sales. Single copy: $6; subscription: $10. **Sample postpaid: $5. No previously published poems. Issue deadlines are June 1 and December 1.** Time between acceptance and publication is 2 months. **Editors alternate as final issue editor. Seldom comments on rejections. Each spring issue has an International Feature Section. Send SASE for guidelines. Reports in 2 months. Pays 2 copies plus subscription. Acquires first North American serial rights.** *AR* also sponsors POETRY 1998, an annual international poetry competition. Prizes are $1,000, $500 and $250, plus 50 International Merit Awards. Winners are announced in leading literary publications. All entries are considered for publication in *Atlanta Review*. Entry fee is $5 for the first poem, $2 for each additional. No entry form or guidelines necessary. Send to POETRY 1998 at the above address. Postmark deadline: May 1, 1998. They say, "We are making a serious effort to give today's poets the international audience they truly deserve." Poetry published here has also been included in the 1996 *Pushcart Prize* anthology.

THE ATLANTIC (II), Dept. PM, 77 North Washington St., Boston MA 02114, phone (617)854-7700, website http://www.theatlantic.com, founded 1857, poetry editor Peter Davison, assistant poetry editor David Barber, publishes 1-5 poems monthly. **Some of the most distinguished poetry in American literature** has been published by this magazine, including work by William Matthews, Mary Oliver, Stanley Kunitz, Rodney Jones, May Swenson, Galway Kinnell, Philip Levine, Richard Wilbur, Tess Gallagher, Donald Hall and W.S. Merwin. The magazine has a circulation of 500,000, of which 5,800 are libraries. They receive some 35,000 poems/year, of which they use 35-40 and have a backlog of 6-12 months. **Sample postpaid: $3. Submit 3-5 poems with SASE. No simultaneous submissions. No fax or e-mail submissions. Publishes theme issues. Always sends prepublication galleys. Pays about $3/line. Buys first North American serial rights only.** Wants "to see poetry of the highest order; we do *not* want to see workshop rejects. **Watch out for workshop uniformity. Beware of the present tense. Be yourself.**" Poetry published here has been included in the 1992, 1993, 1995 and 1996 volumes of *The Best American Poetry*.

✦**ATLANTIS: A WOMEN'S STUDIES JOURNAL (V-Feminist)**, Dept. PM, Institute for the Study of Women, Mount Saint Vincent University, Halifax, Nova Scotia B3M 2J6 Canada, phone (902)457-6319, fax (902)443-1352, founded 1975, appears twice a year using "a little" **poetry "certainly no longer than five ms pgs.; should have a feminist perspective, preferably academic."** They have published poetry by Liliane Welch. The editor describes it as 150 pgs., magazine-sized, flat-spined with card cover. They accept about 5-10% of submissions. Press run is 1,000 for 600 subscribers of which 55% are libraries. Subscription: Canada: individual $20, institution $40; US: individual $30, institution, $50; international: individual $35, institution $55 (all in Canadian dollars). **Sample postpaid: $12 Canadian. Currently not accepting poetry submissions.**

ATOM MIND (II); MOTHER ROAD PUBLICATIONS (V), P.O. Box 22068, Albuquerque NM 87154-2068, first founded 1968-70, reestablished 1992, editor Gregory Smith. *Atom Mind* is a quarterly journal of "alternative literature, mostly influenced by the Beats, Steinbeck, John Fante and Bukowski. **Narrative, free verse, 20-80 lines preferred, although length restrictions are not set in stone. No light verse, inspirational poetry, doggerel, 'moon-spoon-June' rhyming verse."** They have published poetry by Lawrence Ferlinghetti, Charles Plymell and Wilma Elizabeth McDaniel. The editor says *AM* is 120 pgs., 8½×11, offset, with illustrations and photographs. They receive approximately 2,000 submissions annually, publish perhaps 5%. Press run is 1,000 for 750 subscribers of which 25 are libraries. Subscription: $20. **Sample postpaid: $6. Prefers to consider submissions of 5-8 poems at a time, rather than 1 or 2 poems. Previously published poems OK; no simultaneous submissions.** Time between acceptance and publication is 8-12 months. "*Atom Mind* **is very much a one-man operation; therefore, submissions are subject to the whims and personal biases of the editor only." Often comments on rejections. Send SASE for guidelines. Reports in 1-2 months. Pays copies, number varies. Acquires first or one-time rights.** Mother Road Publications also publishes 2 paperback and 2 hardback collections of poetry/year. **"Book-length poetry manuscripts considered by invitation only." Send SASE for catalog.**

AURA LITERARY/ARTS REVIEW (II), Dept. PM, Box 76, Hill University Center, University of Alabama at Birmingham, Birmingham AL 35294-1150, phone (205)934-3216, founded 1974, editor Steve Mullen, is a semiannual magazine that publishes "fiction and art though majority of acceptances are poetry—90-100 per year. **Length open, style open, subject matter open. We are looking for quality poetry. Both first-time and often-published poets are published here."** *Aura* has published work by Lyn Lifshin, Adrian C. Louis and William Miller. The 6×9 magazine is 100-140 pgs., perfect-bound, printed on white matte with b&w photos, lithography and line art. Circulation is 500, of which 40-50 are subscriptions; other sales are to students and Birmingham residents. Subscription: $6. **Sample postpaid: $3. Writers should submit "3-5 poems, with SASE, no simultaneous submissions, will even take neatly handwritten." Send SASE for guidelines. Reports in 2-3 months. Pays 2 copies.**

THE AUROREAN: A POETIC QUARTERLY; ENCIRCLE PUBLICATIONS (II), P.O. Box 219, Sagamore Beach MA 02562, phone (508)833-0805, press founded 1992, magazine founded 1995, editor Cynthia Brackett-Vincent. *The Aurorean*, which appears in March, June, September and December, seeks to publish "poetry that is inspirational, meditational or reflective of the Northeast. Strongly encouraged topics: positiveness, recovery and nature. Maximum length: 36 lines. Typographical oddities are OK as long as we can reproduce them on our page. No hateful, overly religious or vulgar poetry." They have recently published poetry by Daniel Green, Timothy Hodor and Errol Miller. As a sample the editor selected these lines from "Dew" by Dawn Goodrich:

> At night,
> when we're asleep,
> the Gods & Goddesses come out
> and weep
> at what we've done.

The Aurorean is 24-32 pgs., 5½×8½, professionally printed and saddle-stapled with 65 lb. cover. Press run is 300. Subscription: $14. **Sample postpaid: $4. Make checks payable to Encircle Publications. Submit 3-5 poems at a time. No previously published poems or simultaneous submissions. Cover letter preferred. Often comments on rejections. Send SASE for guidelines.** "I notify authors of receipt of manuscripts immediately and report on decisions in one week to three months." Always sends prepublication galleys. Pays 3 copies/poem. Also features a "Poet-of-the-Quarter" each issue with publication of up to 3 poems and an extended bio (100 words). The "Poet-of-the-Quarter" receives 10 copies and a 1-year subscription. The editor says, "Study *Poet's Market*. If possible, request a sample before you submit. Always have a ms out there. Stop saying you want to be a writer. You are a writer if you write. Remember, editors are people too. What one editor rejects one day, another may jump at the next. Invest in small presses with samples. Invest in yourself with postage. Always include enough postage for the return/reply process!!! Read more poetry than you write, and read your poetry out loud."

‡AVISSON PRESS, INC. (III), 3007 Taliaferro Rd., Greensboro NC 27408, founded 1995, editor M.L. Hester. Seeks high literary quality work only and publishes 5 paperbacks/year. They have recently published poetry by Charles Fishman, Janet McCann, Joanne Lowery and Sonya Hess. Books are usually 64-120 pgs., 5½×8½, perfect-bound, offset printed with line art. **Submit 5-6 poems at a time. Previously published poems and simultaneous submissions OK. Cover letter required with bio, publication credits and SASE.** Time between acceptance and publication is 4-6 months. **Seldom comments on rejections. Replies to queries in 2-4 weeks, to mss in 2 months. Pays 8% royalties or 30 author's copies (out of a press run of 300). Obtain sample books by sending $10.**

‡AVOCET; AVOCET PRESS (IV-Nature, spirituality), 3802 N. Lupine Lane #P, Calabasas CA 91302, e-mail jayt79b@prodigy.com, first issue published Fall 1997, editor Patricia Swenson. *Advocet* is a new quarterly poetry journal "focusing on nature/spiritual." **They want "poetry that shows man's interconnectedness with nature; discovering the Divine in nature."** The editor says *Advocet* is 20-30 pgs., 4¼×5½, professionally printed and saddle-stapled with card cover, some illustrations. "We will try to publish one poem from each submission." Press run is 200. **Submit up to 5 poems at a time. Previously published poems OK if acknowledged; no simultaneous submissions. Cover letter required including brief bio and SASE.** Time between acceptance and publication is 3 months. **Often comments on rejections. Reports in 2-3 weeks. Pays 1 copy.**

‡AXE FACTORY REVIEW; CYNIC PRESS (I, II), P.O. Box 40691, Philadelphia PA 19107, *Axe Factory* founded 1986, Cynic Press founded 1996, editor/publisher Joseph Farley. *Axe Factory* is published 1-4 times/year and its purpose is to "spread the disease known as literature. The content is mostly poetry and essays." **They want "eclectic work. Will look at anything but suggest potential contributors purchase a copy of magazine first to see what we're like. No greeting card verse."**

● We highly recommend obtaining a sample before submitting as the editor has displayed, in his answers to our questionnaire, a quirky sense of humor.

They have recently published poetry by Taylor Graham, Charles O'Hay and Kimberly Brittingham. As a sample the editor selected these lines from "Starting Over" by Louis McKee:

> I kept the doll I found
> in the yard, a Barbie with matted
> blond hair and not a stitch
> of clothing. A new wife,
> I thought, and I proposed to her

Axe Factory is 20-40 pgs., 8½×11, saddle-stitched, neatly printed with light, colored card cover. Press run is 100. Single copy: $5; subscription: $20 for 5 issues. **Sample postpaid: $3. Make checks payable to Joseph**

● **A BULLET** introduces comments by the editors of *Poet's Market* indicating special information about the listing.

Farley. Submit up to 10 poems. Previously published poems "sometimes, but let me know up front"; simultaneous submissions OK. Cover letter preferred "but not a form letter, tell me about yourself." Often comments on rejections. Pays 1-2 copies. Reserves right to anthologize poems under Cynic Press; all other rights returned. Reviews books of poetry in 10-1,000 words. Open to unsolicited reviews. Poets may also send books for review consideration. Cynic Press occasionally publishes chapbooks. Send SASE for details before submitting. The editor says, "Writing is a form of mental illness, spread by books, teachers, and the desire to communicate."

BABYSUE (I), P.O. Box 8989, Atlanta GA 30306-8989, founded 1985, editor/publisher Don W. Seven, appears twice a year publishing obtuse humor for the extremely open-minded. **"We are open to all styles, but prefer short poems." No restrictions.** They have published poetry by Edward Mycue, Susan Andrews and Barry Bishop. The editor says *babysue* is 32 pgs., offset. "We print prose, poems and cartoons. We usually accept about 5% of what we receive." Single copy: $3; subscription: $12 for 4 issues. **Sample postpaid: $2. Previously published poems and simultaneous submissions OK. Deadlines are March 30 and September 30 of each year. Seldom comments on rejections. Reports "immediately, if we are interested." Pays 1 copy.** "We do occasionally review other magazines." The editor adds, "We have received no awards, but we are very popular on the underground press circuit and sell our magazine all over the world."

BACKSPACE (IV-Gay/lesbian/bisexual), 25 Riverside Ave., Gloucester MA 01930-2552, e-mail charkim@ti ac.net, website http://www.tiac.net/users/charkim, founded 1991, managing editor Kim Smith. *Backspace*, published 3 times a year, is a collection of queer poetry and fiction, provides a forum for gay/lesbian writers to share their work with their peers." **They want any kind of poetry, prefer gay and lesbian themes, but nothing more than 50 lines. "No explicitly sexual or violent works."** The editor says *Backspace* is about 48 pgs., digest-sized, laser-printed and saddle-stitched with glossy cover stock. They receive 30-50 poems a year, accept approximately 35%. Press run is 400. Single copy: $4; subscription: $7.50/year. **Sample postpaid: $2. Make checks payable to Charlotte Stratton. Submit 6 poems at a time. E-mail and diskette submissions OK. No previously published poems; simultaneous submissions OK. Cover letter with brief bio (no more than 30 words) required. Send SASE for guidelines. Reports immediately. Pays 1 copy.** Reviews books of poetry. Open to unsolicited reviews. Poets may also send books for review consideration to Charlotte Stratton, assistant managing editor. The editor says, "Don't hold yourself back—share your work."

‡❁BADLANDS PRESS; SANDSTONE (IV-Science fiction/fantasy, horror), 304-314 Broadway Ave., Winnipeg, Manitoba R3C 0S5 Canada, founded 1993, editor Anna Boudneau. *Sandstone*, first published in Spring 1997, is dedicated to expanding Canadian horror, science fiction and fantasy. **They want "no poems longer than 100 words; free verse on the subjects of horror, science fiction or fantasy. No bad, moody and self-depressing poetry."** They have recently published poetry by Karen Blicker. The editor says *Sandstone*'s format is similar to a chapbook. Single copy: $6. **Submit 3 poems at a time. No previously published poems or simultaneous submissions. Cover letter required. Reads submissions February 1 through March 15.** Time between acceptance and publication is 3 months. **Often comments on rejections. Publishes theme issues. Send SASE for guidelines and upcoming themes. Reports in 1 month. Pays $5/poem. Buys "publishing rights only."** BadLands Press's purpose is "to explore undeveloped talent, and expand the appreciation of a neglected genre in literature." Books are formatted "to enhance the imagery of material." **Query first with a few sample poems and a cover letter with brief bio and publication credits. Replies to queries in 2 months, to mss in 3 weeks. Pays $5 honorarium and 1 author's copy (out of a press run of 100).** The editor says, "Always proofread. Don't stop at a rejection, keep trying. Writers and books are poorly advertized by publishers. The same is true for small press, self-promotion is important. I welcome working with my contributors to promote their work in *Sandstones*."

‡BANGTALE INTERNATIONAL (II), P.O. Box 83984, Phoenix AZ 85071-3984, founded 1989, editor William Edward Dudley, appears twice a year. **They want "poetry that is telling and doesn't complicate itself through evasive word salad but seeks understanding and gives emotion. Use quality in language that is humane, humorous, passionate, culturally forward and unexpected. Above all we encourage writing as an instrument that disentangles your thought process."** They have published poetry by Mary Winters, Stephen R. Roberts, Lyn Lifshin and Thomas Dorsett. *Bangtale* is 50 pgs., digest-sized, offset and saddle-stapled, with glossy card cover and b&w art. Press run is 450. Subscription: $8. **Sample: $5. Sometimes sends prepublication galleys. Pays 1 copy.**

BANTAM DOUBLEDAY DELL PUBLISHING GROUP (V), 1540 Broadway, New York NY 10036, phone (212)354-6500, **only accepts mss from agents.**

‡BARBARIC YAWP; BONEWORLD PUBLISHING (I, II), 3706 County Route 24, Russell NY 13684, founded 1996, editor John Berbrich. *Barbaric Yawp*, appears biannually, "publishing the best fiction, poetry and essays available"; encourages beginning writers. "We are not preachers of any particular poetic or literary school. **We publish any type of quality material appropriate for our intelligent and wide-awake audience; 50 lines maximum. We do not want any pornography, gratuitous violence, or any whining, pissing or moaning."**

They have recently published poetry by Tim Hodor, Mark Spitzer and Jade. As a sample the editor selected these lines from this untitled poem by J. Patrick:

> *The shadow tosses in a mist of snow*
> *Sparkling, now Ruby!*
> *Hunter springs! Lunge after lunge!*
> *His wide padded paws-feet race madly.*
> *Club held high as he approaches*
> *The beast furiously wrestling against its fate . . .*

The editor says *BY* is a 50-page booklet, stapled with 24 lb. cover, line drawings. They receive 120 poems a year, accept approximately 20%. Press run is 100 for 20 subscribers. Single copy: $4; subscription: $7.50/year. **Sample postpaid: $3. Make checks payable to John Berbrich. Submit up to 5 poems at a time, no more than 50 lines each. Previously published poems and simultaneous submissions OK. One-page cover letter preferred, include a short publication history (if available) and a brief bio. Submission deadlines: March 15 for summer issue, September 15 for winter.** Time between acceptance and publication is 2-6 months. **Often comments on rejections. Send SASE for guidelines. Reports in 1-2 months. Pays 1 copy. Acquires one-time rights.** The editor says, "We are primarily concerned with work that means something to the author but which is able to transcend the personal into the larger more universal realm. Send whatever is important to you. We will use yin and yang. We really like humor."

‡*BATS AND RED VELVET MAGAZINE (IV-Horror/gothic/vampire), Flat 1, 112 St. George's Terrace, Newcastle Upon Tyne NE2 2DP United Kingdom, e-mail batsvelvet@aol.com, founded 1991, is a bimonthly "gothic/darkwave music magazine which features supernatural/horror articles." **They want gothic/vampire/horror genres only. "Must be quite short—limited space."** They say the magazine is about 52 pgs., A4, offset printed, stapled, with glossy "spot colour" cover, includes illustrations, photos and ads. They receive about 100 poems a year, accept approximately 90%. Press run is 1,000 for 500 subscribers, 500 shelf sales. Subscription: $30. **Sample postpaid: $5. "We cannot accept US cheques." Submit up to 4 poems at a time. No previously published poems or simultaneous submissions. Cover letter preferred.** Time between acceptance and publication can be up to 18 months. **Always comments on rejections. Reports in 1-6 weeks.**

WILLIAM L. BAUHAN, PUBLISHER (V, IV-Regional), P.O. Box 443, Old County Rd., Dublin NH 03444, phone (603)563-8020, fax (603)563-8026, founded 1959, editor William L. Bauhan, publishes poetry and art, especially New England regional books. **Currently accepts no unsolicited poetry.** They have published books of poetry by Sarah Singer, Anne Marx, Phoebe Barnes Driver and May Sarton.

BAY AREA POETS COALITION (BAPC); POETALK (I), P.O. Box 11435, Berkeley CA 94712-2435, founded 1974, direct submissions to Editorial Committee. Coalition sends bimonthly poetry journal, *Poetalk*, to over 300 people. They also publish an annual anthology (19th—180 pgs., out in February 1998), giving one page to each member of BAPC (minimum 6 months) who has had work published in *Poetalk* during the previous year. *Poetalk* publishes approximately 90 poets each issue. BAPC has 160 members, 70 subscribers, but *Poetalk* is open to all. **No particular genre. Short poems (under 35 lines). "Rhyme must be well done."** Membership: $15 for 12 months of *Poetalk*, copy of anthology and other privileges; extra outside US. Also offers a $50 patronage, which includes a subscription and anthology for another individual of your choice, and a $25 beneficiary/memorial, which includes membership plus subscription for friend. Subscriptions: $6/year. As a sample the editors selected this complete poem, "Technology" by Margaret Finch:

> *We do not stroke cats*
> *we do not stroke horses*
> *we do not stroke dogs*
> *we only stroke*
> *computer keys.*

Poetalk is 24 pgs., 5½×8½, photocopied, saddle-stapled with heavy card cover. **Send SASE with 55¢ postage for a free complimentary copy. Submit up to 4 poems, typed and single-spaced, 35 lines maximum, with SASE, no more than twice a year. Simultaneous and previously published work OK, but must be noted. "All subject matter should be in good taste." Response time is 2 weeks to 4 months. Pays 1 copy.** BAPC holds monthly readings, yearly contest, etc.; has mailing list open to local members. BAPC's annual contest, established in 1980, awards a $40 first prize, $25 second prize, $10 third prize, certificate for honorable mention, plus publication in and 1 copy of BAPC's annual anthology. Submissions must be unpublished. Submit 2 copies of up to 8 poems on any subject of 15-35 lines (blank lines count), with SASE for winners list. Include name, address and whether member or nonmember on 1 copy only. Send SASE in September for guidelines. Entry fee: $1/poem for members. Submission period: October 1 through November 15, 1997. Winners will be announced by mail in January 1998. People from many states and countries have contributed to *Poetalk* or entered their annual contests. Send SASE in early September for contest guidelines. The editors say, "We differ from many publishers in that we are very actively involved in working with the poets to make their poems publishable. We try to help people get to the point where we can publish their work, i.e., we make editorial comments on almost everything we reject. If you don't want suggested revisions you need to say so clearly in your cover letter."

BAY WINDOWS (IV-Gay/lesbian), 1523 Washington St., Boston MA 02118, phone (617)266-6670 ext. 211, fax (617)266-5973, e-mail rudyk@aol.com or rkikel@tiac.com, founded 1983, poetry editor Rudy Kikel. *Bay Windows* **is a weekly gay and lesbian newspaper** published for the New England community, regularly using **"short poems of interest to lesbians and gay men. Poetry that is 'experiential' seems to have a good chance with us, but we don't want poetry that just 'tells it like it is.' Our readership doesn't read poetry all the time. A primary consideration is giving** *pleasure*. **We'll overlook the poem's (and the poet's) tendency not to be informed by the latest poetic theory, if it** *does* **this: pleases. Pleases, in particular, by articulating common gay or lesbian experience, and by doing that with some attention to form. I've found that a lot of our choices were made because of a strong image strand. Humor is** *always* **welcome—and hard to provide with craft. Obliquity, obscurity? Probably not for us. We won't presume on our audience."** They have recently published poetry by Jeff Walt, Judith Saunders, Mark Hallman and Kate Adams. As a sample the editor selected these lines from "In the Kingdom of Honey" by Jessica Jopp:

> *We put the jar of slow liquid*
> *where it will quicken when the air gets cold.*
> *And when we sleep, there it will be*
> *below us on the kitchen sill,*
> *the memory of bees*
> *faintly in the chambered dark*
> *drinking in then giving away their gold.*

"We try to run four poems each month." They receive about 300 submissions/year, use 1 in 6, have a 3-month backlog. Press run is 13,000 for 700 subscribers of which 15 are libraries. Single copy: 50¢; subscription: $40. **Sample postpaid: $2. Submit 3-5 poems at a time, "5-25 lines are ideal; include short biographical blurb and SASE. No submissions via e-mail, but poets may request info via e-mail." Reports in 2-3 months. Pays 1-2 copies. Acquires first rights. Editor "often" comments on rejections.** They review books of poetry in about 750 words—"Both single and omnibus reviews (the latter are longer)."

BEACON (IV-Regional), Southwestern Oregon Community College, 1988 Newmark Ave., Coos Bay OR 97420-2956, phone (541)888-7335, editor changes yearly. *Beacon* is a small, college literary magazine that appears twice a year and publishes the work of local writers and artists. **They want poetry only from those who have had their beginnings or currently reside in Southwestern Oregon. No specifications as to form, length, subject matter or style. "Submissions limited to five poems per term, prefer non-saga poems; one story per term, maximum 3,000 words."** The editor says *Beacon* is 75-100 pgs., 5½×8, professionally printed with color cover and b&w art within; no ads. They receive about 400 poems a year, accept approximately 25%. Press run is 300, all shelf sales. **Sample postpaid: $3.50. No previously published poems or simultaneous submissions. Cover letter required. Reads submissions December 1 through January 15 and March 1 through April 15.** Time between acceptance and publication is 2 months. **Seldom comments on rejections. Reports "on publication." Pays 1 copy. Acquires first rights.** The editor says, "We encourage poets to visit for readings and bring works to offer for sale. We do not compensate in any way for these readings. The purpose of our magazine is to heighten the value of literature in our community."

THE BEAR ESSENTIAL (IV-Nature/rural/ecology), P.O. Box 10342, Portland OR 97296-0342, phone (503)242-1047, fax (503)243-2645, e-mail orlo@teleport.com, website http://www.teleport.com/~orlo/, founded 1993, editor Tom Webb, is a semiannual that "provides a fresh voice amid often strident and polarized environmental discourse. Street-level, non-dogmatic and solution-oriented, *The Bear Essential* presents lively creative discussion to a diverse readership. **They want poetry with "innovative environmental perspectives, not much longer than 50 lines. No rants."** They have recently published poetry by Mary Winters, Stephen Babcock, Carl Hanni and Derek Sheffield. As a sample the editor selected these lines from "Smoking" by Leanne Grabel:

> *I wonder what I*
> *think's going to*
> *happen if I*
> *breath only*
> *air.*

The Bear Essential is 76 pgs., 11×14, newsprint with brown Kraft paper cover, saddle-stitched, with lots of original graphics and b&w photos. They receive about 400 poems a year, publish 20-30. Press run is 15,000 for 750 subscribers of which 10 are libraries, 14,000 distributed free on the streets of the Western US and beyond. Subscription: $10. **Sample postpaid: $3. Make checks payable to Orlo. Submit 3-5 poems at a time. Previously published poems and simultaneous submissions OK. Poems are reviewed by a committee of 7-9 people. Publishes theme issues. Send SASE for guidelines and upcoming themes. Reports in 6-8 weeks. Pays $10/poem, 5-20 copies, subscription and "invitation to great events." Buys first or one-time rights.** Note: *The Bear Essential* is published by Orlo, a nonprofit organization exploring environmental issues through the creative arts.

‡BEAUTY FOR ASHES (I, II), 1000 Charles St., Mechanicsburg PA 17055-3944, e-mail beauty/ashes@geocities.com, website http://www.geocities.com/paris/2729/, founded 1996, editor C.R. Cain, appears 3 times/year. "Our desire is to spark the reader into a personal debate with himself. The topic? 'How do I see the spiritual when the mundane stands in my way?' **We consider free verse first but, please note, this does not mean abstract. We will consider well-written rhyme. No erotica, vulgar or profane poems. If 'I' or 'me' is used too often, consider sending your poems elsewhere. Better yet, rewrite it then submit here."** They have recently published poetry by Marc Awodey, Richard Fein and Barbara Bradshaw. As a sample the editor selected these lines from "Hockey Players" by Ryan Johnson:

> *as the boys began their dance on the denim-blue ice,*
> *writing their own poetry with each shift of weight—*
> *so casual it seems as if they had just dreamed the movement—*
> *and one boy, no taller than your hip, a mere swallow,*
> *guided the puck, which moves like a frightened mouse,*
> *through the flock and into the net,*
> *his cry of triumph a bell echo in the cold.*

BFA is 30-40 pgs., digest-sized, desktop-published and saddle-stitched with card cover with pen & ink drawings. "We are interested in receiving artwork for future covers. We will also carry ads for chapbooks. Send SASE for details. They accept approximately 5% of poems received. Press run is 150 for 5 subscribers, 75-100 shelf sales. Subscription: $10. **Sample postpaid: $4. Submit up to 5 poems at a time. Previously published poems OK, but "must state when and where published and author must own the rights to publish again"; simultaneous submissions OK if notified. Cover letter strongly preferred including bio. Electronic submissions OK, "but this option does not always allow for proper line breaks in the poems."** Time between acceptance and publication is 3-6 months. **Often comments on rejections. Send SASE for guidelines or obtain via website. Reports in 4-6 weeks, "occasionally longer." Pays 2 copies. Acquires first or one-time rights. "Some poems are held in archive at our website. After publication in print, poets may request their poem be removed from the website."** Reviews books and chapbooks of poetry. Open to unsolicited reviews. Poets may also send books for review consideration. Sponsors annual contest. Contest submissions are accepted from November 1 to February 15. Subject is open. Reading fee: $3 for 1 poem, $5 for up to 3 poems. First place: $50, 1-year subscription and "featured" poet on website for 30 days. The editor says, "Too many poets write but don't read poetry. And all too often poets go to open readings to read and not to listen. How can you hear a poem when the one you're holding is screaming to be read? Go to a reading empty handed, you will hear some uncommonly good works from others—and learn something."

BEGGAR'S PRESS; THE LAMPLIGHT; RASKOLNIKOV'S CELLAR; BEGGAR'S REVIEW (I), 8110 N. 38th St., Omaha NE 68112-2018, phone (402)455-2615, founded 1977, editor Richard R. Carey. *The Lamplight* is a semiannual (more frequent at times) publication of short stories, poetry, humor and unusual literary writings. **"We are eclectic, but we like serious poetry, historically orientated. Positively no religious or sentimental poetry. No incomprehensible poetry."** They have published poetry by Fredrick Zydek and John J. McKernan. As a sample the editor selected these lines (poet unidentified):

> *Lord, why did you curse me with doubt!*
> *I'm a shot discharged in a wood without trees,*
> *like a scream that began as a shout.*
> *Never too far from famine or mire;*
> *hunger and cold, and all creatures turn bold—*
> *But, Lord, why did you give me desire!*

The Lamplight is 40-60 pgs., 8½×11, offset printed and perfect-bound with 65 lb. cover stock. They receive about 600 poems a year, use approximately 10-15%. Press run is 500 for 300 subscribers of which 25 are libraries. Single copy: $9.50. **Sample: $7 plus 9×12 SASE. No previously published poems; simultaneous submissions OK. Cover letter required—"must provide insight into the poet's characteristics. What makes this poet different from the mass of humanity?"** Time between acceptance and publication is 4-12 months. **Often comments on rejections. Also offers "complete appraisals and evaluations" for $4/standard sheet, double-spaced. Brochure available for SASE. Reports in 2 to 2½ months. Pays 2 copies plus discount on up to 5. Acquires first North American serial rights.** *Raskolnikov's Cellar* is an irregular magazine of the same format, dimensions and terms as *The Lamplight*. However, it deals in **"deeper psychologically-orientated stories and poetry.** It is more selective and discriminating in what it publishes. Guidelines and brochures are an essential to consider this market." **Send SASE and $1 for guidelines. Brochures require only SASE.** *Beggar's Review* is 20-40 pgs., 8½×11, offset printed and saddle-stitched. It lists and reviews books, chapbooks and other magazines. "It also lists and reviews unpublished manuscripts: poetry, short stories, book-length, etc. Our purpose is to offer a vehicle for unpublished work of merit, as well as published material. We like to work with poets and authors who have potential but have not yet been recognized." Lengths of reviews range from a listing or mere caption

---

MARKET CATEGORIES: (I) Beginning; **(II)** General; **(III)** Limited; **(IV)** Specialized; **(V)** Closed.

to 1,000 words, "according to merit." Single copy: $6. Beggar's Press also plans to publish 4-6 paperbacks/year—some on a subsidy basis. **"In most cases, we select books which we publish on a royalty basis and promote ourselves. Borderline books only are author-subsidized."** Query first with a few sample poems and a cover letter with brief bio and publication credits. **"We also like to know how many books the author himself will be able to market to friends, associates, etc."** Replies to queries in 1 month, to mss in 2½ months. Pays 10-15% royalties and 3 author's copies. Terms vary for subsidy publishing. **"Depending on projected sales, the author pays from 20% to 60%."** The editor says, "Our purpose is to form a common bond with distinguished poets whose poetry is marketable and worthy. Poetry is difficult to market, thus we sometimes collaborate with the poet in publishing costs. But essentially, we look for poets with unique qualities of expression and who meet our uncustomary requirements. We prefer a royalty arrangement. Beggar's Press is different from most publishers. We are impressed with concrete poetry, which is without outlandish metaphors. Keep it simple but don't be afraid to use our language to the fullest. Read Poe, Burns and Byron. Then submit to us. There is still a place for lyrical poetry."

‡**BEHIND BARS (II)**, P.O. Box 2975, Tempe AZ 85280-2975, founded 1996, editor-in-chief Stephanie Owen, is a biannual "literary magazine of poetry, fiction, essays, reviews and art based on quality by both known and undiscovered writers." **They want "any subject, any length, in any voice but strong in image and emotion. We only want poets who are obsessed with their poetry to submit based on quality not bio information. No cliché-bound, worn-out language; no punctuation, no capital letters."** They have recently published poetry by Martha Modena Vertreace, William Greenway, Rane Arroyo and Barbara Daniels. As a sample the editor selected these lines from "Like A Knife Into The Heart of Morpheus (for John Berryman)" by Joseph Allgren:

> The leap provides the certainty of change,
> and stops the chance some god will take
> you while you dream. The sky, enameled, pure
> and starless, flies back as you roll and, like
> a knife into the heart of Morpheus,
> descend toward the waking, the crack of ice.

BB is 40-50 pgs., 5½×8½, professionally printed and saddle-stapled with colored card cover, b&w art and photos. They accept less than 5% of poetry received. Press run is 60-70, 50% shelf sales. Subscription: $6. **Sample (including guidelines) postpaid: $3. Make checks payable to Stephanie Owen. Submit 3-5 poems at a time. No previously published poems or simultaneous submissions. Cover letter preferred.** "Make sure name and address are on every page; only interested in reading cover letters that are three lines or less." Seldom comments on rejections. Reports in 2-3 months. Pays 1 copy. "All rights revert to the author upon publication." Sponsors a poetry/fiction contest. Send SASE for details.

BELHUE PRESS (III, IV-Gay), 2501 Palisade Ave., Suite A1, Riverdale, Bronx NY 10463, founded 1990, editor Tom Laine, is a small press **specializing in gay male poetry**, publishing 3 paperbacks/year—no chapbooks. **"We are especially interested in anthologies, in thematic books, in books that get out of the stock poetry market."** They want **"hard-edged, well-crafted, fun and often sexy poetry. No mushy, self pitying, confessional, boring, indulgent, teary or unrequited love poems—yuck! Poets must be willing to promote book through readings, mailers, etc." Query first with 6 pgs. of poetry and cover letter. Previously published poems and simultaneous submissions OK.** Time between acceptance and publication is 1 year. **Often comments on rejections. Will request criticism fees "if necessary." Replies to queries and submitted mss "fast." No payment information provided. Sample: $7.95.** "The only things we find offensive are stupid, dashed off, 'fortune cookie' poems that show no depth or awareness of poetry. We like poetry that, like good journalism, tells a story."

THE BELLINGHAM REVIEW; THE SIGNPOST PRESS; 49TH PARALLEL POETRY AWARD (II), M.S. 9053, Western Washington University, Bellingham WA 98225, founded 1975, editor Robin Hemley, publishes *The Bellingham Review* twice a year, runs an annual poetry competition and publishes other books and chapbooks of poetry occasionally. **"We want well-crafted poetry but are open to all styles,"** no specifications as to form. They have recently published poetry by David Shields, Tess Gallagher, Gary Soto, Jane Hirshfield, Albert Goldbarth, R.T. Smith and Rebecca McClanahan. As a sample the editor selected these lines from "Sitting at Dusk in the Back Yard After the Mondrian Retrospective" by Charles Wright:

> Form imposes, structure allows—
>   the slow destruction of form
> So as to bring it back resheveled, reorganized,
> Is the hard heart of the enterprise.
>   Under its camouflage,
> The light, relentless shill and cross-dresser, pools and deals.
> Inside its short skin, the darkness burns.

The *Review* is 6×9, perfect-bound, with art and glossy cover. Each issue has about 60 pgs. of poetry. They have a circulation of 1,500 with 500 subscriptions. Subscription: $10/year, $19/2 years. **Sample postpaid: $5. Submit up to 10 poems at a time. Simultaneous submissions OK. Reads submissions September 1 through May 1** only. Reports in 1-4 months. Pays 1 copy, a year's subscription plus monetary payment (if funding allows). **Acquires first North American serial rights.** Reviews books of poetry. Send books for review consideration also between September 1 and May 1. Query regarding book publication before sending a ms. The 49th Parallel Poetry Award, established in 1983, awards a $500 first prize, $250 second prize and $100 third prize, plus a year's subscription to the *Review*. Submissions must be unpublished and may be entered in other contests. Send any number of poems on any subject, in any form. The author's name must not appear on the manuscript. Enclose with each poem a 3×5 index card with the poem's title, first line of poem, author's name and address, phone/fax number, e-mail address (if any). Manuscripts will not be returned. Include SASE for winners list. Send SASE for guidelines. Entry fee: $5/poem. Submission period: October 1 through November 30. Most recent award co-winners were Beth Simon and Judith H. Montgomery (1996). Judge was Albert Goldbarth. Winners will be announced in March. Copies of previous winning poems may be obtained by sending for a sample copy of the *Review*'s winners issue ($5 postpaid).

BELLOWING ARK (II); BELLOWING ARK PRESS (V), P.O. Box 45637, Seattle WA 98145, phone (206)545-8302, founded 1984, editor Robert R. Ward. *Bellowing Ark* is a bimonthly literary tabloid that **"publishes only poetry which demonstrates in some way the proposition that existence has meaning or, to put it another way, that life is worth living. We have no strictures as to length, form or style; only that the work we publish is to our judgment life-affirming."** They do not want **"academic poetry, in any of its manifold forms."** They have recently published poetry by Benjamin Green, Jay Udall, Paula Milligan, Lucas Poolin, Muriel Karr and Teresa Noelle Roberts. As a sample the editor selected these lines from ''Photography'' by Leslie Goerner:

> *Even in darkest dark, the camera*
> *shutters open, gathers*
> *remnant light,*
> *long seconds worth*
> *of evidence that what primarily*
> *we cannot see*
> *surrounds us, embered*
> *in the ash, and subtle-stirred*
> *inspires vision.*

The paper is 32 pgs., tabloid-sized, printed on electrobright stock with b&w photos and line drawings. It is a lively publication. Almost every poem is accessible, enjoyable and stimulating. All styles seem to be welcome—even long, sequence poems and formal verse. Circulation is 1,000, of which 275 are subscriptions and 500 are sold on newsstands. Subscription: $15/year. **Sample postpaid: $3. Submit 3-6 poems at a time. "Absolutely *no* simultaneous submissions."** They reply to submissions in 2-12 weeks and publish within the next 1 or 2 issues. Occasionally they will criticize a ms if it seems to **"display potential to become the kind of work we want."** Sometimes sends prepublication galleys. Pays 2 copies. Reviews books of poetry. Send books for review consideration. Bellowing Ark Press publishes collections of poetry by invitation only.

BELL'S LETTERS POET (I, IV-Subscribers), P.O. Box 2187, Gulfport MS 39505-2187, founded 1956, publisher and editor Jim Bell, is a quarterly which **you must buy ($5/issue, $20 subscription) to be included.** The editor says ''many say they stop everything the day it arrives,'' and judging by the many letters from readers, that seems to be the case. **Though there is no payment for poetry accepted, many patrons send awards of $5-20 to the poets whose work they especially like. Poems are "four to 20 lines in good taste."** They have recently published poetry by Najwa Brax, Anita Broiles, Ruby Phillipy and Denver Stull. As a sample the editor selected these lines from ''Their Love'' by Ruth Phillips:

> *She wanted to give so much*
> *he asked for so little.*
> *She was scared*
> *he was brave.*
> *She was afraid of broken hearts*
> *he said don't sweat the small stuff*
> *She was worried about children*
> *he said they could adopt*
> *She loved him*
> *He loved her*

BL is about 64 pgs., digest-sized, photocopied on plain bond paper (including cover) and saddle-stitched. **Sample (including guidelines) postpaid: $5. Submit 4 poems a year. Ms must be typed. No simultaneous submissions.** Previously published poems OK "if cleared by author with prior publisher." **Accepted poems by subscribers go immediately into the next issue. Deadline for poetry submissions is 3 months prior to publication.** Reviews books of poetry by subscribers in ''one abbreviated paragraph.'' ''The Ratings'' is a competition in each issue. Readers are asked to vote on their favorite poems, and the ratings are announced in the next issue, along with awards sent to the poets by patrons. *BL* also features a telephone exchange among poets and a birth-date listing. The editor asks, ''Tired of seeing no bylines this year? Subscription guarantees a byline in each issue.''

THE BELOIT POETRY JOURNAL; CHAD WALSH POETRY PRIZE (II), RFD 2, Box 154, Ellsworth ME 04605-9616, phone (207)667-5598, website http://zinnia.umfacad.maine.edu/~sharkey/bpj, founded 1950, editor Marion K. Stocking, is a well-known, long-standing quarterly of quality poetry and reviews. **"We publish the best poems we receive, without bias as to length, school, subject or form.** It is our hope to discover the growing tip of poetry and to introduce new poets alongside established writers. **We publish occasional chapbooks to diversify our offerings."** They want **"fresh, imaginative poetry, with a distinctive voice. We tend to prefer poems that make the reader share an experience rather than just read about it, and these we keep for up to three months,** circulating them among our readers, and continuing to winnow for the best. At the quarterly meetings of the Editorial Board we read aloud all the surviving poems and put together an issue of the best we have." They have recently published poetry by Bei Dao, Molly Tenenbaum, Albert Goldbarth and Sherman Alexie. As a sample the editor selected the poem "titled" by Xiang He:

> for an eternal moment i was so still
> that i almost saw the word still
> standing there still
> with its motionless l-like legs
> and slightly waving s of tail
>
> for an eternal moment it gazed into my soul
> quizzically, with a face long and narrow
> until i gave up and galloped away—
> being, of course
> outstared by a beautiful black horse

The journal is 48 pgs., digest-sized, saddle-stapled, and attractively printed with tasteful art on the card cover. All styles of verse—providing they articulate ideas or emotions intelligently and concisely—are featured. The editor is also keen on providing as much space as possible for poems and so does not include contributors' notes. They have a circulation of 1,600 for 575 subscribers of which 325 are libraries. **Sample (including guidelines) postpaid: $4. Send SASE for guidelines alone. Submit any time, without query, any legible form.** *"No previously published poems or simultaneous submissions.* **Any length of ms, but most poets send what will go in a business envelope for one stamp. Don't send your life's work."** **Pays 3 copies. Acquires first serial rights.** Staff reviews books by and about poets in an average of 500 words, usually single format. Send books for review consideration. The journal awards the Chad Walsh Poetry Prize ($4,000 in 1996) to a poem or group of poems published in the calendar year. "Every poem published in 1998 will be considered for the 1998 prize." Poetry published in *The Beloit Poetry Journal* has also been included in *The Best American Poetry* (1994 and 1996) and *Pushcart Prize* anthologies. The editor says, "We'd like to see more strong, imaginative, experimental poetry; more poetry with a global vision; and more poetry with fresh, vigorous language."

✦**BENEATH THE SURFACE (II)**, % The Dept. of English, Chester New Hall, McMaster University, Hamilton, Ontario L8S 4L9 Canada, e-mail schryese@muss.cis.mcmaster.ca, founded 1911, editor changes yearly, is a biannual using **"top quality poetry/prose that achieves universality through individual expression."** They want **"quality poetry; any form; no restrictions." Also interested in short stories.** They have recently published poetry by Janice Knapp and Jeffrey Donaldson. As a sample the editor selected these lines from "Kristallnacht" by Jonathan M. Berkowitz:

> Haphazard whispers scream in the ears of the three
> mad prophets soothsaying time, place, and purpose
> Awake!! Awake!! I spit upon the sacred
>
> floor. I have six million good reasons to pray
> as mother cries and I Herr Doctor write
> incompetent pornographic prescriptions.

BTS is 30-50 pgs., professionally printed, saddle-stapled, with cover art, drawings and b&w photographs. They receive about 250 submissions/year, use approximately 10%. Press run is 150 for 8 subscribers of which 3 are libraries, 92 shelf sales. Subscription: $8/year. **Sample postpaid: $4. No previously published poems or simultaneous submissions. Submit poems with cover letter, including short bio and summary of previous publications, if any. Reads submissions September through April only. Pays 1 copy. Acquires first North American serial rights.** Rarely reviews books of poetry, "though we do include literary essays when submitted."

BENNETT & KITCHEL (IV-Form), P.O. Box 4422, East Lansing MI 48826, phone (517)355-1707, founded 1989, editor William Whallon, publishes 1-2 hardbacks/year of **"poetry of form and meaning. No free verse or blank verse."** As an example of what he admires, the editor selected these lines by Rhina P. Espaillat:

> Aloof from self, the apple tree
> regretless shall unbloom to death;
> my epitaph's in every breath:
> "Remember me, remember me."

Bennett & Kitchel published *Severe* by Anthony Lombardy. **Sample postpaid: $8. Submit 6 poems at a time. Simultaneous submissions and previously published poems OK if copyright is clear. Minimum volume for** a book "might be 750 lines." Time between acceptance and publication is 9 months. **Seldom comments on submissions. Reports in 2 weeks. Terms are "variable, negotiable."** The editor says, "To make a bad rhyme not from incompetence but willfully is like stubbing your toe on purpose."

‡*BEYOND THE BOUNDARIES; WELSH SPECULATIVE WRITERS FOUNDATION (IV-Horror, science fiction/fantasy)**, 16 Queenwood Close, Cyncoed, Cardiff CF3 7JH United Kingdom, contact Gerry Moreton, is a quarterly "collection of stories, articles, poems and cartoons of science fact and fiction, fantasy and horror. **We are looking for poems of various speculative genres to publish. They should be original works, able to fit within the general scope of our magazine: science fiction, horror, ghost, murder, or just plain weird."** *BTB* is about 40 pgs., magazine-sized, printed on bond paper and saddle-stitched with glossy card cover, b&w illustrations. Single copy: £1.90; subscription: £7. **Make checks payable to W.S.W.F. No previously published poems. Submit poems on 3.5 disk in ASCII or Word for Windows format. "Persons overseas should send a disposable manuscript (marked as such) and a small SAE with 2 IRCs. Please do not send foreign stamps." Send SASE (or SAE with IRC) for further details.** The Welsh Speculative Writers Foundation meets at the Cardiff Central Library on the first Thursday of each month. They say, "We have no specific guidelines for poetry, except that it should be speculative in nature. However, your chances of publication increase if it is 30 lines or less or no more than 300 words."

‡BIBLE ADVOCATE (I, IV-Religious)**, P.O. Box 33677, Denver CO 80233, website http://www.denver.net/~baonline, founded 1863, assistant editor Sherri Langton, published monthly, features "Christian content—to proclaim the gospel of Christ and the truths of His Word." **They want "free verse, some traditional; 5-25 lines, with Christian/Bible themes." They do not want "avant garde poetry."** The editor says *Bible Advocate* is 20-28 pgs., 8×10 with most poetry set up with 4-color art. They receive about 30-50 poems a year, accept 10-20. Press run varies for 12,500 subscribers with all distributed free. **Submit 5 poems at a time. Previously published poems (with notification) and simultaneous submissions OK. Cover letter preferred.** Time between acceptance and publication is 3-12 months. **Poems are circulated to an editorial board.** "I read them first and reject those that won't work for us. I send good ones to editor for approval." **Seldom comments on rejections. Publishes theme issues. Send SASE for guidelines. Reports in 4-6 weeks. Pays $10. Buys first, reprint and one-time rights.** The editor says, "Avoid trite, or forced rhyming. Be aware of the magazine's doctrinal views (send for doctrinal beliefs booklet)."

BILINGUAL REVIEW PRESS; BILINGUAL REVIEW/REVISTA BILINGÜE (IV-Ethnic/Hispanic, bilingual/Spanish), Hispanic Research Center, Arizona State University, Box 872702, Tempe AZ 85287-2702, phone (602)965-3867, journal founded 1974, press in 1976. Managing editor Karen Van Hooft says they are "a small press publisher of U.S. Hispanic creative literature and of a journal containing poetry and short fiction in addition to scholarship." The journal, published 3 times/year, contains some poetry in each issue; they also publish flat-spined paperback collections of poetry. **"We publish poetry by and/or about U.S. Hispanics and U.S. Hispanic themes. We do not publish translations in our journal or literature about the experiences of Anglo Americans in Latin America. We have published a couple of poetry volumes in bilingual format (Spanish/English) of important Mexican poets."** They have published poetry by Alberto Ríos, Martín Espada, Judith Ortiz Cofer and Marjorie Agosín. The editor says the journal is 96 pgs., 7×10, offset and flat-spined, with 2-color cover. They use less than 10% of hundreds of submissions received each year. Press run is 2,000 for 1,200 subscribers. Subscriptions: $18 for individuals, $32 for institutions. **Sample postpaid: $6 individuals/ $11 institutions. Submit "two copies, including ribbon original if possible, with loose stamps for return postage." Cover letter required. Pays 2 copies. Acquires all rights.** Reviews books of US Hispanic literature only. Send books, Attn: Editor, for review consideration. **For book submissions, inquire first with 4-5 sample poems, bio and publication credits. Pays $200 advance, 10% royalties and 10 copies.** Over the years, books by this press have won 5 American Book Awards and 2 Western States Book Awards.

‡BIRCH BROOK PRESS (III)**, P.O. Box 81, Delhi NY 13753, phone (212)353-3326, founded 1982, contact Tom Tolnay, "is a small letterpress book printer/typesetter/designer that uses monies from these activities to publish a few titles of its own each year." Publishes 4-6 paperbacks and hardbacks/year. **The press specializes** "mostly in anthologies with specific subject matter. BBP publishes one or two books by individuals with high-quality literary work, on a co-op basis." Books are "handset letterpress editions printed in our own shop." **Query first. Occasionally comments on rejections. Obtain sample books by sending for catalog.**

‡BIRD WATCHER'S DIGEST (IV-Nature)**, P.O. Box 110, Marietta OH 45750, founded 1978, editor William H. Thompson, III, is a specialized but promising market for **poems of "true literary merit" in which birds figure in some way, at least by allusion.** They have published poetry by Susan Rea, Nancy G. Westerfield, Suzanne Freemans and William D. Barney. **"Preferred: no more than 20 lines, 40 spaces, no more than 3 poems at a time, no queries." Sample postpaid: $3.50. Reports in 2 months. Pays $10/poem.** They have up to 2 year's backlog and use 2-6 of the approximately 500 poems received each year.

BIRMINGHAM POETRY REVIEW (II, IV-Translations), English Dept., University of Alabama at Birmingham, Birmingham AL 35294, phone (205)934-8573, founded 1988, co-editors Robert Collins and Randy

Blythe. The review appears twice a year using poetry of **"any style, form, length or subject. We are biased toward exploring the cutting edge of contemporary poetry. Style is secondary to the energy, the** *fire* **the poem possesses. We don't want poetry with cliché-bound, worn-out language."** They have published poetry by Hague, Hopes, McDonald, Richards, Call and Miltner. They describe their magazine as 50 pgs., 6×9, offset, with b&w cover. Press run is 700 for 300 subscribers. Subscription: $4/year; $7/2 years. **Sample postpaid: $2. Submit 3-5 poems, "no more. No cover letters. We are impressed by good writing; we are unimpressed by publication credits." SASE required. No simultaneous or multiple submissions, and previously published poems only if they are translations. Editor sometimes comments on rejections. Send SASE for guidelines. Reports in 1-4 months. Pays 2 copies and one-year subscription.** They say, "Advice to beginners: Read as much good contemporary poetry, national and international, as you can get your hands on. Then be persistent in finding your own voice."

BISHOP PUBLISHING CO. (IV-Specialized), 2131 Trimble Way, Sacramento CA 95825, phone (916)971-4987, professor Roland Dickison, is a "small press publisher of **folklore in paperbacks, including contemporary** and out-of-print."

‡**THE BITTER OLEANDER; FRANCES LOCKE MEMORIAL AWARD (II)**, 4983 Tall Oaks Dr., Fayetteville NY 13066-9776, phone (315)637-3047, fax (315)637-5056, e-mail bones44@ix.netcom.com, founded 1974, editor/publisher Paul B. Roth. *The Bitter Oleander* appears biannually, publishing "imaginative poetry; poetry in translation; serious language." **They want "highly imaginative poetry whose language is serious. We prefer short poems of no more than 25 lines. We are not interested in very long poems and prefer not to receive poems about the common values and protests of society."** They have recently published poetry by Robert Bly, Alan Britt and Silvia Scheibil. As a sample the editor selected these lines from "Sawdust" by Duane Locke:

> *No luminous helicopter will fly low*
> *to search among these piles*
> *of sawdust, once a swamp.*
> *All the trees have been sawed*
> *to build houses for the new born*
> *coming off the assembly line,*
> *I'm alone, no trees, no companions.*

The Bitter Oleander is 80-100 pgs., digest-sized, offset printed, perfect-bound with glossy 2-color cover, cover art and ads. They receive about 2,500 poems a year, accept approximately 4%. Press run is 1,000, 500 shelf sales. Subscription: $12. **Sample postpaid: $6. Make checks payable to Bitter Oleander Press. Submit 8 poems at a time with name and address on each page. No previously published poems or simultaneous submissions. Cover letter preferred. Does not read mss during July.** Time between acceptance and publication is 4-6 months. **"All poems are read by the editor only and all decisions are made by this editor."** Often comments on rejections. **Reports within a month. Pays 2 copies. Also sponsors the Frances Locke Memorial Award, awarding $500 and publication. Submit any number of poems. Entry fee: $2/poem. Submission period: March 1 through June 1.** The editor says, "We simply want poetry that is imaginative and serious in its performance of language. So much flat-line poetry is written today that anyone reading one magazine or another cannot tell the difference."

BKMK PRESS (II), University House, University of Missouri-Kansas City, 5101 Rockhill Rd., Kansas City MO 64110-2499, phone (816)235-2558, fax (816)235-2611, founded 1971, associate editor Michelle Boisseau, managing editor Kelly Freeman, generally publishes 4-5 paperbacks. BkMk Press seeks to publish "well-known and beginning poets fairly and equally." **They have no specifications regarding form, length or subject matter but do not want to see "pretentious, unserious poetry."** They have published books of poetry by Howard Schwartz and Neal Bowers. Their books are generally 64 pgs., 5½×8½, professionally printed and perfect-bound with laminated covers with art and photographs. **Query first with sample poems and a cover letter with brief bio and publication credits. Previously published poems and simultaneous submissions OK. Seldom comments on rejections. Replies to queries in 1 month, to mss in 2-6 months. Pays 10% royalties and 20 author's copies (out of a press run of 600).** Call or write for catalog to order samples.

BLACK BEAR PUBLICATIONS; BLACK BEAR REVIEW (II, IV-Social issues), 1916 Lincoln St., Croydon PA 19021-8026, email bbreview@aol.com, website http://members.aol.com/bbreview/index.htm, founded 1984, poetry and art editor Ave Jeanne, review editor Ron Zettlemoyer. *Black Bear Review* is a semiannual international literary and fine arts magazine that also publishes chapbooks and holds an annual poetry competition. **"We like well-crafted poetry that mirrors real life—void of camouflage, energetic poetry, avant-garde, free verse and haiku which relate to the world today. We seldom publish the beginner, but will assist when time allows. No traditional poetry is used. The underlying theme of** *BBR* **is social and political, but the review is interested also in environmental, war/peace, ecological and minorities themes. We would like to receive more ideas on AIDS awareness, life styles and current political topics."** They have recently published poetry by Livio Farallo, Raven, B.L. Niditch, Rick Duffey and Michael Gregg Michaud. As a sample the editor selected these lines from "Optimism" by Bruce Williams:

> *But in some dark*
> *it strokes its claws*
> *through the ocean,*
>
> *smiling*
> *with bright teeth*

BBR is 64 pgs., digest-sized, perfect-bound, offset from typed copy on white stock, with line drawings, collages and woodcuts. Circulation is 500 for 300 subscribers of which 15 are libraries. Subscription: $10, $15 overseas. **Sample postpaid: $5; back copies when available are $4. Submit 5 poems at a time, one to a page. "Please have name and address on each page of your submissions." Simultaneous submissions are not considered. "Submissions without SASE will be discarded." E-mail submissions OK.** Time between acceptance and publication is 6 months. **Send SASE for guidelines. Reports in 2 weeks. Pays 1 copy. Acquires first North American serial rights and electronic rights, "as work may appear on our website."** Considers reviews of books of poetry and recent issues of literary magazines, maximum 250 words. Send books for review consideration. **They also publish 2 chapbooks/year.** They have published *Rubato Jitter* by John Sullivan. **Chapbook series requires a reading fee of $5, complete ms and cover letter. Send SASE for guidelines.** For book publication, they require that "*BBR* has published the poet and is familiar with his/her work." **Author receives one-half print run.** They say, "We appreciate a friendly, brief cover letter. Tell us about the poet; omit degrees or any other pretentious dribble. All submissions are handled with objectivity and quite often rejected material is directed to another market. If you've not been published before, mention it. We are always interested in aiding those who support small press. We frequently suggest poets keep up with the current edition of *Poet's Market* and read the listings and reviews in issues of *Black Bear*. Most recent issues of *BBR* include reviews on small press markets, outlets on the Internet for poets, current releases of chapbooks and the latest literary magazines. We make an effort to keep our readers informed and on top of the small press scene. Camera-ready ads are printed free of charge as a support to small press publishers. We also run an ad page on the Internet, "InterActions," for all interested poets and writers to advertise. We do suggest poets and artists read issues before submitting to absorb the flavor and save on wasted postage. Send your best! Our yearly poetry competition offers cash awards to poets." Deadline: November 1. Send SASE for guidelines. The editors add, "We are currently at work on our website. *Black Bear* will continue to print in our paperback format as well as art and poems online."

‡**BLACK BELT PRESS (III)**, P.O. Box 551, Montgomery AL 36111, website http://www.blackbeltpress.com, founded 1989, editors Jeff Slaton and Ashley Gordon, publishes literature, poetry, history and biography— "primarily examining the culture and history of the Deep South." They publish 2 hardbacks/year. **Their preferred subjects are the South, civil rights, women, ethnic minorities. No religious, romantic or pastoral work.** As a sample the editor selected these lines from "Someone Will Go On Owing" by Andrew Glaze:

> *For the first time in my life, I had neither shield nor friend,*
> *no place, no enemy, no time.*
> *I crouched there counting the holes in my pockets.*
> *The wind was cold, there was no wall nor roof*
> *nor any fire to keep me warm.*
> *I began to dance.*

Submit 5-15 poems at a time. Previously published poems and simultaneous submissions OK. Cover letter preferred. Time between acceptance and publication is 1-3 years. **Poems are circulated to an editorial board. "They are reviewed by the two in-house editors with final approval going to the editor-in-chief." Seldom comments on rejections. Replies to queries within 1 month, to mss within 6 months. Pays 5-15% royalties and 10 author's copies. For sample books "order from us or through bookstores (1-800-959-3245)."** Their book *Witness*, by Jeanie Thompson, won the 1995 PMA Ben Franklin Award.

BLACK BOUGH (II, IV-Form), 7 Park Ave., Flemington NJ 08822, founded 1991, editor Charles Easter, is a triannual that publishes "haiku and related poetry that uses the Eastern form in the Western milieu." **They want "haiku, senryu, tanka, haibun (in particular) and sequences. No academic essays or extremely long poems."** They have published work by Nasira Alma, Jim Kacian and Yvonne Hardenbrook. As a sample the editor selected this haiku by Tom Clausen:

> *last ray of sun*
> *in the feeder*
> *a sparrow*

USE THE GENERAL INDEX to find the page number of a specific publisher. Also, if a publisher from last year's edition is not included in this edition, the General Index will tell you why.

bb is 30 pgs., digest-sized, professionally printed, saddle-stitched, with photos, no ads. They receive about 5,200 poems a year, use 5-10%. Press run is 200 for 100 subscribers. Subscription: $16.50. **Sample postpaid: $6. "Submit no more than 20 haiku; prefer several haiku/page." No previously published poems or simultaneous submissions.** Time between acceptance and publication is 3-6 months. **Comments on rejections "if requested." Reports in 6-10 weeks. Pays $1/verse, up to $4 for a long poem or haiku sequence. Buys first rights.**

BLACK BUZZARD PRESS; BLACK BUZZARD REVIEW; VISIONS—INTERNATIONAL, THE WORLD JOURNAL OF ILLUSTRATED POETRY; THE BLACK BUZZARD ILLUSTRATED POETRY CHAPBOOK SERIES; INTERNATIONAL—VISIONS POETRY SERIES (II), 1007 Ficklen Rd., Fredericksburg VA 22405, founded 1979, poetry editor Bradley R. Strahan, associate editor Shirley G. Sullivan. "We are an independent nonsubsidized press dedicated to publishing fine accessible poetry and translation (particularly from lesser-known languages such as Armenian, Gaelic, Urdu, Vietnamese, etc.) accompanied by original illustrations of high quality in an attractive format. **We want to see work that is carefully crafted and exciting, that transfigures everyday experience or gives us a taste of something totally new; all styles except concrete and typographical 'poems.' Nothing purely sentimental. No self-indulgent breast beating. No sadism, sexism or bigotry. No unemotional pap. No copies of Robert Service or the like. Usually under 80 lines but will consider longer."** They have published poetry by Ted Hughes, Michael Mott, Louis Simpson, Marilyn Hacker, James Dickey, Naomi Shihab Nye and Lawrence Ferlinghetti. *Visions*, a digest-sized, saddle-stapled magazine finely printed on high-quality paper, appears 3 times a year, uses 56 pages of poetry in each issue. Circulation 800 with 400 subscribers of which 50 are libraries. **Sample postpaid: $4. Current issue: $5.** They receive *well* over 1,000 submissions each year, use 150, have a 3- to 18-month backlog. "*Visions* is international in both scope and content, publishing poets from all over the world and having readers in 48 U.S. states, Canada and 24 other countries." *Black Buzzard Review* is a "more or less annual informal journal, dedicated mostly to North American poets and entirely to original English-language poems. In *BBR*, we are taking a more wide-open stance on what we accept (including the slightly outrageous)." **Sample postpaid: $4. Current issue: $5.** It is 36 pgs., magazine-sized, side-stapled, with matte card cover. **Submit 3-6 poems at a time. "Poems must be readable (not faded or smudged) and *not* handwritten. We resent having to pay postage due, so use adequate postage! No more than six pages, please." No previously published poems or simultaneous submissions. Publishes theme issues. Send SASE for upcoming themes. Reports in 3 days to 3 weeks. Pays 1 copy or $5-10 "if we get a grant." Buys first North American serial rights.** Staff reviews books of poetry in "up to two paragraphs." Send books for review consideration. **To submit for the chapbook series, send samples (5-10 poems) and a *brief* cover letter "pertinent to artistic accomplishments." Reports in 3 days to 3 weeks. Pays in copies. Usually provides criticism. Send $4 for sample chapbook.** They also publish the International-Visions Poetry Series. Send SASE for flyer describing titles and order information. Bradley Strahan adds that in *Visions* "We sometimes publish helpful advice about 'getting published' and the art and craft of poetry, and often discuss poets and the world of poetry on our editorial page."

BLACK CROSS (I), 3121 Corto Place #2, Long Beach CA 90803, e-mail wstien@csulb.edu, or wraith@gte.net, website http://www.csulb.edu/~wstien, founded December 1995, editors Jim Guess and Erik Jensen, is a quarterly that features poetry and art "with a heavy-metal edge and mild touches of psychosis and perversion. **We want image-heavy work, any length, subject, style or form. No greeting card rhymes. Don't be boring or lame."** They have recently published poetry by Jay Alamares, Andrew Demcak, Charles Ellik, Gerald Locklin, Raindog, Kristine Sanders and T. Thrasher. As a sample the editors selected "Poppa Got a Brand Name Whore" by Ben Ohmart:

> *she was self-servicing, self-lubricating.*
> *dad kept her under the bed to sort of hide her from me.*
> *but she had to eat sometimes and came*
> *out for food. then i'd get her pregnant*
> *from behind while she tried to decide*
> *whether her Chunky needed a fork or a spoon.*

Black Cross is 70 pgs., about 5½ × 8½, photocopied and saddle-stapled, with heavy card stock cover with b&w art and b&w cartoon-like art and collages inside. They receive about 1,000 poems a year, accept approximately 10%. Press run is 200 for 50 shelf sales. Subscription: $7.50/year. **Sample postpaid: $2. Make checks payable to James Guess. Submit 2-5 poems at a time. No previously published poems or simultaneous submissions. "Cover letters are appreciated, but not required. Electronic submissions are welcome. Postal submissions should be typed or at least legible." Comments on rejections if requested. Publishes theme issues. Send SASE for guidelines and upcoming themes. Brief guidelines are also included inside the magazine or can be obtained via e-mail or website. Reports in 2-3 months. Pays 1 copy. Acquires first rights.** Jim Guess says, "Particularly good submissions are featured on the *Black Cross* website. Online, poets can discover other Internet resources relating to poetry, view art and poetry samples from various issues of the magazine, and find submission guidelines and updates." He adds, "The end result of any poem should be heavy images and killer lines that dismay your loved ones. Remember, fear your government, not your genitals."

‡**BLACK MOON: POETRY OF IMAGINATION (II)**, 233 Northway Rd., Reisterstown MD 21136, founded 1994, contact Alan Britt, appears annually and publishes the "most imaginative, outspoken poetry available. Experimental poetry and essays welcome." They have recently published poetry by Robert Bly, Donald Hall, Andrei Codrescu, John Haines, David Ignatow, Louis Simpson and David Ray. As a sample the editor selected these lines from "Walking" by Silvia Scheibli:

> We wash the moon
> in olive oil
> Rays separate on the water
> like belly dancers
> Night stains
> our skin

Black Moon is about 200 pgs., 6×9, professionally printed and perfect-bound, with glossy card cover, ads. They accept 10% of work received. Press run is 2,000 for 200 subscribers of which 20 are libraries, 1,500 shelf sales. Single copy: $8.95. **Sample postpaid: $10.70. No previously published poems; simultaneous submissions OK. Cover letter preferred. Reads submissions March 1 through September 30 only. Has backlog of work through January '98.** Time between acceptance and publication is 1-3 months. **Poems are circulated to an editorial board. "Some poems are accepted by various consultants for *Black Moon*." Often comments on rejections. Send SASE for guidelines. Reports in 1-3 months. Pays 1 copy. Does not acquire rights, however, "we would like to be recognized for having published the piece."** They say, "We would like to see more submissions that reflect political and social consciousness."

BLACK MOUNTAIN REVIEW; LORIEN HOUSE (IV-Themes), P.O. Box 1112, Black Mountain NC 28711-1112, founded 1969, editor David A. Wilson. Lorien House is a small press publishing many books (poetry on a subsidy basis) and the literary periodical, *Black Mountain Review*. The review focuses on **work about American authors. "Poetry is an important part of each issue, but must be on the theme. If not, please do not send it."** Recent themes have included William Faulkner and Margaret Mitchell. As a sample the editor selected these lines from "Thoughts on Reading *The People, Yes*" by Wally Kennicutt, in issue #10 on Carl Sandburg:

> The yarns and folk jests
> and the lingo
> his friend and rival Robert Frost
> called "a box of exclamation points!!!"
> all the big sprawling contradiction
> called America
> packed into one book.

BMR is 36 pgs., about 5½×8½, neatly printed and saddle-stitched with card cover, b&w drawings and photos. **Send SASE for guidelines and upcoming themes. Themes for March 1998, September 1998 and March 1999 are Sidney Lanier, Erskine Caldwell and Carson McCullers, respectively. Reports in 1-2 months. Pays small monetary amount plus 2 copies. Query regarding subsidized book publication. Editor comments on submissions "occasionally," and offers "full analysis and marketing help" for $1/typed page of poetry. "Only material with full return postage will be returned."** The editor says, "Many poets do not include return postage and expect an answer. I apologize to all . . . what to you is 32¢ is several thousand dollars at this end."

BLACK RIVER REVIEW (II, IV-Translations), Dept. PM, 855 Mildred Ave., Lorain OH 44052-1213, phone (216)244-9654, e-mail brr@freenet.lorain.oberlin.edu, founded 1985, poetry contact Kaye Coller, editorial contact Kaye Coller or Deb Gilbert, is a literary annual using **"contemporary poetry, any style, form and subject matter, 50 line maximum (usually), poetry with insight, energy and a distinctive voice. Do *not* want Helen Steiner Rice, greeting card verse, poetry that mistakes stilted, false or formulaic diction for intense expression of feeling. We receive too many well-written, polished poems that have nothing to distinguish them from the thousands of other well-written, polished poems we've read over the years."** They have recently published poetry by Adrian Louis, Diane Glancy, Timothy Russell, B.Z. Niditch, Nathaniel Smith and Lyn Lifshin. As a sample the editor selected these lines from "The River's Wife" by Sandra Reiff:

> The River's Wife
> was dry as a hymn
> he was deep   cunning
> able to shed his skin
>   they were fated for each other
> She'd sit and watch the traffic
> in lost souls
> recede across his muscles
>   an enigma
> she couldn't hold him   he was slippery
> fleeting   fascinating how
> he got into her mind
> and out came gates   fences   walls
>   whole cities

INSIDER REPORT

Poetry requires passion and conviction

Alan Britt

"I'm trying to bring a passion and intensity back to American poetry," says Alan Britt, poet and editor of *Black Moon: Poetry of Imagination*. "That's what it's all about. You've got to love this stuff even in the most melancholy mood. So much of today's poetry seems to me to be flat, uninteresting; there's an absence of real joy. It's as if people are trying to get as many poems published as they can and get their names out there."

This passion and intensity are ably showcased in Britt's poems and essays. His work has appeared in such wide-ranging publications as *Duckabush Journal*, *Blank Gun Silencer*, *New Letters*, *Exquisite Corpse*, *Kansas Quarterly*, *Santa Barbara Review*, *Epoch* and *Christian Science Monitor*. CypressBooks has also published a collection of his work entitled *Bodies of Lightning*, and he has contributed poems to the anthologies *For Neruda, For Chile* (published by Beacon Press) and *Poems from A to Z* (published by Swallow Press).

Even though Britt's own publication didn't premier until 1994, his desire to publish originated in the late '60s when his older brother convinced him to attend the University of Tampa, Florida. "He said, 'You've got to come here to college. There's this poet teaching here who's very exciting.' Hearing this from my brother, who was practically a juvenile delinquent, I thought he had to be kidding." However, Britt did enroll and studied under southern poet Duane Locke.

Britt also assisted with Locke's magazine, *Poetry Review*. "He was a fine editor, publishing many poets who went on to prominence, David Ignatow and John Haines, for example." In addition to this exposure, the sample magazines that flooded the office gave Britt a real sense of what was going on in the contemporary poetry scene. "Since then I've always had this drive to gather as many interesting poems as I could find, put them into magazine form and send them out there, hoping people will enjoy them as much as I do."

Now, for *Black Moon*, Britt selects whatever material strikes him as interesting. Robert Bly, David Ray, Marjorie Agosin, Steve Sleboda and Silvia Scheibli are a small sampling of poets to be found in the journal's pages. "I'm not looking for a specific style. I don't want the editorial focus so narrow that each issue is predictable. I like the idea of diversity and excitement." Britt produces *Black Moon* as a glossy paperback journal and showcases new as well as prominent writers. As with his poems, *Black Moon*'s title "just came" to him and, like the journal's contents, conveys opposites, the unexpected—the unanticipated that jumps out at you.

When the journal was recently picked up by four new distributors, placing it in bookstores across the country, submissions skyrocketed. Despite this, Britt still tries to send a handwritten reply to each poet. "People I've never heard of have seen the issues and are

INSIDER REPORT, *Britt*

sending me poems from all over the place. I think that's exciting." Equally exciting are the possibilities for exposure on the Internet. "It's incredible to think a single ad may be seen by millions of readers and poets around the world who might otherwise never know of a publication."

In regard to his own poetry, Britt's role as husband/father and his full-time job don't allow him the freedom to set a daily writing schedule, nor would one be conducive to his individual style. He feels ideas come from everywhere and creativity cannot be put on a timetable. Bits and pieces of experience are his essential building blocks. "I'm not so much inspired by ideas as by internal emotion. Like the silt on a lake bottom, daily experiences settle emotions one on another. Stir them and you don't know which direction they'll go. In the morning some agitation will get my soul churning this silt and by the afternoon I have to put it on paper; a television show will rile or fascinate me; metaphors will jump into my brain or a leisurely, pastoral feeling comes over me while watching a wasp fly around a wild rose and I'll start writing."

"Crossing the Walt Whitman Bridge"

They have named a bridge after Walt.
A massive extension of steel
& persistent weight.

This bridge connects daily lives,
supports the multitudes
nonstop 24 hours a day.

Walt would surely be proud.

But the true bridge,
the one he created
from our loves to the infinite,
is the one I'm crossing now
between the shores of my solitude.

(originally published in *Black Moon: Poetry of Imagination*, Issue Two; reprinted by permission of the author)

Rewriting is an important part of Britt's style. He wastes very little of what he writes. Unfinished poems are placed in a folder kept close by. "I might not open it for five nights in a row, but the next three nights I'll pull out 20 poems in progress and the changes will come flying out of my pen."

Britt's writing style was shaped early on during his years at the University of Tampa. "I'd only been writing poetry for a year and a half when my brother gave me a copy of ***Love Poems: From Spain and Spanish America*** [translated by Perry Higman and published by City Lights]. One poem, 'Brown and Agile Child,' by Pablo Neruda, just knocked my socks off. I'd never read the Spanish poets and this marvelous poem, in all seriousness, not only changed my writing style, it changed my soul. I didn't immediately drop everything and begin imitating Neruda, but it really got inside my blood and I more or less gravitated to a style similar to the Latin poets."

Along with Neruda, Latin poets Cesar Vallejo, Federico García Lorca and Miguel

INSIDER REPORT, *continued*

Hernandez showed Britt that poetry could be highly imaginative, profound, sad, happy and extremely enjoyable at the same time. "It's so different from the 'academic' poetry so prevalent in U.S. workshops. I feel they make far too little use of not only the Latin but the European style. In the 1920s and '30s Europe underwent a profound surreal movement that passed through these countries like a freight train, adding richness to their literature. Unfortunately, surrealism never really passed through the American tradition and, in my opinion, we've suffered because of it."

In addition, Britt feels contemporary poetry lacks conviction, that it is mired in a prosy, autobiographical language that's simplistic and naive rather than profound. "It has no linguistic energy, no spiritual force either intellectual or social. Poetry should at least be a language of conviction. It should be interesting, unique, your blood should get into the words. I like to see a poem rise up on its hind legs and say something, not abstractly or intellectually blow a lot of hot air."

With that sentiment in mind, Britt offers this advice to the beginning poet: "Don't expect a workshop to teach you everything about poetry. Take responsibility yourself. Start at the library. Select 100 different books of poetry from all over the world. Half a dozen isn't enough. Read them three, four, five times each. Then write 100 poems imitating as many styles as you can. Then you've got a beginning. Don't worry about developing your own voice; over the years that individual voice inside you will find its way out.

"Look for poets who exhibit strong imagination. That's where our true wisdom is housed. Inside the imagination you can create several worlds with one image. Read and write with a healthy diversity. It's joyful to write prose poems alongside condensed, highly imagistic poems. It's taken me a long time to be able to do so with any sense of accomplishment, but nobody said it wasn't going to be work. It is work. You have to learn to enjoy that work."

—*Glenn L. Marcum*

BRR is about 60 pgs., magazine-sized, offset printed on quality stock, saddle-stapled with glossy cover with art. Circulation is 400 (sold in college and area bookstores and by mail). **Sample: $3.50 (back copy); $4 (current issue); plus $1.50 p&h. Prefers no simultaneous submissions but will consider with the understanding that no submission may be withdrawn after May 1. Previously published poems OK if acknowledged. Submit between January and May 1. Send SASE for guidelines or request via e-mail. Pays 1 copy.** Reviews books of poetry. Kaye Coller comments, "We want strong poems that show a depth of vision beyond the commonplace. We don't care if a poet is well-known or not, but we don't publish amateurs. An amateur is not necessarily a new poet, but one who doesn't believe in revision, tends to be preachy, writes sentimental slush, tells the reader what to think and/or concludes the poem with an explanation in case the reader didn't get the point. If we think we can use one or more of a poet's poems, we keep them until the final choices are made in June; otherwise, we send them back as soon as possible. Follow the ms mechanics in *Poet's Market*. **We are also looking for poems written in Spanish. If selected, they will be published with English translation by either the poet or one of our staff."**

‡**BLACK ROSES (I)**, 305 South Main St., Torrington CT 06790, founded 1996, editor Sheryl J. Miller, appears quarterly and publishes "dark, sexy poetry mixed with personal ramblings." **They want "any style, 5-75 lines on the subjects of bad love, vampires, death, sex, murder, darkness, the bizarre. Nothing too happy or with an abundance of rhyme."** As a sample the editor selected these lines from "The Value of Revenge" by Christa Jacaruso:

> *Justice, are you finally mine?*
> *my partner in dance forevermore?*
> *or the macabre display I have just witnessed,*
> *As the angel of death awaits at the door . . .*

> *Sweet irony, you've kissed my face,*
> *now its me looking down.*

Black Roses is 20-30 pgs., 8½×11 (folded in half), photocopied. Press run is 50 for 25 subscribers; 20 distributed free to friends and local coffeehouse. Single copy: $2; subscription: $6.50. **Sample postpaid: $1.50. Make checks payable to Sheryl J. Miller. Submit up to 5 poems at a time. Previously published poems and simultaneous submissions OK. Cover letter preferred.** Time between acceptance and publication is 2-6 months. **Often comments on rejections. Publishes theme issues ("but I'm flexible"). Send SASE for guidelines. Reports in 1 month. Pays 1-2 copies. Acquires one-time rights.** The editor says, "Don't be discouraged by a rejection. I love my pile of rejection slips. It shows I've been trying."

THE BLACK SCHOLAR; THE BLACK SCHOLAR PRESS (IV-Ethnic), P.O. Box 2869, Oakland CA 94618, founded 1969, publisher Robert Chrisman, uses **poetry "relating to/from/of the black American and other 'Third World' experience."** The quarterly magazine is basically scholarly and research-oriented. They have published poetry by Ntozake Shange, Jayne Cortez, Andrew Salkey and D.L. Smith. The editor says it is 64 pgs., 7×10, with 10,000 subscribers of which 60% are libraries, 15% shelf sales. "We only publish one issue every year containing poetry." Subscription: $30, institutions, $60; foreign $45, foreign institutions $75. **Sample issue: $6, institutions $10. Enclose "letter and bio or curriculum vita, SASE, phone number, no originals." Send SASE for guidelines. Pays 10 copies and subscription.** Reviews books of poetry. They also publish 1-2 books a year, average 100 pgs., flat-spined. **Send query letter. For sample books, send 8½×11 SASE for catalog, average cost $10.95 including p&h.** The publisher says, "Please be advised—it is against our policy to discuss submissions via telephone. Also, we get a lot of mss, but read *every single one,* thus patience is appreciated."

‡BLACK THISTLE PRESS (I), 491 Broadway 6th Floor, New York NY 10012, phone (212)219-1898, website http://www.blackthistlepress.com, founded 1990, publisher Ms. Hollis Melton. "Our goals are to publish people's dreams, visions, stories in the way that is most appropriate to each work." They publish 1 paperback/year. **They want "good, fresh, authentic poetry." No pornographic work.** They have recently published poetry by Jonas Mekas and Vyt Bakaitis. As a sample the editor selected this poem from *Miss Laughinghouse and the Reluctant Mystic* by Judith Morley:

> *Should you put*
> *the fingerling goldfish*
> *in a tiny glass bowl*
> *on the table*
> *it would remain tiny*
> *and swim its life away*
> *going in circles.*
> *Put in a big pond*
> *it would continue to grow*
> *until it was awesome in size.*
>
> *Are we, too,*
> *limited by the walls*
> *of the container?*
> *Were our pond the universe . . .?*

Submit up to 10 typed poems. Simultaneous submissions OK. Cover letter preferred. Time between acceptance and publication is at least 1 year. **Seldom comments on rejections. Replies to queries in 2 weeks, to mss in 2 months. "Payment agreements vary depending on press run. This would be negotiated with each author."** The publisher says, "We are very small, and are limited to the amount of poetry we can publish. We have to really like the poems, believe in them, want to commit to them as a book. However, we are always looking for good poets and poetry. We are setting up a website and will have a place for new writing, with permission we will put poems submitted up on the web; we hope this will be interactive, a forum."

BLACK TIE PRESS (III), P.O. Box 440004, Houston TX 77244-0004, fax (713)789-5119, founded 1986, publisher and editor Peter Gravis. "Black Tie Press is committed to publishing innovative, distinctive and engaging writing. We publish books; we are not a magazine or literary journal. We are not like the major Eastern presses, university presses or other small presses in poetic disposition. To get a feel for our publishing attitude, we urge you to buy one or more of our publications before submitting." He is **"only interested in imaginative, provocative, at risk writing. *No rhyme.*"** They have published poetry by Steve Wilson, Guy Beining, Sekou Karanja, Craig Cotter, Harry Burrus and Jenny Kelly. As a sample the editor selected these lines from "Late November, Los Angeles" in *Steaming* by Donald Rawley:

> *In this rubbed dusk,*
> *the false fall sky*
> *silvers itself*
> *into a pale, nude witch,*
> *a sun of mother's cologne,*

> *and a neck of distanced chill*

Sample postpaid: $8. "We have work we want to publish, hence, unsolicited material is not encouraged. However, we will read and consider material from committed, serious writers as time permits. Query with four sample poems. Write, do not call about material. *No reply without SASE.***" Cover letter with bio preferred. Reports in 2-6 weeks. Always sends prepublication galleys. Author receives percent of press run.** Peter Gravis says, "Too many writers are only interested in getting published and not interested in reading or supporting good writing. Black Tie hesitates to endorse a writer who does not, in turn, promote and patronize (by actual purchases) small press publications. Once Black Tie publishes a writer, we intend to remain with that artist."

BLACK WARRIOR REVIEW (II), P.O. Box 862936, Tuscaloosa AL 35486-0027, founded 1974, contact poetry editor, is a semiannual review. They have recently published poetry by Yusef Komanyakaa, Lee Upton, Lucia Maria Perillo and Tony Hoagland. As a sample the editor selected these lines from "The Life of a Baby Boomer" by Dave Smith:

> *But people look at you, even make remarks.*
> *Windows and mirrors loom everywhere. The worst*
> *days point fingers, nothing's color stays, no voice*
> *turns you around, even birds, and she won't call.*

BWR is 200 pgs., 6 × 9. Circulation is 2,000. **Sample postpaid: $8. Submit 3-6 poems at a time. Simultaneous submissions OK if noted. Send SASE for guidelines. Reports in 1-4 months. Pays $30-45/poem plus 2 copies. Buys first rights.** Awards one $500 prize annually to a poet whose work appeared in either the fall or spring issue. Reviews books of poetry in single or multi-book format. Open to unsolicited reviews. Poets may also send books for review consideration to Christopher Chambers, editor. Poetry published in *BWR* has been included in the 1993 and 1997 volumes of *The Best American Poetry*. The editor says, "We solicit a nationally-known poet for a chapbook section. The remainder of the issue is chosen from unsolicited submissions. Many of our poets have substantial publication credits, but our decision is based simply on the quality of the work submitted."

‡*BLADE MAGAZINE; BLADE PRESS (I, II), 'Maynrys'/Glen Chass, Port St. Mary, Isle of Man IM9 5PN Great Britain, fax (01624)836459, founded 1995, editor Jane Holland, appears 3 times/year in April, August and December and publishes poetry and poetry reviews "intended to sharpen poets." **They want "sharp vibrant work that raises the hairs on the back of a reader's neck, without being consciously sensationalist. No obscure, self-involved work from poets who do not widely read contemporary poetry."** They have recently published poetry by Brendan Kennelly, Maura Dooley, Paul Violi and Tony Towle. As a sample the editor selected these lines from "Nathan Whiting" by Robert Hershon:

> *. . . So they waited until Nathan Whiting*
> *came to visit and they asked him*
> *What is the difference between*
> *poetry and prose and Nathan said*
> *Prose-writers go to prose-writers'*
> *parties and poets go to poets' parties.*

Blade is about 44 pgs., A5, professionally printed and saddle-stapled with colored card cover, few graphics, ⅔ poetry, the rest reviews. They receive about 500 poems a year, accept approximately 5-10%. Press run is 300 for 150 subscribers of which 5 are libraries, 20 shelf sales. Single copy: $7; subscription: $20. **Sample postpaid: $5. Make checks payable to Blade Press Magazine ("cash preferred if payment is in dollars"). Submit 4-6 poems at a time. No previously published poems or simultaneous submissions. Cover letter required with short bio.** Time between acceptance and publication is 3-6 months. **Often comments on rejections. Publishes theme issues. Reports "within one month to U.S., less for Europe." Pays 1 copy. Acquires all rights. Returns rights upon publication.** Reviews books of poetry in 500-2,500 words. Poets may also send books for review consideration. They also operate The Isle of Man Poetry Society. Send SASE for details. The editor says, "Read, read, read, and accept criticism openly."

BLANK GUN SILENCER; BGS PRESS (II), 1240 William St., Racine WI 53402, phone (414)639-2406, founded 1991, editor Dan Nielsen, is "an independent art/lit mag" which appears twice a year "publishing Buk-heads, post-Dada freaks and everything in between." **They want poetry that is "tight, concise, startling, funny, honest, causing leaps of recognition—a good solid kick in the head. Nothing flowery, overly 'poetic,' too academic, rhyming or blatantly pointless."** They have published poetry by Charles Bukowski, Gerald Locklin, Fred Voss and Ron Androla. As a sample the editor selected these lines from "Edge" by Mark Weber:

> *where are my John Coltrane records?*
> *o, i sold them when*
> *i was a junkie*
> *they sold good*
> *but now i want to hear them*
> *need to hear the cycle of 5ths played backwards*
> *on "Giant Steps"*

one of the purest musicians ever

The editor says *BGS* is 60-80 pgs., digest-sized, photocopied and saddle-stapled with card stock cover and b&w art. They accept approximately 200 poems a year. Press run is 300 for 50 subscribers of which 7 are libraries. Single copy: $4; subscription: $8. **Sample postpaid: $3. Submit 6 poems at a time. Fresh copies preferred. Previously published poems OK, if notified. No simultaneous submissions. Cover letter required.** Time between acceptance and publication is up to 1 year. **Often comments on rejections. Send SASE for guidelines. Reports within 3 months. Pays up to 3 copies. Acquires first or one-time rights.** Reviews books of poetry in up to 3 pages. Open to unsolicited reviews. Poets may also send books for review consideration. BGS Press **publishes 4 chapbooks/year. Query first with sample poems and cover letter with bio and publication credits. Replies to queries in 1 week, to mss within 1 month. Sometimes sends prepublication galleys. Pays 30 copies. Obtain sample chapbook by sending $2.**

BLIND BEGGAR PRESS; LAMPLIGHT EDITIONS; NEW RAIN (IV-Ethnic, anthology, children), P.O. Box 437, Williamsbridge Station, Bronx NY 10467, phone/fax (914)683-6792, founded 1976, literary editor Gary Johnston, business manager C.D. Grant, publishes **work "relevant to Black and Third World people, especially women."** *New Rain* is an annual anthology of such work. Lamplight Editions is a subsidiary that publishes "educational materials such as children's books, manuals, greeting cards with educational material in them, etc." They want to see **"quality work that shows a concern for the human condition and the condition of the world—art for people sake."** They have published work by Judy D. Simmons, A.H. Reynolds, Mariah Britton, Kurt Lampkin, Rashidah Ismaili, Jose L. Garza and Carletta Wilson. *New Rain* is a 60- to 200-page chapbook, digest-sized, finely printed, saddle-stapled or perfect-bound, with simple art, card covers. **Sample postpaid: $5.** They also publish about 3 collections of poetry by individuals each year, 60-100 pgs., flat-spined paperback, glossy, color cover, good printing on good paper. **Sample: $5.95. For either the anthology or book publication, first send sample of 5-10 poems with cover letter including biographical background, philosophy and poetic principles. Considers simultaneous submissions. Reads submissions January 15 through September 1 only. Replies to queries in 3-4 weeks, to submissions in 2-3 months. Pays copies (the number depending on the print run). Acquires all rights. Returns them "unconditionally."** Willing to work out individual terms for subsidy publication. Catalog available for SASE.

THE BLIND HORSE REVIEW (II), P.O. Box 81305, Lincoln NE 68501-1305, founded 1992, editor Todd Kalinski, is a poetry and prose publication that appears about twice a year. **They do not want poetry that is "overtly sentimental in nature. No particular qualms as to length, and subject matter or language may be what it may [and they mean that]. No academic writing for the sake of strictly writing it, and no globs of despair for no sensible reason."** They have recently published poetry by Steve Richmond, Gerald Locklin, Barbara Peck, James Magorian and Hugh Fox. As a sample the editor selected these lines from "Locked Out" by Chris Mortenson:

> It would be preferable to contemplate
> and to discuss important things
> but most people don't.
>
> Humanity more easily accepts the insubstantial,
> though some have a bit more depth,
> it is not much.

The Blind Horse Review is 36-48 pgs., digest-sized and saddle-stapled with heavy, colored, matte paper cover. They accept about 5% of the poetry received and feature 11-14 writers in each issue. Press run is 300 for 50 subscribers. Subscription: $15 for 3 issues. **Sample postpaid: $6. Make checks payable to Todd Kalinski. Submit 10 poems at a time. No previously published poems or simultaneous submissions. Include SASE "and, if you may, a cover letter without awards and publications, but a letter of interest, something maybe of insight." Often comments on rejections. Send SASE for guidelines. Reports in up to 1 month. Pays 1 copy. Rights revert to authors.** The editor says, "Type yourself into a certain sensibility that one can actually persevere in this vocation; because it doesn't seem to come easily to most of the writers writing today."

‡**BLIND MAN'S RAINBOW (I)**, P.O. Box 1557, Erie PA 16507-0557, founded 1993, editor Melody Sherosky, a quarterly publication whose focus is to create a diverse collection of quality poetry and art." They want "all **forms of poetry, though excessively long poems are less likely to be accepted. All subject matter accepted."** They do not want **"anything graphically sexual or violent."**
   • This is a poetry and art zine; rough but containing some interesting work.

THE SUBJECT INDEX, located before the General Index, can help you select markets for your work. It lists those publishers whose poetry interests are specialized.

As a sample the editor selected these lines from "Spines and Minds" by Lou Hertz:

> *In Haverwood, where willows grow*
> *On landscaped hillocks, row on row,*
> *The bent and twisted folk reside*
> *In bodies they can barely bide.*

BMR is 16 pgs., 8½×11, photocopied and side-stapled with contents ⅔ poetry, ⅓ art, paper cover with art, line drawings inside, back cover reserved for ads. (The issue we received contained market listings on the back cover). They receive about 800 poems a year (200 submissions). "We print at least one poem from 75% of submissions. Single copy: $2; subscription: $10, $14 (outside the US). **Sample postpaid: $3, $4 (outside the US), back issues $2. Make checks payable to Melody Sherosky. Submit 2-10 poems at a time with name and address on each poem. Previously published poems and simultaneous submissions OK. Cover letter preferred. "Submissions only returned if requested and with adequate postage. Disk submissions must be in ASCII format on a 720k or 1.44M DOS formatted diskette."** Time between acceptance and publication is 1-3 months. **Often comments on rejections. Send SASE for guidelines (also included in magazine.) Reports in 1-6 weeks. Pays 1 copy, 2 by request. Acquires one-time rights.** The editor says, "Graphics submitted must include directions about their relationship to the poetry (Do they go with a poem? Which one?). We look for poetry that reaches inside, captures the feeling and mood of the author."

BLOCK'S MAGAZINE; BLOCK PUBLICATIONS (III),

(formerly *Block's Poetry Collection*), 1419 Chapin St., Beloit WI 53511-5601, founded 1993, editor Alan J. Block, is a quarterly. **"Poems of shorter length (one page or less), high quality and unique perspective have a home here. We also publish poetry-related reviews and b&w artwork." They do not want erotica or religious verse.** They have recently published poetry by Lyn Lifshin, David Robson and Robert Bunzer. As a sample the editor selected these lines from "Mother" by Corrine DeWinter:

> *How many stars can I offer*
> *To retract the pain,*
> *How many late night*
> *Conversations with God?*

The editor says *Block's* is 50 pgs., 5½×8½, offset and saddle-stapled with card cover containing art, b&w photos and ads inside. Press run is 100 for 40 subscribers. Subscription: $20. **Sample postpaid: $6. Submit 5 poems at a time. No previously published poems or simultaneous submissions.** Time between acceptance and publication is 6-8 months. **Always comments on rejections. Reports in 1-3 months. Pays 1 copy/poem.** Awards 1-issue subscription to best poem in each issue; 1-year subscription and cash award to poet of the year. The editor says, "I am open to most kinds of poetry. I see too much trite verse. If you submit, be prepared to receive critical comments with returned poems."

‡BLOOD AND FIRE REVIEW (II),

P.O. Box 89, Cassville GA 30132-0089, founded 1996, editor Valerie Gilreath, is a biannual (November and May) and "provides an outlet for quality poetry and short fiction. Contains mostly poetry with usually one short story per issue." **They want "poetry that speaks from experience, but is concise with a strong sense of imagery. No limit on length, subject matter or style."** No epic poetry or sentimental Hallmark verse. They have recently published poetry by Mildred Greear and Anselm Brocki. As a sample the editor selected these lines from "My Mother at Seventy Nine" by Lyn Lifshin:

> *her dark eyes losing their*
> *mahogany. Someone in the hollow*
> *of her cheeks whispers the night*
> *aid with an accent is a murderer,*
> *a monster and she hisses her out*
> *of the room, . . .*

BAFR is 40-50 pgs., digest-sized, attractively printed and saddle-stapled with 2- or 3-color card cover. No artwork. They receive about 1,300 poems a year, accept approximately 5%. Press run is 75 for 12 subscribers, 20-25 shelf sales. Subscription: $7. **Sample postpaid: $3.75. Make checks payable to Valerie Gilreath, BFR. Submit 5 poems at a time. No previously published poems; simultaneous submissions OK. Cover letter preferred, "include a bio that can be used if work is accepted. No electronic submissions."** Time between acceptance and publication is "no longer than 7 months, usually sooner." **Seldom comments on rejections. Occasionally publishes theme issues. Send SASE for guidelines and upcoming themes. Reports in 6-8 weeks. Pays 1 copy and a discount on additional copies. Acquires first rights.** The editor says, "We use a lot of free verse, but we like to see forms as well when they are done right. Just send us your best. Also, we do provide guidelines, but my advice is just to go ahead and submit or buy a sample instead."

‡BLUE INK PRESS (II),

P.O. Box 21037, Columbus Circle Station, New York NY 10023, founded 1996, publisher/editor Lisa Zuckerman, is published biannually. **They want "poems that have a certain something, an unexplainable quality that makes them 'a poem.' "** They have recently published poetry by Nancy Sirianni, Max Chandler, Tina Chang and Lyn Lifshin. As a sample the editor selected these lines from "Old Lovers" by Albert Huffstickler:

> *In the night*

he would turn to her
and put his hands in the old places
and leave them there
and there was no stirring in either of them—
a flickering warmth perhaps—like memory—

Blue Ink Press is 20 pgs., 6 × 8½, offset printed in blue ink on 70 lb. paper, saddle-stitched with glossy, heavy card cover. They receive about 500 poems a year, accept approximately 11. Press run is 250; all distributed free in New York City. Subscription: $8. **Sample postpaid: $4. Submit any number of poems with SASE. Previously published poems not preferred. Simultaneous submissions OK. "Cover letters, although sometimes interesting, are not necessary." Seldom comments on rejections. Send SASE for guidelines. Reports in a few days to 1 year. Pays 3 copies. Authors retain all rights to their work.**

BLUE LIGHT PRESS (II), P.O. Box 642, Fairfield IA 52556, phone (515)472-7882, founded 1988, editor Diane Frank, publishes 2 paperbacks, **3 chapbooks/year. "We like poems that are imagistic, emotionally honest and uplifting poems where the writer pushes through the imagery to a deeper level of insight and understanding. No rhymed poetry or dark poetry." Send SASE for submission deadlines.** They have published poetry by Rustin Larson, Nancy Berg, Viktor Tichy, Tom Centolella and Meg Fitz-Randolph. As a sample the editor selected these lines from "Seven Messages" from *Collecting Moon Coins* by Jane Oliver:

Checking your mail for a letter,
you find it full of white sand.
The wind leaves patterns
that look like words in your hand,
but they have no meaning.
Take care how you dispose of them.

That book is 120 pgs., digest-sized, professionally printed and flat-spined with elegant matte card cover: $10 plus $1.50 p&h. They have also published 3 anthologies of Iowa poets. They have an editorial board, and "work in person with local poets, have an ongoing poetry workshop, give classes, and will edit/critique poems by mail— $30 for 4-5 poems." They sponsor a poetry contest and a chapbook contest. Send SASE for more information.

BLUE MESA REVIEW (II, IV-Themes), Dept. of English, Humanities Bldg. #217, University of New Mexico, Albuquerque NM 87131-1106, phone (505)277-6347, fax (505)277-5573, e-mail: psprott@unm.edu, website http://www.unm.edu/~english/bluemesa/, founded 1989 by Rudolfo Anaya, managing editor Patricia Lynn Sprott, faculty editor Dr. David Johnson, is an annual review of poetry, short fiction, creative essays and book reviews. **They want "all kinds of free, organic verse; poems of place encouraged. No length limits; no greeting card verse."** They have published poetry by Virgil Suarez, David Axelrod and Brian Swann. As a sample they selected these lines from "Que Milagro" by Melissa Flores:

a poco piensas que you can hold
back the swelling tide with one hand
leading the pledge of allegiance with the other
then you believe
in the power la fuerza
of miracles

BMR is about 250 pgs., 6 × 9, professionally printed and flat-spined with glossy cover, photos and graphics. This hefty publication includes a number of long poems—several spanning 3 pages. They receive about 1,000 poems a year, accept 10% or less. Press run is 1,600 for 600 shelf sales. Single copy: $10. **Sample postpaid: $12. "Please submit two copies of everything with your name, address and telephone number on each page. Fax numbers and e-mail addresses are also appreciated." No previously published poems or simultaneous submissions. Cover letter required. Accepts mss from May 15 through October 31 only. Poems are then passed among readers and voted on. Seldom comments on rejections. Publishes special theme sections. Send SASE for upcoming themes. Reports on mss by mid-December. Pays 2 copies.** Reviews books of poetry. Open to unsolicited reviews. Poets may also send books for review consideration.

BLUE MOUNTAIN ARTS, INC. (IV-Specialized: greeting cards), Dept. PM, P.O. Box 1007, Boulder CO 80306-1007, e-mail bma@rmii.com, founded 1971, contact editorial staff. Blue Mountain Arts is a publisher of greeting cards, calendars, prints and mugs. They are looking for poems, prose and lyrics ("**usually nonrhyming**") appropriate for publication on greeting cards and in poetry anthologies. "Poems should reflect a message, feeling or sentiment that one person would want to share with another. We'd like to receive **sensitive, original submissions about love relationships, family members, friendships, philosophies and any other aspect of life. Poems and writings for specific holidays (Christmas, Valentine's Day, etc.) and special occasions, such as graduation, anniversary and get well, are also considered.** Only a small portion of the material we receive is selected each year and the review process can be lengthy, but be assured every manuscript is given serious consideration." **Submissions must be typewritten, one poem/page or sent via e-mail. Simultaneous submissions "discouraged but OK with notification." Submit seasonal material at least 4 months in advance. Send SASE for guidelines or request via e-mail. Reports in 3-6 months. Pays $200/poem for the worldwide, exclusive right, $25/poem for one-time use in an anthology.** They advise, "We strongly suggest that you familiarize yourself with our products before submitting material, although we caution you not to study them too hard. We do not need more poems that sound like something we've already published. Overall, we're looking for poetry that expresses real emotions and feelings."

BLUE PENNY QUARTERLY (II), Metronetics Publications, 1517 University Ave., P.O. Box 1888, Charlottesville VA 22903, phone (804)295-2407, fax (804)295-8129, e-mail publications@comet.net (best way to contact), website http://www.blue.comet.net, founded 1994, editor Andria Thomas, poetry editor Susan Imhof (address submissions to "Poetry Editor"), is a quarterly designed to promote fine literature in the electronic communities. **They want "Originality. Depth. Music. Image. We accept lyric, narrative, formal, experimental, or any hybrid, as long as it is well-crafted and imaginative."** They have published poetry by Ioana Ieronim (in translation), Wendy Battin, Eva Shaderowfsky and Robert Klein Engler. *BPQ* is an electronic publication, more than 100 pgs., using full-color artwork. It is printable by the reader's home computer and readers are encouraged to pass the software along to others. They accept 10% of the poetry received. **No previously published poems; simultaneous submissions OK. Cover letter required. Submissions via e-mail recommended as regular mail address may change.** Time between acceptance and publication is 1 month to 1 year. **Guidelines available via website. Reports in up to 3 months. Acquires first North American or one-time rights and electronic rights. Electronic rights returned upon request.** Reviews books of poetry in about 1,000 words. Open to unsolicited reviews. Poets may also send books for review consideration, attn: Andria Thomas. They also offer Readers' Choice Awards of $50 for the best poem of the issue and an Editor's Choice Award of $100 for the best poem published during the year.

‡THE BLUE SKUNK COMPANION (I, IV-Regional), P.O. Box 8400, MSU 59, Mankato MN 56002-8400, phone (507)625-7176, website http://krypton.mankato.musus.edu/~dsbs/bskunk.html, founded 1994, co-editors Scott Welvaert and Josh Lukkes, is a biannual publishing poetry, fiction, nonfiction, essays and art by emerging and veteran writers from Minnesota. **They want "any length of poetry utilizing language that creates images inside the reader's head. We don't want poetry that overuses abstractions and 'poet's language.' "**
  • *The Blue Skunk Companion* is the publication of The Blue Skunk Society, the official student organization of Mankato State University.
They have recently published poetry by Angelica Kauti, Leo Dangel, Susan Shulka and Jen Studer. As a sample the editor selected these lines from "Note Found Inside a Barrel" by Philip Dacey:

> But I will set that word,
> that coffin-boat, floating
> last home, upon some water
> that will take it and its
> voluble captain
>
> up and down and around
> some bend, a rudderless thing,
> whirl it till language itself
> dizzies, becomes its own
> rapids, its own falls.

BSC is 35-45 pgs., 8½ × 11, attractively printed, saddle-stapled with glossy cover, b&w line art, sketches, drawings. They receive about 100 poems a year, accept approximately 20%. Press run is 500-1,000 for 100 subscribers of which 12 are libraries, 200 shelf sales. Single copy: $3.75; subscription: $7. **Sample postpaid: $3. Make checks payable to The Blue Skunk Society Inc. Submit 4-6 poems at a time. No previously published poems; simultaneous submissions OK. Cover letter required. Include name and address on each poem. Submission deadlines: June 1 (summer), December 1 (winter).** Time between acceptance and publication is 6 months. **Poems are circulated to an editorial board. "Our staff comments, critiques and votes on each piece of poetry and fiction." Always comments on rejections. Send SASE for guidelines. Reports in 1-2 months. Sometimes sends prepublication galleys. Pays 1 copy. Acquires first rights.** The editors say, "We like to see poetry and prose inspired by life, not other literature or styles/periods. The author's voice is best when it's a 'human being' and not a 'writer.' "

BLUE UNICORN, A TRIQUARTERLY OF POETRY; BLUE UNICORN POETRY CONTEST (II, IV-Translations), 22 Avon Rd., Kensington CA 94707, phone (510)526-8439, founded 1977, poetry editors Ruth G. Iodice, Martha E. Bosworth and Fred Ostrander, wants **"well-crafted poetry of all kinds, in form or free verse, as well as expert translations on any subject matter. We shun the trite or inane, the soft-centered, the contrived poem. Shorter poems have more chance with us because of limited space."** They have published poetry by James Applewhite, Kim Cushman, Charles Edward Eaton, Patrick Worth Gray, Joan LaBombard, James Schevill, John Tagliabue and Gail White. As a sample the editors selected this poem, "Three Tercets for Harold Witt" by Stanley Noyes:

> One by one you die, my friends.
> Now, Harold. Farewell.
> Black ink leaks on my shirt.

Limestone slabs in new grass—
walked in Sandías, Harold,
all day, seeing only tombstones.

Was "Keats" ever "writ in water"?
On Newport Beach, Harold,
Pacific waves scribble your name.

Blue Unicorn is "**distinguished by its fastidious editing, both with regard to contents and format.**" It is 56 pgs., narrow digest-sized, finely printed, saddle-stapled, with some art. It features 40-50 poems in each issue, all styles, with the focus on excellence and accessibility. They receive over 35,000 submissions a year, use about 200, have a year's backlog. **Sample postpaid: $5. Submit 3-5 typed poems on 8½ × 11 paper. No simultaneous submissions or previously published poems. "Cover letter OK, but will not affect our selection." Send SASE for guidelines. Reports in 1-3 months (generally within 6 weeks), sometimes with personal comment. Pays 1 copy.** They sponsor an annual contest with small entry fee, with prizes of $100, $75, $50 and sometimes special awards, distinguished poets as judges, publication of 3 top poems and 6 honorable mentions in the magazine. Entry fee: $4 for first poem, $3 for others to a maximum of 5. Write for current guidelines. **Criticism occasionally offered**. The editors add, "We would advise beginning poets to read and study poetry—both poets of the past and of the present; concentrate on technique; and **discipline yourself by learning forms before trying to do without them**. When your poem is crafted and ready for publication, study your markets and then send whatever of your work seems to be compatible with the magazine you are submitting to."

BLUE VIOLIN (II, IV-Form/style), P.O. Box 1175, Humble TX 77347-1175, founded 1995, editor Mary Agnes Dalrymple, is a biannual publication of free verse poetry. **The editor wants "free verse poetry *only*, no longer than 60 lines. Shorter poems have a better chance of being accepted."** *Blue Violin* is 40 pgs. (including cover), digest-sized, neatly printed and saddle-stapled with colored card cover and graphics done by the editor. She receives about 5,000 poems a year, accepts 50-60. Press run is 200-300. Subscription: $10. **Sample postpaid: $5. Submit 3-7 poems at a time, typed 1 to a page, name and address on each. "Please include SASE with proper postage." Previously published poems and simultaneous submissions OK. Cover letter and letter-sized envelope preferred.** Time between acceptance and publication is 6-12 months. **Often comments on rejections. Reports in 2-4 weeks. "Poets who are accepted receive a free copy of the issue in which their poem appears.** Patron donations are accepted (and greatly appreciated). Patrons receive a free copy and are named in subsequent issues. These funds help pay printing and postage costs."

BLUELINE (IV-Regional), Dept. PM, English Dept., Potsdam College, Potsdam NY 13676, fax (315)267-3256, e-mail tylerao@potsdam.edu, founded 1979, editor-in-chief Anthony Tyler, and an editorial board, "is an annual literary magazine dedicated to prose and **poetry about the Adirondacks and other regions similar in geography and spirit.**" They want "**clear, concrete poetry pertinent to the countryside and its people. It must go beyond mere description, however. We prefer a realistic to a romantic view. We do not want to see sentimental or extremely experimental poetry.**" They usually use poems of 75 lines or fewer, though "occasionally we publish longer poems" on "**nature in general, Adirondack Mountains in particular. Form may vary, can be traditional or contemporary.**" They have published poetry by Phillip Booth, George Drew, Eric Ormsby, L.M. Rosenberg, John Unterecker, Lloyd Van Brunt, Laurence Josephs, Maurice Kenny and Nancy L. Nielsen. It's a handsomely printed, 112-page, 6×9 magazine with 40-45 pgs. of poetry in each issue. Circulation is 400. **Sample copies: $4 for back issues. Submit 5 poems at a time. Include short bio. No simultaneous submissions. Submit September 1 through November 30.** They have a 3- to 11-month backlog. **Occasionally comments on rejections. Send SASE for guidelines or request via e-mail. Reports in 2-10 weeks. Pays 1 copy. Acquires first North American serial rights.** Reviews books of poetry in 500-750 words, single and multi-book format. "We are interested in both beginning and established poets whose poems evoke universal themes in nature and show human interaction with the natural world. We look for **thoughtful craftsmanship rather than stylistic trickery.**"

BOA EDITIONS, LTD. (III), 260 East Ave., Rochester NY 14604, phone (716)546-3410, e-mail boaedit@frontiernet.net, founded 1976, poetry editor A. Poulin, Jr. They have published some of the major American poets, such as W.D. Snodgrass, John Logan, Isabella Gardner, Richard Wilbur and Lucille Clifton, and they publish introductions by major poets of those less well-known. For example, Gerald Stern wrote the foreword for Li-Young Lee's *Rose*. Send SASE for guidelines.

BOGG PUBLICATIONS; BOGG (II), 422 N. Cleveland St., Arlington VA 22201-1424, founded 1968, poetry editors John Elsberg (USA), George Cairncross (UK: 31 Belle Vue St., Filey, N. Yorkshire YO 14 9HU England) and Sheila Martindale (Canada: P.O. Box 23148, 380 Wellington St., London, Ontario NGA 5N9 Canada). "We publish *Bogg* magazine and occasional free-for-postage pamphlets." The magazine uses a great deal of poetry in each issue (with several featured poets)—"**poetry in all styles, with a healthy leavening of shorts (under ten lines). Prefer original voices. Our emphasis is on good work per se and Anglo-American cross-fertilization. We are always looking for American work with British/Commonwealth themes/references.**" This is one of the liveliest small press magazines published today. It started in England and in 1975 began including a supplement of American work; it now is published in the US and mixes US, Canadian, Australian and UK work with reviews of small press publications from all of those areas. It's thick (68 pgs.), typeset, saddle-stitched, in a 6×9 format that leaves enough white space to let each poem stand and breathe alone. They have recently published work by Ann Menebroker, Miriam Segan, Robert Peters and Ann Erickson. As a sample the editors selected these lines from "Bondi Afternoons" by Australian poet Peter Bakowski:

> *I hear children and seagulls squeal,*
> *the clock leisurely licks its paws.*
> *There is rust and washing and tin chimneys.*
> *It's timeless, lazy, beautiful.*
> *An acoustic guitar and mist can still*
> *break your heart.*

They accept all styles, all subject matter. "Some have even found the magazine's sense of play offensive. Overt religious and political poems have to have strong poetical merits—statement alone is not sufficient. Submit six poems at a time. Prefer typewritten manuscripts, with author's name and address on each sheet. We will reprint previously published material, but with a credit line to a previous publisher." No simultaneous submissions. Cover letters preferred. "They can help us get a 'feel' for the writer's intentions/ slant." SASE required for return of ms. There are about 50 pgs. of poetry/issue. Press run is 850 for 400 subscribers of which 20 are libraries. Single copy: $4.50; subscription: $12 for 3 issues. **Sample postpaid: $3.50.** They receive over 10,000 American poems/year, use 100-150. "We try to accept only for next two issues. SASE required or material discarded (no exceptions)." **Send SASE for guidelines. Reports in 1 week. Pays 2 copies. Acquires one-time rights.** Reviews books and chapbooks of poetry in 250 words, single format. Open to unsolicited reviews. Poets may also send books to relevant editor (by region) for review consideration. Their occasional pamphlets and chapbooks are by invitation only, the author receiving 25% of the print run, and you can get **chapbook samples free for 6×9 SASE.** Better make it at least 2 ounces worth of postage. John Elsberg advises, "Become familiar with a magazine before submitting to it. Long lists of previous credits irritate me. Short notes about how the writer has heard about *Bogg* or what he or she finds interesting or annoying in the magazine I read with some interest."

BOHEMIAN BRIDGE (II, IV-Regional), P.O. Box 1780, Shepherdstown WV 25443, e-mail bohemian@acces s.mountain.net, founded 1993, is a quarterly publication devoted to promoting the work of writers of the Appalachian region. It contains poetry, short stories and quotes. **They want poetry from Appalachian writers. "Unlimited as to style or perspective; prefer less than 100 lines; new styles and innovation welcome. No sentimental love poetry or religious poetry."** *Bohemian Bridge* is 60 pgs., approximately 7×8½, photocopied and saddle-stapled with card stock cover and b&w graphics and ads. They receive about 500 poems a year, accept approximately 10%. Press run is 300-500 for about 100 subscribers, 20-40 shelf sales. Subscription: $7.95 for 6 months, $15.95 yearly. **Sample postpaid: $3.50. Submit up to 3 poems at a time, typed with name and address on each page. Previously published poems and simultaneous submissions OK. Cover letter preferred. Often comments on rejections. Send SASE for guidelines or request via e-mail. "However, we will need an address (physical) to respond." Reports in approximately 2 months. Pays 1 copy plus discount on additional copies. Acquires one-time rights.**

BOMB MAGAZINE (III), 594 Broadway, Suite 905, New York NY 10012, phone (212)431-3943, fax (212)431-5880, e-mail bomb@echonyc.com, website http://www.bombsite.com, founded 1981, senior editor Jenifer Berman, is a quarterly magazine that "encourages a dialogue among artists of various media. **Experiments with form and language are encouraged. No limericks, inspirational verse, clever or greeting card styles."** They have published poetry by David Mamet, Harold Pinter and A.C. Purcell. *Bomb* is 108 pgs., saddle-stitched with 4-color cover. "We receive about 100 manuscripts a month; we accept 2 or 3 every 4 months." Press run is 12,000 for 2,000 subscribers of which 600 are libraries. Single copy: $4.50; subscription: $18/year. **Sample postpaid: $5. No previously published poems; simultaneous submissions OK. Cover letter including name, address, telephone number and previous publications required. "Poetry should be legibly typed."** Time between acceptance and publication is 4-6 months. **Reports in 4 months. Pays $50. Buys first North American serial rights.**

BOOG LITERATURE; BOOGLIT (I, II), P.O. Box 150570, Brooklyn NY 11215-0570, e-mail booglit@aol. com, founded 1991, editor/publisher David Kirschenbaum. BOOG Literature publishes *BOOGLIT*, a quarterly arts and culture magazine with journalism, poetry, prose and arts reviews, as well as 5-10 chapbooks/year and

---

THE GEOGRAPHICAL INDEX, located before the Subject Index, can help you discover the publishers in your region. Publishers often favor poets (and work) from their own areas.

occasional broadsides. The editor says he **would like to see more "honest poetry written from personal experience."** They have published poetry by Bob Holman, Anselm Berrigan, Quincy Troupe, Bernadette Mayer and Anne Waldman. As a sample the editor selected these lines from "The Day the War Started" by Lee Ann Brown:

> *My cat catches a baby mouse.*
> *I take birth control pill number three.*
> *Kim says a cloud in the shape of a cross was spotted over Washington, D.C.*
> *   and that Barbara Bush's broken leg is a sign.*

BOOGLIT is 48 pgs., 8½ × 11 offset printed on white paperstock with a glossy wraparound, includes art, graphics and small press ads. "We accept 10-15 poems per issue, sometimes more, never less." Press run is 2,000; distributed nationally and internationally. **Sample postpaid: $3.50. Make all checks payable to BOOG Literature. Submit up to 5 poems; 6 short poems can count as 1 poem or page of poetry. Previously published poems and simultaneous submissions OK. "A friendly cover letter is always appreciated. Most small presses have low circulations, so if your piece was (or may be) published elsewhere, but you think it deserves/needs to be read by more people, send it along (but please tell us when and where it was or will be published)."** Time between acceptance and publication is "usually no more than six months." **Often comments on rejections. Send SASE for guidelines. Reports within 3 months. Pays 2 copies. Acquires first North American serial or reprint rights.** "We welcome and will write reviews of either chaps or mags in 50-1,000 words, single or multi-book format." **For chapbook or broadside publication, query with sample poems and cover letter including brief bio and publication credits. Replies to queries within 2 months, to mss within 6 months. Pays 10% of press run; first printing is 100-200 copies.** Recent chapbook authors include Amiri Baraka, Wanda Phipps, Todd Colby and Barry Gifford. For sample chapbook, "send check or money order for $5, and we will select a chap to send in return." The press also publishes occasional spoken word cassette compilations. Query before sending tapes. The editor says, "The job of the small press is to get the word out. If it's solid, we will publish it. It's quality, not résumé."

THE BOOKPRESS: THE NEWSPAPER OF THE LITERARY ARTS (III), The DeWitt Bldg., 215 N. Cayuga St., Ithaca NY 14850, phone (607)277-2254, founded 1990, editor/publisher Jack Goldman, associate editor Isaac Bowers, appears 8 times/year, each month except January and June, July and August. As for poetry, the editor says, **"The only criterion is a commitment to the aesthetic power of language. Avoid the hackneyed and formulaic."** They have recently published poetry by Phyllis Janowitz, Kathleen Gemmell and A.R. Ammons. The editor says *The Bookpress* is a 12-page tabloid. They receive about 50 poems a year, accept approximately 10%. Press run is 7,500 for 300 subscribers of which 15 are libraries. Subscription: $12/year. **Sample copies free. No previously published poems or simultaneous submissions. Cover letter preferred. Reads submissions August 1 through April 1 only. SASE required.** Time between acceptance and publication is 1 month. **Often comments on rejections. Send SASE for guidelines. Reports in 3 months. Pays 2 copies. Acquires first North American serial rights.** Reviews books of poetry. Length of reviews varies, typically between 1,500-2,000 words, sometimes longer. Poets may also send books for review consideration.

BORDERLANDS: TEXAS POETRY REVIEW (II), % Austin Writer's League, 1501 W. Fifth St., Suite E-2, Austin TX 78703-5155, founded 1992, appears twice a year publishing "high-quality, outward-looking poetry by new and established poets, as well as brief reviews of poetry books and critical essays. Cosmopolitan in content, but particularly welcomes Texas and Southwest writers." They want **"outward-looking poems that exhibit social, political, geographical, historical or spiritual awareness coupled with concise artistry. We also want poems in two languages (one of which must be English), where the poet has written both versions. Please, no introspective work about the speaker's psyche, childhood or intimate relationships."** They have recently published poetry by Walter McDonald, Charles Behlen, Marlys West, Lyn Lifshin and Edward Byrne. As a sample the editors selected these lines from "Body Music" by Marilynn Talal:

> *Their bodies sing, music*
>
> *of wingbeat hour after hour, dreamless streaming*
> *   to great salt marshes toothed with grass, white blaze flying*
> *   snow capped peaks, air so blue it hurts.*

Borderlands is 80-120 pgs., 5½ × 8½, offset, perfect-bound, with 4-color cover, art by local artists. They receive about 2,000 poems a year, use approximately 120. Press run is 800. Subscription: $17/year; $33/2 years. **Sample postpaid: $10. Submit 5 typed poems at a time. No previously published poems or simultaneous submissions. Include SASE (or SAE and IRCs) with sufficient postage to return poems and a response. Seldom comments on rejections. Reports in 4-6 months. Pays 1 copy. Acquires first rights.** Reviews books of poetry in one page. Also uses 3- to 6-page essays on single poets and longer essays (3,500-word maximum) on contemporary poetry in some larger context (query first). They say, "We believe it's possible—though not easy—for poetry to be both involved with the world and high-quality."

♣**BOREALIS PRESS; TECUMSEH PRESS LTD.; JOURNAL OF CANADIAN POETRY (V)**, Dept. PM, 9 Ashburn Dr., Nepean, Ontario K2E 6N4 Canada, founded 1972. Borealis and Tecumseh are imprints for books, including **collections of poetry, by Canadian writers only, and they are presently not considering**

unsolicited submissions. Send SASE (or SAE with IRCs) for catalog to buy samples. Poets published include Carol Shields and Diane Dawber. As a sample the editor selected this poem, "Uncle," by Shields:

> When he speaks
> it is with the privileged
> angular paragraphs
> of old essays,
> his phrases antique
> and shapely as jewelry.
>
> But when he laughs
> he touches new territory
> somewhere sad between
> language and breath
> just missing the edge
> of what he really
> means.

The *Journal* is an annual that publishes articles, reviews and criticism, not poetry. **Sample postpaid: $15.95.**

BOSTON REVIEW (II), E53-407, MIT, 30 Wadsworth St., Cambridge MA 02139-4307, phone (617)253-3642, fax (617)252-1549, website http://www.polisci.mit.edu/BostonReview/, founded 1975, poetry editors Mary Jo Bang and Timothy Donnelly, is a bimonthly tabloid format magazine of arts, culture and politics which uses about 25 poems a year, for which they receive about 1,000 submissions. **"We are open to both traditional and experimental forms. What we value most is originality and a strong sense of voice."** They have recently published poetry by Lynn Emanuel, Jorie Graham, John Peck, Kay Ryan, Donald Revell and Charles Simic. They have a 4- to 6-month backlog. Circulation is 20,000 nationally including subscriptions and newsstand sales. Single copy: $3; subscription: $15. **Sample postpaid: $4.50. Submit 3-5 poems at a time. Simultaneous submissions OK with notification. Cover letter listing recent publications encouraged. Submissions and inquiries are accepted via regular mail only. Reports in 1-3 months. Pays $40/poem. Buys first serial rights.** Reviews books of poetry. Only using *solicited* reviews. Publishers may send books for review consideration. Poetry published by this review has been included in *The Best American Poetry 1993*.

BOTTOMFISH (II), De Anza College, 21250 Stevens Creek Blvd., Cupertino CA 95014, founded 1976, editor David Denny. This college-produced magazine appears annually. They have recently published poetry by Chitra Divakaruni, Walter Griffin and Robert Cooperman. As a sample the editor selected the opening stanza from "In the Parking Lot of the Funeral Home" by Susan Grimm:

> Slick as a dance floor under the sky.
> the smooth black asphalt shines
> liquid with rain.
> Giddy, I want to twirl on the mirror,
> head bent, rain falling in my hair.

Bottomfish is 80 pgs., 7 × 8¼, well-printed on heavy stock with b&w graphics, perfect-bound. Circulation is 500, free to libraries, but **$5/copy to individual requests. "Before submitting, writers are strongly urged to purchase a sample copy." Best submission times: September through February. Deadline: February 15 each year. Reports in 1-6 months, depending on backlog. Pays 2 copies.**

BOUILLABAISSE (I, IV-Form/style), % Alpha Beat Press, 31 Waterloo St., New Hope PA 18938-1210, phone (215)862-0299, founded 1991, editors Dave Christy and Ana Christy, is a biannual using **"poetry that reflects life and its ups and downs."** They want **"modern, Beat poetry; poetry from the streets of life—no limit. No rhythm, Christian or sweet poetry."** They have recently published poetry by Jan Kerouac, Allen Ginsberg, elliott, Steve Richmond and Joseph Verrilli. The editors say *Bouillabaisse* is 160 pgs., 8½ × 11, offset, saddle-stitched, with graphics. They accept 200 submissions a year, accept 40%. Press run is 500 for 350 subscribers of which 9 are libraries. Subscription: $17. **Sample postpaid: $10. Submit 5 poems at a time. Previously published poems and simultaneous submissions OK. Cover letter required. Always comments on rejections. Send SASE for guidelines. Reports "immediately." Pays 1 copy.** Reviews books of poetry in 250-500 words. Open to unsolicited reviews. Poets may also send books for review consideration. They publish 2 paperbacks and 10 chapbooks/year. "We work with each individual on their project." **Replies to queries "immediately," to mss within 3 weeks. Always sends prepublication galleys for chapbooks. Pays author's copies.** Also see the listings for *Alpha Beat Soup* and *Cokefish*.

BOULEVARD (II), % editor Richard Burgin, 4579 Laclede Ave. #332, St. Louis MO 63108-2103, phone (314)361-2986, founded 1985, appears 3 times a year. **"We've published everything from John Ashbery to Howard Moss to a wide variety of styles from new or lesser known poets. We're eclectic. Do not want to see poetry that is uninspired, formulaic, self-conscious, unoriginal, insipid."** They have published poetry by Amy Clampitt, Molly Peacock, Jorie Graham and Mark Strand. *Boulevard* is 200 pgs., digest-sized, professionally printed, flat-spined, with glossy card cover. Poetry herein—mostly free verse but wide-ranging in content, length and tone—is accessible and exciting. Poems have one thing in common: careful attention to craft (particularly line, stanza and voice). Their press run is 3,000 with 700 subscribers of which 200 are libraries. Subscription: $12. **Sample postpaid: $7. "Prefer name and number on each page with SASE. Encourage cover letters but don't require them. Will consider simultaneous submissions but not previously published poems." Reads submissions October 1 through May 1 only. Editor sometimes comments on rejections. Pays $25-150/poem, depending on length, plus 1 copy. Buys first-time publication and anthology rights.** Open to unsolicited reviews. Poetry published in *Boulevard* has also been included in the 1992, 1993, 1994 and 1995 volumes of *The Best American Poetry*. Richard Burgin says, "We believe the grants we have won from the National Endowment for the Arts, etc., as well as the anthologies that continue to recognize us, have rewarded our commitment. My advice to poets: 'Write from your heart as well as your head.' "

‡BRANCH REDD BOOKS; BRANCH REDD REVIEW; BRANCH REDD POETRY BROAD-SHEETS; BRANCH REDD POETRY CHAPBOOKS (V), 9300 Atlantic Ave., Apt. 218, Margate NJ 08402, phone (609)822-7050, editor Bill Sherman, is a "small press publisher of poetry" that **discourages unsolicited mss.** He has published poetry by Allen Fisher, Asa Benveniste, Eric Mottram, Kate Ruse-Glason and Shreela Ray. As a sample the editor selected these lines (poet unidentified):

> *Her hair, her blue nightslip, more*
> *Frustration. Earlier*
> *news of Bunting's death.*

The *Branch Redd Review* appears irregularly in varied formats with a press run of 500. **Pays at least 10 copies.** Staff reviews books of poetry. Send books for review consideration.

(the) BRAVE NEW TICK (I, IV-Gay/lesbian/bisexual), P.O. Box 24, S. Grafton MA 01560, phone/fax (508)754-0963, e-mail tick@ma.ultranet.com, website http://www.ultranet.com/~tick/, founded 1985, editor Paul N. Dion-Deitch, is a gay bimonthly, art and literary publication designed for networking. **They want gay and lesbian work. No Christian "religious right" material or "hard core" porn.** They have published poetry by Brian Duley, Kevin Hibshman and John Mark Ivey. The editor says it is 10-12 pgs., 8½×11, photocopied. They receive 200-300 poems a year, "try to publish most." Press run is 100. Subscription: $10/year. **Sample postpaid: $1. Make checks payable to Paul N. Dion-Deitch. Cash also OK. Previously published poems and simultaneous submissions OK. Cover letter with bio preferred. Electronic submissions OK. "Submissions on disk (PC) are much appreciated!" Often comments on rejections, if asked. Publishes theme issues. Guidelines are included inside the publication or may be obtained via website. Reports in about a month. Pays 1 copy.**

‡*BREAKFAST ALL DAY (I), 43 Kingsdown House, Amhurst Rd., London E8 2AS United Kingdom, founded 1995, editor Philip Boxall, appears quarterly and publishes "satire, humor, general interest; special interest in art and language; includes short fiction and graphic work." **They want "4-15 lines average (not more than 30 lines); any subject matter; humor appreciated." No concrete poems, sentimental verse or long poems.** As a sample the editor selected these lines from "Dedicated Modeler of Fashion" by RJ Ritchie:

> *With a sassy sashay of her classy chassis*
> *she cakewalks down the catwalk*
> *in a sequence of sequined mannequins;*
> *she is known for her temper and tantrums,*
> *hauteur and extravagent shenanigans;*
> *imposingly posing enclothed in haute couture . . .*

BAD is 36-40 pgs., A4, litho printed, saddle-stitched with paper cover, b&w graphics, strip cartoons, photographs. They receive about 150 poems a year, accept approximately 20%. Press run is 500 for 70 subscribers, 100 shelf sales. Subscription: $10/4 issues. **Sample postpaid: $2.50. Make checks payable to Bad Press. Submit 5 poems at a time, "preferably on 3.5 disk, as a text (ASCII) file, or in clear black type." Previously published poems OK. Cover letter preferred. Seldom comments on rejections. Publishes theme issues. Send SASE (or SAE and IRC) for guidelines and upcoming themes. Reports in 2 month. Pays 1-3 copies on request. Acquires one-time rights.** Staff reviews small press books in 30-50 words in multi-book format.

THE BRIAR CLIFF REVIEW (II, IV-Regional), Briar Cliff College, 3303 Rebecca St., Sioux City IA 51104-2340, website http://www.briar-cliff.edu/www/bcchomep/publicat/bccrevie/bcreview.htm, founded 1989, poetry editor Jeanne Emmons, is an attractive annual "eclectic literary and cultural magazine focusing on (but not limited to) Siouxland writers and subjects." **They want "quality poetry with strong imagery; especially interested in regional, Midwestern content with tight, direct, well-wrought language. No allegorical emotional landscapes."** They have recently published poetry by Clif Mason, M. Elvis Mauch and Pat Underwood. As a sample the editor selected these lines from "Someone on the Stairs" by David Wyatt:

> *He will meet a woman there*
> *who's already sitting in a booth.*
> *Together they'll smoke and talk,*
> *while their reflections*
> *in the window pay no attention*
> *to the falling snow.*

BCR is 64 pgs., 8½×11, professionally printed on 70 lb. matte paper, saddle-stapled, four-color cover on 10 pt. coated stock, b&w photos inside. They receive about 100 poems a year, accept 12. Press run is 500, all shelf sales. Single copy: $5. **Sample postpaid: $6. No previously published poems; simultaneous submissions OK. "We will assume that submissions are not simultaneous unless notified." Cover letter with short bio required. "No manuscripts returned without SASE." Reads submissions August 1 through November 1.** Time between acceptance and publication is 5-6 months. **Seldom comments on rejections. Reports in 6 months. Pays 2 copies. Acquires first serial rights.** *Briar Cliff Review* was awarded the Gold Crown Award from the Columbia Scholastic Press Association in 1993 and 1994 and the National Pacemaker Award from the Associated Collegiate Press in 1995.

‡BRICKHOUSE BOOKS, INC.; THE NEW POETS SERIES, INC./CHESTNUT HILLS PRESS (III); STONEWALL SERIES (IV-Gay/lesbian/bisexual), 541 Piccadilly Rd., Baltimore MD 21204, phone (410)828-0724, e-mail e7e4ray@toe.towson.edu, founded 1970, editor/director Clarinda Harriss. NPS, along with Chestnut Hills Press and Stonewall, is now a division of BrickHouse Books. BrickHouse publishes 64-112 page works. The New Poets Series, Inc. brings out **first books by promising new poets. Poets who have previously had book-length mss published are not eligible. Prior publication in journals and anthologies is strongly encouraged. They want "excellent, fresh, nontrendy, literate, intelligent poems. Any form (including traditional), any style." BrickHouse Books and NPS pay 20 author's copies (out of a press run of 1,000), the sales proceeds going back into the corporation to finance the next volume.** "BrickHouse has been successful in its effort to provide writers with a national distribution; in fact, The New Poets Series was named an Outstanding Small Press by the prestigious Pushcart Awards Committee, which judges some 5,000 small press publications annually." Chestnut Hills Press publishes author-subsidized books—"High quality work only, however. CHP has achieved a reputation for prestigious books, printing only the top 10% of mss CHP and NPS receive." **CHP authors receive proceeds from sale of their books.** Stonewall publishes work with a **gay, lesbian or bisexual perspective.** NPS/CHP has recently published books by Patricia Adams, Richard Fein, Donald Menaker and Gerald George. As a sample the editor selected these lines by Nancy Adams from *So Close*:

> My mother had a vanity.
> It stood against the wall and flanking either side
> were other mirrors, framed in ornate wood.
>
> She searched her face.
> What if the mirror lied?
>
> I searched but never found that magic bond.

Send a 50- to 55-page ms, $10 reading fee and cover letter giving publication credits and bio. Indicate if ms is to be considered for BrickHouse, NPS, CHP or Stonewall. **Simultaneous submissions OK. Cover letters should be very brief, businesslike and include an accurate list of recently published work. Editor sometimes comments briefly on rejections. Reports in 6 weeks to 1 year. Mss "are circulated to an editorial board of professional, publishing poets.** BrickHouse is backlogged, but the best 10% of the mss it receives are automatically eligible for Chestnut Hills Press consideration," a subsidy arrangement. **Send $5 and a 7×10 SASE for a sample volume.** Stonewall Series offers a chapbook contest whose winner is published by NPS. Send 20-30 poems with $20 entry fee, postmarked no later than August 15. Rane Arrogo's *The Naked Thief* is a recent Stonewall winner.

‡THE BRIDGE: A JOURNAL OF FICTION AND POETRY (II), 14050 Vernon St., Oak Park MI 48237, founded 1990, editor Jack Zucker, appears twice a year using **"exciting, largely mainstream poetry."** They have published poetry by Ruth Whitman and Daniel Hughes. It is 192 pgs., digest-sized, perfect-bound. Press run is 700. Subscription: $13. **Sample postpaid: $7. Poems are circulated to an editorial board. Three consider mss; decision made by editor and 1 special editor. Editor rarely comments on submissions. Pays 2 copies. Acquires first rights.** Reviews books of poetry and prose in 1-10 pgs. Poetry published in *The Bridge* has been selected for inclusion in *The Best American Poetry 1994*.

‡BRIGHT HILL PRESS (V); NATIONAL POETRY BOOK COMPETITION; NATIONAL CHAP-BOOK COMPETITION (II), P.O. Box 193, Treadwell NY 13846, e-mail wordthurs@aol.com, founded 1992, director/editor-in-chief Bertha Rogers. Bright Hill Press publishes 2-3 paperbacks and **1 chapbook/year** through their competitions. **They want "intelligent, well-crafted poetry—traditional or experimental."** They have recently published poetry by Richard Foerster, Maurice Kenny, Hal Sirowitz, Richard Frost and Robert Bensen. As a sample the director selected these lines from "Scorn" by Carol Frost:

> She thought of no wilder delicacy than the starling eggs she fed him for breakfast,
> and if he sat and ate like a farmhand and she hated him sometimes,
> she knew it didn't matter: that whatever in the din of argument
> was harshly spoken, something else was done, soothed and patted away

Chapbooks are usually 24-36 pgs., 5½×8½, stapled-bound; full-length books are 48-64 pgs., 5½×8½, perfect-bound. For the annual Poetry Book Competition, winner receives $500, publication and 25 copies. **Submit 48-64 pgs. including bio, table of contents and acknowledgments page. Poems may be previously published** in journals or anthologies. Mss will be judged blindly by nationally-known poet. **Send SASE for complete guidelines. Entry fee: $15; $10 for Word Thursdays/Bright Hill Press members. Postmark deadline: September 15.** Winner announced winter of the following year. Winning ms of the 1995-96 competition was *My Own Hundred Doors* by Pam Bernard. For the Chapbook Competition (poetry in odd-numbered years; fiction in even-numbered years), winner receives $100, publication and 25 copies. **Submit 16-24 pgs. including bio, table of contents, acknowledgments page and title page. Poems may be previously published but not required. Send SASE for complete guidelines. Entry fee: $8; $5 Word Thursday/Bright Hill Press members. Postmark deadline: May 31 of odd-numbered years.** Winner announced in late fall. The 1995 competition winner was *The Man Who Went Out for Cigarettes* by Adrian Blevins-Church. **Obtain sample books or chapbooks by sending SASE for catalog.** Bright Hill Press also sponsors a large variety of activities throughout the year, including a bimonthly reading series and an annual festival. Write for details. The director says, "Revise, revise, revise! Read other poets to learn how good poetry is crafted."

‡BRILLIANT CORNERS: A JOURNAL OF JAZZ & LITERATURE (II, IV-Specialized: jazz-related literature)

‡**BRILLIANT CORNERS: A JOURNAL OF JAZZ & LITERATURE (II, IV-Specialized: jazz-related literature)**, Lycoming College, Williamsport PA 17701, fax (717)321-4090, e-mail feinstei@lycoming.edu, founded 1996, editor Sascha Feinstein, a biannual, publishes jazz-related poetry, fiction and nonfiction. **"We are open to length and form, but want work that is both passionate and well crafted—work worthy of our recent contributors. No sloppy hipster jargon or improvisatory nonsense. Jazz is serious music; jazz poetry should be serious, too."** They have recently published poetry by Jayne Cortez, Philip Levine, William Matthews, Al Young and Paul Zimmer. As a sample the editor selected these lines from "Rhythm Method" by Yusef Komunyakaa:

> *If you can see blues*
> *in the ocean, light & dark,*
> *can feel worms ease through*
> *a subterranean path*
> *beneath each footstep,*
> *Baby, you got rhythm.*

BC is 100 pgs., 6×9, commercially printed and perfect-bound with color card cover with original artwork, ads. They accept approximately 5% of work received. Press run is 400 for 200 subscribers. Subscription: $12. **Sample postpaid: $7. Submit unlimited number of poems at a time. Previously published poems "very rarely, and only by well established poets"; no simultaneous submissions. Cover letter preferred. Reads submissions September 1-May 15 only. Seldom comments on rejections. Send SASE for guidelines. Reports in 2 months. Pays 2 copies; $5/page; $10-25 (when possible). Acquires first North American serial rights.** Staff reviews books of poetry. Poets may also send books for review consideration.

BRILLIANT STAR (IV-Children, religious)

BRILLIANT STAR (IV-Children, religious), % Baha'i Subscriber Service, Baha'i National Center, 1233 Central St., Evanston IL 60201, is a Baha'i bimonthly for children, appearing in a magazine-sized format. **"Poems are always illustrated, so think about how your poem will look. Our readers are ages 5-14. Write for *them* not for yourself. We do not want to see Christmas themes in any form. If you are not familliar with the Baha'i Faith, research is encouraged."** As a sample the editor selected these lines from "Hooray for Skin" by Susan Engle:

> *Suppose, when God created skin,*
> *He turned the skinside outside in*
> *So when you talk to Mrs. Jones,*
> *Your eyes meet over fat and bones*
> *And tissues, blue and white and red,*
> *That stretch from toe to hand to head.*
> *It makes me glad to have a skin*
> *To keep the outside boneside in.*

Sample $2 with 9×12 SASE (sufficient postage for 5 oz.); objectives are printed in the masthead. Considers simultaneous submissions. Pays 2 copies. The editor urges children who wish to write poetry to avoid "writing about tired subjects like 'dogs as friends' and being 'afraid of the dark.' Write about today's world in fun, exciting language. Write about a realistic fear—guns, drugs, the school dance, my ugly feet, will my parents divorce. Make your poem an engaging short story." This is also good advice for adults who wish to write children's poetry for this publication.

*BRITISH HAIKU SOCIETY; BLITHE SPIRIT (IV-Form/style, translations)

*****BRITISH HAIKU SOCIETY; BLITHE SPIRIT (IV-Form/style, translations)**, (formerly listed under Equinox Press), 44 Romsgill Dr., Ilford, Essex 1G2 7TR England, phone 0181-924-3186, founded 1990, secretary Susan Rowley. BHS publishes a quarterly journal, *Blithe Spirit*, a quarterly newsletter and other occasional publications (pamphlets, folios); address: Farnley Gate Farmhouse, Riding Mill, Northumberland NE44 6AA England, phone 01434-682-465, editor Jackie Hardy. *Blithe Spirit* **publishes mainly haiku, senryu and tanka sent in by society members,** but one section, "The Pathway," accepts **originals in any language plus a translation in one of English, French or German, and is open to non-members.** Staff reviews books of poetry. Send books for review consideration. The Museum of Haiku Literature, Tokyo, gives a quarterly best-of-issue award (£50). In addition, BHS administers the annual James W. Hackett Haiku Award (currently £100). Rules of entry are available annually in the spring. Send SASE (or SAE and IRC from outside England) to J.W. Hackett Award, % R. Goring, 27 Park St., Westcliff-on-Sea, Essex SS0 7PA England.

BROKEN STREETS (I, IV-Religious), 57 Morningside Dr. E., Bristol CT 06010, founded 1979, editor Ron Grossman, is a **"Christian-centered outreach ministry to poets."** The editor wants **"Christian-centered poetry, feelings, etc., usually 5-15 lines, but also haiku. No more than three poems at a time. Not necessary to query, but helpful."**
● This is an attractive publication.
He has recently published Maude Carolan and N.S. Rhoades. The magazine, which appears twice a year, is 40-80 pgs., digest-sized, photocopied typescript with heavy card cover includes some ads. Uses about 300 of the 500 poems submitted/year—by folks of all ages, including children and senior citizens. Press run is 1,000. Subscription: $10 (includes "all mailings and current chapbook"). **Sample postpaid: $4. No previously published poems. Cover letter required. Reports in 1 week. Pays 1 copy.** Reviews books of poetry. Open to unsolicited reviews. Poets may also send books for review consideration.

BROODING HERON PRESS (V), Bookmonger Rd., Waldron Island WA 98297, founded 1984, co-publishers Sam and Sally Green, **publishes 3 chapbooks/year.** They have **"no restriction other than excellence."** They do not want **"prose masquerading as poetry or poems written for form's sake."** However, **"we're too backlogged to look at anything new until 1999."** They have published poetry by Denise Levertov, James Laughlin and Gary Snyder. **Query in late 1998 to determine when the press will be reading again. If open to submissions, submit complete ms of 16-20 poems; no query. Previously published poems OK; no simultaneous submissions. Cover letter required.** Time between acceptance and publication varies. **Always comments on rejections. Reports within 6 weeks. "We print 300 books per title, bound in paper and cloth. Payment is 10% of the press run. Author retains copyright."** This press has received many awards for fine printing. Write for catalog to order samples.

BROOKLYN REVIEW (II), 2900 Bedford Ave., Brooklyn College, Brooklyn NY 11210, founded 1974, editors change each year, address correspondence to poetry editor. They have recently published such poets as Sapphire, John Ashbery, Joan Larkin and L.S. Asekoff. *BR* is an annual, 128 pgs., digest-sized, flat-spined, professionally printed with glossy color cover and art. Circulation is 750. **Sample postpaid: $6. "Please send no more than four poems." Cover letter with brief history required. Reads submissions September 1 through December 1 only. Reports in 6 weeks to 6 months. Pays 2 copies.** Poetry published in *BR* has also been selected for inclusion in *The Best American Poetry 1992*.

‡BROUHAHA; GREEN BEAN PRESS (I), 22 Strathmore Village Dr., South Setauket NY 11720, founded 1993, editor Ian Griffin. *Brouhaha* appears 2 times/year. **They want "fearless but unpretentious poetry. Rather, fearless AND unpretentious. However, I don't like to see poems by people who think they are tougher than they really are."**
● The format for *Brouhaha* is very unusual. We suggest you obtain a sample copy.
They have recently published poetry by Joe R, Ana Christy, A.D. Winans and Daniel Crocker. As a sample the editor selected these lines from "anorexia xi" by joe r:

> yu'd
> be
> bettrrr
> offf
> blind

The issue we received of *Brouhaha* is approximately 35 pgs., 8½ × 8½ (many of the individual pages are smaller and larger than 8½ × 8½ with the excess of the larger sheets folded in), photocopied on a variety of colored and white paper and side-stapled, colored construction paper cover, line drawings inside. They receive about 750 poems a year, accept approximately 15%. Press run is 150. Subscription: $9. **Sample postpaid: $5. Make checks payable to Ian Griffin. Submit 3-5 poems at a time. Previously published poems OK; no simultaneous submissions. Cover letter preferred.** Time between acceptance and publication is "one to two issues" (about 1 year). **Seldom comments on rejections. Reports in 1-2 weeks. Pays 1 copy.** Green Bean Press **publishes 3-4 chapbooks/year.** Chapbooks are usually 25-30 pgs., no graphics, occasional cover art, "but each one is different." **Query first, with 5-10 sample poems and cover letter with brief bio and publication credits. Replies to queries and mss in 1 month. Pays 35% author's copies (out of a press run of "whatever.")** "Each

---

THE CHAPBOOK INDEX, located before the Geographical Index, lists those publishers who consider chapbook manuscripts. A chapbook, a small volume of work, is often a good middle step between magazine and book publication.

arrangement is different. Some authors have helped with costs, others have not."

THE BROWNSTONE REVIEW (II), 331 16th St. #2, Brooklyn NY 11215, phone (718)788-6220, e-mail dawson@quicklink.com, founded 1995, poetry editor Aaron Scharf, appears twice a year. **"We will consider poems of any form, length and style as long as the language is fresh and vivid."** They do not want to see **"anything trite or pretentious—nor generic workshop poems."** The editor says the review is 60 pgs., $7 \times 8\frac{1}{2}$, side-stapled, and receives 300-400 poems a year. Press run is 100. Single copy: $6; subscription: $10. **Make checks payable to Keith Dawson. Submit 3-5 poems at a time. E-mail submissions OK, "but poets should not expect a dramatically quicker response." No previously published poems; simultaneous submissions OK. Cover letter preferred. Seldom comments on rejections. Send SASE for guidelines. Reports within 3 months. Pays 2 copies.**

BRUNSWICK PUBLISHING CORPORATION (I), 1386 Lawrenceville Plank Rd., Lawrenceville VA 23868, phone (804)848-3865, founded 1978, poetry editor Dr. Walter J. Raymond, is a **partial subsidy publisher. Query with 3-5 samples. Response in 2 weeks with SASE. If invited, submit double-spaced, typed ms. Reports in 3-4 weeks, reading fee only if you request written evaluation. Always sends prepublication galleys. Poet pays 50-80% of cost, gets same percentage of profits for market-tester edition of 500-1,000, advertised by leaflets mailed to reviewers, libraries, book buyers and bookstores**. Books are usually 54 pgs., digest-sized, flat-spined, neatly printed, glossy cover with photo. **Send SASE for catalog to order samples and "Statement of Philosophy and Purpose," which explains terms**. That Statement says: "We publish books because that is what we like to do. Every new book published is like a new baby, an object of joy! We do not attempt to unduly influence the reading public as to the value of our publications, but we simply let the readers decide that themselves. We refrain from the artificial beefing up of values that are not there. . . . We are not competitors in the publishing world, but offer what we believe is a needed service. We strongly believe that in an open society every person who has something of value to say and wants to say it should have the chance and opportunity to do so."

‡BUENO; IN ONE EAR PUBLICATIONS (IV-Bilingual/foreign language), 29481 Manzanita Dr., Campo CA 91906-1128, phone (619)478-5619, fax (619)478-5363, founded 1989 (In One Ear), 1991 (*Bueno*), contact Eli Reid. *Bueno* is a quarterly friendly foreign language learning zine. **They want "short poems; must be in two languages (English and one other) either side-by-side translation or incorporate foreign words. No erotic, political, violent, vulgar or pagan work."** They have recently published poetry by Dick Hayman, Hugh Fox and Matt Welter. As a sample the editor selected these lines from "La Rana" by Dick Hayman:

> *The frogs of neighbor Mexico*
> *Hop and hop wherever they go*
> *Croaking, "tomorrow, tomorrow,"*
> *Mañana, Mañana*

> *And call themselves, as frogs,*
> La rana.

Bueno is 16 pgs., $5\frac{1}{2} \times 8\frac{1}{2}$, offset printed, saddle-stitched, contains some art, (Aztec, Maya or Inca Indian—noncopyrighted), no ads. They receive about 25 poems a year, accept approximately 8. Press run is 5,000 for 3,000 subscribers of which 1,000 are libraries; 1,000 distributed free to inquiries and at book/curriculum fairs. Single copy: $3; subscription: $10. **Sample postpaid: $1. Purchase of sample strongly encouraged. Submit up to 6 poems at a time. Previously published poems and simultaneous submissions OK. Cover letter preferred. "If possible, submit on IBM diskette (either size) in WordPerfect or ASCII with hard copy."** Time between acceptance and publication is 6 months. **Often comments on rejections. Charges criticism fees if extensive critique is desired or if translation is desired. Reports in 1-2 months. Pays $10 plus 5 copies. Buys first or second North American serial rights.** Includes brief staff reviews of books or magazines (50-75 words) "which we also sell." Poets may also send book for review consideration. In One Ear Publications publishes friendly foreign language learning books, chapbooks, magazine and greeting cards. It publishes 1 hardback and **1 chapbook/year.** Chapbooks are usually 32 pgs., $5\frac{1}{2} \times 8\frac{1}{2}$, offset printed and saddle-stitched with 10 pt. CS1 cover, illustrated "when appropriate." **Replies in 1-2 months. Pays $5/poem and 10 author's copies (out of a press run of 1,000). For samples "request zine and ordering instructions are included."** The editor says, "The world's full of beauty and ugliness—poetry that we are interested in will focus on the beauty."

BUFFALO BONES (II), Evergreen Poets & Writers, P.O. Box 714, Evergreen CO 80437, founded 1994, contact editors (editorial staff rotates), appears 2 times/year, is a nonprofit publication containing "nothing elitist. Poems by known and unknown poets stand side by side. We look for high quality." **They want "any form of poetry, 40-line limit, strong imagery, narratives with a new twist, and a bit of fun once in awhile. No profanity, graphic/sexual, or woe-is-me poems."** They have published poetry by Robert Cooperman, Judith Herschemeyer, Donna Park, Carolyn Campbell and Lyn Lifshin. *Buffalo Bones* is 40 pgs., digest-sized, nicely printed on quality paper. They receive about 4,000 poems a year, accept approximately 150. Press run is 1,000 for 80 subscribers, 75% distributed free to libraries and bookstores. Subscription: $12. **Sample postpaid: $5. Make checks payable to Evergreen Poets & Writers. Submit up to 5 poems at a time with a $1/poem**

reading fee. "Poems are not returned." Previously published poems and simultaneous submissions OK. Reads submissions September 1 through May 1. Poems are circulated to an editorial board. "We have a rotating editorship in order to ensure variety and a fresh look in every issue." Send SASE for guidelines. Reports in 3 months. Pays 2 copies. Acquires first or one-time rights. The editors say, "Every poem gets attention from several readers. There are many fine poems—so little space. Our editorial staff rotates for each issue, therefore, try us again."

BUFFALO SPREE MAGAZINE (II), 4511 Harlem Rd., Buffalo NY 14226, founded 1967, poetry editor Janet Goldenberg, is the quarterly regional magazine of western New York. It has a controlled circulation (21,000) in the Buffalo area, mostly distributed free (with 3,000 subscriptions, of which 25 are libraries). Its glossy pages feature general-interest articles about local culture, plus book reviews, fiction and poetry contributed nationally. It receives about 300 poetry submissions/year and uses about 25, which have ranged from work by Robert Hass and Carl Dennis to first publications by younger poets. They use 5-7 poems/issue, **these are selected 3-6 months prior to publication. Sample postpaid: $3.75. Submit up to 6 poems at a time. Considers simultaneous submissions, "but we must be advised that poems have been or are being submitted elsewhere." Pays $25/ poem on publication.**

‡**BURNING BUSH PUBLICATIONS; PEOPLE BEFORE PROFITS POETRY PRIZE (I, II)**, P.O. Box 7361, Santa Cruz CA 95061, phone (408)426-9172, founded 1996, contact acquisitions editor, serves "voices that are underserved by mainstream presses." Publishes 1 paperback/year. **They want "uplifting writing that believes in a more harmonious and equitable world with an emphasis on social justice and conscience." They do not want "any work that is degrading to humans or other lifeforms."** They have recently published poetry by Morton Marcus, Lyn Lifshin, David Kherdian and Opal Palmer Adisa. As a sample the editor selected these lines from "like a red tail" by Abby Bogomolny:

> i scope out your canyon
>   clearing the ridge and view your landscape,
>   a shifting of your desire
>   steaming, brown, dusty
>   and ride the hot wind high

Books are usually 144 pgs., 5½ × 8½, offset, stapled with medium card cover and photographs. **"Send ten sample poems with a description of the audience you wish to reach. Explain the scope of work in a cover letter and include any previous publications including references." Charges $45 fee for book-length mss that have passed the 10-poem approval phase. Previously published poems OK; no simultaneous submissions.** Time between acceptance and publication is 1 year. **Poems are circulated to an editorial board. "Board meets once per month and reviews all submissions that have passed our acquisitions editors approval."** Seldom comments on rejections. **Charges critism fees "only under special circumstances: if the author can benefit from it, agrees to it and if we love their work enough to provide it. They must first send ten-poem sample for approval." Replies to queries and mss in 2 months. Authors are paid by individual contract.** Sponsors People Before Profits Poetry Prize which awards a $100 first prize, $75 second prize and a Honorable Mention. Submit up to 3 poems in any style or form, attach index card with name, address and phone with every entry. Entry fee is $10 per poem, maximum length 50 lines. Poems accepted through May 15, 1998. Send SASE for guidelines.

‡**BURNING LIGHT: A JOURNAL OF CHRISTIAN LITERATURE (I, II, IV-Religious)**, 59 Treetop Court, Bloomingdale NJ 07093-1016, phone (201)283-9516, founded 1993, editor/publisher Carl Simmons, is a quarterly literary magazine with a Christian viewpoint. **They want "poetry rich with imagination, insight and belief—form, length, et. al. are no object. Write something good, that's it. No Helen Steiner Rice clones."** They have recently published poetry by David Craig, Diane Glancy and David Middleton. As a sample the editor selected this poem, "Adam's Second Fall," by T.H.S. Wallace:

> Imperfect light fills the sky
> and the garden's beyond hope.
>
> It's a ravaged season, all loose
> and fall about, the collapse
>
> of singalong work, the birds
> in ragged flight beating their way south
>
>   from this cold unwinding year.

BL is 32-48 pgs., digest-sized, professionally printed and saddle-stitched with card cover containing art, some illustrations, ads. They receive about 500 poems a year, accept approximately 50-60. Press run is 200-300 for 100 subscribers of which about 10 are libraries. Subscription: $14, $16 (foreign). **Sample postpaid: $4. Make checks payable to Burning Light Press. Submit 3-6 poems at a time. Rarely accepts previously published poems; simultaneous submissions OK. Cover letter preferred.** Time between acceptance and publication is 2-6 months. **Often comments on rejections. Send SASE for guidelines. Reports in 1-2 months. Pays 5-6** copies. **Acquires all rights, "but it's negotiable."** Reviews books of poetry in 200-400 words. Open to unsolicited reviews. Poets may also send books for review consideration. Through Burning Light Press, they offer editorial/critiquing services. Write for details.

BUTTON MAGAZINE; THIMBLE PRESS (I, II), P.O. Box 26, Lunenburg MA 01462, e-mail symboline@ju no.com, founded 1993, poetry editor D.E. Bell, "is New England's tiniest magazine of fiction, poetry and gracious living." **They want "poetry about the quiet surprises in life, not sentimental, and true moments carefully preserved. Brevity counts."** They have recently published poetry by William Corbett, David Barber, Amanda Powell and Norah Dooley. As a sample the editor selected these lines from "Barnum in Nantucket" by David Barber:

> Here's the rub: the Republic's archetypal shark
> was just another rube that afternoon, a gaping epigone
> caught up in Leviathan's maw.
>
> Was he awestruck? Delectable to think him so.
> Here was a jaw wide as a double churchdoor,
> grand as a robber baron's balustrade, a spectacle that spoke for itself.

Button appears twice a year and is 30 pgs., 4¼ × 5½, saddle-stitched, card stock 4-color cover with illustrations that incorporate one or more buttons (our favorite shows the Statue of Liberty holding needle and thread). *The Boston Globe* called it charmingly homemade in feel and liked "its lack of pretension and its quirky humor." Press run is 1,200 for more than 450 subscribers; 750 shelf sales. Subscription: $5/2 years. **Sample postpaid: $1. Submit up to 3 poems at a time. No previously published poems. Cover letter required.** Time between acceptance and publication is 6-12 months. **Poems are circulated to an editorial board. Often comments on rejections.** Send SASE for guidelines or request via e-mail. **Reports in 2-3 months. Pays $10/poem, 2-year subscription and author's copies. Acquires first North American serial rights.** Thimble Press **publishes 1 chapbook/year. Query first, with sample poems and cover letter with brief bio and publication credits. Replies to queries in 2 months. Pays half net profit and 30 author's copies. For sample, send $1.** The editor says, "*Button* was started so that a century from now when people read it they'll say, 'Gee, what a wonderful time to have lived. I wish I lived back then.' Our likes include wit and humanity, intelligence and eccentricity. We dislike whining, cheap sentimentality and 'writing as therapy,' and strongly recommend you spring the buck to see what's in the magazine. All correspondence handled with graciousness and consideration."

BYLINE MAGAZINE (IV-Writing), P.O. Box 130596, Edmond OK 73013-0001, phone (405)348-5591, founded 1981, editor Marcia Preston, poetry editor Betty Shipley, is a **magazine for the encouragement of writers and poets, using 8-10 poems/issue about writers or writing.** As a sample the editor selected these lines from "Cone" by Darrell Fike:

> The crimson-tipped calligraphy
> of the morning glory vine
> scrawled across the top of the fence rail
> spells out a message perhaps
> the lost instruction manual for this world

ByLine is magazine-sized, professionally printed, with illustrations, cartoons and ads. They have about 3,000 subscriptions and receive about 2,500 poetry submissions/year, of which they use 144. Subscription: $20. **Sample postpaid: $4. Submit up to 4 poems at a time, no reprints. Send SASE for guidelines. Reports within 6 weeks. Pays $5-10/poem. Buys first North American serial rights.** Sponsors monthly poetry contests. Send #10 SASE for details. Marcia Preston advises, "We are happy to work with new writers, but please read a few samples to get an idea of our style. We would like to see more serious poetry about the creative experience (as it concerns writing)."

‡*CADMIUM BLUE LITERARY JOURNAL; PRECIOUS PEARL PUBLICATIONS (II), 71 Harrow Crescent, Romford, Essex RM3 7BJ England, founded 1991 (Precious Pearl Publications), 1994 (*Cadmium Blue Literary Journal*), editor/publisher Peter Geoffrey Paul Thompson. *Cadmium Blue* is a biannual journal of traditional poetry of the romantic school. **They want "traditional romantic/lyrical poetry, any length, in the Wordsworth and Shelley tradition."** They have recently published poetry by Pamela Constantine, Stella Browning and Peter Russell. As a sample the editor selected these lines by Peter Geoffrey Paul Thompson:

> Light breaks! Behold, a cycle new alights,
> The whole within the group of pensive soul.
> We waited long in exile, destined heights
> Already are upon us, to make whole
> Romantic longing, new champagne we pour.

The editor says *Cadmium Blue* is 32 pgs., laser printed and stapled with a cover design. They receive over 500 poems a year, use less than 10%. Press run is 500 for 300 subscribers of which 10 are libraries; 50 distributed free to libraries, reviewers and bookshops. Subscription: £10. **Sample postpaid (including guidelines): £5. Make checks payable to Precious Pearl Publications. "Purchase of subscription advised for consideration." Submit 3 poems at a time. Previously published poems OK; no simultaneous submissions. Cover letter** required. **Submit typed sheets of paper, one poem per sheet.** Time between acceptance and publication is between 2-12 months. **Poems are selected by the editor. Often comments on rejections. Reports in 1 month. Pays 1 copy.** Copyright remains with poet. Staff reviews books of poetry for subscribers, up to 200 words.

‡**CAFE EIGHTIES MAGAZINE (II)**, F.D.R. Station, P.O. Box 8068, New York NY 10150, phone (212)802-4528, founded 1995, publisher/editor-in-chief Kimberly Brittingham. *Cafe Eighties*, published quarterly, "caters to a readership that grew out of the quirky early 1980s with identifiable images in fiction, poetry, commentary, humor pieces and celebrity profiles." **They want poems "no more than one page in length; generally open to form and subject matter." They do not want "New Age, vampire, poems not directed toward an audience under 40."** They have recently published poetry by B.Z. Niditch, Rick Wormwood and Daniel Nester. *Cafe Eighties* is 36 pgs., 8½×11, offset printed with glossy cover, some ads, graphics and b&w photos. They receive about 200 poems a year, use approximately 5%. Press run is 2,500 for 2,100 subscribers, 300 shelf sales. Subscription: $18. **Sample postpaid: $5. Submit up to 4 poems at a time. Previously published poems and simultaneous submissions OK. Cover letter preferred. Address and phone number must be included on every page of poetry.** Time between acceptance and publication is 1 year. **Poems are circulated to an editorial board. Selections are forwarded to editor-in-chief for final decision. Often comments on rejections. Send SASE for guidelines. Reports in 1-8 weeks. Pays 1 copy. Buys one-time rights.** Reviews books and chapbooks of poetry, sometimes single, sometimes multi-book format, length varies. Open to unsolicited reviews. Poets may also send books for review consideration.

THE CAFÉ REVIEW (III), c/o Yes Books, 20 Danforth St., Portland ME 04101, e-mail writer@mainelink.net, website http://www.mainelink.net/~writer/cafehtml/index.html, founded 1989, editors Steve Luttrell and Wayne Atherton, is a quarterly which has grown out of open poetry readings held at a Portland cafe. The editors say they aim "to print the best work we can!" **They want "free verse, 'beat' inspired and fresh. Nothing clichéd."** They have published poetry by Charles Bukowski, Robert Creeley, Janet Hamill and Diane Wakoski. *The Review* is 70-80 pgs., 5½×8½, professionally printed and perfect-bound with card cover, b&w art, no ads. They receive over 1,000 submissions a year, accept approximately 15%. Press run is 300 for 70 subscribers of which 10 are libraries, 75-100 shelf sales. Subscription: $20. **Sample postpaid: $6. No previously published poems or simultaneous submissions. Cover letter with brief bio required. "Poems only may be sent via e-mail. All other requests should be sent via U.S. mail. We usually respond with a form letter indicating acceptance or rejection of work, seldom with additional comments." Reports in 2-4 months. Pays 1 copy.** They also publish 1-2 chapbooks/year.

CALAPOOYA COLLAGE; $1,000 CAROLYN KIZER POETRY AWARDS (V), P.O. Box 309, Monmouth OR 97361, phone (503)838-6292, founded 1981, editor Thomas L. Ferte. *CC* is a literary annual using **"all kinds" of poetry.** They have published poetry by Robert Bly, Joseph Bruchac, Octavio Paz, Marge Piercy, Etheridge Knight, Vassar Miller, William Stafford, Ursula K. LeGuin, Patricia Goedicke, David Wagoner and David Ray. It is 48 pgs., tabloid-sized. Press run is 1,500 for 250 subscribers of which 16 are libraries. They receive about 6,000 poems/year, accept approximately 6%. **Sample postpaid: $5. Reads submissions September 1 through June 1 only. Best times for submissions are January and February. Reports in 1-2 months. Pays 2 copies.** Reviews books of poetry in 600-1,000 words. Open to unsolicited reviews. Poets may also send books for review consideration. All poems accepted for publication are eligible for annual $1,000 Carolyn Kizer Poetry Awards.

*****CALDER PUBLICATIONS LTD.; RIVERRUN PRESS INC.; ASSOCIATION CALDER (V)**, 179 Kings Cross Rd., London WC1X 9BZ England, phone 0171-833-1300, publisher John Calder, is a literary book publisher. On their list are Samuel Beckett, Breyten Breytenbach, Erich Fried, Paul Eluard, Pier Paolo Passolini and Howard Barker. **"We do not read for the public,"** says John Calder, and he wants **no unsolicited mss.** "Any communication which requires a response should be sent with a SAE."

CALLALOO (IV-Ethnic), Dept. PM, Dept. of English, 322 Bryan Hall, University of Virginia, Charlottesville VA 22903, phone (804)924-6616, fax (804)924-1478, founded 1976, editor Charles H. Rowell. Devoted to **poetry dealing with North America, Europe, Africa, Latin and Central America, South America and the Caribbean.** They have published poetry by Rita Dove, Jay Wright, Alice Walker, Yusef Komunyakaa, Aimé Césaire, Nicolás Guillén and Jimmy Santiago Baca. Visually beautiful and well-edited with thematic, powerful poems in all forms and styles, this thick quarterly journal features about 15-20 poems in each issue (along with concise and scholarly book reviews). Circulation is 1,400, for 1,400 subscribers of which half are libraries. Subscription: $27, $54 for institutions. **"We have no specifications for submitting poetry except authors should include SASE." Reports in 6 months. Pays copies.** Poetry published in *Callaloo* has been included in the 1992, 1994, 1995 and 1996 volumes of *The Best American Poetry*.

CALYX, A JOURNAL OF ART & LITERATURE BY WOMEN (IV-Women, lesbian); CALYX BOOKS (V), P.O. Box B, Corvallis OR 97339-0539, phone (541)753-9384, fax (541)753-0515, founded 1976, managing editor M. Donnelly, is a journal edited by a collective editorial board, **publishes poetry, prose, art, book reviews and interviews by and about women.** They want **"excellently crafted poetry that also has**

excellent content." They have published poetry by Diane Glancy, Robin Morgan, Carole Boston Weatherford and Eleanor Wilner. As a sample the editor selected these lines from "Comiendoselo a los muertos (Eating Your Dead)" by Alma Garcia:

> *You can't cut your eyes away*
> *from the naked shrivel on velvet pillows,*
> *mouths open like baby birds.*
> *tongues writing names in the space between lips,*
> *the tracings half scrutable, wrapped,*
> *the color of mummy.*

Calyx appears 3 times every 18 months and is 7×8, handsomely printed on heavy paper, flat-spined, glossy color cover, 125-200 pgs., of which 50-60 are poetry. Poems tend to be lyric free verse that makes strong use of image and symbol melding unobtrusively with voice and theme. Single copy: $9.50. **Sample postpaid: $11.50. In 1998, *Calyx* is open to submissions October 1 through November 15 only. Mss received when not open to reading will be returned unread. Send up to 6 poems with SASE and short bio. "We accept copies in good condition and clearly readable. We focus on new writing, but occasionally publish a previously published piece." Simultaneous submissions OK, "if kept up-to-date on publication." Send SASE for guidelines. Reports in 2-6 months. Pays 1 copy/poem and subscription.** Open to unsolicited reviews. Poets may also send books for review consideration. *Calyx* received a Special Merit Award for Editorial Content from the 1995 American Literary Magazine Awards and a 1996 Oregon Governor's Award for the Arts. Calyx Books publishes 1 book of poetry a year. All work published is by women. Recently published: ***Another Spring, Darkness: Selected Poems by Anuradha*** translated by Carolyne Wright et al. **However, they are not accepting book submissions at this time.** They say, "Read the publication and be familiar with what we have published."

CAMELLIA; CAMELLIA PRESS INC. (II), P.O. Box 417, Village Station, New York NY 10014-0417, editor Tomer Inbar, associate editor Beth Stevens. *Camellia* is published biannually as a fold-out magazine/poster "available for free in New York City, the San Francisco/Oakland Bay area, Seattle, Ithaca, D.C., Northern Virginia and Baltimore, or by sending 55¢ postage. **We publish poetry in the W.C. Williams tradition. The poetry of things, moment and sharpness. We encourage young writers and like to work with the writers who publish with us. Our main goal is to get the poetry out. We do not want to see poetry where the poem is subordinate to the poet or poetry where the noise of the poetic overshadows the voice. We look for poetry that is honest and sharp and unburdened."** *Camellia*'s exact dimensions, the theme for a given issue and the mix of poetry and other art will be determined on an issue by issue basis. "We will keep the basic graphic design consistent with the style we have used for the past seven years, however we will be inviting guest designers to work with that design, bringing something new to each issue. We will continue to publish special project issues from time to time using various formats and mediums. We receive approximately 300-350 poems/issue and publish about 20." Press run is 1,000-2,000. Subscription: $5/year, $7 overseas. **Sample: 55¢ postage. Submit 8 poems at a time. Simultaneous submissions and previously published poems OK. "Cover letters are helpful, but shouldn't go overboard. Sometimes the cover letters are more interesting than the poetry received." Reports "ASAP." Pays 2 copies. Editor comments on submissions "if asked for or if I want to see more but am not satisfied with the poems sent."** A chapbook of poems by Jerry Mirskin, entitled *Picture A Gate Hanging Open And Let That Gate Be The Sun*, is available for $5 from Camellia Press Inc. Also available is a poster of poetry, photographs and design using poems from the first 6 years of *Camellia*. **They send prepublication galleys only for chapbooks.**

♣CANADIAN AUTHOR; CANADIAN AUTHORS ASSOCIATION (III), Box 419, Campbellford, Ontario K0L 1L0 Canada, phone (705)653-0323, fax (705)653-0593, e-mail canauth@redden.on.ca, poetry editor Roo Borson. *Canadian Author*, a quarterly, is 28 pgs., magazine-sized, professionally printed, with paper cover in 2 colors. It contains articles useful to writers at all levels of experience. **Sample postpaid: $4.75. Buys 40 poems a year. "The trend is toward thematic issues and profiles of featured poets, so query letters are recommended." Pays $15 plus one copy.** (See also Canadian Authors Association Literary Awards in the Contests and Awards section.)

♣CANADIAN DIMENSION: THE MAGAZINE FOR PEOPLE WHO WANT TO CHANGE THE WORLD (III, IV-Political), 91 Albert St., Room 2-B, Winnipeg, Manitoba R3B 1G5 Canada, phone (800)737-7051, fax (204)943-4617, e-mail info@canadiandimension.mb.ca, website http://www.canadiandimension.mb.ca/cd/index.html, founded 1964, editorial contact Brenda Austin-Smith, appears 6 times/year, using **"short poems on labour, women, native, gay/lesbian and other issues. Nothing more than one page."** They have published

---

SENDING TO A COUNTRY other than your own? Be sure to send International Reply Coupons (IRCs) instead of stamps for replies or return of your manuscript.

poetry by Tom Wayman and Milton Acorn. It is 48-56 pgs., magazine-sized, slick, professionally printed, with glossy paper cover. Press run is 3,500 for 2,500 subscribers of which 800 are libraries, 1,000 shelf sales. Subscription: $30.50 US ($24.50 Canadian). **Sample postpaid: $2. Submit up to 5 poems at a time. Previously published poems are unlikely to be accepted. Simultaneous submissions OK, if notified. Editor comments on submissions "rarely." Publishes theme issues. Send SASE (or SAE and IRC) for upcoming themes.** Reviews books of poetry in 750-1,200 words, single or multi-book format. They say, "We are broadly political—that is, not narrowly sloganeering, but profoundly sensitive to the connections between words and the state of the world. Topics can be personal as well as political. Also, American writers are reminded to include Canadian return postage or its equivalent in reply coupons, etc."

✿**CANADIAN LITERATURE (IV-Regional),** 167-1855 West Mall, University of British Columbia, Vancouver, British Columbia V6T 1Z2 Canada, phone (604)822-2780, fax (604)822-5504, website http://www.swifty. com/cdn_lit, founded 1959, editor E.M. Kröller, is a quarterly review which publishes **poetry by Canadian poets. "No limits on form. Less room for long poems."** They have published poetry by Atwood, Ondaatje, Layton and Bringhurst. As a sample the editor selected these lines from "Forerunners" by Elizabeth Brewster:

> *Before the king comes, he sends messengers.*
> *Tyrant or liberator, which is he?*
> *How judge the message that the postman brings?*
> *Promise or threat? true? false? ambiguous?*
> *Loveletter or a summons to a trial?*

Each issue is professionally printed, digest-sized, flat-spined, with 175-200 pgs., of which about 10 are poetry. They receive 100-300 submissions/year, use 10-12. Circulation is 1,200, two-thirds of which are libraries. **Sample for the cover price: $15 Canadian plus postage and GST. No simultaneous submissions or reprints. Cover letter and SASE (or SAE and IRC) required. Reports within the month. "Accepted poems must be available on diskette." Pays 1 copy. Buys first rights.** Reviews books of poetry in 500-1,000 words.

✿**CANADIAN WRITER'S JOURNAL (IV-Writing); WIND SONGS (IV-Form/style),** White Mountain Publications, Box 5180, New Liskeard, Ontario P0J 1P0 Canada, phone (705)647-5424, fax (705)647-8366, e-mail dranchuk@aol.com, owner Deborah Ranchuk, is a small quarterly, publishing mainly short "how-to" articles of interest to writers at all levels. They use a few **"short poems or portions thereof as part of 'how-to' articles relating to the writing of poetry and occasional short poems with tie-in to the writing theme."** The Wind Songs column of *CWJ* accepts **unpublished poems including haiku, senryu, tanka, sijo, one-liner renga and sequences. Maximum 15 lines.** Subscription: $15/year, $25/2 years. **Sample: $4. Submit up to 5 poems (identify each form)** to Elizabeth St. Jacques, Poetry Editor, 406 Elizabeth St., Sault Ste. Marie, Ontario P6B 3H4 Canada. **Include SASE ("U.S. postage accepted; do not affix to envelope"). Token payment. Pays $2-5 and 1 copy/poem.** The magazine runs an annual poetry competition with closing date June 30. Send SASE for current rules.

CANDLELIGHT POETRY JOURNAL; ARMADILLO POETRY PRESS (I, II), P.O. Box 3184, St. Augustine FL 32085-3184, phone (904)794-0294, e-mail clight96@aol.com, founded 1995, editors Carl Heffley and Robin Heffley. *Candlelight Poetry Journal* is a quarterly **"seeking an eclectic mix of form, free verse and avant-garde work from the poets of today. Limit 30 lines, though this may be relaxed for exceptional work. Form poetry is preferred, but please no cliché, hearts-and-flowers, moon-June poetry."** They have recently published poetry by Delphine LeDoux, Kerry Lowes Coleman, Fontaine Falkoff, Robert Gaurnier and Ruth Gillis. As a sample the editors selected these lines from "Food For Thought" by William J. Middleton:

> *We poets write the words that others read:*
> *At times it seems on us the "others" feed*
> *To fill their hunger for a metaphor*
> *Or simile that lets their dull minds soar*
> *To see the things we poets clearly see;*
> *To feel emotions poets know to be;*
> *And this is good, for if we are not read*
> *Our hard won works of poetry are dead.*

CPJ is 56-64 pgs., 8½×11, offset and saddle-stapled with a full-color, coated card cover with art. They accept about 30% of the poetry received. Press run is 800 for 400 subscribers of which 14 are libraries. Subscription: $30. **Sample postpaid: $7.50. Make checks payable to Armadillo Poetry Press. Submit 5 poems at a time. Previously published poems OK ("after a period of two years"); no simultaneous submissions. Cover letter with brief bio preferred. "Poems are selected on a basis of form, imagery, creativity and originality." Always comments on rejections. Send SASE for guidelines. Reports in 2-4 weeks. Pays byline and "publication," which means you must purchase a copy if you want to see your work in print. However, they also offer 4 Editors' Choice Awards of $10 and give $10 to "the poet receiving the most votes from readers in each issue." Acquires first (or occasionally reprint) rights.** Always includes market listings and articles on writing poetry. Also reviews books of poetry. Poets may also send books for review consideration. **Also publishes chapbooks.** Send SASE for information. Armadillo Poetry Press also offers a series of contests (with reading fees of $2 for the first poem and $1 for each additional poem and prizes ranging from $25 to $200) and publishes perfect-bound and saddle-stitched collections, 80-120 pgs., which entrants may purchase if they want to see their work in print.

CANNEDPHLEGM (I), 37 Lafayette, San Francisco CA 94103, phone/fax (415)252-8768, founded 1995, editor Jeff Fleming. *CannedPhlegm*, which appears every 6 weeks, is a literary magazine containing poetry, short fiction, columns, sketches and a few b&w photos. **The editor says he is open to any type of poetry—no specifications.** He has recently published poetry by Tim Scannel, Barbara Cooper and Nicholas J. Gardiner. As a sample the editor selected these lines from "Paint Creek," a poem of his own:

> *There are ghosts in the orchard*
> *picking fruit, telling stories*
> *of cider and donuts*
> *and crisp fall*
> *days where you*
> *can bite the air like an apple.*

CannedPhlegm is 24-36 pgs., $7 \times 8\frac{1}{2}$, photocopied and saddle-stapled with paper cover. They receive 400-500 poems a year, accept approximately 50%. Press run is 175 for 75 subscribers. Subscription: $10 for 6 issues. **Sample postpaid: $2. Make checks payable to Jeff Fleming. Submit up to 3 poems at a time. Fax submissions OK. No previously published poems or simultaneous submissions. Cover letter required. Often comments on rejections. Send SASE for guidelines. Reports within 2 weeks. Pays 1 copy.** Sponsors annual poetry competition. Deadline January 31, 1998. Send SASE for more information. The editor says, "One rejection to one poem could just as easily indicate a poor editor as a poor poem."

THE CAPE ROCK (II), Dept. of English, Southeast Missouri State University, Cape Girardeau MO 63701, phone (314)651-2500, founded 1964, editor Dr. Harvey Hecht, appears twice yearly and consists of **64 pgs. of poetry and photography, with a $200 prize for the best poem in each issue and $100 for featured photogra-phy. "No restrictions on subjects or forms. Our criterion for selection is the quality of the work. We prefer poems under 70 lines; no long poems or books; no sentimental, didactic or cute poems."** They have published poetry by Stephen Dunning, Joyce Odam, Judith Phillips Neeld, Lyn Lifshin, Virginia Brady Young, Gary Pacer-nick and Laurel Speer. It's a handsomely printed, flat-spined, digest-sized magazine. Circulation is about 500 for 200 subscribers of which half are libraries. Single copy: $5; subscription: $7/year. **Sample: $4. Submit 3-7 poems at a time. Do not submit mss in May, June or July. Send SASE for guidelines.** They have a 2- to 8-month backlog and **report in 1-3 months. Pays 2 copies.** This is a solid publication that features a wide selection of forms and styles, leaning in recent years toward free verse that establishes a mood or milieu.

❧**CAPERS AWEIGH MAGAZINE (I, IV-Regional)**, P.O. Box 96, Sydney, Nova Scotia B1P 6G9 Canada, founded 1992, publisher John MacNeil, is a quarterly of **poetry and short fiction "of, by and for Cape Bretoners at home and away." They want work by Cape Bretoners only. Nothing profane.** The publisher says it is 50-60 pgs., 5×8, desktop-published, stapled, including computer graphics and trade ads. Press run is 500. Subscription: $20. **Sample postpaid: $5. No simultaneous submissions. Cover letter required. Seldom comments on rejections. Pays 1 copy.**

❧**THE CAPILANO REVIEW (III)**, 2055 Purcell Way, North Vancouver, British Columbia V7J 3H5 Canada, fax (604)983-7520, e-mail erains@capcollege.bc.ca, website http://www.capcollege.bc.ca, founded 1972, editor Robert Sherrin, is a literary and visual media review appearing 3 times/year. **They want avant-garde, experimen-tal, previously unpublished work, "poetry of sustained intelligence and imagination."** They have recently published poetry by Bernice Friesen, Tony Lopez and John Barton. *TCR* comes in a handsome digest-sized format, 150 pgs., flat-spined, finely printed, semi-glossy stock with a glossy full-color card cover. Circulation is 1,000. **Sample: $9 prepaid. Do not submit mss during June and July. No simultaneous submissions. Reports in up to 5 months. Pays $50-200, subscription, plus 2 copies.**

CAPPER'S (I, IV-Nature, inspirational, religious, humor), 1503 SW 42nd St., Topeka KS 66609-1265, fax (913)274-4305, founded 1879, editor Nancy Peavler, is a biweekly tabloid (newsprint) going to **270,000 mail subscribers, mostly small-town and farm people. Uses 6-8 poems in each issue. They want short poems (4-10 lines preferred, lines of one-column width) "relating to everyday situations, nature, inspirational, humorous."** They have published poetry by Elizabeth Searle Lamb, Robert Brimm, Margaret Wiedyke, Helena K. Stefanski and Claire Puneky. As a sample the editor selected this poem, "Sugar maple matinee," by Linda Roth:

> *Forty thousand sun-*
> *burned hands,*
> *Applaud them-*
> *selves*
> *Then drop down*
> *into autumn's*
> *lap.*

Send $1.50 for sample. Not available on newsstand. "Most poems used in *Capper's* are upbeat in tone and

offer the reader a bit of humor, joy, enthusiasm or encouragement." Submit 4-6 poems at a time. No simultaneous submissions. Returns mss with SASE. Publishes theme issues. Send SASE for upcoming themes. Reports in 2-3 months. Pays $10-15/poem. Buys one-time rights. The editor says, "Poems chosen are upbeat, sometimes humorous, always easily understood. Short poems of this type fit our format best."

THE CARIBBEAN WRITER; THE DAILY NEWS PRIZE; THE CHARLOTTE AND PAIEWON-SKY PRIZE (IV-Regional), University of the Virgin Islands, RR 02, P.O. Box 10,000, Kingshill, St. Croix, USVI 00850, phone (809)692-4152, fax (809)692-4026, e-mail ewaters@uvi.edu, founded 1987, editor Dr. Erika Waters, is an annual literary magazine **with a Caribbean focus. The Caribbean must be central to the literary work or the work must reflect a Caribbean heritage, experience or perspective.** They have published poetry by Derek Walcott, Kamaw Brathwaite and Opal Palmer Odisa. The magazine is 250 pgs., 6×9, handsomely printed on heavy pebbled stock, flat-spined, with glossy card cover, using advertising and b&w art by Caribbean artists. Press run is 1,000. Single copy: $10 plus $1.50 postage; subscription: $20/2 years. **Sample: $5 plus $1.50 postage. Send SASE for guidelines. (Note: Postage to and from the Virgin Islands is the same as within the US.) Simultaneous submissions OK. Blind submissions only: name, address, phone number and title of ms should appear in cover letter along with brief bio. Title only on ms. Deadline is September 30 of each year.** The annual appears in the spring. **Pays 2 copies. Acquires first North American serial rights.** Reviews books of poetry and fiction in 500 words. Open to unsolicited reviews. Poets may also send books for review consideration. The magazine annually awards The Daily News Prize of $300 for the best poem or poems and The Charlotte and Paiewonsky Prize of $100 for first-time publication.

❦**CARLETON ARTS REVIEW (II)**, Box 78, 18th Floor, Davidson Dunton Tower, Carleton University, Ottawa, Ontario K1S 5B6 Canada, phone (613)520-2310, founded 1982, co-ordinating editor Steve Zytveld, is a 60-page semiannual publishing poetry, prose, visual art (b&w) and reviews. **"All kinds of poetry accepted and encouraged."** They have published poetry by Stan Rogal, Brian Burke, Calvin White and Alan Packwood. They receive 200-300 poems a year, publish about 10%. Press run is 400 for 50 subscribers most of which are libraries, 150 shelf sales. Subscription: $8. **Sample postpaid: $4. No previously published poems or simultaneous submissions. "Please include a short biography and list of publications plus a SASE or SAE and IRC." Always comments on rejections. Reports in 1-2 months. Pays 2 copies.**

*****CARN; THE CELTIC LEAGUE (IV-Ethnic, foreign language)**, 11 Hilltop View, Braddan, Isle of Man, phone/fax (UK)(0)1624-627128, founded 1973, general secretary Bernard Moffatt, is a magazine-sized quarterly, circulation 2,000. "The aim of our quarterly is to contribute to a **fostering of cooperation between the Celtic peoples,** developing the consciousness of the special relationship which exists between them and making their achievements and their struggle for cultural and political freedom better known abroad. Contributions to *Carn* come **through invitation to people whom we know as qualified to write more or less in accordance with that aim. We would welcome poems** *in the Celtic languages* **if they are relating to that aim.** If I had to put it briefly, we have a political commitment, or, in other words, *Carn* **is not a literary magazine."** Reviews books of poetry only if in the Celtic languages.

CARNEGIE MELLON MAGAZINE (II, IV-Specialized: university affiliation), Carnegie Mellon University, Pittsburgh PA 15213, phone (412)268-2132, editor Ann Curran, is the **alumni magazine** for the university and **limits selections to writers connected with the university. Submit 3 poems at a time (typed, double-spaced, with SASE) to Gerald Costanzo, poetry editor. No payment.** Only uses staff-written reviews.

THE CAROLINA QUARTERLY; THE CHARLES B. WOOD AWARD (II), 510 Greenlaw Hall, CB #3520, University of North Carolina, Chapel Hill NC 27599-3520, phone (919)962-0244, founded 1948, poetry editor Robert West, appears 3 times a year primarily publishing fiction and poetry. **They have no specifications regarding form, length, subject matter or style of poetry.** They have recently published poetry by Denise Levertov, Richard Wilbur, Robert Morgan and Diane Wakoski. *TCQ* is about 90 pgs., 6×9, professionally printed and perfect-bound with one-color matte card cover, a few graphics and ads. They receive about 6,000 poems a year, accept less than 1%. Press run is 1,500 for 200 library subscriptions and various shelf sales. Single copy: $4; subscription: $10. **Sample postpaid: $5. No previously published poems or simultaneous submissions. Poems are circulated to an editorial board. "Every manuscript is read by at least two people. Manuscripts that make it to the meeting of the full poetry staff are discussed by all. Any poem with strong support of one or more people is accepted." Seldom comments on rejections. Reports in 4 months. "Poets are welcome to write or phone about their submission's status, but please wait about four months before doing so." Pays 4 copies. Acquires first rights.** Reviews books of poetry. Poets may also send books for review consideration (attn: Editor). The Charles B. Wood Award for Distinguished Writing is given to the author of the best poem or short story published in each volume of *The Carolina Quarterly.* Only those writers *without* major publications are considered and the winner receives $500.

CAROLINA WREN PRESS (V, IV-Women, ethnic, gay/lesbian, social issues), 120 Morris St., Durham NC 27701, phone (919)560-2738, founded 1976, publishes 1 book/year, **"primarily women and minorities, though men and majorities also welcome."** They have published poetry by Jaki Shelton Green, Mary Kratt

and Steven Blaski. **They currently are not accepting any unsolicited mss. Reports in 2-4 months. Pays 10%
of print run in copies. Send 9½×12 SASE for catalog and guidelines (include postage for 3 ounces).**

CAROUSEL MAGAZINE (III), Room 274, University Centre, University of Guelph, Guelph, Ontario N1G
2W1 Canada, founded 1983, editors Dan Evans and Amber Wilson, is an annual which features "the best in
North American fiction, poetry, essays and visual art by both established and emerging talent." They have
published poetry by Timothy Findley, Leon Rooke, Lorna Crozier, Terry Griggs and Steven Heighton. It is 200
pgs., flat-spined. Their press run is 500. **Sample postpaid: $12. Type name and address on each page. Cover
letter with short bio and info on past publications required. Pays 1 copy.** Also sponsors a contest. Send SASE
(or SAE and IRCs) for more information.

CAT FANCY (IV-Animals), P.O. Box 6050, Mission Viejo CA 92690, phone (714)855-8822, founded 1965,
editor Jane Calloway. *Cat Fancy* is a magazine-sized monthly that uses **poems on the subject of cats. "No
more than 30 short lines; open on style and form, but a conservative approach is recommended. In our
children's department we occasionally use longer, rhyming verse that tells a story about cats. No eulogies
for pets that have passed away."** Circulation is 300,000. Subscription: $25.97. **Sample postpaid: $5.50. Submit
ms with SASE; editors do not respond to submissions without SASE. Reports in 10-12 weeks. Pays $20/
poem plus 2 copies.**

CATAMOUNT PRESS; COTYLEDON (II, IV-Anthology), 2519 Roland Rd. SW, Huntsville AL 35805,
founded 1992, editor Georgette Perry. *Cotyledon*, founded in 1997, published several times a year is a miniature
magazine. **They want poems about nature and the environment of up to 8 lines.** Poets recently published
include Peggy Heinrich, Leonard Cirino and Jervey Bauer. Catamount Press publishes **1-2 chapbooks** or antholo-
gies/year. **During 1998, Catamount will continue to use short to mid-length poems on nature and conservation.** As a sample the editor selected these lines from "The Wounded Muskrat" by Fred Boltz from the chapbook-
anthology *Star Nose*:

> *Heading toward*
> *the north shore*
> *of the moon, he drags*
> *a small chain of ice*
> *across a sky made of stone.*

It is 12 pgs., 3½×4¼, photocopied, saddle-stapled, with bond cover and b&w art. **Submit 3-6 poems at a time.
Previously published poems OK. Cover letter required. "Before submitting a chapbook ms, send three
unattached 32¢ stamps for guidelines and sample, so your submission will fit the format." Previously
published poems OK if author holds copyright. Reports in 1 month. Pays copies.**

CAVEAT LECTOR (III), 400 Hyde St., Apt. 606, San Francisco CA 94109, founded 1989, editors Christopher
Bernard, James Bybee and Andrew Towne, appears 2 times/year. "*Caveat Lector* is devoted to the arts and to
cultural and philosophical commentary. We publish visual art and music as well as literary and theoretical texts."
**They want poetry that "has authenticity of emotion and high craft, whether raw or polished, that rings
true—if humorous, actually funny, or at least witty. Classical to experimental. 400-line limit."** They have
recently published poetry by Lyn Lifshin, Jerry Sexton, Christian C. Thompson and Yvette Flaten. The editors
say *CL* is 32-36 pgs., 4¼×11, offset and saddle-stitched. They receive about 600-800 poems a year, accept less
than 2%. Press run is 300 for 30 subscribers of which 12 are libraries, 200 shelf sales. Single copy: $2.50;
subscription: $10/4 issues. **Sample postpaid: $3. Simultaneous submissions OK.** Time between acceptance
and publication is 1 year. **Sometimes comments on rejections. Reports in 1 month. Pays 5 copies. Acquires
first publication rights.** Christopher Bernard says, "The two rules of writing are: 1. Rewrite it again. 2. Rewrite
it again. The writing level of most of our submissions is pleasingly high. A rejection by us is not always a
criticism of the work, and we try to provide comments to our more promising submitters."

WM CAXTON LTD. (I, IV-Regional), 12037 Hwy. 42, Ellison Bay WI 54210, phone (414)854-2955,
founded 1986, publisher K. Luchterhand. **"About 50% of our books involve an author's subvention of production costs with enhanced royalties and/or free copies in return,"** and the publisher acquires all rights. They
want **"any serious poetry, not children's or doggerel."** Poetry must have Northern Midwest author or
subject. They have published books of poetry by David Koenig (*Green Whistle*), Marilyn Taylor (*Shadows Like
These*), William Olson (*North of Death's Door*) and Caroline Sibr (*Moon Gold*). Write or call to purchase sample
copies.

FOR INFORMATION ON ENTERING the *1999 Poet's Market* Poetry Contest, see
page 2.

‡CC MOTORCYCLE NEWS MAGAZINE (IV-Sports/recreation), P.O. Box 1046, New York NY 10960, phone (914)353-6686, fax (914)353-5240, e-mail motomag@aol.com, website http://www.motomag.com, founded 1990, is a monthly containing regional motorcycle news and features. **They want motorcycle-related poetry.** They say *CCMNM* is 44 pgs., tabloid-sized and printed on newsprint. Press run is 25,000 for 2,000 subscribers of which 25 are libraries; 5,000 distributed free to bike shops. Single copy: $1.95; subscription: $25. **Sample postpaid: $2. Make checks payable to Motomag Corp. Submit up to 5 poems at a time. Previously published poems and simultaneous submissions OK. Cover letter required including SASE.** Time between acceptance and publication is 1-4 months. **Often comments on rejections. Publishes theme issues. Send SASE for guidelines and upcoming themes. Reports in 1 month. Pays $10-25. Buys one-time regional rights.**

THE CENTENNIAL REVIEW (II), 312 Linton Hall, Michigan State University, East Lansing MI 48824-1044, phone (517)355-1905, e-mail cenrev@pilot.msu.edu, founded 1957, editor R.K. Meiners, appears 3 times/year. **They want "that sort of poem which, however personal, bears implications for communal experience."** They have published poetry by David Citino and Dimitris Tsaloumas. It is 240 pgs., 6×9, desktop-published, perfect-bound, with 3-color cover, art, graphics and ads. They receive about 500 poems a year, accept about 2%. Press run is 1,000 for 800 subscribers. Subscription: $12/year. **Sample postpaid: $6. Submit 5 poems at a time. No previously published poems or simultaneous submissions. Seldom comments on rejections. Publishes theme issues. Send SASE for guidelines and upcoming themes or request via e-mail or fax. Reports in about 2 months. Pays 2 copies plus 1-year subscription. Acquires all rights. Returns rights "when asked by authors for reprinting."**

CENTER PRESS; MASTERS AWARD (III), Box 16452, Encino CA 91416-6452, founded 1980, editor Gabriella Stone. Center Press is "a small press presently publishing 6-7 works per year including poetry, photo-journals, calendars, novels, etc. We look for quality, freshness and that touch of genius." In poetry, **"we want to see verve, natural rhythms, discipline, impact**, etc. We are flexible but **verbosity, triteness and saccharine make us cringe. We now read and publish only mss accepted from the Masters Award."** They have published books by Bebe Oberon, Walter Calder, Exene Vida, Carlos Castenada and Claire Bloome. As a sample the editor selected these lines from "Mostly the Moon" by Scott Alejandro Sonders (the 1996 Masters Award Winner):

> It is mostly the moon
> she said, so let's not talk
> of love as the crescent
> rolls slowly to silver
> and luminous shadows
> wove jasmine over
> coats of night.

Their tastes are for poets such as Charles Bukowski, Sylvia Plath, Erica Jong and Bob Dylan. **"We have strong liaisons with the entertainment industry and like to see material that is media-oriented and au courant.** We sponsor the Masters Awards, established in 1981, including a poetry award with a $1,000 grand prize annually plus each winner (and the five runners up in poetry) will be published in a clothbound edition and distributed to selected university and public libraries, news mediums, etc. There is a one-time only $10 administration and reading fee per entrant. Further application and details available with a #10 SASE." The editor says, "Please study what we publish before you consider submitting."

UNIVERSITY OF CENTRAL FLORIDA CONTEMPORARY POETRY SERIES (II), % English Dept., University of Central Florida, Orlando FL 32816-1346, phone (407)823-2212, founded 1968, poetry editor Judith Hemschemeyer, publishes **two 50- to 80-page hardback or paperback collections each year**. **"Strong poetry on any theme in the lyric-narrative tradition."** They have published poetry by Robert Cooperman, Katherine Soniat and John Woods. **Submit complete paginated ms with table of contents and acknowledgment of previously published poems. Simultaneous submissions OK. "Please send a reading fee of $7, a SASE for return of ms, and a self-addressed postcard for acknowledgment of receipt of ms." Reads submissions September through April only. Reports in 3 months.** Time between acceptance and publication is 1 year.

‡CHACHALACA POETRY REVIEW (II), English Dept., UT-Brownsville, Brownsville TX 78521, phone (210)544-8239, e-mail mlewis@utb1.edu, founded 1997, contact Marty Lewis, is a biannual. "We're looking for quality work in theme and craftsmanship." **They want "crafted work, thematic substance, quality in line and word." They do not want "greeting card stuff, intrusive rhymes, meaningless forms."** The editor says *Chachalaca* is 50-100 pgs., professionally printed and perfect-bound with no ads. Press run is 500 with 100 distributed free to libraries, 100 shelf sales. Single copy: $8; subscription: $12. **Submit 3-6 poems at a time. No previously published poems; simultaneous submissions OK. Cover letter preferred.** Time between acceptance and publication varies. **Poems are circulated to an editorial board of 3 readers. Seldom comments on rejections. Reports in 2 months. Sometimes sends prepublication galleys. Pays 2 copies. Buys all rights. Returns rights.** They say, "*Chachalaca* is new, but its editors are experienced and the journal is well supported."

CHAFF (I), 1061 NW 84th Ave., Plantation FL 33322, fax (954)474-6629, e-mail jordan5450@aol.com, founded 1996, first issue 1997, editor Jordan Taylor Young, is a semiannual publication "for the express purpose of uniting **Christian** poets through the publication of their work." **They want "free verse poetry—rhyme and meter only if exceptional quality—humor, romance, nature, aging, friendship and family life. Nothing satanic, obscene, violent, sensual, erotic or homosexual."** As a sample the editor selected these lines from "Through The Garden Gate" by Daniel Harr:

> *On the other side we find*
> *a place where peace can fill the mind*
> *and all the others there*
> *are kind and gentle loving folk.*
> *I believe 'twas heaven that did await us*
> *   through the garden gate*

The editor says *Chaff* is 20-24 pgs., 5½×8, laser-printed and stapled. Estimated press run is 50-100. **Submit 5 poems at a time with $2/reading fee per poem. Make checks payable to the editor, Jordan Taylor Young. Previously published poems and simultaneous submissions OK. E-mail and fax submissions OK. Cover letter required. Publishes theme issues. Send SASE for upcoming themes. Reports in 3-4 weeks. Pays 2 copies.** The editor says, "Often poets are not recognized for their artistry, separated like chaff from wheat. We intend to provide a stronger link to self, helping new and aspiring poets to find their own voices through the publication of their work."

CHAMINADE LITERARY REVIEW (II, IV-Regional), 3140 Waialae Ave., Honolulu HI 96816, founded 1986, editor Loretta Petrie, appears annually giving **special consideration to Hawaii's writers or Hawaii subject matter. "No jingles or pop poetry."** They have recently published poetry by Eleanor Wilner, William Heyen and Ian MacMillan. *CLR* features the work of many well-known creative writers and thus, at first blush, seems like a mainstream literary magazine. But poems, prose and artwork play off each other for added effect and unify such themes as ecology, love, nature, etc. The handsomely printed magazine averages over 200 pgs., 6×9, flat-spined with glossy card cover. They receive about 500 poems a year, accept approximately 25%. Press run is 500 for 350 subscribers of which 6 are libraries. Subscription: $10/year, $18/2 years. **Sample postpaid: $4. Previously published poems OK. Pays one year subscription**. Open to unsolicited reviews.

CHAMPION BOOKS, INC.; NEW SHOES SERIES (IV-Style), P.O. Box 636, Lemont IL 60439, phone (800)230-1135 or (630)257-9655, founded 1993, president Rebecca Rush, publishes 3-12 flat-spined paperback books of poetry/year through their New Shoes Series. They say, "In their prime, Kerouac and Ginsberg were never literary stars; they were the unknown and the unheard, speaking their minds and breaking new literary ground. But, now, decades after their heyday, they have become the pantheon for the mainstream of today's youth. Combined with the crossover between music and literature by such artists as Henry Rollins, William Burroughs and Jim Morrison, this has created a new era of readers with an appreciation for the great authors of the past as well as an interest in the direction of writing in the future. **Champion Books seeks neo-Beat, obscure and unrenowned authors interested not in following in the footsteps of others, but in creating their own new shoes to walk in." Query first, with 5-10 sample poems, cover letter with brief bio. Previously published poems and simultaneous submissions OK. Replies to queries in 1-3 months. Pays 7-10% royalties and about 4 author's copies. Write for catalog to order samples.** Rebecca Rush says, "As an editor I am more interested in the content and tone of the poetry rather than the number of periodicals in which the poems have previously appeared. I am also impressed with authors who take initiative to promote their own works through self-published chapbooks and readings; it's always helpful if an author is willing to extend their own time and effort in order to get their works out to the public."

CHANTRY PRESS (III), P.O. Box 144, Midland Park NJ 07432, founded 1981, poetry editor D. Patrick, publishes **perfect-bound paperbacks of "high quality" poetry. No other specifications**. They have published work by Laura Boss, Anne Bailie, Ruth Lisa Schechter, Susan Clements and Joanne Riley. Books from this press are usually 72 pgs., flat-spined, glossy cover, good printing on heavy paper, author's photo on back, $5.95. **Don't send complete ms. Query first, with sample poems and SASE, no cover letter necessary. Simultaneous submissions OK. Submission period October through April. Replies in 4 months. Always sends prepublication galleys. Pays 15% royalties after costs are met and 10 author's copies. Very short comment "sometimes" on rejected mss.**

CHANTS (II, IV-Translations), Dept. of English, Kennesaw State College, 1000 Chastain Rd., Kennesaw GA 30144-5591, founded 1988, editors Austin Hummell and Michael Fournier, appears twice a year. The editors "publish the **best translations and the most ambitious lyric poetry we can find. We encourage all poets, particularly younger ones, for whom poetry is a ruling passion."** They have published poetry by Jorie Graham, Ron Rash and Ricardo Pau-Llosa. *Chants* is 64 pgs., digest-sized, professionally printed and flat-spined with photo or graphic on cover but no inside art. They accept about 5% of poems received. Single copy: $4. **Sample: $4 plus $1 postage. No previously published poems or simultaneous submissions.** Time between acceptance and publication is up to 6 months—occasionally longer. **Sometimes comments on rejections. Reports in 1-3 months. Pays 2 copies.** The editors say, "We favor the lyric above other modes, but will publish any poem, formal or informal, that has heart and imagination. We discourage timid and anecdotal verse, and bloodless experiment. We publish poetry exclusively, and are fond of translation. We feature one poet per issue, and try to include a brief essay to accompany each feature."

THE CHARITON REVIEW PRESS; THE CHARITON REVIEW (II), Truman State University, Kirksville MO 63501, phone (816)785-4499, founded 1975, editor Jim Barnes. *The Chariton Review* began in 1975 as a twice yearly literary magazine and in 1978 added the activities of the press, producing "limited editions (not chapbooks!) of **full-length collections . . . for the purpose of introducing solid, contemporary poetry to readers**. The books go free to the regular subscribers of *The Chariton Review*; others are sold to help meet printing costs." The poetry published in both the books and the magazine is, according to the editor, **"open and closed forms—traditional, experimental, mainstream. We do not consider verse, only poetry in its highest sense, whatever that may be. The sentimental and the inspirational are not poetry for us. Also, no more 'relativism': short stories and poetry centered around relatives."** They have published poetry by Michael Spence, Neil Myers, Sam Maio, Andrea Budy, Charles Edward Eaton, Wayne Dodd and J'laine Robnolt. There are 40-50 pages of poetry in each issue of the *Review*, a 6×9, flat-spined magazine of over 100 pages, professionally printed, glossy cover with photographs. Circulation is about 600 for 400 subscribers of which 100 are libraries. They receive 8,000-10,000 submissions/year, of which they use 35-50, with never more than a 6-month backlog. Subscription: $9/1 year, $15/2 years. **Sample postpaid: $5. Submit 5-7 poems at a time, typescript single-spaced. No simultaneous submissions. Do *not* write for guidelines. Always sends prepublication galleys. Pays $5/printed page. Buys first North American serial rights. Contributors are expected to subscribe or buy copies.** Open to unsolicited reviews. Poets may also send books for review consideration. *The Chariton Review* continues to be a lively magazine open to all styles and forms with only one criterion: excellence. Moreover, response times here are quick, and accepted poems often appear within a few issues of notification. **To be considered for book publication, query first. Samples of books: $3. Payment for book publication: $500 with 20 or more copies. Usually no criticism is supplied.**

THE CHATTAHOOCHEE REVIEW (II), DeKalb College, 2101 Womack Rd., Dunwoody GA 30338, phone (770)551-3166, founded 1980, editor-in-chief Lamar York, poetry editor (Mr.) Collie Owens, is a quarterly of poetry, short fiction, essays, reviews and interviews, published by DeKalb College. **"We publish a number of Southern writers, but *CR* is not by design a regional magazine. In poetry we look for vivid imagery, unique point of view and voice, freshness of figurative language, and attention to craft. All themes, forms and styles are considered as long as they impact the whole person: heart, mind, intuition and imagination."** They have published poetry by Peter Meinke, David Kirby, Allan Peterson, Bin Ramke, Peter Wild and Cory Brown. *The Review* is 90 pgs., 6×9, professionally printed on white stock with b&w reproductions of artwork, flat-spined, with one-color card cover. Its reputation as a premiere literary magazine continues to grow. Recent issues feature a wide range of forms and styles augmenting prose selections. Circulation is 1,250, of which 300 are complimentary copies sent to editors and "miscellaneous VIPs." Subscription: $16/year. **Sample postpaid: $5. Writers should send 1 copy of each poem and a cover letter with bio material. No simultaneous submissions.** Time between acceptance and publication is 3-4 months. **Publishes theme issues. Send SASE for guidelines. Queries will be answered in 1-2 weeks. Reports in 3 months. Pays $50/poem and 2 copies. Acquires first rights.** Staff reviews books of poetry and short fiction in 1,500 words, single or multi-book format. Send books for review consideration.

CHELSEA; CHELSEA AWARD COMPETITION (III, IV-Translations), P.O. Box 773, Cooper Station, New York NY 10276-0773, founded 1958, editor Richard Foerster, associate editors Alfredo de Palchi and Andrea Lockett, is a long-established, high-quality literary biannual aiming to promote intercultural communication. **"We look for intelligence and sophisticated technique in both experimental and traditional forms. We are also interested in translations of contemporary poets. Although our tastes are eclectic, we lean toward the cosmopolitan avant-garde. We would like to see more poetry by writers of color. Do not want to see 'inspirational' verse, pornography or poems that rhyme merely for the sake of rhyme."** They have recently published poetry by Timothy Liu, William Dickey, Kay Murphy, Chim Nwabueze and Marjorie Stelmach. As an example of "the kind of attention to language and imagery" wanted for *Chelsea*, the editor selected these lines from "The Eye-mote" by Sylvia Plath:

> *What I want back is what I was*
> *Before the bed, before the knife,*
> *Before the brooch-pin and the salve*
> *Fixed me in this parenthesis;*
> *Horses fluent in the wind,*
> *A place, a time gone out of mind.*

Chelsea is 192-240 pgs., 6×9, flat-spined, offset, cover art varies, occasional photos, ads. Circulation is 1,400 for 800 subscribers of which 200 are libraries. Subscription: $13 domestic, $16 foreign. **Sample: $7. Submissions of 5-7 pgs. of poetry are ideal; long poems should not exceed 10 pgs.; must be typed; include brief bio. No previously published poems or simultaneous submissions. "We try to comment favorably on above-average mss; otherwise, we do not have time to provide critiques." Reports within 3 months. Always sends prepublication galleys. Pays $15/page and 2 copies. Buys first North American serial rights and one-time nonexclusive reprint rights.** Guidelines for their annual Chelsea Award Competition (deadline December 15), $750 for poetry, available for SASE to P.O. Box 1040, York Beach ME 03910. Work published in *Chelsea* has been included in the 1993, 1994, 1995 and 1997 volumes of *The Best American Poetry*. Richard Foerster, editor, comments: "Beginners should realize editors of little magazines are always overworked and that it is necessary haste and not a lack of concern or compassion that makes rejections seem coldly impersonal."

CHERRY STREET GRILL (I, II), P.O. Box 278, Alamo CA 94507-0278, phone (510)930-6762, e-mail cherryst rt@aol.com, founded 1995, editor Mark Hoehner, is a quarterly "eclectic collection of lively, unpredictable poetry that makes the reader think, feel, and want to read the magazine cover to cover, and then go back to the beginning and do it again." **They want "well-crafted, down-to-earth, accessible poetry on any subject. Put away your rhyming dictionary and avoid clichés. Don't send in a poem you wrote today—good poetry takes time to mature. Prefer poems under 50 lines in length. No love sonnets, overly sentimental verse or 'inspirational' poetry. Only about 5% of accepted poems rhyme."** They have published poetry by Romola Robb Allrud, Caron Andregg and Raphael Seth. As a sample the editor selected this poem, "To Be in the Same Room with Beauty," by Robert Klein Engler:

> The overhead fans mill their portions of smoky air.
> Paintings hang like ash on the edge of glaciers.
>
> You are reading in the corner—asleep and awake.
>
> Once, when you turn to look at a noise in the street,
> I feel the lance of your eyes wind by.

Cherry Street Grill is 24-32 pgs., digest-sized, photocopied from laser-printed originals and saddle-stapled, with colored card stock cover. They receive approximately 350 poems a year, accept about 20%. Press run is 150 for 45 subscribers. Single copy: $3; subscription: $10. **Sample (including guidelines) postpaid: $2. Make checks payable to Mark Hoehner. Submit 5 poems at a time, typed with name and address on each page. Previously published poems and simultaneous submissions OK. Cover letter preferred. E-mail submissions OK. If submitting via e-mail, save work as "text" prior to sending. Poems are read by the editor and 2 assistant editors. Seldom comments on rejections. Send SASE for guidelines or request via e-mail. Reports in 6-8 weeks. Pays 3 copies.**

CHICAGO REVIEW (III, IV-Translations), 5801 S. Kenwood, Chicago IL 60637-1794, phone/fax (773)702-0887, e-mail org_crev@orgmail.uchicago.edu, website http://www.humanities.uchicago.edu/humanit ies/review/, founded 1946, poetry editor Devin Johnston. **"We publish high quality poetry. About 20% of the work we select is unsolicited; the remainder is solicited from poets whose work we admire. Translations are welcome, but please include a statement of permission from the original publisher if work is not in the public domain."** They have recently published poets as diverse as Alice Fulton, Yusef Komunyakaa, Turner Cassity, Nathaniel Mackey, August Kleinzahler, Meena Alexander and Anne Carson. Editors seem to prefer lyric free verse—some of it leaning toward avant-garde and some quite accessible. Circulation is 2,800. **Sample postpaid: $6. Queries and guideline requests may be sent/requested via fax and e-mail. No electronic submissions. Reports in 3 months, longer in some cases. Sometimes sends prepublication galleys. Pays 3 copies and one-volume subscription.** Occasionally reviews books of poetry. Open to unsolicited reviews.

✤**CHICKADEE MAGAZINE; THE YOUNG NATURALIST FOUNDATION (IV-Children, nature)**, 179 John St., Suite 500, Toronto, Ontario M5T 3G5 Canada, website http://www.owl.on.ca, founded 1979, editor Susan Berg, is a magazine **for children 6-9 about science and nature** appearing 9 times/year. **They want "evocative poetry; poems that play with words; humorous poetry; no longer than 50 lines. Nothing religious, anthropomorphic; no formal language; no poetry that is difficult to understand."** As a sample the editor selected this complete poem, "Winter Bows" by Beverly J. Letchworth:

> The world lies cold in ice and snow.
> Every creature is lying low.
> Except the birds who come to feed—
> From every direction, in they speed.
> They wrap the feeder like colourful bows,
> Making it spring with their cheery "Hellos."

Chickadee is 32 pgs., magazine-sized, professionally printed in full-color, with paper cover. They accept 1-2% of every 500 poems received. Circulation: 25,800 within US and 100,000 within Canada. Subscription: $14.95 US. **Sample postpaid: $3.75. Submit up to 10 poems at a time. Simultaneous submissions considered. Send SASE (or SAE and IRC) for writers' guidelines. Pays $10-75/poem plus 2 copies. Buys all rights.** The editor says, "*Chickadee* is a 'hands-on' science and nature publication designed to entertain and educate 6- to 9-year-olds. Each issue contains photos, illustrations, an easy-to-read animal story, a craft project, puzzles, a science experiment and a pullout poster."

CHICORY BLUE PRESS (IV-Women, senior citizens), 795 East St. N., Goshen CT 06756, phone (860)491-2271, fax (860)491-8619, founded 1988, publisher Sondra Zeidenstein, **publishes 2-3 chapbooks/year. She is currently open to receiving queries for chapbooks by women poets over age 60. Submit 5-7 poems**

and cover letter with only "a brief introduction of self and work." Replies to queries and mss (if invited) in 3 months. Seldom comments on rejections. Pays royalties, honorarium or 5-10 author's copies. She has recently published poetry by Honor Moore, Pattiann Rogers, Joan Swift and Nelly Wong. **Obtain sample books by ordering from the press.**

CHINOOK PRESS (IV-Regional); THE CHINOOK QUARTERLY (I, II), 1432 Yellowstone Ave., Billings MT 59102, phone (406)245-7704, founded 1996, editor/publisher Mary Ellen Westwood. *The Chinook Quarterly* is a literary magazine containing prose, poetry, art and nonfiction "combining the traditional values and the contemporary spirit of the West. **I am open to work of any kind, but want real human themes with some purpose and message about life. As a Westerner, I favor themes of change and redemption, nature and harmony. I will also take some poems on seasonal themes. I do not want poems that shock, just for the sake of shocking. But I am willing to take on difficult themes of human importance."** In their first issue, they published poetry by Josephine Jones, Mela Mlekush and Dan Burke. As a sample the editor selected these lines from "Luck of the Draw" by Paul Zarzyski:

> high above the Missouri River's silent swirls,
> the flicking together of leaves
> is the applause of small green hands, children
> thrilled by a winning ride, by their wildest wish
> beginning, as everything begins, with luck
> of the draw, with a breeze in the heat . . .

The editor says *TCQ* is 60-80 pgs., $7 \times 8\frac{1}{2}$, flat-spined with glossy cover, some color. They accept 48-60 poems a year. Subscription: $20. **Sample postpaid: $7. Submit 4-6 poems at a time, name and address on each page. No previously published poems; simultaneous submissions OK with notification. Cover letter required; include brief bio and brief statement about why you wrote the work.** Time between acceptance and publication is 2-12 months. **Always comments on rejections. Send SASE for guidelines. Reports within 2 months. Always sends prepublication galleys. Pays $5/poem plus 4 copies.** Reviews books and chapbooks and includes general literary criticism. Open to unsolicited reviews. Poets may also send books for review consideration. Chinook Press, which has a Northwest regional bias, also plans to publish 2 paperback books of poetry/year. **Prefers to see complete ms. Replies to mss in 2-6 months. As for payment, "individual arrangements will be made with each poet based on the book and the market. All poet will contribute is promotion time." Call or write to purchase sample.** The editor says, "I want real, true-to-life poetry commenting on and challenging change in the human condition. I do not want a lot of 'ivory tower' musings. I admire risk-takers because I am one, and I will publish both new and established writers who take a risk with their work."

CHIRON REVIEW; CHIRON BOOKS; CHIRON REVIEW POETRY CONTEST (I, II), 522 E. South Ave., St. John KS 67576-2212, phone (316)549-3933, e-mail mshauers@midusq.net, founded 1982 as the *Kindred Spirit*, editor Michael Hathaway, assistant editor Jane Hathaway, contributing editor (poetry) Gerald Locklin, is a quarterly tabloid using photographs of featured writers. **No taboos.** They have recently published poetry by Charles Bukowski, Marge Piercy, Denise Duhamel, Charles Plymell and Vivian Shipley. As a sample the editor selected this complete poem, "Poem for Jeffrey Dahmer" by Micki Myers:

> Someone asked me once how his victims could
> have gone for him, given what he did. He was
> cute, I said. Yeah, appearances & all that. Still.

Each issue is 24-32 pgs. and "contains dozens of poems." Their press run is about 1,000. **Sample postpaid: $4 ($8 overseas or institutions). Submit 3-6 poems at a time, "typed or printed legibly." No simultaneous submissions or previously published poems. Very seldom publishes theme issues. Send SASE for guidelines and any upcoming themes or request via e-mail. Reports in 2-8 weeks. Pays 1 copy. Acquires first-time rights.** Reviews books of poetry in 500-900 words. Open to unsolicited reviews. Poets may also send books for review consideration. **For book publication submit complete ms.** They publish 1-3 books/year, flat-spined, professionally printed, **paying 25% of press run of 100-200 copies.** Their annual poetry contest offers awards of $100 plus 1-page feature in Winter issue, $50, and 5 free subscriptions and a Chiron Press book. Entry fee: $5/poet.

THE CHRISTIAN CENTURY (II, IV-Religious, social issues), Dept. PM, 407 S. Dearborn St., Chicago IL 60605, phone (312)427-5380, founded 1884, named *The Christian Century* 1900, founded again 1908, joined by *New Christian* 1970, poetry editor Jill Peláez Baumgaertner. This "ecumenical weekly" is a liberal, sophisti-

---

MARKET CONDITIONS are constantly changing! If you're still using this book and it is 1999 or later, buy the newest edition of *Poet's Market* at your favorite bookstore or order directly from Writer's Digest Books.

cated journal of news, articles of opinion and reviews from a generally Christian point-of-view, **using approximately 1 poem/issue, not necessarily on religious themes but in keeping with the literate tone of the magazine. "No pietistic or sentimental doggerel, please."** They have published poetry by Robert Beum, Joan Rohr Myers, Ida Fasel, Kathleen Norris, Luci Shaw, David Abrams, James Worley, J. Barrie Shepherd and Wendell Berry. As a sample the editor selected this poem, "Rapture" by Ashley Mace Havird:

> *In a straight-backed pew*
> *on the balcony's front row,*
> *I keep my distance.*
> *Still, the sunburst*
> *of red-hot gladiolus,*
> *fireball mums,*
> *spikes me blind. . . .*

The journal is magazine-sized, printed on quality newsprint, using b&w art, cartoons and ads, about 30 pgs., saddle-stapled. **Sample postpaid: $2. No simultaneous submissions. Submissions without SASE or SAE and IRCs will not be returned. Pays usually $20/poem plus 1 copy and discount on additional copies. Acquires all rights. Inquire about reprint permission.** Reviews books of poetry in 300-400 words, single format; 400-500 words, multi-book.

‡***CHRISTIAN POETRY REVIEW; GRENDON HOUSE (IV-Religious)**, 67 Walsall Rd., Lichfield, Staffordshire WS13 8AD England, phone 01543 411015, fax 01543 411015, founded 1995, editor F.T. Lewis, is a quarterly. "*Christian Poetry Review* **is a platform for Christians writing poetry, e.g., life experiences."** They have recently published poetry by Tom Daly, Andrew Hawthorne, Tom Lewis and Bryn Fortey. The editor says *CPR* is approximately 35 pgs., A5, as paperback. They receive about 336 poems a year, use approximately 72. Press run is 100 for 55 subscribers of which 14 are libraries, 25 shelf sales. Single copy: £1.35; subscription: £5.40 (4 issues). **Sample postpaid: £2. Make checks payable to Grendon House. Submit 3-6 poems at a time. Previously published poems and simultaneous submissions OK. Cover letter preferred. SAE must be enclosed. Closing dates for issues are January 1, April 1, July 1 and October 1.** Time between acceptance and publication is up to 1 month from selection which is after the closing dates." **Seldom comments on rejections. Send SASE (or SAE and IRC) for guidelines. Reports in 1-3 months, "always within two weeks of closing date."** Staff reviews books of poetry. Poets may also send books for review consideration.

THE CHRISTIAN SCIENCE MONITOR (II), The Home Forum Page, 1 Norway St., Boston MA 02115, phone (617)450-2474, founded 1908, is an international daily newspaper. **Poetry used regularly in The Home Forum, poetry editor Elizabeth Lund.** They want "**finely crafted poems that celebrate the extraordinary in the ordinary. Seasonal material always needed. Especially interested in poems about life in the city. No violence, sensuality or racism. Short poems preferred.**" They have published work by William Stafford, Diana der-Hovanessian, Steven Ratiner and Lyn Lifshin. **Submit up to 5 poems at a time, single-spaced. SASE must be included. No previously published poems or simultaneous submissions. Usually reports within 1-2 months. Pays varying rates, upon publication.**

CHRISTIANITY AND THE ARTS (I, II, IV-Religious), P.O. Box 118088, Chicago IL 60611, phone (312)642-8606, fax (312)266-7719, e-mail chrnarts@aol.com, founded 1994, editor/publisher Marci Whitney-Schenck, poetry editor Robert Klein Engler **(and submissions should go directly to him at Richard J. Daley College, 7500 S. Pulaski, Chicago IL 60652)**. *Christianity and the Arts* is a quarterly magazine designed "to celebrate the revelation of God through the arts and to encourage excellent Christian artistic expression." **They want poetry of "excellence—open to all styles—with a Christian viewpoint."** It is 56 pgs., 8½ × 11, professionally printed on coated stock and saddle-stapled, with b&w and color photos. They accept 20% of the poetry received. Press run is 5,000 for 3,000 subscribers, 700 shelf sales. Single copy: $5.95; subscription: $21. **Sample postpaid: $6. Simultaneous submissions OK.** Time between acceptance and publication is 6 months. **Publishes theme issues. Send SASE for upcoming themes. Themes for November 1997 and February 1998 are Sacred Spaces and Resurrection, respectively, Reports within 2 weeks. Always sends prepublication galleys. Pays 2 copies. Acquires first or one-time rights.** The editor says, "We wish to support the efforts of Christian poets, however we get more poetry than any other type of writing. We can't publish everyone's wonderful efforts but we do try to include as many poems as possible, especially when the poems concern our themes. Many submissions read more like prayers than poems. We are looking for quality verse."

THE CHRONICLE OF THE HORSE (IV-Animals), P.O. Box 46, Middleburg VA 22117, phone (540)687-6341, founded 1937, assistant editor Tricia Booker, is a weekly magazine using **short poetry related to horses "the shorter the better. No free verse."** The magazine is devoted to English horse sports, such as horse shows and steeplechasing. It averages 68 pgs., magazine-sized. Subscription: $47. **Sample postpaid: $2. No simultaneous submissions. Summer "is not a good time" to submit. 1-3 editors read poems. Reports in 4-6 weeks. Pays $20/poem. Buys first North American rights.** "We review books submitted to us but do not accept reviews for publication."

CHRYSALIS READER (II, IV-Spirituality, themes), Rt. 1 Box 184, Dillwyn VA 23936-9616, fax (804)983-1074, e-mail lawson@aba.org. founded 1985, editor Carol S. Lawson, poetry editor Robert F. Lawson. *Chrysalis*

Reader is published by the Swedenborg Foundation as a "contribution to the search for spiritual wisdom." It appears intermittently and is now a "book series that draws upon diverse traditions to engage thought on questions that challenge inquiring minds. Each issue addresses a topic from varied perspectives using literate and scholarly fiction, essays and poetry dealing with spiritual aspects of a particular theme." **They want poetry that is "spiritually related and focused on the particular issue's theme. Nothing overly religious or sophomoric."** They have recently published poetry by Jan Frazier, Linda Pastan and Robert Bly. As a sample the editor selected these lines from "I'm Told" by Tom O'Grady:

> I'm told there are stars beneath the sea,
> that their dust, a handful of it, is as dense as Everest
> and all those stories there, those scattered bones,
> and the bright scarfs of the women on the shore
> follow like the barren obsequy
> that grips you as you sink beneath the sea.

CR is 160 pgs., 7×10, professionally printed on archival paper and perfect-bound with coated cover stock, illustrations, photos and ads for other literary publications. They receive about 150 poems a year, use 8-10%. Press run is 3,500. **Sample postpaid: $10. Submit no more than 6 poems at one time. No previously published poems or simultaneous submissions. Submissions via fax OK.** Time between acceptance and publication is 18 months maximum. **Seldom comments on rejections. Send SASE for themes and guidelines or request via fax or e-mail. Themes for Winter 1997, Summer 1998 and Winter 1998 are Symbols, Choices and Education, respectively. Reports in 2 months. Always sends prepublication galleys. Pays $25 and 3 copies. Buys first-time rights. "We like to be credited for reprints."** The editor says *Chrysalis Reader* is devoting more attention and space to poetry.

♣THE CHURCH-WELLESLEY REVIEW; XTRA! (IV-Gay/lesbian), 491 Church St., Suite 200, Toronto, Ontario M4Y 2C6 Canada, fax (416)925-6503. *The Church-Wellesley Review* is the annual supplement for *Xtra!* (Canada's largest gay/lesbian newspaper.) **"We want wild humour, fast-paced drama, new takes on old themes, gays and lesbians in other contexts. Our aim is always quality, not style. Although we prefer non-traditional poetry,** we have in the past published a contemporary 30-line 'up-dating' of Chaucer called 'Provincetown Tales.' **Amaze us or amuse us, but just don't bore us."** They have published Patrick Roscoe, Jane Rule, Timothy Findley, Chocolate Waters and David Watmough. The magazine receives over 1,000 submissions/year. Press run is 37,000 in Toronto plus 22,000 in Vancouver and is distributed free. **Poetry can be any length ("no epics, please"), but no more than 10 poems per writer per year. Mss should include 8 poems with name on every page, daytime phone number and 50-word bio. Submissions are accepted March 1 through July 1. "We do not respond at other times. We report as soon as possible, definitely by publication in early fall." Payment is made in Canadian funds within one month of publication.** Staff reviews books of poetry. Send books for review consideration to the attention of Fiction Editor. *Xtra!*, the review's parent magazine, has received several community awards as well as a journalism award for a column on Living with AIDS.

CIMARRON REVIEW (II), 205 Morrill Hall, Oklahoma State University, Stillwater OK 74078-0135, phone (405)744-9476, founded 1967, poetry editors Doug Martin, Mark Cox, Lisa Lewis, James Cooper and Todd Fuller, is a quarterly literary journal. **"We take pride in our eclecticism. We like evocative poetry (lyric or narrative) controlled by a strong voice. No sing-song verse. No quaint prairie verse. No restrictions as to subject matter. We look for poems whose surfaces and structures risk uncertainty and which display energy, texture, intelligence, and intense investment."** Among poets they have published are Dorothy Barresi, Cesare Pauese, Mark Doty, Tess Gallagher, David Rivard and Albert Goldbarth. This magazine, 100-150 pgs., 6×9, perfect-bound, boasts a handsome design, including a color cover and attractive printing. Poems lean toward free verse, lyric and narrative, although all forms and styles seem welcome. There are 15-25 pages of poetry in each issue. Circulation is 500 of which most are libraries. Single copy: $3; subscription: $12/year ($15 Canada), $30/3 years ($40 Canada), plus $2.50 for all international subscriptions. **Submit to Poetry Editor, anytime, 3-5 poems, name and address on each, typed single- or double-spaced. No simultaneous submissions. Send SASE for upcoming themes. Reports within 3 months. Pays $15 for each poem published, 1 copy and a subscription. Buys all rights. "Permission for a reprinting is granted upon request."** Reviews books of poetry in 500-900 words, single-book format, occasionally multi-book. All reviews are assigned.

CINCINNATI POETRY REVIEW; CINCINNATI WRITERS' PROJECT (II, IV-Regional), Humanities Dept., College of Mount St. Joseph, 5701 Delhi Rd., Cincinnati OH 45233, fax (513)244-4222, e-mail jeff_hillard @mail.msj.edu, founded 1975, editor Jeffrey Hillard, "attempts to set local poets in a national context. Each issue includes **a quarter to a third of work by local poets (within about 100 miles of Cincinnati)**, but most are from all over." They use **"all kinds" of poetry** and have published such poets as Enid Shomer, Lynne Hugo deCourcy, Pat Mora, Marilyn Krysl, David Citino, Jeff Worley, Harry Humes, Walter Pavlich and Ray Gonzalez. They publish 1 issue/year, usually a fall/winter issue. *CPR* is 64 pgs., digest-sized, handsomely printed and flat-spined, all poems with art on the glossy card cover. They receive about 2,500 submissions a year, use 40-60. Circulation is about 1,000 for 130 subscribers of which 30 are libraries. Subscription: $9 for 4 issues. **Sample: $2. Submit typed mss with address on each poem. "No poems by fax or e-mail. Must be mailed only. However, requests for guidelines may be made through fax or e-mail." "Occasionally" publishes themes**

in a special section of the journal. Themes for recent issues include special sections on Sri Lanka and Hiroshima. Note, however, that the editor solicits material for special sections. **Reports in 1-3 months. Pays 2 copies.** *CPR* is published by the Cincinnati Writers' Project. Other publications include *Pieces of Fernald: Poems & Photographs of a Place* by Jeffrey Hillard and Jon Hughes, *The Kansas Poems* by Dallas Wiebe, *Dismal Man* by Jon Christopher Hughes, *River Dwellers—Poems on the Settling of the Ohio River* by Jeffrey Hillard, *Living in Cincinnati* by Kevin Walzer and *Down the River—A Collection of Fiction & Poetry on the Ohio River Valley*, edited by Dallas Wiebe.

THE CINCINNATI POETS' COLLECTIVE (II), 716 Maple Ave., Newport KY 41071, founded 1988, editor Rebecca M. Weigold, is an annual poetry magazine **accepting only well-crafted poems, and wants more poetry concerning political issues with conservative themes. No rhyme or greeting card verse; no cartoons or artwork, "no sexually explicit or violent content that is gratuitous in nature."** *TCPC* is digest-sized, saddle-stapled. Circulation is approximately 150 through bookstore sales and subscriptions. **Submit up to 5 camera-ready poems at a time. SASE required for consideration. No previously published poems. Simultaneous submissions OK, if noted. Reads submissions October 1 through April 1 only. Reports in 4-6 months. Pays 1 copy.** They have recently published poetry by James Proffitt, Mary Winters and Lyn Lifshin. The editor says, "Always check spelling and grammar and make corrections before sending. Make absolutely sure the poem is *completely* finished, that every word belongs and serves its purpose."

CITY LIGHTS BOOKS (III), 261 Columbus Ave., San Francisco CA 94133, phone (415)362-1901, founded 1955, edited by Lawrence Ferlinghetti and Nancy J. Peters, is a paperback house that achieved prominence with the publication of Allen Ginsberg's *Howl* and other **poetry of the "Beat" school.** They publish **"poetry, fiction, philosophy, political and social history." Simultaneous submissions OK. "All submissions must include SASE." Reports in 2 months. Payment varies.**

THE CLASSICAL OUTLOOK (IV-Specialized, translations), Classics Dept., Park Hall, University of Georgia, Athens GA 30602-6203, fax (706)542-8503, e-mail mricks@uga.cc.uga.edu, website http://www.classic s.uga.edu/journals.html, founded 1924, poetry editors Prof. David Middleton (original English verse) and Prof. Jane Phillips (translations and original Latin verse), "is an internationally circulated quarterly journal (4,200 subscriptions, of which 250 are libraries) for high school and college Latin and Classics teachers, published by the American Classical League." **They invite submissions of "original poems in English on classical themes, verse translations from Greek and Roman authors, and original Latin poems. Submissions should, as a rule, be written in traditional poetic forms and should demonstrate skill in the use of meter, diction and rhyme if rhyme is employed. Original poems should be more than mere exercise pieces or the poetry of nostalgia. Translations should be accompanied by a photocopy of the original Greek or Latin text. Latin originals should be accompanied by a literal English rendering of the text. Submissions should not exceed 50 lines."** They have recently published work by Sarah Ruden. As a sample the editors selected these lines from "Gaia" by R.H. Morrison:

> Or does she store for them, as in a void,
> seeds of the fruit of some unripe abyss
> that we call future? With that patient gait
> through silvered darknesses and golden joys
> we go from the emblazoned to the hidden
> as once, out of the hidden, Gaia came.

There are 2-3 magazine-sized pgs. of poetry in each issue, and they use 20% of the approximately 350 submissions they receive each year. They have a 12- to 18-month backlog, 4-month lead time. **Submit 2 anonymous copies, double-spaced, no more than 5 poems at a time. Receipt is acknowledged by letter. Poetry is refereed by poetry editors. Send SASE for guidelines or request via e-mail or fax. Reports in 6-9 months. Pays 2 copies.** Sample copies are available from the American Classical League, Miami University, Oxford OH 45056 for $10. Reviews books of poetry "if the poetry is sufficiently classical in nature." The editors add, "Since our policy is to have poetry evaluated anonymously, cover letters, names and addresses on poems, etc., just make work at this end. Also, we never knowingly publish any works which have been or will be published elsewhere."

CLEANING BUSINESS MAGAZINE; CLEANING CONSULTANT SERVICES, INC. (IV-Specialized), P.O. Box 1273, Seattle WA 98111, phone (206)622-4241, fax (206)622-6876, e-mail wgriffin@seanet.com, website http://www.cleaningconsultants.com, founded 1976, poetry editor William R. Griffin. *CBM* is "a monthly magazine **for cleaning and maintenance professionals" and uses some poetry relating to their interests. "To be considered for publication in *Cleaning Business*, submit poetry that relates to our specific audience— cleaning and self-employment."** He has published poetry by Don Wilson, Phoebe Bosche, Trudie Mercer and Joe Keppler. The editor says it is 100 pgs., 8½×11, offset litho, using ads, art and graphics. They receive about 50 poems a year, use approximately 10. Press run is 5,000 for 3,000 subscribers of which 100 are libraries, 500 shelf sales. Single copy: $5; subscription: $20. **Sample postpaid: $3. Send SASE and $3 for guidelines. Simultaneous submissions OK; no previously published poems. Pays $5-10 plus 1 copy.** William Griffin suggests "poets identify a specific market and work to build a readership that can be tapped again and again over a period of years with new books. Also write to a specific audience that has a mutual interest. We buy poetry about cleaning, but seldom receive anything our subscribers would want to read."

CLEVELAND STATE UNIVERSITY POETRY CENTER; CSU POETRY SERIES (II); CLEVELAND POETS SERIES (IV-Regional), Cleveland State University, Cleveland OH 44115, fax (216)687-6943, coordinator Rita Grabowski, editors Leonard Trawick, David Evett and Ted Lardner. The Poetry Center was founded in 1962, first publications in 1971. **The Poetry Center publishes the CSU Poetry Series for poets in general and the Cleveland Poets Series for Ohio poets. "Open to many kinds of form, length, subject matter, style and purpose. Should be well-crafted, clearly of professional quality, ultimately serious (even when humorous). No light verse, devotional verse or verse in which rhyme and meter seem to be of major importance."** They have recently published poetry by Jared Carter, Richard Jackson, Jan Freeman and Susan Firer. **Books are chosen for publication from the entries to the CSU Poetry Center Prize contest. (Write for free catalog and sampler of some 75 Poetry Center books.) Deadline: March 1. Entry fee: $15. The winner receives $1,000 and publication. They publish some other entrants in the Poetry Series, providing 50 copies (out of a press run of 1,000) and 10% royalty contract. The Cleveland Poets Series (for Ohio poets) offers 100 copies of a press run of 600. To submit for all series, send ms between December 1 and March 1. Reports on all submissions for the year by the end of July. Mss should be for books of 50-100 pgs., pages numbered, poet's name, address and phone number on cover sheet, clearly typed. Poems may have been previously published (listed on an acknowledgment page). Simultaneous submissions OK, if notified and "poet keeps us informed of change in status." Send SASE for guidelines.** The Center also publishes other volumes of poetry, including chapbooks (20-30 pgs.), with a **$10 reading fee for each submission (except for Ohio residents)**.

THE CLIMBING ART (IV-Sports/recreation), 6390 E. Floyd Dr., Denver CO 80222, phone (303)757-0541, founded 1986, editor Ron Morrow, is a biannual journal **"read mainly by mountain enthusiasts who appreciate good writing about mountains and mountaineering. We are open to all forms and lengths. The only requirement is that the work be fresh, well-written and in some way of interest to those who love the mountains."** They have published poetry by Terry Gifford, Allison Hunter, Paul Willis, Denise K. Simon and Barry Govenor. *TCA* is 160 pgs., digest-sized, professionally printed on heavy stock with glossy card cover. They use 12-20 poems/issue, receive 50 submissions/month. Press run is 1,500 for 700 subscribers of which 10 are libraries, 500 shelf sales. Subscription: $18. **Sample postpaid: $4. Simultaneous submissions and previously published poems OK. Reports in 6 months. Sometimes sends prepublication galleys. Pays 2 copies and subscription. Acquires one-time rights.** Reviews books of poetry only if they concern mountains. Open to unsolicited reviews.

*CLÓ IAR-CHONNACHTA (IV-Bilingual/foreign language), Indreabhán, Co. Galway, Ireland, phone (091)593307, fax (091)593362, e-mail cic@iol.ie, website http://www.wombat.ie/cic, founded 1985, contact Nóirín Ní Ghrádaigh, publishes paperback books of **Irish language poetry**, one of which is selected through a competition. They have published collections of poetry by Cathal Ó Searcaigh and Gabriel Rosenstock. **Query with 20 sample poems and a cover letter with brief bio and publication credits. Mss are read by an editorial panel. Often comments on rejections. No payment information provided.** The poetry competition offers a £5,000 first prize in addition to publication. Deadline: December 1. Send SASE (or SAE and IRC) for details.

CLOCKWATCH REVIEW (I, II), Dept. of English, Illinois Wesleyan University, Bloomington IL 61702, phone (309)556-3352, founded 1983, editor James Plath, associate editors Lynn Devore, James McGowan, Robert Bray, Brian Burt and Pamela Muirhead. "We publish a variety of styles, leaning toward poetry which goes beyond the experience of self in an attempt to SAY something, without sounding pedantic or strained. **We like a strong, natural voice, and lively, unusual combinations in language. *Something fresh, and that includes subject matter as well*. It has been our experience that extremely short/long poems are hard to pull off.** Though we'll publish exceptions, we prefer to see poems that can fit on one published page (digest-sized) which runs **about 32 lines or less**." They have published poetry by Peter Wild, Martha Vertreace, John Knoepfle, Rita Dove and Peter Meinke. Asked for a sample, the editors say "trying to pick only four lines seems like telling people what detail we'd like to see in a brick, when what we're more interested in is the design of the *house*." The 80-page, semiannual *CR* is printed on glossy paper with colored, glossy cover. They receive 2,080 submissions/year, use 20-30. They use 7-10 unsolicited poems in each issue, with 1 featured poet. Circulation is 1,400 for 150 subscribers, of which 25 are libraries; 300 distributed free and "the balance is wholesale distribution and single-copy sales." **Sample postpaid: $4. Submit 5-6 poems at a time.** "We are not bowled over by large lists of previous publications, but brief letters of introduction or sparse bios are read out of curiosity. One poem per page, typed, single-spacing OK." **Comments on rejections "if asked, and if time permits." Reports in 4 months. Pays 3 copies and, when possible, small cash awards—currently $5/poem.** Only uses staff-written or solicited reviews. Send books for review consideration if not self-published. Poetry published here has also been included in *The Best American Poetry 1997*.

CLOUD RIDGE PRESS (V), 815 13th St., Boulder CO 80302, founded 1985, editor Elaine Kohler, is a "literary small press for unique works in poetry and prose." They publish letterpress and offset books in both paperback and hardcover editions. In poetry, they publish **"strong images of the numinous qualities in authentic**

experience grounded in a landscape and its people." The first book, published in 1985, was *Ondina: A Narrative Poem* by John Roberts. The book is 6×9¼, handsomely printed on buff stock, cloth bound in black with silver decoration and spine lettering, 131 pgs. 800 copies were bound in Curtis Flannel and 200 copies bound in cloth over boards, numbered and signed by the poet and artist. This letterpress edition, priced at $18/cloth and $12/paper, is not available in bookstores but only by mail from the press. The trade edition was photo-offset from the original, in both cloth and paper bindings, and is sold in bookstores. The press plans to publish 1-2 books/year. **Since they are not accepting unsolicited mss, writers should query first. Queries will be answered in 2 weeks and mss reported on in 1 month. Simultaneous submissions are acceptable. Royalties are 10% plus a negotiable number of author's copies. A brochure is free on request; send #10 SASE.**

CLUBHOUSE; YOUR STORY HOUR (V, IV-Children, teens), Dept. PM, P.O. Box 15, Berrien Springs MI 49103, poetry editor Krista Phillips-Hainey. The publication is printed in conjunction with the **Your Story Hour** radio program, founded 1949, which is designed to teach the Bible and moral life to children. The magazine, *Clubhouse*, started with that title in 1982, but as *Good Deeder*, its original name, it has been published since 1951. The editor says, **"We do like humor or mood pieces. Don't like mushy-sweet 'Christian' poetry. We don't have space for long poems. Best—16 lines or under."** They have published poetry by Lillian M. Fisher, Audrey Osofsky, Sharon K. Motzko, Bruce Bash and Craig Peters. *Clubhouse*, published monthly, is 20 pgs. The magazine has a circulation of 500, all for subscribers of which maybe 5 are libraries. Subscription: $5/year. **Sample cost: 3 oz. postage. They are closed to submissions until 1999. Simultaneous submissions OK. The** "evaluation sheet" for returned mss gives reasons for acceptance or rejection. **Writer's guidelines available for SASE. Pays about $12 for poems under 24 lines plus 2 copies. Negotiates rights.**

CLUTCH (III), 147 Coleridge St., San Francisco CA 94110, founded 1991, editors Dan Hodge and Lawrence Oberc, is an irregular (1 or 2 issues/year) "alternative/underground literary review." **They want "poetry which explores or reveals an edge, societal edges especially.** *Take chances.* **Academic, overly-studied poems are not considered."** They have published poetry by Charles Bukowski, Lorri Jackson, Todd Moore and Robert Peters. As a sample the editors selected these lines from "1492" by Mitchel Cohen:

> *and the syringe is the size of a lover, O yes!*
> *and the kisses, and the bodies,*
> *and the fleshy zipless hallucinations*
> *that pass for lovers*
> *are no cure, no cure at all . . .*

The editors describe *Clutch* as 60-70 pgs., approximately 5½×8½. "Printing, binding and graphics vary with each issue. We receive approximately 300 unsolicited submissions a year, but we accept less than 10% of unsolicited material. The majority of material is solicited." Press run is 200-500 for 40 subscribers of which 6 are libraries, approximately 70 shelf sales. Subscription: $5/issue for as many future issues as specified. **Sample postpaid: $5. Make checks payable to Dan Hodge. Simultaneous submissions OK. Cover letter required. Seldom comments on rejections. Reports in 1-6 months. Pays 1 copy. Rights revert to authors.** "Open to publishing reviews of books/magazines from underground press." Poets may also send books for review consideration. The editors say, "We advise obtaining a sample copy or otherwise becoming familiar with the kind of poetry we've previously published before considering a submission."

COAL CITY REVIEW (II), English Dept., University of Kansas, Lawrence KS 66045, founded 1989, editor Brian Daldorph, is an annual publication of poetry, short stories, reviews and interviews—"the best material I can find." **As for poetry, the editor quotes Pound: " 'Make it new.' " They do not want to see " 'experimental' poetry, doggerel, five-finger exercises or beginner's verse."** They have published poetry by Taylor Graham and Elliot Richman. As a sample the editor selected these lines from "photograph" by Steve Dolgin:

> *i ate donuts with coke and vodka*
> *and was not privileged*
>
> *except for one smile*
> *that i won't give back*

CCR is 60 pgs., 5×8, professionally printed on recycled paper and saddle-stapled with light card cover. They accept approximately 5% of the material received. Press run is 200 for 50 subscribers of which 5 are libraries. Subscription: $6. **Sample postpaid: $4. Submit 6 poems at a time. Accepts previously published poems occasionally; prefers not to receive simultaneous submissions. Seldom comments on rejections. Send SASE for guidelines. Reports in 1-3 months. Pays 1 copy.** Reviews books of poetry in 300-1,000 words, mostly

---

✝ **THE DOUBLE DAGGER** before a listing indicates that the listing is new in this edition. New markets are often the most receptive to submissions.

single format. Open to unsolicited reviews. Poets may also send books for review consideration. *CCR* also **publishes occasional chapbooks** as issues of the magazine but does not accept unsolicited chapbook submissions. Their most recent chapbook is *Under a Flare-lit Sky: Vietnam Poems* by John Musgrave. The editor says, "Care more (much more) about writing than publication. If you're good enough, you'll publish."

COCHRAN'S CORNER (I, IV-Subscribers), 1003 Tyler Court, Waldorf MD 20602-2964, phone (301)870-1664, founded 1985, poetry editor Billye Keene, is a **"family type" quarterly open to beginners, preferring poems of 20 lines or less. You have to be a subscriber to submit. "Any subject or style (except porn)."** She has recently published poetry by Jean B. York, Brian Duthins, C.J. Villiano and Annette Shaw. As a sample the editor selected this poem "Journey" (poet unidentified):

> *You take me to places*
> *Within myself*
> *Where I have never been—*
> *foreign places*
> *Timidly I follow you through*
> *Subterranian chambers*
> *And*
> *Undiscovered essences*
> *to the*
> *mainstream*
> *that*
> *is*
> *I*

CC is 58 pgs., desktop-published, saddle-stapled, with matte card cover. Press run is 500. Subscription: $20. **Sample: $5 plus SASE. Submit 5 poems at a time. Simultaneous submissions and previously published poems OK. Cover letter welcome. Send SASE for guidelines. Reports in average of 3 months. Pays 2 copies. Acquires first or one-time rights.** Reviews books of poetry. Send books for review consideration. Sponsors contests in March and July; $5 entry fee for unlimited poems "if sent in the same envelope. We provide criticism if requested at the rate of $1 per page." The editor says, "Write from the heart, but don't forget your readers. You must work to find the exact words that mirror your feelings, so the reader can share your feelings."

THE COE REVIEW (II), Coe College, 1220 First Ave. NE, Cedar Rapids IA 52402, phone (319)399-8760, founded 1972, is "a diverse annual magazine, **valuing innovation and originality, preferring well-developed and tasteful content, but eclectic in selection."** They have published poetry by James Galvin and Jan Weissmiller. The annual is 100-150 pgs., flat-spined, digest-sized with matte card cover. "Each issue includes 4-8 reproductions of works of art, usually photographs, lithography and etched prints." Circulation is about 500. **Sample postpaid: $4. Submit 3-5 poems at a time. No simultaneous submissions. Accepted work appears in the next issue, published in April. Include "brief cover letter with biographical information and SASE. We only accept submissions from August 31 through March 15 due to the academic school year." Send SASE for guidelines. Pays 1 copy.**

COFFEE HOUSE PRESS (III), 27 N. Fourth St., Suite 400, Minneapolis MN 55401, phone (612)338-0125, founded 1984, associate editor Chris Fischbach, publishes 15 books/year, 6 of which are poetry. **They want poetry that is "challenging and lively; influenced by the Beats, the NY School or Black Mountain."** They have published poetry collections by Victor Hernandez Cruz, Anne Waldman, Andrei Codrescu and Linda Hogan. **Submit 8-12 poems at a time. Previously published poems OK. Cover letter required. "Please include a SASE for our reply and/or the return of your ms." Seldom comments on rejections. Replies to queries in 1 month, to mss in 6 months. Always sends prepublication galleys. Send SASE for catalog to order sample.** Coffee House Press books have won numerous honors and awards. As an example, *The Book of Medicines* by Linda Hogan won the Colorado Book Award for Poetry and the Lannan Foundation Literary Fellowship. The editor says, "We'd like to see more books by writers of color."

COKEFISH; COKEFISH PRESS (I), 31 Waterloo St., New Hope PA 18938-1210, phone (215)862-0299, founded 1990, editor Ana Christy, is an irregular journal **with an entry fee of $1/3 poems. "I want to see work that has passion behind it. From the traditional to the avant-garde, provocative to discreet, trivial to the significant. Am interested in social issues, alternative, avant-garde, erotica and humor for people with nothing to hide."** They have recently published poetry by David Whitacre, Paul Weinman, Ralph Haselman, Joan Reid and Dan Crocker. The format is 60 pgs., side-stapled on heavy paper with a cover printed on both sides on colored photocopy paper. They accept 30% of mss received. Press run is 300 for 150 subscribers. Subscription: $15. **Sample postpaid: $4. Submit 5-7 poems at a time. Note entry fee: $1/3 poems, additional $1 for additional poems. Simultaneous submissions and previously published poems OK. Cover letter "explaining why the poet chose *Cokefish*" required. Send SASE for guidelines. Reports in 1 week. Sometimes sends prepublication galleys. Pays 1 copy.** "We publish a mostly poetry broadside and will work with poets on publishing their chapbooks and audiotapes through Cokefish Press. Manuscript length up to 40 pages— $5 reading fee." Cokefish Press also **publishes cooperative chapbooks**. Write for details. The editor advises,

"Spread the word; don't let your poems sit and vegetate in a drawer. Send me stuff that will make my hair stand up on end." Also see the listings for *Alpha Beat Soup* and *Bouillabaisse*.

COLD MOUNTAIN REVIEW (II), English Dept., Appalachian State University, Boone NC 28608, phone (704)262-2154, editor Maria Tabor. *CMR* is published twice a year by students in the English Department at Appalachian State University and features poetry, short fiction, b&w line drawings and photographs. **They have no specifications regarding form, length, subject matter or style of poetry.** They have recently published poetry by Deanne Bayer, William Purcell and Carol Frith. As a sample the editors selected these lines from "A Resurrection Proposal" by Frederick Wilbur:

> *The oak screen once covered the cathedral's organ pipes;*
> *its wheat no longer golden, its grapes yeasted by years of neglect.*
> *Below the carved lattice is a panel of figures*
> *perpetually beginning a last supper.*

CMR is about 60 pgs., 6×9, neatly printed with 1 poem/page (or 2-page spread), saddle-stitched, with light card stock cover. They publish about 10% of the submissions received. **For sample, send SASE or make donation to ASU Visiting Artist Series. Previously published poems and simultaneous submissions OK. "Please include short biographical description." Reads submissions September 1 through November 20 and January 10 through March 15 only. Send SASE for guidelines. Reports within 6 weeks. Pays 3 copies.**

COLLAGES & BRICOLAGES, THE JOURNAL OF INTERNATIONAL WRITING (II, IV-Translations, feminist, political, social issues, themes), P.O. Box 86, Clarion PA 16214, e-mail fortis@vaxa.clarion. edu, founded in 1986, editor Marie-José Fortis. *C&B* is a "small literary magazine with **a strong penchant for literary, feminist, avant-garde work.** Strongly encourages poets and fiction writers, as well as essayists, whether English-speaking or foreign. (**Note: Writers sending their work in a foreign language must have their mss accompanied by an English translation.**) We are presently looking for **poetry that is socially aware—politically engaged. No sexism, racism or glorification of war. We are going towards focus-oriented issues."** As a sample the editor selected these lines by Gary Wiener:

> *If promised a pen and a cartridge of blood,*
> *would you cast them away and make that easy leap*
> *or, like Tennyson's eagle, soar down toward*
> *that murky Molochian underworld, armed like*
> *Achilles, resolved to work your black magic below.*

The annual is 100-150 pgs., magazine-sized, flat-spined, with card cover. They accept 7% of 900 poetry submissions/year. Press run is 800. **Sample postpaid: $8.50 (postage not included for orders outside the U.S.), $3 for back issue. Submit up to 5 poems at a time, no more. Reads submissions August 15 through November 30 only. Publishes theme issues. Send SASE for upcoming themes. Racial Tensions is the theme for the 1998-1999 issue; deadline for submissions is November 30, 1997. Reports in 1-3 months. Always sends prepublication galleys. Pays 2 copies with 50% off additional copies. Acquires first rights.** "It is recommended that potential contributors order a copy, so as to know what kind of work is desirable. We understand that nobody's budget is unlimited, but remember that most lit mags' back issues are half price. *C&B*'s are only $3. Be considerate to editors, as many of them work on a voluntary basis and sacrifice much time and energy to encourage writers. And please, do not send a tiny SASE in which we will have to fold material a zillion times— use at least a 9½×4 envelope." Marie-José Fortis says, "Show me that you write as if nothing else mattered."

COLLEGE ENGLISH; NATIONAL COUNCIL OF TEACHERS OF ENGLISH (II), Dept. of English, University of Massachusetts-Boston, 100 Morrissey Blvd., Boston MA 02125-3393, e-mail collengl@umbsky.cc. umb.edu (for queries only), editor Louise Z. Smith, poetry editor Thomas O'Grady. This journal, which is sent 8 times/year to members of the National Council of Teachers of English (membership: $40, includes subscription to *CE*), is a scholarly journal for the English discipline, but includes poems in each issue. They have published poetry by Sherman Alexie, W.D. Ehrhart and Catherine Phil MacCarthy. As a sample the editor selected these lines from "In Praise of Ravens" by Charles Hood:

> *They praise the horizon by using it,*
> *going from cloud to noon like hawks*
> *or peregrine angels, and when the light*
> *is right they can row white with each*
> *wing beat, flashing silver as they cut*
> *tinsel from the sun, beating home.*

CE is 100 pgs., perfect-bound, with matte card cover, 7½×9½, circulation 18,000. Poems tend to be wide-ranging in style, form and content. **Sample postpaid: $6.25, from NCTE, 1111 W. Kenyon Rd., Urbana IL 61801-1096. Submit a "letter-quality copy" of each poem with cover letter including titles of poems submitted. Reports in 2 months maximum, except for summer submissions. Pays 2 copies.**

COLOR WHEEL; MINK HILLS JOURNAL (II, IV-Nature/ecology, spiritual); SUGAR MOUNTAIN PRESS (V), 36 W. Main St., Warner NH 03278-9202, phone (603)456-3036, e-mail colorwheel@juno.com, founded 1990, editor Frederick Moe, "*Color Wheel* is now an online journal available at The Creative Spirit venue on firefly (http://www.ffly.com), uses high-quality prose and **poetry related to spiritual, ecological and mythological themes. We want poetry that explores more deeply and intensely our relationships with the earth and one another. All forms of poetry are welcome, including longer poems (2-4 pages). No rhymed verse."** They have published poetry by R.D. Savage, Lynn Kozma, David Sparenberg, Janine Canan and Walt Franklin. **Sample back issue postpaid (print version): $6. Make checks payable to Frederick Moe. Cover letter required—include "something that does not keep the writer 'anonymous'!" No e-mail submissions. Reads submissions September through May only. Comments on "close" rejections. Publishes theme issues. Send SASE for guidelines and publication list or request via e-mail. Reports in up to 2 months. Pays copies. Retains one-time reprint rights for special editions.** Sugar Mountain Press publishes an annual titled *Mink Hills Journal* which publishes poetry and creative nonfiction **"with a focus on the Northeast region."** The premier issue was published autumn 1995. Subscription: $12 (2 issues). Frederick Moe says, "*Mink Hills Journal* is esoteric yet focused in content. Poets should be familiar with the evolution of the magazine and type of material we publish before sending work. I encourage 'new' voices and appreciate creative approaches to the material. I am annoyed by poets who enclose postcards for response rather than a SASE and expect me to recycle their manuscript. I do not respond to such submissions. Inclusion of a SASE allows me to return press information with response and demonstrates concern on the part of the writer for their work. It is worth the extra expense! Also, *Color Wheel* is now available only on the Internet. This is a major advantage to my small press as *Color Wheel* did not have the financial resources available to continue as a print journal." Sugar Mountain Press is known for publishing "deeply ecological poetry, with intricate in-depth exploration of self in relation to nature." **However, the press is currently not open to submissions.**

COLORADO REVIEW (II, IV-Translations, themes); COLORADO PRIZE FOR POETRY, Dept. of English, 359 Eddy Bldg., Colorado State University, Ft. Collins CO 80523, phone (970)491-5449, fax (970)491-5601, founded 1955 as *Colorado State Review*, resurrected 1967 under "New Series" rubric, renamed *Colorado Review* 1985, editor David Milofsky, poetry editor Jorie Graham. *Colorado Review* is a journal of contemporary literature which appears twice annually; it combines short fiction, poetry, interviews with or articles about significant contemporary poets and writers, articles on literature, culture and the arts, translations of poetry from around the world and reviews of recent works of the literary imagination. **"We're interested in poetry that explores experience in deeply felt new ways; merely descriptive or observational language doesn't move us. Poetry that enters into and focuses on the full range of experience, weaving sharp imagery, original figures and surprising though apt insight together in compressed precise language and compelling rhythm is what triggers an acceptance here."** They have recently published poetry by Barbara Guest, James Tate and Stephen Berg. Circulation is 1,500 for 300 subscribers of which 100 are libraries. They receive about 500-1,000 submissions a year, use approximately 10%. Subscription: $15/year. **Sample postpaid: $8. Submit about 5 poems at a time. Reads submissions September 1 through May 1 only. "When work is a near-miss, we will provide brief comment and encouragement." Reports in 3-6 months. Pays $10/printed page for poetry. Buys first North American serial rights.** Reviews books of poetry, both single and multi-book format. Open to unsolicited reviews. Poets may also send books for review consideration. Also sponsors the Colorado Prize for Poetry, established in 1995, offering an annual honorarium of $1,000. Submissions must be unpublished. Submit a book-length ms on any subject in any form. Send SASE for guidelines. Entry fee: $22. Deadline: January 10. Most recent award winner was Bruce Beasley (1996). Judge was Charles Wright. The judge for upcoming award will be Jane Miller. Winner will be announced in June. Poetry published in *Colorado Review* has been included in the 1993, 1994, 1995, 1996 and 1997 volumes of *The Best American Poetry*. They say, "Our attitude is that we will publish the best work that comes across the editorial desk. We see poetry as a vehicle for exploring states of feeling, but we aren't interested in sentimentality (especially metaphysical)."

‡*COMME ÇA ET AUTREMENT (V); L'IMPERTINENTE, 19 Rue des jardins, 58 160 IMPHY France, founded 1995, publisher J.C. Belleveaux, is a quarterly of poetry, literature (short stories) and criticism (books, magazines). **They want "free, inventive poetry, short texts." They do not want "classic poetry."** They have recently published poetry by Ted Hughes, Peter Härtling, Phan Kim Dien and Jean-Pierres Georges. As a sample the editor selected these lines from "Les méduses" by Eric Sautou:

> *la pomme tombe*
> *j'écris des mots sur l'ardoise*
> *je les efface*
> *la pomme est dans l'herbe*
> *l'herbe remue*

The editor says *Comme Ça et Autrement* is 52 pgs., compo laser printed, stapled with b&w cover (4-color once a year), graphics, pictures. They receive about 200 poems a year, accept approximately 30%. Press run is 200 for 120 subscribers of which 5 are libraries, 20 shelf sales; 50 distributed free to publishers and authors. Single copy: $5-6; subscription: $20. **Sample postpaid: $5. Currently not accepting unsolicited submissions. Query for status. When accepting mss, submit 10 poems at a time. Previously published poems and simultaneous submissions OK. Cover letter preferred.** Time between acceptance and publication is 6 months. **Poems are circulated to an editorial board. Often comments on rejections. Publishes theme issues. Reports in 3 months. Pays 2 copies.** Reviews book of poetry. Open to unsolicited reviews. Poets may also send books for review consideration. L'Impertinente publishes poetic prose. **Publishes 4 chapbooks/year.** Chapbooks are usually 4 pgs., compo laser, turn down, b&w cover. **Query with complete ms. Replies to queries in 1 month, to mss in 2 weeks. Pays 20 author's copies (out of a press run of 200).** The editor says, "Read [our publication] before sending anything."

COMMONWEAL (III, IV-Religious), 475 Riverside Dr., New York NY 10115, poetry editor Rosemary Deen, appears every 2 weeks, circulation 20,000, is a general-interest magazine for college-educated readers **by Catholics. Prefers serious, witty, well-written poems of up to 75 lines. Does not publish inspirational poems.** In the issues we reviewed, editors seemed to favor free verse, much of it open with regard to style and content, appealing as much to the intellect as to the emotions. **Sample: $3. Considers simultaneous submissions. Reads submissions September 1 through June 30 only. Pays 50¢ a line. Buys all rights. Returns rights when requested by the author.** Reviews books of poetry in 750-1,000 words, single or multi-book format.

COMMUNICATIONS PUBLISHING GROUP; CAREER FOCUS, FOR TODAY'S RISING PROFESSIONAL; COLLEGE PREVIEW, A GUIDE FOR COLLEGE-BOUND STUDENTS; DIRECT AIM, A GUIDE TO CAREER ALTERNATIVES; JOURNEY, A SUCCESS GUIDE FOR COLLEGE AND CAREER-BOUND STUDENTS; VISIONS, A SUCCESS GUIDE FOR NATIVE AMERICAN STUDENTS; FIRST OPPORTUNITY, A GUIDE FOR VOCATIONAL TECHNICAL STUDENTS (IV-Youth, themes, ethnic), 3100 Broadway #660, Kansas City MO 64411-2413, phone (816)960-1988, fax (816)960-1989, editor Georgia Clark. These 6 publications are 40% freelance written. All are designed to inform and motivate their readers in regard to college preparation, career planning and life survival skills. All except *First Opportunity*, which is quarterly, appear in spring and fall. *Career Focus* is for Blacks and Hispanics, ages 21-50. Circ. 250,000. *College Preview* is for Black and Hispanic young adults, ages 16-21. Circ. 600,000. *Direct Aim* is for Black and Hispanic young adults, ages 18-25. Circ. 500,000. *Journey* is for Asian-American high school and college students, ages 16-25. Circ. 200,000. *Visions* is for Native American students and young adults, ages 16-25. Circ. 100,000. *First Opportunity* is for Black and Hispanic young adults, ages 16-21. Circ. 500,000. **Sample copy of any for 9 × 12 SAE with 4 first-class stamps. Simultaneous and previously published submissions OK. Submit seasonal/holiday material 6 months in advance.** "Include on manuscript your name, address, phone and Social Security numbers." They use free verse. **Each magazine buys 5 poems/year. Submit up to 5 poems at one time. Length: 10-25 lines. Writer's guidelines for #10 SASE. Reports in 2 months. Pays $10-25/poem on acceptance.**

COMMUNITIES: JOURNAL OF COOPERATIVE LIVING (IV-Specialized), P.O. Box 169, Masonville CO 80541-0169, phone/fax (970)593-5615, founded 1972, editor Diana Christian, is a "quarterly publication on **intentional communities and cooperative living**," occasionally using poetry relevant to those topics. It is 76 pgs., magazine-sized, professionally printed on recycled white stock with 2-color glossy paper cover, saddle-stapled. **Submit any number of poems at a time. SASE required. Previously published poems and simultaneous submissions OK. Publishes theme issues. Send SASE for upcoming themes.** Themes for Fall '97, Winter '97 and Spring '98 are Food & Meal Sharing, 25th Anniversary and Money, respectively. **Pays 4 copies and subscription.** They also publish the *Communities Directory*. The editor says, "Poets rarely 'get' who we are and what our publication is about, so I reject good poems for wrong content. We're about cooperation and intentional community living."

A COMPANION IN ZEOR (IV-Science fiction/fantasy), 307 Ashland Ave., Egg Harbor Township NJ 08234-5568, phone (609)645-6938, founded 1978, editor Karen Litman, is a **science fiction, fantasy fanzine** appearing *very* irregularly (last published issue November 1994; hopes to publish again this year). "Material used is now limited to creations based solely on works (universes) of Jacqueline Lichtenberg. No other submission types considered. Prefer nothing obscene. Homosexuality not acceptable unless very relevant to the piece. Prefer a 'clean' publication image."** It is magazine-sized, photocopied from typescript. Press run is 100. **Send SASE for guidelines. Cover letter preferred with submissions; note whether to return or dispose of rejected mss. Sometimes sends prepublication galleys. Pays 1 copy, "but can negotiate." Acquires first rights.** "Always willing to work with authors or poets to help in improving their work." Reviews books of poetry. Open to unsolicited reviews. Poets may also send books for review consideration. The editor says, "Future issues may not be in paper form, but posted on the Internet."

THE COMSTOCK REVIEW; COMSTOCK WRITERS' GROUP INC. (II), 907 Comstock Ave., Syracuse NY 13210, phone (315)475-0339, founded 1987 as *Poetpourri*, published by the Comstock Writers' Group, Inc., co-editors Jennifer B. MacPherson and Kathleen Bryce Niles, appears biannually. **They use "work that is clear and understandable to a general readership, that deals with issues, ideas, feelings and beliefs common to us all—well-written free and traditional verse. No obscene, obscure, patently religious or greeting card verse."** They have published poetry by Gayle Elen Harvey, Katharyn Howd Machan, Robert Cooperman, Michael Scofield and Susan A. Manchester. As a sample they selected these lines from "Just This One Thing Lost" by William Preston:

> *We pack away valuables:*
> *peaches, cherries, blueberries sealed in jars,*
> *the heart's discernment sealed away for winter,*

>   the meat a heavy sight from days of butchering.
>   Avoid naming animals, I say.

The Comstock Review is 100 pgs., digest-sized, professionally printed, perfect-bound with raised cover. Circulation 550. Subscription: $10. **Sample postpaid: $5. Submit 3-6 poems at a time, name and address on each page, unpublished poems only. Cover letter with short bio of poet preferred. Return time is about 6 weeks. Editors usually comment on returned submissions. Pays copies. Acquires first North American serial rights.** They offer a yearly contest with over $400 in prizes, $3/poem fee, 40-line limit.

CONCHO RIVER REVIEW; FORT CONCHO MUSEUM PRESS (II), Department of English, Angelo State University, San Angelo TX 76909, phone (915)942-2252, founded 1984, poetry editor Chris Ellery. "The Fort Concho Museum Press is entering another year of publishing *Concho River Review*, a literary journal published twice a year. **Prefer shorter poems, few long poems accepted; particularly looking for poems with distinctive imagery and imaginative forms and rhythms. The first test of a poem will be its imagery."** Short reviews of new volumes of poetry are also published. *CRR* is 120-138 pgs., digest-sized, flat-spined, with matte card cover, professionally printed. They use 35-40 of 600-800 poems received/year. Press run is 300 for about 200 subscribers of which 10 are libraries. Subscription: $14. **Sample postpaid: $5. "Please submit 3-5 poems at a time. Use regular legal-sized envelopes—no big brown envelopes; no replies without SASE. Type must be letter-perfect, sharp enough to be computer scanned." Reports in 1-2 months. Pays 1 copy. Acquires first rights.** The editor says, "We're always looking for good, strong work—from both well-known poets and those who have never been published before."

CONDUIT (II), 510 Eighth Ave. NE, Minneapolis MN 55413, e-mail conduit@bitstream.net, founded 1993, editors William D. Waltz and Brett Astor, is a triquarterly designed "to explore language, art, life without ulterior motives; to publish work that is 'essential.' " **They want "lively, honest poetry that is attuned to language."** They have published poetry by Richard Jones, Daniil Kharms and Dara Wier. *Conduit* is 52 pgs., 4¼×11, neatly printed on recycled paper and saddle-stapled with matte card cover and art. They receive about 2,000 poems a year, publish about 50. Press run is 600-1,000 for 100 subscribers, 100-200 shelf sales. Subscription: $12. **Sample postpaid: $4. Submit 3-5 poems at a time. No previously published work.** Time between acceptance and publication is 6-12 months. **Seldom comments on rejections. Send SASE for guidelines or request via e-mail. Reports in 6-10 weeks. Pays 3 copies. Rights revert to authors upon publication.** Reviews books of poetry in 500 words. Open to unsolicited reviews. Poets may also send books for review consideration. The editors say, "*Conduit* is dedicated to the work of poets and artists who wear the stains of a life lived and whose edges are neither affected nor accidental. *Conduit* will grow and evolve, but one thing will remain constant: quality writing that risks annihilation."

CONFLUENCE; OHIO VALLEY LITERARY GROUP (II), P.O. Box 336, Belpre OH 45714, phone (304)422-3112, e-mail dprather@prodigy.com, founded 1983 as *Gambit*, 1989 as *Confluence*, editor J. Scott Bond, assistant editor David Prather. *Confluence* is an annual "credible platform for established/emerging authors and outstanding student work. This literary magazine is published at Marietta College, Marietta, Ohio, and was named to represent the merging of the Ohio and Muskingum Rivers as well as the collaboration of the Ohio Valley Literary Group with Marietta College." They have recently published poetry by Charles Edward Mann, Phebe Davidson, A.E. Stringer and Lois Marie Harrod. As a sample the editor selected these lines from "Bell" by Edward Haworth Hoeppner:

>   . . . When the young girl in bed
>   upstairs moves her hand beneath the quilts,
>   stillness, stillness. Concentration
>
>   fills the drawer, the house, the marsh
>   where an egret steps, curved white
>   in the darkness, a hunting spike.

Confluence is 96-112 pgs., digest-sized, professionally printed and perfect-bound with 2-color matte card cover and b&w graphics. They receive 800-1,000 submissions a year, accept approximately 2%. Press run is 500 for 300 subscribers of which 10 are libraries, about 150 shelf sales. Single copy: $5. **Sample: $3 plus $1.25 postage. No previously published poems or simultaneous submissions. Cover letter with brief bio required. Reads submissions September 1 through March 1 only.** Time between acceptance and publication is 6 months. **Seldom comments on rejections. Send SASE for guidelines or request via e-mail. Reports in 3 months. Pays 1-3 copies. Returns rights upon publication.**

 THE MAPLE LEAF symbol before a listing indicates a Canadian publisher, magazine, conference, contest or organization.

‡**CONFLUENCE PRESS (II, IV-Regional)**, Lewis-Clark State College, Lewiston ID 83501, phone (208)799-2336, founded 1975, poetry editor James R. Hepworth, is an "independent publisher of fiction, poetry, creative nonfiction and literary scholarship. **We are open to formal poetry as well as free verse. No rhymed doggerel, 'light verse,' 'performance poetry,' 'street poetry,' etc. We prefer to publish work by poets who live and work in the northwestern United States.**" They have published poetry by John Daniel, Greg Keeler, Nancy Mairs and Sherry Rind. They print about 2 books a year. **"Please query** *before* **submitting manuscript." Query with 6 sample poems, bio, list of publications. Replies to queries in 6 weeks. Pays $100-500 advance and 10% royalties plus copies. Buys all rights. Returns rights if book goes out of print. Send SASE for catalog to order samples.**

CONFRONTATION MAGAZINE (II), English Dept., C.W. Post Campus of Long Island University, Brookville NY 11548-0570, phone (516)299-2391, fax (516)299-2735, founded 1968, editor-in-chief Martin Tucker, is "a semiannual literary journal with **interest in all forms. Our only criterion is high literary merit.** We think of our audience as an educated, lay group of intelligent readers. **We prefer lyric poems. Length generally should be kept to two pages. No sentimental verse.**" They have published poetry by Karl Shapiro, T. Alan Broughton, David Ignatow, Philip Appleman, Jane Mayhall and Joseph Brodsky. *Confrontation* is 250 pgs., digest-sized, professionally printed, flat-spined, with a circulation of about 2,000. A well-edited, visually beautiful journal, each issue features about 30-40 poems of varying lengths. The magazine is recommended not only for its "showcase" appeal, but also for the wide range of formal and free styles, displaying craft and insight. They receive about 1,200 submissions/year, publish 150, have a 6- to 12-month backlog. **Sample postpaid: $3. Submit no more than 10 pgs., clear copy. No previously published poems. Do not submit mss June through August. "Prefer single submissions." Publishes theme issues. Send SASE for upcoming themes. Reports in 6-8 weeks. Sometimes sends prepublication galleys. Pays $5-50 and copy of magazine.** Staff reviews books of poetry. Send books for review consideration. Basically a magazine, they do on occasion publish "book" issues or "anthologies." Their most recent "occasional book" is *Clown at Wall*, stories and drawings by Ken Bernard.

CONJUNCTIONS (III), Dept. PM, Bard College, Annandale-on-Hudson NY 12504, founded 1981, managing editor Michael Bergstein, editor Bradford Morrow, is an elegant journal appearing twice a year, using work that is "**stylistically innovative. Potential contributors should be familiar with the poetry published in the journal.**" They have published poetry by John Ashbery, Robert Kelly, Charles Stein, Michael Palmer, Ann Lauterbach and Fanny Howe. This publication is distributed by Consortium. It is 350 pgs., 6×9, flat-spined, professionally printed. Issues reviewed feature mostly lyric free verse with occasional sequences and stanza patterns (some leaning toward the avant-garde). Poems compete with prose, with more pages devoted to the latter. Press run is 5,500 for 1,000 subscribers of which 250 are libraries. Subscription: $18. **Sample postpaid: $12. Pays $100-175.**

THE CONNECTICUT POETRY REVIEW (II), P.O. Box 818, Stonington CT 06378, founded 1981, poetry editors J. Claire White and Harley More, is a "small press that puts out an annual magazine. **We look for poetry of quality which is both genuine and original in content. No specifications except length: 10-40 lines.**" The magazine has won high praise from the literary world; they have published such poets as John Updike, Robert Peters, Diane Wakoski and Marge Piercy. Each issue seems to feature a poet. As a sample the editors selected these lines by Gabriela Mistral (translated by Christiane Jacox Kyle):

> We ourselves are her exhausted chest,
> her bloodless pale skin, the wild shout
> thrown toward the setting sun and the rising,
> the red fever of her veins,
> God's forgetfulness of his children.

The flat-spined, large digest-sized journal is "printed letterpress by hand on a Hacker Hand Press from Monotype Bembo." Most of the 45-60 pgs. are poetry, but they also have reviews. Editors seem to favor free verse with strong emphasis on voice (and judicious use of image and symbol). They receive over 1,200 submissions a year, use about 20, have a 3-month backlog. Press run is 400 for 80 subscribers of which 35 are libraries. **Sample postpaid: $3.50. Reports in 3 months. Pays $5/poem plus 1 copy.** The editors advise, "Study traditional and modern styles. Study poets of the past. Attend poetry readings. And write. Practice on your own."

‡**CONNECTICUT REVIEW (II)**, Southern Community State University, 501 Crescent St., New Haven CT 06473, phone (203)392-6737, founded 1968, editor Dr. Vivian Shipley, published biannually, contains essays, poetry, articles, fiction and artwork. They have recently published poetry by James Fowler, Laurence Goldstein, Stephen Gardner, Margot Schilpp, Robert Stewart and Geraldine Connolly. *Connecticut Review* is 160 pgs., digest-sized, offset, perfect bound, with glossy 4-color cover and 8-color interior art. They receive about 2,500 poems a year, accept approximately 5%. Press run is 3,000 of which 400 are libraries, with 1,000 distributed free to Connecticut State libraries and high schools. **Sample postpaid: $6. Make checks payable to Connecticut State University. Submit 3-5 typed poems at a time, 2 copies of each with name, address and phone in the upper left-hand corner on 8½×11 paper with SASE. Pays 2 copies. Acquires first or one-time rights.**

CONNECTICUT RIVER REVIEW; BRODINE CONTEST; CONNECTICUT POETRY SOCIETY (II), 35 Lindsley Place, Stratford CT 06497, founded 1978, appears twice yearly, editor Norah Christianson.

They are looking for **"original, honest, diverse, vital, well-crafted poetry. Translations and long-poems accepted."** They have recently published poetry by Rennie McQuilkin, Paul Petrie, John Kennedy, Thomas Michael McDade and Michael Stein. As a sample the editor selected these lines from "Blue Point Collie" by Len Krisak:

> *Let slip then, on the gauntness came (though who*
> *Had led it out to freedom wasn't clear).*
> *Its jagged markings—ashen greys and blues—*
> *Ran down a hunting snout whose ragged spears*
> *Of silver made us look at them askance.*
> *Alone, the unleashed carnivore advanced. . . .*

Each of the attractively printed, digest-sized issues contains about 40 pgs. of poetry, has a circulation of about 500 with 175 subscriptions of which 5% are libraries. They receive about 2,000 submissions a year, use approximately 80. Subscription: $12. **Sample postpaid: $6. Submit up to 3 poems at a time. No previously published poems or simultaneous submissions. Guidelines available with SASE. Pays 1 copy.** The Brodine Contest has a $2 entry fee/poem and 3 cash awards plus publication in the *Connecticut River Review*. Entries must be postmarked between May 1 and July 31. Connecticut Poetry Society, 24 Commerce St., Clinton CT 06413, phone (860)669-7300, president Thomas Morris. Founded in 1974 to encourage the art of Poetry. State-wide organization open to all who are interested in poetry. Affiliated with the National Federation of State Poetry Societies. Currently has 150 members. Sponsors conferences, workshops. Publishes *Poets at Work*, for members only, appearing irregularly; and *Newsletter*, a bimonthly publication, also available to nonmembers for SASE. Members or nationally known writers give readings that are open to the public. Sponsors open-mike readings. Membership dues are $20/year. Members meet monthly. Send SASE for additional information.

CONSCIENCE (II), CFFC, 1436 U St. NW, Suite 301, Washington DC 20009-3997, founded 1980, poetry editor Andrew Merton, is a quarterly newsjournal of prochoice Catholic opinion, published by Catholics for a Free Choice. **They want poetry up to 45 lines maximum. "We're topically broad and broadminded. However, no polemics (about abortion/choice/religion) nor poems in conflict with a prochoice—albeit not stiflingly politically correct—organization."** They have published poetry by Mekeel McBride and Romana Huk. As a sample the editor selected these lines from "Autobiography" by Lysa James:

> *Sometimes they tell me I lie.*
> *I am only trying to find*
> *which story is mine.*
> *This pattern of moving*
> *away from all memory*
> *did not stop*

Conscience is 48 pgs., $8 \times 10\frac{1}{2}$, web press newsprint, saddle-stitched with some b&w art and photos. They accept less than 10% of poetry received. Press run is 10,000. Single copy: $3.50; subscription: $10/year. **Sample free for 9×12 SAE with $1.01 postage. Submit 3-5 poems at a time. No previously published poems; simultaneous submissions OK, if noted.** Time between acceptance and publication is 1-8 months. **Seldom comments on rejections. Pays $10 and 5 copies. Buys first serial rights.** Interested poets are strongly urged to read a few issues of this publication before submitting. The editor says, "*Conscience* explores ethical and social policy dimensions of sexuality and reproductive health and decision-making, church-state dynamics and related topics. CFFC is a nonprofit educational organization that shapes and advances sexual and reproductive ethics that are based on justice, reflect a commitment to women's well-being, and respect and affirm the moral capacity of women and men to make sound and responsible decisions about their lives."

CONSERVATIVE REVIEW; NEWCOMB PUBLISHERS, INC.; CARDINAL FIRST BOOK COMPETITION (II), 1307 Dolley Madison Blvd., Room #203, McLean VA 22101, phone (703)893-7302, fax (703)893-7273, founded January 1990, poetry editor Mattie F. Quesenberry, is a bimonthly magazine that includes "political articles, political statistics, political cartoons and especially strong articles on foreign affairs. **We want to see poetry of any form exploring our relationship to religion and the natural world, especially poems exploring the impact of 20th century science and technology on traditional values. We do not want to see any political poetry. Poetry transcends political divisions because it captures universal experiences."** They have recently published poetry by Keats Jaynes, Maro Lorimer, Barbara N. Ewell, Jay Liveson and Madeline Hoffer. As a sample the editor selected these lines from "Modern Physics" by Jill M. Tress:

> *laser prisms*
> *splice their iconic images*
> *into perfect patterns*
> *and fractured fractals*
> *where godlike children*
> *splinter unsuspected:*
> *mathematical metaphors*
> *for eternity.*

CR is 40 pgs., $8\frac{1}{2} \times 11$, offset printed and saddle-stitched with glossy card cover. They use one page of poetry in each issue. Press run is 900 for 700 subscribers of which 150 are libraries. Subscription: $29/year. **Sample** postpaid: $5. Submit 3 poems at a time. Simultaneous submissions OK. "Unsolicited manuscripts must be accompanied by a letter certifying the material is the original work of the author and involves no contravention of copyright or unauthorized use of another author's material." Time between acceptance and publication is up to a year. **Often comments on rejections. Send SASE for guidelines. Reports in 1-2 months. Pays 3 copies. Acquires all rights. Returns rights upon request.** "We will review books and chapbooks, and print short critical essays." Open to unsolicited reviews. Poets may also send books for review consideration. Newcomb Publishers also sponsors the annual Cardinal First Book Competition. Established in 1997, the competition awards publication to a first book of poetry. Submit 50-100 pages on any subject, in any form. "We prefer for the poet to have numerous poems published in publications." Send SASE for complete guidelines. Entry fee: $12 (make check payable to Newcomb Publishers Inc.). Deadline: April 15. Winner is announced in July by letter to all entrants. The editor says, "There is no real division between poetry and our 20th century science and technology. Even the most specialized specialists live their lives with consciences housed in flesh and blood. Even our most unscientific writers and poets must live and react in the modern world."

‡✤CONTEMPORARY VERSE 2; THE LENA CHARTRAND AWARD (II), P.O. Box 3062, Winnipeg, Manitoba R3C 4E5 Canada, phone (204)949-1365, founded 1975, contact Janine Tschuncky, appears quarterly. "We publish poetry, prose, essays, interviews, reviews and art by women and men." They want **"writing which in its diversity represents a range of social and cultural experience, with a particular focus on the experience of women." They do not want racist, sexist, homophobic poems.** They have recently published poetry by Di Brandt, Gail Scott, Claire Harris and Beth Goobie. As a sample the editor selected these lines from "By Way of Oceans" by A. Synento:

> *Disappearing under*
> *the cool ripple of her stroke,*
> *laurels of aquatic plants*
> *divide their long tassels*
> *separate sleep from shore.*

CV2 is 76 pgs., 6×9, with cover art, inside art, exchange ads. They receive about 800-1,000 poems a year, accept approximately 160. Press run is 700 for 480 subscribers of which 50 are libraries, 130 shelf sales; 80 distributed free at readings and events. Single copy: $6; subscription: $21.98. **Sample postpaid: $6. Submit 4-6 poems at a time. No previously published poems or simultaneous submissions. Cover letter required with a 3-line bio and SASE.** Time between acceptance and publication is 6 weeks. **Poems are circulated to an editorial board. Poems go to the editorial collective; usually 3 out of 6 editors work on an issue and make those decisions. Often comments on rejections. Publishes theme issues. Send SASE (or SAE and IRC) for guidelines and upcoming themes. Reports in 4-6 weeks. Always sends prepublication galleys. Pays $20/poem.** Reviews books and chapbooks in 800 words. Open to unsolicited reviews. Poets may also send books for review consideration. Sponsors 3 annual contests, and administers the Lena Chartrand award recognizing the outstanding work of one poet over the year. The award is the amount collected on the interest, which is around $400/year. The editor says, "Familiarize yourself with the publication you are submitting to, it saves time and money."

CONTEXT SOUTH (III), 2100 Memorial Blvd., #4504, Kerrville TX 78028, e-mail drpoetry@ktc.com, website http://www.Zilker.net/business/web/context/index.html, founded 1988, editor/publisher David Breeden, appears once a year using **"any form, length, subject matter. Looking for strong rhythms, clear vision. Nothing sentimental."** They have recently published poetry by Kirpal Gordon, Simon Perchik and Marth Minford Meas. As a sample the editor selected these lines from "At the Museum of the Revolution, Moscow" by Carol Coffee Reposa:

> *All the Russian elegies and catalogues*
> *That Whitman never wrote,*
> *Where he might have placed*
> *The star, lilac, thrush*
> *Measureless with love*
> *In the life or death forever*

CS is 65 pgs., digest-sized, saddle-stapled, using fiction, criticism and book reviews as well as poetry. They accept less than 1% of poems received. Press run is 500 for 60 subscribers of which 6 are libraries. **Sample: $5. Simultaneous submissions OK. Reads submissions January 1 through March 31 only. Publishes theme issues. Pays 1 copy. Acquires first serial rights.** Reviews books of poetry in 500 words maximum. Open to unsolicited reviews. Poets may also send books for review consideration. The editor advises, "Read every poem you can find from the beginning of time. Every poem encapsulates the tradition."

COPPER BEECH PRESS (III), P.O. Box 2578, Providence RI 02906, phone (401)351-1253, founded 1973, editor Randy Blasing, publishes **books of all kinds of poetry**, about three 64-page, flat-spined paperbacks a year. They have published Phillis Levin, Jeffrey Harrison, Robert B. Shaw and Kay Ryan. **Query with 5 poems, biographical information and publications. Simultaneous submissions OK. Do not submit queries from Memorial Day to Labor Day. Replies to queries in 1 month, to mss in 3 months. Always sends prepublication galleys. Pays 5% royalties. Obtain sample books by calling or writing for free catalog.**

COPPER CANYON PRESS (III), P.O. Box 271, Port Townsend WA 98368, phone (360)385-4925, fax (360)385-4985, founded 1972, editor Sam Hamill, publishes books of poetry. They have published books of poetry by Lucille Clifton, Hayden Carruth, Carolyn Kizer and Olga Broumas. **Query first with sample poems and cover letter with brief bio and publication credits. Include SASE. No queries via fax. Replies to queries and mss (if invited) in 1 month.** Time between acceptance and publication is 2 years. **Write for catalog to order samples.**

‡**COPPER MOON PUBLISHING; WOMAN MAGAZINE (I, IV-Women)**, P.O. Box 1348, Meadville PA 16335, phone (814)336-4132, e-mail bwalton@toolcity.net, website http://www.toolcity.net/~lmassung/woman.html, founded 1996, editor Babs Walton. *Woman*, published monthly, features articles, fiction and poetry for women—"not fashion/beauty oriented." **They want "woman-oriented poetry; preferably 32 lines or less." They do not want "erotic, man-bashing (if that's the only purpose)."** They have recently published poetry by Paul Raymond Martin and Nadia Giordana. *Woman* is 24 pgs., 8½×11, desktop-published with colored paper cover, clip art and ads. They receive about 200 poems a year, accept approximately 36. Press run is 300 for 100 subscribers, 100 shelf sales. Single copy: $1.25; subscription: $12. **Sample postpaid: $1.50. Make checks payable to Copper Moon Publishing. Submit up to 3 poems at a time. Previously published poems OK; no simultaneous submissions. Cover letter preferred. E-mail submissions OK.** Time between acceptance and publication is 2 months. **"The editor selects from everything that comes in, then if anyone else has specific objections, we discuss it." Seldom comments on rejections. Publishes theme issues. Send SASE for guidelines and upcoming themes or obtain via e-mail or website. Reports in 1 month. Pays 1 year subscription. Acquires first North American serial or one-time rights.**

CORNERSTONE (IV-Religious), Jesus People USA, 939 W. Wilson, Chicago IL 60640-5706, phone (773)561-2450 ext. 2088, poetry editor Tammy Boyd, is a mass-circulation (50,000), low-cost ($2.50/copy) publication appearing 2-4 times/year, **directed at young adults (20-35), covering "contemporary issues in the light of Evangelical Christianity." They use avant-garde, free verse, haiku, light verse, rarely traditional— "no limits except for epic poetry. (We've not got the room.)"** As a sample the editor selected these lines by Beth Wagler:

> she lies like a young man's tie thin and pressed
> holding her own hand
> open-mouthed
> baby robin-like
> waiting for Bigness to drop in
> something that'll make her strong enough to fly

They buy 10-25 poems/year, use 1-2 pgs./issue, and have a 6- to 9-month backlog. **Sample: $2.50. Submit maximum of 5 poems at a time. Cover letter required. Send SASE for guidelines. Pays 6 copies and $10 for poems having 1-15 lines, $25 for poems having 16 lines or more. Buys first or one-time rights.** Open to unsolicited reviews. Poets may also send books for review consideration. In past years, *Cornerstone* has received numerous awards from the Evangelical Press Association (including second place for poetry) as well as a Medal of Distinctive Merit from the Society of Publication Designers and a Certificate of Design Excellence from *Print* magazine.

CORONA (II), Dept. of History and Philosophy, Montana State University, Bozeman MT 59717, phone (406)994-5200, founded 1979, poetry editors Lynda and Michael Sexson, "is an interdisciplinary occasional journal bringing together reflections from those who stand on the edges of their disciplines; those who sense that insight is located not in things but in relationships; those who have deep sense of playfulness; and those who believe that the imagination is involved in what we know." In regard to poetry they want **"no sentimental greeting cards; no slap-dash."** They have published poetry by Wendy Battin, William Irwin Thompson, Frederick Turner and James Dickey. The journal is 125-140 pgs., perfect-bound, professionally printed. They use about 20-25 pgs. of poetry/issue. Press run is 2,000. **Sample postpaid: $7. Submit any number of pages. No simultaneous submissions. Reports in 1 week to 9 months. Payment is "nominal" plus 2 copies.** The editors advise, "Today's poet survives only by the generous spirits of small press publishers. Read and support the publishers of contemporary artists by subscribing to the journals and magazines you admire."

♣**COSMIC TREND; PARA*PHRASE (I, IV-Themes, love/romance/erotica)**, Sheridan Mall Box 47014, Mississauga, Ontario L5K 2R2 Canada, founded 1984, Cosmic Trend poetry editor George Le Grand, *PARA*phrase* editor Tedy Asponsen. Cosmic Trend annually **publishes 1 chapbook anthology** and 1 special project with narrated music cassettes of **"New Age, and Post-New-Age, sensual and mind-expanding short material of any style, but preferably unrhymed; also: humorous, unusual or zany entries (including graphics) with deeper meaning. We ignore epics, run-of-a-mill romantic and political material. Would like to publish more free verse."** They have recently published poetry by Shula Robin and Heather Fraser. As a sample the editor selected these lines by Susan Benischek:

> All things
> —of beauty
> —of love

> *go beyond dimension*
>   *and only in relation*
>   *to eternity*
>   *are balanced!*

PARA*phrase—Newsletter of Cosmic Trend (irregular: 2-3 times a year)—publishes "poetry related to our major anthologies advertised there." For both Cosmic Trend and **PARA*phrase**, submit up to 10 poems at a time with name and address on each sheet. Submission fee: $1 for each 2 poems submitted, plus $1 for postage. Minimum fee is $2 plus postage. ("No U.S. postal stamps, please.") They will consider simultaneous submissions and previously published poems "with accompanied disclosure and references." Publishes theme issues. Theme for Fall 1998 and Summer 1999 are "Infinitely Whispering Surfs" (deadline: May 15, 1998) and "Beyond Dimensions of Truth" (deadline: September 15, 1998), respectively. Send $1 for guidelines and upcoming themes or $6 for sample publication, guidelines and upcoming themes. Response time is usually less than 3 weeks. Editor "often" comments on submissions. Poets purchase a copy of the publication in which their work appears for the "discounted price" of $6. Rights revert to authors upon publication.** Reviews books of poetry. Open to unsolicited reviews. Poets may also send books for review consideration, attn. Tedy Asponsen. Cosmic Trend publishes electronic music cassette tapes in addition to their poetry/music anthology accompaniments. They say, "Share your adventure of poetry beyond the usual presentation! Cosmic Trend can choose your poems for narration with music and inclusion into our cassette accompaniments to our illustrated anthologies."

✤**COTEAU BOOKS; THUNDER CREEK PUBLISHING CO-OP (III, IV-Regional, children)**, 2206 Dewdney Ave. #401, Regina, Saskatchewan S4R 1H3 Canada, phone (306)777-0170, fax (306)522-5152, e-mail coteau@coteau.unibase.com, website http://www.coteau.unibase.com/welcome.html, founded 1975, publisher Geoffrey Ursell, managing editor Nik L. Burton, is a "small literary press that publishes poetry, fiction, drama, anthologies, criticism, young adult novels—**only by Canadian writers.**" They have recently published poetry by Kim Morrissey, Armand Garnet Ruffo, Bruce Rice and William Robertson as well as 2 anthologies of Saskatchewan poetry. As a sample they selected these lines from "Lian Lian" from **White Crane Spreads Wings** by Gary Hyland:

> *Day four she starts to moult. They pull silken*
> *husks of skin, one a buttock perfectly*
> *curved. Her hand hanging gossamer from*
> *the nurse's hand. During the third, the last*
> *moult Lian Lian, her fever gone, eyes open,*
> *does not speak but sings, in throaty wobble,*
> *love songs to the serpent.*

"We publish theme anthologies occasionally." However, writers should submit 30-50 poems "and indication of whole ms," typed; simultaneous and American submissions not accepted. E-mail submissions OK. Cover letter required; include publishing credits and bio and SASE (or SAE and IRC) for return of ms. Queries will be answered in 2-3 weeks and mss reported on in 3-4 months. Always sends prepublication galleys. Authors receive 10% royalty and 10 copies. Their attractive catalog is free for 9 × 12 SASE (or SAE and IRC), and sample copies can be ordered from it. The editor says: "Generally, poets should have a number of publishing credits, single poems or series, in literary magazines and anthologies before submitting a manuscript." Coteau Books published *Voice*, by Anne Szumigalski, winner of the 1995 Governor General's Award for Poetry; *Beyond My Keeping*, by Elizabeth Philips, winner of the 1995 Saskatchewan Book Award; and *Clay Birds*, by Tonja Gunvaldsen Klassen, winner of the 1996 Saskatchewan Book Award.

COTTONWOOD; COTTONWOOD PRESS (II, IV-Regional), Box J, 400 Kansas Union, University of Kansas, Lawrence KS 66045, phone (913)864-3777, e-mail cottonwd@falcon.cc.ukans.edu, website http://www.falcon.cc.ukans.edu/~cottonwd, founded 1965, poetry editor Philip Wedge. **The press "is auxiliary to** *Cottonwood Magazine* **and publishes material by authors in the region. Material is usually solicited."** The press published *Violence and Grace* by Michael L. Johnson and Victor Contoski's *Midwestern Buildings* is forthcoming. **For the magazine they are looking for "strong narrative or sensory impact, non-derivative, not 'literary,' not 'academic.' Emphasis on Midwest, but publishes the best poetry received regardless of region. Poems should be 60 lines or fewer, on daily experience,** *perception.*" They have recently published poetry by Simon Perchik, Denise Low, Gloria Vando, Walter Griffin and David Starkey. As a sample the editors selected these lines from "The World Remade" by Lyn Plath:

> *Sunlight becomes a room in the city,*
> *an angle of windows, a bar of gold on the floor.*
> *In a white vase on a table in the corner*
> *flowers open, pulling the day into themselves,*
> *into the rush and flutter of yellow petals*
> *the way one body draws another body into itself.*

The magazine, published 3 times/year, is 112 pgs., 6 × 9, flat-spined, printed from computer offset, with photos, using 15-20 pages of poetry in each issue. They receive about 2,000 submissions/year, use about 30, have a maximum of 1-year backlog. They have a circulation of 500-600, with 150 subscribers of which 75 are libraries.

Single copy: $6.50. **Sample postpaid: $4. Submit up to 5 pgs. of poetry at a time. No simultaneous submissions. Sometimes provides criticism on rejected mss. Reports in 2-5 months. Pays 1 copy.** The editors advise, "Read the little magazines and send to ones you like."

‡**COUNTRY CONNECTIONS (II)**, 14431 Ventura Blvd., #407, Sherman Oaks CA 91423, phone (818)501-1896, fax (818)501-1897, e-mail countryink@igc.apc.org, website http://www.igc.apc.org/cocomag/, founded 1995, associate editor Britt Leach, published bimonthly, "discusses Seeking The Good Life—For The Common Good by presenting creative, hopeful alternatives in the areas of lifestyle, politics, culture, community, ecology and ethics. Sometimes outrageous, often outspoken, our independent 'Plain Talk for Interesting Times' is for those reconsidering the status quo. **Topics range from progressive politics and environmental and animal protection to social activism, civil liberties and economic democracy.** An original in the land of the ditto." **They want "anything if the submitting poet has read the journal." They do not want "very long poems."** They have recently published poetry by Leonard J. Cirino, Crawdad Nelson and Mary Winters. As a sample the editor selected these lines from "Reckoning" by Victoria Ford:

> Where the currents cross, a man
>   gloves an oil-slick loon,
>   tossing it like a bag of salt
>   over his shoulder; another
> pitches a blackened grebe like a cat

Country Connections is 16 pgs., tabloid-sized, printed on "agri-pulp" paper, b&w inside, ads, graphics. They receive about 300 poems a year, accept approximately 4%. Press run is 2,000 for 500 subscribers of which 3% are libraries; 50 distributed free, "balance" shelf sales. Single copy: $3; subscription: $22. **Sample postpaid: $4. Submit 4 poems at a time. Previously published poems (sometimes) and simultaneous submissions OK. Cover letter is undesired except for name, address and phone number or e-mail address.** Time between acceptance and publication is 2 weeks to 4 months. **Editor and associate editor read all submissions. Seldom comments on rejections. Send SASE for guidelines or request via e-mail. Reports in 2-8 weeks. Buys first North American serial or one-time rights.** Named one of nine "Best Magazines of 1995" by *Library Journal*.

COUNTRY WOMAN; REIMAN PUBLICATIONS (IV-Women, humor), P.O. Box 643, Milwaukee WI 53201, founded 1970, managing editor Kathy Pohl. *Country Woman* "is a bimonthly magazine dedicated to the lives and interests of country women. Those who are both involved in farming and ranching and those who love country life. In some ways, it is very similar to many women's general interest magazines, and yet its subject matter is closely tied in with rural living and the very unique lives of country women. **We like short (4-5 stanzas, 16-20 lines) traditional rhyming poems that reflect on a season or comment humorously or seriously on a particular rural experience. Also limericks and humorous four- to eight-line filler rhymes. No experimental poetry or free verse. Poetry will not be considered unless it rhymes. Always looking for poems that focus on the seasons. We don't want rural putdowns, poems that stereotype country women, etc. All poetry must be positive and upbeat. Our poems are fairly simple, yet elegant. They often accompany a high-quality photograph."** They have published poetry by Hilda Sanderson, Edith E. Cutting and Ericka Northrop. *CW* is 68 pgs., magazine-sized, glossy paper with much color photography. They receive about 1,200 submissions of poetry/year, use 40-50 (unless they publish an anthology). Their backlog is 1 month to 3 years. Subscription: $16.98/year. **Sample postpaid: $2. Submit up to 6 poems at a time. Photocopy OK if stated not a simultaneous submission. Reports in 2-3 months. Pays $10-25/poem plus 1 copy. Buys first rights (generally) or reprint rights (sometimes).** They hold various contests for subscribers only. One of their anthologies, *Cattails and Meadowlarks: Poems from the Country*, is 90 pgs., saddle-stapled with high-quality color photography on the glossy card cover, poems in large, professional type with many b&w photo illustrations. The editor says, "We're always welcoming submissions, but any poem that does not have traditional rhythm and rhyme is automatically passed over."

THE COVENANT COMPANION; COVENANT PUBLICATIONS (II, IV-Religious), 5101 N. Francisco Ave., Chicago IL 60625, phone (773)784-3000, founded 1923, executive secretary of publications John E. Phelan Jr., is a monthly designed to "gather, stimulate and enlighten the church it serves—The Evangelical Covenant Church—on the way to promoting Christ's mission in the world." **They want brief poems with Christian viewpoint. Nothing sing-songy.** The editor says it is 40 pgs., 8 × 10, some 4-color, some 2-color, some b&w, with self cover, pictures, graphics and ads. They receive about 200 poems a year, use 5-10. Press run is 21,000 for about that many subscribers. Subscription: $26. **Sample postpaid: $2.25. Submit 3-6 poems**

 AN ASTERISK before a listing indicates an overseas publisher, magazine, contest, conference or organization.

at a time. Previously published poems and simultaneous submissions OK. Time between acceptance and publication is 3 months. **Seldom comments on rejections. Reports on submissions "as we get around to them." Pays $10-15 and 3 author's copies. Buys first or one-time rights.**

COVER MAGAZINE (II), P.O. Box 1215, Cooper Station, New York NY 10276, phone (212)673-1152, founded 1986, editor/publisher Jeffrey C. Wright, poetry editor Lita Hornick, is a "broad-based arts monthly covering all the arts in every issue, a 64-page magazine sold on newsstands and in select bookstores nationwide." They want **"shorter poems—2-24 lines generally, modern, favoring new romantic work. Nothing stodgy or simplistic."** They have published poetry by John Ashbery, Lawrence Ferlinghetti, Allen Ginsberg, Robert Creeley and Molly Peacock. *Cover* tries "to reach a cutting-edge/front-line audience in touch with the creative fields." They receive about 1,000 poems a year, accept approximately 50. Entirely supported by subscriptions, sales and ads. Press run is 20,000 for 3,400 subscribers of which 20 are libraries, 4,000 shelf sales. Subscription: $18/2 years. **Sample postpaid: $5. Submit 4 poems with cover letter.** Time between acceptance and publication is 4-6 months. **Editor often comments on submissions. Send SASE for upcoming themes. Reports in 4 months. Pays nothing, not even a copy.** Open to unsolicited reviews. Poets may also send books for review consideration. Offers annual poetry contest, for subscribers only.

CQ (CALIFORNIA STATE POETRY QUARTERLY); CALIFORNIA STATE POETRY SOCIETY (II), P.O. Box 7126, Orange CA 92863-7126, phone (714)854-8024, founded 1972, editorial board chair Julian Palley. *CQ* is the official publication of the California State Poetry Society (an affiliate of the National Federation of State Poetry Societies) and is designed "to encourage the writing and dissemination of poetry." **They want poetry on any subject, 60 lines maximum. "No geographical limitations. Quality is all that matters."** They have published poetry by Michael L. Johnson, Lyn Lifshin and Robert Cooperman. *CQ* is 50-60 pgs., 5½ × 8½, offset and perfect-bound, heavy paper cover with art. They receive 3,000-4,000 poems a year, accept approximately 5%. Press run is 500 for 300 subscribers of which 24 are libraries, 20-30 shelf sales. Membership in CSPS is $12/year and includes a subscription to *CQ*. **Sample (including guidelines) postpaid: $4. Send SASE for guidelines alone. Submit up to 6 "relatively brief" poems at a time; name and address on each sheet. Generally no previously published poems or simultaneous submissions. Reports in 1-4 months. Pays one copy. Acquires first rights.** CSPS also sponsors an annual poetry contest. Awards vary. All entries considered for *CQ*. They say, "Since our editor changes with each issue, we encourage poets to resubmit. Also, we are not opposed to rhyme, but it should be used with great discretion."

CRAB CREEK REVIEW (II, IV-Themes), 7265 S. 128th St., Seattle WA 98178, founded 1983, editorial collective Kimberly Allison, Harris Levinson, Laura Sinai and Terri Stone. Published biannually, *CCR* publishes **"an eclectic mix of energetic poems, free or formal, and more interested in powerful imagery than obscure literary allusion. Wit? Yes. Punch? Sure. Toast dry? No thank you. Translations are welcome—please submit with a copy of the poem in its original language, if possible."** They have recently published poetry by Yehuda Amichai, Naomi Shihab Nye, Jim Bodeen, Olga Popova, David Romtvedt and Israeli, Eastern European, Japanese, Chinese and Latin American writers. The editor says *CCR* is a 80-page, perfect-bound paperback. Subscription: $15 (3 issues). **Sample postpaid: $6. Submit up to 5 poems at a time. Publishes theme issues. Pays 2 copies. Send SASE for guidelines and upcoming themes.** They also sponsor contests. Send SASE for details.

CREAM CITY REVIEW (II), P.O. Box 413, Dept. of English, University of Wisconsin at Milwaukee, Milwaukee WI 53201, editor Staci Leigh O'Brien, poetry editors Laura Micciche and Karen Howland, is a nationally distributed literary magazine published twice a year by the university's Creative Writing Program. The editors will consider **any poem that is well-crafted.** They have published poetry by Albert Goldbarth, Audre Lorde, Marge Piercy, May Sarton, Philip Dacey, Amiri Baraka, Tess Gallagher, Cathy Song, Mary Oliver and Philip Levine. They do not include sample lines of poetry; "We prefer not to bias our contributors. We strive for variety—vitality!" *CCR* is averaging 200 pgs., 5½ × 8½, perfect-bound, with full-color cover on 70 lb. paper. This journal is lovely to look at—one of the most attractive designs around—with generous space devoted to poems, all styles (but favoring free verse). Press run is 1,000 for 450 subscribers of which 40 are libraries. **Sample postpaid: $5. "Include SASE when submitting and please submit no more than five poems at a time." Simultaneous submissions OK when notified. Reads submissions September 1 through April 30 only. Editors sometimes comment on rejections. Send SASE for guidelines. Reports in 4 months. Payment includes choice of 2 copies or 1-year subscription. Buys first rights.** Reviews books of poetry in 1-2 pgs. Open to unsolicited reviews. Poets may also send books to the poetry editors for review consideration. Sponsors an annual contest for poems under 100 lines. Submit 3-5 poems/entry. Entry fee is $5. Awards $100 plus publication and one-year subscription for first place; publication and one-year subscription for second through fifth place. Poetry published in this review has been included in the 1996 and 1997 volumes of *The Best American Poetry*.

‡CREATIVE JUICES; FORESTLAND PUBLICATIONS (I, II), 423 N. Burnham Highway, Canterbury CT 06331, founded 1989 (Forestland Publications), editor Geraldine Hempstead Powell, published bimonthly, features poetry, arts, photos, "something to inspire everyone's creative juices." **They want "any style or subject,**

50 lines or less." They do not want "pornography." They receive about 100-1,000 poems a year, accept approximately 350. Press run is 100 for 65 subscribers, 30 shelf sales. Single copy: $3; subscription: $15 (6 issues). **Sample postpaid: $1.50. Make checks payable to Geraldine Powell. Submit 3-5 poems at a time. Previously published poems (with credits) and simultaneous submissions OK. Cover letter preferred.** Time between acceptance and publication is 1-3 months. **Submissions reviewed by editor. Often comments on rejections. Publishes theme issues. Send SASE for guidelines and upcoming themes. Reports in 1-4 weeks. Sometimes sends prepublication galleys. Pays 1 or more copies. Acquires first North American serial or one-time rights. Always returns rights.** Reviews books of poetry. Open to unsolicited reviews. Poets may also send books for review consideration. Forestland Publications **publishes 3 chapbooks/year.** Chapbooks are usually 5×7, 20 pgs. **Query first with sample poems and cover letter with brief bio and publication credits. Replies to queries in 1 week, to mss in 1 month. Obtain sample chapbooks by sending SASE.**

CREATIVE WITH WORDS PUBLICATIONS (C.W.W.); SPOOFING (IV-Themes); WE ARE WRITERS, TOO (I, IV-Children, seniors), P.O. Box 223226, Carmel CA 93922, phone (408)655-8627, founded 1975, poetry editor Brigitta Geltrich, **offers criticism for a fee**. It focuses "on furthering **folkloristic tall tales** and such; creative writing abilities in **children** (poetry, prose, language art); creative writing in **senior citizens** (poetry and prose)." The editors publish on a wide range of themes relating to human studies and the environment that influence human behaviors. **$5 reading fee/poem, includes a critical analysis.** The publications are anthologies of children's poetry, prose and language art; anthologies of special-interest groups such as senior citizen poetry and prose; *Spoofing: An Anthology of Folkloristic Yarns and Such*; and anthologies with announced themes (nature, pets, love, sports, etc.). **"Want to see: folkloristic themes; poetry for and by children; poetry by senior citizens; special topic (inquire). Do not want to see: too mushy; too religious; too didactic; expressing dislike for fellow men; political; pornographic; death and murder poetry." Send SASE for guidelines and upcoming themes. Themes for November, December, 1997 and January, February, March, April, May and June, 1998 are Gardens & Anything Associated with Them, Travel, Let's Have Fun!, Another Turn at Love, Angels, Gifts—The Gift of Giving, History (Past & in the Making), and More Animals, respectively. Deadlines are the last day of the previous month.** They have recently published poetry by Patsy Lowe, Brad Hengehold, Ruth Margarete Boehnke and Becky Novack. As a sample the editor selected these lines by Maura Roosevelt:

> My name is my title,
> But I am the book.
> It's the heading line to many chapters
> And many stories . . .

Spoofing! and *We are Writers, Too!* are low-budget publications, photocopied from typescript, saddle-stapled, card covers with cartoon-like art. **Samples: $8-12 plus p&h. Submit 20-line, 40 spaces wide maximum, poems geared to specific audience and subject matter. "Query with sample poems (one poem/page, name and address on each), short personal biography, other publications, poetic goals, where you read about us, for what publication and/or event you are submitting. Also include SASE for response." Queries via fax OK.** They have "no conditions for publication, but C.W.W. is dependent on author/poet support by purchase of a copy or copies of publication." They offer a 20% reduction on any copy purchased. Sponsors "Best of the Month" contest, awards publication and 1 copy. The editor advises, "Trend is proficiency. Poets should research topic; know audience for whom they write; check topic for appeal to specific audience; should not write for the sake of rhyme, rather for the sake of imagery and being creative with the language. Feeling should be expressed (but no mushiness). Topic and words should be chosen carefully; brevity should be employed; and author should proofread for spelling and grammar. We would like to receive more positive and clean, family-type poetry."

‡CREATIVITY UNLIMITED PRESS; ANNUAL CREATIVITY UNLIMITED PRESS POETRY COMPETITION (I), 30819 Casilina, Rancho Palos Verdes CA 90274, phone (213)541-4844, founded 1989, editor Shelley Stockwell, publishes annually a collection of poetry submitted to their **contest, $5 fee for 1-5 poems; prizes of $50, $35 and $25 and possible publication. Deadline: December 31. "Clever spontaneous overflows of rich emotion, humor and delightful language encouraged. No inaccessible, verbose, esoteric, obscure poetry. Limit three pgs. per poem, double-spaced, one side of page."** They also accept submissions for book publication. **Query first. "Poems previously published will be accepted provided writer has maintained copyright and notifies us."** They often use poems as chapter introductions in self help books. **Always comments on rejections. Publishes theme issues. Send SASE for upcoming themes. Sometimes sends prepublication galleys. Pays 2-5 copies.** The editor says, "We are interested in receiving more humorous poetry."

*CRESCENT MOON PUBLISHING; PASSION (II, IV-Anthology, gay/lesbian, love/romance/erotica, occult, religious, spirituality, women/feminism), 18 Chaddesley Rd., Kidderminster, Worcestershire DY10 3AD England, founded 1988, editor Jeremy Robinson, **publishes about 25 books and chapbooks/year on arrangements subsidized by the poet.** He wants **"poetry that is passionate and authentic. Any form or length."** Not "the trivial, insincere or derivative. We also publish a quarterly magazine, *Passion* ($4 each, $17 subscription). It features poetry, fiction, reviews and essays on feminism, art, philosophy and the media. Many American poets are featured, as well as British poets such as Jeremy Reed, Penelope Shuttle, Alan Bold,

D.J. Enright and Peter Redgrove. **Contributions welcome. We are also publishing two anthologies of new American poetry each year entitled *Pagan America*.**" They have also published studies of Rimbaud, Rilke, Cavafy, Shakespeare, Beckett, German Romantic poetry and D.H. Lawrence. Books are usually about 76 pgs., flat-spined, digest-sized. Anthologies now available ($8.99 or $17 for 2 issues of *Pagan America*) include: *Pagan America: An Anthology of New American Poetry*; *Love in America: An Anthology of Women's Love Poetry*; *Mythic America: An Anthology of New American Poetry*; and *Religious America: An Anthology of New American Poetry*. **Submit 5-10 poems at a time. Cover letter with brief bio and publishing credits required ("and please print your address in capitals"). Send SASE (or SAE and IRCs) for upcoming anthology themes. Replies to queries in 1 month, to mss in 2 months. Sometimes sends prepublication galleys.** The editor says, "Generally, we prefer free verse to rhymed poetry."

CRICKET; SPIDER, THE MAGAZINE FOR CHILDREN; LADYBUG, THE MAGAZINE FOR YOUNG CHILDREN; BABYBUG, THE LISTENING AND LOOKING MAGAZINE FOR INFANTS AND TODDLERS (IV-Children), P.O. Box 300, Peru IL 61354-0300, *Cricket* founded 1973, *Ladybug* founded 1990, *Spider* founded 1994, *Babybug* founded 1995, editor-in-chief Marianne Carus. *Cricket* (for ages 9-14) is a monthly, circulation 78,000, **using "serious, humorous, nonsense rhymes" for children and young adults. They do not want "forced or trite rhyming or imagery that doesn't hang together to create a unified whole." They sometimes use previously published work.** The attractive 8×10 magazine is 64 pgs., saddle-stapled, with color cover and full-color illustrations inside. *Ladybug*, also monthly, circulation 140,000, is similar in format and requirements but is aimed at younger children (ages 2-6). *Spider*, also monthly, circulation 92,000, is for children ages 6-9. Format and requirements similar to *Cricket* and *Ladybug*. *Babybug*, published at 6-week intervals, circulation 44,000, is a read-aloud magazine for ages 6 months to 2 years; premier issue published January 1995. It is 24 pgs., $6\frac{1}{4} \times 7$, printed on cardstock with nontoxic glued spine and full-color illustrations. The magazines receive over 1,200 submissions/month, use 25-30, and have up to a 2-year backlog. **Do not query. Submit no more than 5 poems—up to 50 lines (2 pgs. max.) for *Cricket*; up to 20 lines for *Spider* and *Ladybug*, up to 8 lines for *Babybug*, no restrictions on form. Sample of *Cricket*, *Ladybug* or *Spider*: $4; sample of *Babybug*: $5. Guidelines available for SASE. Reports in 3-4 months. Payment for all is up to $3/ line and 2 copies. "All submissions are automatically considered for all four magazines."** *Cricket* and *Spider* hold poetry contests every third month. *Cricket* accepts entries from readers of all ages; *Spider* from readers ages 10 and under. Current contest themes and rules appear in each issue. *Cricket* has received Parents' Choice Awards every year since 1986 and the Golden Lamp Award in 1995. *Ladybug*, launched in 1990, has received Parents' Choice Awards every year since 1991 and the EdPress Golden Lamp Award in 1994.

‡***CROOKED STARE; PAPER TIGERS; KIDS OF DELUSION; DIVING FOR ALIENS; NUMBER SEVEN POETS (II)**, Flat 2, 47 Shortlands Rd., Bromley, Kent BR2 0JJ England, founded 1993. The zines, published irregularly, feature poetry, prose, art, photos, etc. **"Anything that is punk. Has to be good, offbeat, quirky, different." They want "Thoughtscrawl—stream of consciousness. Prose rather than poetry. Style: introverted, offbeat, intriguing." They do not want "standard conventional stuff."** As a sample the editor selected these lines from *Kids of Delusion* (poet unidentified):

> *It gets dark in November*
> *The daylight gets beaten to pulp and temperature drops like an Eskimo's dream*
> *In November I can think, the wind cuts slivers of ice across my face, forcing me into remission*
> *Now comes safety, the refuge of hibernation*

The editor says the zines are 20 pgs., A5/A6, photocopied with colored ink, aesthetic use of graphics, visuals, etc. They receive about 50-100 poems a year, accept approximately 5%. Press run is 300, 50-100 shelf sales; 50 distributed free as promo material. **Sample postpaid: $2 (£1) or send 3 IRCs. For checks, leave payee name blank. Submit up to 5 poems at a time. No previously published poems; simultaneous submissions OK. Cover letter preferred.** Time between acceptance and publication varies, with a 5 issue backlog. **Often comments on rejections. Send SASE (or SAE and IRC) for guidelines. Reports in 1-4 weeks. Sometimes sends prepublication galleys.** The editor says, "We don't easily fit into any genre or style. We advise folks to sample our stuff first before submitting."

CROSS-CULTURAL COMMUNICATIONS; CROSS-CULTURAL REVIEW OF WORLD LITERA-TURE AND ART IN SOUND, PRINT, AND MOTION; CROSS-CULTURAL MONTHLY; CROSS-CULTURAL REVIEW CHAPBOOK ANTHOLOGY; INTERNATIONAL WRITERS SERIES (II, IV-Translations, bilingual), 239 Wynsum Ave., Merrick NY 11566-4725, phone (516)868-5635, fax (516)379-1901, founded 1971, Stanley H. and Bebe Barkan. Stanley Barkan began CCC as an educational venture, a program in 27 languages at Long Island University, but soon began publishing collections of poetry translated into English from various languages—some of them (such as Estonian) quite "neglected"—in bilingual editions. During the '70s he became aware of Antigruppo (a group against groups), a movement with similar international focus in Sicily, and the two joined forces. **CCR** began as a series of chapbooks (6-12 a year) of collections of poetry translated from various languages and continues as the **Holocaust, Women Writers, Latin American Writers, African Heritage, Asian Heritage, Italian Heritage, International Artists, Art & Poetry, Jewish, Israeli, Yiddish, Cajun, Dutch, Finnish, Swedish, Scandinavian, Turkish,** and **Long Island** and **Brooklyn Writers Chapbook Series** (with a number of other permutations in the offing)—issued simultaneously in palm-sized and regular paperback and cloth-binding editions and boxed and canned editions, as well as audiocassette and videocassette. **Cross-Cultural International Writers Series,** focusing on leading poets from various countries, includes titles by Leo Vroman (Holland) and Pablo Neruda (Chile). **All submissions should be preceded by a query letter with SASE. The Holocaust series is for survivors. Send SASE for guidelines. Pays 10% of print run.** In addition to publications in these series, CCC has published anthologies, translations and collections by dozens of poets from many countries. As a sample the editor selected the beginning of a poem by Rainer Maria Rilke, as translated by Stephen Mitchell:

> *She was no longer that woman with blue eyes*
> *who once had echoed through the poet's songs,*
> *no longer the wide couch's scent and island,*
> *and that man's property no longer.*
>
> *She was already loosened like long hair,*
> *poured out like fallen rain,*
> *shared like a limitless supply.*

That's from the bilingual limited poetry and art edition, *Orpheus. Eurydice. Hermes*: *Notations on a Landscape*, published in 1996. It is 35 pgs., 10½×13½, smythe-sewn cloth. **Sample chapbook postpaid: $10.** *Cross-Cultural Monthly* focuses on bilingual poetry and prose. Subscription (12 issues/editions): $50. **Sample postpaid: $7.50. Pays 1 copy.** CCC continues to produce the International Festival of Poetry, Writing and Translation with the International Poets and Writers Literary Arts Week in New York. CCC won the Poor Richards Award "for a quarter century of high-quality publishing," presented by The Small Press Center in New York.

CRUCIBLE; SAM RAGAN PRIZE (I, II), Barton College, College Station, Wilson NC 27893, phone (919)399-6456, founded 1964, editor Terrence L. Grimes, is an annual using **"poetry that demonstrates originality and integrity of craftsmanship as well as thought. Traditional metrical and rhyming poems are difficult to bring off in modern poetry. The best poetry is written out of deeply felt experience which has been crafted into pleasing form. No very long narratives."** They have published poetry by Robert Grey, R.T. Smith and Anthony S. Abbott. It is 100 pgs., 6×9, professionally printed on high-quality paper with matte card cover. Good type selection and point sizes highlight bylines and titles of poems. Press run is 500 for 300 subscribers of which 100 are libraries, 200 shelf sales. **Sample postpaid: $6. Send SASE for guidelines for contests (prizes of $150 and $100), and the Sam Ragan Prize ($150) in honor of the Poet Laureate of North Carolina. Submit 5 poems at a time between Christmas and mid-April. No previously published poems or simultaneous submissions. Reports in 3 months or less. "We require three unsigned copies of the manuscript and a short biography including a list of publications, in case we decide to publish the work."** Editor leans toward free verse with attention paid particularly to image, line, stanza and voice. However, he does not want to see poetry that is "forced."

CUMBERLAND POETRY REVIEW; THE ROBERT PENN WARREN POETRY PRIZE (II, IV-Translations), Dept. PM, P.O. Box 120128, Acklen Station, Nashville TN 37212, founded 1981, is a biannual journal presenting poets of diverse origins to a widespread audience. "Our aim is to support the poet's effort to keep up the language. We accept special responsibility for reminding American readers that not all excellent poems in English are being written by U.S. citizens. We have published such poets as Debra Marquart, Richard Tillinghast, Rachel Hadas and Yves Bonnefoy (in translation)." *CPR* is 75-100 pgs., 6×9, flat-spined. Circulation 500. **Sample postpaid: $9. Send poetry, translations or poetry criticism with SASE or SAE with IRC. Submit up to 6 poems at a time. No previously published poems. "We accept, but do not like to receive simultaneous submissions." Cover letter with brief bio required. Reports in 6 months. Pays 2 copies. Acquires first rights. Returns rights "on request of author providing he acknowledges original publication in our magazine."** They award The Robert Penn Warren Poetry Prize annually. Winners receive $500, $300 and $200 and publication in the review. For contest guidelines, send SASE.

CURRICULUM VITAE LITERARY SUPPLEMENT; SIMPSON PUBLICATIONS (I), Grove City Factory Store, P.O. Box 1309, Grove City PA 16127, e-mail mdittman@owl.engl.sru.edu, website http://www.well.com/user/ruz/cv/cv3toc.html, founded 1995, editor Amy Kleinfelder. *Curriculum Vitae Literary Supplement* appears 2 times a year. **"We'd like to see more metrical work, especially more translations, and well-crafted narrative free verse is always welcome. However, we do not want to see rambling Bukowski-esque free verse or poetry that overly relies on sentimentality.** We are a relatively new publication and focus on unknown poets." As a sample the editor selected these lines from "Faye's Loose Hair" by Andy Krackow:

● **A BULLET** introduces comments by the editors of *Poet's Market* indicating special information about the listing.

Grandma called you Susan,
But Mom I named you Faye
To my ninth grade classmates
Because it was romantic and I wanted you
To be a movie star with a murderous man.

The editor says *CVLS* is 26 pgs., digest-sized, photocopied and saddle-stitched with a 2-color card stock cover. They receive about 350 poems a year, accept about 40. Press run is 1,000 for 300 subscribers of which 7 are libraries, 200 shelf sales. Subscription: $6 (6 issues). **Sample postpaid: $3. Submit 3 poems at a time. Previously published poems and simultaneous submissions OK. Cover letter preferred. E-mail submissions OK.** Time between acceptance and publication is 8 months. **Poetry is circulated between 3 board members. Often comments on rejections. Publishes theme issues. Send SASE for guidelines and upcoming themes. Reports within a month. Pays 3 copies.** Simpson Publications also **publishes about 5 chapbooks a year.** Interested poets should query.

CUTBANK; THE RICHARD HUGO MEMORIAL POETRY AWARD (II), English Dept., University of Montana, Missoula MT 59812, phone (406)243-5231, founded 1973, has revolving editors. *Cutbank* is a biannual literary magazine which publishes regional, national and international poetry, fiction, reviews, interviews and artwork. It also offers 2 annual awards for best poem and piece of fiction, The Richard Hugo Memorial Poetry Award and The A.B. Guthrie, Jr. Short Fiction Award. Winners are announced in the spring issue. They have published poetry by Seamus Heaney, Norman Dubie, James Tate, Amiri Baraka and Gerald Stern. There are about 100 pgs. in each issue, 50 pgs. of poetry. Circulation is 400 for 250 subscribers of which 30% are libraries. Single copy: $6.95; subscription: $12/2 issues. **Sample postpaid: $4. Submit 3-5 poems at a time, single-spaced. Simultaneous submissions discouraged but accepted with notification. "We accept submissions from August 15 through March 15. Deadlines: Fall issue, November 15; Spring issue, March 15." Send SASE for guidelines. Reports in 2 months. Pays 2 copies. All rights return to author upon publication.** Staff reviews books of poetry in 500 words, single or multi-book format.

‡*CYPHERS (III)**, 3 Selskar Terrace, Dublin 6 Ireland, phone 01-4978866, founded 1975, appears 2-3 times yearly. They have published poetry by Pearse Hutchinson, Paul Durcan, Medbh McGuckian and P.J. Kavanagh. The editor says it is 52 pgs., A5. Press run is 650 for 250 subscribers of which 20 are libraries. Subscription: $20 US (3 issues). **Sample postpaid: $6. No previously published poems or simultaneous submissions. Seldom comments on rejections. Reports in 3-4 months. Pays £10/page.**

DAGGER OF THE MIND; K'YI-LIH PRODUCTIONS; BREACH ENTERPRISES (IV-Science fiction/fantasy, horror), 1317 Hookridge Dr., El Paso TX 79925-7808, phone (915)591-0541, founded 1989, executive editor Arthur William Lloyd Breach, wants **"poetry that stirs the senses and emotions. Make the words dance and sing, bring out the fire in the human soul. Show flair and fashion. No four-letter words, nothing pornographic, vulgar, blasphemous, obscene and nothing generally in bad taste."** They have published poetry by Jessica Amanda Salmonson. The quarterly *DOTM* is magazine-sized, saddle-stapled, with high glossy covers. They receive about 300-450 poems a year, use approximately 75. Press run is 4,000-5,000 for 400 subscribers. Subscription: $8/half year, $16/year. **Sample postpaid: $3.50. "Send in batches of ten. I will consider simultaneous submissions only if told in advance that they are such. Include cover letter with published credits, a very brief bio and kinds of styles written. Length is open as is style. Be creative and try to reflect something about the human condition. Show me something that reflects what is going on in the world. Be sensitive but not mushy. Be intelligent not sophomoric. Don't try to carbon copy any famous poet. You lead the way—don't follow. I don't like the trend toward blood and gore and obscenity. Report back in three months tops." Pays $1-5/poem plus 1 copy. Buys first North American serial rights and reprint rights.** "*DOTM* is devoted to *quality* horror. The key word is quality. *DOTM* is a publication under the division of K'yi-Lih Productions." The editor will evaluate work and review books of poetry for a fee, depending on length and quantity. Send books for review consideration. He says, "I'm planning an anthology of Lovecraftian related material. The paperback will be predominantly Cthulhu Mythos fiction, but I do intend to publish some poetry."

‡**DAMAGED GOODS; GODDESSDEAD, PUBLICATIONS (I, II)**, P.O. Box 46277, Los Angeles CA 90046, phone (213)850-0067, magazine founded 1997, publishing co. founded 1996, editor Tracey Lee Williams. *Damaged Goods* is a bimonthly designed to "shake up the poetry world—to introduce poetry and writing to non-poetry buying people." **They want poetry "the riskier, the better, show me your guts and/or your balls—make me feel. No kitty cat, daffodil or grandma's baking cookies poems; nothing boring or unrisky."** They have recently published poetry by Pleasant Gehman and Jimmy Jazz. The editor says *DG* is 75 pgs., magazine-sized and staple-bound with glossy cover, contains articles, photographs and reviews. Press run is 10,000, 2,000 shelf sales; 5,000 distributed free. Single copy: $2.95; subscription: $20/year. **Sample postpaid: $2. Submit 3-5 poems at a time. Previously published poems and simultaneous submissions OK. Cover letter preferred.** Time between acceptance and publication is 3-4 months. **Poems are circulated to an editorial board. Sometimes comments on rejections. Send SASE for guidelines. Reports in "a couple of months." Sometimes sends prepublication galleys. Pays 1 copy. Rights revert back to author upon publication.** Open to unsolicited

reviews. Poets may also send books for review consideration to Book Review, Franc Gabusi, P.O. Box 46277, Los Angeles CA 90046. GoddessDead, Publications strives to be the Starbucks of Books. They say "This ain't your momma's poetry." They publish 3 paperbacks/year. Books are usually 100 pgs., 5½×8½, perfect-bound with 4-color "beautifully photographed" covers. **"Send query and sample of work and we will respond." Replies to queries in 2-3 months, to mss in 6 months. Pays 7-10% royalties and 10 author's copies (out of a press run of 1,000). Write to obtain samples of books or chapbooks.** The editor says, "Do not follow trends; follow your instinct; just do what you do and never waver—and if all else fails, start a publishing company."

DANCING JESTER PRESS; ONE NIGHT IN PARIS SHOULD BE ENOUGH (II, III), 3411 Garth #208, Baytown TX 77521, phone (713)427-9560, e-mail djpress@aol.com, founded 1994, acquisitions editor Shiloh Daniel. Dancing Jester Press publishes "in order to promote tolerance, cooperation and understanding." They publish 5 paperbacks a year. They recently published *The Pharoah's Falcon* by Ramzi Najm. As a sample the editor selected these lines from that book:

> *Disciple, our only hope is to bridge the rift,*
> *extend the hand & smile back.*
> *Share the meal & the sorrow.*
> *Together lay the foundation; gently take the stranger's arm.*
> *Make room in the limited shade &*

The editor says books are usually 60 pgs., soft flat-spined, with fine art graphic covers. They also publish audiobooks. **Query with 3 sample poems, a cover letter with short bio and publication credits. "Please include all illustrations connected with the writing."** Previously published poems and simultaneous submissions OK. Time between acceptance and publication is 18 months. **Poems are circulated to an editorial board. Replies to queries in 3-6 months. Pays 14% royalties and 5 author's copies (out of a press run of 500).** For a catalog, mail a request along with SASE plus $2.50 p&h. They also sponsor the "One Night in Paris Should Be Enough" contest, for poems of any style or form, no more than 300 lines total. First prize is one night in Paris, France (airfare and accommodations included). Entry fee: $15; 3 poems/entry. Entries are not returned. Deadline: December 22.

DANCING SHADOW PRESS; DANCING SHADOW REVIEW (I, II), P.O. Box 9778, Baldwin MD 21013, phone (410)557-0110, founded 1992, editors Alan C. Reese, Sam Schmidt and Virginia Crawford. *Dancing Shadow Review* is a biannual "dedicated to publishing outstanding poetry and fiction without regard for political, ideological, social or stylistic constraints." **They want "poetry in which the form and language hammer home the poet's vision. We want to see it all, but tend to shy away from preachy or sentimental claptrap."** They have published poetry by Harvey Lillywhite and Richard Peabody. *DSR* is 80-100 pgs., digest-sized and perfect-bound with glossy card cover and b&w artwork. Press run is 500 for 100 subscribers, 50 shelf sales. Single copy: $6.95; subscription: $14. **Sample postpaid: $8. Submit 3-5 poems at a time with a biographical sketch. Previously published poems OK; no simultaneous submissions. Reads submissions September 1 through June 30 only. Often comments on rejections. Pays 1 copy.** Dancing Shadow Press also **publishes 2-4 chapbooks/year. Query first with sample poems and cover letter with brief bio and publication credits. Replies to queries in 4-6 weeks, to mss in 2-4 months. Pays author's copies, 10% of the press run.**

‡*DANDELION ARTS MAGAZINE; FERN PUBLICATIONS (I, IV-Membership/subscription), 24 Frosty Hollow, East Hunsbury, Northants NN4-OSY England, founded 1975, editor/publisher Mrs. Jacqueline Gonzalez-Marina M.A. *Dandelion Arts Magazine*, published biannually, is "a platform for new and established poets to be read throughout the world." **They want poetry "not longer than 35-40 lines. Modern but not wild." They do not want "bad language poetry, religious or political, nor offensive to any group of people in the world."**
● Fern Publications subsidizes costs for their books, paying no royalties.
They have recently published poetry by Andrew Duncan, Donald Ward, Andrew Pye, John Brander and Diane Moore. As a sample the editor selected these lines from her own poem:

> *. . . The human spirit without a planned path*
> *to follow, is a sad landscape,*
> *only grass and weeds, and nothing more*
> *to expect.*

The editor says *Dandelion* is 25 pgs., A4, thermal binding with b&w illustrations, original cover design, some ads. They receive about 200-300 poems a year, accept approximately 15%. Press run is up to 1,000 for 100 subscribers of which 10% are libraries, some distributed free to chosen organizations. Single copy: £9; subscription: £18. **Sample postpaid: £10. Make checks payable to J. Gonzalez-Marina. Poets must become member-subscribers of *Dandelion Arts Magazine* and poetry club in order to be published. Submit 4-6 poems at a time. No previously published poems; simultaneous submissions OK. Cover letter required. "Poems must be typed out clearly and ready for publication, if possible, accompanied by a SAE or postal order to cover the cost of postage for the reply. Reads submissions preferably March through May and September through November, but there are no restrictions.** Time between acceptance and publication is 4-6 months. **"The poems are read by the editor when they arrive and a decision is taken straight away." Seldom comments on rejections. Send SASE (or SAE and IRC) for guidelines. Reports "straight away."** Reviews books of poetry.

Open to unsolicited reviews. Poets may also send books for review consideration. *Dandelion* includes information on poetry competitions and events. Fern Publications is a subsidy press of artistic, poetic and historical books and publishes 2 paperbacks/year. Books are usually 50-80 pgs., A5 or A4, "thermal bound" or hand finished. **Query first with 6-10 poems. Requires authors to subscribe to *Dandelion Arts Magazine*.** Replies to queries and mss in 1-2 weeks. **"All publications are published at a minimum cost agreed beforehand and paid in advance."** The editor says "Consider a theme from all angles and to explore all the possibilities, never forgetting grammar! Stay away from religious or political or offensive issues."

JOHN DANIEL AND COMPANY, PUBLISHER; FITHIAN PRESS (II), a division of Daniel & Daniel, Publishers, Inc., P.O. Box 21922, Santa Barbara CA 93121-1922, phone (805)962-1780, founded 1980, reestablished 1985. John Daniel, a general small press publisher, specializes in literature, both prose and poetry. Fithian Press is a subsidy imprint open to all subjects. **"Book-length mss of any form or subject matter will be considered, but we do not want to see pornographic, libelous, illegal or sloppily written poetry."** He has recently published *The Lug of Days to Come*, by Daniel Haberman; *Granite Underwater*, by Jeanne Lohmann; *Traveling Light*, by Norma Almquist. As a sample John Daniel selected "Would you linger to Suppose" from the book *The Lug of Days to Come*, by Daniel Haberman:

> Would you linger to suppose
> Venus orbits as the Rose
> Yields its fold to patterned Time;
> Though we declaim on the sublime.

He publishes 10 flat-spined paperbacks, averaging 64 pgs., each year. **For free catalog of either imprint, send #10 SASE. To submit material send 12 sample poems and bio. Reports on queries in 2 weeks, on mss in 2 months. Simultaneous submissions OK. Always sends prepublication galleys. Pays 10-75% royalties of net receipts. Buys English-language book rights. Returns rights upon termination of contract. Fithian Press books (50% of his publishing) are subsidized, the author paying production costs and receiving royalties of 50-75% of net receipts. Books and rights are the property of the author, but publisher agrees to warehouse and distribute for one year if desired.** John Daniel advises, "Poetry does not make money, alas. It is a labor of love for both publisher and writer. But if the love is there, the rewards are great."

‡*DARK HORIZONS; THE BRITISH FANTASY SOCIETY (IV-Science fiction/fantasy, horror), 46 Oxford Rd., Birmingham, W. Midlands B27 6DT United Kingdom, founded 1971, editor Peter Coleborn, appears approximately 2 times/year and contains "fiction/articles on fantasy, science fiction and horror fiction; few poems (2-3/issue). Our poetry editor is very demanding." They want **"almost any style/form to a maximum of 50-60 lines in general. Usually based in the fantasy, science fiction, horror field, but interpretation is vast (e.g., to include social issues)." No haiku.** They have recently published poetry by Joel Lane, Mark McLaughlin and Brian Maycock. As a sample the editor selected these lines from "The Outer Districts" by Joel Lane:

> A mother ate her children. She lived
> in one of those buildings. When you say
> this is where evil lives, you only mean
> that this is where humanity dies.

The editor says *DH* is 60 pgs., A5, litho printed with b&w cover art and interior illustrations. Press run is 700 for 500 subscribers of which 50 or less are libraries, 100-200 shelf sales. Single copy: $4; subscription: $32 in US. **Sample postpaid: $5. Make checks payable to British Fantasy Society. No requirements—although we encourage contributors to join the B.F.S. Submit 6 poems at a time. Previously published poems OK; no simultaneous submissions. Brief cover letter required.** "If a reprint, ensure original publication details are included. If a disk is sent, I require IBM/PC ASCII format—and no computer viruses!" Poems are circulated to an editorial board. "Poems first read by poetry editor—then 'accepted' poems shown to rest of the editors (three in total)." Seldom comments on rejections. Reporting time is flexible, "sorry to say." Pays 1-2 copies. **Acquires first or one-time rights.**

DEAD METAPHOR PRESS (II), P.O. Box 2076, Boulder CO 80306-2076, phone (303)939-0268, e-mail wilmartr@colorado.edu, founded 1985, contact Richard Wilmarth, **publishes 1-3 chapbooks of poetry and prose a year** through an annual chapbook contest. **"No restrictions in regard to subject matter and style."** They have published poetry by Anselm Hollo, Jack Collom and Aimée Grunberger and prose by Tracy Davis.

ALWAYS include a self-addressed, stamped envelope (SASE) when sending a ms or query to a publisher within your own country. When sending material to other countries, include a self-addressed envelope and International Reply Coupons (IRCs), available for purchase at many post offices.

As a sample we selected these lines from "The Bed" by Tree Bernstein from her chapbook, *Journal of the Lingering Fall*:

> We lay down together mother, father, and I
> between them, on the crack between the beds,
> our hands folded across our chests
> dress rehearsal for a mausoleum dance
>
> Small now, like a deflated balloon,
> her body nearly spent of air
> her thin cold hand reaches for mine as she dreams
> of the stranger who offers his bed and rest at last

Chapbooks are usually 24-60 pgs., 6×9, printed or photocopied, saddle-stitched, some with illustrations. **Submit 24 pgs. of poetry or prose with a bio, acknowledgments and SASE. "Entries must be typed or clearly reproduced and bound only by a clip. Do not send only copy of manuscript." Previously published poems and simultaneous submissions OK. Reading fee: $8. Deadline: October 31. Winner will be announced in** *Poets & Writers* and *The Small Press Review*. **Winner receives 10% of press run plus discounted copies.** For sample chapbooks, send $6.

DEFINED PROVIDENCE; DEFINED PROVIDENCE PRESS (II), P.O. Box 16143, Rumford RI 02916, founded 1992, editor Gary J. Whitehead. *Defined Providence* is an annual that aims to publish "unknown poets alongside some of those poets considered to be the best in America." They want **"well-crafted lyrical or narrative poems grounded in experience. No overly religious, pornographic; singsong or conspicuous rhyme. Nothing too long. Shorter poems have a better chance."** They have recently published poetry by Peter Cooley, Mark Doty, Neal Bowers, X.J. Kennedy, Jack Myers and Kathleen Spivack. *DP* is an average of 72 pgs., digest-sized, photocopied from laserprint, perfect-bound with colored card cover and exchange ads. "I receive about 2,000 poems per year and accept about 40 of them." Press run is 300 for 60 subscribers, 40 shelf sales. Subscription: $4, $7/2 years. **Sample postpaid: $3. Submit no more than 4 poems at a time, single-spaced. No previously published poems or simultaneous submissions. Cover letter preferred. Comments on rejections that show promise. Reports in 1-3 weeks. Pays 1 copy.** The magazine also includes book reviews (in both single and multi-book format), and considers essays and interviews. Defined Providence Press occasionally **publishes chapbooks** through a contest. Winner receives stipend and 25 copies of a perfect-bound book, 24-56 pgs. $10 reading fee required. They also hold an individual poem contest ($3/poem fee, any number of poems, 3 prizes, judged by a well-known poet). The editor says, "I see too much poetry that is hurried and uninteresting. I like poems surprising in their use of language, unpredictable, that have closure. I encourage poets to read a copy prior to submitting, and I remind poets that small mags stay alive through subscriptions."

DENVER QUARTERLY; LYNDA HULL POETRY AWARD (II), Dept. of English, University of Denver, Denver CO 80208, phone (303)871-2892, fax (303)871-2852, founded 1965, editor Bin Ramke, is a quarterly literary journal that publishes fiction, poems, book reviews and essays. **There are no restrictions on the type of poetry wanted.** Poems here focus on language and lean toward the avant-garde. Length is open, with some long poems and sequences also featured. They have recently published poetry by S. Ben-Tov, Alice Fulton, Gary Soto and John Hollander. *Denver Quarterly* is about 130 pgs., 6×9, handsomely printed on buff stock and flat-spined with two-color matte card cover. Press run is 1,600 for 700 subscribers of which 300 are libraries, approximately 700 shelf sales. Subscription: $20/year to individuals and $18 to institutions. **Sample postpaid: $6. Submit 3-5 poems at a time. Simultaneous submissions discouraged. No submissions read between May 15 and September 15 each year. Publishes theme issues. Send SASE for guidelines and upcoming themes. Reports in 2-3 months. "Will request diskette upon acceptance." Pays 2 copies and $5/page.** Reviews books of poetry. The Lynda Hull Poetry Award is awarded annually for the best poem published in a volume year. All poems published in the *Denver Quarterly* are automatically entered. Poetry published here has also been included in the 1992 and 1997 volumes of *The Best American Poetry*.

DEPTH CHARGE; JOURNAL OF EXPERIMENTAL FICTION (II), P.O. Box 7037, Evanston IL 60201, phone (888)Depth-Ch, e-mail egerdes@artic.edu, website http://www.idis.com/Depthcharge, founded 1986, editor Eckhard Gerdes. The *Journal of Experimental Fiction*, which appears irregularly (approximately twice a year), is a "literary and scholarly journal focusing on the limits of fiction, especially areas where it interfaces other art forms, including poetry, visual art and music." They want **"poetry from the interface zone, where it meets experimental fiction and the avant-garde."** They have published poetry by Richard Kostelanetz, Arthur W. Knight and Tim W. Brown. The editor says it is 100 pgs., 5½×8½, perfect-bound with a 2-color cover (occasionally 4-color), some b&w artwork and ads. They receive 100-200 submissions a year, accept 5-10. Press run is 500 for 250 subscribers of which 100 are libraries, 100 shelf sales. **Sample postpaid: $9. No previously published poems or simultaneous submissions. Cover letter required. E-mail submissions OK.** Time between acceptance and publication is 2 months to 1 year. **Usually comments on rejections. Send SASE for guidelines. Reports in 2 weeks to 2 months. Pays 3-5 copies. Acquires first North American serial rights.** Reviews books of poetry in 100-200 words. Open to unsolicited reviews. Poets may also send books for review consideration. Depth Charge also publishes 2-4 paperback books of poetry a year. **Query first, with sample poems and**

cover letter with brief bio and publication credits. **Replies to queries and mss (if invited) in 2 weeks to 2 months. Pays 10% royalties and 20 author's copies.** The editor says, "Please familiarize yourself with our publications before submitting. We have become so delayed with inappropriate material that we ask you spend the $9 to see what we are doing before submitting."

❀**DESCANT (III, IV-Regional)**, Box 314, Station P, Toronto, Ontario M5S 2S8 Canada, phone (416)593-2557, founded 1970, editor-in-chief Karen Mulhallen, is "a quarterly journal of the arts committed to being the finest in Canada. **While our focus is primarily on Canadian writing we have published writers from around the world.**" Some of the poets they have published are Lorna Crozier, Stephen Pender and Libby Scheier. *Descant* is 140 pgs., over-sized digest format, elegantly printed and illustrated on heavy paper, flat-spined with colored, glossy cover. They receive 1,200 unsolicited submissions/year, of which they use less than 10, with a 2-year backlog. Circulation is 1,200 for 800 subscribers of which 20% are libraries. **Sample postpaid: $13. Submit typed ms of no more than 6 poems at a time, name and address on first page and last name on each subsequent page. Include SASE with Canadian stamps or SAE and IRCs. No previously published poems or simultaneous submissions. Send SASE (or SAE and IRC) for guidelines and upcoming themes. Reports within 4 months. Pays "approximately $100." Buys first rights.** Karen Mulhallen says, "Best advice is to know the magazine you are submitting to. Choose your markets carefully."

DESCANT: FORT WORTH'S JOURNAL OF POETRY AND FICTION (II), English Dept., Box 297270, Texas Christian University, Fort Worth TX 76129, phone (817)921-7240, fax (817)921-7722, e-mail descant@tcu.edu, founded 1956, editor Neil Easterbrook, appears twice a year. **They want "well-crafted poems of interest. No restrictions as to subject matter or forms. We usually accept poems 40 lines or fewer but sometimes longer poems."** It is 80 pgs., 6×9, professionally printed and saddle-stapled with matte card cover. Poems in issues we read tended to be lyric free verse under 50 lines with short line lengths (for added tension). "We publish 30-40 pgs. of poetry per year. We receive probably 4,000-5,000 poems annually." Their press run is 500 for 350 subscribers. Single copy: $6; volume: $12, $18 outside US. **Sample postpaid: $4. No simultaneous submissions. Reads submissions September through May only. Reports in 6 weeks. Pays 2 copies.**

THE DEVIL'S MILLHOPPER PRESS; THE DEVIL'S MILLHOPPER; KUDZU POETRY CONTEST; SAND RIVER POETRY CONTEST (II), English Dept., Box 26, University of South Carolina at Aiken, 171 University Parkway, Aiken SC 29801-6309, phone/fax (803)641-3239, e-mail gardner@vm.sc.edu, founded 1976, editor Stephen Gardner, publishes 1 magazine issue of *The Devil's Millhopper* each year and **1 chapbook**, winner of an annual competition. **They want to see any kind of poetry, except pornography or political propaganda, up to 100 lines.** They have published poetry by Susan Ludvigson, Ann Darr, Lynne H. deCourcy, Ricardo Pau-Llosa, Dorothy Barresi and Richard Frost. The magazine is 32-48 pgs., digest-sized, printed on good stock and saddle-stapled with card cover and uses beautiful b&w original drawings inside and on the cover. The print run of *Devil's Millhopper* is 500. The annual chapbook has a print run of 600, going to 375 subscribers of which 20 are libraries. **Sample postpaid: $4. Submit 5-6 poems at a time. Send regular, non-contest submissions September and October only. They want name and address on every page of submissions; simultaneous submissions acceptable. Sometimes the editor comments on rejected mss. Reports usually in 2 months. Sometimes sends prepublication galleys. Pays 2 copies. Acquires first North American serial and reprint rights. Rights automatically revert to author upon publication.** Send SASE for their annual Kudzu Poetry Contest rules (prizes of $150, $100 and $50/poem entry fee), annual Sand River Contest for poetry in traditional fixed forms (prizes of $250, $150 and $50, $3/poem entry fee), chapbook competition rules, and guidelines for magazine submissions. Send Kudzu Contest submissions September 1 to October 31; Sand River Contest submissions June 1 to July 31; chapbook contest submissions January 1 to February 28. Chapbook competition requires $10 reading fee (which includes a one-year subscription). Pays $50 plus 50 copies. The editor advises, "There is no substitute for reading a lot and writing a lot or for seeking out tough criticism from others who are doing the same."

DIAL BOOKS FOR YOUNG READERS (V, IV-Children), 375 Hudson St., New York NY 10014, publishes some illustrated **books of poetry for children. "Poetry should be fairly straight forward." Do not submit unsolicited mss. Query first with sample poems and cover letter with brief bio and publication credits. SASE required with all correspondence. No previously published poems; simultaneous submissions OK. Send queries to Attn: Submissions. Replies to queries in 1-2 months. Payment varies.**

‡*DIALOGOS: HELLENIC STUDIES REVIEW (II)**, Dept. of Byzantine and Modern Greek Studies, King's College, London WC2R 2LS England, phone/fax 0171-8732330, founded 1994, co-editors Michael Silk and David Ricks, is an annual of "Greek language and literature, history and archaeology, culture and thought, present and past." **They want "poems with reference to Greek or the Greek world, any period (ancient, medieval, modern), translations of Greek poetry." They do not want "watery mythological musings."** They have recently published poetry by Homer (translated by Oliver Taplin) and Nikos Enganopoulos (translated by Martin McKinsey). As a sample the editor selected these lines by C. Haim Goui, translated by Ari Sharon:

"Error always returns" said Odysseus to his weary heart
and came to the crossroads of the next town

to find that the way home was not water.

The editor says *Dialogos* is 130 pgs., professionally printed and bound. They receive about 30 poems a year, accept approximately 5%. Press run is 500 for 150 subscribers of which 100 are libraries. Subscription: $55. **Sample postpaid: $40. Make checks payable to Frank Cass & Co. Ltd. Submit 6 poems at a time. No previously published poems or simultaneous submissions. Cover letter preferred.** Time between acceptance and publication is 1 year. **Poems are circulated to an editorial board of 2 editors. Seldom comments on rejections. Send SASE (or SAE and IRC) for guidelines. Reports within 6 weeks. Always sends prepublication galleys. Pays 1 copy and 25 offprints. Acquires all rights. Returns rights.** Staff reviews books of direct Greek interest, in multi-book review. Open to unsolicited reviews. Poets may also send books for review consideration.

JAMES DICKEY NEWSLETTER (III), 1753 Dyson Dr., Atlanta GA 30307, fax (404)373-2989, e-mail j.pair @worldnet.att.net, founded 1984, editor Joyce M. Pair, is a biannual newsletter devoted to critical articles/studies of James Dickey's works/biography and bibliography. They **"publish a few poems of** *high* **quality. No poems lacking form or meter or grammatical correctness."** It is 30 pgs. of ordinary paper, neatly offset (back and front), with a card back-cover, stapled top left corner. The newsletter is published in the fall and spring. Subscription to individuals: $12/year (includes membership in the James Dickey Society), $14 to institutions. **Sample available for $3.50 postage. Contributors should follow MLA style and standard ms form, sending 1 copy, double-spaced. Cover letter required. E-mail submissions OK. Pays 5 copies. Acquires first rights.** Reviews "only works on Dickey or that include Dickey." Open to unsolicited reviews. The editor's advice is: "Acquire more knowledge of literary history, metaphor, symbolism and grammar, and, to be safe, the poet should read a couple of our issues."

‡THE DIDACTIC (II), 11702 Webercrest, Houston TX 77048, founded 1993, editor Charlie Mainze, is a monthly publishing **"only, only didactic poetry. That is the only specification. Some satire might be acceptable as long as it is didactic."** The editor is still experimenting with the format of the magazine. **Previously published poems and simultaneous submissions OK.** Time between acceptance and publication is about a year. "Once it is determined that the piece is of self-evident quality and is also didactic, it is grouped with similar or contrasting pieces. This may cause a lag time for publication." **Reports "as quickly as possible." Pay is "nominal." Buys one-time rights.** Considering a general review section, only using staff-written reviews. Poets may send books for review consideration.

‡*DIEHARD (III), 3 Spittal St., Edinburgh EH3 9DY Scotland, phone (031)229-7252, founded 1990, editors Ian King and Sally Evans. Publishes Scottish and international poetry; maximum 1 American book a year. Recently published Martha Modena Vertreace. "A book is a book. Write me a book rather than ply me with a heap of scraps from magazines. **No reply unless interested, do not send SAE. Use your own name, keep it accurate, keep it legible." Reporting is "slow." They pay 5% royalties plus 6 copies. Send IRC for catalog.** The editor says, "Anyone attempting subsidy will be booted out the door that fast and it might cause an international incident. We are actually quite a major antiquarian bookshop (Grindles of Edinburgh) with a bindery and letterpress printing facilities (for shop use only). As most of our staff are writers or former publishers of some description, we like to keep Diehard going as a sideline where quality of production really matters."

‡DIRIGIBLE (II), 101 Cottage St., New Haven CT 06511, founded 1994, co-editors David Todd and Cynthia Conrad. "*Dirigible* is a quarterly avant garde journal of language art which publishes prose, poetry, selective reviews, translations, and hybrid genres. **We seek language-centered poetry, controlled experiments, fiction that is postmodern, paraliterary, nonlinear or subjective, and work that breaks with genre, convention or form. Hybrid forms of writing and essays on aesthetics, poetics, reader experience and writing processes are also of interest to us. No social issues, no inspirational, scatological or emotional work; no exhibitionism."** They have recently published poetry by Sheila E. Murphy, W.B. Keckler, J.M. Bennett, Laurel Speer, Lyn Lifshin, Albert Huffstickler and John Grey. As a sample the editor selected these lines from "Weights and Measures" by Morgan Avery Sispoidis:

> *I hold your steadfastness*
> *like a spirit level*
> *to keep a balance that*
> *does not fall*
> *to guide me past the worn down chairs*
> *away from spoon-faces and kitchen knives*
> *and things that linger in thin curtains*
> *sharp and white like razor blades.*

Dirigible is 40-48 pgs., 4¼×7, photocopied, saddle-stapled with buff card cover, in-house graphics; "will swap ads with similar publications." They accept approximately 10% of poems received each year. Press run is 500-800, 60% shelf sales. Subscription: $7/year. **Sample postpaid: $2. Make checks payable to David Todd. Submit up to 8 poems at a time. No previously published poems or simultaneous submissions. Cover letter preferred.** Time between acceptance and publication is 1 month. **Reports in 1-3 months. Pays 2 copies. Acquires first rights.** Staff reviews books of poetry—"selective reviews; length and type vary." The editors say, "We are interested in a phenomenological lyricism which recreates the texture and logic of interior experience. We are grinding an aesthetic ax and acceptance is dependent upon our editorial vision."

‡*DISSIDENT EDITIONS (IV-Specialized: non-anecdotal, dissident, metaphysical verse), 71 Bally-culter Rd., Down Patrick, Northern Ireland BT30 7BD United Kingdom, website http://www.gmtnet.co.uk/indigo/dissiden/, founded 1994, editor Frederik Wolff, publishes 2 paperbacks/year. **They want "short metaphysical, dissident, anticapitalist, antimaterialist verse with punch and/or zap, and/or humor."** As a sample the editor selected these lines from "Beyond the form" in *Dispatches from the War against the World* by Anthony Weir:

> *Beyond the form*
> *of growls or barks*
> *& all things mauled, devoured or bitten,*
> *the sheerest poetry is composed by dogs,*
> *the most shimmering symphonies by sharks.*
> *The finest human poetry, says the worm,*
> *is not just unpublished, but unwritten.*

Books are usually A5, perfect-bound or stapled. **"Submit no more than ten poems, no biography or other crap."** Time between acceptance and publication is 6 months. **Always comments on rejections. Replies to queries and mss in 2 weeks. Obtain samples of books or chapbooks by ordering through booksellers or directly from press.** Dissident Editions is an "extremely small, non-profit-making publisher." From submissions, they require high quality work with individuality. When queried about the current literary scene, the editor said, "What current literary scene? There are only self-therapists and ego-wavers!"

DJINNI (V), 29 Front St., #2, Marblehead MA 01945, fax (617)631-8595, e-mail kaloclarke@aol.com, founded 1990, editors Kalo Clarke and Kim Alan Pederson, is an annual international magazine publishing contemporary poetry, short fiction, short drama, essays and drawings by well-knowns and new talent. **As this edition went to the printer, we were notified that** *Djinni* **had ceased publication.** *Djinni* is published "when sufficient quality material has been selected—usually late fall or early winter." The handsome magazine is 60-100 pgs., digest-sized, professionally printed and perfect-bound with matte card cover. Subscription or **sample: $5. Reads submissions May through November only. Reports in 1-3 months. Pays 1 copy.**

DOC(K)S; EDITIONS NEPE; ZERROSCOPIZ; ANTHOLOGIES DE L 'AN 2.000; LES ANARTISTES (II, IV-Bilingual/foreign language), Le Moulin de Ventabren, 13122 Ventabren, France 13122, uses **"concrete, visual, sound poetry; performance; mail-art; metaphysical poetry,"** not "poesie à la queue-leu-leu" ... **whatever that means.** They have published work by J.F. Bory, Nani Balestrini, Bernard Heidsieck, James Koller, Julien Blaine and Franco Beltrametti. The magazine *Doc(k)s* is published 4 times a year and has a circulation of 1,100, of which 150 are subscriptions. It is an elegantly produced volume of over 300 pgs., 7×10, flat-spined, using heavy paper and glossy full-color card covers. Most of it is in French. "We cannot quote a sample, because concrete poetry, a cross between poetry and graphic art, requires the visual image to be reproduced." **There are no specifications for submissions. Pays 5 copies.** Nepe Editions publishes collections of poetry, mostly in French.

DOLPHIN LOG (IV-Children, themes); THE COUSTEAU SOCIETY, 777 United Nations Plaza, New York NY 10017-3585, phone (212)949-6290, fax (212)949-6296, founded 1981, editor Lisa Rao, is a bimonthly educational publication for children offered by The Cousteau Society. "Encompasses all areas of science, ecology and the environment as they relate to our global water system. Philosophy of magazine is to delight, instruct and instill an environmental ethic and understanding of the interconnectedness of living organisms, including people." They want to see **"poetry related to the marine environment, marine ecology or any water-related subject matter to suit the readership of 7- to 13-year-olds and which will fit the concept of our magazine. Short, witty poems, thought-provoking poems encouraged. No dark or lengthy ones (more than 20 lines). No talking animals."** It is 20 pgs., magazine-sized, saddle-stapled, offset, using full-color photographs widely throughout, sometimes art, no advertising. It circulates to 80,000 members, approximately 860 library subscriptions. Membership: $35/year for a Cousteau Society family membership, $15/year for *Dolphin Log* only. **Sample: $2.50 plus 9×12 SAE with 3 first-class stamps. Prefers double-spaced submissions. Publishes theme issues. Reports within 2 months. Always sends prepublication galleys. Pays $25-100 on publication and 3 copies. Rights include one-time use in** *Dolphin Log*, **the right to grant reprints for use in other publications, and worldwide translation rights for use in other Cousteau Society publications.** The editor advises, "Become familiar with our magazine by requesting a sample copy and our guidelines. We are committed to a particular style and concept to which we strictly adhere and review submissions consistently. We publish only a very limited amount of poetry each year. We are looking for longer poetry about entire ecosystems rather than one specific animal. For example, a poem about the wetlands or tidepools would be great."

DOLPHIN-MOON PRESS; SIGNATURES (II, IV-Regional), P.O. Box 22262, Baltimore MD 21203, founded 1973, president James Taylor, is **"a limited-edition (500-1,000 copies) press which emphasizes quality work (regardless of style), often published in unusual/'radical' format."** The writer is usually allowed a strong voice in the look/feel of the final piece. "We've published magazines, anthologies, chapbooks, pamphlets, perfect-bound paperbacks, records, audio cassettes and comic books. **All styles are read and considered, but the work should show a strong spirit and voice. Although we like the feel of 'well-crafted' work, craft for its own sake won't meet our standards either."** They have published work by Michael Weaver, John Strausbaugh, Josephine Jacobsen and William Burroughs. They have also previously published a collection by the late Judson Jerome, *The Village: New and Selected Poems*, $10.95 paperback, $15.95 hardcover. **Send SASE for catalog and purchase samples or send $15 for their 'sampler' (which they guarantee to be up to $25 worth of their publications). To submit, first send sample of 6-10 pgs. of poetry and a brief cover letter. Replies to query or to submission of whole work (if invited) in 2-4 weeks. Always sends prepublication galleys. Pays in author's copies, negotiable, though usually 10% of the run. Acquires first edition rights.** Three of the books published by this press have been nominated for the Pulitzer Prize and another for a National Book Award. "Our future plans are to continue as we have since 1973, publishing the best work we can by local, up-and-coming and nationally recognized writers—in a quality package."

THE DOMINION REVIEW (II), Bal 220, English Dept., Old Dominion University, Norfolk VA 23529-0446, phone (804)683-3991, website http://www.cais.net/aesir/fiction/dreview, founded 1982, supervising editor Scott Cairns, "is an annual literary journal of poetry, fiction, and artwork, featuring writers from around the world." They have published poetry by Donald Morrill, Ioanna-Veronika Warwick, Peter Spiro and Brighde Mullins. *TDR* is 150 pgs., digest-sized, professionally printed and flat-spined. They have 500 subscriptions. **Sample: $5. They will not consider previously published poems. Cover letter and brief bio requested. Submissions read from August through December; allow to March 15 for replies. Sometimes sends prepublication galleys. Pays 2 copies. Acquires first North American serial rights.**

DOMINO; CEDAR BAY PRESS, LLC (I, II), (formerly *Literary Fragments*), P.O. Box 751, Beaverton OR 97075-0751, e-mail domino@cedarbay.com, website http://www.teleport.com/~cedarbay/index.html, anthology founded 1997, press founded 1980, editor Susan Roberts, is a printed and electronic quarterly anthology **open to all forms, lengths, styles and subjects of poetry as well as related articles.** *Literary Fragments* is still being published but now is only open to short stories. As a sample of work accepted in *Domino*, the editor selected this poem, "Essentials," by Diana Watanabe:

> *The pierced heart*
> *The pulsating pain*
> *The provoked waves of poignant feelings*
> *Mental polarity struggling for identity*
> *Searching for trust . . . a trust in the process.*

The editor says *Domino* is 48-88 pgs., 5½×8½, saddle-stitched (occasional expanded editions are 100-200 pgs., 8½×11, perfect-bound), with b&w art/graphics and display ads. Includes "500-1,500 word tutorials for emerging poets, poetry book/magazine and poetry reviews, opportunities and contests for poets/calls for submissions, and poet-to-poet contacts." They receive approximately 1,000 poems a year. **Sample postpaid: $7 for current issue and guidelines. Send SASE for guidelines alone. Submit up to 10 poems "on a nonreturnable PC-compatible 3.5 disk in either WordPerfect or Word (either up to version 6) with #10 SASE. On disk label and poetry text, in upper left corner list your real name, address, phone, e-mail address (if available) and Social Security number." Previously published poems and simultaneous submissions OK. Queries via e-mail OK.** Time between acceptance and publication is 6 months. **Usually comments on rejections. Reports in 1-2 months. Pays 80% of the net profit for the life of the anthology on an annual basis. Acquires world rights. "Poems of notable merit may be published in 'Best of' anthology."** Reviews books of poetry in 350-1,200 words, single or multi-book format. Open to unsolicited reviews on PC-compatible disk. Poets may also send books for review consideration. Cedar Bay Press **publishes chapbooks** in print and electronic format. Send SASE for information or view website.

‡DOUBLEBUNNY PRESS; OMNIVORE (I, II), P.O. Box 3094, Worcester MA 01613, e-mail bunnyx2@earthlink.net, editor-in-chief Sou Macmillan. *Omnivore*, published 7 times/year, features regular and guest columns, Slam column, poetry, fiction, b&w art and photos and the occasional puzzle. **They want "free verse, 1-2 pages/work. We are excited by interesting/unorthodox use of the page, including concrete poetry, though will consider new twists on the old canons. Haikus are cool too. No classic style or canon-bound. No Hallmark cards, please."** They have recently published poetry by Taylor Mali, Daniel Grey-Kontar, Daniel McGinn and Hillary Thomas. *Omnivore* is 24 pgs., 11×17, offset, staple-bound with b&w graphics and photos, occasional ads. They receive about 200 poems a year, accept approximately 50%. Press run is 100-400 for 103 subscribers of which 2 are libraries; 10-20 distributed free "to people we hope will submit work." Single copy: $3; subscrip-

---

MARKET CATEGORIES: (I) Beginning; **(II)** General; **(III)** Limited; **(IV)** Specialized; **(V)** Closed.

tion: **$10. Sample postpaid: $3.50. Make checks payable to S. Macmillan. Submit up to 4 poems at a time with name and address on each page. Previously published poems and simultaneous submissions OK. Cover letter preferred.** Time between acceptance and publication is 2 months. **Poems are circulated to an editorial board where "we sit around and read 'em, pass 'em around." Often comments on rejections. Publishes theme issues. Send SASE for guidelines. Reports in 1-2 months. Sometimes sends prepublication galleys. Pays 1 copy.** Reviews books of poetry and other magazines in 50-1,500 words, multi-book format. Open to unsolicited reviews. Poets may also send books for review consideration. doublebunny press specializes in "living writers, preferably authors who tour, authors who stray from the classical canons yet remain intelligible," publishes 3 paperbacks, 1 hardback and **6 chapbooks/year.** Chapbooks are usually up to 36 pgs., 8½×5 or 8½×7, some double, "flip" books; paperbacks up to 50 pgs., 8½×5½ or 5½×4¼, all hand bound by glue press or stitching; hardcover up to 200 pgs., 8½×7, hand stitched and bound. Hand-bounds are in small runs (50-200). **Query first, include literary résumé. Prefers a publication in** *Omnivore* **first. Replies to queries in 1-2 months, to mss in 3 months. Pay is "negotiable as runs are small."** The editor says, "Chapbooks are usually projects with New England authors."

‡DOWN UNDER MANHATTAN BRIDGE (III), 114 E. First St. #23, New York NY 10009, e-mail dumbzine@tiac.net, website http://www.dumbmagazine.com, founded 1979, re-established in 1995, editor Elizabeth Morse, published biannually, is an "art and literary magazine with art, fiction and personal essays as well as poetry." **They want "any bold work. We're eclectic and humanistic. We like irony and prose poems." They do not want "greeting card verse."** They have recently published poetry by Hal Sirowitz, Lou Reed, Barry Yourgrau, Wanda Phipps and Dean Kostos. As a sample the editor selected these lines from "Bomb" by Sparrow:

> *My father gave me a bomb and a walkie talkie. "Carry this walkie talkie at all times. When I call you, pull this string and detonate the bomb," he said.*

The magazine is 34 pgs., digest-sized, desktop published, offset, saddle-stapled, with b&w glossy cover, art, photographs and illustrations. Press run is 1,000. Subscription: $8/year, $15/2 years. **Sample postpaid: $4.89. Make checks payable to Longhall Productions. Submit 5 poems at a time. No previously published poems; simultaneous submissions OK. Cover letter preferred.** "Submission on disk is a plus." Time between acceptance and publication is up to 6 months. **Poems are circulated to an editorial board. Seldom comments on rejections. Publishes theme issues. Send SASE for upcoming themes. Reporting time "varies—please be patient." Pays 5-10 copies. Rights revert to poet upon publication.** May review books of poetry in the future. Open to unsolicited reviews.

DRAGON'S TEETH PRESS; LIVING POETS SERIES (III), El Dorado National Forest, 7700 Wentworth Springs Rd., Georgetown CA 95634, founded 1970, poetry editor Cornel Lengyel. Published poets include Francis Weaver, Marcia Lee Masters and Stanley Mason. Dragon's Teeth Press **"subsidy publishes 25% of books** if book has high literary merit, but very limited market"—which no doubt applies to books of poetry. They publish other books on 10% royalty contract. **Simultaneous submissions OK. Reports in 2 weeks on queries, 1 month on mss.**

DREAM INTERNATIONAL QUARTERLY (I, IV-Specialized), ℅ Tim Scott, 4147 Kedvale Ave., Chicago IL 60641, phone (773)794-5287, founded 1981, senior poetry editor Tim Scott, associate poetry editor Carmen M. Pursifull. **"Poetry must be dream-inspired and/or dream-related. This can be interpreted loosely, even to the extent of dealing with the transitory as a theme. Nothing written expressly or primarily to advance a political or religious ideology. We have published everything from neo-Romantic sonnets to stream-of-consciousness, ala 'the Beat Generation.'"** They have recently published poetry by Lladoow S. Shevshenko, Nancy Berg and Leighton B. Watts. As a sample the editor selected these lines from "For Tania and Her World," by Erroll Miller:

> *Wherever you are*
> *in your palace of smoky ice*
> *there must be music, desolate strands euphoric*
> *Time moves slowly without you, mornings*
> *fusing into long dark nights . . .*

DIQ is 120-150 pgs., 8½×11, with vellum cover and drawings. They receive about 300 poems a year, accept about 30. Press run is 300 for 200 subscribers of which 4 are libraries. Subscription: $30 for 1 year. **Sample postpaid: $8. Submit up to 5 typed poems at a time. Previously published poems and simultaneous submissions OK. Disk submissions welcome (details available in guidelines). Cover letter including publication history, if any, and philosophy of creation required.** "As poetry submissions go through the hands of two readers, poets should enclose one additional first-class stamp, along with the standard SASE." Do not submit mss September or October. Time between acceptance and publication is 1-2 years. **Comments on rejections if requested. Send SASE for guidelines. Reports in 1-2 weeks. Sometimes sends prepublication galleys. Pays 1 copy, "less postage."** Also, from time to time, "exceptionally fine work has been deemed to merit a complimentary subscription." **Acquires first North American serial or reprint rights.** Tim Scott says, "Don't get discouraged. Discouragement is the beginning writer's biggest enemy. If you are good at your craft, you will eventually find an outlet for it. Know your literary predecessors and the tradition in which you are working. Read everything from Shakespeare and Donne to Baudelaire and Rimbaud, from Crane and Hopkins to Plath and Sexton."

THE DREAM SHOP; VERSE WRITERS' GUILD OF OHIO; OHIO HIGH SCHOOL POETRY CONTESTS (IV-Membership, students), 233 E. North St., Medina OH 44256-1947, founded 1928, editor J.A. Totts. The Verse Writers' Guild of Ohio (Amy Jo Zook, treasurer, 3520 St. Rte. 56, Mechanicsburg OH 43044) is a state poetry society open to members from outside the state, an affiliate of the National Federation of State Poetry Societies. *The Dream Shop* is their poetry magazine, appearing twice a year. **Only members of VWG may submit poems. They do not want to see poetry which is highly sentimental, overly morbid or porn—and nothing over 40 lines. "We use beginners' poetry, but would like it to be good, tight, revised. In short, not first drafts. Too much is sentimental or prosy when it could be passionate or lyric. We'd like poems to make us think as well as feel something."** They have published poetry by Yvonne Hardenbrook, Betsy Kennedy, Rose Ann Spaith and Dalene Workman Stull. As a sample the editor selected these lines from "In Dubiis" by Timothy Russell:

> . . . as the boy practices the limited part
> for tenor sax of a popular theme
> for the twentieth time tonight.
> He's had it perfect for two days.
> Warped images dance in the bell
> of the boy's polished instrument:
> his father sitting like a gargoyle
> on the wooden steps, wiping his eye.

The magazine is 52 pgs., digest-sized, computer typeset, with matte card cover. "Ours is a forum for our members, and we do use reprints, so new members can get a look at what is going well in more general magazines." Annual dues including *The Dream Shop*: $15. Senior (over 65): $12. Single copies: $2. **Previously published poems OK, if "author is upfront about them. All rights revert to poet after publication."** The Verse Writers' Guild sponsors an annual contest for unpublished poems written by high school students in Ohio with categories of traditional, modern, and several other categories. March deadline, with 3 money awards in each category. For contest information write Verse Writers' Guild of Ohio, % Elouise Postle, 115 Beekin Dr., Hillsboro OH 45133.

DREAMS AND NIGHTMARES (IV-Science fiction/fantasy), 1300 Kicker Rd., Tuscaloosa AL 35404, phone (205)553-2284, e-mail dkm.alageol@genie.com, founded 1986, editor David C. Kopaska-Merkel, is published twice a year. The editor says, **"I want to see intriguing poems in any form or style under about 60 lines (but will consider longer poems). All submissions must be either science fiction, fantasy or horror (I prefer supernatural horror to gory horror). Nothing trite or sappy, no very long poems, no poems without fantastic content, no excessive violence or pointless erotica. Sex and/or violence is OK if there is a good reason."** He has published poetry by Charlee Jacob, Herb Kauderer, D.F. Lewis, Wendy Rathbone, Greg Stewart and John Grey. As a sample the editor selected these lines from "out by the airport" by W. Gregory Stewart:

> there's a joint
> called the Mobius Strip
> where the girls
> take it off
> and take it off
> and take it off again

Dreams and Nightmares is 24 pgs., digest-sized, photocopied from typescript and saddle-stapled with a colored card stock cover and b&w illustrations. They accept about 80 of 1,000-1,500 poems received. Press run is 250 for 90 subscribers. Subscription: $10/6 issues. Lifetime subscription: $100 (includes available back issues). **Samples: $2. Submit up to 5 poems at a time. "Rarely" uses previously published poems. No simultaneous submissions. Send SASE for guidelines. Information requests and comments via e-mail are welcome; e-mail submissions are accepted but not encouraged. Reports in 2-10 weeks. Pays $3/poem plus 2 copies. Buys first North American serial rights.** The editor reviews books of poetry. Send books for review consideration. *Dreams and Nightmares* received an award from the Professional Book Center for "advancing the field of speculative poetry." The editor says, "There are more magazines publishing fantastic poetry than ever before, and more good fantastic poetry is being written, sold for good money and published. The field is doing very well."

‡DREAMS OF DECADENCE: VAMPIRE POETRY AND FICTION (I, IV-Specialized); ABSOLUTE MAGNITUDE (I, IV-Science fiction); DNA PUBLICATIONS, INC., P.O. Box 13, Greenfield MA 01302, phone/fax (413)772-0725, founded 1995 (*Dreams of Decadence*), 1993 (*Absolute Magnitude* and DNA Publications), editor Angela Kessler, editor-in-chief Warren Lapine, *Dreams of Decadence* and *Absolute Magnitude* are published quarterly. *DOD* features vampire poetry and fiction. **They want "all forms; however, the less horrific and more explicitly vamperic a poem is, the more likely it is to be accepted."** They have recently published poetry by Denise Dumars and Nancy Ellis Taylor. *AM* is one of the largest science fiction magazines in America and is looking to **use poetry as a filler; wants only science fiction-related poetry.** *DOD* is 64 pgs., digest-sized, web offset, saddle-stapled, desktop-published, with full-color slick cover, illustrations and clip art. *AM* is

96 pgs., 8½ × 11, newsprint paper, offset printed on web press, saddle-stapled, with glossy 4-color cover, cover art, b&w illustrations and ads. *DOD* receives about 1,000 poems a year, accepts approximately 100; *AM* accepts approximately 20 poems. *DOD* press run is 2,000 for 200 subscribers, 1,000 shelf sales. *AM*'s press run is 9,000 for 1,000 subscribers of which 5% are libraries, the remaining are shelf sales. Subscriptions: $16. **Samples postpaid: $5. Make checks payable to DNA Publications. Submit 5 poems at a time. No previously published poems; simultaneous submissions with notification OK. Cover letter preferred.** Time between acceptance and publication is 6 months. **Often comments on rejections. Send SASE for *DOD*'s guidelines. Reports in 1 month. Sometimes sends prepublication galleys. *DOD* pays 1 copy; *AM* pays 10¢ per line and 1 copy. Acquires or buys first North American serial rights.** *DOD*'s staff reviews books or chapbooks of poetry. Poets may also send book for review consideration to Angela Kessler at the above address. The editor of *AM* says, "Write as often as you can. Send your work out and keep it out. A helpful hint: as we pay by the line many poets are tempted to truncate their lines to maximize their payment. This is not a good idea. Each line of a poem has a natural length and if it is truncated this will affect your poems' chances."

‡THE DRINKIN' BUDDY MAGAZINE; PIMPERIAL PRODUCTIONS (I), P.O. Box 7615, Laguna Niguel CA 92677, phone (714)452-8720, e-mail kc@kaiwan.com, website http://www.kaiwan.com/~kc/, founded 1994, contact Poetry Dept. *The Drinkin' Buddy Magazine*, published quarterly, is "a magazine for art and words." **They want "shorter, concise work."** *Drinkin' Buddy* is 30 pgs., 5½ × 8½, photocopied, stapled, graphics intensive with art and ads. They receive about 100 poems a year, "use what I can." Press run is 1,000 for 200 subscribers. Single copy: free; subscription: $8. **Sample postpaid: $1. Make checks payable to K.C. Bradshaw. Previously published poems and simultaneous submissions OK. Cover letter preferred. Accepts 3.5 IBM format disk with poems in DOS/ASCII text along with a printout/copy of the work on paper.** Time between acceptance and publication "depends on when we can use it." **Seldom comments on rejections. Acquires first North American serial or one-time rights.** Reviews books of poetry. Open to unsolicited reviews. Poets may also send books for review consideration.

‡DRY BONES PRESS; THE COMPLEAT NURSE (I, IV-Specialized: nursing), P.O. Box 640345, San Francisco CA 94164, phone (415)292-7371, fax (415)292-7314, founded 1992 (Dry Bones Press), editor/publisher Jim Rankin, RN, MSN, *the Compleat Nurse*, a monthly newsletter, "is a voice of independent nursing featuring matters of interest to nurses—a very broad range, indeed." They have recently published poetry by James Snydal. *the Compleat Nurse* is 4 pgs., 8½ × 11, desktop-published, folded with clip art; occasionally published as an anthology. They receive about 10-20 poems a year, "accept most, if in our range." Press run is 500-1,000 with all distributed free. **Sample postpaid for SASE. Submit 2-3 poems at a time. Previously published poems and simultaneous submissions OK. Cover letter preferred.** Time between acceptance and publication "varies greatly; 1 month to 2 years." **Poems are selected by editor with consideration of space availability. Always comments on rejections. Reports "within 30 days." Sometimes sends prepublication galleys. Pays 4 copies. Acquires "one-time, plus right to include in anthology."** Reviews books or chapbooks of poetry. Open to unsolicited reviews. Poets may also send books for review consideration. Dry Bones Press seeks "to encourage nurses, or just do things we like, or want to take a flyer on." Publishes 1-3 paperbacks and **2-3 chapbooks/year.** Books are usually 5½ × 8½, offset, stapled or "fine wire-O" bound with glossy, b&w cover. Replies to queries and mss in 1 month. **Pays 10 author's copies.**

THE DRY CREEK REVIEW (II), Aims Community College, Loveland Center, 104 E. Fourth, Loveland CO 80537, founded 1990, faculty advisor Tony Park, is an annual. "We accept creative nonfiction, fiction, translations and quality poetry." **They are open to all forms/styles. "We want poems built around vivid imagery, rich language and risk. We do not want to see the abstract based on the insignificant."** They have recently published poetry by Carolyn Forché, Joy Harjo, Evan Oakley, Jack Martin, Alissa Reardon and Deanna Kern Ludwin. As a sample the editor selected these lines from "antonio" by aaron a abeyta:

> *waiting for a candle to be lit*
> *here at the edge of the llano*
> *where the grass begins to take over*
> *like a migrant pulse*
> *thumping in the wind*
> *every april*

The attractive *Review* is 95-150 pgs., 6 × 9, professionally printed and perfect-bound with 4-color light card cover with art and occasional b&w art and photos inside. They receive 300-400 poems a year, accept 10-15%. Press run is 750, all distributed free. **No previously published poems; simultaneous submissions OK. Reads submissions September 15 through April 30 only. Poems are circulated to an editorial board. Seldom comments on rejections. Reports in 3-6 months. Rights revert to author on publication.** Open to unsolicited reviews. Poets may also send books for review consideration.

DUSTY DOG PRESS (V), (formerly listed as *Dusty Dog Reviews*), 6901 S. McClintock Dr. #0138, Tempe AZ 85283, phone (602)755-8831, founded 1990, editor/publisher John Pierce. *Dusty Dog Press* publishes 1-2 **chapbooks of poetry per year by invitation only,** usually by poet Simon Perchik. Chapbooks are usually 24 pgs., 5½ × 8½, desktop published and saddle-stapled.

DWAN (I, IV-Gay/lesbian, translations), Box 411, Bellefonte PA 16823, founded 1993, editor Donny Smith, appears every 2 to 3 months. *Dwan* is a "queer poetry zine; some prose; some issues devoted to a single poet or a single theme ('Jesus' or 'Mom and Dad,' for instance)." The editor wants **"poetry exploring gender, sexuality, sex roles, identity, queer politics, etc. If you think Charles Manson is cool—or even Charles Bukowski—you might not feel welcome at *Dwan*."** They have recently published poetry by Janell Moon, Brent Wade Smith and Vernon "Mikki" Maulsby. As a sample the editor selected these lines from "Brothers" by Michael Gregg Michaud:

> *dreaming so softly of two brothers*
> *who would love each others body,*
> *singing music that*
> *lingers on the tongue like anger,*
> *who disappeared into each other*
> *which was a dream*

Dwan is 20 pgs., 5½×8½, photocopied on plain white paper, and stapled. They receive 400-500 pgs. of poetry/year ("that's no exaggeration!"), accept less than 10%. Press run is 75. **Sample available for 64¢ (free to prisoners). Submit 5-15 poems typed. Previously published poems and simultaneous submissions OK. Cover letter required.** Time between acceptance and publication is 6-18 months. **Often comments on rejections. Send SASE for upcoming themes. Reports in 1-3 months. Pays copies.** The editor reviews books, chapbooks and magazines usually in 25-150 words. Poets may also send books for review consideration. "Heterosexuals usually welcome."

EAGLE'S FLIGHT; EAGLE'S FLIGHT BOOKS (I, IV-Translations), P.O. Box 465, Granite OK 73547, phone (405)535-2452, founded 1989, editor/publisher Shyamkant Kulkarni, is a quarterly "platform for poets and short story writers—new and struggling to come forward." **They want "well-crafted literary quality poetry, any subject, any form, including translations. Translations should have permission of original poets."** They have recently published poetry by Robert O. Schulz, Amrita Kulkarni and Kim Klemm. As a sample the editor selected these lines from "Midnight" by Camille E. Torok:

> *Midnight calls, I respond.*
> *The force of nature beckons*
> *me from constraint. Dawn is a lifetime away*
> *and the darkness lasts forver.*

Eagle's Flight is 8-12 pgs., 7×8½, printed on colored paper and saddle-stapled, including simple art, few ads. They receive about 200 poems/year, accept 10%. Press run is 200 for 100 subscribers. Subscription: $5. **Sample postpaid: $1.25. Submit up to 5 poems at a time, no more than 21 lines each. No previously published poems or simultaneous submissions. Cover letter required; include short bio, up to 4 lines. Reads submissions January 1 to June 30.** Time between acceptance and publication is 1-3 years. **Seldom comments on rejections. Send SASE for guidelines. Reports in 2-3 months. Pays 1 copy. Acquires first publication rights.** Reviews books of poetry in 250-750 words, single format. Sponsors the "Poem of the Year" award for the best poem published in *Eagle's Flight* in the previous year. Under Eagle's Flight Books, they publish 1 paperback/year. "Up to now we have been publishing our own books, but **if somebody wants to share publishing cost, we can help or undertake publishing a book/anthology. We don't have selling organizations. Anybody interested in this may enquire." Replies to queries in 1 month.** The editor says, "We expect poets to be familiar with our publication and our expectations and our limitations. To be a subscriber is one way of doing this. Everybody wants to write poems and, in his heart, is a poet. Success lies in getting ahead of commonplace poetry. To do this one has to read, to be honest, unashamed and cherish decent values of life in his heart. Then success is just on the corner of the next block."

‡EARSPANK (I), 2250 Center Lane, Dixon IL 61021, founded 1996, contact Wayne Wilkinson, is an audio journal appearing every 2 months. *earspank's* purpose is to "let the poetry be heard and expose new poets to a wider market. It is a multicultural coffee house experience that can be listened to over and over. **It's not so much what we want to see but what we want to hear. As long as the work is intelligible we welcome it."**
   ● The issue we received contained mostly commentary and poetry by Mr. Wilkinson. Much of the poetry was accompanied by music and sound effects. The recording quality was good.
As a sample Mr. Wilkinson selected these lines from his poem "My Demon":

> *The ghost of my demon grows a face like Bogart.*
> *Dreaming of one more LUCKY STRIKE on the shores of Morocco.*
> *. . . He knows too well the tale of silver bullets*
> *crucifixes and garlic.*
> *Dust in the wind covers all.*

earspank is an audio cassette format usually 30-60 minutes. Cover art provided by subscribers is sometimes used. They receive about 200 poems on tape and nearly 500 that had been typed. Use almost every one on tape and half of the typed poems. Press run is 50 for 40 subscribers. Single copy: $5; subscription: $20. **Sample postpaid: $3.50. Make checks payable to Wayne Wilkinson. "Anyone can contribute but those who submit typed mss are required to pay for the volume in which their work appears." Submit 5 poems at a time. Previously published poems OK; no simultaneous submissions. Cover letter preferred. "Our format is** audio tape, any submissions should be made on a tape with the author's voice. Typed submissions will be considered but if chosen will be read by our staff and put on tape." Time between acceptance and publication is 2-8 weeks. **Always comments on rejections. Publishes theme issues. Send SASE for guidelines and upcoming themes. Reports "usually the same week." Sometimes send prepublication galleys.** Staff reviews books in up to 200 words, single book reviews with possible publication on cassette. Open to unsolicited reviews. Poets may also send books for review consideration. Mr. Wilkinson says, "Poetry was made to be heard. Let us hear it!"

EARTH'S DAUGHTERS: A FEMINIST ARTS PERIODICAL (IV-Women/feminism, themes), P.O. Box 41, Central Park Station, Buffalo NY 14215, founded 1971. The "literary periodical **with strong feminist emphasis**" appears 3 times a year, irregularly spaced. Its "format varies. Most issues are flat-spined, digest-sized issues of approximately 60 pgs. We also **publish chapbooks**, magazine-sized and tabloid-sized issues. Past issues have included broadsheets, calendars, scrolls and one which could be assembled into a box." **Poetry can be "up to 40 lines (rare exceptions for exceptional work), free form, experimental—we like unusual work. All must be strong, supportive of women in all their diversity. We like work by new writers, but expect it to be well-crafted. We want to see work of technical skill and artistic intensity. We rarely publish work in classical form, and we never publish rhyme or greeting card verse."** They have recently published poetry by Christine Cassidy, Diane di Prima, Janine Pommy Vaga, Joseph Bruchak, Lyn Lifshin, Susan Fantl Spivack, "and many fine 'unknown' poets, writers and artists." They publish poetry by men if it is supportive of women. As a sample the editor selected "Sweet Dream" by Tori Gallagher:

> *I woke from dreaming the smooth arctic*
> *wasteland of your skin which I have haunted*
> *slowly, again and again. The cliffs*
> *of your face soared above me, the sea*
> *washing green to blue in your*
> *tropic eyes . . .*

"Our purpose is to publish primarily work that otherwise might never be printed, either because it is unusual, or because the writer is not well known." Subscription: $14/3 issues for individuals; $22 for institutions. **Sample postpaid: $5. Simultaneous submissions OK. "Per each issue, authors are limited to a total of 150 lines of poetry, prose or a combination of the two. Submissions in excess of these limits will be returned unread. Business-size envelope is preferred, and use sufficient postage—we do not accept mail with postage due." Send SASE for guidelines. Some issues have themes, which are available for SASE after March of each year. Length of reporting time is atrociously long if ms is being seriously considered for publication, otherwise within 3 weeks. Pays 2 copies and reduced prices on further copies. Editor comments "whenever we have time to do so—we want to encourage new writers."** The collective says: "Once you have submitted work, please be patient. We only hold work we are seriously considering for publications, and it can be up to a year between acceptance and publication. If you must contact us (change of address, notification that a simultaneous submission has been accepted elsewhere), be sure to state the issue theme, the title(s) of your work and enclose SASE."

EASTERN CARIBBEAN INSTITUTE (I, IV-Regional), P.O. Box 1338, Frederiksted, U.S. Virgin Islands 00841, phone (809)692-4109, fax (809)772-3463, e-mail sjonesh@gecko.uvi.edu, founded 1982, editor S.B. Jones-Hendrickson, editorial contact Cora Christian, is a "small press publisher" **especially interested in poetry of the Caribbean and Eastern Caribbean.** Their books are softcover, averaging 60 pgs. Sample copies available for purchase. **Submit 5 sample poems and cover letter with bio and previous publications. Simultaneous submissions and previously published poems OK. Reads submissions January to May only. Reports in 1 month. Pays 50 copies.** The editor says, "In our part of the world, poetry is moving on a new level. People who are interested in regional poetry should keep an eye on the Caribbean region."

ECHOES MAGAZINE (I, II), P.O. Box 3622, Allentown PA 18106-0622, fax (610)776-1634, e-mail echoesmag@aol.com or 73200.1446@compuserve.com, website http://users.aol.com/echoesmag/, founded 1993, is a bi-monthly designed to "provide a forum for people in all walks of life to share their experiences and perspectives in creative ways—poetry, stories, plays, drawings. **We want poems that speak to the reader, sharing the writer's unique perspective and inspiring new insights or understanding. We look for imaginative use of imagery, metaphor, and language that is meaningful to the average reader.**" They have published poetry by

---

USE THE GENERAL INDEX to find the page number of a specific publisher. Also, if a publisher from last year's edition is not included in this edition, the General Index will tell you why.

both well-known poets and talented newcomers. As a sample we selected these lines from "After the Battle" by John Grey:

> The bruising of an August morning.
> Hoping the sun will peel away the
> bad tissue. He stands to lonely attention
> at the French windows, too ashamed for warming.
> Her pain makes her feel out of place
> in a slight, see-through nightdress.

Echoes is 64 pgs., 6×9, offset printed and perfect-bound with card stock cover and original drawings and artwork. They receive about 1,500 poems a year, accept less than 10%. Press run is 1,200. Subscription: $24 (6 issues). **Sample postpaid: $5. Submit 4-5 poems at a time, name and address on each page. Previously published poems OK, "if publication was to a limited audience." No simultaneous submissions. Cover letter required; include brief description of background and writing experience. "We also accept ASCII text files via e-mail or on 3.5 computer disks, Mac or DOS."** Time between acceptance and publication is 2-5 months. **Poems are circulated to 2-3 members of an editorial review panel and to each editor. Often comments on rejections. Send SASE for guidelines, also available via website. Reports in 3-4 weeks for subscribers, 2-3 months for nonsubscribers. Pays 5 copies. "We ask all writers of accepted work to authorize the Library of Congress to include their work in its programs of Braille and sound recordings for the handicapped. We also request exclusive magazine, reprint, and anthology rights for one year, including the right to publish audio or electronic issues, and nonexclusive rights thereafter. All negotiable to fit author's situation."** The editor says, "We see too much poetry that is full of abstractions, or deals with familiar subjects in an all-too-familiar way, or delights in its own obscurity. The result is not interesting or meaningful to the average reader."

‡ECHOES POETRY MAGAZINE (I), 445 Rowland Rd., Swannanoa NC 28778, founded 1995, co-editors Tennille McElrath and Christie Wild, published once or twice a year, "strives to publish poetry of all kinds, and to be of help to unpublished poets as well as published." **They want "quality poetry. We have no specific preference."** As a sample the editor selected these lines by Laura Shoemaker:

> My fervor
> seeps through my breath,
> and my brain,
> drags like a sullen child behind my heart's hand
> following the pull of encompassing acceptance.

Echoes is 50 pgs., 5½ × 8½, photocopied, stapled, medium card cover with one page of ads. They accept approximately 75% of what they receive. Press run varies. **Sample postpaid: $4. Make checks payable to Tennille McElrath. Submit any number of poems. Previously published poems OK; no simultaneous submissions. Cover letter preferred. "Computer printouts and copies are fine."** Time between acceptance and publication is 2-6 months. **Poems are circulated to an editorial board. Often comments on rejections. Reports in 2-4 months.**

EDICIONES UNIVERSAL (IV-Ethnic, foreign language, regional), 3090 SW Eighth St., Miami FL 33135, phone (305)642-3234, founded 1964, general manager Marta Salvat-Golik, is a small press subsidy publisher of **Spanish language books. "We specialize in Cuban authors and themes."** They have published books of poetry by Olga Rosalo and Amelia del Castillo. **Poets "must be able to purchase in advance 75% of the copies, due to the fact that poetry does not sell well." Poets receive the copies they paid for. Submit sample, bio, publications. Reports in 1 month.**

EIDOS MAGAZINE: SEXUAL FREEDOM & EROTIC ENTERTAINMENT FOR WOMEN, MEN & COUPLES (IV-Erotica, women), P.O. Box 96, Boston MA 02137-0096, phone (617)262-0096, fax (617)364-0096, e-mail eidos@eidos.org, website http://www.eidos.org, founded 1982, poetry editor Brenda Loew. "Our press publishes erotic literature, photography and artwork. Our purpose is to provide an alternative to women's images and male images and sexuality depicted in mainstream publications like *Playboy, Penthouse, Playgirl*, etc. We provide a forum for the discussion and examination of two highly personalized dimensions of **human sexuality: desire and satisfaction. We do not want to see angry poetry or poetry that is demeaning to either men or women. We like experimental, avant-garde material that makes a personal, political, cultural statement about sensu-sexuality."** They have published poetry by Sheree Anne Slaughter, Lorraine A. Williams, Corrine DeWinter and Frank Moore. As a sample we selected this poem, "Source Mythology," by John Hulse:

> When I was young someone told me
> that to really please a woman
> I had to learn how to balance a nickel
> on the tip of my tongue.

Eidos is a newsprint tabloid, professionally printed with photography and art. They receive hundreds of poems/ year, use about 100. Readership is 12,000. Subscription: $25 for 4 issues. **Sample postpaid: $7. Only accepts sexually-explicit material. 1 page limit on length, format flexible. Must be 18 or over; age statement required. Camera-ready, "scannable" poems preferred, but not required. No previously published poems;**

simultaneous submissions OK. "Poets must submit their work via regular 'snail' mail. No faxes or e-mail submissions accepted." Do not send computer disks. Publishes bio information as space permits. Comment or criticism provided as often as possible. Send SASE for guidelines. Reports in 1 month. Pays 1 copy. Acquires first North American serial rights. Open to unsolicited reviews. Poets may also send books for review consideration. The editor advises, "There is so much poetry submitted for consideration that a rejection can sometimes mean a poet's timing was poor. We let poets know if the submission was appropriate for our publication and suggest they resubmit at a later date. Keep writing, keep submitting, keep a positive attitude."

1812 (III), P.O. Box 1812, Amherst NY 14226, e-mail box1812@aol.com, website http://members.aol.com/box1812/, founded 1993, editors Dan Schwartz and Richard Lynch, is an annual electronic, literary arts publication **"looking for material with a *bang*."** They receive about 1,000 poems a year, accept 1-3%. **Previously published poems OK; no simultaneous submissions. E-mail submissions OK; "do not use attached files." Cover letter required. "Submission may be arranged by e-mail with permission."** Time between acceptance and publication is 6-12 months. **Sometimes comments on rejections. Send SASE for guidelines. Payment is "arranged." Buys one-time rights.** Open to unsolicited reviews. Sponsors New Writing Awards with $3,000 in prizes plus publication. Entry fee: $10. Send SASE for guidelines.

THE EIGHTH MOUNTAIN PRESS; EIGHTH MOUNTAIN POETRY PRIZE (IV-Women/feminism), 624 SE 29th Ave., Portland OR 97214, founded 1985, editor Ruth Gundle, is a "small press publisher of **feminist literary works by women.**" They have recently published poetry by Lucinda Roy, Maureen Seaton, Irena Klepfisz and Elizabeth Woody. They publish 1 book of poetry averaging 128 pgs., every other year. **"We publish poetry *only* through the Eighth Mountain Poetry Prize." Pays 8-10% royalties. Buys all rights. Returns rights if book goes out of print.** The Eighth Mountain Poetry Prize is a biennial award of a $1,000 advance and publication for a ms of 50-120 pgs. written by a woman; no restrictions as to subject matter. Send SASE for rules. **Submit during January in even-numbered years. Postmark deadline: February 1.** Entry fee: $20. "The selection will be made anonymously. Therefore, the ms must have a cover sheet giving all pertinent information (title, name, address, phone number). No identifying information except the title should appear on any other ms page. The contest will be judged by a different feminist poet each year, whose name will be announced after the winning ms has been chosen." Previous judges have included Audre Lorde, Linda Hogan, Marilyn Hacker, Judy Grahn, Lucille Clifton and Naomi Shihab Nye.

‡EKPHRASIS (II, IV-Specialized: ekphrastic verse); FRITH PRESS (II), P.O. Box 161236, Sacramento CA 95816-1236, *Ekphrasis* founded Summer 1997, Frith Press 1995, editors Laverne Frith and Carol Frith. *Ekphrasis* is a biannual "outlet for the growing body of poetry focusing on individual works from the other arts." **They want "poetry whose main content is based on individual works from the other arts. Poetry should transcend mere description. Form open. No poetry without ekphrastic focus. No poorly crafted work. No archaic language."** The editors say *Ekphrasis* is 40-50 pgs., digest-sized, photocopied and saddle-stapled with matte cover. Subscription: $12/year. **Sample postpaid: $6. Make checks payable to Laverne Frith. Submit up to 7 poems at a time. Accepts previously published poems "occasionally, must be credited"; no simultaneous submissions. Cover letter required including short bio with representative credits and phone number.** Time between acceptance and publication is up to 1 year. **Seldom comments on rejections. Send SASE for guidelines. Reports in 2-16 weeks. Pays 1 copy. Acquires first North American serial or one-time rights.** Frith Press (a.k.a. Laverne Frith, Publishing) publishes well-crafted poems—all subjects and forms considered—through their annual chapbook competition. **Submit 14-22 pages of poetry with $8 entry fee. Previously published poems must be credited. No simultaneous submissions. Deadline: September 30. Winner receives $50, publication and 50 copies of their chapbook.** The editors say, "With the focus on ekphrastic verse, we are bringing attention to the interconnections between various artistic genres and dramatizing the importance and universality of language. Study in the humanities is essential background preparation for the understanding of these interrelations."

‡EL DORADO POETRY REVIEW (I, II), 23792 Calle Ganador, Mission Viejo CA 92691, phone (714)855-2737, founded 1997 (first issue will appear in November 1997), editor Katherine Hageland, appears biannually in the spring and fall. "Send to *El Dorado* if you are tired of being turned down by elitist, academic journals and magazines published by poetry cliques. We promise you a fair reading. Remember, El Dorado is the land of opportunity." **They want "concise, accessible free verse driven by strong concrete images. Narrative and lyric; personal experience and erotica welcome. Verse must be well crafted and show strong attention to correct capitalization, punctuation and grammar."** The editor says *EDPR* is 40 pgs., digest-sized, saddle-stapled with matte card cover, computer-generated with clip art graphics, no ads. Press run for first issue is 200. Subscription: $10/year. **Sample (including guidelines) postpaid: $4 "when available." Make checks payable to Katherine Hageland. Submit 5 poems at a time. No previously published poems or simultaneous submissions. Cover letter required including short bio with credits. Provide name, address and telephone number on each page.** Time between acceptance and publication is 6-12 months. **Often comments on rejections. Reports in 6-8 weeks. Sometimes sends prepublication galleys. Pays 1 copy. Acquires first rights.** The editor says, "Read, read, read: the classics as well as the best of the moderns. Write, revise and revise again. Always read your work aloud. Go to readings, attend poetry workshops, join a writers' group. Peer criticism is essential."

ELF: ECLECTIC LITERARY FORUM (ELF Magazine) (II), P.O. Box 392, Tonawanda NY 14150, phone/fax (716)693-7006, e-mail neubauer@buffnet.net, website http://www.pce.net/elf, founded 1990, editor C.K. Erbes, is a quarterly. **"Subject matter and form are open, but we are looking for well-crafted poetry. We prefer poems of 30 lines or less, but will consider longer poems. We look for music, meaning and memorability."** They have published poetry by Gail White, Hayden Carruth, John Dickson, Dana Gioia, X.J. Kennedy, Rachel Hadas and John Haines. As a sample the editor selected these lines from "Space" by George Lober:

> So this is where we have landed,
> this gray quiet in every other
> afternoon where for one hour
> skin slips as easily into silence
> as it once slipped from grace,

ELF is 56 pgs., magazine-sized, professionally printed and saddle-stapled with semi-gloss cover. They use approximately 140 poems/year. Circulation 5,000. Subscription: $16. **Sample postpaid: $5.50. Submit 3 poems at a time. Hard copy with SASE required for submission. Send SASE for guidelines or obtain via e-mail or website.** "Accepted writers are asked to submit a bio of 25 words or less." Poems are circulated to an editorial board of professional poets and writers. Editor comments when possible. **Reports in 1-2 months. Always sends prepublication galleys. Pays 1 copy. Acquires first North American serial rights.** Staff reviews books of poetry. Publishers only may send books for review consideration. They also sponsor the Ruth Cable Memorial Prize for Poetry (annual deadline March 31). Send SASE for guidelines.

♣**ELLIPSE (V, IV-Translations, bilingual)**, C.P. 10, FLSH Université de Sherbrooke, Sherbrooke, Quebec J1K 2R1 Canada, phone (819)821-7000 ext. 3268, fax (819)821-7285, founded 1969, editors M. Grandmangin and C. Bouchara, **publishes Canadian poetry in translation.** That is, on facing pages appear either poems in English and a French translation or poems in French and an English translation. **Currently they are not accepting unsolicited mss.** They have published poetry by Erin Mouré and John Thompson. As a sample, the editors selected these lines from "St. Catherine Street East" by Raymond Souster:

> [. . .] Every face in every window
> of each building watching as we go
> down the steaming pavement, on, out of this jungle
> where the dead are never buried by the living, [. . .]

translated by Charly Bouchara:

> [. . .] Chaque visage derrière chaque fenêtre
> de chaque immeuble nous regarde presser le pas
> sur ce trottoir fumant et laisser derrière nous cette jungle
> où les vivants n'enterrent jamais leurs morts [. . .]

The magazine appears twice yearly in an elegant, flat-spined, 6×9 format, professionally printed, 120 pgs. Subscription: $12. **Sample postpaid: $6.**

ELLIPSIS MAGAZINE (II), Westminster College of Salt Lake City, 1840 S. 1300 East, Salt Lake City UT 84105, phone (801)488-4158, website http://www.wcslc.edu, founded 1967, appears twice a year using **"good literary poetry and fiction. Limited on space."** They have published work by Wyn Cooper, Penelope Austin, David Lee, Dixie Partridge and Ron Carlson. The editor describes it as 90 pgs., digest-sized, perfect-bound. Subscription: $18/year. **Sample postpaid: $10. Send ms with SASE and contributor notes. Does not read submissions from April 15 through August 31. Responds within 4 months. Pays $10/poem, plus 1 copy.**

EMERALD COAST REVIEW; WEST FLORIDA LITERARY FEDERATION; FRANCIS P. CASSIDY LITERARY CENTER; THE LEGEND; BACK DOOR POETS; WISE (WRITERS IN SERVICE TO EDUCATION) (IV-Regional), 400 S. Jefferson St., Pensacola Cultural Center, Pensacola FL 32501, phone (904)435-0942. The WFLF was founded in 1987 and began the Cassidy Literary Center, a regional writers' resource and special collection library. One of their programs is WISE, which provides over 50 area writers who volunteer their time to share their writing and writing experiences with local students. They sponsor a Student Writers Network for students in grades 9-12 and scholarships for area college student writers. WFLF also sponsors a PEN-WISE poetry contest for grades 1-12. The contest awards publication in a chapbook. They publish *The Legend*, a newsletter bringing literary arts news to 800-1,000 area writers and their supporters. Back Door Poets, one of their subgroups, conducts open microphone poetry readings the third Saturday of each month. Also, WFLF hosts a writing workshop the first Saturday of every month. Membership in WFLF ranges from $10/year for students to $500 and up for life-time memberships. The *Emerald Coast Review* is an **annual limited to Gulf Coast regional writers. Sample postpaid: $12. Send SASE for guidelines. Submit with required form (included in guidelines) January 1 to May 15. Pays copies.**

‡♣**EMPLOI PLUS; DGR PUBLICATION (V)**, 125 Principle N. St. #13, L'Annonciation, Quebec J0T 1T0 Canada, phone (819)275-3293, founded 1988 (DGR Publication), 1990 (*Emploi Plus*), publisher Daniel G. Reid. *Emploi Plus*, published irregularly, features poems and articles in French or English. **However, they do not accept unsolicited submissions.** They have recently published poetry by Robert Ott. As a sample the editor selected this excerpt from "A Delicious Summer" by D.G. Reid:

MY, MY, . . .
Reading, swimming, running, walking,
drinking cold beer on hot summer days,
dreaming, living, growing with trees
and flowers, loving a beautiful girl
having a breath as sweet as the honey of bees . . .

Emploi Plus is 12 pgs., 7 × 8½, photocopied, stapled, with b&w drawings and pictures, no ads. Press run is 500 for 400 subscribers; 100 distributed free to friends and relatives. **Sample postpaid: $10. Make checks payable to Daniel Reid.**

EMRYS JOURNAL (V), P.O. Box 8813, Greenville SC 29604, founded 1982, editor Jeanine Halva-Neubauer, is an annual. They have published poetry by Jan Bailey, Gil Allen and Cecile Goding. As a sample the editor selected the first stanza from "Motor without a Boat" by Mary Matthews:

An enormously wealthy oil company
had thousands of things to sell and so
they took their things to an enormously
barren lot where no wildflowers or
weeds would grow and where the prints
of a working man's shoes left no impression.

EJ is up to 120 pgs., 6 × 9, handsomely printed, flat-spined. Press run is 400 for 250 subscribers of which 10 are libraries. **Sample postpaid: $12.** "The 1997-98 *Emrys Journal* is a special theme issue, 'Women, Women, Women: Artists, Objects, Icon,' a joint publication with the Greenville County Museum of Art. Only solicited work will be included. Open submissions of a non-theme issue will resume in August 1998."

THE EMSHOCK LETTER (IV-Subscribers), Randall Flat Rd., P.O. Box 411, Troy ID 83871-0411, phone (208)835-4902, founded 1977, editor Steve Erickson, appears 3-12 times/year, occasionally with **poetry and other writings by subscribers. It is "a philosophical, metaphysical, sometimes poetic expression of ideas and events. It covers a wide range of subjects and represents a free-style form of expressive relation. It is a newsletter quite unlike any other."** The editor describes it as 5-7 pgs., magazine-sized, photocopied from typescript on colored paper. Subscription: $25. **"Poets (who are subscribers) should submit poetry which contains some meaning, preferably centering on a philosophic theme and preferably 50 lines or less. Any good poetry (submitted by a subscriber) will be considered for inclusion and will receive a personal reply by the editor, whether or not submitted material is published in *The Emshock Letter*. Editor will promptly discard any and all material submitted by nonsubscribers. Poets must become subscribers prior to submitting any material!"** Reviews books of poetry only if written by subscribers.

ENCODINGS: A FEMINIST LITERARY JOURNAL (IV-Women/feminism), P.O. Box 6793, Houston TX 77265, founded 1989, co-editors Jacsun Shah and Biobé Ngozi, with occasional guest editors. *Encodings* appears "randomly, once or twice a year," using **"high-quality poetry with a feminist perspective; especially interested in women's ways of knowing, women's invention and use of language."** As a sample the editors selected these lines from "Gertrude Stein Visits a Health Food Store" by Kathleen Bogan:

Granola. Sunny sunny little tongues. Sweet clasp together. Wrinkling.
Brown ready round bready all around. A sweet sweet sound.

Tofutti.   The moon she said please the moon, not knowing the moon on a plate
is a brick. No no whipping. Not knowing. A decline in cows, a reclining
cow. It is gliding. It is a smooth sliding. It is all the same it is a square
come air it is not a plate it is a swollen lightly.

Encodings is 40-60 pgs., 7 × 8½, photocopied from typescript and saddle-stapled with glossy card cover. Subscription: $10. **Sample postpaid: $5. Submit up to 5 poems at a time. Cover letter with brief bio preferred. Send SASE for guidelines. Reports in 2-3 months. Pays 2 copies.**

*ENITHARMON PRESS (V), 36 St. George's Ave., London N7 0HD England, phone (0171)607-7194, fax (0171)607-8694, founded 1969, poetry editor Stephen Stuart-Smith, is a publisher of fine editions of poetry and literary criticism in paperback and some hardback editions, about 15 volumes/year averaging 100 pages. They have published books of poetry by John Heath-Stubbs, Phoebe Hesketh, David Gascoyne, Jeremy Hooker, Frances Horovitz and Ruth Pitter. **"Substantial backlog of titles to produce, so no submissions possible before 1999."**

THE SUBJECT INDEX, located before the General Index, can help you select markets for your work. It lists those publishers whose poetry interests are specialized.

*ENVOI (II), 44 Rudyard Rd., Biddulph Moor, Stoke-on-Trent, Staffs ST8 7JN United Kingdom, founded 1957, editor Roger Elkin, appears 3 times/year using poetry, articles about poetry and poets, and reviews. "1) *Envoi* does not subscribe to any one particular stable, school or style of contemporary poetry writing and has catholic tastes; 2) To be selected, **poetry must be sincere in its emotional and intellectual content, strongly integrated in form and contemporary in its subject matter—while a poem may be set in classical times or depend heavily on mythic archetypes, its overall 'texture' must have contemporary relevance; 3) *Envoi* requires writing that is daring in its subject matter and challenging in its expressive techniques—in short, work that takes risks with the form, the language and the reader; 4) *Envoi* is, however, still interested in traditional verse structures (the villanelle, pantoum, sonnet) but these must subscribe to the points listed in 2);** and 5) *Envoi* is looking for writing that sustains its creative strengths over a body of poems, or sequence. These criteria are prescriptive, rather than proscriptive; gates rather than hurdles. The over-riding concern is the creation of access for writers and readers to as wide a variety of contemporary poetry as space will allow." *Envoi* is 176 pgs., digest-sized, professionally printed and perfect-bound with matte card cover. "The emphasis is on giving space to writers so the reader can begin to assess the cumulative strengths of any one author over a body of work. This means competition for space is very keen. I handle between 300 and 500 poems per week and can only feature the equivalent of 100 poems three times a year!" Press run is 1,000 including 20 library subscriptions. Single copy: £4 ($10); subscription: £15 ($30—"U.S. funds preferably in bills rather than checks because of the high cost of conversion rates"). **Sample: £3 ($8). Submit no more than 6 poems, or a long poem of up to 6 sides; each poem on a separate page, bearing name and address; an accompanying SAE with 3 IRCs for return. Reports in 1-2 months. Pays 2 copies.** Roger Elkin says "*Envoi* presents the work of any one poet by a group of poems, up to six. Space is given to long(er) poems and short sequences, or extracts from longer sequences. We have a First Publication Feature for writers who have not appeared in national publications previously, and each issue contains a 'reading' of a modern poem or an article on poetic style. The Review section has been expanded in length to feature more comprehensive articles. Each issue also features a competition with prizes totalling £200; prize-winning poems are published along with a full adjudicator's report. We also feature poems in collaboration, as well as translations."

EPICENTER (II), P.O. Box 367, Riverside CA 92502, e-mail pozo@aol.com, founded 1994, is a quarterly poetry and short story forum **open to all styles.** They have published poetry by Mike Cluff, Max Berkovitz, Stan Nemeth and Vicki Solheid. *Epicenter* is 24 pgs., digest-sized and saddle-stapled with semi-glossy paper cover and b&w graphics. They receive about 300 submissions a year, use approximately 15%. Press run is 400 for 250 shelf sales. Single copy: $3. **Sample postpaid: $3.50. Make checks payable to Rowena Silver. Previously published poems and simultaneous submissions OK. Seldom comments on rejections. Send SASE for guidelines. Pays 1 copy. Acquires one-time rights.** The editors add, "*Epicenter* is looking for ground-breaking poetry and short stories from new and established writers. No angst-ridden, sentimental or earthquake poetry."

EPOCH; BAXTER HATHAWAY PRIZE (III), 251 Goldwin Smith, Cornell University, Ithaca NY 14853, phone (607)255-3385, founded 1947, has a distinguished and long record of publishing **exceptionally fine poetry** and fiction. They have published work by such poets as Ashbery, Ammons, Eshleman, Wanda Coleman, Molly Peacock, Robert Vander Molen and Alvin Aubert. The magazine appears 3 times/year in a 6×9, professionally printed, flat-spined format with glossy color cover, 100 pgs., which goes to 1,000 subscribers. They use less than 1% of the many submissions they receive each year, have a 2- to 12-month backlog. Mostly lyric free verse, with emphasis on voice and varying content and length, appears here (and, occasionally, avant-garde or "open" styles)—some of it quite powerful. **Sample postpaid: $5. "We *don't read* unsolicited mss between April 15 and September 15." Reports in 2 months. Occasionally provides criticism on mss. Pays $5-10/page. Buys first serial rights.** The annual Baxter Hathaway prize of $1,000 is awarded for a long poem or, in alternate years, a novella. At this time, however, the Baxter Hathaway Prize has been temporarily suspended. Poetry published in *Epoch* has also been included in the 1992 and 1993 volumes of *The Best American Poetry*. The editor advises, "I think it's extremely important for poets to read other poets. I think it's also very important for poets to read the magazines that they want to publish in. Directories are not enough."

‡EQUILIBRIUM[10]; EAGLE PUBLISHING PRODUCTIONS (I, IV-Specialized), Box 162, Golden CO 80402, website http://ourworld.CompuServe.com/homepages/POBox162, founded 1982, publisher Gary S. Eagle. We publish everything and I mean everything **dealing with equilibrium: balance, opposites, pairs, equality, opposite and equal reactions, etc."** They are open to "all types, lengths and styles. Very lenient!" on themes given above. The following sample is from "The Supposition of Opposition" by Caral Davis:

> The sun rises, just to fall.
> It's all for one and one for all.
> It rains on the rich and on the poor,
> The rich get richer and the poor get poorer.
> Winter withers summer away, only to revive
> another day.

The quarterly is striking in appearance, photocopied on pocket-edition 4¼×8½ sheets of various colors, about 70 pgs., saddle-stapled with glossy b&w paper cover, using many photos, drawings and cartoons throughout. One page is devoted to "Poems," each with an illustration. Circulation 10,000. Single copy: $4. **Sample: $4**

"As an editor, I am most interested in the work of people when they feel free to experiment and express themselves in the medium and style they feel is most innovative for them," says Mindi Englart, editor of the biannual publication *Etcetera*. In fact, Englart commissioned the computer-drawn image on this issue's cover from illustrator/graphic designer Barbara Kagan because she enjoyed the work Kagan did for the local daily newspaper and was interested in what Kagan would draw if she had no outside constraints. "*Etcetera*'s main goal is to encourage creative thought, action and risk-taking, and also to provide a respectful and editorially-supportive element to the submission process." The Connecticut-based journal contains about 70 percent poetry, mostly free verse, and accepts work by writers and artists of all ages, backgrounds, and professional levels.

plus 5 (regular) stamps. Backlog 1-12 months. "We prefer to hold in files until needed!" Editor sometimes comments on rejections. Reports in 6 months. Pays $15 and up plus 1 copy. He says, "We prefer for poets to keep a photocopy and send us the original for our files. They may be handwritten if you wish for your poem printed as such. It is best for the poet (even youngsters) to include art, pictures, etc., too. Letter and queries arriving at our office will become the property of our company and material may and will be published 'as-is.' "

‡ETCETERA (II), P.O. Box 8543, New Haven CT 06531, e-mail iedit4you@aol.com, founded 1995, editor Mindi Englart, a biannual journal of "art, literature and ideas designed to encourage creative thought, action and risk-taking." **They want "avant-garde work, linguistics, word play and experimental poetry; humor, thought-provoking and deep work. No rhyming (in most cases) or traditional poetry."** They have recently published poetry by John M. Bennett, Albert Huffstickler, Michael Estabrook and Sheila E. Murphy. As a sample the editor selected these lines from "When America Starts Seeping" by David Todd:

> *When America starts seeping*
> *into my skin I quickly shake myself*
> *like a wet dog and run*
> *into another state of mind.*

Etcetera is 28 pgs., 5½ × 8½, photocopied and staple-bound with b&w art and photography. They receive about 250 poems a year, accept approximately 50. Press run is 400 for about 200 subscribers, about 50 shelf sales; about 150 distributed free "to those who wouldn't/couldn't get it otherwise." **Sample postpaid: $3. Submit 2-3 poems at a time. Previously published poems and simultaneous submissions OK. Cover letter preferred. "E-mail submissions accepted. Please include 30-35 word biography with all submissions. Send SASE with snail mail."** Time between acceptance and publication is 1-5 months. **Always comments on rejections if requested. Send SASE for guidelines or request via e-mail. Reports receipt of work in 2-4 weeks; final acceptance/rejection in March and September. Sometimes sends prepublication galleys. Pays in 1 copy plus a 1-year subscription.** Staff reviews chapbooks of poetry and other magazines. Poets may also send books for review consideration.

‡ETHEREAL GREEN (II), 5937 Shaw St. #8, Haslett MI 48840-8439, founded 1996, contact Sarah Hencsie, published quarterly, strives "to feed readers' unknown talent. Contains poetry, art and articles." **They want "the avant-garde, spiritual and the unknown. Poems should be less than 40 lines."** They do not want "children's, ethnic or edited poems." They have recently published poetry by Jaime Morrison. As a sample the editor selected these lines by Jaime Morrison:

> *Because it's raining . . . you're*
> *falling from the sky, from*
> *your soul being drained . . .*

Ms. Hencsie says *Ethereal Green* is 30-70 pgs., approximately 6 × 8, with cover art. They receive hundreds of poems a year, accept approximately 50%. Press run is 250 for about 70 subscribers, 60% shelf sales. Subscription:

$27. **Sample postpaid: $7. Make checks payable to Sarah C. Hencsie. Submit 3-7 printed or typed poems at a time. Previously published poems and simultaneous submissions OK. Cover letter preferred.** Time between acceptance and publication is 3-7 months. **Poems are circulated to an editorial board with "poems edited twice; once by publisher and again by select editors on board." Always comments on rejections. Send SASE for guidelines. Reports within 1 month. Sometimes sends prepublication galleys. Pays 2 copies. Acquires first North American serial or one-time rights.** Open to unsolicited reviews.

*EUROPEAN JUDAISM (III, IV-Religious, ethnic), Kent House, Rutland Gardens, London SW7 1BX England, founded 1966, poetry editor Ruth Fainlight, is a "twice-yearly magazine with emphasis on European Jewish theology/philosophy/literature/history, with **some poetry in every issue. It should preferably be short and have some relevance to matters of Jewish interest.**" They have published poetry by Linda Pastan, Elaine Feinstein, Daniel Weissbort and Dannie Abse. As a sample the editor selected these lines from a poem by Michael Heller:

> *I took silence into time, marking the absence*
> *of our late vocabularies in their conspirings,*
> *these new mythologies, as they fell from on high*
>
> *through our skies and through our roofs*
> *scouring the mind as cosmic rays leave*
> *traceries in the cool white lime of tunnels.*

It is a glossy, elegant, 6×9, flat-spined magazine, rarely art or graphics, 110 pgs. They have a press run of 950, about 50% of which goes to subscribers (few libraries). Subscription: $27. **Submit 3-4 poems at a time. SASE (or SAE with IRCs) required. "We cannot use American stamps. Also, I prefer unpublished poems, but poems from published books are acceptable." Cover letter required. Pays 1 copy.**

‡EVANGEL; LIGHT AND LIFE COMMUNICATIONS (III, IV-Religious), P.O. Box 535002, Indianapolis IN 46253-5002, founded 1897, editor J. Innes, is a weekly adult Sunday school paper. "Devotional in nature, it lifts up Christ as the source of salvation and hope. **The mission of *Evangel* is to increase the reader's understanding of the nature and character of God and the nature of a life lived for Christ. Material that fits this mission that isn't more than one page will be considered." No rhyming work.** *Evangel* is 8 pgs., 5½×8½ (2 8½×11 sheets folded), photocopied, unbound with photos and graphics used. They accept approximately 5% of poetry received. Press run is approximately 20,000 for 19,000 subscribers. Subscription: $1.85/quarter (13 weeks). **Submit 3 poems at a time. Simultaneous submissions OK. Cover letter preferred. Seldom comments on rejections. Send SASE for guidelines Reports in 4-6 weeks. Pays $10 plus 2 copies. Buys one-time rights.** The editor says, "Poetry is used primarily as filler. Send for sample and guidelines to better understand what and who the audience is."

♣EVENT (II, IV-Themes), Douglas College, P.O. Box 2503, New Westminster, British Columbia V3L 5B2 Canada, founded 1971, editor Calvin Wharton, appears 3 times/year and is "a literary magazine publishing **high-quality contemporary poetry**, short stories and reviews. **In poetry, we tend to appreciate the narrative and sometimes the confessional modes. In any case, we are eclectic and always open to content that invites involvement. We publish mostly Canadian writers."** They have recently published poetry by Tom Wayman, Patricia Young and Tom Bowling. *Event* is 140 pgs., 6×9, finely printed and flat-spined with glossy cover. Circulation is 1,000 for 700 subscribers of which 50 are libraries. **Sample postpaid: $8. Submit 5 poems at a time. No previously published poems. Brief cover letter with publication credits required. Include SASE or SAE and IRCs. "Tell us if you'd prefer your manuscript to be recycled rather than returned."** Time between acceptance and publication is within 1 year. **Comments on some rejections. Reports in 3-4 months. Pays honorarium. Buys first North American serial rights.** Sometimes they have special thematic issues, such as: work, feminism, peace and war, coming of age.

THE EVER DANCING MUSE; WHO WHO WHO PUBLISHING (II), P.O. Box 7751, East Rutherford NJ 07073-1624, founded 1993, editor John Chorazy, is a "semiannual collection of poetry and short prose, publishing fine work in a small press format." **The editor wants "thinking, feeling poetry; poems no longer than two typed pages, prose no longer than four typed pages. Does not use rhyming poetry. I like short, tight poems, from 1-20 lines, but will consider everything sent. Submit three to five poems that you care deeply about, and want me to care about as well as the readers."** They have recently published poetry by Mary Winters, Gina Grega and Mary DeBow. As a sample the editor selected these lines from "Biblical Lessons" by Laura Deromedi:

> *I am an enormous bundle*
> *Of appetites and aversions.*
> *They stuffed me in a corset*
> *To suck out my breath*
> *While filling my head with shame*
> *And visions of mother worship.*

The Ever Dancing Muse is 20 pgs., 5½×8½, saddle-stapled with light card cover. Press run is 150 for 50 subscribers. Subscription: **$8 for 3 issues, 1 back issue free. Sample postpaid: $3. Previously published poems and simultaneous submissions OK, "if stated as such, and author holds the rights to the work. Cover letters are interesting and appreciated but not required." Seldom comments on rejections. Reports in 2-8 weeks. Pays 2 copies. Acquires one-time rights.** The press has started a "broadside" series with the publication of Oliver Hydon's poem "Samsara," and will continue to consider poems for future broadsides. The editor reminds poets, "This magazine, and all small press publications, need the support of poets and poetry readers to continue. Read a sample issue!"

THE EVERGREEN CHRONICLES (IV-Gay/lesbian/bisexual), P.O. Box 8939, Minneapolis MN 55408, phone (612)823-6638, e-mail evgrnchron@aol.com, is "a triannual journal of arts and cultures dedicated to presenting the best of lesbian, gay, bisexual, and transgender literary and visual artists. **The artistry presented is not limited to gay or themes, but extends to life, in all its dimensions."** Subscription: $20. **Sample postpaid: $8.95. "Send four copies of your work, up to ten pgs. of poetry. Please include cover letter with short biographical paragraph describing yourself and your work. Deadlines: July 1 and January 1." Send SASE for guidelines and upcoming themes or request via e-mail. Pays 1 copy and honorarium. Acquires first rights.** Staff reviews books of poetry in 500 words, single format. Send books for review consideration.

EXCURSUS LITERARY ARTS JOURNAL (II), P.O. Box 1056, Knickerbocker Station, New York NY 10002, e-mail malchiodi-excursus@worldnet.att.net, founded 1994, publisher Giancarlo Malchiodi, is an annual "eclectic collection of quality work from both new and established poets. **All literary excursions are welcome ... from the idyllic to the rebellious, formal and traditional to free form and avant-garde, imagistic to concrete to narrative to 'language' to Beat, to everything in between and beyond." However, they do not want "religious poetry nor any romantic pablum."** As a sample the publisher selected these lines from "Face" by Tina Chang:

> *In America, I give them my face*
> *heedful of hair singed to thin wire*
> *my mouth but a box of broken teeth*
> *eyes ebb in cataract clouds of pastel blue*

Excursus is about 128 pgs., 8½ × 11, offset printed and perfect-bound, with glossy card stock cover and b&w art and photos. They receive upwards of 2,500 submissions a year, accept 5-10%. Press run is 1,000. **Sample postpaid: $10. Submit up to 3 poems at a time, "not to exceed 170 lines total," addressed "Attn: Poetry." Simultaneous submissions and previously published poems OK, "if notified of previous placement." Personalized cover letter preferred. Reads submissions September 1 through June 30 only. "Publisher initially screens all submissions and forwards quality work to Editorial Collective." Seldom comments on rejections. Send SASE for guidelines or request via e-mail. Reports within 5 months. Pays 1 copy. Acquires one-time rights.** They sponsor an annual contest. Entry fee: $5 for 5 poems, addressed "Attn: Contest." Deadline: June 30. The winner receives $200, 4 pages of dedicated space in the magazine, 5 copies, and an invitation to join the Editorial Collective. The publisher says "Don't be concerned with 'fads' in poetry, whether 'formal,' 'performance,' or whatever ... write from your instincts. Assimilate what you read and enjoy, but don't copy."

EXIT 13 (IV-Specialized: geography/travel), % Tom Plante, 22 Oakwood Ct., Fanwood NJ 07023-1162, phone (908)889-5298, founded 1987, editor Tom Plante, is a "contemporary poetry annual" using **poetry that is "short, to the point, with a sense of geography."** They have recently published poetry by William Borden, L.L. Ollivier, Maggie McKirgan, Mary E. Grow and Emilie Luria. As a sample the editor selected these lines by Askold Skalsky:

> *We saw egrets by the exit ramps,*
> *tigers lazing on small islands*
> *guarded by pines and the purple waters*
> *of amusement parks. The brave*
> *innuendos of love went unanswered.*

Exit 13, #8, was 64 pgs. Press run is 300. **Sample postpaid: $6. They accept simultaneous submissions and previously published poems. Send SASE for guidelines. Reports in 4 months. Pays 1 copy. Acquires one-time and possible anthology rights.** Staff reviews books of poetry and magazines in a "Publications Received" column, using 25-30 words/listing. Send books for review consideration. The editor advises, "Write about what you know. Study geography. *Exit 13* looks for adventure. Every state and region is welcome. Send a snapshot of an 'Exit 13' road sign and receive a free copy of the issue in which it appears."

EXPEDITION PRESS (III, IV-Love, religious), 105 E. Walnut St., #2306, Kalamazoo MI 49007-5253, phone (616)345-6067, publisher Bruce W. White, **publishes chapbooks of love poems and religious poems. "I dislike violence."** He likes to use **"experimental, fresh new approaches, interesting spatial relationships, as well as quality artwork. I dislike political diatribes."** He has recently published poetry by J. Kline Hobbs, Robin Reish, Todd Zimmerman, Margaret Tyler, Martin Cohen and C. VanAllsburg. As a sample the publisher selected these lines from "Central Park" by Margaret Tyler:

> *. . . . By the zoo, maids push patriarchs in wheelchairs.*
> *They nod like the shadows, dapple grey and dancing.*

The monkey strikes the hour on the Delacourte clock.
Brass animals glide in stately circles and then stop.

Submit typed ms of 20-30 pgs. and cover letter with brief bio. No previously published poems or simultane-ous submissions. Ms on cassette OK. Reports in 1 month. Sometimes sends prepublication galleys. Pays 100 copies. Bruce White provides "much" criticism on rejected mss.

EXPLORATIONS (II), UAS, 11120 Glacier Highway, Juneau AK 99801-8761, phone (907)465-6418, fax (907)465-6406, e-mail jnamp@acadl.alaska.edu, founded 1980, editor Professor Art Petersen, is the annual liter-ary magazine of the University of Alaska, Southeast. **"The editors respond favorably to 'language really spoken by men' and women. Standard form and innovation are encouraged as well as appropriate and fresh aspects of imagery (allusion, metaphor, simile, symbol . . .)."** *Explorations* is digest-sized, nicely printed and saddle-stapled, with front and back cover illustration in one color. The editors tend to go for smaller-length poems (with small line breaks for tension) and often print two on a page—mostly lyric free verse with a focus on voice. **Sample postpaid: $4.** In 1997, they again offered first prizes of $500 for poetry and prose and published the best of the submissions received. Each year a prominent poet or writer serves as judge (1997: John Haines). **An entry/reading fee is required: $5 for 1 or 2 poems (60 lines/poem maximum), $2/poem for 3-5 poems (5 maximum, no more than 60 lines each); those paying reader/contest entry fees receive a copy of the publication. Checks should be made payable to "UAS Explorations." Mss must be typed with name, address, and 3- or 4-line biography on the back of each first page. Simultaneous submissions OK. Submit January through March. Mss are not returned. Send SASE for guidelines. Submissions are reported on in May or June, publication is annual, out in May or June. Pays 2 copies. Acquires one-time rights.**

EXPLORER MAGAZINE; FLORY LITERARY FOUNDATION (I, IV-Inspirational, nature, love), P.O. Box 210, Notre Dame IN 46556-0210, phone (219)277-3465, founded 1960, editor/publisher Raymond Flory, is a semiannual magazine that contains **short inspirational, nature and love poetry** as well as prose. The editor wants **"poetry of all styles and types; should have an inspirational slant but not necessary. Short poems preferred—up to 20 lines—the shorter the better. Good 'family' type poetry always needed. Seasonal material also welcome. No real long poetry or long lines; no sexually explicit poetry or porno."** He has published poetry by Joan Olivieri, Terry Peterson, L.J. Cardin, Rita Collura and Philip Huss. As a sample the editor selected "Christmas Eve" by Rosemary Lauturner:

Christmas eve
Snowflakes falling,
Late night
Cosmic peacefulness,
As the moon rises.

Explorer is 32-48 pgs., digest-sized, photocopied from typed copy in a variety of fonts (some of it dot-matrix) and saddle-stapled with card cover. Circulation is 250-400. Subscription: $6/year. **Sample available for $3, guidelines for SASE. Subscribers vote for the poems or stories they like best and prizes are awarded; 4 prizes each issue: $25, $20, $15 and $10; first-prize winner in each issue receives a plaque along with the cash prize. In addition to the regular cash prizes, there is also an editor's choice award, the Joseph Flory Memorial Award, named after the editor's late father. Award is $10 and a plaque.** The editor also awards the Angel Light Award, given to the author whose prose or poetry most emphasizes the "spiritual." Award is $10 and a plaque. **Writers should submit 3-4 poems, typed, camera-ready. Material must be previously unpublished; simultaneous submissions OK. Submit seasonal material 8 months to 1 year in advance. Reports in 1-2 weeks. Time between acceptance and publication is 1-2 years. Pays 1 copy only to those appearing in the magazine for the first time.** The editor says, "Over 90% of the poets submitting poetry to *Explorer* have not seen a copy of the magazine. Order a copy first—then submit. This will save poets stamps, frustration, etc. This should hold true for whatever market a writer is aiming for!"

EXPRESSIONS (I, IV-Health concerns), P.O. Box 16294, St. Paul MN 55116-0294, phone (612)552-1209, fax (612)451-1209 "call first," e-mail expmag@aol.com, founded 1993, editor Sefra Kobrin Pitzele, is a non-profit semiannual, subtitled "Literature and Art by People with Disabilities and Ongoing Health Problems," designed "to provide a place for talented people to be published." **They are open to any topic provided entry is written by people with disabilities and/or ongoing health problems.**
● Before sending e-mail submissions, contact editor regarding reading fee.
They have published poetry by Mark Franz, Stephanie R. Bird and Susan Dion. As a sample the editor selected these lines from "Your Picture, Which Cannot Fade" by Daniel J. McCaffrey:

While I was going blind,
I made it a point to check you out.
I would take every opportunity
I could to see you naked.
In the shower or slowly getting dressed,
Openly, checking you out.
This picture of you,
in all your beauty,

is mine forever now.

Expressions is 80 pgs., 5½ × 8½, perfect-bound with 60 lb. glossy card cover. They publish about 25% of the poetry received. Press run is 700 for 120 subscribers. Subscription: $12 US, $17 foreign and institutions. **Sample postpaid: $6. Submit no more than 5 poems at a time with $5 reading fee. Previously published poems and simultaneous submissions OK. Cover letter with 4- to 5-line bio and statement of ownership required. "No submissions by fax, although we are ready to try e-mail submissions." Do not submit mss from December 15 to January 15. "Six others read each submission and grade it—independently—from 1 to 5. Most 5's are published." Often comments on rejections. Send SASE for guidelines and upcoming themes. Reports in 4-6 months. Pays 2 copies. Acquires one-time rights.** They sponsor an annual poetry contest. Deadline: March 15. Write for details. "At the end of each issue, we print book reviews appropriate to our audience. We only review informational books on disability or illness." However, they are open to unsolicited reviews of such materials.

EXQUISITE CORPSE (II), P.O. Box 25051, Baton Rouge LA 70894, e-mail corpse@linknet.net, website http://www.corpse.books.com, founded 1983, editor Andrei Codrescu (whom you can often hear in commentary segments of "All Things Considered," The National Public Radio news program). This curious and delightful monthly ($30/year), when you unfold it, is 6" wide and 16" long, 48 pgs., saddle-stapled, professionally printed in 2 columns on quality stock. The flavor of Codrescu's comments (and some clues about your prospects in submitting here) may be judged by this note: "A while ago, alarmed by the number of poems aimed at the office—a number only the currency inflation and Big Macs can hold candles to—we issued an edict against them. Still they came, and some even came live. They came in the mail and under the door. We have no poetry insurance. If we are found one day smothered under photocopy paper, who will pay for the burial? The *Corpse* wants a jazz funeral. Rejections make poets happy. Having, in many cases, made their poems out of original, primal, momentary rejections, the rejection of these rejections affirms the beings forced to such deviousness." He has published poetry by Carol Bergé, Charles Plymell, Lawrence Ferlinghetti, Alice Notley and many others. **You'll find all styles and forms here, even short light verse. Most examples are freestyle, leaning toward expressionism (effective use of symbol), and accessible, too. Translations are also welcome. Pays 10 copies plus 1 year subscription. You take your chances inserting work into this wit machine. Their policy is: ". . . we are abolishing the SASE-based privacy system . . . Your submissions will be answered directly in the pages of our publication. Look for your name and for our response to your work in the next *Corpse*. We will continue returning your submissions by SASE if you wish, but as to what we think of your *écriture*, please check 'Body Bag,' our editorial column."** Here's an example: "We were excited by 'The Wind Got Excited' until the puppy-hero got too excited and leapt off the 13th floor. That was cruel . . ." Comments you want, comments you get! Poetry published in this magazine has been included in the 1992 and 1997 volumes of *The Best American Poetry*.

FABER AND FABER, INC. (V), 53 Shore Rd., Winchester MA 01890, phone (617)721-1427, editor-in-chief Dan Weaver, senior editor Valerie Cimino, has a distinguished list of poetry publications but is **not accepting mss.**

FARMER'S MARKET; MIDWEST FARMER'S MARKET, INC. (II), Elgin Community College, 1700 Spartan Dr., Elgin IL 60123-7193, fax (847)888-7995, founded 1981, poetry editor Joanne Lowery, is a biannual seeking **high quality poems: "Do not be fooled by our name—we have wide tastes, though are not interested in light verse, rhyme, street language or overtly political/trendy subject matter. Admire distinctive poetic voice, unique imagery, gutsy juxtaposition. Prefer surreal poems over realistic accounts of childhood experiences. Short poems stand a better chance with us, though occasionally we publish longer ones."** They have recently published poetry by Robert Cooperman, Kenneth Pobo, Kim Bridgford, Bob Hicok, Philip Dacey, Kristy Nielsen, Patrick Moran and Peter Huggins. As a sample the editor selected these lines from "Backyard: Letter to the Dead" by Rane Arroyo:

> *I'm easily distracted by green peas*
> *in their canoes against the dying light.*

FM is 80-150 pgs., digest-sized, perfect-bound with card cover, handsomely printed with graphics and photos. The poems are almost always accessible . . . clear, crafted lyric free verse. All in all, this is an enjoyable read. They receive about 1,000 submissions/year, of which they use 40-50, have a 6-month backlog. Circulation 850 for 250 subscribers, of which 25 are libraries. **Sample: $4.50 plus $1 p&h. Submit 4-6 poems at a time, typed. "Cover letters do more harm than good; we dislike bragging and flattery. Your work is more important**

THE GEOGRAPHICAL INDEX, located before the Subject Index, can help you discover the publishers in your region. Publishers often favor poets (and work) from their own areas.

than your credentials. New poets are welcome to submit." Would rather not have simultaneous submissions. Reads submissions September through November and March through May. Often comments on rejections. Reports in 1-2 months. Pays 2 copies plus 1-year subscription. Acquires one-time rights. This publication has received numerous Illinois Arts Council Literary Awards and poetry published here has also been included in *The Best American Poetry 1996*.

FARRAR, STRAUS & GIROUX/BOOKS FOR YOUNG READERS (II, IV-Children), 19 Union Square W., New York NY 10003, phone (212)741-6900, founded 1946, contact Editorial Dept./Books for Young Readers. They publish one book of children's poetry "every once in awhile," in both hardcover and paperback editions. **They are open to book-length submissions of children's poetry only.** They have published collections of poetry by Valerie Worth and Deborah Chandra. **Query first with sample poems and cover letter with brief bio and publication credits. Poems previously published in magazines and simultaneous submissions OK. Seldom comments on rejections. Send SASE for reply. Replies to queries in 1-2 months, to mss in 1-4 months. "We pay an advance against royalties; the amount depends on whether or not the poems are illustrated, etc." Also pays 10 copies.**

FAT TUESDAY (II), 560 Manada Gap Rd., Grantville PA 17028, phone (717)469-7159, founded 1981, editor-in-chief F.M. Cotolo, other editors Kristen von Oehrke, B. Lyle Tabor, Thom Savion and Lionel Stevroid, is an annual which calls itself "**a Mardi Gras of literary and visual treats featuring many voices, singing, shouting, sighing and shining, expressing the relevant to irreverent**. On Fat Tuesday (the Tuesday before Ash Wednesday, when Lent begins) the editors hold The Fat Tuesday Symposium. In over ten years no one has shown up." **They want "prose poems, poems of irreverence, gems from the gut. Usually shorter, hit-the-mark, personal stuff inseparable from the voice of the artist. Form doesn't matter, but no rhyming greeting-card stuff. Also particularly interested in hard-hitting 'autofiction.'** " They have published poetry by Mark Cramer, Mary Lee Gowland, Chuck Taylor, Patrick Kelly, Charles Bukowski, Gerald Locklin and Kilgore Rimpau. The digest-sized magazine is typeset (large type, heavy paper), 36-60 pgs., saddle-stapled, card covers, (sometimes magazine-sized, unbound) with cartoons, art and ads. Circulation 200 with 20-25 pgs. of poetry in each issue. They receive hundreds of submissions each year, use 3-5%, have a 3- to 5-month backlog. **Sample postpaid: $5. Submit 4 poems at a time. "Handwritten OK; we'll read anything." No previously published poems or simultaneous submissions. "Cover letters are fine, the more amusing the better." Reads submissions June through December only. Reports in 1-2 weeks. Pays 1 copy. Rights revert to author after publication.** The editors say, "Our tip for authors is simply to be themselves. Poets should use their own voice to be heard. Publishing poetry is as lonely as writing it. We have no idea about current trends, and care less. We encourage all to buy a sample issue to see what they have which best fits our style and format, and also to help support the continuation of our publication. We rely on no other means but sales to subsidize our magazine, and writers should be sensitive to this hard fact which burdens many small presses."

FAULTLINE (II), P.O. Box 599-4960, Irvine CA 92716-4960, fax (714)824-2916, e-mail faultline@uci.edu, founded 1991, is an annual journal of art and literature occasionally edited by guest editors and published at the University of California, Irvine. **"We are looking for top, top quality poetry from poets who are obviously acquainted with contemporary poetry."** They have published poetry by Thomas Lux, Heather McHugh and Sabina Grogan. As a sample we selected the opening lines of "Gravediggers" by Linda Thomas:

> At first I am sure
> the sea once covered our backyard.
> With each spadeful of dirt
> come cones and sea slippers,
> the dry dishes of scallops and jackknives,
> and I am sure
> this neglected plot of hard clay
> once served as the ocean floor.

Faultline is approximately 120 pgs., 6×9, professionally printed on 60 lb. paper, perfect-bound with 80 lb. cover stock and featuring color and b&w art and photos. They receive about 1,500 poems a year, accept approximately 5%. Press run is 500 for 50 subscribers, 175 shelf sales. Single copy: $10. **Sample postpaid: $5. Submit up to 5 poems at a time. Simultaneous submissions OK. Cover letter preferred. Do not include name and address on ms to assist anonymous judging. Reads submissions October 1 to March 30 only. Poems are selected by a board of up to 6 readers. Seldom comments on rejections. Send SASE for guidelines. Reports in 3 months. Always sends prepublication galleys. Pays 2 copies. Buys first or one-time rights.** Poetry published by this journal has also been selected for inclusion in a *Pushcart Prize* anthology.

FAUQUIER POETRY JOURNAL (I, II), P.O. Box 68, Bealeton VA 22712-0068, founded 1994, managing editor D. Clement, is a quarterly that contains poetry and poetry comment. **They want "fresh, creative, well-crafted poetry, any style. Due to format, longer poems over 40 lines are not often used. Do not want overly sentimental or religious themes, overdone subjects, or overly obscure work."** They have recently published poetry by Sean Brendan-Brown, B.R. Culbertson, Marty Walsh, Nancy Ryan and Robert Deluty. As a sample the editor selected these lines from "JENN" by Peter Layton:

> *we sort of talk*
> *exchange these*
> *cryptic-vague-poem-responses*
> *with holes the*
> *air passes between,*
> *wind*

FPJ is 40-50 pgs., digest-sized, laser-printed on plain white paper and saddle-stapled with bright colored paper cover. Press run is more than 100 for 50 subscribers. Subscription: $20. **Sample postpaid: $5. The editor encourages subscriptions by requiring a reading fee for nonsubscribers ($5 for 1-5 poems); no reading fee for subscribers. Submit poetry with name and address in the upper left corner of each page and include SASE. Simultaneous submissions OK. Rarely accepts previously published poems. Often comments on rejections. Send SASE for guidelines. Reports in 2-6 weeks. Offers Editor's Choice Awards of $5-25 for the best entries in each issue. Pays 1 copy to remainder of published poets. Acquires one-time rights.** They sponsor quarterly poetry contests, explained in the journal. Entry fee: $5. Prizes range from $15-75, and winners are published in the following issue. In addition to poetry, *FPJ* occasionally prints articles by guest columnists. Articles should deal with some aspect of poetry, the writing experience, reactions to particular poems or poets, the mechanics (how to), etc. No reading fee, no guidelines other than word limit (around 1,000 words). "Pretty much anything goes as long as it's interesting and well-written." Pays 2¢/word. The editor says, "Let us see a variety in your submission; what one editor likes, another won't. Send a range of work that illustrates the breadth and depth of your talent; this helps us decide if there's something we like. We encourage submissions from anyone who is writing mature, well-crafted poetry."

‡*FEATHER BOOKS; THE POETRY CHURCH MAGAZINE; CHRISTIAN HYMNS & SONGS (I, IV-Religious)**, Fairview, Old Coppice, Lyth Bank, Shrewsbury, Shropshire SY3 0BW United Kingdom, phone/fax (01763)872177, Feather Books founded 1982, *Poetry Church Magazine* founded 1996, contact Rev. John Waddington-Feather. *The Poetry Church Magazine* appears quarterly and contains Christian poetry and prayers. **They want "Christian or good religious poetry—usually around 20 lines, but will accept longer." They do not want "unreadable blasphemy."** They have recently published poetry by M.A.B. Jones, Joan Smith, Bruce James and Idris Caffrey. *TPCM* is 20 pgs., digest-sized, photocopied, saddle-stapled with laminated cover and b&w cover art. They receive about 1,000 poems a year, accept approximately 500. Press run is 1,000 for 400 subscribers of which 10 are libraries. Single copy free; subscription: suggested donation of £5 ($10 US). **Sample postpaid: $5. Make checks payable to Feather Books. Submit 2 typed poems at a time. Previously published poems and simultaneous submissions OK. Cover letter preferred with information about the poet.** Time between acceptance and publication is 4 months. **"The editor does a preliminary reading; then seeks the advice of colleagues about uncertain poems." Always comments on rejections. Send SASE (or SAE and IRC) for guidelines. Reports within a week. Pays 1 copy. Poets retain copyright.** Feather Books publishes the Feather Books Poetry Series, books of Christian poetry and prayers. Books are usually photocopied and saddle-stapled with laminated covers. **"Poets' works are selected for publication in collections of around 20 poems in our Feather Books Poetry Series. We do not insist, but most poets pay for small run-offs of their work, e.g., around 50-100 copies for which we charge $200 per fifty. If they can't afford it, but are good poets, we stand the cost. We expect poets to read our *Poetry Church Magazine* to get some idea of our standards." Pays 5% royalty "where we sell copies of poetry" or 1 author's copy (out of a press run of 50) "if we pay cost."** Feather Books also publishes *Christian Hymns & Songs*, a quarterly supplement by Grundy and Feather. The editor says, "We find it better for poets to master rhyme and rhythm before trying free verse. Many poets seem to think that if they write 'down' a page they're writing poetry, when all they're doing is writing prose in a different format."

FEELINGS: AMERICA'S BEAUTIFUL POETRY MAGAZINE; ANDERIE POETRY PRESS (II), P.O. Box 85, Easton PA 18044-0085, phone (610)559-9287, fax (610)559-3927, e-mail feelings@itw.com, website http://www.silo.com/FEELINGS, founded 1989, editor Carole J. Heffley, submission editor Michael Steffen, a quarterly magazine, uses **"high-quality poetry in both free verse and form, rhyme and non-rhyme, no more than 30 lines." Any theme that is well written, no pornography.** They have recently published poetry by Elaine Preston, Albert Huffstickler and Walter Inman. As a sample the editor selected the opening lines from "Song For A Survivor" by Judith E. Miles:

> *She was a shooting star*
> *which sparked in the heavens*
> *before falling to the sea:*
> *she was a flash of lightning*
> *which split the summer stormclouds*

Feelings is magazine-sized, professionally printed on lightweight paper, saddle-stapled with heavy glossy paper cover, using "photography appropriate to the season or subject." Subscription: $24. **Sample postpaid: $6.50. Cover letter with background, credits ("something about the writer") required. "SASE must accompany all correspondence." Send SASE for guidelines. Reports in 6 weeks. Acquires first rights.** Also runs several contests throughout the year with prizes ranging from $20-500. **"We publish chapbooks; info/price list upon request with SASE."** Mss on "how-to" write/publish poetry welcome. Payment for articles varies.

FELLOWSHIP IN PRAYER (IV-Religious), 291 Witherspoon St., Princeton NJ 08542, phone (609)924-6863, fax (609)924-6910, founded 1950, contact Editor, is an interfaith bimonthly **"concerned with prayer, meditation and spiritual life" using short poetry "with deep religious (or spiritual) feeling."** It is 48 pgs., digest-sized, professionally printed, saddle-stapled with glossy card cover. They accept about 2% of submissions received. Press run is 10,000. Subscription: $16. **Sample free. Submit 5 poems at a time, double-spaced. Simultaneous submissions and "sometimes" previously published poems OK. Cover letter preferred. Reports in 1 month. Pays 5 copies.** Staff reviews books of poetry in 75 words, single format.

FEMINIST STUDIES (IV-Women/feminism), % Dept. of Women's Studies, University of Maryland, College Park MD 20742, e-mail femstud@umail.umd.edu, website http://www.inform.umd.edu/femstud, founded 1969, poetry editor Alicia Ostriker, **"welcomes a variety of work that focuses on women's experience, on gender as a category of analysis, and that furthers feminist theory and consciousness."** They have published poetry by Janice Mirikitani, Paula Gunn Allen, Cherrie Moraga, Audre Lorde, Judith Small, Valerie Fox and Diane Glancy. The elegantly printed, flat-spined, 250-page paperback appears 3 times a year in an edition of 8,000, goes to 7,000 subscribers, of which 1,500 are libraries. There are 4-10 pgs. of poetry in each issue. **Sample postpaid: $12. No simultaneous submissions; will only consider previously published poems under special circumstances. Manuscripts are reviewed twice a year, in May and December. Deadlines are May 1 and December 1. Authors will receive notice of the board's decision by June 30 and January 30. Always sends prepublication galleys. No pay.** Commissions reviews of books of poetry. Poets may send books to Claire G. Moses for review consideration.

‡*FENICE BROADSHEETS; NEW BROOM PRIVATE PRESS (II), 78 Cambridge St., Leicester LE 3 0JP England, founded 1968, poetry editor Cynthia A. Savage (assumed the press after Toni Savage's death in 1994), **publishes chapbooks**, pamphlets and broadsheets on a small Adana Horizontal Hand Press. The editor wants poetry which is **"descriptive—not too introvert or modern, not erotica or concrete, up to 12 lines (for the sheets).** Also some personal background of the poet." Recently published poets include Jack Woolgar, Paul Humphrey and Alix Weisz. As a sample the editor selected this poem, "Dartmoor Pony," by Edward Murch (Fenice Broadsheet No. 34):

> The November sun, spring-warm, is very low
> And casts around this pony, in a golden glow,
> An aureole of mystic morning light,
> That makes him seem like Pegasus just landed from the night.

The broadsheets are letterpress printed on tinted paper (about 5×8) with graphics. "Some sheets are hand coloured." **Submit no more than 3 poems with cover letter giving "personal background and feelings." Poet receives 20-30 copies.** Broadsheets are given away in streets, hospitals and leisure groups. This is a hobby and strictly part-time, production is therefore erratic." *Fenice Broadsheets* may be obtained by sending adequate postage (IRCs), approximately $1.50 (cash—no cheques) for 5 or more sheets.

♣THE FIDDLEHEAD (I, II, IV-Regional, students), Campus House, University of New Brunswick, P.O. Box 4400, Fredericton, New Brunswick E3B 5A3 Canada, founded 1945, poetry editors Robert Gibbs, Robert Hawkes and Don MacKay. From its beginning in 1945 as a local little magazine devoted mainly to student writers, **the magazine retains an interest in poets of the Atlantic region and in young poets** but prints poetry from everywhere. It is **open to excellent work of every kind, looking always for vitality, freshness and surprise.** They have recently published poetry by Edmond Chow and Walter McDonald. As a sample, the editors selected these lines by Tara J. Hoag:

> it is written in blood and credit card statements: I am
> a grown women. There are days now
> when I refuse to speak with my father. he calls and
> the days go by. I cultivate my anger.
> I take my mother to lunch. Her ribs
> spread sad and wide as angel wings.

The Fiddlehead is a handsomely printed, 6×9, flat-spined paperback (120 pgs.) with b&w graphics, colored cover, paintings by New Brunswick artists. They use less than 10% of submissions. Circulation is 1,000. Subscription: $20/year plus $6 postage (US). **Sample: $7 (US). Submit 3-10 poems at a time. No simultaneous submissions. For reply or return of ms, send SAE with Canadian stamps, IRCs or cash. Reporting time is 2-6 months, backlog 6-18 months. Pay is $10-12/printed page.** Reviews books of poetry by Canadian authors only.

FIELD; FIELD TRANSLATION SERIES; FIELD POETRY PRIZE; CONTEMPORARY AMERICAN POETRY SERIES; O.C. PRESS (II, IV-Translations), Rice Hall, Oberlin College, Oberlin OH 44074, phone (216)775-8408, fax (216)775-8124, founded 1969, editors Stuart Friebert, David Young, Alberta Turner and David Walker, is a literary journal appearing twice a year with "emphasis on poetry, translations and essays by poets." **They want the "best possible" poetry.** They have published poetry by Thylias Moss, Yusef Komunyakaa, Charles Simic and Sharon Olds. The handsomely printed, digest-sized journal is flat-spined, has 100 pgs., rag stock with glossy card color cover. Although most poems fall under the lyrical free verse category, you'll find narratives and formal work here on occasion, much of it sensual, visually appealing and resonant. Circulation

2,500, with 800 library subscriptions. Subscription: $14/year, $24/2 years. **Sample postpaid: $7. Reports in 2 weeks, has a 3- to 6-month backlog. Always sends prepublication galleys. Pays $20-30/page plus 2 copies.** They publish books of translations in the Field Translation Series, averaging 150 pgs., flat-spined and hardcover editions. **Query regarding translations. Pays 7½-10% royalties with some advance and 10 author's copies.** They also have a Contemporary American Poetry Series. This series is by invitation only. Write for catalog to buy samples. Sponsors the *Field* Poetry Prize, the winning ms will be published in their poetry series; submit mss of 50-80 pgs. with a $22 reading fee in December only. Contest guidelines available for SASE. Work published in *Field* has also been included in the 1992, 1993, 1994 and 1995 volumes of *The Best American Poetry*. The editors say they would like to see more poetry from "minority" poets "of any and all cultures."

5TH GEAR; TWELVE CONTEST (V), 724 Humphries Lane, Chesapeake VA 23322-3414, founded 1994, first issue September 1995, editor/publisher Andy Fogle. **Currently not accepting unsolicited manuscripts.** "*5th Gear* comes out several times a year in a variety of formats: one-page folded or unfolded leaflets, 12-page homemade side-stapled booklets, and someday I hope to publish a large perfect-bound beautiful anthology of poets previously appearing in *5th Gear*. Occasional reviews of books and records, little pieces of artwork or serial fiction may be included. It's distributed for free at record stores, bookstores and through the mail. **As for poetry, I'll consider absolutely anything and have fairly wide tastes, but I also have my biases. I am leaning more and more toward surrealism, experimental and prose poems.**" He has recently published poetry by Mary Winters, Mark Wallace, Andy Fenwick, Dennis Saleh and Graham Foust. They receive about 2,000 poems a year, accept 100. Press run is 112 for 20 subscribers. Subscription (at least 12 leaflets, large annual issue and several supplements): $10. **Make checks payable to Paul A. Fogle. Send up to 5 pages of poems at a time. No previously published poems; simultaneous submissions OK.** Time between acceptance and publication can run up to a year. **Reports in 4 months. Pays 1-12 copies depending on format. Acquires first rights and requests mention "if poem later appears somewhere else."** Offers critique service for 25¢/line; include SASE; work will be returned within 1 month. Sponsors annual Twelve Contest, awarding $100 and publication in *5th Gear*. Sponsors annual chapbook contest awarding $100, publication of chapbook and 50 copies. **Not currently accepting entries for either contest.** When accepting submissions, the editor says, "Guidelines are available with a SASE, but I'd rather you just send the poetry. I'd like submissions to be typed, but will consider handwritten poems. I'd rather not see any staples, paper clips or separately folded poems but those are just tics. I comment on rejections whenever possible and like to think I can be helpful at times, but I can also be blunt, so be prepared either way. The best advice I can give is Jack Kerouac's: 'Be in love with your life.' "

✤**FILLING STATION (II)**, P.O. Box 22135, Bankers Hall, Calgary, Alberta T2P 4J5 Canada, phone/fax (403)252-8185, e-mail hefitzge@acs.ucalgary.ca, website http://www.cadvision.com/Home.Pages/accounts/tmuir, founded 1993, appears 3 times/year (February, June and October). *Filling Station* is a magazine of contemporary writing featuring poetry, fiction, interviews, reviews and other literary news. **"We are looking for all forms of contemporary writing. No specific objections to any style."** They have recently published poetry by Camilla Pickard, Doug Beardsley, Bert Almon and Peter Bakowski. As a sample the editor selected these lines from "First Word" by Richard Harrison:

> *"foreword the word we wait for is always the first, origin issue, book of hope, opening element in the*
> *list off what she says and what we say, bX in overlapping circles of logic, treasure map, gold in*
> *the chest, breather out, the mystery of names in her mouth . . ."*

FS is 48 pgs., 8½ × 11, saddle-stapled with card cover and includes photos, artwork and ads. They receive about 100 submissions for each issue, accept approximately 10%. Press run is 500 for 100 subscribers, 250 shelf sales. Subscription: $15/1 year, $25/2 years. **Sample postpaid: $6. Submit typed poems with name and address on each page. No previously published poems; simultaneous submissions OK. Fax and e-mail submissions OK (include mailing address). Cover letter required. Deadlines are November 15, March 15 and July 15. Seldom comments on rejections. Send SASE (or SAE with IRC) for guidelines. Reports in 3 months. Pays 1 year subscription. Acquires first North American and second reprint rights.** Reviews books of poetry in both single and multi-book format. Open to unsolicited reviews. Poets may also send books for review consideration. Here's what the collective has to say about *Filling Station* and the philosophy behind this publication: "You stop between these 'fixed' points on the map to get an injection of something new, something fresh that's going to get you from point to point. . . . We want to be a kind of connection between polarities: a link. We'll publish any poem or story that offers a challenge: to the mind, to the page, to writers and readers."

FINE MADNESS (II), P.O. Box 31138, Seattle WA 98103-1138, website http://www.scn.org/arts/finemadness, founded 1982, editors Sean Bentley, C. Deavel, John Malek and J.W. Marshall. *Fine Madness* publishes 3 issues every 2 years (a new issue roughly every 8 months). **They want "contemporary poetry of any form and subject. We look for highest quality of thought, language and imagery. We look for the mark of the individual: unique ideas and presentation; careful, humorous, sympathetic. No careless poetry, greeting card poetry, poetry that 10,000 other people could have written."** They have published poetry by Pattiann Rogers, Albert Goldbarth and Caroline Knox. As a sample we selected these lines from "Sugar" by Alan Ridenour:

> *The piñata explodes like a beehive.*
> *Amid the sound of clubs,*

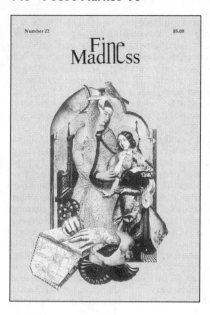

Appearing approximately every eight months, *Fine Madness* looks for unique, high-quality ideas in the work accepted for publication whether that be poetry or art. "What appealed to us about Carlo Levy's collage [on this issue's cover] is what often appeals to us about the poems we choose to print: it is unusual, textured, iconoclastically reverential, somewhat disconcerting but in no way derogatory," says co-editor Christine Deavel. "The form and content serve each other well, a beneficient relationship we look for in poetry as well as cover art." And because the Seattle-based publication is comprised almost entirely of poetry, the editors feel collage is a particularly appropriate cover art for the magazine. Says Deavel, "To produce both [art and poetry], skillful selection from other, often prosaic, sources is required, and equally skillful assembling of the pieces into a transcendant whole." Cover artist Carlo Levy has recently completed a collage novel and has had poetry published in *Fine Madness*.

> its candy is trampled into diamonds
> while paper crowns are whirled through
> blind rage and love of chocolate.

Fine Madness is 64 pgs., digest-sized, perfect-bound, offset with color card cover. They accept about 40 of 1,500 poems received. Their press run is 1,000 for 100 subscribers of which 10 are libraries. Subscription: $9. **Sample postpaid: $4. Guidelines available for SASE. Submit 2-5 poems, preferably originals, not photocopy, 1 poem/page. No previously published poems or simultaneous submissions. Reports in 1-4 months. Pays 1 copy plus subscription.** *Fine Madness* has had poetry selected for inclusion in the 1990, 1991, 1992, 1993 and 1994 volumes of *The Best American Poetry* and a *Pushcart Prize* anthology. Editor Sean Bentley says, "If you don't read poetry, don't send us any."

FIREBRAND BOOKS (IV-Feminist, lesbian, ethnic), 141 The Commons, Ithaca NY 14850, phone (607)272-0000, founded 1984, editor and publisher Nancy K. Bereano, "is a **feminist and lesbian** publishing company committed to producing quality work in multiple genres by ethnically diverse women." They publish both quality trade paperbacks and hardbacks. Books are usually 94 pgs., flat-spined, elegantly printed on heavy stock with a glossy color card cover, a photo of the author on the back. **Simultaneous submissions acceptable with notification. Replies to queries within 2 weeks, to mss within 1 month. Pays royalties.** Send for catalog to buy samples.

‡*FIREWATER PRESS INC.; VARIOUS ARTISTS; WORKING TITLES (II), 65 Springfield Ave., Bristol BS7 9QS United Kingdom, founded 1989, contact editor Tony Lewis-Jones for *Various Artists* and editor Claire Williamson for *Working Titles*. Both *Various Artists* and *Working Titles* appear annually and intend "to encourage good accessible poetry by new and established writers. *Working Titles* also has a brief to encourage women's writing." **They want any format/style "so long as the work is not anti-minority. Prefer short poems (up to 40 lines)."** They have recently published poetry by Sophie Hannah, Robert Etty, Michael Daugherty and Jessica Freeman. As a sample the editor selected this poem, "The Lady of Shalott—Abridged," by Alison Wade:

> The Lady of Shalott
> died
> because she fancied Lancelot.
> Did he notice?
> Not a jot!

The editors say *VA* is A5, saddle-stitched with graphics; *WT* is A5, saddle-stitched. Both publications accept 10% of poems received a year (2,000 for *VA*, 1,500 for *WT*). Press run is 250 for 100 subscribers of which 10 are libraries. Single copy: $5; subscription: $10. **Sample postpaid: $3. Make checks payable to A. Lewis-Jones (they prefer currency from the US). Submit 6 poems at a time. No previously published poems or simultaneous submissions. Cover letter preferred.** Time between acceptance and publication is 1-12 months. **Always comments on rejections. Send SASE (or SAE and IRC) for guidelines. *VA* reports in 2 weeks; *WT* in 1 month. Pays 2 copies. Returns rights upon publication.** Staff reviews books of poetry. Poets may also send books for review consideration. Firewater Press also sponsors Poetry in the Parks and Poems on the Buses "aimed at making poetry more accessible to a wider public." The editors say, "Write from the heart, don't compromise and keep trying. If you're good enough, you'll make it."

FIREWEED: POETRY OF WESTERN OREGON (IV-Regional), 1330 E. 25th Ave., Eugene OR 97403, founded 1989, is a quarterly publishing the work of **poets living in Western Oregon or having close connections to the region. However, poems need not be regional in subject; any theme, subject, length or form is acceptable.** They have published poetry by Jane Glazer, Charles Goodrich, Wes Vollmer and Stephanie Van Horn. As a sample they selected these lines from "Memory for a City Dweller" by Michael Spurlin:

> *Recall this day when the world*
> *spoke its center in you,*
> *when a glacier's movement into water*
> *was the rapid motion of earth*
> *and your eye roved around*
> *the world's stillness, bounded*
> *by mountain, river and open range.*

Fireweed is 44 pgs., digest-sized, laser printed and saddle-stapled with card cover. "We receive several hundred poems and publish about ¼ or ⅓ of them." Press run is 250 for 180 subscribers of which 20 are libraries, 25 shelf sales. Subscription: $10. **Sample postpaid: $2.50. Submit 3-5 poems at a time, name and address on each page. No previously published poems; simultaneous submissions OK. Cover letter with brief bio required. Often comments on rejections. They do not publish guidelines for poets but will answer inquiries with SASE. Reports in 2-4 months. Pays 2 copies. Acquires first North American serial rights.** Reviews books of poetry by Oregon poets in 500-750 words, single format. Open to unsolicited reviews. Oregon poets may also send books for review consideration. They add, "We occasionally have special issues organized by theme, compiled by a guest editor or focused on newcomers to *Fireweed*. Support your local magazines by sending work and buying subscriptions! Submit to the smaller publications *first!*"

✤FIRM NONCOMMITTAL: AN INTERNATIONAL JOURNAL OF WHIMSY (II, IV-Humor), 5 Vonda Ave., North York, Ontario M2N 5E6 Canada, founded 1995, editors Brian Pastoor and Jeff Bersche, is an annual forum for international light verse and humorous, short fiction and nonfiction. **"Short poems under 40 lines are preferred, in all forms and styles from visual to villanelle. There is a morass of morose writing out there. We seek writers who find the sunshine in the saturnine, who 'take the utmost trouble to find the right thing to say and then say it with the utmost levity'—G.B. Shaw."** They have recently published "levity" by bill bissett (Canada), K.V. Skene (England), Michael Shuval (Israel) and Francine Porad (U.S.). As a sample the editors selected these lines from "Pre-Dawn Aphorisms" by Libby Scheier (Canada):

> *I accidentally planted the garden twice this year,*
> *there will be a war of the seeds*
> *and the fittest will survive.*

Firm Noncommittal is 40-48 pgs., 6¼ × 8¼, professionally printed and perfect-bound with matte card cover, using mirthful, b&w art. They accept "nearly 10%" of the submissions received. Circulation is 100 and growing, "thanks to support from *Krax* and other light-minded magazines." **Sample postpaid: $5 (Canadian funds). Make checks payable to Brian Pastoor. Submit up to 6 poems in May or June only. Previously published poems OK; no simultaneous submissions. Cover letter required; include a brief bio, "preferably under 50 words, preferably factual. Unless of edificial genius, mss without SASE or SAE and IRCs will be binned (sorry)." Often comments on rejections. Send SASE (or SAE and IRCs) for guidelines. Reports in 2 months. Sometimes sends prepublication galleys. Pays 2 copies.** Brian Pastoor says, "While we do admit a bias to the ironist here, we shy away from satire that is too heavy. We're after light, perspicuous writing that reveals a quickness of mind about the spiritual or mundane (all themes universal), writing that is characterized by imagination, ingenuity and/or self-conscious verbal artifice. Tom Robbins, as always, put it best: 'Those who fail to see the whimsy of things will experience rigor mortis before death.' "

‡FIRST CLASS; FOUR-SEP PUBLICATIONS (I), P.O. Box 303, Butler WI 53007, founded 1994, contact editor. *First Class* appears 3-4 times/year and "publishes excellent/odd writing for intelligent/creative readers." **They want "short post-modern poems, also short fiction." No traditional work.** They have recently published poetry by Antler, McDaris, Locklin, DeWitt and Bennett. *FC* is 40-48 pgs., digest-sized, photocopied and saddle-stitched with colored card cover. They receive about 150 poems a year, accept approximately 15. Press run is

---

THE CHAPBOOK INDEX, located before the Geographical Index, lists those publishers who consider chapbook manuscripts. A chapbook, a small volume of work, is often a good middle step between magazine and book publication.

200-400. **Sample (including guidelines) postpaid: $4. Make checks payable to Christopher Meyer. Submit 5 poems at a time. Previously published poems and simultaneous submissions OK. Cover letter preferred.** Time between acceptance and publication is 2-4 months. **Often comments on rejections. Reports in 2-3 weeks. Pays in 1 copy. Acquires one-time rights.** Will be reviewing books of poetry "in near future." Open to unsolicited reviews. Poets may also send books for review consideration. The editor says, "Belt out a good, short, thought-provoking, graphic, uncommon piece."

*FIRST TIME; NATIONAL HASTINGS POETRY COMPETITION (I, II), Burdett Cottage, 4 Burdett Place, George St., Hastings, East Sussex TN34 3ED England, phone/fax 01424 428855, founded 1981, editor Josephine Austin, who says the biannual magazine is **open to "all kinds of poetry—our magazine goes right across the board—which is why it is one of the most popular in Great Britain."** As a sample the editor selected these lines from "Why a Poet?" by R.M. Griffiths:

> *Of all types of people*
> *and all their differences in depth,*
> *the poet is the deepest,*
> *Or is it just the most vacuous?*

The digest-sized magazine, 24 pgs., saddle-stapled, contains several poems on each page, in a variety of small type styles, on lightweight stock, b&w photographs of editor and 1 author, glossy one-color card cover. Subscription: $13. **Sample: $2 plus postage. "Please send dollars." Submit 10 poems with name and address of poet on each. Poems submitted must not exceed 30 lines. No previously published poems. Cover letter required.** Time between acceptance and publication is up to 2 months. "Although we can no longer offer a free copy as payment, we can offer one at a discounted price of $3." The annual National Hastings Poetry Competition for poets 18 and older offers awards of £150, £75 and £50, £2/poem entry fee. Editor Josephine Austin has received The Dorothy Tutin Award "for services to poetry." She advises, "Keep on 'pushing your poetry.' If one editor rejects you then study the market and decide which is the correct one for you. Try to type your own manuscripts as longhand is difficult to read and doesn't give a professional impression. Always date your poetry — ©1997 and sign it. Follow your way of writing, don't be a pale imitation of someone else—sooner or later styles change and you will either catch up or be ahead."

FISH DRUM (II), P.O. Box 966, Murray Hill Station, New York NY 10156, founded in 1988 by Robert Winson (1959-1995), now edited by Suzi Winson, is a literary magazine appearing once a year. They want **"West Coast poetry, the exuberant, talky, often elliptical and abstract 'continuous nerve movie' that follows the working of the mind and has a relationship to the world and the reader. Philip Whalen's work, for example, and much of *Calafia, The California Poetry*, edited by Ishmael Reed. Also magical-tribal-incantatory poems, exemplified by the future/primitive *Technicians of the Sacred*, ed. Rothenberg. *Fish Drum* has a soft spot for schmoozy, emotional, imagistic stuff. Literate, personal material that sings and surprises, OK?"** They have published poetry by Philip Whalen, Joy Harjo, Arthur Sze, Nathaniel Tarn, Alice Notley, John Brandi, Steve Richmond, Jessica Hagedorn and Leo Romero. As a sample the editor selected these lines from "Glossolalia" by Kate Bremer:

> *Everywhere I look I see amino acids on the ground.*
> *When I close my eyes, I see molecules and pieces of Sanskrit:*
> *I hear syllables and alphabets.*

FD is approximately 80 pgs., perfect-bound, professionally printed. "Of 300 or so unsolicited submissions, accepted fewer than twenty." Press run is 500 for 100 subscribers of which 10 are libraries, 400 shelf sales. Subscription: $20/4 issues. **Publishes theme issues. Sometimes sends prepublication galleys. Pays 2 copies. Acquires first serial rights.** Reviews books or chapbooks of poetry in long essays and/or capsule reviews. Open to unsolicited reviews. Poets may also send books for review consideration. The editor says, **"We're looking for prose, fiction, essays, what-have-you, and artwork, scores, cartoons, etc.—just send it along. We are also interested in poetry, prose and translations concerning the practice of Zen. We publish chapbooks, but solicit these from our authors."** She also adds, "It is my intention to complete Robert's work and to honor his memory by continuing to publish *FishDrum*."

‡5 AM (III), 1109 Milton Ave., Pittsburgh PA 15218, founded 1987, editors Patricia Dobler, Lynn Emanuel, Ed Ochester and Judith Vollmer, is a poetry publication that appears twice a year. They are **open in regard to form, length, subject matter and style. However, they do not want poetry that is "religious or naive rhymes."** They have published poetry by Rita Dove, Elton Glaser, Alicia Ostriker and Alberto Rios. The editors describe *5 AM* as a 24-page, offset tabloid. They receive about 3,000 poems a year, use approximately 2%. Press run is 1,000 for 550 subscribers of which 22 are libraries, about 300 shelf sales. Subscription: $10/4 issues. **Sample postpaid: $3. No previously published poems or simultaneous submissions. Each editor chooses 25% of the magazine. Seldom comments on rejections. Reports within 3 months. Pays 2 copies. Acquires first rights.**

‡*FLAMBARD (II), 4 Mitchell Ave., Newcastle upon Tyne NE2 3LA England, founded 1990, contact Peter Lewis, "is particularly sympathetic to new or neglected writers from the North of England, and is keen to nourish developing talent." But open to all. They publish 5 paperbacks/year. Books are usually 64 pgs., 234×156mm, disk to plate printing, limp-sewn binding, 4-color cover, art work sometimes included. **Submit 15 poems at a time. Previously published poems and simultaneous submissions OK. Cover letter required. "If accepted, we expect the text on a disk we can read."** Time between acceptance and publication is 12-15 months. **Often comments on rejections. Replies to queries and mss in 1 month. Pays honorarium and 6 author's copies. Obtain samples of books or chapbooks "by direct mail purchase or through shops."** Peter Lewis says, "Not much point thinking about book publication until a reasonable level of magazine publication has been achieved."

‡***FLAMING ARROWS (II)**, County Sligo VEC, Riverside, Sligo, Ireland, phone (+353)7145844, fax (+353)7143093, founded 1989, arts education organizer Leo Regan, published yearly, features poetry, prose, interviews, graphics and photographs. **They want "cogent, lucid, coherent, technically-precise poetry. Poems of the spirit, mystical, metaphysical but sensuous, tactile and immediate to the senses." They do not want "loose rambling emotional release."** They have recently published poetry by Sydney Bernard Smith, Medbh McGuckian, James Liddy and Ciaran O'Driscoll. As a sample the editor selected these lines from "The Summons" by Peter Van Belle:

> Sacred hawk, descend from your heights,
> star clenched in beak, your eyes, my diamonds,
> your mind, a twine of steel.
> From this roof I speak to you,
> holding one foot over the abyss.
> I relish the dizziness.

Flaming Arrows is 80-102 pgs., A5, offset, perfect-bound or saddle-stapled, with 2-color cover stock, and b&w interior photos and graphics used in conjunction with the written work. They receive about 500 poems a year, accept approximately 6%. Press run is 500 for 150 subscribers of which 30 are libraries, 180 shelf sales; 100 distributed free to writer's groups, contributors, literary events. **Sample postpaid: $10. Make checks payable to Co. Sligo VEC. Submit 5 poems "typed, A4, in 10 or 12 pt. for scanning or discs for Word 7 in Windows 95." Previously published poems and simultaneous submissions OK. Cover letter required.** Time between acceptance and publication is 1 year. **Reports in 3 months. Pays $25/poem and 1-3 copies.** They receive financial assistance from the Arts Council of Ireland. The editor says, "We seek a distributor in the U.S. from whom we receive regular submissions."

‡**FLEDGLING (I)**, 65 John Mooney Rd., Revere MA 02151, founded 1994, editor/publisher Mary-Margaret Mulligan, appears twice a year. "*Fledgling* is dedicated to publishing poetry by new and emerging writers." **They want to see "descriptive, tactile poetry, with tastes and smells and sounds. Two pages maximum, any form. No rhyming for no reason, no sickly-sweet poems, no love poems, no poor-me poems."** They have recently published poetry by Rick Agran, Carol Frith and B.Z. Niditch. As a sample the editor selected these lines from "Louisiana State Penitentiary" by Greg Heilshorn:

> If I had his Stetson,
> I'd turn it over, climb in
> ride down the rest of the Mississippi.
> Paddle to Florida.
> Maybe just float in the Gulf awhile,
> catch me a fish whenever I got hungry.

Fledgling is 32 pgs., 5½×8½, photocopied and saddle-stapled, card stock cover with b&w illustrations. They publish 18-20 poems each issue. Press run is 100 for 28 subscribers, more than 30 shelf sales. Single copy: $3; subscription: $5/2 issues. **Sample postpaid: $2. Submit no more than 5 poems at a time. No previously published poems; simultaneous submissions OK. Often comments on rejections (when asked or when the work is close to what she's looking for). Reports within 3 months. Pays 1 copy.** Reviews books of poetry. Open to unsolicited reviews. Poets may also send books for review consideration. *Fledgling* also sponsors a reading to celebrate each issue. Poets published in that issue are invited to read.

FLIPSIDE (II), 109 Dixon Hall, California University of Pennsylvania, California PA 15419, founded 1987, poetry editors Cindy Speer and Derek C.F. Pegritz, is a literary tabloid appearing twice a year. **"We publish highly imageable poetry about concrete people, places and things. We tend to publish poems that deal with a darker, more unusual side of life. We don't publish melodramatic love poems or mushy ballads, nor do we publish bitter poetry."** They have published poetry by Charles Bukowski and Arthur Winfield Knight. The tabloid is 48 pgs., professionally printed on newsprint with b&w photos and line drawings inside, some ads. They accept less than 5% of hundreds of poems submitted. Press run is 5,000, distributed free to the public, libraries, writing schools, colleges, advertisers, poets, etc. **Sample postpaid: $2. Send SASE for guidelines. Reports in 2 months. Pays as many copies as you want.**

FLOATING BRIDGE PRESS (IV-Regional), P.O. Box 18814, Seattle WA 98118, founded 1994, **publishes limited edition chapbooks by Washington state poets, selected through an annual contest.** They have published chapbooks by Nance Van Winckel and Joannie Kervran. As a sample the editors selected these lines from "Love Apples" in Kervran's chapbook, *A Steady Longing for Flight*:

> Each cut and push of the shovel sings inside her

> *and she imagines the summer garden*
> *awash in lavender and meadow rue.*
> *In the darkest corner she'll plant a bleeding heart,*
> *fleshy pendants dripping ruby in the shade.*

That chapbook is 32 pgs., digest-sized and offset printed on acid-free recycled paper with a letterpress linocut matte cover. **Sample postpaid: $6. For consideration in the contest, Washington poets (only) should submit a chapbook ms of 20-24 pgs. of poetry with $10 reading fee and SASE (for results only) between September and January. Previously published individual poems and simultaneous submissions OK. Author's name must not appear on the ms; include a separate page with title, name, address, telephone number and acknowledgments of any previous publication. Deadline: February 1.** Mss are judged anonymously and will not be returned. **In addition to publication, the winner receives $250 (minimum), 50 copies and a reading in the Seattle area. All entrants receive a copy of the winning chapbook. Send SASE for guidelines.**

THE FLORIDA REVIEW (II), Dept. of English, University of Central Florida, Box 25000, Orlando FL 32816, phone (407)823-2212, founded 1972, editor Russ Kesler, is a "literary biannual with emphasis on short fiction and poetry." **They want "poems filled with real things, real people and emotions, poems that might conceivably advance our knowledge of the human heart."** They have published poetry by Knute Skinner, Elton Glaser, Silvia Curbelo and Walter McDonald. It is 128 pgs., professionally printed, flat-spined, with glossy card cover. Press run is 1,500 for 500 subscribers of which 50 are libraries, 300 shelf sales. **Sample postpaid: $4.50. Submit no more than 6 poems at a time. Simultaneous submissions OK. Editor comments on submissions "occasionally." Send SASE for guidelines. Reports in 1-3 months. Always sends prepublication galleys. Pays 3 copies, small honorarium occasionally available. Acquires all rights. Returns rights "upon publication, when requested."** Reviews books of poetry in 1,500 words, single format; 2,500-3,000 words, multi-book. Send books for review consideration. The editor says they would like more formal verse.

FLUME PRESS (II), 773 Sierra View, Chico CA 95926, phone (916)342-1583, founded 1984, poetry editors Casey Huff and Elizabeth Renfro, **publishes poetry chapbooks. "We have few biases about form, although we appreciate control and crafting, and we tend to favor a concise, understated style, with emphasis on metaphor rather than editorial commentary."** They have published chapbooks by Tina Barr, Randall Freisinger, Leonard Kress, Carol Gordon, Gayle Kaune, Luis Omar Salinas, Judy Lindberg, Ava Leavell Haymon, Martha M. Vertreace, Mary Matthews and Lynne Kuderko. As a sample the editors selected these lines from "Hopeless Love" by Joanne Allred:

> *I sit on a porch wearing nothing*
> *but hot ambition under a cool cotton shift, waiting*
> *for a boy who never shows. He can't get a car,*
> *or off work, or the nerve, or some needed luck*
> *circumstance won't grant in its plot to keep me pure.*
> *My virginity aches like a loose milk tooth.*

Chapbooks are chosen from an annual competition, March 1 through May 30. $7 entry fee. Submit 20-24 pgs., including title, contents and acknowledgments. Considers simultaneous submissions. Brief cover letter preferred. "Flume Press editors read and respond to every entry." Sometimes sends prepublication galleys. Winner receives $100 and 25 copies. Sample: $7.

‡FLY BY NIGHT MAGAZINE; ATTIC CHAPBOOKS; COYOTE PUBLICATIONS (I, II), P.O. Box 101, Harveyville KS 66431, founded 1996, editor John C. Leonard. *Fly by Night Magazine*, published biannually (for now), "strives to publish quality literature and some art (as space allows) without regard for the publishing experience of the author." **They want "richness of language and texture as well as unique interpretations of events, emotions, and form. I do not wish to enforce any specific limitations on the kind of poetry I will publish. Due to size limitations, poems over three pgs. may be published sequentially by** *FBNM*.**" They do not want "monolithic, heaving-brain epics without plots and opaque, infinitesimal word-gatherings without titles."** They have recently published poetry by Brian S. Dyer and Mike Catalano. As a sample the editor selected these lines from "On Going Anywhere" by D.L. Cox:

> *It is tough to know that absence is impossible,*
> *that even in a vacuum leptons appear*
> *and disappear seemingly from nowhere;*
> *nothing into something that I believed was absence.*

FBNM is 32 pgs., 7 × 8½, offset printed and/or photocopied, saddle-stitched, colored card cover with art, graphics and "ads only to literary magazines or other publications of literary interest." They accept approximately 10-25% of poems received. Press run is 100-250 for 20 subscribers, 25 shelf sales; most distributed free to contributors and staff. Single copy: $2.50; subscription: $4/2 issues. **Sample postpaid: $2. Submit 5-10 poems at a time with name and address on each page of ms. Previously published poems and simultaneous submissions OK. Cover letter preferred.** Time between acceptance and publication is 6-12 months. **"Each poem is considered on an individual basis, however, I prefer to publish more than one poem from each author and also look for natural groupings within a submission." Always comments on rejections. Send SASE for guidelines. Reports within 1 month. Sometimes sends prepublication galleys. Pays 1 copy. Acquires one-time and**

single reprint (for "Best of" anthology). "I review books and chapbooks, no magazines, in 50-250 word reader response reviews and occasionally some heavier critical approaches." Open to unsolicited reviews. Poets may also send books for review consideration. Attic Chapbooks "publishes high-quality literature which is unique or controversial enough to cause reluctance with more profit-oriented presses," **publishes 2-5 chapbooks/year. "I call it a contest, publishing as many winners as funds allow, but mss are read year-round. Mss submitted can also be considered for partial inclusion in *FBNM*."** Books are usually 32 pgs., 5½×8½ or 7×8½, saddle-stapled or stitched, often photocopied on interior/offset cover (card) with graphics or art on front cover, photo and bio on back. **Submit entire ms with $5 reading fee. "If ms is not to be considered for partial publication in *FBNM*, please indicate in cover letter. Include brief bio with credits in ms, not in cover letter." Replies to queries in 1-6 weeks, to mss in 1-6 months. Pays 25% royalty or 25% of run (length of run varies).** The editor says, "Every day a literary magazine closes its doors forever and a new one takes its place. Everyday an author gives up writing and ten more take his/her place. Keep your sense of humor and don't ever quit trying to improve your writing. The most valuable tool of any writer is not taught in any school: stubbornness."

FLYWAY (II), 203 Ross Hall, Iowa State University, Ames IA 50011-1201, fax (515)294-6814, e-mail flyway@ iastate.edu, founded 1961, editor Stephen Pett, appears 3 times a year. *Flyway* "is one of the best literary magazines for the money; it is packed with some of the most readable poems being published today—all styles and forms, lengths and subjects." The editor shuns elite-sounding free verse with obscure meanings and pretty-sounding formal verse with obvious meanings. It is 6×9, 76 pgs., professionally printed and perfect-bound with matte card cover with color. Circulation is 600 for 400 subscribers of which 100 are libraries. Subscription: $18. **Sample postpaid: $8. Submit 4-6 poems at a time. Cover letter preferred. "We do not read mss between the end of May and mid-August." May be contacted by fax or e-mail, but "work should come by mail." Reports in 4-6 weeks (often sooner). Pays 1 copy. Acquires first rights.**

FOOTWORK: THE PATERSON LITERARY REVIEW; HORIZONTES; ALLEN GINSBERG POETRY AWARDS; THE PATERSON POETRY PRIZE; PASSAIC COUNTY COMMUNITY COLLEGE POETRY CENTER LIBRARY (II, IV-Regional, bilingual/foreign language), Poetry Center, Passaic County Community College, Cultural Affairs Dept., 1 College Blvd., Paterson NJ 07505-1179, phone (201)684-6555. A wide range of activities pertaining to poetry are conducted by the Passaic County Community College Poetry Center, including the annual literary magazine *Footwork*, founded 1979, editor and director Maria Mazziotti Gillan, using **poetry of "high quality" under 100 lines; "clear, direct, powerful work."** They have published poetry by David Ray, Diane Wakoski, William Stafford, Sonia Sanchez, Laura Boss and Marge Piercy. *Footwork: The Paterson Literary Review* is 240 pgs., magazine-sized, saddle-stapled, professionally printed with glossy card 2-color cover, using b&w art and photos. Circulation 1,000 with 100 subscribers of which 50 are libraries. **Sample postpaid: $10. Send up to 5 poems at a time. Simultaneous submissions OK. Reads submissions September through January only. Reports in 1 year. Pays 1 copy. Acquires first rights.** *Horizontes*, founded in 1983, editor José Villalongo, is an annual Spanish language literary magazine using **poetry of high quality no longer than 20 lines. Will accept English translations, but Spanish version must be included.** They have published poetry by Nelson Calderon, Jose Kozer and Julio Cesar Mosches. *Horizontes* is 120 pgs., magazine-sized, saddle-stapled, professionally printed with full-color matte cover, using b&w graphics and photos. Circulation 800 with 100 subscribers of which 20 are libraries. **Sample postpaid: $4. Accepts simultaneous submissions. "On occasion we do consider published works but prefer unpublished works." Reads submissions September through January only. Reports in 3-4 months. Pays 2 copies. Acquires first rights.** Staff reviews books of poetry. Send books for review consideration. The Poetry Center of the college conducts The Allen Ginsberg Poetry Awards Competition each year. Entry fee: $12. Prizes of $300, $150 and $100. Deadline: April 1. Send SASE for rules. They also publish a *New Jersey Poetry Resources* book, the *PCC Poetry Contest Anthology* and the *New Jersey Poetry Calendar*. The Paterson Poetry Prize of $1,000 is awarded each year (split between poet and publisher) to a book of poems published in the previous year. Publishers should write with SASE for application form to be submitted by February 1. Passaic County Community College Poetry Center Library has an extensive collection of contemporary poetry and seeks small press contributions to help keep it abreast. The Distinguished Poetry Series offers readings by poets of international, national and regional reputation. Poetryworks/USA is a series of programs produced for UA Columbia-Cablevision.

THE FORMALIST; HOWARD NEMEROV SONNET AWARD (II, IV-Form, translations), 320 Hunter Dr., Evansville IN 47711, founded 1990, editor William Baer, appears twice a year, **"dedicated to contemporary *metrical* poetry written in the great tradition of English-language verse."** This is one of a handful of magazines that publish formal (metered, rhymed) poetry *exclusively*. The poems here are among the best in the genre—a joy to read—tastefully edited so each verse plays off the other. They have published poetry by Richard Wilbur, Donald Justice, Mona Van Duyn, Derek Walcott, John Updike, Maxine Kumin, James Merrill, Karl Shapiro, X.J. Kennedy, May Swenson, W.S. Merwin, W.D. Snodgrass and Louis Simpson. As a sample the editor chose the opening stanza from "The Amateurs of Heaven" by Howard Nemerov:

> *Two lovers to a midnight meadow came*
> *High in the hills, to lie there hand in hand*
> *Like effigies and look up at the stars,*
> *The never-setting ones set in the North*

INSIDER REPORT

Commenting on rejections keeps editor human

"Quandary of the Writer"

He wasn't ready. He had not
made the world safe.
But his son squirmed
in his arms anyway.
His own eyes looked up
from that too big tiny head.
Miniature fingers
grasped one of his, and
suddenly, on that evening
drive back home, he saw
the beauty of this world
and knew
he could never express it.

Photo by Wendy Roberts

John C. Leonard

"I have come to the conclusion there are far too many ogres in the world of publishing, and I don't want to become one of them," says John C. Leonard of Coyote Publications. A writer of short stories, essays, poetry and a novel, Leonard knows what it's like to submit to publications and wait for a reply.

After being on staff at literary magazines—including editor-in-chief at *Tripe Magazine*—and studying literature and creative writing at the collegiate level, in 1996 Leonard started Coyote Publications, comprised of Attic Chapbooks and the biannual *Fly by Night Magazine*. The idea of running a magazine had always intrigued him and was the result of an "organic process" rather than something prompted by a specific event. Leonard explains, "The idea for Attic Chapbooks hit me at a time when my 'office' was relegated to our attic. The name *Fly by Night* accurately represents the spirit of independence which makes the magazine possible."

This independence carries over to the physical side of putting out the publications. Leonard does everything except the actual printing. A typical day includes reviewing submissions, typesetting, writing reviews, updating the subscriber database, spending time on his own writing and individually drafting acceptances and rejections. "For me, the easiest part of being an editor is sitting in my easy chair and reading submissions. I find 'discovering' great poems and stories to be very rewarding."

Having been on both sides of the submission process, the distinction Leonard strives for in publishing is the amount of individual attention he gives to the manuscripts. He comments on all rejections, aiming to make the poem publishable. "I know that's a terrible liberty for me to take with someone else's writing, but it's also a valuable self-check: if I should want to reject a piece just because I'm in a bad mood—there's a little ogre in every

---

INSIDER REPORT, *Leonard*

editor—I will be less likely to send a stock rejection and let it go at that."

Subscribers to *FBNM* are generally well-educated Gen-Xers, but the magazine is aimed at anyone who has an interest in literature without a real slant. When reading submissions Leonard looks for "emotional impact, unique methods of image presentation and competence in whatever form the poem takes. I evaluate each poem according to its individual merits." He publishes poetry based on the poem and not the poet because he considers any press requiring a list of publication credits to be "at best guilty of elitism or at worst guilty of incompetence—by not making up their own minds." Leonard believes he is in the minority when it comes to adopting this guideline as he sees many magazines "paying it lip service" but not following through.

Leonard advises poets to provide a variety of work in a submission package with less emphasis on cohesion within the group of poems, and more concentration on craft. He suggests beginning poets "read the classics, read the Beats, read the obscure poets no one has ever heard of. Then read Goldbarth, Brommage, Howell, Lyons and anyone who's not white and is still alive. And then question everything you've read."

Finally, he recommends not submitting too soon but revising, revising, revising, letting the poem sit a month and then revising again. "I see learning patience as the most difficult task a poet can face. The desire to write poetry becomes such a driving force in a poet's life they want to declare themselves 'Poet!' instead of waiting for the whispers of the word to come floating across the room unbidden."

—*Tara A. Horton*

To circle the Pole in idiot majesty,
And wonder what was given them to wonder.

"We're looking for well-crafted poetry in a contemporary idiom which uses meter and the full range of traditional poetic conventions in vigorous and interesting ways. We're especially interested in sonnets, couplets, tercets, ballads, the French forms, etc. We're also interested in metrical translations of the poetry of major, formalist, non-English poets—from the ancient Greeks to the present. We're not, however, interested in haiku (or syllabic verse of any kind) or sestinas. Only rarely do we accept a poem over two pages, and we have no interest in any type of erotica, blasphemy, vulgarity or racism. Finally, like all editors, we suggest that those wishing to submit to *The Formalist* become thoroughly familiar with the journal beforehand." *The Formalist* is 128 pgs., digest-sized, offset printed on bond paper, perfect-bound, with colored card cover. Subscription: $12/year; $22/2 years. **Sample postpaid: $6.50. Submit 3-5 poems at a time. No simultaneous submissions, previously published work, or disk submissions. A brief cover letter is recommended** and a SASE is necessary for a reply and return of ms. **Reports within 2 months. Pays 2 copies. Acquires first North American serial rights.** The Howard Nemerov Sonnet Award offers $1,000 and publication in *The Formalist* for the best unpublished *sonnet*. The final judge for 1997 was Donald Justice. Entry fee: $3/sonnet. Postmark deadline: June 15. Send SASE for guidelines. See also the contest listing for the World Order of Narrative and Formalist Poets. Contestants must subscribe to *The Formalist* to enter. Work published in *The Formalist* also appears in *The Best American Poetry 1992*.

‡*FORTNIGHT MAGAZINE (II), 7 Lower Crescent, Belfast, County Antrim BT7 1NR Northern Ireland, phone 01232-232353, fax 01232-232650, e-mail mairtin@fortnite.dnet.co.uk, founded 1970, contact Medbh McGuckian or Mairtin Crawford, published monthly, covers current affairs, culture, arts, books, poetry of Northern

---

SENDING TO A COUNTRY other than your own? Be sure to send International Reply Coupons (IRCs) instead of stamps for replies or return of your manuscript.

Irish interest. **They want any style or content. They do not want "doggerrel or beginners."** They have recently published poetry by Seamus Heaney, Paul Muldoon and Michael Longley. *Fortnight* is 44 pgs., A4, offset printed, saddle-stitched, colored cover stock with photos and ads. Press run is 4,500 for 1,500 subscribers of which 300 are libraries, with 100 distributed free. Subscription: £39 sterling. **Sample postpaid: £1.80. Make checks payable to Fortnight Publications. Submit 6 poems at a time. No previously published poems or simultaneous submissions. Cover letter required with photo and bio.** Time between acceptance and publication is 6 months. **Poems are circulated to an editorial board of literary editor, assistant editor and editor. Seldom comments on rejections. Publishes theme issues. Reports ASAP. Sometimes sends prepublication galleys. Pays on arrangement. Copyright remains with author.** Reviews books in 400-750 words. Open to unsolicited reviews. Poets may also send books for review consideration.

FOUND STREET PRESS; FOUND STREET (II, IV-Form/style), 2260 S. Ferdinand Ave., Monterey Park CA 91754, founded 1991, editor Larry Tomoyasu. *Found Street* is a *"visual* exploration of language and meaning" appearing 1-2 times a year. The editor says, **"I would like to see truly 'creative' writing; writing that expands the boundaries of what writing *is*; poems that are almost drawings and drawings that are almost words. Nothing seen; nothing taught; nothing approved."** He has recently published experimental and verbal/visual poetry by John M. Bennett, Patrick Mullins, Jessica Freeman and Kevin Friend. The format of the publication changes from issue to issue. One issue we received was $3 \times 4\frac{1}{4}$ with foldout pages; another issue was $5\frac{1}{2} \times 8\frac{1}{2}$. The editor receives about 200 poems a year, accepts approximately 20%. Press run is 40. **Sample postpaid: $2. Make checks payable to Larry Tomoyasu. Submit 3-5 poems at a time. "All verbal/visual work should be camera-ready (b&w only)." No previously published poems or simultaneous submissions. Cover letter preferred.** Time between acceptance and publication is 3 months to 1 year. **Seldom comments on rejections. Send SASE for guidelines. Reports usually within 1 month. Pays 1-2 copies. Acquires first rights.** The editor says, "Found Street Press specializes in small publications and gets its name from where most people find our publications: on the street." He adds, "My advice to beginners: If you can't get your work published, start your own zine. Give it away free to all your friends and anyone who will take it, and send it to other poets and publishers, because if people aren't interested when it's free, they sure as hell aren't gonna pay for it. Read poetry, write poetry and *buy* poetry—we are our own market."

‡FOURTEEN HILLS: THE SFSU REVIEW (II), Creative Writing Dept., San Francisco State University, 1600 Holloway Ave., San Francisco CA 94132, (415)338-3083, fax (415)338-7030, e-mail hills@sfsu.edu, website http://www.mercury.sfsu.edu/~hills/14hills.html, founded 1994, contact poetry editor, is a biannual. **"We are seeking high quality, innovative work."** They have recently published poetry by Alice Notley, Kate Braverman, Leslie Scalapino and Jane Hirshfield. As a sample the editor selected these lines from "Striptease #3" by Kate Braverman:

> *Full moon in New York.*
> *I am three days without you.*
> *I decipher dialects of stone*
> *and the gestures of boulevards*
> *in a granite autumn.*

FH is 170 pgs., 6×9, professionally printed and perfect-bound with glossy card cover. They receive about 600 poems a year, accept approximately 5-10%. Press run is 600 for 125 subscribers of which 25 are libraries. Single copy: $7; subscription: $12/year, $21/2 years. **Sample postpaid: $5. Submit 5 poems at a time. No previously published poems; simultaneous submissions OK. Cover letter preferred. Reads submissions August-September for the fall issue; January-February for the spring. "The editorial staff is composed entirely of graduate students from the Creative Writing Program at SFSU." Seldom comments on rejections. Send SASE for guidelines. Reports in 3-6 months. Always sends prepublication galleys. Pays 2 copies.** Work published in this review has been included in *The Best American Poetry 1996*. The editor says, "Please read an issue of *Fourteen Hills* before submitting."

‡THE FRACTAL (IV-Science fiction/fantasy), 4400 University Dr., MS 2D6, Fairfax VA 22030, (703)993-2874, e-mail fractal@gmu.edu, website http://www.gmu.edu/org/fractal, founded 1993, submissions: poetry editors, inquiries/guidelines: attn. submission guidelines, is a semiannual journal "presenting the literary market with the best in science fiction, fantasy and the fantastic." **They want "well-crafted and meaningful poems of any style dealing with science fiction, fantasy, and the fantastic. Experimental forms and ideas are encouraged. Nothing media-based (Star Trek, Star Wars, etc.). Nothing preachy, pointless or forced."** They have recently published poetry by Todd Eckliardt, Nancy Ellis Taylor, Amber J. Smiley and Thomas Morrissey. As a sample the editor selected these lines (poet unidentified):

> *The game is won.*
> *I have often sweated between the stone walls,*
> *bounding on jaguar feet, glistening, tawny red,*
> *monkey-quick, eluding my enemies*
> *to cup the prize and win the right to reach for the sun.*

Fractal is 60 pgs., $8\frac{1}{2} \times 5\frac{1}{2}$, desktop-produced and photocopied, saddle-stitched with card cover, b&w art, scholarly journal ads. They receive about 50-100 poems a year, accept approximately 10-15%. Press run is 1,500 for 5 subscribers, 50 shelf sales; 500 distributed free to Georg Mason University students and at conventions. Subscription: $8/year. **Sample: $5 plus 6×9 SASE. Submit up to 10 poems at a time. No previously published poems; simultaneous submissions OK. Cover letter preferred. E-mail submissions in ASCII format OK. "Submissions should be on 8½×11 white paper, with double-spaced text and one-inch margins, printed on one side of the page. Name and address should appear in the upper right corner of the first page. Name, the title and the page number should appear on all subsequent pages."** Time between acceptance and publication is 2-8 months. **Poems are circulated to an editorial board. "All editors read and comment; poetry editor has weighted vote; senior editor has final say, but often defers to poetry editor." Often comments on rejections. Send SASE for guidelines or obtain via e-mail or website. Reports within 3-4 months, "slower in summer." Pays $5 plus 1 copy. Buys first rights.**

BENJAMIN FRANKLIN LITERARY AND MEDICAL SOCIETY, INC.; HUMPTY DUMPTY'S MAGAZINE; TURTLE MAGAZINE FOR PRESCHOOL KIDS; CHILDREN'S DIGEST; CHILDREN'S PLAYMATE; JACK AND JILL; CHILD LIFE (IV-Children), (formerly listed as Children's Better Health Institute), 1100 Waterway Blvd., P.O. Box 567, Indianapolis IN 46206-0567. This publisher of magazines stressing health for children has a **variety of needs for mostly short, simple poems.** For example, *Humpty Dumpty* is **for ages 4-6;** *Turtle* is for preschoolers, similar emphasis, uses many stories in rhyme—and action rhymes, etc.; *Children's Digest* is for preteens (10-13); *Jack and Jill* is for ages 7-10. *Child Life* is for ages 9-11. *Children's Playmate* **is for ages 6-8.** All appear 8 times/year with cartoon art, very colorful. **Sample postpaid: $1.25. Send SASE for guidelines. Reports in 8-10 weeks. Pays $15 minimum.** Staff reviews books of poetry. Send books for review consideration. The editors suggest that writers who wish to appear in their publications **study current issues carefully.** "We receive too many poetry submissions that are about kids, not for kids. Or, the subject matter is one that adults think children would or should like. We'd like to see more humorous verse."

FREE FOCUS (I, IV-Women/feminist); OSTENTATIOUS MIND (I, IV-Form/style), P.O. Box 7415, JAF Station, New York NY 10116, *Free Focus* founded 1985, *Ostentatious Mind* founded 1987, poetry editor Patricia D. Coscia. *Free Focus* "is a literary magazine **only for creative women, who reflect their ideas of love, nature, beauty and men and also express the pain, sorrow, joy and enchantment that their lives generate.** *Free Focus* **needs poems of all types on the subject matters above. Nothing X-rated, please. The poems can be as short as two lines or as long as two pages.** The objective of this magazine is to give women poets a chance to be fullfilled in the art of poetry, for freedom of expression for women is seldom described in society." They have published poetry by Helen Tzagoloff, Elizabeth Hahn Ph.D., Patricia A. Pierkowski, D.R. Middleton, Crystal Beckner, Carol L. Clark and Mary Anderson. *Ostentatious Mind* "is a co-ed literary magazine **for material of stream of consciousness and experimental poems. The poets deal with the political, social and psychological.**" They have published poetry by Paul Weinman, Rod Farmer, L. Mason, Dr. John J. Soldo, Carl A. Winderl, James W. Penha and Joe Lackey. Both magazines are printed on 8×14 paper, folded in the middle and stapled to make a 10-page (including cover) format, with simple b&w drawings on the cover and inside. The two magazines appear every 6-8 months. **Sample of either is $3.50 postpaid. Submit only 3 poems at a time. Poems should be typed neatly and clearly on white typing paper. Simultaneous submissions and previously published poems OK. Publishes theme issues. Send SASE for guidelines and upcoming themes. Reports "as soon as possible." Sometimes sends prepublication galleys. Pays 1-2 copies.** The editor says, "I think that anyone can write a poem who can freely express intense feelings about their experiences. A dominant thought should be ruled and expressed in writing, not by the spoken word, but the written word."

FREE LUNCH (II), P.O. Box 7647, Laguna Niguel CA 92607-7647, founded 1988, editor Ron Offen, is a **"poetry journal interested in publishing the whole spectrum of what is currently being produced by American poets. Occasionally offers a 'Reprise Series' in which an overlooked American poet is reexamined and presented. Among those who have been featured are Kenneth Patchen, Maxwell Bodenheim, Stephen Vincent Benet, Kenneth Fearing and Lola Ridge.** Also features a 'Mentor Series,' in which an established poet introduces a new, unestablished poet. Mentors have included Maxine Kumin, James Dickey, Lucille Clifton, Kenneth Koch, Carolyn Forché and Wanda Coleman. **Especially interested in experimental work and work by unestablished poets. Hope to provide all serious poets living in the US with a free subscription. For details on free subscription send SASE. No restriction on form, length, subject matter, style, purpose. Don't want cutsie, syrupy, sentimental, preachy religious or aggressively 'uplifting' verse. No aversion to form, rhyme."** Poets recently published include Sherman Alexie, Lyn Lifshin, Mekeel McBride and Paul Violi. As a sample the editor selected these lines from "Training Camp" by Neal Bowers:

> *I am coaching my heart to quit,*
> *calling it "fat boy," "loser,"*
> *feeding it greasy fries*
> *and the lonely fast food of 3 a.m.,*
> *saying, "Stay down! Stay down!"*
> *like a manager who has money*
> *on the other fighter, . . .*

FL, published 2-3 times a year, is 32-40 pgs., digest-sized, attractively printed and designed, saddle-stapled, featuring free verse that shows attention to craft with well-knowns and newcomers alongside each other. Press run is 1,200 for 200 subscribers of which 15 are libraries. Subscription: $12 ($15 foreign). **Sample postpaid: $5 ($6 foreign). "Submissions must be limited to three poems and are considered only between September 1 and May 31. Submissions sent at other times will be returned unread. Although a cover letter is not mandatory, we like them. We especially want to know if a poet is previously unpublished, as we like to work with new poets." They will consider simultaneous submissions. Editor usually comments on rejections and tries to return submissions in 2 months. Send SASE for guidelines. Occasionally publishes theme issues. They will publish a special issue of prisoner poetry in 1998 (submit 3 poems, poetry not returned). Pays 1 copy plus subscription.** Work published in *Free Lunch* has been included in *The Best American Poetry 1993*. The editor quotes Archibald MacLeish, " 'A poem should not mean/ But be.' I have become increasingly leery of the ego-centered lyric that revels in some past wrong, good-old-boy nostalgia, or unfocused ecstatic experience. Poetry is concerned primarily with language, rhythm and sound; fashions and trends are transitory and to be eschewed; perfecting one's work is often more important than publishing it."

‡FREE SPIRIT (I, IV-Specialized: traveling on two-wheeled motor vehicles), 755 NE Circle Blvd. Space #1, Corvallis OR 97330, phone (541)758-5564, founded 1996, editor Andrew E. Muench, published monthly. "Our goal is to capture the essence of travel by those of us who continue to cherish the two-wheel motor vehicle. **We want poetry that captures the essence of traveling, particularly on two-wheeled motor vehicles. Poems must be rich in imagery. No preaching. We do not want poetry from people who have no knowledge of grammar, punctuation and mechanics."** They have recently published poetry by Jaton Rash and Tony Curtis. As a sample the editor selected these lines from his poem "Travels with Fran Fipple":

> The road wound itself 'round a bend,
> Mercilessly delivering me to the edge of the world
> Where the Great Hand descended from the firmament
> To create an unprecedented masterpiece
> Where the beasts and flocks held a perfect sanctuary . . .

The editor says *Free Spirit* is 30 pgs., 8½×11 with art, photos and computer prints. They receive about 20 poems a year, accepts all. Press run is 100 for 40 subscribers, 60 shelf sales. Single copy: $2.50; subscription: $20. **Sample postpaid: $1. Make checks payable to Andrew Muench. Submit up to 3 poems. Previously published poems and simultaneous submissions OK. Cover letter and SASE required.** Time between acceptance and publication is 1 month. **Always comments on rejections. Send SASE for guidelines. Reports in 1 week. Always sends prepublication galleys. Pays 1 copy. Acquires first rights.** "This magazine is designed specifically for beginners who want their work read. Because our magazine is young and small, you have to exert an effort to not get published in *Free Spirit*."

‡FREE THOUGHT CONCEPTIONS (I), P.O. Box 432, Glen Echo MD 20812, phone (800)542-8194, e-mail concepts@wam.umd.edu, website http://www.wam.umd.edu/~concepts, founded 1990, contact Eric Smith, published quarterly, is "a zine devoted to circulating articles and information. A state of intellect, perceptiveness, and inspiration." **They want "nature-related/surrealistic poetry—almost any style considered." They do not want "anger poetry and death."** They have recently published poetry by Mike Catalano, Paul Weinman, Christopher Stolle and Michael Morain. As a sample the editor selected these lines from "The Fly" (poet unidentified):

> The buzzes and
> The whizzes
> Whirling about—
> The wings of life
> Are suddenly folded with the
> Volatile gesture of a swat.

The editor says *Free Thought Conceptions* is 24-32 pgs., 8½×11, saddle-stitched with cover art and graphics. They receive about 300-400 poems a year, accept approximately 10-20%. Press run is 3,500. Single copy free. **Sample "free if available." Submit 5 poems at a time. Previously published poems and simultaneous submissions OK. Cover letter preferred. E-mail submissions OK.** Time between acceptance and publication is 4-6 months. **"Poems are circulated among three people, most favorable ones published." Seldom comments on rejections. Send SASE for guidelines. Reports in 1-2 months. Pays 1 copy. Acquires one-time rights.** Reviews chapbooks of poetry in 350-500 words or other magazines in 50-150 words. Open to unsolicited reviews. Poets may also send books for review consideration.

FREEZER BURN MAGAZINE (I, IV-Science fiction/fantasy, horror), 10 Becket St. #3, Salem MA 01970, phone (508)745-7379, e-mail freezburn2@aol.com, founded 1994, editors David G. Rogers and Teresa C. Cerrato, is a quarterly of science fiction, horror and fantasy short stories, poetry and artwork. **They want science fiction, horror and fantasy poetry. "Avoid epic length poems. Poems under 30 lines stand the best chance. Nothing pornographic."** They have recently published poetry by Mary Winters, William Kopecky and Glenna Holloway. As a sample the editors selected these lines from "The Dead" by Mary Winters:

> You know who's a real pain in the neck?
> the dead.
> just when you think you've got them

> *stuffed in a box*
> *they're reading over your shoulder*
> *spying on you in bed*
> *scaring the bejesus out of some poor kid*
> *selling Girl Scout cookies*

Freezer Burn is 80 pgs., 7 × 8½, photocopied and saddle-stapled with 70 lb. color cover, b&w art and ads from other publications. They receive "hundreds" of poems a year, accept approximately 10%. Press run is 125 for 25 subscribers, 60 shelf sales. Subscription: $12. **Sample postpaid: $4. Make checks payable to David G. Rogers. Submit 5 poems at a time. Previously published poems and simultaneous submissions OK. Cover letter strongly preferred. "Give us a sense of who you are."** Time between acceptance and publication is 3-9 months. **Always comments on rejections. Send SASE for guidelines. Reports in 3 weeks. Pays $20 (flat fee) and 1 copy. Acquires first or one-time rights.**

FRENCH BROAD PRESS (V), Dept. PM, The Asheville School, Asheville NC 28806, phone (704)255-7909, founded 1989, publishers Jessica Bayer and J.W. Bonner, publishes 20- to 40-page chapbooks. French Broad Press **does not accept unsolicited material.**

FRIENDS JOURNAL (IV-Specialized: Quakerism), 1501 Cherry St., Philadelphia PA 19102-1497, phone (215)241-7277, founded 1827 as *The Friend*, 1844 as *Friends Intelligencer,* 1955 as *Friends Journal,* appears monthly, magazine-sized, circulation 9,500. Subscription: $25/year. **"We seek poetry that resonates with Quakerism and Quaker concerns, such as peace, nonviolence and spiritual seeking." No multiple or simultaneous submissions. Pays 2 copies/poem.**

‡FRISSON: DISCONCERTING VERSE; SKULL JOB PRODUCTIONS (I, IV-Form/style), 1012 Pleasant Dale Dr., Wilmington NC 28412-7617, phone (910)799-3356, founded 1995, editor Scott H. Urban. *frisson: disconcerting verse*, published quarterly, "presents poetry that is disturbing, haunting, macabre, yet subtle—poetry that attempts to elicit 'frisson.' " **They want "poetry that takes readers past the edge of comfort and into disturbing realms of experience. Poems should attempt to elicit the delicate sensation of 'frisson.' Any form or length, although shorter poems stand better chance." They do not want "light verse, romantic verse, inspirational verse, humorous verse."** They have recently published poetry by Robert Perchan, John Grey, D.F. Lewis and Thomas Wiloch. As a sample the editor selected these lines from "Flight" by Corrine DeWinter:

> *Awakened before dawn*
> *I turned to see you*
> *sprawled*
> *as if you had crawled*
> *onto the ledge of the fortieth floor*
> *and leapt*

frisson is 16-20 pgs., digest-sized, photocopied, saddle-stapled with cardstock cover, original artwork on cover and in interior with limited ads. They receive about 150-200 poems a year, accept approximately 10-15%. Press run is 100 for 50 subscribers, with 15 distributed free to reviewers. Subscription: $8. **Sample postpaid: $2. Make checks payable to Scott H. Urban. Submit 4-5 poems at a time in standard poem ms format. No previously published poems; simultaneous submissions OK. Cover letter preferred.** Time between acceptance and publication is 3-5 months. **Poems chosen "solely according to editor's personal taste—how well each individual poem is applicable to the concept of 'disconcerting verse.' " Often comments on rejections. May publish theme issues in the future. Send SASE for guidelines. Reports within a week. Sometimes sends prepublication galleys. Pays 2 copies or "short" subscription. Acquires first North American serial rights.** There is no review column as such, although editor recommends material in the introductory 'Foreshadowings' article. Poets may also send books for review consideration. The editor advises, "Open others' perceptions to that shadowy, half-glimpsed world that you as a poet are aware lurks just at the edge of each dream. . . ."

*FROGMORE PAPERS; FROGMORE POETRY PRIZE (III), 42 Morehall Ave., Folkestone, Kent CT19 4EF England, founded 1983, poetry editor Jeremy Page, is a biannual literary magazine with emphasis on new poetry and short stories. **"Quality is generally the only criterion, although pressure of space means very long work (over 100 lines) is unlikely to be published."** They have recently published poetry by Carole Satyamurt, John Mole, Katherine Pierpoint, Elizabeth Garrett, R. Nikolas Macioci and John Latham. As a sample the editor selected these lines by Tobius Hill:

> *if I stand just here, just right*
> *and look up, I can see the rain*
> *coming, and light on aeroplanes*
> *high and certain, crossing time zones.*

The magazine is 42 pgs., saddle-stapled with matte card cover, photocopied in photoreduced typescript. They accept 3% of the poetry received. Their press run is 300 for 120 subscribers. Subscription: £6 ($12). **Sample postpaid: £2 ($5). (US payments should be made in cash, not check.) Submit 5-6 poems at a time. Considers simultaneous submissions. Editor rarely comments on rejections. Reports in 3-6 months. Pays 1 copy.** Staff reviews books of poetry in 2-3 sentences, single format. Send books for review consideration to Sophie Hannah, reviews editor, 127 Horton Rd., Manchester M14 7QD England. They also publish *Crabflower* pamphlets and have published collections by Geoffrey Holloway, Robert Etty, Sophie Hannah and Giles Goodland as well as several anthologies. Write for information about the annual Frogmore Poetry Prize. The editor says, "My advice to people starting to write poetry would be: Read as many recognized modern poets as you can and don't be afraid to experiment."

FRONTIERS: A JOURNAL OF WOMEN STUDIES (IV-Feminist), % Susan Armitage, Wilson 12, Washington State University, Pullman WA 99164-4007, founded 1975, is published 3 times/year and **uses poetry on feminist themes.** They have published work by Audré Lorde, Janice Mirikitani, Carol Wolfe Konek and Opal Palmer Adisa. The journal is 200-208 pgs., 6×9, flat-spined. Circulation 1,000. **Sample: $9. No simultaneous submissions. Reports in 3-5 months. Pays 2 copies.** "We are not currently publishing reviews of books, poetry, essays or otherwise."

‡FUCK DECENCY (II, IV-Erotica, science fiction), 5960 S. Land Park Dr., Suite 253, Sacramento CA 95822, phone (916)429-8522, e-mail roller666@aol.com, website http://members.aol.com/nnd6/fuckdecency.h tml/, founded 1986, publisher Andrew L. Roller. This electronic newsletter appears daily. **They want experimental and/or erotic poetry. Any type is acceptable, but they must have some literary merit.** Also willing to look at **"occult or science fiction poetry (political or comics related)."** As a sample the publisher selected these lines by Alan Freer:

> *Crow spies Wogg huddled*
> *over a small writhing shape;*
> *curious*
> *Crow jutts down.*
>
> *Crow lands atop the fuzzbaby head,*
> *pecks the scalp with a questing beak.*
> *In annoyance*
> *Patchwork grabs a tuft of feathers*
> *and stuffs Crow into his gaping maw;*
> *burps a muffled caw.*

The newsletter is 8 pgs., e-mailed to 300 subscribers, plus newsgroups, BBS's, FTP sites and web pages. **Submit two to three poems at a time. "Poems should be well typed for camera ready reproduction." E-mail submissions preferred. Reports "at once." Pays 1 copy. Acquires first North American serial rights.** Reviews loose poetry, books of poetry and zines. Open to unsolicited reviews. Poets may also send chapbooks for review consideration. The editor says, "Just send me 2-3 poems. If I like them, I'll publish them. Currently I need a new poem every day and I publish (almost) every day. I'd love to just run Shakespeare and Milton but that would be useless since they are readily available at any bookstore. So I need new high-quality poetry, from you!"

THE FUDGE CAKE (I, IV-Children/teens), P.O. Box 197, Citrus Heights CA 95611-0197, founded 1994, editor/publisher Jancarl Campi, is a bimonthly children's newsletter designed to showcase the work of young writers. **They want poetry and short stories written by children ages 6-17. "Any form is fine. Open to any style or subject matter. Poetry: 30 lines or less. Short stories: 300-400 words."** As a sample we selected these lines from "The Sentry of the Highway" by Alice Martin:

> *The sentry of the highway*
> *Stands guard over the desert*
> *Mankind glides by*
> *Not pausing to fight.*

The Fudge Cake is 20 pgs., 5½×8½, desktop-published and saddle-stapled with colored paper cover and computer-generated graphics. Press run is 300 for 100 subscribers; 150 distributed free to libraries and bookstores. Subscription: $10 US, $12 Canada, $15 overseas. **Sample postpaid: $3. Submit 1-4 poems at a time. "Submissions should be typed or neatly printed on 8½×11 white paper." Previously published poems OK. Cover letter required with #10 SASE for notification. "Copies of poems and stories are not returned."** Often comments on rejections or suggests revisions. Send #10 SASE for guidelines. Reports in 2 months. Pays 1 copy. Authors retain all rights. Holds bimonthly contests. Winners are published in the winners' section of the next edition. The editor adds, "We value the work of today's children and feel they need an outlet to express themselves."

FUGUE (II), Room 200, Brink Hall, University of Idaho, Moscow ID 83844-1102, website http://www.uidaho. edu/LS/Eng/Fugue, founded 1989, is a biannual literary digest of the University of Idaho. **They have "no limits" on type of poetry. "We're not interested in trite or quaint verse. Nothing self-indulgent or overly metaphoric to the point of being obscure."** They have recently published poetry by Ricardo Sanchez and Jack Myers. As a sample the editor selected these lines from "Sister Shirt" by Brenda Hillman:

> *. . . I said what*

> *do you think of him? With his beautiful face,*
> *we lay like a saint without god, candle*
> *without fire—*
> *no translation for tomorrow—*

The editor says *Fugue* is 96 pgs., digest-sized, perfect-bound. They receive approximately 400 poems/semester, use 5-10 poems/issue. Press run is 250 plus an electronic version on the World Wide Web. **Sample postpaid: $5. No previously published poems or simultaneous submissions. Reads submissions September 1 through April 1 only. Reports in 1-3 months. Pays at least 1 copy and honorarium. Buys first North American serial rights.** The editor says, "Proper manuscript format and submission etiquette is expected; submissions without proper SASE will not be read or held on file."

FULL-TIME DADS (IV-Specialized), P.O. Box 577, Cumberland ME 04021, phone (207)829-5260, e-mail fulltdad@pipeline.com, website http://www.parentsplace.com/readroom/fulltdad, founded 1991, editor/publisher Stephen Harris, is an electronic magazine that seeks "to encourage and support men in their work as fathers." **They want material about fathers, fatherhood, and parenting from a father's perspective. As for poetry, "short is better. Not overly sentimental, but must come from the heart. Humor a plus. Absolutely no violence or anti-child, anti-male attitudes."** *Full-Time Dads* is only available on the Internet. Send e-mail for more information. **They accept about 10 poetry submissions a year. Previously published poems and e-mail submissions OK; no simultaneous submissions. Always comments on rejections. Send SASE for guidelines. Reports in 2 weeks. Acquires one-time rights.** Reviews books, etc., that deal with fatherhood. Open to unsolicited reviews. Poets may also send related books for review consideration.

‡**GAFF PRESS (III)**, P.O. Box 1024, Astoria OR 97103-3051, phone (503)325-8288, founded 1987, publisher Paul Barrett, publishes **2 chapbooks/year. They want "anything well-crafted, meaningful, extensively polished. Anything with heart and balls. Only your best." They do not want "inchoate poetry."** They have recently published poetry by C.B. Doran-Maurer, Harrison Smith and S.W. Gilbert. Format of chapbooks varies. **Submit "unlimited" poems at a time. Previously published poems and simultaneous submissions OK.** Time between acceptance and publication varies. **Always comments on rejections. Reports ASAP to queries and mss. Pay varies widely. Obtain samples of chapbooks by writing to the above address.** The publisher says, "We sometimes pass poems on to one of several alternative newspapers—friends who use good poems, with permission of course. No typos. Poems must sing! Please don't send anything unpolished, unedited. Only your best, nothing less. Always include a SASE."

*****GAIRM; GAIRM PUBLICATIONS (IV-Ethnic, foreign language)**, 29 Waterloo St., Glasgow G2 6BZ Scotland, phone/fax (0141)221-1971, editor Derick Thomson, founded 1952. *Gairm* is a quarterly that uses **modern/cosmopolitan and traditional/folk verse in Scottish Gaelic only.** It has published the work of all significant Scottish Gaelic poets, and much poetry translated from European languages. An anthology of such translations, *European Poetry in Gaelic*, is available for £7.50 or $15. *Gairm* is 96 pgs., digest-sized, flat-spined with coated card cover. Circulation is 2,000. **Sample: $3.50. Submit 3-4 poems at a time. Reads submissions October 1 through July 31 only.** Staff reviews books of poetry in 500-700 words, single format; 100 words, multi-book format. Occasionally invites reviews. Send books for review consideration. **All of the publications of the press are in Scottish Gaelic.** Catalog available.

‡**GARNET (II)**, P.O. Box 655, Hampden-Sydney VA 23943, (804)223-6786, e-mail purcellm@tiger.hsc.edu, website http://www.hsc.edu, founded 1937, editor Lem Purcell, is a semiannual journal of literature and the creative arts published by Hampden-Sydney College. **"We like to see most anything—forms, free verse, light verse. Poems must, of course, be of the highest quality. No trash. No erotica, juvenile, religious or romantic work."** They have recently published poetry by Craig Challender, Jaroslav Seifert, Grace Simpson and Louis Simpson. As a sample the editor selected these lines from "Who Knows" by Richard Stern:

> *Such the enzymes that decayed*
> *the sugars of life and laid*
> *him youthful in the ground, amazed, decayed.*

Garnet is 80-100 pgs., 6×9, professionally printed, perfect-bound with glossy card cover, photography and art included. They receive about 500 poems a year, accept approximately 5-10%. Press run is 1,000 for 400 subscribers of which 20 are libraries, 100-200 shelf sales; about 500 distributed free to students, professors, alumni and contributors. Single copy: $3.95; subscription: $6. **Sample postpaid: $5. Submit 2-5 poems at a time. No previously published poems; simultaneous submissions OK. Cover letter required.** "Double space poems;

FOR INFORMATION ON ENTERING the *1999 Poet's Market* Poetry Contest, see page 2.

include name, address and phone number on ms; include 3-5 line bio; electronic submissions accepted—contact editor for details." Time between acceptance and publication is 6-8 months. **Poems are circulated to an editorial board. "Poems are read by the editor and two poetry editors." Often comments on rejections. Send SASE for guidelines or request via e-mail. Reports in 6-8 weeks. Sometimes sends prepublication galleys. Pays 2 copies. Acquires one-time rights.** Reviews books or chapbooks in 1,000-2,000 words in single book format. Open to unsolicited reviews. Poets may also send books for review consideration. Sponsors several contests awarding a total of $1,000. All submissions are automatically eligible. The editor says, "We have published both beginners and Pulitzer Prize recipients. We're not looking for names; we're looking for outstanding poetry. Show us you care for your work."

GASLIGHT: TALES OF THE UNSANE (IV-Horror, science fiction/fantasy), P.O. Box 21, Cleveland MN 56017, founded 1992, editor Melissa Gish, published annually. **All poetry must be related to the genres of horror, dark fantasy, or sci-fi and must be under 3 pages. No high fantasy, sword and sorcery, or gaming themes."** They have published poetry by Ruth Berman and Herb Kauderer. The editor says *Gaslight* is 100 pgs., digest-sized and perfect-bound with b&w art. They receive about 500 poems a year, accept approximately 8%. Press run is 500 for 400 subscribers. Single copy: $10. **Sample postpaid: $3 (for back issue in previous format). Submit 3 poems at a time. No previously published poems or simultaneous submissions. Cover letter preferred.** Time between acceptance and publication is up to 1 year. **Always comments on rejections. Send SASE for guidelines before submitting. Reports in 1 month. Pays up to 10¢/line and 1 copy. Buys first North American serial rights.** Includes brief reviews of genre material. Open to unsolicited reviews. Poets may also send related books for review consideration. The editors are organizing a contest for female poets who have published less than 5 poems. Send SASE for guidelines and dates.

‡A GATHERING OF THE TRIBES; FLY BY NIGHT PRESS (II), P.O. Box 20693, New York NY 10009, phone (212)674-3778, e-mail tribes@interport.net, website http://www.interport.net/~tribes, founded 1991, managing editor Renée McManus. *A Gathering of the Tribes*, published biannually, "showcases established and emerging poets, writers, artists and forums." **They want poetry 30 lines maximum. They do not want "third-rate poetry."**

● Fly By Night Press is a subsidy publisher, expecting the author to pay 50% of the publishing costs.
They have recently published poetry by Jayne Cortez, Nikki Giovanni, Victor Cruz and Kimiko Hahn. As a sample the editor selected these lines from "How I Love Ya" by Tracie Morris:

> Sweat like grease running
> As if away from slavery
> Smothered grandmother.

The editor says *A Gathering of the Tribes* is 89 pgs., 8 × 10, glossy cover, with ads in back pages. They receive about 600 poems a year, accept approximately 5%. Press run is 2,000 for 100 subscribers of which 10 are libraries, 100 shelf sales; 200 distributed free. Subscription: $22.50. **Sample postpaid: $10. Submit 3 poems at a time. Previously published poems and simultaneous submissions OK. Cover letter preferred. E-mail submissions OK.** Time between acceptance and publication is 3 months. **Always comments on rejections. Publishes theme issues. Send SASE for guidelines. Reports immediately. Always sends prepublication galleys. Pays 1 copy.** Staff reviews books of poetry or other magazines. Poets may also send books for review consideration. Fly By Night Press publishes "excellence in poetry from a diverse perspective (topics of the author's choosing)." Books are usually 70 pgs., 5½ × 7½. **Replies to queries in 3 months. Pays 12-15% royalties and 500 author's copies (out of a press run of 1,000). Offers subsidy arrangements: Tribes puts up 50% fee, author puts up 50% and sells their half. Obtain sample books by writing to the above address.** Sponsors annual poetry contest. Deadline: April. Send up to 3 poems, no poem to exceed 30 lines with a $10 fee. First place prize of $500 and publication. They were awarded third place for their contest by the American Magazine Society. The editor says, "We believe the United States should celebrate its diversity from a global perspective. *Tribes* tries to achieve the same through excellence in the arts."

GAZELLE PUBLICATIONS (V), 11650 Red Bud Trail, Berrien Springs MI 49106, phone (800)650-5076 (orders only), e-mail kivu@juno.com, website http://www.goshen.net/Gazelle/, founded 1976, editor Ted Wade, is a publisher for home schools and compatible markets including **books of verse for children but is not currently considering unsolicited manuscripts. Obtain guidelines via e-mail or website.**

GENERATOR; GENERATOR PRESS (V), 3203 W. 14th St. #13, Cleveland OH 44109-1810, founded 1987, poetry editor John Byrum, is an annual magazine "devoted to the presentation of **all types of experimental poetry, focusing on language poetry and 'concrete' or visual poetic modes."** They have published poetry by Susan Smith Nash, Jessica Grim, Jane Reavill Ransom, Deborah Meadows, Liz Waldner and Carla Bertola. As a sample the editor selected these lines from "Edifice Wrecks" by Ross Martin:

> The purpose of this listing is
> simply to help investigators in this field
> to locate scattered references to data that
> might be useful to them in their work.

Generator is magazine-sized, photocopied, side-stapled, using b&w graphics, with matte card cover. Press run is 200 copies for 25 subscribers of which 20 are libraries. **Sample postpaid: $8. Pays 1 copy.** Generator Press also publishes the **Generator Press chapbook series. Approximately 2-4 new titles/year. They are currently not accepting unsolicited manuscripts for either the magazine or chapbook publication.** Together with Score (see listing in this section), Generator Press has published *CORE: A Symposium on Contemporary Visual Poetry*, described as "an international survey of the methods, opinions and work of over 75 contemporary visual poets" (photocopy version available for $25). The editor adds, "Worthwhile writers do not need advice and should not heed any but their own."

THE GENTLE SURVIVALIST (I, IV-Ethnic, nature, inspirational), Box 4004, St. George UT 84770, website http://www.infowest.com/gentle/, founded 1991, editor/publisher Laura Martin-Bühler, publishes "Eleven issues over a 13-month period" (not published in February and August). *The Gentle Survivalist* is a newsletter of "harmony—timeless truths and wisdom balanced with scientific developments. For Native Americans and all those who believe in the Great Creator." **They want poetry that is "positive, inspirational, on survival of body and spirit, also man's interconnectedness with God and all His creations. Nothing sexually oriented, occult, negative or depressing."** They have published poetry by Keith Moore and C.S. Churchman. *TGS* is 8 pgs. (two 11×17 sheets folded in half). The issues we have received warn readers about the dangers of aluminum and formaldehyde, discuss herbal medicine, and offer spice and food alternatives for those "stuck in a rut." They also offer money-saving tips and ideas on writing a personal history. "We print four poems average per issue." Press run is 200. Subscription: $20. **Sample postpaid: $2. Submit 4 poems at a time. Previously published poems and simultaneous submissions OK. Cover letter required; "just a note would be fine. I find noteless submissions too impersonal."** Time between acceptance and publication is 3-4 months. **Send SASE for guidelines. Reports within 2 months. Does not return poetry. Pays 1 copy.** Sponsors annual contest. Awards a 1-year subscription to the winner. Winner announced in December issue. Send SASE for details. The editor says, "To succeed, one must not seek supporters, but seek to know whom to support. *TGS* receives a great deal of poetry that is general in nature. We seek poems of inspiration about God, Man and our interconnectedness with all living."

GEORGE & MERTIE'S PLACE: ROOMS WITH A VIEW (I, II), P.O. Box 10335, Spokane WA 99209-1335, phone (509)325-3738, founded 1995, editors George Thomas and Mertie Duncan, appears monthly except for January. *GMP* is "a Spokane home for wayward literature, a monthly journal of opinion and imagination or any realm between. **We are open to any form but our limited format prohibits long poetry. Social realism is just one interest."** They have recently published poetry by Tom Gribble, Iris Neal and Tom Hunley. As a sample the editors selected these lines from "Why I Don't Vote" by Geoff Peterson:

> *Some columnist said it best.*
> *He said remember the shiny boys and girls*
> *who courted your vote*
> *to be president*
> *when you were horny and failing math*
> *and too crazy to drive a car? . . .*

GMP is a 4- to 8-page, 8½×11, "micromagazine," printed (unbound) on colored paper with b&w graphics. In addition to poetry it may contain essays, short short stories, letters, opinions and "tidbits with a twist." Press run is 50 for 20 subscribers, 20 shelf sales. Single copy: $1.50; subscription: $12/year. **Sample postpaid: $2. Submit 3 poems at a time. No previously published poems or simultaneous submissions. Cover letter preferred, "but not a long list of credits; we're looking for personal historical comments to personalize our content."** Time between acceptance and publication is 3 months. **Seldom comments on rejections. Reports in 1-2 months. Pays 1¢/word ($2 minimum) and 1 copy.** A $10 "Best of Issue" prize is awarded each month; poetry, fiction and essays compete. They say, "We think much poetry is sterile and not attached to the world where men and women struggle to survive in an ever more alienating environment."

GEORGETOWN REVIEW (II), P.O. Box 6309, Southern Station, Hattiesburg MS 39406-6309, phone/fax (601)583-6930, e-mail jsfulmer@whale.st.edu, website http://www.2.digimag.net/~georgetownreview/, founded 1992, is a biannual literary journal publishing fiction and poetry—no criticism or reviews. **They want "honest, quality work; not interested in tricks."** They have published poetry by Fred Chappell, John Tagliabue, William Greenway, Elton Glaser, X.J. Kennedy, Peter Wild, Michael Cadnum and Alan Feldman. *GR* is 100-120 pgs., 5½×8½, perfect-bound, with heavy stock cover with art. They receive about 1,000 submissions a year, "take maybe 10%." Press run is 1,000. Subscription: $10/year. **Sample postpaid: $5. Submit no more than 5 poems at a time, name and address on each page. No previously published poems; simultaneous submissions OK. Reads submissions September 1 through May 1 only. Poems are read by at least 3 readers. Sometimes comments on rejections. Reports in 2-4 months. Always sends prepublication galleys. Pays 2 copies. Acquires all rights. Returns rights provided "our name is mentioned in any reprint."** Sponsors annual poetry contest. $500 first prize; runners-up receive publication and subscription. Entry fee: $5 for the first poem, $2 each additional poem. Deadline: October 1. Winner and runners-up announced in fall issue each year.

GEORGIA JOURNAL (IV-Regional), P.O. Box 1604, Decatur GA 30031-1604, phone (404)377-4275, poetry editor Janice Moore. *Georgia Journal* is a bimonthly magazine covering the state of Georgia. **They use poetry**

"from Georgia writers or poetry about Georgia. It should be suitable for the general reader." They have published poems by former President Jimmy Carter, Stephen Corey, Blanche Farley and Adrienne Bond. As a sample the editor selected these lines from "Next Door" by John Stone:

> of a sudden
> with no fanfare
> but much finesse
>
> the gingko that
> has blazed all month
> has acquiesced

Georgia Journal is 80 pgs., 8½ × 11, saddle-stapled and professionally printed on glossy paper with color cover. Circulation is 15,000. Recent issues feature accessible narrative and lyric free verse. Content is genuinely open and varied, from nature and personal poems to war and meditative verse. About 4 poems appear in each issue. Single copy: $3.95. **Submit 3-4 poems at a time, maximum length 30 lines. "A brief cover letter with previous publications is fine, but keep it brief." Send SASE for guidelines. Reports in 2-3 months. Pays copies. Acquires first rights.** Staff selects books by Georgia authors to review.

UNIVERSITY OF GEORGIA PRESS; CONTEMPORARY POETRY SERIES (II), 330 Research Dr., Suite B100, University of Georgia, Athens GA 30602-4901, phone (706)369-6140, press founded 1938, series founded 1980, series editor Bin Ramke, publishes 4 collections of poetry/year, **2 of which are by poets who have not had a book published,** in paperback editions. They have published poetry by Martha Collins, Marjorie Welish, Arthur Vogelsang and C.D. Wright. **"Writers should query first for guidelines and submission periods. Please enclose SASE." There are no restrictions on the type of poetry submitted,** but "familiarity with our previously published books in the series may be helpful." **$10 submission fee required.** Manuscripts are *not* returned after the judging is completed. **Always sends prepublication galleys.**

THE GEORGIA REVIEW (II), The University of Georgia, Athens GA 30602-9009, phone (706)542-3481, founded 1947, editor Stanley W. Lindberg, associate editor Stephen Corey, assistant editor Janet Wondra. They have recently published poetry by Philip Booth, Brendan Galvin, Maurya Simon and Peter Meinke. "Also have featured first-ever publications by many new voices over the years, but encourage all potential contributors to become familiar with past offerings before submitting." As a sample the editor selected these lines from "Autumn Leaves" by Jeff Mock:

> The maples are speaking their off-
> Colored tongue. It's luscious
> In her ear, the red weather
> Licking from ear to spine
> And down. It's a promise to be
> Unfaithful.

This distinguished quarterly is 208 pgs., 7 × 10, professionally printed, flat-spined with glossy card cover. They use 60-70 poems a year, less than one-half of one percent of those received. Circulation is 6,000. Subscription: $18/year. **Sample postpaid: $6. Submit 3-5 poems at a time. No simultaneous submissions. Rarely uses translations. No submissions accepted during June, July and August. Publishes theme issues occasionally. Reports in 1-3 months. Always sends prepublication galleys. Pays $3/line. Buys first North American serial rights.** Reviews books of poetry. "Our poetry reviews range from 500-word 'Book Briefs' on single volumes to 5,000-word essay reviews on multiple volumes." *The Georgia Review* is one of the best literary journals around. It respects its audience, edits intelligently and has won or been nominated for awards in competition with such slicks as *The Atlantic*, *The New Yorker* and *Esquire*. Work appearing here has also been included in the 1992 and 1995 volumes of *The Best American Poetry*. Needless to say, competition is extremely tough. All styles and forms are welcome, but response times can be slow during peak periods in the fall and late spring. Yet the editors say they would like to receive "the very best work from an even wider slate of poets."

GERBIL: A QUEER CULTURE ZINE; GERBIL PRESS (II, IV-Gay/lesbian/bisexual), P.O. Box 10692, Rochester NY 14610, phone (716)262-3966, e-mail gerbilzine@aol.com, website http://www.multicom.org/ger bil/gerbil.htm, founded 1994, editors Tony Leuzzi and Brad Pease. *Gerbil* is a quarterly designed to provide "an open forum for lesbian/gay-identified writers and artists to express themselves and their work." **They seek poetry with gay/lesbian content but are not limited to that. They are "open to all forms as long as the poetic voice is honest and clear. We look for lively, personal material of literary merit. No angst, pointless experimenta-tion or abstraction."** They have recently published poetry by Rane Arroyo, David Trinidad, Beth Bailey, Horehound Stillpoint and Deborah Moore. As a sample the editors selected these lines from "Randy Poem" by Glenn Sheldon:

> At first six hands busy themselves
> unwinding time's new tonight; you say
> you've thrown caution to the wind,
> let it rain cats and dogs, let me be judged or
> not, *but then you flip on yourself, toss us*

out of the bed you borrowed.

Gerbil is 28 pgs., about 7½ × 9½, offset and saddle-stitched with coated paper cover and b&w photos and graphics and lots of spot color inside. They receive about 500 poems a year, accept about 20. Press run is 2,000 for 100 subscribers, 700 shelf sales. Subscription: $10/4 issues. **Sample postpaid: $3. Submit 3-5 poems at a time. No previously published poems. "Friendly" cover letter preferred. Disk submissions (for Mac) welcome. E-mail submissions OK.** Time between acceptance and publication is up to 1 year. **Always comments on rejections. Publishes theme issues occasionally. Reports in 1-3 months. Pays 2 copies. Acquires first rights.** Reviews books of poetry and other magazines. Open to unsolicited reviews. Poets may also send books for review consideration. Occasionally sponsors poetry contests; watch website or zine for details. Gerbil Press also occasionally publishes **chapbooks on a cooperative basis. They usually work with poets who first published in the magazine, and their publishing arrangements vary based on the writer and project.** As for the zine, they say, "If you're a beginning writer, don't be afraid to submit work! We publish a wide range of work of literary merit."

‡GESTALTEN [EXPERIMENTAL POETRY]; BROKEN BOULDER PRESS (II, IV-Form), 1207 W. 19th St., Lawrence KS 66046, e-mail psilvia@stat1.cc.ukans.edu, founded 1996, editor Paul Silvia. *gestalten: [experimental poetry]* is an annual "devoted solely to poetry that is experimental in content, form or any other aspect." **They want "poems that are aggressively experimental; poems that are to mainstream poetry as the Mahavishnu Orchestra is to mainstream jazz. We'll read everything but are suspicious of most religious, 'love,' and 'my girl/boyfriend dumped me' poetry."**

- When asked for a list of recently published poets and a sample poem, they noted they preferred not to include this information to avoid biasing submissions.

The editor says *gestalten* is 40-60 poems enclosed in a digest-sized envelope with small press ads. They receive about 500 poems a year; accept approximately 10%. Press run is 100 for 40 subscribers, 20 shelf sales. Single copy: $4; subscription: $3/1 year; $5/2 years. **Sample postpaid: $3. Make checks payable to Paul Silvia. Submit up to 25 poems at a time. Previously published poems and simultaneous submissions OK, if stated in cover letter. Cover letter required including brief bio and publication credits. E-mail for electronic submission guidelines.** Time between acceptance and publication varies. **Often comments on rejections. Reports in 1 month maximum. Sometimes sends prepublication galleys. Pays 1 copy. Acquires one-time rights.** "We do not write reviews but are very receptive to unsolicited reviews (200-300 words)." Broken Boulder Press publishes "chapbooks of experimental and inventive poetry, fiction and nonfiction." They publish **1-2 chapbooks/year.** Chapbooks are usually 12-20 pgs., 5½ × 8½, photocopied, and saddle-stapled with card stock cover, occasional graphics. **Query first with 6-10 sample poems and cover letter with brief bio and publication credits. Replies to queries in 2-4 weeks, to mss in 1 month. Pays 25% of a minimum press run of 100. Obtain samples of chapbooks by sending $4.** The editor says, "Most chapbook rejections are due to a lack of resources, not a lack of respect for the work, so don't be discouraged if your manuscript isn't accepted. We're receptive to beginning and unpublished poets. We occasionally solicit work. We try to keep things friendly and informal and hope that contributors do likewise."

THE GETTYSBURG REVIEW (II), Gettysburg College, Gettysburg PA 17325, phone (717)337-6770, founded 1988, editor Peter Stitt, is a multidisciplinary literary quarterly considering **"well-written poems of all kinds."** They have published poetry by Rita Dove, Donald Hall, Susan Ludvigson, Pattiann Rogers, Charles Wright and Paul Zimmer. As a sample the editor selected these lines by Thomas Rabbitt:

> *My father nods again and does not speak.*
> *This is Boston. He is thirty-six. The war is over.*
> *The good times have begun. And yet, overhead,*
> *Floating in the oaks above Hyde Park, there is*
> *This blimp, round as a breast, gray as death,*
> *Slow as a mortgage, going nowhere overhead.*

They accept 1-2% of submissions received. Press run is 4,500 for 2,700 subscriptions. **Sample postpaid: $7. Submit 3-5 poems at a time, with SASE. No previously published poems or simultaneous submissions. Cover letter preferred. Reads submissions September through May only. Publishes theme issues occasionally. Pays $2/line.** Essay-reviews are featured in each issue. Open to unsolicited essay-reviews. Poets may also send books for review consideration. Editor Peter Stitt, a leading literary critic and reviewer, has created a well-edited and respected journal that features a tantalizing lineup of poems in all styles and forms. Competition is keen, and response times can be slow during heavy submission periods, especially in the late fall. Work appearing in *The*

MARKET CONDITIONS are constantly changing! If you're still using this book and it is 1999 or later, buy the newest edition of *Poet's Market* at your favorite bookstore or order directly from Writer's Digest Books.

Gettysburg Review has been included in *The Best American Poetry* (1993, 1994, 1995 and 1997) and *Pushcart Prize* anthologies. As for the editor, Peter Stitt won the first PEN/Nora Magid Award for Editorial Excellence.

GINGER HILL (II), c/o English Dept., Room 314, Spotts World Cultures Building, Slippery Rock University, Slippery Rock PA 16057, founded 1963, is an annual literary magazine using **"academic poetry, with preference for excellent free verse, but all forms considered. 27-line limit. No greeting card verse, no sentimentality, no self-serving or didactic verse."** They have published poetry by Elizabeth R. Curry, B.Z. Niditch, Lyn Lifshin and Robert Cooperman. It is digest-sized, "varies in format and layout every year," perfect-bound, with 2,000 distributed free. **Submit 3 poems at a time in duplicate. No previously published poems. Submissions must be postmarked on or before December 1 of each year. Send SASE for guidelines. Pays 2 copies.** They say, "We choose about 5-10% of all submissions. Excellence is stressed."

THE GLASS CHERRY PRESS; THE GLASS CHERRY (II), 901 Europe Bay Rd., Ellison Bay WI 54210-9643, founded 1994, editor Judith Hirschmiller. *The Glass Cherry* is a quarterly literary magazine composed primarily of contemporary poetry. **They want "original poetry that is stunning; poetry that clings, leaves a scar. Any form, length, style or subject matter, except pornographic."** They have published poetry by Simon Perchik and James Liddy. As a sample the editor selected the poem "Time's Shaft" by Philip C. Kolin:

> *Crumbling tomestones*
> *Redneck trailer parks*
> *Silver mines*
> *For eternity*

The Glass Cherry is 40-60 pgs., 5½×8½, saddle-stapled with card stock cover. Each issue has a featured poet whose work comprises approximately 40% of the issue, and a photo of the featured poet appears on the back cover. They receive about 2,000 poems a year, accept less than 10%. Press run is 500 for 25 subscribers ("and growing"), 5% shelf sales. Single copy: $5; subscription: $15. **Sample postpaid: $6. Make checks payable to Judith Hirschmiller. Submit up to 5 poems at a time, name and address on each page. Previously published poems OK, "only if requested." No simultaneous submissions. Cover letter with brief bio required. Seldom comments on rejections. Send SASE for guidelines and upcoming themes. Reports in 1 month. Pays 1 copy. Acquires first or one-time rights. Requests acknowledgment and notification from author when work is reprinted elsewhere.** Reviews books of poetry. Open to unsolicited reviews. Poets may also send books for review consideration. The Glass Cherry Press also plans to publish 3 books of poetry a year. Previously published: *My Mother's Fire* by Lyn Lifshin. **Poems included in book-length mss need not be previously published. The editor reads book-length submissions (20-60 pgs.) from January through April only. Send SASE for guidelines. Reports in 1-4 months. Samples are available from the press for $10 and a SASE.** The editor says, "Writers are encouraged to read back issues of *The Glass Cherry* prior to submitting."

GLB PUBLISHERS (III, IV-Gay/lesbian/bisexual), P.O. Box 78212, San Francisco CA 94107-8212, phone (415)621-8307, founded 1990, associate editor John Hanley. "We are **cooperative publishers. Founded for gay, lesbian and bisexual writers. Authors share cost of printing and promotion but have much control over cover design, typefaces, general appearance."** They publish 2-4 paperbacks and 1-2 hardbacks/year. **They want "book-length collections from gay, lesbian or bisexual writers. Nothing antagonistic to gay, lesbian or bisexual life-styles."** They have published poetry by Robert Peters, Paul Genega and Thomas Cashet. **Previously published poems OK; no simultaneous submissions. Cover letter required. "Author should explain intention for poems and expectations for sales of books." Often comments on rejections. Replies to queries in 10 days, to mss in 1 month. Always sends prepublication galleys. Pays 15-25% royalties and 20 author's copies. Check bookstores for samples.**

*GLOBAL TAPESTRY JOURNAL; BB BOOKS (II), Spring Bank, Longsight Rd., Copster Green, Blackburn, Lancs, BB1 9EU United Kingdom, founded 1963, poetry editor Dave Cunliffe. **"Experimental, avant-garde—specializing in exciting high-energy new writing. Mainly for a bohemian and counter-culture audience. Poetry in the Beat tradition. Don't want contrived, traditional, pompous and academic or pretentious mainstream."** Also considers sexually explicit material. In addition to the magazine, *Global Tapestry Journal*, BB Books publishes chapbooks. "We want honest, uncontrived writing, strong in form and content. We don't want 'weekend hobby verse' and poetry without energy." They have published poetry by David Tipton, Kenneth Patchen, Jeff Cloves and Joy Walsh. As a sample the editor selected these lines by Liza Kucharski:

> *the system doesn't fit where our*
> *body's going to*
> *we make square corners*
> *and walk around them in curves*

GTJ is 72 pgs., 9×6, saddle-stapled, typeset in a variety of mostly small sizes of type, rather crowded format, casual pasteup, with b&w drawings, photos, collages, display and classified ads, with a 2-color matte card cover. Circulation 1,150 with 450 subscribers of which 50 are libraries. Subscription: £8 sterling for 4 issues mailed seamail to USA. **Sample postpaid: $3. Previously published poems OK. Cover letter, with clear address, telephone number and short publishing history, required. Send SASE (or SAE and IRC) for guidelines. Responds "soon," has an 18-month backlog. Pays 1 copy.** Open to unsolicited reviews. Poets may also send books for review consideration. BB Books publishes about **4 chapbooks of poetry/year. To submit for chapbook publication send 6 samples and cover letter giving publication credits. Pays 10% of press run in copies. Obtain sample chapbooks by sending SASE (or SAE with IRCs if foreign) for catalog.** David Cunliffe comments, "The United Kingdom has a limited number of magazines and small press ventures publishing poetry from unknowns. Many little mags are self-publishing cliques or small-time vanity operations. Simultaneous submissions and simultaneous publication are often resented. There is much readership crossover among the non-poet subscribers and they resent seeing the same work in many magazines over a short period. We typeset for a few United Kingdom mags and publishers and we see this in the setting jobs we do every week. Many of the editors circulate poet blacklists to help prevent this tendency from spreading."

DAVID R. GODINE, PUBLISHER (V), P.O. Box 9103, Lincoln MA 01773, website http://www.godine.com. They have published *New and Selected Poems* by Ron Padgett and *The Stonecutter's Hand* by Richard Tillinghast. They say, **"Our poetry program is completely filled through 1998, and we do not accept any unsolicited materials."**

GOLDEN ISIS MAGAZINE; GOLDEN ISIS PRESS; POEM OF THE YEAR CONTEST (I, IV-Mystical/occult), P.O. Box 525, Fort Covington NY 12937, founded 1980, editor Gerina Dunwich. "*Golden Isis* is a quarterly New Age/Neo-Pagan journal of Goddess-inspired poetry, Pagan art, Wiccan news and announcements, reviews, networking services, Witchy recipes, ritual outlines and ads. Positive magick for solitaries and covens of all traditions, and a literary forum in which individuals from around the world can share poetic visions and their special love for the Goddess and Horned God. **Occult, Egyptian, cosmic, euphonic and Goddess-inspired poems, mystical haiku and magickal chants are published. We are also interested in New Age spiritual poetry, astrological verses and poems dealing with peace, love and ecology. All styles considered; under 60 lines preferred. We do not want to see pornographic, Satanic, sexist or racist material."** They have recently published poetry by Lee Prosser, Reed Dunwich, Sheryl J. Miller and Anne Wilson. As a sample the editor selected these lines from "Transformation (A Circle Prayer)" by Gerina Dunwich:

> *Learn, learn, the magick of the Earth,*
> *the spiral dance of life,*
> *the cauldron of re-birth.*
> *Yearn, yearn, for the old forgotten days;*
> *return, return to our ancient Pagan ways.*

The magazine is 15-20 pgs., digest-sized, desktop-published, saddle-stapled with paper cover. International circulation is 5,000. Single copy: $3; subscription: $10/year. "No postal money orders, please." **Submit 1 poem/page, typed single-spaced, name and address on upper left corner and the number of lines on upper right corner. No limit on number of poems submitted. Previously published poems and simultaneous submissions OK. Occasionally comments on rejected material. Reports within 2-3 weeks. No payment or free copies. "We can no longer afford it." All rights revert to author upon publication.** Reviews books of poetry, "length varies." Open to unsolicited reviews. Poets may also send books for review consideration. Golden Isis Press **currently accepts mss for chapbook publication. Send complete ms and $5 reading fee. "Please make checks payable to Golden Isis. We offer a small advance, ten free copies of the published work, and 10% royalty on every copy sold for as long as the book remains in print." Sample chapbook (***Circle of Shadows*** by Gerina Dunwich): $3.95.** The magazine sponsors an annual "Poem of the Year" contest that offers cash prizes. Entry fee: $1/poem. Deadline: December 1. No limit on number of poems entered. Poems should be up to 60 lines, any form, with author's name and address on upper left corner of each page. Free guidelines and contest rules for SASE. *Golden Isis* is a member of W.P.P.A. (Wiccan/Pagan Press Alliance).

✤**GOOSE LANE EDITIONS (V)**, 469 King St., Fredericton, New Brunswick E3B 1E5 Canada, phone (506)450-4251, acquisitions editor L. Boone, founded 1956, is a small press publishing Canadian fiction, poetry and literary history. **Writers should be advised that Goose Lane considers mss by Canadian poets only.** They receive approximately 400 mss/year, publish 10-15 books yearly, 2 of these being poetry collections. Writers recently published include Gary Geddes, winner of the 1995 Gabriela Mistral Prize, and Douglas Lochhead. **They are not currently reading submissions. "Call to inquire whether we are reading submissions after January 1998."** Always sends prepublication galleys. Authors may receive royalty of up to 10% of retail sale price on all copies sold. Copies available to author at 40% discount.

‡**GORTDAY REVIEW (I)**, P.O. Box 170249, San Francisco CA 94117, founded 1993, editor Don Clog, is a monthly arts and literary journal. **They indicate no specifications or preferences as to the kind of poetry they are interested in.** They have recently published poetry by John Grey, Pete Lee, Mahdy H. Kaiyat and D. Castleman. The editor says *GR* is 8½×11, photocopied with color cover. They receive about 100-150 poems a year, accept all. Press run is 650 for 200 subscribers, 50 shelf sales; 300 distributed free to "science fiction cafe clubs, etc." Single copy: $2; subscription: $12/6 months. **Sample postpaid: $1.** Make checks payable to Don Clog. **Submit 4 poems at a time. Previously published poems and simultaneous submissions OK. Cover letter preferred.** Time between acceptance and publication is 2 months. **Poems are circulated to an editorial board. Seldom comments on rejections. Send SASE for guidelines. Reports "ASAP." Pays 1-3 copies.**

GOSPEL PUBLISHING HOUSE (IV-Religious); PENTECOSTAL EVANGEL (V); LIVE (IV-Religious); TEEN LIFE (V); WOMAN'S TOUCH (V); TAKE FIVE; JUNIOR TRAILS (IV-Religious, children/teens), The General Council of the Assemblies of God, 1445 Boonville Ave., Springfield MO 65802-1894, phone (417)831-8000 ext. 4276, fax (417)862-7566. **Gospel Publishing House produces the Spirit of Praise Bulletin Series. Poems accepted for back cover of bulletins. For more information, call or write to Promotions.** *Pentecostal Evangel* is a weekly magazine containing **inspirational articles and news of the Assemblies of God for members of the Assemblies and other Pentecostal and charismatic Christians,** circulation 250,000. **"Presently, the** *Pentecostal Evangel* **is not accepting poetry."** *Live* is a weekly **for adults in Assemblies of God Sunday schools,** circulation 125,000. **Traditional free and blank verse, 12-20 lines. "Please do not send large numbers of poems at one time." Submit seasonal material 1 year in advance; do not mention Santa Claus, Halloween or Easter bunnies. Sample copy and writer's guidelines for 7×10 SAE and 2 first-class stamps. Letters without SASE will not be answered. Pays $15/line on acceptance. Buys first and/or second rights.** *Teen Life* is a quarterly magazine of **Christian fiction and articles for teenagers, 12-19,** circulation 50,000. *Woman's Touch* is a bimonthly **inspirational magazine for women,** circulation 21,000. **However,** *Woman's Touch* **is currently not accepting poetry.** *Take Five* is a youth devotional **accepting poetry written by teens. Poetry should be typed, double-spaced, and must include the teen's name, complete address, church and age. Pays $15 upon acceptance.** *Junior Trails* is a weekly tabloid covering **religious fiction and biographical, historical and scientific articles with a spiritual emphasis for boys and girls ages 10-11,** circulation 38,000. **Buys 10-15 poems/year. Free verse and light verse. Submit seasonal/holiday material 15 months in advance. Simultaneous and previously published submissions OK. Sample copy and writer's guidelines for #10 SAE and 2 first-class stamps. Reports in 2-4 weeks. Pays $5-10 on acceptance. Buys first and/or second rights.** "We like poems showing contemporary children positively facing today's world. **For all our publications, submit one to two poems at a time."**

GOTTA WRITE NETWORK LITMAG; MAREN PUBLICATIONS (I, IV), 612 Cobblestone Circle, Glenview IL 60025, fax (847)296-7631, e-mail netera@aol.com, founded 1988, editor/publisher Denise Fleischer, features "contemporary poetry, articles, short stories and market listings. *GWN* now spans 40 states, Canada, England and Japan. Half of the magazine is devoted to science fiction and fantasy in a section called 'Sci-Fi Galleria.' **A short checklist of what I look for in all poems and stories would be: drawing the reader into the protagonist's life from the beginning; presenting a poem's message through powerful imagery and sensory details; and language that is fresh and dynamic. I prefer free verse. Would also like to receive experimental, multicultural, feminist, humor, contemporary and translations. The poetry we publish expresses today's society openly and honestly. Our contributors dive into the subjects where others turn away. They speak of moments before the bomb hit the Japanese, life in prison, anorexia, suicide attempts, and life in a nursing home."** She has published poetry by Mary Gallagher, Lyn Lifshin, Robin Bayne, Roxanne Sadovsky and Debbie McIntyre. As a sample the editor has selected the poem "Street Games" by Sharon Anderson:

> *Children tossing stones on bloodstained chalk*
> *drawings. . . . a new kind of hopscotch*
> *played in alleys of bullet-ridden tenements.*

The semiannual is 48-64 pgs., magazine-sized, desktop-published, saddle-stapled. "*Gotta Write Network* subscribers receive more than a magazine. In subscribing, they become part of a support group of both beginners and established poets. Readers are from all walks of life. I'm striving to give beginners a positive starting point (as well as promote the work of established writers and editors) and to encourage them to venture beyond rejection slips and writer's block. Publication can be a reality if you have determination and talent. There are over a thousand U.S. litmags waiting for submissions. So take your manuscripts out of your desk and submit them today!" Subscription: $12.75. **Sample postpaid: $5. Submit up to 5 poems at a time. Name and address on each page. No previously published poems or simultaneous submissions. Include a cover letter and SASE. Accepts poetry submissions via fax "at night" or via e-mail "any hour." Reports in 2-4 months. Sometimes sends prepublication galleys. Pays 1 copy, offers second copy at a discount. Acquires first North American serial rights.** Pays $5 for assigned by-mail interviews with established big press authors and small press editors. Maren Publications now offers a small press magazine distribution service." She adds, "Write the way you feel the words. Don't let others mold you into another poet's style. Poetry is about personal imagery that needs to be shared with others."

‡GRAFFITI RAG; GRAFFITI RAG POETRY AWARD (I, II), 5647 Oakman Blvd., Dearborn MI 48126, founded 1995, editors Hayan Charara and Erik Fahrenkopf, published annually, is a "poetry journal that seeks to publish work of well-known and gifted unknown poets on the urban experience." **They want "poetry of the highest quality that brings a unique perspective on the shifting and limitless themes of urban life—economic, ethnic, intellectual, political, sexual."** They have recently published poetry by Philip Levine, Hayden Carruth, Sherman Alexie and Naomi Shihab Nye. As a sample the editor selected these lines from "Fire" by Bob Hicok:

> *A survivor*
> *of Auschwitz wrote in a knuckle-*
> *thick book he was jealous of the smoke*

> *because it left. And no, he said when asked,*
> *shame is not out of the question.*

Graffiti Rag is approximately 96 pgs., 6×9, perfect-bound, professionally printed with a colored matte cover. They receive about 300-500 poems a year, accept approximately 5-10%. Press run is 750, 400 shelf sales. Single copy: $9.95; subscription: $9.95 plus $1.50 p&h. **Sample issue: $7.95 plus $1.50 p&h. Submit 3-5 poems at a time. Previously published poems OK; no simultaneous submissions. Cover letter preferred.** Time between acceptance and publication is 2-8 weeks. **Poems are circulated to an editorial board. "Guest editor (usually poets) assist in editorial process. Final decisions are made by main editor, Charara and Fahrenkopf." Often comments on rejections. Send SASE for guidelines. Reports in 2-8 weeks. Pays 1 copy. Acquires first North American serial or one-time rights.** Sponsors the annual Graffiti Rag Poetry Award. Submit 3-5 unpublished poems from February 1 through April 30. Enclose reading fee of $10 (check or money order) and a SASE. Winning poet is featured in the anthology and receives cash award of $500. The editor says, "Advise yourself— be your hardest critic."

‡✦**GRAFFITO, THE POETRY POSTER (II)**, Dept. of English, University of Ottawa, Ottawa, Ontario K1N 6N5 Canada, fax (613)738-1929, e-mail graffito@uottawa.ca, website http://www.cyberperk.com/graffito, founded 1994, managing editor b stephen harding, is a monthly poster/zine. **They want any style of poetry, maximum 32 lines.** They have recently published poetry by R.M. Vaughan, George Elliot Clark, Michael Dennis, John B. Lee and Susan McMaster. *graffito* is an 11×17 sheet of colored paper folded in half to allow for a front cover and back cover containing reviews. Press run is 250; half distributed free within the local area of Ottawa. Subscription: $12 in Canada, $20 in US. **Sample postpaid: $1. Make checks payable to b stephen harding. Submit 5-8 poems at a time. Previously published poems OK "only in special cases;" no simultaneous submissions. Cover letter preferred. Reads submissions the 15th of every month.** Time between acceptance and publication is 2-3 months. **"We have a guest editor who is responsible for the content of their issues. However, final approval rests with the managing editor." Often comments on rejections. Send SASE (or SAE and IRC) for guidelines or obtain via website. Reports in 2-3 months. Pays 2 copies.** "We review books and chapbooks with preference for chapbooks." Poets may also send books for review consideration.

✦**GRAIN; SHORT GRAIN CONTEST (II)**, Box 1154, Regina, Saskatchewan S4P 3B4 Canada, phone (306)244-2828, fax (306)244-0255, e-mail grain.mag@sk.sympatico.ca, website http://www.sasknet.com/corporate/skwriter, founded 1971, is a literary quarterly. "*Grain* strives for artistic excellence and seeks poetry that is **well-crafted, imaginatively stimulating, distinctly original.**" *Grain* is digest-sized, professionally printed, 128-144 pgs. Circulation is 1,500, with 1,100 subscriptions of which 100 are libraries. They receive about 1,200 submissions of poetry/year, use 80-140 poems. Subscription: $23.95 (Canadian), $27.95 for US, $29.95 for other foreign destinations (includes postage). **Sample: $6.95 plus IRC. Submit up to 8 poems, typed on 8½×11 paper, single-spaced, one side only. No previously published poems or simultaneous submissions. Cover letter required. Include "the number of poems submitted, address (with postal or zip code) and phone number. Submissions accepted by regular post only. No e-mail submissions." Send SASE (or SAE and IRC) for guidelines or request via e-mail or website. Reports in 3 months. Pays $30+/poem plus 2 copies. Buys first North American serial rights.** Holds an annual Short Grain Contest. Entries are either prose poems (a lyric poem written as a prose paragraph or paragraphs in 500 words or less), dramatic monologues, or postcard stories (also 500 words or less). Prizes in each category, $500 first, $300 second, $200 third and honorable mentions. All winners and honorable mentions receive regular payment for publication in *Grain*. Entry fee of $20 allows up to two entries in the same category, and includes a 1-year subscription. Additional entries are $5 each. "U.S. and International entrants send fees in U.S. funds ($20 for two entries in one category plus $4 to help cover postage)." Entries are normally accepted between September 1 and January 31. The editor comments, "Only work of the highest literary quality is accepted. Read several back issues."

GRAND STREET (III), 131 Varick St., Room 906, New York NY 10013, is a quarterly magazine publishing poetry, fiction, nonfiction and art. **"We have no writer's guidelines, but publish the most original poetry we can find—encompassing quality writing from all schools."** They have published poetry by John Ashbery, Nicholas Christopher, Fanny Howe, Robert Kelly, August Kleinzahler and Charles Simic. **Sample postpaid: $15. Submit 5 poems at a time. Publishes theme issues. Reports in 2 months.** Work published in *Grand Street* has been included in the 1992, 1993, 1994, 1995 and 1997 volumes of *The Best American Poetry*.

GRASSLANDS REVIEW (I, II), P.O. Box 626, Berea OH 44017, founded 1989, editor Laura B. Kennelly, is a magazine **"to encourage beginning writers and to give adult creative writing students experience in editing fiction and poetry; using any type of poetry; shorter poems stand best chance."** They have recently published poetry by Richard Pearse, Gale Acuff, Colin Morton, Claude Wilkinson, Judy Blevins and Dan Cheifetz. As a sample the editor selected these lines from "How Edgar Became a Kite" by K.J.H. Berland:

> *How Edgar became a kite:*
> *his shoulderblades grew first*
> *and stretched along his arms*
> *out to his wrists where a stout length*
> *of cartilage joined them*

> *and the marrow faded easily from his bones*
> *and the heavy flesh of his thighs dissolved*

GR is 80 pgs., digest-sized, professionally printed, photocopied, saddle-stapled with card cover. They accept 60-70 of 500 submissions received. Press run is 300. Subscription (2 issues): $10 for individuals, $20 institutions. **Sample postpaid: $3.50. Submit only during October and March, no more than 5 poems at a time. No previously published poems or simultaneous submissions. Short cover letter preferred. Send #10 SASE for response. Editor comments on submissions "sometimes." Reports in 3-4 months. Sometimes sends prepublication galleys. Pays 2 copies.**

GRAYWOLF PRESS (V), 2402 University Ave., Suite 203, Saint Paul MN 55114, phone (612)641-0077, website http://www.graywolfpress.org, founded 1975, director Fiona McCrae, **does not read unsolicited mss.** They have published poetry by Jane Kenyon, David Rivard, Vijay Seshadri, John Haines, Carl Phillips, Eamon Grennan, Tess Gallagher, Linda Gregg, Sophie Cabot Black and Dana Gioia. **Sometimes sends prepublication galleys. Pays 7½-10% royalties, 10 author's copies, advance negotiated.** Their book *The Misunderstanding of Nature*, by Sophie Cabot Black, received the Poetry Society of America's Norma Farber First Book Award and their book *Wise Poison*, by David Rivard, won the 1996 James Laughlin Award of the Academy of American Poets. In conjunction with *Agni* magazine (see listing in this section), they also publish a new annual series introducing emerging poets, called *Take Three*. Graywolf Press does not take direct submissions for this series.

‡**THE GREAT LAWN; THE PALM COURT PRESS (II, IV-Gay)**, P.O. Box 170251, St. Louis MO 63117-7951, phone (314)621-6721, e-mail greatlawn@aol.com, founded 1997, editor/publisher David Olin Tullis, is a quarterly art and literary journal for gay men. "Our goal is to publish a superlative, brilliantly written and illustrated collection of short fiction, poetry, art, and photography. *The Great Lawn* is designed to showcase the talents of gay men, but we welcome *all* submissions." **They want work of interest to gay men. "Principle characters must be gay men. The overall tone must be positive and uplifting."**
  ● The inaugural issue of this journal (Spring 1997) was very elegant and nicely produced.
GL is 56-64 pgs., 7½ × 10½, professionally printed on glossy paper and saddle-stitched, with glossy paper cover, uses fine art and fine art photography. Subscription: $24/year. **Sample postpaid: $7. Make checks payable to The Palm Court Press. No previously published poems; simultaneous submissions OK. Cover letter preferred. Often comments on rejections. Send SASE for guidelines or request via e-mail. Reports in 2-4 weeks. Pays 5 copies. Acquires one-time rights.**

‡**GREAT MIDWESTERN QUARTERLY (II)**, 7816 Foxtrot Dr., North Bend OH 45052, founded 1996, editor James S. Proffitt, is "a journal of poetry, fiction, art and book reviews." **They want to see "poetry that explores the world in deeply-moving new ways or at least, inasmuch as possible, deeply-moving new language. We do not want mere descriptions but rather, lines and stanzas and poems that enter the mind and linger with anger, lust, remorse, etcetera. No specifications other than excellence. No visual, greeting card, high school love/suicide poems, social activism, haiku or form poetry."** They have recently published poetry by Lyn Lifshin and Diana Der-Hovanessian. As a sample the editor selected these lines from "Birth" by Linda Nemez Foster:

> *In mid-sentence, my friend is startled by a moth*
> *the color of dusk. The dark wings seem to flutter*
> *right out of her shoulder. If we were in a dream,*
> *she whispers, this small act of flight*
> *would be a good sign. Tonight I cannot sleep.*
> *Instead, I watch the heavy rain change*

GMQ is 48-64 pgs., 4½ × 5¼, offset printed, saddle-stapled, with card cover and b&w cover art. They receive about 2,000 poems a year, accept approximately 70. Press run is 300 for 50 subscribers of which 2 are libraries, 100 shelf sales; 50 distributed free to contributors, reviewers, arts organizations. Subscription: $15. **Sample postpaid: $4. Make checks payable to James S. Proffitt. Submit 5 poems at a time. No previously published poems; simultaneous submissions OK. Cover letter optional.** Time between acceptance and publication is 6 months. **Poems are circulated to an editorial board. Three editors review all material. Often comments on rejections. Send SASE for guidelines. Reports within 1 month. Pays 2 copies. Acquires first North American serial rights.** Staff reviews books or chapbooks of poetry in 50-200 words. Poets may also send books for review consideration. *GMQ* sponsors annual poetry awards of $200, $100 and $50. Entry fee: $3 for first poem, $1 each additional. No limit on number of poems, no style or line limit. Deadline: December 31. Winners are announced in January and published in the spring issue. Send SASE for guidelines. The editor says, "Beginning poets should

---

✝ **THE DOUBLE DAGGER** before a listing indicates that the listing is new in this edition. New markets are often the most receptive to submissions.

read as much as they can of classics as well as current small press material. Support the publications you submit to and encourage others to do the same."

THE GREEN HAT (I, II), P.O. Box 8023, Des Moines IA 50301, founded 1995, editor Guillaume Williams, is an annual designed to publish "**poets who have material that is difficult to market** due to length, theme, darkness, or any other reason." **They want "well-crafted poetry that leaves the reader's ability for interpretation. Strong forms are OK. No limit to length or subject, except no short poems (six lines or less), no preaching, no cute poetry, and no rhymes (unless strict forms)."** They have recently published poetry by Ruth Doty, Simon Perchik, B.Z. Niditch and Lyn Lifshin. The editor says *The Green Hat* is about 70 pgs., digest-sized, professionally printed and flat-spined with stock cover, no art or ads. Press run is 500-700. Single copy: $8. **Submit 3 poems at a time, double-spaced. Previously published poems and simultaneous submissions OK. Cover letter preferred. Seldom comments on rejections. Publishes theme issues. Upcoming themes are Social Issues, deadline August 20, 1997 and Pastoral Poems, deadline August 20, 1998. Reports in 1-4 weeks. Sometimes sends prepublication galleys. Pays 1 copy, sometimes 2. Acquires first or one-time rights.** The best poem each issue (selected by panel) may be subtitled on the cover of the magazine and the author of the poem will receive $50. The editor says, "We like poetry that doesn't spell it out. Thought provoking material is desired and things rich in images. If you get material returned that an editor liked but didn't publish, we want to see it."

GREEN HILLS LITERARY LANTERN (II), P.O. Box 375, Trenton MO 64683, phone (816)359-3948 ext. 324, fax (816)359-2211, e-mail jsmith@ncmc.cc.mo.us, editors Jack Smith and Ken Reger, poetry editor Joe Benevento, is the annual journal of the North Central Missouri College and the North Central Missouri Writer's Guild and is open to short fiction and poetry of "exceptional quality." **They want "the best poetry, in any style, preferably understandable. No haiku, limericks or anything over three pages."** They have recently published poetry by Jim Thomas, Mary Winters and Chris Dungey. As a sample the editor selected these lines from "Exotic Dancer" by Stephanie Dickinson:

> The racks of elk branch over the men.
> Cigarettes glow in the eyes of prongtails,
> Javelina, moose. The mounted birds swirl like shawls:
> An African gray with shellacked beak, a macaw,
> A golden vulture. . . .

Green Hills is 150-160 pgs., 5½ × 8½, perfect-bound with good quality card cover. They receive work by more than 200 poets a year and publish 2-3 poems by about 10% of the poets submitting—less than 10% of all poetry received. Press run is 225. Subscription or **sample postpaid: $5.95. Submit 4-7 poems at a time. No previously published poems; simultaneous submissions OK but not preferred. Cover letter with list of publications preferred. Often comments on rejections. Send SASE for guidelines or request via e-mail. Reports in 3 months. Always sends prepublication galleys. Pays 2 copies. Acquires one-time rights.** The editor says, "Read the best poetry and be willing to learn from what you encounter."

GREEN MOUNTAINS REVIEW (II), Johnson State College, Johnson VT 05656, phone (802)635-2356 ext. 1350, founded 1975, poetry editor Neil Shepard, appears twice a year and includes poetry (and other writing) by well-known authors and promising newcomers. **"We publish quality work; formal or free verse, realistic or surrealistic, narrative-based or language poetry."** They have recently published poetry by Galway Kinnell, Derek Walcott, Maxine Kumin, Stephen Dunn, David Mura, Naomi Shihab Nye and Elizabeth Spires. *GMR* is digest-sized, flat-spined, 150-200 pgs. Of 1,000 submissions they publish 30 authors. Press run is 1,500 for 200 subscribers of which 30 are libraries. Subscription: $12/year. **Sample postpaid: $7. Submit no more than 5 poems at a time. No simultaneous submissions. Reads submissions September 1 through May 15 only. Editor sometimes comments on rejection slip. Publishes theme issues. Send SASE for guidelines and upcoming themes. Reports in 2-3 months. Pays 1 copy plus 1-year subscription. Acquires first North American serial rights.** Send books for review consideration. Poetry published in *GMR* has been selected for inclusion in *The Best American Poetry* (1994 and 1997) and *Pushcart Prize* anthologies.

GREENHOUSE REVIEW PRESS (V), 3965 Bonny Doon Rd., Santa Cruz CA 95060, founded 1975, publishes a series of poetry chapbooks and broadsides. **"Unsolicited mss are not accepted."** Send SASE for catalog to buy samples.

♣**GREEN'S MAGAZINE (II)**, P.O. Box 3236, Regina, Saskatchewan S4P 3H1 Canada, founded 1972, editor David Green. *Green's Magazine* is a literary quarterly with a balanced diet of short fiction and poetry. They publish **"free/blank verse examining emotions or situations." They do not want greeting card jingles or pale imitations of the masters.** They have recently published poetry by Robert L. Tener, Russ Savage, Robert Cooperman, Sheila Hyland, Doreen Gandy Wiley and Nancy G. Westerfield. As a sample the editor selected these lines from "Reflections in a Hubcap" by Howard Prescott:

> My vision transcends a time warp
> Into a cosmic corridor parallel to our own universe
> Where mighty mutant beings stare with horror and disbelief,

Into their side of a large, shiny hubcap,
And see us as strange mutant species on planet Earth.

The magazine is 92 pgs., digest-sized, typeset on buff stock with line drawings, matte card cover, saddle-stapled. Circulation is 300. Subscription: $12. **Sample postpaid: $4. Submit 4-6 poems at a time. The editor prefers typescript, complete originals. No simultaneous submissions. "If © used, poet must give permission to use and state clearly the work is unpublished."** Time between acceptance and publication is usually 3 months. **Comments are usually provided on rejected mss. Send SASE (or SAE and IRCs) for guidelines. Reports in 2 months. Pays 2 copies. Acquires first North American serial rights.** Occasionally reviews books of poetry in "up to 150-200 words." Send books for review consideration. The editor says, "Would-be contributors are urged to study the magazine first."

THE GREENSBORO REVIEW; GREENSBORO REVIEW LITERARY AWARDS (II), English Dept., Room 134, McIver Bldg., University of North Carolina, Greensboro NC 27412, phone (910)334-5459, fax (910)334-3281, e-mail clarkj@fagan.uncg.edu, website http://www.uncg.edu, founded 1966, editor Jim Clark. *TGR* appears twice yearly and showcases well-made verse in all styles and forms, though shorter poems (under 50 lines) seem preferred. They have recently published poetry by Bruce Smith, Jeffrey Skinner, David Rivard, Thomas Lux and Gail Mazur. As a sample the poetry editor selected these lines from "Tornado Warnings" by Jeff Mock:

Somewhere
Tornadoes touch down and snap pines to kindling,
But not in this field. That's what we really need,
Isn't it? Face to face with a danger real
Enough it will swirl round us and lift the ever-
Perfect past completely away.

The digest-sized, flat-spined magazine, 120 pgs., colored matte cover, professional printing, uses about 25 pgs. of poetry in each issue, about 2.5% of the 2,000 submissions received each year. Circulation is 500 for 300 subscribers of which 100 are libraries. **Sample postpaid: $4. "Submissions (no more than five poems) must arrive by September 15 to be considered for the Winter issue (acceptances in December) and February 15 to be considered for the Summer issue (acceptances in May). Manuscripts arriving after those dates will be held for consideration with the next issue." No simultaneous submissions. Cover letter not required but helpful. Include number of poems submitted. Reports in 2-4 months. Always sends prepublication galleys. Pays 3 copies. Acquires first North American serial rights.** They sponsor an open competition for *The Greensboro Review* Literary Awards, $250 for both poetry and fiction each year. Deadline: September 15. Send SASE for guidelines.

GROVE ATLANTIC (V), 841 Broadway, New York NY 10003. Grove Press and Atlantic Monthly Press merged in February 1993. **They currently do not accept unsolicited mss.**

♣GUERNICA EDITIONS INC.; ESSENTIAL POET SERIES, PROSE SERIES, DRAMA SERIES; INTERNATIONAL WRITERS (IV-Regional, translations, ethnic/nationality), P.O. Box 117, Toronto, Ontario M5S 2S6 Canada, founded 1978, poetry editor Antonio D'Alfonso. "We wish to bring together the **different and often divergent voices that exist in Canada and the U.S. We are interested in translations. We are mostly interested right now in poetry and essays on pluriculturalism.**" They have recently published work by Mary Melfi, Fulvio Caccia, Gianna Patriarca (Canada), Peter Carravetta, Scott Rollins (US); and Leonardo Sinsigalli (Italy). **Query with 1-2 pgs. of samples. Send SASE (Canadian stamps only) or SAE and IRCs for catalog.** The editor comments, "We are interested in promoting a pluricultural view of literature by bridging languages and cultures through our specialization in international translation."

GULF COAST: A JOURNAL OF LITERATURE AND FINE ART (II), Dept. of English, University of Houston, Houston TX 77204-3012, founded 1986, poetry editors Corey Marks and Cate Marvin, is published twice a year in the winter and summer. While the journal features work by a number of established poets, editors are also interested in "providing a forum for new and emerging writers who are producing well-crafted work that takes risks." Each issue includes poetry, fiction, essays, interviews, and color reproductions of work by artists from across the nation. They have recently published poetry by Heather McHugh, Kevin Young, Billy Collins, Cathleen Calbert, Pattiann Rogers and Amy Gerstler. As a sample the editors selected these lines from "Answer to Crowd" by Ed Skoog:

You have to ask, what was your war crime?
This is social work, walking around the crowd,
wanting to tell the woman who left hours ago
that her scarf still lies across the bench,
another coworker at a crossroad like yours.
At the end of the world one feels worldlier.

The editor says *Gulf Coast* is 140 pgs., 6×9, offset, perfect-bound. Single copy: $7; subscription: $12/year, $22/2 years. **Submit up to 4 poems at a time. No previously published poems; simultaneous submissions OK with notification. Cover letter with previous publications, "if any," and a brief bio required. Does not read** submissions May through July. Send SASE for guidelines. Reports in 2-6 months. Pays copies. Returns rights upon publication.

GULF STREAM MAGAZINE (II), English Dept., Florida International University, North Miami Campus, North Miami FL 33181, phone (305)919-5599, founded 1989, editor Lynne Barrett, associate editors Mark Martin and Guo Liang, is the biannual literary magazine associated with the creative writing program at FIU. They want **"poetry of any style and subject matter as long as it is of high literary quality."** They have published poetry by Gerald Costanzo, Naomi Shihab Nye, Jill Bialosky and Catherine Bowman. The handsome magazine is 90 pgs., digest-sized, flat-spined, printed on quality stock with glossy card cover. They accept less than 10% of poetry received. Press run is 750. Subscription: $7.50. **Sample postpaid: $4. Submit no more than 5 poems. No simultaneous submissions. Reads submissions September 15 through April 30 only. Editor comments on submissions "if we feel we can be helpful." Publishes theme issues. Send SASE for guidelines. Reports in 2-3 months. Pays 2 copies and 2 subscriptions. Acquires first North American serial rights.**

GUT PUNCH PRESS (III), P.O. Box 105, Cabin John MD 20818, founded 1987, editor Derrick Hsu, publishes 1-2 paperbacks/year. **They want "free verse with an innovative edge and possibly a sense of humor. No language school or formal narrative style."** They have published poetry collections by Richard Peabody, Sunil Freeman and Rose Solari, and an anthology of African-American poetry edited by Alan Spears. No poems previously published in book form or simultaneous submissions. Time between acceptance and publication is 1 year. **Replies to mss (if invited) in 3 months. Pays royalties ("determined on an individual basis") and 50 author's copies. For sample books, send SASE for list and order form.** Most books are $7.95 postpaid.

HABERSHAM REVIEW (III, IV-Regional), P.O. Box 10, Demorest GA 30535, fax (706)776-2811, founded 1991, poetry editor Dr. Stephen R. Whited, is a biannual, general interest, regional journal published by Piedmont College. **"While we are interested in publishing regional poets, we will publish a good poem no matter where the poet lives. We accept all styles, and we prefer a range of subject matter."** They have published poetry by Judson Mitcham, R.T. Smith, Paul Ramsey, William Miller and Simon Perchik. As a sample we selected these lines from "When I Survey the Wondrous Cross" by David Bottoms:

> A heavy odor of flowers
> rode the fans,
> and I sat with my bare feet dangling over a bench.
> Light from an open window fell across the face
> of a brown guitar, dust twisting like worms in that light,
> as the pail of water
> slid across the splintered floor.

HR is about 100 pgs., 6¾ × 10, perfect-bound, offset, with color art and photographs on the cover, some b&w art and photographs inside, and ads. It receives 250 poems a year, accept 40. Press run is 1,000 for 300 subscribers of which 10% are libraries, 50-100 shelf sales. Subscription: $12. **Sample postpaid: $6. Make checks payable to Piedmont College. Submit up to 5 poems at a time. No previously published poems or simultaneous submissions. Cover letter preferred. Reads submissions September through May only.** Time between acceptance and publication is 1-2 years, "in some cases." **Send SASE for guidelines. Reports in 3-6 months. Pays 5 copies. Acquires first rights. Requires acknowledgment if reprinted elsewhere.** Staff reviews books of poetry in 200-500 words, single or multi-book format. Poets may send books for review consideration.

HAIGHT ASHBURY LITERARY JOURNAL (II, IV-Social issues, themes), 558 Joost Ave., San Francisco CA 94127, phone (415)221-2017, founded 1979-1980, editors Joanne Hotchkiss, Alice Rogoff and Conyus, is a newsprint tabloid that appears 1-3 times/year. They use **"all forms and lengths, including haiku. Subject matter sometimes political, but open to all subjects. Poems of background—prison, minority experience— often published, as well as poems of protest and of Central America. Few rhymes."** They have published poetry by Joyce Odam, Jack Micheline, Edgar Silex, Lonnie Hull Dupont, Bill Shields and Ina Cumpiano. As a sample the editors selected these lines from "Parecer" by Arlene Biala:

> When you lie awake nights straining
> to put her face in a place to define
> all those words, you pick up a pen
> and bleed her expression onto the page.

The tabloid has a photo of its featured poet on the cover, uses graphics, ads, 16 pgs., circulation 2,000-3,000. $35 for a lifetime subscription, which includes 3 back issues. Subscription: $12/4 issues. **Sample postpaid: $3. Make checks payable to Alice Rogoff. Submit up to 6 poems. Prefers poems under 2 pages long. "Please type one poem to a page, put name and address on every page and include SASE." No previously published poems. Each issue changes its theme and emphasis. Send SASE for guidelines and upcoming themes. Reports in 2-6 months. Pays 3 copies. Rights revert to author.** An anthology of past issues, *This Far Together*, is available for $15. *HAL* received a 1996 American Literary Magazine Award of Second Place for Tabloids.

HAIKU HEADLINES: A MONTHLY NEWSLETTER OF HAIKU AND SENRYU (IV-Form), 1347 W. 71st St., Los Angeles CA 90044-2505, phone (213)778-5337, founded 1988, editor/publisher Rengé/David

Priebe. *HH*, "America's only monthly publication dedicated to the genre," uses **haiku and senryu only. The editor prefers the 5/7/5 syllabic discipline, but accepts irregular haiku and senryu which display pivotal imagery and contrast.** They have published haiku by Dorothy McLaughlin, Jean Calkins, Günther Klinge, George Knox and Mark Arvid White. Here are examples of haiku and senryu by Rengé:

> Low clouds gathering
> over the ocean . . . sunbeams
> glare and disappear.

> Catching a moth
> and setting it free outdoors
> . . . gold dust in my hand.

The newsletter is 8 pgs., 8½×11, corner-stapled and punched for a three-ring binder. "Each issue has a different color graphic front page. The back page showcases a Featured Haiku Poet with a photo-portrait, biography, philosophy and six of the poet's own favorite haiku." *HH* publishes 88-98 haiku/senryu a month, including, on the average, work from 6 newcomers. They have 225 subscribers of which 3 are libraries. Single copy: $1.75 US, $2 Canada, $2.50 overseas; subscription: $21 US, $24 Canada, $30 overseas. **Haiku/senryu may be submitted with 12 maximum/single page. Unpublished submissions from subscribers will be considered first. Nonsubscriber submissions will be accepted only if space permits and SASE is included. Reports in about 2 months. Pays subscribers half price rebates for issues containing their work—credits applicable to subscription. Nonsubscribers are encouraged to prepay for issues containing their work.** Monthly Readers' Choice Awards: The Awards Kitty (average $50-75—contributions of postage stamps and money by the voters) is shared by the top three favorites. The "First Timer" with the most votes receives an Award of Special Recognition ($5). *HH* sponsors an annual contest (prizes $100, $75, $50) and publishes the results in a calendar book, *Timepieces: Haiku Week At-A-Glance*, which the selected contributors can purchase at half the market price. The contest is open to the public and accepts entries from April 1 through July 31. Write for details.

‡**A HALF RIDGE PRESS (I, II)**, 607 Ridge Rd., P.O. Box 605, Creede CO 81130, founded 1996, editor W.K. Sheldrake, publishes "high-quality chapbooks featuring 2-4 poets. Our mission is to provide the aspiring and serious poet with an attractive forum through which to present his/her work." Publishes **"as many chapbooks as finances allow"/year. They want "poetry that fits on a page (35 lines or less). Poetry that is about specific unusual or quirky individuals or relationships/emotions/events; even nature poetry should have someone in it. Subject matter may be very typical if approached with subtlety. Humor OK. Sarcasm OK, but not for its own sake."** They do not want **"cowboy poetry, end rhyming, themes that scream out with your agenda or begs a specific audience. No brutality without beauty."** They have recently published poetry by Samuel Mills, Dyan Sublett and Jodie Ryan. As a sample the editor selected these lines from "Dead Work" by David Hayden:

> One day God sent a message directly to me.
> Said: You stand around, You stop for doughnuts, You leer
> At the help, You loiter at the Nymph church, You are fired.
> Fired, by God. They took my wings. They operated.
> So here I begin again, living in these Wonderful Earplugs.
> God was a tough boss. He sees it all.

Chapbooks are usually 24 pgs., 8½×5½, offset, saddle-stapled, with heavy card cover and b&w cover art. **Submit 5-8 poems with a $3 reading fee, 1 poem/page. Previously published poems and simultaneous submissions OK. Cover letter preferred.** Time between acceptance and publication is 1-3 months. **Often comments on rejections. Replies to queries in 6 weeks. Pays 65-75 author's copies (out of a press run of 300). Obtain sample chapbooks by sending $3 with your request.** The editor says, "We hope the poet will find the chapbooks useful as commercial and personal promotion. We envision the active poet reading from and selling copies in the local community, sending copies to editors, as well as giving them away to friends and family. We want our poets to be proud to say, 'I am a poet,' and proud to see their important work with the work of two or three others just as good and important."

HALF TONES TO JUBILEE (II), English Dept., Pensacola Junior College, 1000 College Blvd., Pensacola FL 32504, phone (904)484-1418, founded 1986, faculty editor Walter Spara, is an annual literary journal featuring poetry and short fiction. They have published poetry by R.T. Smith, Sue Walker, Larry Rubin and Simon Perchik. *HTTJ* is 100 pgs., digest-sized, perfect-bound with matte card cover, professionally printed. They receive about 1,000 poems a year, use 50-60. Press run is 500. Subscription: $4. **Sample: $4. Submit 5 poems at a time. No previously published work or simultaneous submissions. SASE mandatory. Cover letter with bio and/or publication history preferred. Reads submissions August 1 through May 15 only. Reports in 2-3 months, faster when possible. Pays 1 copy. Acquires first rights.** *HTTJ* sponsors an annual poetry competition ($300 first prize, $200 second, $100 third. Entry fee: $2/poem. Send SASE for rules, deadlines. In addition to numerous awards from the Florida Press Association, *Half Tones to Jubilee* has received 2 national awards, a first place with merit from the American Scholastic Press Association, and first place, Southern division, literary magazine competition, Community College Humanities Association.

HAMMERS; DOUBLESTAR PRESS (III), 1718 Sherman, #203, Evanston IL 60201, founded 1989, editor Nat David. *Hammers*, "an end of millennium irregular poetry magazine," appears once or twice a year. Many of the poets they have published are from the Chicago area, although each issue also includes the work of poets from a variety of other geographical regions. **They want "honest, well-written poetry from the depths of the**

poet's universe and experience, which is cognizant of our interconnectedness." They have recently published poetry by Mike Puican, John Dickson, Suzanne Frank, Lisa Alvarado and Susen James. As a sample the editor selected these lines from "one breath" by Andy Nettles:

> *And I drift into a dream*
> *where it is my hand she's holding*
> *like a soft morning squash*
> *and I notice she is my mother then*
> *she is my daughter, and*
> *then she is my sister*
> *and I'm twisting sweet in her hand.*

Hammers is 88 pgs., 6⅞ × 8½, professionally printed and saddle-stapled with matte card cover. Single copy: $5; subscription: $15/4 issues. **Sample postpaid: $7. Submit 5-10 poems at a time. Editor seldom comments on submissions. Reports ASAP. Pays 1 copy.** In 1999, the editor intends to publish in book form *The Best of Hammers*.

‡*HANDSHAKE; THE EIGHT HAND GANG (IV-Science fiction), 5 Cross Farm, Station Rd., Padgate, Warrington, Cheshire WA2 OQG United Kingdom, founded 1992, contact J.F. Haines. *Handshake*, published irregularly, "is a newsletter for science fiction poets. It has evolved into being one side of news and information and one side of poetry." **They want "science fiction/fantasy poetry of all styles. Prefer short poems." They do not want "epics or foul language."** They have recently published poetry by Steve Sneyd, Andrew Darlington, J.C. Hartley and Neil K. Henderson. As a sample the editor selected these lines from "Report on Arriving at the First Colony" by Brian Maycock:

> *most died it seems on impact*
> *those left we found insane*
> *mapping craters to prove a theory*
> *on the origin of their race*

Handshake is 1 sheet of A4 paper, photocopied with ads. They receive about 50 poems a year, accept approximately 50%. Press run is 60 for 30 subscribers of which 5 are libraries. Subscription: SAE with IRC. **Sample postpaid: SAE with IRC. Submit 2-3 poems, typed and camera-ready. No previously published poems or simultaneous submissions. Cover letter preferred.** Time between acceptance and publication varies. **Editor selects "whatever takes my fancy and is of suitable length." Seldom comments on rejections. Publishes theme issues. Reports ASAP. Pays 1 copy. Acquires first rights.** Staff reviews books or chapbooks of poetry or other magazines of very short length. Poets may also send books for review consideration. *Handshake* is also the newsletter for The Eight Hand Gang, an organization for British science fiction poets, established in 1991. They currently have 60 members. Information about the organization is found in their newsletter.

*HANDSHAKE EDITIONS (V); CASSETTE GAZETTE (II), Atelier A2, 83 rue de la Tombe Issoire, Paris, France 75014, phone 33-1-4327-1767, fax 33-1-4320-4195, e-mail jim_haynes@msn.com, founded 1979. *Cassette Gazette* is an audiocassette issued "from time to time. We are interested in **poetry dealing with political/ social issues and women/feminism themes.**" Poets published include Ted Joans, Yianna Katsoulos, Judith Malina, Elaine Cohen, Amanda Hoover, Jayne Cortez, Roy Williamson and Mary Guggenheim. **Pays in copies. Handshake Editions does not accept unsolicited mss for book publication.** Jim Haynes, publisher, says, "I prefer to deal face to face."

HANGING LOOSE PRESS (V); HANGING LOOSE (I, II, IV-Teens/students), 231 Wyckoff St., Brooklyn NY 11217, founded 1966, poetry editors Robert Hershon, Dick Lourie, Mark Pawlak and Ron Schreiber. **The press does not accept unsolicited book mss, but welcomes work for the magazine,** which appears 3 times/year. The magazine has published poetry by Paul Violi, Donna Brook, Kimiko Hahn, Ron Overton, Jack Anderson and Frances Phillips. *Hanging Loose* is 120 pgs., flat-spined, offset on heavy stock with a 2-color glossy card cover. One section contains **poems by high-school-age poets. The editor says it "concentrates on the work of new writers." Sample postpaid: $8.50. Submit 4-6 "excellent, energetic" poems. No simultaneous submissions.** "Would-be contributors should read the magazine first." **Reports in 1-12 weeks. Pays small fee and 3 copies.** Poetry published in *Hanging Loose* has been included in the 1993, 1995, 1996 and 1997 volumes of *The Best American Poetry*.

*HANGMAN BOOKS (I), 2 May Rd., Rochester, Kent ME1 2HY England, founded 1982, editor Jack Ketch, publishes selected books of poetry on a cooperative basis. **They want "personal" poetry, "underground"**

 AN ASTERISK before a listing indicates an overseas publisher, magazine, contest, conference or organization.

writing, "none rhyming, none political, bla bla bla." They have published poetry by Chris Broderick and Neil Sparkes. As a sample the editor selected these lines from "dead funny" by Billy Childish from his book, *Big Hart and Balls*:

> and with every poem i rite
> my fame grows
> another nail in my coffin
> people feel embarrassed for me
> everything i utter becomes a cliche
>
> when oh when the people ask
> will billy shut up?

When submitting a ms, send sufficient IRCs for return. Editor always sends prepublication galleys. 60% of press run belongs to poet.

♣**HARBOUR PUBLISHING (IV-Regional)**, P.O. Box 219, Madeira Park, British Columbia V0N 2H0 Canada, founded 1972, president Howard White, publishes poetry collections by **"Canadian authors—citizens or permanent residents—with an emphasis on West Coast themes."** They have recently published collections by Al Purdy, Patrick Lane, Tom Wayman, Anne Cameron and Peter Trower. They say their books are typically 80 pgs., perfect-bound. **Canadian poets should query first, with 15 sample poems and a cover letter with brief bio and publication credits. Previously published poems and simultaneous submissions OK. Seldom comments on rejections. Replies to queries and mss (if invited) in 3-6 months. Pays standard industry royalties.** They say, "If Canadian poets want to buy a Harbour catalog to get a better idea of the titles we publish, please send $3 and an 8½×11 SASE to our address with your request."

HARCOURT BRACE & COMPANY; HB CHILDREN'S BOOKS; GULLIVER BOOKS; BROWN-DEER PRESS; SILVER WHISTLE (V), 525 B St., Suite 1900, San Diego CA 92101, phone (619)231-6616. HB Children's Books, Gulliver Books, Browndeer Press and Silver Whistle publish hardback and trade paperback books for children. They have published books of children's poetry by Jane Yolen, Arnold Adoff, Douglas Florian, e.e. cummings, Lee Bennett Hopkins and Carl Sandburg. **They do no accept unsolicited material.**

HARP-STRINGS POETRY JOURNAL; EDNA ST. VINCENT MILLAY AWARD; ROBERT FROST BLANK VERSE AWARD (II); POETS' FORUM MAGAZINE (I), ELIZABETH B. BROWNING SONNETS AWARD; WILLIAM STAFFORD "GOLDEN STRING" AWARD; DYLAN THOMAS "DO NOT GO GENTLY INTO THAT GOOD NIGHT" AWARD; JOSEPH V. HICKEY "RIGHTS AND RESPONSIBILITIES" AWARD, P.O. Box 640387, Beverly Hills FL 34464, founded 1989, editor Madelyn Eastlund. *Harp-Strings* appears biannually. **They want poems of "14-80 lines, narratives, lyrics, ballads, sestinas, rondeau, redouble, blank verse. Nothing 'dashed off,' trite, broken prose masquerading as poetry."** Occasionally they have a profile and selection of poems from one featured poet. They have published poetry by Walter Griffin, Patricia Higginbotham, Norman Kraeft and June Owens. As a sample the editor selected these lines from "Reassembling" by Elsie Pankowski:

> A shadow in an empty house, a star
> without a play, she could not stand alone
> or cope without him there. Within the blur
> of passing days, she focused on the pain,
> until a morning when she came to know
> his absence from the house had made her whole.

Harp-Strings is 40 pgs., digest-sized, saddle-stapled, professionally printed on quality colored matte stock with matte card cover. She accepts 5-10% of poems received. Press run is 125 for 75 subscribers. Subscription: $11. **Sample postpaid: $6. Submit 3-5 poems at a time. Cover letters that provide information about poet or poem ("a few interesting lines to use in contributor's notes") welcome. Reports in 2-3 weeks. Pays 1 copy. Acquires one-time rights. "I am interested in seeing poems that have won awards but have not been published."** Sponsors 2 contests each year: Edna St. Vincent Millay Award (narrative from 36 to 80 lines, deadline August 15); Robert Frost Blank Verse Award (deadline February 15). Poems must be unpublished and not have won awards of more than $10. Entry fee for each contest: $2/poem, $5/3 poems. Cash awards of $10-40 and publication. They also publish the quarterly *Poets' Forum Magazine*, which includes poet profiles; instruction on poetry forms and patterns; information on submitting work, organizations for poets and entering contests. **They want poems "no longer than 24 lines and no more than 45 characters across."** Single copy: $4.50; subscription: $16. **(For both *Harp-Strings* and *Poets' Forum*, make checks payable to Madelyn Eastlund.) Submit 3-5 poems at a time. No simultaneous submissions. "We are especially pleased to see poems in recognized forms.** Sponsors 4 contests each year: Elizabeth B. Browning Sonnets Award (Shakespearean or Petrarchan Sonnet, deadline June 15); William Stafford "Golden String" Award (poems of 28-40 lines, deadline August 15); Dylan Thomas "Do Not Go Gently Into That Good Night" Award (villanelle, deadline November 15); Joseph V. Hickey "Rights and Responsibilities" Award (narrative poetry of 30-40 lines, deadline April 19). Stanley Kunitz once said, 'Poetry today has become easier to write but harder to remember.' We want poetry to remember, poetry that haunts, poetry the reader wants to read again and again."

THE HARVARD ADVOCATE (IV-Specialized: university affiliation), Dept. PM, 21 South St., Cambridge MA 02138, phone (617)495-0737, founded 1866, is a quarterly literary magazine, circulation 4,000, that publishes **poetry, fiction and art only by those affiliated with Harvard University; open to outside submissions of essays. Sample: $4. In submitting state your exact relationship to Harvard. Does not pay.** Reviews books, including poetry.

HAUNTS (IV-Science fiction/fantasy, horror), Nightshade Publications, P.O. Box 8068, Cranston RI 02920-0068, phone (401)781-9438, fax (401)943-0980, is a "literary magazine geared to those fans of the 'pulp' magazines of the 30s, 40s and 50s, with tales of **horror, the supernatural and the bizarre. We are trying to reach those in the 18-35 age-group.**" They use free verse, light verse and traditional, about 12-16 poems a year. Circulation: 2,750. **Sample: $4.95 plus $1 postage. Send a maximum of 3 poems. Cover letter including "brief introduction of the writer and the work submitted" required. Send SASE for guidelines. Pays $3/ poem.**

HAWAII PACIFIC REVIEW (II), 1060 Bishop St., Honolulu HI 96813, phone (808)544-0214, e-mail efischel @hpu.edu, founded 1986, editor Elizabeth Fischel, is an annual literary journal "publishing quality poetry, short fiction and personal essays from writers worldwide. **Our journal seeks to promote a world view that celebrates a variety of cultural themes, beliefs, values and viewpoints. Although we do publish beginning poets on occasion, we do not publish amateurish poetry. We wish to further the growth of artistic vision and talent by encouraging sophisticated and innovative poetic and narrative techniques.**" They have published poetry by Robert Cooperman and Mary Kay Rummel. *HPR* is 80-120 pgs., 6×9, professionally printed on quality paper, perfect-bound, with coated card cover; each issue features original artwork. Mostly free verse, poems here tend to be insightful, informative and well-made with an emphasis on cultural diversity. They receive 800-1,000 poems a year, accept 30-40. Press run is approximately 1,000 for 200 shelf sales. Single copy: $5-6. **Sample postpaid: $4. No previously published poems; simultaneous submissions OK. Cover letter with 5-line professional bio including prior publications required.** Seldom comments on rejections. **Send SASE for guidelines or request via e-mail. Reports within 3 months. Pays 2 copies. Acquires first North American serial rights.** The editor says, "We'd like to receive more experimental verse. Many of the poems we receive are more personal therapy than true art. Good poetry is eye-opening; it investigates the unfamiliar or reveals the spectacular in the ordinary. Good poetry does more than simply express the poet's feelings; it provides both insight and unexpected beauty."

HAYDEN'S FERRY REVIEW (II), Box 871502, Arizona State University, Tempe AZ 85287-1502, phone (602)965-1243, founded 1986, is a handsome literary magazine appearing twice a year. They have published poetry by Dennis Schmitz, Raymond Carver, Maura Stanton, Ai, and David St. John. *HFR* is 6×9, 120 pgs., flat-spined with glossy card cover. Press run is 1,300 for 200 subscribers of which 30 are libraries, 800 shelf sales. They accept about 3% of 5,000 submissions annually. Subscription: $10. **Sample postpaid: $6.** "No specifications other than limit in number (six) and no simultaneous submissions. We would like a brief bio for contributor's note included." **Submissions circulated to two poetry editors. Editor comments on submissions "often." Send SASE for guidelines. Reports in 8-10 weeks of deadlines. Deadlines: February 28 for Spring/Summer issue; September 30 for Fall/Winter. Sends contributors galley proofs. Pays 2 copies.**

‡THE HEALING WOMAN (IV-Specialized: women survivors of childhood sexual abuse), P.O. Box 1210, Sutter Creek CA 95685, phone (408)246-1788, fax (408)247-4309, e-mail healingw@aol.com, website http://members.aol.com/healingw/healingw.htm, founded 1992, editor Brenda Anderson, "is a monthly newsletter written by and for women survivors of childhood sexual abuse, their friends and supportive family members, and the professionals who help them heal. Its purpose is to provide information, self-help, and support to women in recovery from childhood sexual abuse." **They want 50 lines maximum.** "Our focus is on healing, not on suffering. We look for poetry that shows some promise of healing; while we do not minimize the pain, we prefer poetry that offers hope to our readers. No graphic depictions of sexual abuse." *Healing Woman* is 12 pgs., 8½×11, attractively printed and saddle-stitched with colored paper cover, line drawings and clip art. Press run is about 4,200 for 3,000 subscribers. Subscription: $30/year, $55/2 years. **Submit 5 poems at a time. Previously published poems OK; no simultaneous submissions. Cover letter preferred. They require a permission-to-publish form to be completed before publication. Send SASE for form and guidelines.** Time between acceptance and publication is 4-12 months. **Pays copies.**

THE HEARTLANDS TODAY (II, IV-Regional, themes), Firelands College, 901 Rye Beach Rd., Huron OH 44839, phone (419)433-5560, fax (419)433-9696, founded 1990, editors Deb Benko and David Shevin. *The Heartlands Today* is an annual publication of the Firelands Writing Center at Firelands College. They want work **by Midwestern writers about the Midwest Heartlands, "writing and photography that is set in the Midwest today and deals revealingly and creatively with the issues we face—good writing and art that documents our lives." Each issue has a specific theme.** They have published poetry by Alberta Turner, David Baker, Chris Llewellyn and James Bertolino. The editors describe it as 160 pgs., 6×9, perfect-bound with 30-40 b&w photos. They accept 10-20% of the poetry received. Press run is 850-900. Single copy: $8.50. **Sample postpaid: $5. Submit up to 5 poems at a time. Simultaneous submissions OK. Cover letter with brief bio required.**

Reads submissions January 1 to July 1 only. Often comments on rejections. Send SASE for guidelines and upcoming themes. Reports in 2 months once reading period begins. Pays $10 and 2 copies. Buys first or second rights. They also sponsor an annual chapbook contest. Send up to 10 poems ("a unified whole") with a $10 reading fee; writer receives a critique and a copy of the magazine. Winner receives $100 and publication in *The Heartlands Today.*

HEAVEN BONE MAGAZINE; HEAVEN BONE PRESS; HEAVEN BONE PRESS INTERNATIONAL CHAPBOOK COMPETITION (II, IV-Spiritual, nature/rural/ecology), P.O. Box 486, Chester NY 10918, phone (914)469-9018, e-mail 71340.520@compuserve.com, founded 1986, poetry editor Steve Hirsch, publishes poetry, fiction, essays and reviews with **"an emphasis on spiritual, metaphysical, esoteric and ecological concerns."** They have published poetry and fiction by Charles Bukowski, Marge Piercy, Kirpal Gordon, Diane di Prima and Michael McClure. As a sample the editor selected these lines from "Message of Hope" by G. Sutton Breiding:

> *The screech owl's call*
> *Is vertical: a tower*
> *Rippling in the mist,*
> *A door of oracles*
> *Hung between night*
> *And dawn that opens*
> *And shuts softly*
> *In the white places*
> *Of sleep.*

Heaven Bone is 96 pgs., magazine-sized, saddle-stapled, using b&w art, photos and ads, on recycled bond stock with glossy 4-color recycled card cover. Of 500-800 poems received they accept 18-30. They have a press run of 2,500. Subscription: $16.95. **Sample postpaid: $6. Submit 3-10 poems at a time. "I will not read submissions without SASEs." Simultaneous submissions and previously published poems OK, "if notified."** Time between acceptance and publication is up to 1 year. **Occasionally publishes theme issues. Send SASE for upcoming themes. Reports in 2 weeks to 6 months. Sometimes sends prepublication galleys. Pays 2 copies. Acquires first North American serial rights.** Reviews books of poetry. Open to unsolicited reviews. Poets may also send books for review consideration. The press sponsors the annual Heaven Bone Press International Chapbook Competition which awards $100 plus publication to an original, unpublished poetry ms of 30 pgs. or less. Requires $10 reading fee. Send SASE for guidelines. Editor advises, "Please be familiar with the magazine before sending mss. We receive too much religious verse. Break free of common 'poetic' limitations and speak freely with no contrivances. No forced end-line rhyming please. Channel the muse and music without being an obstacle to the poem."

HELICON NINE EDITIONS (V); MARIANNE MOORE POETRY PRIZE (III), 3607 Pennsylvania Ave., Kansas City MO 64111, phone (816)753-1095, fax (816)753-1090, founded 1977, editor Gloria Vando Hickok. Helicon Nine publishes poetry, including winners of the annual Marianne Moore Poetry Prize. **The editor reads no unsolicited mss for Helicon Nine Editions.** They have recently published poetry by David Ray, Robley Wilson, Martha McFerren, Albert Goldbarth and Judy Longley. As a sample the editor selected these lines from "Night Ritual" by Marjorie Stelmach from her book *Night Drawings*:

> *Finger things: a silver hook*
> *lifted and lowered on the screen-porch door,*
> *a lamp-key turned to lower the flame,*
> *a gown's hem lifted for stairs, one*
> *slippered foot suspended.*

The Marianne Moore Poetry Prize awards $1,000 and publication for an unpublished poetry ms of at least 50 pgs. **Manuscripts are not returned, and there is a $15 reading fee for all contest entries. Deadline for entry: May 1.** Send SASE for guidelines.

HELIKON PRESS (V), 120 W. 71st St., New York NY 10023, founded 1972, poetry editors Robin Prising and William Leo Coakley, **"tries to publish the best contemporary poetry in the tradition of English verse. We read (and listen to) poetry and ask poets to build a collection around particular poems. We print fine editions illustrated by good artists. Unfortunately we cannot encourage submissions."**

‡HELIOTROPE (I, II), P.O. Box 9517, Spokane WA 99209-9517, website http://www.ior.com/heliotrope, founded 1996, editors George Thomas, Jan Stever, Iris Gribble-Neal, Jan Lindholm and Tom Gribble, published annually, is "an outlet for poetry, fiction, prose and criticism." **They want "poetry of any form, length, subject matter, style or purpose with no restrictions."** The editor says *Heliotrope* is 100 pgs., 8½ × 11, offset, saddle-stapled with 2-color slick paper cover with art. Press run is 100, 100 shelf sales. Subscription: $10. **Make checks payable to Tom Gribble. Submit 5 poems at a time. No previously published poems or simultaneous submissions. Cover letter preferred. E-mail submissions OK. Reads submissions June 21 through September 21 only. Poems are circulated to an editorial board. Seldom comments on rejections. Send SASE for**

guidelines. **Reports in 1 month. Sometimes sends prepublication galleys. Pays 1 copy.** The editors say, "We are open to all writers."

HELLAS: A JOURNAL OF POETRY AND THE HUMANITIES; THE HELLAS AWARD; THE ALDINE PRESS, LTD.; THE NEW CLASSICISTS (II, IV-Form), 304 S. Tyson Ave., Glenside PA 19038, phone (215)884-1086, founded 1988, editor Gerald Harnett. *Hellas* is a semiannual published by Aldine Press that wants poetry of **"any kind but especially poems in meter. We prize elegance and formality in verse, but specifically encourage poetry of the utmost boldness and innovation, so long as it is not willfully obscurantist; no ignorant, illiterate, meaningless free verse or political poems."** They have published poetry by Hadas, Steele, Moore, Butler, Kessler, Gioia and many others. *Hellas* is 172 pgs., 6×9, flat-spined, offset, using b&w art. Press run is 1,000. Subscription: $16/year, $28/2 years. **Sample postpaid: $9. Submit 3-5 poems at a time. No simultaneous submissions or previously published poems. Editor comments on rejections "happily if requested. If I don't understand it, I don't print it. On the other hand, we don't want obvious, easy, clichéd or sentimental verse." Send SASE for guidelines. Reports in 3-4 months. Pays 1 copy. Acquires first North American serial rights.** The *Hellas* Award ($200) is open to *Hellas* subscribers only and is awarded annually to the finest poem entered in the contest. Poems may be submitted to both *Hellas* and the contest simultaneously at any time throughout the year, but the annual deadline is December 31. Winner is published in spring issue of *Hellas*. Enclose SASE if submission is to be returned. The New Classicists is a Society of friends of the Aldine Press that publishes a quarterly newsletter for members. In addition to *Hellas*, the press publishes Lyrica, an ongoing series of metrical poetry chapbooks, in conjunction with sponsoring The Lycidas Award offered to the best chapbook of that series. They also plan to publish The New Classicists, "the only permanent and ongoing series of new books of metrical poetry." In addition, they sponsor the *Hellas* readings, held at various locations in Philadelphia, New York and elsewhere. Send SASE for guidelines. Their flyer says, **"*Hellas* is a lively and provocative assault on a century of modernist barbarism in the arts. A unique, Miltonic wedding of *paideia* and *poiesis*, engaging scholarship and original poetry, *Hellas* has become the forum of a remarkable new generation of poets, critics and theorists committed to the renovation of the art of our time . . . Meter is especially welcome, as well as rhymed and stanzaic verse. We judge a poem by its verbal artifice and its truth. Lines should not end arbitrarily, diction should be precise: We suggest that such principles can appear 'limiting' only to an impoverished imagination. To the contrary, we encourage any conceivable boldness and innovation, so long as it is executed with discipline and is not a masquerade for self-indulgent obscurantism. . . . We do not print poems about Nicaragua, whales or an author's body parts. We do specifically welcome submissions from newer authors."**

HEN'S TEETH (V), P.O. Box 87945, Sioux Falls SD 57105, founded 1988, editor Janice H. Mikesell, expects to publish a book every 2 years but **will not be open for submissions. "I publish material that I have written or co-edited only. Unsolicited material, unless accompanied by a SASE, will not be returned."** She has published *Women Houses & Homes: an anthology of prose, poetry and photography*, $8 plus $1.25 p&h, a 52-page, saddle-stapled book, cut with a roof-line top, professionally printed with a cover photograph of a "painted lady" Victorian house and now in its fifth printing. As a sample the editor selected these lines from her second book, *A Survivor's Manual: a book of poems*:

> my godmother
> so long ago
> her arms
> her lap
> her strokes that calmed the night

That book is a 52-page, perfect-bound paperback with an arresting cover photo (also $8 plus $1 p&h), now in its second printing.

HERALD PRESS; PURPOSE; STORY FRIENDS; ON THE LINE; WITH; CHRISTIAN LIVING (IV-Religious, children), 616 Walnut Ave., Scottdale PA 15683-1999, phone (412)887-8500. **Send submissions or queries directly to the editor of the specific magazine at address indicated.** Herald Press (formerly Mennonite Publishing House), the official publisher for the Mennonite Church in North America, seeks also to serve a broad Christian audience. **Each of the magazines listed has different specifications, and the editor of each should be queried for more exact information.** *Purpose*, editor James E. Horsch, a "religious young adult/adult monthly in weekly parts," circulation 14,000, its focus: "action oriented, discipleship living." It is 5⅜×8⅜, with two-color printing throughout. **They buy appropriate poetry up to 12 lines.** *Purpose* uses 3-4 poems/week, receives about 2,000/year of which they use 150, has a 10- to 12-week backlog. **Send SASE for guidelines and free sample. Mss should be typewritten, double-spaced, one side of sheet only. Simultaneous submissions OK. Reports in 6-8 weeks. Pays $7.50-20/poem plus 2 copies.** *On the Line*, edited by Mary C. Meyer, a monthly religious magazine, for children 9-14, "that reinforces Christian values," circulation 6,000. **Sample free with SASE. Wants poems 3-24 lines. Submit poems "each typed on a separate 8½×11 sheet." Simultaneous submissions and previously published poems OK. Reports in 1 month. Pays $10-25/poem plus 2 copies.** *Story Friends*, edited by Rose Mary Stutzman, is for **children 4-9**, a "story paper that reinforces Christian values," also a monthly magazine, circulation 6,500, uses poems **3-12 lines. Send SASE for guidelines/sample copy. Pays $5-10.** *With*, Editorial Team, Box 347, Newton KS 67114, phone (316)238-5100, is for **"senior**

highs, ages 15-18," focusing on empowering youth to radically commit to a personal relationship with Jesus Christ, and to share God's good news through word and actions." Circulation 5,800, uses **a limited amount of poetry. Poems should be 4-50 lines. Pays $10-25.** *Christian Living*, edited by Stephen Kriss, published 8 times/ year, is "for people and faith today," uses poems **up to 30 lines.** They have recently published poetry by Julia Kasdorf. As a sample the editor selected these lines from "Sometimes Hope" by Jean Janzen:

> But sometimes hope
> is a black ghost
> in a fantastic twist,
> an old dream that flickers
> in the wind.

The editor says *Christian Living* is 28-44 pgs., 8 × 10, 1-3 color with photos and artwork. They receive about 75 poems a year, accept approximately 15-20. Press run is 5,200 for 5,000 subscribers of which 8-10 are libraries, 10-20 shelf sales; 100-300 distributed free. Single copy: $3.10; subscription: $21.95. **Sample postpaid: $2.50. Make checks payable to *Christian Living*. Submit 3-5 poems at a time. Previously published poems and simultaneous submissions OK. Cover letter preferred with information about previous publications.** Time between acceptance and publication is 2-14 months. **Seldom comments on rejections. Publishes theme issues. Send SASE for guidelines. Reports in 1-6 months. Pays $1/line plus 2 copies. Buys first or one-time rights.** Staff reviews books or chapbooks of poetry in 200-800 words. Poets may also send books for review consideration.

THE HERB NETWORK (IV-Specialized), P.O. Box 12937, Albuquerque NM 87195, fax (505)452-8615, founded 1995, editor Kathleen O'Mara, is a quarterly newsletter of information for herbal enthusiasts. **They want poetry related to herbs or plants—real or folklore. Short poems to 250 words.** They have recently published poetry by Michael Drayton and William Shenstone. As a sample the editor selected "Dandelions" by Elizabeth Willis DeHuff:

> Slim little girls with green flounced dresses,
> Dandelions stand with yellow shaggy hair.
> Soon they grow to gray haired ladies,
> Whose locks sail away through the air.
> Ashamed of their baldness, each of these dears,
> Fringes a cap which she always wears.

The newsletter is 12 pgs., 8½ × 11, neatly printed on plain white paper with a few b&w graphics. The issue we received included recipes, information about herbs used by midwives, an article focusing on lavender, book reviews and classified ads. Press run is 2,500 for 2,000 subscribers. Subscription: $25/year. **Sample postpaid: $5. Submit 1-3 poems at a time, typed double-spaced, one poem/page, name and address on each. Previously published poems and simultaneous submissions OK. Submissions via fax OK. Cover letter preferred. Send SASE for guidelines. Reports in 3-6 months. Sometimes sends prepublication galleys. Pays by barter, offering free advertisements or copies. Acquires first or one-time rights.**

‡HERETIC HOLLOW (IV-Psychic/occult), P.O. Box 5511, Pasadena CA 91117, phone (818)584-0008, founded 1996, editor Capella, is a monthly newsletter "intended as a forum of expression for diverse magical, Pagan and Wiccan concerns, issues, facts, fantasy and opinion." **They want "occult, magick, wicca, metaphysical and druidical work and ritual chants. No Christian fundamentalist poetry or channeled material."** *HH* is 14 pgs., 8½ × 11, photocopied and saddle-stitched, b&w drawings and clip art, ads. They receive about 5 poems a year, accept approximately 10%. Press run is 250 for 10 subscribers; 240 distributed free to the general public. **Sample (including guidelines) postpaid: $2. Make checks payable to Pat W. Submit 5 poems at a time. Previously published poems and simultaneous submissions OK. Cover letter preferred. May submit on 5.25 disk, MSDOS ASCII format. Seldom comments on rejections. Publishes theme issues. Send SASE for upcoming themes. Sometimes sends prepublication galleys. Pays 1-year subscription. Acquires first and reprint rights.**

‡HERON QUARTERLY OF HAIKU AND ZEN POETRY; THINKING POST PRESS (I, IV-Form/ style), 17825 Bear Valley Lane, Escondido CA 92027, founded 1997, editor Carolyn Thomas. *Heron Quarterly of Haiku and Zen Poetry* strives to "bring the spirit of haiku and Zen poetry together in one place." **They want "Zen poems no more than 32 lines in length; haiku 1-4 lines. Spirit is more important than syllable count; I like season-words; nature relating to itself; the insignificant becoming significant; a spirit of enlightenment; I like poems that feel fresh and real as a sudden wind gust, or cool and weighty as a small round stone in the palm of the hand. No erotic poems or profanity, please. Nothing sentimental."** They have recently published poetry by Randy M. Brooks, Emily Romano and Dion O'Donnol. As a sample the editor chose her own poem:

> lake water
>   moves
>   with no sound;
> even the crows are silent
>   this cold grey evening

Heron Quarterly is 24 pgs., 8½ × 5⅜, professionally printed, saddle-stapled, with card stock cover of different color for each seasonal issue and heron brush-drawing on cover. Subscription: $16, $20 overseas. **Sample postpaid: $4, $5 overseas. Make checks payable to Thinking Post Press. Submit up to 10 haiku; up to 5 Zen poems on 8½ × 11 paper, single-spaced with name (and pseudonym, if desired) in left-hand corner of all pages. No previously published poems or simultaneous submissions.** Time between acceptance and publication is "within one year; I try to fit poems to the season." **Often comments on rejections. Send SASE for guidelines. Reports in 1-4 weeks. Pays 1 copy. Acquires first rights.** The editor says, "Keep images simple and clear, no flowery language. When you write haiku, that gong like a temple bell, you have hit your mark. It is the same with Zen poetry."

HIGH PLAINS PRESS (IV-Regional), P.O. Box 123, Glendo WY 82213, phone (307)735-4370, founded 1985, poetry editor Nancy Curtis, considers books of **poetry "specifically relating to Wyoming and the West, particularly poetry based on historical people/events or nature. We're mainly a publisher of historical nonfiction, but do publish one book of poetry every year."** They have recently published poetry by Charles Levendosky, Robert Roripaugh and Jane Candia Coleman. As a sample the editor selected these lines from "Gathering Mint" from the book *Glass-eyed Paint in the Rain* by Laurie Wagner Buyer:

> *He returned at dusk, drunk on solitude, singing*
> *in time with the gelding's rocky trot,*
> *moccasined feet wet with mud,*
> *the burlap bag he tossed me*
> *stuffed full of mint*
> *from the beaver slough.*

Query first with 3 sample poems (from a 50-poem ms). Reports in 2 months, publication in 18-24 months. Always sends prepublication galleys. Pays 10% of sales. Buys first rights. Catalog available on request; sample books: $5. Their book, *The Red Drum: Poetry of the American West*, by Jane C. Coleman, won the Wrangler Award for "accuracy and literary merit in portraying the West" in the poetry category from the National Cowboy Hall of Fame in 1995.

HIGH/COO PRESS; MAYFLY (IV-Form), 4634 Hale Dr., Decatur IL 62526, phone (217)877-2966, founded 1976, editors Randy and Shirley Brooks. High/Coo is a small press publishing nothing but **haiku in English.** "We publish haiku poemcards, minichapbooks, anthologies and a bibliography of haiku publications in addition to paperbacks and cloth editions and the magazine *Mayfly*, evoking emotions from contemporary experience. We are not interested in orientalism nor Japanese imitations." **They publish no poetry except haiku.** They have published haiku by Virgil Hutton, Lee Gurga and Wally Swist. *Mayfly* is 16 pgs., 3 × 5, professionally printed on high-quality stock, saddle-stapled, one haiku/page. It appears in January and August. They publish 32 of an estimated 1,800 submissions. Subscription: $8. **Sample postpaid: $4; or send $17 (Illinois residents add 7½% tax) for the *Midwest Haiku Anthology* which includes the work of 54 haiku poets. A Macintosh computer disk of haiku-related stacks is available for $10 postpaid. Submit no more than 5 haiku/issue. No simultaneous submissions or previously published poems. Send SASE for guidelines. Pays $5/poem; no copies.** High/Coo Press **considers mss "by invitation only."** Randy Brooks says, "Publishing poetry is a joyous work of love. We publish to share those moments of insight contained in evocative haiku. We aren't in it for fame, gain or name. We publish to serve an enthusiastic readership."

HIGHLIGHTS FOR CHILDREN (IV-Children), 803 Church St., Honesdale PA 18431, phone (717)253-1080, founded 1946, appears every month using **poetry for children ages 2-12. They want "meaningful and/or fun poems accessible to children of all ages. Welcome light, humorous verse. Rarely publish a poem longer than 16 lines, most are shorter. No poetry that is unintelligible to children, poems containing sex, violence or unmitigated pessimism."** They have published poetry by Bobbi Katz, Myra Cohn Livingston, Eileen Spinelli and Carl Sandburg. As a sample the editor selected "Instead of Buying You a Valentine, I Looked Out My Kitchen Window" by Barbara Crooker:

> *In February, trees are bare,*
> *snowflakes lace the frosted air*
> *and make the ground a clean white sheet*
> *of paper, scrawled by tiny feet*
> *of juncoes, titmice, chickadees,*
> *who write their names with practiced ease,*
> *and on a branch of snowy pine,*
> *two cardinals sit—a valentine.*

 THE MAPLE LEAF symbol before a listing indicates a Canadian publisher, magazine, conference, contest or organization.

It is generally 42 pgs., magazine-sized, full-color throughout. They receive about 300 submissions/year, purchase 6-10. Press run is 3.3 million for approximately 2.8 million subscribers. Subscription: $26.04/year (reduced rates for multiple years). **Submit typed ms with very brief cover letter. Please indicate if simultaneous submission. Editor comments on submissions "occasionally, if ms has merit or author seems to have potential for our market." Reports "generally within 1 month." Always sends prepublication galleys. Payment: "money varies" plus 2 copies. Buys all rights.** The editor says, "We are always open to submissions of poetry not previously published. However, we purchase a very limited amount of such material. We may use the verse as 'filler,' or illustrate the verse with a full-page piece of art. Please note that we do not buy material from anyone under 16 years old."

*HILLTOP PRESS (V, IV-Science fiction), 4 Nowell Place, Almondbury, Huddersfield, West Yorkshire HD5 8PB England, founded 1966, editor Steve Sneyd, publishes **"mainly science fiction poetry nowadays," but does not accept unsolicited mss. Query (with SAE/IRC) with proposals for relevant projects.** Publications include *Star-Spangled Shadows: Poetry in American SFanzines*, the 1930s to 1960s, including A-Z of writers/publications and poem extracts; *The Fantastic Muse*, reprinting a 1938 article and 1939 poem by science fiction giant Arthur C. Clarke; and *AE—The Seven Wonders of the Universe* by Mike Johnson. As a sample the editor selected these lines from "Lobster Quadrille" by Andrew Darlington:

> *my eyes*
> *on stalks*
> *follow delicate traceries of*
> *silver across rumpled canvas*
> *in the gutter*
> *a sea-horse attacks and consumes*
> *a drowned alley-cat*

Some Hilltop titles are distributed in the USA by the New Science Fiction Alliance. For full list of UK publications, including those NSFA distributes, send SAE/IRC to A. Marsden, 31192 Paseo Amapola, San Juan Capostrano CA 92675-2227. "My advice for beginning poets is (a) persist—don't let any one editor discourage you. 'In poetry's house are many mansions,' what one publication hates another may love; (b) be prepared for long delays between acceptance and appearance of work—the small press is mostly self-financed and part time, so don't expect it to be more efficient than commercial publishers; (c) *always* keep a copy of everything you send out, put your name and address on *everything* you send and *always* include adequately stamped SAE."

*HIPPOPOTAMUS PRESS (IV-Form); OUTPOSTS POETRY QUARTERLY; OUTPOSTS ANNUAL POETRY COMPETITION (II), 22 Whitewell Rd., Frome, Somerset BA11 4EL England, phone/fax 01373-466653, *Outposts* founded 1943, Hippopotamus Press founded 1974, poetry editor Roland John, who explains, "*Outposts* **is a general poetry magazine that welcomes all work either from the recognized or the unknown poet. The Hippopotamus Press is specialized, with an affinity with Modernism. No Typewriter, Concrete, Surrealism.**" They have published in *OPQ* poetry by John Heath-Stubbs, Peter Dale and Elizabeth Jennings. *Outposts* is 70-100 pgs., digest-sized, flat-spined, litho, in professionally set small type, using ads. Of 60,000 poems received he uses about 300. Press run is 3,000 for 2,800 subscribers of which 10% are libraries, 2% of circulation through shelf sales. Subscription: $32. **Sample postpaid: $8. Submit 5 poems at a time. "IRCs must accompany U.S. submissions." Simultaneous submissions and previously published poems OK. Cover letter required. Reports in 2 weeks plus post time. Sometimes sends prepublication galleys. Pays $8/poem plus 1 copy. Copyright remains with author.** Staff reviews books of poetry in 200 words for "Books Received" page. Also uses full essays up to 4,000 words. Send books for review consideration, attn. M. Pargitter. The magazine also holds an annual poetry competition. Hippopotamus Press publishes 6 books a year, averaging 80 pgs. **For book publication query with sample poems. Simultaneous submissions and previously published poems OK. Reports in 6 weeks. Pays 10% royalties plus 20 paper copies, 6 cloth. Send for book catalog to buy samples.**

HIRAM POETRY REVIEW (I, II), P.O. Box 162, Hiram OH 44234, founded 1967, poetry editor Hale Chatfield, is a semiannual with occasional special supplements. **"We favor new talent—and except for one issue in two years, read** *only* **unsolicited mss." They are interested in "all kinds of high quality poetry"** and have published poetry by Grace Butcher, David Citino, Michael Finley, Peter Wild, Jim Daniels, Peter Klappert and Harold Witt. There are 30 pgs. of poetry in the professionally printed, digest-sized, saddle-stapled magazine (glossy cover with b&w photo). Circulation is 400 for 300 subscriptions of which 150 are libraries. They receive about 7,500 submissions/year, use 50, have up to a 6-month backlog. Although most poems appearing here tend to be lyric and narrative free verse under 50 lines, exceptions occur (a few longer, sequence or formal works can be found in each issue). Single copy: $4; subscription: $8. **Sample: free! No simultaneous submissions. "Send four to five fresh, neat copies of your best poems." Reports in 2-6 months. Pays 2 copies plus 1-year subscription. Acquires first North American serial rights; returns rights upon publication.** Reviews books of poetry in single or multi-book format, no set length. Send books for review consideration.

‡HODGE PODGE POETRY (II), P.O. Box 11107, Shorewood WI 53211, e-mail tallpoet@aol.com, founded 1995, contact Kenneth P. Gurney, published quarterly, "to promote poetry in my community and for the fun of it." They want "typed, original, unpublished work. Hodge podge describes it. I take the best of what comes in." They do not want "poems that have excessive violence, swearing or prejudice." They have recently published poetry by Antler, Lyn Lifshin, Eileen Tabios and Matt Welter. *Hodge Podge* is 48 pgs., 5½ × 8½, desktop-published, saddle-stapled with medium card cover with art, no ads. They receive about 2,400 poems a year, accept approximately 160. Press run is 100 for 12 subscribers of which 1 is a library; 30 distributed free. Subscription: $19. **Sample postpaid: $5. Make checks payable to Hodge Podge Press. Submit up to 5 poems at a time. No previously published poems; simultaneous submissions OK. No electronic submissions. Poems should be typed, 1 to a page, name and address on each page, work is not returned. "First five poems read for free, $1 per poem after that." Deadlines are: March 31 (summer), June 30 (autumn), September 30 (winter) and December 31 (spring).** Time between acceptance and publication is 2 months. "I read. I decide. (I read every poem that comes in.)" **Charges criticism fees of $2 per poem, $10 minimum; response in 3-6 weeks. Send SASE for guidelines. Reports 1 month after deadline. Pays 1 copy. Acquires first rights.** Reviews books or chapbooks of poetry or other magazines. Open to unsolicited reviews. Poets may also send books for review consideration.

HOLIDAY HOUSE, INC. (III, IV-Children), 425 Madison Ave., New York NY 10017, founded 1936, editor-in-chief Regina Griffin, is a trade children's book house. They have published hardcover books for children by Myra Cohn Livingston. They publish 1 poetry book a year averaging 32 pages. The editor says, "acceptance of complete book ms. of high-quality children's poetry is limited."

THE HOLLINS CRITIC (II), P.O. Box 9538, Hollins College, Roanoke VA 24020-1538, phone (540)362-6275, founded 1964, editor R.H.W. Dillard, appears 5 times/year, publishing critical essays, poetry and book reviews. **They use a few short poems in each issue, interesting in form, content or both.** They have recently published poetry by John Engels, William Miller, Stephen Herz and John Cassels. As a sample the editor selected these lines from "Carving the Salmon" by John Engels:

> And then it is recognizable, a fish,
>   and ready for finishing. It quivers

> a little at the skew chisel, flinches
>   at the spoonbit. With the straight gouge
>   I give it eyes, and with the veiner, gills,

> and it leaps a little in my hand.

The Hollins Critic is 20 pgs., magazine-sized. Circulation is 500. **Sample: $1.50. Submit up to 5 poems, none over 35 lines, must be typewritten, to Cathryn Hankla, poetry editor. Cover letter preferred. Reports in 6 weeks (slower in the summer). Pays $25/poem plus 5 copies.** Traditionally, verse here has been open as to form and style with poems that please the mind, eye and senses.

HENRY HOLT & COMPANY (V), 115 W. 18th St., New York NY 10011, **accepts no unsolicited poetry.**

HOME TIMES (I), P.O. Box 16096, West Palm Beach FL 33416, phone (561)439-3509, founded 1988, editor/publisher Dennis Lombard, is a monthly "independent, conservative, pro-Christian, pro-Jewish," 20-page newsprint tabloid of local, national and world news and views, including information in the areas of home and family, arts and entertainment, and religion. **They want poetry that is "humorous or spiritual—not 'religious'; for a general audience."** As a sample we selected these lines from "Heritage" by Paul Swope:

> And, overwhelmingly, I realize
> That, trying to be different,
> I have become my father
> Then, relieved, I remember
> That as he grew older,
> he seemed quite intelligent
> And before he died
> We agreed on almost everything
> My son is a different story . . .

The editor says they receive about 200 poems a year, accept 2-3%. Press run is 5,000. Single copy: $1. **Samples: $3 for 3 current issues. Submit 3 poems at a time. Previously published poems and simultaneous submissions OK.** Time between acceptance and publication is 1-6 months. **Sometimes comments on rejections. Send SASE for guidelines. Reports in 2-4 weeks. Pays $5 "generally"; a 6-month subscription, if requested. Buys one-time rights.** The editor says, "*Home Times* is very different! Please read guidelines and sample issues."

HOPSCOTCH: THE MAGAZINE FOR GIRLS; BOYS' QUEST (IV-Children), P.O. Box 164, Bluffton OH 45817-0164, phone (419)358-4610, founded 1989, editor Marilyn B. Edwards. *Hopscotch* is a bimonthly magazine for **girls 6-12. "In need of short traditional poems for various holidays and seasons. (Limit to 21 lines if possible, 700-1,000 words.) However, we do not want Halloween-related material. Nothing abstract, experimental."** They have published poetry by Lois Grambling, Judy Nichols, Leila Dornak, Judith Harkham

Semas and Maggie McGee. The editor describes *Hopscotch* as "full-color cover, 50 pgs. of 2-color inside, 7×9, saddle-stapled." They use about 30-35 of some 2,000 poems received/year. Press run is 11,000 for 10,000 subscribers of which 7,000 are libraries, 200 to inquiring schools and libraries. Subscription: $15. **Sample postpaid: $3. Submit 3-6 poems/submission. Cover letter preferred; include experience and where published. Publishes theme issues. Send SASE for upcoming themes. Themes include Sports (August/September 1997), Teeth (October/November 1997), Cooking (December/January 1998), Our Health (February/March 1998), Diaries & Journals (April/May 1998), Summertime (June/July 1998) and Other Countries-Other Cultures (August/September 1998). Reports in 2-4 weeks. Pays $10-40. Buys first American serial rights.** The few poems in this children's magazine occasionally address the audience, challenging young girls to pursue their dreams. To see how, order a sample copy (or check one out at the library) because it is too easy for poets who write children's verse to forget that each magazine targets a specific audience . . . in a specific way. They also publish *Boys' Quest*, a bimonthly magazine for **boys 6-13.** Similar in format to *Hopscotch*, the magazine premiered in June/July 1995. **Upcoming themes include: Insects (August/September 1997), Communication (October/November 1997), Pets (December 1997/January 1998), Animals (February/March 1998), Gardening (April/May 1998), Sports (June/July 1998) and Water Creatures (August/September 1998). Send SASE for details.**

‡*HORIZON (III)**, Stationsstraat 232A, 1770 Liedekerke, Belgium, founded 1985, editor Johnny Haelterman, published semiannually, is a "cultural magazine with prose and illustrations, in Dutch and a few pages in English." **Preference is given to "poems with punctuation, metre and rhyme but that is not a hard and fast rule. If a poem is not published after a year, it means that it couldn't be used. *Horizon* takes poems only as a filler."** The editor says *Horizon* is 29.7×21cm, "reprographic," saddle-stapled with color cover. They receive about 200 poems (in English) a year, accept approximately 3%. Press run is 100. Single copy: $10; subscription: $20/2 issues. **Pays 1 copy.**

HOUGHTON MIFFLIN CO. (V), 222 Berkeley St., Boston MA 02116, founded 1850, poetry editor Peter Davison. Houghton Mifflin is a high-prestige trade publisher that puts out both hardcover and paperback books, but **poetry submission is by invitation only and they are not seeking new poets at present.** They have published poetry books by Donald Hall, May Swenson, Rodney Jones, Geoffrey Hill, Galway Kinnell, Thomas Lux, Erica Funkhouser, William Matthews, Margaret Atwood, Linda Gregerson, Mary Oliver and Andrew Hudgins. **Always sends prepublication galleys. Authors are paid 10% royalties on hardcover books, 6% royalties on paperbacks (minimum), $1,000 advance and 12 author's copies.**

✦**HOUSE OF ANANSI PRESS (II, IV-Regional)**, 1800 Steeles Ave. W., Concord, Ontario L4K 2P3 Canada, phone (905)660-0611, fax (905)660-0676, e-mail anansi@irwin-pub.com, website http://www.irwin-pub.com/irwin/anansi, founded 1967, publisher Michael Davis, editor Martha Sharpe, publishes literary fiction and poetry **by Canadian writers. "We seek to balance the list between well-known and emerging writers, with an interest in writing by Canadians of all backgrounds. We publish Canadian poetry only, and poets must have a substantial publication record—if not in books, then definitely in journals and magazines of repute. No children's poetry and no poetry by previously unpublished poets."** They have published *Power Politics* by Margaret Atwood and *More Watery Still* by Patricia Young. As a sample they selected these lines from "The Ecstasy of Skeptics" in the book *The Ecstasy of Skeptics* by Steven Heighton:

> This tongue
> is a moment of moistened dust, it must learn
> to turn the grit of old books
> into hydrogen, and burn
> The dust of the muscles must burn
> down the blood-fuse of the sinews, . . .

Their books are generally 96-144 pgs., trade paperback with French sleeves, a matte finish cover and full-color cover art. **Canadian poets should query first with 10 sample poems (typed double-spaced) and a cover letter with brief bio and publication credits. Previously published poems and simultaneous submissions OK. Poems are circulated to an editorial board. Often comments on rejections. Replies to queries within 3 months, to mss (if invited) within 4 months. Pays 8-10% royalties, a $500 honorarium and 10 author's copies (out of a press run of 1,000).** To learn more about their titles, check their website or write to the press directly for a catalog. They say, "We strongly advise poets to build up a publishing résumé by submitting poems to reputable magazines and journals. This indicates three important things to us: One, that he or she is becoming a part of the Canadian poetry community; two, that he or she is building up a readership through magazine subscribers; and three, it establishes credibility in his or her work. There is a great deal of competition for only three or four spots on our list each year—which always includes works by poets we have previously published."

HOUSEWIFE-WRITER'S FORUM (IV-Women, humor), P.O. Box 780, Lyman WY 82937, phone (307)782-7003, founded 1988, editor/publisher Emma Bluemel, is a magazine of "prose, poetry, information and open forum communication for and by housewives or any woman or man who writes while juggling a busy schedule. **We have no specifications as to form, subject, style or purpose. Length maximum 30 lines. We publish both serious poetry and humorous. Nothing pornographic, but erudite expression is fine."** Emma

Bluemel describes the magazine as "a small market for women who aspire to write for larger women's markets or support each other in the quest for finding time and energy to write." It is 48 pgs., desktop-published, using some art, graphics and ads, appearing bimonthly. Press run is 2,000. **Sample postpaid: $3. "Simultaneous submissions are OK."** Send SASE for guidelines. **Reports in 2 months. Pays 1 copy plus $1-2/poem. Buys first-time rights.** She holds an annual contest with $4/poem fee, June 1 deadline. *Housewife-Writer's Forum* received a first place award for magazine editing from Wyoming Media Professionals. The editor adds, "I like to see poems that have a strong central purpose and use the language to express it beautifully, powerfully. I also like to see poems that make me laugh."

HOWLING DOG (V), 2913 Woodcock Court, Rochester MI 48306, founded 1985, poetry editor Wipee Zippie. *Howling Dog*, a literary journal, is **not accepting unsolicited manuscripts at this time.**

*HQ: THE HAIKU QUARTERLY; THE DAY DREAM PRESS (II), 39 Exmouth St., Kingshill, Swindon, Wiltshire SN1 3PU England, phone 01793-523927, founded 1990, editor Kevin Bailey, is "a platform from which new and established poets can speak and/or experiment with new forms and ideas." They want **"any poetry of good quality."** They have published poetry by Peter Redgrove, Alan Brownjohn, James Kirkup and Cid Corman. The editor says *HQ* is 48-64 pgs., A5, perfect-bound with art, ads and reviews. They accept approximately 5% of poetry received. Press run is 500-600 for 500 subscribers of which 30 are libraries. Subscription: £9 UK, £12 foreign. **Sample postpaid: £2.50. No previously published poems or simultaneous submissions. Cover letter and SASE (or SAE and IRCs) required.** Time between acceptance and publication is 3-6 months. **Often comments on rejections. Reports "as time allows." Pays 1 copy.** Reviews books of poetry in about 1,000 words, single format. Open to unsolicited reviews. Poets may also send books for review consideration.

*HRAFNHOH (IV-Form, religious); BLACK EAGLE (IV-Ethnic, translations), 32 Strŷd Ebeneser, Pontypridd, CF 37 5PB Wales via GB, founded 1987, editor Joseph Biddulph, *Hrafnhoh* is a small press magazine seeking **"metrical verse."** They use **"poetry in traditional verse forms with a Christian inspiration and purpose, with an active concern for metrical technique and conveying a serious message in an evocative and entertaining style."** They have published poetry by John Waddington-Feather, M.A.B. Jones, Joe Keysor and many others. The editor describes *Hrafnhoh* as 24-40 pgs., digest-sized, occasionally typeset, illustrated with carefully-researched heraldic illustrations and other sketches. He accepts about 1 of 6-10 poems received, but is not always able to publish even if accepted. Press run is 100-500. *Hrafnhoh* includes a supplement, *Black Eagle,* which seeks **short, preferably metrical verse on the living experience of Africa or the African diaspora, or translations of African languages in English, French, Spanish or Creole. Sample copy free worldwide. Submit up to 7 poems at a time. Simultaneous submissions and previously published poems OK. Publishes theme issues. Reports as soon as possible. Pays up to 10 copies, "depending on circumstances."** The editor says, "Many unsolicited manuscripts are in one form—free verse—and without substance, i.e., without a definite purpose, message or conclusion. I am anxious to obtain verse with a strong technique, particularly on Pro-Life and Christian subjects."

*HU (HONEST ULSTERMAN) (II, IV-Regional), 49 Main St., Greyabbey, County Down BT22 2NF United Kingdom, founded 1968, editor Tom Clyde, is a literary magazine appearing 3-4 times a year using **"technically competent poetry and prose and book reviews. Special reference to Northern Irish and Irish literature. Lively, humorous, adventurous, outspoken."** They have published poetry by Seamus Heaney, Paul Muldoon, Gavin Ewart, Craig Raine, Fleur Adcock and Medbh McGuckian. As a sample the editor selected these lines from "Badger With Ursa Minor" by Frankie McGurk:

> You can see this fire in a badger's eyes,
> it blazes in the white of his mask.
> The pole star is in his nose.
> With a bouncing gait
> he moves through space
> in the vast and fertile
> galaxy of a field.

HU is 128 pgs., A5 (digest-sized), photolithographic, phototypeset, perfect-bound with photographs and line drawings and loose, inserted ads with an "occasional color cover." Press run is 1,000 for 350 subscribers. Subscription: $28. **Sample postpaid: $7. "Potential contributors are strongly advised to read the magazine before submitting their work." Submit 6 poems at a time. Editor comments on submissions "occasionally." Publishes theme issues. Send SAE and IRCs for upcoming themes. Pays "a nominal fee" plus 2 copies.** Reviews books of literary and cultural interest in 500-1,000 words, single or multi-book format. Open to unsolicited reviews. Poets may also send books for review consideration. They also publish occasional poetry pamphlets.

HUBBUB (III), 5344 SE 38th Ave., Portland OR 97202, founded 1983, editors L. Steinman and J. Shugrue, appears once a year. *Hubbub* is designed "to feature a multitude of voices from interesting contemporary American poets. **We look for poems that are well-crafted, with something to say. We have no single style, subject or length requirement and, in particular, will consider long poems. No light verse."** They have published

Meaning noise, uproar or confusion, the title of **Hubbub** represents the type of work sought for this publication: poetry with something to say. Says co-editor Lisa M. Steinman, "**Hubbub** is designed to feature a multitude of voices from interesting, contemporary American poets. We look for voices that couple craft with having something to say." Likewise, the cover selected for this Oregon-based annual's thirteenth edition says much about the work represented inside. "This cover illustration offers a visual equivalent of our magazine's title," says Steinman. The cover is from "Harvest Spin," a pen and ink drawing by Portland, Oregon, resident Stan Wood.

poetry by Madeline DeFrees, William Matthews, Cecil Giscombe, Carolyn Kizer, Agha Shahid Ali and Alice Fulton. The editors describe **Hubbub** as 60-65 pgs., 5½ × 8½, offset, perfect-bound, cover art only, usually no ads. They receive about 1,200 submissions/year, use approximately 2%. Press run is 350 for 100 subscribers of which 12 are libraries, about 150 shelf sales. Subscription: $5/year. **Sample postpaid: $2.65 (volumes 1-8), $3.15 (volumes 9 and 11), $6.25 (volume 10, 12 and following). Submit 3-6 typed poems (no more than 6). No previously published poems or simultaneous submissions. Send SASE for guidelines. Reports in 2-4 months. Pays 2 copies. Acquires first North American serial rights.** "We review two to four poetry books a year in short (three-page) reviews; all reviews are solicited. We do, however, list books received/recommended." Send books for consideration. Outside judges choose poems from each volume for two awards: Vi Gale Award ($100) and Adrienne Lee Award ($50). There are no special submission procedures or entry fees involved.

THE HUDSON REVIEW (III), 684 Park Ave., New York NY 10021. *The Hudson Review* is a high-quality, flat-spined quarterly of 704 pgs., considered one of the most prestigious and influential journals in the nation. Editors welcome all styles and forms. However, competition is extraordinarily keen, especially since poems compete with prose. **Sample postpaid: $7. Nonsubscribers may submit poems only between April 1 and July 31. "Simultaneous submissions are returned unread." Reports in 6-8 weeks. Always sends prepublication galleys. Pays 50¢/line for poetry.** Work published in this review has also been included in the 1993, 1994 and 1997 volumes of *The Best American Poetry*.

‡HULA MAGAZINE (II), 7706 W. Lake Dr., Springfield IL 62707, phone (217)529-8971, e-mail winterlady@ aol.com, website http://www.gfaphoto@midwest.net, founded 1995, contact Jenny Gillespie, published quarterly, features "poetry and stories from Generation Y—ages 14-21." **They want "moving pieces with unique styles— ages 14-21 preferred." They do not want "death, hate, racist, erotic."** They have recently published poetry by Todd Campbell. As a sample the editor selected these lines from "Love Brings Ants" by Leanne Laux-Bachard:

> there is a girl i know
> she has stucco thighs
> heart of cotton
> her will power is soft like dough
> a shell of her true righteous self

The editor says *Hula* is 25-30 pgs., photocopied, stapled with art and graphics. They receive about 30-50 poems a year, use approximately 10. Press run is 100. Single copy: $1.50. **Sample postpaid: $1. Make checks payable to Jenny Gillespie. Submit 3-4 poems at a time. Previously published poems and simultaneous submissions OK. Cover letter preferred. Include name, age and address.** Time between acceptance and publication is 1-2 months. **Seldom comments on rejections. Obtain guidelines via e-mail or website. Reports in 2-3 weeks.** Reviews books of poetry or other magazines. Open to unsolicited reviews. Poets may also send books for review consideration.

THE HUMAN QUEST (IV-Political), (formerly *The Churchman's Human Quest*), 1074 23rd Ave. N., St. Petersburg FL 33704-3228, editor Edna Ruth Johnson, is a "humanistic bimonthly dealing with society's problems, especially peace. We use practically no poetry." It is magazine-sized and appears 6 times a year. Circulation is 10,000, of which 1,000 go for library subscriptions. **Send for free sample. Pays copies.**

THE HUNTED NEWS; THE SUBOURBON PRESS (I, II), P.O. Box 9101, Warwick RI 02889, phone (401)826-7307, founded 1990, editor Mike Wood. *The Hunted News* is an annual "designed to find good writers and give them one more outlet to get their voices heard." As for poetry, the editor says, **"The poems that need to be written are those that need to be read."** They do not want to see **"the poetry that does not need to be written or which is written only to get a reaction or congratulate the poet."** The editor says *THN* is 25-30 pgs., 8½×11, photocopied, unstapled. "I receive over 200 poems per month and accept perhaps 10%." Press run is 150-200. **Sample free with SASE. Previously published poems OK; no simultaneous submissions. Always comments on rejections. Send SASE for guidelines. Reports in 1 month. Pays 2-5 copies, more on request.** "I review current chapbooks and other magazines and do other random reviews of books, music, etc. Word count varies." The editor says, "I receive mostly beginner's poetry that attempts to be too philosophical, without much experience to back up statements, or self-impressed 'radical' poems by poets who assume that I will publish them because they are beyond criticism. I would like poets to send work whose point lies in language and economy and in experience, not in trite final lines, or worse, in the arrogant cover letter."

HYACINTH HOUSE PUBLICATIONS; BROWNBAG PRESS; PSYCHOTRAIN; THE CROW-BAIT REVIEW (V), P.O. Box 120, Fayetteville AR 72702-0120, founded 1989, contact Shannon Frach. *Brownbag Press*, *The Crowbait Review* and *PsychoTrain* are semiannual magazines. **Currently, however, all three magazines are not accepting unsolicited submissions.** *Brownbag Press* publishes "forceful writing full of spark and vigor for a widely diverse, intelligent, fairly left-of-center audience." *PsychoTrain* uses "bizarre, avant-garde material with a delightfully psychotic edge. Heady and chaotic." *The Crowbait Review* is a poetry-only publication "using a wide stylistic mix, from the abrasive and gut-level to the deliciously surreal. It comes out more often than our other publications and is cheaper to produce, hence allowing us to publish far more poetry than we used to. This is a zine in the rawest sense of the word; do not expect to see a perfect-bound, coffee-table edition. The editors feature **poetry that is "avant-garde, confessional, contemporary, erotic, experimental, gay/lesbian, pagan/occult or punk. Also Dada, surrealism and decadent writing at its best. No rhyming poetry, mainstream poetry, academic poetry. We are interested in free verse. No traditional 'horror' or vampire poetry. We're looking for what would typically be considered 'underground' or 'alternative' writing. Morbid humor is always a plus here. We prefer two-fisted, dynamic, very intense poetry."** They have published poetry by Andrew Lucariello, Marty Evans, Lawrence Carradini, Noelle Kocot, Kimberly J. Bright and C.F. Roberts. As a sample the editors selected these lines from "condoms are doggie bags of soul" by Randal Seyler:

> . . . she tilts her head back at the neck
> laughs like christ on the cross
> like jekyll taking a crap . . .
> her hand crouched on my thigh like a spider
> waiting for a love letter

Brownbag is 24 pgs. and *PsychoTrain* is 20 pgs., magazine-sized. Both are photocopied and stapled with card covers. *The Crowbait Review* is 14 pgs., photocopied and stapled. Press run for each is 300 for 100 subscribers, 125 shelf sales. **Sample postpaid: $4 for *Brownbag*, $4 for *PsychoTrain*, $2 for *The Crowbait Review*. Make checks payable to Hyacinth House Publications. "Cash is also OK."** They are not currently accepting submissions. Hyacinth House also has **a chapbook series. "Presently we're using solicited material only—please don't send us unsolicited chapbook mss at this time.** We will be doing approximately seven chapbooks this year, all from authors who have first appeared in our magazines. We don't take chapbook submissions 'out of the blue'—we like to know who we're working with." Hyacinth House Publications also sponsors the Richard A. Seffron Memorial Poetry Prize. "This is an ongoing competition with an annual deadline of May 1. Winners receive chapbook copies and a small cash prize. Send SASE for details and any queries concerning the Seffron Prize.

I.E. MAGAZINE, A JOURNAL OF LITERATURE AND THE ARTS; POET'S JOURNEY; I.E. PRESS (I, II), P.O. Box 9873, The Woodlands TX 77387-6873, phone (713)901-2750 (voice mail, can only return calls collect), publisher/managing editor Yolande Gottlieb. Founded in 1990, the biannual *i.e. magazine* contains poetry, fiction, nonfiction, poetry translations and art. **"We are committed to furthering excellence in literature**

and the arts." **They want "well-crafted, thought-provoking poetry that is crisp, vivid and imaginative; poetry of irresistible brilliance, writing that makes a difference."** They have recently published poetry by André de Korvin, Robert Haas, A.B. Telyachenk and Martina Reisz. As a sample the editor selected these lines from "Grieving A Garden" by Lora Dewey Finley:

> She did not understand the anarchy
> of bones that claimed poetry as my life.
> She did not know how this dark river
> swallows sound. Instead, she claimed soil
> rode a plow over a poisoned hexagon of red land.

i.e. magazine is 40-48 pgs., 5½×8½, professionally printed on coated stock, saddle-stitched, with b&w photos and graphics. They receive about 500 poems a year, accept 8-10/issue. Press run is 500. Single copy: $4.50; subscription: $12/year US, $16/year for libraries and institutions, $16/year foreign (US funds only). **Sample postpaid: $6. Submit 3-5 poems at a time. Name on upper right hand corner. Cover letter with name, address, phone number, titles of poems, brief biography, writing credits and photograph. No previously published poems or simultaneous submissions. "Please label envelopes with genre." Disk (3.5 IBM compatible) submissions OK.** Time between acceptance and publication is 2-12 months. **Seldom comments on rejections. Send SASE for guidelines. Reports in 2-6 months. Pays 1 copy. Acquires first rights.** Reviews books and chapbooks of poetry. Open to unsolicited reviews. Poets may also send books for review consideration. i.e. press also publishes *Poet's Journey*, a biannual magazine containing "poetry, poetry translations, articles on the life and poetry of famous poets, articles about poetics and art. **We look for imagination, well-constructed, outstanding poetry; one page maximum. Open form and subject matter. No religious, juvenile or greeting card verse."** The editor says *PJ* is 40-48 pgs., digest-sized with colored card cover. Press run is 200. Subscription: $12 US, $16 foreign. **Submit 3-5 poems at a time with $1 reading fee per poem, essay, article or art. No previously published poems; simultaneous submissions OK if noted. Often comments on rejections. Send SASE for guidelines. Pays 1 copy. Acquires first rights.** Awards $20, $10, $5 and 3 honorable mentions to the best work in each issue. Sponsors annual poetry and poetry chapbook contests. Send SASE for details. The editors say, "We advise new poets to read as much contemporary poetry as possible, small literary magazines, contemporary anthologies, prestigious magazines. See what is being published everywhere. Daily writing time is most important. Seek poetry groups and participate in their programs."

‡**IBIS REVIEW (II)**, P.O. Box 133, Falls Village CT 06031, phone (860)824-7636, e-mail ibisbooks@aol.com, founded 1995, contact the editors, is an annual publication of poetry and short fiction. **They want any kind of poetry, but have a preference for free verse.** They have recently published poetry by James Laughlin, Simon Perchik and Richard Kostelanetz. The editors say *IBIS* is 116 pgs., 5½×8½ staple-bound with original art on paper cover. Single copy: $8.95. **Submit 1 poem to a page, 15 pages maximum. No previously published poems; simultaneous submissions OK. Cover letter preferred including short bio. Reads submissions January through April only. Poems are circulated to an editorial board. "Four editors read all mss." Seldom comments on rejections. Send SASE for guidelines or request via e-mail. Sometimes sends prepublication galleys. Pays 2 copies. Rights revert to author upon publication. "However, we require acknowledgement of first publication."**

ICON; HART CRANE AWARD (II), Kent State University-Trumbull, 4314 Mahoning Ave., NW, Warren OH 44483-1998, phone (330)847-0571, e-mail lynchm@trumbull.kent.edu, website http://www.trumbull.kent.edu/icon.html/, founded 1966, is a biannual, "eclectic" literary and art magazine. **"We prefer short lyric poems, although all forms are considered. Originality and innovation are appreciated. Sentimental or angst-ridden poems should send themselves elsewhere."** They have published poetry by Gay Brewer and William Greenway. The editor says *Icon* is 48-60 pgs., saddle-stapled with b&w photos and graphics. They receive 1,200 poems a year, publish about 90. Press run is 500 for 75 subscribers of which 15 are libraries, 400 distributed half-price to students. Single copy: $4; subscription: $6. **Sample postpaid: $2. Submit 5 poems at a time. No previously published poems; simultaneous submissions OK. Cover letter preferred. Reads submissions September 15 through April 15 only. Poems are circulated to an editorial board. Often comments on rejections. Reports in 2-6 months. Pays 2 copies.** They also offer the Hart Crane Award, an annual poetry award of $100. The winner is published in the spring issue. Send SASE for details.

THE ICONOCLAST (II), 1675 Amazon Rd., Mohegan Lake NY 10547-1804, founded 1992, editor/publisher Phil Wagner, is a general interest literary publication appearing 8 times/year "for those who find life absurd and profound." **They want "poems that have something to say—the more levels the better. Nothing sentimental, religious, obscure or self-absorbed. Our poetry is accessible to a thoughtful reading public."** *The Iconoclast* is 32 pgs., 5½×8½, double-stapled, typeset and photocopied on 20 lb. white paper, with b&w art, graphics and ads. They receive about 1,000 poems a year, use 5%. Press run is 500 for 240 subscribers. Subscription: $13 for 8 issues. **Sample postpaid: $2. Submit 3-4 poems at a time. Previously published poems and simultaneous submissions OK, though they say "previously published and simultaneous submissions must be demonstrably better than others."** Time between acceptance and publication is 1-9 months. **"Poems are subject to the extremely fallible judgments of the editor-in-chief." Often comments on rejections. Reports in 2-4 weeks.**

Pays 1 copy per published page or poem, 40% discount on extras. **Acquires one-time rights.** Reviews books of poetry in 250 words, single format.

‡**IDEALS MAGAZINE; IDEALS PUBLICATIONS INC. (II)**, Suite 250, 535 Metroplex Dr., Nashville TN 37211, founded 1944, contact editorial department. *Ideals Magazine* appears 6 times/year and publishes "light poetry and short articles with a nostalgic theme. Issues are seasonally oriented." **They want "traditional forms and subjects, such as home, family, nature, holidays, patriotic. No limericks, erotica, haiku."** They have recently published poetry by Edna Jaques, Edgar A. Guest and Patience Strong. They say *Ideals* is 88 pgs., 8½ × 11, perfect-bound with 4-color glossy cover, old-fashioned artwork, no ads. They receive about 2,000 poems a year, accept approximately 5%. Press run is 190,000 for 170,000 subscribers of which 6,000 are libraries, 40,000 shelf sales. Single copy: $5.95; subscription: $19.95. **Sample postpaid: $4. Make checks payable to Ideals Publications Inc. Submit 10 poems at a time. Previously published poems and simultaneous submissions OK. Cover letter preferred. Publishes theme issues. Send SASE for guidelines. Reports in 6-8 weeks. Pays $10/poem and 1 copy. Buys first North American serial or one-time rights.**

THE IDIOT (IV-Humor), 1706 S. Bedford St., Los Angeles CA 90035, founded 1993, editor Sam Hayes, is a biannual humor magazine. "We mostly use fiction, articles and cartoons, but **will use anything funny, including poetry. Nothing pretentious."** They have recently published poetry by Horace Hauermeyer, Mark Von Lafferty and Rodrigo Pendergast. As a sample the editor selected these lines from "Buttermilk Pancake Batter" by Freud Pachenko:

> *Why do you scorn me?*
> *Do I not sew mittens to keep your testicles warm on*
> > *cold winter nights.*
> *Wait, those aren't mittens, those are mousetraps!*
> *No wonder you scorn me.*

The Idiot is 48 pgs., 5½ × 8½, professionally printed and staple-bound with glossy cover. They receive about 30 submissions a year, accept 3-4. Press run is 300. Single copy: $4. **Sample postpaid: $5. Previously published poems and simultaneous submissions OK. Seldom comments on rejections. Reports in 2-6 months. Pays 1 copy. Acquires one-time rights.** The editor says, "If it ain't funny, don't send it! I mean it! We're talkin' belly laughs, damn it!"

UNIVERSITY OF ILLINOIS PRESS (III), 1325 S. Oak St., Champaign IL 61820, phone (217)333-0950, founded 1918, poetry editor Laurence Lieberman, publishes **collections of individual poets, 65-105 pgs.** They have published *Walt Whitman Bathing* by David Wagoner, *Honorable Amendments* by Michael Harper and poetry collections by Sydney Lea, Dave Smith and Kevin Stein. **Send SASE for guidelines. Offers royalty contract and 10 copies.**

ILLYA'S HONEY (I, II), 432 Greenridge, Coppell TX 75019-5717, phone (972)462-7186, e-mail swbrodie@aol.com, website http://members.aol.com/swbrodie/honey/, founded 1994, editor Stephen W. Brodie, is a quarterly journal of poetry and b&w artwork, occasionally using very short stories. **"All subjects and styles of poetry are welcome. Poems can be up to 60 lines and should be interesting, imaginative and thought-provoking. Different is good. No forced rhyme or overly religious verse, please."** They have published poetry by Liza Bachman, Clebo Rainey, Julie Irsch and Douglas Spangle. As a sample the editor selected these lines from "The Werewolf's Daughters" by Bob Zordani:

> *another flawless bloom who fills her field*
> *with song. My daughters waltz about the town*
> *so carelessly they will not guess whose voice*
> *has bid them dance, whose tune will deem them ripe,*
> *whose undulating claws will gleam like death*
> *personified and carve them into ghosts . . .*

Illya's Honey is 50-60 pgs., 5½ × 8½, desktop-published and saddle-stitched with glossy card cover and b&w artwork throughout. They receive about 2,400 poems a year, use approximately 125. Press run is 250 for 80 subscribers, 50 shelf sales. Subscription: $18. **Sample postpaid: $5. Submit 5 poems at a time. Previously published poems and simultaneous submissions OK. Cover letter preferred. Seldom comments on rejections. Send SASE for guidelines or request via e-mail. Reports in 2 months, usually sooner. Sometimes sends prepublication galleys. Payment is publication. Contributors must purchase a copy if they want to see their work in print.**

‡**IMAGE: A JOURNAL OF ARTS & RELIGION (III, IV-Religious)**, P.O. Box 674, Kennett Square PA 19348, phone (610)444-8065, e-mail 73424.1024@compuserve.com, founded 1989, publisher Gregory Wolfe, published quarterly, "explores and illustrates the relationship between faith and art through world-class fiction, poetry, essays, visual art, and other arts." **They want "poems with a religious theme, usually Judeo-Christian."** They have recently published poetry by Philip Levine, Edward Hirsch, Denise Levertov and Annie Dillard. As a sample we selected these lines from "Receptionism" by Marjorie Maddox:

> *Does our kneeling*

bring him down
again, from the wood,
unhinge his stone,
trumpet for ourselves
our catalytic salvation?

Image is 136 pgs., 10×7, perfect-bound, acid free paper with glossy 4-color cover, averages 10 pgs. of 4-color art/issue (including cover), ads. They receive about 800 poems a year, accept approximately 2%. They have 4,000 subscribers of which 50 are libraries. Subscription: $30. **Sample postpaid: $10. Submit up to 4 poems at a time. No previously published poems. Cover letter preferred.** Time between acceptance and publication is 1 year. **Reports in 3 months. Always sends prepublication galleys. Pays 4 copies plus a variable honorarium. Acquires first North American serial rights.** Reviews books of poetry in 1,000-1,300 words, single and multi-book format. Open to unsolicited reviews. Poets may also send books for review consideration.

*IMAGO: NEW WRITING; CITY OF BRISBANE POETRY AWARD (II, IV-Regional), School of Media & Journalism, Q.U.T., GPO Box 2434, Brisbane 4001 Queensland, Australia, fax (07)3864-1810, founded 1988, appears three times a year, publishing "the best **Australian writing, placing particular emphasis on Queensland writing and culture, but also welcoming submissions from overseas. Poems preferably short— up to about 50 lines, most from 12-25 lines. Our main criterion is good writing.**" They have published poetry by Tom Shapcott, Peter Rose and Philip Hammial. *Imago* is 160 pgs., digest-sized, with glossy card cover. They accept about 10% of 500 poems from about 150 writers. Press run is 1,000 for 450 subscribers of which 36 are libraries. Subscription: $A21 in Australia; $A28, overseas (airmail). **Sample postpaid: $A9.50. Submit 6-8 poems at a time. "A brief biography (few lines) of the writer accompanying the submission saves time if the work is accepted. We have a Notes on Contributors column." Comments if requested. Reports in 1-6 months. Never sends prepublication galleys "unless specifically asked for by contributor." Pays $A30-40 plus 1 copy. Buys first Australian serial rights. They publish the winning poems of the City of Brisbane Poetry Award (annual).** Reviews books of poetry in 600 words—"usually commissioned. Unsolicited reviews would have to be of books relevant to *Imago* (Queensland or writing)." Send books for review consideration.

IMPLOSION PRESS; IMPETUS (I, II, IV-Erotica, women), 4975 Comanche Trail, Stow OH 44224-1217, phone/fax (216)688-5210, e-mail impetus@aol.com, founded 1984, poetry editor Cheryl Townsend, publishes *Impetus*, a "somewhat" quarterly literary magazine, chapbooks, special issues. The editor would like to see **"strong social protest with raw emotion. No topic is taboo. Material should be straight from the gut, uncensored and real. Absolutely no nature poetry or rhyme for the sake of rhyme, oriental, or 'Kissy, kissy I love you' poems. Any length as long as it works. All subjects OK, providing it isn't too rank.** *Impetus* **is now publishing annual erotica and all-female issues. Material should reflect these themes."** They have published poetry by Ron Androla, Kurt Nimmo, Lyn Lifshin and Lonnie Sherman. The magazine varies in size and is photocopied from typescript, saddle-stapled. Press run is about 1,000, with 300 subscriptions. Generally a 5-month backlog. Subscription: $15 for 4 issues; $20 for 4 issues plus chapbooks. **Sample postpaid: $5; make checks payable to Cheryl Townsend. Submit 3-8 poems at a time. The editor says, "I prefer shorter, to-the-point work." Include name and address on each page. Previously published work OK if it is noted when and where. "I always like a cover letter that tells me how the poet found out about my magazine." E-mail submissions OK. Send SASE for guidelines. Usually reports within 3 months. Pays 1 copy. Acquires first or one-time rights.** In her comments on rejections, the editor usually refers poets to other magazines she feels would appreciate the work more. Reviews books of poetry. Open to unsolicited reviews. Poets may also send books for review consideration. Implosion Press hosts "The Last Friday Poetry Readings" at Borders Books & Music in Fairlawn, Ohio. The editor says, "Bear with the small press. We're working as best as we can and usually harder. We can only do so much at a time. Support the small presses!"

IN YOUR FACE! (I), P.O. Box 174, Manasquan NJ 08736, e-mail mcluff@exit109.com, website http://www.exit109.com/~mcluff/inyour face, founded 1992, editors Gina Grega and Ronda Matthews, is a quarterly that publishes art, poetry, essays and reviews, "whatever strikes our fancy and knocks the wind out of us." **They want "anything bold, confrontative, risky and/or risqué, funny, political, personal, sexual, unpretentious, honest, real-life language. No PC multicultural whinings, phony pseudo-emotionalism, rhyming poems, unintelligible manifestos filled with 50-cent words. No women-hating spewage."** They have recently published poetry by Jennifer Helms, Michael Estabrook, Charles Rammelkamp, Chriss-Spike Quatrone and Larissa Shmailo. As a sample the editor selected this poem "Bad Seeds" by Carl Alessi:

Poe, Poe! Your books are poisonous . . .
too many homicidal dandies,
too many incestuous lovers,
too many sets of feminine teeth
being yanked out by sleepwalking maniacs.

IYF! is 50-60 pgs., 5½×8½, saddle-stapled, with colored card cover, b&w art and ads. They receive about 2,000 pieces a year, accept 5%. Press run is 350 for 100 subscribers. Subscription: $16. **Sample postpaid: $4. Make checks payable to Gina Grega. Submit no more than 5 pgs. at a time. Previously published poems OK; no simultaneous submissions. "Be friendly, drop us a note, not a pretentious bio! SASE with appropriate** postage a must. Also, if you don't want your writings returned, let us know." Often comments on rejections. **Send SASE for guidelines or obtain via e-mail or website. Reports in 3-4 months. Pays 1-2 copies.** Reviews books, chapbooks, zines, "whatever else we can get our hands on," in roughly 75-100 words each. Open to unsolicited reviews. Poets may also send books for review consideration. The editor says, "*In Your Face!* isn't afraid to offend. We look for gut-punching work—not big names. We especially encourage beginners as they haven't been polished by the cold, impersonal 'name' magazines and are usually still humble enough to send a 'hi' with their submissions. We *recommend* that contributors see a copy of our publication, but this is not a requirement."

INDEFINITE SPACE (II), P.O. Box 40101, Pasadena CA 91114, founded 1992, editors Marcia Arrieta and Kevin Joy, is a poetry journal published annually or biannually, "depending on finances." **They want "experimental, minimalistic, imagistic, philosophical poetry not exceeding two pages. No rhyming poetry."** They have published poetry by Dan Campion, Alan Catlin, Simon Perchik and W.B. Keckler. As a sample the editors selected the poem "reason" by Denise Enck:

> :in winter,
> your hair across the sky.
>
> (underneath
> the balance
> flotsam in the gills)

Indefinite Space is 32-40 pgs., 5½×8½, neatly printed and saddle-stapled with matte card cover with b&w art, no ads, poems appearing one to a page. Press run is 125-150 for 20 subscribers of which 5 are libraries. Subscription: $7. **Sample postpaid: $4. "Please make checks payable to editors." No previously published poems; simultaneous submissions OK. Seldom comments on rejections. Send SASE for guidelines. Reports usually within a month. Pays 1 copy. Rights remain with poet.**

INDIA CURRENTS (IV-Ethnic, regional), P.O. Box 21285, San Jose CA 95151-1285, phone (408)274-6966, e-mail editor@indiacur.com, website http://www.indiacur.com/indiacur/, founded 1987, editor Arvind Kumar, is a monthly magazine about Indian culture in the U.S. They want **"poetry that offers an insight into India, Indians, Indian Americans; very brief works stand a better chance of acceptance." They do not want "poetry that exploits mystery or exoticism about India or long poems (over 300 words). Readership is 70% Indian, 30% non-Indian."** They have published poetry by Chitra Divakaruni. It is 136 pgs., 8½×11, offset, newsprint, saddle-stitched. They receive 50-75 submissions a year, "accept fewer than 12." Press run is 24,000 for 4,000 subscribers. Rest distributed free at stores, restaurants and libraries. Single copy: $1.95; subscription: $19.95. **Sample postpaid: $3. Previously published poems and simultaneous and e-mail submissions OK. Cover letter with brief bio and background required.** Time between acceptance and publication is 6-12 months. **Send SASE for guidelines. Reports in 3 months.** Reviews books of poetry in 300 words maximum. Open to unsolicited reviews. Poets may also send books for review consideration. The editor says, "*India Currents* has a heavy tilt in favor of arts. We feel that arts can contribute to global understanding and peace by bringing it about at a personal level. America needs to learn about India just as India needs to learn about America."

‡INDIAN HERITAGE PUBLISHING; INDIAN HERITAGE COUNCIL QUARTERLY; NATIVE AMERICAN POETRY ANTHOLOGY (I, IV-Ethnic/nationality); P.O. Box 2302, Morristown TN 37816, phone (423)581-4448, founded 1986, CEO Louis Hooban. *Indian Heritage Council Quarterly* devotes 1 issue to poetry with a Native American theme. **They want "any type of poetry relating to Native Americans, their beliefs or Mother Earth." They do not want "doggerel."** They have recently published poetry by Running Buffalo and Angela Evening Star Dempsey. As a sample the editor selected these lines from his poem "the Powwow":

> And listen! You can
> hear it
> as the drum beats tune in
> to the heartbeats of
> Mother Earth

ALWAYS include a self-addressed, stamped envelope (SASE) when sending a ms or query to a publisher within your own country. When sending material to other countries, include a self-addressed envelope and International Reply Coupons (IRCs), available for purchase at many post offices.

> *giving birth to life*
> *in the center*
> *of the Dance Circle.*

IHCQ is 6 pgs., 5½×8½ (8½×11 folded sheet with 5½×8½ insert), photocopied. They receive about 300 poems a year, accept approximately 30%. Press run and number of subscribers vary, 50% shelf sales; 50 distributed free to Indian reservations. Subscription: $10. **Sample: "negotiable." Make checks payable to Indian Heritage council. Submit up to 3 poems at a time. Previously published poems (author must own rights only) and simultaneous submissions OK. Cover letter required.** Time between acceptance and publication is 3 months to 1 year. **"Our editorial board decides on all publications." Seldom comments on rejections. Charges criticism fees "depending on negotiations." Publishes theme issues. Send SASE for guidelines and upcoming themes. Reports within 3 weeks. Pay is negotiable. Acquires one-time rights.** Staff reviews books or chapbooks of poetry or other magazines. Poets may also send books for review consideration. Indian Heritage Publishing publishes Native American themes and/or Native American poets. Format of chapbooks varies. Query first, with a few sample poems and cover letter with brief bio and publication credits. **Replies to queries within 3 weeks, varies for mss. Pays 33-50% royalties. Offers subsidy arrangements that vary by negotiations, number of poems, etc. For sample books or chapbooks, write to the above address.** Sponsors a contest for their anthology "if approved by our editorial board. Submissions are on an individual basis—always provide a SASE." Louis Hooban was named Native American Poet Laureate and the company has received awards from reservations and Indian groups. The editor says, "any poet interested in Native American themes or any Native American poet expressing poems of any theme is invited to submit to us. If you have strong feelings for Native American people, culture, religion or ideas, express yourself through your poetry and let us help you get published."

INDIANA REVIEW (II), Indiana University, 465 Ballantine Hall, Bloomington IN 47405, phone (812)855-3439, founded 1982, editor Bob King, is a biannual of prose, poetry and visual art. **"In general the *Review* looks for fresh, original poems of insight, poems that are challenging without being obtuse. We'll consider all types of poems—free verse, traditional, experimental. Reading a sample issue is the best way to determine if *IR* is a potential home for your work. Any subject matter is acceptable if it is written well."** They have published poetry by Philip Levine, Taslimā Nāsreen, Sherman Alexie, Charles Simic, Mark Strand and Alberto Rios. As a sample the editor selected these lines from "Dull Weather" by Lucie Brock-Broido:

> *Rises, sets, by my own hand, dog days end.*
> *Even my self reminds me of you.*
>
> *I cannot refrain from Ruin.*
> *Your boys practice violence, even in peculiar*
>
> *Heat. They are hairless, clean as copper*
> *Coins made in a New England mint, doomed*
>
> *To be spent.*

The magazine uses about 50-70 pgs. of poetry in each issue (6×9, flat-spined, 200 pages, color matte cover, professional printing). They receive about 10,000 submissions a year, use approximately 60. The magazine has 1,000 subscriptions of which 120 are libraries. **Sample postpaid: $7. Submit 3-5 poems at a time, do not send more than 8-10 pages of poetry per submission. Pays $5/page ($10 minimum/poem), plus 2 copies and remainder of year's subscription. Buys first North American serial rights only. "We try to respond to manuscripts in 2-3 months. Reading time is often slower during summer and holiday months."** This magazine's reputation continues to grow in literary circles. It is generally accepted as one of the best publications, featuring all styles, forms and lengths of poetry (much of it exciting or tense). Brief book reviews are also featured. Send books for review consideration. Poetry published in *IR* has also been selected for inclusion in the 1996 and 1997 volumes of *The Best American Poetry*.

INKSLINGER (I, IV-Subscription), 8661 Prairie Rd. NW, Washington Court House OH 43160-9490, founded 1993, publisher/editor Nancy E. Martindale, appears 3 times/year (in March, July and November) to "provide an additional market for poets and to further the poetic arts." **They want poetry from subscribers only. Any subject, any format, no longer than 30 lines. "No porn or erotica. Also no translations or foreign language poetry."** They have published poetry by Geraldine Zeigler, Ryan Trauman, Katherine Brooks and A.M. Roman. *Inkslinger* is 20 pgs., digest-sized, saddle-stapled with 60 lb. colored paper cover. They receive 200-300 poems a year, accept 54 or more if short in length. Subscription: $12/year, $23/2 years, $35/3 years. **Sample postpaid: $4. "Purchase of a one-year subscription is required to submit at present time—hoping to change this policy soon." Send no more than 5 poems at a time. Previously published poems OK if author still owns copyright; no simultaneous submissions.** Time between acceptance and publication is 1 month. "Poems arriving too late for one issue will be held for the next issue's consideration. Poems are judged according to imagery, style, creativity, originality and sincerity (5 points each). Poems with most points are accepted. One(s) with the highest is named 'Editor's Choice' and poet receives $10." **Seldom comments on rejections. Send SASE for guidelines and list of upcoming themes. Reports in 5 months maximum. Pays no money at present (except**

to "Editor's Choice"), **"but hoping to pay soon." Poets retain all rights.** The editor says, "Novices and experienced poets welcome. We're small, but open. *Always read guidelines first.* Failure to meet even one will result in unread, returned manuscripts."

‡**INNER VOICE (IV-Specialized: prisoners)**, P.O. Box 4500 #219, Bloomington IN 46226, founded 1995, editor C.N. Williams, published biannually, is a "monograph of prison literature." **They want "any form, subject or style. We try for balance and eclecticism. Keep it under a few pages." They do not want "midnight meditations, religious works and love poetry. We get a lot so the odds are not as good for these works."** *Inner Voice* is 50 pgs., 5½×8½, photocopied, saddle-stapled with medium card cover, graphic art accepted, occasional color, trade ads with closely related organizations or businesses. They receive about 150 poems a year, use approximately 20. Press run is 200 for 30 subscribers, 30 shelf sales. Subscription: $8 ($5 for prisoners). **Sample postpaid: $4. Authors must be prisoners (or occasionally their loved-ones or ex-prisoners). Submit up to 10 poems at a time. Previously published poems OK; no simultaneous submissions. Cover letter preferred with a brief bio or personal statement of about 100 words.** Time between acceptance and publication varies. **Poems are circulated to an editorial board. Seldom comments on rejections. Theme issues possible in the future. Send SASE for guidelines. Reports ASAP. Pays 2 copies. Acquires first North American serial or one-time rights.** Reviews books of prison poetry or journals. Open to unsolicited reviews. Poets may also send books for review consideration.

INSECTS ARE PEOPLE TWO; PUFF 'N' STUFF PRODUCTIONS (I, IV-Specialized), P.O. Box 146486, Chicago IL 60614-6400, phone (773)772-8686, founded 1989, publisher H.R. Felgenhauer, an infrequent publication focusing solely on **"poems about insects doing people things and people doing insect things."** They have recently published poetry by Bruce Boston, Steve Sneyd, Paul Wieneman and Lyn Lifshin. *Insects* is 8½×11, stapled down the side, with card cover, b&w art and graphics. Press run is 400. **Sample postpaid: $5. Previously published poems and simultaneous submissions OK. Often comments on rejections. Reports "immediately." Pay varies.** Open to unsolicited reviews. Poets may also send books for review consideration. Puff 'N' Stuff Productions publishes **1 chapbook/year. Replies to queries and mss in 10 days. Pay is negotiable.** H.R. Felgenhauer says, "Hit me with your best shot. Never give up—editors have tunnel-vision. The *BEST* mags you almost *NEVER* even hear about. Don't believe reviews. Write for yourself. Prepare for failure, not success."

THE INTERCULTURAL WRITER'S REVIEW; THE INTERCULTURAL WRITER'S ASSOCIATION (I, II); MERLANA'S MAGICKAL MESSAGES (I, IV-Spirituality/inspirational, psychic/occult); POETRY BREAK JOURNAL (I, II); NAVARRO PUBLICATIONS (I, II, IV-Anthology), P.O. Box 1107, Dept. PM, Blythe CA 92226-1107, phone (888)922-0835, managing editor Marjorie (Merlana) Navarro, executive editor/art director Richard LeJose Navarro. *The Intercultural Writer's Review*, first published in April 1995, is the official publication of The Intercultural Writer's Association and is published quarterly. **They welcome poetry on any subject, any length.** Short stories and articles, up to 3,500 words, are also used. They have recently published work by Sister Mary Ann Henn, Reggie Rendon, Ted Elden, Anne Marie Bruum and Anthony Garavente. The editor describes *TIWR* as 8½×11 with soft cover. Subscription: $29.95/year and includes membership. **Sample: $8. Make checks or money orders payable to Navarro Publications. Payment is in contributor's copies.** *Poetry Break Journal*, first published in 1984, appears 3 times/year. **They want poetry on any subject, any length.** The editor describes *PBJ* as digest-sized with card cover. Deadline for January issue is November 17, deadline for July issue is May 17. **Pays copies.** Their publication *Merlana's Magickal Messages*, first published in March 1995, is "a metaphysical, spiritual, New Age publication" which appears in March, July and October. They have recently published work by Diane Scott, Thomas Wells, Anne Wallace Sharp, John F. Zurn and Gurattan Khalsa. As a sample the editor selected these lines from "Wild Rose of My Heart" by their executive editor Richard LeJose Navarro:

> *You are the hyacinth of all my senses;*
> *Your enchanting beauty obviates my defenses*
> *With you there is no need for pretenses,*
> *And I fully accept my actions consequences*
> *You are, indeed, the Wild Rose of my Heart.*

The editor says *MMM* is digest-sized desktop-published with card cover. Subscription: $20. **Sample postpaid: $7. Make checks or money orders payable to Navarro Publications. Submit any number of poems with a cover letter and brief bio. Occasionally publishes theme issues. Theme for July 1998 issue is Gods, Goddesses and Angels (deadline May 10, 1998). Reports "as soon as possible." Pays 1 copy.** Navarro Publications publishes **chapbooks. Offers subsidy arrangements.** The author pays 50% of publishing costs and Navarro helps with promotion. Send SASE for details. Sponsors an annual poetry contest and an ongoing poetry chapbook contest. Send SASE for details. The editor says, "We welcome new, established writers who have a fresh, originality and conciseness to their work. Read *Poet's Market* listings *carefully* and send for sample copies to avoid sending material not suitable for various markets. When you can, subscribe, donate to the publications who work so hard to bring your work to the reading public."

INTERIM (II), Dept. of English 5034, University of Nevada—Las Vegas, Las Vegas NV 89154, phone (702)895-3458, founded in Seattle, 1944-55, revived 1986, editors James Hazen, Joseph B. McCullough and Timothy

Erwin, English editor John Heath-Stubbs. Member CLMP, New York. Indexed in *Index of American Periodical Verse*. Biannual magazine, **publishing the best poetry it can find, no specific demands in form, new and established writers.** They have recently published poetry by William Stafford, Walter McDonald, Faye George, Stephen Stepanchev and Mary Winters. As a sample the editor selected these lines from "A Photograph" by Maurice Lindsay:

> . . . *Acres of the heart*
> *lay unexplored behind that photo-smile*
> *happiness, satisfactions, failures, halts*
> *that tolerant age has learnt to reconcile.*
> *As wonder cadences its dying fall*
> *old photograph, I turn you to the wall.*

Interim is 60 pgs., 6×9, professionally printed and perfect-bound with coated card cover. Press run is 600. Individual subscription: $7/year, $12/2 years, $15/3 years; libraries: $14/year. **Sample copy: $5. Submit 3-5 poems at a time, SASE and brief biographical note. No simultaneous submissions. Reports in 3 months. Pays 2 copies and a 2-year subscription. Acquires first serial rights. Poems may be reprinted elsewhere with a permission line noting publication in** *Interim*.

INTERNATIONAL POETRY REVIEW (II, IV-Translations), Dept. of Romance Languages, UNC-Greensboro, Greensboro NC 27412, phone (910)334-5655, fax (910)334-5358, website http://www.uncg.edu/rom/ipr, founded 1975, editor Mark Smith-Soto, is a biannual primarily publishing **translations of contemporary poetry with corresponding originals (published on facing pages) as well as original poetry in English.** They have published work by Jasha Kessler, Lyn Lifshin, Pureza Canelo, Jaime Sabines and Fred Chappell. *IPR* is 100 pgs., 5½×8½, professionally printed and perfect-bound with 2-3 color cover. "We accept 5% of original poetry in English and about 30% of translations submitted." Press run is 500 for 250 subscribers of which 100 are libraries. Subscription: $10 individuals, $15 institutions. **Sample postpaid: $5. Submit no more than 5 pages of poetry. No previously published poems; simultaneous submissions OK. Seldom comments on rejections. Send SASE for guidelines. Reports in 2-4 months. Pays 1 copy. All rights revert to authors and translators.** Occasionally reviews books of poetry. Open to unsolicited reviews. Poets may also send books for review consideration. The editor says, "We strongly encourage contributors to subscribe. We prefer poetry in English to have an international or cross-cultural theme."

INTERNATIONAL QUARTERLY (II, IV-Translations), P.O. Box 10521, Tallahassee FL 32302-0521, phone (904)224-5078, fax (904)224-5127, e-mail vbrock@mailer.fsu.edu, website http://www.mailer.fsu.edu/~vbrock/, founded 1993, editor-in-chief Van K. Brock. **"We welcome outstanding writing in all genres, in original English and in translation, quality work that transcends cultural givens. No one-dimensional views of people or place, work that is amateurish or lacks complexity."** They are also interested in work addressing international concerns. They have published work by S a adi Yusuf, David Bottoms and Miroslav Holub. As a sample the editor selected these lines by Anna Akhmatova, translated by Judith Hemschemeyer:

> *I came here without a child, without a knapsack,*
> *Without so much as a walking stick,*
> *Accompanied only by the ringing voice*
> *Of yearning.*

IQ is 200 pgs., 7½×10, offset, perfect-bound, with full-color artwork on the coated card cover and an 8-page, 4-color insert. They receive about 800 mss/year, accept a quarter. Press run is 5,000 for 1,000 shelf sales. Single copy: $10; subscription: $30/year. **Sample postpaid: $6. Submit up to 8 poems, name on each. No previously published poems; simultaneous submissions OK. Cover letter welcomed. Accepts submissions, requests for information, or any sort of query via phone, fax or e-mail.** Time between acceptance and publication is 3-9 months. **Poems go from multiple readers to poetry editor to editorial board and editor-in-chief. Often comments on rejections. Send SASE for upcoming themes or request via e-mail. Reports within 4 months. Pays 2 copies plus subscription. Acquires first serial rights.** Reviews books of poetry. Open to unsolicited reviews; query first. Poets may also send books for review consideration. Sponsors an annual contest called Crossing Boundaries. Awards $500 in each of 4 categories: poetry, fiction, nonfiction and "Crossing Boundaries." Send SASE for guidelines. The editor says, "Writers who have not published elsewhere are welcome to submit, but rarely have the polish necessary to be published in *IQ*."

‡*INTERPRETER'S HOUSE; BEDFORD OPEN POETRY COMPETITION (II, IV-Regional), 10 Farrell Rd., Wootton, Bedfordshire MK43 9DU United Kingdom, founded 1996, contact Merryn Williams, appears 3 times/year (February, June, October) and publishes short stories and poetry. "We are particularly open to writers from our area. **They want "good poetry (and short stories), not too long. No Christmas-card verse or incomprehensible poetry."** They have recently published poetry by Dannie Abse, Tony Curtis, Pauline Stainer and R.S. Thomas. As a sample the editor selected these lines from "Metrics" by R.S. Thomas:

> *There should be no*
> *introit into a poem.*
>
> *The listener should come*

> *to and realise*
> *verse has been going on*
> *for some time. . . .*

Merryn Williams says *TIH* is 56 pgs., A5 with attractive cover design. They receive about 1,000 poems a year, accept approximately 10%. Press run is 220 for 80 subscribers. Subscription: £8.50. **Sample postpaid: £2.50 plus 31 p. Submit 5 poems at a time. No previously published poems or simultaneous submissions. Cover letter preferred.** Time between acceptance and publication is 2 weeks to 8 months. **Often comments on rejections. Send SASE (or SAE and IRC) for guidelines. Reports "fast." Pays 1 copy.** Sponsors the Bedford Open Poetry Competition. Send SAE and IRC for details.

INTERTEXT (III, IV-Translations), 2633 E. 17th Ave., Anchorage AK 99508-3207, founded 1982, editor Sharon Ann Jaeger, publishes "full-length collections by poets of demonstrated achievement" and is "devoted to producing lasting works in every sense. We specialize in poetry, translations and short works in the fine arts and literary criticism. **We publish work that is truly excellent—no restrictions on form, length or style. Cannot use religious verse. Like both surrealist and realist poetry, poetry with intensity, striking insight, vivid imagery, fresh metaphor, musical use of language in both word sounds and rhythm. Must make the world—in all its dimensions—come alive."** To give a sense of her taste she says, "I admire the work of Sarah Kirsch, William Stafford, Eavan Boland, António Ramos Rosa, Gary Snyder, W.S. Merwin, Bob Perelman and Rainer Maria Rilke." Forthcoming: *Karasuyama Poems* by Brenda Jaeger. They have recently published *Pelted with Petals: The Burmese Poems and Tibetan Tanka* by Burmese poet Kyi May Kaung. As a sample the editor selected these lines from *The Mirror Dance* by Louis Hammer:

> *Out of nowhere a fly buzzes the lamp*
> *then returns to the nowhere*
> *from which it has drawn its body.*
> *The evening has hardly begun,*
> *it's too early to crave to be human.*

Query first with 3-5 samples and SASE sent by first-class mail. Simultaneous queries OK. She says, **"Cover letter optional—the sample poems are always read first—but no form letters, please. If sample poems are promising, then the complete book ms will be requested." Always sends prepublication galleys. Pays 10% royalty after costs of production, promotion and distribution have been recovered; plus 10% of print run for printed works.** "We also send out review copies if the work appears in a print medium." The editor says, "As we are moving into electronic publishing, the Intertext has become even more selective. Please do not send a complete manuscript unless we specifically ask to see it. Intertext is not grant-supported, and each poet published represents a heavy investment of time, money, and life moments on the part of the staff."

INVERTED-A, INC.; INVERTED-A HORN (I), 401 Forrest Hill, Grand Prairie TX 75052, phone (214)264-0066, founded 1977, editors Amnon Katz and Aya Katz, is a very small press that evolved from publishing technical manuals for other products. "Our interests center on freedom, justice and honor." *Inverted-A Horn* is a periodical, magazine-sized, offset, usually 9 pages, which appears irregularly; circulation is 300. **The editors do not want to see anything "modern, formless, existentialist."** As a sample the editors selected these lines by F.L. Light:

> *Like propositions we endure the proof.*
> *Not lightened of probation, we must learn*
> *How merit may proceed to our behoof*
> *From manly testors, who would men discern.*

Replies to queries in 1 month, to mss in 4 months. Simultaneous submissions OK. Pays 1 copy plus a 40% discount on additional copies. Samples: SASE with postage for 2 ounces (subject to availability). They publish 1 chapbook/year. The editor says, "I strongly recommend that would-be contributors avail themselves of this opportunity to explore what we are looking for. Most of the submissions we receive do not come close."

*IOTA (II), 67 Hady Crescent, Chesterfield, Derbyshire S41 0EB Great Britain, phone 01246-276532, founded 1988, editor David Holliday, is a quarterly wanting **"any style and subject; no specific limitations as to length, though, obviously, the shorter a poem is, the easier it is to get it in, which means that poems over 40 lines can still get in if they seem good enough. No concrete poetry (no facilities) or self-indulgent logorrhea."**
● *Iota*'s design is simple and straight-forward, but the poetry included is quality thought-provoking work. They have recently published poetry by H.H. Bolero, William Greenway, Dylan Pugh, Virginia Rounding, Kim Taplin, Emily Wills and Peter Wyton. As a sample the editor selected this poem, "Remembrance" by Janet Faraday:

> *Small plot, iron-railed,*
> *Stained and stunted cenotaph,*
> *Starkly listed names—*
> *Little is of glory here,*
> *And less of Owen's pity.*

Iota is 44 pgs., professionally printed and saddle-stapled with light colored card cover. They publish about 250 of 5,000 poems received. Their press run is 400 with 200 subscribers of which 6 are libraries. Subscription: $15

(£8). **Sample postpaid: $2 (£1)** "but sometimes sent free." **Submit 4-6 poems at a time. The editor prefers name and address on each poem, typed,** "but provided it's legible, am happy to accept anything." **Simultaneous submissions OK, but previously published poems** "only if outstanding." **First report in 1-3 weeks (unless production of the next issue takes precedence) but final acceptance/rejection may take up to a year. Pays 2 copies. Acquires first British serial rights only. Editor usually comments on rejections,** "but detailed comment only when time allows and the poem warrants it." Reviews books of poetry in about 200 words, single or multi-book format. Open to unsolicited reviews. Poets may also send books for review consideration. He says, "I am after crafted verse that says something; self-indulgent word-spinning is out. All editors have their blind spots; the only advice I can offer a beginning poet is to find a sympathetic editor (and you will only do that by seeing their magazines) and not to be discouraged by initial lack of success. Keep plugging!"

THE IOWA REVIEW (II), Dept. PM, 308 EPB, University of Iowa, Iowa City IA 52242, phone (319)335-0462, founded 1970, editors David Hamilton and Mary Hussmann, appears 3 times/year. The editors say, "We simply look for poems that at the time we read and choose, we admire. **No specifications as to form, length, style, subject matter or purpose**. There are around 40 pgs. of poetry in each issue and we like to give several pages to a single poet. Though we print work from established writers, we're always delighted when we discover new talent." *IR* is 200 pgs., professionally printed, flat-spined. They receive about 5,000 submissions/year, use about 100. Editors of this influential journal do seem open to all styles and lengths, with most poems falling into the lyric free verse category. Diction, for the most part, is accessible although some examples show degrees of experimentation with form. In all, poems evoke intriguing situations or ideas. Circulation is 1,200-1,300 with 1,000 subscribers of which about half are libraries. Subscription: $18. **Sample postpaid: $6. Submit 3-6 poems at a time. Reads submissions September 1 through May 1 only.** Time between acceptance and publication is "around a year. Sometimes people hit at the right time and come out in a few months." **Occasionally comments on rejections or offers suggestions on accepted poems. Reports in 1-4 months. Pays $1 a line, 2-3 copies and a 1-year subscription. Buys first North American serial rights.** Poetry published in *The Iowa Review* has also been included in the 1992, 1993, 1994, 1995, 1996 and 1997 volumes of *The Best American Poetry* and the *Pushcart Prize* anthology for 1994.

IOWA WOMAN (IV-Women), P.O. Box 680, Iowa City IA 52244, founded 1979, poetry editor Debra Marquart. "We are a literary quarterly publishing fiction, essays and poetry of interest to women. This is a literary magazine that has received national recognition for editorial excellence. We are publishing work **by women, about women and for women. Prefer contemporary poetry that is clear and concise. Prefer narrative and lyric. No greeting card verse.**" They have published poetry by Lyn Lifshin, Alice Friman and Enid Shomer. *Iowa Woman* is elegantly printed, 48 pgs., magazine-sized, 4-color cover with "original cover art and illustrations." Of 2,000 poems received "I accept about 30." Press run is 2,500 for subscriptions and national newsstand sales. **Sample postpaid: $6. Submit 4-5 poems at a time. No simultaneous submissions. Send SASE for guidelines. Pays 2 copies and $5/poem. Buys first rights.** Reviews books of poetry in 500-1,000 words. Open to unsolicited reviews. Poets may also send books to Book Editor for review consideration. "No guarantee that books sent will be reviewed; this is at the discretion of our reviewers." They hold an annual poetry contest with first-place prize of $100. $10 entry fee, 3 poems, for non-subscribers. Contest guidelines available after May. Deadline: December 31. The editor says, "We would like to receive more poetry from minority women about their life experiences."

‡IRIS: A JOURNAL ABOUT WOMEN (III, IV-Translations, women/feminism), Women's Center, Box 323, HSC, University of Virginia, Charlottesville VA 22908, founded 1980, poetry editor Margo Andrea Figgins, is a semiannual magazine that **"focuses on issues concerning women worldwide. It also features quality poetry, prose and artwork—mainly by women, but will also accept work by men if it illuminates some aspect of a woman's reality. It also publishes translations. Form and length are unspecified.** The poetry staff consists of experienced poets with a diversity of tastes who are looking for new and original language in well-crafted poems." Poets who have appeared in *Iris* include Sharon Olds, Elaine Terranova, Mary Oliver, Lisel Mueller, Linda Pastan, Naomi Shihab Nye and Gregory Orr. As a sample the editor selected these lines from "Flash Flood" by Kelli Rae Patton:

> *Those berries*
> *were so lucid before the rain. Swollen and swelling.*
> *All over town the smells were good. Vibrant.*
> *Vine-ripened, we shrink from the introduction*
> *of new substances. Bodies float away unbeknownst*
> *in floodtime, bridges wash out. One learns*

MARKET CATEGORIES: (I) Beginning; **(II)** General; **(III)** Limited; **(IV)** Specialized; **(V)** Closed.

to rely on word of mouth. Road closed.
This isn't the end of it, *they say. Three straight days.*
Iris is 72 pgs., magazine-sized, professionally printed on heavy, glossy stock, saddle-stapled with a full-color glossy card cover, using graphics and photos. It has a circulation of more than 3,000, with over 50 library subscriptions, 1,000 shelf sales. Single copy: $5; subscription: $9/year; $17/2 years. **Sample postpaid: $6.50. Submit 1-5 poems at a time. Simultaneous submissions are discouraged. Pays 1 copy and subscription. Acquires first rights. Reports in 3-6 months. Name, address, phone number should be listed on every poem. Cover letter should include list of poems submitted and a brief bio.** The editor says, "Because *Iris* is a feminist magazine, it receives a lot of poetry that tends to focus on the political experience of coming to consciousness. The editor is interested in *all* aspects of the reality of women's lives and because many poems are on similar topics, freshness of imagery and style become even more important."

ITALIAN AMERICANA; JOHN CIARDI AWARD (IV-Ethnic), URI/CCE, 80 Washington St., Providence RI 02903-1803, phone (401)277-5306, fax (401)277-5100, founded 1974, editor Carol Bonomo Albright, poetry editor Dana Gioia, appears twice a year using **8-10 poems "on Italian-American subjects, no more than three pgs. No trite nostalgia; no poems about grandparents."** It is 150-200 pgs., 7×9, professionally printed and flat-spined with glossy card cover. Press run is 1,000 for 900 subscribers of which 175 are libraries, 175 shelf sales. Subscription: $20. **Sample postpaid: $7.50. Submit 3 poems at a time. No previously published poems or simultaneous submissions. Cover letter not required "but helpful." Name on first page of ms only. Do not submit poetry in July, August or September. Occasionally comments on rejections. Reports in 4-6 weeks. Acquires first rights.** Reviews books of poetry in 600 words, multi-book format. Poets may send books for review consideration to Prof. John Paul Russo, English Dept., University of Miami, Coral Gables FL 33124. Along with the National Italian American Foundation, *IA* co-sponsors the annual $1,000 John Ciardi Award for Lifetime Contribution to Italian American Poetry. Send SASE for details. The editor says, "Single copies of poems for submissions are sufficient."

ITALICA PRESS (IV-Bilingual/foreign language), 595 Main St., #605, New York NY 10044-0047, phone (212)935-4230, fax (212)838-7812, e-mail italica@aol.com, founded 1985, publishers Eileen Gardiner and Ronald G. Musto, is a small press publisher of **English translations of Italian works** in Smyth-sewn paperbacks, averaging 175 pgs. They have published *Guido Cavalcanti, The Complete Poems*, a dual-language (English/ Italian) book with English translation and introduction by Marc Cirigliano, and *Women Poets of the Italian Renaissance*, a dual-language anthology, edited by Laura Anna Stortoni and translated by Laura Anna Stortoni and Mary Prentice Lillie. **Query with 10 sample translations of medieval and Renaissance Italian poets. Include cover letter, bio and list of publications. Simultaneous submissions OK, but translation should not be "totally" previously published. No submissions via fax or e-mail; however, queries via fax or e-mail are OK. Reports on queries in 3 weeks, on mss in 3 months. Always sends prepublication galleys. Pays 7-15% royalties plus 10 author's copies. Buys English language rights.** Sometimes comments on rejections.

‡JACK MACKEREL MAGAZINE; ROWHOUSE PRESS (I, II), P.O. Box 23134, Seattle WA 98102-0434, founded 1992, editor Greg Bachar. *Jack Mackerel*, published quarterly, features poetry, fiction and art. They have recently published poetry by Bill Knott, William D. Waltz, Ann Miller and Frank Gaard. *Jack Mackerel* is 40-60 pgs., 5½×8½, printed on bond paper, with glossy card cover stock, b&w illustrations and photos. Press run is 500. Subscription: $12. **Sample postpaid: $5. Make checks payable to Greg Bachar. No previously published poems or simultaneous submissions. Cover letter preferred. Poems are circulated to an editorial board. Seldom comments on rejections. Publishes theme issues. Reports in 2-4 weeks. Pays 2 copies.** Staff reviews chapbooks, books and magazines of poetry. Poets may also send books for review consideration. Send SASE for information on Rowhouse Press or to obtain sample book.

JANUS, A JOURNAL OF LITERATURE; COLLINGS HOUSE PRESS (III), P.O. Box 376, Collingswood NJ 08108, editor David Livewell, appears semiannually in the spring and fall. The editor says, **"We seek well-crafted verse in forms that are necessary to the content. Both metrical and free verse are considered."** They have recently published poetry by Fred Chappell, Dana Gioia, Rachel Hadas, Anthony Hecht, X.J. Kennedy, Thomas Kinsella, Medbh McGuckian, Edwin Morgan and Louis Simpson. *Janus* is 72 pgs., 5½×8½, neatly printed and saddle-stapled, with colored card cover and b&w graphics. They receive approximately 1,000 poetry submissions a year, accept about 12. Press run is 700. Subscription: $12/3 issues, $15 for institutions. **Sample postpaid: $5. Submit 3-5 poems at a time. "Submissions cannot be returned." Include SASE for response. No previously published poems or simultaneous submissions. Cover letter and short bio required. Seldom comments on rejections. Reports in 2-3 months. Pays in copies.** "We review books of poetry and other books of literary merit." Open to unsolicited reviews and essays provided "they are serious and relevant to contemporary poetry." The editor says, "We do not want to discourage submissions, but since we publish so few unsolicited poems, it is important that authors submit their very best work. In particular, we do not see enough attention paid to the intricacies of meter and form."

‡JAVA SNOB REVIEW (II), P.O. Box 54, Bellevue MI 49021, e-mail javasnob@aol.com, founded 1996, editor D. Foley, published quarterly, features poetry, short fiction and b&w art/photos. **They want "just about**

anything, so long as the work is compelling. It must have bite, wit or attitude." They have recently published poetry by Lois Marie Harrod and Mary Winters. As a sample the editor selected these lines from "The Mad Girl Thinks How Sometimes A Tongue Just Isn't Enough" by Lyn Lifshin:

> . . . A penis could stir
> up its own juice and like a little god,
> make out of what seems a marshy little
> hole, a whole life.

Java Snob is 75 pgs., 5½×9, perfect-bound with medium card cover, b&w art, photos. They receive about 1,000 poems a year, accept approximately 15%. Press run is 1,000 for 200 subscribers of which 20 are libraries, 300 shelf sales. Subscription: $20. **Sample postpaid: $6. Submit 3-5 poems at a time. No previously published poems; simultaneous submissions OK. Cover letter preferred with brief bio. Include name and address at the top of each page.** Time between acceptance and publication is 3 months. **Poems are circulated to an editorial board. "Work is initially screened and weeded out. Promising work is considered by editorial board." Seldom comments on rejections. Send SASE for guidelines. Reports in 1-4 months. Pays 2 copies. Acquires first rights.**

‡*JEWISH AFFAIRS (I, IV-Ethnic), P.O. Box 87557, Houghton 2082, Johannesburg, South Africa, phone (27)(11)486-1434, fax (27)(11)646-4940, e-mail 071jos@muse.arts.wits.ac.za, founded 1941, executive editor professor Joseph Sherman, is a "quarterly journal of Jewish interest containing scholarly essays on all aspects of Jewish history, culture, thought and religion." **All poetry is welcome; poetry with Jewish themes or subject matter especially so. We do not accept previously published material."**
- Note: South Africa does not use IRC coupons. Therefore, *JA* cannot return submissions. A letter will be sent if work is accepted.
They have recently published poetry by Sinclair Beiles, Lionel Abrahams and Frieda Freeman. *JA* is 84 pgs., A4 size, perfect-bound, professionally printed with glossy 4-color cover, cover art, and b&w and color ads. They receive about 100 poems a year, accept approximately 20%. Press run is 2,000 for 1,500 subscribers of which 100 are libraries. Subscription: $40. **Sample (including guidelines) postpaid: $10. Make checks payable to South African Jewish Board of Deputies. No previously published poems or simultaneous submissions. Cover letter required.** Time between acceptance and publication is 6-8 months. **Poems are circulated to an editorial board. "Poems are considered by two members of the editorial board before being accepted." Publishes theme issues. Write for list of upcoming themes. Reports within 2 months. Acquires first rights. Requests acknowledgement of first publication in *Jewish Affairs*.** Reviews books of poetry in up to 2,500 words depending on significance of the book." Open to unsolicited reviews. Poets may also send books for review consideration. The editor says, "We welcome all submissions, especially from poets never published before."

JEWISH CURRENTS (II, IV-Themes), 22 E. 17th St., Suite 601, New York NY 10003-1919, phone/fax (212)924-5740, founded 1946, editor Morris U. Schappes, is a magazine appearing 11 times a year that publishes **poetry on Jewish subjects and themes, including translations from the Yiddish and Hebrew** (original texts should be submitted with translations). The editor says it is 48 pgs., 5×8, offset, saddle-stapled. Press run is 2,600 for 2,300 subscribers of which about 10% are libraries. Subscription: $30/year. **Sample postpaid: $2. Submit 1 poem at a time, typed, double-spaced, with SASE. No previously published poems or simultaneous submissions. Cover letter required. Publishes theme issues.** Time between acceptance and publication is 2 years. **Seldom comments on rejections. Themes for September, December, 1997 and February, March, April, May, July, 1998 are Jewish New Year, Honuka, Black-Jewish Relations, Purim/Jewish Music Month/ International Women's Day, Pesach/Holocaust/Resistance, Israel, and Murdered Soviet Jewish Writers, respectively. Deadlines for themes are 6 months in advance. Reports in 6-12 months. Always sends prepublication galleys. Pays 6 copies plus 1-year subscription.** Reviews books of poetry.

JEWISH SPECTATOR (IV-Religious), 4391 Park Milano, Calabasas CA 91302, phone (818)591-7481, fax (818)591-7267, e-mail jewishspec@aol.com, founded 1935, editor Robert Bleiweiss, poetry editor Charles Muñoz. *Jewish Spectator* is a 68-page Judaic scholarly quarterly that **welcomes poetry on Jewish themes.** They have recently published poetry by Rodger Kamenetz, Louis Daniel Brodsky, Barbara Brent Brower, Lynn Levin and Robert Deluty. Subscribers: 1,400. **Cover letter with brief bio (2-3 lines) required. Reports in 6 weeks. Returns mss only with SASE. Pays 2 copies.** Open to unsolicited reviews. Poets may also send books for review consideration.

JEWISH VEGETARIANS NEWSLETTER; JEWISH VEGETARIANS OF NORTH AMERICA (I, IV-Religious, specialized), 6938 Reliance Rd., Federalsburg MD 21632, phone (410)754-5550, e-mail mossman@ skipjack.blueetab.org, founded 1983, editor Eva R. Mossman. *Jewish Vegetarians Newsletter* is a quarterly publication of the Jewish Vegetarians of North America, a nonprofit organization. It is designed to promote vegetarianism within the Judaic tradition and includes various articles, recipes and short book reviews. **They want poetry that is "Jewish related and/or about vegetarianism, veganism, animal rights and/or the environment."** As a sample the editor selected these lines from "Humankind?" by Susan Holdridge, Ph.D:

> Silently

they stand condemned,
prisoners without a crime,
lost because
we cannot see
these gentle beasts
are all our brothers.

The newsletter is 16 pgs., 8½×11, printed on recycled paper and saddle-stapled. Press run is 1,200 for 700 subscribers. Subscription: $12/year. **Sample available free with #10 SAE and 2 first-class stamps. Previously published poems and simultaneous submissions OK. Cover letter required. "Please include permission to print." E-mail inquiries OK. No e-mail submissions. Often comments on rejections. Send SASE for upcoming themes. Reports in no more than 3 months. "We do not pay for literary contributions." However, copies are available free for the cost of postage and all poetry remains the property of the author.** The editor says, "We encourage everyone to obtain a sample issue."

JEWISH WOMEN'S LITERARY ANNUAL; JEWISH WOMEN'S RESOURCE CENTER (IV-Ethnic, women), 9 E. 69th St., New York NY 10021, phone (212)751-9223, fax (212)935-3523, founded 1994, editor Henny Wenkart, publishes poetry and fiction **by Jewish women. They want "poems by Jewish women on any topic, but of the highest literary quality."** They have published poetry by Alicia Ostriker, Lyn Lifshin, Grace Herman, Enid Dame, Marge Piercy and Lesléa Newman. As a sample the editor selected these lines from "Remembrance" by Lori A. Roth:

She . . . selected a fish as it swam in a tank.
I tried not to think of its strong wild black tail
switching fiercely
as it traced the confines of the tank.
Later, when we returned to collect the tidy white package,
I tried not to think of death.

The annual is 160 pgs., 6×9, perfect-bound with a laminated card cover, b&w art and photos inside. They receive about 500 poems a year, publish approximately 15%. Press run is 1,500 for 480 subscribers. Subscription: $18/3 issues. **Sample postpaid: $7.50. No previously published poems. Prefers to receive submissions by "snail mail." Poems are circulated to an editorial board. Often comments on rejections. Reports in 3-5 months. Pays 3 copies plus a small honorarium. Rights remain with the poet.** The Jewish Women's Resource Center holds a monthly workshop, sponsors occasional readings and **also publishes a few books of poetry.** "We select only 1 or 2 manuscripts a year, use approximately 20 submitted. But although authors then receive editing help and publicity, they bear the cost of production. Members of the workshop we conduct and poets published in our annual receive first attention." The editor says, "It would be helpful, but not essential, if poets would send for a sample copy of our annual before submitting."

THE JOHNS HOPKINS UNIVERSITY PRESS (V), 2715 N. Charles St., Baltimore MD 21218, founded 1878. "One of the largest American university presses, Johns Hopkins is a publisher mainly of scholarly books and journals. We do, however, publish short fiction and poetry in the series Johns Hopkins: Poetry and Fiction, edited by John Irwin. **Unsolicited submissions are not considered."**

THE JOURNAL (III), Dept. of English, Ohio State University, 164 W. 17th Ave., Columbus OH 43210, phone (614)292-4076, fax (614)292-7816, e-mail thejournal05@postbox.acs.ohio-state.edu, website http://www.cohums.ohio-state.edu/english/journals/the_journal/hompage.htm, founded 1972, co-editors Kathy Fagan and Michelle Herman, appears twice yearly with reviews, essays, quality fiction and poetry. **"We're open to all forms; we tend to favor work that gives evidence of a mature and sophisticated sense of the language."** They have published poetry by Brigit Kelly, Lucia Perillo, Timothy Liu and Heather McHugh. *The Journal* is 6×9, professionally printed on heavy stock, 80-120 pgs., of which about 50 in each issue are devoted to poetry. They receive about 4,000 submissions a year, use approximately 200, and have a 3- to 6-month backlog. Press run is 1,500. Subscription: $8. **Sample: $5. No submissions via fax. On occasion editor comments on rejections. Pays 2 copies and an honorarium of $25-50 when funds are available. Acquires all rights. Returns rights on publication.** Reviews books of poetry. Contributing editor David Citino advises, "However else poets train or educate themselves, they must do what they can to know our language. Too much of the writing we see indicates poets do not in many cases develop a feel for the possibilities of language, and do not pay attention to craft. Poets should not be in a rush to publish—until they are ready." (Also see Ohio State University Press/*The Journal* Award in Poetry.)

‡JOURNAL OF AFRICAN TRAVEL-WRITING (IV-Specialized), P.O. Box 346, Chapel Hill NC 27514, website http://www.unc.edu/~ottotwo, founded 1996, contact editorial board, published biannually, "presents and explores past and contemporary accounts of African travel." **They want "poetry touching on any aspect of African travel. Translations are also welcome."** As a sample the editor selected these lines from "A Spring of Bullets" by José Craveirinha:

I take hold of
My last humiliation

> *And without leaving my land*
> *I emigrate to the North of Mozambique*
> *With a spring of bullets on my shoulder.*

JATW is 96 pgs., 7×10, professionally printed, perfect-bound, coated stock cover with cover and illustrative art, ads. Press run is 600. Single copy: $5; subscription: $10. **Sample postpaid: $6. Submit up to 6 poems at a time. No previously published poems; simultaneous submissions OK. Cover letter preferred.** Time between acceptance and publication is 3-6 months. **"The editor usually makes these selections." Often comments on rejections. Send SASE for guidelines. Reports in 2-6 weeks. Always sends prepublication galleys. Pays 4 copies. Acquires first international publication rights.** Reviews books, chapbooks or magazines of poetry. Open to unsolicited reviews. Poets may also send books for review consideration.

JOURNAL OF ASIAN MARTIAL ARTS (IV-Sports/recreation), 821 W. 24th St., Erie PA 16502-2523, phone (814)455-9517, fax (814)838-7811, e-mail viamedia@ncinter.net, website http://www.ncinter.net/~viamedia, founded 1991, editor-in-chief Michael A. DeMarco, is a quarterly "comprehensive journal on Asian martial arts with high standards and academic approach." **They want poetry about Asian martial arts and Asian martial art history/culture. They have no restrictions provided the poet has a feel for, and good understanding of, the subject. They don't want poetry showing a narrow view. "We look for a variety of styles from an interdisciplinary approach."** The editor says the journal is 128 pgs., 8½×11, perfect-bound, with soft cover, b&w illustrations, computer and hand art and ads. Press run is 8,000 for 1,500 subscribers of which 50 are libraries, the rest mainly shelf sales. Single copy: $9.75; subscription: $32/year, $55/2 years. **Sample postpaid: $10. Previously published poems OK; no simultaneous submissions. Cover letter required. Often comments on rejections. Send SASE for guidelines. Reports in 1-2 months. Sometimes sends prepublication galleys. Pays $1-100 and/or 1-5 copies on publication. Buys first and reprint rights.** Reviews books of poetry "if they have some connection to Asian martial arts; length is open." Open to unsolicited reviews. Poets may also send books for review consideration. The editor adds, "We offer a unique medium for serious poetry dealing with Asian martial arts. Any style is welcome if there is quality in thought and writing."

‡*JOURNAL OF CONTEMPORARY ANGLO-SCANDINAVIAN POETRY (II, IV-Ethnic/nationality, translations)**, 11 Heatherton Park, Bradford on Tone, Taunton, Somerset TA4 1EU England, phone 01823 461725, founded 1994, contact Sam Smith, published biannually, features English poetry or English translations of Scandinavian poems and interviews with Scandinavian poets. **They want "new poetry howsoever it comes, translations from Scandinavian and original English language poems." They do not want "staid, generalized, all form no content."** They have recently published poetry by Tomas Tranströmer, Staffan Söderblom, Olav H. Hange and Alexis Lykiard. As a sample the editor selected these lines from "We Too Are Laymen, Said the Waves" by Werner Aspenström, translated by Robin Fulton:

> *Two nights in a row setting out from Stavanger*
> *I made my way on foot over the Atlantic*
> *between icebergs and oil-rigs*
> *to the accompaniment*
> *of excited conversations with the waves*
> *who comforted me saying:*
> *"We too are laymen."*

JoCA-SP is 50-60 pgs., A5, offset printed, perfect-bound with CS1 cover stock. They receive about 500 poems a year, accept approximately 5%. Press run is 100-150 for 50 subscribers of which 8 are libraries. Single copy: £6; subscription: £11. **Sample postpaid: £2 or £3 (sterling). Make checks payable to Sam Smith. Submit up to 6 poems. Previously published poems and simultaneous submissions OK. Cover letter preferred.** "If a reply is required, include IRCs or $1 (no checks, please)." Time between acceptance and publication is 6-8 months. **Often comments on rejections. Send SASE (or SAE and IRC) for guidelines. Reports in 2-4 weeks. Always sends prepublication galleys. Pays 1 copy.**

JOURNAL OF NEW JERSEY POETS (II, IV-Regional), English Dept., County College of Morris, Randolph NJ 07869-2086, phone (201)328-5471, fax (201)328-5425, founded 1976, editor Sander Zulauf. This biannual periodical uses poetry from **current or former residents of New Jersey. They want "serious work that is regional in origin but universal in scope." They do not want "sentimental, greeting card verse."** They have published poetry by Amiri Baraka, X.J. Kennedy, Brigit Pegeen Kelly, Kenneth Burke, Gerald Stern,

---

USE THE GENERAL INDEX to find the page number of a specific publisher. Also, if a publisher from last year's edition is not included in this edition, the General Index will tell you why.

Renée and Ted Weiss, and Michael Bugeja. As a sample the editor selected these lines from "In My Universe There is No Hope (A Poem of Joy)" by Joe Weil:

> *In my universe, there is no hope,*
> *only an old blue-gray cat,*
> *dreaming its version*
> *of valhalla—birds swift, but not overly so,*
> *familiar well-marked laps, the scent of catnip*
> *wafting every breeze.*
> *Soon, I'll be nearing an exit I always miss.*

The journal is published in Summer (May) and Winter (December), and is digest-sized, offset, with an average of 64 pgs. Press run is 900. Subscription: $7/year, $12/2 years. **Sample: $4. There are "no limitations" on submissions; SASE required. Faxed submissions will not be returned. Reports in 3-6 months.** Time between acceptance and publication is within 1 year. **Pays 2 copies/published poem. Acquires first North American serial rights.** Only using solicited reviews. Send books for review consideration.

JOURNAL OF POETRY THERAPY (IV-Health concerns), Dept. PM, Human Sciences Press, 233 Spring St., New York NY 10013-1578, phone (212)620-8069 or (800)221-9369, founded 1987. **Poetry mss should be sent to journal editor,** Dr. Nicholas Mazza, School of Social Work, Florida State University, Tallahassee FL 32306-2024. They use **"poems that could be useful in therapeutic settings, prefer relatively short poems; no sentimental, long poems."** They have published poetry by Ingrid Wendt and Virginia Bagliore. "The *Journal* is devoted to the use of the poetic in health, mental health, education and other human service settings." The quarterly is 64 pgs., digest-sized, flat-spined, using 3-6 pgs. for poetry. They accept approximately 10% of 100 poems received. There are 500 subscriptions. Subscription: $44 (US), $51 (international) for individuals; $195 (US), $230 (international) for institutions. **Write publisher for free sample. Submit up to 3 poems, 4 copies of each with name on only 1 of them. "Due to a large number of submissions, manuscripts are not acknowledged or returned. Reports on accepted poems in 2-4 months."** Pays 1 copy.

JOURNAL OF THE AMERICAN MEDICAL ASSOCIATION (JAMA) (II, IV-Health concerns, themes), 515 N. State, Chicago IL 60610, phone (312)464-2417, fax (312)464-5824, founded 1883, associate editor Charlene Breedlove, has a "Poetry and Medicine" column and publishes **poetry "in some way related to a medical experience, whether from the point-of-view of a health care worker or patient, or simply an observer. No unskilled poetry."** They have published poetry by Aimée Grunberger and Jack Coulehan. As a sample the editor selected these lines from "Storm in the Morning" by Floyd Skloot:

> *All I have to do is wait here.*
> *Yes, I know I do not know where*
> *I am now, so I must be near*
> *the source of peace. Across the years*
> *to this bed blazed by a long skein*
> *of dreams, I find myself at ease.*

JAMA, magazine-sized, flat-spined, with glossy paper cover, has 360,000 subscribers of which 369 are libraries. They accept about 7% of 550 poems received/year. Subscription: $66. **Sample free. No previously published poems; simultaneous submissions OK, if identified. "I always appreciate inclusion of a brief cover letter with, at minimum, the author's name and address clearly printed. Mention of other publications and special biographical notes are always of interest." Publishes theme issues.** Theme issues include managed care, medical education, ethics/human rights, allergy and immunology, and science reporting. **"However, we would rather that poems relate obliquely to the theme." Pays 1 copy, more by request. "We ask for a signed copyright release, but publication elsewhere is always granted free of charge."**

JOYFUL NOISE: THE JOURNAL OF CHRISTIAN POETRY (IV-Subscription, religious), P.O. Box 401, Bowling Green KY 42102, e-mail jim.erskine@bgamug.com, editor Jim Erskine, appears quarterly. **They want "poetry with a Christian outlook, any style—free verse, rhyme, haiku, etc. Maximum length: 25 lines. We ask all authors whose work is accepted for publication to subscribe."** The journal is 24 pgs., 8½×11, saddle-stapled with a card stock cover and a few b&w graphics. Single copy: $5; subscription: $18/year. **Sample postpaid: $5. Submit no more than 3 poems at a time. "Simultaneous submissions OK, but previously *un*published poems preferred." Reports in 1 month. Pays copies.** Also awards 3 Editor's Choice Awards ranging from $10-25. The editor says, "Avoid political, social, New Age and broad, universal topics—love, brotherhood, peace, etc. We think the smaller in scope and more personal your subject, the better the poem."

JUGGLER'S WORLD (IV-Sports/recreation), % Ken Letko, College of the Redwoods, 883 W. Washington Blvd., Crescent City CA 95531-8361, phone (707)464-7457, founded 1982, literary editor Ken Letko, is a quarterly magazine, **using poems about juggling. "Only restriction is that all content is focused on juggling."**
● *JW* is a publication of the International Jugglers' Association and is intended "as a forum for the exchange of information and ideas on juggling." If you're not a juggler, or an enthusiast of the sport, we suggest reading a few issues before submitting.
They have recently published poetry by Mary Winters, Anita Endrezze, Barbara Goldberg, Robert Hill Long,

A Christian publication devoted solely to poetry, *Joyful Noise* seeks poetry that "has a small, personal quality and which also glorifies the Lord." Says editor/publisher Jim Erskine, "In this cover illustration, the singer is singing from the heart; that's where we want our poems to come from as well. The illustration captures the spirit of inspirational poetry as a song or praise to the Lord." The quarterly, based in Bowling Green, Kentucky, is open to any style of poetry as long as it is no more than 25 lines, but now requires all those accepted for publication to subscribe. Cover artist: Will H. Bradley, a decorative illustrator during the Art Nouveau Movement of the 1890s. This particular illustration was originally printed on the cover of *Harper's Bazaar* in March 1896.

Lucien Stryk and Margo Wilding. As a sample the editor selected these lines from "Juggling" by Theresa Hemmer:

> Red balls briefly fill
> the palms of my hands;
> solid slap of a rhythm
> sensed, not measured,
> balance of three into two.
> A triangle flips end over end.

JW is 40 pgs., magazine-sized, professionally printed on glossy stock and saddle-stapled, with 2-color glossy paper cover, contains b&w photos, cartoons and ads. They receive 50-100 poetry submissions/year, use 4-8 poems. Press run is 3,500, circulated to more than 3,000 jugglers in more than 20 countries. Subscription: $30. **Sample: $8. They will consider previously published poems. Editor sometimes comments on rejections, suggesting some revision. Reports in 1-4 months. Pays 1 copy. Acquires first or one-time rights.** The editor urges poets to "provide insights and remember that the theme is always juggling!"

JUNCTION PRESS (II), P.O. Box 40537, San Diego CA 92164, phone (619)282-0371, fax (619)282-0297, founded 1991, publisher Mark Weiss, aims to publish "overlooked non-mainstream poetry." The press publishes 2 paperback books of poetry a year. **They want "modern or postmodern work, any form or length. No academic, Iowa school or formal poetry."** They have recently published poetry by Stephen Vincent, Rochelle Owens, Luisa Futoranski, José Kozer and Mervyn Taylor. They say their books are typically 72-96 pgs., 5½×8½, offset and perfect-bound with coated covers with graphics. **Query first with 10-15 pgs. of poetry and a cover letter (bio unnecessary). Previously published poems OK; no simultaneous submissions. Often comments on rejections. Replies to queries in 6 months, to mss (if invited) "immediately." Pays 100 copies (out of a press run of 1,000).** The publisher says, "While I don't dismiss the possibility of finding a second Rimbaud, please note that all of my authors have been in their 50s and have written for many years."

JUNIPER PRESS; NORTHEAST; JUNIPER BOOKS; THE WILLIAM N. JUDSON SERIES OF CONTEMPORARY AMERICAN POETRY; CHICKADEE; INLAND SEA SERIES; GIFTS OF THE PRESS (III, IV-Form), 1310 Shorewood Dr., La Crosse WI 54601, e-mail juniperpr@juno.com, founded 1962, poetry editors John Judson and Joanne Judson, is one of the oldest and most respected programs of publishing poetry in the country. *Northeast* is an annual little magazine, digest-sized, saddle-stapled. **"Poets published in our books have first appeared in *Northeast* and are invited to submit mss. Any other book mss sent will be returned without being read. No submissions by fax or e-mail." Reports in 2-4 months.** A subscription to *Northeast/Juniper Press* is $33/year ($38 for institutions), which brings you 1 issue of the magazine and the Juniper Books, Chickadees, WNJ Books and some gifts of the press, a total of about 3-5 items. (Or send SASE for catalog to order individual items; orders can be placed via e-mail. **Sample postpaid: $2.50.**) The Juniper Books are chapbooks of poetry; the WNJ Books are letterpress poetry books by one author; Chickadees are 12-

24 pgs. each, in wrappers; Inland Sea Series is for larger works; Gifts of the Press are usually given only to subscribers or friends of the press. The editors say, "Please read us before sending mss. It will aid in your selection of materials to send. If you don't like what we do, please don't submit."

JUST ABOUT HORSES (II, IV-Animals), 14 Industrial Rd., Pequannock NJ 07440, founded 1975, editor Stephanie Macejko, is a magazine which appears 6 times/year and provides information about both the model horse hobby and real horses. **"Our magazine contains information on model horses and real horses. Any style of poetry will be read as long as the style suits the subject matter."** *Just About Horses* is 40 pgs., digest-sized, saddle-stapled, professionally printed on glossy paper with b&w and color photos. Press run is 15,000 for 12,500 subscribers. Subscription: $12. **Sample postpaid: $2.50.**

‡KAIMANA: LITERARY ARTS HAWAII; HAWAII LITERARY ARTS COUNCIL (III, IV-Regional), P.O. Box 11213, Honolulu HI 96828, founded 1974, editor Tony Quagliano. *Kaimana*, a semiannual, is the magazine of the Hawaii Literary Arts Council. **Poems with "some Pacific reference are preferred—Asia, Polynesia, Hawaii—but not exclusively."** They have published poetry by Howard Nemerov, John Yau, Reuben Tam, Reuel Denney, Tony Friedson, Lyn Lifshin, Haunani-Kay Trask, Anne Waldman and Joe Stanton. *Kaimana* is 64-76 pgs., 7½×10, saddle-stapled, with high-quality printing. Press run is 1,000 for 600 subscribers of which 200 are libraries. Subscription: $12. **Sample postpaid: $7. Cover letter with submissions preferred. Sometimes comments on rejections. Reports with "reasonable dispatch." Pays 2 copies.** The editor says, "Hawaii gets a lot of 'travelling regionalists,' visiting writers with inevitably superficial observations. We also get superb visiting observers who are careful craftsmen anywhere. *Kaimana* is interested in the latter, to complement our own best Hawaii writers."

KALEIDOSCOPE: INTERNATIONAL MAGAZINE OF LITERATURE, FINE ARTS, AND DIS-ABILITY (IV-Specialized, themes), 326 Locust St., Akron OH 44302-1876, phone (330)762-9755, fax (330)762-0912, founded 1979, editor-in-chief Dr. Darshan C. Perusek, consulting poetry editor Christopher Hew-itt. *Kaleidoscope* is based at United Disability Services, a nonprofit agency. **Poetry should deal with the experience of disability but not limited to that when the writer has a disability. "***Kaleidoscope* **is interested in high-quality poetry with vivid, believable images and evocative language. Works should not use stereotyping, patronizing or offending language about disability."** They have published poetry by Margaret Robison, Sheryl L. Nelms and Sandra J. Lindow. As a sample the editors selected these lines from "Anniversary" by Patricia Ranzoni:

> *This morning*
> *we stood*
> *watching swallows flirt*
>
> *beyond the glass*
> *and I swear.*
> *watching us, they*
>
> *might be saying*
> *in swallow conjugation*
> *the same as we: look*
>
> *dear, what an exciting pair!*

Kaleidoscope is 64 pgs., 8½×11, professionally printed and saddle-stitched with 4-color semigloss card cover, b&w art inside. Circulation is 1,500, including libraries, social service agencies, health-care professionals, universities and individual subscribers. Single copy: $5; subscription: $9 individual, $14 agency. **Sample: $4. Submit photocopies with SASE for return of work. Limit 5 poems/submission. Previously published poems and simultaneous submissions OK, "as long as we are notified in both instances." Cover letter required. All submissions must be accompanied by an autobiographical sketch. Deadlines: March and August 1. Publishes theme issues. Theme for 1998 is "Disability: The Lighter Side." Reports in 3 weeks; acceptance or rejection may take 6 months. Pays $10-125. Rights return to author upon publication.** Staff reviews books of poetry. Send books for review consideration to Gail Willmott, senior editor.

KALLIOPE, A JOURNAL OF WOMEN'S ART (IV-Women, translations, themes); SUE SANIEL ELKIND POETRY CONTEST, 3939 Roosevelt Blvd., Jacksonville FL 32205, phone (904)381-3511, founded 1978, editor Mary Sue Koeppel, is a literary/visual arts journal published by Florida Community College at Jacksonville; the emphasis is on women writers and artists. The editors say, **"We like the idea of poetry as a sort of artesian well—there's one meaning that's clear on the surface and another deeper meaning that comes welling up from underneath. We'd like to see more poetry from Black, Hispanic and Native American women. Nothing sexist, racist, conventionally sentimental. We will have one special theme issue each year. Write for specific guidelines."**

• The Jacksonville Branch of National League of American Pen Women selected *Kalliope* to award the

1996 Frances Buck Sherman Award. The winner was chosen from Florida women with work published in *Kalliope* during the previous year. The 1996 winner was Debra Bokur.

Poets published include Rosemary Daniell, Marge Piercy, Martha M. Vertreace, Karen Subach and Tess Gallager. As a sample the editor selected the following lines by Melanie Richards:

> With dried orange rind,
> fragrant sage, and a blue
>
> branch of coral, I seal
> this package full of artifacts
>
> in case the wild horses
> all vanish from the earth,
>
> or the red throat of the hummingbird
> lies to us about summer;

Kalliope calls itself "a journal of women's art" and publishes fiction, interviews, drama and visual art in addition to poetry. The magazine, which appears 3 times/year, is 7¼ × 8¼, flat-spined, handsomely printed on white stock, glossy card cover and b&w photographs of works of art. Average number of pages is 80. Poems here are lively, celebratory and varied in form, style and length. The circulation is 1,500, of which 400-500 are subscriptions, including 100 library subscriptions, and 800 are copies sold on newsstands and in bookstores. Subscription: $12.50/year or $22/2 years. **Sample: $7. Submit poems in batches of 3-5 with brief bio note, phone number and address. No previously published poems. Reads submissions September through April only. SASE required. Because all submissions are read by several members of the editing staff, response time is usually 3-4 months. Publication will be within 6 months. Criticism is provided "when time permits and the author has requested it." Send SASE for guidelines and upcoming themes. Pays $10 or subscription. Acquires first publication rights.** Reviews books of poetry, "but we prefer groups of books in one review." Open to unsolicited reviews. Poets may also send books for review consideration. They sponsor the Sue Saniel Elkind Poetry Contest. 1997 judge was Maxine Kumin. First prize: $1,000; runners up published in *Kalliope*. Deadline: November 1. Send SASE for details. The editor says, "*Kalliope* is a carefully stitched patchwork of how women feel, what they experience, and what they have come to know and understand about their lives . . . a collection of visions from or about women all over the world. Send for a sample copy, to see what appeals to us, or better yet, subscribe! We have increased our circulation and can pay our contributors a bit."

KANSAS QUARTERLY/ARKANSAS REVIEW; SEATON AWARD (II, IV-Regional), Dept. of English and Philosophy, P.O. Box 1890, Arkansas State University, State University AR 72467, editor Norman Lavers, published under the combined name of *Kansas Quarterly/Arkansas Review* since 1996, the magazine "seeks to continue the fine 25-year tradition of the *Kansas Quarterly*. *KQ/AR* publishes almost entirely fiction and creative nonfiction. However, each issue contains, at most, the poetry of two or three people. (An occasional all-poetry issue may be published.) And, since part of *KQ/AR*'s funding comes from the Arkansas State University Delta Studies Project, the magazine will preserve a corner to showcase the art and culture of the lower Mississippi Delta." **They are "wide open" as far as submission guidelines, but seek "quality. We just want good work."** They have recently published poetry by Susan Wicks, Craig Raine, Walter McDonald and Laurence Lieberman. The editor says *KQ/AR* is 90 pgs., 8½ × 11, saddle-stitched with 4-color cover. **Submit up to 4 poems at a time. No previously published poems; simultaneous submissions OK.** Time between acceptance and publication is 1 year. **Often comments on rejections. Send SASE for guidelines. Pays $10/page (minimum $25) plus 2 copies. Buys first North American serial rights.** Sponsors the Seaton Award, a $1,000 award to "the best work (in any genre) published in the magazine during the year by a Kansas-connected writer. No application procedure."

KARAMU (II), Dept. of English, Eastern Illinois University, Charleston IL 61920, phone (217)581-5614, founded 1966, editor Peggy Brayfield, is an annual whose "goal is to provide a forum for the best contemporary poetry and fiction that comes our way. We especially like to print the works of new writers. **We like to see poetry that shows a good sense of what's being done with poetry currently. We like poetry that builds around real experiences, real images and real characters and that avoids abstraction, overt philosophizing and fuzzy pontifications. In terms of form, we prefer well-structured free verse, poetry with an inner, sub-surface structure as opposed to, let's say, the surface structure of rhymed quatrains. We have definite preferences in terms of style and form, but no such preferences in terms of length or subject matter. Purpose, however, is another thing. We don't have much interest in the openly didactic poem. If the poet wants to preach against or for some political or religious viewpoint, the preaching shouldn't be so strident that it overwhelms the poem. The poem should first be a poem."** They have recently published poetry by Barbara Crooker, Allison Joseph, Katharine Howd Machan and Joanne Mokosh Riley. As a sample the editor selected these lines from "Musica Dolce" by Mary A. Hood:

> Women playing Renaissance music in a brown spiked desert?
> Women who comfort crying children, scrub floors, stir pots?
> Are they water bearers pouring liquid from vessel to vessel,

the more they pour, the more there is to flow?
Are they the ones who know the songs of creation?
Yes. Blessed are the women who among the dust make music.

The format is 120 pgs., 5×8, matte cover, handsomely printed (narrow margins), attractive b&w art. They receive submissions from about 300 poets each year, use 40-50 poems. Never more than a year—usually 6-7 months—between acceptance and publication. They have a circulation of 350 with 300 subscribers of which 15 are libraries. **Sample: $5. Poems—in batches of no more than 4-6—may be submitted to Peggy Brayfield. "We don't much care for simultaneous submissions. We read September 1 through June 30 only, for fastest decision submit February through May. Poets should not bother to query. We critique a few of the better poems. We want the poet to consider our comments and then submit new work." Publishes theme issues occasionally. Send SASE for upcoming themes. Pays 1 copy. Acquires first serial rights.** *Karamu* received an Award of Merit in 1996 from American Literary Magazine Awards. The editor says, "Follow the standard advice: Know your market. Read contemporary poetry and the magazines you want to be published in. Be patient."

KATYDID BOOKS (V), 1 Balsa Rd., Santa Fe NM 87505, founded 1973, editors/publishers Karen Hargreaves-Fitzsimmons and Thomas Fitzsimmons, publishes 3 paperbacks and 3 hardbacks/year. "We publish three series of poetry: Asian Poetry in Translation (distributed by University of Hawaii Press), European Writing in Translation (distributed by Wayne State University Press), and American Poets." They have recently published *Beneath the Sleepless Tossing of the Planets—Selected Poems 1972-1989* by Makoto Oska, *Map of Days* by Shuntaro Tanikawa, and *Stages and Views* by Penny Harter. **However, they are currently not accepting submissions.**

*KAWABATA PRESS; SEPIA POETRY MAGAZINE (I, II, IV-Anthology), Knill Cross House, Millbrook, Torpoint, Cornwall, United Kingdom, founded 1977, poetry editor Colin David Webb, publishes **"nontraditional poetry, prose and artwork (line only), open to all original and well thought-out work. I dislike rhymes, traditional poems and 'genre' stories. I want original and thought-provoking material."** *Sepia* is published 3 times/year in an inexpensively produced, 32-page, digest-sized, saddle-stapled format, photoreduced from typescript, with narrow margins and bizarre drawings. They receive 500 submissions a year, use approximately 50. Press run is 150 for 75 subscribers of which 5-6 are libraries. Subscription: £2 ($5) a year. **Sample: 75p. ($2). Submit 6 poems at a time, typed. Prefers not to use previously published poems. Simultaneous submissions OK. "Letter with poems is polite." Reports in 3 weeks. Sometimes sends prepublication galleys. Pays 1 copy.** Reviews books of poetry in 50-100 words. Open to unsolicited reviews. Poets may also send books for review consideration. Under the imprint of Kawabata Press, Colin Webb also publishes anthologies and collections. **However, publication of these has been temporarily suspended. Query with 6-10 poems and "maybe a brief outline of intent." Poet gets 50% of profits (after cost of printing is covered) and 5 copies.** A book catalog of Kawabata Press publications is on the back of *Sepia*, for ordering copies. The editor **always comments on rejections** and advises, "Strike out everything that sounds like a cliché. Don't try any tricks. Work at it, have a feeling for what you write, don't send 'exercise' pieces. Believe in what you send."

KELSEY REVIEW (IV-Regional), Mercer County Community College, P.O. Box B, Trenton NJ 08690, phone (609)586-4800, fax (609)586-2318, e-mail kelsey.review@mccc.edu, founded 1988, editor-in-chief Robin Schore, is an annual published by Mercer County Community College. It serves as **"an outlet for literary talent of people living and working in Mercer County, New Jersey only."** They have **no specifications as to form, length, subject matter or style, but do not want to see poetry about "kittens and puppies."** As a sample the editor selected these lines from "Why Poems Are Better Than" by Valerie L. Egar:

> *Poems*
> *slip into pockets*
> *tuck neatly*
> *behind dollar bills*
> *ride lightly*
> *in memory*

Kelsey Review is 82 glossy pgs., 7×11, with paper cover and line drawings; no ads. They receive about 60 submissions a year, accept 6-10. Press run is 2,000. All distributed free to contributors, area libraries and schools. **Submit up to 6 poems at a time, typed. No previously published poems or simultaneous submissions. Deadline: May 1. Always comments on rejections. May request information via e-mail or fax. Reports in May of each year. Pays 5 copies.** All rights revert to authors.

THE KENYON REVIEW (II); THE WRITERS WORKSHOP, Kenyon College, Gambier OH 43022, phone (614)427-5208, fax (614)427-5417, e-mail kenyonreview@kenyon.edu, founded 1939, editor David Lynn, is a triquarterly review containing poetry, fiction, criticism, reviews and memoirs. It is **one of the country's leading literary publications.** Under David Lynn's editorship, this magazine continues to blossom, featuring all styles and forms, lengths and subject matters—a real openness. But this market is more closed than others because of the volume of submissions typically received during each reading cycle. Issues contain work by such poets as Cyrus Cassells, Judith Ortiz Cofer, Joy Harjo, Richard Howard, Josephine Jacobsen, Alicia Ostriker, Sherod Santos and Quincy Troupe. The elegantly printed, flat-spined, 7×10, 180-page review has a circulation of 4,000 for 3,200 subscribers of which 1,100 are libraries. They receive about 3,000-4,000 submissions a year, use 50-

60 (about 50 pgs. of poetry in each issue), have a 1-year backlog. The editor urges poets to read a few copies before submitting to find out what they are publishing. **Sample postpaid: $8. Unsolicited submissions are read from September 1 through November 1 and February 1 through March 31 *only*. "However, submissions from subscribers who identify themselves will be read year round." Writers may contact by phone, fax or e-mail, but may submit mss by mail only. Reports in 3 months. Pays $15/page for poetry, $10/page for prose. Buys first North American serial rights.** Reviews books of poetry in 2,500-7,000 words, single or multi-book format. "Reviews are primarily solicited—potential reviewers should inquire first." Also sponsors The Writers Workshop, an annual 10-day event. 1997 dates: June 24 through July 4. Location: the campus of Kenyon College. Average attendance is 12. **Open to writers of fiction, short short-story fiction, plays and poetry. Conference is designed to provide intensive conversation, exercises and detailed readings of participants' work.** Speakers at last conference were Allison Joseph, Wendy McLeod, Pamela Painter, Nancy Zafris, David Baker and Reginald McKnight. Other special features include a limited-edition anthology produced by workshop writers and *The Kenyon Review* that includes the best writing of the session. College and non-degree graduate credit is offered. Cost for 1997 conference was $1,450, including meals, a room and tuition. Send SASE for application. Early application is encouraged as the workshops are limited to 12 participants. Poetry published in *The Kenyon Review* was also selected for inclusion in the 1992, 1993, 1994, 1996 and 1997 volumes of *The Best American Poetry* and several *Pushcart Prize* anthologies.

‡**THE KERF (II, IV-Nature/ecology)**, College of the Redwoods, 883 W. Washington Blvd., Crescent City CA 95531, founded 1995, editor Ken Letko, annually published, features "poetry that speaks to the environment and humanity." **They want "poetry that exhibits an environmental consciousness."** They have recently published poetry by Philip Dacey, Ray Gonzalez, Laurel Speer and Ann Struthers. As a sample the editor selected these lines from "The Stones" by Janine Canan:

>Along the beach, stones
>exposed by the retreating tide
>greet me like friends from long ago.
>And I bend to gather eggs
>mounds, ovals, crescents
>smoothed by life in the tumbling sea.

The Kerf is 40 pgs., 8½×5½, offset printed, saddle-stitched with CS2 cover stock. They receive about 2,000 poems a year, accept approximately 1-3%. Press run is 400, 150 shelf sales; 100 distributed free to contributors and writing centers. **Sample postpaid: $5. Make checks payable to College of the Redwoods. Submit up to 5 poems (up to 7 pgs.) at a time. No previously published poems; simultaneous submissions OK. Reads submissions January 15 through March 31 only.** Time between acceptance and publication is 3 months. **Poems are circulated to an editorial board. "Our editors debate (argue for or against) the inclusion of each manuscript." Seldom comments on rejections. Send SASE for guidelines. Reports in 1-2 months. Sometimes sends prepublication galleys. Pays 1-2 copies. Acquires first North American serial rights.**

‡❧**KICK IT OVER (IV-Political)**, P.O. Box 5811, Station A, Toronto, Ontario M5W 1P2 Canada, e-mail kio@web.apc.org, founded 1981, editor Bob Melcombe, published 1-2 times/year is an "anarchist magazine—to furthering ideas of radical social change." **They want "political, radical poetry." They do not want "love sonnets and the like."** *Kick It Over* is 60-80 pgs., 8½×11, web printed on newsprint with glossy cover, ads, photos and art. They receive about 25-50 poems a year, accept approximately 6-12%. Press run is 2,000 for 350 subscribers of which 10 are libraries, 800-1,000 shelf sales; 400 distributed free to prisoners and contributors. Subscription: $14. **Sample postpaid: $3.50. Submit up to 10 poems at a time. Previously published poems and simultaneous submissions OK. Cover letter preferred.** Time between acceptance and publication is 2 months to 1 year. **"There are two of us who read submissions. I decide based primarily on my perceptions, but will defer to the other reader if I'm ambivalent." Publishes theme issues. Send SASE (or SAE and IRC) for upcoming themes. Reports in 1-4 months. Pays 3 copies.**

‡**KIDS' WORLD; DREAMS & NIGHTMARES (I, IV-Children/teen/young adult)**, 1300 Kicker Rd., Tuscaloosa AL 35404, e-mail d.kopasks-me@genie.com, founded 1992, editor Ms. Morgan Kopaska-Merkel. *Kids' World*, published quarterly, features "poems, art, stories by kids for children's entertainment and to provide an entrance to poetry for young poets." **They want "poetry less than a page long. Fantasy, science fiction, rhyming or freestyle. Age-appropriate for children and of interest to kids." They do not want "horror, erotic or religious."** As a sample the editor selected these lines from "The Mountain" by Alexis Miseyko:

>If you fall the rocks below
>Will split you like a knife,
>But if you make it to the top
>You have won your life.

The editor says *Kids' World* is 12-16 pgs., digest-sized, photocopied, stapled with b&w art, no ads. They receive about 20-25 poems a year, accept approximately 10-20. Press run is 100 for 35 subscribers of which 7 are libraries, 1 shelf sales; 23 distributed free to libraries, reviewers, friends and schoolteachers. Single copy: $1; subscription: $3. **Sample postpaid: $1. Make checks payable to David Kopaska-Merkel. Poets must be 16 years or younger. Submit any number of poems. Cover letter preferred. "State whether you'd like an illustration."** Time between acceptance and publication is 3-6 months. **"I read them and decide to accept/ reject based on merit, available space, etc."** Seldom comments on rejections. Send SASE for guidelines. **Reports 2-4 weeks. Pays 1 copy. Acquires first North American serial rights.** "I will criticize your work free on request." The editor says, "I am looking for poetry that's freestyle. If rhyming, rhyme and meter must be perfect. Check spelling, grammar and punctuation (or have an adult do it.)"

‡**KIMERA: A JOURNAL OF FINE WRITING (II)**, 1316 Hollis, Spokane WA 99201, e-mail kimera@ on-ramp.ior.com, website http://www.ior.com/kimera, founded 1996, publisher Jan Strever, is a biannual online journal (appears yearly in hard copy) and "attempts to address John Locke's challenge—'where is the head with no chimeras.' " **They want poetry that "attempts to 'capture the soul in motion.' No flabby poems."** They have recently published poetry by Wendy Battin, Colin Morton and N. Palmer Hall. They accept approximately 10% of poems/year. Press run is 300 for 200 subscribers. Single copy: $10; subscription: $20. **Sample postpaid: $5. Submit 3-6 poems at a time. No previously published poems; simultaneous submissions OK. Cover letter required. "Poets can send either e-mail or hard copy submissions."** Poems are circulated to an editorial board. **Seldom comments on rejections. Obtain guidelines via website. Reports in 3 months. Pays 2 copies. Acquires first rights.**

KINESIS (II), P.O. Box 4007, Whitefish MT 59937-4007, e-mail kinesis@eworld.com, founded 1992. *Kinesis* is a monthly that calls itself "the literary magazine for the rest of us" and includes fiction, poetry, essays and reviews. **They want any type of poetry—"as long as it moves."** They have published poetry by Lucy Shaw, John Leax, Ross Talarico, Simon Perchik and Rick Newby. *Kinesis* is 48 pgs., 8½ × 11, printed on recycled paper and saddle-stitched with spot color and artwork, graphics and ads inside. They accept about 10% of the poetry received. Press run is 2,000 for 1,600 subscribers of which 10 are libraries, 500 shelf sales. Single copy: $3; subscription: $20. **Sample postpaid: $4. Previously published poems and simultaneous submissions OK. Send SASE for guidelines. Reports in 1 month. Pays 5 copies and a subscription. Acquires one-time rights.** Reviews books of all kinds in 1,000-2,000 words and offers a page of "Book Briefs" in addition. Poets may also send books for review consideration. They sponsor an annual "If It Moves . . . Contest" for both poetry and fiction. $10 reading fee covers 3 poems or 1 story. All entrants receive a year's subscription. Poetry winners receive prizes of $200, $100 and $50 (fiction: $200, $100 and $50) in addition to publication. Send SASE for details.

‡**KINGS ESTATE PRESS (III)**, 870 Kings Estate Rd., St. Augustine FL 32086-5033, phone (800)249-7485, founded 1993, publisher Ruth Moon Kempher, "publishes the best contemporary poetry available; all books are illustrated." They publish about 3 paperbacks/year. **They want any well-crafted work.** They have recently published poetry by Gerald Locklin, Laurel Speer, Michael Hathaway, John Elsberg and Wayne Hogan. Books are usually 50-120 pgs., perfect-bound, 7 × 8½, with b&w drawings. **Query first with 6-10 sample poems "unless it's a long poem—then 6-10 pgs. of excerpts. Previously published poems OK. Cover letter required.** Time between acceptance and publication is 6 months to 2 years. **Often comments on rejections. Replies to queries in 2-6 months; to mss immediately. Pay is "individually negotiated." Obtain samples of books by writing or calling 1-800-249-7485.** The publisher says, "Unless you're willing to wait two years for publication, please wait to query us."

KIOSK (II), 306 Clemens Hall, SUNY, Buffalo NY 14260, phone (716)645-2578, founded 1985, editor Lia Vella, poetry editor Loren Godman, is an annual literary magazine using **poetry of "any length, any style, especially experimental."** They have published poetry by Raymond Federman, Sheila Murphy, Lyn Lifshin, Carl Dennis and Charles Bernstein. The editor describes *Kiosk* as flat-spined, digest-sized. They receive about 400 poems a year, accept approximately 10-15. **Sample free (if available) with SAE and 6 first-class stamps. Submit poems in batches of 3. Cover letter not required, "but we suggest one be included." Reads submissions September 1 through April 30 only. Reports within 4 months. Pays in copies.**

KITCHEN TABLE: WOMEN OF COLOR PRESS (III, IV-Women/feminism, lesbian, ethnic, political), P.O. Box 40-4920, Brooklyn NY 11240-4920, phone (718)935-1082, fax (718)935-1107, founded 1981, is "the only publisher in North America committed to producing and distributing the **work of women of color of all racial/cultural heritages, sexualities and classes. We publish work of the highest literary quality that**

THE SUBJECT INDEX, located before the General Index, can help you select markets for your work. It lists those publishers whose poetry interests are specialized.

INSIDER REPORT

Perseverance helps poets achieve their dreams

David Starkey

Photo by Melodie Starkey

"The great thing about writing is that, in a sense, it doesn't occur in real time," says poet and professor David Starkey. "If you're a musician or an actor or even a salesman, for that matter, you can't take back your performance. But a poet can return, over and over, to his poem until it becomes something like he imagined it would be."

Of course, striving to reach one's vision requires persistence, Starkey says. And that's exactly what he has exhibited not only with his poetry but also with his career. Though at one time ashamed to admit his dream because he thought it was "hopeless," Starkey wanted to be a writer. Instead of writing, however, he pursued a Ph.D. in literature.

Unprepared to be a "literary critic," Starkey opted for a Master's degree and accepted a position as a claims adjuster, the first decent-paying job he could find. "I was incredibly naive," he says. "I didn't know about the academic creative writing world. I thought all writers lived in garrets and supported themselves with odd jobs."

Once Starkey secured his "mind-numbing" insurance job, he devoted his real energy to writing, not poetry, but fiction, his main interest growing up. "I wrote a miserable autobiographical novel. Halfway through my second draft, I realized it was going nowhere. So, at the encouragement of my friend David Case, I started writing poetry and mailing it off."

At first, his approach was less than scientific. "I didn't know anything about books like *Poet's Market*. I just scanned the address lists in the back of old copies of *The Pushcart Prize* and sent to any magazine that had a name I liked." Soon, however, he was discovering directories and reading everything he could find in the poetry stacks of public libraries.

After a year or so, Starkey had published a handful of poems and was on his way to a Master of Fine Arts at Louisiana State University, where he would focus on reading, writing and thinking about poetry. Since then he has gone from an instructorship to a tenure-track professorship. He also has numerous publications, including more than 200 poems in literary journals, and his most recent book, *Open Mike Night at the Cabaret Voltaire*, was published by Kings Estate Press in 1996.

Now an assistant professor of English at North Central College in Naperville, Illinois, Starkey credits perseverance for his success in getting published. "If a magazine didn't accept the first batch of poems, I tried them again later. Even if I didn't go directly from graduate school to a tenure-track job, I ended up with an instructorship that later became something better. There were countless opportunities along the way for me to quit. Yet my experience has been that if a poet works hard enough at his or her craft and career, sooner or later, that person will succeed."

INSIDER REPORT, *Starkey*

"Epilogue: The Minor Poet's Ars Poetica"

Visual artists have it made,
I mean made, *right there in front of them.*
They spread paint thick
as cookie dough across a canvas.
They pry rhinestones and glass beads
from costume jewelry, cover a cuckoo clock
with glue and—Voila!—their art.
Even if nothing comes
of an afternoon spent gouging
and caressing a wet lump of clay,
they still have the flecks of earth
dried to their face and arms,
the warm water and soap
on their hands.
            But imagine
you are a young black man from Oklahoma
come to New York to play guitar.
Imagine you are Charlie Christian
breathing the smoke of Minton's
into your tubercular lungs, red-hot
and burning out fast,
yet your genius going all but unrecorded.
Your audience sees your fingers moving
across the frets, but there is no accounting
for the proud, gut-stricken slur
coming from your amplifier.
Imagine emptying your life into the invisible.
Willingly.

Now that *would be something like poetry.*

(first published in *Grasslands Review*; also published in *Adventures of the Minor Poet*, by David Starkey, published by I*D Books of Great Britain, 1994)

He also acknowledges the encouragement of literary magazine editors, which is what inspired him to give up the insurance job and try something he really wanted to do in the first place. "I've never had the opportunity to live in the center of the poetry world, so I've always relied on the judgment of magazine editors. They've acted as my de facto writers' group," he says. "If a stranger is willing to invest money to bring your poetry to other people, that's a sincere compliment."

Knowing how important outside validation is for writers, Starkey requires students in his advanced poetry class to submit their work. In fact, **Poet's Market** is a required text and Starkey personally takes students' submissions to the post office. "Before they submit their poetry, we read through a few sample entries together. I emphasize how unlikely it is to be published in a magazine which lists Pulitzer Prize winners as recent contributors and claims to publish less than one percent of its submissions."

INSIDER REPORT, *continued*

Starkey also urges students to read editors' remarks very carefully. "For instance, if an editor says he hates poems that end with rhetorical questions, take him at his word. And it just makes sense to begin by submitting to magazines marked with a (**I**). There's nothing more discouraging to a beginning poet than to receive a dozen form rejections, even if they're all from *The New Yorker*."

Much to Starkey's delight, the first year he mailed out his students' work, six out of the 14 students had poetry accepted for publication. Besides presenting their work in a professional manner, students who found their work being accepted were very attentive to the specific needs of the magazine, he says. They tried to find an editor who would accommodate their work, rather than tailor their work to the editor's taste.

The most difficult task for any poet today is not to give up in the face of the overwhelming apathy he or she is likely to receive from friends, family and acquaintances, not to mention the general public, says Starkey. "You have to believe what you're doing is important, even if no one else seems to agree.

"I also think poets shouldn't dwell too much on their present circumstances, no matter how miserable they are. I'm basically a hard-nosed pragmatist, but I'm convinced we have to believe what we're doing has some greater spiritual significance than just being published in a little magazine with 500 readers. We write for the ages, whether we want to or not."

Starkey says when it comes to offering advice to his students and other beginning poets, Joseph Campbell was right: "Follow your bliss. If you love it, do it. Don't let anybody stop you, and never give up."

—*Christine Martin*

also contributes to furthering the liberation struggles of all women of color. Many writers do not take the time to understand that we are a book publisher and cannot publish single poems." They publish flat-spined paperback collections and anthologies—an average of one book of poetry every other year and have published four anthologies, three of which contain poetry. They have recently published poetry by Chrystros, Janice Gould, Nellie Wong and Sonia Sanchez. All books are published simultaneously in hardback for library sales. **Submit a query or complete manuscript with SASE. "Material without a SASE will be held 2 months, then destroyed. No queries by phone or fax and no handwritten submissions." Send SASE for guidelines. Reports in 3-6 months. "We strongly suggest reading one of our publications first. No romance, beauty, pornography, or simplistic rhymed material. We are an undercapitalized and understaffed operation. Please be patient." Write for catalog to purchase samples.** The editors say, "We are particularly interested in publishing work by women of color which would generally be overlooked by other publishers, especially work by Native American, Latina, Asian American, Caribbean, Arab and African American women who may be working class, lesbian, disabled or older writers."

‡**KNOCKED (II)**, P.O. Box 98, Swarthmore PA 19081-0098, website http://www.ash.swarthmore.edu/knocked/, founded 1994, editor Eric Behrens, appears semiannually in January and July. **They have "no restrictions as to form, length, subject matter, etc. We prefer concise, hard-hitting verse. Have a soft-spot for poets with a deep sense of irony, love of language. No 'penis poems;' maudlin, sentimental verse; self-pity; pompous, footnoted works; nothing the writer sent out the same day he wrote it."** They have recently published poetry by Dennis Saleh, Taylor Mali, Kate Krautkramer and Brent Askari. As a sample the editor selected these lines from "Mother" by Janet McCann:

> In "Calling Your Name," you call out your own name, then wait a minute, then call again. Then you
>   wait a half a minute and call. Then a quarter of a minute. You continue this until you find yourself
>   calling your name out twice at once.

Knocked is 48 pgs., digest-sized, saddle-stapled with glossy card cover and professional cover art. They receive about 2,000 poems a year, accept approximately 2-3%. Press run is 300 for 80 subscribers of which 5 are libraries; many distributed free as "random acts of artistic kindness." Subscription: $8. **Sample postpaid: $4. Make** checks payable to Eric Behrens. Submit 3-6 poems at a time. No previously published poems; simultaneous submissions OK. Cover letter preferred. "In cover letter, we care more about personal history than we do about previous credits. We don't print bios, so poets needn't go to the trouble of writing them for us." Time between acceptance and publication is 2-7 months. **Often comments on rejections. Send SASE for guidelines. Reports in 1-12 weeks. Pays subscription. Acquires serial rights for print and electronic editions. "We request authors note source with future publication."** The editor says, "We're looking for those writers of uncommon style, not bogged down by heady, ethereal notions of poetry who can, on the first reading, make us squeal in literary delight."

ALFRED A. KNOPF (V), 201 E. 50th St., New York NY 10022, poetry editor Harry Ford. Over the years Knopf has been one of the most important and distinguished publishers of poetry in the United States. **"The list is closed to new submissions at this time."**

KONOCTI BOOKS (V), 23311 County Rd. 88, Winters CA 95694, phone (916)662-3364, founded 1973, editor/publisher Noel Peattie, **publishes poetry by invitation only.**

*KRAX (II, IV-Humor), 63 Dixon Lane, Leeds, Yorkshire LS12 4RR England, founded 1971, poetry editors Andy Robson et al. *Krax* appears twice yearly, and publishes contemporary poetry from Britain and America. They want poetry which is **"light-hearted and witty; original ideas. Undesired: haiku, religious or topical politics." 2,000 words maximum. All forms and styles considered.** As a sample the editor selected these lines from ". . . ER . . ." by Dave Pruckner:

> *Then the tall blonde said 'I'm sorry,'*
> *And flashed her eyes of blue*
> *'You're right—you're not who I thought you were*
> *He was much better looking than you.'*

Krax is 6×8, 48 pgs. of which 30 are poetry, saddle-stapled, offset with b&w cartoons and graphics. They receive up to 1,000 submissions a year of which they use approximately 6%, have a 2- to 3-year backlog. Single copy: £2.25 ($4.50); subscription: £8 ($16). **Sample: $1 (75p). "Submit maximum of six pieces. Writer's name on same sheet as poem. SASE or SAE with IRC encouraged but not vital."** No previously published poems or simultaneous submissions. **Brief cover letter preferred. Reports within 2 months. Pays 1 copy.** Reviews books of poetry (brief, individual comments; no outside reviews). Send books for review consideration. During the 1996 Hastings National Poetry Festival, editor Andy Robson received an award for his service to poetry publishing. The editor says, "Before sending your poems, always add your address to the piece—we can't always place everyone's pseudonym."

KUMQUAT MERINGUE; PENUMBRA PRESS (I, II), P.O. Box 736, Pine Island MN 55963, phone (507)367-4430, e-mail moodyriver@aol.com, founded 1990, editor Christian Nelson, appears approximately 2 times/year using **"mostly shorter poetry about the small details of life, especially the quirky side of love and sex. We want those things other magazines find just too quirky. Not interested in rhyming, meaning of life or high-flown poetry."** They have published works by Gina Bergamino, T. Kilgore Splake, Antler, Monica Kershner, Lynne Douglass and Ianthe Brautigan. As a sample the editor selected these lines from "Leaping Lizards" by Emile Luria:

> *After we made love . . . Kate said,*
> *"You're so weird, really,*
> *Even weirder than I thought."*
> *And I thought, could she taste the salt,*
> *Feel the sea lapping on my back?*
> *I went to sleep wondering*
> *About dinosaurs and lungfish*
> *And the deepest reaches of the sea*

KM is 40-48 pgs., digest-sized, "professionally designed with professional typography and nicely printed." Press run is 600 for 250 subscribers. Subscription: $8/3 issues. **Sample postpaid: $4. "We like cover letters but prefer to read things about who you are, rather than your long list of publishing credits. Previously published and simultaneous submissions are OK, but please let us know."** Often comments on submissions. **"Please don't forget your SASE or you'll never hear back from us. E-mail address is only for those who want to say 'Hi.' " Send SASE for guidelines. Usually reports in 2 months. Pays 1 copy. Acquires one-time rights.** The magazine is "dedicated to the memory of Richard Brautigan." The editor advises, "Read *Kumquat Meringue* and anything by Richard Brautigan to get a feel for what we want, but don't copy Richard Brautigan, and don't copy those who have copied him. We just want that same feel. We also have a definite weakness for poems written 'to' or 'for' Richard Brautigan. Reviewers have called our publication iconoclastic, post-hip, post-beat, post-antipostmodern; and our poetry, carefully crafted imagery. When you get discouraged, write some more. Don't give up. Eventually your poems will find a home. We're very open to unpublished writers, and a high percentage of our writers had never been published anywhere before they submitted here."

KUUMBA (IV-Ethnic, gay/lesbian, love/romance/erotica), Box 83912, Los Angeles CA 90083-0912, phone (310)410-0808, fax (310)410-9250, e-mail newsroom@blk.com, website http://www.blk.com/blk, founded

1991, editor Mark Haile, is a biannual poetry journal of the black lesbian and gay community. **They want subject matter related to black lesbian and gay concerns.** "Among the experiences of interest are: coming out, interacting with family and/or community, substance abuse, political activism, oral histories, AIDS and intimate relationships." **They do not want to see "gay-only subjects that have no black content, or black-only subjects with no gay content."** They have published poetry by David Frechette, Assotto Saint, Sabrina Sojourner and Eric S. Booth. As a sample we selected these lines from "The Sweetest Taboo" (for Gene) by Richard D. Gore:

> Forbidden,
> But I loved you anyway
> Dark, smouldering, and sweet
> Luminous Black skin and Sloe-eyes. . .

Kuumba is 48 pgs., 8½ × 11, offset and saddle-stitched, with b&w cover drawing and ads. They receive approximately 500 poems a year, accept approximately 25%. Press run is 3,000 for 750 subscribers of which 25 are libraries, 2,000 shelf sales. Subscription: $7.50/year. **Sample postpaid: $4.50. Make checks payable to BLK Publishing Company. Submit 3 poems at a time. No previously published poems; simultaneous submissions OK, if notified. Cover letter preferred. Electronic submissions OK. Seldom comments on rejections. Send SASE for guidelines or obtain via e-mail or website. Reports in 6 weeks. Pays 5 copies. Acquires first North American serial rights and right to anthologize.** The editors add, "Named for one of the Nguzo Saba (Seven Principles) which are celebrated at Kwanzaa, Kuumba means creativity." This poetry journal is not only dedicated to the celebration of the lives and experiences of black lesbians and gay men, but it is also intended to encourage new and experienced writers to develop their poetic craft.

‡LA PIERNA TIERNA (I), P.O. Box 100, Shartlesville PA 19554, phone (610)488-6894, founded 1992, submissions editor Mary M. Towne, published bimonthly, features "poetry with annotation by staff." **They want "any poetry, 24 lines maximum (query for longer)." They do not want "smut, cruelty to identifiable groups or persons."** They have recently published poetry by Patricia Prime, John Binns, Gary Allen and Ram Krishna Singh. As a sample the editor selected these lines from "Fra Serra" by Dorotéo Estrago:

> Fra Serra rings the bell
> Bronze and polished Jesus-gong.
> We go in now, to thank
> His new God with all the Magic.
> We starve? It makes us strong.
> Strong, but God, how long?

La Pierna Tierna is 48 pgs., digest-sized, photocopied, saddle-stitched, with light card cover. They receive about 600 poems a year, accept approximately 40%. Press run is 40 for 25 subscribers. Subscriptions: $18. **Sample postpaid: $2. Make checks payable to L.D. Emery. Submit any number of poems at a time "single spaced and both sides of sheet if legible (use scanning where possible)." Previously published poems and simultaneous submissions OK. Cover letter preferred.** Time between acceptance and publication is 3-6 months. **Poems are circulated to an editorial board. "All members of staff (three) read and sort by quality—roundtable selects from top of piles for paste-up." Always comments on rejections. Send SASE for guidelines. Reports in 1 month. Pays 1 copy. Acquires one-time rights.**

LACTUCA (II, IV-Translations), 159 Jewett Ave., Jersey City NJ 07304-2003, phone/fax (201)451-5411, e-mail lactuca@mindspring.com, founded 1986, editor/publisher Mike Selender, usually appears 0-3 times a year. **"Our bias is toward work with a strong sense of place, a strong sense of experience, a quiet dignity and an honest emotional depth. Dark and disturbing writings are preferred over safer material. No haiku, poems about writing poems, poems using the poem as an image, light poems or self-indulgent poems. Readability is crucial. We publish poetry that readily transposes between the spoken word and printed page. First English language translations are welcome provided that the translator has obtained the approval of the author."** They have published poetry by Sherman Alexie, Joe Cardillo, Christy Beatty and Kathleen ten Haken. *Lactuca* is 72 pgs., digest-sized, saddle-stapled, laser printed or offset on 24 lb. bond with matte card cover, no ads. They receive "a few thousand poems a year of which less than 5% are accepted." Circulation 500 for 100 subscribers, 200 store sales. Subscription: $10/3 issues, $17/6 issues. **Sample postpaid: $4. "We plan to resume publication the second half of 1998 as an annual with a new format (200 pgs., perfect-bound). We are not accepting new material until late 1998. Query before submitting work to find out if we're accepting new submissions." Queries accepted via e-mail. Submit 4-5 poems at a time. "We do not print previously published material nor do we accept simultaneous submissions. We comment on rejections when we can. However the volume of mail we receive limits this." Reports within 3 months, "usually within one." Always sends prepublication galleys. Pays 2-5 copies "depending on length." Acquires first rights.** Reviews books of poetry. Open to unsolicited reviews. Poets may also send books for review consideration. He says, "The purpose of *Lactuca* is to be a small literary magazine publishing high-quality poetry, fiction and b&w drawings. Much of our circulation goes to contributors' copies and exchange copies with other literary magazines. *Lactuca* is not for poets expecting large circulation. Poets appearing here will find themselves in the company of other good writers."

LACUNAE MAGAZINE (I), P.O. Box 827, Clifton Park NY 12065, e-mail lacunaemag@aol.com, website http://www.loginet.com/cfd/lacunae.htm, founded 1994, editor Pamela Hazelton, is a bimonthly featuring comics, fiction, poetry, music, reviews and interviews. "*Lacunae* is *the* showplace to feature independent talent." The magazine's content is aimed at **"mature audiences" and ranges from humor to horror to science fiction to crime. They do not want romance.** They have published poetry by Hart D. Fisher, Jaime Hill, James Russell and Sean Kelley McKeever. *Lacunae* is 48 pgs., 6¾×10¼, professionally printed and saddle-stapled with full-color glossy cover and b&w art inside. They receive 100-200 poems a year, accept approximately 20-30%. Press run is about 5,000 for 50 subscribers, approximately 3,000 shelf sales. Single copy: $2.50; subscription: $14/year. **Sample postpaid: $3.25. Submit up to 10 poems at a time. Previously published poems and simultaneous submissions OK. Cover letter required. E-mail submissions OK.** Time between acceptance and publication is 1-4 months. **Poems are circulated to an editorial board. Always comments on rejections. Publishes theme issues. Send SASE for guidelines and upcoming themes or request via e-mail. Reports in 2-6 weeks. Pays 5-15 copies.** Reviews books of poetry. Open to unsolicited reviews. Poets may also send books for review consideration to Attn: Reviews. "Include price and address [with review copy] for ordering direct." Sponsors contest. Send SASE for details.

LAKE SHORE PUBLISHING; SOUNDINGS (I, IV-Anthology), 373 Ramsay Rd., Deerfield IL 60015, phone (847)945-4324, founded 1983, poetry editor Carol Spelius, is an effort "to put out decent, economical volumes of poetry." **Reading fee: $1/page. They want poetry which is "understandable and *moving*, imaginative with a unique view, in any form. Make me laugh or cry or think. I'm not so keen on gutter language or political dogma—but I try to keep an open mind. No limitations in length."** They have published poetry by Bob Mills, Constance Vogel and Dona Goldman. The editor selected these sample lines from "Slow Miracle" by Christine Swanberg:

> There were times when walking here
> would not have been enough, times
> my restless spirit needed an ocean,
> not this river, serene and simple.

The first 253-page anthology, including over 100 poets, is a paperback, at $7.95 (add $1 p&h), which was published (in 1985) in an edition of 2,000. It is flat-spined, photocopied from typescript, with glossy, colored card cover with art. **Submit 5 poems at a time, with $1/page reading fee, and a cover letter telling about your other publications, biographical background, personal or aesthetic philosophy, poetic goals and principles. Simultaneous submissions OK. Any form or length. "Reads submissions anytime, but best in fall." Send SASE for upcoming themes. Reports in 1 year. Pays 1 copy and half-price for additional copies. "All rights return to poet after first printing."** The editor will read chapbooks, or full-length collections, with the possibility of sharing costs if Lake Shore Publishing likes the book ($1/page reading fee). "I split the cost if I like the book." **Sample copy of anthology or random choice of full-length collections to interested poets: $5.**

THE LAMP-POST (I, II, IV-Religious, form/style), 29562 Westmont Court, San Juan Capistrano CA 92675-1221, fax (714)364-7009, e-mail lamppost@ix.netcom.com, founded 1977, senior editor James Prothero, is the quarterly publication of the Southern California C.S. Lewis Society and "echoes his thoughts in scholarly essays, informal essays, fiction and poetry as well as reviews. **We look for (1) formal, (2) literary quality poetry with (3) an orthodox Christian slant. Will look at free verse, but prefer formal."** They have published poetry by John Brugaletta, Paul Willis and Joe Christopher. As a sample the editor selected these lines from "Aesthete's Dictum" by David Drake:

> The beauties most enjoyed are those
> That offer some resistance;
> God placed the thorn upon the rose
> To keep us at a distance.

The Lamp-Post is 40 pgs., digest-sized, professionally printed and saddle-stapled with card cover and b&w line drawings. They receive 100 poems a year, use about 20. Press run is 300 for 250 subscribers of which 5 are libraries. Subscription: $12, $8 students, seniors and libraries. **Sample postpaid: $3. For subscriptions and sample back issues, write to Edie Dougherty, managing editor/secretary, 1212 W. 162nd St., Gardena CA 90247. Previously published poems accepted "cautiously." No simultaneous submissions. E-mail submissions OK; "if sending long ms, also mail hard copy." Cover letter not required, "but we like them." No SASE, no reply.** Time between acceptance and publication is about 1 year. **Sometimes comments on rejections. Send SASE for guidelines. Reports in 6-8 weeks. Pays 3 copies. Acquires first serial or reprint rights.** Reviews books of poetry "if the poet is a Lewis scholar or the poetry has some connection to C.S. Lewis." Open to unsolicited reviews. Poets may also send books for review consideration and scholarly articles to M.J. Logsdon, 2294 N. Main St., Salinas CA 93905. The editor says, "We exist to echo the thought of C.S. Lewis in contemporary writing. Quality, literary poetry only, please. Read John Donne, George Herbert, Gerard Manley Hopkins and Francis Thompson and give us that sort of formal, literary and Christian quality—**no 'inspirational' please;** inspire us with quality and depth."

*LANDFALL: NEW ZEALAND ARTS AND LETTERS (IV-Regional), University of Otago Press, P.O. Box 56, Dunedin, New Zealand, phone 0064 3 479 8807, fax 0064 3 479 8385, founded 1947, originally published by Caxton Press, then by Oxford University Press, now published by University of Otago Press, appears twice a year (in May and November). They say, "Apart from occasional commissioned features on aspects of international literature, *Landfall* focuses primarily on **New Zealand literature and arts.** It publishes new fiction, poetry, commentary, and interviews with New Zealand artists and writers, and reviews of New Zealand books." Subscription: \$39.95 NZ for 2 issues for New Zealand subscribers, \$30 A for Australian subscribers, \$30 US for other overseas subscribers. **Pays (for poetry) \$15 NZ/printed page and 1 copy. New Zealand poets should write for further information.**

PETER LANG PUBLISHING, INC. (IV-Translations), 275 Seventh Ave., 28th Floor, New York NY 10001, phone (212)647-7700, fax (212)647-7707, editor Owen Lancer, publishes primarily scholarly monographs in the humanities and social sciences. List includes **critical editions of great poets of the past. Submit descriptive cover letter and *curriculum vita.* Accepts no original poetry.**

‡VINCENT LASPINA; BATH AVENUE REVIEW; ONE CENT STAMP REVIEW; PATRICK HENRY NEWSLETTER (I, II), 1980 65th St., 3D, Brooklyn NY 11204, e-mail laspina@msn.com, founded 1986, director of publications Rhett Moran. *Bath Avenue Review* published monthly, *One Cent Stamp Review* published quarterly and *Patrick Henry Newsletter* published 3 times/year, feature "the best work we receive." **They want "any style, any length poetry."** They have recently published poetry by Wanda Coleman, Robert Peters, Peter Wild and Rhett Moran. The editor says, *BAR, OCSR* and *PHN* are 24-32 pgs., 8½ × 11, offset printed with art, graphics and ads. They receive about 1,000 poems a year, accept approximately 10%. Press run is 2,500 for 500 subscribers of which 200 are libraries; 1,000 distributed free to neighborhoods in New York City. Single copy: \$2.95; subscription: \$24. **Sample postpaid: \$3.73. Make checks payable to Vincent LaSpina. Submit up to 5 poems at a time. No previously published poems; simultaneous submissions OK. Cover letter preferred with short bio and recent publications.** Time between acceptance and publication is 1-12 weeks. **"Rhett Moran is the final editor. Others read and comment." Seldom comments on rejections. Send SASE for guidelines. Reports in 1-12 weeks. Pays 2-5 copies. Acquires first rights.** Reviews books of poetry in 200-1,000 words. Open to unsolicited reviews. Poets may also send books for review consideration to Rhett Moran ℅ Vincent LaSpina. Vincent LaSpina, publisher of "individual voices who've obviously experienced life," publishes **10 chapbooks/year.** Chapbooks are usually 24-36 pgs., offset printed, saddle-stapled. **Replies to queries in 1-8 weeks, to mss in 1-12 weeks. Pays 10% author's copies (out of a press run of 26-50).** "We offer publishing services separately from our publishing program." **Obtain sample chapbooks by sending \$5.** "We also provide printing services, typesetting services and distribution and publishing advice for self-publishers on a fee basis. We do not subsidy publish." The editor advises, "read, write, experience, submit."

‡LAUGHING BOY REVIEW (II), 910 Minnesota Ave., South Milwaukee WI 53172, phone (414)764-8081, founded 1996, editor Nikki Morawski, appears 3-4 times/year. "An all poetry magazine whose purpose is to publish poetry of interest to all kinds of people." **They want "all kinds of poetry; prefer shorter poems but will not reject others solely on length." No greeting card rhyme.** They have recently published poetry by Sherman Alexie, James Liddy, Susan Firer and Lyn Lifshin. *LBR* is 35-40 pgs., digest-sized, photocopied and saddle-stitched, card stock cover with original artwork, no ads. Press run is 200, 50 shelf sales; 50 distributed free to people in the poetry community. Subscription: \$12/4 issues. **Sample postpaid: \$3. Submit 3 poems at a time. No previously published poems; simultaneous submissions OK if noted. Cover letter preferred.** Time between acceptance and publication is 1-5 months. **Seldom comments on rejections. Send SASE for guidelines. Reports in 1-2 weeks. Pays 2 copies. Acquires first rights.** The editor says, "*Laughing Boy* is committed to publishing quality poetry by unknown poets as well as the well-known."

THE LAUREATE LETTER; WRITERS GAZETTE (I), 899 Williamson Trail, Eclectic AL 36024-6131, e-mail bren666@aol.com, founded 1993, editor Brenda Williamson. *The Laureate Letter* is a sporadically published newsletter open to submissions of poetry. **They want "simple, easy-to-understand poems which stretch the mind to remember their lives, the hopes of others and the dreams that exist amongst us. Any form, but prefer titled, 20 lines maximum. No jibberish or extremely mushy garbage."** As a sample the editor selected the poem "Spider," by Kimberly L. Coulter:

> *A spider is like a nightmare*
> *crawling into your mind in the dark of night*
> *tickling your senses*
> *Like a memory you are scared of*
> *And try to kill.*

LL is one 8½ × 11 colored sheet, printed on both sides. They receive 1,500-2,000 poems a year, accept 25%. Press run is 250. Single copy: \$2. **Sample postpaid: \$2 plus #10 SASE. Submit 3 poems at a time. Previously published poems and simultaneous submissions OK.** "No e-mail submissions are accepted for this publication." Time between acceptance and publication is 1-2 months. **Send SASE for guidelines. Reports in 1-4 weeks "most of the time." No pay in cash or copies, but no fee required for publication. Acquires one-time rights.** They also publish *Writers Gazette.* Founded in 1980, the publication appears 4 times/year and is designed "for writers, by writers, about writing." It includes poetry, fiction, nonfiction, art, cartoons, occasional photos, market listings, contest information and news on related writing subjects. **They want poems of "any style, subject or length, but prefer short verses of under 24 lines. Always looking for shorter poems of 4-12 lines. New writers are always encouraged and regularly published, even children."** They have published poetry by Carl Dietrich, Ann Boger and Denise Clinton. As a sample the editor selected these lines from "Reflection" by Paul Devine:

> . . . *I stare at the crack in the mirror*
> *distorting the true reflection*
> *I've been looking for all my life.*

WG is approximately 12 pgs., 8½ × 11, corner stapled, with some ads. They receive 1,200 poems a year, accept 10%. Press run is 500 for 250 subscribers. Subscription: $15. **Sample postpaid: $4. Previously published poems and simultaneous submissions OK. E-mail submissions OK, "but remember to include your real name and mailing address." Seldom comments on rejections. Send SASE for guidelines. Reports in 1-2 months. No pay in cash or copies. Acquires one-time rights.** Reviews books and chapbooks of poetry. Poets may also send books for review consideration. The editor says, "I read everything that crosses my desk and reply as soon as possible. Be creative and unusual. Don't query—send entire manuscripts. Also, we check for SASE before ever considering poems. If authors cannot consider sending SASE, we cannot consider their work."

LAUREL REVIEW (III); GREENTOWER PRESS, Dept. of English, Northwest Missouri State University, Maryville MO 64468, phone (816)562-1265, founded 1960, co-editors William Trowbridge, David Slater and Beth Richards. *LR* is a literary journal appearing twice a year using **"poetry fiction, and creative nonfiction of the highest literary quality."** They have published poetry by Patricia Goedicke, Paul Zimmer, Miller Williams, Albert Goldbarth, David Citino and Nancy Willard. As a sample the editors selected these lines from "Wheel" by Jim Simmerman:

> *Don't fall in love before you've made the wheel*
> *your study. See how it crushes and churns*
> *unsullied on to the next disaster.*
> *See how it burns like the hoop an animal*
> *learns to leap through for its supper. Study*
> *the heart and its demolition derby.*

This handsome journal (128 pgs., 6 × 9) features excellent poems—usually more than 20 each issue—in all styles and forms. Press run is 900 for 400 subscribers of which 53 are libraries, 100 shelf sales. Subscription: $8/year. **Sample postpaid: $5. Submit 4 poems at a time. No previously published poems or simultaneous submissions. Reads submissions September 1 through May 31 only. Editor "does not usually" comment on submissions. Reports in 1 week to 4 months. Always sends prepublication galleys. Pays 2 copies plus 1-year subscription.** Rights revert to author upon publication.

‡LAURELS; WEST VIRGINIA POETRY SOCIETY (I, IV-Membership), Rt. 2, Box 13, Ripley WV 25271, e-mail mbush814@aol.com, founded 1996, editor Jim Bush, is the quarterly journal of the West Virginia Poetry Society containing 95% poetry/5% art. **Only considers work from WVPS members. They want traditional forms and good free verse. "If it's over 100 lines it must be very, very good. No porn, foul language, shape poems; no 'broken prose.' "** They have recently published poetry by Amy Jo Schoonover, Ida Fasel and June Gilbaugh. The editor says *Laurels* is 40 pgs., digest-sized, photocopied and saddle-stapled with paper cover, some pen-and-ink art, no ads. They receive about 500 poems a year, accept approximately 50%. Press run is 200 for 150 subscribers. Subscription: $10. **Sample postpaid: $4. Make checks payable to the West Virginia Poetry Society for a subscription, to Jim Bush for a sample. Requires contributors be members. For membership in WVPS, send $10 to Larry Bloomfield, 617-A Boggs Hollow Rd., Benwood WV 26031. Submit 4-5 poems at a time. Previously published poems and simultaneous submissions OK. Cover letter preferred including brief bio. E-mail submissions OK.** Time between acceptance and publication is 3-12 months. **Always comments on rejections. Send SASE for guidelines. Reports "next day, usually." Sometimes sends prepublication galleys. Pays 1 copy. Acquires one-time rights.** Staff briefly reviews 3-4 books a year if author is a member. Poets may also send books for review consideration. Sponsors a 35-category annual contest for members. The editor says, "Our purpose is to encourage and aid amature poets who believe that words can be used to communicate meaning and to create beauty."

THE LEDGE (II), 78-08 83rd St., Glendale NY 11385, founded 1988, editor-in-chief/publisher Timothy Monaghan, co-editors George Held and Laura M. Corrado. **"We publish the best poems we receive. No biases.**

THE GEOGRAPHICAL INDEX, located before the Subject Index, can help you discover the publishers in your region. Publishers often favor poets (and work) from their own areas.

Excellence is the only criterion." Recent contributors include Sherman Alexie, Terri Brown-Davidson, David Kirby, Kevin Pilkington and Vivian Shipley. As a sample the editor-in-chief selected these lines from "Crossed Lines" by Elton Glaser:

> *If you were at hand, and the night warm,*
> *And all the crossed lines clear,*
> *Would we undo Newton and confuse the physical,*
>
> *Proving that two bodies can enclose*
> *The same space at the same time, . . .*

The Ledge is 160 pgs., digest-sized, typeset and perfect-bound with b&w glossy cover. They accept 5% of poetry submissions. Circulation is 1,000, including 400 subscribers. Subscription: $12/2 issues, $22/4 issues or $30/6 issues. **Current issue postpaid: $7. Submit 3-6 poems at a time. No previously published work. Simultaneous submissions OK. Do not submit mss in July or August. "Submissions received during those months will be returned unread." Reports in 3 months. Pays 2 copies. Acquires one-time rights.** *The Ledge* sponsors an annual poetry chapbook contest, as well as an annual poetry contest. Send SASE for details. Timothy Monaghan says: "I believe the strongest poems appeal to the widest audience and consider *The Ledge* a truly democratic publication in that regard."

LEFT CURVE (II, IV-Social issues), P.O. Box 472, Oakland CA 94604-0472, phone (510)763-7193, e-mail leftcurv@wco.com, website http://www.wco.com/~leftcurv, founded 1974, editor Csaba Polony, appears "irregularly, about every ten months." **They want poetry that is "critical culture, social, political, 'post-modern,' not purely formal, too self-centered, poetry that doesn't address in sufficient depth today's problems."** They have recently published poetry by Devorah Major, W.K. Buckley and Seamus Carraher. As a sample the editor selected these lines by Christos Tsiokas:

> *The great God money has dominion all over this globe. West, East. North,*
> *South. Air, fire, water, earth. I could walk this planet, roam the last desert,*
> *sail the lost sea searching for my Authentic Man. And find instead*
> *Only Narcissus gazing into my reflection.*

Left Curve is 136 pgs., 8½×11, offset, perfect-bound with Durosheen cover, photos and ads. Press run is 2,000 for 200 subscribers of which 50 are libraries, 1,500 shelf sales. Subscription: $25/3 issues (individuals). **Sample postpaid: $8. Submit up to 5 poems at a time. Cover letter stating "why you are submitting" required. Publishes theme issues. Send SASE for guidelines and upcoming themes. Reports in 3-6 months. Pays 3 copies.** Open to unsolicited reviews. Poets may also send books for review consideration.

LIBERTY HILL POETRY REVIEW (II), P.O. Box 426967, San Francisco CA 94142-6967, founded 1994, editor Ken Butler, is a biannual designed to publish local and national poets, both experienced writers and talented newcomers. **They want "well-crafted free verse which exhibits a thorough knowledge of and love for language and content. Poetry that is carefully thought-out with proper punctuation, spelling and grammar. No subject matter is taboo, except those which promote racism, homophobia, and the humiliation of any race, gender or orientation. No prose poetry, no haiku; visual and verbal gymnastics are discouraged."** They have recently published poetry by Simon Perchik, Eileen Tabios, Walter McDonald, Mark Halperin, Barbara F. Lefcowitz and Robert Cooperman. As a sample the editor selected these lines from "The Cremation" by Sarah Sorenson:

> *the moon moves over you in vicious cycles.*
> *you're luna, in the tide, filled with sand dollars*
> *and bug eyed jellyfish. some half dead, legs ripped*
> *by undertow, still flopping and stinging.*

LHPR is 56-60 pgs., digest-sized, attractively designed, saddle-stapled with matte card stock cover featuring original art. They receive about 3,100 poems a year, accept 80. Press run is 250. Single copy: $4; subscription: $7. **Sample postpaid: $3. Submit up to 5 typed poems of no more than 60 lines each in length. Include name and address on each page. SASE required. Simultaneous submissions OK if noted. No previously published poems. Cover letter encouraged. Reads submissions July through August (for Fall/Winter issue) and January through February (for Spring/Summer issue). Often comments on rejections. Send SASE for guidelines. Reports in 2-8 weeks. Pays 2 copies. Acquires one-time rights.** The editor says, "Above all, please support your local small presses and readings. Read as much poetry as you write. And always read a copy of the magazine to which you are submitting."

LIBIDO: THE JOURNAL OF SEX AND SEXUALITY (II, IV-Erotica, humor, gay/lesbian/bisexual), P.O. Box 146721, Chicago IL 60614-6721, phone (773)275-0842, fax (773)275-0752, e-mail rune@mcs.com, website http://www.indrd.com/libido, founded 1988, editors Marianna Beck and Jack Hafferkamp, is published 6 times/year. **"Form, length and style are open. We want poetry of any and all styles as long as it is erotic and/or erotically humorous. We make a distinction between erotica and pornography. We want wit, not dirty words."** They have published poetry by Stuart Silverman, Alan Isler, Lani Kaahumanu, Anne MacNaughton, Chocolate Waters, Robert Perchan, Bruce Lennard and Bill Vickers. *Libido* is 88 pgs., digest-sized, professionally printed, flat-spined, with 2-color varnished card cover. They accept about 5% of poetry received. Press

A biannual published in San Francisco, **Liberty Hill Poetry Review** is flourishing in its fifth year of publication. And Ken Butler, the editor and publisher of the poetry-only review, enthusiastically showcases the work of local and national poets, new talents and experienced writers. Since **LHPR**'s first issue in the fall of 1994, Butler has read over 5,000 poems and, yet, still encourages new contributors and subscribers. Of the cover of his latest issue, Butler says, "I like its simple beauty and grace and the way the figure interacts with the magazine's new logo. The cover represents joy, grace, and balance—the poetry I choose is always a joy to read and represents a diverse and balanced selection of talented poets." Cover illustrator Cea Korb teaches special education in Minneapolis, Minnesota.

run is 9,500 for 3,500 subscribers, 3,500 shelf sales and 1,500 single issues by mail. Subscription: $30 in US, $40 in Canada and Mexico (US funds), $50 in Europe and $60 elsewhere. **Sample postpaid: $8. Submit 2-3 poems at a time. Cover letter including "a one-sentence bio for contributors' page" required with submission. "Please, no handwritten mss and do not submit via fax or e-mail." Reports in 4-6 months. Pays $0-25 plus 2 copies.** Send books for review consideration "only if the primary focus is love/eroticism."

LIBRA PUBLISHERS, INC. (I), 3089C Clairemont Dr., Suite 383, San Diego CA 92117, phone/fax (619)571-1414, poetry editor William Kroll, publishes two professional journals, *Adolescence* and *Family Therapy*, plus books, primarily in the behaviorial sciences but also some general nonfiction, fiction and poetry. "At first we published books of poetry on a standard royalty basis, paying 10% of the retail price to the authors. Although at times we were successful in selling enough copies to at least break even, we found that we could no longer afford to publish poetry on this basis. Now, unless we fall madly in love with a particular collection, **we offer professional services to assist the author in self-publishing."** They have published books of poetry by Martin Rosner, William Blackwell, John Travers Moore and C. Margaret Hall. **Prefers complete ms but accepts query with 6 sample poems, publishing credits and bio. Replies to query in 2 days; to submissions in 2-3 weeks. Mss should be double-spaced. Sometimes sends prepublication galleys. Send 9×12 SASE for catalog. Sample books may be purchased on a returnable basis.**

THE LICKING RIVER REVIEW (II), Dept. of Literature and Language, Northern Kentucky University, Highland Heights KY 41099, faculty editor Phil Paradis, general editor Charles Wheatley, poetry editor Wendy Elam, founded 1991, is an annual designed "to showcase the best writing by Northern Kentucky University students alongside work by new or established writers from the region or elsewhere." **They have no specifications regarding form, subject matter or style of poetry. "No long poems (maximum 60 lines)."** They have published poetry by Ron Wallace, Jim Barnes, Ann Struthers, Jack Meyers, Allison Joseph and William Greenway. The review is 96 pgs., 7×10, offset on recycled paper and perfect-bound with a 16-page artwork inset (all art solicited). They accept 5% of the poetry received. Press run is 1,500. **Sample postpaid: $5. Submit up to 4 poems at a time. No previously published poems or simultaneous submissions. Reads submissions September through January only. Poems are circulated to an editorial board. Reports in up to 6 months. Pays in copies. Rights revert to author. Requests acknowledgment if poem is later reprinted.**

‡LIFTOUTS MAGAZINE; PRELUDIUM PUBLISHERS (V), Dept. PM, 1414 S. Third St., Suite 102, Minneapolis MN 55454, fax (612)305-0655, founded 1971, poetry editor Barry Casselman, is a "publisher of **experimental literary work and work of new writers in translation from other languages." Currently not accepting unsolicited material.** *Liftouts* appears irregularly. It is 5½×8, offset, 50-150 pgs. Press run is 1,000. Reviews books of poetry.

LIGHT (II), Box 7500, Chicago IL 60680, founded 1992, editor John Mella, is a quarterly of **"light and occasional verse, satire, wordplay, puzzles, cartoons and line art."** They do not want "greeting card verse, cloying or sentimental verse." The editor says *Light* is 32 pgs., stapled, including art and graphics. Single copy: $5; subscription: $16. **Sample postpaid: $4. Submit 1 poem on a page with name, address, poem title and page number on each page. No previously published poems or simultaneous submissions. Seldom comments on rejections. Publishes theme issues. Send #10 SASE for guidelines and upcoming themes. Reports in 3 months or less. Always sends prepublication galleys. Pays 2 copies to domestic contributors, 1 copy to foreign contributors.** Open to unsolicited reviews; query first. Poets may also send books for review consideration.

LILITH MAGAZINE (IV-Women, ethnic), 250 W. 57th St., Suite 2432, New York NY 10107, phone (212)757-0818, fax (212)757-5705, e-mail lilithmag@aol.com, founded in 1976, editor-in-chief Susan Weidman Schneider, poetry editor Alicia Ostriker, "is an independent magazine with a Jewish feminist perspective" which uses **poetry by Jewish women "about the Jewish woman's experience. Generally we use short rather than long poems. Run four poems/year. Do not want to see poetry on other subjects."** They have published poetry by Irena Klepfisz, Lyn Lifshin, Yael Messinai, Sharon Neemani, Marcia Falk and Adrienne Rich. It is glossy, magazine-sized. "We use colors. Page count varies. Covers are very attractive and professional-looking (one has won an award). Generous amount of art. It appears 4 times a year, circulation about 10,000, about 6,000 subscriptions." Subscription: $18 for 4 issues. **Sample postpaid: $5. Send up to 3 poems at a time; advise if simultaneous submission. Editor "sometimes" comments on rejections. Send SASE for guidelines.** She advises: "(1) Read a copy of the publication before you submit your work. (2) Be realistic if you are a beginner. The competition is *severe*, so don't start to send out your work until you've written for a few years. (3) Short cover letters only. Copy should be neatly typed and proofread for typos and spelling errors."

LILLIPUT REVIEW (II, IV-Form), 282 Main St., Pittsburgh PA 15201-2807, founded 1989, editor Don Wentworth, is a tiny ($4\frac{1}{2} \times 3.6$ or $3\frac{1}{2} \times 4\frac{1}{4}$), 12- to 16-page magazine, appearing irregularly and **using poems in any style or form no longer than 10 lines.** They have published poetry by Albert Huffstickler, Lonnie Sherman, Lyn Lifshin and Jennifer Besemer. As a sample the editor selected these lines by Jack Greene:

> Flowers once bled from my hands;
> Now even the stems are gone

LR is laser-printed on colored paper and stapled. Press run is 250. **Sample: $1 or SASE. Make checks payable to Don Wentworth. Submit up to 3 poems at a time. Currently, every fourth issue is a broadside featuring the work of one particular poet. Send SASE for guidelines. Reports usually within 2 months. Pays 2 copies/poem. Acquires first rights. Editor comments on submissions "occasionally—always at least try to establish human contact."** He started the Modest Proposal Chapbook Series in 1994, publishing **1-2 chapbooks/year**, 18-24 pgs. in length. **Chapbook submissions are by invitation only. Query with standard SASE. Sample chapbook: $3.** Recent chapbook publications include *Getting Across* by David Chorlton. The editor says, "A note above my desk reads 'Clarity & resonance, not necessarily in that order.' The perfect little poem for *LR* is simple in style and language and elusive/allusive in meaning and philosophy. *LR* is open to all short poems in both approach and theme, including any of the short Eastern forms, traditional or otherwise."

‡LIME GREEN BULLDOZERS (I, IV-Themes), P.O. Box 4333, Austin TX 78765, e-mail oystapress@tab. com, founded 1986, an annual theme-based publication whose purpose is "to expose new, young writers and to communicate." **They want "anything honest and without pretense. No boring academic crap."** They have recently published poetry by Judson Crews, Lyn Lifshin, Edward Mycue and Alan Catlin. They say the format "depends on the number of submissions that make it in." Press run is 500 for 50 subscribers, 400 shelf sales. **Sample postpaid: $5. Make checks payable to Alaina Duro. "It is recommended that contributors purchase a sample copy before contributing." Submit 5 poems at a time. Previously published poems and simultaneous submissions OK. Cover letter preferred. Reads submissions November through January 1 only. Has a large backlog of work. Seldom comments on rejections. Publishes theme issues. Send SASE for upcoming themes. Obtain guidelines via e-mail. Reports "as soon as I can." Pays 1 copy. Acquires one-time rights.** They say, "I'm very choosy about what I include. I'm struggling to maintain a personal publication that has a 'community' feel to it. I can't stand getting an envelope full of poetry from someone who has no idea or care for what *Lime Green Bulldozers* is about."

LIMESTONE: A LITERARY JOURNAL (II), Dept. of English, 1215 Patterson Office Tower, University of Kentucky, Lexington KY 40506-0027, phone (606)257-7008, founded as *Fabbro* in 1979, as *Limestone* in 1986, editor Jennifer Stimson, is an annual seeking **"poetry that matters, poetry that shows attention to content and form. We're interested in all poetics, but we do watch for quality of thought and a use of language that will wake up readers and resonate in their minds."** They have published poetry by Wendell Berry, Guy Davenport, Michael Cadnum, Kelly Ellis and James Baker Hall. It is 6×9, perfect-bound, offset. They receive about 1,100 poems a year, use approximately 40-50. Press run is 300. **Sample postpaid: $3. Simultaneous submissions OK. Submit 1-10 pgs. at a time. Reports in 3-6 months. Pays 2 copies.** The editor advises, "If you're considering publication, work over your poems till you're sick of them."

LIMITED EDITIONS PRESS; ART: MAG (III), P.O. Box 70896, Las Vegas NV 89170, phone (702)734-8121, founded 1982, editor Peter Magliocco, "have become, due to economic and other factors, more limited to a select audience of poets as well as readers. We seek to expel the superficiality of our factitious culture, in all its drive-thru, junk-food-brain, commercial-ridden extravagance—and stylize a magazine of hard-line aesthetics, where truth and beauty meet on a vector not shallowly drawn. Conforming to this outlook is an operational policy of **seeking poetry from solicited poets primarily, though unsolicited submissions will be read, considered and perhaps used infrequently. Sought from the chosen is a creative use of poetic styles, systems and emotional morphologies other than banally constricting."** They have recently published poetry by David P. Kozinski, B. Chown, Laura Joy Lustig, Lyn Lifshin and John Grey. As a sample the editor selected these lines from "After the First Birth" by David Joseph Passey:

> This is not the girl who fished the crescent
> moon, casting toward the mystery of trout,
> speaking of the children in her blood, the bare
> springing wheat of them, the hunger
> and ache; neither is she the waking bride
> who spoke the slow stones of my name. . . .

ART: MAG, appearing in 1-2 large issues of 100 copies/year, is limited to a few poets. **Sample postpaid: $5 or more. Submit 5 poems at a time with SASE. "Submissions should be neat and use consistent style format (except experimental work). Cover letters are optional."** No previously published poems; simultaneous submissions OK. Sometimes comments on rejections. Publishes theme issues. Send SASE for guidelines and upcoming themes. Reports within 3 months. Pays 1 copy. Acquires first rights.** Staff occasionally reviews books of poetry. Send books for review consideration. The press also occasionally **publishes chapbooks** (such as *Neo-Runes*, by Alan Catlin). The editor says, "The mag is seeking a futuristic aestheticism where the barriers of fact and fiction meet, where inner- and outer-space converge in the realm of poetic consciousness in order to create a more productively viable relationship to the coming 'cyberology' of the 21st century."

LINCOLN SPRINGS PRESS (II), P.O. Box 269, Franklin Lakes NJ 07417, founded 1987, editor M. Gabrielle, publishes 1 paperback and 1 hardback book of poetry each year. They have published poetry by Maria Mazziotti Gillan, Justin Vitiello and Abigail Stone. **Query first with sample poems and cover letter with brief bio and publication credits. Send SASE for response. No previously published poems; simultaneous submissions OK. Accepts submissions October through April only. Seldom comments on rejections. Replies to queries in 2-4 weeks, to mss in 2-3 months. Always sends prepublication galleys. Pays 15% royalties.**

LINES N' RHYMES (I), 5604 Harmeson Dr., Anderson IN 46013, phone (765)642-1239, founded 1989, editor Pearl Clark, appears every other month using **"some 4-line poetry, most between 12-20 lines. I like poems concerning life, belief in God's guidance, especially seasonal/holiday poetry. Nothing pornographic or occult."** They have recently published poetry by Hugh Alexander, C. David Hay and Rosina Clifford. As a sample the editor selected these lines from "Exit" by Evalyn Torrant:

> Summer went so quickly
> I never saw her leave.
> She merely left her calling card
> And tugged upon my sleeve.

It is photocopied on 3 legal-sized colored sheets. Press run is 70, 3-5 shelf sales. Subscription: $7/6 issues. **Sample: $2. Submit 3 poems at a time. "A brief cover letter is OK but not essential. I receive 170 poems/ year—accept 70%. I pay nothing for poetry used. I award 'Editor's Choice' to two poets/issue at $2. I give preference to subscribers. However, I sometimes use poetry from non-subscribers." Previously published poems and simultaneous submissions OK.** Reviews books of poetry and comments in current issue. She holds a contest for limericks each September with 3 prizes of $5 each, open only to subscribers.

*LINES REVIEW (III, IV-Regional), Edgefield Rd., Loanhead, Edinburgh EH20 9SY Scotland, founded 1952 ("the oldest continuing Scottish literary magazine"), editor Tessa Ransford. *LR* is a quarterly that **gives priority to poets living in Scotland** and the editor says, "is generally receiving too much from elsewhere at present. **I like to accept from 4-6 poems in traditional page format, though with energy and intelligence in use of language, form and content. No unusual typography, concrete, sensation-seeking, nostalgic, dully descriptive or fanatically political poetry."** They have recently published poetry by Tom Leonard, Brian McCabe and WN Herbert. *LR* is known for well-written, thoughtful, lucid poetry that is intelligible to the educated reader. Press run is 750 for 500 subscribers of which 100 are libraries, 100 shelf sales. **Sample postpaid: £3 sterling. Submit 4-6 poems at a time. No previously published poems. Cover letter required; include information relevant to the work. "Double spacing helps, and clear indication whether a page break is or is not also a stanza break, and careful attention to punctuation—that it is as it will be printed." Reports in 2-3 weeks. Pays £10/page plus 1 copy.** Includes "good review section." *LR* often has special issues devoted, for example, to poetry from Glasgow, Japan, India and Italy. They also publish translations. Tessa Ransford is also director of Scottish Poetry Library (see listing under Organizations) and offers a School of Poets and Critical Service through the library.

LINGO: A LANGUAGE ART JOURNAL (I, IV-Form/style), 502 S. Laurel St., Richmond VA 23220, founded 1995, editor Kara J. West, is a quarterly publication of both language poetry and poetry about language.

"Our purpose is to take language to a point where it is broken and undeniably whole at the same time." **They want language-oriented, experimental work, "anything that challenges the conventional uses of language. No sentimental, rhyming, confessional poetry; no greeting card or light verse."** They have recently published poetry by Tod Thilleman. As a sample the editor selected these lines by Ethel Rackin:

> *The moon offers no despair except for that which I make*
> *up in order to move asterisk to center stage. Tell me a story.*
> *The light is fallen that way on its stubby sides flat*
> *on our play's purpose*

Lingo is 12-24 pgs., 8½ × 11 (folded lengthwise), photocopied and unbound with line drawings. To be distributed, the journal is folded down to 4 × 5½ and stapled. Press run is 500. Subscription: $6/year. **Sample postpaid: 2 first class stamps. Make checks payable to Kara J. West. Submit 2-4 poems at a time. Previously published poems and simultaneous submissions OK. Cover letter preferred. "Include a brief philosophy of poetry and language in cover letter." Often comments on rejections. Send SASE for guidelines. Reports in 1-3 months. Pays 3 copies. Acquires first and reprint rights.** Reviews books of language-oriented poetry. Open to unsolicited reviews. Poets may also send books for review consideration. Poetry published in *Lingo* has been included in *The Best American Poetry 1996*. The editor says, "*Lingo* is interested in de-solving language into art. Send us your visceral celebrations of language, your vivid exploitations."

*LINQ (II), c/o English Dept., James Cook University, Townsville, Queensland 4811 Australia, phone (077)815097 or (077)814451, fax (077)815655, e-mail jcu.linq@jcu.edu.au, founded 1971, administrator Tina Langford. *LiNQ* is a 100-page biannual that "aims to publish works of a high literary standard, encompassing a wide and varied range of interest." **They do not want to see "overtly naive and self-consciously subjective poetry."** They have published poetry by Mark O'Connor, Alison Croggon, Aileen Kelly, Eve Stafford and Rebecca Edwards. As a sample they selected these lines from "Sign Me In" by Peter Porter:

> *The private truth I kept within*
> *Grew as a cancer undisclosed,*
> *My books were bound in my dead skin,*
> *My patent brilliances opposed*
> *The ordinariness of life: I said*
> *I'll show up brighter when I'm dead.*

They receive about 250 poems a year, use approximately 20/edition. Press run is 350 for 160 subscribers of which 30 are libraries, 180 shelf sales. Single copy: $10 (within Australia), $15 (overseas); subscription: $20 individual (within Australia), $25 institution (within Australia), $30 overseas (for individual and institution). Since the journal is published in May and October, all subscriptions are due by November 1. **Sample back issue postpaid: $6 (Australian). Poems must be typed, 1 to a page, and contain title, page number and writer's name and address. No previously published poems; simultaneous submissions OK. Cover letter with brief bio required. Submissions via fax or e-mail OK. Submission deadlines: September 30 (May edition) and April 30 (October edition). Send SASE (or SAE and 3 IRCs) for return of work. Author retains copyright.** The editors say, "*LiNQ* aims for a broadly-based sympathetic approach to creative work, particularly from new and young Australian writers."

LINTEL (II), 24 Blake Lane, Middletown NY 10940, phone (212)674-4901, founded 1977, poetry editor Walter James Miller, who says, **"We publish poetry and innovative fiction of types ignored by commercial presses. We consider any poetry except conventional, traditional, cliché, greeting card types, i.e., we consider any artistic poetry."** They have published poetry by Sue Saniel Elkind, Samuel Exler, Adrienne Wolfert and Edmund Pennant. As a sample the editor selected these lines by Nathan Teitel:

> *loneliness*
> *is a Mexican earring*
> *and fear*
> *a crushed cigarette*

The book from which this was taken, *In Time of Tide*, is 64 pgs., digest-sized, professionally printed in bold type, flat-spined, hard cover stamped in gold, jacket with art and author's photo on back. Walter James Miller asks that you **query with 5 sample poems. Reads submissions January and August only. He replies to the query within a month, to the ms (if invited) in 2 months. "We consider simultaneous submissions if so marked and if the writer agrees to notify us of acceptance elsewhere." Ms should be typed. Always sends prepublication galleys. Pays royalties after all costs are met and 100 copies. Buys all rights. Offers usual subsidiary rights: 50%/50%. To see samples, send SASE for catalog and ask for "trial rate" (50%).** The

---

SENDING TO A COUNTRY other than your own? Be sure to send International Reply Coupons (IRCs) instead of stamps for replies or return of your manuscript.

editor says, "Form follows function! We accept any excellent poem whose form—be it sonnet or free verse—suits the content and the theme. We like our poets to have a good publishing record in literary magazines, before they begin to think of a book."

‡LIPS (III), Box 1345, Montclair NJ 07042, founded 1981, poetry editor Laura Boss, "is a quality poetry magazine that is published twice a year and takes pleasure in publishing previously unpublished poets as well as the most established voices in contemporary poetry. **We look for quality work: the strongest work of a poet; work that moves the reader; poems take risks that work. We prefer clarity in the work rather than the abstract. Poems longer than six pages present a space problem.**" They have published poetry by Michael Benedikt, Gregory Corso, Allen Ginsberg, Richard Kostelanetz, Lyn Lifshin, Theodore Weiss, Marge Piercy, Warren Woessner, Maria Gillan, Nicholas Christopher, Stanley Barkan, David Ignatow and Ishmael Reed. As a sample the editor selected these lines from "The Dark" by Ruth Stone:

> In the dark of the moon
> under the shadow of our local hydrogen fluff,
> I look out of my worn eyes
> and see the bright new Pleiades
> My sister lies in a box
> in a New England graveyard.

Lips is 70 pgs. (average), digest-sized, flat-spined. They receive about 8,000 submissions/year, use less than 1%, have a 6-month backlog. Circulation 1,000, 200 subscriptions, approximately 100 are libraries. **Sample postpaid: $6. Occasional double issues are $10. Poems should be submitted between September and March only, 6 pgs., typed, no query necessary. She tries to respond in 1 month but has gotten backlogged at times. Sometimes sends prepublication galleys. Pays 1 copy. Acquires first rights. Send SASE for guidelines.** Her advice to poets is, "Remember the 2 T's: Talent *and* Tenacity."

THE LISTENING EYE (II), Kent State Geauga Campus, 14111 Claridon-Troy Rd., Burton OH 44021, phone (216)286-3840, e-mail hy151@cleveland.freenet.edu, website http://www.geocites.com/Athens/3716, founded 1970 for student work, 1990 as national publication, editor Grace Butcher, is an annual publication of poetry, short fiction, creative nonfiction and art that welcomes both new and established poets and writers. **They want "high literary quality poetry. Prefer shorter poems (less than two pages) but will consider longer if space allows. Any subject, any style. No trite images or predictable rhyme."** They have published poetry by William Stafford, Walter McDonald, Timothy Russell, Ann Menebroker and John Knoepfle. As a sample the editor selected these lines from "Casualties" by Dean Blehert:

> Some conversations are like sending my best men
> on suicide missions.
>
> Afterwards I must write hurtful letters
> to their Greek, Latin, Sanskrit,
> Hebrew and Old English parents,
> and I just don't know what to say.

The Listening Eye is 52-60 pgs., 5½ × 8½, professionally printed and saddle-stapled with card stock cover with b&w art. They receive about 200 poems a year, accept approximately 5%. Press run is 300. Single copy: $4. **Sample postpaid: $4.50. Make checks payable to Kent State University. Submit up to 4 poems at a time with SASE for return of work. Previously published poems occasionally accepted; no simultaneous submissions. Cover letter preferred. Reads submissions January 1 through April 15 only.** Time between acceptance and publication is 4-6 months. **Poems are circulated to the editor and 2 assistant editors who read and evaluate work separately, then meet for final decisions. Occasionally comments on rejections. Send SASE for guidelines or obtain via e-mail or website. Reports in 3 months. Pays 2 copies. Acquires first or one-time rights.** Also awards $30 to the best sports poem. The editor says, "I look for tight lines that don't sound like prose, unexpected images or juxtapositions; the unusual use of language, noticeable relationships of sounds; a twist in viewpoint, an ordinary idea in extraordinary language, an amazing and complex idea simply stated, play on words and with words, an obvious love of language. Poets need to read the 'Big 3'—cummings, Thomas, Hopkins—to see the limits to which language can be taken. Then read the 'Big 2'—Dickinson to see how simultaneously tight, terse, and universal a poem can be, and Whitman to see how sprawling, cosmic and personal. Then read everything you can find that's being published in literary magazines today and see how your work compares to all of the above."

LITERAL LATTÉ; LITERAL LATTÉ POETRY AWARDS (II), 61 E. Eighth St., Suite 240, New York NY 10003, phone (212)260-5532, e-mail litlatté@aol.com, founded 1994, editor Jenine Gordon Bockman, is a bimonthly tabloid of "pure prose, poetry and art," distributed free in coffeehouses and bookstores in New York City, and by subscription. **They are "open to all styles of poetry—quality is the determining factor."** They have published poetry by Allen Ginsberg, Carol Muske and John Updike. As a sample we selected these lines from "O.R." by Roberta Swann:

> I watched a boy so pale he disappeared
> into the sandbox. His name was Alexander.

> He was the Sisyphus of kids, scooping
> up dirt, climbing out and over to a step,
> dumping and tamping it down, tumbling back
> into the box and starting again.

LL is 24-28 pgs., 11×17, neatly printed on newsprint and unbound with b&w art, graphics and ads. They receive about 3,000 poems a year, accept approximately 2%. Press run is 20,000 for distribution in over 200 bookstores and coffeehouses. Subscription: $15. **Sample postpaid: $5. No previously published poems; simultaneous submissions OK. Cover letter with bio and SASE required. E-mail submissions OK.** Time between acceptance and publication is 6 months. **Often comments on rejections. Send SASE for guidelines or request via e-mail. Reports in 2-3 months. Pays 10 copies and 3 subscriptions (2 gift subscriptions in author's name). All rights return to author upon publication.** They also sponsor the *Literal Latté* Poetry Awards, an annual contest for previously unpublished work. Entry fee: $10 for 3 poems (or buy a subscription and the entry fee for 3 poems is included). A past contest was judged by Carol Muske and offered $500 in awards, and publication. Send SASE for current details.

‡LITERARY FOCUS POETRY PUBLICATIONS; ANTHOLOGY OF CONTEMPORARY POETRY; INTERNATIONAL POETRY CONTESTS: FALL CONCOURS, SPRING CONCOURS, SUMMER CONCOURS (I, IV-Anthology), P.O. Box 36242, Houston TX 77236-6242, phone/fax (281)568-8780, website http://www.A.Davieson.com, founded 1988, editor-in-chief Adrian A. Davieson. **Purchase of anthology may be required of poets accepted for publication.** Literary Focus publishes anthologies compiled in contests, 3 times/year, with prizes of $200, $100 and $50, plus "Distinguished Mention" and "Honorable Mention." **"Contemporary poetry with no restriction on themes. 20-line limit. Maximum submission 15 poems, minimum three poems. No abusive, anti-social poetry."** The digest-sized anthologies are either flat-spined or saddle-stapled, 70 pgs., typeset. **Previously published poems and simultaneous submissions OK. "In order to evaluate serious entries, a $5 entry fee is required for the first three poems. Poems are evaluated on an individual basis by a panel of five editors chaired by editor-in-chief. Poets are notified of acceptance two weeks after deadlines." Send SASE for guidelines or obtain via website. Pays up to 5 copies.** Reviews books of poetry.

THE LITERARY REVIEW: AN INTERNATIONAL JOURNAL OF CONTEMPORARY WRITING (III), Fairleigh Dickinson University, 285 Madison Ave., Madison NJ 07940, phone/fax (201)443-8564, e-mail tlr@fdu.edu, website http://www.cais.com/aesir/fiction/tlr, founded 1957, editor-in-chief Walter Cummins, a quarterly, seeks **"work by new and established poets which reflects a sensitivity to literary standards and the poetic form." No specifications as to form, length, style, subject matter or purpose.** They have published poetry by Jesse Lee Kercheval, Gary Fincke, Tom Hanson, Jeff Worley and Beth Houston. The magazine is 128 pgs., 6×9, flat-spined, professionally printed with glossy color cover, using 20-50 pgs. of poetry in each issue. Circulation is 2,500 with 900 subscriptions of which one-third are overseas. They receive about 1,200 submissions a year, use approximately 100-150, have a 6- to 12-month backlog. Poems appearing here show careful attention to line, image and form—largely lyric free verse. Editors of recent issues also seem particularly open to translations. **Sample postpaid: $5, request a "general issue." Submit up to 5 poems at a time, clear typed. Simultaneous submissions OK. At times the editor comments on rejections. Publishes theme issues. Send SASE for upcoming themes or request via e-mail. Reports in 2-3 months. Always sends prepublication galleys. Pays 2 copies. Acquires first rights.** Reviews books of poetry in 500 words, single format. Open to unsolicited reviews. Poets may also send books for review consideration. They advise, "Read a general issue of the magazine carefully before submitting."

LITERATURE AND BELIEF (II, IV-Religious), 3076-E Jesse Knight Humanities Building, Brigham Young University, Provo UT 84602, phone (801)378-3073, fax (801)378-4720, e-mail cracrftr@jhkbhrc.byu.edu, founded 1981, editor Richard H. Cracroft, is the "biannual journal of the Center for the Study of Christian Values in Literature." **It uses "carefully crafted, affirmation poetry in the Judeo-Christian tradition."** They have published poetry by Ted Hughes, Donnel Hunter, Leslie Norris, William Stafford, Susan Elizabeth Howe and Lance Larsen. As a sample the editor selected these lines from "Cycle" by Cyd Adams:

> The air bears the heaviness
> of creation's spawning,
> for Christ has borne the dogwood
> to scale the last escarpment
> so a risen sun can silver
> the cobalt sky.

It is handsomely printed and flat-spined. Single copy: $5 US, $7 outside US. **Submit 3-4 poems at a time. No previously published poems. Publishes theme issues. Send SASE for upcoming themes. Pays 5 copies and 10 "offprints."** The center also publishes religious monographs, most recently *Toward the Solitary Star*, selected poems by Östen Sjöstrand.

LITTLE RIVER PRESS (V), 10 Lowell Ave., Westfield MA 01085, phone (413)568-5598, founded 1976, editor Ronald Edwards, publishes **"limited editions of poetry collections, chapbooks and postcards of New**

England poets." They have published poetry by Steven Sossaman, Wanda Cook and Frank Mello. **However, they currently do not accept unsolicited submissions.**

LODESTAR BOOKS (V, IV-Children/teen), 375 Hudson St., New York NY 10014, phone (212)366-2627, fax (212)366-2011, a member of Penguin/Putnam Inc., founded 1980, editorial director Virginia Buckley, is a trade publisher of **juvenile and young adult nonfiction, fiction and picture books. "We are not currently accepting unsolicited submissions."**

*LONDON MAGAZINE (II), 30 Thurloe Place, London SW7 England, founded 1954, poetry editor Alan Ross, is a literary and art monthly using **poetry "the best of its kind."** Editors seem open to all styles and forms, including well-made formal works. Some of the best poems in England appear here. It is a 6 × 8½, perfect-bound, elegant-looking magazine, with card cover, averaging about 150 pages six times/year. They accept about 150 of 2,000 poems received each year. Press run is 5,000 for 2,000 subscribers. Subscription: £28.50 or $67. **Sample postpaid: £4.75. Cover letter required. Reports "very soon." Pays £20/page. Buys first British serial rights.** Reviews books of poetry in up to 1,200 words. Open to unsolicited reviews. Poets may also send books for review consideration. Alan Ross says, "Quality is our only criterion."

‡LONE STARS MAGAZINE (I, II), 4219 Flinthill, San Antonio TX 78230, founded 1992, editor/publisher Milo Rosebud, published 3 times/year, features "contemporary poetry." **They want poetry that holds a continuous line of thought. No profanity.** They have recently published poetry by Ralph E. Martin, Ken Jones, Theresa Bonner and Terry Lee. As a sample the editor selected this line from "The Book Shelf" by Ron Ribble:

> *I've browsed these long and timeless lines of utterings . . .*

Lone Stars is 25 pgs., 8½ × 11, photocopied, with some hand-written poems, saddle-stapled, bound with tape, with clip art. Press run is 200 for 100 subscribers of which 3 are libraries. Single copy: $5; subscription: $15. **Sample postpaid: $4.50. Submit 3-5 poems at a time with "the form typed the way you want it in print." Charges reading fee of $1 per poem. Previously published poems and simultaneous submissions OK. Cover letter preferred.** Time between acceptance and publication is 2 months. **Publishes theme issues. Send SASE for guidelines and upcoming themes. Reports within 3 months. Acquires one-time rights.** Sponsors annual "Songbook" (song-lyric poems) Poetry Contest.

LONE WILLOW PRESS (III), P.O. Box 31647, Omaha NE 68131-0647, founded 1993, editor Dale Champy, publishes **2-3 chapbooks/year. "We publish chapbooks on single themes and we are open to all themes. The only requirement is excellence. However, we do not want to see doggerel or greeting card verse."** They have recently published *The Border Life* by Philip Arnold. That book is 20 pgs., digest-sized, neatly printed on gray paper and saddle-stapled with a light, gray card stock cover. **Query first with 5 sample poems and cover letter with brief bio and publication credits. Previously published poems OK; no simultaneous submissions.** Time between acceptance and publication is 6 months. **Seldom comments on rejections. Send SASE for guidelines. Replies to queries in 1 month, to mss (if invited) in 2-3 months. Pays 25 author's copies. "We also pay a small royalty if the book goes into a second printing." For a sample chapbook, send $7.95 in check or money order.** The editor says, "If you don't know the work of Roethke, DeFrees and Hugo, don't bother sending work our way. We work with no more than two poets at a time."

LONG ISLAND QUARTERLY (IV-Regional), P.O. Box 114, Northport NY 11768, founded 1990, editor and publisher George Wallace, is a quarterly using **poetry by people on or from Long Island. "Surprise us with fresh language. No conventional imagery, self-indulgent confessionalism, compulsive article-droppers."** They have published poetry by Edmund Pennant and David Ignatow. As a sample the editor selected this poem, "The Willow," by William Heyen:

> *Crazy Horse counted the leaves of willows along the river.*
> *He realized one leaf for each buffalo,*
> *& the leaves just now appearing in the Moon of Tender Grass*
> *were calves being born. If he could keep the trees*
> *from the whites, the herds would seed themselves.*
> *He watched the buffalo leaves for long, & long,*
> *how their colors wavered dark & light in the running wind.*
> *If he could keep his rootedness within this dream,*
> *he could shade his people to the end of time.*

LIQ is a handsome publication whose clean design (28 pgs., digest-sized, saddle-stapled, professionally printed on quality stock with matte card cover) enhances the image-based, mostly lyric free verse inside. Most contributions show attention to craft and structure. Press run is 250 for 150 subscribers of which 15 are libraries, 50-75 shelf sales. Subscription: $15. **Sample postpaid: $4. Submit 3 poems at a time. Name and address on each page. Cover letter including connection to Long Island region required. Submissions without SASE are not returned. Responds in 3 months. Sometimes sends prepublication galleys. Pays 1 copy.** Sponsors an annual open poetry competition with deadline of March 31. The winner and runners up are awarded cash prizes. Entrants may send up to 5 original, unpublished poems for consideration. No restrictions on theme or length. Entry fee: $5. No mss will be returned. Winners announced 3 months after closing date. For competition results, include SASE. Send submissions to: Long Island Quarterly Poetry Prize at the above address. The editor advises: "(1) Go beyond yourself; (2) Don't be afraid to fictionalize; (3) Don't write your autobiography—if you are worth it, maybe someone else will."

LONG ISLANDER; WALT'S CORNER (II), 322 Main St., Huntington NY 11743, phone (516)427-7000, fax (516)427-5820, founded 1838 by Walt Whitman, poetry editor George Wallace, is a weekly newspaper, 25,000 circulation, using **unrhymed poetry up to 20 lines "grounded in personal/social matrix; no haiku, inspirational."** They have published poetry by David Ignatow, David Axelrod and R.B. Weber. It is "48 pgs., newsprint." They receive about 1,000 poems a year, use approximately 52. Subscription: $18. **Sample postpaid: $2.50. Submit 3 poems at a time. Simultaneous submissions OK. "Cover letter should be simple, not effusive. SASE missing? Then we won't reply or return copy."** Editor "normally" comments on rejections. **Pays 1 copy.** Staff reviews books of poetry. Send books for review consideration.

LONG SHOT (III), P.O. Box 6238, Hoboken NJ 07030, founded 1982, edited by Danny Shot, Nancy Mercado, Lynne Breitfeller and Michael Kramer, is, they say, "writing from the real world." They have published poetry by Adrienne Rich, Gregory Corso, Jayne Cortez, Allen Ginsberg, Amiri Baraka, Reg E. Gaines and June Jordan. As a sample the editors selected these lines from "Telephone booth number 73237" by Pedro Pietri:

> *fuck the circus*
> *i get my rocks off*
> *seeing people going*
> *to work in the morning*
> *on my way to the bar!*

Long Shot is 192 pgs., flat-spined, professionally printed with glossy card cover using b&w photos, drawings and cartoons. It comes out twice a year. Press run is 2,000. Subscription: $24/2 years (4 issues). **Sample: $8. No previously published poems; simultaneous submissions OK. Reports in 2 months. Pays 2 copies.** Unlike other publishers, Danny Shot says they receive "too many requests for writer's guidelines. Just send the poems."

‡LONGHOUSE (II); SCOUT (V); ORIGIN PRESS (V), Green River R.F.D., Brattleboro VT 05301, founded 1973, editor Bob Arnold. *Longhouse* is a literary annual using **poems "from the serious working poet"** from any region in any style. They have recently published poetry by Hayden Carruth, Janine Pommy-Vega, Bobby Byrd, Sharon Doubiago, George Evans, Marie Harris, John Mactone and James Koller. Its format is unusual: a thick packet of looseleaf 8½×14 sheets, photocopied from typescript, in a handsomely printed matte cover. Press run is 200. **Sample postpaid: $12. Pays 2 copies.** Reviews books of poetry. **They publish chapbooks and books (solicited manuscripts only) under the imprints of Longhouse and Scout.** "We are also a bookshop and mail-order business for modern first editions and modern poetry and small presses. We encourage poets and readers looking for collectible modern first editions and scarce—and not so scarce—books of poetry and small press magazines to send a donation for our catalog; whatever one can afford." Bob Arnold says, "Origin Press is best known as Cid Corman's press. One of the quiet giants in American poetry plus the wide scope of international work. Established in the early 1950s in Boston, it has moved around as Cid went with his life: France, Italy, Boston, for many years now in Kyoto, Japan. Cid has merged with Longhouse in that we now edit and publish a few items together. He continues to edit, translate and publish from Kyoto. His own books are heavily based in our bookshop and mail-order catalog."

THE LONGNECK (I, II), P.O. Box 659, Vermillion SD 57069, phone (605)624-4837, fax (605)624-5562, e-mail sonsofthor@aol.com, founded 1993, poetry editor Michael Tidemann, assistant editor J.D. Erickson, is an annual publication of the Northbank Writers Group. "We publish established and new authors side by side." **They want poetry with "fresh, strong imagery, both visually and intellectually. No tired, ineffectual meanderings or greeting card work."** They have published poetry by Joseph Ditta, Corrine DeWinter and Norma Wilson. As a sample the editor selected these lines from "The Cold Dark Age Ahead" by Errol Miller:

> *Oh Lord, we are all innocent and guilty, framed*
> *by someone Else's uniform method*
> *of loveliness and loneliness,*
> *enacting the same selfsame play*
> *over and over among the sawbriar and the thorn*

The Longneck is 48 pgs., 11×17, professionally printed on 50# white paper with b&w photos and illustrations. They receive about 250 poems a year, use approximately 25%. Press run is 1,000 for 700-800 shelf sales. Single copy: $3. **Sample postpaid: $4.95. Submit up to 5 poems at a time, name and address on each page.**

FOR INFORMATION ON ENTERING the *1999 Poet's Market* Poetry Contest, see page 2.

Previously published poems and simultaneous submissions OK. Cover letter with brief bio preferred. Submission deadline: February 1. Poems are circulated to an editorial board. Often comments on rejections. Send SASE for guidelines or request via e-mail ("please, no spamming"). Pays 2 copies. Acquires first or one-time rights. The editor says, "Read and write a lot of poetry. Bloom late if that's the way it is—share your work—listen to your critics. Find your images and then fine-tune them. As we are an annual publication with volunteer staff, please be patient in having your work returned. If we take an extended period to return your work, that is good news. It means we are seriously considering your work."

♣**THE LONSDALE: THE INTERNATIONAL QUARTERLY OF THE ROMANTIC SIX (IV-Specialized)**, 6044 Leeside Crescent, Mississauga, Ontario L5M 2K6 Canada, phone/fax (905)821-9878, founded 1993, editor Michael L. Jabri-Pickett, is a quarterly journal devoted to the works of William Blake, William Wordsworth, Samuel Taylor Coleridge, Lord Byron, Percy Bysshe Shelley and John Keats. **"Content must be relevant to one of the six writers with which the publication is devoted. Poems of any length and style may be considered, but no haiku."** *The Lonsdale* is 16 pgs., 8½×11, professionally printed and saddle-stitched. They receive 10-20 poems a year, "to date none have been published." Press run is 1,500, most distributed free to museums and libraries throughout the UK. Single copy: $10; subscription: $19/year. **Sample free. Make checks payable to Michael L. Jabri-Pickett. Submit 3 poems at a time, typed double-spaced, one poem/page. No previously published poems or simultaneous submissions. Cover letter required. Reports in 4-6 weeks. Pays 30 copies.** Reviews anything of relevance; limitless word count, single or multi-book reviews. Open to unsolicited reviews. Poets may also send related books for review consideration.

LOOM PRESS (III), P.O. Box 1394, Lowell MA 01853-1394, founded 1978, editor/publisher Paul Marion, is a small press publisher of books with **an emphasis on publishing poets from New England**. Poets recently published include Ed Croke, George Chigas, Kathleen Aponick and Doug Flaherty. Books are usually perfect-bound, 6×9, with an average page count of 64. **Sample postpaid: $10. Writers should query first for book publication, sending cover letter, credits, 5 sample poems and bio. "Do not send book-length mss." Queries will be answered in 1 month, mss reported on in 3 months. Simultaneous submissions will be considered.** Time between acceptance and publication is 12-18 months. **The editor comments on mss "when time allows." Always sends prepublication galleys. Pays royalties of 10%, plus 5% of print run.** The editor says, "Please support the small publishers who make poetry available. We are especially interested in poems that address issues related to place and history and American culture."

LOONFEATHER; LOONFEATHER PRESS (II, IV-Regional), P.O. Box 1212, Bemidji MN 56619-1212, phone (218)751-4869, founded 1979, poetry editors Betty Rossi, Mark Christensen and Gail Rixen, is a small press publisher of the literary magazine *Loonfeather* appearing 2 times a year, **"primarily but not exclusively for Minnesota writers. Prefer poems of not over 42 lines, accepts some traditional forms if well done, no generalizations on worn-out topics."** They have published poetry by Spencer Reece, Joyce Penchansky, Thom Ward and Mary Winters. As a sample the editors selected these lines from "The Owl" by Malcolm Moos:

> Who was it that I saw moving through the language of the rain?
> Was it my grandmother, lingering?
> Something heard and forgotten, deep in the forest of my body,
> something I am always trying to remember . . . .

Loonfeather is 48 pgs., 5½×8½, saddle-stapled, professionally printed in small type with matte card cover, using b&w art and ads. Single copy current issue: $5; back issues: $2.50, subscription: $7.50/year. **Pays 2 copies.** Loonfeather Press publishes a limited number of quality poetry books. They published *Feast* by Carol Ann Russell and *Notes of an Ancient Chinese Poet* by Philip Dacey. **Query with 2-3 sample poems, cover letter and previous publications. "Please do not query until after January 1998." Replies to queries in 6 months.** Time between acceptance and publication is 1-1½ years. **Pays 10% royalties.**

‡**LOS (III)**, 150 N. Catalina St., No. 2, Los Angeles CA 90004, founded 1991, published biannually, features poetry. As a sample the editor selected these lines from "cunctator" by C. Mulrooney:

> like throwing pieces of himself
> to wolves says Kafka
> is this writing craft
> to delay them

The editor says *Los* is 5×8½ and saddle-stapled. **Submit any number of poems at a time. Previously published poems and simultaneous submissions OK.** Time between acceptance and publication is up to 6 months. **Reports in 1-2 weeks. Pays 1 copy. Sample postpaid: $1. Make checks payable to Heather J. Lowe.** Press run is 100 for 25 subscribers of which 1 is a library; 15 distributed free to local bookstores.

‡**THE LOST LIBRARY OF ALEXANDRIA MAGAZINE (II)**, P.O. Box 2981, Citrus Heights CA 95611, e-mail conrel@ns.net, website http://www.ns.net/~conrel/lostlib.htm, founded 1996, editor Alexandra Storm-Wycoff, appears 3-6 times/year, is "an electronic magazine featuring poetry, humor, reviews, opinion, links to other sites and more." **They want "longer poems with no limit on length. Blank and free verse is fine but we are especially interested in looking at poems that follow other conventions, such as sonnets, pantoums,**

etc." They do not want "pornographic (as opposed to erotic) verse or work that is racist." They have recently published poetry by Marc Awodey, Riki Anne Wilchins, Michael Estabrook and Cheryl Townsend. As a sample the editor selected these lines from "The Rain" by Holly Day:

> But I just want to go outside and play in the rain, put on
> my huge rubber coat and Splash! in the puddles, chase
> the birds pulling up worms, ruffled feathers bright and all shiny
> glorious mud filling up every tread in bright yellow boots.

TLLOAM is a series of hypertext pages connected to a main page. Each page has art "with an eye toward illuminating the text." They receive about 400-450 poems a year, accept approximately 15%. They have 262 subscribers, however the site gets about 300 "hits" per month. **Submit up to 10 poems at a time. E-mail submissions are preferred; hard copies are not returned without SASE. Previously published poems OK; no simultaneous submissions. Cover letter preferred.** Time between acceptance and publication is 1-6 months. **Seldom comments on rejections. Reports in 2-4 weeks. Always sends prepublication galleys. Acquires one-time rights.** Reviews books or chapbooks of poetry or other magazines in single/multi book format. Open to unsolicited reviews. Poets may also send books for review consideration. The magazine usually has references/links to other sites of interest to poets, and which also publish poetry. The editor says, "Take advantage of the space available in the better web magazines. It is often much easier to break into print on the web than in a paper publication. There are also opportunities to develop personal relationships with editors in a way that is impossible or at best much more difficult when dealing with the postal service. We are exploring the possibility of becoming a paying market by mid-1998."

LOTHROP, LEE & SHEPARD BOOKS (V), 1350 Avenue of the Americas, New York NY 10019, founded 1894, editor-in-chief Susan Pearson. Publishes 30 hardback children's books/year. **"We do not accept unsolicited mss."**

LOTUS PRESS, INC.; LOTUS POETRY SERIES; NAOMI LONG MADGETT POETRY AWARD (IV-Ethnic), P.O. Box 21607, Detroit MI 48221, phone (313)861-1280, fax (313)861-4740, founded 1972, editor Naomi Long Madgett. "With one exception of a textbook, we publish books of **poetry by individual authors,** although we have published three anthologies. We occasionally sponsor readings. **Most, but not all, of our authors are black. We publish only two books of poetry a year. We now have a backlog. The manuscripts we are currently considering are for publication in 1998 or 1999."** They have published poetry by Adam David Miller, Robert Chrisman and Alvin Aubert. As a sample we selected these lines from "Thinking About Medusa" from *Walking North* by Beverly V. Head:

> she must have been lonely
> watching all those possible lovers
> turn into beautiful stone
> horror painted perfectly
> across their faces. . .

Submit 5-10 sample poems, typed. Poems previously published in magazines OK; no simultaneous submissions. Time between acceptance and publication is 12-18 months. **Poems are circulated to an editorial board.** **"Senior editor reads manuscripts first, then passes on the best with names removed to other editors." Seldom comments on rejections. Response is usually within 6 weeks. SASE required for response. Pays 10% royalties plus author's copies. Poets are not expected to contribute to the cost of publication. "Copies may be ordered from our catalog, which is free upon request. We do not give samples."** They also sponsor the Naomi Long Madgett Poetry Award. The award goes to a manuscript by an African-American poet. "Those who recognize poetry as an art form which must be developed will stand the best chance for consideration." Awards $500 and publication by Michigan State University Press as part of its Lotus Poetry Series. Submit 3 complete copies of 60-80 pages of poetry, exclusive of a table of contents or other optional introductory material, with a $15 reading fee. Any number of poems in the collection may be previously published individually in newspapers, magazines, journals or anthologies. Do not include author's name on any page of the ms. Include with each copy a cover sheet with the title of the collection only and no other information. Also enclose a sheet with the title of the ms, author's name, address, phone and brief statement, signed, indicating all the poems are original and uncollected. Mss will not be returned. Include a stamped, self-addressed postcard for acknowledement of receipt. Submission period: February 1 through April 1. Winners will be announced no later than July 1. Send SASE for more information. The editor says, "Beginners should read a great deal of contemporary poetry and recognize what is and what is not usually being done. That does not rule out experimentation, but styles of bygone eras and imitation of other poets' styles are discouraged."

LOUISIANA LITERATURE; LOUISIANA LITERATURE PRIZE FOR POETRY (II, IV-Regional), SLU-792, Southeastern Louisiana University, Hammond LA 70402, phone (504)549-5022, fax (504)549-5021, e-mail dhanson@selu.edu, editor David Hanson, appears twice a year. They say they **"receive mss year round although we work through submissions more slowly in summer. We consider creative work from anyone though we strive to showcase our state's talent. We appreciate poetry that shows firm control and craft, is sophisticated yet accessible to a broad readership. We don't use highly experimental work."** They have published poetry by Claire Bateman, Kate Daniels, Elton Glaser, Gray Jacobik, Al Maginnes, Vivian Shipley,

Richard Katrovas, D.C. Berry and Judy Longley. As a sample the editor selected these lines from "Notre Dame" by Alison T. Gray:

> *Today Grandmama is as wide as Paris*
> *and engulfs the city like smoke.*
> *She is looking for you, sister.*
> *You think for a moment it's raining.*
>
> *but it's a trick of the dead: how*
> *in certain light smoke can seem water. . . .*

The magazine is 100 pgs., 6¾ × 9¾, flat-spined, handsomely printed on heavy matte stock with matte card cover. Single copies: $5 for individuals; subscription: $10 for individuals, $12.50 for institutions. **Submit up to 5 poems at a time. Send cover letter, including bio to use in the event of acceptance. No simultaneous submissions. Enclose SASE specifying whether work is to be returned or discarded. No submissions via fax. Publishes theme issues. Send SASE for details. Sometimes sends prepublication galleys. Pays 2 copies.** Open to unsolicited reviews. Poets may also send books for review consideration; include cover letter. The Louisiana Literature Prize for Poetry offers a $400 award. Send SASE for guidelines. The editor says, "It's important to us that the poets we publish be in control of their creations. Too much of what we see seems arbitrary."

LOUISIANA STATE UNIVERSITY PRESS (V), P.O. Box 25053, Baton Rouge LA 70894-5053, phone (504)388-6294, fax (504)388-6461, founded 1935, poetry editor L.E. Phillabaum, is a highly respected publisher of collections by poets such as Lisel Mueller, Margaret Gibson, Fred Chappell and Henry Taylor. **Currently not accepting poetry submissions; "fully committed through 1999."**

THE LOUISVILLE REVIEW (II, IV-Children/teen), Dept. PM, 315 Bingham Humanities, University of Louisville, Louisville KY 40292, phone (502)852-6801, founded 1976, faculty editor Sena Jeter Naslund, appears twice a year. **They use any kind of poetry except translations, and they have a section of children's poetry (grades K-12).** They have published poetry by Richard Jackson, Jeffrey Skinner, Maura Stanton, Richard Cecil, Roger Weingarten and Greg Pape. *TLR* is 200 pgs., flat-spined, 6 × 8¾. They receive about 700 submissions a year, accept approximately 10%. **Sample postpaid: $4. "Poetry by children must include permission of parent to publish if accepted. In all of our poetry we look for the striking metaphor, unusual imagery and fresh language. We read in fall only. Poems are read by three readers; time to publication is two to three months." Pays 1 copy.**

‡L'OUVERTURE: A LITERARY CALL TO ACTION (I), P.O. Box 8565, Atlanta GA 31106, phone (404)572-9141, e-mail louveatl@aol.com, founded 1996, published bimonthly, features "multicultural exchange of ideas meant to provoke thought." **They want "sociological/political and/or avant garde poetry." They do not want "romantic poems."** They have recently published poetry by Dr. Juba and David R. Bunch. As a sample the editor selected these lines by Stephanie Siegel:

> *I'm gonna get the whip*
> *do you want a whippin*
> *and according to the law*
> *he must be crucified*
> *discipline's the thing*
> *Mr. Christian*

L'ouverture is currently 44 pgs., digest-sized, offset printed, saddle-stitched with glossy b&w cover, art, photos and ads. They receive 150 poems a year, accept approximately 20%. Press run is 600 for 200 subscribers, 160 shelf sales; 40 distributed free to other publications and prisoners. Subscription: $15. **Sample postpaid: $3.50. Submit up to 4 poems at a time. Previously published poems and simultaneous submissions OK. Cover letter preferred.** Time between acceptance and publication is 6-12 months. **Often comments on rejections. Send SASE for guidelines. Reports in 1-2 months. Pays 2 copies.** The editor says, "We are on a mission to re-marry arts and politics. If it doesn't provide thought it will only provoke our anger."

‡THE LOWELL REVIEW (II), P.O. Box 184, Struthers OH 44471, e-mail rita@etext.org, founded 1994, managing editor Rita Chapman, published annually, features "poetry, fiction, essays with special emphasis on issues surrounding post-industrial mill cities of Youngstown, Ohio and Lowell, Massachusetts." **They want "anything—even genre work—if it is well done." They do not want "greeting card poetry, angst-ridden nihilism, gratuitous vulgarity."** They have recently published poetry by Lola Haskins, Jim Daniels, William Greenway and Jacquelne Malone. As a sample the editor selected these lines from "Equinox" by Liz Abrams-Morley:

> *a living room of teenagers:*
> *July, 1969. What did we think*
> *we would become, strung out*
> *then across a friend's frayed*
> *sofa, wide eyes lined black*

with drugstore mascara

The Lowell Review is 135 pgs., 5½×8, perfect-bound with b&w glossy cover, cover art and ads. They receive about 200 poems a year, accept approximately 10%. Press run is 500 for 15 subscribers of which 4 are libraries, 100 shelf sales; 100 distributed free as back issues to other presses, etc. Single copy: $7; subscription: $7. **Sample postpaid: $5. Make checks payable to IK Press. Submit up to 3 poems at a time. No previously published poems; simultaneous submissions OK. Cover letter preferred. Reads submissions January through May. "Please submit only once per reading period unless otherwise invited."** Time between acceptance and publication is 6 months. **"We reject what we don't like, forward 'maybes' to the other. Decisions are made from combined 'maybe' piles with both having input, but Ms. Dickeman-Nelson has final say." Seldom comments on rejections. Send SASE for guidelines. Reports in 2-24 weeks. Sometimes sends prepublication galleys. Pays 1 copy. Acquires first North American serial rights.** The editor says, "I do not believe there is anything better than the slush pile to gauge what is going on in poetry today. Every year, without fail, we see themes emerge from the random chaos in the mailbox that mirror those of society in general. These themes do not often survive editors to manifest themselves in the small press at large."

LOW-TECH PRESS (V), 30-73 47th St., Long Island City NY 11103, founded 1981, editor Ron Kolm, has published work by Hal Sirowitz, John Yau and Jennifer Nostrand. As a sample the editor selected "Business District" by Mike Topp:

> *Advice*
> *Lemonade*
> *Toy hats*
> *Closed.*

This poem is from *Six Stories & Seven Short Poems*, 16 pgs., 3¼×4⅓, offset, on bond paper and saddle-stapled. **"I am only interested in short poems with clear images. Since almost nobody gets paid for their work, I believe in multiple submissions and multiple publishings. Even though we only publish solicited mss, I respond right away to any mail the press receives."**

‡**LUCID MOON (I)**, 67 Norma Rd., Hampton NJ 08827, founded 1997, editor Ralph Haselmann Jr., published monthly, their goal is "to publish lively, moving, humorous poems and to keep the magazine in the public eye." **They want "post beat, independent, modern poetry—no restrictions."**
● The format of their premiere issue is similar to that of many 'zine publications.
They have recently published poetry by Ana Christy, Pete Lee and Kevin M. Hibshman. As a sample the editor selected these lines from his poem "Lucid Moon":

> *Traveling across America in all its terrible beauty, hitchhiking through history*
> *the miles of highways and open roads a typewriter ribbon of future stories we could tell . . .*

Lucid Moon is 60 pgs., 8½×11, photocopied, side-stapled with some hand-written poems, cartoons and drawings. They receive about 600 poems a year, accept approximately 95%. Press run is 30 for 6 subscribers; "a few" distributed free to friends. Single copy: $5; subscription: $30/6 issues. **Make checks payable to Ralph Haselman Jr. "Contributors are encouraged to buy a subscription." Submit up to 6 poems at a time, must be "photocopy ready." Previously published poems and simultaneous submissions OK. Cover letter preferred.** Time between acceptance and publication is 6 months. **"I choose poems that are honest and moving in some way. Humor is good." Often comments on rejections. Send SASE for guidelines. Reports same day. Rights revert to author upon publication.** "We will be seeking authors to write chapbook reviews in the future." Open to unsolicited reviews. Poets may also send books for review consideration. The editor advises, "read other poets and back issues of *Lucid Moon* to get a feel for the style wanted. Send poems you are proud of."

‡**THE LUCID STONE (II)**, P.O. Box 940, Scottsdale AZ 85252-0940, founded 1994, managing editor Pauline Mounsey, is a quarterly publishing "quality poetry and a small amount of quality artwork. We focus on poetry with complimentary artwork." **They want "unpublished quality poetry of any style and length. We are interested in poetry in the full poetic range, including formal, traditional and experimental poems." Nothing trite or didactic.** They have recently published poetry by Ida Fasel, Will Inman, Margaret Randall and Alberto Alvaro Rios. As a sample the editor selected these lines from "Loneliness" by Perry Sams:

> *And so you trekked to that strange*
> *country of whistling white falling*
> *on red bricks, of soundless gray smoke,*
> *and took off your coat of silence.*
> *When you opened your mouth lumps*
> *of coal burned in your throat.*

LS is 64-72 pgs., 7×8½, professionally offset printed and saddle-stitched with 80 lb. Tahoe dull cover with one halftone of artwork, 5-7 b&w pieces of artwork and photography, no ads. They receive about 5,000 poems a year, accept less than 200. Press run is 250-300 for 125 subscribers. **Sample postpaid: $6. Submit 3-5 poems at a time. No previously published poems or simultaneous submissions. Cover letter preferred including "short personal biographical sketch other than the usual vita. No manuscripts or art will be returned nor queries answered unless accompanied by an SASE with adequate postage."** Time between acceptance and publication is 1-6 months. **Poems are circulated to an editorial board. "We have a staff of readers who** individually review a group of approximately 50 poems at a time." Seldom comments on rejections. Send SASE for guidelines. Reports in 1-4 months. Pays 1 copy. Acquires first rights. The editor says, "We look for fresh language and use of images."

LUCIDITY; BEAR HOUSE PUBLISHING (I), Route 2, Box 94, Eureka Springs AR 72631-9505, phone (501)253-9351, e-mail tbadger@ipa.net, website http://www.ipa.net/~tbadger, founded 1985, editor Ted O. Badger. *Lucidity* is a quarterly of poetry. **Submission fee required—$1/poem for "juried" selection by a panel of judges or $2/poem to compete for cash awards of $15, $10 and $5. Other winners paid in both cash and in copies. In addition, the editor invites a few guest contributors to submit to each issue. Contributors are encouraged to subscribe or buy a copy of the magazine.** The magazine is called *Lucidity* because, the editor says, "I have felt that too many publications of verse lean to obscurity." They are **"open as to form. 36-line limit due to format. No restriction on subject matter except that something definitive be given to the reader. We look for poetry that is life-related and has clarity and substance."** Purpose: **"to give a platform to poets who can impart their ideas with clarity."** He does not want **"religious, nature or vulgar poems."** Recently published poets include Esther Towns, Maryl Shackett, Eve J. Blohm, Winnie Fitzpatrick and Marian Ford Park. As a sample of the type of verse sought, the editor offers these lines from his own work:

> *Of all*
> *mistakes we make,*
> *presuming tomorrow*
> *is ours to speak, write, or love is*
> *the worst.*

The magazine is 76 pgs., digest-sized, photocopied from typescript, saddle-stapled, with matte card cover. It's a surprisingly lively small press magazine featuring accessible narrative and lyric poetry, with almost equal space given to free and formal verse. Press run is 350 for 220 subscribers. Subscription: $10. **Sample postpaid: $2.50. Submit 3-6 poems at a time. Simultaneous submissions OK.** Time between acceptance and publication is 3 months. **Send SASE for guidelines or request via e-mail. Reports in 2-3 months. Buys one-time rights.** Bear House Press is a self-publishing arrangement by which poets can pay to have booklets published in the same format as *Lucidity,* prices beginning at 100 copies of 32 pgs. for $256. Publishes **10 chapbooks/year.** The editor says, "Small press journals offer the best opportunity to most poets for publication."

LUNA BISONTE PRODS; LOST AND FOUND TIMES (IV-Style), 137 Leland Ave., Columbus OH 43214-7505, founded 1967, poetry editor John M. Bennett, may be the zaniest phenomenon in central Ohio. John Bennett is a publisher (and practitioner) of **experimental and avant-garde writing**, sometimes sexually explicit, and art in a bewildering array of formats including the magazine, *Lost and Found Times*, postcard series, posters, chapbooks, pamphlets, labels and audiocassette tapes. You can get a **sampling of Luna Bisonte Prods for $6. Numerous reviewers have commented on the bizarre** *Lost and Found Times,* "reminiscent of several West Coast dada magazines"; "This exciting magazine is recommended only for the most daring souls"; "truly demented"; "Insults . . . the past 3,000 years of literature"; "revolution where it counts, in the dangerous depths of the imagination," etc. Bennett wants to see **"unusual poetry, naive poetry, surrealism, experimental, visual poetry, collaborations—*no* poetry workshop or academic pabulum."** He has recently published poetry by J. Berry, J. Leftwich, S.S. Nash, C. Frost, R. Kostelanetz and B. Heman. As a sample, the editor selected these lines from a poem by Gregory Vincent Saint Thomasino:

> *Off your edgy blonde / stiff / "couch" talk—*
> *cure(-ator's) unsaid (maid) docent, 'er*
>
> *heaven's bent-more norm(atic) jerkings ("leg show")*
> *behind the screen and off the hedge flaunt.*
>
> *I sought, I mouth'd all through EATEN cank'r*
> *for the curator's plastic buttocks. Tall & dominant.*

The digest-sized, 52-page magazine, photoreduced typescript and wild graphics, matte card cover with graphics, has a circulation of 350 with 75 subscribers of which 30 are libraries. Subscription: $25 for 5 numbers. **Sample postpaid: $6. Submit anytime—preferably camera-ready (but this is not required). Reports in 1-2 days. Pays copies. All rights revert to authors upon publication.** Staff reviews books of poetry. Send books for review consideration. **Luna Bisonte also will consider book submissions: query with samples and cover letter (but "keep it brief"). Chapbook publishing usually depends on grants or other subsidies and is usually by solicitation.** He will also consider subsidy arrangements on negotiable terms. The editor says, "I would like to see more experimental and avant-garde material in Spanish and Portuguese, or in mixtures of languages."

LUNA NEGRA (I), Box 26, % Office of Campus Life/Student Activities or English Dept., Kent State University, Kent OH 44242, phone (330)672-2676, editor Tom Sweterlitch, is a student-run, biannual literary and art magazine of the KSU main campus, **open to all forms of poetry and prose.** The editor says it is 40-50 pgs., 8½×11, with art and photography throughout. They receive 400-450 poems a year, accept 40 or 50. Press run is 2,000, most distributed to KSU students. **Submit up to 3 poems at a time. Simultaneous submissions OK.**

The New York City-based **LUNGFULL!** *Magazine* prints the rough drafts of every published poem to connect readers to the creative process. "Hidden within the poem, the monument to creation, is the actual moment of creation," says editor Brendan Lorber. "The magazine tries to make that moment visible." Lorber chose the Statue of Liberty for this issue's cover not only as a symbol of the creative process, but also as a symbol of poetry's struggle for a place in American culture. "Once a symbol of compassion for the heroic lives of everyday people, the statue has become too big to see individuals anymore, let alone the efforts of those individuals. Yet, you can walk inside the skin of the Statue of Liberty and see the struts and girders used to build it. **LUNGFULL!** is a magazine of process, believing that powerful work can be even more powerful if we embrace *work* as a verb as much as a noun. Adding this dimension to the poem makes the writing more engaging, makes it closer to the reader, makes it matter in an entirely new way." Cover design/illustration: Brendan Lorber. Cover poem: Silver.

Reads submissions September 1 through March 30 only. Seldom comments on rejections. Reports in 1 month or so ("depending on school calendar"). Pays 1 copy. "All rights revert to author immediately after publication." The editor adds, "We are also interested in any b&w reproducible artwork or photographs."

‡**LUNGFULL! MAGAZINE (II)**, 126 E. Fourth St., #2, New York NY 10003, e-mail lungfull@interport.net, founded 1994, editor Brendan Lorber, published biannually, prints "the rough draft of each poem, in addition to the final so that the reader can see the creative process from start to finish." **They want "any style as long as its urgent, immediate, playful, probing, showing great thought while remaining vivid and grounded. Poems should be as interesting as conversation." They do not want "empty poetic abstractions."** They have recently published poetry by Hal Sirowitz, Sparrow, Bob Holman and Edwin Torres. As a sample the editor selected "invisible poem" by Suzanne Soloman:

> one day—on a whim—I ripped off my shirt so I could
> write naked, and now
> look at me! ah, the beauty
> is you can't
> until I tell you

LUNGFULL! is 100 pgs., 8½×7, offset printed, perfect-bound, desktop-published, card cover with lots of illustrations (photos in upcoming issues) and a few small press ads. They receive about 500 poems a year, accept approximately 10-20%. Press run is 300 for 20 subscribers of which 1 is a library, 220 shelf sales; 60 distributed free to contributors. Single copy: $4.95; subscription: $10. **Sample postpaid: $6.50. Make checks payable to Brendan Lorber. "We recommend you get a back copy before submitting." Submit up to 6 poems at a time. Previously published poems and simultaneous submissions (with notification) OK. Cover letter preferred. Electronic submissions OK.** Time between acceptance and publication is 2-3 months. **"The editor looks at each piece for its own merit and for how well it'll fit into the specific issue being planned based on other accepted work." Obtain guidelines via e-mail. Reports in 1-12 weeks. Pays 2 copies.** The editor advises, "don't just read books, mark them up, write between the lines, make your own cover, transcribe the pages you love and burn the originals, get paper cuts kissing it, massage its spine, use only the words from the book you're reading in your speech, or none of them."

‡**LUZ EN ARTE Y LITERATURA; CARPETAS DE POESÍA LUZ; CARPETAS DE POESÍA LUZ BILINGÜE; LUZ BILINGUAL PUBLISHING, INC. (IV-Translations, bilingual/spanish)**, P.O. Box 571062, Tarzana CA 91357-1062, phone (818)907-1454, founded 1991, director Veronica Miranda. *Luz en Arte y Literatura*, published annually is an "international bilingual magazine with the purpose to promote art and literature throughout U.S.A. and foreign countries." **They want "Latin American literature, poetry translation from Spanish to English and English to Spanish."** They have recently published poetry by Luis Benitez, Alima Galliano, Martha Cerda and Eduardo Liendo. As a sample the editor selected these lines from "El silencia del viento" by Juan Miguel Asensi:

> *El escritorio*
> *la mosca en el tintero*
> *zapatos negros*

and translated by Kirk Anderson:

> *The writing table*

> *the fly in the inkpot*
> *little black shoes*

Luz en Arte y Literatura is 100-200 pgs., 8½ × 6½, professionally printed, perfect-bound, CS1 cover stock with art, photos and ads. They receive about 1,000 poems a year, accept approximately 10%. Press run is 1,000 for 500 subscribers of which 300 are libraries, 200 shelf sales; 300 distributed free to reviewers, collaborators, cultural institutions. Single copy: $19; subscription: $25. **Sample postpaid: $8. Make checks payable to Luz Bilingual Publishing, Inc. Submit up to 10 poems at a time. Previously published poems and simultaneous submissions OK. Cover letter required with curriculum vitae.** Time between acceptance and publication is 6-12 months. **Poems are circulated to an editorial board. "There is a preselection a year before publication and a final selection upon publication." Publishes theme issues. Send SASE for guidelines and upcoming themes. Reports in 6-12 months. Pays 1 copy.** Staff reviews books or chapbooks of poetry or other magazines in 1-3 pages. Poets may also send books for review consideration. Luz Bilingual Publishing, Inc., publishes poetry translations: Spanish/English, English/Spanish and Spanish poetry in the form of poetry folders as the result of 2 annual poetry contests, Carpetas de Poesía Luz and Carpetas de Poesía Luz Bilingüe. Send SASE for entry form and guidelines. Entry fee: $10. Deadline for entry, December 31. Winners will be announced in *Luz en Arte y Literatura*, the works will be published in the spring and distributed with the magazine and made available to the public. The translator and/or author will receive a free magazine subscription. Poetry folders are 20-40 pgs., 9 × 7½, professionally printed. Replies to queries and mss in 3-6 months. Pays author's copies. For sample books or chapbooks, write to the above address.

LYNX, A JOURNAL FOR LINKING POETS; AHA BOOKS; INTERNATIONAL TANKA SPLENDOR AWARD (IV-Form), P.O. Box 1250, Gualala CA 95445, e-mail ahabooks@mcn.org, website http://www.faximum.com/aha!poetry, founded as *APA-Renga* in 1986, later the name was changed to *Lynx* "to link an endangered species of poetry with an endangered animal and to inspire the traditional wit of renga," says Jane Reichhold, who co-edits the publication with Werner Reichhold. *Lynx*, published 3 times/year (February, June and October) "is **based on the ancient craft of renga, linked verse with origins in Zen and Japanese culture, and now publishes both renga and tanka.** A renga is a non-narrative series of linked images as a group effort. Tanka is the most popular poetry form in Japan and the oldest continued form." As a sample the editor selected this poem by Sanford Goldstein:

> *heaven and earth,*
> *I do remember*
> *the long long delicate*
> *contradictions*
> *of done, not done*

Lynx is 90 pgs., 4½ × 11, neatly printed and comb-bound with card cover. It also publishes essays, book reviews, articles, interviews, experimental linked forms, linked prose, art, commentaries and "whatever encourages poets to link ideas." They currently have 300 subscribers. Subscription: $15 US and Canada, $20 elsewhere. **Sample (including guidelines) postpaid: $6. Make checks payable to AHA Books. Submit 1 renga and/or 6-10 tanka at a time.** *Lynx* **encourages submissions by those experienced and experimenting with collaborative forms. Subscribers participate in ongoing renga, start trends and otherwise determine the content. All submissions should include a brief bio with the title of the work. E-mail submissions are welcome. E-mail information requests are welcome, however, poets need to include an address as info is sent via regular mail. "I send a packet of info too large to attach to e-mail." Most information is available on the website. "Please send us copies that do not need to be returned." Include SASE for reply. Editor responds to all who submit. Reports in 1 week.** AHA Books publishes online books. Access through the above website (click on "read online books") or at http://www.faximum.com/aha.d/onlinebk.htm. The press also sponsors the International Tanka Splendor Award. Winning entries will be published in *Tanka Splendor*. Deadline: September 30. Send SASE for details.

LYNX EYE; SCRIBBLEFEST LITERARY GROUP (I, II), 1880 Hill Dr., Los Angeles CA 90041-1244, phone (213)550-8522, founded 1994, co-editors Pam McCully and Kathryn Morrison. *Lynx Eye* is the quarterly publication of the ScribbleFest Literary Group, an organization dedicated to the development and promotion of the literary arts. *Lynx Eye* is "**dedicated to showcasing visionary writers and artists, particularly new voices." Each issue contains a special feature called Presenting, in which an unpublished writer of prose or poetry makes his/her print debut. They have no specifications regarding form, subject matter or style of poetry, but poems should be 30 lines or less.** They have recently published poetry by Elizabeth Morse, Kel Munger,

---

MARKET CONDITIONS are constantly changing! If you're still using this book and it is 1999 or later, buy the newest edition of *Poet's Market* at your favorite bookstore or order directly from Writer's Digest Books.

Simon Perchik and Donald Rawley. As a sample the editors selected these lines from "The Need for Saturday Poetry" by Bruce Curley:

> but the baby has always to be fed
> not only the sweet
> and nutritious mother's milk,
> but the poetry and song
> and gentle mental caress
> of the word well turned

Lynx Eye is about 120 pgs., 5½ × 8½, perfect-bound with b&w artwork. They receive about 2,000 poetry submissions a year and have space for about 75. Press run is 500 for 150 subscribers, 200 shelf sales. Single copy: $7.50. Subscription: $20/year. **Sample postpaid: $5. Make checks payable to ScribbleFest Literary Group. No previously published poems; simultaneous submissions OK. Name, address and phone number on each piece. Always comments on rejections. Send SASE for guidelines. Reports in 2-3 months. Pays $10/piece and 3 copies. Buys first North American serial rights.**

THE LYRIC (II), 307 Dunton Dr. SW, Blacksburg VA 24060-5127, founded 1921 ("the oldest magazine in North America in continuous publication devoted to the publication of **traditional poetry**"), poetry editor Leslie Mellichamp, uses about 65 poems each quarterly issue. **"We use rhymed verse in traditional forms, for the most part, with an occasional piece of blank or free verse. Forty lines or so is usually our limit. Our themes are varied, ranging from religious ecstasy to humor to raw grief, but we feel no compulsion to shock, embitter or confound our readers. We also avoid poems about contemporary political or social problems— grief but not grievances, as Frost put it. Frost is helpful in other ways: If yours is more than a lover's quarrel with life, we're not your best market. And most of our poems are accessible on first or second reading. Frost again: Don't hide too far away."** They have published poetry by Anne Barlow, Tom Riley, Michael J. Bugeja, Rhina P. Espaillat, Richard Moore, Barbara Loots, Alfred Dorn, Sharon Kourous, Gail White, Neill Megaw and Maureen Cannon. As a sample the editor selected these lines from "Evening" by R.L. Cook:

> Now nature rests and smoky darkness
>   Laces purple frills
> Along the road that leads to nightfall
>   In the velvet hills.

The Lyric is 36 pgs., digest-sized, professionally printed with varied typography, matte card cover. It has a circulation of 700 of which 290 go to libraries. They receive about 5,000 submissions a year, use approximately 250, have an average 3-month backlog. Subscription: $12 US, $14 Canada and other countries (in US funds only). **Sample postpaid: $3. Submit up to 5 poems at a time. No previously published poems; simultaneous submissions OK. "Cover letters often helpful, but not required." Send SASE for guidelines. Reports in 2 months (average). Pays 1 copy, and all contributors are eligible for quarterly and annual prizes totaling over $750.** Leslie Mellichamp comments, "Our raison d'être has been the encouragement of form, music, rhyme and accessibility in poetry. We detect a growing dissatisfaction with the modernist movement that ignores these things and a growing interest in the traditional wellsprings of the craft. Naturally, we are proud to have provided an alternative for 75 years that helped keep the true roots of poetry alive."

M.I.P. COMPANY (IV-Foreign language, erotica), P.O. Box 27484, Minneapolis MN 55427, phone (612)546-7578, fax (612)544-6077, e-mail mp@mipco.com, website http://www.mipco.com, founded in 1984, contact Michael Peltsman, publishes 3 paperbacks/year. **They only publish Russian erotic poetry and prose written in Russian.** They have published poetry collections by Mikhail Armalinsky and Aleksey Shelvakh. **No previously published poems; simultaneous submissions OK. Replies to queries in 1 month. Seldom comments on rejections.**

M.O.O.N. MAGAZINE; MOON SHADOW PUBLICATIONS (I, IV-Membership/subscription); "FINISH THIS POEM CONTEST" (I), P.O. Box 1302, Covington KY 41012-1302, phone (606)291-2642, founded 1992, editor/publisher B.C. Mullikin. *M.O.O.N. Magazine* (Muse Odyssey Orbital News), a quarterly appearing in January, April, July and October, "was created as an alternative answer for poets, writers and artists who are seeking to be published and promoted. *M.O.O.N.* is an open format, literary and art membership publication." **They want to see "more humorous poetry and free verse relating to contemporary issues, 25 lines or less. We do not want to see submissions promoting any form of discrimination or containing pornographic content."** They have published poetry by Martha Calloway, Irma Wassall, Jane Stuart and William T. Masonis. *M.O.O.N.* is about 20 pgs., 8½ × 11, saddle-stitched, colored card cover with artwork, b&w cartoons and drawings, and ads. They receive about 300 poems a year, accept 50%. Press run is 300 for 50 subscribers. Subscription: $20. **Sample (including guidelines) postpaid: $6. Nonmember submissions, if selected, will be published one time only. For future submissions to be considered, contributors must then become a member by purchasing a subscription. Submit 3-6 poems at a time. Previously published poems OK; no simultaneous submissions. Cover letter preferred.** Time between acceptance and publication is 3-6 months. **Seldom comments on rejections. Send SASE for guidelines only. Reports in 1-3 months. Sometimes sends prepublication galleys. Pays 1 copy. Acquires one-time rights.** Reviews books of poetry in their "Moon Market" section. Open to unsolicited reviews. Poets may send books for review consideration to Attn: Madame Zonka.

They also sponsor the "Finish This Poem Contest." First Place: $75, Second Place: $35, and Third Place: 1-year subscription (4 issues). The three top winners, and a select group of honorable mentions, also receive publication in *M.O.O.N.* The contest is open to everyone. Entry fee: $5 for the first poem, $1 each additional. Each entrant receives a copy of *M.O.O.N.* containing the contest results. Send SASE for details. The editor says, "Be bold, original and explore new ideas."

THE MACGUFFIN; NATIONAL POET HUNT (II), Schoolcraft College, 18600 Haggerty Rd., Livonia MI 48152-2696, phone (313)462-4400 ext. 5292, fax (313)462-4558, founded 1983, editor Arthur Lindenberg, who says, "*The MacGuffin* is a literary magazine which appears three times each year, in April, June and November. We publish the best poetry, fiction, nonfiction and artwork we find. We have no thematic or stylistic biases. **We look for well-crafted poetry. Long poems should not exceed 300 lines. Avoid pornography, trite and sloppy poetry. We do not publish haiku, concrete or light verse.**" They have published poetry by Kathleen Ripley Leo, Stephen Dunning, Jim Daniels and Daniel James Sundahl. *The MacGuffin* is 144 pgs., digest-sized, professionally printed on heavy buff stock, with matte card cover, flat-spined, with b&w illustrations and photos. Circulation is 600 for 215 subscriptions and the rest are local newsstand sales, contributor copies and distribution to college offices. Single copy: $4.50; subscription: $12. **Sample postpaid: $4. "The editorial staff is grateful to consider unsolicited manuscripts and graphics." Submit up to 5 poems at a time of no more than 300 lines; poems should be typewritten. "We discourage simultaneous submissions." Prefers submissions to be sent through the mail. Publishes theme issues. Send SASE for guidelines and upcoming themes or request via fax. Reports in 10-12 weeks; publication backlog is 6 months. Pays 2 copies,** "occasional money or prizes." Also sponsors the National Poet Hunt, established in 1996, offering annual awards of $500 first prize, $250 second prize, $100 third prize, 3 honorable mentions and publication. Submissions may be entered in other contests. Submit 5 typed poems on any subject in any form. Put name and address on separate 3×5 index card only. Send SASE for guidelines. Entry fee: $15/5 poems. Deadline: May 31. Judge for 1996 contest was Jim Daniels. Winners will be announced June 30, and in *Poets and Writers* in the fall. Poetry published in *The MacGuffin* has been selected for inclusion in *Pushcart Prize* anthologies. The editor says, "We will always comment on 'near misses.' Writing is a search, and it is a journey. Don't become sidetracked. Don't become discouraged. Keep looking. Keep traveling. Keep writing."

MACMILLAN PUBLISHING CO.; SCRIBNER; ATHENEUM, 1633 Broadway, New York NY 10019. Publishes 60-100 paperbacks and hardbacks/year. Prefers not to share information.

‡MAD POETS REVIEW; MAD POETS REVIEW POETRY COMPETITION; DELAWARE COUNTY POETS COOPERATIVE (II), P.O. Box 1248, Media PA 19063-8248, founded 1987, editor Eileen M. D'Angelo, associate editor Camelia Nocella. *Mad Poets Review* is published annually. "Our primary purpose is to promote thought-provoking, moving poetry, and encourage beginning poets. We don't care if you have a 'name' or a publishing history, if your poetry is well-crafted." They are **"anxious for work with 'joie de vivre' that startles and inspires." No restrictions on subject, form or style. "We are not interested in porn or obscenities used for the sake of shock value."** They have recently published poetry by Louis McKee, Valentina Sinkevich, Ray Greenblatt and June King. As a sample the editor selected these lines from "Rescue" by Francine Witte:

> They had said goodbye for years
> before the moving van parked
> its undeniable weight outside their house.
> He touched the curtains she let him keep
> and waited for answers to fall from their folds.

MPR is about 70 pgs., digest-sized, attractively printed and perfect-bound with textured card cover. They receive about 400-600 poems a year, use approximately 50-60. Press run is 200. Subscription: $10. **Sample postpaid: $5. Make checks payable to either Delco Poets Cooperative or *Mad Poets Review*. Submit 6 poems at a time. Previously published poems and simultaneous submissions OK. Cover letter preferred. "Mark envelope 'contest' or 'magazine.' " Reads submissions January 1 through June 1 only.** Time between acceptance and publication is 7-8 months. **Often comments on rejections. Send SASE for guidelines. Reports in 6-8 weeks. Pays 1 copy. Acquires one-time rights.** Sponsors the annual *Mad Poets Review* Poetry Competition. "All themes and styles of poetry are welcome, no line limit, previously unpublished work only. Send 2 copies of each poem with identification only on 1 copy." Deadline: May 1. Entry fee: $3 for up to 5 poems. Winners published in *MPR*. Cash prizes awarded—amount depends on number of entries. Send SASE for guidelines. "The Delco Poets Cooperative is an active organization in Pennsylvania. We run five poetry series; have monthly meetings for members for critique and club business; coordinate a children's contest through Del. Co. School system; run an annual poetry festival the first Sunday in October; sponsor Mad Poets Bonfires for local poets and musicians; publish an annual literary calendar listing local arts events; send quarterly newsletters to members." Membership fee: $15. The editor says, "It is advised that if someone is going to submit they see what kind of poetry we publish. We sometimes receive poetry that is totally inappropriate of our mag and it is obvious the poet does not know *MPR*."

MAD RIVER PRESS (V), State Road, Richmond MA 01254, phone (413)698-3184, founded 1986, editor Barry Sternlieb, publishes 3 broadsides and **1 chapbook/year, "all types of poetry, no bias," but none unsolicited.** They have published poetry by Gary Snyder, Hayden Carruth, W.S. Merwin, Louise Glück, Linda Gregg and Richard Wilbur. Call or write for information.

♣**MADAME BULL'S TAVERN (I, II)**, Box 60369, U. of A. Postal Outlet, Edmonton, Alberta T6G 2S6 Canada, phone (403)439-6816, founded 1995, editors Jocko, Tom Emmens and Gail Sídonie Sobat, is a biannual literary magazine "with publicly-engaged poetry, genre fiction (with a strong literary grounding), topical essays and staff reviews." **They want "any form of poetry, up to 100 lines. Prefer poetry with some form of narrative. Subject matter: urban, social, political. Prefer poetry that has something to say, and it should have, where possible, public and personal dimensions. No purely personal or purely experimental poetry. No purely formal exercises."** They have published poetry by S.K. Kelen, Anna Mioduchowska and Matt Santateresa. As a sample the editors selected these lines from "The moon of magpies quarrelling" by Alice Major:

> The moon of magpies quarrelling
> shimmers in the pale sky of early morning
> like a court reporter's screen. It records
> the magpies' proceedings—litigious birds
> with ermine draped across their shoulders,
> their bellies drooped in prosperous curves.

The editors describe *MBT* as 64 pgs., digest-sized, high-quality photocopied and saddle-stapled with offset card stock cover and some graphics. They accept 10% of the material received. Press run is 200. Single copy: $6. **Submit 5-8 poems at a time. Cover letter preferred. Poems are screened by two readers and narrowed down for the five-person editorial board. Often comments on rejections. Send SASE (or SAE and IRCs) for guidelines. Reports in 2-4 months. Pays 1 copy. Acquires first North American serial rights.** Staff reviews books of poetry. Poets may send books for review consideration. The editors add, "We like to see writers who know how to think, as well as how to feel. Poets we enjoy are able to see beyond themselves and engage the surroundings and issues of their time. And it never hurts to be able to tell a good story and so begin to create the new myths for our society."

THE MADISON REVIEW; PHYLLIS SMART YOUNG PRIZE IN POETRY (II), Dept. of English, Helen C. White Hall, University of Wisconsin, 600 N. Park St., Madison WI 53706, phone (608)263-0566, founded 1978, poetry editor Michelle Ephraim, want **poems that are "smart and tight, that fulfill their own propositions. Spare us: love poems, religious or patriotic dogma, light verse. We'd like to see poetry in ethnic/nationality, form/style, gay/lesbian, humor (not light verse, though), political, social issues and women/feminism categories."** They have recently published work by Lise Goett, Ben Passikoff, Anne Caston, Lisa Steinman and Richard Tillinghast. *The Madison Review* is published in May and December, with 15-20 poems selected from a pool of 750. **Sample postpaid: $2.50. Submit up to 6 poems at a time. No simultaneous submissions.** Usually reports in 4 months, may be longer in summer. **Pays 2 copies. "We do require a concise cover letter with short bio information."** The Phyllis Smart Young Prize in Poetry is for $500 and publication in *TMR*, for "the best group of three unpublished poems submitted by a single author." Send SASE for rules before submitting for prize or see announcement for guidelines in *AWP* or *Poets & Writers* magazines. Submissions must arrive during September—winner announced December 15. The editor says, "Contributors: Know your market! Read before, during and after writing. Treat your poems *better* than job applications!"

THE MAGAZINE OF SPECULATIVE POETRY (IV-Science fiction), P.O. Box 564, Beloit WI 53512, founded 1984, editor Roger Dutcher, is an irregularly published magazine that features **"the best new speculative poetry. We are especially interested in narrative form, but interested in variety of styles, open to any form, length (within reason), purpose. We're looking for the best of the new poetry utilizing the ideas, imagery and approaches developed by speculative fiction and will welcome experimental techniques as well as the fresh employment of traditional forms."** They have published poetry by Brian Aldiss, Jane Yolen, Bruce Boston and Steve Rasnectem. As a sample Roger Dutcher chose these lines from "To Dine with Poetry and Mathematics" by Bruce Boston:

> when poetry and mathematics
> sit down to dinner
> the evening is vintage,
> the conversation moves
> by leaps and starts,
> like time or evolution

The digest-sized magazine, 20-24 pgs., is offset from professional typesetting, saddle-stapled with matte card cover. They accept less than 5% of some 500 poems received/year. Press run is 100-200, going to nearly 100 subscribers of which 4 are libraries. Subscription: $11. **Sample postpaid: $3.50. Submit 3 poems at a time, double-spaced. No previously published poems or simultaneous submissions. "We like cover letters but they aren't necessary. We like to see where you heard of us; the name of the poems submitted; a statement if the poetry ms is disposable; a big enough SASE; and if you've been published, some recent places."**

Editor comments on rejections "on occasion." Send SASE for guidelines. Reports in 1-2 months. Pays 3¢/word, minimum $3, plus copy. Buys first North American serial rights. Reviews books of speculative poetry. Query on unsolicited reviews. Send speculative poetry books for review consideration.

MAIL CALL JOURNAL (IV-Specialized: American Civil War); DISTANT FRONTIER PRESS, P.O. Box 5031, South Hackensack NJ 07606, phone (201)296-0419, e-mail mailcall1@aol.com, founded 1990, managing editor Anna Pansini, appears 6 times/year with the purpose of "keeping the spirit of the Civil War soldier alive." **They want poetry with unique Civil War themes in first or third person.** As a sample the editor selected these lines from "Colors" by Jim Boring:

> *"Now," he said*
> *And the boys fell down*
> *Down fell the blue and the gray*
> *Down fell the stars*
> *From the noble stripes*
> *Down from the proud blue bars.*

Mail Call Journal is 8 pgs., 8½ × 11, offset printed on colored paper and corner stapled. They receive about 100 poems a year, accept approximately 10. Press run is 500 for 450 subscribers of which 5 are libraries. Subscription: $24.95/year. **Sample postpaid: $5. "We prefer contributors order a writer's packet for $5 which includes a sample copy before submitting, but it is not required." Previously published poems and simultaneous submissions OK. Cover letter optional.** "If poet is a descendant of a Civil War soldier or a member of any Civil War organizations, please provide details for publication." Time between acceptance and publication is 6-12 months. **Often comments on rejections. Send SASE for guidelines or request via e-mail. Reports in 6-12 months. Pays 2 copies, but "open to negotiation."** Distant Frontier Press publishes book excerpts, narratives, diary entries, poems and editorial think pieces. Send SASE for details. Sponsors a biannual history poetry competition, established in 1997. Awards 3 prizes of "publication on website plus percentage of proceeds." Submissions may be entered in other contests. Submit 3 typed poems per category (American Civil War poetry; United States history poetry; and world history poetry). Indicate whether the poem is fictional or non-fictional. Entry fee: $5/category (3 poems). Deadlines: September 15 (for Fall), March 15 (for Spring). The judge for upcoming contest will be Anna Pansini. Winners will be announced October 15 and April 15 on website; winners will be notified by mail. The editor says, "Don't make a Civil War movie into a poem. Write with feeling from your heart."

‡MAIN STREET RAG POETRY JOURNAL (II), P.O. Box 25331, Charlotte NC 28229-5331, phone (704)535-1918, founded 1996, publisher/editor M. Scott Douglass, published quarterly, aims "to bring poetry back to the main streets and living rooms of America." **They want "any style, any subject, with emphasis on grittier material (open raincoats and unnecessary foul language are not grit, they're stupid)." They do not want "poetry containing derogatory language directed toward race, religion, gender or sexual orientation. Pissing off politicians, corporations, religious zealots and lawyers is acceptable and in fact, encouraged."** They have recently published poetry by Anthony S. Abbott, John Grey, Livio Farallo and Linda Lerner. As a sample the editor selected these lines from "Vanitas" by Sharon Scholl:

> *It all boils down*
> *to a urine-scented room*
> *and the blue glow*
> *of Lucy show reruns.*

The editor says *MSR* is 52-60 pgs., digest-sized, saddle-stapled with 100 lb. stock glossy cover, photos, art and ads. They receive about 3,000 poems a year, accept approximately 300. Press run is 500 for 100 subscribers, 40% shelf sales; 10% distributed free to perspective vendors and advertisers. Subscription: $12. **Sample postpaid varies but most are $3.50. Submit 6 pages of poetry at a time. No previously published poems or simultaneous submissions. Cover letter preferred with a brief bio "about the poet, not their credits." Reads submissions year-round, "but only accepts unsolicited work from non-subscribers June 1 to September 1." Has backlog of 6-12 months. Poems are circulated to an editorial board of chief editor, then associate and/or contributing editors. Often comments on rejections "if requested and time allows." Send SASE for guidelines. Reports in 2-3 weeks. Pays 1 copy and contributor's discount for the issue in which they appear. Acquires one-time rights.** Staff plans to review books and chapbooks of poetry in the future. Open to unsolicited reviews. Poets may also send books for review consideration. The editor says, "Rejection is an obstacle in the road—nothing personal—just drive around it. Always drive around it."

‡*MAKING WAVES (IV-Translations), P.O. Box 226, Guildford, Surrey GU1 4NW United Kingdom, phone/fax (01483)567182, founded 1986, editor Anthony Selbourne, publishes 2 paperbacks/year of translation from the Nordic/Arctic regions and minority cultures/natives. Traveling exhibitions of illustrated work accompany the books. **They do not want "poetry of a general racist, sexist or extremist nature or immature writing."** They have recently published poetry by Ilpo Tiihonen and Eeva-Liisa Manner. Books are usually 70 pgs., 8½ × 5¾, offset with 2- to 3-color cover and mixed media illustrations. **Query first with 10 sample poems and cover letter with brief bio, publication credits and proposed illustrations and artists if applicable. Previously published poems OK; no simultaneous submissions.** Time between acceptance and publication is 6 months.

Poems are circulated to an editorial board. Replies to queries and mss in 2-3 weeks. Pays $500-1,000 honorarium and 20 author's copies (out of a press run of 500.) Obtain samples of books by writing to the above address.

‡**MALACHITE & AGATE (IV-Lesbian)**, 6558 Fourth Section Rd. #149, Brockport NY 14420, e-mail mmilto n@frontiernet.net, founded 1997, editor Marianne Milton, published annually, contains **"lesbian poetry and related prose."** They have recently published poetry by May Swenson, Adrian Oktenberg, Laurel Speer, Ellen Bass and Alexandra Grilikhes. As a sample the editor selected these lines from "Handprints" by E.M. Lauricella:

> Now the sunflower has begun to seed,
> and her hand reaches my mouth.
> The sky is ribbed with pink and red
> as I lower myself among her.

The editor says *Malachite & Agate* is 104 pgs., 5½×8½, perfect-bound, professionally printed with 2-color card cover and ads. They receive about 300-400 poems a year, accept approximately 10%. Press run is 500 for 50 subscribers, 10% shelf sales; 10 distributed free to lesbian archives. Subscription: $15/2 years. **Sample postpaid: $9.95. Submit up to 6 poems at a time. Previously published poems and simultaneous submissions OK. Time between acceptance and publication is 1 year. "Editor selects poetry." Send SASE for guidelines. Reports "promptly." Always sends prepublication galleys. Pays 1 copy. Acquires one-time rights.** Reviews books or chapbooks of recent lesbian poetry in 500-3,000 words in single/multi book format. Open to unsolicited reviews. Poets may also send books of lesbian poetry for review consideration.

✤**THE MALAHAT REVIEW (II); LONG POEM PRIZES (II, IV-Form)**, P.O. Box 1700, University of Victoria, Victoria, British Columbia V8W 2Y2 Canada, phone (604)721-8524, founded 1967, editor Derk Wynand, is "a high quality, visually appealing literary quarterly which has earned the praise of notable literary figures throughout North America. Its purpose is to publish and promote poetry and fiction of a very high standard, both Canadian and international. **We are interested in various styles, lengths and themes. The criterion is excellence."** They have recently published poetry by Margaret Atwood and P.K. Page. As a sample the editor selected these lines from "relay" by Jan Zwicky and Don McKay:

> . . . Sleep
> is a ship whose rigging keeps coming
> undone in the rain,
> and the self who wakes is the self who walks
> its deck, its pockets stuffed
> with all the letters you have never mailed.

They use 50 pgs. of poetry in each issue, have 1,500 subscribers of which 300 are libraries. They receive about 2,000 poems a year, use approximately 100. Topics and length in this handsome publication are particularly open, though editors show a distinct taste for free verse exhibiting craft and focus. Subscription: $35 Canadian (or US equivalent). **Sample postpaid: $8 US. Submit 5-10 poems, addressed to Editor Derk Wynand. The editors comment if they "feel the ms warrants some attention even though it is not accepted." Send SASE (or SAE and IRC) for guidelines. Reports within 3 months. Pays $25 per poem/page plus 2 copies and reduced rates on others.** Reviews books of poetry. The Long Poem Prizes of $400, plus publication and payment at their usual rates (entry fee is a year's subscription), is for a long poem or cycle 5-15 pgs. (flexible minimum and maximum), deadline March 1 of alternate years (1999, 2001, etc.).

MALEVOLENCE PUBLICATIONS; BLOOD & FEATHERS MAGAZINE; BLOOD & FEATHERS CHAPBOOK SERIES CONTEST (I, II), P.O. Box 55, Willoughby OH 44096-0055, founded 1995, editor Jennifer Helms. *blood & feathers magazine*, a quarterly publication, is "a testimony of survival. The poetry reflects our strength and resilience despite the slings and arrows of every day life." **They want "poems of strength and survival; intelligent with clear and strong imagery. No longer than one typed page. Free verse preferred. No gore, preachy religious or experimental work."** They have recently published poetry by W. Gregory Stewart, Lyn Lifshin, James Mackie and Cindy Main. As a sample the editor selected these lines from "Vignette" by Scott H. Urban:

> The sunset looked like
> a spreading scarlet wound
> on the high blue shirt of God
> and when He fell back,
> staining the treetops pink,
> He left only darkness behind Him.

b&f is 40 pgs., photocopied, digest-sized and saddle-stapled with color card cover, and ads inside. They receive about 2,000 poems a year, publish 80. Subscription: $12. **Sample postpaid: $3. Submit 3-5 poems at a time. Previously published poems and simultaneous submissions OK. Cover letter preferred including 3- to 5-line bio. Often comments on rejections. Publishes theme issues. Send SASE for guidelines and upcoming themes. Reports in 2-6 weeks. Pays 2 or more copies. All rights returned upon publication.** Malevolence Publications publishes **1 chapbook/year** through its blood & feathers chapbook series contest. Winning poet receives **$50 and 20 chapbooks.** Submit 25-35 pgs. of poetry, any style or subject. Poems may be previously published or entered in other contests. Entry fee: $5, includes a recent issue of *blood & feathers magazine*. Deadline: November 31. Send SASE for complete guidelines. The editor says, "We try very hard to make our publications accessible to all people. Poetry is not just for poets; it's for everyone. Be honest when writing. The important part of publishing for me is not profit, but getting your words out into the world. We want people to be able to read and identify with your work. I do this because poetry is in my soul. I hope it's in yours."

‡*MANCHESTER POETS PRESS; TARANTULA PUBLICATIONS (III), 122 Petersburg Rd., Edgeley Park, Stockport SK3 9RB United Kingdom, founded 1976, contact Dave Tarrant. Manchester Poets' Press, under their imprint Tarantula Publications, publishes 3-4 paperbacks/year. **They want "the 'well-made poem'— mature writing, thoughtful with originality."** They do not want "juvenile or therapy poems." They have recently published poetry by John Ward. Books are usually 90 pgs., A5, perfect-bound with soft cover and occasional graphics. **Previously published poems OK; no simultaneous submissions. Cover letter required.** Time between acceptance and publication is up to 3 months. **Poems are circulated to an editorial board. Always comments on rejections. Replies to queries and mss ASAP. Pays 150-250 copies, "according to demand."** Sponsors annual contest. Write for details. The editor says, "We only publish what we feel has to be published. We try to spare poets the embarrassment of being published before they are ready."

‡*MANDRAKE POETRY REVIEW; THE MANDRAKE PRESS (III, IV-Translations), ul. Wielkiej Nied-źwiedzicy 35/8, Gliwice 44-117 Poland, or Box 792, Larkspur CA 94977-0792, founded 1993 in New York, European editor Leo Yankevich, North American editor David Castleman, appears twice a year, in April and October. The editors say, **"We look at anything, but accept very little."** They have recently published poetry by Madison Cawein, Michael Daugherty, Roy Clark Dickson, William Linville, Stanley Mason and Czeslaw Milosz. As a sample the editor selected these lines from "By A Philosopher's Tomb" by Cornel (Adam) Lengyel:

> How may one thank in fitting terms the maker
> of new and taller windows for the soul?
> I turn my transient eyes without and see
> the world's great ghostly wheels of change reduce
> our mortal home to essences eternal—
> the terror and the grandeur, all within.

Mandrake Poetry Review is 12-32 pgs., A4, offset printed and saddle-stapled with white card cover. The editors say they accept about 2% of the poetry received. Press run is 500 for 100 subscribers from 3 continents. Single copy: $3 (by airmail); subscription: $10/2 years. **Make checks payable to David Castleman at the California address. Submit 1-7 poems at a time. Previously published poems and simultaneous submissions OK. Cover letter preferred. "Send only copies of your poems, as we do not return poems with our reply." Reports in 1-2 months. Pays 2 copies "sometimes more." All rights revert to author.** The Mandrake Press also publishes 1 perfect-bound collection of poems, averaging 36 pgs., each year. Press runs vary from 60 to 300. "I should at least be familiar with a poet before publishing a book. If he's published poems in magazines and has a modest readership, it certainly helps." **Query first with sample poems and cover letter with brief bio and publication credits. Pays copies.** They have recently published *A Foggy Morning* by Richard Alan Bunch, *Selected Poems* by David Castleman, *Epistle From The Dark* by Leo Yankevich and *A Lookout's Letter* by Cornel (Adam) Lengyel.

‡MANGROVE (II), University of Miami, Dept. of English, P.O. Box 248145, Coral Gables FL 33124-4632, founded 1994, contact poetry editors, published annually, is a "high-quality literary magazine." **They want "high-quality poetry of no more than five pgs. No restrictions on form."** They do not want "children's poetry." They have recently published poetry by Maxine Kumin, Nelida Pinon, Christina Garcia, Lyn Lifshin, Fred D'Aguiar and Jim Daniels. The editor says *Mangrove* is 125 pgs. They receive about 1,000 poems a year, accept approximately 3%. Press run is 500 for 50 subscribers of which 25 are libraries, 100 shelf sales; 35 distributed free to contributors. **Sample postpaid: $5. Make checks payable to Mangrove/Dept. of English. Submit up to 5 poems at a time. No previously published poems; simultaneous submissions OK. Cover letter preferred. Time between acceptance and publication is 3-6 months. Poems are circulated to an editorial board.** "Panel of readers vote on the poetry. A majority decision is accepted." **Send SASE for guidelines. Reports in 3-6 months. Pays 1 copy. Acquires first North American serial rights.**

THE MANHATTAN REVIEW (II, IV-Translations), 440 Riverside Dr., Apt. 45, New York NY 10027, phone (212)932-1854, founded 1980, poetry editor Philip Fried, tries **"to publish American and foreign writers, and we choose foreign writers with something valuable to offer the American scene. We like to think of**

---

‡   **THE DOUBLE DAGGER** before a listing indicates that the listing is new in this edition. New markets are often the most receptive to submissions.

poetry as a powerful discipline engaged with many other fields. We want to see ambitious work. Interested in both lyric and narrative. Not interested in mawkish, sentimental poetry. We select high-quality work from a number of different countries, including the U.S." They have recently published poetry by Wistawa Szymborska, Baron Wormser, D. Nurkse, Penelope Shuttle and Peter Redgrove. The *MR* is now "an annual with ambitions to be semiannual." The magazine is 64 pgs., digest-sized, professionally printed with glossy card cover, photos and graphics. Press run is 500 for 400 subscribers of which 250 are libraries. It is also distributed by Bernhard DeBoer, Inc. and Fine Arts Distributors. They receive about 300 submissions a year, use few ("but I do read everything submitted carefully and with an open mind"). "I return submissions as promptly as possible." Single copy: $5; subscription: $10. **Sample: $6.25 with 6×9 envelope. Submit 3-5 pgs. of poems at a time. No simultaneous submissions. Cover letter with short bio and publications required. Editor sometimes comments "but don't count on it." Reports in 10-12 weeks. Pays copies.** Staff reviews books of poetry. Send books for review consideration. Philip Fried advises, "Don't be swayed by fads. Search for your own voice. Support other poets whose work you respect and enjoy. Be persistent. Keep aware of poetry being written in other countries."

MANKATO POETRY REVIEW (II), Box 53, English Dept., Mankato State, Mankato MN 56001, phone (507)389-5511, founded 1984, editor Roger Sheffer, is a semiannual magazine that is **"open to all forms of poetry. We will look at poems up to 60 lines, any subject matter."** They have published poetry by Edward Micus, Judith Skillman and Walter Griffin. The magazine is 5×8, typeset on 60 lb. paper, 30 pgs., saddle-stapled with buff matte card cover printed in one color. It appears usually in May and December and has a circulation of 200. Subscription: $5/year. **Sample postpaid: $2.50. Submit 3-5 poems at a time. However, do not submit mss in summer (May through August). No previously published poems or simultaneous submissions. Cover letter required. Send SASE for guidelines. Reports in about 2 months; "We accept only what we can publish in next issue." Pays 2 copies.** The editor says, "We're interested in looking at longer poems—up to 60 lines, with great depth of detail relating to place (landscape, townscape)."

MANNA; MANNA FORTY, INC. (IV-Nature/ecology, religion, psychology/science), Box 548, Rt. 1, Sharon OK 73857-9761, phone (405)254-2660, fax (405)256-2416, founded 1986, literary format 1991, editor Richard D. Kahoe. As their "Mission Statement" says: "*manna*, a quarterly literary-professional journal, advances and publishes interests of manna forty, inc., a not-for-profit corporation. *manna* promotes ideals of a holistic view of truth and beauty, expressed in poetry, appropriate prose and pen sketches. It focuses on nature (natural living, ecology, environmental issues), religion (Christian and ecumenical) and psychology (and related sciences), and especially the interfaces of these areas." **They are open to all styles of poetry up to 50 lines, "but prefer shorter (under 25 lines) and will be publishing no more than 35% free verse." They want poetry related to religion, nature and psychology. "Prefer integrating two or three of these areas. No mushy sentimentality, highly obscure verse or doggerel (except possibly in short humorous context)."** They have published poetry by C. David Hay, Marian Ford Park and Howard F. Stein. As a sample the editor selected these lines from "A Covenant Kept" by Marian Ford Park:

> If fears rush in with wicked banshee howl
> And threaten love and lifestyle with their cries,
> My faith, unshaken, I still climb aboard,
> Ignoring panic's wild and ugly growl.
> I search for rainbows in more sunny skies
> And write my memos to our Blessed Lord.

manna is 8 pgs., 8½×11, desktop-published and professionally printed on 70 lb. recycled stock, with line drawings. Press run is 350 for 110 subscribers of which 6 are libraries; 200 distributed free to community groups and to contributors. Subscription: free ("donation encouraged"). **Sample available for 1 first-class stamp.** "Contributors who can are asked (but not required) to make donation toward costs, generally $7.50-15, depending on length of poem." **Previously published poems and simultaneous submissions OK. SASE and cover letter required. "Prefer to receive two to six poems on separate pages." Deadlines: February 15, May 15, August 15 and November 15. Publication appears one month later. Comments on rejections with SASE. Publishes occasional theme issues. Send SASE for guidelines and subscribe for upcoming themes. Themes are announced 1 issue in advance. Reports in 1-3 months. Pays at least 2 copies but for minimal donation pays 5 copies direct to poet, 10 mailed to addresses provided by poet.** The editor says, "Poets and prose contributors should observe our subject guidelines. Beginners are encouraged, but we prefer poems not to *sound* like beginners."

MANOA: A PACIFIC JOURNAL OF INTERNATIONAL WRITING (II), 1733 Donaghho Rd., Honolulu HI 96822, e-mail mjournal@hawaii.edu, website http://www2.hawaii.edu/uhpress/Journals/MA/MAHome.html (publication) and http://www2.hawaii.edu/mjournal (editorial office), founded 1989, poetry editor Frank Stewart, appears twice a year. **"We are a general interest literary magazine, open to all forms and styles. We are not for the beginning writer, no matter what style. We are not interested in Pacific exotica."** They have recently published poetry by Arthur Sze, Linda Hogan and John Haines. It is 240 pgs., 7×10, offset, flat-spined using art and graphics. They receive about 3,000 poems a year, accept approximately 2%. Press run is 2,000 for 1,000 subscribers of which 30 are libraries, 700 shelf sales. Subscription: $22/year. **Sample postpaid: $10. Query by**

mail or e-mail. Submit 3-5 poems at a time. Send SASE for guidelines. Reports in 6 weeks. Always sends prepublication galleys. Pay "competitive" plus 2 copies. Seldom comments on rejections. They review current books and chapbooks of poetry. Open to unsolicited reviews. Poets may also send books for review consideration, attn. reviews editor. This magazine has become well known for the quality and diversity of its verse. It has also received a Design Excellence Award from the American Association of University Presses and Best Journal of the Year Award (honorable mention) from the Council of Editors of Learned Journals. Poetry published in *Manoa* has also been selected for inclusion in the 1995 and 1996 volumes of *The Best American Poetry*. The editor says, "We welcome the opportunity to read poetry submissions from throughout the country. We are not a regional journal, but we do feature work from the Pacific and Asia, especially in our reviews and essays. We are not interested in genre or formalist writing for its own sake, or picturesque impressions of the region."

MANY MOUNTAINS MOVING; MANY MOUNTAINS MOVING LITERARY AWARDS (II), 420 22nd St., Boulder CO 80302, phone (303)545-9942, fax (303)444-6510, e-mail mminc@concentric.net, website http://www.concentric.net/mmminc/, founded 1994, co-editors Naomi Horii and Marilyn Krysl, published biannually, *Many Mountains Moving* is "a literary journal of diverse contemporary voices that welcomes previously published fiction, poetry, nonfiction, and art from writers and artists of all walks of life. We publish the world's top writers as well as emerging talents." **They are open to any style of poetry, but they do not want any "Hallmark-y" poetry.** They have published poetry by Robert Bly, Lorna Dee Cervantes, Allen Ginsberg and Adrienne Rich. As a sample they selected these lines from "Bathing Susan" by Sarah Wolbach:

> *Her vertebrae are little apples softening in the heat, rocks on the river*
> *bottom that shimmer and dissolve in the light, little tumors like the*
> *ones within her, spreading through her lungs and glands like a flood*
> *of mold, a village of tiny fists. Touching her body is like reading*
> *Braille, but nothing is explained. Lifted from the water, she is wood*
> *dripping life, she is air with light breathing through.*

The attractive journal is about 200 pgs., $6 \times 8\frac{3}{4}$, web offset and perfect-bound with four-color cover and b&w art and photos inside. They receive 4,000 poems a year, accept about 1%. Press run is 2,000 for 400 subscribers. Single copy: $6.50; subscription: $18/year, $15/year for students and teachers. **Submit 3-10 poems at a time, typed with SASE. E-mail submissions OK. No previously published poems; simultaneous submissions OK.** Cover letter preferred. Poems are circulated to an editorial board. "Poems are first read by several readers. If considered seriously, they are passed to the poetry editor for final decision." Seldom comments on rejections. Publishes theme issues occasionally. Send SASE for guidelines. Reports in 1-4 weeks, "if we are seriously considering a submission, we may take longer." Sends prepublication galleys upon request. Pays 3 copies, additional copies available at $3/copy. Acquires first North American serial rights and "rights to publish in a future edition of the *Best of Many Mountains Moving Anthology*." They sponsor the annual Many Mountains Moving Literary Awards which awards $200 plus publication in the categories of poetry, fiction and essay. Entry fee: $15 (includes subscription). Send SASE for details. Poetry published in *Many Mountains Moving* has also been included in the 1996 and 1997 volumes of *The Best American Poetry*. The editors say, "Although we have featured a number of established poets, we encourage new writers to submit. However, we recommend that poets read through at least one issue to familiarize themselves with the type of work we generally publish."

‡THE MARLBORO REVIEW; MARLBORO PRIZE FOR POETRY (II), P.O. Box 243, Marlboro VT 05344, e-mail marlboro@cybergate.net, website http://www.cyberdrive.net/~marlboro/mr.htm, founded 1995, editor Ellen Dudley, poetry editor Ruth Anderson Barnett, published biannually, is a "literary magazine containing poetry, fiction, essays, reviews and translations." **They want "long poems." They do not want "greeting card verse."** They have recently published poetry by William Matthews, Brenda Hillman, Heather McHugh and Stephen Dobyns. The *Marlboro Review* is 80-112 pgs., 6×9, perfect-bound, offset printed with laminated colored cover and ads. They receive about 1,000 poems a year, accept approximately 7%. Press run is 1,000 for 350 subscribers of which 25 are libraries, 300 shelf sales; 50-70 distributed free to writers and institutions. Single copy: $8; subscription: $16. **Sample postpaid: $8.75. Submit up to 5 typed, near letter quality or better poems at a time. No previously published poems; simultaneous submissions OK "if we are notified." Send SASE for guidelines. Reports in up to 3 months. Sometimes sends prepublication galleys. Pays 2 copies. Acquires all rights. Returns rights on publication.** Reviews books of poetry in 500-1,000 words in single book format. Open to unsolicited reviews. Poets may also send books for review consideration. Sponsors the Marlboro Prize for Poetry. Awards a $500 honorarium and publication in fall issue. Submit $10 reading fee for up to 5 poems. Deadline June 30th. Include name on cover letter only, not on ms. All entrants receive the Marlboro Prize issue and are considered for publication.

MARYLAND POETRY REVIEW; MARYLAND STATE POETRY AND LITERARY SOCIETY (I, II), P.O. Drawer H, Catonsville MD 21228, founded 1985, edited by Rosemary Klein, "is interested in promoting the literary arts in Maryland as well as nationally and internationally. **We are interested in strong, thoughtful poetry with a slight bias to free verse. All submissions are read carefully. *MPR* is open to good poets who have not published extensively as well as to those who have."** They have published poetry by Josephine

Jacobsen, Richard Jackson, Gary Finke and Walter McDonald. As a sample the editor selected these lines from "House of Forgotten Names" by Michael Fallon:

> *This house is made of wineglasses*
> *Made of friends and bright words*
> *This house is built on goodbye*

MPR is 75 pgs., 7×11, professionally printed in small type on quality eggshell stock, saddle-stapled with a glossy b&w card cover. It appears yearly with periodic theme issues. In the past they have done special issues on confessional, Irish, Hispanic and Australian poetry. **Query about possible future special issues.** Subscription and Maryland State Poetry and Literary Society membership is $20 ($15 for students and senior citizens; $25 for institutions). **Sample postpaid: $8. Submit up to 5 poems at a time with brief bio. No simultaneous submissions. "We read submissions only in January, April and September but accept all year." Send SASE for guidelines and upcoming themes. Reports in 3-6 months. Pays 1 copy.** Staff reviews books of poetry. Poets may also send books for review consideration, attn. Hugh Burgess. MSPLS sponsors the Michael Egan Memorial Poetry Contest for poetry of any length. Entry fee: $3/poem, $13/5 poems. Contest runs from September 1 through October 28. Cash prizes and magazine publication. Send SASE for guidelines.

MARYLAND REVIEW (II), Dept. of English and Modern Languages, Wilson Hall, UMES, Princess Anne MD 21853, phone (410)651-6552, fax (410)651-6550, founded 1986, is an annual literary journal of poetry and short fiction. "*MR* is looking for insightful work, historical or contemporary in perspective." **They want all kinds of poetry. "Special emphasis on black literature, entertaining, original themes, believable characters, widely appealing. Nothing that is clearly autobiographical."** They have published poetry by Errol Miller and Stephen Cushman. As a sample the editor selected these lines from "Sieve" by Steven Duplij:

> *Turning over pages of streets split*
> *Of alien cities' warped bodies,*
> *I asked the Shadow over them swirling*
> *Whence execution of dreams comes.*
>
> *The meaning bespattered cuts off the meeting*
> *With blows of beggars and lashes of gods . . .*

The editor says *MR* is 100-200 pgs., 6×9, typeset and professionally bound with 1-6 pgs. of graphics or art, no ads. They receive 50-100 poems a year, accept 10-30%. Press run is 500-1,000 for 75-100 subscribers of which 15 are libraries. Subscription: $6/year, $11.50/2 years. **Sample (including guidelines) postpaid: $6. Submit 2-5 poems at a time. No previously published poems; simultaneous submissions OK. Cover letter with brief bio (no more than 75 words) required. "All text must be in laser quality/scannable type. Manuscripts submitted on Macintosh or PC disks should be written using Macwrite. WordPerfect, or Microsoft Word. Hard copy should accompany disks." Reads submissions September through May only. Reports in up to 1 year, average 6 months. Sometimes sends prepublication galleys. Pays 2 copies. Acquires first serial rights only.** The editor says they want "writing that broadens the reader's sensitivities to aspects of the human experience. The writing should be substantive—not flippant or 'empty' i.e., much said about nothing. Racial minority writers are particularly encouraged to share their work with *MR*."

MASONIA ROUNDUP (I), 200 Coolwell Rd., Madison Heights VA 24572, e-mail dcmanson@pen.klz.va.us, founded 1990, editors Ardis and Dan Mason, is a quarterly "personal magazine of general interest written by real people about what has happened to them, their thoughts and ideas." **They want humor, short poetry (up to 30 lines), and family/children-oriented work. "Nothing too profound."** As a sample the editors selected these lines from "October Days" by Harold Wilson:

> *October days, the glow*
> *of summer's fire,*
> *Do embers come*
> *To warm the searching soul,*
> *In squirrel's joy,*
> *In scarlet flame,*
> *Do maples have their show.*

Masonia Roundup is 16 pgs. (including cover), 7×8½ (four 8½×14 sheets folded in half), offset printed. They receive about 100 poems a year, accept 4-8. Press run is 150 for 92 subscribers. Subscription: $5. **Sample postpaid: $1.50. Make checks payable to Ardis or Dan Mason. Submit 10 poems at a time, typed with SASE. Previously published poems and simultaneous submissions OK. Cover letter preferred.** Time between acceptance and publication is 6 months to 1 year. **Seldom comments on rejections. Send SASE for guidelines or request via e-mail. Reports in 1-2 months. Pays 2 copies. Acquires first or one-time rights.** Staff reviews books of poetry. Poets may also send books for review consideration.

THE UNIVERSITY OF MASSACHUSETTS PRESS; THE JUNIPER PRIZE (II), P.O. Box 429, Amherst MA 01004-0429, phone (413)545-2217, fax (413)545-1226, website http://www.umass.edu/umpress, founded 1964. The press offers an annual competition for the Juniper Prize, in alternate years to first and subsequent books. In even-numbered years (1998, 2000, etc.) only subsequent books will be considered: mss whose authors have had at least one full-length book or chapbook of poetry published or accepted for publication. In odd-numbered years (1997, 1999, etc.) only "first books" will be considered: mss by writers whose poems may have appeared in literary journals and/or anthologies but have not been published, or been accepted for publication, in book form. Such chapbooks must be at least 30 pages, and self-published work is not considered to lie within this "books and chapbooks" category. They have published *At the Site of Inside Out* by Anna Rabinowitz; *After Frost: An Anthology of Poetry from New England* edited by Henry Lyman; and *Cities and Towns: Poems* by Arthur Vogelsang. "Poetry books are approximately $14 for paperback editions and $24 for cloth." **Submissions must not exceed 60 pgs. in typescript (generally 50-55 poems). Include paginated contents page; provide the title, publisher and year of publication for previously published volumes. A list of poems published or slated for publication in literary journals and/or anthologies must also accompany the ms. Such poems may be included in the ms and must be identified.** "Mss by more than one author, entries of more than one ms simultaneously or within the same year, and translations are not eligible." **Entry fee: $10 plus SASE for return of ms or notification. Entries must be postmarked not later than September 30.** The award is announced in April/May and publication is scheduled for the following spring. The amount of the prize is $1,000 and is in lieu of royalties on the first print run. Poet also receives 12 copies in one edition or 6 copies each if published in both hardcover and paperbound editions. **Fax, e-mail or send SASE for guidelines and/or further information to the above address. Entries are to be mailed to Juniper Prize, University of Massachusetts, Amherst MA 01003.**

THE MASSACHUSETTS REVIEW (II), South College, Box 37140, University of Massachusetts, Amherst MA 01003, phone (413)545-2689, founded 1959, editors Paul Jenkins and Mary Heath. Mostly free verse, all lengths and topics, appears here, with emphasis in recent issues on narrative work. An interesting feature: Editors run poems with long-line lengths in smaller type, to fit on the page without typographical interruption (as in other journals). They have published poetry by Marge Piercy, Michael Benedikt and Eavan Boland. As a sample the editor selected these lines from "What They Did" by Vern Rutsala:

> What they decided to do was so hard
> we marvelled at their courage.
> It was like trying to tie knots
> with two fingers inside a matchbox
> the way surgeons do, practicing.
> Like that only much harder.

The Massachusetts Review is 308 pgs., 6×9, offset on bond paper, perfect-bound with 4-color card cover and 4-color pages of art. They receive about 2,500 poems a year, use about 50. Press run is 1,600 for 1,100-1,200 subscribers of which 1,000 are libraries, the rest for shelf sales. Subscription: $18 (US), $30 outside US, $24 for libraries. **Sample postpaid: $7. No simultaneous submissions or previously published poems. Read submissions October 1 through June 1 only. Send SASE for guidelines. Reports in 6 weeks. Pays minimum of $10, or 35¢/line, plus 2 copies.** Work published in this review has been included in the 1995 and 1997 volumes of *The Best American Poetry*.

‡MATCHBOOK; MATCHBOOK PRESS; LCPH MEDIA SERVICES (II), 242 N. Broad St., Doylestown PA 18901, e-mail matchbookpress.com, website http://www.matchbookpress.com, founded 1994, editor Debrie Stevens, published biannually, "presents intriguing poetry and reviews to readers interested in same." **They want "most any form, length, subject, style with the following restrictions, query first on long poems or translations." They do not want "rhymed verse, traditional forms, concrete poems."** They have recently published poetry by Simon Perchik, Cid Corman and Robert Peters. The editor says *Matchbook* is 64 pgs., tabloid-sized, offset printed with cover art and ads. They receive about 500 poems a year, accept approximately 20%. Press run is 300 for 12 subscribers of which 2 are libraries; 25 distributed free to area bookstores. Subscription: $11.95. **Sample postpaid: $6.95. Make checks payable to LCPH Media Services. "Copy purchase suggested but not mandatory." Submit 5-6 poems at a time typewritten, printed out, or legible copies. No previously published poems; simultaneous submissions OK "if noted." Cover letter preferred. Time between acceptance and publication is 6 months. Seldom comments on rejections. Publishes theme issues, "announced in previous issues, plus on website." Send SASE for guidelines or obtain via e-mail or website. Reports in 1 month. Sometimes sends prepublication galleys. Pays 2 copies. Acquires first North American serial rights.** Staff reviews books, chapbooks, magazines and zines in 200 words, single format. Poets may also send books for review consideration.

*MATTOID (II), School of Literary & Communication Studies, Deakin University, Geelong, Victoria, Australia 3217, fax (052)272484, founded 1977, contact Dr. Brian Edwards, appears 2 or 3 times/year. **"No special requirements but interesting complexity, quality, experimentation. No naive rhyming verse."** They have published poetry by Lauris Edmond, Kevin Hart and Judith Rodriguez. It is 200 pgs., flat-spined with 2-color cover. They receive about 800 poems a year, publish 10-15%. Press run is 650 for 400 subscribers of which 10 are libraries, 50-100 shelf sales. **Sample postpaid: $15 overseas. Publishes theme issues. Send SASE (or SAE and IRC) for upcoming themes. Reports in 2-3 months. Pays 1 copy.** Reviews books of poetry in 1,000-2,000 words, single format.

MATURE YEARS (IV-Senior citizen, religious), P.O. Box 801, 201 Eighth Ave. S., Nashville TN 37202, phone (615)749-6292, founded 1954, editor Marvin W. Cropsey, is a quarterly. "The magazine's purpose is to help persons understand and use the resources of Christian faith in dealing with specific opportunities and problems related to aging. **Poems are usually limited to 16 lines and may, or may not, be overtly religious. Poems should not poke fun at older adults, but may take a humorous look at them. Avoid sentimentality and saccharine. If using rhymes and meter, make sure they are accurate."** *MY* is 112 pgs., magazine-sized, perfect-bound, with full-color glossy paper cover. Circulation 70,000. **Sample postpaid: $3.95. Submit season and nature poems for spring during December through February; for summer, March through May; for fall, June through August; and for winter, September through November. Send SASE for guidelines. Reports in 2 months; sometimes a year's delay before publication. Pays 50¢-$1/line upon acceptance.**

THE MAVERICK PRESS; SOUTHWEST POETS SERIES ANNUAL CHAPBOOK CONTEST (II, IV-Regional, themes), Rt. 2 Box 4915, Eagle Pass TX 78852-9605, phone/fax (210)773-1836, founded 1991, editor Carol Cullar, publishes a biannual of "outstanding Texas writers and other mavericks whose works represent the contemporary scene. Each issue is individually named (e.g., the April 1996 issue was titled *Jack Rabbit*)." They are **looking for "strong, uncluttered figurative language to 100 lines. No diatribes on current events or political posturings, no smut."** They have published poetry by Errol Miller, Gina Tabasso, Jo LeCoeur and Duane Locke. As a sample the editor selected these lines from "The View She Promised" by Larry L. Fontenot:

> . . . *The hawk sears the sky,*
> *its shadow lost in the blur of flight.*
> *Its cry promises her the next journey.*
> *She leaves her old voice at the top of the view,*
> *trades tongue for talon,*
> *feels the breeze of rising wings. . . .*

The editor says it is 120 pgs., 7×10, perfect-bound. Cover is an original block print by the editor, inside illustrations include b&w line drawings or block prints by contributors. They receive 1,000-2,000 poems a year, accept 4-8%. Press run is 250 for 100 subscribers of which 12 are libraries, 120 shelf sales. Subscription: $15. **Sample postpaid: $8. Submit up to 6 poems at a time. "Author's name and address must appear on every page submitted. Prefer standard size paper and envelopes 6×9 or larger." No previously published poems; simultaneous submissions OK with notification up front and a phone call if ms is accepted elsewhere. Cover letter with brief bio required.** Time between acceptance and publication is a year and a half maximum. **"All entries are sorted into Texans/Non-Texans, then read impartially. Outstanding pieces are reread and resorted later with slight consideration made to Texas writers. Final selections are made after consultation with Rio Bravo Literary Arts Council." Often comments on rejections. Criticism provided, if requested. Fee negotiated on a job-by-job basis, minimum $25. Publishes one theme issue each year in November. Send SASE for guidelines and upcoming themes. Reports in 6-8 weeks. Sometimes sends prepublication galleys. Pays 1 copy. All rights retained by authors.** They also sponsor the Southwest Poets Series Annual Chapbook Contest, for residents of Arizona, California (Southern), Colorado, Nevada, New Mexico, Oklahoma, Texas and Utah. Entry fee: $10, includes copy of winning chapbook published in February of following year. Deadline: October 31. Write for details. The editor says, "We are looking for strong, uncluttered, figurative language and prefer free verse, although the exception is considered. I would like to see more poems that 'push the envelope'—test the limits of what is poetic. Main criterion is excellence. Beginners: Presentation is important, but content is paramount."

‡*MAYPOLE EDITIONS (II), 22 Mayfair Ave., Ilford, Essex IG1 3DQ England, (0181)252-0354, contact Barry Taylor, publishes 3 hardbacks/year of fiction and poetry, as well as anthologies. **They want "poems broadly covering social concerns, ethnic minorities, feminist issues, romance, lyric." They do not want** "politics." They have recently published poetry by A. Lee Firth, Samantha Willow, Brian Jeffry, Mindy Cresswell, Denise Bell and Paul Amphlet. **Query first with a few sample poems approximately 30 lines long and cover letter with brief bio and publication credits. Obtain samples of books by sending £1 and an A5 SAE for a catalog.**

MEADOWBROOK PRESS (IV-Anthologies, children, humor), 5451 Smetana Dr., Minnetonka MN 55343, founded 1975, contact Children's Poetry Editor. Meadowbrook Press publishes one anthology a year as part of a series of funny poetry books for children. **They want humorous poems aimed at children ages 6-12. Length limit: 45 lines. "Poems should be fun, light and refreshing. We're looking for new, hilarious, contemporary voices in children's poetry that kids can relate to."** They have published poetry by Shel

---

✳ **AN ASTERISK** before a listing indicates an overseas publisher, magazine, contest, conference or organization.

"Poetry is a significant form of expression for both healthcare workers and patients," says Eugene D. Radice, M.D., editor of *Mediphors*, a literary journal of the health professions. "The interest in *Mediphors'* poetry continues to increase, paralleling the national trend in medicine which includes poetry as a form of therapy for those experiencing illness and an emotional outlet for medical practitioners." The biannual, published in Bloomsburg, Pennsylvania, seeks work showing the artistic side of medicine: "finding images of beauty, an oasis in the often harsh and adverse nature of disease." In fact, the image for this issue's cover was selected because of its dual representation of nature and disease. "Besides being an intriguing nature photograph of trees, the image could also represent the pattern made by arteries on the back of a damaged eye (retinopathy)," says Radice. Cover photo by Peter S. Petropoulos, M.D., a resident in Emergency Medicine at the State University of New York at Syracuse.

Silverstein, Jack Prelutsky, Jeff Moss and Bruce Lansky. Anthologies have included *Kids Pick the Funniest Poems*; *A Bad Case of the Giggles*; and *Miles of Smiles*. Forthcoming will be *No More Homework! No More Tests!* "Submit your best work." One poem to a page, name and address on each. Include SASE with each submission. Previously published poems and simultaneous submissions OK. Cover letter required "just to know where the poet found us." Time between acceptance and publication is 1-2 years. Poems are tested in front of grade school students before being published. Send SASE for guidelines. Pays $50-100/poem plus 1 copy.

‡*MEANJIN (II)**, 99 Barry St. Carlton, Melbourne, Victoria 3053 Australia, phone (613)9344-6950, e-mail meanjin@unimelb.edu.au, founded 1940, poetry editor Laurie Duggan, published quarterly, features "English literature and cultural studies." **They want "skillfully crafted poetry, any subject." They do not want "self-indulgent, long or incomprehensible poems."** They have recently published poetry by Philip Hammial, John Kinsella, Alan Wearne and π0. The editor says *Meanjin* is 200 pgs., 200×140mm, perfect-bound with 4-color cover and graphics. They receive about 2,000 poems a year, accept approximately 2-3%. Press run is 2,500 for 1,200 subscribers of which 30% are libraries, 500-800 shelf sales; 150 distributed free to subscribers, funding bodies and press. Single copy: $9.95; subscription: $36. **Sample postpaid: $8.50. Submit 2 poems at a time. No previously published poems; simultaneous submissions OK. Time between acceptance and publication is 3-6 months. Always comments on rejections. Publishes theme issues. Send SASE (or SAE and IRC) for guidelines. Reports in 1-2 months. Always sends prepublication galleys. Pays $80 minimum plus 2 copies.** Acquires "50% of copying rights to published version of poems."

MEDICINAL PURPOSES LITERARY REVIEW; POET TO POET, INC. (II), 86-37 120th St., #2D, Richmond Hill NY 11418, phone (718)776-8853, e-mail scarptp@worldnet.att, founded 1994, executive editor Robert Dunn, managing editor Thomas M. Catterson, poetry editor Leigh Harrison. *Medicinal Purposes* appears 3 times/year and **wants "virtually any sort of quality poetry (3 poems or 100 lines, whichever comes first). Please, no pornography, gratuitous violence or hate mongering."** They have published poetry by D.H. Melhem, X.J. Kennedy, Rhina P. Espaillat, W.R. Elton, Chocolate Waters and t. kilgore splake. *Medicinal Purposes* is 64 pgs., 8½×5½ (landscape format), professionally printed and perfect-bound with card stock cover with b&w illustration, b&w illustrations also inside. They receive 800 poems a year, accept 10%. Press run is 1,000 for 120 subscribers, 30% shelf sales. Subscription: $16/year. **Sample postpaid: $6. Make checks payable to Poet to Poet. Submit 3 poems at a time, up to 60 lines per poem, typed with SASE. E-mail submissions OK (1 poem per electronic page). No previously published poems or simultaneous submissions. Cover letter preferred.** Time between acceptance and publication is 4-16 months. **Often comments on rejections. Send SASE for guidelines. Reports in 3 months. Always sends prepublication galleys. Pays 2 copies. Acquires first rights.** They produce a poetry/folk music public access cable show called "Poet to Poet." They also sponsor an annual poetry contest, first prize $100. Submit 3 poems of 6-16 lines each with a $5 entry fee by May 1st. Winners will be published in the Fall issue. The editors say, "Poetry cannot be created out of a vacuum. Read the work of others, listen to performances, and most important—Get A Life! Do Things! Only then do you stand a chance of finding your own voice."

MEDIPHORS (I, II, IV-Health concerns), P.O. Box 327, Bloomsburg PA 17815-0327, founded 1992, editor Eugene D. Radice, M.D. *Mediphors* is a biannual literary journal of the health professions that publishes literary work in medicine and health, including poetry, short story, humor, essay, drawing, art/photography. **They want "fresh insights into illness and those caregivers with the burden and joy of working in the fields of medicine and health. Optimism in the face of adversity and overwhelming sorrow. The day-to-day feelings of health-care workers in diverse settings from hospitals in cities to war zones in military hot spots."** *Mediphors* is 72 pgs., 8½ × 11, offset and saddle-stapled with color cover and b&w art, graphics and photos throughout. They receive about 2,000 poetry submissions a year, accept approximately 100. Press run is 1,200 for 300 subscribers of which 20 are libraries, 450 shelf sales. Single copy: $6.95; subscription: $15. **Sample postpaid: $5.50. Submit "two copies of each poem that we can keep; 6 poems maximum, 30 lines each. We do not accept previously published poems or simultaneous submissions, and it is upsetting to find out that this has occurred when we accept a poem." Cover letter not required "but helpful."** Time between acceptance and publication is 10-12 months. **Seldom comments on rejections. Send SASE for guidelines. Reports in 1-3 months. Pays 2 copies. "We require authors to sign a very tight contract for first North American serial rights that makes them legally responsible for plagiarism, libel, copyright infringement, etc."** The editor says, "Our goal is to place in print as many new authors as possible, particularly those working within the health/medical fields (such as doctors, nurses, technologists, therapists, etc.). We encourage unsolicited manuscripts."

MELLEN POETRY PRESS (II), P.O. Box 450, Lewiston NY 14092-0450, phone (716)754-2266, fax (716)754-4056, e-mail mellen@moran.com, founded 1973, poetry editor Patricia Schultz, is a scholarly press. "We do not have access to large chain bookstores for distribution, but depend on direct sales and independent bookstores." **They pay 2 copies, no royalties. "We require no author subsidies. However, we encourage our authors to seek grants from Councils for the Arts and other foundations because these add to the reputation of the volume." They want "original integrated work—living unity of poems, preferably unpublished, encompassable in one reading."** They have published poetry by W.R. Elton and Albert Cook. Their books are 64 pgs., 6 × 9, softcover binding, no graphics. Price: $12.95. **Submit 30-60 sample poems with cover letter including bio and publications. "We do not print until we receive at least 100 prepaid orders. Successful marketing of poetry books depends on the author's active involvement.** We send out up to 15 free review copies to journals or newspapers, the names of which may be suggested by the author. An author may (but is not required to) purchase books to make up the needed 100 prepublication sales." The editor says, "We seek to publish volumes unified in mood, tone, theme."

MELTING TREES REVIEW (II, IV-Ethnic, ecology), 2026 Mt. Meigs Rd. #2, Montgomery AL 36107, founded 1995, editor Mike Catalano, associate editor Suzanne Catalano. *Melting Trees Review*, "The Peoples' Park of Poetry," appears quarterly and "encourages the ethnic, the disillusioned, and the ecologist to explore their different drummers." **They want "free verse, vivid imagery; risk-taking and ethnic work; apocalyptic and anarchistic poetry. No academic work; prose chopped into poetry; boring, obscure or rhyming poetry."** They have recently published poetry by John Grey, Daniel Green, Rosemary Hildebrandt, Tim Scannell, Richard E. Reeve and Annie Hubbard. As a sample they selected these lines from "Suffer The Little Children" by Dawn Zapletal:

> *I was filled with the fear*
> *that my life would be this way*
> *forever and ever, until I died,*
> *and I wondered if this lonely,*
> *bitter pain was what Jesus felt*
> *when He was crucified.*

MLTR is 52 pgs., digest-sized, saddle-stapled with card stock cover and b&w cover art. They receive about 2,000 poems a year, use 10-15%. Press run is 300. **Sample postpaid: $3. Make checks payable to Mike Catalano. Submit 3-5 typed poems at a time. No previously published poems or simultaneous submissions. Cover letter preferred. "Unanimous concensus needed for acceptance." Always comments on rejections. Send SASE for guidelines. Reports in 2-3 weeks. Pays 1 copy. Acquires first rights.** The editors say, "We are a father/daughter team, not husband/wife. We are ethnic-friendly and community-involved. In our opinion, there is too much unimaginative, formalistic poetry. Our readers want bite, sustenance. Few mainstream poets take risks anymore. And unfortunately, poets seem more interested in their free copy than giving back to the community in which they reside."

‡*THE MENTOR (IV-Science fiction), P.O. Box K940, Haymarket, NSW 1240 Australia, founded 1964, editor Ron Clarke, published 2-3 times/year is a science fiction "genzine." **They want "poetry with a science fiction subject." They do not want "speculative" poetry.** They have recently published poetry by Steve Sneyd and John Light. As a sample the editor selected these lines from "Dragons Wake!" by Bridh Hancock:

> *Once upon a time*
> *beaten and knowing their time was over*
> *they layd and buryd sad last eggs*
> *then, wishing their young a much better morrow,*
> *died—to all but lejend and myth.*

The editor says *The Mentor* is 40 pgs., A4, photocopied, saddle-stapled with art. They receive about 50 poems a year, accept approximately 20. Press run is 200 for 3 subscribers of which 6 are libraries, 10 shelf sales; 180

distributed free. Single copy: $4 (AU); subscription: $5 (AU). **Sample postpaid: $5 (US). Submit 5 poems at a time. No previously published poems or simultaneous submissions. Cover letter preferred.** Time between acceptance and publication is 3 weeks. **Poems are selected by the editor. Often comments on rejections. Reports in 3 weeks. Pays 1 copy. Acquires first rights.** Staff reviews books of poetry in 40 words. Poets may also send books for review consideration.

MERLYN'S PEN: THE NATIONAL MAGAZINE OF STUDENT WRITING, GRADES 6-12 (IV-Students, young adults), Dept. PM, Box 1058, East Greenwich RI 02818, phone (401)885-5175, founded 1985, editor R. Jim Stahl. Each issue is 40 pgs., magazine-sized, professionally printed with glossy paper, color cover. Press run is 40,000 for 38,000 subscribers of which 5,000 are libraries. Subscription: $21. **Sample postpaid: $3. Send SASE for guidelines. Reports in 3 months. Pays 3 copies plus $5-10/piece.**

MERRIMACK BOOKS; PALACE CORBIE (II), P.O. Box 83514, Lincoln NE 68501-3514, e-mail we45927 @navix.net, website http://www.para-net.com/~palace_corbie, founded 1986, editor/publisher Wayne Edwards. *Palace Corbie* is an annual fiction and poetry anthology. **They want nontraditional poetry containing misery, angst and anguish. No rhyming poetry.** The editor says *Palace Corbie* is 224 pgs., 5½×8½, perfect-bound with 4-color cover. They receive approximately 1,000 poems a year, accept less than 1%. Press run is 1,000. Single copy: $9.95. **Submit any number of poems. Previously published poems OK if noted; no simultaneous submissions. Seldom comments on rejections. Send SASE for guidelines or obtain via e-mail. Reports in 1 month. Sometimes sends prepublication galleys. Pay varies, but "usually one copy." Acquires one-time rights.** Merrimack Books looks for "unusual emotive poems" and publishes 1-2 paperbacks and **3-5 chapbooks a year**. Chapbooks are usually 32-44 pgs. and saddle-stitched. **Submit entire ms. Replies in 1 month.** Send SASE for more information.

‡MESECHABE: THE JOURNAL OF SURRE(GION)ALISM (III), 1539 Crete St., New Orleans LA 70119-3006, phone (504)944-4823, founded 1988, editor Dennis Formento, published annually, exists "to surre(gion)alize the earth." **They want "poetry seriously committed to changing the language, the world, or both." They do not want "poetry by poets who don't read the publications they submit to." They have published poetry by Di Palma, Di Prima, di Michele and Max Cafard.** *Mesechabe* is 24 pgs., 8½×11, saddle-stapled with b&w photos, collages, computer graphics and drawings. They accept approximately 5% of poems received. Press run is 700 for 200 subscribers, 250-400 shelf sales; 50 distributed free to writers, friends and artists. Subscription: $20 individual, $30 institution. **Sample postpaid: $4. Submit 5-10 poems at a time. No previously published poems; simultaneous submissions OK. Cover letter required. Time between acceptance and publication is "unpredictable." Poems are circulated to an editorial board. "There is an editorial board of two; we read separately and compare findings." Always comments on rejections.** Publishes theme issues. Send SASE for upcoming themes. **Reports within 2 weeks. Sometimes sends prepublication galleys. Pays 2-5 copies.** Staff reviews books in 200-700 words. Poets may also send books for review consideration.

‡MESSAGES FROM THE HEART (I, II), P.O. Box 64840, Tucson AZ 85728, phone (520)577-0588, fax (520)529-9657, e-mail lsbsmith@aol.com, founded 1993, editor Lauren B. Smith, published quarterly, offers "writings, specifically letters (letters, journal entries, poems, essays), which nurture understanding between people." **They want "poems no more than 800 words, accessible to mainstream readers, which contain an element of hope." They do not want "explicit sexuality, hopelessness, 'cute.' "** They have recently published poetry by Sheila Bender, David Citino, John Levy and W.H. Auden. As a sample the editor selected these lines from "Blessings" by Sheila O'Connor:

> *You have taught me to taste the world again,*
> *swallow the dry snow,*
> *smell the surprise of the January sun.*
> *You, my small scientists of beauty,*
> *recover the wonder of life*
> *in your open, astonished hands.*

Messages From the Heart is 16 pgs., 4¼×10½, offset printed, saddle-stapled with medium card cover. They receive about 500-600 poems a year, accept approximately 2-4%. Press run is 600 for 300 subscribers; 50 distributed free for public relations. Single copy: $3.50; subscription: $12. **Sample postpaid: $3. Submit up to 6 poems at a time with SASE. Previously published poems and simultaneous submissions OK. Cover letter preferred. Time between acceptance and publication is 1 year. Poems are circulated to an editorial board. "Poems are selected by one editor and then reviewed by two others." Seldom comments on rejections. Publishes theme issues. Send SASE for guidelines. Reports in 1-3 weeks. Pays 3 copies. Acquires one-time rights.** "We review books about letter writing in 300-600 words." Open to unsolicited reviews. Poets may also send books for review consideration "only if about or including letters."

‡MIAMI UNIVERSITY PRESS (III), English Dept., Miami University, Oxford OH 45056, phone (513)529-5110, founded 1992, editor James Reiss, publishes 2 books/year in paperback and cloth editions. **They want "book manuscripts by poets who have already published at least one full-length book of poems."** They have recently published poetry by Ralph Angel, Judith Baumel, Steve Orlen and Hugh Seidman. Time between

INSIDER REPORT

To achieve publication, get into poetry "for the long haul"

"I think beginning writers focus too much on getting published, and not enough on learning to write well," says award-winning poet Aleda Shirley. "Like most poets I know, I blush when I think of some of the early poems of mine that were published, and are probably still available in dusty stacks of libraries."

Since the time of those first blush-inducing poems, Shirley's writing has come a long way. She has had her work published in numerous journals, including *The American Poetry Review*, *Prairie Schooner*, *The Georgia Review* and *Poetry*. She has been awarded grants from the National Endowment for the Arts, the Kentucky Foundation for Women, the Kentucky Arts Council and the Mississippi Arts Council. Two collections of Shirley's poetry have been published as well: *Chinese Architecture* (University of Georgia Press, 1986) and *Long Distance* (Miami University Press, 1996).

Aleda Shirley

Photo by Kay Holloway

Shirley started writing poetry as a response to the almost nomadic aspect of her childhood. "I was a military brat, and all that moving around probably only enhanced my natural tendency toward introspection," she says. "I remember reading Robert Frost when I was around ten and liking those poems very much. I probably started writing poems then. I became more serious about it as an adolescent, and I began reading Hart Crane and Wallace Stevens and Ezra Pound. I don't remember ever choosing, or deciding, to write; it was just something always with me."

For Shirley, getting her poems published came easy—in the beginning. "I started sending out poems when I was 17. I had a poem immediately accepted, and for a brief period I was under the impression getting published was easy. It is not easy; I was lucky. It wasn't until several years later I had poems accepted by good magazines."

Even though most of the responses she received in the beginning were form rejection letters, Shirley didn't let that discourage her. "I just figured I was in this—poetry I mean—for the long haul and I tried to see it as a part of my job, to send things out and, when they were rejected, to send them out again. As my poems got better, they started getting published."

Once a considerable number of her poems were accepted in magazines, Shirley felt it was time to put together a collection of her work. "I didn't really put together a manuscript until I'd had a number of poems published in magazines, and I didn't send that manuscript out until I felt pretty confident it was a finished book. I submitted my first collection of poems to the poetry series Princeton University used to sponsor, and they sent back a nice comment. I submitted it to the Yale Series of Younger Poets and got a form rejection. Then I submitted it to the University of Georgia Press and it was taken. I had no connections

INSIDER REPORT, *Shirley*

"Shades"

It takes more than a door painted blue
to keep the ghosts away. All you have to do
is live long enough and they will come.

Beside the interstate the old road still ran,
though it ended abruptly in a field of sage and mist.
That road seemed like the future: an emptiness

that could turn, at any moment, into beauty.
I stopped in a small town in Oklahoma—
a liquor store in a bad neighborhood,

old men and teenagers standing around out front,
a radio crackling in the dry wind.
Did the old men come this far and stop?

Smoke from their cigarettes disappeared an instant later.
In the darkness nothing was visible but the darkness.
By dawn the road was the color of silk

gone orchid or violet when tilted to the light,
the trees on the side of the road permanently twisted
from the wind off the plains. On that leg they bent

toward me. I stood some distance from the car and felt
the dry air whipping my skirt around my legs.
I realized I'd forgotten too little about my life,

that there was in sleep and inattention a kind of salvation
and I wanted to be saved because I no longer believed
any one place was different from any other.

Being haunted means you never feel wholly abandoned,
and as I drove past the blinded diners and the shells of old trucks,
I gathered it close to me, all of it, and went on.

(from *Long Distance*, 1996, Miami University Press; reprinted by permission of the author)

INSIDER REPORT, *continued*

with anyone there. I'd just researched which presses had contests for first books and sent my manuscript to them." That first book, ***Chinese Architecture***, won the Norma Farber First Book Award in 1987.

For those considering entering poetry competitions, Shirley stresses the importance of following the guidelines set up by the competition, and notes the quality of the presentation counts just as much as the quality of the poetry. "Submit a clean, easy-to-read manuscript. You want it to look like you care about your work and the impression it makes. That means going to some pains to choose a readable font, to use a good photocopying machine or printer, and to make sure your manuscript looks like you know what you're doing. You don't want to submit a manuscript of poems that looks as though you have never read a book of poetry."

Many of Shirley's revealing, intimate poems may seem to be reflections of events in her life but that isn't always the case. Her poems are inspired not only by her own life but by the lives of those around her and those she reads about. "A poem is a public act," she says. "And a very difficult thing to do, when you are learning to write, is to give up what you might want to express personally even if it's in the best interest of the poem. I suppose many of the things in my poems are from my personal experience, but just as many are invented. This doesn't make them less true, because I'm not after narrative truth or biographical accuracy; rather, I'm trying to express the particular truth of a particular poem."

By taking her time with her poems Shirley doesn't rush them into being. "I have a notebook and I write things down as they occur to me—lines and images and ideas. I don't really have a way to jumpstart myself into writing." Once those ideas form themselves into a poem, however, along comes the hard part—the revisions. "The only way to write a poem is to start writing and then keep working on it even if it seems impossible. I'm a pretty obsessive reviser of my own work; before I got a computer, I'd have 50 or 60 versions of a poem I'd typed out before it felt finished. With a computer, it's a bit harder to tell how many drafts a poem goes through."

Shirley recognizes many poets find it difficult to maintain a sense of honesty in their writing. "The whole 'business' of poetry is so competitive, and the rewards [as in money and fame] so negligible, it's easy to get bitter or write for the wrong reasons or compromise yourself somehow." Staying honest and writing for the love of the poem, not just to get published, is what poets should strive for.

"I think the real terrible truth of the matter is this: the way to learn how to write is to read and to write and then to read some more and then to write some more. There aren't any shortcuts."

—*Cindy Laufenberg*

acceptance and publication is 1-2 years. **"Poems are circulated to an editorial board where votes are tallied." Sometimes comments on rejections. Replies to queries and mss vary. Pays 10% royalties and 10 author's copies (out of a press run of 1,000). For sample books or chapbooks, purchase in bookstores or order from publisher.** Their book *Neither World* is the winner of the 1995 James Laughlin Award of The Academy of American Poets. *Selected Poems: 1965-1995* was chosen as one of the *Village Voice*'s "25 Favorite Books of 1995."

MICHIGAN QUARTERLY REVIEW (III), Dept. PM, 3032 Rackham Bldg., University of Michigan, Ann Arbor MI 48109, phone (313)764-9265, founded 1962, editor-in-chief Laurence Goldstein, is "an interdisciplinary, general interest academic journal that publishes mainly essays and reviews on subjects of cultural and literary interest." They use **all kinds of poetry except light verse. No specifications as to form, length, style, subject matter or purpose.** They have recently published poetry by Diane Ackerman, Thylias Moss, Sharon Olds and Yusef Komunyakaa. As a sample the editor selected these lines from "To the One Upstairs" by Charles Simic:

> *Boss of all bosses of the infinite universe,*
> *Wheeler-dealer, wire-puller, know-it-all,*
> *Or whatever else they call you?*
> *Go ahead, make the wind count the zeros tonight,*
> *Paper-clip the comets' tails,*
> *Staple everything with your star-light.*

The *MQR* is 160 pgs., 6×9, flat-spined, professionally printed with glossy card cover, b&w photos and art. They receive about 1,500 submissions a year, use approximately 30, have a 1-year backlog. Circulation is 2,000, with 1,500 subscribers of which half are libraries. Single copy: $5; subscription: $18. **Sample postpaid: $2.50. They prefer typed mss. No previously published poems or simultaneous submissions. Publishes theme issues. Reports in 4-6 weeks. Always sends prepublication galleys. Pays $8-12/page. Buys first rights only.** Reviews books of poetry. "All reviews are commissioned." Poetry published in the *Michigan Quarterly Review* was also selected for inclusion in the 1992, 1994 and 1995 volumes of *The Best American Poetry*. Laurence Goldstein advises, "There is no substitute for omnivorous reading and careful study of poets past and present, as well as reading in new and old areas of knowledge. Attention to technique, especially to rhythm and patterns of imagery, is vital."

MID-AMERICAN REVIEW; JAMES WRIGHT PRIZE FOR POETRY (II, IV-Translations), Dept. of English, Bowling Green State University, Bowling Green OH 43403, phone (419)372-2725, founded 1980, editor-in-chief George Looney, poetry editor Tony Gardner, appears twice a year. **"Poetry should emanate from strong, evocative images; use fresh, interesting language; and have a consistent sense of voice. Each line must carry the poem, and an individual vision should be evident. We encourage new as well as established writers. There is no length limit."** They have published poetry by Stephen Dunn, Catherine Sasanov, Albert Goldbarth, Naomi Shihab Nye, Greg Pape and Frankie Paino. The review is 100 pgs., offset printed, flat-spined, using line drawings, laminated card cover. They receive over 1,000 mss a year, use approximately 40-60 poems. Press run is 1,000. Single copy: $7; subscription: $12. **Sample postpaid: $5. Reads submissions September 1 through May 30 only. Send SASE for guidelines. Sometimes sends prepublication galleys. Pays $10/printed page when possible plus 2 copies. Rights revert to authors on publication.** Reviews books of poetry. Open to unsolicited reviews. **They also publish chapbooks in translation** and award the James Wright Prize for Poetry to a ms published in regular editions of *MAR*, when funding is available.

MIDDLE EAST REPORT (IV-Regional, ethnic, themes), 1500 Massachusetts Ave. NW, Suite 119, Washington DC 20005, phone (202)223-3677, founded 1971, editor Geoff Hartman, is "a magazine on contemporary political, economic, cultural and social developments in the Middle East and North Africa and U.S. policy toward the region. We occasionally publish **poetry that addresses political or social issues of Middle Eastern peoples."** They have published poetry by Dan Almagor (Israeli) and Etel Adnan (Lebanese). It is 48 pgs., magazine-sized, saddle-stapled, professionally printed on glossy stock with glossy paper cover, 4 issues/year. Press run is 7,500. Subscription: $32. **Sample postpaid: $6 domestic; $8 airmail overseas. Simultaneous submissions and previously published poems OK.** The editor says, "We key poetry to the theme of a particular issue. Could be as long as 6 months between acceptance and publication." **Editor sometimes comments on submissions. Reports in 6-8 weeks. Pays 3 copies.**

MIDLAND REVIEW (II), English Dept., Morrill Hall, Oklahoma State University, Stillwater OK 74078, phone (405)744-9474, founded 1985, is a literary annual that publishes "poetry, fiction, essays, ethnic, experimental, women's work, contemporary feminist." The editors say, **"style and form are open." They do not want "long or religious poetry."** They have published poetry by Amy Clampitt, William Stafford, Bill Knott, Tom Lux and Richard Kostelanetz. *Midland Review* is 100-120 pgs., digest-sized, with photography, artwork and ads. Circulation is 500 for 470 subscribers. Single copy: $6. **Sample postpaid: $5. Submit 3-5 poems at a time, typed ms in any form. "We no longer read during the summer (May 1 through August 31)."** Time between acceptance and publication is 6-12 months. **Reports in 3-6 months. Pays 1 copy.**

‡MIDMARCH ARTS PRESS; WOMEN ARTISTS NEWS (IV-Women), 300 Riverside Dr., New York NY 10025, founded 1979, editor Sylvia Moore. They have published poetry by Muriel Rukeyser, Eve Merriam and Jane Cooper. *WAN* is a 72-page magazine focusing **on women in the arts**, using some poetry. **Sample postpaid: $3.75. Send SASE for guidelines. Reports in 6 weeks. Pays 5 copies.** Midmarch Arts Press publishes 4 paperbacks/year.

MIDSTREAM: A MONTHLY JEWISH REVIEW (IV-Ethnic), 110 E. 59th St., New York NY 10022, phone (212)339-6040, editor Joel Carmichael, is an international journal appearing 8 times a year. **They want short poems with Jewish themes or atmosphere.** They have published poetry by Yehuda Amichai, James Reiss, Abraham Sutzkever, Liz Rosenberg and John Hollander. The magazine is 48 pgs., approximately 8½×11, saddle-stapled with colored card cover. Each issue includes 4 to 5 poems (which tend to be short, lyric and freestyle expressing seminal symbolism of Jewish history and Scripture). They receive about 300 submissions a year, use approximately 5-10%. Circulation: 10,000. Single copy: $3; subscription: $21. **Submit 3 poems at a time. Publishes theme issues. Reports in 3 months. Pays $25/poem. Buys all rights.**

MIDWEST POETRY REVIEW (II), P.O. Box 20236, Atlanta GA 30325-0236, phone (404)350-0714, fax (404)352-8417, founded 1980, editor/publisher John K. Ottley, Jr., is a quarterly, with no other support than subscriptions, contest entry fees and an occasional advertisement. **They are looking for "quality accessible verse. Great imagery with powerful adjectives and verbs. Poetry that opens the door to the author's feelings through sensory descriptions.** We are attempting to encourage the cause of poetry by purchasing the best of modern poetry. **No jingly verses or limericks. Forty-line limit. Any subject is considered, if handled with skill and taste. No pornography."** They have recently published poetry by Louis Brodsky, Ray Johnson, Norbert Krapf, Anna-Margaret O'Sullivan, B.R. Culbertson and Katherine Marsh. As a sample the editor selected these lines from "Snow Horse" by Glenna Holloway:

> *My tan legs pressed her flanks,*
> *her whiteness steaming in leaf-lit morning,*
> *peach groves shimmering on the horizon.*
> *I still can see the ignis fatuus in her eye,*
> *the arch of her fringed neck in bias sunshafts.*

MPR is 40 pgs., professionally printed in Univers type, digest-sized, saddle-stapled with matte card cover. Subscription: $20 ($25 Canadian, $30 foreign, both in US funds). **Sample postpaid: $5.78 (when available). Submit up to 5 poems at a time. Fax submissions OK. Send SASE and $1 for guidelines. Reports in 3-4 weeks. Pays $5/poem. Buys first rights.** They have varied contests in each issue, with prizes ranging from $10-250, with "unbiased, non-staff judges for all competitions." Contests have entry fees. Send SASE for details. A 20-point self-analysis survey to assist poets in analyzing their own work is offered free to new subscribers.

THE MIDWEST QUARTERLY (II), Pittsburg State University, Pittsburg KS 66762, phone (316)235-4689, fax (316)235-4686, e-mail smeats@pittstate.edu, founded 1959, poetry editor Stephen Meats, "publishes articles on any subject of contemporary interest, particularly literary criticism, political science, philosophy, education, biography and sociology, and each issue contains a **section of poetry usually 15 poems in length.** I am interested in **well-crafted, though not necessarily traditional poems that explore the inter-relationship of the human and natural worlds in bold, surrealistic images of a writer's imaginative, mystical experience. Sixty lines or less (occasionally longer if exceptional)."** They have recently published poetry by Ronald Wallace, Fleda Brown Jackson, Lyn Lifshin, Jeanne Murray Walker and William Kloefkorn. The magazine is 130 pgs., digest-sized, flat-spined, matte cover, professionally printed. A nice mix of poems appears here, most of it free verse with room for an occasional formal or narrative piece. Circulation is 650, with 600 subscribers of which 500 are libraries. They receive about 4,000 poems a year, use approximately 60. "My plan is to publish all acceptances within 1 year." Subscription: $12. **Sample: $3. Mss should be typed with poet's name on each page, 10 poems or fewer. No previously published poems; simultaneous submissions OK. E-mail and fax submissions OK. Send SASE for guidelines and upcoming themes or request via fax or e-mail. Publishes theme issues occasionally. Reports in 2 months, usually sooner. "Submissions without SASE cannot be acknowledged." Pays 3 copies. Acquires first serial rights. Editor comments on rejections "if the poet or poems seem particularly promising."** Reviews books of poetry by *MQ* published poets only. He says, "Keep writing; read as much contemporary poetry as you can lay your hands on; don't let the discouragement of rejection keep you from sending your work out to editors."

MIDWEST VILLAGES & VOICES (V, IV-Regional), P.O. Box 40214, St. Paul MN 55104, phone (612)822-6878, founded 1979, is a cultural organization and small press publisher of **Midwestern poetry and prose.** They have published books of poetry by Ethna McKiernan, Florence Chard Dacey, Kevin FitzPatrick and Sue Doro. A collection of poetry and prose by Irene Paull is their most recent offering. The flat-spined books are generally 48 pgs., professionally printed with glossy card covers, selling for $5-12. **"We encourage and support Midwestern writers and artists. However, at this time submissions are accepted by invitation only. Unsolicited submissions are not accepted."**

MIDWIFERY TODAY (IV-Specialized: childbirth), P.O. Box 2672, Eugene OR 97402-0223, phone (541)344-7438, fax (541)344-1422, e-mail mtedit@aol.com, founded 1986, editor Jan Tritten, is a quarterly that "provides a voice for midwives and childbirth educators. **We are a midwifery magazine. Subject must be birth or profession related."** They do not want poetry that is "off subject or puts down the subject." *MT* is 56 pgs., 8½×11, offset, saddle-stapled, with glossy card cover with b&w photo and b&w artwork photos, and ads inside. They use about 1 poem/issue. Press run is 5,000 for 3,000 subscribers, 1,000 shelf sales. Subscription: $35. **Sample postpaid: $9. No previously published poems or simultaneous submissions. Cover letter required.** Time between acceptance and publication is 1-2 years. **Seldom comments on rejections. Publishes theme issues. Send SASE for writer's guidelines and upcoming themes. Reports in 2-6 weeks. Pays 2 copies. Acquires first rights.** The editor says, "With our publication *please* stay on the subject."

MILKWEED EDITIONS (II), 430 First Ave. N., Suite 400, Minneapolis MN 55401-1743, phone (612)332-3192, fax (612)332-6248, founded 1979, poetry editor Emilie Buchwald. Three collections published annually. **Unsolicited mss are only accepted from writers who have previously published a book-length collection of poetry or a minimum of 6 poems in commercial or literary journals.** One of the leading literary presses in the country, Milkweed publishes some of the best poets composing today in well-made, attractively designed collections. Published books of poetry include: *Invisible Horses* by Patricia Goedicke; and *Night Out: Poems About Hotels, Motels, Restaurants and Bars* edited by Kurt Brown and Laure-Anne Bosselaar. **Submit 60- to 200-page ms with SAS return bookmailer (or the ms will not be returned). Include SAS postcard for notification of ms arrival. Indicate in cover letter if ms is to be recycled. Unsolicited mss read in January and June; please include return postage. Send submissions to Poetry Readers. Send SASE for guidelines. Reports in 1-6 months.** Catalog available on request, with $1.50 in postage.

MIND IN MOTION: A MAGAZINE OF POETRY AND SHORT PROSE (I, II), P.O. Box 7070, Big Bear Lake CA 92315-7070, founded 1985, editor Céleste Goyer, is a quarterly wanting **poetry "15-60 lines. Explosive, provocative. Images not clichéd but directly conveyant of the point of the poem. Use of free association particularly desired. We encourage free verse, keeping in mind the essential elements of rhythm and rhyme. Traditional forms are acceptable if within length restrictions. Meaning should be implicit, as in the styles of Blake, Poe, Coleridge, Stephen Crane, Emily Dickinson, Leonard Cohen. Not interested in sentimentality, emotionalism, simplistic nature worship, explicit references.** *MIM* is known for thoughtful poetry that explores the timeless themes of philosophy and human nature." She has recently published poetry by Robert E. Brimhall, Sean Brendan-Brown, Dave J. Fergerson, Joseph Hart and Michael Swofford. As a sample she selected these lines from "The Mind of Man" (poet unidentified):

> For the mind of man will
> never admit that it inhabits
> a fragile body lives too
> short a course of years or
> that it must hopelessly try
> to measure the universe
> from an uncharted piece of
> teeming real estate located
> God only knows where.

MIM is 54 pgs., digest-sized, saddle-stapled, photocopied from photoreduced typescript with a heavy matte cover with b&w photos. Of approximately 2,400 poems/year she accepts about 200. Press run is 525 for 350 subscribers. Subscription: $14 (overseas $18). **Sample postpaid: $3.50 (overseas: $4.50). Submit 6 poems at a time. No previously published poems; simultaneous submissions OK, if notified. "Please have name and address on each poem. We also use dates of composition; it would help if these were provided with submissions." Editor usually comments on rejected mss. Send SASE for guidelines. Reports in 1-6 weeks. Pays 1 copy. Magazine is copyrighted; all rights revert to author.** The editor says, "Please do not submit further material until your last submission has been responded to. Please be patient and don't overwhelm the editor."

MIND MATTERS REVIEW (III), 2040 Polk St., #234, San Francisco CA 94109, founded 1988, phone (415)775-4545, e-mail bonwilly@aol.com, website http://www.home.earthlink.net/~openbook, editor Carrie Drake, poetry editor Bunny Williams **(and submissions should be sent directly to her at 158-21 78th Ave., Flushing NY 11366)**, is a **"literary annual with emphasis on use of science as a tool for responsible organization of information;** analysis of the role of language in consciousness, knowledge and intelligence; and social criticism particularly of metaphysics. Also includes book reviews, poetry, short stories, art and essays." **They want "short poems for fillers."** They have published poetry by Russell Eisenmann and Robert L. Brimm. As a sample the editor selected these lines by an anonymous poet:

> Poetic wisdom is one thing
> But it is only in prose
> That truth has sting.
> After all, it is the sound effect
> Which poets are after
> Not the sober reality.

MMR is magazine-sized, desktop-published, includes graphics, sketches, b&w photos. Subscription: $15 US, $20 foreign. **Sample postpaid: $3.50. Poets are encouraged to buy a copy before submitting. Submit 3 poems at a time. E-mail submissions OK. No simultaneous submissions; previously published poems OK. Cover letter required; include publishing credits and note if submissions have been previously published or accepted for publication elsewhere. Publishes theme issues. Send SASE for guidelines and upcoming themes. Sometimes sends prepublication galleys. Pays 1 copy.**

MIND PURGE (I, II), NT Box 5471, Denton TX 76203, e-mail jivan@anet-dfw.com, founded 1994, editors Jason Hensel and Cheryl Doughty, is a biannual literary and art magazine publishing poetry, short fiction, one-act plays, short screenplays, essays, book reviews and art. **They want poetry that is "well-crafted, insightful, imagistic. No specifications as to form, length, subject matter or style. However no greeting card verse,**

hackneyed themes or poetry that says nothing or goes nowhere." They have published poetry by Cannon, Ben Omhart and Christopher Stolle. As a sample the editors selected these lines from "Boquillas" by Chad Forbes:

> *And we rode to Boquillas in the back of a rusted brown truck*
> *that snaked up the gravel road. A Mexican child who was probably*
> *five stood on the open tailgate and swayed at fifty with one hand gripping,*
> *worrying us Americans until someone said, "He's here to keep us from falling."*

Mind Purge is 36-52 pgs., 7 × 8½, neatly printed and saddle-stapled with matte card stock cover with b&w photo and b&w photos inside. They receive about 100 poems a year, accept approximately 10%. Press run is 100 for 10 subscribers. Single copy: $3; subscription: $5. **Sample postpaid: $2. Make checks payable to Jason Hensel. Submit up to 5 poems at a time, name and address on each page. E-mail submissions OK. No previously published poems or simultaneous submissions. Cover letter preferred. Seldom comments on rejections. Reports within 3 months. Pays 1 copy.** Reviews books of poetry in 200 words, single format. Open to unsolicited reviews. Poets may also send books for review consideration. Jason Hensel's advice: "Don't give up, just keep submitting. And read, not only poetry, but everything you can get your hands on."

THE MINNESOTA REVIEW (II), English Dept., East Carolina University, Greenville NC 27858-4353, phone (919)328-6388, founded 1960, editor Jeffrey Williams, is a biannual literary magazine wanting **"poetry which explores some aspect of social or political issues and/or the nature of relationships. No nature poems, and no lyric poetry without the above focus."** As a sample the editors selected the opening lines from "In Historic Perspective" by Charlotte Mayerson:

> *Without the women of the Holocaust*
> *Who saw their children ripped asunder*
> *I could not go on.*
> *Without the women*
> *Of eighteen hundred and five*
> *Who bore eight children and raised five*
> *I would go under. . . .*

TMR is 200 pgs., digest-sized, flat-spined, with b&w glossy card cover and art. Mostly free verse (lyric and narrative) poems here tend to have strong themes and powerful content, perhaps to coincide with the magazine's subtitle: "a journal of committed writing." Circulation: 1,500 for 800 subscribers. Subscription: $12 to individuals, $36 to institutions. **Sample postpaid: $7.50. Address submissions to "Poetry Editor" (not to a specific editor). Cover letter including "brief intro with address" preferred. Publishes theme issues. Send SASE for upcoming themes. Reports in 2-4 months. Pays 2 copies. Acquires all rights. Returns rights upon request.** Reviews books of poetry in single or multi-book format. Open to unsolicited reviews.

MINORITY LITERARY EXPO (IV-Membership, ethnic), 216 Avenue T, Pratt City, Birmingham AL 35214-5308, phone (205)798-9083, founded 1990, editor/publisher Kervin Fondren, is an annual literary professional publication featuring minority poets, novices and professionals. **"Organization membership open to all minority poets nationally. I want poems from minority poets that are holistic and wholesome, less than 24 lines each, no vulgar or hate poetry accepted, any style, any form, any subject matter. Poetry that expresses holistic views and philosophies is very acceptable. Literary value is emphasized. Selected poets receive financial awards, certificates, honorable mentions, critiques and special poetic honors."** No fee is charged for inclusion. As a sample the editor selected his poem "It's Lonely at the Top":

> *No Man Can*
> *Reach the Top of the Mountain*
> *With Hate, Greed and Despair.*
>
> *Because in Reaching the Top*
> *He Soon Will Find Out that*
> *he is the only one There.*

Send SASE for guidelines and upcoming themes. Pays 1 copy. They also sponsor an annual poetry chapbook contest and an annual "Analyze the Poem" contest. Send SASE for details. The editor says, "We seek novices and unpublished poets to breathe the new life every poetry organization needs."

MINOTAUR PRESS; MINOTAUR (II), P.O. Box 470, Burlingame CA 94010, e-mail 102552.1253@compuserve.com, founded 1974, editor Jim Gove. *Minotaur* is a "small press literary quarterly **with emphasis on**

 THE MAPLE LEAF symbol before a listing indicates a Canadian publisher, magazine, conference, contest or organization.

contemporary and experimental styles. **Must be relevant. No rhymed and/or traditional verse."** They have published poetry by Judson Crews, Mark Weber, Alan Catlin, Will Inman, Hugh Fox and Duane Locke. As a sample the editor selected these lines from "Y esterRrdayy myy television set caught om firrre" by Mark Neville:

> SHE HAD
> she had
> EXTRACTED A
> wish from
> FROM FROSTY HALOS
> AND MADE
> she made the
> MOON WALK BACK OUT
> OF THE WINDOW- HIS HAIR
> TOUSLED INTO HER ROOM

The editor describes it as digest-sized, offset, saddle-stapled, "stock cover—cover graphics—sometimes use interior graphics, but rarely." They receive about 100 poems a year, accept approximately 5. Press run is 300 for 200 subscribers of which 30 are libraries. Subscription: $18. **Sample postpaid: $3.50. "Submissions via e-mail OK if clean ASCII text files." Send SASE for guidelines. Submit 4-8 poems at a time with name and address on each page. Sends prepublication galleys "with exception of submissions via e-mail." Reports in 3-6 weeks, faster for e-mail submissions. Pays 1 copy. Editor comments on submissions "if requested only."** Open to unsolicited reviews. They also award a $50 prize for the best poem in each issue by a subscribing poet. However, "you do not need to subscribe to be published." The editor says, "Subscribe to the magazines that publish your work. Few poetry magazines run in the black. We would like to see more experimental, leading edge, borderline poetry."

THE MIRACULOUS MEDAL (IV-Religious), 475 E. Chelten Ave., Philadelphia PA 19144-5785, phone (215)848-1010, founded 1928, editor Rev. William J. O'Brien, C.M., is a religious quarterly. **"Poetry should reflect solid Catholic doctrine and experience. Any subject matter is acceptable, provided it does not contradict the teachings of the Roman Catholic Church. Poetry must have a religious theme, preferably about the Blessed Virgin Mary."** They have published poetry by Gladys McKee. The editor describes it as 32 pgs., digest-sized, saddle-stapled, 2-color inside and cover, no ads. *The Miraculous Medal* is used as a promotional piece and is sent to all clients of the Central Association of the Miraculous Medal. Circulation is 340,000. **Sample and guidelines free for postage. Poems should be a maximum of 20 lines, double-spaced. No simultaneous submissions or previously published poems. Reports in 6 months to 3 years. Pays 50¢ and up/line, on acceptance. Buys first North American rights.**

‡MISC. PROJ.: A POETRY NEWSLETTER (II), 641 N. Highland Ave., NE #11, Atlanta GA 30306, founded 1996, editor Mark Prejsnar, appearing quarterly, is a newsletter publishing new poetry, and commentary and theory about poetry. **"We suggest poets read Zukofsky, Stein, Oppen, Vallejo, Char, Eigner, Olson and Coolidge. This suggests the range of our interests. Short is better due to our limited format."** *Misc. Proj.* is 20 pgs., 8½ × 11, photocopied on colored paper, desktop-published, corner stapled. They receive about 100 poems a year, accept approximately 25%. Press run is 100 for 100 subscribers of which 3 are libraries; 50 distributed free "to various poets we admire." Subscription: $3.50/4 issues. **Sample postpaid: $1. Make checks payable to M. Prejsnar. Submit 5-10 short poems at a time. Previously published poems and simultaneous submissions OK. Cover letter preferred.** Time between acceptance and publication is 4 months. **Poems are circulated to an editorial board with "decision made by editor and input on about 50% of submissions from 3 or 4 associates." Seldom comments on rejections. Send SASE for guidelines. Reports in 5 weeks. Pays 3 copies. Acquires one-time rights.** Reviews books or chapbooks of poetry or other magazines in single and multi-book formats. Open to unsolicited reviews. Poets may also send books for review consideration. The editor says, "Poetry still needs more venues that admit modernism (including objectivism, surrealism, Black Mountain) actually happened; academe and other well-funded institutions don't admit that; this is why a group of poets felt this publication was necessary."

MISSISSIPPI MUD (III), 1505 Drake Ave., Austin TX 78704, phone (512)444-5459, founded 1973, editor Joel Weinstein, published irregularly, features fiction, poetry and artwork which "portray life in America as the 20th century crashes and burns." As for poetry **they want "smart, contemporary themes and forms, free verse preferred."** They do not want "anything stodgy, pathetic or moralistic; the self-consciously pretty or clever; purely formal exercises." They have published poetry by Ivan Arguelles, Christy Sheffield Sanford and Simon Perchik. *MM* is 96 pgs., 7¾ × 10, perfect-bound, with 4-color glossy paper cover, full-page graphics and display ads. They receive 100-200 poems a year, accept less than 10%. Press run is 1,500 for 150 subscribers of which 16 are libraries, 1,000 shelf sales; about 200 distributed free to galleries, museums and critical media. Subscription: $12/2 issues. **Sample postpaid: $6. Submit up to 6 poems at a time. No previously published poems; simultaneous submissions OK.** Time between acceptance and publication is a year or more. **Seldom comments on rejections. Reports in 4-6 months. Pays $25 and 2 copies. Buys first North American serial rights.**

MISSISSIPPI REVIEW (II), University of Southern Mississippi, Box 5144, Hattiesburg MS 39406-5144, phone (601)266-4321, fax (601)266-5757, e-mail fb@netdoor.com, website http://www.sushi.st.usm.edu\MRW, editor Frederick Barthelme, managing editor Rie Fortenberry. Literary publication for those interested in contemporary literature. Poems differ in style, length and form, but all have craft in common (along with intriguing content). **Sample: $8. Query first, via mail, e-mail or their website. Does not read manuscripts in summer. Pays 3 copies.** Sponsors contests. Send SASE for guidelines.

MISSOURI REVIEW (II), 1507 Hillcrest Hall, University of Missouri, Columbia MO 65211, phone (573)882-4474, fax (573)884-4671, founded 1978, poetry editor Greg Michalson, general editor Speer Morgan, is a quality literary journal, 6×9, 208 pgs., which appears 3 times/year, **publishing poetry features only—6-12 pages for each of 3 to 5 poets/issue.** By devoting more editorial space to each poet, *MR* provides a fuller look at the work of some of the best writers composing today. However, the number of poets whose work appears here has decreased significantly, limiting your chances in a prestigious market where competition has become even keener than in the past. **Sample: $7. Submit 6-12 poems at a time. No previously published poems or simultaneous submissions. Reports in 8-10 weeks. Sometimes sends prepublication galleys. Pays $125-250/feature. Buys all rights. Returns rights "after publication, without charge, at the request of the authors."** Staff reviews books of poetry. Awards the Tom McAfee Discovery Feature once or twice a year to an outstanding young poet who has not yet published a book; poets are selected from regular submissions at the discretion of the editors. Also offers the Larry Levis Editors' Prize Contest in Poetry. Deadline: October 15. $1,500 first prize and publication. Three finalists named in addition. Write for details. The editors add, "We think we have enhanced the quality of our poetry section and increased our reader interest in this section. We remain dedicated to publishing at least one younger or emerging poet in every issue."

MKASHEF ENTERPRISES; PRISONERS OF THE NIGHT (V, IV-Psychic/occult, science fiction/ fantasy, horror, erotica); POETIC LICENSE; NIGHT VISIONS; MONUMENTAL MOMENTS, P.O. Box 688, Yucca Valley CA 92286-0688, poetry editor Alayne Gelfand. *Prisoners of the Night*, founded 1987, **focusing on vampire erotica, uses poetry that is "erotic, unique, less horrific and more romantic, non-pornographic, original visions of the vampire."** Poets who have appeared recently in *POTN* include Ann K. Schwader, Corrine DeWinter, Bobbi Sinaha-Morey, Elizabeth Wein, John Grey and Wendy Rathbone. As a sample the editor selected these lines from "Falling In The Garden of Angels" by Tippi N. Blevins:

> we know our faces
> by shadow alone,
> grotesque gray things,
> lithic masks of gargoyles
> with angels' wings

The intent of *POTN* is "to show the erotic, the romantic, rather than the horrific aspects of the vampire." It is 70-90 pgs., magazine-sized, perfect-bound, with color cover, produced by high-speed photocopying. Most poems are illustrated. It appears annually, usually in August. They receive about 300 poems a year, accept approximately 10-20. It has an initial press run of 3,000, but each issue is kept in print. **Sample postpaid: $15 each (for #1-4), $12 (#5), $9.95 each (#6-9).** *Note: The editor is currently not accepting submissions as POTN is on hiatus until September 1997 when issue #10 will appear, which is closed to all submissions. The August 1998 issue will feature the work of poet Wendy Rathbone and will not be open to other poetry. However, beginning in September 1998, she will be accepting submissions for the 1999 issue.* **Send SASE for guidelines. When *POTN* is open to submissions, submit up to 6 poems at a time. No simultaneous submissions or previously published poems, "unless they've only appeared in your own chapbook." Editor sometimes comments on rejections. Reports "within 1 month." Pays $5/poem plus 1 copy. Buys first serial rights. *POTN* wants unusual visions of the vampire, not stereotypical characterizations.** Also sponsors Poetic License, a biannual poetry contest awarding $500 first prize, $100 second prize and $50 third prize, plus publication in anthology and 2 copies. Ten honorable mentions receive 1 copy; other poems of exceptional interest will also be included in the anthology. Sponsors the contest Night Visions. Submit any number of poems on dreams, visions, stars or anything to do with the night, any style, of up to 50 lines/poem. Include name, address and phone on each poem. Enclose an SASE, for notification of winners. "Judges prefer original, accessible and unforced works." Entry fee: $5/poem or $10/3 poems. Deadline: February 1. Sponsors the contest Monumental Moments, awarding $500 first place, $100 second place, $50 third place, plus publication and 2 copies. 10 honorable mentions receive 1 copy. Submit poems "that speak about those moments or events that changed your life forever." Deadline: August 1. Also sponsors annual chapbook contest. Send SASE for guidelines and more detailed information for all their contests. The editor says, "Be original! Find new ways of saying things, explore the infinite possibilities of words and images. Do not rely on stereotypical visions of the vampire; the use of clichés is the quickest road to rejection. I'm not looking for your typical 'count' or 'countess,' no loners in ruined castles. I'm looking for the unusual image and sharp word usage. I want you to make my heart race with both the structure and subject of your poem. Non-rhyming, unstructured poems much prefered."

MÖBIUS (I, II), P.O. Box 674, St. Clair Shores MI 48080, founded 1982, editor Jean Hull Herman. She looks for "the informed mind responding to the challenges of reality and the expression of the imagination in poetry that demonstrates intelligence and wit. **Poets should say significant, passionate things about the larger world**

and galaxies outside themselves, using all the resources of the English language. Consideration is given to poetry using meter, rhyme, dramatic and narrative structures, traditional, blank and free verse and all that pleases the ear as well as the intellect and soul. General topics include the philosophical questions; love and romance; relationships; war; science and technology; and humor (for which the editor has a weakness)." They have recently published poetry by Ace Boggess, Richard Davignon and Robert Cooperman. As a sample the editor selected these lines from her poem "When A Wise Woman Dies," inspired by Joanna Linsalata:

> There are exceptional women.
> There have always been exceptional women:
> Women who knew the effect of every cause, saw the web and its center,
> Women who could read the colors of the skies and knew
> That while blue skies were good, red, purple, and golden glows were also necessary;
> That while rain was needed, so was time for drying of lands and eyes . . .

Möbius is published twice a year, at Memorial Day and Thanksgiving. It is magazine-sized, 60 pgs., professionally printed, saddle-stapled with matte card cover. Subscription: $12/year. **Sample postpaid: $7. Submit up to 5 poems at a time. Send SASE for guidelines. "Response time is two weeks to two months, as editor does read submissions all year round. Printed authors receive one copy free. Editor will comment on all rejections."**

‡*MOCK FROG PUBLISHING (I, IV-Specialized: regional history, feminism); FOE AMPHIBIAN QUARTERLY (I), P.O. Box 2, Newcastle Univ. Union, Callaghan, NSW 2308 Australia, phone 0419-316-625, e-mail maitiu@usa.net, website http://www.geocites.com/soho/3766, founded 1996, editor Matthew Glenn Ward. *Foe Amphibian Quarterly*, is "at present a variety of poetry and illustrations." **They want "any length, most styles. We love non-rhyme and Beat stream-of-consciousness-poetry." They do not want "haiku, non-English language, science fiction or medieval D&D stuff."** As a sample the editor selected "Dream of Me" from *des éclairs de fantaisie* by Valerie Mai:

> May subtle phantoms seep themselves
> Into your vision,
> And twist themselves around you
> Like a mist.

The editor says *FAQ* is 30 pgs., A4, photocopied, center stapled with graphics. They receive about 200 poems a year, accept approximately 70%. Press run is 500 for 100 subscribers, 400 shelf sales. Single copy: $5; subscription: $4. **Sample postpaid: $2.50. Make checks payable to Matthew Glenn Ward. Purchase of copy required for consideration. Submit 6 poems, single spaced on white paper. Disk submissions OK. Previously published poems and simultaneous submissions OK. Cover letter preferred.** Time between acceptance and publication is 2-5 months. **Seldom comments on rejections. Publishes theme issues. Send SASE (or SAE and IRC) for guidelines and upcoming themes. Reports in 2 months. Pays 1 copy.** Reviews books or chapbooks of poetry or other magazines. Open to unsolicited reviews. Poets may also send books for review consideration to The Review Section at the above address. Mock Frog Publishing publishes 6 paperbacks/year on feminist poetry and poetry dealing with local history. Books are usually 45 pgs., A5, perfect-bound with laminated or non-laminated covers and graphics and illustrations if required. **Query first with 6 poems and cover letter and bio. Replies to queries and mss in 2 months. Pays 10-15% royalties and 5 author's copies (out of a press run of 100).** They also provide services for the self-published poet: layout and editing, plus proofreading and presentation pre-submission." The editor says, "Mock Frog believes it is the poet's duty to record the history of the world through the writing of poetry. Those new to poetry should read a lot of poetry from others, established and ancient as well as contemporary."

MOCKINGBIRD; ROBERT FRANCIS MEMORIAL PRIZE (II), P.O. Box 761, Davis CA 95617, founded 1994, co-editors C.G. Macdonald and Joe Aimone (with frequent guest editors as well). *Mockingbird* is a biannual journal of poetry and reviews. **They are looking for "craft and inspiration; also we value clarity and intensity. We want form, but not witless conformity; innovation, but not convenient ignorance of tradition."** They have recently published poetry by Sandra McPherson, Annie Finch, Jared Carter, David Alpaugh, Klip Schutz and Crawdad Nelson. As a sample the editors selected these lines from "Mortician's Secrets" by Rigobento Gonzalez:

> The most righteous part of the body
> is the armpit with its delicate growth of hair.
> The armpit has withheld more gossip. It has kept quiet
> more than our privates, complacent
> in a corner that when exposed we choose to ignore.
> That's how it became so respected:
> it took advantage of our faces turned sideways, our embarrassed
> looks, and then imitated that humility.

Mockingbird is 48 pgs., 5½ × 8½, photocopied from desktop-published originals and saddle-stapled with matte card cover with b&w art. They receive about 1,000-1,200 poems a year, use approximately 50-60 (not counting a few solicited works). Press run is 250 for 125 subscribers of which 4 are libraries, 20 shelf sales. Subscription: $7.50/year, $12/2 years. **Sample postpaid: $4. Submit up to 5-6 pages of poetry at a time. No previously** published poems or simultaneous submissions. **Cover letter preferred. Sometimes comments on rejections. Send SASE for guidelines. Reports usually within 2 months, "3-4 months on acceptances and near misses." Pays 1 copy. Acquires first serial rights. Requests acknowledgment if work is reprinted elsewhere.** Reviews books and chapbooks of poetry as well as other magazines in up to 1,500 words. Open to unsolicited reviews. Poets may also send books for review consideration. They also sponsor the Robert Francis Memorial Prize which awards a total of $350 to one first place winner and two seconds. The contest runs from July 4 to Halloween. Entry fee: $2/poem. An $8 entry includes a one-year subscription. Send SASE for details. The editor says, "We are a unique magazine. Reading a sample copy could be very helpful to submitting poets. We are eclectic but especially interested in formal poetry, West Coast and other marginalized writers, wit, and a flair for the vernacular. We encourage real world referents, especially to the natural, personal, sensual and political worlds."

MODERN BRIDE (IV-Love/romance), 249 W. 17th St., New York NY 10011, phone (212)462-3400, executive editor Mary Ann Cavlin, a slick bimonthly, occasionally buys **poetry pertaining to love and marriage. Pays $30-40 for average short poem.**

MODERN HAIKU; FOUR HIGH SCHOOL SENIOR SCHOLARSHIPS (IV-Form, students), P.O. Box 1752, Madison WI 53701-1752, phone (608)233-2738, founded 1969, poetry editor Robert Spiess, "is the foremost international journal of English language haiku and criticism. We are devoted to publishing only the very best haiku being written and also publish articles on haiku and have the most complete review section of haiku books. Issues average 88 pages." **They want "contemporary haiku in English (including translations into English) that incorporate the traditional aesthetics of the haiku genre, but which may be innovative as to subject matter, mode of approach or angle of perception, and form of expression. Haiku only. No tanka or other forms."** They have published haiku by Wally Swist, Phyllis Walsh, Lee Gurga and Gary Hotham. As a sample the editor selected this haiku (poet unidentified):

> the field's evening fog—
>   quietly the hound comes
>   to fetch me home

The digest-sized magazine appears 3 times/year, printed on heavy quality stock with cover illustrations especially painted for each issue by the staff artist. They receive about 12,000-14,000 submissions a year, use approximately 800. There are over 260 poems in each issue. Circulation 650. Subscription: $16.85. **Sample postpaid: $5.75. Submit on "any size sheets, any number of haiku on a sheet; but name and address on each sheet." Include SASE. No previously published haiku or simultaneous submissions. Send SASE for guidelines. Reports in 2 weeks. Pays $1/haiku (but no contributor's copy). Buys first North American serial rights.** Staff reviews books of haiku in 350-1,000 words, single format. Send books for review consideration. They offer 4 annual scholarships for the best haiku by high school seniors. Scholarships range from $200-500 (total $1,400). Deadline is mid-March. Send SASE for rules. The editor says, "Haiku achieve their effect of felt-depth, insight and intuition through juxtaposition of perceived entities, not through intellective comment or abstract words."

‡*MODERN POETRY IN TRANSLATION (II, IV-Translations), King's College London, Strand, London WC2 R2LS United Kingdom, (171)873-2360, fax (171)873-2415, founded 1965 (original series), 1992 (new series), editor Daniel Weissbort, advisory and managing editor Professor Norma Rinsler, published biannually, features "translations of poems from any language into English, and essays on translation (practice rather than theory). Our aim is to further international cultural understanding and exchange and to awaken interest in poetry." **They want "only translations from any language into English—'modern' refers to translation (which should be unpublished), not to original." They do not want "self-translation by those not familiar with English; work by translators who are not poets or not familiar with a range of works in the original language rarely succeed (unless they work with original authors)."** *MPIT* is 200-240 pgs., 5⅝×8½, offset, perfect-bound with illustrated 2-color cover on scanchip board, matte laminated. Accept approximately 50% of the poems they receive. Press run is 500 for 350 subscribers of which 50% are libraries, 50 shelf sales. Single copy: £20 (individuals), £32 (institutions); subscription: £25, $40 (individuals), £40, $65 (institutions). **Sample (including guidelines) postpaid: $9.50. Make checks payable to King's College London. Submit 5-6 poems at a time "unless very long, in which case 1 or 2". Disk submissions (in Word) OK. Originals should accompany translation. No previously published poems or simultaneous submissions. Cover letter required.** Time between acceptance and publication is 3-9 months. **The editor and managing/advisory editor discuss submissions and consult individual members of advisory board if expertise required. Often comments on rejections. Publishes theme issues. Send SASE (or SAE and IRC) for upcoming themes. Reports "as soon as possible—within weeks." Sometimes sends prepublication galleys. Pays £10/poem or £12/page plus 1 copy to translator, 1 for original author. "Copyright on selection as printed—general rights remain with contributors."** Features reviews of poetry books often commissioned from experts in the field. Poets may also send books for review consideration (translations only).

MODERN WORDS (IV-Gay/lesbian), 350 Bay St., #100, Box 325, San Francisco CA 94133, press founded 1984, journal 1994, editor/publisher Garland Richard Kyle. *modern words,* "a thoroughly queer international literary journal," appears annually. *"modern words* is eclectic and no specific theme or style is required. Work should be original and reflect the diversity of our voices. Non-American-born writers and international-themed work is especially encouraged." They have recently published poetry by Blaine Marchand, Gerry Gomez Pearlberg, Jules Mann and Terry Wolverton. *modern words* is about 200 pgs., 4½×7, professionally printed and perfect-bound with 1-2-color coated card cover with b&w photo and b&w photos of the authors inside. They receive 200 poems a year, use approximately 10-15%. Press run is 500 for 100 subscribers of which 6 are libraries, 25-50% shelf sales. Subscription: $20, $200 for lifetime. **Sample postpaid: $10** (back issue). **Submit no more than 10 pgs. of poetry at a time. No previously published poems; simultaneous submissions OK. Cover letter preferred. Seldom comments on rejections. Send SASE for guidelines. Reports** "promptly." **Always sends prepublication galleys. Pays 2 copies. Acquires first serial rights.**

‡**MOJO RISIN' MAGAZINE (II)**, P.O. Box 268451, Chicago IL 60626, founded 1995, editor Josh Samuels, published quarterly, features "poetry, prose, short stories and some sort of contest in each issue." **She wants "any form or style."** She does not want "**corpse worshippers, incest, racism, blatant sex or anything written for shock value.**" She has recently published poetry by Michael McNeilley, Lyn Lifshin, Ana Christy and Cheryl Townsend. As a sample the editor selected these lines from "Only Fair" by Dan Nielsen:

> i knew she would
> never be unfaithful
> to me
> so i hired
> a friend of mine
> to rape her

mojo risin' is 32 pgs., 8½×11, photocopied, saddle-stapled or spiraled, with colored paper cover, b&w drawings and art. She receives about 300 poems a year, accepts half. Press run is 500 for 150 subscribers. Subscription: $15. **Sample postpaid: $5. The editor strongly encourages subscription, though not required for acceptance. Submit 3-5 poems (1 page maximum) at a time. No previously published poems or simultaneous submissions. Cover letter preferred.** Time between acceptance and publication is 1-3 months. **The editor is solely responsible for all aspects of editing and publishing. Send SASE for guidelines. Reports within 10 days. Acquires first North American serial rights.** Sponsors a contest each issue.

‡**MOONRABBIT REVIEW; LIFTING BELLY (I, II, IV-Ethnic)**, 2525 Arapahoe Ave., E4-230, Boulder CO 80302, phone (303)439-7285, fax (303)439-8362, e-mail jhlee@ucsub.colorado.edu, website http://www.spot .Colorado.edu/~jangd/moonrabbit, founded 1994, editor Jackie Lee, published biannually, is "a literary journal of Asian American writers." **They want "poems that are vivid, organic, original, provocative and concise." They do not want "sloppy, over-bloated lines that read too listy or mechanical."** They have recently published poetry by Eileen Tabios. As a sample the editor selected these lines from "Three Days of Spirits" by Mariko Nagai:

> Listen: my father is calling the unwilling
> spirits home, lighting the bonfire to guide
> their way. Making a horse out of a cucumber,
> a bull from an eggplant, he welcomes the past
> into our house, a reminder that we cannot
> forget what we have lived through. Their feet leaving

The editor says *MoonRabbit* is 144 pgs., 6×9, perfect-bound with artwork and a variety of media. Press run is 1,000 for 500 subscribers of which 25% are libraries. Single copy: $10; subscription: $17 individual; $27 institution; $13 student. **Sample postpaid: $7.** "Contributors are encouraged to purchase a sample copy prior to submitting, but are not required." **Submit 3-10 poems at a time. No previously published poems; simultaneous submissions OK. Cover letter required with a brief bio.** "We like to see poems in whatever format the poet chooses so long as we can read them clearly and is pleasing to the eyes." Time between acceptance and publication is 2-4 months. Poems are circulated to an editorial board. "Readers make their selections then pass them to the managing editor, who then makes recommendations to the editor-in-chief." **Seldom comments on rejections. Publishes theme issues. Send SASE for guidelines and upcoming themes. Reports** "immediately." **Pays 3 copies. Acquires first North American rights with anthology publication rights.** Reviews books of poetry. Open to unsolicited reviews. Poets may also send books for review consideration. Sponsors Lifting Belly, an annual poetry/fiction writing contest. $10 entry fee. Deadline October 1. First prize: $200 plus publication; second prize: $75 plus publication; and third prize is publication. For information call (800)985-6602 or visit their website listed above.

MOOSE BOUND PRESS (I), P.O. Box 111781, Anchorage AK 99511-1781, founded 1995, editor Sonia Walker, publisher Robert L. Walker, publishes a quarterly journal which appears under various titles. "We provide positive and energetic poetry, short stories and essays; and promote creative writing, literacy and family reading. Our reading audience includes elementary school children to senior citizens. Therefore, we ask that material sent be something **the entire family can enjoy reading. Our tastes are general and eclectic**." They have recently published poetry by Celine Rose Mariotti, James Ryan, "Uncle Mickey" and Linda Creech. As a sample the editor selected these lines from "Whispering Angels" by Dusty Niendam:

> I heard a whisper as I walked by—
> From whom or where I know not why—

> *The gentle murmur of a voice on high—*
> *The sound of softly fluttering wings—*
> *My mind raced back to angel things—*
> *The whisper-whispered . . .*

The journal we received, entitled ***Friendship Clouds***, was 113 pgs., 8½×11, desktop published, spiral-bound with b&w clip art, photos and drawings inside. Press run is 500 for 100 subscribers of which 20 are libraries, 200 shelf sales. Subscription: $24/year. **Sample postpaid: $8. Make checks payable to Sonia Walker. Submit 5 poems at a time, no more than 30 lines each, 1 poem to a page. Previously published poems and simultaneous submissions OK. Cover letter preferred.** Time between acceptance and publication is 6-12 months. **Often comments on rejections. Publishes theme issues. Send SASE for guidelines and upcoming themes. Reports in 3-6 months. "No payment other than publication." Acquires one-time rights.** Sponsors an Editor's Choice Award. They also publish a quarterly newsletter which contains poetry, general interest articles and announcements of themes for future editions of their quarterly journals. The newsletter is included with the cost of an annual subscription. They will begin publishing a biennial anthology in March of 1998. Write for information. The editor says, "Moose Bound Press encourages and is receptive to new writers of all ages. Do not be afraid of rejection—MBP believes there is a poem or story that wants to be shared and enjoyed by the reading world."

WILLIAM MORROW AND CO. (V), 1350 Avenue of the Americas, New York NY 10019, phone (212)261-6500, publishes poetry on standard royalty contracts **but accepts no unsolicited mss. Queries with samples should be submitted through an agent.**

✿**(m)ÖTHÊR TØÑGUÉ PRESS (I, II, IV-Regional)**, 290 Fulford-Ganges Rd., Salt Spring Island, British Columbia V8K 2K6 Canada, founded 1990, editor/publisher Mona Fertig, holds an annual poetry chapbook contest for the best Canadian ms of poetry. The 1st place winner receives $400 plus publication, 2nd place winner receive $200 plus publication of a "beautiful limited edition chapbook." **Canadian poets send 15 pgs. of unpublished poetry with short bio and $20 entry fee. SASE must be included. Mss will not be returned. Send SASE for details. Deadline: November 30.**

‡**MOUNT OLIVE COLLEGE PRESS; MOUNT OLIVE REVIEW; LEE WITTE POETRY CONTEST (II)**, 634 Henderson St., Mount Olive NC 28365, phone (919)658-2502, founded 1987 (*Mount Olive Review*), 1990 (Mount Olive College Press), editor Dr. Pepper Worthington, published annually, features "literary criticism, poetry, short stories, essays and book reviews." **They want "modern poetry."** The editor says *Mount Olive Review* is 7½×10. They receive about 2,000 poems a year, accept approximately 8%. Press run is 1,000. Single copy: $25. **Make checks payable to Mount Olive College Press. Submit 6 poems at a time. No previously published poems or simultaneous submissions. Cover letter preferred. Time between acceptance and publication varies. Poems are circulated to an editorial board. Seldom comments on rejections. Publishes theme issues. Send SASE for guidelines and upcoming themes. Reports in 3 months. Sometimes sends prepublication galleys. Acquires first rights.** Reviews books or chapbooks of poetry or other magazines. Open to unsolicited reviews. Poets may also send books for review consideration. Mount Olive Press publishes **6 chapbooks/year. Selected through the Lee Witte Poetry Contest. Write to above address for guidelines.** Chapbooks are usually 5½×8. **Submit 12 sample poems. Replies to queries and mss in 3 months. Obtain sample chapbooks by writing to the above address.**

MOVING PARTS PRESS (V), 10699 Empire Grade, Santa Cruz CA 95060-9474, phone (408)427-2271, fax (408)458-2810, founded 1977. Poetry editor Felicia Rice says they are a "fine arts literary publisher using letterpress printing and printmaking to produce handsome and innovative books, broadsides and prints in limited editions." Moving Parts has published books of poetry by Francisco X. Alarcón, Elba Rosario Sánchez, Nathaniel Mackey and Henri Michaux. **They do not accept unsolicited mss. Pay 10% of the edition in copies.** The book *De Amor Oscuro/Of Dark Love* received one of 18 international design awards from among the "600 Best Designed Books in the World" exhibit mounted by Stiftung Buchkunst at the Leipzig Book Fair.

MS. MAGAZINE (V), 135 W. 50th St., New York NY 10020, founded 1972, is a bimonthly "feminist source of national and international news, politics, arts, scholarship and book reviews." **They are currently not accepting unsolicited poetry.** They have published poetry by Alice Walker, Maya Angelou and May Swenson. Circulation is 150,000. Single copy: $5.95 (available on newsstands); subscription: $30. They say, "Due to the volume of the material received, we cannot accept, acknowledge or return unsolicited poetry or fiction. We cannot discuss queries on the phone and cannot be held responsible for manuscripts sent to us."

● **A BULLET** introduces comments by the editors of *Poet's Market* indicating special information about the listing.

MUDFISH; BOX TURTLE PRESS (I, II), 184 Franklin St., New York NY 10013, phone (212)219-9278, founded 1983, editor Jill Hoffman. *Mudfish*, published by Box Turtle Press, is a journal of poetry and art that appears once a year and is looking for **free verse with "energy, intensity, and originality of voice, mastery of style, the presence of passion."** They have published poetry by Charles Simic, Jennifer Belle, Hal Sirowitz, Doug Dorph and John Ashbery. As a sample the editor selected these lines from "Quince" by Shannon Hamann:

> *When you're God, eternity is already over,*
> *but at the Cloisters, Jenny gives me*
> *a quince she plucked from a tree in the courtyard,*
> *her eyes like eightballs, eyes*
> *that could heat Russia, shining with the mischief*
> *of every woman who ever offered a boy fruit . . .*

Press run is 1,200. **Sample copies are available for $10 plus $2.50 shipping and handling. Submit 4-6 poems at a time. They will not consider simultaneous submissions or previously published poems. Reports from "immediately to 3 months." Sends prepublication galleys. Pays 1 copy.** Sponsors the Mudfish Poetry Prize Award: $500. Submit up to 3 poems for $10, $2 for each additional poem. Deadline: November 12. Send SASE for further guidelines.

MURDEROUS INTENT (IV-Mystery), Madison Publishing Company, P.O. Box 5947, Vancouver WA 98668-5947, phone (360)695-9004, fax (360)693-3354, e-mail madison@teleport.com, website http://www.teleport.com/~madison, founded 1994, editor Margo Power, is a quarterly magazine of mystery and suspense using mystery-related poetry, limericks and such as fillers. **The editor says all poetry (including humorous verse) must be mystery-related and must easily entertain. They do not want poetry with "deep, convoluted meaning" and the shorter the work, the better. "Four-liners are always good though we occasionally buy a longer, ballad-type poem—always mystery-related."** The editor says *Murderous Intent* is 64 pgs., 8½×11, saddle-stapled, with 2-color cover and b&w interior including art, graphics and ads. Press run is 9,500 for 1,425 subscribers, 85% shelf sales. Single copy: $5; subscription: $18. **Sample postpaid: $6.24. Make checks payable to Madison Publishing Company. Submit 6-10 poems at a time. No previously published poems; simultaneous submissions OK. Cover letter preferred. "If accepted, we would like poetry sent on a 3.5 disk."** Time between acceptance and publication can be 1-2 years, "usually less." **Occasionally comments on rejections. Reports in 3-4 months. Pays $2 and 1 copy. Buys first or one-time rights.**

MUSE OF FIRE (I, II), 21 Kruse Rd., Port Angeles WA 98362-8900, founded 1996, editor/publisher Tim Scannell, appears at least 8 times/year "when the editor receives a score of worthy poems." **"All forms welcome: lyric, fixed, narrative, etc. No taboos. Craftsmanship is the only requirement."** As a sample the editor chose this poem "JJ" (poet unidentified):

> *Bless you, John James Audobon*
> *in those lean years keeping on*
> *with the rainbow of your brush*
> *of feathered worlds—miraculous.*

Muse Of Fire is 6 pgs., 8½×11, unbound with b&w clip art. Press run is 50. **Sample available for $1 and #10 SASE. Previously published poems and simultaneous submissions OK. Cover letter required. Seldom comments on rejections. Send SASE for guidelines. Reports in 1 week. Pays 1 copy. Acquires one-time rights.** The editor says, "There are nine musae and so nine grand areas for poetry. Write in all nine areas, in every traditional and untraditional form! And, remember, words become a poem only after eight to twelve revisions."

MUSE PORTFOLIO (II), 25 Tannery Rd., Unit Box 8, Westfield MA 01085-4800, founded 1992, editor Haemi Balgassi, appears 2-4 times/year. *Muse Portfolio* is a "casual magazine for sincere, eloquent, earnest writers who crave forum to share work with others." **They want poetry of "any structure, formal or free, 25 lines maximum. Poetry with writing themes welcome. No forced rhymes, nothing profane. We also publish short stories and nonfiction."** They have recently published poetry by Pandora Deichert, Ed Brindle and Cara Trittipoe. As a sample the editor selected these lines from "A Meadow Song" by David J. Madden:

> *Just before dusk gave way to dark,*
> *when stars pierced the deepening blue,*
> *I heard the song of a solitary lark*
> *coming from the fragrant meadow rue.*

Muse Portfolio is 40 pgs., 5½×8½, saddle-stapled, printed on 20 lb. paper with heavier stock cover, b&w artwork, occasional ads. They receive about 300 poems a year, accept approximately 5%. Press run is 150 for 100 subscribers. Subscription: $5. **Sample postpaid: $3. Submit up to 3 poems at a time. Previously published poems and simultaneous submissions OK. Cover letter required. "Include a biographical paragraph— need not list published credits if author prefers to write something else." Seldom comments on rejections. Send SASE for guidelines. Reports in 3-4 months. Pays 1 copy. Acquires one-time rights.** The editor says, "Please remember to include a SASE with submissions."

♣**MUSICWORKS (IV-Themes)**, 179 Richmond St. W., Toronto, Ontario M5V 1V3 Canada, phone (416)977-3546, founded 1978, editor Gayle Young, is a triannual journal of contemporary music. The editor says, "**The poetry we publish only relates directly to the topics discussed in the magazine or relates to contemporary sound poetry**—*usually* **it is poetry written by the (music) composer or performers we are featuring.**" Poets published include bpnichol, Colin Morton and Jackson Mac Low. The magazine is 64 pgs., 8½×11, with b&w visuals, b&w photography, some illustrative graphics and scores and accompanied by 60-minute cassette. Circulation is 1,600 for 500 subscribers. Price is $5/issue or $11 for the magazine plus CD. **Sample postpaid: $15 for magazine and CD. Simultaneous submissions OK. Reports within 2 months, and there is no backlog before publication. The magazine pays Canadian contributors variable rate.**

THE MUSING PLACE (IV-Specialized: poets with a history of mental illness), 2700 N. Lakeview, Chicago IL 60614, phone (773)281-3800 ext. 2470, fax (773)281-8790, founded 1986, editor Laurie Peters, is an annual magazine "**written and published by people with a history of mental illness. All kinds and forms of poetry are welcome.**" The editor says *The Musing Place* is 32 pgs., 8½×11, typeset and stapled with art also produced by people with a history of mental illness. They receive about 300 poems/year, publish about 40. Press run is 1,000. Single copy: $3. **Fax submissions OK. No previously published poems; simultaneous submissions OK. Cover letter required.** "**Poets must prove and explain their history of mental illness.**" Time between acceptance and publication is 6 months to 1 year. "**The board reviews submissions and chooses those that fit into each issue of the publication.**" Seldom comments on rejections. **Reports within 6 months. Pays 1 copy (additional copies at a discount).**

‡♣**MUSK GLAND SALLY (II, IV-Women/feminism)**, 150 Barrington Ave., Toronto, Ontario M4C 4Z2 Canada, website http://www.express@the-wire.com, founded 1995, editors Sigrun Wister and Yuki Hayashi, published 3 times/year, provides "entertaining reading for smart, with-it, hip feminists and riot grrrls. Contents: political/social commentary, arts reviews (music, film, literary, etc.), poetry/prose." **They want "a good slug in the gut."** They do not want "rambling exercises in excess, superficial weltsmerz, sound or picture/concrete poetry." They have recently published poetry by Lyn Lifshin and Pheasant Ellakowski. As a sample the editor selected these lines by Ibi Kaslik:

> . . . *there have been trains made*
> *to take you away from here*
> *i have heard them bearing away*
> *at night speeds. entrance.*
> *metal down*
> *on wayward corpse*

Musk Gland Sally is 50 pgs., 11×8½ white 20 lb bond, photocopied, desktop published, side-stapled with graphics and photos. "We use a high-quality laser printer for originals." They receive about 75-100 poems a year, use approximately 10-35. "We use 2-3 poets per issue each featuring 1-4 of her poems." Press run is 200, 60 shelf sales; 20 distributed free to record companies and literary reviews. Single copy: $3. **Sample postpaid: $4. Make checks payable to Yuki Hayashi and Sigrun Wister. Submit up to 5 poems at a time. Previously published poems and simultaneous submissions OK. Cover letter required with a brief bio and listing of where poet has been previously published.** "**Please note that submissions with return American postage will not be returned.**" Time between acceptance and publication is up to 4 months. "One editor reads the poems and pulls out the weaker ones for return to sender. The better poems are then read by the other editor and some are approved, the rest are rejected." Seldom comments on rejections. **Publishes theme issues. Send SASE (or SAE and IRC) for guidelines and upcoming themes. Reports in 1 month. Pays 2 copies.** Reviews books or chapbooks of poetry in 500 words. Open to unsolicited reviews. Poets may also send books for review consideration. The editor says, "Review a copy first, so you know what kind of work has a better chance of being accepted. Too many writers today are trying to imitate poets like Charles Bukowski or 'pay homage in verse' to artists like Kurt Cobain and other tragic pop-culture heroes. Try to find your own voice, not borrow someone else's formula."

MYSTERY TIME (I, IV-Mystery); RHYME TIME (IV-Subscribers), P.O. Box 2907, Decatur IL 62524, poetry editor Linda Hutton, founded 1983. *Mystery Time* is a semiannual containing 3-4 pages of **humorous poems about mysteries and mystery writers** in each issue. As a sample the editor selected the limerick "You Can't Take It With You" by Kristine E. Jagusch:

> *A convict awaiting Death Row*
> *On the way to The Chair stubbed his toe;*
> *Now he's suing the State*
> *While delaying his fate,*
> *But he'll fry once he's gotten his dough.*

Mystery Time is 44 pgs., digest-sized, stapled with heavy stock cover. They receive up to 15 submissions a year, use approximately 4-6. Circulation 100. **Sample: $4. Submit 3 poems at a time, "typed in proper format with SASE." Previously published poems OK. Does not read mss in December. Guidelines available for #10 SASE. Pays $5 on acceptance.** Hutton's other publication, *Rhyme Time*, is a quarterly newsletter **publishing only the work of subscribers. No length limit or style restriction.** Subscription: $24. **Sample: $4.** Cash prize of $10 awarded to the best poem in each issue. She also sponsors an annual poetry contest that awards a $10 cash prize for the best poem in any style or length. Submit typed poem with SASE. No entry fee; one entry/person. Deadline: November 1.

NADA PRESS; BIG SCREAM (II, IV-Form/style), 2782 Dixie SW, Grandville MI 49418, phone (616)531-1442, founded 1974, poetry editor David Cope. *Big Scream* appears annually and is **"a brief anthology of mostly 'unknown' poets. We are promoting a continuation of objectivist tradition begun by Williams and Reznikoff. We want objectivist-based short works; some surrealism; basically short, tight work that shows clarity of perception and care in its making."** They have published poetry by Antler, Richard Kostelanetz, Andy Clausen, Allen Ginsberg, John Steinbeck, Jr., Jim Cohn and Marcia Arrieta. *Big Scream* is 35 pgs., magazine-sized, xerograph on 60 lb. paper, side-stapled, "sent gratis to a select group of poets and editors." They receive "several hundred (not sure)" unsolicited submissions a year, use "very few." Press run is 100. Subscription to institutions: $6/year. **Sample postpaid: $6. Submit after July. Send 10 pgs. No cover letter. "If poetry interests me, I will ask the proper questions of the poet." Simultaneous submissions OK. Comments on rejections "if requested and ms warrants it." Reports in 1-14 days. Sometimes sends prepublication galleys. Pays as many copies as requested, within reason.** The editor advises: "Read Pound's essay, 'A Retrospect,' then Reznikoff and Williams; follow through the Beats and NY School, especially Denby & Berrigan, and you have our approach to writing well in hand. I expect to be publishing *BS* regularly ten years from now, same basic format."

NASSAU REVIEW (III), English Dept., Nassau Community College, Garden City NY 11530-6793, phone (516)572-7792, founded 1964, managing editor Dr. Paul A. Doyle, is an annual "creative and research vehicle for Nassau College faculty and the faculty of other colleges." **They want "serious, intellectual poetry of any form or style. No light verse or satiric verse." Submissions from adults only. "No college students; graduate students acceptable."** They have published poetry by Patti Tana, Dick Allen, Louis Phillips, David Heyen and Simon Perchik. *NR* is about 150 pgs., digest-sized, flat-spined. They receive 1,000-1,200 poems a year, use approximately 20-25. Press run is 1,200 for about 1,200 subscribers of which 300 are libraries. **Sample free. Submit only 3 poems per yearly issue. No previously published poems or simultaneous submissions. Reads submissions October 1 through March 1 only. Reports in 3-8 months. Pays copies.** They sponsor occasional contests with $100 or $200 poetry awards, depending on college funding. Well-edited and visually appealing, *Nassau Review* tends to publish free verse emphasizing voice in well-crafted lyric and narrative forms. The editor says, "Each year we are more and more overwhelmed by the number of poems submitted, but many are of an amateur quality."

THE NATION; "DISCOVERY"/THE NATION POETRY CONTEST (III), 72 Fifth Ave., New York NY 10011, founded 1865, poetry editor Grace Schulman. *The Nation*'s **only requirement for poetry is "excellence,"** which can be inferred from the list of poets they have published: Marianne Moore, Robert Lowell, W.S. Merwin, Maxine Kumin, Donald Justice, James Merrill, Richard Howard, May Swenson, Amy Clampitt, Edward Hirsch and Charles Simic. **Pay for poetry is $1/line, not to exceed 35 lines, plus 1 copy.** The magazine co-sponsors the Lenore Marshall Prize for Poetry which is an annual award of $10,000 for the outstanding book of poems published in the US in each year. For details, write to the Academy of American Poets, 584 Broadway, #1208, New York NY 10012. They also co-sponsor the "Discovery"/*The Nation* Poetry Contest ($200 each plus a reading at The Poetry Center, 1395 Lexington Ave., New York NY 10128. Deadline: mid-February. Send SASE for application). Poetry published in *The Nation* has been included in the 1993 and 1995 volumes of *The Best American Poetry*.

NATIONAL ENQUIRER (II, IV-Humor), Lantana FL 33464, filler editor Kathy Martin, is a weekly tabloid which uses **short poems, most of them humorous and traditional rhyming verse. "We want poetry with a message or reflection on the human condition or everyday life. Avoid sending obscure or 'arty' poetry or poetry for art's sake. Also looking for philosophical and inspirational material. Submit seasonal/holiday material at least three months in advance. No poetry over eight lines will be accepted." Submit 1-5 poems at a time. Requires cover letter from first-time submitters; include name, address, social security and phone numbers. "Do not send SASE; filler material will not be returned." Pays $25 after publication; original material only. Buys first rights.**

ALWAYS include a self-addressed, stamped envelope (SASE) when sending a ms or query to a publisher within your own country. When sending material to other countries, include a self-addressed envelope and International Reply Coupons (IRCs), available for purchase at many post offices.

NATIONAL FORUM: THE PHI KAPPA PHI JOURNAL (III), 129 Quad Center, Mell St., Auburn University AL 36849-5306, phone (334)844-5200, website http://www.auburn.edu/academic/societies/phi_kappa_phi/natforum.html, founded 1915, editor James P. Kaetz, is the quarterly of Phi Kappa Phi using **quality poetry.** *NF* is 48 pgs., magazine-sized, professionally printed, saddle-stapled, with full-color paper cover and two-color interior. They receive about 300 poems a year, accept approximately 20. Press run is 120,000 for 117,000 subscribers of which 300 are libraries. Subscription: $25. **Submit 3-5 poems at a time, including a biographical sketch with recent publications. Reads submissions approximately every 3 months. Reports in about 4 months. Pays 10 copies.**

NATURALLY: NUDE RECREATION FOR ALL AGES; EVENTS UNLIMITED PUBLISHING CO. (IV-Specialized), P.O. Box 317, Newfoundland NJ 07435-0317, phone/fax (201)697-8313, e-mail naturally@nac.net, website http://www.tiac.net/users/nat, founded 1981, editor/publisher Bern Loibl. *Naturally* is a quarterly magazine devoted to family nudism and naturism. **They want poetry about the naturalness of the human body and nature, any length.** As a sample the editor selected these lines from "On a Woman who is Busy Deliberating her Liberation" by Wolfgang Somary:

> *I bet: you wouldn't dare yet*
> *to walk bare in the wet*
> *glare of the moon*
> *or just for fun*
> *under the sun*
> *in the nudeness of noon—*

Naturally is 48 pgs., 8½×11, printed on glossy paper and saddle-stitched with b&w and full-color photos throughout. They receive about 30 poems a year, use 5-10. Press run is 13,000 for 5,500 subscribers, 6,500 shelf sales. Single copy: $6.50; subscription: $21.95. **Sample postpaid: $9. Previously published poems and simultaneous submissions OK. Often comments on rejections. Send SASE for guidelines or obtain via e-mail. Reports in 2 months. Pay is negotiable. Buys first North American serial or one-time rights.** Events Unlimited Publishing Co. is planning a poetry/photography book for 1998. Poems must have a natural/nudism theme. Write for more information.

NEBO: A LITERARY JOURNAL (II), English Dept., Arkansas Tech University, Russellville AR 72801-2222, phone (501)968-0256, founded 1982, poetry editor Michael Ritchie, appears in May and December. Regarding poetry they say, **"We accept all kinds, all styles, all subject matters and will publish a longer poem if it is outstanding. We are especially interested in formal poetry."** They have published poetry by Jack Butler, Turner Cassity, Wyatt Prunty, Charles Martin, Julia Randall and Brenda Hillman. *Nebo* is 50-70 pgs., digest-sized, professionally printed on quality matte stock with matte card cover. Press run "varies." **Sample postpaid: $6. Submit 3-5 poems at a time. Simultaneous submissions OK. "Please no offbeat colors." Cover letter with bio material and recent publications required. Do not submit mss between May 1 and August 15.** Editor comments on rejections "if the work has merit but requires revision and resubmission; we do all we can to help." **Reports at the end of November and February respectively. Pays 1 copy.** Staff reviews books of poetry. Send books for review consideration.

THE NEBRASKA REVIEW; TNR AWARDS (II), Creative Writing Program, FA, University of Nebraska, Omaha NE 68182-0324, phone (402)554-2771, fax (402)554-3436, founded 1973, co-editor Art Homer, poetry editor Susan Aizenberg, is a semiannual literary magazine publishing fiction and poetry with occasional essays. The editors want **"lyric poetry from 10-200 lines, preference being for under 100 lines. Subject matter is unimportant, as long as it has some. Poets should have mastered form, meaning poems should have form, not simply 'demonstrate' it."** They don't want to see "concrete, inspirational, didactic or merely political poetry." They have published poetry by Erin Belieu, Michael Bugeja, Stuart Dybek and Carl Phillips. As a sample, they selected these lines from "Crickets" by Pamela Stewart:

> *In every small place the eye, toe, or caught breath turns,*
> *crickets are singing. From that shin*
> *just above the ground they fling an edge of sound*
> *straight through what's left of wilderness.*
> *It swings out across the trees and yards,*
> *up to the warm sills of September.*

The magazine is 6×9, nicely printed, 60 pgs., with flat-spined, glossy card cover. It is a publication of the Writer's Workshop at the University of Nebraska. Some of the most exciting, accessible verse is published in this magazine. All styles and forms are welcome here, although relatively few long poems are used. Circulation is 500, for 380 subscribers of which 85 are libraries. Single copy: $5; subscription: $9.50/year. **Sample postpaid: $3.50. Submit 4-6 poems at a time. "Clean typed copy strongly preferred." Reads open submissions January 1 through April 15 only. Reports in 3-4 months.** Time between acceptance and publication is 3-12 months. **Pays 2 copies and 1-year subscription. Acquires first North American serial rights.** Submissions for The Nebraska Review Awards are read from September 1 through November 30. The TNR Awards of $500 each in poetry and fiction are published in the spring issue. Entry fee: $9, includes discounted subscription. You can enter as many times as desired. Deadline: November 30. The editor says, "Your first allegiance is to the poem.

Publishing will come in time, but it will always be less than you feel you deserve. Therefore, don't look to publication as a reward for writing well; it has no relationship."

NEDGE (II), P.O. Box 2321, Providence RI 02906, website http://www.wings.buffalo.edu/epc/mags/nedge, founded 1969, co-editors Henry Gould and Janet Sullivan, is a biannual published by The Poetry Mission, a nonprofit arts organization. It includes poetry, fiction, reviews and essays. **They want work that "exhibits originality, talent, sincerity, skill and inspiration."** The purpose of *Nedge* is "to aim toward a Rhode Island literary standard, both local and international in scope." Circulation is 300. **Sample postpaid: $5. No simultaneous submissions. SASE required. Reports in 2-3 months. Pays 1 copy.**

NEGATIVE CAPABILITY; NEGATIVE CAPABILITY PRESS; EVE OF ST. AGNES COMPETITION (III), 62 Ridgelawn Dr. E., Mobile AL 36608-2465, fax (334)344-8478, e-mail negcap@datasync.com, founded 1981, poetry editor Sue Walker. *Negative Capability* is a tri-quarterly of verse, fiction, commentary, music and art. The press publishes broadsides, **chapbooks**, perfect-bound paperbacks and hardbacks. They want **both contemporary and traditional poetry. "Quality has its own specifications—length and form."** They have published poetry by John Brugaletta, Marge Piercy, John Updike, Pat Schneider, Vivian Shipley and Diana Der Hovanessian. As a sample Sue Walker selected these lines from "As If Corn Could Invent Itself" by Vivian Shipley:

> *I've come back, father, though to a day I didn't want*
> *to see. I walk right on around*
> *your porch tunneled like stands*
> *put on the road where you laid corn in double rows*
>
> *and piled up the tomatoes I sold for you. I lean over*
> *your face boxed in ivory silk.*

The editor says, "Reaching irritably after a few facts will not describe *Negative Capability*. Read it to know what quality goes to form creative achievement. Shakespeare had negative capability, do you?" This journal has indeed achieved a major prominence on our literary scene. It is an elegantly printed, flat-spined, digest-sized format of 200 pgs., glossy card color cover with art, circulation 1,000. About 60 pgs. of each issue are devoted to poetry. They receive about 1,200 unsolicited submissions a year, use approximately 350. Single copy: $5; subscription: $15. **Sample postpaid: $4. Submit 3-5 poems at a time. Fax and e-mail submissions OK. Reads submissions September 1 through May 30 only. Send SASE for guidelines and upcoming themes. Reports in 6-8 weeks. Pays 1 copy. Acquires first rights.** Reviews books of poetry. Negative Capability Press has published *Little Dragons*, by Michael Bugeja and *The Mouse Whole*, by Richard Moore. **For book publication, query with 10-12 samples and "brief letter with major publications, significant contributions, awards. We like to know a person as well as their poem." Replies to queries in 3-4 weeks, to submissions (if invited) in 6-8 weeks. Payment arranged with authors. Editor sometimes comments on rejections.** They offer an annual Eve of St. Agnes Competition with major poets as judges. Send SASE for details. The editor says, "Poets should keep abreast of current books, know who the contemporary poets are and learn from them. Reading stimulates the muse."

‡NEOLOGISMS (I, II), 1102 Pleasant St. #869, Worcester MA 01602, founded 1996, editor/publisher Jim Fay, published quarterly, is a journal of the written word covering all aspects of writing. **They want "unusual, new styles or modern styles that have character." They do not want "sentimental 'love' poetry; all love-struck sonnet writers should stay away."** They have recently published poetry by Vincent Ferrini, Greg St. Thomasino and Jim Leftwich. *Neologisms* is 60-70 pgs., 8½ × 11, spiral-bound, with b&w card cover, photos and artwork. They receive about 500 poems a year, accept approximately 100. Press run is 150 for 20 subscribers of which 3 are libraries, 25 shelf sales; 20 distributed free to other publishers. Single copy: $5; subscription: $20/4 issues. **Make checks payable to Jim Fay. Submit any number of poems at a time. Previously published poems and simultaneous submissions OK. Cover letter required and "although I do not request it, I do like to know how someone found out about us."** Time between acceptance and publication is 6-8 months. **Poems are selected by editor. Often comments on rejections. Publishes theme issues. Send SASE for guidelines and upcoming themes. Reports in 2-12 weeks. Send prepublication galleys only on request. Pays 1 copy. Acquires one-time rights with an option for second.** Reviews books or chapbooks of poetry or other magazines in 300-500 words. Open to unsolicited reviews. Poets may also send books for review consideration. The editor advises, "Check out our magazine before sending anything in. It makes you look like you've done your homework."

‡THE NEOVICTORIAN/COCHLEA (I, II), P.O. Box 55164, Madison WI 53705, founded 1995, editor Esther Cameron, appears biannually and "seeks to promote a poetry of introspection, dialogue and social concern." **They want "poetry of beauty and integrity with emotional and intellectual depth, commitment to subject matter as well as language, and the courage to ignore fashion. Formal verse preferred; social comment welcome. No over-workshopped poetry that refuses to take risks; no profanity."** They have recently published poetry by Hadassah Haskale, Richard Moore, Carolyn Stoloff and Martha Modena Vertreace. As a sample the editor selected these lines from "Roots" by Rose Rosberg:

> *The groping tendrils find their way*

NERVE COWBOY

Number 2, Fall 1996

A national publication based in Austin, Texas, **Nerve Cowboy** focuses on publishing accessible, narrative poetry. Each issue features 50-60 poems from about 40 different poets and 2-3 "particularly strong" short stories. "Wayne Hogan's drawing, 'Rowboats in the Desert,' hit us just right for the cover of **Nerve Cowboy** #2," says Joseph Shields, co-editor of the biannual literary journal. "Besides the Southwestern motif in this drawing, Hogan uses ordinary images to create an extraordinary situation. We strive to do the same in **Nerve Cowboy** by publishing writing that is direct, accessible, and with a bit of an edge to it." Cover illustrator Wayne Hogan lives in Cookeville, Tennessee, and contributes work to books published by Kings Estate Press and several other literary journals.

> *around the stones which lie between*
> *and block their words, blindly cling,*
> *wordless to each other sing*
>
> *how nerves of all the kindred meet*
> *beneath the surface, reaching forth*

N/C is 28-32 pgs., 8×11, photocopied and saddle-stapled with cardstock cover, occasional graphics, no ads. They receive about 900 poems a year, accept approximately 180. Press run is 250 for 30 subscribers, 20 shelf sales; 100 distributed free to friends, 10-15 to reviewers. Single copy: $6; subscription: $10. **Sample postpaid: $4. Submit 3-5 poems at a time. Previously published poems and simultaneous submissions OK. Cover letter "not necessary. We prefer that poets not cite their publication record in cover letter. Poets whose work is accepted will be asked for titles of books available, to be published in the magazine."** Time between acceptance and publication is 6-12 months. **Often comments on rejections. Does not offer guidelines because "the tradition is the only 'guideline.' We do encourage contributors to write for sample." Reports in 3-8 weeks. Pays 2 copies. Acquires first rights.** *N/C* publishes the addresses of poets who would welcome correspondence. The editor says, "Like all our social functioning, poetry today suffers from a loss of community, which translates into a lack of real intimacy with the reader. Poets can work against this trend by remaining in touch with the poetry of past generations and by forming relationships in which poetry can be employed as the language of friendship. Publication should be an afterthought."

‡NERVE BUNDLE REVIEW (II), 1240 William St., Racine WI 53402, phone (414)639-2406, founded 1996, editor Dan Nielsen, appears 3 times/year. **They want "short, startling, imaginative, accessible, funny poetry." They do not want "poetry that makes the reader feel stupid rather than smart."** They have recently published poetry by Charles Bukowski, Kitrell Dadis, Lisa Glatt and Joel Dailey. As a sample the editor selected these lines from "In the Midst of It" by Frances Heart:

> *my eyes blinked open*
> *to see his closed*
> *all maleness captured*
> *in that*
> *faraway sneer*

NBR is 32 pgs., digest-sized, photocopied, saddle-stapled with card cover and b&w art. Press run is 300 for 50 subscribers of which 10 are libraries. Subscription: $9. **Sample postpaid: $3. Make checks payable to Dan Nielsen. Submit 6 poems, typed, one poem/page with name and address on each sheet. No previously published poems or simultaneous submissions. Cover letter required.** Time between acceptance and publication is "less than six months." **Often comments on rejections. Send SASE for guidelines. Reports "within a month." Always sends prepublication galleys. Pays 1 copy.** Reviews books or chapbooks of poetry or other magazines. Open to unsolicited reviews. Poets may also send books for review consideration.

NERVE COWBOY (I, II); LIQUID PAPER PRESS (V), P.O. Box 4973, Austin TX 78765,website http://www.eden.com/~JWHAGINS/nervecowboy, founded 1995, editors Joseph Shields and Jerry Hagins. *Nerve Cowboy* is a biannual literary journal featuring contemporary poetry, short fiction and b&w drawings. **The editors are "open to all forms, styles and subject matter preferring writing that speaks directly, and minimizes literary devices. We want to see poetry of experience and passion which can find that raw nerve and ride**

it." They have recently published poetry by Michael Estabrook, Mary Winters, Gerald Locklin, Patrick McKinnon, Dawn McGuire and Fred Voss. As a sample the editors selected these lines from "My Inheritance" by Catfish McDaris:

> *I asked if I could touch*
> *the hole where his eye used to be*
> *he looked at me for awhile*
> *then lifted his patch*
> *his gnarled hand guided*
> *my little fingers over*
> *the scarred socket*
> *grandpa said, "even your*
> *granny's never done that."*

Nerve Cowboy is 48-52 pgs., $7 \times 8\frac{1}{2}$, attractively printed and saddle-stapled with matte card cover with b&w cover art. They currently accept 5-10% of the submissions received. Press run is 200-300 for 50 subscribers. Subscription: $14/4 issues. **Sample postpaid: $4. Submit 3-5 poems at a time, name on each page. Previously published poems with notification OK; no simultaneous submissions. Informal cover letter with bio credits preferred. Seldom comments on rejections. Send SASE for guidelines. Reports in 2-4 weeks. Pays 1 copy. Acquires first or one-time rights.** Liquid Paper Press publishes **2-3 chapbooks/year but will not be accepting unsolicited chapbook mss in the foreseeable future.** Chapbooks are 24-40 pgs., $5\frac{1}{2} \times 8\frac{1}{2}$, photocopied with some b&w artwork. Recent publications include *Hindsight, Or How I Survived the Depression* by Albert Huffstickler; *Born Not to Laugh at Tornadoes* by Joan Jobe Smith; and *Wisconsin Daze* by Joseph Shields. Send SASE for a list of available titles.

NEW COLLAGE MAGAZINE (II), 5700 N. Tamiami Trail, Sarasota FL 34243-2197, phone (941)359-5605, founded 1970, poetry editor A. McA. Miller. *New CollAge* provides "a forum for contemporary poets, both known and undiscovered. We are **partial to fresh slants on traditional prosodies and poetry with clear focus and clear imagery. No greeting card verse. We prefer poems shorter than five single-spaced pages. We like a maximum of three to five poems per submission."** They have published poetry by Peter Meinke, Yvonne Sapia, Lola Haskins, J.P. White, Peter Klappert, Peter Wild, Stephen Corey and Malcolm Glass. The magazine appears 2 times a year, 28-32 pgs. of poetry in each issue, circulation 500 with 200 subscribers of which 30 are libraries. They receive about 5,000 poems a year, use approximately 90. Subscription: $6. **Sample: $2. No simultaneous submissions. Publishes theme issues. Send SASE for upcoming themes. Reports in 6 weeks. Pays 2 copies. Editor sometimes comments on rejections.** "We review books and chapbooks in 1,000-2,000 words." Editor "Mac" Miller advises, "Sending a ms already marked 'copyright' is absurd and unprofessional. Mss may be marked 'first North American serials only,' though this is unnecessary. Also, quality is the only standard. Get a sample issue to see our taste."

THE NEW CRITERION (III), The Foundation for Cultural Review, Inc., 850 Seventh Ave., New York NY 10019, poetry editor Robert Richman, is a monthly (except July and August) review of ideas and the arts, which uses **poetry of high literary quality**. They have published poetry by Donald Justice, Andrew Hudgins, Elizabeth Spires and Herbert Morris. It is 90 pgs., 7×10, flat-spined. Poems here truly are open, with structured free verse and formal works highlighted in the issues we critiqued. Much of it was excellent, and book reviews were insightful. **Sample postpaid: $4.75. Cover letter required with submissions. Reports in 2-3 months. Pays $2.50/line ($75 minimum).** Poetry published in this review was selected for inclusion in the 1992 and 1994 volumes of *The Best American Poetry*. The editor says, "To have an idea of who we are or what we stand for, poets should consult back issues."

‡NEW DELTA REVIEW; THE EYSTER PRIZE (II), English Dept., Louisiana State University, Baton Rouge LA 70803-5001, contact poetry editor. They **"publish works of quality, many of them by young writers who are building their reputations."** They have recently published poetry by George Cooney and Doug Martin. *NDR* appears twice a year, 6×9, 90-120 pgs., flat-spined, typeset and printed on quality stock with glossy card cover with art. Press run is 500 for 100 subscribers of which 20 are libraries; the rest are for shelf sales. Subscription: $7. **Sample postpaid: $4. No simultaneous submissions or previously published poems. Cover letter with biographical information required. Mss read in summer. Poetry editor sometimes comments on rejections, often suggesting possible revisions. Reports in 3-4 months. Sometimes sends prepublication galleys. Pays 2 copies. Acquires first North American serial rights.** Reviews books of poetry in no more than 2,000 words, single or multi-book format. Open to unsolicited reviews and interviews. Poets may also send books to poetry editor for review consideration. The Eyster Prize of $25 is awarded to the best story and best poem in each issue. The editor says, "Our only criterion is quality: work that has obviously resulted from much care and respect for the poetic arts."

‡NEW DIGRESSIONS ART AND LITERARY MAGAZINE (I, II), P.O. Box 2640, Stuyvesant Station, New York NY 10009, e-mail elda1@aol.com, founded 1993, contact editors, published 1-2 times/year, "is an art and literary magazine publishing poetry, short stories, b&w graphic art and photography. *New Digressions* encourages, but is not exclusive to, emerging authors and artists ages 18-29 and welcomes all submissions from diverse cultural, social and creative bends." **They want "typewritten only, no identification on pages, only on cover letter, ten pgs. mss only or less." They do not want "handwritten submissions."** They have recently published poetry by Tina Chang, Alan Kaufman, Lyn Lifshin, Ben Passikoff and Mark Zimmermann. *New Digression* is 44-68 pgs., 8½ × 7, saddle-stitched, offset printed, medium card cover with photography, graphic art and ads. They receive about 300 poems a year, accept approximately 20%. Press run is 500 for 250 subscribers of which 1% are libraries, 30% shelf sales; 10% distributed free to reviewers and donors. **Sample (with guidelines) postpaid: $3.50. Make checks payable to Elda Rotor. Submit 3 unidentified copies of up to 10 pgs. of poetry. Previously published poems and simultaneous submissions OK. Cover letter required with name, address, phone number, e-mail and short bio. Entries on disk (Mac or PC) welcomed with hard copy. Manuscripts not returned but recycled. Include SASE for editorial response.** Backlog of 10-12 months. Time between acceptance and publication is 3 months. **Poems are circulated to an editorial board. "All submissions reviewed are masked (anonymously) by editorial staff and voted on."** Seldom comments on rejections. **Send SASE for guidelines or request via e-mail. Reports in 10-12 months. Pays 2 copies. Acquires first rights.**

NEW EARTH PUBLICATIONS (V, IV-Spiritual, political, translations), 1921 Ashby Ave., Berkeley CA 94703, phone (510)549-0176, fax (510)549-1514, e-mail newearth@sirius.com, founded 1990, editors Clifton Ross and Dave Karoly, publishes **"books (up to 96 pgs.) dealing with the struggle for peace and justice, revolutionary anarchism, quality poetry, prose and translations. Some publications are author subsidized."** They publish 1-2 paperbacks, **2-3 chapbooks/year. They are currently not accepting unsolicited submissions.**

NEW ENGLAND REVIEW (II), Middlebury College, Middlebury VT 05753, phone (802)443-5075, e-mail nereview@mail.middlebury.edu, founded 1978, editor Stephen Donadio. *New England Review* is a prestigious literary quarterly, 160 pgs., 7 × 10, flat-spined, elegant make-up and printing on heavy stock, glossy cover with art. All styles and forms are welcome in this carefully edited publication. They have recently published poetry by Alfred Corn, Sandra McPherson, Eric Pankey, Carl Phillips, Cathy Sung and Richard Tillinghast. Sample copies or subscriptions may be ordered through the University Press of New England, 23 S. Main St., Hanover NH 03755; (800)421-1561. Subscription: $23. **Sample postpaid: $7. Submit up to 6 poems at a time. Address submissions to Poetry Editor. No previously published poems. "Brief cover letters are useful. All submissions by mail. Questions by e-mail OK." Reads submissions September 1 through May 31 only. Response times can be exceptionally slow here, far exceeding published limits of 6-8 weeks. Always sends prepublication galleys. Pays $10/page, $20 minimum per poem, plus 2 copies.** Also features essay-reviews. Publishers may send books for review consideration. Work published in this review was included in the 1992, 1993 and 1994 volumes of *The Best American Poetry*.

NEW ERA MAGAZINE (I, IV-Religious, teen/young adult), 50 E. North Temple St., Salt Lake City UT 84150-0001, phone (801)240-2951, fax (801)240-5997, founded 1971, managing editor Richard M. Romney, appears monthly. *New Era* is an "official publication for youth of The Church of Jesus Christ of Latter-day Saints; it contains feature stories, photo stories, fiction, news, etc." **They want "short verse in any form, particularly traditional—must pertain to teenage LDS audience (religious and teenage themes). No sing-songy doggerel, gushy love poems or forced rhymes."** *New Era* is 52 pgs., approximately 8 × 10½, 4-color offset, saddle-stitched, quality stock, top-notch art and graphics, no ads. They receive 200-300 submissions a year, accept approximately 2-5%. Press run is 220,000 for 205,000 subscribers, 10,000 shelf sales. Single copy: $1.50; subscription: $8/year. **Sample: $1.50 plus postage. Send up to 5 poems at one time. No previously published poems or simultaneous submissions.** Time between acceptance and publication is a year or longer. "We publish one poem each month next to our photo of the month." **Sometimes comments on rejections. Publishes 1-2 theme issues each year, one of which is geographically themed (LDS youth in one country). Theme deadlines are 6 months minimum to 1 year in advance. Send SASE for guidelines and upcoming themes. Reports in 6-8 weeks. Sometimes sends prepublication galleys. Pays $10 minimum. "LDS church retains rights to publish again in church publications—all other rights returned."** They also offer an annual contest—including poetry—for active members of the LDS church between ages 12-23. Poetry entries should consist of one entry of 6-10 different original poems (none of which exceeds 50 lines) reflecting LDS values. Deadline: January. Winners receive either a partial scholarship to BYU or Ricks College or a cash award. Send SASE for rules. The editor says, "Study the magazine before submitting. We're a great market for beginners, but you must understand Mormons to write well for us. Just because a subject is noble or inspirational doesn't mean the poetry automatically is noble or inspirational. Pay attention to the craft of writing. Poetry is more than

---

MARKET CATEGORIES: (I) Beginning; **(II)** General; **(III)** Limited; **(IV)** Specialized; **(V)** Closed.

just writing down your thoughts about an inspirational subject. Poetry needs to communicate easily and be readily understood—it's too easy to mistake esoteric expression for true insight."

NEW FRONTIERS OF NEW MEXICO (II), P.O. Box 1299, Tijeras NM 87059, phone (505)281-1990, fax (505)281-2300, founded 1993, editor/publisher Wally Gordon, is a quarterly publication of "poetry, fiction, journalism and commentary dealing with New Mexico and the Southwest." **They want poems under 60 lines, light verse and "prefer, but do not require, a Southwestern theme. No touristic poems about sunsets and blue skies."** They have published poetry by Lyn Lifshin, Wayne Hogan, Jay Udall and Francis DiPietro. As a sample the editor selected these lines from "Loneliness is not silent" by Diana L. Martinez:

> *Loneliness is not silent*
> *Its screams compound*
> *And bounce violent*
> *Down*
> *Halls that shriek you're gone.*

The editor says *New Frontiers* is 32 pgs., 8×11, with 2-color cover, photos, cartoons and drawings inside. They receive about 400 poems a year, use approximately 50. Press run is 3,000 for 1,000 subscribers of which 25 are libraries, 1,000 shelf sales. Subscription: $9.50/year. **Sample postpaid: $2.95. Simultaneous submissions OK. Cover letter including brief bio with publication credits preferred. Seldom comments on rejections. Send SASE for guidelines. Reports in 2 months. Pays up to $25 and 1 copy. Buys first North American serial rights, "but will consider republication if not in competing magazine."** Sponsors an annual contest in collaboration with PEN. Send SASE for details. The editor says, "Poets in the Southwest sometimes think scenery is an appropriate subject in and of itself. It's not—unless the writer puts something unusual in the scene."

*NEW HOPE INTERNATIONAL (III), 20 Werneth Ave., Gee Cross, Hyde, Cheshire SK14 5NL United Kingdom, founded 1969, editor Gerald England, includes *"NHI Writing*, **publishing poetry, short fiction, artwork, literary essays and reports. All types of poetry from traditional to avant-garde, from haiku to long poems, including translations (usually with the original).** *NHI Review* **carries reviews of books, magazines, cassettes, CDs, records, PC software, etc. Special Edition Chapbooks with a theme or individual collections also included."** *NHI Poetry Forum* **is a poetry magazine on disk with original poetry and articles from 10 countries.** They have recently published poetry by Nilofar Hussain, Coral Hull, Thomas Land, H.F. Noyes, Damion Quinn and John Waddington-Feather. As a sample the editor selected these lines from "Perfumed Night" by Maureen Weldon:

> *My love who wore his hair in bright beads*
> *died suddenly like the wind.*
> *The tall tree tells this*
> *with the moon in her eye.*
>
> *Yet—somewhere a rose blooms*
> *in a perfumed night.*

The digest-sized magazine, 36-40 pgs., is printed offset-litho from computer typesetting, saddle-stapled, color card cover, using b&w artwork. Press run is 600 for 300 subscribers of which 25 are libraries. Subscription: £20/ 6 issues (*NHI Writing, NHI Review* and **S.E. Chapbooks** as published). **Sample postpaid: £4.** *NHI Poetry Forum* **is available on 3.5-inch PC compatible disk for £2/issue in UK and £3/issue outside UK. Make checks payable to Gerald England. "Non-sterling cheques no longer accepted. Payment by International Giro (available from Post Offices worldwide) preferred. Currency notes to the sterling equivalent accepted as a last resort." Submit up to 6 poems at a time; put name and address on each sheet; simultaneous submissions *not* encouraged. Cover letter required. Translations should include copy of original. Disk submissions with hard copy OK for *NHI Poetry Forum*. Full guidelines available for IRC (3 for airmail). Send 1 IRC for reply if return of mss not required. Reports "usually fairly prompt, but sometimes up to 4 months." Always sends prepublication galleys.** *NHI Writing* and *NHI Review* **pay 1 copy (***NHI Poetry Forum* **does not pay its contributors). Acquires first British serial rights.** Staff reviews books of poetry. Send books for review consideration. **For chapbooks, query first.** The editor advises, "Long lists of previous publications do not impress; perceptive, interesting, fresh writing indicative of a live, thinking person makes this job worthwhile."

NEW HORIZONS POETRY CLUB (II, IV-Membership), Box 5561, Chula Vista CA 91912, phone (619)474-4715, fax (619)474-8060, founded 1984, poetry editor Alex Stewart (recent past president of the California Federation of Chaparral Poets). This organization offers poetry contests of various sorts for experienced writers, publishing winners in an anthology. They also offer newsletters and critiques and publish anthologies of members' poetry. Membership (includes 4 newsletters): $14/year or $12.50 plus 4 SASEs/year. They have published poetry by Alice Mackenzie Swaim, Glenna Holloway, Pegasus Buchanan and Emery Campbell. Prizes in their Annual Poetry Day Contest are "$250 and down. We offer other cash awards, prizes and trophies, and certificates for honorable mentions. 'Mini-manuscript' winners are offered trophies, cash prizes and anthologies." Entry fees are $5/2 poems, $10/5 poems. **"We expect poets to know technique, to be familiar with traditional forms and to be able to conform to requirements regarding category, style and length and to show original-**

ity, imagery and craftsmanship. Nothing amateurish, trite or in poor taste." Alex Stewart offers critiques at reasonable rates. (Discounts on critiques and books to members.) She says, "Poets need to study technique before *rushing to get published!* (*Where* is what counts!) The current trend seems to be a wide range of traditional forms and comprehensible free verse. The sonnet is making a real comeback!" (Book list, including *The Poet's Art*, the editor's complete handbook on the craft of poetry writing, available on request.)

NEW LETTERS; NEW LETTERS POETRY PRIZE (II), University of Missouri-Kansas City, Kansas City MO 64110, phone (816)235-1168, fax (816)235-2611, founded 1934 as *University Review*, became *New Letters* in 1971, managing editor Bob Stewart, editor James McKinley, "is dedicated to publishing the best short fiction, best contemporary poetry, literary articles, photography and artwork by both established writers and new talents." They want **"contemporary writing of all types—free verse poetry preferred, short works are more likely to be accepted than very long ones."** They have recently published poetry by Joyce Carol Oates, Amiri Baraka, Nancy Willard, Margaret Randall, Gary Gildner and Trish Reeves. The 6×9, flat-spined, professionally printed quarterly, glossy 2-color cover with art, uses about 40-45 (of 120) pgs. of poetry in each issue. Circulation is 2,500 with 1,800 subscriptions of which about 40% are libraries. They receive about 7,000 submissions a year, use less than 1%, have a 6-month backlog. Poems appear in a variety of styles exhibiting a high degree of craft and universality of theme (rare in many journals). Subscription: $17. **Sample postpaid: $5. Send no more than 6 poems at a time. No previously published poems or simultaneous submissions. Short cover letter preferred. "We strongly prefer original typescripts and we don't read between May 15 and October 15. No query needed." Reports in 4-10 weeks. Pays a small fee plus 2 copies. Occasionally James McKinley comments on rejections.** The New Letters Poetry Prize of $750 is given annually for a group of 3-6 poems, entry fee $10 (check payable to New Letters Literary Awards). Send SASE for entry guidelines. Deadline: May 15. They also publish occasional anthologies, selected and edited by McKinley. Work published in *New Letters* appeared in the 1992 and 1997 volumes of *The Best American Poetry*.

NEW METHODS: THE JOURNAL OF ANIMAL HEALTH TECHNOLOGY (IV-Animals), P.O. Box 22605, San Francisco CA 94122-0605, phone (415)664-3469, founded as *Methods* in 1976, poetry editor Ronald S. Lippert, AHT, is an irregular 4-page newsletter, "a networking service in the animal field, active in seeking new avenues of knowledge for our readers, combining animal professionals under one roof." They want poetry which is **"animal related but not cutesy, two pages maximum."** They receive about 50 poems a year, accept approximately 5. Press run is 5,000 for 4,000 subscribers of which 100 are libraries. Subscription: $32. **Sample: $3.20. A listing of all back issues and the topics covered is available for $5, and there is a 20% discount on an order of 12 or more mixed copies. No previously published poems or simultaneous submissions. Dated cover letter required. Everything typed, double-spaced with 1-inch margins. Often comments on rejections. Send SASE for guidelines. Reports in 2-4 weeks. Pays 10 copies.** Reviews books of poetry "pertaining to our subject matter."

‡NEW MILLENNIUM WRITINGS; NEW MILLENNIUM AWARD FOR POETRY (III), P.O. Box 2463, Knoxville TN 37901, founded 1996. *New Millenium Writings*, published biannually, features "forward-looking fiction, essays and poetry of exceptional literary merit." **They want "upbeat, witty, alliterative poetry of fewer than 50 lines." They do not want** "confessional, medical, political or sentimental poetry." They have recently published poetry by Marily Kallet and Sallie Bingham. *New Millennium Writings* is 160 pgs., 6×9, professionally printed, perfect-bound with color cover, illustrations and photos. They receive about 3,000 poems a year, accept approximately 1%. Press run is 2,500 for 1,000 subscribers, 1,000 shelf sales; 100 distributed free for public relations. Single copy: $7.95; subscription: $14.95. **Sample (including guidelines) postpaid: $7. Submit 3 poems at a time with a $5 reading fee. No previously published poems; simultaneous submissions OK "if so noted." Cover letter preferred. Reads submissions July through August and February through March only**. Time between acceptance and publication is 3 months. **Seldom comments on rejections. Reports in 3 months. Pays 2 copies. Acquires first North American serial rights.** Sponsors the New Millenium Award for Poetry, awarded biannually, pays $1,000 and publication in *NMW*. Deadline: January 5. Send SASE for guidelines.

NEW NATIVE PRESS (III), P.O. Box 661, Cullowhee NC 28723, phone (704)293-9237, founded 1979, publisher Thomas Rain Crowe, is a publisher of "new, original and innovative work by American and foreign authors with an emphasis on translated material." They publish 2 paperbacks/year. **They want lyric poetry and translations. "No one-dimensional rhymed metric, confessional, political or issue-oriented poetry."** They have recently published *Seizures of the Sun* by Meschach McLaclan. As a sample the publisher selected these lines from his own poem "Learning to Dance":

> . . . *I have given up the toys of my childhood and my ambitions for old age*
> *and have moved deep within the walls of her silver skin.*
> *I am through with my love of suffering and the words that describe that love.*
> *I am going to carry on a magnificent affair with the wind*
> *from the inside of her body, where we both sleep.*

Books are typically 80 pgs., offset and perfect-bound with glossy 120 lb. cover with graphics. **Query first with 10 sample poems and cover letter with brief bio and publication credits. Previously published poems and**

simultaneous submissions OK. Time between acceptance and publication is 6-12 months. **Always comments on rejections. Reports in 2 weeks. Pays copies, "amount varies with author and title."** The publisher says, "Manuscripts for books accepted are most often solicited—with the possible exception of rare talent and translations. I am always looking for unique and original voices using language experimentally and symbolically."

NEW ORLEANS POETRY JOURNAL PRESS (III), 2131 General Pershing St., New Orleans LA 70115, phone (504)891-3458, founded 1956, publisher/editor Maxine Cassin, co-editor Charles deGravelles. **"We prefer to publish relatively new and/or little-known poets of unusual promise or those inexplicably neglected." They do not want to see "cliché or doggerel, anything incomprehensible or too derivative, or workshop exercises. First-rate lyric poetry preferred (not necessarily in traditional forms)."** They have published books by Vassar Miller, Everette Maddox, Charles Black, Raeburn Miller and Martha McFerren. As a sample the editor selected these lines from "The Truck Driver's Hands" from *The Well-Governed Son* by Charles de Gravelles:

> *Just before the truck rumbles over, these hands*
> *rise and float mysteriously as handkerchiefs*
> *during the brief madness*
>
> *of motion before they descend, settling like dust,*
> *like the delicate decision to resume the struggle*
> *for control of a difficult journey.*

Query first. They do not accept unsolicited submissions for chapbooks, which are flat-spined paperbacks. **Unsolicited mss will not be returned. The editors report on queries in 2-3 months, mss in the same time period, if solicited. Simultaneous submissions will possibly be accepted. Sometimes sends prepublication galleys. Pays copies, usually 50-100.** Ms. Cassin does not subsidy publish at present and does not offer grants or awards. For aspiring poets, she quotes the advice Borges received from his father: "1) Read as much as possible! 2) Write only when you *must*, and 3) Don't rush into print!" As a small press editor and publisher, she urges poets to read instructions in *Poet's Market* listings with utmost care! She says, "No poetry should be sent without querying first! Publishers are concerned about expenses unnecessarily incurred in mailing manuscripts. *Telephoning is not encouraged.*"

NEW ORLEANS REVIEW (II), Box 195, Loyola University, New Orleans LA 70118, phone (504)865-2295, fax (504)865-2294, e-mail noreview@beta.loyno.edu, founded 1968, editor Ralph Adamo. They have recently published poetry by Jack Gilbert, Rodney Jones, Besmilr Brigham, Hank Lazar and Joy Lahem. *New Orleans Review* publishes **"lyric poetry of all types,** fiction that is strongly voiced and essays." It is 120 pgs., perfect-bound, elegantly printed with glossy card cover. Circulation is 1,700. **Sample postpaid: $10. Submit 3-6 poems at a time. No previously published work. Brief cover letter preferred. Publishes theme issues. Send SASE for upcoming themes. Reports in 3 months. Pays 5 copies. Acquires first North American serial rights.**

THE NEW PRESS LITERARY QUARTERLY; THE NEW PRESS POETRY CONTEST (II), 63-44 Saunders St., Suite 3, Rego Park NY 11374-2039, phone (718)459-6807, fax (718)275-1646, founded 1984, poetry editor Evie-Ivy Biber, is a quarterly magazine using **poems "less than 100 lines, accessible, imaginative. No doggerel, sentimentality."** They include a multilingual section for poetry. **They want poems in Spanish, Italian, Portuguese, Japanese, Chinese, Russian, Hungarian, German, Icelandic and French, accompanied by their English versions/translations. Each poem must list the author's and translator's names and addresses.** They have published poetry by Allen Ginsberg, Lawrence Ferlinghetti, Louise Jaffe, Mary Winters, D.H. Melhem, Les Bridges and Gina Bergamino. It is magazine-sized, 32-48 pgs., desktop-published, with glossy cover, saddle-stapled. They receive 500-1,000 poems a year, accept approximately 10%. Press run is 2,000 for 350 subscribers. Subscription: $15/year, $29/2 years (add $5/year for overseas). **Sample postpaid: $5.50. "Payable by check or money order in U.S. funds only." Submit 6 poems at a time. Nonsubscribers are required to pay a reading fee of $2 (1-3 poems) or $4 (4-6 poems). "Include name and address on the top of each page." Publishes theme issues. Send SASE for upcoming themes. Reports in 4 months. Always sends prepublication galleys. Pays 2 copies. Acquires first-time rights.** The New Press Poetry Contest is annual, deadline is July 1, entry fee of $5 for up to 3 poems or 100 lines, has prizes of $100, $75 and five 2-year subscriptions. They also sponsor poetry readings in Brooklyn and Manhattan. Send SASE for details.

THE NEW RENAISSANCE (II, IV-Translations, bilingual), 26 Heath Rd. #11, Arlington MA 02174, founded 1968, editor-in-chief Louise T. Reynolds, poetry editor Frank Finale. *the new renaissance* is "intended for the 'renaissance' person—the generalist, not the specialist. Publishes the best new writing and translations. Offers a forum for articles on political, sociological topics, features established as well as emerging visual artists and writers, and highlights reviews of small press books and other books of merit. **We are open to traditional as well as other types of poetry and usually receive samples of every kind during our submission periods."** They have recently published poetry by Stephen Booker, Marc Hudson and Allen C. Fisher, and translations of Umberto Saba (by Christopher Merrill) and Domokos Szilagyi (by Len Roberts). As a sample the editor selected these lines from "My Mother Gardens II" by Dashka Slater:

> *My mother is forgetful now, not with age.*

> Her mind returns to her own concerns.
> Before, her attention
> dangled, a baited line
> and any of the world's hungry fishes
> could gobble it.

tnr is flat-spined, professionally printed on heavy stock, glossy, color cover, 144-186 pgs., using 24-40 pgs. of poetry in each issue. They receive about 750 poetry submissions a year, use 15-23, have about a 1½- to 2-year backlog. Usual press run is 1,500 for 710 subscribers of which approximately 132 are libraries. Subscriptions: $24/3 issues US, $26 Canada, $28 all others. **"We're an unsponsored, independent small litmag. All poetry submissions are tied to our Awards Program for best poetry published in a three-issue volume. Entry fee $15 for nonsubscribers, $10 for subscribers, for which they may receive either of the following: two back issues or a current issue or extend their subscription." Submit 3-6 poems at a time, "unless a long poem— then one." No previously published poems "unless magazine's circulation was under 300"; simultaneous submissions OK, if notified. Reads mss January through June 1st and September and October. Send SASE for guidelines. Reports in 3-6 months. Pays $15-22, more for the occasional longer poem, plus 1 copy/poem. Buys all rights. Returns rights provided *tnr* retains rights for any *tnr* collection, anthology, etc. Reviews** books of poetry. The Awards Program gives 3 awards of $250, $125 and $50, with 3 Honorable Mentions of $20. Poetry published in *the new renaissance* has been included in the 1995-1996 *Anthology of Magazine Verse & Yearbook of American Poetry*. The editor says, "We believe that poets should not only be readers but lovers of poetry. We're looking for 'literalists of the imagination—imaginary gardens with real toads in them.' **Our range is from traditionalist poetry to post-modern, experimental (the latter only occasionally, though) and street poetry. We also like the occasional 'light' poem and, of course, have an emphasis on translations. We're especially interested in the individual voice. We aren't interested in greeting card verse or prose set in poetic forms. If you're querying us about anything, please include a SASE. We can't answer unless there is one."**

THE NEW REPUBLIC (II), 1220 19th St. NW, Washington DC 20036, phone (202)331-7494, founded 1914, poetry editor Mark Strand. *The New Republic*, a weekly journal of opinion, is magazine-sized, printed on slick paper, 42 pgs., saddle-stapled with 4-color cover. Subscription: $69.97/year. **Sample postpaid: $3.50. Include SASE with submissions. Always sends prepublication galleys. Pays $100/poem.** Poetry published in *The New Republic* has also been included in the 1993, 1994, 1995 and 1997 volumes of *The Best American Poetry*.

NEW RIVERS PRESS; MINNESOTA VOICES PROJECT (II, IV-Regional, translations), 420 N. Fifth St., Suite 910, Minneapolis MN 55401, founded 1968, publishes collections of poetry, novels or novellas, translations of contemporary literature, collections of short fiction. **Write for free catalog or send SASE for guidelines/ inquiries. New and emerging authors living in Iowa, Minnesota, North and South Dakota, and Wisconsin are eligible for the Minnesota Voices Project. Book-length mss of poetry,** short fiction, novellas or familiar essays are all accepted. **Send SASE for entry form. Winning authors receive a stipend of $500 plus publication by New Rivers. Second and subsequent printings of works will allow 15% royalties for author. Postmark deadline: April 1.**

NEW SPIRIT PRESS; POEMS THAT THUMP IN THE DARK/SECOND GLANCE MAGAZINE (II), 82-34 138 St., #6F, Kew Gardens NY 11435, phone (718)847-1482, e-mail newspirit@aol.com, website http://members.aol.com/nsp97, founded 1991, editor Ignatius Graffeo. *Poems That Thump in the Dark/Second Glance* appears 2 times a year and publishes poetry, poetry book reviews and poetry magazine reviews. **They want "all styles and forms of fine-crafted poetry on mythology, folklore, gothic, erotica, humor, history, contemporary people and/or experiences; poetry with good metaphors, form and feeling. No greeting card verse, cascading stanzas, political ravings, gratuitous violence or sex."** They have published poetry by Stephen Dunn, Colette Inez, Donna Masini and William Pitt Root. As a sample the editor selected these lines from "Vulcan & Venus" by LindaAnn Loschiavo:

> The first time he saw Venus Vulcan loved.
> She was a flower, petals arching back,
> Intent on showing off its pollen tease.
> Without her in his life he'd be a dead sea
> That's drying up. Without her as his wife,
> The god of fire suspects he will amount
> To merely supervisor of the clowns.
> His smithy's flames were never this intense.
> Those passions of extremity, he knows,
> Have rendered subsequent existence pale,
> Her image driven into him, hard nailed.

It is 72 pgs., digest-sized, laser-printed and saddle-stapled with heavy card cover with b&w art, b&w graphics and ads inside. Press run is 300 for 100 subscribers of which 10 are libraries, 30 shelf sales. Subscription: $20. **Sample postpaid: $6. Make checks payable to New Spirit Press. Submit 4 poems at a time. No previously published poems; simultaneous submissions OK. Cover letter including brief bio, publication credits and**

SASE preferred. **"Windows/IBM compatible diskette submissions OK."** Time between acceptance and publication is up to 1 year. **Seldom comments on rejections. Send SASE for guidelines. Reports in 3-6 months. Pays 1 copy plus 33% discount on additional copies.** Staff reviews books and magazines of poetry in 3,000 words. Poets may also send books for review consideration. New Spirit Press also **publishes chapbooks** through their quarterly chapbook contests. The winner receives 50 copies of chapbook. Submit mss of 16-20 pgs. Deadlines: March 31, June 30, September 30 and December 31. Entry fee: $10, includes copy of winning chapbook. Send SASE for guidelines.

NEW THOUGHT JOURNAL (II, IV-Inspirational), 2520 Evelyn Dr., Kettering OH 45409, phone/fax (937)293-9717, e-mail ntjmag@aol.com, founded 1993, editor/publisher Jeffrey M. Ohl, is a quarterly art and literary magazine including stories (fiction and nonfiction), poetry, art and reviews "focusing on arts, humanities, metaphysics, creativity, transformation, personal growth and spiritual themes." **They want poetry of any form, any length, but "subject matter to be inspirational, moving readers to change the world and/or the way they look at the world, to bring people together. No hatred or negativity, nothing prejudicial."** They have recently published poetry by Mary Winters, Michael Steffen, Armin Wilson and David Romtvedt. As a sample the editor selected this poem by Therese Halscheid:

> I woke early and recorded a dream about a man
> who wouldn't write about the sea.
> He did it this way. He would listen,
> and water had words.
> The same words over and over.
> I don't remember what they were,
> but I heard them. I saw them too.

NTJ, subtitled "The Beat of a Thousand Drummers," is about 40 pgs., 8½×11, offset and saddle-stitched with a high quality 4-color glossy cover and b&w photos, illustrations and ads inside. They receive about 400 poems a year, accept 100-150. Press run is 5,000. Single copy: $3.95; subscription: $15. **Sample (including guidelines) postpaid: $5. Submit 4 poems at a time. Previously published poems and simultaneous submissions OK. Cover letter preferred; include "background, author biography—inspiration for poem." Seldom comments on rejections. Reports upon publication by sending 2 copies to the author. Acquires one-time rights.** Open to unsolicited reviews.

‡**NEW VIRGINIA REVIEW (II)**, 1312 E. Cary St., Richmond VA 23219, phone (804)782-1043, founded 1978, poetry editor Margaret Gibson, appears 3 times/year publishing both fiction and poetry. **They want "seriously written poetry addressing any subject matter, in any variety of styles. No greeting card verse or haiku."** They have published poetry by Mona Van Duyn, Mary Oliver, Philip Booth and Norman Dubie. *NVR* is 160 pgs., 6¾×10, offset, perfect-bound, with color cover, no graphics. They receive over 6,000 mss a year, accept approximately 10%. Press run is 2,500 for 1,500 subscribers of which 20% are libraries, 250 shelf sales. Subscription: $15. **Sample postpaid: $6. No previously published poems or simultaneous submissions. Reads submissions September 1 through May 31 only. Seldom comments on rejections. Send SASE for guidelines. Reports in 3-6 weeks. Pays $25/poem on publication, plus $10 for additional printed pages. Buys first North American serial rights.**

***NEW WELSH REVIEW (II, IV-Ethnic)**, Chapter Arts Centre, Market Rd., Cardiff CF5 1QE Wales, United Kingdom, phone 0222-665529, founded 1988, editor Robin Reeves. *NWR* is a literary quarterly publishing articles, short stories and poems. The editor describes it as an average of 100 pgs., glossy paper in three colors, laminated cover, using photographs, graphics and ads. Press run is 1,100. Subscription: £15 (£17 overseas surface mail). **Sample postpaid: £4.20. Submit poems double-spaced. No simultaneous submissions or previously published poems. Reports in 3 months. Publication within 1-7 months.** Reviews books of poetry.

NEW WRITER'S MAGAZINE (I, II, IV-Humor, writing), P.O. Box 5976, Sarasota FL 34277-5976, phone (941)953-7903, e-mail newriters@aol.com, founded 1986, editor George J. Haborak, is a bimonthly magazine "for aspiring writers, and professional ones as well, to exchange ideas and working experiences." **They are open to free verse, light verse and traditional, 8-20 lines, reflecting upon the writing lifestyle. "Humorous slant on writing life especially welcomed." They do not want poems about "love, personal problems, abstract ideas or fantasy."** *NWM* is 28 pgs., 8½×11, offset, saddle-stapled, with glossy paper cover, b&w photos and ads. They receive about 300 poems a year, accept approximately 10%. Press run is 5,000. Subscription:

USE THE GENERAL INDEX to find the page number of a specific publisher. Also, if a publisher from last year's edition is not included in this edition, the General Index will tell you why.

$15/year, $25/2 years. **Sample postpaid: $3. Submit up to 3 poems at a time. No previously published poems or simultaneous submissions.** Time between acceptance and publication is up to 1 year. **Send SASE for guidelines or request via e-mail. Reports in 1-2 months. Pays $5/poem. Buys first North American serial rights.** Each issue of this magazine also includes an interview with a recognized author, articles on writing and the writing life, tips and markets.

NEW YORK QUARTERLY (II), P.O. Box 693, Old Chelsea Station, New York NY 10113, founded 1969, poetry editor William Packard, appears 3 times/year. They seek to publish "a cross-section of the best of contemporary American poetry" and, indeed, **have a record of publishing many of the best and most diverse of poets**, including W.D. Snodgrass, Gregory Corso, James Dickey and Judson Jerome. It appears in a 6×9, flat-spined format, thick, elegantly printed, glossy color cover. Subscription: $15. **Submit 3-5 poems at a time with your name and address; include SASE. Simultaneous submissions OK with notification. Reports within 2 weeks. Pays copies.**

THE NEW YORKER (III, IV-Translations, humor), 20 W. 43rd St., New York NY 10036, founded 1925, poetry editor Alice Quinn, circulation 640,000, uses **poetry of the highest quality (including translations). Sample: $2.95 (available on newsstands). Mss are not read during the summer. Replies in 6-8 weeks. Pays top rates.** Poems appearing in *The New Yorker* have also been selected for inclusion in the 1992, 1993, 1994, 1995, 1996 and 1997 volumes of *The Best American Poetry*.

NEWSLETTER INAGO (I), P.O. Box 26244, Tucson AZ 85726-6244, phone (520)294-7031, founded 1979, poetry editor Del Reitz, is a monthly newsletter. **"Free verse and short narrative poetry preferred although other forms will be read. Rhymed poetry must be truly exceptional (nonforced) for consideration. Due to format, 'epic' and monothematic poetry will not be considered. Cause specific, political or religious poetry stands little chance of consideration. A wide range of short poetry, showing the poet's preferably eclectic perspective is best for** *NI*. **No haiku, please."** They have published poetry by Chloe Heuch, Rose Marie Hunold, Elizabeth Zibas, Holly Lalena Day, Simon Perchik, Albert Huffstickler and Kirsten Fox. As a sample the editor selected these lines from "Feathers And Strings" by Mark J. Isham:

> The Bell-Ringer and the Elephant Man
> were pissing away another afternoon
> in a West Hollywood bar
> Safe from paparrazzi and People
>   Magazine
> Hunched over another round
> mumbling about feathers and strings
> and the unbearable lightness of being
> Charles Bukowski would've been proud
> Tom Waits too

NI is 4-5 pgs., corner-stapled. Press run is approximately 200 for that many subscriptions. **No price is given for the newsletter, but the editor suggests a donation of $3.50 an issue or $17.50 annually ($3.50 and $21 Canada, £8 and £21 UK). Make checks payable to Del Reitz. Submit 10-15 poems at a time. "Poetry should be submitted in the format in which the poet wants it to appear, and cover letters are always a good idea." Simultaneous submissions and previously published poems OK. Sometimes comments on rejections. Send SASE for guidelines. Reports ASAP (usually within 2 weeks). Pays 4 copies.** The first and second audio anthologies of poetry (on audiotapes) are available. These anthologies present selections from the poetry published in *Newsletter Inago* during the first and second 5 years, respectively. Write for current price and details.

NEXUS (II), WO16A Student Union, Wright State University, Dayton OH 45435, phone (937)775-5533, founded 1967, editor Larry Sawyer. "*Nexus* is a student operated magazine of mainstream and street poetry; also essays on environmental and political issues. **We're looking for truthful, direct poetry. Open to poets anywhere. We look for contemporary, imaginative work."** *Nexus* appears 3 times a year—fall, winter and spring, using about 40 pgs. of poetry (of 80-96) in each issue. They receive about 1,000 submissions a year, use approximately 30-50. Circulation 1,000. **For a sample, send a 10×15 SAE with 5 first-class stamps and $5. Submit 4-6 pgs. of poetry with bio. Reads submissions September through May only. Simultaneous submissions OK, "but due to short response time we want to be told it's a simultaneous submission."** Editor sometimes comments on rejections. **Send SASE for guidelines. Reports in 15-20 weeks except summer months. Pays 2 copies. Acquires first rights.**

NIGHT ROSES (I, IV-Teen/young adult, love/romance, nature, students, women/feminism); MOONSTONE BLUE (I, IV-Anthology, science fiction/fantasy), P.O. Box 393, Prospect Heights IL 60070-0393, phone (847)392-2435, founded 1986, poetry editor Allen T. Billy, appears 2-4 times/year. "*Moonstone Blue* is a science fiction/fantasy anthology, but we have no set dates of publication. We do an issue every 14-24 months as items, time and funds allow. We look for women/feminism themes for our *Cocktail Shakers* series." For *Night Roses* they want **"poems about dance, bells, clocks, nature, ghost images of past or future, romance and flowers (roses, wildflowers, violets, etc.). Do not want poems with raw language."** They have published poetry by Emma J. Blanch, M. Riesa Clark, Joan Payne Kincaid, Lyn Lifshin and Alice Rogoff. As a sample the editor selected these lines from "secret light" by Cathy Drinkwater Better:

> *she looked into his eyes*
> *and saw all of eternity*
> *staring back at her*
> *with the face of an enchanter*

Night Roses is 44 pgs., saddle-stapled, photocopied from typescript on offset paper with tinted matte card cover. Press run is 200-300. Subscription: $10/3 issues. **Sample postpaid: $4 for *Night Roses*, $3.75 for *Moonstone Blue*. Submit up to 8 poems at a time. "Desire author's name and address on all sheets of ms. If previously published—an acknowledgment must be provided by author with it." No simultaneous submissions; some previously published poems used. "I prefer submissions between March and September." Reports in 1-4 months. "Material is accepted for current issue and two in progress." Sometimes sends prepublication galleys. Pays 1 copy. Acquires first or reprint rights.** Staff reviews books of poetry. Send books for review consideration. The editor says, "We are more interested in items that would be of interest to our teen and women readers and to our readership in the fields of dance, art and creative learning. We are interested in positive motives in this area."

NIGHTSUN (II), Dept. of English, Frostburg State University, Frostburg MD 21532, phone (301)687-4221, fax (301)687-4495, e-mail dzpcsl@fra00.ump.fsu.edu, founded 1981, co-editors Keith Schlegel, Barbara Hurd and Karin Zealand, is a literary annual of poetry, fiction and interviews. **They want "highest-quality poetry." Subject matter open. Publishes mostly free verse. Prefers poems not much longer than 40 lines. Not interested in the "extremes of sentimental, obvious poetry on the one hand and the subjectless 'great gossamer-winged gnat' school of poetry on the other."** They have published poetry by Diane Wakoski, Philip Dacey, Walter McDonald, David Citino, Stephen Perry and Robert Cooperman. Interviews include Lucille Clifton, Sharon Olds, Galway Kinnell, Stephen Dobyns, Maxine Kumin, Marvin Bell and Marge Piercy. As a sample the editor selected these lines from "Looking Into the Ether" by Dina Coe:

> *I close the door on the highways*
> *lit like an underground:*
> *arteries of the same rough heart*
> *that has born two to climb*
> *towards bedtime in the window*
> *of Earth's obtuse dark.*

Nightsun is 68 pgs., 6×9, printed on 100% recycled paper and perfect-bound with card cover, b&w print on front. This attractive journal features well-known poets alongside relative newcomers. Editors take free verse mostly with attention paid to line, stanza and shape of poem. They accept about 1% of poetry received. **Subscription/sample postpaid: $6.50. Submit 3-5 poems at a time. Fax submissions OK. No simultaneous submissions. Do not submit mss during summer months. Send SASE for guidelines or request via e-mail. Reports within 2-3 months. Pays 2 copies. Acquires first rights. "Contributors encouraged to subscribe."**

NIMROD: INTERNATIONAL JOURNAL OF CONTEMPORARY POETRY AND FICTION; RUTH G. HARDMAN AWARD: PABLO NERUDA PRIZE FOR POETRY (I, II), University of Tulsa, 600 S. College, Tulsa OK 74104-3189, phone (918)631-3080, fax (918)631-3033, e-mail ringoldfl@centum.utulsa.edu, website http://www.si.umlch.edu/~jringold/nimrod/nimrod.html, founded 1956, editor-in-chief Francine Ringold, "is an active 'little magazine,' part of the movement in American letters which has been essential to the development of modern literature. *Nimrod* publishes 2 issues/year: an awards issue in the fall featuring the prize winners of our national competition and a thematic issue each spring." **They want "vigorous writing that is neither wholly of the academy nor the streets, typed mss."** They have published poetry by Wendy Wirth-Brock, Jan Beatty, Ruth Schwartz and Terry Ehret. The 6×9, flat-spined, 160-page journal, full-color glossy cover, professionally printed on coated stock with b&w photos and art, uses 50-90 pgs. of poetry in each issue. It is an extraordinarily lovely magazine with one of the best designs in the lit world. Poems in non-award issues range from formal to freestyle with several translations. They receive about 2,000 submissions a year, accept approximately 1%, have a 3- to 6-month backlog. Circulation is 3,500 of which 200 are public and university libraries. Subscription: $17.50/year inside USA; $19 outside. **Sample postpaid: $8 for a recent issue, $6.95 for an issue more than 2 years old. Submit up to 10 poems at a time. Request submission guidelines via e-mail. Send SASE for upcoming themes. Reports in 3-4 weeks. Pays $5/page up to $25 (when funds are available) and 2 copies plus reduced cost on additional copies. "Poets should be aware that during the months that the Ruth Hardman Awards Competition is being conducted, reporting time on non-contest manuscripts will be longer."** Send business-sized SASE for guidelines and rules for the Ruth G. Hardman Award: Pablo Neruda Prize for Poetry ($1,000 and $500 prizes). Entries accepted January 1 through April 17 each year. The $20 entry fee includes 2 issues. This annual poetry contest is considered one of the most prestigious in the publishing world, and your material is still considered for publication if you lose in the contest! Poetry published in *Nimrod* has been included in *The Best American Poetry 1995*.

96 INC MAGAZINE (I, II); BRUCE P. ROSSLEY LITERARY AWARDS (IV-Regional), P.O. Box 15559, Boston MA 02215, founded 1992, editors Julie Anderson, Vera Gold and Nancy Mehegan. *96 Inc* is a biannual literary magazine that focuses on new voices, "connecting the beginner to the established, a training center for the process of publication." **They want all forms and styles of poetry, though "shorter is better."** They have recently published poetry by Ace Boggess, Stephen Cushman, Stephanie Kaplan Cohen and Barbara A. Rouillard. As a sample the editors selected this poem by John Tsoumas:

> *when I write*
> *I think of the trees*
> *who gave their lives*
> *for what I write on*
>
> *it helps me to*
> *concentrate*

96 Inc is 38-50 pgs., 8½×11, saddle-stapled with coated card cover and b&w photos and graphics. They receive around 2,000 submissions a year, accept approximately 5%. Press run is 3,000 for 500 subscribers of which 50 are libraries, 1,500 shelf sales. Single copy: $4; subscription: $13. **Sample postpaid: $5.50. No previously published poems; simultaneous submissions OK.** Time between acceptance and publication is 1 year or longer. **Poems are circulated to an editorial board. Send SASE for guidelines. Reports in 6 months. Pays 4 copies, subscription and modest fee (when funds are available). Copyright reverts to author 2 months after publication.** Occasionally, staff reviews books of poetry. Send books for review consideration, attn: Andrew Dawson. The Bruce P. Rossley Literary Awards are given to previously under-recognized writers (of poetry or fiction) in New England. Writers can be nominated by anyone familiar with their work. Send SASE for further information. The editors add, "**96 Inc** is an artists' collaborative and a local resource. It often provides venues and hosts readings in addition to publishing a magazine."

NINETY-SIX PRESS (V, IV-Regional), Furman University, Greenville SC 29613-0438, founded 1991, editors William Rogers and Gilbert Allen, publishes 1-2 paperback books of poetry/year. "The name of the press is derived from the old name for the area around Greenville, South Carolina—the Ninety-Six District. The name suggests our interest in the writers, readers and culture of the region. In 1994, we published an anthology of South Carolina poetry, including the work of more than 40 poets. **We currently accept submissions by invitation only. At some point in the future, however, we hope to be able to encourage submissions by widely published poets who live in South Carolina.**" They have published *Fly with the Puffin* by Dorothy Thompson and *Paying the Anesthesiologist* by Starkey Flythe. Books are usually 58 pgs., 6×9, professionally printed and perfect-bound with coated stock cover. **For a sample, send $10.**

NITE-WRITER'S INTERNATIONAL LITERARY ARTS JOURNAL (I, II), 3101 Schieck St., Suite 100, Pittsburgh PA 15227-4151, phone (412)882-2259, founded 1993, editor/publisher John A. Thompson Sr., is a quarterly open to beginners as well as professionals. *Nite-Writer's* is " 'dedicated to the emotional intellectual' with a creative perception of life." **They want strong imagery and accept free verse, avant-garde poetry, haiku and senryu. Open to length and subject matter. No porn or violence.** They have published poetry by Lyn Lifshin, Rose Marie Hunold, Peter Vetrano, Carol Frances Brown and Richard King Perkins II. As a sample we selected these lines from "Argument" by Julia McSweeney:

> *With a single flick*
> *of a deftly turned phrase*
> *She spread his anger*
> *across the table*
> *And set it for dinner,*
> *Using only the finest silver.*

The editor says the journal is 30-50 pgs., 8½×11, laser-printed, stock cover with sleeve, some graphics and artwork. They receive about 1,000 poems a year, use approximately 10-15%. Press run is about 100 for more than 60 subscribers of which 10 are libraries. Single copy: $6; subscription: $20. **Sample postpaid (when available): $4. Previously published poems and simultaneous submissions OK. Cover letter preferred. "Give brief bio, state where you heard of us, state if material has been previously published and where. Always enclose SASE if you seek reply and return of your material."** Time between acceptance and publication is within 1 year. **Always comments on rejections. Send SASE for guidelines. Reports in 2-4 weeks.** The editor says, "Don't be afraid to submit your material. Take rejection as advice—study your market. Create your own style and voice, then be heard. 'I am a creator, a name beneath words' (from my poem, 'unidentified-Identified')."

NO EXIT (II), P.O. Box 454, South Bend IN 46624-0454, founded 1994, editor Mike Amato, is a quarterly forum "for the experimental as well as traditional excellence." **The editor says he wants "poetry that takes chances in form or content. Form, length, subject matter and style are open. No poetry that's unsure of why it was written. Particularly interested in long (not long-winded poems)."** They have recently published poetry by Lyn Lifshin, Ken McCullough, Stephen Berry and Ron Offen. As a sample the editor selected these lines from "Hill Sermon" by Stephen R. Roberts:

> *When the old concrete truck*
> *tipped over slowly*

like one of those
great beasts of Africa
going belly-up from a 30-06
between the eyes, I thought
my forty-foot double-wide
was history. . . .

NE is 32 pgs., saddle-stapled, digest-sized, card cover with art. They accept 10-15% of the submissions received. Press run is less than 500 for 65 subscribers of which 6 are libraries. Subscription: $12. **Sample postpaid: $4. Submit up to 5 poems ("send more if compelled, but I will stop reading after the fifth"), 1 poem/page on 8½×11 paper.** "No handwritten work, misspellings, colored paper, multiple type faces, typos, long-winded cover letters and lists of publication credits." **No previously published poems; simultaneous submissions OK.** Time between acceptance and publication can vary from 1 month to 1 year. **Sometimes comments on rejections, "if the poem strikes me as worth saving." Send SASE for guidelines. Reports in 1-3 months. Pays 1 copy plus 4-issue subscription. Acquires first North American serial rights plus right to reprint once in an anthology.** Reviews books of poetry. "Also looking for articles, critical in nature, on poetry/poets." Open to unsolicited reviews. Poets may also send books for review consideration. The editor says, "Presentation means something; namely, that you care about what you do. Don't take criticism, when offered, personally. I'll work with you if I see something solid to focus on."

NOCTURNAL LYRIC, JOURNAL OF THE BIZARRE (I, IV-Horror), P.O. Box 115, San Pedro CA 90733-0115, phone (310)519-9220, founded 1987, editor Susan Moon, is a quarterly journal "featuring bizarre fiction and poetry, primarily by new writers." **They want "poems dealing with the bizarre: fantasy, death, morbidity, horror, gore, etc. Any length. No 'boring poetry.'"** They have recently published poetry by Ishroud Maakua, prologue and Jennifer Tobkin. As a sample the editor selected these lines from "Do or Die" by Jeromy John Visser:

Enter Again my hatred
Feed on my time
Take my soul
and kill my mind.

NL is 40 pgs., digest-sized, photocopied, saddle-stapled, with trade ads and staff artwork. They receive about 200 poems a year, use approximately 35%. Press run is 250 for 40 subscribers. Subscription: $10. **Sample postpaid: $3, $2 for back issues. Make checks payable to Susan Moon. Submit up to 4 poems at a time. Previously published poems and simultaneous submissions OK. Seldom comments on rejections. Reports in 4-6 months. Pays 50¢ "discount on subscription" coupons. Acquires one-time rights.** The editor says, "Please send us something really wild and intense!"

NOMAD'S CHOIR (II), % Meander, P.O. Box 232, Flushing NY 11385-0232, founded 1989, editor Joshua Meander, is a quarterly. **"Subjects wanted: love poems, protest poems, mystical poems, nature poems, poems of humanity, poems with solutions to world problems and inner conflict. 9-30 lines, poems with hope. Simple words, careful phrasing. Free verse, rhymed poems, sonnets, half-page parables, myths and legends, song lyrics. No curse words in poems, little or no name-dropping, no naming of consumer products, no two-page poems, no humor, no bias writing, no poems untitled."** They have published poetry by Brenda Charles, Joseph Gourdji, Dorothy Wheeler and Jeff Swan. *Nomad's Choir* is 10 pgs., 8½×11, typeset and saddle-stapled with 3 poems/page. They receive about 150 poems a year, use approximately 50. Press run is 400; all distributed free. Subscription: $5. **Sample postpaid: $1.25. Make checks payable to Joshua Meander. Reports in 6-8 weeks. Pays 1 copy.** The editor says, "Stick to your guns; however, keep in mind that an editor may be able to correct a minor flaw in your poem. Accept only minor adjustments. Go to many open poetry readings. Respect the masters. Read and listen to other poets on the current scene. Make pen pals. Start your own poetry journal. Do it all out of pure love."

NORTH AMERICAN REVIEW (III), University of Northern Iowa, Cedar Falls IA 50614, phone (319)273-6455, founded 1815, poetry editor Peter Cooley, is a slick magazine-sized bimonthly of general interest, 48 pgs. average, saddle-stapled, professionally printed with glossy full-color paper cover, **publishing poetry of the highest quality.** They have published poetry by Francine Sterle, Cynthia Hogue and Marvin Bell. They receive about 15,000 poems a year, use approximately 20-30. Press run is 6,400 for 2,200 subscribers of which 1,100 are libraries, some 2,800 newsstand or bookstore sales. Subscription: $18. **Sample postpaid: $4. No simultaneous submissions or previously published poems.** Time between acceptance and publication is up to 1 year. **Send SASE for guidelines. Reports in 1-2 months. Always sends prepublication galleys. Pays 50¢/line and 2 copies.** Work published in the *North American Review* has been included in the 1992, 1995, 1996 and 1997 volumes of *The Best American Poetry*.

NORTH DAKOTA QUARTERLY (III), Box 7209, University of North Dakota, Grand Forks ND 58202-7209, phone (701)777-3322, fax (701)777-3650, founded 1910, poetry editor Jay Meek, is a literary quarterly published by the University of North Dakota that includes material in the arts and humanities—essays, fiction, interviews, poems and visual art. **"We want to see poetry that reflects an understanding not only of the**

difficulties of the craft, but of the vitality and tact that each poem calls into play." They have recently published poetry by John Allman, Lorna Crozier, Martin Espada and Leslie Andrienne Miller. The poetry editor says *North Dakota Quarterly* is 6×9, about 200 pgs., perfect-bound, professionally designed and often printed with full-color artwork on a white card cover. You can find almost every kind of poem here—avant-garde to traditional. Typically the work of about 10 poets is included in each issue. Circulation is 850, of which 650 are subscribers. Subscription: $20/year. **Sample postpaid: $8. Submit 5 poems at a time, typed, double-spaced. No previously published poems or simultaneous submissions.** Time between acceptance and publication varies. **Reports in 4-6 weeks. Always sends prepublication galleys. Pays 2 copies.**

NORTHEAST ARTS MAGAZINE; BOSTON ARTS ORGANIZATION, INC. (III), P.O. Box 94, Kittery ME 03904, founded 1990, publisher/editor Mr. Leigh Donaldson, is a biannual using **poetry that is "honest, clear, with a love of expression through simple language, under 30 lines. Care for words and craftsmanship are appreciated."** They have published poetry by S.P. Lutrell, Eliot Richman, Elizabeth R. Curry and Alisa Aran. It is 32 or more pgs., digest-sized, professionally printed with 1-color coated card cover. They accept 20-25% of submissions. Press run is 500-1,000 for 150 subscribers of which half are libraries, 50 to arts organizations. An updated arts information section and feature articles are included. Subscription: $10. **Sample postpaid: $4.50. Reads submissions September 1 through February 28 only.** "A short bio is helpful." Send SASE for guidelines. **Reports in 2-3 months. Pays 2 copies. Acquires first North American serial rights.**

‡**NORTHEAST CORRIDOR (II, IV-Regional)**, English Dept., Beaver College, Glenside PA 19038, founded 1993, contact Janna King, published semiannually, is "devoted to **writers living in or writing about Northeast region of America.**" They want "**poetry that pays attention to fresh language, well-crafted structure and emotional resonance.**" **They do not want "sappy poetry."** They have recently published poetry by Ted Kooser, Dana Gioia, Charity Hume and Stephen Dobyns. The editor says *NC* is 120-180 pgs., 6×8, perfect-bound, with color cover. They receive about 300 poems a year, use approximately 30-40. Press run is 1,000 for 200 subscribers of which 5 are libraries, 700 shelf sales; a few distributed free to contributors and donors. Single copy: $7; subscription: $20. **Sample postpaid: $6. Submit 3-5 poems with name and address on each page/poem. No previously published poems; simultaneous submissions OK. Cover letter preferred. Reads submissions September through May only.** Time between acceptance and publication is 9 months. **Poems are circulated to an editorial board. Often comments on rejections. Publishes theme issues.** Send SASE for guidelines and upcoming themes. **Reports in 3-4 months. Always sends prepublication galleys. Pays $10/poem plus 2 copies. Buys first rights.** Occasionally sponsors contest issues.

NORTHWEST LITERARY FORUM; IRVING ST. PRESS, INC.; PORTLANDIA REVIEW OF BOOKS (II, IV-Form), 3439 NE Sandy Blvd. #143, Portland OR 97232, e-mail forumnw@aol.com, founded 1992, editor Ce Rosenow. *Northwest Literary Forum* is a quarterly publication of poetry, short fiction, interviews, short plays and essays. *Portlandia Review of Books*, 3439 NE Sandy Blvd. #174, Portland OR 97232, e-mail poxia@aol.com, editor Tami Parr, is a quarterly published by Irving St. Press featuring book reviews, poetry, fiction, essays and interviews. **They are open to all types of poetry and have a special section for haiku and related forms.** They have recently published poetry by John Martone and Charlie Mehrhoff. As a sample the editors selected these two haiku by Sabine Miller:

> sunlight through the trees
> white violets
> bloom in sidewalk cracks

> midnight bath—
> stream on the window
> blurs the moon

NLF is 40 pgs., 5½×8½, offset printed and saddle-stapled with card cover and b&w cover art. Press run is 150. Subscription: $15. **Sample postpaid: $4. E-mail submissions OK. No previously published poems or simultaneous submissions.** Time between acceptance and publication is 1-3 months. **Seldom comments on rejections. Reports in 1-3 months. Acquires first North American serial rights.** Does not review books of poetry, but lists publications received with ordering information. Poets may send books for listing consideration.

NORTHWEST REVIEW (II), 369 PLC, University of Oregon, Eugene OR 97403, phone (503)346-3957, founded 1957, poetry editor John Witte. They are "seeking excellence in whatever form we can find it" and use **"all types" of poetry.** They have published poetry by Alan Dugan, Olga Broumas, William Stafford and Richard Eberhart. *NR*, a 6×9, flat-spined magazine, appears 3 times/year and uses 25-40 pgs. of poetry in each issue. They receive about 3,500 submissions a year, use approximately 4%, have up to a 4-month backlog. Press run is 1,300 for 1,200 subscribers of which half are libraries. **Sample postpaid: $4. Submit 6-8 poems clearly reproduced. No simultaneous submissions.** The editor comments "whenever possible" on rejections. Send

---

THE SUBJECT INDEX, located before the General Index, can help you select markets for your work. It lists those publishers whose poetry interests are specialized.

SASE for guidelines. Reports in 8-10 weeks. Pays 3 copies. Poetry published in this review has been included in *The Best American Poetry 1994*. The editor advises poets to "persist."

NORTHWOODS PRESS; NORTHWOODS JOURNAL: A MAGAZINE FOR WRITERS; C.A.L. (II), P.O. Box 298, Thomaston ME 04861-0298, phone (207)354-0998, fax (207)354-8953, e-mail olrob@midcoast.com, Northwoods Press founded 1972, C.A.L. (Conservatory of American Letters) 1986 and *Northwoods Journal* 1993. *Northwoods Journal* is a quarterly literary magazine. **"The journal is interested in all poets who feel they have something to say and who work to say it well. We have no interest in closet poets, or credit seekers. All poets seeking an audience, working to improve their craft and determined to 'get it right' are welcome here. Please request submission guidelines before submitting."** Send SASE for guidelines or request via e-mail or fax. Subscription: $12/year, free to C.A.L. members. **Sample: $5. Deadlines are the 1st of April, July, October and January for seasonal publication. Reports within 2 weeks after deadline, sometimes sooner. Pays $4/page, average, on acceptance.** "For book-length poetry manuscripts, submit to Northwoods Press, designed for the excellent *working poet* who has a following which is likely to create sales of $3,000 or more. Without at least that much of a following and at least that level of sales, no book can be published. Request 15-point poetry program. **Please do not submit manuscripts until you have read our guidelines." Northwoods Press will pay a minimum of $250 advance on contracting a book.** C.A.L. is a nonprofit tax-exempt literary/educational foundation; up to 4 anthologies of poetry and prose are published each year. **There is a $1 (cash—no checks) reading fee for each poetry submission to their anthologies, which goes to readers, not to the publisher.** Poets are paid $4/page or more on acceptance, shorter poems pro-rata page rate. **"Payment is advance against 10% royalties on all sales we can attribute to the influence of the author. To be considered for our next anthology, send #10 SASE and request guidelines for Next Anthology."** Robert Olmsted regards his efforts as an attempt to face reality and provide a sensible royalty-contract means of publishing many books. He says, "If you are at the stage of considering book publication, have a large number of poems in print in respected magazines, perhaps previous book publication, and are confident that you have a sufficient following to ensure very modest sales, send SASE for descriptions of the Northwoods Poetry Program and C.A.L." His advice is, "Poetry must be non-trite, non-didactic. It must never bounce. Rhyme, if used at all, should be subtle. One phrase should tune the ear in preparation for the next. They should flow and create an emotional response." Bob Olmsted "rarely" comments on rejections, but he offers commentary for a fee, though he says he "strongly recommends *against* it." Membership in C.A.L. is $24 a year, **however, membership is not required.** Members receive the quarterly *Northwoods Journal* plus 10% discount on all books and have many services available to them. The *Northwoods Journal* sponsors an annual poetry contest, first prize royalty publication with $500 advance. Unpublished poems only. $12 entry fee to C.A.L. members, $20 non-members. Send SASE for contest guidelines.

W.W. NORTON & COMPANY, INC. (III), 500 Fifth Ave., New York NY 10110, phone (212)354-5500, founded 1925, poetry editor Jill Bialosky. W.W. Norton is a well-known commercial trade publishing house that publishes only original work in both hardcover and paperback. **They want "quality literary poetry"; no "light or inspirational verse."** They have published books by Rita Dove, Marilyn Hacker, Joy Harjo, Martin Espada, Stephen Dunn and Eavan Boland. W.W. Norton publishes approximately 10 books of poetry each year with an average page count of 64. They are published in cloth and flat-spined paperbacks, attractively printed, with 2-color glossy card covers. **Query first. Simultaneous submissions will be considered if the editor is notified. Norton will consider only poets whose work has been published in quality literary magazines. They report on queries in 2-3 weeks and mss in 4 months. Catalog is free on request.**

NOSTALGIA: A SENTIMENTAL STATE OF MIND (II), P.O. Box 2224, Orangeburg SC 29116, founded 1986, poetry editor Connie Lakey Martin, appears spring and fall using **"nostalgic poetry, style open, prefer *non* rhyme, but occasional rhyme OK, relatively short poems, never longer than one page, no profanity, no ballads."** *Nostalgia* is 24 pgs., digest-sized, offset typescript, saddle-stapled, with matte card cover. Press run is 1,000. Subscription: $8. **Sample postpaid: $5. "Most poems selected from contest."** There are contests in each issue with award of $150 and publication for outstanding poem, publication and $25 for Honorable Mentions. Entry fee of $5 reserves future edition, covers 3 entries. Deadlines: June 30 and December 31 each year. **No previously published poems or simultaneous submissions. Guidelines available for SASE. Sometimes sends prepublication galleys. All rights revert to author upon publication.** Reviews books of poetry. Open to unsolicited reviews. Poets may also send books for review consideration. Connie Martin says, "I offer criticism to most rejected poems, but I suggest sampling before submitting. More poets seem to be sampling and getting a better idea of what type of poetry I use. That's great. Sending a poem to a publisher without sampling is like dropping a message in a bottle and tossing it out to sea. Don't you care where it lands?"

‡NOVA EXPRESS (IV-Science fiction/fantasy, horror), P.O. Box 27231, Austin TX 78755, e-mail lawrence@bga.com, founded 1987, editor Lawrence Person, appears "irregularly (at least once a year) with coverage of cutting edge science fiction, fantasy and horror literature, with an emphasis on post-cyperpunk and slipstream." **They want "poetry relating to literature of the fantastic in some way."** They have recently published poetry by Alison Wimsatt. The editor says *Nova Express* is 36 pgs., 8½×11, stapled, desktop-published with b&w graphics and line art. They receive about 10-20 poems a year, use approximately 1-2. Press run is 750 for 200 subscribers, 200 shelf sales; 200-300 distributed free to science fiction industry professionals. Subscription: $12. **Sample postpaid: $4. Submit up to 5 poems at a time. No previously published poems or simultaneous submissions. Cover letter preferred. E-mail submissions OK, "they get the quickest response."** Time between acceptance and publication is 3 months. **Often comment on rejections. Publishes theme issues. Send SASE for guidelines or obtain via e-mail. Reports in 1-3 months. Sometimes sends prepublication galleys. Pays 2-4 copies plus subscription. Acquires one-time rights.** The editor says, "We are not interested in any poetry outside the science fiction/fantasy/horror genre. *Nova Express* is read widely and well regarded by genre professionals."

NOW AND THEN (IV-Regional, themes), ETSU, P.O. Box 70556, Johnson City TN 37614-0556, phone (423)439-5348, fax (423)439-6340, e-mail woodsidj@etsu-tn.edu, founded 1984, editor-in-chief Jane Woodside, poetry editor Linda Parsons, is a regional magazine that covers Appalachian issues and culture. **The editor specifically wants poetry related to the region. "We want genuine, well-crafted voices, not sentimentalized stereotypes."** They have published poetry by Fred Chappell, Rita Quillen, Michael Chitwood, Jim Wayne Miller and George Ella Lyon. *Now and Then* appears 3 times/year and is 42 pgs., magazine-sized, saddle-stapled, professionally printed, with matte card cover. Its press run is 1,250-1,500 for 900 members of the Center for Appalachian Studies and Services, of which 200 are libraries. They accept 6-10 poems an issue. Center membership is $15; the magazine is one of the membership benefits. **Sample: $4.50 plus $1.50 postage. They will consider simultaneous submissions; they occasionally use previously published poems. Submit up to 5 poems, with SASE and cover letter including "a few lines about yourself for a contributor's note and whether the work has been published or accepted elsewhere." Deadlines: March 1, July 1 and November 1. Publishes theme issues. Send SASE for guidelines and upcoming themes. Editor prefers fax or e-mail to phone calls. Reports in 4 months. Sometimes sends prepublication galleys. Pays $10/poem plus 2 copies. Acquires all rights.** Reviews books of poetry in 750 words. Open to unsolicited reviews. Poets may also send books for review consideration to Sandy Ballard, book review editor, Dept. of English, Carson-Newman College, Box 2059, Jefferson City TN 37760.

NUTHOUSE; TWIN RIVERS PRESS (I, IV-Humor), P.O. Box 119, Ellenton FL 34222, press founded 1989, magazine founded 1993, editor D.A. White. *Nuthouse*, "amusements by and for delightfully diseased minds," appears every 6 weeks using humor of all kinds, including homespun and political. **They simply want "humorous verse; virtually all genres considered."** They have published poetry by Holly Day, Daveed Garstenstein-Ross and Don Webb. The editor says *Nuthouse* is 12 pgs., digest-sized and photocopied from desktop-published originals. They receive about 100 poems a year, accept approximately 25. Press run is 100 for 50 subscribers. Subscription: $5/5 issues. **Sample postpaid: $1. Previously published poems and simultaneous submissions OK.** Time between acceptance and publication is 6-12 months. **Often comments on rejections. Reports within 1 month. Pays 1 copy/poem. Acquires one-time rights.**

‡O!!ZONE (III, IV-Specialized: visual poetry, photography, collage), 1266 Fountain View, Houston TX 77057-2204, e-mail hgburrus@msn.com, founded 1993, editor/publisher Harry Burrus. *O!!Zone* is "an international literary-art zine featuring visual poetry, travel pieces, interviews, manifestos, and art. We are particularly intrigued by poets who also do photography (or draw or paint). We also do broadsides, publish small, modest saddle-stitched collections, and will consider full book collections (on a collaborative basis) as time and dinero permits." **They want visual poetry and collage. "I am interested in discovery and self-transcendence." No academic, traditional or rhyming poetry.** They have recently published poetry by Ruggero Maggi, Alberto Rizzi, Hiroshi Tanabu and Arelino De Aranjo. The editor did not offer sample lines of poetry because he says, "*O!!Zone* needs to be seen." The editor says *O!!Zone* is 80 pgs., 8½×5½, desktop-published, loaded with graphics. Single copy: $5; add $1 for Mexico and Canada, $3 or 6 IRCs for overseas. **Sample postpaid: $6. Make checks payable to Harry Burrus. Submit 3-6 poems at a time. No previously published poems or simultaneous submissions. Cover letter preferred.** They have a large backlog, "but always open to surprises." **Seldom comments on rejections. Send SASE for guidelines. Reports "soon." Pays 1-2 copies.**.

THE OAK (I); PHANTASM (I, IV-Fantasy, horror, mystery); THE ACORN (I, IV-Children); THE GRAY SQUIRREL (I, IV-Senior citizens); THE SHEPHERD (I, IV-Inspirational), 1530 Seventh St., Rock Island IL 61201, phone (309)788-3980, poetry editor Betty Mowery. *The Oak*, founded 1990, is a "publication for writers with poetry and fiction (no more than 500 words)." They want poetry **"no more than 32 lines. No restrictions as to types and style, but no pornography."** *The Oak* appears quarterly and includes *Phantasm*, founded 1993, which publishes **soft horror, fantasy and mystery.** Founded 1991, *The Gray Squirrel* is now included in *The Oak* and **takes poetry of no more than 20 lines only from poets 60 years of age and up.** They take more than half of about 100 poems received each year. Press run is 250, with 10 going to libraries. Subscription: $10. **Sample: $2. Submit 5 poems at a time. Simultaneous submissions and previously published poems OK. Reports in 1 week. "The Oak does not pay in dollars or copies but you need not purchase to be published." Acquires first or second rights.** *The Oak* holds an Orange Blossom Poetry Contest February 1 through August 1. *The Acorn*, founded 1988, is a "newsletter for young authors and teachers or anyone else interested in our young authors. **Takes mss from kids K-12th grades. Poetry no more than 32 lines.** It also takes fiction of no more than 500 words." It appears 4 times/year and "we take well over half of submitted mss." Press run is 100, with 6 going to libraries. Subscription: $10. **Sample postpaid: $2. Submit 5 poems at a time. Simultaneous submissions and previously published poems OK. Reports in 1 week.** *"The Acorn* does not pay in dollars or copies but you need not purchase to be published." Acquires first or second rights. Young authors, submitting to *The Acorn*, should put either age or grade on manuscripts. *The Shepherd*, founded 1996 is a quarterly publishing **inspirational poetry of up to 35 lines.** Subscription: $10. **Sample postpaid: $2.** Send SASE for contest guidelines. *The Gray Squirrel* sponsors the Minnie Chezum Memorial Contest December through April. Editor Betty Mowery advises, "Beginning poets should submit again as quickly as possible if rejected. Study the market: don't submit blind. Always include a SASE or rejected manuscripts will not be returned. Please make checks for *all* publications payable to *The Oak*."

‡**OASIS (II)**, P.O. Box 626, Largo FL 33779-0626, phone (813)449-2186, founded 1992, editor Neal Storrs, is a quarterly forum for high quality literary prose and poetry. **They want "to see original poetry of stylistic beauty. No superficial sentimentality, old-fashioned prosody."** They have recently published poetry by David Lunde, Fredrick Zydek and Nancy G. Westerfield. As a sample the editor selected these lines from "The Lightning Speech of Birds" by Corrinne DeWinter:

> *But now I must comply, twisting away from the clawed*
> *lovers, shrinking from the familiar habits*
> *of all three wives who have built cities and spires*
> *under my skin*
> *from the expectant crucifixions on the shoulder of the roads,*
> *from the blessed damned on Venus' blushing sands.*

Oasis is about 75 pgs., 7×10, attractively printed on heavy book paper, perfect-bound with medium-weight card cover, no art. They receive about 1,200 poems a year, accept approximately 3%. Press run is 300 for 90 subscribers of which 6 are libraries. Subscription: $20/year. **Sample postpaid: $7.50. Submit any number of poems. Rarely accepts previously published poems; simultaneous submissions OK. Cover letter preferred.** Time between acceptance and publication is 4 months. **Seldom comments on rejections. Send SASE for guidelines. Reports "the same or following day more than 99% of the time."** Sometimes sends prepublication galleys. **Pays $5/poem. Buys one-time rights.**

***OASIS BOOKS; OASIS MAGAZINE (III)**, 12 Stevenage Rd., London SW6 6ES England, founded 1969, editor/publisher Ian Robinson. *Oasis Magazine* is a bimonthly of short fiction and poetry as well as occasional reviews and other material. **"No preference for style or subject matter; just quality. No long poems;** *Oasis* **is a very short magazine. Also, usually no rhyming poetry."** They have published poetry by John Ash, Lee Harwood, George Evans and Roy Fisher. The editor says *Oasis* is international A5 size, litho, folded sheets. They receive 500-600 poems a year, use about 4 or 5. Press run is 500 for 400 subscribers of which 10 are libraries. **Sample postpaid: $3.50 (US). Make checks payable to Robert Vas Dias. Submit up to 6 poems at a time. Previously published poems sometimes OK; simultaneous submissions OK "if work comes from outside the U.K." Include SAE and 4 IRCs for return (US postage is not valid). Seldom comments on rejections. Publishes theme issues. Send SAE and IRC (US postage is not valid) for a list of upcoming themes. Reports in 1 month. Pays 2 copies.** Staff reviews books of poetry. Send books for review consideration. Oasis Books publishes 2-3 paperbacks and **2-3 chapbooks/year.** They have recently published *Flecks* by Ralph Hawkings; *Anxious to Please* by Nicholas Moore; and *3,600 Weekends* by Ken Edwards. **Replies to queries and mss in 1 month. For sample books or chapbooks, write for catalog.** Ian Robinson says, "One IRC (U.S. postage is not valid) is not enough to ensure return airmail postage; four will, provided manuscript is not too thick. No return postage will ensure that the ms is junked. It's best to write first before submitting (include IRCs for reply)."

OATMEAL AND POETRY; APRON STRINGS; VOYAGER PUBLISHING (I, IV-Subscribers), P.O. Box 2215, Dept. PM, Stillwater MN 55082-2215, phone (612)578-9589, founded 1994, editor Demitra Flanagan. A quarterly magazine of short stories and verse "from the country side of life, *Oatmeal and Poetry* is a product of a dream; to keep alive the integrity and beauty of traditional, metric poetry as an art form." **They want "traditional rhyme and form poetry; sonnets, haiku, senryu and tanka; poetry with strong use of meter and rhyme combined with visualization, metaphor, etc.; country and family themes; poems should be no longer than 30 lines. Free and blank verse are considered, but must be exceptional to be published. No experimental garble dealing with overly explicit sexual connotations; no satanic or cult themes; no profanity."** They have recently published poetry by George Barrie Carlson, Mary Stickney Strand, Mark E. Priest and Marlene Meehl. *Oatmeal and Poetry* is 48 pgs., $8\frac{1}{2} \times 11$, desktop-published and saddle-stapled with parchment cover and b&w art, photos and graphics inside. They receive more than 3,000 poems a year, publish 50-60 poems/issue. Press run is 500. Subscription: $21.95. **Sample postpaid: $5.50. Make checks payable to Voyager Publishing. There is a $1/poem reading fee for nonsubscribers. Submit 3 poems at a time, typed or legibly printed. One poem to a page (3/page for haiku/senryu/tanka) with name and address on each page. "Submissions which do not include SASE or required fee will be discarded without response." Previously published poems OK; no simultaneous submissions. Cover letter preferred.** Time between acceptance and publication is 2 months to 1 year. **Poems are circulated to an editorial board. Seldom comments on rejections. Publishes theme issues. Send SASE for guidelines and upcoming themes. Reports in 2 weeks to 3 months. Pays 1 copy. Acquires first North American serial or reprint rights.** *Apron Strings*, published in December and June, is companion publication of *Oatmeal & Poetry*. They also sponsor quarterly contests plus an annual anthology contest. Send SASE for details. The editor says, "All submissions are considered for publication based on their own merit. The best way to see what will get published is to obtain a copy of our journal. Because we are a family magazine, we do not consider any works which are profane, or excessively violent."

OBLATES (IV-Religious, spirituality/inspirational), Missionary Association of Mary Immaculate, 9480 N. De Mazenod Dr., Belleville IL 62223-1160, phone (618)398-4848, editor Christine Portell, is a bimonthly magazine circulating free to 500,000 benefactors. **"We use well-written, perceptive traditional verse, average 16 lines. Avoid heavy allusions. Good rhyme and/or rhythm a must. We prefer a reverent, inspirational tone, but not overly 'sectarian and scriptural' in content. We like to use seasonal material. We like traditional poetry (with meter) and are always on the lookout for good Christmas poetry."** They have published poetry by Jean Conder Soule, Carlton J. Duncan and Claire Puneky. *Oblates* is 20 pgs., digest-sized, saddle-stapled, using color inside and on the cover. **Sample and guidelines for SAE and 2 first-class stamps. Submit up to 2 poems at a time. Considers simultaneous submissions.** Time between acceptance and publication "is usually within 1 to 2 years." **Editor comments "occasionally, but always when ms 'just missed or when a writer shows promise.' " Reports within 4-6 weeks. Pays $30 plus 3 copies. Buys first North American serial rights.** She says, "We are a small publication very open to mss from authors—beginners and professionals. We do, however, demand professional quality work. Poets need to study our publication, **and to send no more than one or two poems at a time. Content must be relevant to our older audience to inspire and motivate in a positive manner."**

‡OF UNICORNS AND SPACE STATIONS (IV-Science fiction/fantasy, form), P.O. Box 97, Bountiful UT 84011-0097, founded 1994, editor Gene Davis, published quarterly, features science fiction/fantasy literature. **"Material written in traditional fixed forms are given preference."** As a sample the editor selected these lines from "Sick Satellite" by John Grey:

> *its orbit decays*
> *like flesh and bone,*
> *even in space*

OUASS is 60 pgs., digest-sized, offset, saddle-stitched with 1-color illustrated card cover. They receive about 30 poems a year, accept approximately 25%. Press run is 100 for 100 subscribers of which 2 are libraries; 2-3 distributed free to convention organizers and critics. Subscription: $16. **Sample postpaid: $4. Make checks payable to Gene Davis. Submit 3 poems, with name and address on each page. Previously published poems OK; no simultaneous submissions. Cover letter preferred.** Time between acceptance and publication is 6-9 months. **Poems are circulated to an editorial board of 2 editors. "Both have veto power over every piece." Seldom comments on rejections. Send SASE for guidelines. Reports in 2-3 months. Pays 1 copy. Acquires one-time rights.**

‡OFF THE ROCKS (IV-Gay/lesbian), 921 West Argyle #1 West, Chicago IL 60640, e-mail offtherock@aol. com, website http://www.Lionwood.com/Newtown/, founded 1982, president (Newtown Writers) Randy Greshaw, editor (*Off The Rocks*) Greg Anderson. *Off The Rocks*, a publication of Newtown Writers, is an annual and publishes poetry focused on gay/lesbian subjects. **They want "all forms, 30 lines or less."** They have recently published poetry by Robert Klein Engler, Adrian Ford, Gerald Wozek and Judy McCormick. As a sample the editor selected these lines from "Door Colmel" (poet unidentified):

> *You rang my bell*
> *later on we lay*
> *in the light of the alien t.v.*
> *at 5:00*
> *alone I heard the self-same note*
> *float in my dream . . .*

The editor says *OTR* is about 50 pgs., 8×11, staple-bound with art/graphics, no ads. They receive about 100 poems a year, accept approximately 20%. Press run is 1,000, almost all shelf sales. Single copy: $5. **Sample postpaid: $2. Make checks payable to Newtown Writers, Inc. Submit 5 poems at a time. Previously published poems and simultaneous submissions OK. Cover letter preferred including bio and list of previously published work. Reads submissions March 1 through June 1 only.** Time between acceptance and publication is 1 year. **Poems are circulated to an editorial board. "There is discussion of poem's merits, debate, rebuttal, then voting on poems to be published." Often comments on rejections. Obtain guidelines via e-mail or website. Reports in 3 months. Sometimes sends prepublication galleys. Pays 2 copies.**

OFFERINGS (I, II, IV-Students), P.O. Box 1667, Lebanon MO 65536-1667, founded 1994, editor Velvet Fackeldey, is a poetry quarterly. **"We accept traditional and free verse from established and new poets, as well as students. Prefer poems of less than 30 lines. No erotica."** They have published poetry by Michael Estabrook, Kent Braithwaite, Jocelyne Kamerer and Robert Hentz. As a sample the editor selected these lines from "Reading" by Eric Colburn:

> *Love isn't something to be lost,*
> *but rather how we lose ourselves.*

> *Because you didn't want me then,*
> *I changed. That change was love.*
> *Because you talked to me, I changed.*
> *That change was part of love.*

Offerings is 50-60 pgs., digest-sized, neatly printed (one poem to a page) and saddle-stapled with paper cover. They receive about 500 poems a year, accept approximately 25%. Press run is 100 for 75 subscribers, 25 shelf sales. Single copy: $5; subscription: $16. **Sample postpaid: $3. Submit typed poems with name and address on each page. Students should also include grade level. SASE required. No simultaneous submissions. Seldom comments on rejections. Send SASE for guidelines. Reports in 1 week. All rights revert to author after publication.** The editor says, "We are unable to offer payment at this time (not even copies) but hope to be able to do so in the future. We welcome beginning poets."

OFFICE NUMBER ONE (I, IV-Form), 1708 S. Congress Ave., Austin TX 78704, e-mail onocdingus@aol. com, founded 1988, editor Carlos B. Dingus, appears 2-4 times/year. *ONO* is a "humorous, satirical zine of news information and events from parallel and alternate realities." In addition to stories, they want **limericks, 3-5-3 or 5-7-5 haiku and rhymed/metered quatrains. "Poems should be short (2-12 lines) and make a point. No long rambling poetry about suffering and pathos."** As for a sample, the editor says, "No one poem provides a fair sample." *ONO* is 12 pgs., 8½×11, computer set in 10 pt. type, saddle-stitched, with graphics and ads. They use about 20 poems a year. Press run is 2,000 for 75 subscribers, 50 shelf sales; 1,600 distributed free locally. Single copy: $1.85; subscription: $8.82/6 issues. **Sample postpaid: $2. Submit up to 5 pgs. of poetry at a time. Previously published poems and simultaneous submissions OK. E-mail submissions OK. "Will comment on rejections if comment is requested." Publishes theme issues occasionally. Send SASE for guidelines and upcoming themes or request via e-mail. Reports in 1-2 months. Pays "23¢" and 1 copy. Buys "one-time use, and use in any *ONO* anthology."** The editor says, "Say something that a person can use to change his life."

THE OHIO REVIEW (II); OHIO REVIEW BOOKS (V), 209C Ellis Hall, Ohio University, Athens OH 45701-2979, phone (614)593-1900, founded 1959, editor Wayne Dodd, attempts "to publish the best in contemporary poetry, fiction and reviews" in the *Review* and in chapbooks, flat-spined paperbacks and hardback books. They use **"all types"** of poetry and have published poems by David Baker, William Matthews, Lynn Emanuel and Robin Behn. *The Ohio Review* appears 2 times/year in a professionally printed, flat-spined format of 200 pgs., matte cover with color and art, circulation 3,000, featuring about 28 poets/issue. One of the respected "credits" in the literary world, this magazine tends to publish mostly lyric and narrative free verse with an emphasis on voice. Content, structure and length seem open, and voices tend to complement each other, evidence of careful editing. Moreover, you'll find top-name writers appearing with relative newcomers. They receive about 3,000 submissions a year, use approximately 1% of them, and have a 6- to 12-month backlog. Subscription: $16. **Sample postpaid: $6. Reads submissions September 15 through March 30 only. Editor sometimes comments on rejections. Send SASE for guidelines. Reports in 1 month. Always sends prepublication galleys. Pays $1/line for poems and $5/page for prose plus copies. Buys first North American serial rights.** Reviews books of poetry in 5-10 pgs., single or multi-book format. Send books to Robert Kinsley for review consideration. **They are not currently accepting unsolicited submissions of book mss. Query with publication credits, bio.** Work published in *The Ohio Review* has been included in *The Best American Poetry* (1992 and 1993) and *Pushcart Prize* anthologies.

OHIO STATE UNIVERSITY PRESS/THE JOURNAL AWARD IN POETRY (II), 180 Pressey Hall, 1070 Carmack Rd., Columbus OH 43210-1002, phone (800)437-4439, fax (614)292-2065, poetry editor David Citino. Each year *The Journal* (see listing also in this section) selects for publication by Ohio State University Press for the Ohio State University Press/Journal Award **one full-length (at least 48 pgs.) book ms submitted during September, typed, double-spaced, $15 handling fee (payable to OSU).** Send SASE for return of ms; self-addressed, stamped postcard for notification of ms receipt. **Some or all of the poems in the collection may have appeared in periodicals, chapbooks or anthologies, but must be identified. Along with publication,** *The Journal* Award in Poetry pays **$1,000 cash prize from the Helen Hooven Santmyer Fund "in addition to the usual royalties."** Each entrant receives a subscription (2 issues) to *The Journal.*

OLD CROW REVIEW (III), P.O. Box 403, East Hampton MA 01027-0403, founded 1990, editors John Gibney and Tawnya Kelley, is a biannual magazine with mythic concerns, "visions or fragments of visions of a

---

THE GEOGRAPHICAL INDEX, located before the Subject Index, can help you discover the publishers in your region. Publishers often favor poets (and work) from their own areas.

new myth." It includes novel fragments, short stories, poems, essays, interviews, photography and art. **They have no specifications regarding form, length, subject matter or style of poetry.** They have published poetry by Michael Ventura, Simon Perchick and Patricia Martin. *Old Crow* is 100 pgs., digest-sized, neatly printed and perfect-bound with card cover. They receive about 1,000 submissions a year, accept 2-3%. Press run is 500. Subscription: $9/year. **Sample postpaid: $5. (A portion of the sale price from each review goes to Food For All, a nonprofit organization benefiting the hungry and homeless.) Submit 3-6 poems at a time. Previously published poems and simultaneous submissions OK. Cover letter with brief bio (for Contributor's Notes) required. Reads submissions February 1 through July 30 and October 1 through December 15. Poems are screened by editorial assistants then the editorial board then the editor-in-chief (John Gibney). Seldom comments on rejections. Reports in 2 months. Pays 1 copy. Copyright reverts to poet at publication.** Open to unsolicited reviews.

THE OLD RED KIMONO (I, II), P.O. Box 1864, Rome GA 30162, phone (706)295-6312, founded 1972, poetry editors Jon Hershey, Jeffrey Mack and Ed Sharp, a publication of the Humanities Division of Floyd College, has the "sole purpose of putting out a magazine of original, high-quality poetry and fiction. *ORK* **is looking for submissions of three to five short poems. Poems should be very concise and imagistic. Nothing sentimental or didactic."** They have published poetry by Walter McDonald, Peter Huggins, Midred Greear, John C. Morrison, Jack Stewart, Kirsten Fox and Al Braselton. The magazine is an annual, circulation 1,400, 72 pgs., 8½×11, professionally printed on heavy stock with b&w graphics, colored matte cover with art, using approximately 40 pgs. of poetry (usually 1 or 2 poems to the page). They receive about 1,000 submissions a year, use approximately 60-70. **Sample: $3. Reads submissions September 1 through March 1 only. Reports in 3 months. Pays copies. Acquires first publication rights.**

OLYMPIA REVIEW; ZERO CITY PRESS; ZERO CITY POETRY WEBZINE; THE HAWK (III), 3430 Pacific Ave. SE, Suite A-6254, Olympia WA 98501, e-mail mmichael@olywa.net, website http://www.CRU ZIO.com/~zerocity/, founded 1992, editor Michael McNeilley, appears irregularly, publishing "the best available contemporary writing, without regard for rules, conventions or precedent. **No taboos, beyond 'reasonably' good taste; style and talent, significance and artistry are our only criteria. Seldom use rhyme. Nothing incidental, religious or sentimental. Prefer poems under 50 lines or so."** They have published poetry by Charles Bukowski, Ronald Wallace, Albert Huffstickler, Errol Miller, Virgil Hervey, Mere Smith, Antler, Cat Townsend and Gerald Locklin. As a sample the editor selected these lines from "Legacy" by Renay:

> *I have daddy's eyes*
> *blue like the weld on a muffler*
> *his maroon hair*
> *his unsmiling lip*
> *a mole on my hip*
> *toes that can peel a banana*

The editor says *OR* is 60-100 pgs., professionally-printed, with art, graphics, photos and ads. Press run is 750-1,000. Subscription: $9.50/2 issues. **Sample postpaid: $4.95. Submit up to 6 poems at a time. Previously published poems ("tell us where") and simultaneous submissions OK. Cover letter and short bio required. E-mail submissions OK. Seldom comments on rejections. Pays 1 copy. Acquires first North American serial or one-time rights.** Reviews books of poetry and magazines in up to 700 words, single or multi-book format. *Zero City Poetry WebZine*, contact co-editors Michael McNeilley and J.J. Webb at zcity@cruzio.com, publishes poetry and art, and hosts the Small Press Bulletin Board, with submission and ordering information on a variety of small press publications, and links to Internet poetry sites around the world. "*Zero City* attracted more than 1,000 readers in its first month of operation, billing itself as 'ground zero for explosive poetry.' " Recently published writers include Janet Bernichon. Regular mail for *Zero City* can be addressed to the *Olympia Review* above. *The Hawk* (http://www.cruzio.com/~hawk), is "an arts and literary eZine for the World Wide Web, accepting submissions of fiction up to 5,000 words, poetry, essays, reviews and graphics." It has published writers such as Robert Anton Wilson, Nick Herbert, Ralph Abraham, Donald Rawley and Robert Sward, and has a quarterly circulation in excess of 20,000. **Reports in 1 week to 8 months. Pays $5-10/published piece.** Contact editor J.J. Webb or fiction editor Michael McNeilley at hawk@cruzio.com, or write *The Hawk*, 240A Sylvan Way, Boulder Creek CA 95006. Michael McNeilley advises poets to "start with the classics, to see where poetry has been. Then read more poetry, and fiction, in the little magazines, where today's writing is found. Develop your own voice, write a clean line, edit mercilessly and you may help determine where poetry is going. Read an issue, see firsthand what we're up to, then submit."

♣ON SPEC: THE CANADIAN MAGAZINE OF SPECULATIVE WRITING (IV-Regional, science fiction/fantasy), P.O. Box 4727, Edmonton, Alberta T6E 5G6 Canada, e-mail onspec@freenet.edmonton.ab.ca, website http://www.greenwoods.com/onspec/, founded 1989, is a quarterly featuring Canadian science fiction writers and artists. **They want work by Canadian poets only and only science fiction/speculative poetry. 100 lines maximum.** They have published poetry by Alice Major and Eileen Kernaghan. As a sample the editor selected these lines from "Spiritworld" by Peter Koens:

> *The shaman's drum brings anachronisms back, televised if*
> *necessary*

A quarterly magazine of science fiction/speculative writing, **On Spec** devotes most of its pages to fiction. However, the Canadian-based publication tries to publish 2-3 poems, by Canadian poets only, in each issue. And although the poetry they publish is selected by their editorial collective, the cover art is selected solely by the art director. The cover art for **On Spec**'s Winter 1996 issue is by Jean-Pierre Normand, a freelance illustrator and winner of the 1996 Aurora Award for Science Fiction Art. In addition to seven short stories, two poems, a writing column and a list of Canadian science fiction conventions, four pieces of Mr. Normand's work are showcased within this issue's pages.

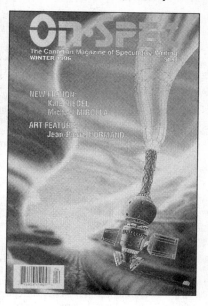

to live in you and in me.
And yet?
In the inukshuk, in the enuksos, living stone columns which are
built in the form of a man, the past comes to life.

On Spec is 96 pgs., digest-sized, offset printed on recycled paper and perfect-bound with color cover, b&w art and ads inside. They receive about 100 poems a year, accept approximately 5%. Press run is 1,750 for 800 subscribers of which 10 are libraries, 600 shelf sales. Single copy: $4.95; subscription: $19.95 (both in Canadian funds). **Sample postpaid: $6. Submit up to 5 poems at a time, in "competition format" (author's name should not appear on the ms).** No previously published poems or simultaneous submissions. **Cover letter with poem titles and 2-sentence bio required.** Time between acceptance and publication is 6 months. **Poems are circulated to an editorial board. Seldom comments on rejections. Publishes theme issues. Send SASE for guidelines and upcoming themes or request via fax or e-mail. Reports in 5 months maximum. Pays $15/poem and 1 copy. Acquires first North American serial rights.**

ONCE UPON A WORLD (IV-Science fiction/fantasy), 646 W. Fleming Dr., Nineveh IN 46164-9718, e-mail 107753.2174@compuserve.com, founded 1988, editor Emily Alward. **"All poetry submitted should relate to science fiction or fantasy in concept and/or imagery. This does not mean it has to be 'about' space travel or dragons. None with a nihilistic outlook, extremely avant-garde style or formats."** They have published poetry by John Grey, W. Gregory Stewart and Laura Vess. As a sample the editor selected these lines from "Instant Icons" by Gary Every:

I remember watching Neil Armstrong
step onto the moon
as my family gathered around
the electronic oracle at my grandfather's
summer lodge outside Detroit. The television
newscaster narrated events as they unfolded,
the Stars and Stripes unfurled,
but I was 9 years old and unimpressed.
It was lame compared to Sunday Afternoon
Science Fiction Theatre . . .

Once Upon A World is 80-100 pgs., magazine-sized, with heavy card stock colored covers, spiral-bound. They receive about 50 submissions a year, accept approximately 5-10. Press run is 120. **Sample postpaid: $8.50. Make checks payable to Emily Alward. Publishes theme issues. Theme for Spring 1998 is Ethical & Philosophical Implications of "Other" Worlds. Reports in 1-4 months. Pays 1 copy. "We strongly recommend purchase of a copy before submitting both to give some idea of the content and tone and to help keep the magazine solvent. But this is not a requirement."** The editor says, "Our major interest is in presenting science fiction and fantasy *short* stories with well-worked-out alternate world settings and an emphasis on ideas and/or character interaction. We use poetry for fillers. Where possible we try to match a poem with an adjacent story that it somewhat resembles in subject matter or tone. As the editor's major interest is fiction, she does not feel qualified to give in-depth critiques of poetry."

ONIONHEAD; ARTS ON THE PARK, INC. (THE LAKELAND CENTER FOR CREATIVE ARTS); WORDART, THE NATIONAL POETS COMPETITION; ESMÉ BRADBERRY CONTEMPORARY POETS PRIZE (II), 115 N. Kentucky Ave., Lakeland FL 33801-5044, phone (941)680-2787, editors Susan Crawford, Dot D. Davis and Brenda Patterson. Arts on the Park founded 1979; *Onionhead* founded 1988. *Onionhead* is a literary quarterly. **"Our focus is on provocative political, social and cultural observations and hypotheses. International submissions are welcome. We have no taboos, but provocation is secondary to literary excellence. No light verse please."** They have published poetry by Alan Catlin, Corrine DeWinter, and Judith Tate O'Brien. As a sample the editors selected these lines from "The Wake" by Kristin Bock:

> *My fingers frost and lace at your still hem,*
> *I tell you that I cannot reweave your tunic*
> *blood-appled and drip-dried in sunshine.*
> *I cannot cleave to your*
> *waist like a skin apron.*
> *There is no hope to high march . . .*

The magazine is 40-50 pgs., digest-sized, photocopied from typescript, saddle-stapled with glossy card cover. They receive about 2,500 submissions a year, accept approximately 100. Press run is 250. Complimentary distribution to universities, reviews and libraries worldwide. Subscription: $8 US, $16 other. **Sample postpaid: $3. Submit 3-8 poems at a time, maximum 60 lines each. No previously published poems or simultaneous submissions. Short cover letter preferred. Poet's name, address and title of poems should appear in the upper right-hand corner of each page. Poem "should be submitted exactly as you intend it to appear if selected for publication." SASE required for return of material.** Poems are reviewed by an Editorial Board. **"Rarely" comments on rejections. Reports in 10 weeks.** Time between acceptance and publication is "normally within 1 year." **Pays 1 copy. Acquires first serial and electronic rights.** WORDART, The National Poets Competition, established 1983, is open to all American authors. Cash awards, "including the prestigious Esmé Bradberry Contemporary Poets Prize and chapbook, are announced at a reading and reception during the first part of March." $8 reading fee. For guidelines and specific dates send SASE to the sponsoring organization, Arts on the Park, Inc., at the above address.

ONTHEBUS; BOMBSHELTER PRESS (II), P.O. Box 481266, Bicentennial Station, Los Angeles CA 90048, founded 1975, *ONTHEBUS* editor Jack Grapes, Bombshelter Press poetry editors Jack Grapes and Michael Andrews. *ONTHEBUS* uses **"contemporary mainstream poetry—no more than six poems (ten pgs. total) at a time. No rhymed, 19th Century traditional 'verse.' "** They have published poetry by Charles Bukowski, Albert Goldbarth, Ai, Norman Dubie, Kate Braverman, Stephen Dobyns, Allen Ginsberg, David Mura, Richard Jones and Ernesto Cardenal. As a sample Jack Grapes selected "Splitting Hairs" by Joyce Elaine Ross:

> *After I poured my blocks onto the floor and shuffled them,*
> *then made one last attempt to attain some form of poetic*
> *fusion, like William Grant Still's Afro-American Symphony*
> *of classical blues on jazz, I realized that I've never been*
> *able to get others to understand me; that my words always*
> *seem to turn into fishbones and sawdust whenever I tried*
> *to talk about it. And if I could, I would drink my own*
> *skin, erase the stain of my colors.*

ONTHEBUS is a magazine appearing 2 times/year, 275 pgs., offset, flat-spined, with color card cover. Press run is 3,500 for 600 subscribers of which 40 are libraries, 1,200 shelf sales ("500 sold directly at readings"). Subscription: $28/3 issues; Issue #8/9, special double issue: $15. **Sample (including guidelines) postpaid: $12. Submit 3-6 poems at a time to the above address** (send all other correspondence to: 6684 Colgate Ave., Los Angeles CA 90048. **Simultaneous submissions and previously published poems OK, "if I am informed where poem has previously appeared and/or where poem is also being submitted. I expect neatly-typed, professional-looking cover letters with list of poems included plus poet's bio. Sloppiness and unprofessional submissions do not equate with great writing." Do not submit mss between November 1 and March 1 or between June 1 and September 1. Submissions sent during those times will be returned unread. Reports in "anywhere from two weeks to two years." Pays 1 copy. Acquires one-time rights.** Reviews books of poetry in 400 words (chapbooks in 200 words), single format. Open to unsolicited reviews. Poets may also send books for review consideration. This exciting journal seems a cross between *The Paris Review* and *New York Quarterly* with a distinct West Coast flavor that puts it in a league of its own. Editor Jack Grapes jam-packs each issue with dozens upon dozens of poems, mostly free verse (lyric, narrative, dramatic)—some tending toward avant-garde and some quite accessible—that manages somehow to reach out and say: "Read Me." Poetry published in *ONTHEBUS* has been included in *The Best American Poetry 1993*. Bombshelter Press publishes 4-6 flat-spined paperbacks and **5 chapbooks/year. Query first. Primarily interested in Los Angeles poets. "We publish very few unsolicited mss." Reports in 3 months. Pays 50 copies.** They also publish the *ONTHEBUS* Poets Anthology Series. Send SASE for details. Jack Grapes says, "My goal is to publish a democratic range of American poets and ensure they are read by striving to circulate the magazine as widely as possible. It's hard work and a financial drain. I hope the mag is healthy for poets and writers, and that they support the endeavor by subscribing as well as submitting."

‡**THE OPEN BONE (I, II)**, P.O. Box 3096, Port Angeles WA 98362, founded 1996, editor Susan S. Hahn, published quarterly, features "accessible, quality poetry." **They want "poems that say something. Poetry that is fresh, energetic, enigmatic, but accessible, with strong imagery," no longer than 20-30 lines. They do not want "clichéd, rhymed, trivial poems. No sentimental! No pornography, obscene, filthy language."** They have recently published poetry by Lyn Lifshin and Patrick Loafman. As a sample the editor selected these lines from "The Sounding Line" by Melanie Falcioni:

> *I will brave the shallows of this moonlit*
> *harbor. I will wade out backwards, cast*
> *at your instruction towards a chill*
> *submersion, holding to the timbre*
> *and intonation*
>
> *of your voice unfurled across the ebbing*
> *water, sure and irresistible as any siren's.*
> *Let the North Star falter. I will keep*
> *my bearings, trusting only words*
> *to reel me back in after.*

OB is 15-20 pgs., 5½×8½, photocopied, saddle-stapled, with colored paper cover and b&w cover art. They receive about 40-60 poems a year, accept approximately 15-20%. Press run is 40-60. Subscription: $11. **Sample postpaid: $2. Make checks payable to Susan S. Hahn. Submit 4-6 poems at a time. Previously published poems OK; no simultaneous submissions. Cover letter "acceptable but not required."** Time between acceptance and publication is 6-12 months. **"As editor, I make the final decision; occasionally I get input from a panel of local poets I work with." Often comments on rejections. Send SASE for guidelines. Reports ASAP. Pays 1 copy. Acquires one-time or first rights.**

OPEN HAND PUBLISHING INC. (V), P.O. Box 22048, Seattle WA 98122-0048, phone (206)323-2187, fax (206)323-2188, founded 1981, publisher P. Anna Johnson, is a "literary/political book publisher" bringing out flat-spined paperbacks as well as cloth cover editions about African-American and multicultural issues." They have published ***Puerto Rican Writers at Home in the USA***, "an anthology of seventeen of the most well-known Puerto Rican writers"; ***Where Are the Love Poems for Dictators?*** by E. Ethelbert Miller; and ***Stone on Stone/Piedra Sobre Piedra***, a bilingual anthology edited by Zoë Anglesey. As a sample the editor selected "Kira's Tanka" from *Old Woman of Irish Blood* by Pat Andrus:

> *Fragrant pea blossom,*
> *why do your scent and color*
> *wake me at sunrise?*
> *Daughter's breath sweet after birth.*
> *Her small body light rose tones.*

They do not consider unsolicited mss. Send SASE for catalog to order samples.

ORACLE POETRY; ASSOCIATION OF AFRICAN WRITERS; RISING STAR PUBLISHERS (I, IV-Ethnic), 2105 Amherst Rd., Hyattsville MD 20783, phone (301)422-2665, fax (301)422-2720, founded 1989, editorial director Obi Harrison Ekwonna. *Oracle Poetry* and *Oracle Story and Letters* appear quarterly using works **"mainly of African orientation; must be probing and must have meaning—any style or form. Writers must have the language of discourse and good punctuation. No gay, lesbian or erotic poetry."** Membership in the Association of African Writers is $20/year. *Oracle Poetry* is 46 pgs., digest-sized, saddle-stapled, print run 500. Subscription: $20/year. **No previously published poems or simultaneous submissions. "Poets may submit materials by fax; however, we prefer submissions by disk in WordPerfect 5.1, or in copies." Reports in 4-6 weeks. Pays 1 copy. Acquires first North American serial rights.** Reviews books of poetry. Sponsors contests. Send SASE for details. The editor says, "Read widely, write well and punctuate right."

*ORBIS: AN INTERNATIONAL QUARTERLY OF POETRY AND PROSE (II); RHYME INTERNATIONAL COMPETITION FOR RHYMING POETRY (IV-Form), 199 The Long Shoot, Nuneaton, Warwickshire CV11 6JQ England, founded 1968, editor Mike Shields, considers **"all poetry so long as it's genuine in feeling and well executed of its type."** They have published poetry by Sir John Betjeman, Ray Bradbury, Seamus Heaney and Naomi Mitchison, as well as a US issue including Bukowski, Levertov, Piercy, Stafford and many others, "but are just as likely to publish absolute unknowns." The quarterly is 64 pgs., 6×8½, flat-spined, professionally printed with glossy card cover. They receive "thousands" of submissions a year, use "less than 2%." Circulation is 1,000 with 600 subscribers of which 50 are libraries. Single copy: £3.95 ($6); subscription: £15 ($28). **Sample postpaid: $2 (or £1). Submit 1 poem/sheet, typed on 1 side only. No bio, no query. Enclose IRCs for reply, not US postage. Reports in 1-2 months. Pays $10 or more/acceptance plus 1 free copy. Each issue carries £50 in prizes paid on basis of reader votes. Editor comments on rejections "occasionally—if we think we can help.** *Orbis* is completely independent and receives no grant-aid from anywhere." They sponsor the Rhyme International Competition for Rhyming Poetry. The competition has 2 categories (open class, any rhyming poem up to 50 lines; strict form class) with prizes averaging £500 in each class each year (at least 60% of fees received); minimum entry fee £5 (or $10). They claim to be "the only competition in the world exclusively for rhymed poetry." Write for entry form. Deadline: September 30.

ORCHISES PRESS (III), P.O. Box 20602, Alexandria VA 22320-1602, e-mail rlathbur@osf1.gmu.edu, website http://www.mason.gmu.edu/~rlathbur, founded 1983, poetry editor Roger Lathbury, is a small press publisher of literary and general material in flat-spined paperbacks and in hardcover. **"Although we will consider mss submitted, we prefer to seek out the work of poets who interest us." Regarding poetry he states: "No restrictions, really; but it must be technically proficient and deeply felt. I find it increasingly unlikely that I would publish a ms unless a fair proportion of its contents has appeared previously in respected literary journals."** He has published poetry by L.S. Asekoff and Lia Purpura. He publishes about 4 flat-spined paperbacks of poetry a year, averaging 96 pgs., and some casebound books. **Obtain guidelines via website. Submit 5-6 poems at a time. Poems must be typed. When submitting, "tell where poems have previously been published." Brief cover letter preferred. Reports in 1 month. Pays 36% of money earned once Orchises recoups its initial costs and has a "generous free copy policy."**

OREGON EAST (II, IV-Regional), Hoke Center, Eastern Oregon State College, La Grande OR 97850, phone (541)962-3787, founded 1950, editor changes yearly, is the "literary annual publication of EOSC, open to literary quality off-campus submissions." **"No 'greeting card' verse."** They have published poetry and fiction by Jessica Mills, R.S. Kromwall, Kerri Brostrom, Christine Grey and Mark Shadle. It is approximately 100 pgs., 6×9, flat-spined, book format, typeset, with end papers, using graphics and b&w art. Content tends toward free-verse lyrics. Circulation is 1,000 (300 off-campus) for 100 subscribers of which 30-40 are libraries. Single copy: $5. **Submit 3-5 typed poems at a time of up to 60 lines. No previously published poems or simultaneous submissions. All submissions must be accompanied by SASE and cover letter with brief bio and phone number. "Editors not responsible for returning manuscripts without sufficient postage." Reads submissions September 1 through March 1 only. Notification by May. Send SASE for upcoming themes. Sometimes sends prepublication galleys. Pays 2 copies. Acquires all rights. Returns rights upon publication.** The editor says, "Be fresh. Be daring. Your words should come to life on the page as they're read. We want poetry we can see and feel."

ORTALDA & ASSOCIATES (V), 1208 Delaware St., Berkeley CA 94702-1407, founded 1985, poetry editor Floyd Salas, director/editor Claire Ortalda, publishes quality flat-spined paperbacks of poetry but **is not accepting submissions at this time.** They have published poetry by Czeslaw Milosz, Robert Hass, Ishmael Reed, Gary Soto, Jack Micheline and Carolyn Kizer. As a sample Claire Ortalda selected these lines from "In the Course of My Existence" by Leslie Woodd:

> *I am not some dog*
> *that runs frantically through their minds*
> *I am a gesture*
> *that they see*
> *and think of*

OSIRIS, AN INTERNATIONAL POETRY JOURNAL/UNE REVUE INTERNATIONALE (II, IV-Translations, bilingual), P.O. Box 297, Deerfield MA 01342-0297, phone (413)774-4027, founded 1972, poetry editor Andrea Moorhead, is a semiannual that **publishes contemporary poetry in English, French and Italian without translation and in other languages with translation, including Polish, Danish and German.** They want poetry which is **"lyrical, non-narrative, multi-temporal, post modern, well crafted. Also looking for translations from non-IndoEuropean languages."** They have recently published poetry by Michael Butor (France), Frances Presley (England), Henrik Nordbrandt (Denmark) and Simon Perchik (US). As a sample the editor selected these lines from a poem by Henrik Nordbrandt translated from the Danish by Thom Satterlee:

> *and no shadow*
> *could have been cast by anything*
> *other than itself, just as my own is cast*
> *filling my life's tree*
> *with golden birds and pomegranates.*

Osiris is 40 pgs., 6×9, saddle-stapled with graphics and photos. There are 15-20 pgs. of poetry in English in

---

THE CHAPBOOK INDEX, located before the Geographical Index, lists those publishers who consider chapbook manuscripts. A chapbook, a small volume of work, is often a good middle step between magazine and book publication.

each issue of this intriguing publication. Print run is 500 with 50 subscription copies sent to college and university libraries, including foreign libraries. They receive 200-300 submissions a year, use approximately 12. Single copy: $6; subscription: $12. **Sample postpaid: $3. Submit 4-6 poems at a time. Include short bio and SASE with submission. "Translators should include a letter of permission from the poet or publisher as well as copies of the original text." Reports in 1 month. Sometimes sends prepublication galleys. Pays 5 copies.** If you translate poems from other countries or want to gain an international perspective on the art, you should send for a sample copy. Two poems published in *Osiris* have received Honorable Mentions from *The Pushcart Prize*. The editor advises, "It is always best to look at a sample copy of a journal before submitting work, and when you do submit work, do it often and do not get discouraged. Try to read poetry and support other writers."

‡*OTHER PRESS; ISLINGTON POETRY WORKSHOP (III, IV-Nationality, women)**, 19B Marriott Rd., London N4 3QN England, founded 1992, contact Ms. Frances Presley. The Other Press publishes primarily experimental poetry by British women, though not exclusively. They publish 1 paperback/year. **They do not want traditional poetry by beginners.** As a sample the editor chose this poem by Harriet Tarlo:

> looking up
>
> cloud circle

Books are usually paperback, stapled and sometimes include artwork. **No previously published poems; simultaneous submissions OK. Cover letter required.** Time between acceptance and publication is 1-2 years. **Often comments on rejections. Replies to queries in 1 month. Pays 20 author's copies (out of a press run of 200).**

THE OTHER SIDE MAGAZINE (III, IV-Political, religious, social issues), 300 W. Apsley St., Philadelphia PA 19144, phone (215)849-2178, founded 1965, poetry editor Rod Jellema, is a "magazine (published six times/year) concerned with **social justice issues from a Christian perspective. The magazine publishes one to two poems per issue.** Submissions should be of high quality and must speak to and/or reflect the concerns and life experiences of the magazine's readers. We look for fresh insights and creative imagery in a tight, cohesive whole. Be warned that only 0.5% of the poems reviewed are accepted. Seldom does any published poem exceed 40-50 lines. We do not want to see pious religiosity, sentimental schlock or haiku." They have published poetry by Kathleen Norris, Paul Ramsey, Carol Hamilton and John Knoepfle. *The Other Side* is magazine-sized, professionally printed on quality pulp stock, 64 pgs., saddle-stapled, with full-color paper cover, circulation 13,000 to that many subscriptions. Subscription: $24. **Sample postpaid: $4.50. Submit 3-5 poems at a time. No simultaneous submissions. No previously published poems. Editor "almost never" comments on rejections. Send SASE for guidelines. Pays $15 plus 4 copies and subscription.**

❦OUR FAMILY (IV-Religious)**, Box 249, Battleford, Saskatchewan S0M 0E0 Canada, phone (306)937-7771, fax (306)937-7644, founded 1949, editor Nestor Gregoire, o.m.i., is a monthly religious magazine **for Roman Catholic families. "Any form of poetry is acceptable. In content we look for simplicity and vividness of imagery. The subject matter should center on the human struggle to live out one's relationship with the God of the Bible in the context of our modern world. We do not want to see science fiction poetry, metaphysical speculation poetry, or anything that demeans or belittles the spirit of human beings or degrades the image of God in him/her as it is described in the Bible."** They have published poetry by Nadene Murphy and Arthur Stilwell. *Our Family* is 40 pgs., magazine-sized, glossy color paper cover, using drawings, cartoons, two-color ink. Circulation 10,000 of which 48 are libraries. Single copy: $1.95; subscription: $15.98 Canada, $21.98 US. **Sample postpaid: $2.50. Send SASE or SAE with IRC or personal check (American postage cannot be used in Canada) for writer's guidelines and upcoming themes. Will consider poems of 4-30 lines. Simultaneous submissions OK. Reports within 1 month after receipt. Pays 75¢-$1/line.** The editor advises, "The essence of poetry is imagery. The form is less important. Really good poets use both effectively."

‡OUR JOURNEY (I, IV-Specialized: recovery issues)**, 16016 SE Division #327, Portland OR 97236, e-mail wendy@iccom.com or wendy@zzz.com, founded 1994, editor Wendy Apgar. *Our Journey* is a quarterly newsletter featuring "poetry, articles and occasional book reviews by those and for those involved or interested in the recovery process. This newsletter is a safe way for contributors and readers to address life issues." **They want "recovery-based poetry; all inclusive, not limited to recovery of only one (e.g., addictions, incest, pain, abuse, anger, healing, etc.); will consider any length. Each issue has specific topic. No poetry which is not easily understood or which is inappropriately sexually graphic (accepted only if discussing abuse in general way)."** They have recently published poetry by Carol Michalski and Arthur Slate. As a sample the editor selected these lines from "The Gift of Hope" by Evelyn V. Stankowski, R.N.:

> *Sobriety is a journey . . .*
> *Of broken dreams . . .*
> *Renewed*
> *Of Withered Faith . . .*
> *Revived*
> *Of Self Esteem . . .*
> *Reborn*

Our Journey is about 20 pgs., neatly painted on bond paper and corner stapled, no cover, contains clip art. They receive about 150-200 poems a year, accept approximately 80%. Press run is 200 for 60 subscribers of which 2 are libraries. Single copy: $2; subscription: $8/year, $10 Canada, $14 overseas. **Sample postpaid: $1.50. Submit any number of poems; 1/page, typed with name and address in upper left corner. "Only mss with SASE will be acknowledged or returned."** Previously published poems and simultaneous submissions OK. Cover letter preferred. **"Material may also be submitted via e-mail. If accepted for publication a hard copy must then be submitted via snail mail with the completed release form which will be e-mailed upon acceptance."** Time between acceptance and publication is within 1 year. **Seldom comments on rejections. Publishes theme issues. Send SASE for guidelines. Reports in 4-6 weeks, "usually sooner." Pays 2 copies. Acquires one-time rights.** Reviews chapbooks of poetry. Open to unsolicited reviews. Poets may also send books for review consideration. Sponsors 2-4 annual contests for subscribers. Awards $15 in poetry and essay categories. Send SASE for details.

OUTERBRIDGE (II), English A324, The College of Staten Island, 2800 Victory Blvd., Staten Island NY 10314, phone (718)982-3640, founded 1975, editor Charlotte Alexander, publishes "the most crafted, professional poetry and short fiction we can find (unsolicited except special features—to date rural, urban and Southern, promoted in standard newsletters such as *Poets & Writers, AWP, Small Press Review*), interested in newer voices. **Anti loose, amateurish, uncrafted poems showing little awareness of the long-established fundamentals of verse; also anti blatant PRO-movement writing when it sacrifices craft for protest and message. Poems usually one to four pgs. in length."** They have published poetry by Walter McDonald, Thomas Swiss and Naomi Rachel. The digest-sized, flat-spined annual is 100 pgs., about half poetry, circulation 500-600 for 150 subscribers of which 28 are libraries. They receive about 500-700 submissions a year, use approximately 60. **Sample postpaid: $5. Submit 3-5 poems only, anytime except June and July. Include name and address on each page. "We dislike simultaneous submissions and if a poem accepted by us proves to have already been accepted elsewhere, a poet will be blacklisted as there are many good poets waiting in line." Cover letter with *brief* bio preferred. Reports in 2 months. Pays 2 copies (and offers additional copies at half price). Acquires first rights.** The editor says, "As a poet/editor I feel magazines like *Outerbridge* provide an invaluable publication outlet for individual poets (particularly since publishing a book of poetry, respectably, is extremely difficult these days). As in all of the arts, poetry—its traditions, conventions and variations, experiments—should be studied. One current 'trend' I detect is a lot of mutual backscratching which can result in very loose, amateurish writing. Discipline!"

*OUTREACH: FOR THE HOUSEBOUND, ELDERLY AND DISABLED (IV-Senior citizens, specialized: disabled, religious), 7 Grayson Close, Stocksbridge, Sheffield S30 5BJ England, phone (0114)288-5346, editor J. Kirby, founded 1985, is a quarterly using **"semi-religious poetry and short articles; cowboy, humor, love and romance, mystery, senior citizen and spirituality/inspired poetry. This is a magazine for the housebound, elderly and disabled who need cheering up, not made more depressed or bored!"** As a sample, here are lines from "Stairs to God" by Helen S. Rice:

> *Prayers are the stairs*
> *We must climb every day,*
> *If we would reach God*
> *There is no other way.*

Outreach is photocopied from typescript on ordinary paper, folded and saddle-stapled. **Faxed submissions OK. Send SAE with IRC for upcoming themes.**

OUTRIDER PRESS (I, IV-Women/feminism, gay/lesbian/bisexual, anthology, humor), 1004 E. Steger Rd., Suite C-3, Crete IL 60417-1362, founded 1988, president Phyllis Nelson, publishes 1-2 novels/anthologies/chapbooks annually. **They want "poetry dealing with the terrain of the human heart and plotting inner journeys; growth and grace under pressure. No bag ladies, loves-that-never-were, please."** As a sample the editor selected these lines from "Ice" in *Listen to the Moon* by Whitney Scott:

> *Ice cubes slip, cracking the scalding tea.*
> *It hisses in protest,*
> *waving to go*
> *over the edge.*

That chapbook is 16 pgs., digest-sized, photocopied from typescript with matte card cover, $5. **Submit 3-5 poems at a time with SASE. Include name, address and phone/fax number on every poem. Simultaneous submissions OK, if specified. Cover letter preferred. Responds to queries in 3 months, to submissions in 6 months. Sometimes sends prepublication galleys. Pays 1 copy.** Outrider publishes a themed anthology annually, with cash prizes for best poetry and short fiction. Send SASE for anthology/contest theme and guidelines. The press is affiliated with the Feminist Writers Guild, an organization open to all who support feminist writing. The editor says, "We look for visceral truths expressed without compromise, coyness or cliché. Go for the center of the experience."

"OVER THE BACK FENCE" MAGAZINE (IV-Regional), P.O. Box 756, Chillicothe OH 45601, phone (614)772-2165, fax (614)773-7626, founded 1994, senior editor Barbara Brickey Jividen, is a quarterly regional magazine "serving eighteen counties in southern Ohio. *'Over The Back Fence'* has a wholesome, neighborly style that is appealing to readers from young adults to seniors." **They want rhyming or free verse poetry, 24 lines or less; open to subject matter, "but seasonal works well"; friendly or inspirational work. "Since most of our readers are not poets, we want something simple and likeable by the general public. No profanity, please."** As a sample the editor selected these lines from "Etchings of the Heart" by Charles Clevenger:

> I carved a heart upon this tree
> With cupid's arrow aimed at thee.
> 'Tho time and space keep us apart,
> This etching holds you in my heart.

The editor says it is 68 pgs., published on high gloss paper, saddle-stapled with b&w and color illustrations and photos, includes ads. They receive less than 200 poems a year, publish approximately 4-10. Press run is 15,000 for about 2,000 subscribers, 40% shelf sales. Single copy: $2.95; subscription: $9.97/year. **Sample postpaid: $4. Make checks payable to Back Fence Publishing, Inc. Submit up to 4 poems at a time. Previously published poems and simultaneous submissions OK, "if identified as such." Cover letter preferred. "Since we prefer reader-submitted poetry, we would like for the cover letter to include comments about our magazine or contents."** Time between acceptance and publication is 6-12 months. **Seldom comments on rejections. "We do not publish theme issues, but do feature specific Ohio counties quarterly. Send or call for specific areas." Send SASE for guidelines. Reports in 1-3 months. Pays 10¢/word, $25 minimum. Buys one-time North American print rights.** The editor says, "While we truly appreciate the professional poet, most of our published poetry comes from beginners or amateurs. We strive for reader response and solicit poetry contributions througth the magazine."

THE OVERLOOK PRESS; TUSK BOOKS (V), 149 Wooster St., New York NY 10012, phone (212)477-7162, founded 1972, are trade publishers with about 8 poetry titles. They have published *Disappearances* by Paul Auster, *After a Lost Original* by David Shapiro and *The Boy in the Well* by Daniel Mark Epstein. Tusk/Overlook Books are distributed by Viking/Penguin. **They publish on standard royalty contracts with author's copies. They "are no longer accepting unsolicited poetry submissions."**

‡*OVERSTEPS BOOKS; COMPANY OF POETS BOOKS (III)**, Froude Rd., Salcombe, South Devon T08 8LH United Kingdom, (01548)843713, founded 1989 Company of Poets Books, 1996 Oversteps Books, director Anne Born. Oversteps Books publishes 1 paperback/year. **"I like to publish poets ready for a first collection. I like innovative but obscure work, unsentimental rural themes/settings."** They have recently published poetry by Paul Hyland. As a sample the editor selected these lines from "Littoral" by Giles Goodland:

> A storm from the moment I pitch
> A plane taking off, except it never
> leaves the horizon of hearing.
> Arms hurkled in the downy
> sleepingbag. Woken by a skirr
> of wings.

Books are usually 50-80 pgs., A5, professionally laser printed, perfect-bound, with 4-color glossy cover, photographs, art and graphics. **Submit 6 poems, camera-ready copy preferred. Previously published poems OK; no simultaneous submissions. Cover letter required with short bio and publication details.** Time between acceptance and publication is 1 year. **Often comments on rejections. Replies to queries in 3 months. Pays 6 author's copies (out of a press run of 400), and hopes to pay royalties in the future. Obtain sample books by writing to the above address.**

OVERVIEW LTD. POETRY (I, II), P.O. Box 211, Wood-Ridge NJ 07075, fax (201)778-5111, founded 1990, editor Joseph Lanciotti, is a biannual publication of **"plain good poetry, 10-40 lines."** As a sample the editor selected these lines from "Bridgeport Baseball" by Laura L. Koenig:

> All teams dissolve in the outfield.
> It's all heads up and everyone runs
> regardless of whose game it comes from,
> which
> one of the three
> being played in the park tonight.
> and it's not a big park;
> they're back to back.
> and side to side to side.
> It's baseball season
> in Bridgeport.

Overview Ltd. is 24 pgs., digest-sized, professionally printed and saddle-stapled with matte card cover. Press run is 500 for 150 subscribers, 250 shelf sales. **Sample postpaid: $5. Submit 3-4 poems at a time. No previously published poems; simultaneous submissions OK. Cover letter required. Submit by mail (with SASE) only." Send SASE for guidelines "*before* submitting." Reports in 3 months. Pays 1 copy plus $5-15.** The editor says, "*Overview Ltd.* is published only when a sufficient amount of good poetry has been submitted."

OWL CREEK PRESS; OWL CREEK PRESS POETRY PRIZE; GREEN LAKE CHAPBOOK PRIZE (II), 2693 SW Camano Dr., Camano Island WA 98292, founded 1979, poetry editor Rich Ives. "Owl Creek Press is a nonprofit literary publisher. Selections for publication are based solely on literary quality." They publish full-length poetry books, chapbooks, anthologies. **"No subject or length limitations. We look for poetry that will endure."** They have published poetry by Angela Ball, Art Homer and Laurie Blauner. Owl Creek Press **accepts books and chapbooks for publication only through its 2 annual contests.** The Owl Creek Press Poetry Prize selects 1-3 books for publication. Mss should be a minimum of 50 typed pages and should include an acknowledgments page for previous publications. Deadline: February 15; entry fee: $15; winners receive $750 and 10 copies of published book. The Green Lake Chapbook Prize chooses 1-3 chapbooks for publication. Mss should be under 40 pages and should include an acknowledgments page for previous publications. Deadline: August 15; entry fee: $10; winners receive 5 copies of published chapbook and a cash prize of $500 as an advance against royalties. Additional payment for reprinting. Send SASE for additional information on the contests. The editor says, "It is clear that many would-be poets do not read enough. A hungry mind is a valuable asset. Feed it."

OXFORD MAGAZINE (II), 261 Bachelor Hall, Miami University, Oxford OH 45056, phone (513)529-1954, founded 1984, editors Elizabeth Glass and Bret Johnston, appears annually, in the spring. **"We are open in terms of form, content and subject matter. We have eclectic tastes, ranging from New Formalism to Language poetry to Nuyorican poetry."** They have published poetry by Eve Shelnutt, Denise Duhamel and Walter McDonald. It is 220 pgs., 6×9, professionally printed and flat-spined. Press run is 1,000. **Sample postpaid: $8. Submit 3-5 poems at a time. No previously published poems. Simultaneous submissions OK. Cover letter preferred. Pays copies. Buys first North American serial rights.** *Oxford Magazine* has been awarded two Pushcart Prizes.

*OXFORD POETRY; THE RICHARD ELLMANN PRIZE (I, II), Magdalen College, Oxford, Oxon OX1 4AU England, founded 1983, co-editor Sinead Garrigan, appears 3 times/year. *Oxford Poetry*, designed to promote "new" poets, includes poetry, interviews, reviews and features. **They want "good poetry—not too long, any subject matter, any style except 'therapy' poetry."** They have published poetry by Seamus Heaney, Peter Reading, John Fuller and Jamie McKendrick. The editor says *Oxford Poetry* is about 52 pgs., A5 format, with colored card cover and ads on the back and inside covers. They receive about 800 poems a year, use approximately 70. Press run is 500 for 100 subscribers of which 20 are libraries, 200 shelf sales. Single copy: £2.40. **Sample postpaid: £2. Submit 4-6 poems at a time. No previously published poems; simultaneous submissions OK. Cover letter with brief bio required. Poems are circulated to an editorial board. Seldom comments on rejections. Send SASE (or SAE and IRCs) for guidelines. Reports in 6 months maximum. Pays 1 copy.** Reviews 2 new collections (first publication) in each issue. Poets may send books for review consideration. The Richard Ellmann Prize (established by Seamus Heaney) is awarded to the best poem in 3 issues. They also hold a translation competition in every second issue. Prize: £25. Send SASE (or SAE and IRCs) for details.

OXFORD UNIVERSITY PRESS, 198 Madison Ave., New York NY 10016. See listing in Publications Useful to Poets.

PABLO LENNIS (I, IV-Science fiction/fantasy), 30 N. 19th St., Lafayette IN 47904, founded 1976, editor John Thiel, appears irregularly, is a **"science fiction and fantasy fanzine preferring poems of an expressive cosmic consciousness or full magical approach. I want poetry that rhymes and scans and I like a good rhythmic structure appropriate to the subject. Shorter poems are much preferred. I want them to exalt the mind, imagination, or perception into a consciousness of the subject. Optimism is usually preferred, and English language perfection eminently preferable. Nothing that is not science fiction or fantasy, or which contains morbid sentiments, or is perverse, or does not rhyme or contains slang."** They have recently published poetry by Denny Marshall, Joanne Tolson, Darrin Kidd, W. Gregory Stewart and Todd Tuckey. As a sample the editor selected these lines from "The Tranquil Lament" by Jeromy John Visser:

> *Drawn by intensity, he followed crimson*
> *blossoms out of his abode.*
> *Through the sullen black he approached*
> *the midst of the woods.*
> *consumed by web-like fog . . .*

It is 26 pgs., magazine-sized, photocopied from typescript, side-stapled, using line drawings and hand-lettering. "I get maybe fifty poems a year and have been using most of them." Press run is "up to 100 copies." Subscription: $20/year. **Sample postpaid: $2. No previously published poems or simultaneous submissions. Send SASE for guidelines. Reports "at once. I generally say something about why the poetry was not used, if it was not. If someone else might like it, I mention an address." Pays 1 copy, 2 if requested.** Reviews books of poetry if they are science fiction or fantasy. Open to unsolicited reviews. Poets may also send books for review consideration. The editor says, "Poetry is magic. I want spells, incantations, sorceries of a rhythmic and rhyming nature, loftily and optimistically expressed, and I think this is what others want. People buy poetry to have something that will affect them, add new things to their lives. If they want something to think about, they get prose. See how much magic you can make. See how well-liked it is."

PACIFIC COAST JOURNAL; FRENCH BREAD AWARDS; FRENCH BREAD PUBLICATIONS (II), P.O. Box 23868, San Jose CA 95153-3868, e-mail paccoastj@aol.com, website http://users.aol.com/paccoastj, founded 1992, editor Stillson Graham. *PCJ* is a quarterly "unprofessional" literary magazine. **They want "offbeat poetry, visual poetry, poetry that is aware of itself. We don't rule out rhyming poetry, but rarely do we accept it."** They have published poetry by Joan Payne Kincaid, Errol Miller and Hugh Fox. As a sample the editor selected these lines by C.D. Chase:

> *I am the lie*
> > *that lurks in life,*
> *defubed*
> > *by gray of hair, black*
> *of truth and blue*
> > *of eye. 1*

PCJ is 56 pgs., 5½ × 8½, photocopied and saddle-stitched with a card stock cover and b&w photos and artwork. They receive 400-500 poems a year, accept approximately 15%. Press run is 200 for 75 subscribers, 25 shelf sales. Single copy: $3; subscription: $12. **Sample postpaid: $2.50. Submit 4 poems at a time. No previously published poems; simultaneous submissions OK. Cover letter preferred.** Time between acceptance and publication is 6-12 months. **Seldom comments on rejections. Send SASE for guidelines or request via e-mail. Reports in 3-4 months. Pays 1 copy. Acquires one-time rights.** Reviews novels, short story collections and chapbooks of poetry in 1,500 words, single format. Open to unsolicited reviews (and pays $5 if accepted). Poets may also send books for review consideration. They also sponsor the French Bread Awards for short fiction/poetry. Entry fee: $6 for a group of up to 4 poems (no longer than 8 pgs. total). First prize: $50. Second prize: $25. Deadline: August 1. Send SASE for details. French Bread Publications also occasionally **publishes chapbooks of poetry**, short story collections and short novellas. Books are similar to the journal in format. **Query first with 5 sample poems, a cover letter and a list of credits for all the poems in the ms. Replies to queries in 1-2 months, to mss (if invited) in 3-4 months. Pays royalties and 50 author's copies (out of a press run of 500).** The editor says, "Most poetry looks like any other poetry. We want experiments in what poetry is."

‡PAINTBRUSH: A JOURNAL OF MULTICULTURAL LITERATURE (III), Division of Language & Literature, Truman State University, Kirksville MO 63501, phone (816)785-4185, founded 1974, editor Ben Bennani. *Paintbrush* appears annually and is 5½ × 8½, 250-300 pgs., using **quality poetry.** Circulation is 500. **Sample: $15. No submissions June, July and August. Send SASE with inquiries and request for samples.** Reviews books of poetry.

PAINTED BRIDE QUARTERLY (II), 230 Vine St., Philadelphia PA 19106, editors Kathy Volk Miller and Marion Wrenn, founded 1973, appears quarterly. **"We have no specifications or restrictions. We'll look at anything."** They have published poetry by Robert Bly, Charles Bukowski, S.J. Marks and James Hazen. "*PBQ* aims to be a leader among little magazines published by and for independent poets and writers nationally." The 80-page, digest-sized, perfect-bound magazine uses 40 pgs. of poetry/issue. They receive over 1,000 submissions a year, use approximately 150. Neatly printed, it has a circulation of 1,000 for 850 subscribers, of which 40 are libraries. Subscription: $16. **Sample postpaid: $6. Submit up to 6 poems, any length, typed; only original, unpublished work. "Submissions should include a *short* bio."** Seldom comment on rejections. **They have a 6- to 9-month backlog. Pays 1-year subscription, 1 half-priced contributor's copy and $5/accepted piece.** Publishes reviews of poetry books. "We also occasionally publish critical essays." Sponsors annual poetry contest and chapbook competition. Entry fee required for both. Send SASE for details. Poetry published in *PBQ* has been included in *The Best American Poetry 1995*.

PALANQUIN/TDM; PALANQUIN POETRY SERIES (II), Dept. of English, University of South Carolina-Aiken, 171 University Pkwy., Aiken SC 29801, fax (803)641-3461, e-mail phebed@aiken.sc.edu, founded 1988, editor Phebe Davidson, publishes a pamphlet series 6 times/year featuring one poet/issue. **They do not want "sentimental, religious, consciously academic" poetry.** They have published poetry by Dorothy Perry Thompson, Gregory Jerozal, Danny Romero, Mary Winters and Janet Krauss. As a sample the editor selected these lines by Joe Weil:

> *Above the above ground swimming pools*
> *In backyards of Elizabeth*
> *Gnats swarm at dusk*
> *And always the same girl stands*

The pamphlet we received, featuring poems by Janet Krauss, is professionally printed on heavy paper. Press run is 150 for 80 subscribers. Subscription: $10. **Sample postpaid: $1. Submit 5-10 poems at a time with bio and SASE. No previously published poems. "I read January through March for the following year." Reports in 2-3 months. Pays 25 copies.** *Palanquin* also holds an annual chapbook contest, deadline May 1. Include 20-25 pgs. of poetry (single poems may be previously published), bio, $10 reading fee. SASE for results only.

PALO ALTO REVIEW (I, II, IV-Themes), 1400 W. Villaret Blvd., San Antonio TX 78224, phone (210)921-5255 or 921-5017, fax (210)921-5115, e-mail eshull@accd.edu, founded 1992, editors Ellen Shull and Bob

INSIDER REPORT

Write for the sake of life, not for the sake of publishing

Michael Glaser's poetry deals with the intimate details of life—a child's endless questioning, an aging father's difficulty expressing love, the thrill of observing a topless sunbather, amazement at the continuity of a wife's desire. From the first reading, Glaser's poems pull you deep into the world of a man who looks at life through an artist's eyes and feels with a lover's heart.

"Writing poetry is a way of making sense of life," says Glaser. "It's a way of paying attention to details, of valuing incongruities and complexities, of taking risks and making choices, of watching for connections and seeing things new, of paying attention to the questions that life daily poses. To make time for reading and writing is to make time for exploring the world I live in and for examining that world with wonder."

Michael Glaser

A husband, father of five and literature professor at St. Mary's College of Maryland, Glaser has been consistently publishing his work since the late '60s and, to date, has published approximately 200 individual poems, two chapbooks (*Marmalade*, Seasonings Press, 1977; and *In the Men's Room and other poems*, Painted Bride Quarterly, 1996) and a collection (*A Lover's Eye*, Bunny & Crocodile Press, 1989).

Publishing, however, is not the primary focus of Glaser's work. In fact, he had been writing poetry for nearly ten years before he began submitting his work and, even then, he feels his motivation for submitting was all wrong. "I started submitting my work when I was in graduate school; I knew I'd be looking for jobs. I figured if I got some publication credits, that would help me get a job. So I started sending my poems out and I got a few published. But, in retrospect, I was trying to get published for the wrong reasons. When you write for the sake of a job, or the sake of an ego you are, I think, betraying one of the most significant aspects of any art—the honoring and developing of one's own voice."

Glaser recalls a statement about poetry that poet Stanley Kunitz made during an address he gave at St. Mary's: "The gift of poetry is life sustaining, life enhancing and absolutely unpredictable. Does one live, therefore, for the sake of poetry? No, the reverse is true. Poetry is for the sake of life."

With Kunitz's statement in mind, Glaser says, "My experience has been that when I write poetry to help me make sense of what our lives are about, when I approach the writing of poetry as a process of exploration and discovery, then I also begin discovering my own unique voice. And the more I use my own voice, trying to write as accurately and as truthfully as I can with that voice, the more my poems begin to resonate with the kind of genuineness and honesty that, I believe, has led to them getting published on a more regular basis."

INSIDER REPORT, *Glaser*

To find markets for his work, Glaser spends a lot of time in bookstores, browsing the magazine racks. He does, from time to time, use market directories to place his work. "A good way to discover new magazines is to spend two hours in any lovely bookstore that supports poetry and read through their poetry magazines. The one place I find *Poet's Market* [and other market directories] useful is when I have written highly-specialized poems. I write a lot of poems about my children and so it's helpful to look for magazines seeking poems about children. Or, recently, I've been writing poems about my spiritual life and *PM* helps me identify magazines wanting that kind of poetry. It's a wonderful tool and it is as useful to a writer as a dictionary, but it's just a tool. A dictionary is not going to tell you how to write a poem and *Poet's Market* alone is not going to help you find the markets that, perhaps, are most suited to your writing."

"Losing Branches"

Even of the beauty
of the snow he said only
"it probably won't last"
adding, "it's not good
for the trees you know,
it'll cost some branches"
as though such loveliness
were too much to hold,
as though the burden of it
could not bear the words
or, if he found words
to say what those who love him
long to hear, the sound
might storm white with tears
and stretch his heart to breaking.

(originally published in *Men As We Are*, Summer 1993; reprinted by permission of the author)

In order to really know the poetry market and assist their writing, Glaser believes poets must join the community of writers by reading and buying magazines and books. "Frankly, it is baffling to me why people who write poetry don't want to own more of it. Thoreau said, 'Books are the treasured wealth of the world, the fit inheritance of generations and nations.' I've always loved books; so to buy books by writers whose work I love is just a wonderful thing. I don't think I know any good poets who don't own a lot of books, or who don't subscribe to three, four or five poetry magazines a year. And I would be surprised if that wasn't a pretty accurate generalization."

Most recently Glaser has been submitting his work to book competitions. That's because, he says, presses too often only look at the bottom line and success, for poetry, is selling 2,000 copies. Unfortunately, publishers don't make much of a profit from selling only 2,000 copies. "And for a writer who doesn't have pretensions to fame, and is not famous, I don't imagine I would even get a reading. So my best route, and most poets' best route, is to go through competitions.

"The other thing is there's lots and lots of really good people writing really good poetry

INSIDER REPORT, *continued*

today. It's not that there's a dearth of good poets in the world; there's a dearth of people publishing poetry. I often think getting published is a lot like a crap shoot. What editors and publishers accept for publication is, and probably should be, a very subjective thing." In his own life, however, Glaser has reached a place where neither his job nor his ego depend on publication. And even though he is grateful to be able to share his work with the public, he writes for himself and doesn't invest his work's worth upon getting it published. "Because poetry—reading what others have written as well as my own writing—has become a process for helping me make sense of the world, I view my writing as something I do in my life, and not something I do to get published. I enjoy seeing my work in print, of course, but I think of publication primarily as a means of sharing with and connecting to the world of others. 'Being a poet is something you do, it's not something one can be,' William Meredith said, and the older I get the more I value that understanding of what it means to be a writer."

As well as writing poetry and teaching at St. Mary's College, Glaser is the director of The Literary Festival at St. Mary's, an annual event held the last two weekends in May (see the listing in the Conferences and Workshops section of this book). He also works with the Maryland State Art Council's Poets-in-the-Schools Program, a program supported by the National Endowment for the Arts. The Poets-in-the-Schools Program is designed to encourage school-age children to write poetry by sending poets into the public schools for a week to work with the kids and to teach them about the craft of poetry.

Glaser uses his time with the Poets-in-the-Schools Program to connect the kids to the larger writing community and to get them thinking about the role literature can play in their lives. "I usually organize an assembly at the end [of the week] where I read poems by the kids along with poems by more famous poets to give them a sense that they can join this community of writers. For example, I might read a poem a third grader wrote wondering about justice, and then read a poem by Robert Hayden in which Hayden reflects on justice. Or I might read a poem a son wrote wondering about his relationship with his mother, and then another poem, by a mother, wondering about her relationship with her son. And then the kids say, 'Wow, this is neat. These poets are writing about lives just like mine.'

"To be in a community of writers is to be among people who seek, ultimately, to affirm our shared humanity," says Glaser. "To have the opportunity to nurture that—in other writers as well as in students—is a privilege I am deeply grateful for. I never cease to be amazed by the clarity, energy and humility reading an honest piece of writing can produce in me—whether it comes from a first grader or a celebrated poet."

—*Chantelle Bentley*

Richmond, is a biannual publication of Palo Alto college. "We invite writing that investigates the full range of education in its myriad forms. Ideas are what we are after. The *Palo Alto Review* is interested in connecting the college and the community. We would hope that those who attempt these connections will choose startling topics and find interesting angles from which to study the length and breadth of ideas and learning, a lifelong pursuit." The review includes articles, essays, memoirs, interviews, book reviews, fiction and poetry. **They want "poetry which has something to say, literary quality poems, with strong images, up to 50 lines. No inspirational verse, haiku or doggerel."** They have published poetry by Diane Glancy, Wendy Bishop, Lyn Lifshin and Ruth Daigon. *PAR* is 60 pgs., 8½×11, professionally printed on recycled paper and saddle-stapled with matte card cover with art; b&w photos, art and graphics inside. They publish about 8 poems in each issue (16 poems/year). Press run is 700 for 400 subscribers of which 10 are libraries, 200 shelf sales. Subscription: $10. **Sample postpaid:**

$5. Submit 3-5 poems at a time. No previously published poems; simultaneous submissions OK. Poems are read by an advisory board and recommended to editors, who sometimes suggest revisions. Always comments on rejections. "Although we frequently announce a theme, the entire issue will not necessarily be dedicated to the theme." Send SASE for guidelines and upcoming themes. Reports in 1-3 months. Pays 2 copies. Acquires first North American serial rights. "Please note poems as first published in *Palo Alto Review* in subsequent printings." The editors say there are no requirements for submission, "though we recommend the reading (purchase) of a sample copy."

PANJANDRUM BOOKS; PANJANDRUM POETRY JOURNAL (III, IV-Translations), 6156 Wilkinson Ave., North Hollywood CA 91606, founded 1971, editor Dennis Koran, associate editor David Guss. **The press publishes a distinguished list of avant-garde books. They are interested in translations (especially European) of modern poetry, surrealism, dada and experimental poetry and accept book-length mss only with SASE; query first. Cover letter listing previous publications is required.** *Panjandrum Poetry Journal* is published occasionally. **Submit no more than 10 poems at a time. No simultaneous submissions.** Staff also reviews books of poetry. Send books for review consideration to Dennis Koran.

PANTHEON BOOKS INC., 201 E. 50th St., New York NY 10022, editorial director Dan Frank. Prefers not to share information.

PAPER BOAT MAGAZINE; PAPER BOAT PRESS (I, II), P.O. Box 2615, Poulsbo WA 98370, founded 1995, editor Maura Alia Bramkamp, publisher Paul Bramkamp. *Paper Boat* is a biannual literary magazine. "We aim to publish fresh, new poetry, short-short fiction, personal essays and b&w artwork. We have a slight Pacific Northwest bias—but are open to all. **We like the original, quirky, catch-you-off-guard poems; favor narrative free verse, but are open to other forms. One-page poems have a better chance due to space limitations. No greeting card or religious verse, no haiku, no tiresome pseudo-porn, no violence.**" They have recently published poetry by Jana Harris, Depek Sheffield and Linda Elkin. As a sample the editor selected these lines from "Maui—In Trade" by Naomi Shihab Nye:

> WANTED-free place to live
> where I can bring my large
> quartz healing crystals.
> Giant clusters of ENERGIZERS.
> Must be people who can tolerate
> a large amount of healing energy
> which would be my exchange.

PB is 42-64 pgs., 8½×11, saddle-stapled, glossy card cover with b&w photos, artwork and cartoons. In 1996, they received 2,500 poems, accepted about 2%. Press run is 250 for 60 subscribers of which 3 are libraries. Subscription: $8, $18/year overseas. **Sample postpaid: $4. Make checks payable to Paper Boat Press. Submit 3-5 poems at a time. Very rarely accepts previously published poems; no simultaneous submissions. Cover letter including bio required. Reads submissions September 1 through December 1 and February 1 through May 1. Seldom comments on rejections. Publishes theme issues from time to time. Send SASE for guidelines and upcoming themes. Reports in 1-6 months. Pays 1 copy, offers 40% discount on additional copies. Acquires first North American serial rights.** Paper Boat Press **publishes chapbooks through its biennial contest only.** "We aim to publish new voices as well as those that have 'been around.' We seek fresh, original, surprising poetry." Chapbooks are usually 20-25 pgs., digest-sized, saddle-stapled, card cover with art. **Submit up to 24 pgs., of original poetry with acknowledgement page, bio and SASE.** Entry fee: $10. Winner receives $200; publication and 50 copies of chapbooks. Winner announced in Fall/Winter issue; chapbook published the following Fall. Deadline: June 15, 1998. Send SASE for information. The editor says, "Do not bombard us with inquiries after submitting. We take our time to select quality work. Please be patient. You may send a postcard if you haven't heard from us in six months. Also, we strongly encourage poets to order a sample to get a feel for the magazine. We've had too many people submit one bizarre thing after another without ever reading us."

THE PAPER SALAD ONLINE POETRY JOURNAL (II), P.O. Box 520061, Salt Lake City UT 84152-0061 (for correspondence only), website http://www./gcy.com/users/r/rmoore/salad.htm, founded 1990, editor R.L. Moore, looks for **"poetry that causes something to turn inside you as you read it; that produces a somewhat narcotic buzz in your head, and sings to you. Poetry that takes you to a place, and causes you to experience that place. Poetry that swells."** They have published poetry by Richard Cronshey, Christien

---

SENDING TO A COUNTRY other than your own? Be sure to send International Reply Coupons (IRCs) instead of stamps for replies or return of your manuscript.

Gholson, Gayle Elen Harvey, B.Z. Niditch, Glenn D. Parker, Simon Perchik and Duane Locke. As a sample the editor selected these lines from "Until It Wakes, This Earthworks of Body" by John L. Falk:

> When finally the body becomes the map
> Of earth, the universal geography,
> When the smoking clouds are stroked
> As curled intimacies of sleeping cats,
> And the anemia of airless heights,
> The blue nitrogen dreams of sea depths,
> Are mundane as any swallow of water;

The editor wants to make it clear that the above physical address is for correspondence only. **Submissions will only be accepted by going to the** *PAPER SALAd* **page on the World Wide Web.** "Work is only promised to appear online, however it may possibly be printed up in actual physical form. (about 100 pgs., digest-sized, flat-spined, sometimes color cover, unspecific printing time schedule.)" **Seldom comments on rejections. Reports in 1 month.** "There is no promise of payment for accepted poetry, however payment of one copy will be made if printed." For a sample copy send $7.25 to the physical address above or make order from the web page. The editor says, "Poetry is the music of words. The music in poetry is far more important than the meaning."

‡❤**PAPERPLATES (II)**, 19 Kenwood Ave., Toronto, Ontario M6C 2R8 Canada, phone (416)651-2551, fax (416)651-2910, e-mail paperplates@perkolator.com, website http://www.perkolator.com, founded 1990, publisher/editor Bernard Kelly, published biannually, is a magazine of general interest featuring short stories, poetry, one-act plays, reviews, travel pieces, essays and interviews. **They have no preference for submissions, however they do not want religious poetry.** They have recently published poetry by Richard Ontram and Fraser Sutherland. The editor says *paperplates* is 44 pgs., 8½×11. Press run is 350 for 110 subscribers, 200 shelf sales. Single copy: $4.95; subscription: $14.95. **Sample postpaid: $5. Submit 5 poems at a time. Previously published poems and simultaneous submissions OK. Cover letter preferred. E-mail submissions OK with mailing address and phone number.** Time between acceptance and publication is up to 1 year. **Seldom comments on rejections. Send SASE (or SAE and IRCs) for guidelines. Reports ASAP. Pays 2 copies.** Reviews books of poetry. Open to unsolicited reviews. Poets may also send books for review consideration.

PAPYRUS (III, IV-Ethnic/nationality), P.O. Box 270797, West Hartford CT 06127-0797, e-mail gwhitaker@imagine.com, website http://www.readersndex.com/papyrus, founded 1994, editor Ginger Whitaker, is a quarterly "writer's 'craftletter' featuring the Black experience," published by Papyrus Literary Enterprises, Inc. It includes articles on the art of writing; fiction, nonfiction and poetry; marketplace news; and literary notes for the serious beginning writer. **They want African-American-centered poetry, but will accept good work by anyone. Shorter works preferred, but nothing against any ethnic group.** They have recently published poetry by Lyn Lifshin, John Grey, Lenard D. Moore and Simon Perchik. As a sample we selected these lines from "I Know the Grandmother One Had Hands" by Jaki Shelton Green:

> I know the grandmother one had hands
> but they were always in bowls
> folding, pinching, rolling the dough
> making the bread
> I know the grandmother one had hands
> but they were always under water
> sifting rice
> bluing clothes
> starching lives . . .

Papyrus is 20 pgs., 8½×11, printed in 2 colors and saddle-stitched. They receive about 25 poems a year, publish approximately 50%. Press run is 2,000 for 500 subscribers, 200 shelf sales. Single copy: $2.20; subscription: $8/year. **Sample postpaid: $1. Submit up to 5 poems at a time. No previously published poems or simultaneous submissions. Work may be submitted on a 3.5 disk, with 2 hard copies. "Macintosh users should submit files in ClarisWorks, Microsoft Word, WordPerfect or MacWrite II. IBM users should submit files saved in ASCII. E-mail submissions OK, but submit work within the body of the e-mail only; no attachments. However, we prefer e-mail queries to blind submissions." Poems are reviewed by 2 senior editors and an independent poetry consultant. Often comments on rejections. Send SASE for guidelines or request via e-mail. Reports in 1 month. Pays $10-25 and 2 copies. Buys first rights.** Sponsors annual contest. Entry fee: $5. Awards $100 for winners in each category of fiction, nonfiction and poetry.

PARAMOUR MAGAZINE (I, II, IV-Erotica), P.O. Box 949, Cambridge MA 02140-0008, phone/fax (617)499-0069, e-mail paramour@paramour.com, website: http://www.paramour.com, founded 1993, poetry editor Dan Luft, publisher/editor Amelia Copeland, is a quarterly devoted to "literary and artistic erotica," including short fiction, poetry, photography, illustration and reviews. **They want erotic poetry—"crude, humorous, sweet, all OK. Nothing navel-contemplative."** They have recently published poetry by John Cantey Knight, eve packer, Richard Kostelanetz and Linda Wiggin. *Paramour* is 36 pgs., 9×12, printed 2-color on recycled paper and saddle-stapled with paper cover and b&w photos throughout. Much of the content is sexually explicit. They receive 400-500 poems a year, accept approximately 5%. Press run is 12,000 for 500 subscribers, about 8,000 shelf sales. Single copy: $4.95; subscription: $18. **Submit up to 10 poems each quarter. E-mail submissions OK. Include name, address and phone number on every page. Previously published poems OK, "only if published in obscure publications." Simultaneous submissions OK, "but you must inform us of which publications." Written work will not be returned. Send SASE for guidelines. Reports in 4 months. Pays 3 copies plus a 1-year subscription. Acquires first or second rights.**

THE PARIS REVIEW; BERNARD F. CONNORS PRIZE (III), 541 E. 72nd St., New York NY 10021, phone (212)861-0016, fax (212)861-4504, website http://www.voyagerco.com, founded 1952, poetry editor Richard Howard. This distinguished quarterly (circulation 11,000, digest-sized, 200 pgs.) has published many of the major poets writing in English. Though form, content and length seem open, free verse—some structured, some experimental—tends to dominate recent issues. Because the journal is considered one of the most prestigious in the world, competition is keen and response times can lag. Subscription: $34 (US); $42 (outside US). **Sample: $11. Study publication before submitting.** The Bernard F. Connors prize of $1,000 is awarded annually for the best previously unpublished long poem (over 200 lines). Poetry published in *The Paris Review* was selected for inclusion in the 1992, 1993, 1994, 1995, 1996 and 1997 volumes of *The Best American Poetry*.

PARNASSUS LITERARY JOURNAL (I, II), P.O. Box 1384, Forest Park GA 30051-1384, phone (404)366-3177, founded 1975, editor Denver Stull. "Our sole purpose is to promote poetry and to offer an outlet where poets may be heard. **We are open to all poets and all forms of poetry, including Oriental, 24-line limit, maximum 3 poems.**" They have recently published poetry by Eugene Botelho, Matthew Louviere, Rod Farmer, Jaye Giammarino, Gloria Procsal and Robert Lowenstein. As a sample the editor selected "Visitors" by Diana Kwiatkowski Rubin:

> My children invite them—
> miniscule squatters—
> until the house is full
> to capacity with monarchs,
> laydbugs, lightning bugs,
> grasshoppers, and inch worms.
> Where will they vacation
> when the laughter of their hosts
> bounces down hallways of memory
> and both the young and their mother
> have grown too old for patience?

PLJ, published 3 times/year, is 84 pgs., photocopied from typescript, saddled-stapled, colored card cover, with an occasional drawing. They receive about 1,500 submissions a year, use approximately 350. Currently have about a 1-year backlog. Press run is 300 for 200 subscribers of which 5 are libraries. Circulation includes Japan, England, Greece, India, Korea, Germany and Netherlands. Single copy: $6 US and Canada, $9.50 overseas; subscription: $18 US and Canada, $28 overseas. **Sample postpaid: $5. Offers 20% discount to schools, libraries and for orders of 5 copies or more. Make checks or money orders payable to Denver Stull. Include name and address on each page of ms. "I am dismayed at the haphazard manner in which work is often submitted. I have a number of poems in my file containing no name and/or address. Simply placing your name and address on your envelope is not enough." Previously published poems OK; no simultaneous submissions. Cover letter including something about the writer preferred. "Definitely" comments on rejections. "We do not respond to submissions or queries not accompanied by SASE." Send SASE for guidelines. Reports within 1 week. Pays 1 copy. Acquires all rights. Returns rights.** Readers vote on best of each issue. Also conducts a contest periodically. Staff reviews books of poetry by subscribers only. The editor advises: "Write about what you know. Study what you have written. Does it make sense? A poem should not leave the reader wondering what you are trying to say. Improve your writings by studying the work of others. Be professional."

PARNASSUS: POETRY IN REVIEW; POETRY IN REVIEW FOUNDATION (V), 205 W. 89th St., #8F, New York NY 10024-1835, phone (212)362-3492, fax (212)875-0148, founded 1972, poetry editor Herbert Leibowitz, provides "comprehensive and in-depth coverage of new books of poetry, including translations from foreign poetry. **We publish poems and translations on occasion, but we solicit all poetry. Poets invited to submit are given all the space they wish; the only stipulation is that the style be non-academic.**" They have published work by Alice Fulton, Eavan Boland, Ross Feld, Debora Greger, William Logan, Tess Gallagher, Seamus Heaney and Rodney Jones. Subscriptions are $27/year, $46/year for libraries; they have 1,100 subscribers, of which 550 are libraries. They do consider unsolicited essays. In fact, this is an exceptionally rich market for thoughtful, insightful, technical essay-reviews of contemporary collections. However, it is strongly recommended that writers study the magazine before submitting. **Multiple submissions disliked. Cover letter required. Send SASE for upcoming themes. Reports on essay submissions within 4-10 weeks (response takes longer during the summer). Pays $25-250 plus 2 gift subscriptions—contributors can also take one themselves. Editor comments on rejections—from 1 paragraph to 2 pages.** Send for a sample copy (prices of individual issues can vary) to get a feel for the critical acumen needed to place here. The editor comments, "Contributors should be urged to subscribe to at least one literary magazine. There is a pervasive ignorance of the cost of putting out a magazine and no sense of responsibility for supporting one."

PARTING GIFTS; MARCH STREET PRESS (II), 3413 Wilshire, Greensboro NC 27408, website http://users.aol.com/marchst/msp.html, founded 1987, editor Robert Bixby. **"I want to see everything.** I'm a big fan of Jim Harrison, C.K. Williams, Amy Hempel and Janet Kauffman." He has published poetry by Eric Torgersen, Lyn Lifshin, Elizabeth Kerlikowske and Russell Thorburn. *PG* is 50 pgs., digest-sized, photocopied, with colored matte card cover, appearing twice a year. Press run is 200. Subscription: $12. **Sample postpaid: $6. Submit in groups of 3-10 with SASE. No previously published poems, but simultaneous submissions OK. "I like a cover letter because it makes the transaction more human. Best time to submit mss is early in the year."** Send SASE for guidelines or obtain via website. Reports in 1-2 weeks. Sometimes sends prepublication galleys. Pays 1 copy. March Street Press **publishes chapbooks; $10 reading fee.**

PARTISAN REVIEW (II, IV-Translations, themes), Dept. PM, 236 Bay State Rd., Boston MA 02215, phone (617)353-4260, founded 1934, editor Edith Kurzweil, editor-in-chief William Phillips, is a distinguished quarterly literary journal using **poetry of high quality. "Our poetry section is very small and highly selective. We are open to fresh, quality translations but submissions must include poem in original language as well as translation. We occasionally have special poetry sections on specified themes."** They have published poetry by John Hollander, Czeslaw Milosz, Donald Revell and Rosanna Warren. The journal is 160 pgs., 6×9, flat-spined. Circulation is 8,200 for 6,000 subscriptions and shelf sales. **Sample postpaid: $7.50. Submit up to 6 poems at a time. No simultaneous submissions. Reports in 2 months. Pays $50 and 50% discount on copies.** Work published in this review has also been selected for inclusion in *The Best American Poetry 1995*.

PASSAGER: A JOURNAL OF REMEMBRANCE AND DISCOVERY (I, II, IV-Senior citizen, themes), School of Communications Design, University of Baltimore, 1420 N. Charles St., Baltimore MD 21201-5779, founded 1989, editors Kendra Kopelke and Mary Azrael. *Passager* is published quarterly and publishes fiction, poetry and interviews that give voice to human experience. **"We seek powerful images of remembrance and discovery from writers of all ages. One of our missions is to provide exposure for new older writers."** The journal is 32 pgs., 8×8, printed on white linen recycled paper and saddle-stitched. Includes photos of writers. **Sample postpaid: $4. Submit 3-5 poems at a time, each 30 lines maximum; fiction, 3,000 words maximum. "We like clean, readable typed copy with name, address and phone number on each page."** Simultaneous submissions acceptable if notified. No reprints. **"We prefer cover sheets because it makes it personal. However, we hate pushy cover letters, 'I'm sure you'll find your readers will love my story.' " Does not read mss June through August.** Occasionally does special issues. Send SASE for guidelines and upcoming themes. **Reports in 3 months. Pays 2 copies.** They sponsor an annual spring poetry contest for new poets over 50 years old, with a $500 first prize and honorable mentions; and publication in *Passager*.

PASSAGES NORTH (II), English Dept., 1401 Presque Isle Ave., Northern Michigan University, Marquette MI 49855, phone (906)227-2715, founded 1979, poetry editor Anne Ohman Youngs, is a biannual magazine containing fiction, poetry, essays, interviews and visual art. **"The magazine publishes quality work by established and emerging writers."** They have published poetry by Jim Daniels, Jack Driscoll, Vivian Shipley and Michael Delp. *Passages North* is 100 pgs., perfect-bound. Circulation is at 1,000 "and growing." Single copy: $7; subscription: $13/year, $18/2 years, add $10 for international mail. **Sample postpaid: $2. Prefers groups of 4-6 poems, typed single-spaced. No simultaneous submissions.** Time between acceptance and publication is 6 months. **Reads submissions September through May only. Reports in 6-8 weeks. Pays copies.**

PASSEGGIATA PRESS (III, IV-Ethnic, translations), (formerly Three Continents Press Inc.), P.O. Box 636, Pueblo CO 81002, phone (719)544-1038, fax (719)576-4689, founded 1973, poetry editor Donald Herdeck. **"Published poets only welcomed and only non-European and non-American poets . . . We publish literature by creative writers from the non-western world (Africa, the Middle East, the Caribbean and Asia/Pacific)— poetry *only* by non-western writers or good translations of such poetry if original language is Arabic, French, African vernacular, etc."** They have published poetry by Derek Walcott, Khalil Hawi, Mahmud Darwish, Julia Fields, Hilary Tham, Houda Naamani and Nizar Kabbani. They also publish anthologies and criticisms focused on relevant themes. **Query with 4-5 samples, bio, publication credits. Replies to queries in 5-10 weeks, to submissions (if invited) in 4-5 weeks. Sometimes sends prepublication galleys. Offers 10% royalty contract (5% for translator) with $100-200 advance plus 10 copies. Buys worldwide English rights. Send SASE for catalog to buy samples.**

‡PATCHWORK POEMS (I, IV-Regional), 1528 W. Contour Dr., San Antonio TX 78212, fax (210)684-3050, e-mail rharrell@express-news.net, founded 1995, editor Jeannine Harrell, published monthly "is a creative

---

FOR INFORMATION ON ENTERING the *1999 Poet's Market* Poetry Contest, see page 2.

venture with the sole purpose of extending the art of poetry, increasing its audience and providing a vehicle for its expression." **They want "understandable, sensitive, formal rhyme or free verse, short (30-50 lines) preferred." They do not want "porn or excessive profanity, gay themes or erotica."** They have recently published poetry by Naomi Shihab Nye, Christopher Woods, Albert Huffstickler and Carol Cullar. As a sample the editor selected these lines from "Seminole Canyon" by Mark Smith:

> *They painted these by day*
> *that much seems sure.*
> *How much more vibrant*
> *were these colors then*
> *that they shine yet*
> *four thousand years later*
> *as whole and far as the sun?*

Patchwork Poems is 12-16 pgs., digest-sized, photocopied, saddle-stapled, with colored card cover and graphics. They receive about 300-500 poems a year, accept approximately 50%. Press run is 150. Single copy: $1; subscription: $12. **Sample postpaid: $1.55. Make checks payable to Jeannine Harrell. Contributors must be residents of Texas. Submit 3 poems at a time. Previously published poems and simultaneous submissions OK. Cover letter preferred.** Time between acceptance and publication is 2 months. **The editor determines acceptability based on content, artistic merit, word imagery and length. Always comments on rejections. Reports in 2-3 weeks. Pays "three months of issues."**

PATH PRESS, INC. (IV-Ethnic), 53 W. Jackson Blvd., Suite 724, Chicago IL 60604-3610, phone (312)663-0167, fax (312)663-5318, e-mail bjjIII@aol.com, founded 1969, president Bennett J. Johnson, executive vice president and poetry editor Herman C. Gilbert, is a small publisher of books and poetry primarily **"by, for and about African-American and Third World people." The press is open to all types of poetic forms; emphasis is on high quality. Submissions should be typewritten in ms format. Writers should send sample poems, credits and bio.** The books are "hardback and quality paperbacks."

PAVEMENT SAW (III); PAVEMENT SAW PRESS (II), 7 James St., Scotia NY 12302, founded 1992, editors David Baratier and Tara Pauliny. *Pavement Saw*, which appears annually, **wants "poetry on any subject, especially work. Length: one or two pages. No poems that tell, no work by a deceased writer and no translations."** They have recently published poetry by Jendi Reiter, Sandra Kohler, Timothy Russell and Simon Perchik. The editor says *PS* is 64 pgs., 6×9, perfect-bound. They receive 7,500-9,000 poems a year, publish less than 1%. Press run is 500 for about 250 subscribers, about 250 shelf sales. Single copy: $4; subscription: $6. **Sample postpaid: $3.50. Make checks payable to Pavement Saw Press. Submit 5 poems at a time. "No fancy typefaces." No previously published poems or simultaneous submissions. Cover letter required. Seldom comments on rejections. Send SASE for guidelines. Reports in 3-6 months. Sometimes sends pre-publication galleys. Pays 2 copies. Acquires first rights.** The press also occasionally publishes books of poetry ("most are by authors who have been published in the journal") and sponsors an annual chapbook contest. **For consideration in the contest, submit up to 32 pgs. of poetry with a cover letter and $7 entry fee. The winner will receive $500, publication of the chapbook, and 10% of the press run. Each entrant will receive a copy of the winning chapbook provided a 9×12 SAE with $1.01 postage is supplied. Deadline: December 20. Send SASE for complete details.**

‡*PEACE AND FREEDOM; EASTERN RAINBOW (I), 17 Farrow Rd., Whaplode Drove, Spalding, Lincs PE12 OTS England, editor Paul Rance, founded 1985, is a "small press publisher of poetry, music, art, short stories, reviews and general features," and also is a distributor. *Peace and Freedom* is a magazine appearing 2 times a year. **"We are looking for poems up to 32 lines particularly from U.S. poets who are new to writing, particularly women. The poetry we publish is anti-war, environmental; poems reflecting love; erotic, but not obscene poetry; humorous verse and spiritual, humanitarian poetry. With or without rhyme/metre."** They have recently published poetry by Dorothy Bell-Hall, Matthew Dalby, Bernard Shough, Fay Dickinson, Daphne Richards and Andrew Savage. As a sample the editor selected these lines by Victor West:

> *We became one with Evil, vanquishing ourselves.*
> *Still from its filthy pit beneath crossroads,*
> *thrice-staked, issue demon shrieks gibbering,*
> *promising more Devil's work and professional pride.*

Peace and Freedom has a glossy cover, normally 24 A4 pages. 50% of submissions accepted. "Poetry is judged on merit, but non-subscribers may have to wait longer for their work to appear than subscribers." **Sample: US $4; £1.50 UK. "Sample copies can only be purchased from the above address, and various mail-order distributors too numerous to mention. Advisable to buy a sample copy first. Banks charge the equivalent of $5 to cash foreign cheques in the U.K., so advisable to send bills, preferably by registered post."** Subscription: US $13, U.K. £6/4 issues. **No simultaneous submissions or previously published poems. Poets are requested to send in bios. Reads submissions all through the year. Publishes theme issues. Send SAE with IRC for upcoming themes. Replies to submissions normally under a month, with IRC/SAE. "Work without correct postage will not be responded to or returned until proper postage is sent." Pays 1 copy.** Reviews books of poetry. **Also publishes anthologies.** "*Peace and Freedom* now holds regular contests as does one of our other publications, **Eastern Rainbow**, which is a magazine concerning 20th century popular culture using poetry up to 32 lines. Subscription: U.S. $13, U.K. £6/4 issues. Further details of competitions and publications for SAE and IRC." The editor says, "Too many writers have lost the personal touch and editors generally appreciate this. It can make a difference when selecting work of equal merit."

PEARL; PEARL POETRY PRIZE (II), 3030 E. Second St., Long Beach CA 90803-5163, phone (562)434-4523 or (714)968-7530, founded 1974, poetry editors Joan Jobe Smith, Marilyn Johnson and Barbara Hauk, is a literary magazine appearing 3 times/year. **"We are interested in accessible, humanistic poetry that communicates and is related to real life. Humor and wit are welcome, along with the ironic and serious. No taboos stylistically or subject-wise. Prefer poems up to 35 lines, with lines no longer than 10 words. We don't want to see sentimental, obscure, predictable, abstract or cliché-ridden poetry. Our purpose is to provide a forum for lively, readable poetry, the direct, outspoken type, variously known as 'neo-pop' or 'stand-up,' that reflects a wide variety of contemporary voices, viewpoints and experiences—that speaks to *real* people about *real* life in direct, living language, profane or sublime."** They have recently published poetry by Edward Field, Suzanne Lummis, Gerald Locklin, Donna Hilbert, Fred Voss and Charles Webb. As a sample they selected these lines from "What the Grimm Girl Looks Forward To" by Hayley R. Mitchell:

> *If I am beautiful, they'll call me idle.*
> *If I am smart enough to see the wind come*
> *up the street, they'll say I am proud. If I am*
> *obstinate or inquisitive, they'll take me*
> *for a block of wood and throw me in the fire.*

> *I will waste my youth spinning straw into gold.*

Pearl is 96 pgs., digest-sized, perfect-bound, offset, with glossy cover. Press run is 700 for 100 subscribers of which 7 are libraries. Subscription: $15/year. **Sample postpaid: $6. Submit 3-5 poems at a time. "Handwritten submissions and unreadable printouts are not acceptable." No previously published poems; simultaneous submissions OK. "Cover letters appreciated." Reads submissions September through May only. Send SASE for guidelines. Reports in 6-8 weeks. Sometimes sends prepublication galleys. Pays 2 copies. Acquires first serial rights.** Each issue contains the work of 60-70 different poets and a special 10- to 15-page section that showcases the work of a single poet. "We sponsor the Pearl Poetry Prize, an annual chapbook contest, judged by one of our more well-known contributors. Winner receives publication, $500 and 50 copies. Entries accepted during the months of May and June. There is a $10 entry fee, which includes a copy of the winning chapbook." Send SASE for complete rules and guidelines. Recent books include *Monsters and Other Lovers* by Lisa Glatt, *The Wave He Caught* by Rick Noguchi, *How the Sky Fell* by Denise Duhamel, *Before Our Very Eyes* by Cherry Jean Vasconcellos and *Tattooed Woman* by Carolyn E. Campbell. The editors add, "Advice for beginning poets? Just write from your own experience, using images that are as concrete and sensory as possible. Keep these images fresh and objective, and always listen to the music. . . .'"

THE PEARL (I, II), English Dept., University of Massachusetts at Lowell, University Ave., Lowell MA 01854, founded 1989, is an annual publication designed "to enlighten the readers to other ideas and forms of thinking. **Poetry should be no longer than 50 lines. We accept various styles and forms, but please avoid abstractions. Writing must be well-written and proofed."** The editor says *The Pearl* is 150 pgs., perfect-bound with a limited number of art pgs. They receive about 150 poems a year, accept approximately 25%. Press run is 200. **Sample postpaid: $4. Make checks payable to University of Massachusetts. Submit 3 poems at a time—2 copies of each, 1 without name or identifying marks. Previously published poems and simultaneous submissions OK. Cover letter with bio preferred. Reads submissions September 1 through October 1 for November publication and December 1 through February 1 for March publication. Poems are circulated to an editorial board. Seldom comments on rejections. Send SASE for guidelines. Reports in 2-3 months. Pays 2 copies. Acquires first or one-time rights.** The editor says, "We publish thought-provoking literature which leaves the reader with a sensation of having gained wisdom. *The Pearl* is a student-run organization with changing editors and staffs so if you get rejected once, please submit again."

‡PECAN GROVE PRESS (II), Box AL 1 Camino Santa Maria, San Antonio TX 78228-8608, phone (210)436-3441, fax (210)436-3782, e-mail palmer@netxpress.com, founded 1988, editor H. Palmer Hall, is "interested in fine poetry collections that adhere. A collection should be like an art exhibit—the book is the art space, the pieces work together." They publish 4-6 paperbacks and **2-3 chapbooks/year. They want "poetry with something to say and that says it in fresh, original language. Will rarely publish books of more than 110 pages." They do not want "poetry that lets emotion run over control. We too often see sentiment take precedence over language."** They have recently published poetry by Vince Gotera, Edward Byrne and John Oughton. As a sample the editor selected these lines from Beth Simon's *Out of nowhere, the Body's Shape*:

> *I will not allow you to kneel in your driveway,*
> *Marlboro between your lips,*
> *while you mend your daughter's doll.*
> *These days even the tattooed manage*
> *to own a house, yard littered with bikes.*

Books or chapbooks are usually 50-96 pgs., offset, perfect-bound, one-color plus b&w graphic design or photographic cover on index stock. **Submit complete ms. Previously published poems and simultaneous submissions OK. Cover letter required, with some indication of a poet's publication history and some ideas or suggestions for marketing the book.** Time between acceptance and publication is 8-12 months. **"We do circulate for outside opinion when we know the poet who has submitted a manuscript. We read closely and make decisions as quickly as posisble." Seldom comments on rejections. "We do expect our poets to have a publication history in the little magazines with some acknowledgments." Replies to queries and mss in 1-3 months. After the book has paid for itself, authors receive 50% of subsequent sales and 10 author's copies (out of a press run of 500). "We have no subsidy arrangements, but if author has subvention funds, we do welcome them. Obtain sample books by checking BIP and making purchase. We will send chapbook at random for a fee of $5; book for $10."** The editor says, "We welcome submissions but feel too many inexperienced poets want to rush into book publication before they are quite ready. Many should try the little magazine route first instead of attempting to begin a new career with book publication."

‡*PEER POETRY MAGAZINE; PEER POETRY INTERNATIONAL COMPETITION (I)**, 26 (I) Arlington House, Bath St., Bath, Somerset BA1 1QN United Kingdom, (01225)445298, founded 1995, editor Paul Amphlett. *Peer Poetry Magazine*, published biannually, "is intended to provide poets who have not yet succeeded in 'making their name,' a platform in which they can publish enough of their poetry to allow a number of people in the field to see the quality of their work and at the same time gain an idea of the informed view of a number of poets with a wide range of views, currently practicing their talent." **They want "poetry with natural rhythm, fluent and flowing, having shape and plan; cherishing the sound and beauty of words and ideas. 'Noble sentiments are no substitute for technique and originality.' Highflown language does not make poetry fly high, prose in short lines remains prose; obtrusive rhymes, marching rhythms, produce doggerel!"** They have recently published poetry by Keith Morton, Honour Stedman, Visjna McMaster and Jim Norton. As a sample the editor selected these lines from "Safeguard" by Noel Spence:

> *Time, you're a sneak thief,*
> *stealing my days away*
> *from beneath my very eyes;*
> *and oh! the disbelief,*
> *the numb surprise,*
> *each time I find them gone*

Peer Poetry Magazine is 80 pgs., A4, photocopied, perfect-bound, with colored card cover. They receive about 750 poems a year, accept approximately 33%. Press run is 300 for 80 subscribers. Single copy: £5 plus p&h; subscription: £12 plus p&h. **Submit any number of poems. "We prefer a sufficient quantity of poems to fill either 1 or a maximum of 2 A4 pages within a double column set-up, using approximately 50-60 lines per single column in 10 or 12 pt. font in clear black type." Previously published poems and simultaneous submissions OK. Cover letter preferred.** Time between acceptance and publication is 3-6 months. **Poems are circulated to an editorial board. "Selection is based on originality, comprehensibility and quality of imagination." Often comments on rejections. Send SASE (or SAE and IRC) for guidelines.** Sponsors the Peer Poetry International Competition in each issue of the magazine. Readers vote on the winners; analyzed details of voting reactions and editorial comment given in succeeding issue. Awards prizes of £20, £60 and £30; all qualifying poems are published. Entry fee: £2.50/page. Send 2 copies with SASE (or SAE and IRC). Include name, address, phone and list of titles on the back of each page.

PEGASUS (II), 525 Ave. B, Boulder City NV 89005, founded 1986, editor M.E. Hildebrand, is a poetry quarterly "for serious poets who have something to say and know how to say it using sensory imagery." **Submit 3-5 poems, 3-40 lines. Avoid "religious, political, pornographic themes."** They have recently published poetry by John Grey, Stan Moseley, Nikolas Macioci and Robert K. Johnson. As a sample the editor selected these lines from "A Night of Moon and Stars" by Elizabeth Perry:

> *It is past the hour of long shadows*
> *with time for earth cooling*
> *when the illusion of desert silence shatters.*
>
> *A night of moon and stars.*
> *Silver night pours sky light*
> *over the desert floor as if shedding grace.*

Pegasus is 32 pgs., digest-sized, saddle-stapled, offset from typescript with colored paper cover. Publishes 10-15% of the work received. Circulation is 200. Subscription: $15. **Sample postpaid: $5. Previously published poems OK, provided poet retains rights; no simultaneous submissions. Send SASE for guidelines. Reports in 2 weeks. Publication is payment. Acquires first or one-time rights.**

THE PEGASUS REVIEW (I, II, IV-Themes), P.O. Box 88, Henderson MD 21640-0088, phone (410)482-6736, founded 1980, is a 14-page (counting cover) pamphlet entirely in calligraphy, illustrated on high-quality paper, some color overlays. Editor Art Bounds says, "This magazine is a bimonthly, **based on specific themes. Write to request list of upcoming themes. Because of the calligraphic format, open to all styles, but brevity**

is the key. Uses poetry not more than 24 lines (the shorter the better); fiction that is short short (about 2½ pages would be ideal); essays and cartoons. All material must pertain to indicated themes only. All poetic forms acceptable." They have recently published poetry by Robert H. Deluty, Taylor Reese, Mary Winters, Terry Thomas and Esther Clair Palmenteri. As a sample the editor selected these lines from "RFK" by Barry George:

> *But then when winds blow free again*
> *and jostling dogwoods line the way—*
> *I can't help thinking Bobby died*
> *one fine spring day*

Press run is 160 for 150 subscribers, of which 4 are libraries. Subscription: $10. **Sample: $2.50. Submit 3-5 poems with name and address on each page. "Previously published poems OK, if there is no conflict or violation of rights agreement. Simultaneous submissions OK, but author must notify proper parties once specific material is accepted. Brief cover letter with specifics as they relate to one's writing background welcome."** Query if additional information is needed. Publishes theme issues. Themes for September/October 1997, November/December 1997, January/February 1998, March/April 1998, May/June 1998, July/August 1998 are Books, Holidays, Courage, Nature, Family, America, respectively. **Reports within a month, often with a personal response. Pays 2 copies.** Offers occasional book awards throughout the year. The editor says, "Let guidelines be your guide and adhere to them. Time and postage is money and shouldn't be wasted. Try to support as many small presses as possible. Make your local library aware of them. Also, check out writers organizations in your area and get involved. Keep abreast of certain market needs by means of support and publications such as *Poet's Market*, *Writer's Digest* and numerous others. Above all, persevere."

THE PEKING DUCK; @EVOLUTE.ORG (II), P.O. Box 331661, Corpus Christi TX 78463-1661, e-mail duck@evolute.org, website http://www.evolute.org, founded 1993, editor Edward Cossette. *The Peking Duck*, an electronic magazine, is "a mendicant publication with the aim of promoting experimental or other 'offbeat' forms of writing." **They have no specific guidelines regarding form, length, subject matter or style of poetry—"good work is good work."** They have published poetry by B.Z. Niditch, Lyn Lifshin, Arlene Mandrell and Errol Miller. As a sample we selected these lines from "Creamsicle Lover" by Arlene Mandell:

> *Standing in front*
> *of the frozen food case*
> *I see Creamsicles*
> *and remember*
> *the way you'd suck*
> *the breath out of my body*
> *with your wet kisses*

The Peking Duck is currently in a state of "flux" and will only appear in its "physical" format once a year. Any additional issues will exist in an electronic, computer-based version. In its "physical" format, *The Peking Duck* is 12 pgs., 8½×11, offset printed in 2 colors on 70 lb. glossy paper, saddle-stapled, drawings and graphics throughout. They receive 200-300 poems a year, accept approximately 5%. **Sample postpaid: $5. "We are particularly interested in work that takes advantage of the electronic medium. Submit up to three poems at a time. Poets are encouraged to submit work in html format (send to cossette@evolute.org) and to make hypertext links, graphics and sound files a part of the work."** Publishes theme issues. Send SASE for guidelines and upcoming themes or request via e-mail. @evolute.org publishes **electronic poetry chapbooks.** Visit their website for more information. The editor says, "Read an issue first! Much perfectly 'good' work gets passed over because it doesn't mesh with our outlook/style. Published poets are relentless: submitting often, writing always."

PELICAN PUBLISHING COMPANY (V, IV-Children, regional), Box 3110, Gretna LA 70054-3110, founded 1926, editor-in-chief Nina Kooij, is a "moderate-sized publisher of cookbooks, travel guides, regional books and inspirational/motivational books," which accepts **poetry for "hardcover children's books *only*, preferably with a regional focus. However, our needs for this are very limited; we do five juvenile titles per year, and most of these are prose, not poetry."** They have published *Christmas All Over*, by Robert Bernardini. As a sample the editor selected these lines from *Welcome to Bayou Town!* by Chérie D. Schadler:

> *Here on the bayou, the buildings stand on piers:*
> *businesses, church, and schoolhouse . . . all here.*
> *But today we're on an errand to fill my mama's sack,*

MARKET CONDITIONS are constantly changing! If you're still using this book and it is 1999 or later, buy the newest edition of *Poet's Market* at your favorite bookstore or order directly from Writer's Digest Books.

so we'll tie up right here at Mr. Boudreaux's Seafood Shack.
They are currently not accepting unsolicited mss. Query first with 2 sample poems and cover letter including "work and writing backgrounds, plot summary and promotional connections." No previously published poems or simultaneous submissions. Reports on queries in 1 month, on mss (if invited) in 3 months. Always sends prepublication galleys. Pays royalties. Buys all rights. Returns rights upon termination of contract. These are 32-page, large-format (magazine-sized) books with illustrations. Two of their popular series are prose books about Gaston the Green-Nosed Alligator by James Rice and Clovis Crawfish by Mary Alice Fontenot. They have a variety of books based on "The Night Before Christmas" adapted to regional settings such as Cajun, prairie, and Texas. Typically their books sell for $14.95. **Write for catalog to buy samples.** The editor says, "We try to avoid rhyme altogether, especially predictable rhyme. Monotonous rhythm can also be a problem."

PEMBROKE MAGAZINE (II), UNCP, Box 1510, Pembroke NC 28372-1510, phone (910)521-6358, fax (910)521-6552, founded 1969 by Norman Macleod, edited by Shelby Stephenson, managing editor Frax Oxendine, is a heavy (252 pgs., 6×9), flat-spined, quality literary annual which has published poetry by Fred Chappell, Stephen Sandy, A.R. Ammons, Barbara Guest and Betty Adcock. Press run is 500 for 125 subscribers of which 100 are libraries. **Sample postpaid: $5. Sometimes comments on rejections. Reports within 3 months. Pays copies.** Stephenson advises, "Publication will come if you write. Writing is all."

‡PEMMICAN (II); PEMMICAN PRESS (V), P.O. Box 121, Redmond WA 98073-0121, phone (206)889-0821, founded 1992, editor Robert Edwards, is an annual magazine designed to publish "the best poetry of imagery, imagination and political commitment we can find." **They want "political poetry and poetry of imagery and imagination. No workshop minimalist, right wing or fundamentalist poetry; no greeting card verse. Poets familiar with the work of Thomas McGrath, Meridel LeSeuer and Don Gordon should have no problem understanding what it is we're looking for."** They have published poetry by Adrian C. Louis, Margaret Randall and Patrick Stanhope. *Pemmican* is 60 pgs., $7 \times 8\frac{1}{2}$, saddle-stitched, card stock cover with original art. They receive 1,000-1,200 submissions a year, use less than 10%. Press run is 300 for 100 subscribers of which 17 are libraries, 100 shelf sales. Single copy: $5. **Sample postpaid: $3.50. Submit 6 poems at a time. No previously published poems; simultaneous submissions OK,** "but *Pemmican* expects to be notified if a poem has been accepted elsewhere." **Cover letter required. "Make sure postage on SASE is adequate for full return of submitted materials." Seldom comments on rejections. Send SASE for guidelines. Reports in 1 week to 6 months. Pays 1 copy. Acquires first North American serial rights.** The editor says, "There are no requirements—however, I hope poets realize the importance of small presses and put their money where their mouth is. Advice for beginners? Keep writing. Read everything. Don't write to please an editor or to get published. Follow your own voice."

‡*PEN & KEYBOARD MAGAZINE; THE NEWSLETTER (I, II), 526 Fulham Palace Rd., Fulham, London SW6 6JE United Kingdom, phone 0171-736, founded 1992, contact the editor. *Pen & Keyboard Magazine*, published quarterly, strives "to reflect people's interests, experiences and aspirations." **They want "clear, understandable poetry that has been written to be read."** They have recently published poetry by Kevin McGrath, Sophie Hannah and Yvonne Walus. *P&KM* is 52 pgs., digest-sized, offset, saddle-stapled, with CS1 cover stock. They receive about 100 poems a year, accept approximately 25%. Press run is 100 for 20 subscribers. Subscription: £30. **Sample postpaid: £5. Submit 6 poems at a time. Previously published poems and simultaneous submissions OK. Cover letter required.** Time between acceptance and publication is 3 months. **Always comments on rejections. Send SASE (or SAE and IRC) for guidelines. Pay is "limited." Buys one-time rights.** Reviews books or chapbooks of poetry or other magazines. Open to unsolicited reviews. Poets may also send books for review consideration. Also publishes *The Newsletter*, a monthly 6-page publication providing information about the craft of writing, UK poetry markets and agents. The editor advises, "If writers want to write good poetry then they should get immersed in good poetry. And experience the great tradition of English/American literature."

‡THE PENINSULA REVIEW (II), P.O. Box 436, Winter Harbor ME 04693, phone (207)667-0533, e-mail darthia@acadia.net, founded 1996, poetry editors Carrie Barnard and David Fickett, published biannually, is "a literary journal created by writers to sponsor and showcase other writers." **They want "anything good. No restrictions as to form, length, subject matter or style. We like poems that are original, alive and true."** They have recently published poetry by Robert Chute and Patricia Ranzoni. The editor says *TPR* is 66 pgs., $4\frac{1}{4} \times 5\frac{1}{2}$ and professionally printed. They receive about 250 poems a year, accept approximately 10%. Press run is 300 of which 10 are for libraries, 275 shelf sales. Single copy: $4; subscription: $5. **Sample postpaid: $5. Submit 4 poems at a time. Previously published poems and simultaneous submissions OK. Cover letter preferred.** Time between acceptance and publication is 3-6 months. **Poems are circulated to an editorial board. Often comments on rejections. Send SASE for guidelines. Reports in 3-6 months. Pays 2 copies. Acquires first or one-time rights.** Reviews books or chapbooks of poetry or other magazines. Open to unsolicited reviews. Poets may also send books for review consideration.

*PENNINE INK (I, II), % Mid Pennine Arts, MP The Gallery, Yorke St., Burnley BB11 3JJ Great Britain, founded 1985, appears annually using poems, short prose items and b&w illustrations. They want **"poetry up**

to 40 lines maximum. Consider all kinds." As a sample the editor selected these lines from "Workdays (For Jo)" by Martyn Lowery:

> *Work feels like a hired skin*
> *And each day still*
> *Elopement to a loveless world*
> *Of paper, jumbles, clocks.*
> *Driving in, past fields*
> *Sharpened by your absence*
> *The day tightens*
> *In funereal tie and gloves*

The editor says it is 48 pgs., A5, with b&w illustrated cover, small local ads and 3 or 4 b&w graphics. They receive about 400 poems a year, use approximately 40. Press run is 350. **Submit up to 6 poems at a time. Previously published poems and simultaneous submissions OK. Cover letter preferred. Seldom comments on rejections. Reports in 3 months.** Reviews small press poetry books in about 200 words. The editor adds, "Prose, poetry and illustrations should be accompanied by a suitable stamped, addressed envelope (SASE or SAE with IRCs) for return of work. Contributors wishing to purchase a copy of *Pennine Ink* should enclose £2 ($5 US) per copy plus postage and packing."

*PENNINE PLATFORM (II), 7 Cockley Hill Lane, Kirkheaton, Huddersfield HD5 OHW England, phone (0)1484-516804, founded 1973, poetry editor K.E. Smith, appears 2 times a year. The editor wants **any kind of poetry but concrete ("lack of facilities for reproduction"). No specifications of length, but poems of less than 40 lines have a better chance. "All styles—effort is to find things good of their kind. Preference for religious or sociopolitical awareness of an acute, not conventional kind."** They have published poetry by Elizabeth Bartlett, Anna Adams, John Ward, Ian Caws, John Latham and Geoffrey Holloway. As a sample the editor selected these lines from "A Vision of Cabez De Vaca" by Cal Clothier:

> *Blanched to a skin manned by bones,*
> *we have blood and our breathing*
> *to prove we are men, and the hungry light*
> *jerking our eyes. We are down to mercy,*
> *gratitude, love, down to humanity.*

The 6×8, 48-page journal is photocopied from typescript, saddle-stapled, with matte card cover with graphics, circulation 400, 300 subscriptions of which 16 are libraries. They receive about 300 submissions/year, use about 60, have about a 6-month backlog. Subscription: £8.50 for 2 issues (£12 abroad; £25 if not in sterling). **Sample postpaid: £2. Submit up to 6 poems, typed. Reports in about a month. No pay. Acquires first serial rights. Editor occasionally comments on rejections.** Reviews books of poetry in 500 words, multi-book format. Open to unsolicited reviews. Poets may also send books for review consideration.

PENNSYLVANIA ENGLISH (II), Bloomsburg University, Bloomsburg PA 17815, phone (814)824-2000, founded 1988 (first issue in March, 1989), poetry editor Su Dean, is "a journal sponsored by the Pennsylvania College English Association." They want poetry of **"any length, any style."** The journal is magazine-sized, saddle-stapled, and appears twice a year. Press run is 300. Subscription: $15, which includes membership in PCEA. **Submit 4-5 typed poems at a time. Do not submit mss in the summer. They consider simultaneous submissions but not previously published poems. Reports in 1 month. Pays 2 copies.**

PENNY DREADFUL PRESS; THE PENNY DREADFUL REVIEW (II, IV-Erotica, form/style), 4210 Park Ave., Nashville TN 37209-3650, phone (615)297-1056, e-mail cramcguirt@aol.com, founded November 1993, "maximum domineditrix" Ms. Penelope Dreadful, assistant subeditrix Ms. Shelley Stoker, assistant editor and factotum C Ra McGuirt. *The Penny Dreadful Review* is a quarterly publication of eclectic tastes. "Our motto: Where Poe Meets Bukowski. We accept poetry, short prose, cartoons and b&w photographs. Penny likes **very personal, dark, funny, erotic and/or experimental material; concrete character-driven work preferred."** They have recently published poetry by D. Phillip Caron, James Holder and Jon Taylor. As a sample the editors selected these lines from "Open Mic Night In Music City" by Dan Powers:

> *this is all in the name of something we can't name*
> *some take too long to never say it*
> *others are mercifully brief . . .*

The Penny Dreadful Review is 48 pgs., 5½×8½, photocopied and center-stapled. Press run is 500. Subscription: $10. **Sample copy: $3. Previously published poems and simultaneous submissions OK. Cover letter preferred. "Tell us a little about yourself; communication is its own reward. We will consider any amount of material, but please include sufficient postage for its return if desired and at the least a SASE for our editorial response. We also accept submissions by e-mail as well as information requests."** Time between acceptance and publication is no more than 1 year. **Often comments on rejections. Replies in 1 month. Pays at least 1 copy. All rights remain with poets.** Penny's Dreadful Catalogue, which includes guidelines as well as a complete listing of all chapbooks and back issues of *PDR*, is available for 2 first-class stamps on a SASE.

‡**PENNY DREADFUL: TALES & POEMS OF FANTASTIC TERROR (I, IV-Horror)**, 407 W. 50th St. #16, Hell's Kitchen NY 10019, founded 1996, editor and publisher M. Malefica Grendelwolf Pendragon Le Fay, published 3 times/year, features "fiction and poetry of the horror genre: dark, bloody, disturbing, literary." **They want "any form of poetry, but partial to traditional, rhymed, metered, verse. Would like to see (initiate?) a revival of the Romantic school of poetry. We are, admittedly, not a follower of modern verse. Still, we are often pleasantly surprised by the inclusion of poetic/lyrical elements in many of the submissions we receive, and do not turn down any school of poetry offhand."** *Penny Dreadful* is 28 pgs., 5½×8½, desktop-published, photocopied, saddle-stapled with b&w line art and ads (guidelines) from other magazines. Press run is 500 of which 75 are for libraries; all distributed free to bookstores, organizations and journals. **Sample: 5½×8½ (or larger) SASE with 3 stamps. Submit up to 5 poems with name and address on each. Previously published poems and simultaneous submissions OK. Cover letter preferred.** Time between acceptance and publication is 3 months. **Poems reviewed and chosen by editor. Often comments on rejections. Reports in up to 3 months. Always sends prepublication galleys. Pays 1-3 copies. Acquires one-time rights.**

PENNYWHISTLE PRESS (II), P.O. Box 734, Tesuque NM 87574, phone/fax (505)982-0066, e-mail pnywhistle@aol.com, founded 1986, publisher Victor di Suvero, "was started as a way to present the work of notable poets to the reading public. Known for its Poetry Chapbook Series, which currently features 18 titles by some of the strongest voices of our time: Francisco X. Alarcón, Dennis Brutus, Joyce Jenkins, Jerome Rothenberg, Suzanne Lummis, Judyth Hill and Sarah Blake, the Press has branched out into the anthology market with the publication of *Saludos! Poemas de Nuevo Mexico*, a bilingual collection of 66 poets presenting their diverse views of this unusual tricultural state, which is also a state of being. Poets in this collection run the spectrum from N. Scott Momaday, Luci Tapahonso and Carolyn Forché to Janet Holmes, Reneé Gregorio and Keith Wilson." The press also has a series entitled Sextet, "an anthology of poetry comprised of six chapbooks by new and established voices." They publish 2 paperbacks and 6 chapbooks a year. **They want poetry with "deep, rich imagery; confessional, solid, strong and experimental—generally one page in length." No rhyme.** As a sample the editor selected these lines from "A Love Song from the Chimayó Landfill" by Janet Holmes from the anthology, *Saludos! Poemas de Nuevo Mexico*:

> . . . I had merely
> two bags of garbage to heave into the heap,
> a minor offering beside that of the men
> emptying their truckbeds with shovels. They
> were happy, too; yes, everyone was laughing,
> as if it were Fiesta, not the dump. I wanted to tell you:
> this *is how you make me feel, my darling.*

Chapbooks are usually 32 pgs., 5¼×8⅜, perfect-bound; anthologies are about 200 pgs., 6×9, perfect-bound. **Submit 10 poems at a time. Previously published poems and simultaneous submissions OK. Cover letter preferred. Poems are circulated to an editorial board. "Reviewed by four members of editorial board and then submitted to managing editor and publisher for approval." Always comments on rejections. Replies to queries in 2-4 months, to mss in 1 month. Pays $100 honorarium and 25 author's copies (out of a press run of 1,500). Write to obtain samples of books or chapbooks.**

‡**THE PENWOOD REVIEW (II, IV-Religious)**, P.O. Box 862, Los Alamitos CA 90720-0862, founded 1997, editor Lori M. Cameron, published biannually, "was established to promote excellence in the writing of poetry among students, educators and writers in the Christian community." **They want "serious, disciplined, high-quality, well-crafted poetry on any subject. Prefer poems be less than two pages. Rhyming poetry must be written in traditional forms (sonnets, tercets, villanelles, sestinas, etc.)"** They do not want "light verse, doggerel or greeting card-style poetry. Also, nothing racist, sexist, pornographic or blasphemous." They have recently published poetry by Deborah Oesch, Heather Sellers, Carl Winderl and Priscilla Atkins. As a sample the editor selected these lines from "Afloat at Midnight" by Christopher Salaun:

> This one paddle moves too slowly
> for where I want to go. Even
> in this darkness, where processions
> of trees and muskrats march invisibly by,
> I am reaching for the scent of a wild ache,
> the groan of all blood and root . . .

The editor says *The Penwood Review* has a varying number of pages, 8½×11, saddle-stapled with heavy card cover. Press run is 50-100. **Submit 2-3 poems, 1 per page with the author's full name, address and phone number in the upper right hand corner. No previously published poems or simultaneous submissions. Cover letter preferred.** Time between acceptance and publication is 6-12 months. **"Submissions are circulated among an editorial staff for evaluations." Seldom comments on rejections. Reports in 1-2 months. Pays 1 copy and a discounted subscription. Acquires one-time rights.**

PEOPLENET DISABILITY DATENET (I, IV-Specialized: disabled people, love/romance), P.O. Box 897, Levittown NY 11756-0911, phone (516)579-4043, e-mail mauro@chelsea.ios.com, website: http://chelsea.ios.com/~mauro, founded 1987, editor/publisher Robert Mauro, is a home page (formerly published as a newsletter)

for disabled people focusing on dating, love and relationships. The editor wants **"poetry on relationships, love and romance only. The length should remain ten lines or less. We publish beginners, new poets. Prefer free verse, a lot of good imagery—and very little rhyme."** As a sample the editor selected these lines from his poem "The Geometry of Love":

> *My love she moves in perfect circles*
> *and me isosceles or all right angles.*
> *When we did tend our fertile garden*
> *to Tantalus we never begged his pardon.*
> *The Greeks would be so proud of us:*
> *she a peristyle; me an obelisk.*

PeopleNet DisAbility DateNet appears only on the World Wide Web at the above website. **Submit 3 poems at a time via e-mail only. Poems should be neatly typed with name and e-mail address. No simultaneous submissions. Editor comments on good but rejected mss. Publishes theme issues. Send SASE for upcoming themes. Reports "immediately." Acquires first rights.** He says, "We want to publish poems that express the importance of love, acceptance, inner beauty, the need for love and relationship, and the joy of loving and being loved."

PEP PUBLISHING; LOVING MORE (I, IV-Specialized: "ethical multiple relationships"), P.O. Box 4358, Boulder CO 80306, phone/fax (303)543-7540, e-mail ryampep@aol.com, website http://www.lovemore.c om, founded 1984, editor Ryam Nearing. *Loving More* is a quarterly that "publishes articles, letters, poems, drawings and reviews related to **polyfidelity, group marriage and multiple** *intimacy*.**" They use "relatively short poems, though a quality piece of length would be considered, but topic relevance is essential. Please no swinger or porno pieces. Group marriage should not be equated with group sex."** It is 40 pgs., magazine-sized, few ads. Circulation is 2,500. Subscription: $49/year. **Sample: $6 to poets. Submit up to 10 poems at a time. Ms should be "readable." Considers simultaneous submissions.** Time between acceptance and publication is 2-6 months. **Editor comments on rejections "sometimes—if requested." Publishes theme issues. Send SASE for upcoming themes. Guidelines available via e-mail at writers@lovemore.com. Responds "ASAP." Pays 1 copy.** Open to unsolicited reviews. Poets may also send books for review consideration. The editor says, "We're always looking for good poetry related specifically to our topic. Our readers love it when we find some to include. Writers should read our publication before submitting, and I emphasize no swinger or porno pieces will be published."

PEQUOD: A JOURNAL OF CONTEMPORARY LITERATURE AND LITERARY CRITICISM (III), Dept. of English, New York University, 19 University Place, Room 200, New York NY 10003, phone (212)998-8843, fax (212)995-4019, contact poetry editor, is a semiannual literary review publishing **quality poetry, fiction, essays and translations.** They have published poetry by Sam Hamill, Donald Hall and John Updike. It is 200 pgs., digest-sized, professionally printed, flat-spined with glossy card cover. Subscription: $12. **Sample postpaid: $5. Reads submissions September 15 through April 15 only. Always sends prepublication galleys.** Poetry published in *Pequod* has also been included in the 1993 and 1995 volumes of *The Best American Poetry*.

*PERCEPTIONS: WOMEN'S POETRY FOR A CHANGE (IV-Women), 73 Eastcombe Ave., London SE7 7LL England, founded 1982, poetry editor Temi Rose, is a "small prize-winning **women's poetry magazine for the promotion and development of women's consciousness of peace and hope and freedom to be."** They have published poetry by Chocolate Waters, Lyn Lifshin and Edna Kovacs. As a sample the editor selected these lines by Mary Winters:

> *You know who's a pain in the neck?*
> *the dead*
> *just when you think you've got them*
> *stuffed in a box*
> *they're reading over your shoulder*

Perceptions is 30 pgs., digest-sized, photocopied from typescript and saddle-stitched with paper cover and comes out 3 times/year. They receive about 3,000 poems a year, accept approximately 360. Press run is 300 for 50 subscribers of which 3 are libraries. Subscription: $15 (£10.50). **Sample postpaid: $5 (£3.50). Simultaneous submissions and previously published poems OK. Guidelines available for SASE (or SAE and IRC). Reports in 1-3 months. Pays 1 copy.**

PEREGRINE: THE JOURNAL OF AMHERST WRITERS & ARTISTS (II); AWA CHAPBOOK SERIES (V); THE PEREGRINE PRIZE (II), P.O. Box 1076, Amherst MA 01004-1076, phone (413)253-3307, fax (413)253-7764, *Peregrine* founded 1984, Amherst Writers & Artists Press, Inc., 1987, editor Pat Schneider, poetry editors Anne Brudevold and Mary Beth O'Shea Noonan. *Peregrine*, published annually, features poetry, fiction, poems in translation and reviews. **Open to all styles, forms and subjects except greeting card verse. "Seldom publish poems longer than 70 lines."** They have recently published poetry by Sue Walker and Martin Espada. As a sample the editors selected these lines from "Rain" by Janet Aalfs:

> *Signs of forgetting are everywhere:*
> *names wear off stone,*

stone crumbles. Inside my skin

a stillness I don't know how to touch.
Peregrine is 104 pgs., digest-sized, professionally printed, perfect-bound with matte card cover. Each issue includes at least one poem in translation and several reviews. Press run is 1,000. Single copy: $6. **Sample postpaid: $4. Submit 3-5 poems at a time. Accepts simultaneous submissions. Cover letter is preferred. "We may hold poems for several months, so we encourage simultaneous submissions. Each ms is read by several readers. Final decisions are made by the poetry editors, who read all submissions." Sometimes comments on rejections. Send SASE for guidelines. Pays 2 copies. Acquires first rights.** Reviews books of poetry in 200-500 words. Open to unsolicited reviews. Poets may also send books for review consideration. Sponsors The Peregrine Prize, an annual fiction and poetry contest. First prize is publication in *Peregrine*, copies and $500. Reading fee is $10 per entry. Submit 3-5 poems under 70 lines. Write for guidelines.

PERIVALE PRESS; PERIVALE POETRY CHAPBOOKS; PERIVALE TRANSLATION SERIES (II, IV-Translations, anthology), 13830 Erwin St., Van Nuys CA 91401-2914, phone (818)785-4671, fax (818)904-0512, founded 1968, editor Lawrence P. Spingarn, publishes **Perivale Poetry Chapbooks, Perivale Translation Series**, anthologies. The collections by individuals are usually translations. They publish an average of one 20-page saddle-stapled chapbook, one perfect-bound (20-70 pgs.) collection, one anthology per year, all quality print jobs. Send SASE for catalog. Perivale publishes both on **straight royalty basis (10%, 10 author's copies) usually grant supported, and by subsidy, the author paying 100%, being repaid from profits, if any. "Payment for chapbooks accepted is 60-100 free copies of press run.** Authors should agree to promote books via readings, talk shows, orders and signings with local bookshops. **Contributors are encouraged to buy samples of chapbooks, etc., for clues to editor's tastes." Samples of previous poetry chapbooks: $5.75 postpaid.** They have recently published *Creating the Universe and Other Poems* by George Young. **To submit, query first, with sample of 5 poems, cover letter, bio, previous books. Do not submit mss from June 15 to September 1. Reports in 6 weeks. Always sends prepublication galleys.** Spingarn, a well-known, widely published poet, offers criticism for a fee, the amount dependent on length of book. Sponsors a poetry chapbook contest. Winner receives $100 plus 60 copies of chapbook. Reading fee: $12. Send SASE for details. The editor advises, "Contributors should read samples and guidelines thoroughly before submitting. Also, we would like to see poems with less self-involvement (fewer poems that open with 'I') and a wider world view."

PERMAFROST: A LITERARY JOURNAL (II, IV-Regional), % English Dept., P.O. Box 755720, University of Alaska Fairbanks, Fairbanks AK 99775, e-mail fbprfst@aurora.alaska.edu, founded 1977, contact poetry editor, is an annual publication. *Permafrost* publishes poems, short stories, creative nonfiction and b&w drawings, photographs and prints. "We survive on both new and established writers, and hope and expect to see your best work. **We publish any style of poetry provided it is conceived, written and revised with care. While we encourage submissions about Alaska and by Alaskans, we also encourage and welcome poems about anywhere and from anywhere.** We have published work by Wendy Bishop, John Haines, Naomi Shihab Nye, Peggy Shumaker, Leslie Fields, John Morgan and Patricia Monaghan." The journal is about 150 pgs., 4×6, professionally printed, flat-spined, with b&w graphics and photos. Subscription: $7. **Sample postpaid: $5. Submit 3-6 poems, typed, single or double-spaced, and formatted as they should appear. Considers simultaneous submissions. Deadline: March 15. Does not accept submissions between March 15 and September 1. Editors comment only on mss that have made the final round. Send SASE for further guidelines or request via e-mail. Reports in 3 months. Pays 1 copy; reduced contributor rate on additional copies.** *Permafrost* also sponsors the Midnight Sun Poetry Chapbook Contest, an annual fiction contest, and a nonfiction contest. Send SASE for guidelines. Contest entry fees: $10, includes a subscription to the journal. Deadline: March 15.

‡PERSPECTIVES (II, IV-Religious), P.O. Box 470, Ada MI 49301-0470, co-editors Thomas A. Boogart and Evelyn Diephouse, poetry editor Francis Fike (send poetry submissions to Francis Fike at Dept. of English, Hope College, Holland MI 49422-9000), founded 1986, appears 10 times/year. The journal's purpose is "to express the Reformed faith theologically; to engage issues that Reformed Christians meet in personal, ecclesiastical, and societal life, and thus to contribute to the mission of the church of Jesus Christ." **They want "both traditional and free verse of high quality, whether explicitly 'religious' or not. Prefer traditional form. Publish one or two poems every other issue, alternating with a Poetry Page on great traditional poems from the past. No sentimental, trite, or inspirational verse, please."** They have recently published poetry by Arnold Kenseth, Paul Willis and Paul Zimmer. As a sample the editor selected these lines from "Entering the Kingdom" by Julia Guernsey:

> *So she found Dakota Street, a heap*
> *of trash out back, containers grimed with food,*
> *the third floor balcony on which she stood,*
> *remembering Wordsworth's ode to the shrill beep*
> *of a forklift, which came to strip the mound*
> *and struck a nest of rats. Their whiplike tails*
> *slithered, their bodies scratching separate trails*
> *like dice, a chaos over icy ground.*

Perspectives is 24 pgs., 8½×11, web offset and saddle-stapled, with paper cover containing b&w illustration. They receive about 50 poems a year, accept 6-10. Press run is 3,300 for 3,000 subscribers of which 200 are libraries. Subscription: $19.95. **Sample postpaid: $3.50. No previously published poems or simultaneous submissions. Cover letter preferred.** Time between acceptance and publication is 6 months or less. **Seldom comments on rejections. Reports in 1-3 months. Pays 5 copies. Acquires first rights.**

*PETERLOO POETS (II), 2 Kelly Gardens, Calstock, Cornwall PL18 9SA Great Britain, founded 1977, poetry editor Harry Chambers. They publish collections of "well-made" poetry (rhyming and free verse) under the Peterloo Poets imprint: flat-spined paperbacks, hardbacks and poetry cassettes. They have published *Undark* by John Glenday and *Safe as Houses* by U.A. Fanthorpe (both Poetry Book Society Recommendations). **Query with 10 sample poems, bio and list of publications. Simultaneous submissions and previously published poems OK if they have not been in book form. Always sends prepublication galleys. Pays 10% royalties, $100 advance (for first volume, $200 for subsequent volumes) and 12 copies. Editor "normally, briefly" comments on rejections.** Sponsors an annual open poetry competition. First prize: £4,000 sterling; second prize: £1,000 sterling; four other prizes totaling £1,100 sterling. Entries must be previously unpublished. Deadline: March 1. Send IRC for entry form and rules.

‡PHATI'TUDE; CHIMEARA COMMUNICATIONS, INC. (II), P.O. Box 214, Palisades Park NJ 07650, phone (201)814-1812, fax (201)814-1808, founded 1996, editor G. David, published quarterly, is a "literary publication of poetry, fiction and essays by both emerging and established writers of diverse origins whose works exhibit social, political and cultural awareness." **They want "high quality with emphasis on language and verse. Especially interested in, thought not exclusively devoted to, Native American and African, Hispanic/ Latino, American Indian and Asian descent and their viewpoints. No specifications on form, length or style. Humor is welcome. Translations accepted." They do not want hate poetry, excessive cursing, religious or greeting card stuff.** They have recently published poetry by Lucille Clifton, Linda Ashear, Joseph Bruchac, Leroy Quintana, Louis Reyes Rivera and Eileen Tabios. The editor says *Phati'tude* is 120 pgs., 8½×11, "professionally" desktop published. Press run is 1,000-2,000 for 1,500 subscribers. Single copy: $7; subscription: $25. **Sample postpaid: $5. Submit up to 3 poems with name, address and phone on each page. Previously published poems OK "if so noted"; no simultaneous submissions. Cover letter required, include bio, philosophy and/or poetic principles. Accepts 3.5 disk submissions (IBM-PC compatible) in ASCII or current word processing format.** Time between acceptance and publication is 1 month. **Poems are circulated to an editorial board. Always comments on rejections. Publishes theme issues. Send SASE for list of upcoming themes. "Guidelines not necessary, just send your work." Reports in 1 month. Pays 2 copies.** Reviews books or chapbooks of poetry or other magazines. Open to unsolicited reviews. Poets may also send books for review consideration.

PHILOMEL; PHILOMATHEAN SOCIETY (II), Box 7, College Hall, University of Pennsylvania, Philadelphia PA 19104-6303, phone (215)898-8907, founded in 1813, editor Mr. E.C. Morales. *Philomel* is a literary annual using **"inventive poetry, no more than 300 words or 3 pgs. per poem."** They also use stories, essays and "witty recipes." As a sample they selected these lines from "Tender is the Night" by David Perry Jones:

> *Sweep, sweep; the agony settles shoulder-dust deep in the stillness*
> *Of still bolder enmity:*
> *Red-thundered eyes scream shrill shelter in the pelting.*
> *Weep, weep; unsated escalation*
> *Clears the wiry field; the carpet rims and folds; two minarets afire*
> *Seethe; black-stones scathe, defile the evening sky . . .*

Philomel comes out each spring. It is 80 pgs., 6×9, flat-spined, with glossy card cover. Poems are selected by a committee of the Philomathean Society. Press run is 1,500 for 20 subscribers of which 3 are libraries; 1,400 distributed free to the university community. **Sample postpaid: $5. Submit up to 3 poems at a time. Deadline for submissions: February 1, annually. Pays 1 or more copies.**

PHILOMEL BOOKS (III), 200 Madison Ave., New York NY 10016, phone (212)951-8700, an imprint founded in 1980, editorial director Patricia Gauch. Philomel Books publishes 15-20 hardbacks and **5-7 chapbooks/year.** They say, "Since we're a children's book imprint, **we are open to individual poem submissions—anything suitable for a picture book. However, publication of poetry collections is usually done on a project basis— we acquire from outside through permissions, etc. Don't usually use unpublished material."** They have published poetry by Edna St. Vincent Millay and Walt Whitman. **Query first with 3 sample poems and cover**

 THE DOUBLE DAGGER before a listing indicates that the listing is new in this edition. New markets are often the most receptive to submissions.

letter including publishing history. **Previously published poems and simultaneous submissions OK. Replies to queries in 1 month, to mss in 2. Pay is negotiable.**

PHOEBE (II), George Mason University, 4400 University Dr., Fairfax VA 22030, phone (703)993-2915, website http://www.gmu.edu/pubs/phoebe, founded 1970, poetry editor Christopher Jackson, is a literary biannual **"looking for imagery that will make your thumbs sweat when you touch it."** They have published poetry by C.K. Williams, Mark Doty, Cornelius Eady, Michael Palmer, Leslie Scalapino and Gillian Conoley. As a sample the editor selected these lines from "Semantics of Longing" by Leslie Bumstead:

> *Was he superb in speech*
> *class? Even at parties with women dangling*
> *hunger on their brilliant clavicles, he must*
> *forever look for the just and longest*
> *word (it's Samson through the trees*
> *of high heels) . . .*

Circulation is 3,000, with 30-35 pgs. of poetry in each issue. Single copy: $6; subscription: $12/year. *Phoebe* receives 4,000 submissions a year. **Submit up to 5 poems at a time; submission should be accompanied by SASE and a short bio. No simultaneous submissions. Reports in 2-3 months. Pays copies.** Sponsors an annual poetry contest in the fall. Winners are published. Send SASE for more information. Work published in *Phoebe* was selected for inclusion in *The Best American Poetry 1993*.

‡PHOENIX; PHOENIX POETRY CHAPBOOKS; THE PHOENIX ANTHOLOGY OF POETRY COMPETITION (I, II), 2330 Haste St. #304, Berkeley CA 94704, founded 1996, editor R.C. Poynter, published quarterly, "provides audience for lesser-known poets and publishes work that might be deemed too political or noisy for some magazines." **They want "any subject, any style. I believe confessional poets are going to be the lighthouses of the new century; I would like to see form and old school, as well." They do not want "Hallmark-style verse; but I will read every submission sent in the belief that not all great art is dark and angry. No poetry over 100 lines."** As a sample the editor selected these lines from "the violin" (anonymous):

> *he plays it down off of geary*
> *the money he makes*
> *goes right into smack*
> *i got talking to him one day*
> *said man how can anything so beautiful*
> *come from such   shattered arms*

The editor says *Phoenix* is 64 pgs., 6×9, saddle-stapled, with 2-color cardboard cover and ads. They receive about 300-500 poems per issue, accept approximately 15-20%. Press run is 400 for 100 subscribers of which 10 are libraries, 100 shelf sales; 100 distributed free to prisons and hospices. Subscription: $24. **Sample postpaid: $6. Make checks payable to G.B. Poynter or Phoenix, Inc. Submit 6-8 poems at a time. Previously published poems ("credit must be listed") and simultaneous submissions ("please keep us updated") OK. Cover letter preferred. "We can no longer consider handwritten submissions, sincere apologies. Computer printouts must be dark enough to read! Typewritten submissions can be single spaced but clean them up, please—correction tapes are cheap and your work makes a better impression."** Time between acceptance and publication is 3 months. **Poems are circulated to an editorial board. "Your work goes through four desks; if one likes it, we'll accept. If two or three like it, we might ask to use a few of your poems as a "Poets Page" (separate insert); if all four of us like it, we will come to your house and make you dinner!" Send SASE for guidelines. Reports in 1-3 weeks. Sometimes sends prepublication galleys. Pays 2 copies. Acquires one-time rights.** Reviews chapbooks and books of poetry in a separate insert. Open to unsolicited reviews. "Query." Poets may also send books for review consideration to W. Hall. Phoenix Poetry Chapbooks publishes 1 paperback and **6 chapbooks/year** "of authors we feel would benefit from a larger collection out, rather than one or two poems in a small audience magazine; we publish what we believe is going to be remembered." Chapbooks are usually 24 pgs., 6×9, "copyset," saddle-stitched with cardboard cover and artwork if desired. **Query first, with a few sample poems and a cover letter with brief bio and publication credits. Manuscripts for book publication may include poems previously published in magazines. Replies to queries in 1 week, to mss in 1 month. Pays 10-25% royalty and 50 author's copies (out of a press run of 500). "Chapbooks are the only subsidized work at Phoenix; you cover all costs up front, received listed royalties on copies we sell through mail order. (You will probably recoup $100 of an original $250 input—THINK before you agree to this: Can you afford it at this time?) Send $6 for our choice of in-stock chapbooks."** Sponsors the Phoenix Anthology Poetry Competition. Anthology is perfect-bound with glossy cover. $10 entry fee. Awards 4 cash awards and 50 Honorable Mentions; all included in published anthology: $100 first prize; $75 second prize; $50 third prize; $25 fourth prize; Certificate of Award for fifth through fifty-fourth prizes. The editor says, "We will not reply, in any way, to work that does not include a SASE! Our kind hearts caused a previous magazine to go under, and we will not allow it again. Care about your work, and include enough return postage! I will read beginner's writing! I have no qualms whatsoever of publishing a 14-year-old's first poem, if it is good, next to an author who has been published in hundreds of zines. If you want only to be featured with more settled writers, this is not your magazine. We want, we pray for that newcomer's voice that will make all this worthwhile."

PIEDMONT LITERARY REVIEW; PIEDMONT LITERARY SOCIETY (I, II, IV-Form/style), 3750 Woodside Ave., Lynchburg VA 24503, founded 1976, poetry editor William Reuben Smith. If you join the Piedmont Literary Society, $15 a year, you get the quarterly *Review* and a quarterly newsletter containing current market and contest information. William Smith says, **"I consider all types of poems—lean towards rhyme—up to 42 lines. Each issue has a special section for oriental forms with an emphasis on haiku."** Each also includes short fiction. He wants poems with elegance of style and occasionally accepts humor, but he does *not* want pornographic work. **"Beginners are welcome, but they compete with mature, competent poets."** *PLR* has recently published poetry by Sharon Kourous, Jeanne Heath Heritage, Errol Miller, Carol Hamilton and Georgia Bender. As a sample the editor selected these lines from "Tir Nan Og (after my mother's death from cancer)" by Juilene Osborne-McNight:

> You tunnel the only passageway
> left open in these literal times:
> dreams. Your hair is golden now.
> I must forget your balding, broken body
> for this tawny vision, laughing.
> Cancer has no power
> in the country of the soul.

The quarterly is digest-sized, saddle-stapled, offset from typescript, matte card cover, using b&w graphics, with 40-50 pgs. of poetry in each issue. Circulation is 300 for 200 subscribers of which 10 are libraries. It's a well-established publication with well-made formal and free verse poems. **Sample postpaid: $4 (or $3 prepublication) domestic, $6 foreign. Submit 3-5 poems at a time. Editor often comments on rejections. Send SASE for guidelines. Reports within 3 months. Pays 1 copy. Acquires first rights.** Briefly reviews "a few" books of poetry, "mostly contributors' books," in accompanying newsletter. They also sponsor occasional contests. The editor says he is "interested only in poetry which communicates to the thoughtful reader, with special interest in established verse forms and free verse. Not interested in experimental verse."

PIG IRON; KENNETH PATCHEN COMPETITION (II, IV-Themes), Dept. PM, P.O. Box 237, Youngstown OH 44501, phone (330)747-6932, fax (330)747-0599, founded 1975, poetry editor Jim Villani, is a literary annual devoted to special themes. They want **poetry "up to 300 lines; free verse and experimental; write for current themes."** They do *not* want to see "traditional" poetry. They have published poetry by Wayne Hogan, Laurel Speer, Louis McKee, Lloyd Mills, Marian Steele, Hugh Fox and John Pyros. *Pig Iron* is 128 pgs., magazine-sized, flat-spined, typeset on good stock with glossy card cover using b&w graphics and art, no ads. Circulation is 1,000 for 200 subscribers of which 50 are libraries. Single copy: $10.95. Subscription: $9/year, $16/2 years. **Sample postpaid: $4. No simultaneous submissions. Send SASE for guidelines. Reports in 3 months.** Time between acceptance and publication is 12-18 months. **Pays $5/poem plus 2 copies. Buys one-time rights.** They sponsor the annual Kenneth Patchen Competition. Send SASE for details. The editor says, "We want tomorrow's poetry, not yesterday's."

‡*PIGASUS PRESS; PREMONITIONS; THE ZONE; DRAGON'S BREATH; SCAR TISSUE (II, IV-Science fiction), 13 Hazely Combe, Arreton, Isle of Wight P030 3AJ England, phone (01983)865668, founded 1989, editor Tony Lee. *Premonitions*, published annually features science fiction-horror fiction and poetry. *The Zone*, published 2-3 times/year, features science fiction stories, interviews, feature articles and poetry. **They want "science fiction poetry only. Any length or form."** They do not want **"non-genre, limericks."** They have recently published poetry by Bruce Boston, Don Webb and Andrew Darlington. As a sample the editor selected these lines from "Why We Had to Firststrike First" by Steve Sneyd:

> The creature came right
> down nearly to earth dangling
> his thousand foot long
> penis into town centres
> to catch women's hair
> like midnight bat-myths . . .

The editor says *Premonitions* is 80 pgs., A5 and *The Zone* is 48 pgs., A4, both "litho printed," saddle-stapled with b&w artwork. Press run varies for 300 subscribers; "very few" distributed free to review magazines. Subscription: $35. **Sample postpaid: $9. Make checks payable to Tony Lee (pay by I.M.O. in British currency). "We recommend potential contributors buy copies of our magazines to study contents, but it is not compulsory." Submit 5 poems at a time, one per page with name and address on each. Previously published poems OK; no simultaneous submissions.** Cover letter preferred with brief bio. Time between acceptance and publication is 6 months. **"The first reading is to get on our short list. The second reading is to select best works before final choice to be published." Often comments on rejections. Publishes theme issues. Send SASE (or SAE and IRC) for guidelines and upcoming themes. Reports "usually" within 6 weeks. Pays 1 copy. Acquires first British rights.** "All types of small press books and magazines get brief staff reviews in our *Dragon's Breath* news." Poets may also send books for review consideration to Zine Kat, % Pigasus Press, at the above address. Pigasus Press, publisher of mini-anthologies, aims "to increase the readership of science fiction poetry." Anthologies are usually 24 pgs., A5, litho printed, saddle-stapled with b&w artwork, including unique graphic poems. **Submit up to 5 poems per submission. Introductory letters always welcome.**

Unpublished poetry is preferred. Replies to mss in a few weeks. Sample books or chapbooks available "by mail order only. Send SAE or IRC for our catalog." Also publishes *Dragon's Breath* newsletter for international small press review. Published monthly, with information about latest poetry chapbooks and magazines; also market news updates. The editor says, "All potential contributors (especially beginners) should read and study our magazines before sending any submissions of work. The sort of poetry we publish is unusual and specialized."

PIKEVILLE REVIEW (II), Humanities Dept., Pikeville College, Pikeville KY 41501, phone (606)432-9234, founded 1987, editor James Alan Riley, who says: **"There's no editorial bias though we recognize and appreciate style and control in each piece. No emotional gushing."** *PR* appears once yearly, accepting about 10% of poetry received. Press run is 500. **Sample postpaid: $3. No simultaneous submissions or previously published poems. Editor sometimes comments on rejections. Send SASE for guidelines. Pays 5 copies.** They also sponsor contests.

*PINCHGUT PRESS (V), 6 Oaks Ave., Cremorne, Sydney, NSW 2090 Australia, phone (02)9908-2402, founded 1948, publishes **Australian poetry but is not currently accepting poetry submissions. Send SASE (or SAE and IRCs) for catalog to order samples.**

PINE PRESS (V), RD1 Box 530, Landisburg PA 17040-9739, founded 1978, editor Kerry Shawn Keys, publishes "the finest poetry, especially by younger, less published poets and foreign poets." They publish 2 paperbacks and **3 chapbooks/year** under Pine Press or Format Books. **"Pine Press is in transition to the Czech Republic. Also, our quality is such that, after reviewing the unsolicited manuscripts this past year, it would be better to discourage submissions."** They have recently published poetry by Craig Czury, Gerald Stern, Bill Shields, John Burns and H.T. As a sample the editor selected these lines from "Saint Christopher's Monkey" by Andrew Zec:

> Now I remember my dreams. I race to
> stop the shooting of a wolf
> but am entangled by the bear behind me.
> The young crow asks me for food, he knows
> less about animals than he used to.

Books are usually 32-64 pgs., 5½ × 8½, laser-printed, hand-sewn with flat spine, linen-style cover with artwork. **Pays $5 honorarium and 75 copies, additional copies available at 50% off list price.** The editor says, "No advice, no scene, just let the daimons in and provide the tongue, the breath, the intelligence, the pen."

‡THE PINK CHAMELEON (I, IV-Subscription), 170 Park Ave., Hicksville NY 11801, founded 1985, editor/publisher Dorothy P. Freda, appears biennially, features "rare moments in time, upbeat stories, though not necessarily happy endings; touching emotional pieces, short stories, poetry, short anecdotes, articles, illustrations, cartoons, words of wisdom, **any genre as long as the material submitted is in good taste (family oriented) and gives hope for the future, even in sadness." They do not want "depressing, paranoid, pornographic or violently graphic poetry."** They have recently published poetry by Sister Mary Ann Henn, Paula Freda, Sigmund Weiss, Denise Noe, Irving Kaufman and Uncle River. As a sample the editor selected these lines from "Flowers From the Heart" by Deanne F. Purcell:

> Flowers from the heart, I give my heartfelt thanks.
> There appears no reason, still you have chosen me.
> Perhaps I made you laugh, kind words of comfort from me to you;
> My smile dried your tears, touch of my hand,
> You were no longer lonely.

The Pink Chameleon is approximately 100 pgs., 5½ × 8½, photocopied, spiral bound, some colored paper pgs., with laminated cover, b&w art and inserts. They receive about 50 poems a year, accept approximately 50%. Press run is 100 for 50-100 subscribers of which 2 are libraries. Subscription: $10. **Sample postpaid: $10. Make checks payable to Dorothy P. Freda. "I only publish subscribers." Submit 6-12 poems at a time. Previously published poems OK ("as long as author retains rights"); no simultaneous submissions. Cover letter required.** Time between acceptance and publication is 2 years. **Often comments on rejections. Send SASE for guidelines. Reports in 3-4 months. Pays subscription copy. Acquires one-time rights.**

THE PIPE SMOKER'S EPHEMERIS (I, IV-Specialized), 20-37 120th St., College Point NY 11356-2128, founded 1964, editor/publisher Tom Dunn, who says, "The *Ephemeris* is a limited edition, irregular quarterly

---

● **A BULLET** introduces comments by the editors of *Poet's Market* indicating special information about the listing.

for pipe smokers and anyone else who is interested in its varied contents. Publication costs are absorbed by the editor/publisher, assisted by any contributions—financial or otherwise—that readers might wish to make." **They want poetry with themes related to pipes and pipe smoking.**
- The issue we recently received contained a poetry section with about 15 poems intermixed with line drawings and some notes from the poets. Overall, this is a very accessible publication.

Issues range from 76-96 pgs., and are 8½ × 11, offset from photoreduced typed copy, saddle-stitched, with colored paper covers and illustrations. The editor has also published collections covering the first and second 15 years of the *Ephemeris*. **Cover letter required with submissions; include any credits. Pays 1-2 copies.** Staff reviews books of poetry. Send books for review consideration.

PIRATE WRITINGS; PIRATE WRITINGS PUBLISHING (I, II, IV-Science fiction/fantasy, mystery), P.O. Box 329, Brightwaters NY 11718, founded 1992, editor/publisher Edward J. McFadden. *Pirate Writings: Tales of Fantasy, Mystery & Science Fiction* is a quarterly magazine "filled with fiction, poetry, art and reviews by top name professionals and tomorrow's rising stars." **They want all forms and styles of poetry "within our genres—literary (humorous or straight), fantasy, science fiction, mystery/suspense and adventure. Best chance is 20 lines or less. No crude language or excessive violence. No pornography, horror, western or romance. Poems should be typed with exact capitalization and punctuation suited to your creative needs."** They have published poetry by Nancy Springer and John Grey. *Pirate Writings* is 72 pgs., magazine-sized and saddle-stapled with a full-color cover, interior spot color and b&w art throughout. They receive about 150 poetry submissions a year, use approximately 15-25 poems. Subscription: $15/4 issues, $25/ 8 issues. **Sample postpaid: $4.99. Simultaneous submissions OK. Cover letter required; include credits, if applicable. Often comments on rejections. Send SASE for guidelines. Reports in 1-2 months. Pays 1-2 copies. Acquires first North American serial rights. Also "reserves the right to print in anthology."** Query regarding reviews of chapbooks. Pirate Writings Publishing **publishes chapbooks through various arrangements. Query first. Replies to queries in 1 month, to mss in 2 months. Poets may have to share publication costs. For sample chapbooks, write for flier.**

PITT POETRY SERIES; UNIVERSITY OF PITTSBURGH PRESS; AGNES LYNCH STARRETT POETRY PRIZE (II), 127 N. Bellefield Ave., Pittsburgh PA 15260, founded 1968, poetry editor Ed Ochester, publishes **"poetry of the highest quality; otherwise, no restrictions—book mss minimum of 48 pages." Poets who have previously published books should query. Simultaneous submissions OK. Always sends prepublication galleys.** They have recently published books of poetry by Richard Garcia, Larry Levis, Sharon Doubiago, Jim Daniels and Alicia Ostriker. Their booklist also features such poets as Peter Meinke, Billy Collins, Sharon Olds, Ronald Wallace, David Wojahn and Toi Derricotte. **"Poets who have not previously published a book should send SASE for rules of the Starrett competition ($15 handling fee), the *only* vehicle through which we publish first books of poetry." The Starrett Prize consists of cash award of $3,000 and book publication.**

THE PITTSBURGH QUARTERLY; THE SARA HENDERSON HAY PRIZE (II), 36 Haberman Ave., Pittsburgh PA 15211-2144, phone (412)431-8885, e-mail tpq@city-net.com, website http://www.city-net.com/ ~tpq, founded 1990, editor Frank Correnti, who says, **"Our first criterion is good writing with the variety of content that is common to a broad community interest. Generally, writing with narrative and real-life elements. We don't want doggerel or most rhyme."** They have recently published poetry by Elizabeth Gargano, Richard Fox, Lisa Barnett, Kevin Rippin and Kristin Herbert. It is 76 pgs., digest-sized, professionally printed, saddle-stapled with matte card cover. Press run is 700 for 300 subscribers of which 10 are libraries, 300 shelf sales. Subscription: $12 ($14 Canadian). **Sample postpaid: $5. "We will reply by letter to queries." Editor often comments on submissions. Reports in 3-4 months. Pays 2 copies. Acquires first North American serial rights.** Published books are reviewed as space is available, 1-2/issue. Accepts reviews of 4-6 pages, double-spaced. Send books for review consideration. "We are responding in part to the network of writers whose crafted creativity made the magazine possible, but we also are attempting to provide a readership that will connect more strongly to the community of poets and writers through this quarterly." *The Pittsburgh Quarterly* sponsors an annual prize for poetry: The Sara Henderson Hay Prize. Entry requires current subscription or renewal and is limited to 3 poems up to 100 lines each. Deadline: July 1. Winner receives a cash award and publication of the winning poem in the fall issue.

PIVOT (II), 250 Riverside Dr., #23, New York NY 10025, phone (212)222-1408, founded 1951, editor Martin Mitchell, is a poetry annual that has published poetry by Philip Appleman, William Matthews, Eugene McCarthy, Craig Raine, W.D. Snodgrass and Robert Wrigley. *Pivot* is a handsome, 6 × 9, flat-spined, professionally printed magazine with glossy card cover. Press run is 1,200. Single copy: $5. **Submit 3-7 poems at a time. Brief cover letter preferred. Reads submissions January 1 through June 1 only. Reports in 2-4 weeks. Sometimes sends prepublication galleys. Pays 2 copies.**

THE PLACE IN THE WOODS; READ, AMERICA! (I, IV-Children), 3900 Glenwood Ave., Golden Valley MN 55422, phone (612)374-2120, founded 1980, editor/publisher Roger A. Hammer, publishes *Read, America!*, a quarterly newsletter for reading coordinators. They want **"poems for children that are understand-**

able, under 500 words, unusual views of life. Also, foreign-language poems with English translation. Nothing vague, self-indulgent, erotic. No navel introspection." *Read, America!* is 8 pgs., magazine-sized, professionally printed on yellow paper. "Pages 1-4 are distributed free to some 10,000 programs. Four additional pages go only to readers who support us as subscribers." Most poems appear in the "Subscribers only" insert but poets do not have to be subscribers to submit. Subscription: $25. **No previously published poems or simultaneous submissions. Cover letter "optional and appreciated for insight into poet's background and interests or goals." Always comments on rejections. Pays $10 on publication. Buys all rights.**

PLAINSONG (I, II), Box 8245, Western Kentucky University, Bowling Green KY 42101, phone (502)745-5708, founded 1979, poetry editors Frank Steele, Elizabeth Oakes and Peggy Steele, is an occasional poetry journal. "Our purpose is to print the best work we can get, from known and unknown writers. This means, of course, that we print what we like: poems about places, objects, people, moods, politics, experiences. **We like straightforward, conversational language, short poems in which the marriage of thinking and feeling doesn't break up because of spouse-abuse (the poem in which ideas wrestle feeling into the ground or in which feeling sings alone—and boringly—at the edge of a desert). Prefer poems under 20 lines in free verse—brief, understated lyrics that depend on the image combined with an intimate, conversational voice. No limits on subject matter, though we like to think of ourselves as humane, interested in the environment, in peace (we're anti-nuclear), in the possibility that the human race may have a future."** They have published poetry by Robert Bly, Ted Kooser, Judy Kronenfeld, Laurie Lamon, David Till and Angie Estes. The magazine is 48-56 pgs., 6×9, professionally printed, flat-spined, color matte card cover with photos and graphics. They receive about 2,000 submissions a year, use approximately 100. Press run is 600 for 250 subscribers of which 65 are libraries. Subscription: $7. **Sample postpaid: $3.50. Submit 5-6 poems at a time. "We prefer poems typed, double-spaced. Simultaneous submissions can, of course, get people into trouble, at times." Publishes theme issues occasionally. Send SASE for guidelines. Reports "within a month, usually." Pays copies.** Staff reviews books of poetry. Send books for review consideration to Frank Steele. The editor says, "We receive too many poems in 'the schoolroom voice'—full of language that's really prose. We'd like to see more poems with a voice that feels something without being sentimental or melodramatic."

PLAINSONGS (II), Dept. of English, Hastings College, Hastings NE 68902-0269, phone (402)463-2402 or 461-7352, founded 1980, editor Dwight C. Marsh, is a poetry magazine that **"accepts manuscripts from anyone, considering poems on any subject in any style but free verse predominates. Plains region poems encouraged."** They have recently published poetry by Rebecca Cook, Colin Esler, Eric Gardner, Charlotte Hegg, Walt McDonald and J. Tarwood. As a sample the editor selected these lines from "Parental" a *Plainsongs* Award poem by G.C. Waldrep:

> The girl is in the cornfield. She is
> in the cornfield, or at its far edge, back
> beneath the shed's treelined shadow, and she is sleeping
> or she is dead. Around her throat a necklace of rubies.
> Around her waist a garland. Her blank eyes
> explore the crevices of the moon, from which
> her cheeks drink light:

Plainsongs is 40 pgs., digest-sized, set on laser, printed on thin paper and saddle-stapled with one-color matte card cover with generic black logo. The magazine is supported by the English Dept. of Hastings College and financed primarily by subscriptions. "Contributors who also subscribe receive individual responses to their submissions." The name suggests not only its location on the Great Plains, but its preference for the living language, whether in free or formal verse. It is committed to poems only, to make space without visual graphics, bio or critical positions. Subscription: $9/3 issues. **Sample postpaid: $3. Submit up to 6 poems at a time with name and address on each page. Ms deadlines are August 15 for fall issue; November 15 for winter; March 15 for spring. Notification is mailed about 5 weeks after deadlines. Pays 2 copies and 1-year subscription, with 3 award poems in each issue receiving $25. "A short essay in appreciation accompanies each award poem." Acquires first rights.**

*PLANET: THE WELSH INTERNATIONALIST (III), P.O. Box 44, Aberystwyth, Ceredigion, Wales, phone 01970-611255, founded 1970, editor John Barnie, is a bimonthly cultural magazine, "centered on Wales, but with broader interests in arts, sociology, politics, history and science." **They want "good poetry in a wide variety of styles. No limitations as to subject matter; length can be a problem."** They have published poetry by J.K. Gill and R.S. Thomas. As a sample the editor selected these lines from "On Home Beaches" by Les Murray:

> Back, in my fifties, fatter than I was then,
> I step on the sand, belch down slight horror to walk
> a wincing pit edge, waiting for the pistol shot
> laughter. Long greening waves cash themselves, foam change
> sliding into Ocean's pocket. She turns: ridicule looks down,
> strappy, with faces averted, or is glare and families.

Planet is 128 pgs., A5 size, professionally printed and perfect-bound with glossy color card cover. They receive about 300 submissions a year, accept approximately 5%. Press run is 1,475 for 1,150 subscribers of which about 10% are libraries, 200 shelf sales. Single copy: £2.50; subscription: £12 (overseas: £13). **Sample postpaid: £3.56. No previously published poems or simultaneous submissions. SASE or SAE with IRCs essential for reply.** Time between acceptance and publication is 6-10 months. **Seldom comments on rejections. Send SASE (or SAE and IRCs if outside UK) for guidelines. Reports within a month or so. Pays £25 minimum. Buys first serial rights only.** Reviews books of poetry in 700 words, single and multi-book format. Open to unsolicited reviews. Poets may also send books for review consideration.

*PLANTAGENET PRODUCTIONS (V), Westridge, Andover Rd., Highclere, Nr. Newbury, Royal Berkshire RG 20 9 PJ England, founded 1964, director of productions Miss Dorothy Rose Gribble. Plantagenet issues cassette recordings of poetry, philosophy and narrative (although they have issued nothing new since 1980). Miss Gribble says, "Our public likes classical work . . . We **have published a few living poets, but this is not very popular with our listeners, and we shall issue no more.**" They have issued cassettes by Oscar Wilde, Chaucer and Pope, as well as Charles Graves, Elizabeth Jennings, Leonard Clark and Alice V. Stuart. The recordings are issued privately and are obtainable only direct from Plantagenet Productions; write for list. Miss Gribble's advice to poets is: "If intended for a listening public, let the meaning be clear. If possible, let the music of the words sing."

THE PLASTIC TOWER (II), P.O. Box 702, Bowie MD 20718, founded 1989, editors Carol Dyer and Roger Kyle-Keith, is a quarterly using **"everything from iambic pentameter to silly limericks, modern free verse, haiku, rhymed couplets—we like it all! Only restriction is length—under 40 lines preferred. So send us poems that are cool or wild, funny or tragic—but especially those closest to your soul."** They have published poetry by "more than 400 different poets." It is 38-54 pgs., digest-sized, saddle-stapled; "variety of typefaces and b&w graphics on cheap photocopy paper." Press run is 200. Subscription: $8/year. Copy of current issue: $2.50. **"We'll send a back issue free for a *large* (at least 6×9) SAE with 78¢ postage attached." Submit up to 10 poems at a time. Previously published poems and simultaneous submissions OK. Editors comment on submissions "often." Send SASE for guidelines. Reports in 3-4 months. Pays 1 copy.** Open to unsolicited reviews. Poets may also send books for review consideration. Roger Kyle-Keith says, "*PT* is an unpretentious little rag dedicated to enjoying verse and making poetry accessible to the general public as well as fellow poets. We don't claim to be the best, but we try to be the nicest and most personal. Over the past several years, we've noticed a tremendous upswing in submissions. More people than ever are writing poetry and submitting it for publication, and that makes it tougher for individual writers to get published. But plenty of opportunities still exist (there are thousands of little and literary magazines in the U.S. alone), and the most effective tool for any writer right now is not talent or education, but persistence. So keep at it!"

*THE PLAZA (II, IV-Bilingual), U-Kan, Inc., Yoyogi 2-32-1, Shibuya-ku, Tokyo 151, Japan, phone 81-3-3379-3881, fax 81-3-3379-3882, e-mail u-kan@u-kan.co.jp, website http://u-kan.co.jp/~u-kan, founded 1985, poetry editors Tak Furuya and Roger Lakhani, is a quarterly which "represents a borderless forum for contemporary writers and artists" and includes poetry, fiction and essays published simultaneously in English and Japanese. They want **"highly artistic poetry dealing with being human and interculturally related. Nothing stressing political, national, religious or racial differences. *The Plaza* is edited with a global view of mankind."** They have recently published poetry by Morgan Gibson, Antler and Bun'ichirou Chino. As a sample the editors selected these lines from "Freedom from Heavy Blankets" by Jill Rothstein:

> *Peeking around the corner*
> *a view is offered of his feet*
> *poking out from under the covers*
> *undulating to voiceless music*
> *His body cocooned in terrestrial warmth*
> *Feet left out icy*
> *but free to dance*

The Plaza is 48 pgs., A5, professionally printed and saddle-stapled with card cover. They receive about 2,500 poems a year, accept approximately 4%. Press run is 5,000 for 4,500 subscribers of which 460 are libraries (including 160 overseas), 500 shelf sales. Single copy: 380 yen; subscription: 1,500 yen. **Sample available for 5 IRCs (for overseas airmail). No previously published poems; simultaneous submissions OK. Cover letter required. E-mail and fax submissions OK. "Please include telephone and fax numbers with submissions. As *The Plaza* is a bilingual publication in English and Japanese, it is sometimes necessary, for translation purposes, to contact authors. Japanese translations are prepared by the editorial staff." Seldom comments on rejections. Reports within 1 month. Pays 10 copies plus an additional 10 if self-translated into Japanese.** Reviews books of poetry, usually in less than 500 words. Open to unsolicited reviews. Poets may also send books for review consideration. Roger Lakhani says, "*The Plaza* focuses not on human beings but humans being human in the borderless world. It is not international, but intercultural. And it is circulated all over the world—in the American continents, Oceania, Asia, the Middle East, Europe and Africa."

PLAZM MAGAZINE; PLAZM MEDIA (I, II), P.O. Box 2863, Portland OR 97208-2863, phone (503)222-6389, fax (503)222-6356, founded 1991. *Plazm Magazine* is published 4 times/year by Plazm Media, "a cooperative dedicated to free expression." **They want experimental poetry. Nothing "rudimentary."** They have published poetry by Dan Raphael, Jay Marvin and Bill Shields. The editor says *Plazm* is 9×12, printed offset litho and saddle-stitched, with "much art and design." Press run is 8,000 for 500 subscribers of which 10 are libraries, most shelf sales. Subscription: $16/4 issues. **Sample postpaid: $6. Previously published poems OK (but not preferred). Simultaneous submissions also OK. SASE and biographical statement required. Poems are circulated to an editorial board. Often comments on rejections. Send SASE for guidelines. Reports in 3-4 months. Pays 3 copies and a subscription.** Reviews books of poetry in 25-250 words. Open to unsolicited reviews. Poets may also send books for review consideration.

PLEIADES (II), Dept. of English and Philosophy, Central Missouri State University, Warrensburg MO 64093, phone (816)543-4425, fax (816)543-8006, founded as *Spring Flight* in 1939, reestablished in its present format in 1990, general editor R.M. Kinder, managing editor Kevin Prufer. *Pleiades*, a semiannual journal which publishes poetry, fiction, literary criticism, belles lettres (occasionally) and reviews. It is open to all writers and emphasizes cultural diversity. **They want "avant-garde, free verse and traditional poetry, and some quality light verse. Nothing pretentious, didactic or overly sentimental."** They have recently published poetry by David Citino, Vivian Shipley and William Doreski. As a sample the editor selected these lines from "Bonne Femme" by Barbara J. Orton:

> *Her wrists folded like the wings*
> *of birds: she was hollow-boned.*
> *Between quick cigarettes, her words*
>
> *were nervous as sparrows.*
> *I think she was always straining*
> *to walk on her toes.*

The editor says *Pleiades* is 120 pgs., 5½×8½, perfect-bound with a heavy coated cover and b&w or color cover art. They receive about 1,000 poems a year, accept approximately 3-5%. Press run is 400-500, about 200 distributed free to educational institutions and libraries across the country, about 100 shelf sales. Single copy: $5; subscription: $10. **Sample postpaid: $3.50. Make checks payable to Pleiades Press. Submit 3-5 poems at a time. No previously published poems; simultaneous submissions OK with notification. Cover letter with brief bio preferred.** Time between acceptance and publication can be up to 1 year. **Each poem published must be accepted by 2 readers and approved by the poetry editor. Seldom comments on rejections. Send SASE for guidelines. Reports in 2-12 weeks. Pays $3/poem and 1 copy. Buys first and second serial rights and requests rights for** *Wordbeat*, a TV/radio show featuring work published in *Pleiades*.

PLOUGHSHARES (III), Emerson College, 100 Beacon St., Boston MA 02116, phone (617)824-8753, founded 1971. **The magazine is "a journal of new writing guest-edited by prominent poets and writers to reflect different and contrasting points of view."** Editors have included Carolyn Forché, Gerald Stern, Rita Dove, Chase Twichell and Marilyn Hacker. They have published poetry by Donald Hall, Li-Young Lee, Robert Pinsky, Brenda Hillman and Thylias Moss. The triquarterly is 250 pgs., 5½×8½. Circulation is 6,000. They receive approximately 2,500 poetry submissions a year. Since this influential magazine features different editors with each issue, content varies. As always with prestigious journals, competition is keen. Response times can be slow because submissions are screened inhouse and sent to outside guest editors. Subscription: $21 domestic; $26 foreign. **Sample postpaid: $9.95 current issue, $8 sample back issue. "We suggest you read a few issues before submitting." Simultaneous submissions acceptable. Do not submit mss from April 1 to July 31. Reports in 3-5 months. Always sends prepublication galleys. Pays $50 minimum per poem, $25/printed page per poem, plus 2 copies and a subscription.** Work published in *Ploughshares* appears in the 1992, 1993, 1994, 1995, 1996 and 1997 volumes of *The Best American Poetry*.

❧**THE PLOWMAN (I, II)**, Box 414, Whitby, Ontario L1N 5S4 Canada, phone (905)668-7803, founded 1988, editor Tony Scavetta, appears quarterly using **"didactic, eclectic poetry; all forms. We will also take most religious poetry except satanic and evil. We are interested in work that deals with the important issues in our society. Social and environment issues are of great importance."**
● The most recent issue we received included 3 pages of poetry, 6 pages of classified ads/market listings and 4 pages of chapbooks available through *The Plowman*.
The Plowman is 20 pgs., 8½×11 (17×11 sheet folded), photocopied, unbound, contains clip art and market listings. They accept 70% of the poetry received. Press run is 15,000 for 1,200 subscribers of which 500 are libraries. Single copy: $5; subscription: $10. **Sample free. Previously published poems and simultaneous**

 THE MAPLE LEAF symbol before a listing indicates a Canadian publisher, magazine, conference, contest or organization.

submissions OK. Cover letter required. No SASE necessary. Always comments on rejections. Guidelines available free. Reports in 1 week. Always sends prepublication galleys. Reviews books of poetry. They offer monthly poetry contests. Entry fee: $2/poem. 1st prize: 50% of the proceeds; 2nd: 25%; 3rd: 10%. The top poems are published. "Balance of the poems will be used for anthologies." **They also publish 125 chapbooks/year. Replies to queries and mss in 1 week. Requires $25 reading fee/book. Pays 20% royalties.**

POCAHONTAS PRESS, INC.; MANUSCRIPT MEMORIES (V), P.O. Drawer F, Blacksburg VA 24063-1020, phone (540)951-0467, e-mail mchollim@bev.net, founded 1984, president Mary C. Holliman, publishes chapbook collections of poetry, but **is temporarily not considering new mss** "because I am trying to finish those already accepted." Inquire before submitting. **Prefers Appalachian-related themes and authors only.** "Most of the poetry books I have published have been subsidized to some extent by the author. So far one of those authors' books has sold enough copies that the author has received a significant reimbursement for his investment. We continue to market all of our books as aggressively as possible. The idea is to make a profit for both of us (though we have yet to do so)." She has published books by Leslie Mellichamp, Lynn Kozma, Mildred Nash, Rita Riddle, Preston Newman and Elaine Emans. As a sample the editor selected these lines from "My Friend Built A Bridge" by Sidney Farr:

> Wind words came
> laced with the fragrance of myrtle;
> gypsy winds longing for rain
> in my summer of drought.

Submit 8-10 poems at a time. Always sends prepublication galleys. Pays 10% royalties on all sales receipts, 10 free copies of book, and any number of copies at 50% for resale or "whatever use author wishes. If author helps with printing costs, then an additional percentage of receipts will be paid." She offers editorial critiques for $40/hour. Mary Holliman adds, "There's much more good poetry being written than is getting published, and I only wish I could publish more of it. We are planning to try a new marketing technique—single-fold notecards with one poem from a collection per card, perhaps three poem/cards (two each in a set of six). The full collection and how to order will be given on the back of each card."

POEM; HUNTSVILLE LITERARY ASSOCIATION (II), English Dept., University of Alabama at Huntsville, Huntsville AL 35899, founded 1967, poetry editor Nancy Frey Dillard, appears twice a year, consisting entirely of poetry. **"We are open to traditional as well as non-traditional forms, but we favor work with the expected compression and intensity of good lyric poetry and a high degree of verbal and dramatic tension. We equally welcome submissions from established poets as well as from less-known and beginning poets. We do not accept translations, previously published works or simultaneous submissions. We prefer to see a sample of three to five poems at a submission, with SASE. We generally respond within a month. We are a nonprofit organization and can pay only in copy to contributors. Sample copies are available at $5."** They have published poetry by Robert Cooperman, Andrew Dillon and Scott Travis Hutchison. *Poem* is a flat-spined, $4\frac{3}{8} \times 7\frac{1}{4}$, 90-page journal that contains more than 60 poems (mostly lyric free verse under 50 lines) generally featured 1 to a page on good stock paper with a clean design and a classy matte cover. Circulation is 400 (all subscriptions of which 90 are libraries). Overall, it's a good market for beginners and experienced poets who pay attention to craft.

‡THE POEM & THE WORLD (IV-Anthology, regional), 128 N. 82nd St., Seattle WA 98103, founded 1990, chief editor Sheila Bender. "*The Poem & the World* serves to publish an anthology of **poetry from Seattle and Seattle's sister cities around the world.** The remaining sister cities are Cebu, Philippines; Gdynia, Poland; Kaohsiung, Taiwan; Managua, Nicaragua; Mazatlan, Mexico; Mombasa, Kenya; Surabaya, Indonesia; and Tashkent, Uzbekistan. Poetry from these cities and Seattle (the Puget Sound area) is welcome. They have recently published poetry by Denise Levertov, Heather McHugh, Colleen McElroy and Duane Niatum. As a sample the editor selected these lines from "Silence" by Ilde Arcelli of Perugi, Italy, translated by Giuseppe and Judith Skillman:

> What if a voice
> close to the green fringe of the lawn
> is carried away by the wind . . .
> What if a cicada is suddenly stilled
> by the scorching sun—then
> the silence of things comes to life

Books are usually 96 pgs., digest-sized, offset, perfect-bound, with a 2-color glossy cover and cover art. **Submit 3-6 poems at a time. Previously published poems and simultaneous submissions OK. Cover letter preferred.** Time between acceptance and publication is 6 months. **Poetry is circulated to an editorial board made up of published poets, editors and members of The Poem and the World group. A group decision is made for selection. Replies to queries in 2-3 months, to mss (if invited) in 2-3 weeks. Pays 2-5 copies out of a press run of 500.**

POEMS & PLAYS; THE TENNESSEE CHAPBOOK PRIZE (II), English Dept., Middle Tennessee State University, Murfreesboro TN 37132, phone (615)898-2712, founded 1993, editor Gay Brewer, is an annual "eclectic publication for poems and short plays," published in April. **They have no restrictions on style or content of poetry.** They have recently published poetry by Stephen Dobyns, Billy Collins, Vivian Shipley, Charles Bukowski and Kevin Griffith. As a sample the editor selected these lines from "The Day Before" by Stephen Dunn:

> *Then something sudden, massive, conclusive,*
> *Something gene-driven that comes deeply*
> *from your father, perhaps even tinged*
> *with his goodness, and you're gone.*

Poems & Plays is 88 pgs., 6×9, professionally printed and perfect-bound with coated color card cover and art. "We receive 1,500 poems per issue, typically publish 30-35." Press run is 700. Subscription: $10/2 issues. **Sample postpaid: $6. No previously published poems or simultaneous submissions (except for chapbook submissions). Reads submissions October 1 through January 15 only. "Work is circulated among advisory editors for comments and preferences. All accepted material is published in the following issue." Usually comments on rejections. Reports in 1-2 months. Pays 1 copy. Acquires first publication rights only.** "We accept chapbook manuscripts (of poems or short plays) of 24 pages for The Tennessee Chapbook Prize. The winner is printed as an interior chapbook in *Poems & Plays* and receives 50 copies of the issue. SASE and $10 fee (for one copy of the issue) required. Dates for contest entry are the same as for the magazine (October 1 through January 15). Past winners include Maureen Micus Crisick, David Stark, Steven Sater and Angela Kelly. The 1997 chapbook competition drew 117 manuscripts from the U.S., Taiwan, Australia, Mexico and Guam."

‡THE POET HOUSE (I), P.O. Box 1228, Spring Hill TN 37174-1228, founded 1995, president Michael Salacuse, strives "to bring poetry to a wider audience through the CD format." They produce compact disks of recorded poems. **They want "short poems no longer than one page. All types of poetry accepted." They do not want vulgar poetry. Submit 6-10 poems, printed or typed, with name, address and phone on each page. Previously published poems and simultaneous submissions OK. Cover letter required. Poems are circulated to an editorial board. The Poet House board reads each poem and discusses which fits their needs best. Often comments on rejections. Replies to queries in 6 weeks.**

POET LORE; POET LORE NARRATIVE POETRY COMPETITION (II), The Writer's Center, 4508 Walsh St., Bethesda MD 20815, phone (301)654-8664, website http://www.writer.org, founded 1889, managing editor Sunil Freeman, executive editors Philip Jason and Geraldine Connolly, is a quarterly dedicated "to the best in American and world poetry and objective and timely reviews and commentary. We look for **fresh uses of traditional form and devices, but any kind of excellence is welcome. The editors encourage narrative poetry and original translations of works by contemporary world poets.**" They have recently published poetry by William Matthews, Denise Duhame, R.T. Smith and Cornelius Eady. *Poet Lore* is 6×9, 80 pgs., perfect-bound, professionally printed with matte card cover. Circulation includes 600 subscriptions of which 200 are libraries. Editors are open to all styles (as long as the work is well-crafted and insightful), leaning toward lyric and narrative free verse with an emphasis on voice. They receive about 3,000 poems a year, use approximately 125. Single copy: $5.50; subscription: $15. **Sample postpaid: $4. Submit typed poems, author's name and address on each page. Reports in 3 months. Pays 2 copies.** Reviews books of poetry. Open to unsolicited reviews. Poets may also send books for review consideration. Sponsors the Poet Lore Narrative Poetry Competition (formerly John Williams Andrews Narrative Poetry Competition) for unpublished poems of 100 lines or more. The annual competition awards $350 and publication in *Poet Lore*. Deadline: November 30. Send SASE for entry form and guidelines. Poetry published in *Poet Lore* has also been selected for inclusion in *The Best American Poetry 1994*.

POET MAGAZINE; COOPER HOUSE PUBLISHING INC.; JOHN DAVID JOHNSON MEMORIAL POETRY AWARDS; IVA MARY WILLIAMS INSPIRATIONAL POETRY AWARDS; AMERICAN COLLEGE & UNIVERSITY POETRY AWARDS; AMERICAN HIGH SCHOOL POETRY AWARDS; THE AMERICAN LITERARY MAGAZINE AWARDS (II), P.O. Box 5646, Shreveport LA 71135, founded 1984, managing editor Peggy Cooper, editor Joy Hall, poetry editor Michael Hall. "*Poet* is one of the largest commercial publishers of poetry in the U.S. and is **open to submissions from writers at all levels of experience.**" Michael Hall says, **"I look for poems that display wit, knowledge and skill . . . verse that employs arresting images, poems that make the reader think or smile or even sometimes cry."** They have published poetry by Lewis Turco and H.R. Coursen. *Poet* is 56-80 pgs., magazine-sized, professionally printed, saddle-stitched with glossy cover. Of about 7,000-10,000 submissions, they use a little fewer than 5%. Subscription: $24/year. **Sample postpaid: $6.50 or "check with your bookstore." For guidelines, send 3 loose first-class stamps with request. Submit up to 3 poems at a time. Previously published poems and simultaneous submissions OK. Reports within 3-6 months. Pays 1 copy.** Reviews books of poetry. Open to unsolicited reviews. John David Johnson Memorial Poetry Awards (prizes of $50, $25, $15, special merit and honorable mention awards, award certificates, publication and a copy of the magazine in which the winning poems appear to all winners. Entry fee: $5/poem. March 1 and September 1 deadlines). Iva Mary Williams Inspirational Poetry Awards (prizes of $50, $25, $15 special merit and honorable mention awards, award certificates, publication and a copy of the magazine in which the winning poems appear to all winners. Entry fee: $5/poem. February 1 and August 1 deadlines). American College & University Poetry Awards offers first, second and third place awards, special merit and honorable mention awards, award certificates, publication and copy of the magazine in which the winning poems appear to all winners. No entry fee. Rules and official entry forms may be requested with 2 loose first-class stamps. American High School Poetry Awards offers certificates, publication and copy of the magazine in which the winning poems appear to all winners. No entry fee. Rules and official entry forms may be requested with 2 loose first-class stamps. The American Literary Magazine Awards are engraved plaques, award certificate and free advertising in *Poet Magazine*. All contestants receive a gift. $35 entry fee/title. Deadline: December 31. Send 2 loose first-class stamps with request for rules and entry form.

‡*POETIC HOURS; DREAMLANDS POETRY GROUP (I), 8 Dale Rd., Carlton, Nottingham NG4 1GT England, founded 1993, editor Nicholas Clark, published annually, "is the magazine of the Dreamlands Poetry Group formed to encourage new writers and raise money for charity. The magazine features articles and poetry by members of the group and others." **They want "any subject, rhyme preferred but not essential; suitable for wide ranging readership, 30 lines maximum."** They do not want "gothic, horror, extremist, political, self-interested." As a sample the editor selected these lines from "The Garden Roller" by A.H. Hallwood:

> Can anything be so empty as a view
> Seen by a dead man who will look no more;
> His impromptu seat was home to none save weeds
> That climbing, failed to hold
> His lingering dreams

The editor says *Poetic Hours* is 36 pgs., A4, printed, saddle-stapled and illustrated throughout with Victorian woodcuts. They receive about 500 poems a year, accept up to 40%. Press run is 400 of which 12 are for libraries, 300 shelf sales. Subscription: £5, £7 overseas. **Sample postpaid: £3. Make checks payable to Erran Publishing. "Poets are encouraged to subscribe or buy a single copy, though not required." Submit up to 5 nonreturnable poems at a time. Previously published poems OK; no simultaneous submissions. Cover letter required.** Time between acceptance and publication is 2-3 months. **"Poems are read by editors and if found suitable, are used." Always comments on rejections. Publishes theme issues. Upcoming themes listed in magazine. Reports "immediately, whenever possible." Acquires one-time rights.** Staff reviews books or chapbooks of poetry. Poets may also send books for review consideration. *Poetic Hours* is published solely to encourage and publish new poets, i.e., as a forum where good but little known poets can appear in print and to raise money for Third World charities. Dreamlands Poetry Group is non-profit-making and all proceeds go to various national charities, particularly Oxfam and Amnesty International. A page of *Poetic Hours* is set aside each issue for reporting how money is spent. The editor says, "We welcome newcomers and invite those just starting out to have the courage to submit work. The art of poetry has moved from the hands of book publishers down the ladder to the new magazines. This is where all the best poetry is found."

POETIC PAGE (I, II); OPUS LITERARY REVIEW (II), P.O. Box 71192, Madison Heights MI 48071-0192, phone (810)548-0865, e-mail poeticpage@aol.com., *Poetic Page* founded 1989, *Opus Literary Review* founded 1993, editor Denise Martinson. *Poetic Page* appears quarterly. **Each issue has a contest, $1/poem fee, prizes of $30, $20, $10 and $5. About 90% of the poetry published is that of contest winners, and the rest is used in featured section. "All forms are used except explicit sex, violence and crude. Thirty lines."** They have published poetry by MacDonald Carey, Alice Mackenzie Swaim, T.N. Turner, T. Kilgore Splake, Glenna Holloway and John Grey. *Poetic Page* is 32-36 pgs., magazine-sized, saddle-stapled with coated card cover, desktop-published. Press run is 250-350, sent to libraries, universities, editors and subscribers. Subscription: $20. **Sample postpaid: $5. Simultaneous submissions and previously published poems OK. Cover letter is preferred. E-mail is for information only; no submissions. Send SASE for guidelines. Pays 1 copy to nonsubscribers.** The editor says, "We look for poetry that has something to say. No trite rhyme. Only the very best poems are selected each issue. First place is featured on its own page. We pay copies for articles and cover art, but must be of the highest quality. We ask poets to send us copies of their poetry books for our 'Review' section. Just because we are listed under the I category, does not mean we are an easy magazine to be published in. We want poetry that is well written, poetry that demands to be read. Send your best." *Opus Literary Review* is a biannual. **No specifications as to form, length, style, subject matter or purpose.** They have published poetry by Rudy Zenker, Leonard Cirino, Laurel Speer, Robert S. King, Lyn Lifshin, Pearl Bloch Segall, John Grey and Patricia A. Lawrence. *Opus Literary Review* is desktop-published with matte cover. Subscription: $10. **Sample postpaid: $5. No previously published poems or simultaneous submissions "unless of exceptional quality." Cover letter required. Editor often comments on rejections. Send SASE for guidelines. Pays 1 copy with bio listing. Acquires first rights.** The editor says: "We want poetry that will last the ages. Poetry that is intelligent, well thought out. If you want to write a poem about a flower, go ahead. But make that flower unique—surprise us. Give us your best work. But beginners beware, no trite rhyme here. However, we will publish a well-written rhyme if the rhyme is the poem, not the word endings. Free verse is what we prefer."

POETIC REALM (I); OMNIFIC (I); THE BOTTOM LINE, HC-13, Box 21-AA, Artemas PA 17211-9405, phone (814)458-3102, editor/publisher Kay Weems. *Poetic Realm* is a quarterly of poetry using **36-line, sometimes longer, poems, "anything in good taste"** with an Editor's Choice small cash award for each issue. **No contributor copies.** Subscription: $12/year; $3.50/copy. *Omnific*, a "family-type" quarterly publishes poetry only, 36 lines, sometimes longer; readers vote on favorites, small cash award or copy to favorites. **Send SASE for guidelines. No contributor copies.** Subscription: $16/year; $3.50/copy. She also publishes an annual **Christmas anthology. Poetry only, published/unpublished, 36 lines maximum, Christmas themes. Address to "Christmas Anthology." Deadline: August 31.** *The Bottom Line,* founded 1988, is a monthly newsletter listing over 50 publications and contests for writers, reproducing guidelines of still others. Information is presented in chronological order by deadline date, and then in alphabetical order. Circulation 200-300. Subscription: $21/year; $2.50/copy. Her other publication, *My Legacy,* is still published but now uses only short stories.

‡**THE POETIC SOUL; TPE PRESS (I, IV-Specialized: emotional/human experience)**, 215 Orchard St., Cranston RI 02910, e-mail jcoll37549@aol.com, founded 1995, editor James Collins, published annually, creates "exposure for new and established poets who write emotional poetry—a venue for sharing the human experience." **They want "poetry that conveys strong insight, imagery or emotion as to the human experience. No restrictions as to form, subject or style. Keep length per poem under two pages." They do not want "rhyme unless exceptional. No religious verse."** As a sample the editor selected these lines from "By Way of My Grandmother" by Carol Snow Moon Bachofner:

> *My grandmother fought the war one bead at a time,*
> *Hail Marys and Our Fathers rattling like tank fire*
> *into the minefields of hell to free her son and save*
> *the world. She would not give credence to telegrams.*

The editor says *The Poetic Soul* is 75-100 pgs., typeset, center-stapled with matte stock cover. They accept approximately 10% of poems they receive. Press run is 300, 200 shelf sales; 100 distributed free to contributors. Single copy: $7. **Sample postpaid: $5. Make checks payable to James D. Collins Jr. Submit 3-5 poems at a time. No previously published poems; simultaneous submissions OK. Cover letter preferred with brief bio along with publication credits. E-mail submissions OK (must be contained in the body of the e-mail).** Time between acceptance and publication is 6-12 months. **"All submissions are reviewed for style, intensity, imagery and language." Seldom comments on rejections. Send SASE for guidelines or obtain via e-mail. Reports ASAP (usually within 2 weeks). Pays 1 copy. Acquires all rights; reverts back to individual authors upon publication.** Staff may review chapbooks of poetry. Poets may also send books for review consideration. TPE Press irregularly publishes theme anthologies and publishes 1 paperback/year. Books are usually less than 100 pgs., typeset, flat spined with heavy stock cover. **Query with 10 poems and cover letter. Replies to queries in 1 month, to mss (if invited) in 3 months. Pay will vary depending on circumstances.** The editor advises, "Do not be discouraged by rejections. They do not reflect negatively on your poetic talent. Stay motivated and keep submitting."

POETIC SPACE: POETRY & FICTION (I), P.O. Box 11157, Eugene OR 97440, founded 1983, editor Don Hildenbrand, published biannually, is a nonprofit literary magazine with emphasis on contemporary poetry, fiction, reviews (including film and drama), interviews, market news and translations. Accepts poetry and fiction that is **"well-crafted and takes risks. We like poetry with guts. Would like to see some poetry on social and political issues. We would also like to see gay/lesbian poetry and poetry on women's issues. Erotic and experimental OK." Prefers poems under 1,000 words.** They have published poetry by Crawdad Nelson, Ed Meek, Kell Robertson, Ray Barker, Kit Knight and Lynda S. Silva. The magazine is 30 pgs., 8½ × 11, saddle-stapled, offset from typescript and sometimes photoreduced. They receive about 200-300 poems a year, accept approximately 25%. Press run is 800 for 50 subscribers of which 12 are libraries. Single copy: $4; subscription: $7/2 issues, $13/4 issues. **Send SASE for list of available back issues ($4). Ms should be typed, double-spaced, clean, name/address on each page. "Submissions without SASE will not be considered." Simultaneous submissions and previously published poems OK. Editor provides some critical comments. Send SASE for guidelines. Reports in 2-4 months. Pays 1 copy, but more can be ordered by sending SASE and postage.** Reviews books of poetry in 500-1,000 words. Open to unsolicited reviews. Poets may also send books for review consideration. They have published an *Anthology: 1987-1991 Best of Poetic Space,* $5. Also **publishes one chapbook each spring.** Their first chapbook was *Truth Rides to Work and Good Girls,* poetry by Crawdad Nelson and fiction by Louise A. Blum ($5 plus $1.50 p&h). Don Hildenbrand says, "We like poetry that takes risks—original writing that gives us a new, different perspective."

***POETICAL HISTORIES (III)**, 27 Sturton St., Cambridge CB1 2QG United Kingdom, founded 1985, editor Peter Riley, is a "small press publishing **poetry only." They publish poetry that is "modernist,"** not "experimental, translated, homely." They have recently published poetry by J.H. Prynne, John Kinsella and Tony Baker. **They publish 8-10 hand-printed chapbooks/year averaging 8 pgs. each.** *PH* is also a contact address for The Cambridge Conference of Contemporary Poetry, which takes place annually in late April.

POETRY; THE MODERN POETRY ASSOCIATION; BESS HOKIN PRIZE; LEVINSON PRIZE; EUNICE TIETJENS MEMORIAL PRIZE; FREDERICK BOCK PRIZE; GEORGE KENT PRIZE; UNION LEAGUE PRIZE; J. HOWARD AND BARBARA M.J. WOOD PRIZE; RUTH LILLY POETRY PRIZE; RUTH LILLY POETRY FELLOWSHIP (III), 60 W. Walton St., Chicago IL 60610-3380, founded 1912, editor Joseph Parisi, "is the oldest and most distinguished monthly magazine devoted entirely to verse," according to their literature. "Founded in Chicago in 1912, it immediately became the international showcase that it has remained ever since, publishing in its earliest years—and often for the first time—such giants as Ezra Pound, Robert Frost, T.S. Eliot, Marianne Moore and Wallace Stevens. *Poetry* has continued to print the major voices of our time and to discover new talent, establishing an unprecedented record. There is virtually no important contemporary poet in our language who has not at a crucial stage in his career depended on *Poetry* to find a public for him: John Ashbery, Dylan Thomas, Edna St. Vincent Millay, James Merrill, Anne Sexton, Sylvia Plath, James Dickey, Thom Gunn, David Wagoner—only a partial list to suggest how *Poetry* has represented, without affiliation with any movements or schools, what Stephen Spender has described as 'the best, and simply the best' poetry being written.'' Although its offices have always been in Chicago, *Poetry*'s influence and scope extend far beyond, throughout the US and in over 45 countries around the world. Asked to select 4 lines of poetry "which represent the taste and quality you want in your publication" Joseph Parisi selected the opening lines of "The Love Song of J. Alfred Prufrock" by T.S. Eliot, which first appeared in *Poetry* in 1915:

> *Let us go then, you and I,*
> *When the evening is spread out against the sky*
> *Like a patient etherized upon a table;*
> *Let us go, through certain half-deserted streets . . .*

Poetry is an elegantly printed, flat-spined, 5½×9 magazine. They receive over 80,000 submissions a year, use approximately 300-350, have up to a 9-month backlog. Circulation is 7,700 for 5,700 subscribers of which 53% are libraries. Single copy: $3; subscription: $27, $30 for institutions. **Sample postpaid: $4.50. Submit up to 4 poems at a time. Send SASE for guidelines. Reports in 3-4 months—longer for mss submitted during the summer. Pays $2 a line. Buys all rights. Returns rights "upon written request."** Reviews books of poetry in multi-book formats of varying lengths. Open to unsolicited reviews. Poets may also send books to Stephen Young, senior editor, for review consideration. This is probably the most prestigious poetry credit in the publishing business. Consequently, competition here is extraordinarily keen with more poems received in a year than there are people in some cities in your state. Yet Joseph Parisi is one of the most efficient (and discerning) editors around, and he does much to promote poetry. This is a magazine that you can buy straight off the newsstand to get a feel for the pulse of poetry each month. Seven prizes (named in heading) ranging from $200 to $1,500 are awarded annually to poets whose work has appeared in the magazine that year. *Only verse already published in Poetry is eligible for consideration and no formal application is necessary. Poetry* also sponsors the Ruth Lilly Poetry Prize, an annual award of $75,000, and the Ruth Lilly Poetry Fellowship, two annual awards of $15,000 to undergraduate or graduate students to support their further studies in poetry/creative writing. Work published in *Poetry* was also selected for inclusion in the 1992, 1993, 1994, 1995, 1996 and 1997 volumes of *The Best American Poetry*.

‡**POETRY & PROSE ANNUAL (I)**, P.O. Box 541, Manzanita OR 97130, website http://www.Poetry&ProseAnnual.arts, founded 1996, editor Sandra Claire Foushee, "publishes work with an affirmative appreciation of the universe. Accepted work appears in the American Portfolio section of the journal—poetry, fiction, nonfiction and photography is featured. **We are looking for excellence and undiscovered creative genius in poems of substance. Poems should be original with rhythmic and lyric strength. Innovation and fresh imagery encouraged. Metrical ingenuity recognized. Open to all forms."** They have recently published poetry by Helen Dickinson, Anne Splane Phillips and Barbara Harrah. As a sample the editor selected these lines from "In the Light of Liquid Dreams" by Alwyn Scott Turner:

> *Her body washed in rose water, perfumed with sweet fragrances,*
> *powdered with camphor dust, annointed with palm oil;*
> *The scent of summer flowers and burning sandlewood in the air,*
> *curving around the soft contours of her neck, into fertile soil,*
> *pungent smoke saturating the thick waves of ther auburn hair.*

PPA is approximately 72 pgs., 7×8½, offset-printed and saddle-stitched with glossy card cover, cover photograph, contains line art and photos inside. Press run is about 1,000. Subscription: $15. **"A $20 submission fee is required. A copy of the journal will be sent to anyone submitting, whether or not the work has been accepted." Submit no more than 200 lines of poetry at a time.** Previously published poems and simultaneous submissions OK, "but immediate notice requested if accepted elsewhere." Cover letter preferred with short bio. Electronic submissions accepted through website. **Always comments on rejections. Send SASE for guidelines. Reports as soon as possible. Sometimes sends prepublication galleys. Pays 2 copies. Acquires one-time and reprints rights.** Staff reviews books of poetry in 1-page single-book formats. Poets may send books for review consideration. Work may also appear in the *Poetry & Prose Annual* website.

 AN ASTERISK before a listing indicates an overseas publisher, magazine, contest, conference or organization.

POETRY DIGEST (II), P.O. Box 7692, Port St. Lucie FL 34985-7692, founded 1991, editor John DeStefano, is a national magazine of contemporary poetry which appears 3 times/year. **They want "high-quality poetry by new and established writers. We are open to all forms of contemporary poetry, up to 100 lines. Individuality as well as a skillful crafting with respect to the art must be evident in the framework of the poem. Nothing abstract or political."** They have published poetry by Brendan Galvin, Alfred Dorn, H.R. Coursen, Gerald Locklin, Stuart Friebert, Sanford Pinsker, Walter McDonald and Len Krisak. *POETRY Digest* (formerly known as *The New Review*) is 60-80 pgs. (142 pgs. in their Spring/Summer double issue), 5¾ × 8¾, offset printed and perfect-bound with textured matte cover printed in 2 colors. (Subscribers receive free display/classified ad space for their published chapbooks.) They receive 3,000-3,500 poems a year, accept 35-40%, and publish 40-50 poems in each issue, 80 poems in a double issue. Press run is 450 for 250 subscribers. Subscription: $14.75. **Sample postpaid: $6.75. Make checks payable to John DeStefano. Submit 5-8 poems at a time. No previously published poems; simultaneous submissions OK. Cover letter with brief bio preferred. Seldom comments on rejections. Reports "usually within 15 days." Always sends prepublication galleys. Pays 1 copy.**

POETRY EAST (II), Dept. of English, DePaul University, 802 W. Belden Ave., Chicago IL 60614, phone (773)325-7487, founded 1980, editor Richard Jones, "is a biannual international magazine publishing poetry, translations and reviews. We suggest that authors look through back issues of the magazine before making submissions. **No constraints or specifications; we are open to both traditional forms and free verse.**" They have published poetry by Tom Crawford, Thomas McGrath, Denise Levertov, Galway Kinnell, Sharon Olds and Amiri Baraka. The digest-sized, flat-spined journal is 250 pgs., professionally printed with glossy color card cover. They use 200 pgs. of poetry in each issue. They receive about 50,000 submissions a year, use approximately 10%, have a 4-month backlog. Circulation is 2,500 for 600 subscribers of which 200 are libraries. Single copy: $10; subscription: $15. **Sample postpaid: $8. Reports in 4 months. Pays copies. Editors sometimes comment on rejections.** Open to unsolicited reviews. Poets may also send books for review consideration. This is one of the best-edited and designed magazines being published today. Award-winning editor Richard Jones assembles an exciting array of accessible poems, leaning toward lyric free verse with room for narrative and otherwise well-structured poems in all traditions. He occasionally schedules theme issues and selects poems accordingly. Because competition is keen, response times can exceed stated limits, particularly in the spring. Work published in *Poetry East* has been included in *The Best American Poetry 1993*.

THE POETRY EXPLOSION NEWSLETTER (THE PEN) (I), P.O. Box 4725, Pittsburgh PA 15206, founded 1984, editor Arthur C. Ford, is a "quarterly newsletter dedicated to the preservation of poetry." Arthur Ford wants **"poetry—40 lines maximum, no minimum. All forms and subject matter with the use of good imagery, symbolism and honesty. Rhyme and non-rhyme. No vulgarity."** He has published poetry by Veona Thomas and Rose Robaldo. *The Pen* is 12-16 pgs., saddle-stitched, mimeographed on both sides. They receive about 300 poems a year, accept approximately 80. Press run is 450 for 350 subscribers of which 5 are libraries. Subscription: $15. **Send $4 for sample copy and more information. Make checks payable to Arthur C. Ford. Submit up to 5 poems at a time with $1 reading fee. Also include large SASE if you want work returned. Simultaneous submissions and previously published poems OK. Sometimes publishes theme issues. "We announce future dates when decided. June's issue is usually full of romantic poetry." Send SASE for upcoming themes. Editor comments on rejections "sometimes, but not obligated." Pays 2 copies.** He will criticize poetry for 15¢ a word. Open to unsolicited reviews. Poets may also send books for review consideration. The editor comments: "Even though free verse is more popular today, we try to stay versatile."

‡POETRY FORUM (I, II); THE JOURNAL (IV-Subscription); HEALTHY BODY-HEALTHY MINDS (IV-Health concerns), 5713 Larchmont Dr., Erie PA 16509, phone (814)866-2543 (also fax: 8-10 a.m. or 5-8 p.m.), e-mail 75562.670@compuserve.com, editor Gunvor Skogsholm. *Poetry Forum* appears 3 times/year. **"We are open to any style and form. We believe new forms ought to develop from intuition. Length up to 50 lines accepted. Would like to encourage long themes. No porn or blasphemy, but open to all religious persuasions."** The magazine is 7 × 8½, 38 pgs., saddle-stapled with card cover, photocopied from photoreduced typescript. **Sample postpaid: $3. Simultaneous submissions and previously published poems OK. Electronic submissions OK. Editor comments on poems "if asked, but respects the poetic freedom of the artist." Publishes theme issues. Send SASE for guidelines and upcoming themes or request via fax or e-mail. Sometimes sends prepublication galleys. Gives awards of $25, $15, $10 and 3 honorable mentions for the best poems in each issue. Acquires one-time rights.** Reviews books of poetry in 250 words maximum. Open to unsolicited reviews. Poets may also send books for review consideration. *The Journal*, which appears twice a year, accepts **experimental poetry of any length from subscribers only. Sample: $3.** *Healthy Body-Healthy Minds* is a biannual publication concerned with health issues. **They accept essays, poetry, articles and short-shorts on health, fitness, mind and soul. Send SASE for details.** They offer a poetry chapbook contest. Entry fee: $9. Prize is publication and 20 copies. Send SASE for information. The editor says, "I believe today's poets should experiment more and not feel stuck in the forms that were in vogue 300 years ago. I would like to see more experimentalism—new forms will prove that poetry is alive and well in the mind and spirit of the people."

POETRY HARBOR; NORTH COAST REVIEW (I, II, IV-Regional), P.O. Box 103, Duluth MN 55801-0103, phone (218)728-3728, founded 1989, director Patrick McKinnon. Poetry Harbor is a "nonprofit, tax-exempt organization dedicated to fostering literary creativity through public readings, publications, radio and television broadcasts, and other artistic and educational means." Its main publication, *North Coast Review*, is a regional magazine appearing 3 times/year with **poetry and prose poems by and about Upper Midwest people, including those from Minnesota, Wisconsin, North Dakota, and the upper peninsula of Michigan. "No form/style/content specifications, though we are inclined toward narrative, imagist poetry. We do not want to see anything from outside our region, not because it isn't good, but because we can't publish it due to geographics."** They have published poetry by Mark Vinz, Joe Paddock, Susan Hauser and Jim Northrup. *NCR* is 56 pgs., 7 × 8½, offset and saddle-stapled, paper cover with various b&w art, ads at back. They receive about 500 submissions a year, use 100-150. Press run is 1,000 for 200 subscribers of which 20 are libraries, 300 shelf sales. Subscription: $21.95/2 years. **Sample postpaid: $4.95. Submit 3-5 pgs. of poetry, typed single-spaced, with name and address on each page. Previously published poems and simultaneous submissions OK, if noted. Cover letter with brief bio ("writer's credits") required. "We read three times a year, but our deadlines change from time to time. Write to us for current deadlines for our various projects." Send SASE for guidelines. Reports in 1-5 months. Pays $10 plus copies. Buys one-time rights.** Poetry Harbor also publishes 1 perfect-bound paperback of poetry and **4-8 chapbooks** each biennium. "Chapbooks are selected by our editorial board from the pool of poets we have published in *North Coast Review* or have worked with in our other projects. **We suggest you send a submission to *North Coast Review* first. We almost always print chapbooks and anthologies by poets we've previously published or hired for readings."** Anthologies include *Poets Who Haven't Moved to St. Paul* and *Days of Obsidian, Days of Grace*, selected poetry and prose by four Native American writers. Complete publications list available upon request. Poetry Harbor also sponsors a monthly reading series ("poets are paid to perform"), a weekly TV program (4 different cable networks regionally), various radio programming, a prison workshop series and other special events. They say, "Poetry Harbor is extremely committed to cultivating a literary community and an appreciation for our region's literature within the Upper Midwest. Poetry Harbor projects are in place to create paying, well-attended venues for our region's fine poets. Poets are now OK to people up here, and literature is thriving. The general public is proving to us that they *do* like poetry if you give them some that is both readable and rooted in the lives of the community."

POETRY IN MOTION; NATIONAL POET'S ASSOCIATION (I, IV-Membership), P.O. Box 173, Dept. PM, Bayport MN 55003-0173, phone (612)779-6952, e-mail poem@winternet.com, website http://www.winternet.com/~poem/pim.html, founded 1992, editor Nadia Giordana. *Poetry in Motion* is a quarterly publication "dedicated to showcasing the finest work of emerging and established poets, writers, artists and photographers from across the U.S. and abroad." Each issue includes poetry, short stories, cartoons, artwork and articles. **"Approximately 60% of the material published is by members of the National Poet's Association; 40% is written by nonmembers. Nonmembers must pay a $1 per page reading fee for poetry, but not for stories." They are open to all kinds of poetry, including humorous poems and haiku, 32 lines maximum.** They have published poetry by Clyde Wallin Jr., James S. McLellan, Sara L. Holt and Nancy S. Young. As a sample we selected these lines from "Clavicle" by Sharon F. Suer:

> *Fractured—and an oddly pleasant discomfort,*
> *like the wet sponge inside your head with a cold*
> *or the unrest in every muscle with the flu,*
> *so that you just want to stretch your limbs*
> *in a whole-body yawn. Or the fatigue so intense*
> *that it hurts, every cell trying hard to lie down.*

Poetry in Motion is 64 pgs., 8½ × 11, professionally printed on newsprint with 4-color glossy cover and numerous ads from local supporters. Press run is 3,000. Membership/subscription: $19.99 (4 issues of *Poetry in Motion*). **Sample postpaid: $5. Submit work typed single-spaced, 1 poem (or 3 haiku) to a page, name and address on each. Cover letter (with "interesting information about yourself") required. Nonmembers must include reading fee. Send large SASE for guidelines or request via e-mail. "E-mail submissions OK if they have received a copy of our guidelines. We may keep material for up to three months if it is being seriously considered for publication." Pays 1 copy/accepted piece.** They also publish chapbooks and illustrations, and an occasional full-sized anthology. Send SASE for details. The editor says, "Membership does not ensure publication. All material submitted by members and nonmembers alike is judged and chosen solely on its own merit. Since we publish poetry and stories on a wide variety of subjects, it is always a good idea to review a sample copy to get an idea of what is likely to get published. Please, nothing excessively profane or violent."

‡POETRY INTERNATIONAL (III), Dept. of English, San Diego State University, San Diego CA 92182-8140, phone (619)594-1523, fax (619)594-4998, e-mail fmoramar@mail.sdsu.edu, website http://www.rohan.sdsu.edu/dept/press/poetry.html, founded 1996, editor Fred Moramarco, published annually, is "an eclectic poetry magazine intended to reflect a wide range of poetry being written today." **They want "a wide range of styles and subject matter. We're particularly interested in translations." They do not want "cliché-ridden, derivative, obscure poetry."** They have recently published poetry by Charles Simic, Marge Piercy, Diane Wakoski, Gary Soto and Larry Levis. As a sample the editor selected these lines from "My Muse" by Heinrich Böll, translated by William Pitt Root and Hennelore Quander-Rattee:

My muse stands on the corner
what I don't want
she gives cheap to everyone
when she's happy
she makes a gift of what I want
Seldom have I seen her happy.

The editor says *Poetry International* is 200 pgs. Press run is 1,000. Single copy: $12; subscription: $24/2 years. **Submit up to 5 poems at a time. No previously published poems; simultaneous submissions OK "but prefer not to." Reads submissions September 1 through December 15 only.** Time between acceptance and publication is 6-8 months. **Poems are circulated to an editorial board. Seldom comments on rejections. Reports in 3 months. Pays 2 copies. Acquires all rights. Returns rights "50/50," meaning they split with the author any payment for reprinting the poem elsewhere.** "We review anthologies regularly." The editor says, "We're interested in new work by poets who are devoted to their art. We want poems that matter—that make a difference in people's lives. We're especially seeking good translations and prose by poets about poetry."

*POETRY KANTO (II), Kanto Gakuin University, Kamariya-cho, Kanazawa-Ku, Yokohama 236, Japan, founded 1984, editor William I. Elliott. *Poetry Kanto* is a literary annual published by the Kanto Poetry Center, which also sponsors an annual poetry conference. It publishes **well-crafted original poems in English and in Japanese.** The magazine publishes **"anything except pornography, English haiku and tanka, and tends to publish poems under 30 lines."** They have published work by A.D. Hope, Peter Robinson, Naomi Shihab Nye, Nuala Ni Dhomhnaill and Les Murray. The magazine is 60 pgs., digest-sized, nicely printed (the English poems occupy the first half of the issue, the Japanese poems the second), saddle-stapled, matte card cover. Circulation is 700, of which 400 are distributed free to schools, poets and presses; it is also distributed at poetry seminars. The magazine is unpriced. **Interested poets should query from October through December with SAE and IRCs before submitting. Then, if query is accepted, submit 3-5 poems. No previously published poems or simultaneous submissions. Often comments on rejections. Reports on mss in 1-2 weeks. Pays 3-5 copies.** The editor advises, "Read a lot. Get feedback from poets and/or workshops. Be neat, clean, legible and polite in submissions. *SAE with International Reply Coupons absolutely necessary when requesting sample copy.*"

‡*POETRY LIFE SUPPLEMENT; NOVA POETICA (III, IV-Subscription), 14 Pennington Oval, Lymington, Hampshire 50418BQ England, founded 1994, editor Adrian Bishop. *Poetry Life*, published 3 times/year, describes itself as "Britain's sharpest poetry magazine with serious articles about the poetry scene." **They want "poets who have passion, wit, style, revelation and loads of imagination." They do not want "poems on pets."** They have recently published poetry by James Fenton, Carol Ann Duffy, Le Murray, Benjamin Zephaniah and Simon Armitage. The editor says *Poetry Life* is A4. They accept approximately 1% of the poems they receive. Press run is 1,500. Single copy: £2. **Poets submitting must be subscribers. Submit 6 poems at a time. Previously published poems and simultaneous submissions OK. Cover letter required.** Time between acceptance and publication is 3 months. **Poems are circulated to an editorial board. Send SAE with IRCs for guidelines. Reports in 3 months. Sometimes sends prepublication galleys.** Reviews books or chapbooks of poetry or other magazines. Open to unsolicited reviews. Poets may also send books for review consideration. Sponsors open poetry competitions. Send SAE with IRCs for guidelines.

THE POETRY MISCELLANY (II), English Dept., University of Tennessee at Chattanooga, Chattanooga TN 37403, phone (423)755-4629, e-mail suobodni@aol.com, founded 1971 (in North Adams, MA), poetry editor Richard Jackson. "We publish new and established writers—poems, interviews, essays, translations. We are truly a miscellany: **We look at all schools, types, etc.**" They have published poetry by William Matthews, Marvin Bell, Paula Rankin, Tomaž Šalmun and Donald Justice. The 16-page tabloid appears annually, professionally printed, with black ink on grey paper. Circulation is 750 for 400 subscribers of which 100 are libraries. They receive about 10,000 submissions a year, use approximately 20, have a 6-12 month backlog. Subscription: $5. **Sample postpaid: $2.50. Submit 3-4 clear copies/submission. Editor "rarely" comments on rejections. Send SASE for guidelines. Reports in 3-4 months. Pays 2 copies.** Also publishes chapbooks. Sometimes holds contests "when grants allow."

POETRY MOTEL; POETRY MOTEL WALLPAPER BROADSIDES (I, II), 1911 E. First St., Duluth MN 55812, founded 1984, editors Patrick McKinnon, Bud Backen, Ed Gooder and Ellen Seitz-Ryan aim **"to keep the rooms clean and available for these poor ragged poems to crash in once they are through driving or committing adultery." They want "poems that took longer than ten minutes to author." No other specifications.** They have recently published poetry by Julie Otten, Willie Smith, Albert Huffstickler, Ron Androla, Linda Wing, Tony Moffeit and Todd Moore. As a sample they selected this poem, "Manitowoc" by Carolyn Ahrens:

I did what my father told me to do.
I parked the car off
to an angle, shined the brights
and waited. He told me never
to get too close; they can kick you to death

> *in their dying. And if they come through*
> *the windshield, duck.*

Poetry Motel appears "every 260 days" as a 7 × 8½ digest, with wallpaper cover, 52 pgs. of poetry, prose, essays, literary memoirs and reviews. Circulation is 1,000 for 600 subscribers. They receive about 1,500 submissions a year, accept approximately 150, have a 3- to 24-month backlog. **Sample: $6.95. Submit 3-5 pgs. of poetry at a time, with SASE. Simultaneous submissions OK. Informal cover letter with bio credits required. Reports in "1 week to never." Pay varies.** Reviews books of poetry. Open to unsolicited reviews. Poets may also send books for review consideration. They advise, "Poets should read as much poetry as they can lay their hands on. And they should realize that although poetry is no fraternal club, poets are responsible for its survival, both financially and emotionally. Join us out here—this is where the edge meets the vision. We are very open to work from 'beginners.' "

POETRY NEW YORK: A JOURNAL OF POETRY AND TRANSLATION (II, IV-Translations, themes), P.O. Box 3184, Church Street Station, New York NY 10008, e-mail tunguska@mail.iot.net, founded 1985, editors Burt Kimmelman and Tod Thilleman, is an annual. They have published poetry by Wanda Coleman, Jerome Rothenberg, Enid Dame, Amiel Alcalay and Ann Lauterbach, and translations of Mallarme, Hesiod and Makoto Ooka. The editors describe it as 80 pgs., 6×9, perfect-bound. They accept about 20% of "blind submissions." Press run is 700 for 400 shelf sales. **Submit up to 5 poems at a time. Reports in 6 months. Pays 1 copy.** They sometimes sponsor readings. Work published in *Poetry New York* has been included in the 1993 and 1994 volumes of *The Best American Poetry*.

POETRY NORTHWEST (II), University of Washington, 4045 Brooklyn Ave. NE, JA-15, Seattle WA 98105, phone (206)685-4750, founded 1959, editor David Wagoner, is a quarterly. The magazine is 48 pgs., 5½×8½, professionally printed with color card cover. It features all styles and forms. For instance, lyric and narrative free verse has been included alongside a sonnet sequence, minimalist sonnets and stanza patterns—all accessible and lively. They receive 10,000 poems a year, use approximately 160, have a 3-month backlog. Circulation is 1,500. Subscription: $15. **Sample postpaid: $4. Occasionally comments on rejections. Reports in 1 month maximum. Pays 2 copies. Awards prizes of $500, $100, $50 and $50 yearly, judged by the editors.** Poetry published here has also been included in *The Best American Poetry 1996*.

*POETRY NOTTINGHAM INTERNATIONAL; LAKE ASKE MEMORIAL OPEN POETRY COMPETITION (II); NOTTINGHAM POETRY SOCIETY; QUEENIE LEE COMPETITION (IV-Membership/subscription), 13 Bradmore Rise, Sherwood, Nottingham NG5 3BJ England, founded 1946, editor Cathy Grindrod. Nottingham Poetry Society meets monthly for readings, talks, etc., and publishes quarterly its magazine, *Poetry Nottingham International,* which is open to submissions from anyone. **"We wish to see poetry that is intelligible to and enjoyable by the intelligent reader. We do not want any party politics or religious freaks. Poems not more than 30 lines in length."** They have recently published poetry by William Baer, Brian Daldorph and Walter McDonald from the US. As a sample the editor selected these lines from "Pasta" by Kate Scott:

> *She hangs the frail strips on chairs, on doors.*
>
> *As the dampness lifts they start to flutter.*
> *She hangs them lightly over her arm, padding to the stove.*
>
> *She boils water, opens wine, puts vegetables in pots.*
> *Lights click. Smells blossom.*
> *Everything feels suddenly invited.*

There are 40 pgs. of poetry in each issue of the 6×8 magazine, professional printing with occasional essays, glossy art paper cover. They receive about 1,500 submissions a year, use approximately 120, usually have a 1- to 3-month backlog. Circulation is 275 for 200 subscribers of which 20 are libraries. Single copy: £2 ($8 US); subscriptions: £15 sterling or $30 US. **Sample postpaid: $8 or £1.75. Submit up to 6 poems at any time, not more than 30 lines each, not handwritten, and previously unpublished. Send SAE and 3 IRCs for stamps. No need to query but requires cover letter. Reports "within 2 months plus mailing time." Pays 1 copy.** Staff reviews books of poetry, but space allows only listings or brief review. Send books for review consideration. **Nottingham Poetry Society publishes collections by individual poets who are members of Nottingham Poetry Society.** The Lake Aske Memorial Open Poetry Competition offers cash prizes, annual subscriptions and publication in *Poetry Nottingham.* Open to all. The Queenie Lee Competition is for members and subscribers only, offers a cash prize and publication. The editor says they would like to see "more traditional forms. No disjointed prose under the guise of free verse. Poems most often rejected due to: use of tired language and imagery, use of clichés and inversions, old treatment of an old subject, sentimentality, poor rhythm and scansion, incorrect use of set forms."

POETRY OF THE PEOPLE (I, IV-Humor, love, nature, fantasy, themes), P.O. Box 298, Micanopy FL 32667, phone/fax (352)466-3743, e-mail poetryofthepeople@poetic.com, founded 1986, poetry editor Paul Cohen. *Poetry of the People* is a leaflet that appears 3 times/year. **"We take all forms of poetry but we like**

humorous poetry, love poetry, nature poetry and fantasy. **No racist or highly ethnocentric poetry will be accepted. I do not like poetry that lacks images or is too personal or contains rhyme to the point that the poem has been destroyed.'' They are also accepting poetry written in French and Spanish.** They have published poetry by Max Lizard, Prof. Jerry Reminick, Ian Ayers and Noelle Kocot. The format for *Poetry of the People* varies from 8-32 pgs., 5½×8 to 5½×4⅜, stapled, sometimes on colored paper. Issues are usually theme oriented. It has a circulation between 300 and 2,300. Copies are distributed to Gainesville residents for 25¢ each. **Samples: $4 for 11 pamphlets. "Please send donations, the magazine bank account is overdrawn. Suggested donation: $2." Submit up to 10 poems at a time. Cover letter with biographical information required with submissions. "I feel autobiographical information is important in understanding the poetry." Poems returned within 6 months. Editor comments on rejections "often." Send SASE for upcoming themes. Takes suggestions for theme issues. Sometimes sends prepublication galleys. Pays 10 copies. Acquires first rights.** He advises, ''Be creative; there is a lot of competition out there.''

‡*POETRY REVIEW; NATIONAL POETRY COMPETITION (II), 22 Betterton St., London WC2H 980 United Kingdom, phone (0044)171 240 4810, fax (0044)171 240 4818, e-mail poetrysoc@dial.pipex.com, website http://www.poetrysoc.com, founded 1909, editor Peter Forbes, published quarterly, strives ''to be the leading showcase of UK poetry and to represent poetry written in English and in translation.'' **They want "poems with metaphoric resonance."** They do not want ''**inconsequential disconnected jottings.**'' They have recently published poetry by John Ashbery, Miroslav Holub, Sharon Olds and Paul Muldoon. As a sample the editor selected these lines from ''Addressee Unknown—Retour à L'Expéditeur'' by Hans Magnus Enzensberger:

> *Many thanks for the clouds.*
> *Many thanks for the* well-tempered *clavier*
> *and, why not, for the warm winter boots.*
> *Many thanks for my strange brain*
> *amd for all manner of other hidden organs*

The editor says *Poetry Review* is 96 pgs., 6½×9, paperback, with b&w cartoons and photos. They receive about 30-50,000 poems a year, accept approximately 0.3-0.4%. Press run is 4,750 for 4,000 subscribers of which 400 are libraries, 4 shelf sales; 100 distributed free to contributors and press. Single copy: £5.95; subscription: $56. **Sample postpaid: $13. Submit 4 poems at a time. No previously published poems or simultaneous submissions.** Time between acceptance and publication is 6 months. **Poems are selected by the editor. Seldom comments on rejections. Publishes theme issues. Reports 1-3 months. Sometimes sends prepublication galleys. Pays £40 plus 1 copy. Buys UK first publication rights.** Staff reviews chapbooks of poetry or other magazines in single/multi-book format. Sponsors the National Poetry Competition run by the Poetry Society, £6,000 first prize, send SASE (or SAE and IRC) for guidelines. Offers ''The Script'' reading service: £30 for 100 lines.

*POETRY WALES; SEREN PRESS (II, IV-Ethnic), 2 Wyndham St., First Floor, Bridgend, Mid-Glamorgan CF31 1EF Wales, founded 1965. *Poetry Wales*, a 72-page, 248×177mm quarterly, circulation 1,000, has a primary interest in **Welsh and Anglo-Welsh poets but also considers submissions internationally.** Overseas subscription: £18/year. **Sample: £4. Submit 6 poems at a time. No previously published poems. One-page cover letter required; include name, address and previous publications. SASE (or SAE and IRC) must be included for reply. Pays honorarium and 1 copy.** Staff reviews books of poetry. Send books for review consideration to Amy L. Wack, reviews editor, Wyndham Street address. Seren Press publishes books of **primarily Welsh and Anglo-Welsh poetry**, also biography, critical works and some fiction, distributed by Dufour Editions, Inc., Box 449, Chester Springs PA 19425. They have received several Welsh Arts Council ''Book of the Year'' Prizes. The editor says, ''We would like to see more formal poetry.''

♣POETRY WLU (I, II), Dept. of English, Wilfrid Laurier University, Waterloo, Ontario N2L 3C5 Canada, phone (519)884-1970, ext. 3308, founded 1979, editorial contact E. Jewinski, is an annual literary magazine (published every March) ''with emphasis on *all* poetry and *all* prose *under* 1,000 words. **20-30 lines are ideal; but all kinds and lengths considered.**'' *Poetry WLU* is 6½×8, saddle-stapled, typeset, with matte card cover using b&w art. They receive about 100-120 submissions a year, use approximately 15-20%. Press run is 300. **Sample postpaid: $5. Submit 5 poems at a time. "We strongly discourage simultaneous submissions." Cover letter preferred. Reads submissions September 1 through January 30 only. "When the editorial board has time, comments are made." Reports in 6-8 months. Pays 1 copy.** Staff reviews books of poetry.

POETS AT WORK (I, IV-Subscribers), VAMC 325 New Castle Rd., Box 113, Butler PA 16001, founded 1985, editor/publisher Jessee Poet, **all contributors are expected to subscribe.** The editor says, **"Every poet who writes within the dictates of good taste and within my 20-line limit will be published in each issue. I accept all forms and themes of poetry, including seasonal and holiday, but no porn, no profanity."** He has recently published poetry by Martha Balph, William Middleton, Ann Gasser, Warren Jones and Ralph Hammond. As a sample he selected his poem "An Old Romance":

> *I almost loved you . . . did you know?*
> *Sometimes you still disturb my dreams.*
> *A summer romance long ago*
> *I almost loved you . . . did you know?*
> *We danced to music soft and low*
> *Just yesterday . . . or so it seems*
> *I almost loved you . . . did you know?*
> *Sometimes you still disturb my dreams.*

Poets at Work, a bimonthly, is generally 36-40 pgs., magazine-sized, saddle-stapled, photocopied from typescript with colored paper cover. Subscription: $20. **Sample: $3.50. Submit 5-10 poems at a time. Simultaneous submissions and previously published poems OK. Reports within 2 weeks. Pays nothing, not even a copy.** "Because I publish hundreds of poets, I cannot afford to pay or give free issues. Every subscriber, of course, gets an issue. Subscribers also have many opportunities to regain their subscription money in the numerous contests offered in each issue. Send SASE for flyer for my separate monthly and special contests." He also **publishes chapbooks.** Send SASE for details. The editor adds, "These days even the best poets tell me that it is difficult to get published. I am here for the novice as well as the experienced poet. I consider *Poets at Work* to be a hotbed for poets where each one can stretch and grow at his or her own pace. Each of us learns from the other, and we do not criticize one another. The door for poets is always open, so please stop by; we probably will like each other immediately."

THE POET'S ATTIC QUARTERLY (III), P.O. Box 34273, Philadelphia PA 19101-4273, e-mail poetsattic@ geocites.com, website http://www.geocites.com/Paris/LeftBank/1644, founded 1993, editor William Rothwell, co-editor Anthony Baekaland, assistant editor Ray Reeves. *The Poet's Attic Quarterly* is designed "to expose 'closet' poets that seek a medium for expression." **They welcome young and new writers. "Open to content, enjoy universality. But no verse crippled by conservatism. No teenage angst. No painful rhyme scheme. No poems over 100 lines. Otherwise, we receive you with open arms."** They have recently published poetry by Kenneth Pobo and John Cornwall. As a sample the editor selected these lines from "Letter to Nemo" by Daniela Crasnaru:

> *The bee walled in the hexagonal cell*
> *exudes image of honey having in memory*
> *image of acacia*
> *from a thousand years ago.*
> *"Dead imagination, imagine the fragrance."*

The Poet's Attic Quarterly is 22 pgs., $5\frac{1}{2} \times 8\frac{1}{2}$, photocopied and saddle-stitched with different front and back covers each issue, various b&w graphics (including a few nude photos) "to fit the poems," and ads every other month. They receive about 1,500 poems a year, accept approximately 730. Press run is 500 for 160 subscribers, 290 shelf sales. Single copy: $2; subscription: $14/year ($8 for half a year). **Sample (including guidelines) postpaid: $2.55. Submit 3-5 poems at a time. No previously published poems; simultaneous submissions OK. Cover letter preferred; include** "places of previous publication, mention poems you liked in our last issue, etc." **E-mail submissions OK. Poems are read by each of the editors. Seldom comments on rejections. Brief guidelines are included inside the magazine or can be obtained via website. Reports in 2-6 weeks. Pays 1 copy.** They also sponsor an annual contest with a $250 first prize, $100 second prize. Reading fee: $2/ poem. Deadline: October 15. Send SASE for details.

POET'S FANTASY (I, IV-Fantasy), Dept. PM, 227 Hatten Ave., Rice Lake WI 54868-2030, founded 1991, publisher/editor Gloria Stoeckel, is a quarterly designed "to help the striving poet see his/her work in print." **They want sonnets, haiku and humorous free verse, 4-16 lines. "I accept good, clean poetry. Looking for poems of fantasy, but not exclusively. No profanity or sexual use of words."** They have published poetry by earl jay perel and Gary Michael Lawson. *Poet's Fantasy* is 36 pgs., digest-sized, photocopied from typescript and saddle-stapled with colored paper cover, graphics and ads. They receive about 400 poems a year, accept approximately 90%. Press run is 400 for 450 subscribers. Subscription: $18/year; foreign $24/year. **Sample postpaid: $4. Submit 3-5 poems at a time. No previously published poems or simultaneous submissions. Often comments on rejections. Send SASE for guidelines. Reports within 2 weeks. Pays coupon for $3 off subscription price or greeting card order. (Poets must purchase copy their work is in.) Acquires first North American serial rights.** "I do book reviews if poet sends a complimentary copy of the book and a $3 reading fee. Reviews are approximately 200 to 300 words in length." She holds contests in each issue and also creates greeting cards for poets. "They use verse they wrote and can design their own cover." Send SASE for details.

THE POET'S GUILD (II), P.O. Box 161236, Sacramento CA 95816-1236, phone (916)331-3512, founded 1995, editor Mr. Laverne Frith, associate editor Joyce Odam, art manager Vicki Asp, appears bimonthly. **They want "original poetry that clearly demonstrates an understanding of craft. All styles accepted." However, they do not want to see "poetry which is overtly religious, erotic, inflammatory or demeans the human spirit."** They have published poetry by Lyn Lifshin, John Grey, Ann Menebroker, Jane Blue, Taylor Graham and Geoff Stevens. *The Poet's Guild* is 35-60 pgs., digest-sized, printed on recycled paper and saddle-stapled with a card stock cover with original pen art, interior clip art, and a decorative paper centerfold. They receive 1,800-2,000 poems a year, accept approximately 10%. Press run is 200 of which 5 libraries are subscribers. Single copy: $4; subscription: $16. Send subscription requests to Gary Elton Warrick, publisher, 5836 North Haven Dr., North Highlands CA 95660. **Submit 3-5 poems at a time, "typewritten and presented exactly as you would like them to appear," maximum 49 characters/line. Include name on every page. Previously published poems "occasionally" accepted with publication credits; no simultaneous submissions. Cover letter required; include SASE and 3-10 lines of biographical information and credits. Often comments on rejections. Send SASE for guidelines. Reports in 3 months. Pays 1 copy. Acquires first (or occasionally reprint) rights.** Also annually awards $50 to the best poem (as voted by subscribers) written by a subscriber and published in the magazine during the current calendar year.

‡**POETS ON THE LINE (V)**, P.O. Box 020292, Brooklyn NY 11202-0007, website http://www.echonyc.com/~poets, founded 1995, editor Linda Lerner, is a poetry anthology posted biannually on the Internet. They have recently published poetry by Hayden Carruth, Leo Connellan and Bill Ehrhart. As a sample the editor selected these lines from "Lynx light" by Tess Gallagher:

> *The quilt has slipped*
> *my shoulders. And when*
> *you kiss the knotts*
> *in my fate like that*
> *it's as if a lynx*
> *co-exists with a housecat.*

Currently not accepting unsolicited work. Interested poets should query regarding status. When open to submissions, submit poems on disk or hard copy. Previously published poems OK. Seldom comments on rejections. Sometimes sends prepublication galleys.

THE POET'S PAGE (I), P.O. Box 372, Wyanet IL 61379, founded 1994, editor/publisher Ione K. Pence, is a quarterly "for poets and all who love poetry." **They want poetry of "any subject, any length, any style, but we are not interested in shock poetry or vulgarities."** They have published poetry by Lyn Lifshin, Taylor Reese, Jean Harmon and Duane Locke. *TPP* is 40 pgs., digest-sized and saddle-stapled with colored card stock cover. Subscription: $10. **Sample postpaid: $3. No previously published poems; simultaneous submissions OK, "but we must be notified immediately if work is accepted elsewhere. Also, without a SASE or SAE and IRC, submissions go directly into our wastebasket with no response of any kind to the submitter."** Time between acceptance and publication is 9-12 months. **Send SASE for guidelines. Reports within a month. Pays copies. All rights retained by authors.**

‡**POET'S PARADISE (I, IV-Subscription)**, 158-21 78th Ave., Flushing NY 11366-1907, e-mail bonwilly@aol.com, founded 1991, editor/publisher Bunny Williams, published 3 times/year features essays, articles, tips on grammar, fiction and nonfiction, with two-thirds devoted to verses. **They want "poems that have depth and purpose; nothing trite or forced."** They do not want "salacious material." They have recently published poetry by Kenneth Geisert, Phil Eisenberg and Robert S. Blake. As a sample the editor selected her poem "Metamorphosis":

> *The canvas of life harbors the scent of greed*
> *Where every stroke caterwauls with rage;*
> *Tinsel thrones are painted*
> *And purity . . . now tainted . . .*
> *Writhes in the fallout of an age.*

Poet's Paradise is 92 pgs., 8½ × 11, laser-printed, spiral-bound, with inkjet colored cover and interior, with clip art. They receive about 800 poems a year, accept approximately 80%. Press run is 200 for 85 subscribers of which 15 are libraries, 40 shelf sales. Single copy: $5; subscription: $15. **Editor sends free tearsheets for anyone interested in sampling the magazine. Make checks payable to Bunny Williams. Subscription required for consideration. Submit any number of poems with contest fee of $1/poem (of 2-6 lines) or $2/poem (of 7-40 lines). "All poems are entered in a contest whereby subscribers judge the winning poems." Previously published poems and simultaneous submissions OK. Cover letter preferred. Always comments on rejections. Send SASE for guidelines. Reports in 5-10 days.** Sponsors a subscriber-judged contest in each issue. Every submission is considered an entry. For poems 7-40 lines the entry fee is $2/poem; awards $40, $25 and $10 with 3 honorable mentions. For poems 2-6 lines the entry fee is $1/poem; awards $15, $10 and $5 with 3 honorable mentions. Deadlines: March 1, July 1 and November 1. Include SASE for reply. **Must be a subscriber to enter contests.** The editor says, "Poets should be open to revision. Read your poem aloud for clarity and continuity. Metaphors are a part of poetry, but obscurity is tedious."

POET'S REVIEW (I, IV-Subscribers), P.O. Box I, 806 Kings Row, Varnell GA 30756, phone (706)694-8441, founded 1988, publisher Bob Riemke, is a monthly booklet, using **poetry by subscribers** and making cash awards monthly and annually on basis of votes by subscribers. **"Prefer rhyme. Short poems, 44 lines or less. Open to limericks and humor. Any subject. No porn! No foreign languages."** They have published poetry by Helen Webb, Ashley Anders and J. Alvin Speers. *PR* is 25 pgs., 8½ × 11, neatly printed and spiral-bound with 4-color paper cover. Single copy: $5; subscription: $40. **Sample postpaid: $4. Submit 1 typed poem at a time. "Subscribers are sent a ballot along with their monthly booklet to vote for the poems they believe to be the best." Monthly prizes are $75, $50 and $25, plus 7 honorable mentions. "All $75 winners are presented to the subscribers again at the end of the year and compete for a $500, $250 and $100 prize."** 60-70 poems are printed each month along with the names of winners for the previous month. Their magazine, *Theme Poetry* has ceased publication. However, they now publish *Chicken Soup*, a monthly publication **"with guaranteed publication if guidelines are followed." Send SASE for guidelines.**

POETS' ROUNDTABLE; POETS' STUDY CLUB OF TERRE HAUTE; POETS' STUDY CLUB INTERNATIONAL CONTEST (I, IV-Membership), 826 S. Center St., Terre Haute IN 47807, phone (812)234-0819, founded in 1939, president/editor Esther Alman. Poets' Study Club is one of the oldest associations of amateur poets. It publishes, every other month, *Poets' Roundtable*, a newsletter of market and contest information and news of the publications and activities of its members in a mimeographed, 10-page bulletin (magazine-sized, stapled at the corner), circulation 2,000. They have also published an occasional chapbook-anthology of poetry by members "but do not often do so." **Dues: $6/year. Sample free for SASE. Uses short poems by members only. Simultaneous submissions and previously published poems OK.** They offer an annual Poets' Study Club International Contest, open to all, with no fees and cash prizes—a $25 and $15 award in 3 categories: traditional haiku, serious poetry, light verse. Deadline: February 1. Also contests for members only each 2 months. "We have scheduled criticism programs for members only."

POINT JUDITH LIGHT (IV-Form/style), P.O. Box 6145, Springfield MA 01101, phone (413)746-3294, founded 1992, editor Patrick Frank, creative consultant Liz Fenn, technical editor Larry Kimmel, is a biannual publishing individual haiku/senryu, sequences and essays on Eastern philosophy and creativity theory. They want **haiku/senryu "which explore the relation of the poet to his/her environment and which focus on life as truly lived; 17 syllables maximum."** They have published haiku/senryu by H.F. Noyes, Tom Clausen and Tim Russell. As a sample the editor selected this haiku/senryu by Doratella Cardillo-Young:

> Ringing Tir's school bell
> the sound of its chime
> floating into space forever

PJL is desktop-published in a newsletter format, 20 pgs. maximum. Press run is 300. Subscription: $6/year. **Sample postpaid: $3. Previously published poems OK; no simultaneous submissions. Send 20 haiku/senryu maximum. Submissions should be typed. Cover letter with bio required.** "I want to have some knowledge of the poet behind the work." **Send SASE for guidelines. Reports within 6 months. Pays 1 copy. Acquires first or one-time rights.** The editor says, "Focus on the aspects of life that are immediately before you. Be yourself. Follow your intuition and be willing to explore and experiment. With James J.Y. Liu, I see poetry as a vehicle to explore external and internal worlds, as well as the language in which it is written. I am particularly interested in promoting the development of haiku/senryu sequencing in English. I am also exploring the connection between haiku, Eastern philosophy and creativity theory. Children's haiku are welcome. Politically relevant haiku are welcome, if they are imagistic and grounded in concrete experience. I also publish sports-related haiku."

THE POINTED CIRCLE (II), 705 N. Killingsworth, Portland OR 97217, phone (503)978-5230, fax (503)978-5050, e-mail jranck@pcc.edu, founded 1980, advisor Jefferson Ranck, is an annual. **They want "one-page poems under 60 lines, on any topic which is not hateful or abusive to any group of people."** They have published poetry by Judith Barrington, Lyn Lifshin and Barbara Drake. It is 80 pgs., professionally printed and flat-spined, with card cover and cover art. Press run is 200. **Sample postpaid: $4.50. No simultaneous submissions. Submit up to 6 poems at a time. Cover letter with bio required. Submit mss from December 1 through February 15 only. "Place name, address, etc., on cover sheet only, listing titles of submissions. All submissions are read anonymously by student editorial staff; notification about June 1." Send SASE for guidelines. Pays 1 copy. Acquires one-time rights.**

‡POISON IVY (I, II, IV-Women); POISON OAK (I, II, IV-Specialized: men), 1519 Third Ave., Suite 406, Seattle WA 98101, phone (206)782-9899, founded 1994, editor *Poison Ivy* Leslie Price, editor *Poison Oak* Sean Wheatley. *Poison Ivy*, a quarterly publication of female poets/fiction writers, and *Poison Oak*, of male poets/writers, are each a "literary and arts global forum." **They want "any and all poetry of reasonable length." They do not want "long poems, sonnets."** They have recently published poetry by Wanda Coleman, Brigid Peegen Kelly and Carolyn Forché. The editor says *Poison Ivy* and *Poison Oak* are 80 pgs., "sheet fed," stapled, heavy book stock with glossy cover, b&w photography, art and ads. They receive about 400 poems a year, accept approximately 20%. Press run is 15,000 for 850 subscribers of which 27 are libraries. Subscription: $15. **Sample postpaid: $2. Submit 5 poems at a time. Previously published poems and simultaneous submissions OK. Cover letter preferred with brief bio.** Time between acceptance and publication is 3-6 months.

Poems are circulated to an editorial board. "Four board members meet at a roundtable discussion before final selections are made." Often comments on rejections. Publishes theme issues. Send SASE for guidelines and upcoming themes. Reports "immediately upon approval." Sometimes sends prepublication galleys. Pays 5 copies. Acquires first rights. Reviews books of poetry in 500 words or less. Open to unsolicited reviews. Poets may also send books for review consideration.

‡*POLYGON (III, IV-Bilingual/foreign language), 22 George Square, Edinburgh EH8 9LF Scotland, phone (0131)650 4689, fax (0131)662 0053, e-mail polygon.press@ed.ac.uk, website http://www.ed.ac.uk/~polygon, founded 1969, contact poetry editor, publishes new poets, first-time collections, young voices and Gaelic/English translations. They publish 3 paperbacks and 1 anthology/year. They have recently published poetry by Ian Hamilton Finlay, Aonghas MacNeacail, Raymond Friel and David Kinloch. Books are usually 88 pgs., 194 × 128mm, paperback. Anthologies are 35 pgs., 216 × 138mm, paperback. **Submit 6 poems at a time. No previously published poems or simultaneous submissions. Cover letter required. Reads submissions April, July, October and December only.** Time between acceptance and publication is 6-18 months. **Always comments on rejections. Replies to mss in 2-3 months. Query for payment information.**

‡*POLYPHONIES (III, IV-Translations), 85, rue de la Santé, 75013 Paris, France, founded 1985, editor Pascal Culerrier. Editorial committee: Pascal Boulanger, Laurence Breysse, François Comba, Emmanuelle Dagnaud, Jean-Yves Masson and Alexis Pelletier. Appears twice a year. **"Every case is a special one. We want to discover the new important voices of the world to open French literature to the major international productions. For example, we published Brodsky in French when he was not known in our country and had not yet the Nobel Prize. No vocal poetry, no typographic effects."** They have published poetry by Mario Luzi (Italy), Jeremy Reed (Great Britain), Octavio Paz (Mexico) and Claude Michel Cluny (France). It is about 110 pgs., 6½ × 9½, flat-spined, with glossy card cover, printed completely in French. Press run is 850 for 300 subscribers. **Uses translations of previously published poems. Pays 2 copies.** The editor says, "Our review is still at the beginning. We are in touch with many French editors. Our purpose is to publish together, side-by-side, poets of today and of yesterday."

‡PORCUPINE LITERARY ARTS MAGAZINE (II), P.O. Box 259, Cedarsburg WI 53012, e-mail ppine259 @aol.com, founded 1996, managing editor W.A. Reed, published semiannually, contains featured artists, poetry, short fiction and visual art work. They have recently published poetry by Kimiko Hahn, Thor Ringler, Robert Siegel and Peggy Hong. As a sample, we selected these lines from "Gigue of The Lost Leg" by Cheryl Whitehead:

> When
> the sun comes up, his slurred curses
>
> will lacerate the fragile sigh of dawn.
> Another day, his soul screams, of an age
>
> when a man cannot sleep without fear
> of losing part of himself over and over again.

Porcupine is 100 pgs., 8½ × 5, offset, perfect-bound with 4-color glossy cover and b&w photos and art. They receive about 300 poems a year, accept approximately 5%. Press run is 1,500 for 500 subscribers of which 50 are libraries, 500 shelf sales; 100 distributed free. Single copy: $7.95; subscription: $13.95. **Sample postpaid: $5. Submit up to 3 poems, 1/page with name and address on each. No previously published poems or simultaneous submissions.** Time between acceptance and publication is 6 months. **"Poems are selected by poetry editors and then submitted to managing editor for final approval." Seldom comments on rejections. Send SASE for guidelines. Reports in 10-12 weeks. Pays 1 copy. Acquires one-time rights.**

PORTABLE WALL (V), 215 Burlington, Billings MT 59101, phone (406)256-3588, founded 1977, publisher Daniel Struckman. He publishes, as Ezra Pound described, **"words that throw the object on to the visual imagination and that induce emotional correlations by the sound and rhythm of the speech."** He has published poetry by Dave Thomas and Joe Salerno. As a sample he selected these lines by Kathleen Taylor:

> Lightning rams down
> a cloud-clotted sky;
> the red moon is wasted.

PW, published irregularly, is 60 pgs., saddle-stapled, on heavy tinted stock with 2-color matte card cover. Press

---

MARKET CATEGORIES: (I) Beginning; **(II)** General; **(III)** Limited; **(IV)** Specialized; **(V)** Closed.

Potato Eyes, a semiannual literary arts journal, seeks work "about the land and/or quality of life close to the earth." Though the publication originally began with an Appalachian focus, it now accepts work from throughout the U.S., Canada and overseas. Says co-editor Carolyn Page, "Because we have expanded our focus, we felt this Californian coastal scene, with its ocean breezes and sweeping vistas, would reflect our widening scope." The Maine-based journal primarily publishes poetry but also includes short stories. And, due to the quality of poetry submissions received, the editors have recently begun a chapbook competition to widen the options for the "amazing number of gifted poets." Cover artist: David Kooharian, a line illustrator from N. Falmouth, Massachusetts.

run is 400. Subscription: $18/4 issues. **Sample postpaid: $6.50. Currently not accepting poetry submissions.** The editor says, "I have more poetry than I can print."

POTATO EYES; NIGHTSHADE PRESS; WILLIAM & KINGMAN PAGE POETRY CHAPBOOK COMPETITION (II), P.O. Box 76, Troy ME 04987-0076, phone (207)948-3427, fax (207)948-5088, e-mail potatoeyes@uninet.net, founded 1988, editors Roy Zarucchi and Carolyn Page, is a semiannual literary arts journal **"with a focus on writers who write about the land and/or quality of life close to the earth. We now accept submissions from throughout the U.S., also from Canada, Australia, England, Ireland and Brazil, although much of our poetry is from Appalachian states."** They have published poetry by Daniel Lusk, Barbara Presnell, Jack Coulehan, Julie Kate Howard and Elizabeth Cohen. *PE* is 100 pgs., 5½×8½, flat-spined, professionally printed, with block cut matte paper cover. Circulation is 800. Subscription: $11 ($14 Canadian). **Sample postpaid: $6 or $7 Canadian. The editors say, "those who submit receive a handwritten rejection/ acceptance. We are open to any form other than rhymed, in batches of three to five, but we tend to favor poetry with concrete visual imagery, solid intensity and compression. We respect word courage and risk-taking, along with thoughtful lineation. We prefer rebellious to complacent poetry. We prefer a cover letter with brief bio along with SASE." No e-mail submissions, but queries via e-mail are OK. Reports in 1-2 months. Pays 1 copy. Acquires first North American serial rights.** Reviews books of poetry. Open to unsolicited reviews. Poets may also send books for review consideration. Nightshade Press is the imprint under which they publish about **5 books/chapbooks a year,** each 24-48 pgs. or longer, "usually with block print or pen-and-ink covers, endsheets and recycled 60 lb. text, 80 lb. covers. **Selections come from competitions, mainly, but a few may be from poets who appear first in our magazine." Send SASE for catalog and information and/ or send $6 for sample chapbook.** One of the competitions they sponsor is the annual William & Kingman Page Poetry Chapbook Competition. The award is 50 copies of the chapbook and $500. Deadline: November 15. Send SASE for guidelines. They advise, "Beginning poets should devour as much good poetry as possible in order to delineate their own style and voice. Look for a match between substance and sound. We reject fluff but respect poetry that is multi-layered and which makes a definite statement."

‡POTOMAC REVIEW (II, IV-Regional), P.O. Box 354, Port Tobacco MD 20677, phone (301)934-1412, website http://www.meral.com/potomac, founded 1994, editor Eli Flam, published quarterly. **They want "poetry with a vivid, individual quality that has vision to go with competence, that strives to get at 'the concealed side' of life." They do not want "arch, banal, mannered, surface, flat, self-serving poetry."** They have recently published poetry by Roland Flint, Elisavietta Ritchie, Grace Cavalieri and Simon Perchik. As a sample the editor selected these lines from "Volterra" by Laura Brylawski-Miller:

> *The fields mount toward the rock*
> *in yellow green swells—a tide*
> *of wheat stubbles, olive leaves*
> *rushes up to menace walls that flee*
> *heavenward. You think of Titans*

> *and assaults to the sky.*
> *Or, maybe, Saint Augustine*

Potomac Review is 92 pgs., 5½ × 8½, offset-printed, perfect-bound, with medium card cover, b&w graphic art, photos and ads. They receive about 1,000 poems a year, accept approximately 5%. Press run is 1,500 for 500 subscribers of which 24 are libraries, 500 shelf sales; some distributed free. Subscription: $15/year (MD residents add 5%), $28/2 years. **Sample postpaid: $4. Submit 3-5 poems at a time. Previously published poems and simultaneous submissions OK. Cover letter preferred with brief (i.e., up to two sentences) bio and SASE.** Time between acceptance and publication is up to 1 year. **Poems are circulated to an editorial board, "read by editors; then sent to poetry editor and review her recommendations." Often comments on rejections. Publishes theme issues. Send SASE for guidelines and upcoming themes. Reports in 1-2 months. Pays 1 copy and offers discount on additional copies. Acquires first North American serial rights.** Reviews books or chapbooks of poetry. Open to unsolicited reviews. Poets may also send books for review consideration. Sponsors annual poetry contest, usually open January through March, requires an entry form from the winter issue. $100 first prize; winner's poem and those of runners-up are published in fall.

POTPOURRI (II), P.O. Box 8278, Prairie Village KS 66208, phone (913)642-1503, fax (913)642-3128, founded 1989, poetry editor Terry Hoyland, haiku editor Robert G. Duchouquette, is a quarterly magazine "publishing works of writers, **including new and unpublished writers. We want strongly voiced original poems in either free verse or traditional. Traditional work must represent the best of the craft. No religious, confessional, racial, political, erotic, abusive or sexual preference materials unless fictional and necessary to plot or characterization. No concrete/visual poetry (because of format)."** They have published poetry by X.J. Kennedy, David Ray, Richard Moore, Pattiann Rogers and Tess Gallagher. As a sample the editor selected these lines from "Used Books" by Robert Cooperman:

> *. . . a love gone sour*
> *as the acid-eaten pages.*
> *It's like stumbling*
> *on intimate strangers*
> *when I flip to fly-leaves*
> *and read passion*
> *in flowery hands' flourishes.*

It is 68 pgs., 8½ × 11, professionally printed, saddle-stapled with b&w art on glossy cover, drawings, photos and ads inside. Press run is 1,500 for 675 subscribers. Subscription: $15. **Sample postpaid: $4.95. Submit up to 3 poems at a time, one to a page, length to 75 lines (approximately 30 preferred). Submit seasonal themes 6 months in advance. Address haiku and related forms to Robert G. Duchouquette. Send SASE for guidelines. Reports in 8-10 weeks at most. Pays 1 copy. Acquires first North American serial rights.** The David Ray Poetry Award ($100 or more, depending upon grant monies) is given annually for best of volume. Another annual award is sponsored by the Council on National Literatures and offers $100 and publication in *Potpourri* for selected poem or short story; alternating years (1999 poetry). Send SASE for official guidelines. Deadline: June 30, 1999. The editors advise, "Keep your new poems around long enough to become friends with them before parting. Let them ripen, and, above all, learn to be your own best editor. Read them aloud, boldly, to see how they ripple the air and echo what you mean to say. Unrequited love, children, grandchildren, favorite pets and description that seem to be written for its own sake find little chance here."

‡PRAIRIE DOG: A MAGAZINE FOR THE SOMEWHAT ECCENTRIC (II), P.O. Box 470757, Aurora CO 80047-0757, phone/fax (303)753-0956, e-mail jrhart@pcisys.net. founded 1988, editor-in-chief John R. Hart, is an illustrated "literary quarterly dedicated to presenting emerging and established talent. Staff artists illustrate some of our work, but we encourage submissions from writer-artists, artists and photographers as well." They want poetry that **"traffics in delight as well as agony, that deals both with the 'foul rag and bone shop of the heart,' and 'the sovereign floating of joy.' "** They have published poetry by Terry Thomas, William Nesbit, Hugh Fox and Anthony O. Constantino. As a sample the editor selected the poem "Cuisine" by Kathleen Gunton Deal:

> *Give me a sensitive plate of pasta*
> *with mussels plump as white pillows*
> *bathed in a fragrant wash of white wine,*
> *and I will give you an evening*
> *sliced thin and angel hair*
> *pasta barely dressed.*

Prairie Dog is 64 pgs., magazine-sized, photocopied "on 60 lb. bond with parchment cover (2-3 color)", saddle-stapled, ads, art and appears "more or less biannually, 2 times a year. We receive about 40 submissions per week, use about 40 poems per issue." Press run is 600 for 250 subscribers. Subscription: $15. **Sample $5.95 plus $1 p&h and 9 × 12 SAE. Submit 5-10 poems at a time with $2 reading fee. Simultaneous submissions OK. Fax, e-mail and disk submissions (any format) "are encouraged." Cover letter with "bio info is helpful if work accepted." Send SASE for guidelines. Reports within 6 months, "but we read everything." Editor comments on submissions "if writing or art shows promise." Pays 1 copy. Acquires one-time or first reprint rights.** Open to unsolicited reviews. Poets may also send books for review consideration. The editor says, "We read everything and will respond if you provide a SASE. We accept double-sided and photocopied manuscripts (save the trees) but will not read faint dot-matrix manuscripts. We would like to feature one "youthful new voice" (under 25, just beginning to be published) per issue, but our standards are high. Mass submissions based on class assignments are sure to be rejected."

♣**PRAIRIE FIRE (III)**, 100 Arthur St., Room 423, Winnipeg, Manitoba R3B 1H3 Canada, phone (204)943-9066, fax (204)942-1555, founded 1978, editor Andris Taskans, is a quarterly magazine of new writing including fiction, poetry and reviews. **They want "poetry that articulates a connection between language and ethics, an aesthetic of writing 'from the body,' and open to the nuances of orality, ethnic and racial differences and feminism. No haiku, sonnets or other rhyming forms, nor political or religious treatises in verse form."** They have recently published poetry by George Amolile, Al Purdy and Anne Szumigalski. *Prairie Fire* is 128 pgs., 6×9, offset, perfect-bound, glossy card cover, illustrations and ads. They receive 400-500 submissions (average 6 poems each), accept approximately 2%. Press run is 1,600 for 1,200 subscribers of which 100 are libraries, 150 shelf sales. Single copy: $10.95; subscription: $24 Canadian, $28 US. **Sample postpaid: $10 Canadian. Submissions should be typed, double-spaced, 1 poem to a page, name and address on each page, up to 6 poems at a time. No previously published poems or simultaneous submissions. Cover letter required. Include other publications, brief biographical information, list of poems submitted, name, address and phone number. Reads submissions September 1 through June 30 only.** Time between acceptance and publication is 1 year. **Seldom comments on rejections. Publishes theme issues. Send SASE (or SAE and IRC) for guidelines and upcoming themes. Reports in 4-6 months. Pays $30 for first page, $25 for each additional page, plus 1 copy. Buys first Canadian serial rights only.** Staff reviews books of poetry in 250-750 words, single or multi-book format. Send books for review consideration. The editor says, "Be patient!"

♣**THE PRAIRIE JOURNAL (II); PRAIRIE JOURNAL PRESS (IV-Regional, themes)**, P.O. Box 61203, Brentwood Post Office, 217-3630 Brentwood Rd. NW, Calgary, Alberta T2L 2K6 Canada, founded 1983, editor A. Burke, who wants to see **poetry of "any length, free verse, contemporary themes (feminist, nature, urban, non-political), aesthetic value, a poet's poetry." Does not want to see "most rhymed verse, sentimentality, egotistical ravings. No cowboys or sage brush."** They have published poetry by Mick Burrs, Lorna Crozier, Mary Melfi, Art Cuelho and John Hicks. *Prairie Journal* is 40-60 pgs., 7×8½, offset, saddle-stitched with card cover, b&w drawings and ads, appearing twice a year. They receive about 500 poems a year, accept approximately 4%. Press run is 600 for 200 subscribers of which 50% are libraries, the rest are distributed on the newsstand. Subscription: $6 for individuals, $12 for libraries. **Sample postpaid: $6 ("Use postal money order"). No simultaneous submissions or previously published poems. Guidelines available for postage (but "no U.S. stamps, please"—get IRCs from the Post Office). "We will not be reading submissions until such time as an issue is in preparation (twice yearly), so be patient and we will acknowledge, accept for publication or return work at that time." Sometimes sends prepublication galleys. Pays $10-50 plus 1 copy. Acquires first North American serial rights.** Reviews books of poetry "but must be assigned by editor. Query first." **For chapbook publication, Canadian poets only (preferably from the region) should query with 5 samples, bio, publications. Responds to queries in 2 months, to mss in 6 months. Payment in modest honoraria.** They have published *Voices From Earth*, selected poems by Ronald Kurt and Mark McCawley, and *In the Presence of Grace*, by McCandless Callaghan. "We also publish anthologies on themes when material is available." A. Burke advises, "Read recent poets! Experiment with line length, images, metaphors. Innovate."

PRAIRIE SCHOONER; STROUSSE PRIZE; SLOTE PRIZE; FAULKNER AWARD; HUGH J. LUKE AWARD; STANLEY AWARD; READERS' CHOICE AWARDS (II), 201 Andrews, University of Nebraska, Lincoln NE 68588-0334, phone (402)472-0911, founded 1927, editor Hilda Raz; "one of the oldest literary quarterlies in continuous publication; publishes poetry, fiction, personal essays, interviews and reviews." **They want "poems that fulfill the expectations they set up." No specifications as to form, length, style, subject matter or purpose.** They have recently published poetry by Alicia Ostriker, Marilyn Hacker, Radu Hotinceneasru, Mark Rudman and David Ignatow. As a sample the editor selected these lines from "How to Get in the Best Magazines" by Eleanor Wilner:

> it is time to write
> the acceptable poem—
> ice and glass, with its splinter
> of bone, its pit
> of an olive,
> the dregs
> of the cup of abundance,
> useless spill of gold
> from the thresher, the dust
> of it filling the sunlight, the chum
> broadcast on the black waters
> and the fish
>   —the beautiful, ravenous fish—
> refusing to rise.

The magazine is 176 pgs., 6×9, flat-spined and uses 70-80 pgs. of poetry in each issue. They receive about 4,800 mss (of all types) a year from which they choose 300 pgs. of poetry. Press run is 3,100. Single copy: $7.25; subscription: $22. **Sample postpaid: $5. Submit 5-7 poems at a time. No simultaneous submissions. "Clear copy appreciated." Considers mss from September through May only. Publishes theme issues. Send SASE for guidelines. Reports in 3-4 months; "sooner if possible." Always sends prepublication galleys. Pays 3 copies. Acquires all rights. Returns rights upon request without fee.** Reviews books of poetry. Open to unsolicited reviews. Poets may also send books for review consideration. One of the most influential magazines being published today (often named as such in independent surveys of creative writers), this publication is genuinely open to excellent work in any form: lyric, narrative, dramatic, traditional, etc. Send only your best work, as competition is keen. Brief reviews are an excellent way to break into the journal. Editor Hilda Raz also promotes poets whose work has appeared in her pages by listing their continued accomplishments in a special section (even when their work does not concurrently appear in the magazine). The $500 Strousse Prize is awarded to the best poetry published in the magazine each year. The Slote Prize for beginning writers ($500), Hugh J. Luke Award ($250), the Stanley Award for Poetry ($500) and six other *PS* prizes are also awarded, as well as the Faulkner Award for Excellence in Writing ($1,000) and the Larry Levis Prize for Poetry ($1,000). Also, each year 5-10 Readers' Choice Awards ($250 each) are given for poetry, fiction and nonfiction. Editors serve as judges. All contests are open only to those writers whose work was published in the magazine the previous year. Poetry published in *PS* has also been selected for inclusion in *The Best American Poetry 1996* and a *Pushcart Prize* anthology. Hilda Raz comments, "*Prairie Schooner* receives a large number of poetry submissions; we're not unusual. We don't have time to comment on mss, but the magazine's reputation is evidence of our careful reading. We've been dedicated to the publication of good poems for a very long time and have published work early in the career of many successful poets."

PRAIRIE WINDS (II), Box 536, Dakota Wesleyan University, 1200 W. University Ave., Mitchell SD 57301, phone (605)995-2814, editor James C. Van Oort, is an annual of poetry, fiction, short essays, photos and art. **They are open to all forms, lengths, styles and subjects of poetry except pornographic.** They have published poetry by Simon Perchik, Robert Cooperman, Lyn Lifshin and David Ignataw. The editor says *PW* is 50-60 pgs., 7½×9¼, offset, bound, gloss litho, no ads. They accept approximately 25% of the poetry received each year. Press run is 500 for 50 subscribers of which 10 are libraries. **Sample postpaid: $2. Submit 5-10 poems at a time. No previously published poems; simultaneous submissions OK. Cover letter and SASE required. "We are an annual, published in spring. All submissions must arrive by January 4." Reads submissions January 4 through 31 only. Seldom comments on rejections. Send SASE for guidelines. Reports by end of February. Pays 1 copy.**

*PRAKALPANA LITERATURE; KOBISENA (I, IV-Bilingual, form), P-40 Nandana Park, Calcutta 700034, West Bengal, India, phone (91)(033)478-2347, *Kobisena* founded 1972, *Prakalpana Literature* press founded 1974, magazine 1977, editor Vattacharja Chandan, who says, "We are small magazines which publish only *Prakalpana* (a mixed form of prose and poetry), Sarbangin (whole) poetry, experimental b&w art and photographs, essays on Prakalpana movement and Sarbangin poetry movement, letters, literary news and very few books on Prakalpana and Sarbangin literature. **Purpose and form: for advancement of poetry in the super-space age, the poetry must be really experimental and avant-garde using mathematical signs and symbols and visualizing the pictures inherent in the alphabet (within typography) with sonorous effect accessible to people. That is Sarbangin poetry. Length: within 30 lines (up to 4 poems). Prakalpana is a mixed form of prose, poetry, essay, novel, story, play with visual effect and it is not at all short story as it is often misunderstood. Better send six IRCs to read *Prakalpana Literature* first and then submit. Length: within 16 pages (up to 2 prakalpanas) at a time. Subject matter: society, nature, cosmos, humanity, love, peace, etc. Style: own. We do not want to see traditional, conventional, academic, religious, mainstream and poetry of prevailing norms and forms."** They have published poetry by Dilip Gupta, Rachael Z. Ikins, Bill West and Babloo Roychowdhury. As a sample the editor selected these lines by Norman J. Olson:

> *You are swayed down in the Rains*
> *Far far away far away far away far*
> *You're broken in that secret deep dip duck*
> *!!!! jhir !!!! Jhir !!!! jhir !!!!*
> *!!*

Prakalpana Literature, an annual, is 120 pgs., 7×4½, saddle-stapled, printed on thin stock with matte card cover. *Kobisena*, which also appears once a year, is 16 pgs., digest-sized, a newsletter format with no cover. Both are hand composed and printed by letterpress. Both use both English and Bengali. They receive about 400 poems a year, accept approximately 10%. Press run is 1,000 for each, and each has about 450 subscribers of which 50 are libraries. **Samples: 15 rupees for *Prakalpana*, 4 rupees for *Kobisena*. Overseas: 6 IRCs and 3 IRCs respectively or exchange of avant-garde magazines. Submit 4 poems at a time. Simultaneous submissions and previously published poems OK. Cover letter with short bio and small photo/sketch of poet/writer/ artist required; camera-ready copy (4×6½) preferred.** Time between acceptance and publication is within a year. **After being published in the magazines, poets may be included in future anthologies with translations into Bengali/English if and when necessary. "Joining with us is welcome but not a pre-condition." Editor comments on rejections "if wanted." Send SAE with IRC for guidelines. No reporting time given. Some-**

times sends prepublication galleys. **Pays 1 copy.** Reviews books of poetry, fiction and art, "but preferably experimental books." Open to unsolicited reviews. Poets, writers and artists may also send books for review consideration. He says, "We believe that only through poetry, fiction and art, the deepest feelings of humanity as well as nature and the cosmos can be best expressed and conveyed to the peoples of the ages to come. And only poetry can fill up the gap in the peaceless hearts of dispirited peoples, resulted from the retreat of god and religion with the advancement of hi-tech. So, in an attempt, since the inception of Prakalpana Movement in 1969, to reach that goal in the avant-garde and experimental way we stand for Sarbangin poetry. And to poets and all concerned with poetry we wave the white handkerchief saying (in the words of Vattacharja Chandan), 'We want them who want us.' "

‡**PRAYERWORKS (IV-Religious)**, P.O. Box 301363, Portland OR 97294-9363, phone (503)761-2072, fax (503)760-1184, e-mail jay4prayer@aol.com or 76753.3202@compuserve.com, founded 1988, editor V. Ann Mandeville, appears weekly "to share prayer concerns with others and to encourage prayer. Contents: one devotional and prayer requests, one filler (humorous or catchy)." *PrayerWorks* is 4 pgs., 5½×8, photocopied, desktop-published, folded. They receive about 50 poems a year, accept approximately 25%. Press run is 700 for 700 subscribers. Subscription: free. **Submit 5 poems, 1 per page. Previously published poems and simultaneous submissions OK. Cover letter preferred.** Time between acceptance and publication is 2-6 months. **"I decide if it fits—I print it."** Seldom comments on rejections. **Publishes theme issues relating to the holidays. Send SASE for guidelines. Reports in 1-2 months. Pays 5 or more copies.**

♣**THE PRESBYTERIAN RECORD (IV-Inspirational, religious)**, 50 Wynford Dr., North York, Ontario M3C 1J7 Canada, phone (416)441-1111, fax (416)441-2825, founded 1876, is "the national magazine that serves the membership of The Presbyterian Church in Canada (and many who are not Canadian Presbyterians). We seek to stimulate, inform, inspire, to provide an 'apologetic' and a critique of our church and the world (not necessarily in that order!)." **They want poetry which is "inspirational, Christian, thoughtful, even satiric but** *not* **maudlin. No 'sympathy card' type verse a la Edgar Guest or Francis Gay. It would take a** *very* **exceptional poem of epic length for us to use it. Shorter poems, 10-30 lines, preferred. Blank verse OK (if it's not just rearranged prose). 'Found' poems. Subject matter should have some Christian import (however subtle)."** They have published poetry by Margaret Avison, Joan Dower Kosmachuk, Fredrick Zydek, Robert C. Jones, T.M. Dickey and Charles Cooper. The magazine comes out 11 times/year. Press run is 64,000. Subscription: $15. **Submit 3-6 poems at a time; seasonal work 6 weeks before month of publication. Simultaneous submissions OK; rarely accepts previously published poems. Poems should be typed, double-spaced. Pays $20-50/poem. Buys one-time rights.** Staff reviews books of poetry. Send books for review consideration. *The Presbyterian Record* has won several Canadian Church Press Awards.

PRESCOTT STREET PRESS (V, IV-Regional), Box 40312, Portland OR 97240-0312, phone (503)254-2922, founded 1974, poetry editor Vi Gale: **"Poetry and fine print from the Northwest."** Vi Gale says, "Our books and cards are the product of many hands from poet, artist, printer, designer, typesetter to bookstore and distributor. Somewhere along the line the editor/publisher [herself] arranges to pay one and all in the same way. Sometimes we have had grant help from the NEA and also from state and metropolitan arts organizations. But most of our help has come from readers, friends and the poets and artists themselves. Everyone has worked very hard. And we are immodestly pleased with our labors! **We are not a strictly regional press, although the poets I take on are connected with the Northwest in some way when we bring out the books. We are currently overstocked with poetry through 1998."** Vi Gale publishes a series of postcards, notecards, paperback and hardback books of poetry in various artistic formats with illustrations by nationally known artists. Send SASE for catalog to order copies. **Simultaneous submissions OK. Sometimes sends prepublication galleys. "We pay all of our poets. A modest sum, perhaps, but we pay everyone something."**

‡***PRESENCE (IV-Form)**, One, East View, Galgate, Lancaster, Lancashire LA2 0JT United Kingdom, founded 1995, contact Mr. Martin Lucas, published 2-3 times/year, features haiku, senryu, renga, tanka, etc. **They want "haiku or haiku-related/haiku-influenced work. Maximum length: 16 lines (including title and spaces)." They do not want "anything longer than 16 lines (except renga), anything tortured, absurd or fantastical, even if in 'haiku form.' "** They have recently published poetry by Richard Goring, Gary Hotham, Jean Jorgensen and Hannah Mitte. As a sample the editor selected this haiku by Martin Lucas:

> a gap in the fence—
> next door's cabbage flowers

USE THE GENERAL INDEX to find the page number of a specific publisher. Also, if a publisher from last year's edition is not included in this edition, the General Index will tell you why.

have come through it

The editor says *Presence* is 44 pgs., A5, photocopied, perfect-bound, with brushdrawn art on card cover and illustrations. They receive about 2,000 poems a year, accept approximately 10%. Press run is 150 for 100 subscribers of which 5 are libraries, 10 shelf sales. Subscription: £5 ($10 US). **Sample postpaid: £2 ($5 US). Make checks payable in UK funds to Martin Lucas. Submit 4-12 poems at a time. "Please ensure that separate poems can be identified, and not mistaken for a sequence." No previously published poems or simultaneous submissions. Cover letter preferred.** Time between acceptance and publication is 1-6 months. **Seldom comments on rejections. Send SASE (or SAE and IRC) for guidelines. Reports within 1 month. Pays 1 copy. Copyright remains with authors.** Staff reviews books or chapbooks of poetry or other magazines in 10-500 words, single format. Poets may also send books for review consideration. The editor advises beginners, "The more you read the better you'll write. Those who subscribe to read make better poets than those who are motivated solely by seeing their own name in print."

‡**PRESS (III)**, 2124 Broadway, Suite 323, New York NY 10023, founded 1995, editor Daniel Roberts, published quarterly, is a "cultivation of the written word. **All poems must make sense. That is, all complicated rhythms and fanciful word choices, all emotional and psychological gestures, must have a public value as well as a personal one. We are looking for poems that are thematically and stylistically uniform: meaningful, balanced, and powerful. Loose abstraction, random alliteration, confusion (whether purposeful or not) and any other device or gesture that corrupts meaning is, simply, not for us."** They have recently published poetry by Anthony Hecht, Philip Levine, Paul Muldoon, David Wagoner and Edward Hirsch. The editor says *Press* is 125 pgs., perfect-bound with cover art and some graphics. They receive about 8,000 poems a year, accept approximately 1%. Press run is 15,000. **Sample postpaid: $10. Make checks payable to Press Ltd. Submit up to 3 poems at a time typed on clean paper. No previously published poems or simultaneous submissions.** Time between acceptance and publication is 1-3 months. **Seldom comments on rejections. Send SASE for guidelines. Reports in 3-6 weeks. Sometimes sends prepublication galleys. Pays minimum $50/poem. Buys first or one-time rights.** The editor says, "Sincerity and intense attention to the poems' sound, along with thematic uniformity, capture our attention."

PRESS HERE (IV-Form), P.O. Box 4014, Foster City CA 94404, phone (415)571-9428, e-mail WelchM@aol.com, founded 1989, editor/publisher Michael Dylan Welch (who is also editor/publisher of *Tundra*), **publishes 3 chapbooks/year.** "Press Here was founded to publish fine books of haiku and related forms. Its goal is to present new and established voices through a variety of high-quality publications. Available books include informative interviews with established haiku poets, individual haiku collections and broad-ranging anthologies. **I wish to see manuscripts of poetry, or essays and interviews, related to haiku, senryu or tanka. I am also interested in concrete poetry. Not interested in longer poetry."** They have recently published work by William J. Higginson, Cor van den Heuval, Pat Shelley, Lee Gurga and Stephen Addiss. As a sample the editor selected these lines of his own:

> *after the quake*
> *the weathervane*
> *pointing to earth*

Query first with sample poems and cover letter. Previously published poems OK; no simultaneous submissions. "Queries are acceptable via e-mail, but snail-mail queries are preferred, especially if a catalog is desired." Often comments on rejections. Replies to queries in 1 month, to mss (if invited) in 6-9 months. Pays author's copies. For sample books, write for catalog.

THE PRESS OF THE NIGHTOWL (V), 145 Yorkshire Rd., Bogart GA 30622, phone (706)353-7719, e-mail dagner@typehigh.com, founded 1965, owner Dwight Agner, publishes 1-2 paperbacks and 1-2 hardbacks each year. They have published poetry by Paul Zimmer, Stephen Corey, Mary Anne Coleman and C.K. Williams. **However, they are currently not accepting unsolicited poetry submissions. Pays author's copies. Sample books may be ordered directly from the publisher or located through bookstores.**

THE PRESS OF THE THIRD MIND (IV-Form), 65 E. Scott St., Loft 6P, Chicago IL 60610, phone (312)337-3122, founded 1985, poetry editor "Badly Steamed Lard (anagram of Bradley Lastname)," is a small press publisher of artist books, poetry and fiction. **"We are especially interested in found poems, Dada, surrealism, written table-scraps left on the floors of lunatic asylums by incurable psychotics, etc."** They have published poetry by Anthony Stark, Jorn Barger, Tom Vaultonberg, Kevin Riordan and Eric Forsburg. As a sample the editor selected these lines from "Five Things I Know About the Millipede" by Oscar de la Rentstrike:

> *The spitting millipede is the spitting image of his father the spitting centipede, but does not bear family*
> *resemblances to his winged half-brother, the pissing velocipede.*

They have a press run of 1,000 with books often going into a second or third printing. **Sample for $1.43 postage. For book publication submit up to 20 sample poems. "No anthologized mss where every poem has already appeared somewhere else." Simultaneous submissions OK, if noted. "Cover letter is good, but we don't need to know everything you published since you were age nine in single-spaced detail."** Send SASE for upcoming themes. "Authors are paid as the publication transcends the break-even benchmark." In 1995, the press released an 80-page anthology entitled *Empty Calories* and published a deconstructivist novel about

Breathe fresh air into your haiku by taking it beyond five-seven-five

[haiku]
an old sweater
   taken yarn by yarn
      from a snowbank

[tanka]
all my books collect dust
except the one of love poems
you gave me that day
when the spring rains
kept us indoors

Michael Dylan Welch

"Be your own editor," says Michael Dylan Welch, recalling advice he read in a ***Poet's Market*** interview with Elizabeth Searle Lamb seven years ago. "Don't submit five or six similar haiku expecting the editor to choose the best one. While the editor's perfectly able to select a good poem, it's important for the beginner to take the responsibility of deciding which are the best to submit."

Welch writes haiku and related forms, senryu, tanka and haibun, as well as concrete and longer poetry. He is also the editor of *Woodnotes*, a journal of haiku and related poetry that has included work by Ronan, Cherie Hunter Day, Jeff Witkin and Helen K. Davie. *Woodnotes* recently ceased publication, however, to make way for a new journal, *Tundra*, which showcases all forms of short poetry.

A co-founder of the American Haiku Archive at California State Library and a current first vice-president of the Haiku Society of America, Welch also manages to publish three chapbooks of haiku per year through Press Here, a California small press operation founded in 1989. Recent volumes include the work of William J. Higginson, Sono Uchida and Virginia Brady Young.

Like many others, Welch admits he came to haiku with the superficial understanding that it was a syllabic Japanese form limited to the traditional 17 syllables arranged on three lines in a pattern of five-seven-five. However, he often receives haiku that might have been much more effective had they not been padded or chopped to conform to this syllabic arrangement. "It continues to be, I believe, mistaught this way. In English this strict syllabic notion just doesn't apply. The reason is, simply, that Japanese syllables are not equivalent to those in English. Translate a 17-syllable English haiku into Japanese and it's way too long."

Welch's approach to haiku was reshaped by Zen and Taoism studies that instilled in him an awareness of haiku as a spiritual or transcendent poetry. Thus inspired, he read widely about haiku and discovered a book which had a profound impact on his writing:

Cor Van den Heuvel's *Haiku Anthology* (Fireside/Touchstone, 1986), a collection of North American haiku written in English. "In it there are poems of various lengths, syllables and line counts, and even some concrete poetry. Suddenly I had a dramatic shift from thinking of haiku as a syllabic form to understanding there was something else in the content that made these poems haiku. It was like opening a window for fresh air. I've become more deeply enamored of haiku ever since."

Writing is not a planned activity for Welch. Inspiration comes from any source at any time. It might be a word read in a newspaper or poem, something overheard on an elevator that reverberates or triggers a memory, or he may be literally "stopped" by an incident. "Late for work one morning I rushed downstairs, put my hand on the doorknob and was stopped. It was still cool and dark inside the house but the doorknob was very warm in my hand. I stood there thinking about the bright sun shining on the other side of the door warming the doorknob and later translated it into haiku."

For inspiration he occasionally plays a word game involving randomly opening a copy of *14,000 Things to Be Happy About* by Barbara Kipfer (Workman, 1990), a book containing many concrete, imagistic nouns and phrases. "An entry about the Avon Lady might evoke childhood memories of my mother talking to door-to-door salespeople, a very tactile experience for me, and the poem I'll write will tap the reader's memories of something similar. That's how haiku works—it captures something we've all experienced and the reader finishes the poem, enlarging it."

In the submissions he receives, Welch looks for objectivity and fresh, keen perception. He believes haiku works best when objective words imply a subjective feeling or intuition of the moment. On a practical note, Welch also looks for a SASE, a name on each page of poetry submitted and correct spelling. Unfortunately, he regularly receives submissions that lack these criteria and strike him as unprofessional.

As both poet and editor, Welch finds the skills of each enhanced by the other. Reading 4,000 submissions a year—as well as thousands of haiku for pleasure—has sharpened his understanding of the mechanics of the form. "While reading, I'm constantly thinking, 'How do I feel subjectively? Does this poem touch me?' I try to empathize, express an understanding as to why they do or do not work. The hard part of editing is taking the time necessary to see where the writer is coming from on his own terms. This process of empathy has also helped me clarify my own approach to haiku and its limitations."

Welch developed this empathetic process during his time as editor of *Woodnotes*, a quarterly publication founded in 1989 by the Haiku Poets of Northern California. *Woodnotes* grew out of a regional focus, and under Welch's editorship, which began with Issue 3, rose to the forefront of the haiku community to stand alongside such journals as *Frogpond* and *Modern Haiku*. "In 1996 I took it over as an independent publication because the subscriber base had become so nonregional as to no longer fit the purpose of its founders," says Welch.

The new journal *Tundra* reaches beyond haiku to include all forms of short poetry, up to 12 lines, and drops the regional notion altogether. Haiku will remain a primary focus, but Welch feels broadening that focus will help integrate the "too often insular" haiku community into mainstream poetry. He also looks to improve his own poetry as he reads a wider range of submissions.

Besides Canada and the United States, *Woodnotes*'s readers have hailed from Australia, Japan, England, Romania, Croatia, India and Greece. Once established, Welch expects this international readership to continue and perhaps grow for *Tundra*.

INSIDER REPORT, *continued*

Welch also feels the Internet can be an enormous benefit to the haiku poet, offering everything from serious poetry to science fiction and Spam haiku. However, he warns the beginner that misinformation is common; everything must be taken with a grain of salt. "It's a level playing field where anyone can make a comment, informed or otherwise. The reader has no idea who has authority. I highly recommend the Shiki List, Japan's Matsuyama University discussion list. They also have a website posting the results of a biweekly haiku contest and offering feedback." In addition, Welch is helping develop a website for the Haiku Society of America.

As final words of advice, Welch offers that writing is not enough. "Reading is an essential part of being a poet. Tap into your enthusiasm and broaden it. Read as well as write; process what you read. As a beginner I wrote for myself. I didn't read and, therefore, had no context for my writing."

He recommends William J. Higginson's *Haiku Handbook* (Kodansha, 1992), Bruce Ross's *Haiku Moment* (C E Tuttle, 1993), and Cor Van den Heuvel's *Haiku Anthology* as good introductions to haiku. "If you don't enjoy reading, it's hardly fair to expect others to read your work. But you can't force yourself. If it's not a pleasure then don't bother."

And most importantly: "Edit yourself. What Elizabeth Lamb said was a big influence for me, and I've repeated it to many people. So, if you've just written 20 similar haiku, ask yourself 'Do I want all 20 poems to be published?' Your answer can only be 'I'd rather have the *best* published.' "

—*Glenn L. Marcum*

---

the repetition complusion called *The Squeaky Fromme Gets the Grease*. "The Press of the Third Mind is establishing a fund for all cataract operations heavey net users are going to need 10 or 20 years down the line. Send SASE for details."

PRIMAVERA (II, IV-Women), P.O. Box #37-7547, Chicago IL 60637, phone (773)324-5920, founded 1975, co-editor Ruth Young, is "an irregularly published but approximately annual magazine of poetry and fiction reflecting **the experiences of women. We look for strong, original voice and imagery, generally prefer free verse, fairly short length, related, even tangentially, to women's experience.**" They have recently published poetry by Zsuzsa Rakovszky, Pamela Gemin, Martha Modena Vertreace and Anne Richey. As a sample the editors selected these lines by Rachel Yamagiwa:

> Now the scientist pretends
> to know your soul. Read the fine print
> of the lab report—half
> your heart was never found.

The elegantly printed publication, flat-spined, generously illustrated with photos and graphics, uses 25-30 pgs. of poetry in each issue. They receive over 1,000 submissions of poetry a year, use approximately 25. Circulation is 1,000. Single copy: $10. **Sample postpaid: $5. Submit up to 6 poems anytime, no queries. No simultaneous submissions. Editors comment on rejections "when requested or inspired." Send SASE for guidelines. Reports in 1-3 months. Pays 2 copies. Acquires first-time rights.**

PRINCETON UNIVERSITY PRESS; LOCKERT LIBRARY OF POETRY IN TRANSLATION (IV-Translations, bilingual), 41 William St., Princeton NJ 08540, phone (609)258-4900, e-mail rebrown@pupress. princeton.edu. "In the Lockert Library series, we publish simultaneous cloth and paperback (flat-spine) editions for each poet. Clothbound editions are on acid-free paper, and binding materials are chosen for strength and durability. Each book is given individual design treatment rather than stamped into a series mold. We have published a wide range of poets from other cultures, including well-known writers such as Hölderlin and Cavafy, and those who have not yet had their due in English translation, such as Wistawa Sizymborska. Manuscripts are judged with several criteria in mind: the ability of the translation to stand on its own as poetry in English; fidelity to the tone and spirit of the original, rather than literal accuracy; and the importance of the translated poet to the literature of his or her time and country." The editor says, "All our books in this series are heavily subsidized to break even. We have internal funds to cover deficits of publishing costs. We do not, however, publish books chosen and subsidized by other agencies, such as AWP." **E-mail submissions OK. Simultaneous submissions OK if you tell them. Cover letter required. Send mss only during respective reading periods stated in guidelines. Send SASE for guidelines to submit. Reports in 2-3 months.**

✤**PRISM INTERNATIONAL (II)**, Dept. of Creative Writing, University of British Columbia, Vancouver, British Columbia V6T 1Z1 Canada, phone (604)822-2514, fax (604)822-3616, e-mail prism@unixg.ubc.ca, website http://www.arts.ubc.ca/crwr/prism/prism.html, founded 1959, editors Sioux Browning and Melanie Little, executive editor Shannon McFerran. "*Prism* is an international quarterly that publishes poetry, drama, short fiction, imaginative nonfiction and translation into English in all genres. We have no thematic or stylistic allegiances: Excellence is our main criterion for acceptance of mss. **We want fresh, distinctive poetry that shows an awareness of traditions old and new. We read everything.**" They have published poetry by Floyd Skloot, William Logan, Karen Connelly, Derk Wynard and a translation by Seamus Heaney. As a sample the editors selected these lines from "The Way I Sleep" by Carol Hull:

> The way I sleep is by shyly testing the borders of death.
> My breath is shallow, barely brushing your neck.
> Even when my big tired head is buried there,
> I do not bother you.
>
> Hours later you will feel the space.
> Call out for a coffee from the bed.

Prism is 80 pgs., 6 × 9, elegantly printed, flat-spined with original color artwork on a glossy card cover. Circulation is for 1,000 subscribers of which 200 are libraries. They receive 1,000 submissions a year, use approximately 80, have a 2- to 4-month backlog. Subscription: $16. **Sample postpaid: $5. Submit up to 6 poems at a time, any print so long as it's typed. No previously published poems or simultaneous submissions. Cover letter with brief introduction and previous publications required. "Translations must be accompanied by a copy of the original. Poets may submit by e-mail, or through our website. Include the poem in the main body of the message." Send Canadian SASE or SAE with IRCs for guidelines. Reports in 2-4 months. Pays $20/ printed page plus subscription; plus an additional $10/printed page to selected authors for publication on the World Wide Web. Editors sometimes comment on rejections.** *Prism International* is known in literary circles as one of the top journals in Canada. The editors say, "While we don't automatically discount any kind of poetry, we prefer to publish work that challenges the writer as much as it does the reader. We are particularly looking for poetry in translation."

‡**PROCREATION: A JOURNAL OF TRUTHTELLING IN POETRY & PROSE; SILENT PLANET PUBLISHING, LTD. (I)**, 6300-138 Creedmoor Rd., Suite 260, Raleigh NC 27612, phone/fax (919)510-9010, e-mail slntplanet@aol.com, website http://www.slntplanet.com/procreation, founded 1996, poetry editor Tanya Register, appears 3 times/year. "We are a literary journal devoted to the pursuit and expression of truth. In doing so, we echo the Creator's own imaginative, creative activity and so become more fully human. **We seek poetry that resonates with artfully-encapsulated truth about ultimate reality, including spiritual truth. All forms are acceptable, provided they do not exceed 100 lines. We do not accept propaganda (however truthful), works of maudlin fiction or sentimental verse, or religious verse not rooted in real-life experience. No erotica.**" They have recently published poetry by Luci Shaw, Kathryn Gurkin and Ann O'Donnell. As a sample the editor selected these lines from "Prayer of Keeping" by Aaron Belz:

> My harvest is yours. My dissonance, my thoughts,
> courage, fire, my walking down Hoboken streets
> in the cool of the day, carrying mail to the postbox,
> stopping at Battaglia's for two extra wineglasses,
> this life is yours, this life that is mine, unmine it,
> take it away from me, I want it in your keep.

ProCreation is 24-36 pgs., digest-sized, professionally printed on high-quality paper, saddle-stapled, matte card cover, with graphics, photography and line drawings. They receive about 500 poems a year, accept approximately 20%. Press run is 250 for 50 subscribers, 50 shelf sales; 150 distributed free to media, coffeeshops, independent bookstores and libraries. Subscription: $15/year. **Sample postpaid: $5. Make checks payable to Silent Planet Publishing, Ltd. Submit 5-10 poems at a time. No previously published poems or simultaneous submissions. Cover letter required. "Previous publications, occupation, interests should be in cover letter, and author should indicate if he desires to be contacted by readers who desire to comment on their work."** Time between acceptance and publication is 1-2 months. **Poems are circulated to an editorial board. "Each poem is read by each of three editors. We then meet one to three times to select poems to publish. Each poem is thoroughly discussed." Often comments on rejections. Send SASE for guidelines or obtain via e-mail or website. Reports in 1-2 months. Sometimes sends prepublication galleys. Pays 1 copy. Acquires first North American serial rights.** The editor says, "One of our goals is to feature the work of relatively new poets who show promise alongside the works of more experienced poets. To this end, submit your best work. Select work with strong imagery and good word choice. Avoid the sentimental, preachy, or abstract. Write out of your experience. Find the extraordinary in the ordinary."

‡**PROMETHEUS PRESS (V)**, P.O. Box 1569, Glendale CA 91209-1569, founded 1989. They publish "genuine avant, intelligent poetry" Publishes 2 paperbacks and 2 hardbacks/year. They have recently published poetry by Hakim and Lisa Rafel. Books are usually 48-64 pgs., 8½×5½ or 5½×8½, offset-printed, perfect-bound, coated paper with photos and artwork. **They do not currently accept submissions. "We throw away any submissions." Has a backlog of 5 years. For sample books "send $10 per book."** The editor says, "Keep writing, don't forget to keep reading. Reach within without fear. Be an artist: Don't look away. Dare. Dare to stay. Dare to go. Be yourself. Don't send us any submissions."

PROSE POEM PRESS (III, IV-Form), (formerly *The Prose Poem*), 610 Clyde Court, San Marcos TX 78666-2840, phone (512)353-4998, e-mail swi3@swt.edu, founded 1990, editor Steve Wilson, publishes 2 collections of prose poetry a year. **"I hope and pray the author knows what prose poetry is before submitting to me. For me 'prose poems' run from margin to margin, with no line breaks, and use intense, compact language." Submit ms, SASE and list of previous publications. Submission deadline March 1. Author receives 10% of press run and may purchase additional copies at a discount.** The editor says, "*PPP* is a press focusing on one particular genre and publishing only the best work done in that genre. This does not mean an author cannot experiment. I encourage it. It also does not mean I don't want to see work from new writers. Please send, but only your best. I publish books with my own money, so sales are very important. If you think prose poetry matters and like the idea of a press dedicated to it, please help me keep it going by sending great work and buying our books."

PROSETRY: NEWSLETTER FOR, BY AND ABOUT WRITERS (I), The Write Place, P.O. Box 117727, Burlingame CA 94011, phone (415)347-7613, e-mail prosetry@aol.com, editor P.D. Steele, founded 1986. *Prosetry* is a monthly newsletter featuring "new and newly published poets and prose writers. Our purpose is to provide writers with up-to-date information regarding markets, conferences and contests. To help get the juices flowing, to get the writer's work in the hands of an editor, and to offer the poet a forum in which to 'show their wares.' " As a sample the editor selected this poem, "SOUND and FURY" by Don Havis:

> and the words are clapperless bells
>   jumbled together,
>   struck from the outside,
>   rending senseless clacks
>   with no tune
>   nor any melody.

Prosetry is 4 pgs., 8½×11 (17×11 sheet folded), printed on heavy bond paper and 3-hole punched for home binding. Single copy: $2; subscription: $12/year. **Sample for 2 first-class stamps. Invites new writers. Send up to 3 poems, no more than 20 lines, English only. No profanity. Requires 2-line bio plus latest credits ("tell us if you've never been published"). Publishes theme issues. Send SASE for guidelines and upcoming themes. Themes for February, May and December are Love, Spring and Holidays, respectively. "All deadlines are first of month." Reports in less than 1 month. Pays one-year subscription. Acquires one-time rights; release required.** Reviews books of poetry in 150 words. Open to unsolicited reviews. Poets may also send chapbooks for review consideration. Also publishes "How-to" *CLIPS©* for writers, $2.50 each. Free list for SASE. The editor says, "I'd like to receive less morose poetry and more humor."

PROVINCETOWN ARTS; PROVINCETOWN ARTS PRESS (II), 650 Commercial St., Provincetown MA 02657-1725, phone (508)487-3167, fax (508)487-8634, founded 1985, editor Christopher Busa, is an elegant annual using quality poetry. "*Provincetown Arts* focuses broadly on the artists and writers who inhabit or visit the tip of Cape Cod and seeks to stimulate creative activity and enhance public awareness of the cultural life of the nation's oldest continuous art colony. Drawing upon a century-long tradition rich in visual art, literature and theater, *Provincetown Arts* publishes material with a view towards demonstrating that the artists' colony, functioning outside the urban centers, is a utopian dream with an ongoing vitality." They have published poetry by Bruce Smith, Franz Wright, Sandra McPherson and Cyrus Cassells. *PA* is about 170 pgs., 8¾×11⅞, perfect-bound with full-color glossy cover. Press run is 10,000 for 500 subscribers of which 20 are libraries, 6,000 shelf sales. **Sample postpaid: $10. Submit up to 3 typed poems at a time. All queries and submissions should be via regular mail. Reads submissions September 1 through February 1. Send SASE for guidelines. Reports in 2-3 months. Usually sends prepublication galleys. Pays $25-100/poem plus 2 copies. Buys first rights.** Reviews books of poetry in 500-3,000 words, single or multi-book format. Open to unsolicited reviews. Poets may also send books for review consideration. The Provincetown Arts Press has published 5 volumes of poetry. The Provincetown Poets Series includes *At the Gate* by Martha Rhodes, *Euphorbia* by Anne-Marie Levine, a finalist in the 1995 Paterson Poetry Prize, and *1990* by Michael Klein, co-winner of the 1993 Lambda Literary Award. *Provincetown Arts* has also had work published in *Pushcart Prize XVIII, Pushcart Prize XX* and in *The Best American Poetry* (1991 and 1993, respectively).

*PSYCHOPOETICA (II, IV-Specialized: psychologically-based), Dept. of Psychology, University of Hull, Hull HU6 7RX England, founded 1979, co-editors Dr. Geoff Lowe and Trevor Millum, uses **"psychologically-based poetry."** That is not a very narrow category, and most good poetry is in some sense "psychologically based," as the editors seem to recognize in these comments (from their guidelines): **"We prefer short, experi-**

mental, rhymed and unrhymed, light verse, haiku, etc., (and visual poems). We will read and consider any style, any length, providing it's within the arena of 'psychologically-based' poetry. We're not too keen on self-indulgent therapeutic poetry (unless it's good and original), nor sweetly inspirational stuff. We like poetry that has some (or all!) of the following: humor, vivid imagery, powerful feelings, guts and substance, originality, creative style, punch or twist, word-play, good craftsmanship, etc." Published poets include Sheila E. Murphy, Wes Magee, R. Nikolas Macioci, Allen Renfro, Vi Vi Hlavsa and John Brander. The magazine appears 4 times/year, circulating to "several hundred and increasing." It is A4, perfect-bound. **Sample: £2 ($4). Submit up to 6 poems at a time. Previously published poems ("state where and when") and simultaneous submissions OK. Publishes theme issues. Send SASE (or SAE and IRC) for guidelines and upcoming themes. Theme for an upcoming issue is Portraits (of people, real or imaginary). Editor usually comments on rejections. Pays 1 copy.** Occasionally reviews books of poetry in 25 words, single format. Open to unsolicited reviews. Poets may also send books for review consideration. They say, "Careful presentation of work is most important. But we continue to be impressed by the rich variety of submissions, especially work that shifts boundaries. Also, we now welcome interesting juxtapositions of words and graphics."

THE PUCKERBRUSH PRESS; THE PUCKERBRUSH REVIEW (I, II, IV-Regional), 76 Main St., Orono ME 04473-1430, phone (207)866-4868 or 581-3832, press founded 1971, *Review* founded 1978, poetry editor Constance Hunting, is a "small press publisher of a literary, twice-a-year magazine focused on Maine and of flat-spined paperbacks of literary quality." The editor **looks for freshness and simplicity, but does not want to see "confessional, religious, sentimental, dull, feminist, incompetent, derivative" poetry.** They have published *Claiming* by Patricia Ranzoni and *To a Vanished World* by Lee Sharkey. As a sample the editor selected these lines from "Canvas for Eyes" by Muska Nagel:

> *Our Lady of the Crossroads, stoned by passersby,*
> *mother of all dark lands,*
> *pray for us now:*
> *the numbers,*
> *lost, forgotten, scattered, the nameless dead.*

For the review, submit 5 poems at a time. For book publication, query with 10 samples. Prefers no simultaneous submissions. Offers criticism for a fee: $100 is usual. Pays 10% royalties plus 10 copies.

PUDDING HOUSE PUBLICATIONS; PUDDING MAGAZINE: THE INTERNATIONAL JOURNAL OF APPLIED POETRY; PUDDING HOUSE CHAPBOOK COMPETITIONS; PUDDING HOUSE BED & BREAKFAST FOR WRITERS; PUDDING HOUSE WRITERS RESOURCE CENTER (II, IV-Political, social issues, popular culture), 60 N. Main St., Johnstown OH 43031, phone (614)967-6060, founded 1979, editor Jennifer Bosveld, provides "a sociological looking glass through poems that provide 'felt experience' and share intense human situations. Speaks for the difficulties and the solutions. Additionally a forum for poems and articles by people who take poetry arts into the schools and the human services." They publish *Pudding* every several months, also chapbooks, anthologies, broadsides. They **"want experimental and contemporary poetry—what hasn't been said before. Speak the unspeakable. Don't want preachments or sentimentality. Don't want obvious traditional forms without fresh approach. Long poems happily considered too, as long as they aren't windy. Interested in receiving poetry on popular culture and rich brief narratives, i.e. 'virtual journalism.' "** They have published poetry by Lowell Jaeger, Edward Boccia and Jane Elsdon. *Pudding* **is a literary journal with an emphasis on poetry arts in human service.** They use about 80 pgs. of poetry in each issue—5½ × 8½, 80 pgs., offset composed on IBM 1st choice. Circulation is 1,500 for 1,400 subscribers of which 50 are libraries. Subscription: $18.95/3 issues. **Sample postpaid: $6.95. Submit 4-10 poems at a time with SASE. "Submissions without SASEs will be discarded." No simultaneous submissions. Previously published submissions** *respected* **but include credits. Likes cover letter. Sometimes publishes theme issues. Send SASE for guidelines and upcoming projects. Reports on same day (unless traveling). Pays 1 copy; to featured poet $10 and 4 copies. Returns rights "with** *Pudding* **permitted to reprint."** Staff reviews books of poetry. Send books for review consideration. **Chapbooks considered outside of competitions, no query. $8 reading fee. Send complete ms and cover letter with publication credits and bio. Editor often comments, will critique on request for $4/page of poetry or $60 an hour in person.** Jennifer Bosveld shares, "Editors have pet peeves. I won't respond to postcards or on them. I require SASEs. I don't like cover letters that state the obvious." Pudding House offers 2 annual chapbook competitions—each requires a $10 reading fee with entry. Deadlines: June 30 and September 30. The competitions award $100, publication and 20 free copies. Pudding House Bed & Breakfast for Writers offers "pretty, comfortable, and clean rooms with desk and all the free paper you can use" as well as free breakfast in large comfortable home ½ block from conveniences. Location

---

THE SUBJECT INDEX, located before the General Index, can help you select markets for your work. It lists those publishers whose poetry interests are specialized.

of the Pudding House Writers Resource Center and Library on Applied Poetry. Bed & Breakfast is $65 single or double/night, discounts available. Reservations recommended far in advance. Send SASE for details.

PUEBLO POETRY PROJECT (IV-Regional), Dept. PM, 1501 E. Seventh St., Pueblo CO 81001, phone (719)584-3401, founded 1979, director Tony Moffeit, **publishes poets from the Pueblo area only. If you qualify, inquire.**

PUERTO DEL SOL (II, IV-Translations, regional), Box 3E, New Mexico State University, Las Cruces NM 88003-0001, phone (505)646-2345 or 3517 (poetry editor), founded 1972 (in present format), poetry editor Kathleene West. "We publish a literary magazine twice per year. Interested in poems, fiction, essays, photos, originals and translations from the Spanish. Also (generally solicited) reviews and dialogues between writers. We want **top quality poetry, any style, from anywhere. We are sympathetic to Southwestern writers, but this is not a theme magazine. Excellent poetry of any kind, any form.**" They have published poetry by Judith Sornberger, Ana Castillo, Marilyn Hacker, Virgil Suarez and Lois-Ann Yamanaka. As a sample the editor selected these lines from "And Seeing It" by Valerie Martínez:

> Orange, orange. And the hand arching up
> to hold it. The woman's hand, the arching.
> Up. And the star exploding, seeing it
> where it wasn't, a telescope on the night sky.
> The thermonuclear flash. The explosion.

The 6×9, flat-spined, professionally printed magazine, matte card cover with art, has a circulation of 1,250, 300 subscriptions of which 25-30 are libraries. 40-50 pgs. are devoted to poetry in each 150-page issue, which also includes quite a lot of prose. They use about 50 of the 800 submissions (about 6,000 poems) received each year to fill up the 90 pgs. of poetry the 2 issues encompass. You won't find many literary journals as attractive as this one. It has an award-caliber design (from the selection of fonts to the use of rules and type-size to enhance content). Furthermore, the journal features readable, thought-provoking verse in all styles including translations. It's an exceptional publication. Subscription: $10/2 issues. **Sample copy: $7. Submit 3-6 poems at a time, 1 poem to a page. Simultaneous submissions OK. Cover letter welcome. Reads mss September 1 to March 1 only. Offers editorial comments on most mss. Reports in 3-6 months. Sometimes sends prepublication galleys. Pays 2 copies.** In the past this publication was awarded a NEA Literary Magazine Grant. The editor says, "We're looking for poems that are risk-taking and honest."

‡*PULSAR POETRY MAGAZINE; LIGDEN PUBLISHERS (II), 34 Lineacre, Grange Park, Swindon, Wiltshire SN5 6DA United Kingdom, phone (01793)875941, founded 1994, editor David Pike, editorial assistant Jill Meredith. *Pulsar*, published quarterly, "encourages the writing of poetry from all walks of life. Contains poems, reviews and editorial comments." **They want "hard-hitting, thought-provoking work; interesting and stimulating poetry." They do not want "racist material. Not keen on religious poetry."** They have recently published poetry by Lewis Hosegood, Joy Martin and Gerald England. As a sample the editor selected these lines from "The Stone Bull" by Tim Noble:

> No hunter hauled this bull,
> snorting, to the deep cave:
> he was artist-penned, full
> profile, ochred to a wave
> of soft rock. . . .

Pulsar is 24 pgs., A5, professionally printed, saddle-stapled, glossy 2-color cover with photos and ads. Press run is 250 for 80 subscribers of which 100 are libraries; several distributed free to newspapers, etc. Subscription: $30. **Sample postpaid: $5. Make checks payable to Ligden Publishers. Submit 6 poems at a time "preferably typed." No previously published poems or simultaneous submissions. Cover letter required; include SAE with IRCs.** "Poems can be published in next edition if it is what we are looking for. Otherwise, time between acceptance and publication is up to 1 year. **The editor and assistant read all poems." Seldom comments on rejections. Send SASE (or SAE and IRC) for guidelines. Reports within 3 weeks. Pays 1 copy. Acquires first rights.** Staff reviews poetry books and poetry audio tapes (mainstream); word count varies. Poets may also send books for review consideration. The editor says, "Give explanatory notes if poems are open to interpretation. Be patient and enjoy what you are doing. Check grammar, spelling, etc. (should be obvious). Note: we are a non-profit making society."

PURDUE UNIVERSITY PRESS; VERNA EMERY POETRY PRIZE (II), 1532 S. Campus Courts-E, West Lafayette IN 47907-1532, phone (765)494-2038, founded 1960. They select 1 book/year to publish through the Verna Emery Poetry Prize, which awards $500 on publication plus royalty arrangements. They have published *No Moon* by Nancy Eimers; *The Body Mutinies* by Lucia Perillo; *Desiring Flight* by Christianne Balk; *Fresh Peaches, Fireworks & Guns* by Donald Platt; *Alcatraz* by Richard Cecil; and poetry by Fleda Brown Jackson, whose book, *Fishing With Blood*, won the GLCA New Writers Award. Final judges for the competition have included Gerald Stern, Andrew Hudgins and Ellen Bryant Voigt. **There is a $15 reading fee. Those interested are urged to send SASE for guidelines as particulars vary from year to year. Deadline: April 15.**

‡*PURGE; PUSHTIKA PRESS (V), 11 Hillview Court, Hillview Rd., Woking, Surrey AU22 7QN England, e-mail r.hampson@rhbnc.ac.uk, *purge* founded 1991, pushtika press founded 1978, contact Robert Hampson. *purge*, published annually, features "linguistically innovative poetry." They have recently published poetry by Charles Bernstein, Rosmarie Waldrop and Denise Riley. As a sample the editor selected these lines from "Necessity" by Gavin Selerie:

>   *In a frame called honour,*
>   *no road but the road we've chosen,*
>   *bits come up on autocue:*
>   *mineral perfection, whose black gold*
>   *is saved by a dentant clarion.*

purge is 24-28 pgs., A4, photocopied, saddle-stapled with some graphics. They receive about 100 poems a year, none are usually accepted. Press run is 100. **Sample postpaid: $10. Make checks payable to Robert Hampson. "Currently not accepting submissions: editor doesn't have time to deal with them." Editor usually approaches poets for work.** The editor says, "The magazine was designed to respond quickly to particular occasions—hence the method of printing, the size of circulation, the discouragement of subscribers and contributors."

‡*PURPLE PATCH; THE FIRING SQUAD (I, II), 8 Beaconview House, Charlemont Farm, West Bromwich B7I 3PL England, founded 1975, editor Geoff Stevens, a quarterly poetry and short prose magazine with reviews, comment and illustrations. The editor says, **"All good examples of poetry considered, but prefer 40 lines max. Do not want poor scanning verse, non-contributory swear words or obscenities, hackneyed themes."** They have published poetry by Alex Warner, Sam Smith, Peter Hawkins, Steve Sneyd and "Cato." As a sample the editor selected "Communicating Badly" by Sue Butler:

>   *I'm talking on the telephone*
>   *like a character who is about to buy a bagel*
>   *in the middle of a Frank O'Hara poem,*
>   *which is strange because I've never really read Rilke*
>   *and I don't know a de Kooning from a Hockney. . . .*

Purple Patch is 14-20 pgs., magazine-sized, offset on plain paper, cover on the same stock with b&w drawing, side-stapled. Circulation "varies." Subscription: £3.50 UK/3 issues; US price is $5/issue (submit dollars). **Cover letter with short self-introduction preferred with submissions.** Time between acceptance and publication is 4 months. **Publishes theme issues occasionally. Send SASE (or SAE and IRCs) for upcoming themes. Reporting time is 1 month to Great Britain, can be longer to US. Overseas contributors have to buy a copy to see their work in print. Acquires first British serial rights.** Staff reviews poetry chapbooks, short stories and tapes in 30-300 words. Send books for review consideration. *The Firing Squad* is a broadsheet of **short poetry of a protest or complaint nature**, published at irregular intervals. "All inquiries, submissions of work, etc., must include SASE or SAE and IRCs or $1 U.S./Canadian for return postage/reply."

‡*PUSSY POETRY (IV-Women); SCARS & BRUISES (I), 132 George St., Mablethorpe, Lincolnshire LN12 2BT United Kingdom, founded 1993 (*Scars & Bruises*), 1996 (*Pussy Poetry*), contact Erica. *Pussy Poetry*, published annually, strives "to increase women's confidence in poetry, to get **women's poetry** out into the open." *Scars & Bruises*, published 1-2 times/year, "is about not hiding feelings away." **They want "personal, barefaced feelings with attitude and emotion, no longer than 20 lines in length."** They have recently published poetry by Natasha Morris, Sarah Shoraka and Wendy French. As a sample the editor selected these lines from "Moon" by Caz Blood:

>   *My blood drips and forms a pool,*
>   *Where the moon reflects her silver light.*
>   *Waxing, full and waning,*
>   *She is pure*
>   *Thirteen times a year,*
>   *Hording secrets only a woman knows.*

PP is 44 pgs., *S&B* is 40 pgs., both are A6, photocopied, folded with b&w collages, art, photos and drawings. They receive about 60 poems a year, accept approximately 80%. Press run is 250. **Sample postpaid: $1 plus 2 IRCs. Make checks payable to E. Gilberthorpe. Submit up to 3 poems, with name and address on each page.** The editor says, "I encourage poets to do their own artistic interpretation to accompany their poem on its page." **Previously published poems and simultaneous submissions OK. Cover letter preferred. Seldom comments on rejections. Send SASE (or SAE and IRC) for guidelines. Reports "within 6 weeks."** Reviews books or chapbooks of poetry or other magazines. Open to unsolicited reviews. Poets may also send books for review consideration. The editor says, "Release your inner pains, all your demons, let all that haunts you be set free onto the page."

PYGMY FOREST PRESS; SEMI-DWARF REVIEW (II), P.O. Box 591, Albion CA 95410, phone (707)937-2347, founded 1987, editor/publisher Leonard Cirino, publishes flat-spined paperbacks. **"Forms of any kind/ length to 96 pgs., subject matter open; especially ecology, prison, asylum, Third World, anarchist to far right. Prefer Stevens to Williams. I like Berryman, Roethke, William Bronk; dislike most 'Beats.' Open to anything I consider 'good.' Open to traditional rhyme, meter, but must be modern in subject matter.**

Also open to translations." He has published *From Beirut* by Mahmoud Darwish, translated by Stephen Kessler; *Pagan Fishing & Other Poems* by Walt McLaughlin; *Where the Four Winds Blow* (including epitaphs) by Phillipe Soupault, translated by Pat Nolan; *The Circle & The Line* by Victoria Bouroncle; *Poetry of the Deformed* by Kenn Mitchell; and *Light on The Edge* by Deureaux Baker. **Submit 10-15 poems with bio, acknowledgements, publications. Simultaneous submissions and previously published material OK. Reports on queries in 1-3 weeks, submissions in 2-4 weeks. Usually pays 20% of run ("if author typesets on IBM compatible")—about 30-50 copies. Buys first rights. He comments on "almost every" ms.** Sponsors the Richard A. Seffron Memorial Award given annually to a poet under 30. "No entry, but no prize" money. Send SASE in January 1998 for details. Leonard Cirino says, "I am basically an anarchist. Belong to no 'school.' I fund myself. Receive no grants or private funding. Generally politically left, but no mainline Stalinist or Marxist. Plan to publish one to three books yearly." Also publishes *Semi-Dwarf Review* which accepts poetry, stories, translations, memoirs and essays. Send SASE for details.

PYX PRESS; MAGIC REALISM (II, IV-Fantasy); SHILLELAGH (II, IV-Horror, fantasy); WRITER'S KEEPER (I, II, IV-Writing), P.O. Box 922648, Sylmar CA 91392-2648, founded 1990. *Magic Realism* editor C. Darren Butler, appears quarterly using poetry of **"depth and imagination. *Magic Realism* subverts reality by shaping it into a human mold, bringing it closer to the imagination and to the subconscious. Inner reality becomes empirical reality. We always need good short poems of 3-12 lines."** It is 60-80 pgs., digest-sized, typeset, offset or xerographically printed, with card cover using b&w art. They use 5-15 poems/issue. Press run is 600-800 for 200 subscribers. **Sample postpaid: $5.95. Previously published poems and simultaneous submissions OK. Send #10 SASE for guidelines. Reports in 2-6 months. Always sends prepublication galleys. Pays $3/magazine page on acceptance for poetry and 1 copy. Buys first North American serial or one-time rights and nonexclusive reprint rights; also needs worldwide Spanish language rights for translation which appears 1-2 years after English edition. Editor sometimes comments on rejections.** The editor says, "I am looking for literary work based in exaggerated realism. Fantasy should permeate the reality, give it luster. My needs are somewhat flexible. For example, I occasionally publish genre work, or glib fantasy of the sort found in folktales and fables." *Shillelagh*, editors C. Darren Butler and Lisa S. Laurencot, appears irregularly (1-3 times/year) using **"bizarre, horrific short-shorts and poetry. We are most interested in dreamy, surreal, decadent poetry; intensely imaginative and bizarre works. We try to publish material in any form or category that promotes a sense of wonder or terror or awe, work that transforms the mind and the experience of living. Horror and comedy are closely related. For this reason, we also accept comedic or absurd work when they fit thematically with the magazine."** No obscene, gory, gratuitous, pornographic or trite poetry. Also, no vampires, werewolves, or other horror clichés. The editor says *Shillelagh* is 40-48 pgs., digest-sized, xerographically printed, saddle-stapled with b&w cover and art, ads also included. They use approximately 20 poems/issue. Press run is 400 for 80 subscribers. Subscription: $10.95/3 issues. **Sample postpaid: $4.50. Previously published poems and simultaneous submissions OK. Send SASE for guidelines. Reports in 2-6 months. Pays 1 copy. Acquires first North American serial rights; reprint rights optional.** *Writer's Keeper*, editor C. Darren Butler, is a quarterly publishing poetry, fiction and nonfiction **pertaining to writing. Accepts poetry to 30 lines, any style. "Humorous works especially needed."** *WK* is 2-6 pgs., 8½ × 11, photocopied, corner-stapled. They receive 600-800 submissions a year, accept approximately 2%. Press run 800-1,000 for 40 subscribers; 80% distributed free. Subscription: $5. **Sample postpaid: $1.25 or free for #10 SASE. Previously published poems and simultaneous submissions OK. Send SASE for guidelines. Reports in 3-6 months, "occasionally longer, often sooner." Pays $1 plus contributor's copy and 3-issue subscription. Acquires first North American serial rights.** All three magazines review books of poetry, chapbooks and magazines in ¼ to ½ page as space permits. Poets may send books for review consideration. Pyx Press publishes books and **chapbooks.** "Generally poets we publish first appear in *Magic Realism* or *Shillelagh*." Send SASE for catalog.

‡*QUADRANT MAGAZINE (II), P.O. Box 1495, Collingwood, Victoria 3066 Australia, phone (03)9417 6855, fax (03)9416 2980, founded 1956, contact the editor, published 10 times/year, is a "magazine of literature and ideas; about 10% of pages devoted to poetry." They have recently published poetry by Les Murray, John Ridland, Geoff Page and Kathleen Stewart. *Quadrant* is 88 pgs., 7⅞ × 10¾, professionally printed, newsprint, saddle-stapled, CS2 cover stock with some art and ads. They receive several thousand poems a year, accept approximately 5%. Press run is 8,000 for 3,000 subscribers of which 500 are libraries, 2,500 shelf sales; 130 distributed free. Subscription: $50 (in Australia). **Sample postpaid: $5.50. No previously published poems or simultaneous submissions. Cover letter preferred.** Time between acceptance and publication is 6 months. **"Assessment made by literary editor." Seldom comments on rejections. Send SASE (or SAE and IRCs) for guidelines. Pays $30/poem plus 1 copy. Buys first Australian serial rights.** Reviews books of poetry. Open to unsolicited reviews.

QUARTERLY REVIEW OF LITERATURE POETRY BOOK SERIES; QRL PRIZE AWARDS (II, IV-Subscription, translation), 26 Haslet Ave., Princeton NJ 08540, founded 1943, poetry editors T. Weiss and R. Weiss. After more than 35 years as one of the most distinguished literary journals in the country, *QRL* now appears as the *QRL Poetry Book Series*, in which 4-6 books, chosen in open competition, are combined in one annual volume, each of the 4-6 poets receiving $1,000 and 100 copies. The resulting 300- to 400-page volumes are printed in editions of 3,000-5,000, selling in paperback for $12, in hardback for $20. Subscription—2 paperback volumes containing 10 books: $20. Send SASE for details.

QUARTERLY WEST (II), 317 Olpin Union, University of Utah, Salt Lake City UT 84112, phone (801)581-3938, founded 1976, co-editors Lawrence Coates and Margot Schilpp, poetry editor Jennifer Tonge. *Quarterly West* is a semiannual literary magazine that **seeks "original and accomplished literary verse—free or formal. No greeting card or sentimental poetry." Also publishes translations.** They have recently published poetry by Robert Pinsky, Eavan Boland, Albert Goldbarth, William Matthews, Agha Shahid Ali and Heather McHugh. *QW* is 220 pgs., 6×9, offset with 4-color cover art. They receive 1,250 submissions a year, accept less than 1%. Press run is 1,900 for 500 subscribers of which 300-400 are libraries. Subscription: $12/year, $21/2 years. **Sample postpaid: $7.50. Submit 3-5 poems at a time; if translations, include original. No previously published poems; simultaneous submissions OK, with notification. Seldom comments on rejections. Send SASE for guidelines. Reports in 1-6 months. Pays $15-100. Buys all rights. Returns rights with acknowledgement and right to reprint.** Reviews books of poetry in 1,000-3,000 words. Open to unsolicited reviews. Poets may also send books for review consideration. Poetry published in *Quarterly West* has also appeared in *The Best American Poetry 1997*.

QUEEN OF ALL HEARTS (IV-Religious), 26 S. Saxon Ave., Bay Shore NY 11706, phone (516)665-0726, founded 1950, poetry editor Joseph Tusiani, is a magazine-sized bimonthly that uses **poetry "dealing with Mary, the Mother of Jesus—inspirational poetry. Not too long."** They have published poetry by Fernando Sembiante and Alberta Schumacher. The professionally printed magazine, 48 pgs., heavy stock, various colors of ink and paper, liberal use of graphics and photos, has approximately 4,000 subscriptions at $17/year. Single copy: $2.50. **Sample postpaid: $3.** They receive 40-50 submissions a year, use approximately 2/issue. **Submit double-spaced mss. Reports within 3-4 weeks. Pays 6 copies (sometimes more) and complimentary subscription. Editor sometimes comments on rejections.** His advice: "Try and try again! Inspiration is not automatic!"

‡QUEEN OF SWORDS PRESS (IV-Anthology), P.O. Box 3646, Eugene OR 97403, phone (541)344-0509, e-mail ecqsp@oregon.uoregon.edu, founded 1993, editor Elizabeth Claman, offers "a forum for underrepresented voices on topics of interest primarily to women." **Publishes 1 chapbook** or anthology/year. **They want "the best you have specific to the anthology's subject matter."** They have recently published poetry by Dorianne Laux, Diane Wakoski, Rosmary Waldrop and Gary Young. Anthologies are usually 150-300 pgs., paperback, chapbooks are usually 32-64 pgs. **Query first. Submit 1-5 poems at a time. Previously published poems and simultaneous submissions OK with notification. Cover letter preferred.** Time between acceptance and publication is 3-12 months. **Seldom comments on rejections. Replies to queries and mss (if invited) in up to 1 month. Pays chapbook authors 50 copies out of a press run of 500; pays anthology authors 15 copies out of a press run of 1,000.**

ELLERY QUEEN'S MYSTERY MAGAZINE (IV-Mystery), 1270 Avenue of the Americas, New York NY 10020, founded 1941, appears 11 times/year, primarily using short stories of mystery, crime or suspense. **"We also publish short limericks and verse pertaining to the mystery field."** As a sample the editor selected these lines from "Coffee Olé" by Marie E. Truitt:

> *But once he married, breakfasts were the nastiest of scenes;*
> *On making coffee, Wifie didn't know a hill of beans.*
> *The bitter taste! . . . the inch-deep dregs! . . . he couldn't take much more!*
> *It went from bad to mega-bad, till Fred let out a roar:*
> *"I've had enough! It's Splitsville! There's just no other course!*
> *And I hold within this cup, my Dear, the grounds for our divorce!"*

EQMM is 160 pgs., 5×7¾, professionally printed newsprint, flat-spined with glossy paper cover. Subscription: $33.97. **Sample: $2.95 (available on newsstands). No previously published poems; simultaneous submissions OK. Include SASE with submissions. Reports in 3 months. Pays $5-50 plus 3 copies.**

♣QUEEN'S QUARTERLY: A CANADIAN REVIEW (II, IV-Regional), Queen's University, 184 Union St., Kingston, Ontario K7L 3N6 Canada, phone (613)545-2667, e-mail qquarterly@post.queens.ca, website http://www.info.queensu.ca/quarterly, founded 1893, editor Boris Castel, is "a general interest intellectual review featuring articles on science, politics, humanities, arts and letters, extensive book reviews, some poetry and fiction. **We are especially interested in poetry by Canadian writers. Shorter poems preferred."** They have published poetry by Evelyn Lau, Sue Nevill and Raymond Souster. There are about 12 pgs. of poetry in each issue, 6×9, 224 pgs. Circulation is 3,500. They receive about 400 submissions of poetry a year, use approximately 40. Subscription: $20 Canadian, $25 US for US and foreign subscribers. **Sample postpaid: $6.50 US. Submit up to 6 poems at a time. No simultaneous submissions. E-mail submissions OK. Reports in 1 month. Pays usually $50 (Canadian)/poem, "but it varies," plus 2 copies.**

RADCLIFFE QUARTERLY (IV-Specialized: alumnae), 10 Garden St., Cambridge MA 02138, phone (617)495-8608, production editor Ruth Prince, is an alumnae quarterly that **publishes alumnae poetry.** *RQ* is magazine-sized, with glossy 2-color paper cover. They receive about 50 unsolicited poems/year, use 4 poems/

issue. Press run is 35,000. **Samples free to anyone. No pay.** Reviews books of poetry in 250 words, single format.

RADIANCE: THE MAGAZINE FOR LARGE WOMEN (I, IV-Women), P.O. Box 30246, Oakland CA 94604, phone/fax (510)482-0680, e-mail radmag2@aol.com, website http://www.radiancemagazine.com, founded 1984, publisher/editor Alice Ansfield, appears quarterly. **"Keeping in mind that our magazine is geared toward large women, we look for poetry from women of any size and men who don't accept society's stereotypical standards of beauty and weight—but who celebrate women's bodies, sexuality, search for self-esteem and personal growth."** As a sample she quotes "Homage to My Hips" by Lucille Clifton:

> *these hips are big hips*
> *they need space to*
> *move around in.*
> *they don't fit into little*
> *petty places. these hips*
> *are free hips.*
> *they don't like to be held back.*
> *these hips have never been enslaved,*
> *they go where they want to go*
> *they do what they want to do.*
> *these hips are mighty hips.*
> *these hips are magic hips.*
> *i have known them*
> *to put a spell on a man and*
> *spin him like a top!*

Radiance is 60 pgs., magazine-sized, professionally printed on glossy stock with full-color paper cover, saddle-stapled, 4-color graphics, photos and ads. Circulation is 10,000 for 4,000 subscriptions, 4,000 selling on newsstands or in bookstores; 1,000 distributed free to media and clothing stores for large women. Subscription: $20/year. **Sample postpaid: $3.50. Submit double-spaced, typed ms. Editor usually comments on rejections. Send SASE for guidelines. Reports in 4-6 months. Pays $10-15 plus contributor's copy. Buys one-time rights.** Reviews related books of poetry in 500-800 words.

RAG MAG; BLACK HAT PRESS (I, II), P.O. Box 12, Goodhue MN 55027, phone (612)923-4590, founded 1982, poetry editor Beverly Voldseth, accepts **poetry of "any length or style. No pornographic SM violent crap."** They have recently published poetry by Kenneth Pobo, Trina Zelle and Kerri Brostrom. As a sample the editor selected these lines from "Look at the Tomato Plants" by Sigi Leonhard:

> *We put them in the earth the middle of June*
> *And now, we see the wilderness, the joyous jungle*
> *They have created among themselves!*
> *A cathedral of green, sturdy pillars*
> *And rosettes of gree lace winding*
> *Upward, downward, in vertiginous*
> *Multitude, but not without system.*
> *And we lie in front of them everyday, we see*
> *The sunlight broken and reflected into shades*
> *Of green and the fruit, slowly ripening, now*
> *Turning lighter, now yellow, and orange,*
> *And now, the first flaming reds.*

Rag Mag, appearing twice a year, is 80-112 pgs., perfect-bound, 6×9, professionally printed in dark type with ads for books, matte card cover. The editor says she accepts about 10% of poetry received. Press run is 250 for 80 subscribers of which 8 are libraries. Subscription: $10. **Sample postpaid: $6. "Send three to nine of your best with brief bio. Something that tells a story, creates images, speaks to the heart." Name and address on each page. SASE required for return of work or response. Previously published poems and simultaneous submissions OK, "but please acknowledge both." Send SASE for guidelines. Pays 1 copy. Acquires first or one-time rights.** Reviews books of poetry. Open to unsolicited reviews. Poets may also send books for review consideration. **They may publish chapbook or paperback collections of poetry under the imprint of Black Hat Press. Query first. Simultaneous submissions and previously printed material OK. Reports in 6 weeks.**

THE GEOGRAPHICAL INDEX, located before the Subject Index, can help you discover the publishers in your region. Publishers often favor poets (and work) from their own areas.

Detailed comments provided "sometimes." Financial arrangements for book publication vary. They have recently published *Boom Town* by Diane Glancy and *Poems of Saisseval* by Pierre Garnier. Black Hat Press also publishes a yearly poetry calendar open to submissions from Minnesota poets only. Send SASE for details to Krista Hauenstein, P.O. Box 1076, Eau Claire WI 54702.

THE RAGGED EDGE MAGAZINE (IV-Specialized: disabled community), (formerly *The Disability Rag & Resource*), P.O. Box 145, Louisville KY 40201-0145, fax (502)899-9562, e-mail rgarr@iglou.com, website http://www.iglou.com/uhy/edge, founded 1980, fiction/poetry editor Anne Finger, appears 6 times/year and "is the nation's leading disability rights magazine." **The editors have no restrictions as to form, length or style of poetry. "We are interested in vivid material by disabled writers or about the disability experience. Nothing sappy, sentimental, stereotyped or clichéd."** They have published poetry by Kenny Fries, Margaret Robison, Bill Abrams and Barbara Seaman. The editor says *The Ragged Edge* is approximately 48 pgs., 8 × 10⅝, b&w graphics on newsprint, some advertising. They receive about 300 poems a year, accept approximately 5%. Press run is 5,000 for 4,500 subscribers of which approximately 10% are libraries, 350 shelf sales. Single copy: $3.95; subscription: $17.50 individuals, $35 institutions, $42 international. **Sample postpaid: $4.50. Previously published poems OK, "provided they have not appeared in a publication that circulates to the disabled community." No simultaneous submissions. Cover letter required.** Time between acceptance and publication is 6-12 months. **Often comments on rejections. Send SASE for guidelines or request via e-mail. Reports within 1 month. Pays $25/poem plus 2 copies. Buys first North American serial rights.** "We publish reviews of disability-related poetry collections; our reviews run approximately 250-500 words."

‡RAISED INK; RUTGERS POETRY SOCIETY (II), Sac Box 61, 613 George St., New Brunswick NJ 08903, website http://www.usacs.rutgers.edu/student-orgs/poetry, founded 1994, contact Fred Bicknese and Colin McCaul. *Raised Ink*, published 3 times/year, hopes to "increase interest in poetry, to remove it from the classroom and coffeehouse and allow it to become a mainstream interest. **Our only preference is that it must be interesting. If we are able to stop reading it before the last line, or are otherwise unmoved by the poem, it will likely have the same effect on our readership."** They have recently published poetry by James Nemeth and Aimee Eastwood. As a sample the editor selected these lines from "A Modest Creature" by Jill Cole:

> *Without a shade or shape that can be seen*
> *it simply is;*
> *untroubled by its single state,*
> *it craves to hear the words it speaks,*
> *alone inside a dark and strangling skull.*

Raised Ink is 24 pgs., 4¼ × 5½, offset, saddle-stapled, with full-color cover photo. They receive about 200 poems a year, accept approximately 20%. Press run is 1,000; all distributed free. **Sample postpaid: $1 donation. Make checks payable to Rutgers Poetry Society. Submit up to 9 poems at a time. Previously published poems and simultaneous submissions OK. Reads submissions September through April only.** Time between acceptance and publication is 2 months. **Poems are circulated to an editorial board.** "All editors read all poems and vote. Most popular poems are used." **Often comments on rejections. Reports "within several months." Pays 5 copies. Acquires one-time rights.**

‡RALPH'S REVIEW; RC'S STAMP HOT LINE (II), 129A Wellington Ave., Albany NY 12203, e-mail rcpub@juno.com, website http://members.aol.com/RCPUB/index.html, founded 1988, editor R. Cornell. *Ralph's Review*, published monthly or bimonthly, contains "mostly new writers, short stories and poems." **They want "horror/fantasy, environmental. No more than 30 lines." They do not want "rape, racial, political poems."** They have recently published poetry by Kim Laico and John Grey. The editor says *Ralph's Review* is 20-35 pgs., 8½ × 11, photocopied, sometimes with soft cover, with art, cartoons and graphics. They receive about 80-100 poems a year, accept approximately 40%. Press run is 75-100 for 35 subscribers of which 3 are libraries; 30-40 distributed free to book stores, toy stores, antique and coffee shops. Single copy: $2; subscription: $15. **Sample postpaid: $5. Make checks payable to R. Cornell. Submit up to 5 poems, with a $3 reading fee. Previously published poems and simultaneous submissions OK. Cover letter required.** Time between acceptance and publication is 2-4 months. **Seldom comments on rejections. Publishes theme issues. Send SASE for guidelines and upcoming themes. Reports in 2-3 weeks. Pays 1-2 copies. Acquires all rights. Returns rights 1 year after acceptance.** Reviews books in up to 5,000 words in single-book format. Open to unsolicited reviews. Poets may also send books for review consideration. The editor says, "Books are selling like crazy; keep writing, check out current trends, submit to as many publications as you can afford."

RAMBUNCTIOUS PRESS; RAMBUNCTIOUS REVIEW (II, IV-Regional), 1221 W. Pratt, Chicago IL 60626, founded 1982, poetry editors Mary Alberts, Richard Goldman, Beth Hausler and Nancy Lennon. *Rambunctious Review* appears once yearly. They want **"spirited, quality poetry**, fiction, photos and graphics. **Some focus on local work, but all work is considered."** As a sample the editors selected these lines from "I Grew Up in Arles" by Anne Valdez:

> *I grew up in Arles, South Chicago,*
> *The town where Vincent lived*
> *I never knew the tavern/cafe/bars*

> But I knew the trees and houses
> And people with spider-jointed fingers.

RR is 48 pgs., 7×10, handsomely printed and saddle-stapled. They receive about 500-600 submissions a year, accept approximately 50-60. Circulation is about 500 for 200 subscribers. **Sample postpaid: $4. Will consider simultaneous submissions. No submissions accepted June 1 through August 31. No queries. Occasionally comments on mss. Publishes theme issues. Reports in 9 months. Pays 2 copies.** They run annual contests in poetry, fiction and short drama.

RANGER RICK MAGAZINE (III, IV-Children, nature/ecology), 8925 Leesburg Pike, Vienna VA 22184, founded 1967, senior editor Deborah Churchman, is a monthly nature magazine for children aged 6-12. **They want "short, funny verses for children about nature and the environment. Must be accurate. No religious, preachy or difficult poetry."** They have published poetry by John Ciardi and Charles Ghigna. *RR* is 48 pgs., 8×10, saddle-stitched, glossy paper with numerous full color photos. They receive 100-200 submissions a year, "may accept one." Press run is 900,000. Subscription: $15. **Sample postpaid: $2. Submit up to 5 poems at a time. Previously published poems OK; no simultaneous submissions.** Time between acceptance and publication is 2-5 years. **Seldom comments on rejections. Publishes theme issues. Send SASE for guidelines. Reports in 2 months. Always sends prepublication galleys. Pays $5/line plus 2 copies. Buys all rights. Return is "negotiable."** The editor says, "Think: Will kids understand these words? Will it hook them? Will an eight-year-old want to read this instead of playing Nintendo?"

RARACH PRESS (V), 1005 Oakland Dr., Kalamazoo MI 49008, phone (616)388-5631, founded 1981, owner Ladislav Hanka, is a "small bibliophilic press specializing in hand-printing, hand-binding with original artwork. The material is either in Czech or, if English, dealing with environmentalist subject matter." He has printed books of poetry by Richard Neugebauer, Ben Mitchell and Rainer Maria Rilke. The editor says, "Authors tend to be friends, acquaintances or dead. They are given a portion of the books or a portion of sales after the fact. **I do not care to receive unsolicited mss.** I pity the lot of you. I fully expect most of my books to eventually be taken apart and sold for the artwork when they pass from the present collector of bibliophilia to some philistine. This means the poetry will be lost . . . I really sell my books for the price of the binding and artwork."

RARITAN QUARTERLY (III), Dept. PM, 31 Mine St., New Brunswick NJ 08903, phone (908)932-7887, founded 1982, editor Richard Poirier. **"We publish very little poetry. We publish *almost* no unsolicited poetry, so it would be misleading to encourage submissions."** They have published poetry by J.D. McClatchy, James Merrill, Richard Howard and Robert Pinsky. It is 150 pgs., 6×9, flat-spined, with matte card cover, professionally printed. The few poems appearing here (including sequences and translations) tend toward free verse. Press run is 4,000 for 3,500 subscribers of which 800 are libraries. Subscription: $20. **Sample postpaid: $7. Pays $100/ submission if accepted.** Reviews recent poetry books and chapbooks. Poetry published in this quarterly was included in *The Best American Poetry 1992*.

RATTLE (II), 23440 Ventura Blvd. #200, Sherman Oaks CA 91423, phone (818)788-3232, fax (818)788-2831, founded 1994, editor Alan Fox, poetry editor Stellasue Lee, is a biannual poetry publication which also includes interviews with poets, essays on poetry and brief reviews of poetry books. **They want "high quality poetry of any form, four pages maximum. Nothing unintelligible."** They have published poetry by Charles Bukowski, William Stafford, Charles Webb and Ai. As a sample the editor selected these lines from "The Small Deaths" by Stephanie Mendel:

> Later, I lay my hand on his rib cage,
> bargain with the fist-sized cancer,
> try to soothe it by telling it
> if it grows slowly, it can live longer,
> but I know it's too greedy to care.

Rattle is 122-144 pgs., 5½×8½, neatly printed and perfect-bound with 4-color coated card cover. They receive about 1,000 poems a year, accept approximately 140. Press run is 1,500. Subscription: $20/2 years. **Sample postpaid: $6. Make checks payable to Alan Fox. Submit up to 5 poems at a time. Previously published poems and simultaneous submissions OK. Cover letter with brief bio required. Reads submissions September 1 through May 31 only. Seldom comments on rejections. Reports in 3-5 months. Pays 2 copies. Rights revert to authors upon publication.** Welcomes short essays on poetry and one-page book reviews. Poets may also send books for review consideration.

RAW DOG PRESS; POST POEMS (II, IV-Humor), 151 S. West St., Doylestown PA 18901-4134, phone (215)345-6838, founded 1977, poetry editor R. Gerry Fabian, "publishes Post Poems annual—a postcard series. **We want short poetry (three to seven lines) on any subject. The positive poem or the poem of understated humor always has an inside track. No taboos, however. All styles considered. Anything with rhyme had better be immortal."** They have published poetry by Charles Rossiter, Lyn Lifshin, John Grey, Glen G. Coats and the editor, R. Gerry Fabian, who selected his poem, "Arc Welder," as a sample:

> After years of burning
> he pressed his lips against hers

and sealed out any doubt.

Submit 3-5 poems at a time. Send SASE for catalog to buy samples. The editor "always" comments on rejections. Pays copies. Acquires all rights. Returns rights on mention of first publication. Sometimes reviews books of poetry. He says he will offer criticism for a fee; "if someone is desperate to publish and is willing to pay, we will use our vast knowledge to help steer the ms in the right direction. We will advise against it, but as P.T. Barnum said. . . . Raw Dog Press welcomes new poets and detests second-rate poems from 'name' poets. We exist because we are dumb like a fox, but even a fox takes care of its own." The editor also says, "I get more poems that do not fit my needs. At least one quarter of all poets waste their postage because they do not read the requirements."

‡✤RAW NERVZ HAIKU; PROOF PRESS (IV-Form/style), 67 Court St., Aylmer, Quebec J9H 4M1 Canada, founded 1994, editor/publisher Dorothy Howard. *Raw NerVZ Haiku*, published quarterly, features "haiku and related material." **They want "haiku, senryu, tanka, renga, haiga and haibun."** They have recently published poetry by Marlene Mountain, Janice M. Bostok and LeRoy Gorman. As a sample the editor selected this haiku by Marco Fraticelli:

> *knifethrower*
> *thunderstorm*

The editor says *RNH* is 5½×8½, stapled with graphics and art. Press run is 250 for 150 subscribers of which 10 are libraries. Subscription: $20. **Sample postpaid: $6. Submit up to 10 poems at a time. Previously published poems OK; no simultaneous submissions. Cover letter preferred** "without return envelopes. Cash **preferred to IRCs from non-Canadian contributors for prepaid replies."** Time between acceptance and publication is 1-6 months. **Seldom comments on rejections. Send SASE (or SAE and IRCs) for guidelines. Reports in 2-8 weeks. Sometimes sends prepublication galleys. Acquires one-time rights.** Reviews books or chapbooks of poetry or other magazines in up to 500 words. Open to unsolicited reviews. Poets may also send books for review consideration. proof press publishes **6-10 chapbooks/year** of haiku and renga. Chapbooks are usually under 50 pgs., 4×5½ to 5½×8½, photocopied, saddle-stapled, cover stock with b&w graphics. **Query first with 10-20 sample poems and return postage. Replies to queries in 6 weeks; to mss (if invited) in 2 months. Pays 20 author's copies (out of a press run of 200).** The editor says, "Reading copies of *Raw NerVZ* is useful. We are not interested in run-of-the-mill poetry."

‡RB'S POETS' VIEWPOINT (I), P.O. Box 940, Eunice NM 88231, founded 1989, editor Robert Bennett, published bimonthly, features poetry and cartoons. **They want "general and religious poetry, sonnets and sijo with a 21-line limit." They do not want "vulgar language."** They have recently published poetry by Marion Ford Park, Ruth Ditmer Ream, Ruth Halbrooks and Delphine Ledoux. As a sample the editor selected these lines from "Star Fantasy" by Mary Strand:

> *On the hill where Will-O-Wisps camp*
> *I danced to the chirpings of crickets*
> *by the glow of the lightning-bug's lamp.*
> *When the stars in their celestial thickets*
> *beckoned me with come-hither winks*
> *I climbed a dangling moonbeam*
> *& skipped on heavenly rinks.*

RB's is 34 pgs., digest-sized, photocopied, saddle-stapled with drawings and cartoons. They receive about 3,600 poems a year, accept approximately 90%. Press run is 60 of which 2 are for libraries. Subscription: $8. **Sample postpaid: $2. Make checks payable to Robert Bennett. Submit 3 poems typed single space with a $1.50 per poem reading fee. Previously published poems and simultaneous submissions OK. Reads submissions February, April, June, August, October and December.** Time between acceptance and publication is 1 month. **"Poems are selected by one editor." Often comments on rejections. Send SASE for guidelines. Reports in 1 month. Pays 1 copy. Acquires one-time rights.** Sponsors contests for general poetry, religious poetry, sonnets and sijo with first prizes of $20, $6 and $5, respectively, plus publication in *RB's*. There is a $1.50 per poem entry fee, except the sijo category, which has a 50¢ per poem fee. Deadline October 30. Send SASE for guidelines.

RE:AL—THE JOURNAL OF LIBERAL ARTS (II, IV-Bilingual, translations, humor), Dept. PM, Box 13007, Stephen F. Austin State University, Nacogdoches TX 75962, phone (409)468-2028, e-mail real@sfasu.edu, website http://www.titan.sfasu.edu, founded 1968, editor W. Dale Hearell, is a "Liberal Arts Forum" using short fiction, drama, reviews and interviews; contains editorial notes and personalized "Contributors' Notes"; printed in the winter and summer. They "hope to use from 15 to 35 pages of poetry per issue, one poem per page (typeset in editor's office)." **They receive between 10-35 poems/week. "We presently do not receive enough formal or witty/ironic pieces. We need a better balance between open and generic forms. We're also interested in critical writings on poems or writing poetry and translations with a bilingual format (permissions from original author)."** It is handsomely printed, "reserved format," perfect-bound with line drawings and photos. Simply one of the most readable literary magazines published today, *RE:AL* welcomes all styles and forms that display craft, insight and accessibility. Circulation approximately 400, "more than half of which are major college libraries." Subscriptions also in Great Britain, Ireland, Italy, Holland, Puerto Rico, Brazil and Canada. **Subscription: $10, $15 for institutions. Sample postpaid: $5. Submit original and copy.** "Editors prefer a statement that ms is not being simultaneously submitted; however, this fact is taken for granted when we receive a ms." Writer's guidelines for SASE. They acknowledge receipt of submissions and strive for a 1-month decision. Submissions during summer semesters may take longer. "We will return poems rather than tie them up for more than a one-issue backlog (six to nine months)." **Pays 2 copies.** Reviews are assigned, but queries about doing reviews are welcome.

*REALITY STREET EDITIONS (V), 4 Howard Court, Peckham Rye, London SE15 3PH United Kingdom, phone (0171)639-7297, e-mail 100344.2546@compuserve.com, is the joint imprint of Reality Studios and Street Editions, editors Ken Edwards and Wendy Mulford. They publish 4 paperbacks/year. They have published *Out of Everywhere*, an anthology of innovative poetry by women in North America and the United Kingdom; it is edited by Maggie O'Sullivan and includes Susan Howe, Barbara Guest, Lyn Hejinian, Denise Riley and 26 others. **However, they currently do not accept unsolicited mss.** Their US distributor is Small Press Distribution, 1814 San Pablo Ave., Berkeley CA 94302.

*THE RED CANDLE PRESS; CANDELABRUM (II), 9 Milner Rd., Wisbech PE13 2LR England, founded 1970, editor M.L. McCarthy, M.A., administrative editor Helen Gordon, B.A., was "founded to encourage poets working in **traditional-type verse, metrical unrhymed or metrical rhymed**. We're more interested in poems than poets: that is, we're interested in what sort of poems an author produces, not in his or her personality." They publish the magazine, *Candelabrum*, twice yearly (April and October). They want **"good-quality metrical verse, with rhymed verse specially wanted. Elegantly cadenced free verse is acceptable. No weak stuff (moons and Junes, loves and doves, etc.) No chopped-up prose pretending to be free verse. Any length up to about 40 lines for *Candelabrum*, any subject, including eroticism (but not porn)—satire, love poems, nature lyrics, philosophical—any subject, but nothing racist or sexist."** They have published poetry by Andrea Abraham, Leo Yankevich, John Gurney, Ann Keith, M.L. McCarthy and Peter G.P. Thompson. The editors offer these lines by Paul Look as a sample:

> The moon runs down the rivers of its streets,
> Washing all colour from the ones I meet.
> Malicious voices, delicate and slow,
> Reveal the truths I never wished to know.

The digest-sized magazine, staple-spined, small type, exemplifies their intent to "pack in as much as possible, wasting no space, and try to keep a neat appearance with the minimum expense." They get in about 40 pgs. (some 70 poems) in each issue. They receive about 2,000 submissions a year, use approximately 5% of those, sometimes holding over poems for the next year. Circulation is 900 for 700 subscribers of which 22 are libraries. **Sample: $4 in bills only; checks not accepted. "Submit anytime. IRCs essential for reply and please check the weight if you wish your ms returned. Each poem on a separate sheet please, neat typescripts or neat *legible* manuscripts. *Please* no dark, oily photostats, no colored ink (only black or blue). Author's name and address on each sheet, please." No simultaneous submissions. Reports in about 2 months. Pays 1 copy.** Occasional reviews of books of poetry. Send books for review consideration. The editor comments, "Traditional-type poetry is much more popular here in Britain, and we think also in the United States, now than it was in 1970, when we founded *Candelabrum*. We **always welcome new poets, especially traditionalists, and we like to hear from the U.S.A. as well as from here at home.** General tip: Study the various outlets at the library, or buy a copy of *Candelabrum*, or borrow a copy from a subscriber, before you go to the expense of submitting your work. The Red Candle Press regrets that, because of bank charges, it is unable to accept dollar cheques. However, it is always happy to accept U.S. and Canadian dollar bills."

RED CEDAR REVIEW (II), 17C Morrill Hall, Dept. of English, Michigan State University, East Lansing MI 48824, poetry editor Carrie Preston, founded 1963, is a literary biannual which uses poetry—**"any subject, form, length; the only requirement is originality and vision." The editor encourages work "that shows careful thought and unification of imagery."** They have published poetry by Margaret Atwood, Diane Wakoski, Jim Harrison and Stuart Dybek. As a sample the editor selected these lines from "Late-Night Groceries/Let's Call This The Scarf" by Matthew Thorburn:

> Tells you she's from Italy.
> When she asks where you're from you stretch
> out your hand to make a map of Michigan,
> point to the center of your palm. Here.
>
> She slips off her sandal,
> puts her foot up on the counter.
> I'm from here, *pointing*
> to the show curve of her arch.

The review is 120 pgs., digest-sized. They receive about 500 submissions a year, use approximately 20. Press run is 400 for 200 subscribers of which 100 are libraries. Single copy: $5; subscription: $10. **Sample postpaid: $2.50. Submit up to 4 poems at a time. No previously published poems. Simultaneous submissions are discouraged. Reports in 1-4 months. Pays 2 copies. Sometimes comments on rejections. Send SASE for submission guidelines.**

RED DANCEFLOOR PRESS (III); RED DANCEFLOOR (V), P.O. Box 4974, Lancaster CA 93539-4974, fax (805)948-6121, e-mail dubpoet@as.net, founded 1989, editor David Goldschlag, publishes full-length books, **chapbooks** and poetry audiotapes. **"No restrictions on form, length or subject matter. We want poetry that is well thought out—not a first draft. If you send us rhyme it should have a specific purpose and work."** They have recently published poetry by Michael C. Ford, Laurel Ann Bogen, Annie Reiner and Gary Walton. As a sample the editor selected the first stanza from "A Psycho-confessional in Eight Stanzas" by r.r. Lee Etzwiler:

> *When I was born they brought me home*
> *in a dusty car full of blankets, hugs, and*
> *cigar smoke. Oh beyond their wide eyes*
> *were colors—blue and reds, and heat*
> *tainted by urine. Infinity opened up, I was out*
> *in one fell swoop, an obscene tragedy*
> *pending—I was passive, alone it its arms.*
> > *Infinity my hero.*

He says, the author may want to get a copy of a book, chap or tape before submitting. (Send SAE with first-class stamp for catalog.) **"We openly accept submissions for books, chaps and tapes, but *please* query first with ten samples and a cover letter explaining which area of our press you are interested in. Listing credits in a cover letter is fine, but don't go crazy."** Queries and submissions via e-mail **"strongly encouraged."** The press also publishes the magazine, *Red Dancefloor*. However, the magazine has suspended publication until further notice.

‡**RED DRAGON PRESS (II)**, P.O. Box 19425, Alexandria VA 22320-0425, founded 1993, editor/publisher Laura Qa. *Red Dragon Press* **publishes 3-4 chapbooks/year. They want "innovative, progressive and experimental poetry and prose using literary symbolism, and aspiring to the creation of meaningful new ideas, forms and methods."** They have recently published poetry by Elizabeth Croydon, Laura Qa and Dee Snyder. As a sample the editor selected these lines from "Memorial Day" by Patrick Russell Gibbons:

> *Chiselled granite did not silence me*
> *When I was a springy toddler*
> *Hopping over grandma's gravestone.*
> *Now this polished skyline mutes me,*
> *As I bud in the sunlight,*
> *Agonized by mysteries of birth.*

Chapbooks are usually 64 pgs., 8½ × 5⅜, offset printed, perfect-bound on trade paper with 1-10 illustrations. **Submit up to 5 poems at a time with SASE. Previously published poems and simultaneous submissions OK. Cover letter preferred with brief bio.** Time between acceptance and publication is 8 months. **Poems are circulated to an editorial board. "Poems are selected for consideration by the publisher, then circulated to senior editor and/or poets previously published for comment. Poems are returned to the publisher for further action; i.e., rejection or acceptance for publication in an anthology or book by a single author. Frequently submission of additional works is required before final offer is made, especially in the process for a book by a single author."** Often comments on rejections. Charges criticism fee of $10 per page on request. **Reports on queries in 6-10 weeks, to mss in 6-12 months. For sample books, purchase at book stores, or mail order direct from Red Dragon Press at the above address.** *Tribute to the Hound* (1995) by Laura Qa, was the recipient of the individual artist support grant in literature from the Alexandria Commission for the Arts.

RED HERRING POETS; MATRIX; RED HERRING PRESS; RED HERRING CHAPBOOK SERIES; CHANNING-MURRAY FOUNDATION (IV-Membership), 1209 W. Oregon St., Urbana IL 61801, phone (217)344-1176 or 244-7493, founded 1975, director of Red Herring Poets Steve Kappes. The Red Herring Poets is a workshop that publishes its members' work, after they have attended at least 5 meetings, in their annual magazine, *Matrix*, and, for those who have been members for at least 2 years and given 2 public readings, one chapbook/year.

‡**RED MOON PRESS; THE RED MOON ANTHOLOGY; SOUTH BY SOUTHEAST (IV-Form/ style)**, P.O. Box 2461, Winchester VA 22604-2461, founded 1994, editor/publisher Jim Kacian. *SOUTH by SOUTHEAST*, published triannually, "seeks to publish the finest English-lanuage haiku available, along with

---

THE CHAPBOOK INDEX, located before the Geographical Index, lists those publishers who consider chapbook manuscripts. A chapbook, a small volume of work, is often a good middle step between magazine and book publication.

articles, essays, interviews and retrospectives of what has been done in the form heretofore." **They want "haiku in English (will consider English translations)—require only that the poem be evocative and heartfelt, and that each poem find its own proper form." They do not want "anything else—I do not publish tanka, renga or other oriental forms, nor any western forms."** They have recently published poetry by Anthony J. Pupello, R.A. Stefanac, Tom Clausen and Matthew Louvière. As a sample the editor selected this haiku by John Stevenson:

> luxury car—
> a sparrow's quiet
> thump

SOUTH by SOUTHEAST is 40 pgs., digest-sized, offset-printed on quality bond paper with heavy stock cover with photos and graphics related to haiku and the haiku arts. They receive about 2,000 poems a year, accept approximately 5%. Press run is 250 for 200 subscribers of which 5 are libraries. Subscription: $16. **Sample (including guidelines) postpaid: $5. Make checks payable to Red Moon Press. Submit 5 poems at a time with SASE. No previously published poems or simultaneous submissions.** Time between acceptance and publication is 1 month. **Poems are circulated to an editorial board. "I do have guest readers, but make final decisions myself." Comments on rejections when asked. Send SASE for guidelines. Reports 1 month prior to publication. Pays $1/poem. Buys first North American serial rights.** Reviews books of poetry "irregularly, and only when the book is of overwhelming interest to the haiku community." Open to unsolicited reviews. Poets may also send books for review consideration. Red Moon Press publishes the Red Moon Anthology and seeks to publish the finest English-language haiku published anywhere in the world in the previous 12 months as well as chapbooks of the highest merit. Publishes 2 paperbacks and **3-4 chapbooks/year.** Anthologies are usually 192 pgs., digest-sized, offset-printed, perfect-bound, glossy stock cover with some art. Individual volumes are 64-80 pgs., with varying size and binding, offset, with some art. Chapbooks are "hand-produced volumes in irregular and creative formats appropriate to the material." Query with 30-40 haiku. Replies to queries in 2 weeks, to mss (if invited) in 2-3 months. "Each contract separately negotiated." The editor says, "We strive to give each poem plenty of space in which to breathe, and to place contemporary praxis within the context of the example of finest practitioners of English-language haiku to date."

RED OWL MAGAZINE (I, II), 35 Hampshire Rd., Portsmouth NH 03801-4815, phone (603)431-2691, e-mail redowlmag@aol.com, founded 1995, editor Edward O. Knowlton, is a biannual magazine of poetry and b&w art. **"Ideally, poetry here might stress a harmony between nature and industry; add a pinch of humor for spice. Nothing introspective or downtrodden. Sometimes long poems are OK, yet poems which are 10 to 20 lines seem to fit best." They are also open to poems on the subjects of animals, gay/lesbian issues, horror, psychic/occult, science fiction/fantasy and women/feminisism.** They have published poetry by Lyn Lifshin and John Binns. As a sample the editor selected these lines from "Skippy" by Colby Dorian:

> I'm a guest.
> I'm a pest;
> I'll try to rob your nest . . .
> It's the high school head from Harvard High.
> Would you care to smell a pie?

Red Owl is about 36 pgs., 8½ × 11, neatly photocopied in a variety of type styles and spiral-bound with a heavy stock cover and b&w art inside. "Out of a few hundred poems received, roughly one third are considered." Press run is 100 for 65 subscribers, 5 shelf sales. Subscription: $20. **Sample (including brief guidelines) postpaid: $10. Makes checks payable to Edward O. Knowlton. Submit 4 poems at a time. No previously published poems or simultaneous submissions. Cover letter preferred. "I only use the 'Net to answer questions; I'd prefer to receive the submissions I get via the U.S.P.S. since I feel it's more formal—and I'm not in that big of a hurry, nor do I feel that the world is coming to an end. . . ." Seldom comments on rejections. Reports in 3 weeks to 3 months. Pays 1 copy.** The editor says, "Try and be bright; hold your head up. Yes, there are hard times in the land of plenty, yet we might try to overshadow them. . ."

RED RAMPAN' PRESS; RED RAMPAN' REVIEW; RED RAMPAN' BROADSIDE SERIES (V), 4707 Fielder St., Midland TX 79707-2817, phone (915)697-7689, founded 1981, poetry editor Larry D. Griffin. *RRR* is an "eclectic review quarterly." The editor says it is 48-60 pgs., 6 × 9, with a press run of 300, **"presently not accepting poetry and only using staff-written reviews."**

REED (II), c/o English Dept., San Jose State University, One Washington Square, San Jose CA 95192-0090, founded 1946, is an annual general literary magazine including SJSU student work, Bay Area work, and work from around the US. **They want "any high-quality work. No form or content restrictions."** *Reed* is 120 pgs., 5¼ × 8, professionally printed and perfect-bound with 2-color coated card cover and b&w art inside. They receive about 300 poems a year, publish 25-30. Press run is 500. **Submit 3-5 poems at a time, 40 lines maximum. No previously published poems or simultaneous submissions. Reads submissions May 1 through January 31 only. Poems are circulated to an editorial board. Seldom comments on rejections. Reports in November and December. Pays 2 copies.**

REFLECT (IV-Form/style), 3306 Argonne Ave., Norfolk VA 23509, phone (757)858-4097, founded 1979, poetry editor W.S. Kennedy. They use **"spiral poetry: featuring an inner-directed concern with sound (euphony), mystical references or overtones, and objectivity—rather than personal and emotional poems. No love poems, pornography, far left propaganda; nothing overly sentimental."** They have published poetry by B.Z. Niditch, Lyn Lifshin, Joe Malone, Ruth Wildes Schuler and Stan Proper. As a sample the editor selected these lines from "April Sashays in Lime Heels" by Edward C. Lynskey:

> April sashays across ashy mews,
> in lime heels and lilac breath,
> swells sappy stalks, and shoos
> winter north, the killing guest.
>
> Hyacinths blush and daffodils
> blink as a wisp of apple smoke
> curlicues through screens until
> kale yards wakes in a rainy soak.

The quarterly is 48 pgs., digest-sized, saddle-stapled, typescript. Subscription: $8. **Sample postpaid: $2. Submit 4 or 5 poems at a time. All submissions should be** *single-spaced* **and should fit on one typed page. No previously published poems or simultaneous submissions. Sometimes comments on rejections. Send SASE for guidelines. Reports within a month. Pays 1 copy to nonsubscribers, 2 copies to subscribing contributors. Acquires first rights.** Occasionally reviews books of poetry in 50 words or more.

‡**REFLECTIONS OF YOU® JOURNAL (I)**, P.O. Box 39196, Washington DC 20016-9196, phone/fax (703)913-6172, founded 1995, editor-in-chief Shar'Ron "Maxx" Mahaffey, published 3 times/year, is "a journal for people who are willing to share their vulnerabilities, challenges and laudable successes in order to contribute to the well-being of another. Included are inspiring and thought-provoking personal experience essays, philosophies, uplifting poetry, profiles, ideologies and much more." **They want "10-25 lines, free verse, traditional, conversational. Subject matters: spirituality, relationships, friendship, marriage, parenting, ethnic, moral and social issues, family, love." They do not want material that is religious or preachy.** They have recently published poetry by Carrie Crippen Fisher and Mark Richburg. As a sample the editor selected these lines from her poem "Real Life?":

> . . . Real life is snowflakes
> And even an occasional heartache
> It's the gentle touch of a hand
> A kiss on the lips
> It's a brisk walk on a Fall day
> It's leaves changing colors
> And horses feeding on hay . . .

ROYJ is 34 pgs., 8½×11, offset printed on coated stock, saddle-stapled, with glossy cover, b&w drawings, art, clip art and photos. They receive about 40-75 poems a year, accept approximately 90%. Press run is 2,500-5,000 for 275 subscribers of which 2 are libraries; 2,000 distributed free to mailing lists. Single copy: $5; subscription: $14. **Sample (including guidelines) postpaid: $4. Make checks payable to A&M Publishing Company. Submit 3 poems at a time. No previously published poems or simultaneous submissions.** Time between acceptance and publication is within a year. **Always comments on rejections. Publishes theme issues. Send SASE for upcoming themes. Reports in 2 weeks. Always sends prepublication galleys. Pays 2 copies. Acquires "unconditional rights."** Reviews books or chapbooks of poetry or other magazines. Open to unsolicited reviews. Poets may also send books for review consideration to Poetry Editor, at the above address. The editor advises, "Listen to the rhythm of your heart and let inspiration flow effortless. Speak to the heart of the reader from your heart."

***RENDITIONS: A CHINESE-ENGLISH TRANSLATION MAGAZINE (IV-Translations)**, Research Center for Translation, CUHK, Shatin, NT, Hong Kong, editor Dr. Eva Hung, appears twice a year. **"Contents exclusively translations from Chinese, ancient and modern."** They also publish a paperback series of Chinese literature in English translation. They have published translations of the poetry of Gu Cheng, Shu Ting, Mang Ke and Bei Dao. *Renditions* is 150 pgs., magazine-sized, flat-spined, elegantly printed, all poetry with side-by-side Chinese and English texts, using some b&w and color drawings and photos, with glossy card cover. Annual subscription: $20/2 years: $36/3 years: $50 (US). **Sample postpaid: $15. Publishes theme issues. Reports in 2 months. Pays "honorarium" plus 2 copies. Use British spelling. They "will consider" book mss, for which they would like a query with sample translations. Books pay 10% royalties plus 10 copies. Mss usually not returned. Editor sometimes comments on rejections.**

REPORT TO HELL (I), P.O. Box 44089, Calabash NC 28467, founded 1993, co-editors P. Saur and M. O'Shaughnessy, appears every 2-3 months and features poetry, stories and essays **"on discontent, misery and angst (plus the occasional glimmer of hope)." They want poetry that is "dark but not necessarily morbid; thoughtful without clichés. Nothing flowery or bland."** They have published poetry by James O'Shaughnessy, M. Estabrook, John Grey and Ian Griffin. The editors say *RTH* is 40-60 pgs., digest-sized, simple type, photocopied and staple-bound with graphics included. They accept less than 50% of the poetry received. Press run is 200 for 50 subscribers. Subscription: $10/6 issues. **Sample postpaid: $2. Make checks payable to Paul Saur. Previously published poems and simultaneous submissions OK. Cover letter with brief bio required. Often comments on rejections. Reports within 4-6 weeks. Pays 1 copy.** Reviews books of poetry in 100 words or less. Open to unsolicited reviews.

RESPONSE (IV-Ethnic, students), 27 W. 20th St., Suite 901, New York NY 10011, phone (212)620-0350, fax (212)929-3459, e-mail response@panix.com, founded 1967, poetry editor Pearl Gluck, is a "contemporary Jewish review publishing poetry, fiction and essays **by students and young adult authors." The only specification for poetry is that it be on a Jewish theme and have some significant Jewish content.** They have recently published poetry by Peter Nickowitz, Cassandra Sagan Bell and Joshua Weiner. As a sample the editor chose these lines from "Generation X, Crowe Heights" by Cheryl Fish:

> *Generation X Lubauitch boys*
> *Listening to Sun Ra*
> *and getting high*
> *eating kosher coldcuts by the pound*
> *mingling halakhah and vodka*
> *can you reverse baal t'shuva?*
> *But in the streets near home, they still wear their*
> *yarmulkes*
> *and if momma begs, will straggle into Shul*

They look for "creative, challenging and chutzapadik writing" from young writers. The quarterly is 120 pgs., 6×9, professionally printed on heavy stock, flat-spined, with a glossy "varnished" cover with artwork. Circulation is 2,400 for 600 subscribers of which 30% are libraries; 1,000 distributed through bookstores and newsstands. Subscription: $20 ($12 for students); $25 for institutions. **Sample postpaid: $6. Cover letter with bio and previous publications required with submissions.** Time between acceptance and publication is 6 months. **Reports in about 2 months. Pays 3 copies/poem published. Acquires all rights.** Occasionally reviews books of Jewish poetry. Open to unsolicited reviews. Poets may also send books for review consideration.

REVIEW: LATIN AMERICAN LITERATURE AND ARTS (IV-Ethnic, regional, translations), Dept. PM, 680 Park Ave., New York NY 10021, phone (212)249-8950 ext. 366, fax (212)249-5868, founded 1967, managing editor Daniel Shapiro, is a biannual magazine which serves as a "major forum for Latin American literature in English translation and articles on Latin American visual and performing arts." **They want contemporary Latin American poetry.** They have published poetry by Jose A. Mazzotti, Mateo Rosas de Oquendo and Gregorio de Matos. It is 100 pgs., 8½×11, with b&w photos of Latin American art. They receive 50-100 submissions, accept the work of 1-2 poets. Press run is 10,000 for 6,000 subscribers of which 500 are libraries. Subscription: $18 for individuals, $27 for institutions, $28 for international. Two-year subscription: $32 for individuals, $52 for institutions, $54 for international. **Sample postpaid: $9. Query before submitting work. Previously published poems and simultaneous submissions OK. Cover letter required. Reports in 2-3 months. Pays $100-300.** Reviews books of poetry by Latin Americans. The *Review* is published by the Americas Society, a not-for-profit organization.

REVISTA/REVIEW INTERAMERICANA (IV-Ethnic, regional), Inter-American University of Puerto Rico, Box 5100, San Germán, Puerto Rico 00683, phone (787)892-0100 or 264-1912 ext. 7229 or 7230, fax (787)892-6350, editor Anibal José Aponte. The *Revista/Review* is a bilingual scholarly journal oriented to **Puerto Rican, Caribbean and Hispanic American and *inter-American* subjects, poetry, short stories and reviews.** Press run is 750. **Submit at least 5 poems in Spanish or English, blank verse, free verse, experimental, traditional and avant-garde, typed double-spaced. No simultaneous submissions. Cover letter with brief personal data required. Pays 2 copies.** Open to unsolicited reviews. The editor says, "It is very difficult to really get the feel of a poet's merit when only one or two poems are submitted."

‡RFD: A COUNTRY JOURNAL FOR GAY MEN EVERYWHERE (I, IV-Gay), P.O. Box 68, Liberty TN 37095, phone (615)530-5176, founded 1974, poetry editor Tom Seidner. *RFD* "is a quarterly for gay men with emphasis on lifestyles outside of the gay mainstream—poetry, politics, profiles, letters." **They want poetry with "personal, creative use of language and image, relevant to journal themes, political themes. We try to publish as many poets as we can so tend to publish shorter poems and avoid epics."** They have published poetry by Antler, James Broughton, Gregory Woods and Winthrop Smith. *RFD* has a circulation of 3,800 for 1,300 subscriptions. Single copy: $6.50; subscription: $32 first class, $20 second class. **Sample postpaid: $6. Submit up to 5 poems at a time. Simultaneous submissions OK. Send SASE for guidelines. Editor sometimes comments on rejections. Reports in 6-9 months. Pays copies.** Open to unsolicited reviews. The editor says, "*RFD* looks for interesting thoughts, succinct use of language and imagery evocative of nature and gay men and love in natural settings."

RHINO (II), P.O. Box 554, Winnetka IL 60093, founded 1976, editors Deborah Rosen and Alice George, "is an annually published poetry journal. **We seek poetry and short shorts written in thoughtful and provocative**

voices that speak to the 21st century. Poems no longer than three pgs. double-spaced." They have recently published poetry by Jacqueline Berger, Simon Perchik and M. Eliza Hamilton. The editors chose as a sample the opening lines of "Reclamation" by Lisa Alvarado:

> *In this dream,*
> *I am whole.*
> *I am no longer*
> *saving other people's stories,*
> *scavenging their words;*
> *sifting through their remains.*

Rhino is a 96-page journal, digest-sized, matte card cover with art, offset from typescript on high-quality paper. They receive 1,000 submissions a year, use approximately 70-90. Press run is 300 for 100 subscribers of which 10 are libraries, 200 shelf sales. **Sample: $6 plus $1.24 postage. Submit 3-5 double-spaced poems. Submissions are accepted year-round. Reports in 3-4 months. Pays 1 copy. Acquires first rights only.**

‡**RIDGE RUNNER PRESS; PORTABLE PLATEAU; THUNDERBIRD MOTEL; RIDGE RUNNER PRESS AWARD (I, II, IV-Regional)**, P.O. Box 755, Joplin MO 64802, e-mail bebop@ipa.net, website http://www.ipa.net/~bebop, founded 1996, editor Michael Hoerman, co-editor Kimberly Nicolas. The *Portable Plateau* appears 2-3 times/year and "aims to showcase the poetry and prose of the Ozark Plateau, a geographic region encompassing substantial parts of Missouri, Arkansas and Oklahoma. **We want quality work by Ozark writers or subjects of interest to the people of the region.**" They have recently published poetry by Miller Williams, Frank Stanford, Jack Hambrick and Brent Long. The editor says *PP* is 24-36 pgs., 11×17, features artwork by Ozark artists and photos of featured authors. They receive about 200 poems a year, use approximately 50. Press run is 1,000; all distributed free at libraries, universities and bookstores throughout the Ozarks. **Submit 5 poems at a time. Previously published poems and simultaneous submissions OK. Cover letter preferred. "We prefer not to receive submissions via e-mail." Time** between acceptance and publication is 4 months. **Poems are circulated to an editorial board. "The editorial board is a group of volunteers who are active in Ozark literary arts. Final decisions are made by the editor." Seldom comments on rejections. Send SASE for guidelines. Reports in 6-8 weeks. Pays 6 copies. Acquires first or one-time rights.** "We review any literary material of interest to our readers or editor and staff." Open to unsolicited reviews. Poets may send books for review consideration. They also publish *Thunderbird Motel*, "an electronic forum for experimental or transient work by writers who are defining themselves and their environment with neon words in the pitch black sky of life in transition." The web page utilizes poetry and prose, as well as electronic and other art. Ridge Runner Press publishes collections and anthologies of poetry and prose by Ozark writers. They publish 1 paperback and **2 chapbooks/year—"one chapbook as part of the Ridge Runner Press Award and one as cooperative publishing."** Anthologies are 160 pgs., 8½×5½, perfect-bound, with art and graphics relevant to the Ozark Plateau. Chapbooks are 36-48 pgs., 8½×5½, professionally-printed, saddle-stitched. **"Do not send poems specifically for the anthology. Submit for *Portable Plateau*. The anthology will mostly be drawn from it. Chapbooks are through personal arrangement." Pays 50% royalty and 50 author's copies (out of a press run of 300).** Also sponsors the Ridge Runner Press Award. Submit any combination of poetry and prose up to 5 pieces. Winner receives prizes plus publication of a chapbook. Send SASE for details. The editor says, "Take risks with your writing. Honesty distinguishes the best writers. Avoid literary cliques; write poetry from the heart and when it's appropriate read it to an audience with feeling. At the same time, don't be afraid to challenge your readers with intensity, form, vivid imagery, vision, pathos and subtle intelligence."

RIO GRANDE PRESS; SE LA VIE WRITER'S JOURNAL (I, IV-Themes), P.O. Box 71745, Las Vegas NV 89170, founded 1987, editor Rosalie Avara. *Se La Vie Writer's Journal* is a quarterly journal with articles and cartoons about poetry and writing and monthly contests in poetry and quarterly contests in poetry, essays and short stories. Prizes are $5-25 for poems, entry fee $5 for 3 poems. Publishes 70% of mss received/quarter, **"dedicated to encouraging novice writers, poets and artists; we are interested in original, unpublished mss that reflect the 'life' theme (La Vie). Poems are judged on originality, clarity of thought and ability to evoke emotional response."** They have published poetry by Marian Ford Park, Robert Gaurnier and Angie Monnens. *SLVWJ* is 64 pgs., digest-sized, photocopied from typescript, with blue cover, saddle-stapled. **Sample postpaid: $2. Publishes theme issues. Send SASE for guidelines and upcoming themes.** Staff reviews books of poetry. Send books for review consideration. Also publishes several poetry/short story anthologies annually. "No fee or purchase necessary to enter contests and be published." Cash prizes. Send SASE for guidelines.

‡**RIO GRANDE REVIEW (II)**, 105 East Union, El Paso TX 79968-0622, contact poetry editor, is a biannual student publication from the University of Texas at El Paso. *Rio Grande Review* contains poetry; flash, short,

---

SENDING TO A COUNTRY other than your own? Be sure to send International Reply Coupons (IRCs) instead of stamps for replies or return of your manuscript.

and nonfiction; short drama; photography and line art. They have recently published poetry by Arthur Winfield Knight, James Cooperman, Anne Dean, B.Z. Niditch, Janiece Ward and Anne Marie Mackler. *RGR* is 95 pgs., 6×9, professionally printed and perfect-bound with card cover with b&w line art, b&w line art inside. Subscription: $6/year, $11/2 years. Include bio information with submission. "All submissions must be accompanied by a SASE or they will not be returned." Reads submissions August 1 through October 1 for winter issue; January 1 through March 1 for summer issue. "Those received in other months will be returned unread." Send SASE for guidelines. Pays copies. "Permission to reprint material remains the decision of the author. RGR does not request it be given mention."

RIVER CITY; HOHENBERG AWARD (II), English Dept., University of Memphis, Memphis TN 38152, phone (901)678-4591, fax (901)678-2226, founded 1980, editor Dr. Paul Naylor. *River City* publishes fiction, poetry, interviews and essays. Contributors have included John Updike, Marvin Bell, Philip Levine, Maxine Kumin, Robert Penn Warren, W.D. Snodgrass, Mary Oliver, Fred Busch, Beth Bentley, Mona Van Duyn and Peter Porter. The biannual is 160 pgs., 7×10, perfect-bound, professionally printed with two-color matte cover. Publishes 40-50 pgs. of poetry in each issue. Circulation 1,000. Subscription: $12. **Sample postpaid: $5. Submit no more than 5 poems at a time. Does not read mss June through August. Reports in 2-12 weeks. Pays 2 copies (and cash when grant funds available).** The $100 Hohenberg Award is given annually to the best fiction or poetry selected by the staff. Poetry published here has also been included in *The Best American Poetry 1996*.

‡**RIVER KING POETRY SUPPLEMENT (II)**, P.O. Box 122, Freeburg IL 62243, phone (618)539-5490, fax (618)539-5603, founded 1995, editor Wayne Lanter, published 3 times/year (April, August, December), features "all poetry with commentary about poetry." **They want "serious poetry." They do not want "light verse."** They have recently published poetry by Philip Dacey, John Knoepfle, Philip Miller, Simon Perchik and Katherine Riegel. The editor says *RKPS* is 8 pgs., 17×11 with newsprint. They receive about 500 poems a year, accept approximately 15%. Press run is 2,200 of which 30 are for libraries. **Submit 5 poems at a time. No previously published poems; simultaneous submissions OK. Cover letter preferred.** Time between acceptance and publication is 2 months. **Often comments on rejections. Reports in 1 month. Pays 5 copies.**

RIVER OAK REVIEW (II), P.O. Box 3127, Oak Park IL 60303, phone (708)524-8725, founded 1993, is a biannual literary magazine publishing high quality short fiction, creative nonfiction and poetry. **Regarding work, they say, "quality is primary, but we probably wouldn't publish poems longer than 100 lines or so."** They have recently published poetry by Steven Lautermilch, E. Ethelbert Miller and Maureen Seaton. *ROR* is 112 pgs., 6×9, neatly printed and perfect-bound with glossy 4-color card cover with art. They receive about 1,500-2,500 poems a year, publish approximately 1-2%. Press run is 1,000 for 600 subscribers, 200 shelf sales. Single copy: $6; subscription: $12. **Sample postpaid: $5. Make checks payable to River Oak Arts. Submit 4 poems at a time. No previously published poems; simultaneous submissions OK if notified. Cover letter preferred. Poems are circulated to readers, then an editorial board, then the editor. Seldom comments on rejections. Send SASE for guidelines. Reports in 3 months. Always sends prepublication galleys. Pays $10-50 and 2 copies. Buys first North American serial rights.** They also sponsor a poetry contest in December with an award of $500 and publication in the spring issue of *River Oak Review*. Submit up to 4 poems at a time (maximum 500 lines total); typed, double spaced; with name, address, phone on cover letter only. Entries are not returned. Send postcard for notification of receipt and SASE for winners. Winners will be announced February 15. Send SASE for guidelines. The editor says, "Our advice? Read literary magazines; read new poetry books; only submit if it's excellent."

RIVER STYX MAGAZINE; BIG RIVER ASSOCIATION (II), 3207 Washington Ave., St. Louis MO 63103-1218, founded 1975, editor Richard Newman, senior editors Michael Castro and Quincy Troupe, published 3 times/year, is "an international, multicultural journal publishing both award-winning and previously undiscovered writers. We feature poetry, short prose, interviews, fine art and photography." They want **"excellent poetry— original, energetic and well-crafted."** They have recently published work by Alan Shapiro, Andrew Hudgins, Julia Alvarez, Catherine Bowman, Yusef Komunyakaa, Marilyn Hacker, Anne Caston, Ito Hiromi and Anthony Walton. As a sample the editor selected these lines from "The Dismal Science" by Donald Finkel:

> He could pick up an epic this morning
> from the take-away rack at the local supermarket.
> All over the city young men are scribbling, scribbling,
> and old women, and schoolchildren, and several chimpanzees.
>
> The young man persists in his kitchen, parboiling a dithyramb
> while the sows go farrowing on in Iowa.
> Welcome to the eleventh plague: plenty.

River Styx is 75-100 pgs., 6×9, professionally printed on coated stock, perfect-bound with color cover and b&w art, photographs and ads. They receive about 4,000 mss a year, accept less than 2%. Press run is 1,300 for 1,000 subscribers. **Sample postpaid: $7. Submit 3-5 poems at a time, "legible copies with name and address on each page."** Time between acceptance and publication is within 1 year. **Reads submissions May 1 through November 30 only. Guidelines available for SASE. Editor sometimes comments on rejections. Reports in**

3-5 months. Pays 2 copies plus 1-year subscription. Buys one-time rights. Poetry published in *River Styx* has been selected for inclusion in the 1994 and 1996 volumes of *The Best American Poetry* and *Best of The Small Presses*.

RIVERRUN (II), Glen Oaks Community College, Centreville MI 49032-9719, founded 1974, poetry editor Morgan Rupert Thomlinson, is a literary biannual, using **30-40 magazine-sized pages of poetry in each issue—** "no prejudices. We try to give each issue its own distinct, admittedly subjective personality. We have a special interest in traditional forms (sonnets, villanelles) and rhyme schemes." They receive 1,000 poems/ month, use up to 240/year. Press run is 850. **Sample postpaid: $5. Submit 3-6 poems at a time. Previously published poems and simultaneous submissions OK. Publishes theme issues. Send SASE for upcoming themes. Reports ASAP (usually 2 weeks to 1 month). Pays 1 copy.** The editor says, "We proudly publish an extremely broad range of individuals well-known to small press circles and beyond (for instance, t. Winter-Damon, Bruce Boston, Stuart Friebert, Tom Riley, Lyn Lifshin and Denise Dumars), but we also pride ourselves on devoting occasional space to local poets and as-yet-unpublished poets."

RIVERSIDE QUARTERLY (II, IV-Science fiction/fantasy), Box 12085, San Antonio TX 78212, phone (210)734-5424, founded 1964, editor Leland Sapiro, poetry editor Sheryl Smith **(and submissions should go directly to her at 515 Saratoga #2, Santa Clara CA 95050).** *Riverside Quarterly* is "aimed at the literate reader of science fiction and fantasy. If you've been reared on 'Star Trek,' then *RQ* is not for you. We have no specific subject matter or style preferences. Length: 50 lines maximum. No didactic or 'uplifting' verse." They have published poetry by George Gott, Sue Saniel Elkind, Julia Thomas, Edward Mycue and Denise Dumars. *RQ* is 68 pgs., approximately 5×8, offset, saddle-stapled with paper cover and b&w art. They receive about 1,100 poems a year, accept approximately 3%. Press run is 1,200 for 550 subscribers of which 200 are libraries. Subscription: $8. **Sample postpaid: $2.50. No previously published poems or simultaneous submissions. Cover letter recommended.** Time between acceptance and publication is 15 months. **Usually comments on rejections. Reports in 10 days. Always sends prepublication galleys. Pays 4 copies. Acquires all rights. Returns rights after publication.** "We print reviews of books, movies and magazines—no maximum length." They say, "We advise all contributors (of poetry or prose) to read a copy or two (available at any major public or college library) before sending a mss."

RIVERSTONE, A PRESS FOR POETRY (II), 1184A MacPherson Dr., West Chester PA 19380-3814, founded 1992, publishes **1 or 2 chapbooks a year through an annual contest.** They have published chapbooks by Gia Hansbury, Jefferson Carter, Marcia Hurlow and Cathleen Calbert. As a sample the editor selected these lines from "Night Rising" by Margo Stever:

> When I lie down at night
> above the bitter opening of sleep,
> the sad pines, the sad crooked pines,
> and the birds, listen, hear them,
> as if their song were made in heaven, . . .

That's from the chapbook *Reading the Night Sky*, which won the 1996 Riverstone Poetry Chapbook Award. It is 36 pgs., digest-sized, attractively printed on 80 lb. paper and hand-sewn with spruce green endleaves and a beige card stock cover with matching spruce green ink. **To be considered for the contest, submit $8 reading fee and chapbook ms of 20-24 pgs., "including poems in their proposed arrangement, title page, contents and acknowledgments." Previously published poems OK. Include 6×9 SASE for notification and copy of the winning chapbook. Send SASE for guidelines. Contest deadline: June 30 postmark. Winner receives publication, 50 author's copies and a cash prize of $100.** Sample chapbooks can be ordered from the press for $5 postpaid.

RIVERWIND (II, IV-Regional), General Studies, Hocking College, Nelsonville OH 45764, phone (614)753-3591 ext. 2363, founded 1982, poetry editor J.A. Fuller, is a literary annual publishing **mainly writers from Appalachia.** In addition, one feature poet is published in each issue with a selection of 10-15 poems. They want **"work from serious writers. We are most open to work with serious content, though humor may be the vehicle. Do not want to see poetry from those who view it as a 'hobby.' We have not published limericks."** They have published poetry by Naton Leslie, Gloria Ruth, Charles Semones, John Aber and Greg Anderson. As a sample the editor selected these lines from "Scrub Pines" by Amy Newman:

> Seasons are full of it:
> the buds return in a time they call
> particular to a tree
> or out of their dirt in the pushing green
> a silent child in a corner.

Riverwind is 80-120 pgs., 7×7, flat-spined, offset, with 2-color semiglossy card cover. Of 500 poems received they accept approximately 60. Press run is 500. Single copy: $3.75. **Sample postpaid: $2. Submit 3-5 poems at a time. No previously published poems or simultaneous submissions. Reads submissions September 15 through June 15 only. Submissions received after June 15 will be considered for the following year. Reports in 1-4 months. Pays 2 copies.** Reviews books of poetry.

‡ROANOKE REVIEW (II), English Dept., Roanoke College, Salem VA 24153, founded 1968, poetry editor Robert R. Walter, is a semiannual literary review which uses **poetry that is "conventional; we have not used much experimental or highly abstract poetry."** They have published poetry by Peter Thomas, Norman Russell, Alan Seaburg, Mary Balazs and Irene Dayton. *RR* is 52 pgs., 6×9, professionally printed with matte card cover with decorative typography. They use 25-30 pgs. of poetry in each issue. Circulation is 250-300 for 150 subscribers of which 50 are libraries. They receive 400-500 submissions of poetry a year, use approximately 40-60, have a 3- to 6-month backlog. Subscription: $5.50. **Sample postpaid: $3. Submit original typed mss, no photocopies. Reports in 8-10 weeks. No pay.** The editor advises, "There is a lot of careless or sloppy writing going on. We suggest careful proofreading and study of punctuation rules."

ROCKET PRESS (II), P.O. Box 672, Water Mill NY 11976-0672, e-mail darjohns@suffolk.lib.ny.us, founded 1993, editor Darren Johnson, features "styles and forms definitely for the 21st century." **The editor wants "experimental and eccentric poetry and original ideas expressed in 'a true voice.' I don't want to see hero worship-type poems that drop names. Don't use the words 'poem,' 'love' or 'ode.' "** They have published poetry by Ben Ohmart, Albert Huffstickler and Cheryl Townsend. As a sample the editor selected the poem "The Bovine Photograph" by Brandon Freels:

> At the art museum
> we both stood in front of the
> bovine photograph.
>
> "It's sexy," Kris said.
> "I think it's just a sexy photo!"
>
> "Look at those thighs!"
> Someone in the background
> mumbled.
>
> "You know,"
> I said. "It is kind of sexy."

Rocket Press is a newspaper tabloid, 20 pgs., professionally printed, with a circulation over 2,000. They receive about 1,000 poems a year, accept approximately 1-2%. Press run is 2,000 for 200 subscribers of which 2 are libraries, 400 shelf sales. Subscription: $5. **Sample postpaid: $1.50. Submit 3 poems at a time. E-mail submissions OK. No previously published poems; simultaneous submissions OK.** Time between acceptance and publication is 3 months to 1 year. **Often comments on rejections. "Subscribers get fuller critiques." Reports in less than 3 months. Pays 1 copy. Acquires one-time rights.** Editor includes his own blurb reviews "of anything cool." Send books for review consideration. "Poets are a lot better at buying samples than fiction writers and it's probably more important for a poet to see what's contemporary, what's 'out there.' You can't write 'modern' poetry while only reading Yeats. Poetry is ever-changing."

THE ROCKFORD REVIEW; ROCKFORD WRITERS' GUILD (I, II), P.O. Box 858, Rockford IL 61105, founded 1971, editor David Ross, is a publication of the Rockford Writers' Guild which appears 3 times/year, **publishing their poetry and prose, that of other writers throughout the country and contributors from other countries.** *TRR* seeks experimental or traditional poetry of up to 50 lines. **"We look for the magical power of the words themselves, a playfulness with language in the creation of images and fresh insights on old themes, whether it be poetry, satire or fiction."** They have published poetry by Russell King, David Koenig and Christine Swanberg. *TRR* is 50 pgs., digest-sized, flat-spined, glossy cover with b&w photos. Circulation is 750. Single copy: $5; subscription: $15 (3 issues plus the Guild's monthly newsletter, *Write Away*). **Submit up to 3 poems at a time. No previously published poems; simultaneous submissions OK. Reports in 6-8 weeks. Pays 1 copy and "you will receive an invitation to be a guest of honor at a Contributors' Reading & Reception in the spring." Acquires first North American serial rights.** They offer Editor's Choice Prizes of $25 for prose, $25 for poetry each issue. The Rockford Writers' Guild is a nonprofit, tax-exempt corporation established "to encourage, develop and nuture writers and good writing of all kinds and to promote the art of writing in the Rockford area." They offer lectures by Midwest authors, editors and publishers, and workshops. Membership: $25/year. Write for further information.

ROCKY MOUNTAIN REVIEW OF LANGUAGE AND LITERATURE (IV-Membership, translations), Boise State University English Dept., Boise ID 83725, phone (208)385-1233, fax (208)385-4373, e-mail aaswidma@idbsu.idbsu.edu, founded 1947, editor Jan Widmayer, poetry editor Marcia Southwick. **Contributors to the literary quarterly must be members of Rocky Mountain Modern Language Association. Poetry should be "generally relatively short" and may be in English or other modern languages.** The review has published poetry by Scott P. Sanders and David Faldet and translations of Antonio Cisneros, David Huerta and Viktor Bokov. The 224-page, 6×9, flat-spined semiannual publishes work of interest to college and university teachers of literature and language. Circulation is 1,100-1,200, all membership subscriptions. They accept a few ads from other journals and publishers. **Contributors are not paid and do not receive extra copies; contributors must be RMMLA members. Poets should submit 2 copies, *without author's name*. Reports in 1-2 months.**

Time between acceptance and publication is usually within 6 months but no more than 1 year.

‡ROMANTIC HEARTS (I, IV-Love/romance), P.O. Box 450669, Westlake OH 44145-0612, founded 1996, executive editor Debra Krauss, published bimonthly, "is a magazine dedicated to short romantic fiction. We also publish romantic essays, love poems and short story writing articles." **They want "sweet romantic love poems. Emphasize the lighter side of love. 25 lines or less in length." They do not want "depressing, dark or sexually graphic."** They have recently published poetry by Anna-Maria King, Sheila B. Roark and Mark Richburg. *Romantic Hearts* is 48 pgs., digest-sized, desktop-published, saddle-stapled, 20 lb. paper, 20 lb. color cover with line art graphics and classified ads. They receive about 200 poems a year, accept approximately 25%. Press run is 100 for 50 subscribers; 1 distributed free to Romance Writers of America. Single copy: $3.99; subscription: $22. **Sample postpaid: $4. Submit up to 5 typed poems at a time. No previously published poems; simultaneous submissions OK. Cover letter required with name, address and phone number in upper left corner of all correspondence.** Time between acceptance and publication is 4-12 months. **"The executive editor selects poems." Often comments on rejections. Send SASE for guidelines. Reports 4-6 weeks. Pays 1 copy per poem. Acquires first North American serial rights.**

THE ROMANTIST (IV-Fantasy, horror), Saracinesca House, 3610 Meadowbrook Ave., Nashville TN 37205, phone (615)834-5069, poetry editor Steve Eng, founded 1977, is an "irregular literary magazine of nonfiction articles on fantasy, imaginative and romantic literature, using **lyrical poetry—prefer fantasy content. No homespun, gushy, trite verse with forced rhyme."** They have published poetry by Donald Sidney-Fryer, Joey Froehlich, Stephanie Stearns and Margo Skinner. The editor says *The Romantist* is 100-152 pgs., magazine-sized, letterpress or offset, perfect-bound with b&w illustrations and ads. Press run is 300 numbered copies for 150 subscribers of which 30 are libraries. **Sample postpaid: $15. Submit up to 3 poems at a time, double-spaced. No previously published poems or simultaneous submissions. Cover letter required.** Time between acceptance and publication may be as long as 2-3 years. **Editor sometimes comments on rejections. Reports in 1 month. Contributors may purchase a copy for 50% of its price. Acquires all rights "but grants permission for republication elsewhere upon condition that acknowledgement be made therein."** Open to unsolicited reviews. Poets may also send books for review consideration. The editor says, "Too much contemporary poetry is easy to write and hard to read. We resist the depressed, carefully jaded tone so often fashionable. We prefer lyric verse that reflects some knowledge of traditions of poetry, though we do not require the slavish adherence to any school."

♣RONSDALE PRESS (II, IV-Regional), 3350 W. 21st Ave., Vancouver, British Columbia V6S 1G7 Canada, founded 1988, director Ronald B. Hatch, publishes 3 flat-spined paperbacks of poetry/year—**by Canadian poets only—classical to experimental**. They have published *Phantoms in the Ark* by A.F. Moritz, *Two Shores/Deux rives* by Thuong Vuong-Riddick, and *Burning Stone* by Zoë Landale. As a sample the director selected these lines from "The Process" in *The Edge of Time* by Robin Skelton:

> Begin with listening—the voice
> elsewhere and here, a gleam of brown,
> its movements fluent and its flying leaps
> the sudden judgement of a heart in shock
> at precipices we'd not thought to find.

Query first, with sample poems and cover letter with brief bio and publication credits. Previously published poems and simultaneous submissions OK. Often comments on rejections. Replies to queries in 2 weeks, to mss in 2 months. Pays 10% royalties and 10 author's copies. Write for catalog to purchase sample books. The director adds, "Confessional poetry or even first-person poetry is very difficult to write well."

‡ROSE ALLEY PRESS (V), 4203 Brooklyn Ave. NE #103A, Seattle WA 98105, phone (206)633-2725, founded 1995, publisher David D. Horowitz, publishes 1 paperback of poetry/year. They have recently published poetry by Victoria Ford. As a sample the editor selected these lines from "Love Duet" by William Dunlop:

> Love moves by subtler rhythms, and small sounds:
> a glass set down, clothes shucked, skins' conversation,
> duet of breaths—the orchestration's
> conventional enough, but it abounds
> in touches of a sheer felicity: catch
> in my voice; your chuckle; a struck match.

Books are usually under 100 pgs., 5½ × 8¼, with acid-free paper, saddle-stitched or Smythe-sewn. **"We presently do not read unsolicited manuscripts." Pays 15% royalties and 10 author's copies (out of a press run of 1,000).** "We publish three informative pamphlets, respectively on getting published in journals, self-publishing and improving your writing. They cost $1 apiece or $2.50 as a set of three." The editor says, "Poetry epitomizes condensed, subtle verbal expression. It unites passion and precision. It can guide, heal, inspire and challenge. I recommend that beginning poets study grammar, vocabulary and both classic and contemporary literature; write sincerely and often; revise scrupulously; build a reputation by reading locally and publishing in small journals; and, before submitting poems to journals, review the latest edition of *Poet's Market* and the *International Directory of Little Magazines and Small Presses*."

ROSEBUD (II, IV-Themes), P.O. Box 459, Cambridge WI 53523, phone (608)423-9690, founded 1993, editor Rod Clark, is an attractive quarterly "for people who enjoy good writing." The editor says it is "a writer's feast for the eye, ear and heart" which has rotating themes/departments. **They want contemporary poetry with "strong images, real emotion, authentic voice; well crafted, literary quality. No inspirational verse."** *Rosebud* is 136 pgs., 7×10, offset printed and perfect-bound with full-color coated card cover, art, graphics and ads. They receive about 700 poems a year, accept approximately 10%. Press run is 8,000 for 1,500 subscribers, 6,500 shelf sales. Subscription: $19. **Sample postpaid: $5.95. Submit 3-5 poems at a time. Previously published poems and simultaneous submissions OK. Often comments on rejections. Send SASE for guidelines and explanation of themes/departments. Reports in 3 months. Pays $45/piece and 2 copies. Buys one-time rights.** Each year they also award 3 prizes of $150 for work published in the magazine. The editor says, "We are seeking stories, articles, profiles and poems of love, alienation, travel, humor, nostalgia and unexpected revelation. And something has to 'happen' in the pieces we choose."

THE ROUND TABLE: A JOURNAL OF POETRY AND FICTION (II), P.O. Box 18673, Rochester NY 14618, phone (716)244-0623, founded 1984, poetry editors Alan Lupack and Barbara Lupack. "We publish a journal of poetry and fiction. **However, we are publishing more chapbooks which substitute for our regular issues of *TRT*. Virtually all of our publications focus on the Arthurian legends. Few restrictions on poetry— except high quality. We like forms if finely crafted. Very long poems must be exceptional."** They have published poetry by Kathleene West, John Tagliabue, Wendy Mnookin and Paul Scott. *The Round Table*, now published irregularly, is 64 pgs., digest-sized, perfect-bound, professionally printed (offset) with matte card cover. Circulation is 125 for 75 subscribers of which 3 are libraries. Subscription: $7.50. **Sample postpaid: $5. "We like to see about five poems at a time or complete chapbook (but we read whatever is submitted)." Cover letter required. Simultaneous submissions OK. "But we expect to be notified if a poem submitted to us is accepted elsewhere. Quality of poetry, not format, is most important thing. We try to report in three months, but—especially for poems under serious consideration—it may take longer." Pays copies.** "Usually we will publish a volume of Arthurian poetry or fiction by one author."

ROUTE ONE; MEMO (I), P.O. Box 1375, Mendocino CA 95460, founded 1991, poetry editor William James Kovanda. *Route One* is the centerfold of *Memo*, a bimonthly springboard for writers. The editor says, **"Essentially, I am moved by free form verse. However, I accept other versification if the residual effect of the piece produces thought provocation."** He has published poetry by Del Reitz, John Brander, Esther Leiper and Richard Weekley. As a sample the editor selected the following untitled poem from his own work:

> A woman
> is a gentle giant
> who has allowed man
> to persuade her
> to be smaller
> than his limitations

Memo is a tabloid paper covering "politics, religion, various gripes, wishes, sexual matters, hates and loves. We are open to all forms of writing, but poetry is only published in *Route One*." The editor says he receives 250-600 poems a year and accepts 20-25 poems each issue. Press run is 7,000, most distributed free. Subscription: $30. **Sample postpaid: $2.50. Submit 5 poems at a time** *with $3 reading fee*—**"but if you're broke, send me the poetry because I'm more interested in the manuscript than the fee." Previously published poems and simultaneous submissions OK. Often comments on rejections. Occasionally publishes theme issues. Send SASE for guidelines and upcoming themes. Reports in 2-4 weeks. Generally pays 2 copies. If 3 or more poems are accepted, pays $10 and 2 copies. Or, if a "Featured Poet," pays $20. Buys one-time rights.** The editor says, "Don't buy into any literary scene. Fads in anything come and go but originality stays. Your development as a writer comes from sticking to a plan and working out the kinks. This takes years, sometimes a lifetime. Remember, always be yourself, never a slave to what's hot and what's not. Keep this in mind: Reading is essential."

‡RUBYSHADOW (I, II, IV-Students, regional), P.O. Box 241451, Montgomery AL 36124, founded 1996, editor Dusti R. Worley, assistant editor Nancie Henley, published quarterly, contains "free verse and exceptional traditional verse that relays stories and experiences to sophisticated readers." **They want "poetry from students in Alabama and Ohio about physics, chemistry, Gulf War. Looking for modern stories in traditional forms, especially sestinas and villanelles. Free verse welcomed. Nancie leans toward good confessional; Dusti's favorites are Margaret Atwood and Robert Frost. That's a hint." They do not want "bad poetry, political, teenage screamfests with masses of bleeding flesh or betraying parents, boyfriends, etc."** They have recently published poetry by Jerry Lawrence and Sunny Paulk. As a sample Ms. Worley choose these lines from her poem "What is dead is the truth":

> Where the sirens are is where you go,
> end of story. Someone feeds you a
> late dinner (early breakfast) and in
> the quick flashes of dead light, your
> clothes are on and you're driving

down the highway towards home

The editor says *Rubyshadow* is 30-50 pgs., digest-sized, desktop published, saddle-stapled with light card cover. They receive about 75 poems a year, accept approximately 40%. Press run is 100, 100 shelf sales. Single copy: $2.50; subscription: $8. **Sample postpaid: $3. Make checks payable to Dusti Worley. Submit up to 3 typed poems at a time. No previously published poems or simultaneous submissions. Cover letter required with short bio.** Time between acceptance and publication is 4 months. "We read them and if we life them, we use them. If not, we don't. There are only two of us. We share." **Often comments on rejections. Reports within 1 month. Sometimes sends prepublication galleys. Pays 1-3 copies. Acquires first rights.** Reviews books or chapbooks of poetry or other magazines in less than 500 words. Open to unsolicited reviews. Poets may also send books for review consideration. The editors say, "We're especially interested in work by students. If you don't know the rules (grammatical, mechanical, spelling, form) by all means do not break them. And please—spare us your agendas, whatever side they may come from."

THE RUNAWAY SPOON PRESS (V), Box 3621, Port Charlotte FL 33949-3621, phone (941)629-8045, founded 1987, editor Bob Grumman, is a "photocopy publisher of chapbooks of otherstream poetry & illu-magery." He publishes **"visual poetry, textual poetry mixed with visual matter, verbo-visual collages, infra-verbal poetry and burning poodle poetry. No work in which politics is more important than aesthetics. Standard free-verse is way too traditional for my press."** He has recently published *Reality Slices* by John Vieira and *Silence* by Peter Ganick. As a sample the editor selected this passage by John M. Bennett:

> . . . *Why's your*
> *face like a fish, milky and blurred?*
> *There's a tide in my feet and I can't*
> *get loose.*

The books are usually about $4 \times 5\frac{1}{2}$, printed on good stock with matte card covers. He prints about 10 a year averaging 48 pgs. **Currently not accepting poetry submissions. Pays 25% of first edition of 100. Acquires all rights. Returns rights upon publication. Sample books available for $3 apiece.**

RURAL HERITAGE (I, IV-Rural, humor), 281 Dean Ridge Lane, Gainesboro TN 38562-5039, phone (615)268-0655, e-mail rural_heritage@echo.tfnet.org, founded 1975, editor Gail Damerow, **uses poetry related to draft animal power, livestock, rural living. "Traditional meter and rhyme only. Poems must have touch of humor or other twist. Please, no comparisons between country and city life and no religious, political or issues-oriented material."** As a sample the editor selected this poem, "Mule Headed," by Bonnie Compton Hanson:

> *A man and his mule*
> *Out plowing the field*
> *At the end of the row*
> *Must know which one will yield.*
>
> *You can "gee" all you want*
> *Til you're red in the face*
> *If the mule wants to "haw"*
> *And there's slack in his trace.*

RH is magazine-sized, bimonthly, using b&w photos, graphics and ads, 4-6 poems/issue. Circulation is 3,000. Subscription: $22. **Sample postpaid: $6. Submit up to 3 poems at a time, one/page. "Previously published poems are OK if we are told where and when. Simultaneous submissions must be withdrawn before we publish. We welcome submissions via e-mail—one verse per message please. Don't forget your snail mail address so we'll know where to send the check if your verse is accepted."** Time between acceptance and publication is 4-6 months. "We often group poems by theme, for example plowing, threshing and so forth according to season. Verse may also be coupled with an article of similar theme such as maple sugaring, mule teams, etc." **Send SASE for guidelines. Reports ASAP. Pays on publication, $5 and up (depending on length) and 2 copies.** The editor says, "We receive too much modern poetry (free verse), not enough traditional (true meter & rhyme), not enough humor. We get too much image poetry (we prefer action) and most poems are too long—we prefer 12 lines or less."

‡*RUSTIC RUB (I, II); WOODMAN'S PRESS (V), 14 Hillfield, Selby, North Yorkshire Y08 0ND England, phone (01757)707886, or for magazine sales in the US, Randy Lusk, 903 Ridgewood Rd., Austin TX 78746, founded 1993, editor/publisher Jay Woodman. *Rustic Rub*, published biannually, "concentrates on exciting

---

FOR INFORMATION ON ENTERING the *1999 Poet's Market* Poetry Contest, see page 2.

poetry. Also publishes interviews and information for performers, etc." **They want "originality and vitality, not pretenders. Open to wide variety of styles/forms of any length."** They do not want "uninspired formulaic poetry typically engendered by competitions." They have recently published poetry by Ian Robinson, Albert Huffstickler, Gerald Locklin and Ken C. Steven. As a sample the editor selected these lines from "The Song of Orpheus" by Keith Jafrate:

> *where the trees stand full of sinews*
> *naked fins*
> *of the flying world like*
> *hands sifting rain from rain from*
> *jewelery of rain, and bud*
> *swell fingers undersea shifting*

Rustic Rub is 92 pgs., A5, perfect-bound, desktop-published, medium card cover with b&w artwork and ads. They receive about 700 poems a year, accept approximately 10%. Press run is 350 for 150 subscribers of which 5 are libraries; 100 distributed free to contributors. Single copy: $8/£4; subscription: $5/£7.50. **Sample postpaid: $8. Make checks payable to R. Lusk for USA or J. Woodman for UK. Submit 6 poems at a time. No previously published poems or simultaneous submissions. Cover letter preferred.** Time between acceptance and publication "can be immediate, up to three months." The editor says, "My decisions are mostly personal." **Often comments on rejections. Reports "usually straightaway." Pays 1 copy. Acquires first British serial rights.** Woodman's Press is a subsidy publisher, currently closed to unsolicited mss. Chapbooks vary, usually perfect-bound. **"I expect poets to cover their costs and market their own books. I merely facilitate self-publishing."** The editor advises, "always look at a copy of a magazine before submitting, as that is the best way to guage their needs. Also, please address all mail with the editor's name first."

‡*S.W.A.G., THE MAGAZINE OF SWANSEA'S WRITERS AND ARTISTS; S.W.A.G. NEWSLETTER (I), Dan-y-Bryn, 74 CWM Level Rd., Brynhyfryd, Swansea SA5 9DY Wales, United Kingdom, founded 1992, chairman/editor Peter Thabit Jones. *S.W.A.G.* appears biannually and publishes poetry, prose, articles and illustrations. "Our purpose is to publish good literature." **They want "first-class poetry—up to 40 lines, any style."** They have recently published poetry by Adrian Mitchell, Alan Llwyd, Mike Jenkins and Dafydd Rowlands. As a sample the editor selected these lines from his poem "Castle Gardens, Swansea":

> *In the park, Christmas Eve,*
> *A woman shares her lunch*
> *With a throbbing puddle*
> *Of pigeons at her feet.*

S.W.A.G. is 48 pgs., A4, professionally printed on coated paper and saddle-stitched with glossy paper cover, photos and illustrations. They accept approximately 12-20 poems/issue. Press run is 500 for 120 subscribers of which 50 are libraries. Subscription: £5. **Sample (including guidelines): £2.50 plus postage. "Interested poets should obtain sample beforehand (to see what we offer)." Submit 6 poems, typed. No previously published poems or simultaneous submissions. Cover letter required.** Time between acceptance and publication is 4-6 months. **Poems are circulated to an editorial board. "Editor chooses/discusses choices with board." Send SASE (or SAE and IRC) for guidelines. Reports ASAP. Pays 2 copies plus a copy of S.W.A.G.'s newsletter.** Staff reviews books or poetry (half page to full). Poets may also send books for review consideration. The Swansea Writers and Artists Group (S.W.A.G.) also publishes a newsletter containing information on the group's events. Send SASE for details on the organization. "We also publish Welsh language poetry."

SACHEM PRESS (II, IV-Translations, bilingual), P.O. Box 9, Old Chatham NY 12136-0009, founded 1980, editor Louis Hammer, a small press publisher of poetry and fiction, both hardcover and flat-spined paperbacks. **No new submissions, only statements of projects, until January 1998. Submit mss January through March only.** The editor wants to see **"strong, compelling, even visionary work, English-language or translations."** He has published poetry by Cesar Vallejo, Yannis Ritsos, 24 leading poets of Spain (in an anthology), Miltos Sahtouris and himself. The paperbacks average 120 pgs. and the anthology of Spanish poetry contains 340 pgs. Each poem is printed in both Spanish and English, and there are biographical notes about the authors. The small books cost $6.95 and the anthology $11.95. **Royalties are 10% maximum, after expenses are recovered, plus 50 author's copies. Rights are negotiable.** Book catalog is free "when available," and poets can purchase books from Sachem "by writing to us, 33⅓% discount."

ST. ANDREW PRESS (IV-Religious), P.O. Box 329, Big Island VA 24526, fax (804)299-6148, e-mail raybsosa@aol.com, founded 1986, poetry editor Ray Buchanan, is a "small press publisher of religious material (worship materials, lyrics and music, etc.), **specializing in meditations, lifestyle, church renewal, spirituality, hunger, peace and justice issues." Any form or style up to 64 lines on subjects listed. "No profanity for shock value only; no sickeningly sweet idealism."** They say they will publish **1-2 chapbooks** and flat-spined paperbacks, averaging 64 pgs., each year. They have published *Silence and the Gift* by Richard Beale. **Submit 4-6 samples, bio, other publications. Simultaneous and fax submissions and previously published poems OK. Reports in 2-4 weeks. Payment is usually $10 minimum, averages more.** The editor says, "We are looking forward to doing more with poetry in the next couple of years. The amount we do will be largely determined by quality of submissions we receive. Poetry is not accepted if it is too 'sing-song' with trite rhymes, if it could be rewritten in paragraphs as prose, or if it is so 'stream-of-consciousness' that no one could possibly follow the thought or get any meaning from it."

ST. ANTHONY MESSENGER (IV-Religious), 1615 Republic St., Cincinnati OH 45210-1298, is a monthly 56-page magazine, circulation 345,000, for Catholic families, mostly with children in grade school, high school or college. In some issues, they have a **poetry page that uses poems appropriate for their readership. Their poetry needs are limited but poetry submissions are always welcomed.** As a sample here is "A Valentine for Darby" by Jean M. Syed:

> *Why do I love you, my potbellied love?*
> *Not for your pregnant form or shiny pate.*
> *Were these on tender those decades ago,*
> *would I have been so indiscriminate*
> *as to let you win my heart? No princess*
> *from passion ever took a frog to mate.*

"Submit seasonal poetry (Christmas/Easter/nature poems) several months in advance. Submit a few poems at a time; do not send us your entire collection of poetry. We seek to publish accessible poetry of high quality." Send regular SASE for guidelines and 9×12 SASE for free sample. Pays $2/line on acceptance. **Buys first North American serial rights.** *St. Anthony Messenger* poetry occasionally receives awards from the Catholic Press Association Annual Competition.

ST. JOSEPH MESSENGER AND ADVOCATE OF THE BLIND (I, IV-Religious), 541 Pavonia Ave., P.O. Box 288, Jersey City NJ 07303, founded 1898, poetry editor Sister Ursula Maphet, C.S.J.P., is semiannual, (16 pgs., 8×11). They want **"brief but thought-filled poetry; do not want lengthy and issue-filled."** Most of the poets they have used are previously unpublished. They receive 400-500 submissions a year, use approximately 50. There are about 2 pgs. of poetry in each issue. Circulation 15,000. Subscription: $5. **Sometimes comments on rejections. Publishes theme issues. Send SASE for guidelines, free sample and upcoming themes. Reports within 2 weeks. Pays $5-20/poem and 2 copies.**

ST. MARTIN'S PRESS, 175 Fifth Ave., New York NY 10010. Publishes 1,500 paperbacks and hardbacks/ year. Prefers not to share information.

‡SALMAGUNDI (III), Skidmore College, Saratoga Springs NY 12866, phone (518)584-5000, ext. 2302, founded 1965, edited by Peggy Boyers and Robert Boyers, has long been **one of the most distinguished quarterlies** of the sciences and humanities, publishing poets such as Robert Penn Warren, Louise Glück, John Peck, Howard Nemerov and W.D. Snodgrass. Each issue is handsomely printed, thick, flat-spined, priced at $5-10. Editors here tend to use more lyric free verse than any other style, much of it accessible and usually under 50 lines. Although the magazine is hefty, poems compete with prose (with the latter dominating). They use about 10-50 pages of poetry in each issue, receive about 1,200 submissions a year, use approximately 20 and have a 12- to 30-month backlog. Circulation is 5,400 for 3,800 subscribers of which about 900 are libraries. Subscription: $15/year, $25/2 years. **Sample postpaid: $6. Submissions not accompanied by SASE are discarded. Reads mss November through April only. Reports in 3 months. Pays copies.** Send books for review consideration. Work published in *Salmagundi* has been selected for inclusion in the 1994 and 1995 volumes of *The Best American Poetry*.

SALMON RUN PRESS (III), P.O. Box 231081, Anchorage AK 99523-1081, founded 1991, editor/publisher John E. Smelcer, publishes 2-3 books/year. They want **"quality poetry by established poets, any subject, any style. No poetry that is not representative of the highest achievement in the art."** They have recently published Galway Kinnell, Ursula K. Le Guin, X.J. Kennedy, John Haines, Molly Peacock, Denise Levertov, Denise Duhamel and Luis Omar Salinas. As a sample the editor selected these lines from Kinnell's "The Burn":

> *Twelve years ago I came here*
> *to wander across burnt land,*
> *I had only begun to know*
> *the kind of pain others endure,*
> *I was too full of sorrows.*

Their books are flat-spined and professionally printed on heavy, natural-colored paper with glossy color covers. **Query first with sample poems and cover letter with brief bio. Previously published poems and simultaneous submissions OK. Usually comments on rejections. Replies to queries within 1-3 weeks, to mss in 1-2 months. Pays 10% royalties, sometimes advances and a negotiable number of author's copies.** They also sponsor a pamphlet series ("by invitation only") and an annual poetry contest for book-length mss of 48-96 pgs. $10 reading fee and SASE required. Entries must be postmarked by December 30. The winning ms will be published in book form and nationally distributed.

‡SALOME (II, IV-Gay/lesbian/bisexual), Telling Moment Productions, 2211 NE Halsey #3, Portland OR 97232, founded 1996, editor Bill Olver. *Salome* appears bimonthly and "publishes work by, for, and about queers. Defining 'queer' is up to the contributor. We specifically want non-genre, literary work. Experimental work is encouraged, but should follow a narrative structure. Narrative poetry is preferred, but non-narrative considered." They also publish literary essays, photography, artwork and comics/cartoons. **They want "gay, lesbian, bisexual, transgender, queer, feminist, ethnic/multicultural literary work. No specific themes, but seriously considers holiday material for December issue and erotica/romance for February issue."** *Salome* is 60 pgs., 8½×7, printed on 20 lb. white paper and saddle-stitched with heavy cover, 5-10 photos/illustrations per issue. **Cover letter required, include estimated word count, 50-word bio and publication credits. Send disposable copy of ms.** Time between acceptance and publication is 1-3 months. **Seldom comments on rejections. Reports in 1-3 months. Pays 2 copies. Acquires one-time rights.** The editor says, "The Biblical Salome had a mind for politics and a body for sin, and used both to decapitate an important Christian. Keep that in mind: tell a good story; entertain us; don't be afraid to gut a sacred cow for personal gain. We value work that examines and critiques social, political and cultural standards from an individual's standpoint. Don't be timid in your beliefs, but don't be pigheaded, either. Tell your truths without disrespecting others' lives. Reject political correctness in favor of cultural justice. Above all, have fun. If you're not having fun, it's just not worth it."

‡SALONIKA; CIRCUMSTANCES PRESS; LINEAR ARTS; LINEAR ARTS PRESS (II), P.O. Box 20764, New York NY 10021, founded 1996, editors Jesse Weiner and Victor Asaro, is a monthly magazine of poetry and writing. **"We look at an extensive range—good, serious, innovative—with an awareness of both literature and society; contemporary, sharply defined voices."** They have recently published poetry by Emmy Hunter, Sharon Dolin, Lawrence Mallory and Thad Rutkowski. The editors say *Salonika* is 29 pgs., 7½×11, staple-bound with "strong graphic art component (no photos or drawings)." They receive about 3,200 poems a year, accept approximately 15%. Press run is 250 for 25 subscribers, 30% shelf sales. Single copy: $4; subscription: $20/6 months. **Sample postpaid: $5. Submit 10 typed poems at a time. No previously published poems or simultaneous submissions. Cover letter preferred including phone number.** Time between acceptance and publication is 3-12 months. **Reports in 3 months. Pays 1 copy. Acquires first rights.** Circumstances Press publishes poetry, drama, fiction and nonfiction. "We have a lively commitment to publishing alternative work." They publish 8 paperbacks/year. Books are usually 20-90 pgs., offset and perfect-bound with cardstock cover with art (in-house only). **Query with a few sample poems and letter of "biographical/philosophical/artistic orientation." Reports to queries in 3 months, to mss in 1 month. Pays 12-15% royalties and 15 author's copies (out of a press run of 250). Obtain sample books by requesting a catalog. "Linear Arts runs a Poetry Theater where poetry is read and/or performed. We offer memberships which provide discounts on all our services. We also run workshops."** The editors say, "*Salonika* is itself a medium—it is finely tuned to a great range of voices, registers, venues. We wish to bring disparity into continuity; individuality into community—we feel this is a thesis for all writers. Authenticity and authority remain abject partners in the struggle for expression—publication is an event within a community at expression."

‡SALT HILL JOURNAL; SALT HILL POETRY PRIZE; SALT HILL HYPERTEXT PRIZE (II), English Dept., Syracuse University, Syracuse NY 13244, founded 1994, editor Peter S. Fendrick, published biannually, features "high-quality contemporary writing including poetry, fiction, essays and book reviews." **They want "all kinds of high-quality original work, from four lines to four pages, to free verse and prose poems. We are interested in poetry that does more than simply deliver a tight, well-defined anecdote. We like to see the kind of intellectual and emotional engagement we feel is representative of a mature poetic imagination."** They do not want "badly written sentimental work without soul." They have recently published poetry by Charles Simic, W.S. Merwin, Miroslav Holub, Larry Levis and Jean Valentine. As a sample the editor selected these lines from "2 Bachelard" by Michael Burkard:

> Days go by. 2 Bachelard begins to feel like a street. I
> stare at this weak brown slip called a receipt with its clear
> but incomplete scrawl and an entire world of passion and
> rain and the inner and outer city returns to me. Yes, a
> street. A sign. A smell. A love, a life, a love of life when
> you could not let go of either.

The editor says *Salt Hill Journal* is 80-100 pgs., 5½×8½, perfect-bound, with b&w cover, with art, photography and ads. They receive about 5,000 poems a year, accept approximately 5%. Press run is 700 for 80 subscribers of which 20 are libraries. Subscription: $10. **Sample postpaid: $7. Submit 5 poems at a time. No previously published poems; simultaneous submissions OK. Cover letter preferred with a brief bio. Reads submissions July 1 through March 1 only.** Time between acceptance and publication is 2-8 months. **Poems are circulated to an editorial board. First read by assistant poetry editors and the poetry editor. Stronger work is then considered by associate editor and editor. Seldom comments on rejections. Send SASE for guidelines. Reports in 2-6 months. Always sends prepublication galleys. Pays $25/poem plus 2 copies. Buys one-time rights.** Reviews books or chapbooks of poetry or other magazines in 900-3,000 words and/or essay reviews of single/multi book format. Open to unsolicited reviews. Poets may also send books for review consideration to Book Review Editor, at the above address. Sponsors annual Salt Hill Journal Poetry Prize, awarding $500 first prize and publication, $100 second prize and publication and 3 honorable mentions and publication. Submit unpublished poems with name, address and phone on each. Reading fee is $5 for up to 150 lines (1-3 poems); $3 extra for every additional 100 lines. Include SASE. Postmark deadline May 1. Also sponsors Salt Hill Hypertext Prize, awarding $500 first prize and web publication, $100 second prize and web publication, 3 honorable mentions and web publication. "We are looking for solid literary hypertext poetry, fiction, and design that pushes the boundaries of this as-of-yet undefined space in which to create art." Work incorporating multimedia is preferred, but solely textual submissions will also be considered. Submissions must be viewable over Internet browsers such as Netscape 3.0 and Microsoft Internet Explorer. Accepted work will be posted at http://www-hl.syr.edu/cwp. Reading fee: $10. Address envelope to Web Contest. Send url address, or work as an attachment to jsparker@mailbox.syr.edu, or address envelope with floppy disks to Web Editor (disks will not be returned). Deadline: January 31.

SALT LICK; SALT LICK FOUNDATION, INC.; SALT LICK PRESS; SALT LICK SAMPLERS; LUCKY HEART BOOKS (II), 1900 Hwy. 6 West, Waco TX 76712, phone (817)741-9144, founded 1969, editor James Haining, publishes "new literature and graphic arts in their various forms." They have published poetry by Robert Creeley, Charles Olson, Michael Lally, David Searcy, Julie Siegel, Paul Shuttleworth, Wm. Hart, Robert Slater, Gerald Burns and Sheila Murphy. The magazine-sized journal, 100 pgs., saddle-stapled, matte cover, experimental graphics throughout, appears irregularly. They receive about 400-600 poems a year, use approximately 1-2%. Press run is 1,000. **Sample postpaid: $6. Reports in 1-6 weeks. Pays copies. To submit for book publication under the Lucky Heart Books imprint, send 20 samples, cover letter "open." Simultaneous submissions OK. Always sends prepublication galleys. Pays copies.**

SAMSARA (I, IV-Specialized: suffering/healing), P.O. Box 367, College Park MD 20741-0367, founded 1993, editor R. David Fulcher, is a biannual publication of poetry and fiction dealing with suffering. **"All subject matter should deal with suffering/healing."** They have published poetry by John Grey and Corrine DeWinter. *Samsara* is 80 pgs., 8½ × 11, neatly typeset and stapled down the side with a colored card stock cover and b&w art. They receive about 150 poems a year, accept approximately 7%. Press run is 200 for 35 subscribers. Single copy: $5.50. **Reprints acceptable if 3 years since publication; simultaneous submissions OK, but "if it is a simultaneous submission, a cover letter should be provided explaining this status." Seldom comments on rejections. Send SASE for guidelines. Reports in 1-2 months. Pays 1 copy. Acquires first North American serial rights.** The editor says, "Make me feel anguish, pain and loss—and then some hope—and you'll probably get into *Samsara*."

‡SAN DIEGO POET'S PRESS; AMERICAN BOOK SERIES; LA JOLLA POET'S PRESS; NATIONAL POETRY BOOK SERIES (II), P.O. Box 8638, La Jolla CA 92038. San Diego Poet's Press, a nonprofit press founded 1981 by editor/publisher Kathleen Iddings, has published collections and anthologies that include Galway Kinnell, Carolyn Kizer, Allen Ginsberg, Carolyn Forche, Tess Gallagher and Robert Pinsky, among others. Iddings began publishing individual poets in 1985 and has published 32 poets to date. In 1989, she originated the "American Book Series" wherein she awards the winner $500 and publishes his/her first book of poetry. Past winners include Joan LaBombard, Regina McBride, Charles Atkinson, Michael Cleary and Kevin Griffith. In 1996, through La Jolla Poets Press, Iddings originated the "National Poetry Book Series." She also gives this national contest winner $500 and publishes the winning manuscript. Melissa Morphew was the first winner of this series. As a sample she selected these lines from the poem "Creation" in Morphew's *The Garden Where All Loves End*:

> And God was a green lizard
> sleeping on the edge of the world,
> soaking-in the sun—
>
> and this was before love,
> before the visions of honeysuckle
> and tangerine that would make Him
> lonely, before He wished Himself
> a bird, a snowy egret
> caught on the wind's blade,
> a wisp of grey, . . .

Sample of any winning book, postpaid: $11.50. Watch the *Small Press Review* or *Poets & Writers* for contest information.

SAN FERNANDO POETRY JOURNAL; KENT PUBLICATIONS, INC. (I, IV-Social issues), 18301 Halsted St., Northridge CA 91325, founded 1978, poetry editors Richard Cloke, Shirley Rodecker and Lori Smith. *San Fernando Poetry Journal* uses **poetry of social protest.** According to Richard Cloke, "Poetry, for us, should be **didactic in the Brechtian sense. It must say something, must inform, in the tenor of our time.** We follow Hart Crane's definition of poetry as architectural in essence, building upon the past but incorporating the newest of this age also, including science, machinery, sub-atomic and cosmic physical phenomena as well as the social convulsions wrenching the very roots of our present world." **Send SASE for guidelines which explain this more fully.** For example, we quote this passage for its general usefulness for poets: "In some, the end-line rhyming is too insistent, seeming *forced;* in others the words are not vibrant enough to give the content an arresting framework. Others do not have any beat (cadence) at all and some are simply not well thought out— often like first drafts, or seem like prose statements. Please try reworking again to get some energy in your statement. If your poetry is to succeed in impelling the reader to act, it must electrify, or at least command interest and attention." **They welcome new and unpublished poets.** The flat-spined quarterly, photocopied from typescript, uses 100 pgs. of poetry in each issue. They use about 300 of the 1,000 submissions (the editor rightly prefers to call them "contributions") each year. Press run is 400 for 350 subscribers of which 45 are libraries. **Sample postpaid: $2.50. No specifications for ms form. Simultaneous submissions OK. Reports in 1 week. Pays copies.** The press, under its various imprints, also publishes a few collections by individuals. **Query with 5-6 pgs. of samples.**

SANDPIPER PRESS (V), P.O. Box 286, Brookings OR 97415-0028, phone (541)469-5588, founded 1979, is a small press publisher of large print books. They have published *Poems from the Oregon Sea Coast*; *Unicorns for Everyone*, which includes some poetry; and *Walk With Me*, a book of prayers and meditations. However, **they currently do not accept unsolicited poetry.**

SANSKRIT (I), UNC Charlotte, Cone University Center, Charlotte NC 28223, phone (704)547-2326, e-mail sanskrit@email.uncc.edu, founded 1965, editor Scott Hubbard, is a literary annual using **poetry. "No restrictions as to form or genre, but we do look for maturity and sincerity in submissions. Nothing trite or sentimental."** They have recently published poetry by Kimberleigh Luke-Stallings. As a sample the editor selected these lines from "The World Will Always Be With Us" by Kristina Wright:

> The blues, the scent of lilacs on the tongue, tiny cherries
> softly push from my mouth like the first buds still straining,
>
> Though once I walked stupid-faced: shambling through dairy
> products, putrid flowers, the confusion of menus, guns, women
> skinny as switches on scratch and sniff pages, children with
> tremulous liquid hearts like firing glass vases, . . .

Their purpose is "to encourage and promote beginning and established artists and writers." It is 60-65 pgs., 9×12, flat-spined, printed on quality matte paper with heavy matte card cover. Press run is 3,500 for about 100 subscribers of which 2 are libraries. **Sample postpaid: $6. Submit up to 5 poems at a time. Simultaneous submissions OK. Cover letter with biographical information and past publications required. Reads submissions September through October only. Submission deadline is the first Friday in November.** Editor comments on submissions "infrequently." **Reports in 6-8 weeks. Pays 1 copy.**

SANTA BARBARA REVIEW (V), 104 La Vereda Lane, Santa Barbara CA 93108-2508, founded 1993, editor Patricia Stockton Leddy, is a literary arts journal appearing 3 times/year publishing poetry, fiction and essays, including essays on poetry. **"Due to an over supply of poetry, we will be accepting only submissions for the Phenomena of Place contest."** They have published poetry by Tess Gallagher, Chana Bloch, Stephen Ratcliffe, Marilyn Chandler and John Sanford. As a sample the editor selected these lines from "Jerusalem, 1985" by Yehuda Amichai, translation by Chana Bloch:

> Scribbled wishes stuck between the stones
> of the Wailing Wall:
> bits of crumpled, wadded paper.
>
> And over against them, stuck in an old iron gate
> half hidden by jasmine:
> "Couldn't make it,
> I hope you'll understand."

SBR is 160 pgs., 6×9, professionally printed and perfect-bound with b&w coated card cover and b&w illustrations inside. They use 12-18 poems each issue. Press run is 1,000 for 200 subscribers of which 10 are libraries, 75% shelf sales. Single copy: $7; subscription: $16/1 year. **Sample postpaid: $5.** Sponsors "The Phenomena of Place" contest for poems not more than 28 lines. Awards $100 to winning poem. Reading fee: $1/poem. Deadline: September 16. Send submissions for contest to "Place Contest," P.O. Box 808, Summerland CA 93067. Send SASE for details. The editor says, "The first thing we look for in any submission, whether it is a photograph, essay, poem or story, is voice. Other than a desire to avoid topics for their news value or political correctness, we have no taboo relative to subject matter. So far as length is concerned, make every image, word or trope count."

SANTA MONICA REVIEW (III), Santa Monica College, 1900 Pico Blvd., Santa Monica CA 90405, phone (310)450-5150, founded 1988, editor Lee Montgomery, poetry editor Jenny Cornuelle, appears twice a year publishing fiction and poetry, but is **not interested in traditional forms**. They have recently published poetry by Marc Cohen, Eve Wood and Anna Mortál. Single copy: $7; subscription: $12/year. **No submission information provided.** Poetry published in this review has been included in the 1993 and 1997 volumes of *The Best American Poetry*.

SARABANDE BOOKS, INC.; THE KATHRYN A. MORTON PRIZE IN POETRY (II), 2234 Dundee Rd., Suite 200, Louisville KY 40205, phone (502)458-4028, fax (502)458-4065, e-mail sarabandeb@aol.com, founded 1994, editor-in-chief Sarah Gorham, publishes books of poetry and short fiction. **They want "poetry of superior artistic quality. Otherwise no restraints or specifications."** They have recently published poetry by Sharon Bryan, Dick Allen, Baron Wormser and Belle Waring. **Query with 10 sample poems during the month of September only. No fax submissions. SASE must always be enclosed. Previously published poems OK if acknowledged as such. Simultaneous submissions OK "if notified immediately of acceptance elsewhere." Seldom comments on rejections. Replies to queries in 3 months, to mss (if invited) in 6 months. Pays 10% royalties and author's copies.** The Kathryn A. Morton Prize in Poetry is awarded to a book-length ms submitted between January 1 and February 15. $15 handling fee and entry form required. Send SASE for guidelines beginning in November. Winner receives a $2,000 cash award, publication and a standard royalty contract.

‡**SATIRE (IV-Humor)**, P.O. Box 340, Hancock MD 21750-0340, e-mail satire@intrepid.net, website http://www.intrepid.net/~fanfare/satire.htm, founded 1994, editor Larry Logan, published quarterly, is "the literary quarterly of the satiric." **They want "humor/satire."** They have recently published poetry by Ben Miller, R.A. Burns, G. Sterling Leiby and Joseph Salemi. *Satire* is 95 pgs., digest-sized, offset, perfect-bound with colored medium card cover, cartoons, graphics and some ads. They receive about 100-150 poems a year, use approximately 15-20. Press run is 500 for 200 subscribers, 50 shelf sales; 100 distributed free for promotion. Single copy: $5.25; subscription: $18. **Sample postpaid: $5. Submit up to 5 poems at a time. Accepts previously published poems (but prefer unpublished works); simultaneous submissions OK. Cover letter preferred.** Time between acceptance and publication is 3-6 months. **Editor makes final selections. Seldom comments on rejections. Send SASE for guidelines. Reports in 2 months. Always sends prepublication galleys. Pays 1-2 copies. Acquires one-time rights.** Sponsors periodic writing contest with a $5 entry, 1st, 2nd, and 3rd winners split the accumulated entry fees and are published in *Satire*.

SATURDAY EVENING POST (IV-Humor), 1100 Waterway Blvd., Indianapolis IN 46202, phone (317)636-8881, founded 1728 as the *Pennsylvania Gazette*, since 1821 as *The Saturday Evening Post*, Post Scripts editor Steve Pettinga, P.O. Box 567, Indianapolis IN 46206. *SEP* is a general interest, mass circulation bimonthly with emphasis on preventive medicine, using **"humorous light verse only. No more than 100 words per poem. Stay away from four-letter words and sexually graphic subject matter. No experimental verse (haiku, etc.). Morally, the *Post* is an anachronism of the early 50s; most of its readers are elderly. Other than that, anything goes, as long as it's in good taste."** Subscription: $13.97. **Payment is $15 for all rights.**

SATURDAY PRESS, INC. (V), Box 43548, Upper Montclair NJ 07043, phone (201)256-5053, founded 1975, editor Charlotte Mandel. "Saturday Press, Inc., is a nonprofit literary organization." They have published books of poetry by Janice Thaddeus, Jean Hollander, Anne Carpenter, Anneliese Wagner and Doris Radin. **However, "We do not plan to read manuscripts in the foreseeable future."**

SCAVENGER'S NEWSLETTER; KILLER FROG CONTEST (IV-Science fiction/fantasy, horror, mystery, writing), 519 Ellinwood, Osage City KS 66523-1329, phone (913)528-3538, e-mail foxscav1@jc.net, may seem an odd place to publish poems, but its editor, Janet Fox, uses 1-2 every month. The *Newsletter* is a **booklet packed with news about science fiction and horror publications. Janet prefers science fiction/fantasy, horror and mystery poetry and will read anything that is offbeat or bizarre. Writing-oriented poetry is occasionally accepted but "poems on writing must present fresh ideas and viewpoints. Poetry is used as filler so it must be ten lines or under. I like poems with sharp images and careful craftsmanship."** They have recently published poetry by Marge Simon, Rick Kennet, Dan Crawford and Valerie Hardin. As a sample she selected this poem, "Torture in Heaven" by Scott H. Urban:

> *How many pins can dance on the head of an angel?*

Scavenger's Newsletter is 28 pgs., printed at a quick printing shop for 950 subscribers. Subscription: $17/year; $8.50/6 months. **Sample (including guidelines) postpaid: $2.50. Submit 3-6 poems at a time. Previously published poems and simultaneous submissions OK (if informed)—reprints if credit is given. Send SASE for guidelines or request via e-mail. At last report was "accepting about 1 out of 20 poems submitted. I am currently reading selectively. I put the notice 'reading selectively due to overstock' on my guidelines, so writers will realize that I will be accepting very little during this period." Reports in 1 month or less. Pays $2 on acceptance plus one copy. Buys one-time rights.** Staff reviews science fiction/fantasy/horror and mystery chapbooks, books and magazines only. Send materials for review to either: Jim Lee, 801 - 26th St., Windber PA 15963 or Steve Sawicki, 186 Woodruff Ave., Watertown CT 06795. "I hold an annual 'Killer Frog

---

MARKET CONDITIONS are constantly changing! If you're still using this book and it is 1999 or later, buy the newest edition of *Poet's Market* at your favorite bookstore or order directly from Writer's Digest Books.

Contest' for horror so bad or outrageous it becomes funny. There is a category for horror poetry. Has been opening April 1, closing July 1 of each year. Prizes are $25 each in four categories: poetry, art, short stories and short short stories, plus the 'coveted' Froggie statuette." The last contest had no entry fee but entrants wanting the anthology pay $4 (postpaid). Winners list available for SASE.

‡♣**SCHOLASTIC CANADA LTD.; NORTHWINDS PRESS (V)**, 123 Newkirk Rd., Richmond Hill, Ontario L4C 3G5 Canada, founded 1971, publishes entertaining, high-quality novels and picture books for children. "A good story is prerequisite; very little poetry published. We publish 2 picture books per year that feature poetry. **However, we are not currently accepting unsolicited mss.**"

SCIENCE FICTION POETRY ASSOCIATION; STAR*LINE (IV-Science fiction, horror); THE RHYSLING ANTHOLOGY (V), 1300 Kicker Rd., Tuscaloosa AL 35404, phone (205)553-2284, e-mail dkm.alageol@genie.com, founded 1978, editor David Kopaska-Merkel, the Association publishes *Star*Line*, a bimonthly newsletter and poetry magazine. They are **"open to all forms—free verse, traditional forms, light verse—so long as your poetry shows skilled use of the language and makes a good use of science fiction, science, fantasy, horror or speculative motifs."** The Association also publishes *The Rhysling Anthology*, a yearly collection of nominations from the membership "for the best science fiction/fantasy long and short poetry of the preceding year." The magazine has published poetry by Bruce Boston, Thomas Disch, Denise Dumars, John M. Ford, Robert Frazier and Steve Rasnic Tem. The digest-sized magazine and anthology are saddle-stapled, photocopied, with numerous illustrations and decorations. They have 250 subscribers of which 1 is a library. Subscription: $13/6 issues. **Sample postpaid: $2.** Send requests for copies/membership information to John Nichols, Secretary-Treasurer, 6075 Bellevue Dr., North Olmstead OH 44070. **Submissions to *Star*Line* only.** They receive about 300-400 submissions a year, use approximately 80—**mostly short (under 50 lines). Send 3-5 poems/submission, typed. No simultaneous submissions, no queries. Brief cover letter preferred. Reports in a month. Pays 5¢/line plus 1¢/word and a copy. Buys first North American serial rights.** Reviews books of poetry "within the science fiction/fantasy field" in 50-500 words. Open to unsolicited reviews. Poets may also send books for review consideration to Todd Earl Rhodes, 735 Queensbury Loop, Winter Garden FL 34787-5808. A copy of *The Rhysling Anthology* is $3.

‡**SCIENCE OF MIND (IV-Spirituality/inspirational)**, 3251 W. Sixth St., P.O. Box 75127, Los Angeles CA 90020-5096, phone (213)388-2181, fax (213)388-1926, e-mail edit@scienceofmind.com, website http://www.scienceofmind.com, founded 1927, assistant editor Jim Shea, published monthly, "is a correlation of laws of science, opinions of philosophy, and revelations of religion applied to the needs and aspirations of humankind. A practical teaching, it helps thousands of people experience health, happiness, peace and love." They want **"poems inspirational in theme and characterized by an appreciation of *Science of Mind* principles. Average length is 8-12 lines. Maximum length is 25-30 lines."** They do not want "religious poetry, stuff about Christ and redemption." They have recently published poetry by Terri Glass and Eva Poole-Gilson. As a sample the editor selected these lines from "Such Beauty" by John D. Engle, Jr.:

> There is such beauty in the world today,
> Flowing through me and around me like a current
> Till I am charged and tingling from its force!
> It lives in all I see or hear or touch.
> It glows and sings and dances in its fervor.
> Such beauty! Such forceful beauty in the world, . . .

The editor says *Science of Mind* is 112 pgs., digest-sized, web offset, perfect-bound with 4-color cover and color ads. They receive about 200 poems a year, accept approximately 6-8. Press run is 78,000 for 55,000 subscribers, 15,000 shelf sales. Single copy: $2.50; subscription: $19.95. **Sample postpaid: $5. Submit 5 poems at a time. No previously published poems; simultaneous submissions OK. Cover letter preferred.** Time between acceptance and publication is 1 year (**"each issue has a theme, so we may keep a poem until the right theme comes along"**). **Poems are read by the assistant editor, and if approved, sent to the editor for final decision. Publishes theme issues.** Reports "not soon at all—most are rejected right away, but acceptances may take months." **Pays $25 and 10 copies. Buys first North American serial rights.**

SCOP PUBLICATIONS, INC. (II, IV-Regional), Box 376, College Park MD 20740, phone (301)422-1930, founded 1977, president Stacy Tuthill, publishes approximately 2 paperbacks/year as well as an occasional anthology. They want **"book-length regional manuscripts. No restrictions as to length or form but want well-crafted modern poetry with vivid imagery and skillful use of language with regard to sense impressions and fresh insights."** They have published poetry by Ann Darr, Barbara Lefcowitz and Elisavietta Ritchie. For sample book, send $5. Interested poets should **query with sample poems. Previously published poems and simultaneous submissions OK. Cover letter should include a short biography and recent credits. Seldom comments on rejections. Replies to queries in 6 weeks, to mss in 2-3 months. Pays copies.**

SCORE MAGAZINE; SCORE CHAPBOOKS AND BOOKLETS (II, IV-Form), 1015 NW Clifford St., Pullman WA 99163, phone (509)332-1120, poetry editors Crag Hill and Spencer Selby, is a small press publisher of **visual poetry** in the annual magazine *Score*, booklets, postcards and broadsides. They want **"poetry which**

melds language and the visual arts such as concrete poetry; experimental use of language, words and letters—forms. The appearance of the poem should have as much to say as the text. Poems on any subject; conceptual poetry; poems which use experimental, non-traditional methods to communicate their meanings." They don't want "traditional verse of any kind—be it free verse or rhymed." They have published poetry by Stephen-Paul Martin, A.L. Nielsen, Jonathan Brannen, Larry Eigner and Gregory St. Thomasino. They say that it is impossible to quote a sample because "some of our poems consist of only a single word—or in some cases no recognizable words." **We strongly advise looking at a sample copy before submitting if you are not familiar with visual poetry.** *Score* is 48-72 pgs., magazine-sized, offset, saddle-stapled, using b&w graphics, 2-color matte card cover. Press run is 200 for 25 subscribers, of which 6 are libraries, about 40 shelf sales. **Sample postpaid: $10. Previously published poems OK "if noted." No simultaneous submissions. Send SASE for guidelines. Pays 2 copies.** Open to unsolicited reviews. Poets may also send books for review consideration. **For chapbook consideration send entire ms. No simultaneous submissions. Almost always comments on rejections. Pays 25% of the press run.** They subsidy publish "if author requests it."

‡*SCOTTISH CULTURAL PRESS; SCOTTISH CONTEMPORARY POETS SERIES (III, IV-Nationality), Unit 14, Leith Walk Business Centre, 130 Leith Walk, Edinburgh EH6 5DT Scotland, phone (0131)555 5950, fax (0131)555 5018, e-mail scp@sol.co.uk, founded 1992, director Jill Dick. Scottish Cultural Press publishes **all styles of poetry. Poet should be Scottish or have strong Scottish connections and previously published in magazines, etc.** Publishes 12-15 paperbacks/year. **They do not want "new poets and/or modernistic visual poetry."** They have recently published poetry by Valerie Gillies, John Buchan and Iain Crichton-Smith. Books are usually 64 pgs., A5, "burst-bound," with 2-color cover. **Submit 5-10 poems at a time. Previously published poems and simultaneous submissions OK. Cover letter required and must include bio of poet and indication of whether material is available on disk.** Time between acceptance and publication is up to 9 months. **Poems are circulated to an editorial board. Seldom comments on rejections. Replies to queries in 1 month; to mss in 3 months. Pays 10% of net income royalties and 20 author's copies (out of a press run of 1,000).**

‡UNIVERSITY OF SCRANTON PRESS (IV-Regional), Linden & Monroe, Scranton PA 18510, phone (717)941-4228, fax (717)941-4309, founded 1981, editor Richard W. Rousseau, publishes hardbacks on the culture of Northeastern Pennsylvania and 1 book of poetry/year. **They want "poetry of regional, even ethnic interest." They do not want "deconstructed poetry." Submit 10 poems at a time. Previously published poems OK; no simultaneous submissions. Cover letter required with a brief bio.** Time between acceptance and publication is 2 months. **Poems are circulated to an editorial board. Seldom comments on rejections. Replies to queries in 2 months. Pays 10% royalty and 10 author's copies (out of a press run of 500-1,000). For sample books call the above number.** The editor says, "We publish primarily scholarly works but have published a book of regional poetry which has gone into a second edition, *Coalseam*, edited by Karen Blomain."

‡♥SCRIVENER (II), 853 Sherbrooke St. W., Montreal, Quebec H3A 2T6 Canada, phone (514)398-6588, fax (514)398-8146, founded 1980, is an annual review of contemporary literature and art published by students at McGill University. With a circulation throughout North America, *Scrivener* publishes the best of new Canadian and American poetry, short fiction, criticism, essays, reviews and interviews. **"***Scrivener* **is committed to publishing the work of new and unpublished writers."** As a sample they selected these lines from "Postmodern Magician" by Paul Harrison:

> The magician's union declared him out of order
> And took away his card,
> He had been outrageously postmodern,
> At every show
> Revealing magic's arithmetic—
> This was just not done. . . .

Scrivener is a book-sized review, 120 pgs., printed on natural recycled paper and bound with a flat spine and one color matte card cover; all graphics and ads are black and white. They receive about 1,000 submissions a year, accept approximately 50. **Subscription: $3 Canadian plus $1 for postage. Sample postpaid: $5. January 15 deadline for submissions for April 1st publication; contributors encouraged to submit in early fall. Send 5-10 poems, 1 poem/page; be sure that each poem be identified separately, with titles, numbers, etc. Do not send originals of work as submissions are not returned.** "Poets may contact our editorial staff regarding submission guidelines, deadlines, etc. However, we operate at full capacity only during the academic year; our editors may be difficult to reach during the summer." **Reports in 6 months. Pays 1 copy.**

‡SEA OATS (I, IV-Form), P.O. Box 934623, Margate FL 33093-4623, founded 1993, editor Robert Henry Poulin, assistant editor Maria Flores-Schweinsberg, appears biannually and is published by the Haiku Poets of South Florida. **They want "American genre 'shofo,' haiku, tanka, senryu and Korean sijo. We prefer poetry of explosive moments as seen in nature or felt from the heart with brevity and juxtaposed as a happening event with images expressed in common language."** They have recently published poetry by Robert Spiess, "Mimi" Davis, John Stevenson, Robert Major and Geraldine C. Little. As a sample the editor selected this haiku by H.F. Noyes:

> *Among spring snowflakes*
> *falling blossoms*
> *lose the way*

Sea Oats is 8 pgs., 8½×11, corner-stapled. "We accept at least one from every person who submits." Press run is 300 for 150 subscribers of which 5 are libraries. Single copy: $5; subscription: $10, includes 2 issues, membership and audio recording of each issue on cassette tape. **Make checks payable to Robert Henry Poulin. Submit any number of poems. No previously published poems or simultaneous submissions. Cover letter preferred "of new poets, bio desired with birthday." Send SASE for guidelines. Reports "ASAP." Pays 1 copy.** Sponsors the *Sea Oats* Poet of Year contest. Send SASE for guidelines.

SEASONS OF THE MUSE; CALLIOPE PRESS (I), 2 Jasmine Court, Millbrae CA 94030, founded 1996, editor/publisher Dawn Zapletal, appears quarterly "with the seasons, to give new and established poets a showcase for their work." **They want poetry of all types; "free verse, haiku, rhyme—24 lines or less preferred. No religious, political or pornographic work."** As a sample the editor selected these lines from "Send For Rod" by Rachael Trayar:

> *Time to call in a man with mud on his shoes,*
> *and dirt under his fingernails.*
> *A man with tomatoes and cucumbers*
> *and melons to give away,*
> *and sweet roses for the soul to feed on.*

The editor says *SOTM* is 4-6 pgs., 8½×11, corner stapled, with cover graphics. "No samples or subscriptions available. Only published poets receive copies." **Submit 4 poems at a time with $1 reading fee, "stamps or cash only. No checks, please." Previously published poems and simultaneous submissions OK. Send addressed postal card for reply. Does not return material. Poems are circulated to a 3-member editorial board. Decisions must be unanimous for acceptance. Always comments on rejections. Reports in 1 week to 1 month. Pays $1 plus 1 copy.** Sponsors an Editor's Choice Award in each issue. The best poem from each issue receives $5. The editor says, "No vague inaccessible poetry."

SEATTLE REVIEW (II), Padelford Hall, Box 354330, University of Washington, Seattle WA 98195, phone (206)543-9865, founded 1978, poetry editor Colleen McElroy, appears in the fall and spring using **"contemporary and traditional" poetry.** They have published poetry by William Stafford, Tess Gallagher, Marvin Bell and Walter McDonald. The review is 110 pgs., professionally printed, flat-spined, with glossy card cover. Press run is 800 for 250 subscribers of which 50 are libraries, 400 shelf sales. Single copy: $6; subscription: $10. **Sample postpaid: $3. Reads submissions October 1 through May 31 only. Send SASE for guidelines. Reports in 2-6 months. Pay "varies, but we do pay" plus 2 copies.** The editors offer these "practical suggestions: Cover letters with submissions do help. A cover letter provides something about the author and tells where and for what s/he is submitting. And don't let those rejection letters be cause for discouragement. Rejections can often be a matter of timing. The journal in question may be publishing a special issue with a certain theme (we've done a number of themes—'all-fiction,' 'all-poetry,' 'Asian-American,' 'environmental hazards,' 'Beauty and the Beasts,' etc.). Also, editorial boards do change, and new editors bring their individual opinions and tastes in writing. Good poetry will eventually be published if it is circulated."

*SECOND AEON PUBLICATIONS (V), 19 Southminster Rd., Roath, Cardiff CF2 S4T Wales, phone 01222-493093, founded 1966, poetry editor Peter Finch, is a "small press concerned in the main with **experimental literary works.**" He has published poetry by Bob Cobbing and himself. **Does not accept unsolicited mss. Pays copies.** Reviews poetry as a freelancer for a broad range of publications.

SEEMS (II), P.O. Box 359, Lakeland College, Sheboygan WI 53082-0359, phone (414)565-1276, fax (414)565-1206, founded 1971, published irregularly (32 issues in 25 years). This is a handsomely printed, nearly square (7×8¼) magazine, saddle-stapled, generous with white space on heavy paper. Two of the issues are considered chapbooks, and the editor, Karl Elder, suggests that a way **to get acquainted would be to order *Seems #14, What Is The Future Of Poetry?* for $5**, consisting of essays by 22 contemporary poets, and "If you don't like it, return it and we'll return your $5." *Explain That You Live: Mark Strand with Karl Elder* (#29) is available for $3. There are usually about 20 pgs. of poetry/issue. Elder has recently published poetry by Kim Bridgford, William Greenway, Joanne Lowery, Dave Oliphant and Kelly Shuford. He said it was "impossible" to select 6 illustrative lines. Print run is 350 for 200 subscribers of which 20 are libraries. Single copy: $4; subscription: $16/4 issues. There is a **1- to 2-year backlog. "People may call or fax with virtually any question, understanding that the editor may have no answer." Reports in 1-3 months. Pays 1 copy. Acquires first North American serial rights. Returns rights upon publication.** The editor says, "We'd like to consider more prose poems."

SEGUE FOUNDATION; ROOF BOOKS; SEGUE BOOKS (V), 303 E. Eighth St., New York NY 10009, phone (212)674-0199, president James Sherry, is a small press publisher of avant-garde and experimental poetry, literary criticism, and film and performance texts. Most of their books are flat-spined paperbacks, some hardcover. They have published books by Jackson MacLow, Charles Bernstein, Ron Silliman, Leslie Scalapino and Diane Ward. As a sample the editor selected these lines from "Scatter Matrix" by Abigail Child:

> *Commodity torque*
> *(Still) clackety cups and*
> *Exquisite exceptions requisite meter shock*
> *Genre*
>
> *Dependent on a denotive calculus*
> *A one of a kind*

They do not consider unsolicited mss. Query first.

SENECA REVIEW (II, IV-Translations), Hobart and William Smith Colleges, Geneva NY 14456-3397, phone (315)781-3349, founded 1970, editor Deborah Tall, is a biannual. **They want "serious poetry of any form, including translations. No light verse. Also essays on contemporary poetry."** They have published poetry by Seamus Heaney, Rita Dove, Denise Levertov, Stephen Dunn and Hayden Carruth. *Seneca Review* is 100 pgs., 6×9, professionally printed on quality stock and perfect-bound with matte card cover. You'll find plenty of free verse here—some accessible and some leaning toward experimental—with the emphasis on voice, image and diction. All in all, poems and translations complement each other and create a distinct editorial mood each issue. They receive 3,000-4,000 poems a year, accept approximately 100. Press run is 1,000 for 500 subscribers of which half are libraries, about 250 shelf sales. Subscription: $8/year, $15/2 years. **Sample postpaid: $5. Submit 3-5 poems at a time. No simultaneous submissions or previously published poems. Reads submissions September 1 through May 1 only. Reports in 6-12 weeks. Pays 2 copies.** Poetry published in *Seneca Review* has also been included in *The Best American Poetry 1994 and 1997*.

SENSATIONS MAGAZINE (II, IV-Membership/subscription, themes), 2 Radio Ave., A5, Secaucus NJ 07094, founded 1987, publisher/executive editor David Messineo. **Among the top 15 paying poetry markets in the US.** *Sensations Magazine* is an unusual mix of contemporary poetry, contemporary fiction and historical research. **"Outstanding poetry must take my breath away and make me want to say I wish I had written it myself. We want those writers who are receptive to—in fact, welcome—editorial feedback, and who take their writing seriously enough that they take the time to really research the time period and craft something spellbinding. (With our guidelines, we'll provide a bibliography of reference books that may be helpful.)"** As a sample of their needs for the 1998 issue, the publisher selected these lines from his poem "Witchhunt":

> *snake in the tree on the hanging hill*
> *snake in my dreams, telling me things*
> *Tituba says she can make me fly*
> *and mama promises a piece of rye*
> *says land on the witches' side of town can be mine*
> *if i just lie—but it's not lying cause i'm*
> *feeling snakes upon me in my dreams,*
> *in the trees, but it's not me*
> *on the hanging hill and i smile*
> *one up, seventeen to go*

Sensations Magazine averages over 100 pgs., 8½×11, desktop-published on coated stock, velo-bound, with glossy full-color cover, and b&w and color photos inside. **Mail SASE with brief query letter (tell me a bit about you, including writing and personal background) to above address. Guidelines for preparing manuscript, along with additional background info. about the magazine (including available back issue costs), will be returned in your SASE. Check (or International Money Order) must be made payable to David Messineo. If you send material without a SASE, you will receive no response."** No previously published poems; simultaneous submissions OK. Theme for October 1998 issue is "The 350th Anniversary of the Witchhunt in America 1648-1998." Deadline: August 31, 1998. Release date: Halloween 1998. Pays up to $125/poem minus the difference between the amount of a paid subscription and the cost of the issue in which work appears. Acquires one-time publication rights. *Sensations Magazine* was a first place winner in the 1996 American Literary Magazine Awards. Mr. Messineo says, "We prefer writers who send us material to do so with the hope of developing a long-term editor/writer relationship; we have writers who have sent material to each issue during our ten year history. In many cases, magic has happened. However, if you put misspelled, improperly prepared submissions in an envelope, don't include a SASE, or send poetry without following guidelines, I promise I'll put a hex on you. . . ."

SERPENT & EAGLE PRESS (V), RD#1, Box 29B, Laurens NY 13796, phone (607)432-2990, founded 1981, poetry editor Jo Mish. "Our aim is to print fine limited letterpress editions of titles worth printing in all subject areas." Their chapbooks are elegantly designed and printed on handmade paper with hand-sewn wrappers. **However, they are currently not accepting poetry submissions.**

SEVEN BUFFALOES PRESS; AZOREAN EXPRESS; BLACK JACK; VALLEY GRAPEVINE; HILL AND HOLLER ANTHOLOGY SERIES (IV-Rural, regional, anthologies), Box 249, Big Timber MT 59011, founded 1973, editor Art Coelho, who writes, "I've always thought that rural and working class writers, poets and artists deserve the same tribute given to country singers." These publications all express that interest.

For all of them Art Coelho wants **poetry oriented toward rural and working people, "a poem that tells a story, preferably free verse, not longer than 50-100 lines, poems with strong lyric and metaphor, not romantical, poetry of the heart as much as the head, not poems written like grocery lists or the first thing that comes from a poet's mind, no ivory tower, and half my contributors are women."** He has published poetry by R.T. Smith, James Goode, Leo Connellan and Wendell Berry. *The Azorean Express* is 35 pgs., 5½ × 8½, side-stapled. It appears twice a year. Circulation 200. **Sample postpaid: $6.75. Submit 4-8 poems at a time. No simultaneous submissions. Reports in 1 month. Pays 1 copy.** *Black Jack* is an anthology series on Rural America that uses rural material from anywhere, especially the American West; *Valley Grapevine* is an anthology on central California, circulation 750, that uses rural material from central California; *Hill and Holler*, Southern Appalachian Mountain series, takes in rural mountain lifestyle and folkways. **Sample of any postpaid: $6.75. Seven Buffaloes Press does not accept unsolicited mss but publishes books solicited from writers who have appeared in the above magazines.** Art Coelho advises, "Don't tell the editor how great you are. This one happens to be a poet and novelist who has been writing for 30 years. Your writing should not only be fused with what you know from the head, but also from what you know within your heart. Most of what we call life may be some kind of gift of an unknown river within us. The secret to be learned is to live with ease in the darkness, because there are too many things of the night in this world. But the important clue to remember is that there are many worlds within us."

THE SEWANEE REVIEW; AIKEN TAYLOR AWARD FOR MODERN POETRY (III), University of the South, Sewanee TN 37383-1000, phone (615)598-1246, founded 1892, thus being our nation's oldest continuously published literary quarterly, editor George Core. Fiction, criticism and poetry are invariably of the **highest establishment standards. Most of our major poets appear here from time to time.** *SR* has published poetry by William Logan, Howard Nemerov and Barry Spacks. Each issue is a hefty paperback of nearly 200 pgs., conservatively bound in matte paper, always of the same typography. Truly a magazine open to all styles and forms, issues we critiqued featured formal sequences, metered verse, structured free verse, sonnets, and lyric and narrative forms—all accessible and intelligent. Circulation: 3,200. **Sample: $6.25. Reports in 3-6 weeks. Pays 70¢/line.** Also includes brief, standard and essay-reviews. The Aiken Taylor Award for Modern Poetry is awarded by *The Sewanee Review* and its publisher, the University of the South in Sewanee, TN, "for the work of a substantial and distinguished career." Poetry published in *The Sewanee Review* was also selected for inclusion in *The Best American Poetry 1992*.

‡SHADOWFIRE PRESS; EVERNIGHT (I, IV-Horror, fantasy), P.O. Box 640067, Miami FL 33164-0067, phone (305)651-0187, e-mail tshai@mindspring.com, website http://www.mindspring.com/~stygian/shadowfire, founded 1995, poetry editor Michael Barnette. *evernight: beyond the pale of day lie worlds unending,* published monthly, is a publication specializing in horror/gothic horror and dark urban fantasy. **They want "horror, especially about supernatural creatures/beings." They do not want "humdrum mundane poetry about the vageries of life. No romance, no 'angst.' "** They have recently published poetry by Tippi N. Blevins, William P. Robertson, Charlie Jacob and Wendy Rathbone. As a sample the editor selected these lines from "No Ordinary Zombie" by Valerie Hurdin:

> *Am I nothing but your concubine*
> *To be buried with you at the hour of your death?*
> *I will not be forgotten into shades of grey*
> *I will live for myself until my breath*
> *And the Heavens come for me*

evernight is 24 pgs., digest-sized, offset on 20 lb. bond, saddle-stapled with b&w and greyscale art on cover and interior, ads. Press run is 500. Single copy: $2; subscription: $15. **Sample postpaid: $1.50 (ask for writers discount rate). Make checks payable to Stygian Vortex Publications. Submit up to 8 poems at a time. E-mail submissions OK. Accepts previously published poems occasionally; simultaneous submissions OK. Cover letter required "include a personal biography (not a list of prior credits)."** Time between acceptance and publication is 1-12 months. **Poems are circulated to an editorial board. "We read and consider all submissions and choose those we feel have the greatest merit and will appeal to our readers." Often comments on rejections. Publishes theme issues. Send SASE for guidelines and upcoming themes or obtain via website. Reports in "about 4-6 weeks." Pays 1 copy. Acquires one-time rights.** Reviews books or chapbooks of poetry or other magazines in 600-1,000 words (0-3 reviews each issue). Open to unsolicited reviews. Poets may also send books for review consideration "if they are already in published form." ShadowFire Press publishes **3-6 chapbooks/year** of "horror poetry, particularly vampire related. We strive to create the finest chapbooks we can and use the poetry and accompanying artwork to enhance the appearance of all our books."

---

‡   THE DOUBLE DAGGER before a listing indicates that the listing is new in this edition. New markets are often the most receptive to submissions.

Chapbooks vary in format. The one we saw was 30 pgs., 8½×11, offset, saddle-stapled, with b&w art on the cover and inside. **Requires authors to have published a number of their poems first and they must have a proven track record of numerous sales to other horror markets. Replies to queries in 1-2 weeks; to mss in 4-6 weeks. Pays $10-15 honorarium and 5-15 author's copies (out of a press run of 100).** They offer a poetry formatting guide if requested for a SASE along with their guidelines. Both are also available at their website. The editor advises, "Be familiar with the poets we list in these guidelines as they are among our most popular and well known. If you familiarize yourself with their work, you will have a good idea of the type of material we publish."

SHAMAL BOOKS (IV-Ethnic, anthologies), Dept. PM, GPO Box 16, New York NY 10116, phone (718)622-4426, founded 1976, editor Louis Reyes Rivera. Shamal Books is a small press whose purpose is **"to promote the literary efforts of African-American and Caribbean writers, particularly those who would not otherwise be able to establish their literary credentials as their concerns as artists are with the people."** The press publishes individual and "anthological" books and chapbooks, mostly flat-spined paper texts. They have published poetry by SeKou Sundiata, Sandra Maria Esteves and Rashidah Ismaili. The editor wants to see **"poetry that clearly demonstrates an understanding of craft, content and intent as the scriptural source of the word guiding and encouraging the intellect of the people."** He does not consider unsolicited submissions of individual mss, but will look at work only while anthologies are open. Submit 2 sample poems. Mss should be **"neat and single-spaced." Cover letter "leaning toward personal goals and poetic principles" required. Replies to queries within 2 months. Royalties for book authors are 15%.** The editor says that he will subsidy publish "delicately—depends on resources and interest in work." His projects include "an international anthology; drama; prison anthology; books on language as a weapon; a collectivized publisher's catalog of Third World presses working out of NYC." His advice to poets: "Certainly to study the craft more and to research more into the historical role that has been the hallmark of poetry across class and caste conscious lines that limit younger perspectives. Not to be as quick to publish as to be in serious study, then while looking to publish, looking as well into collective ventures with other poets for publication and distribution. Above all, *read*!"

SHARING THE VICTORY (IV-Spirituality/inspirational, sports), 8701 Leeds Rd., Kansas City MO 64129, phone (816)921-0909, founded 1959, editor John Dodderidge, assistant editor Will Greer, managing editor Kevin Harlan. This monthly magazine is published September through May by the Fellowship of Christian Athletes. **They want free verse on themes of interest to Christian athletes (high school and college, male and female).** They use 2-3 poems/year. Press run is 50,000. **Sample available for $1 with 8½×11 SASE (first-class stamps for 3 ozs.). Reads submissions July 1 through March 1 only.** Time between acceptance and publication averages 3-4 months. **Guidelines available free. Reports in 2 weeks. Pays $25-50. Buys first or second rights.**

SHATTERED WIG REVIEW (II), 425 E. 31st, Baltimore MD 21218, phone (410)243-6888, founded 1988, contact Sonny Bodkin, is a semiannual using **"liquid, messy poetry, oozing the stuff of life. No frustrated English professor poetry."** They have published poetry by John M. Bennett, Cynthia Hendershot, Sheila Murphy and Dan Raphael. *SHW* is approximately 70 pgs., 8½×8½, photocopied, side-stapled with card stock covers with original artwork, art and graphics also inside. They receive about 10 submissions a week, accept about 20%. Press run is 300 for 100 subscribers of which 10 are libraries, 100 shelf sales. Subscription: $9 (2 issues). **Sample postpaid: $4. Previously published poems and simultaneous submissions OK. Seldom comments on rejections. Reports within a month. Pays 1 copy. Acquires one-time rights.** Occasionally reviews books of poetry in 100 words. Open to unsolicited reviews. Poets may also send books for review consideration. The editor says there are no requirements for contributors except "that the contributor include us in their nightly prayers."

HAROLD SHAW PUBLISHERS; WHEATON LITERARY SERIES (V), P.O. Box 567, Wheaton IL 60189, phone (630)665-6700, founded 1967, literary editor Lil Copan, is "small publisher of the Wheaton Literary Series, **works of Christian and literary merit** including fiction, poetry, literary criticism and original prose" in flat-spined paperback and hardback books. They have published poetry by Madeleine L'Engle, John Leax, Sister Maura Eichner and Luci Shaw. **They publish on a 10/5% royalty basis or a flat fee.** They publish a volume in the Wheaton Literary Series approximately every 2 years. "Our work reflects **a Christian evangelical world-view**, though this need not be explicit. In the future we may publish an anthology, rather than single poets." **However, they are currently still not accepting poetry submissions.**

‡**SHEEP MEADOW PRESS (III)**, P.O. Box 1345, Riverdale-on-Hudson NY 10471, founded 1976, publisher/editor-in-chief Stanley Moss, publishes 8-10 paperbacks and 3-4 hardbacks/year. **They want "book-length, high-quality literary poetry."** They have recently published poetry by Grace Schulman, Khaled Mattawa, Diana Der-Hovanessian and Julie Agoos. Books are usually 70-150 pgs., 6×9, perfect-bound (generally) with 4-color covers, "often use art from personal collection." **Do not query—send complete manuscript."** Previously **published poems and simultaneous submissions OK. Cover letter required. "Electronic submission desired upon offer of publication."** Time between acceptance and publication is approximately 1 year. **Seldom comments on rejections. Replies to mss (if invited) in 3-4 months. Pays 6-10% royalties; advance varies and**

10-20 author's copies (out of a press run of 1,000). The publisher says, "We are more likely to accept a poet with a record of publication."

SHEILA-NA-GIG (II), 23106 Kent Ave., Torrance CA 90505, founded 1990, editor Hayley R. Mitchell. *Sheila-Na-Gig* appears once a year as a large general issue. The editor says she is **partial to free verse but accepts many styles and subject matter. She generally does not publish poems over 3 pages, religious poetry or rhyming verse.** They have recently published work by Lyn Lifshin, Gerald Locklin, Michael McNeilley, Denise Duhamel, Joan Jobe Smith and Charles Webb. As a sample the editor selected these lines by Regina O'Melveny:

> *Pressing my ear to the dream*
> *I hear groundwater creep*
> *one-tenth of a mile per year,*
> *hear quakes before they convulse*
> *and jump the slim beak*
> *on the paper cylinder*
> *into jagged black arcs*
> *of astonishment.*

Sheila-Na-Gig is 100-150 pgs., digest-sized, flat-spined, photocopied from laser prints with matte card cover. Subscription: $7/year, $12/2 years. **Sample postpaid: $7 for current issue ($6 for back issues). Submit up to 5 poems with cover letter, short bio and SASE. Reads submissions January through May 31 only. Reports in 6-8 weeks. Pays copies. Acquires first rights.** Sponsors an annual poetry contest. Submit 3 poems with cover letter, SASE and $5 entry fee. Include check number on the bottom of each poem, do not put names on the poems. $50 first prize, copies, and publication of runners-up. Also sponsors an annual chapbook contest. Submit 20-24 poems (25 pgs. maximum) with SASE, cover letter (with name, address, bio, acknowledgments and ms title), a separate cover sheet with ms title only and check number, and $10 entry fee. Prize: $100, publication and 100 copies. All entries receive a copy of the winning chapbook. Deadline for both contests is June 30. Work in *Sheila-Na-Gig* has been nominated for inclusion in *Pushcart Prize XIX: Best of the Small Presses (1994-95 edition)*.

SHENANDOAH (II), Troubadour Theater, 2nd Floor, Washington and Lee University, Lexington VA 24450-0303, founded 1950, editor R.T. Smith, managing editor Lynn L. Leech. Published at Washington and Lee University, it is a quarterly literary magazine which has published poetry by Mary Oliver, Margaret Gibson, Rodney Jones and Brendan Galvin. As a sample the editor selected "The Ghost Orchid" by Michael Longley:

> *Added to its few remaining sites will be the stanza*
> *I compose about leaves like flakes of skin, a colour*
> *Dithering between pink and yellow, and then the root*
> *That grows like coral among shadows and leaf-litter.*
> *Just touching the petals bruises them into darkness.*

The magazine is 120 pgs., 6×9, perfect-bound, professionally printed with full-color cover. Generally, it is open to all styles and forms. Circulation is 1,900. Subscription: $15/year; $28/2 years; $40/3 years. **Sample postpaid: $5. All submissions should be typed on one side of the paper only. Your name and address must be clearly written on the upper right corner of the ms. Include SASE. Reads submissions September 1 through May 30 only. Reports in 3 months. Payment includes a check, 1-year subscription and 1 copy. Buys first publication rights.** Staff reviews books of poetry in 7-10 pages, multi-book format. Send books for review consideration. Most reviews are solicited. A prize is awarded for the best poetry, fiction and nonfiction published in the calendar year. Poetry published in *Shenandoah* has been included in the 1993 and 1997 volumes of *The Best American Poetry*.

SHIP OF FOOLS (II); SHIP OF FOOLS PRESS (V), Box 1028, University of Rio Grande, Rio Grande OH 45674-9989, phone (614)992-3333, e-mail cathart@eurekanet.com, founded 1983, editor Jack Hart, advisory editor Gina Pellegrino-Pines, review editor James Doubleday, is "more or less quarterly." They want **"coherent, well-written, traditional or modern, myth, archetype, love—most types. No concrete, incoherent or greeting card poetry."** They have published poetry by Rhina Espaillat, Paula Tatarunis, Susanna Raxman and Lyn Lifshin. As a sample the editors selected these lines by Elva Lauter:

> *Sipping green tea,*
> *I think, "Now I am there."*
> *I will stay until stars*
> *Streak my eyes*
> *and the cup is empty.*

They describe *Ship of Fools* as digest-sized, saddle-stapled, offset printed with cover art and graphics. Press run is 231 for 44 subscribers of which 6 are libraries. Subscription: $8/4 issues. **Sample postpaid: $2. No previously published poems or simultaneous submissions. Cover letter preferred. Often comments on rejections. Reports in 2-4 weeks. "If longer than six weeks, write and ask why." Pays 1-2 copies.** Reviews books of poetry. Ship of Fools Press publishes chapbooks but does not accept unsolicited mss.

SHOFAR (IV-Children, ethnic, religious), 43 Northcote Dr., Melville NY 11747-3924, phone/fax (516)643-4598, founded 1984, publisher/editor Gerald H. Grayson, is a magazine **for Jewish children 9-13**, appearing monthly October through May (double issues December/January and April/May). It is 32 pgs., magazine-sized, professionally printed, with color paper cover. Press run is 17,000 for 16,000 subscribers of which 1,000 are libraries. Subscription: $14.95. **Sample: $1.01 postage and 9×12 SAE. They will consider simultaneous submissions and "maybe" previously published poems. Send SASE for guidelines. Submit holiday theme poems at least 4 months in advance. Reports in 6-8 weeks. Pays 10¢/word plus 5 copies. Buys first North American serial rights.**

SIDEWALKS (I, II), P.O. Box 321, Champlin MN 55316, founded 1991, editor Tom Heie, is a semiannual anthology of poetry, short prose and art, published to promote the work of emerging and published writers and artists. **They want "poetry that uses strong, original images and language, showing attention to craftsmanship, but not self-conscious; poetry that shows insight. No porno, kinky sex or rhyming verse."** They have published poetry by Mark Vinz, Jay Meek, Michael Dennis Browne and Kenneth Pobo. As a sample the editor selected the last stanza of "The Winter Heart" by Mary Kay Rummel:

> She searches for the bear, remembering
> how she'd watched her roll down the road
> on round haunches. She knows they both
> will wake with lust some morning
> will walk on the ice in shoes of fire.

Sidewalks is 76-80 pgs., 5½×8½, professionally printed and perfect-bound with matte card cover and b&w art. They receive 600-800 poems a year, accept approximately 10%. Press run is 300 for 100 subscribers, 50 shelf sales. Single copy: $6; subscription: $9. **Sample postpaid: $5. Submit 3-6 poems at a time, name and address on each. No previously published poems or simultaneous submissions. Cover letter preferred. Deadlines: May 31 and December 31. Three readers read and vote on submissions; then a group meets to select the best work. Seldom comments on rejections. Send SASE for guidelines. Reports 1 month after deadline. Pays 1 copy. Acquires first rights.** The editor says, "Sidewalks [are] those places where a child first meets the world, [a] place of discovery, of myth, power, incantation . . . a world in itself, places we continue to meet people, ignoring some, smiling at others, preoccupied, on our way somewhere, . . . [places] where we pass with just a glance or smile or protectively turn up our collar on a windy day, . . . paths to and from neighbors, to the corner grocery . . . paths that bring us home."

SIERRA NEVADA COLLEGE REVIEW (I), P.O. Box 4269, Incline Village NV 89450, founded 1990, editor June Sylvester, is an annual literary magazine featuring poetry and short fiction by new writers. **They want "high quality, image-oriented poems that suggest or surprise; no limit on length, style, etc. No light verse, sloppy sentiment, purposeful obscurity, clichés or cuteness."** They have published poetry by Marisella Veiga, Ivanov Y. Reyez, Colleen O'Brien and B.Z. Nidith. As a sample the editor selected these lines from "The Book of Ruth" by Margaret Almon:

> I must not dream of anger.
> Placing a kernel
> in the bend of his knee,
> willing it to sprout into tangles
> around his throat—
> tangles like the ones in my hair
> that break the comb.
> Placing a sheaf beneath his bed,
> his body becoming a field of bruises.

The editor says *SNCR* is approximately 75 pgs., with cover art only. "We receive approximately 500 poems a year and accept approximately 50." Press run is 500. Subscription: $5/year. **Sample postpaid: $2.50. Submit 5 poems at a time. No previously published poems; simultaneous submissions OK. Include brief bio. Reads submissions September 1 through April 1 only. Often comments on rejections. Reports in 3 weeks to 3 months. Pays 2 copies.** The editor says, "We delight in publishing the unpublished or underpublished writer. We look specifically for subtlety and skill."

‡SILHOUETTE MAGAZINE™ (I, II), P.O. Box 53763, Baton Rouge LA 70892-3763, phone (504)358-0617, e-mail cawan@iamerica.net, founded 1995, publisher Candace J. Joseph, is published quarterly. **They want "Spiritual, abstract and/or poetry that reflects society in the most straightforward manner giving voice to the inner conflicts society propogates, poetry offering spirituality as solutions."** They do not want "profane, obscene or vulgar suggestions, innuendos, portraits or statements." They have recently published poetry by William Ashante Hobbs, III, Erica Smith and Tonya Snow. As a sample the editor selected these lines from "Bound" by Michael Duquette:

> I'm a slave to my own creation
> a slave to my own desires
> shackled and bound to a cruel fate
> nailed to my own cross

> *little matters in this state*
> *of minor victories*
> *and forbidden fruits*
> *condemned to a life of pain*
> *where happiness hurts just the same.*

The editor says *Silhouette* is 8 pgs., 8½×11, saddle-stapled, offset with b&w art and ads. Press run is 400 for 50 subscribers, 60 shelf sales; 150 distributed free to organizations and literary agents. Single copy: $2.75; subscription: $14/6 issues. **Sample postpaid: $4. Submit 5-9 poems at a time. Previously published poems and simultaneous submissions OK.** Cover letter preferred. **"Include info about poet such as address, contact number and if applicable, publishing history. Let us know how poet found out about the journal. Typewritten submissions only. May submit on 3.5″ disk in MSWord/MSWorks, MS Publisher or text file."** E-mail submissions OK (no more than 4). Time between acceptance and publication is 2-4 months. **Poems are circulated to an editorial board. Often comments on rejections. Charges criticism fees for book-length ms only; charge/fee based on page numbers. Publishes theme issues. Send SASE for guidelines and upcoming themes. Reports in 3-5 months. Pays 2 copies. Acquires one-time rights.** Staff reviews single books of poetry; no set length. Poets may also send books for review consideration. The editor says, "Literature and art have become the bedrock for releasing society-related anxiety, worries as well as successes and passion (which are often all thrust upon an individual simultaneously). We at *Silhouette Magazine* attempt to allow poets, writers and artists a medium of liberation."

THE SILVER WEB: A MAGAZINE OF THE SURREAL (I, IV-Science fiction, horror), P.O. Box 38190, Tallahassee FL 32315, e-mail annk19@mail.idt.net, founded 1989, editor Ann Kennedy, is a semiannual publication featuring fiction, poetry, art and thought-provoking articles. **They want "works ranging from speculative fiction to dark tales and all weirdness in between; specifically works of the surreal. We are looking for well-written work that is unusual and original. No genre clichés, that is, no vampires, werewolves, zombies, witches, fairies, elves, dragons, etc. Also no fantasy, sword and sorcery. Poems must use standard poetic conventions whether free verse or rhyming."** They have published poetry by Glenna Holloway, Simon Perchik, Tippi N. Blevins and Jacie Ragan. As a sample we selected these lines from "Empty House" by Fabian Peake:

> *You walk the pavement*
> *of my street in your*
> *scuffed black shoes,*
> *dragging behind you*
> *(on lengths of string*
> *tied to your belt),*
> *a hundred paintbrushes*
> *dancing like drumsticks . . .*

The Silver Web is 90 pgs., 8½×11, offset printed, perfect-bound with full-color cover and b&w photos, art and ads. They receive 10-20 poems a week, accept 10-20 a year. Press run is 2,000 for more than 300 subscribers. Subscription: $12. **Sample postpaid: $7.20, $7.95 Canada and overseas. Submit up to 5 poems at a time. Previously published poems OK, but note previous credit. Simultaneous submissions also OK. Reads submissions January 1 through September 30 only. Seldom comments on rejections. Send SASE for guidelines or request via e-mail. Reports in 4-6 weeks. Always sends prepublication galleys. Pays $10-50 and 2 copies. Buys first or one-time rights.** Poetry published in *The Silver Web* has also been included in *The Rhysling Anthology* and *The Year's Best Fantasy and Horror*.

SILVER WINGS (IV-Religious, spirituality/inspirational), P.O. Box 1000, Pearblossom CA 93553-1000, phone (805)264-3726, founded 1983, published by Poetry on Wings, Inc., poetry editor Jackson Wilcox. "As a committed Christian service we produce and publish *Silver Wings*, a quarterly poetry magazine. We want **poems with a Christian perspective, reflecting a vital personal faith and a love for God and man. Will consider poems from 3-20 lines. Quite open in regard to meter and rhyme."** They have published poetry by Elva McAllaster, Mary Ann Henn, Hugh Alexander and C. David Hay. As a sample the editor selected these lines from "The First Step is the Hardest" by Deborah Esling:

> *Eaglets never learn to fly*
> *While clinging to the limb.*
>
> *A lesson gleaned from nature—*
> *When faith outweighs the fear,*
> *First steps can be taken*
> *And miracles appear.*

The magazine is 16 pgs., digest-sized, offset with cartoon-like art. They receive about 1,500 submissions a year, use approximately 260. Circulation is 300 with 250 subscribers, 50 shelf sales. Subscription: $7. **Sample postpaid: $2. Submit typed ms, double-spaced. No previously published poems; simultaneous submissions OK.** Time between acceptance and publication can be up to 2 years. **Send SASE for guidelines and upcoming themes. Reports in 3 weeks, providing SASE is supplied. Pays 1 copy.** "We occasionally offer an award to a poem we consider outstanding and most closely in the spirit of what *Silver Wings* seeks to accomplish." **Acquires first rights.** The editor says, "We have felt that the state of secular poetry today is thrashing in a stagnant pond out of which it cannot extract itself. We want to lift our poetry to a high road where God's sunlight is shining. We even encourage poets with little ability but having an upward mobile commitment."

SILVERFISH REVIEW; SILVERFISH REVIEW PRESS; GERALD CABLE POETRY CONTEST (II), P.O. Box 3541, Eugene OR 97403, phone (503)344-5060, founded 1979, poetry editor Rodger Moody, is a biannual (June and December) literary magazine. **"The only criterion for selection of poetry is quality. In future issues *Silverfish Review* also wants to showcase the short short story."** They have published poetry by Chelsey Minnis, Denise Duhamel, Dick Allen, Ivan Arguelles, Gary Young, Robert Gregory, Kevin Bowen, Richard Jones, Floyd Skloot and Judith Skillman. The magazine is 48 pgs., digest-sized, professionally printed in dark type on quality stock, matte card cover with art. There are 30-34 pgs. of poetry in each issue. They receive about 1,000 submissions of poetry a year, use approximately 20, have a 6- to 12-month backlog. Circulation is 1,000. Subscription for institutions: $12; for individuals: $8. **Sample: $4, single copy orders should include $1.50 for p&h. Submit at least 5 poems to editor. No simultaneous submissions. Reports in about 2-6 months. Pays 2 copies and 1-year subscription, plus small honorarium when grant support permits.** Reviews books of poetry. Open to unsolicited reviews. Poets may also send books for review consideration. Silverfish Review Press sponsors the Gerald Cable Poetry Contest. A $1,000 cash award and publication by SRP is awarded annually to the best book-length ms or original poetry by an author who has not yet published a full-length collection. No restrictions on the kind of poetry or subject matter; translations not acceptable. A $15 reading fee must accompany the ms; make checks payable to Silverfish Review Press. **Send SASE for rules.**

SING HEAVENLY MUSE! (IV-Feminist), Box 13320, Minneapolis MN 55414, founded 1977, editorial circle fosters "the work of women poets, fiction writers and artists. The magazine is **feminist in an open, generous sense: We encourage women to range freely, honestly and imaginatively over all subjects, philosophies and styles. We do not wish to confine women to women's subjects,** whether these are defined traditionally, in terms of femininity and domesticity, or modernly, from a sometimes narrow polemical perspective. We look for explorations, questions that do not come with ready-made answers, emotionally or intellectually." For poetry they have **"no limitations except women's writing or men's writing that reflects awareness of women's consciousness."** They have published poetry by Alexis Rotella, Jill Breckenridge and Amirh Bahati. The magazine appears once a year in a 6×9, flat-spined, 125-page format, offset from typescript on heavy stock, b&w art, glossy card color cover. They receive about 1,500 submissions a year, use approximately 50-60. Press run is 1,000 for 275 subscribers of which 50 are libraries. Single copy: $8 plus $2 p&h; subscription: $15/2 issues, $20/3 issues ($16 low income), $38/6 issues. **Sample postpaid: $4. "Copies are also available in bookstores nationwide that carry small press women's literature." Submit 3-5 poems at a time, name and address on each page. No simultaneous submissions. Editors sometimes comment on rejections. Send SASE for guidelines, information about upcoming reading periods and themes. Reports in 4-5 months. Pays "usually $25 plus 2 copies."**

‡**SINGING HORSE PRESS (III)**, P.O. Box 40034, Philadelphia PA 19106, founded 1976, editor/publisher Gil Ott, publishes an average of 2 new titles/year, primarily poetry. **"We are most interested in work which explores the intersection of poetics and human relation, be that political, cultural or psychological."** Most recent titles: *Muse & Drudge* by Harryette Mullen and *the cairo notebooks* by Ammiel Alcalay. Press run is 1,000. Average page count: 80. Prices average $9.50. **Writers should become acquainted with their publications/editorial preferences and query before submitting. "Most work is solicited."**

SINGULAR SPEECH PRESS (V, IV-Form), 10 Hilltop Dr., Canton CT 06019-2139, phone (860)693-6059, fax (860)693-6338, e-mail dondwilson@aol.com, founded 1976, editor Don D. Wilson. "Singular Speech Press presents examples of our many real poets—probably our most unsupported artists. **And so we tried to publish 5 mss per annum, 48-88 pages. We have just determined to accept no further submissions until 1999, being totally booked up until the millenium. Then we'll publish only formal poetry, for diverse reasons, partly to simplify, because we are inundated by vers libre, partly because we believe it's time to support again the time-honored sonnet, et al."** They have recently published Louise Kennelly's *Tracking God in Italy*, Carol Poster's *Surrounded by Dangerous Things*, Nikolas Macioci's *Why Dance?* and Joel Charell's *Twentieth Century Deaths*. As a sample the editor selected these lines from "The Marakill" in Gray Burr's *Afterlives*:

> How can we love this brook the way it is
> Or love ourselves if we're reflected in
> Its turgid full-length mirror that returns
> A version of ourselves which, like a quiz,
> Asks us who we are and what we've been,
> And how to bear to be the one who learns.

SINISTER WISDOM (IV-Lesbian, feminist), P.O. Box 3252, Berkeley CA 94703, founded 1976, editor Akiba Onáda-Sikwoia, is a lesbian feminist journal. The editor says, **"We want poetry that reflects the diversity of lesbian experience—lesbians of color, Third World, Jewish, old, young, working class, poor, disabled,**

fat, etc.—from a lesbian and/or feminist perspective. **No heterosexual themes. We will not print anything that is oppressive or demeaning to women, or which perpetuates negative stereotypes."** The journal has published work by Gloria Anzaldúa, Sapphire and Betsy Warland. As a sample the editor chose the following lines from Minnie Bruce Pratt's poem "#67 To Be Posted on 21st Street, Between Eye and Pennsylvania":

> *Like a movie, sudden threat*
> *Predictable. I get so tired of this disbelief.*
> *My tongue, faithful in my mouth, said: Yes, we are.*
> *the shout: Lesbians. Lesbians. Trying to curse*
> *us with our name. Me louder: That's what we are.*

The editor says the quarterly magazine is 128-144 pgs., digest-sized, flat-spined, with photos and b&w graphics. Circulation is 3,500 for 1,000 subscribers of which 100 are libraries; newsstand sales and bookstores are 1,500. Single copy: $6; subscription: $20 US, $25 foreign. **Sample postpaid: $7.50. No simultaneous submissions.** Time between acceptance and publication is 6 months to 1 year. **Publishes theme issues. Send SASE for upcoming themes. Reports in up to 9 months. Pays 2 copies.** Reviews books of poetry in 500-1,500 words, single or multi-book format. The editor says they would like "anything *other* than love poetry."

‡SINK FULL OF DISHES (II), P.O. Box 39500, St. Louis MO 63139-8500, founded 1994, contact Ditch Cat, a quarterly zine, "presents a wide range of genuine expression, especially by writers and artists whose work is shunned by academic and mainstream markets." **They want "honest, unpretentious, straight-forward poetry; slice-of-life; confessional; narrative; surreal; humorous; experimental. No pretentious academic styles, 'pity poor me, I'm heartbroken and outcast'-type poetry."** They have recently published poetry by Oberc, Lyn Lifshin, Paul Weinman and Walt Phillips. As a sample the editor selected these lines from "Ocean Goddess" by William Kopecky:

> *Just beneath the starlit face of the water*
> *where moonlight is a blood-fingered song,*
> *she dreams with open eyes*
> *and dances*
> *in the dying arms of the tide.*

SFOD is 28 pgs, 8½×11, photocopied, saddle-stitched, 60 lb. color cover, art, graphics (comics), ads. They receive about 200-300 poems a year, accept approximately 15%. Press run is 200 for 10 subscribers, 20 shelf sales. Subscription: $7/year (4 issues). **Sample postpaid: $2. "No requirements, but suggest purchasing a sample copy." Submit 3-5 poems at a time. Previously published poems and simultaneous submissions OK.** Time between acceptance and publication is 1-10 months. **Seldom comments on rejections. Reports in 1-4 weeks. Sometimes sends prepublication galleys. Pays 1 copy. Rights remain with the author.** Includes brief (50 words or less) reviews of small press (independent) zines and comic books. *Sink Full of Dishes* was chosen to appear in the Seattle Public Library's "Book Art Show" of November 1996. The editor says, "No taboo subjects, language or style restraints; generally, poets receive only one contributor's copy regardless of the number of poems published in an issue (due to the font size used on poetry); avoid pretension at all costs."

THE SIREN (II), Campus Box 1514, Eckerd College, 4200 54th Ave. S., St. Petersburg FL 33711, e-mail siren@eckerd.edu, founded 1993, is the annual, nationally-distributed literary magazine of Eckerd College which publishes high-quality poetry, fiction and color and b&w artwork. **"We want to see poems of a wide range of content, length and tone from poets who pay particular attention to craft (particularly line, stanza and voice). Nothing sentimental or cliché, nor poems that are needlessly obscure or Beat."** They have published poetry by Kathryn Stripling Byer, Fred Chappell and R.T. Smith. As a sample the editor selected these lines from "First Snake in Five Years" by Robert Wrigley:

> *After all, the rattler's half asleep*
> *under the sun and a cool spring breeze,*
> *a green so true he looks to be pure*
> *chlorophyl himself, his taper of rattles closing*
> *on a nub red and swollen*
> *as an in-grown nail . . .*

The editor says *Siren* is 100 pgs., perfect-bound with full-color cover and art. "We receive 200-300 poems a year and usually accept 1%." Press run is 1,400 for 800 shelf sales. **Sample postpaid: $6. Submit 4 poems at a time. No previously published poems or simultaneous submissions. Cover letter required. Reads submissions September 1 through January 15 only. Poems are first read by a staff of 20. Final decisions are made by an editorial board. Seldom comments on rejections. Send SASE for guidelines. Reports in 6 weeks. Pays**

 THE MAPLE LEAF symbol before a listing indicates a Canadian publisher, magazine, conference, contest or organization.

1 copy. **Acquires first rights.** Staff reviews books of poetry and fiction in 900 words, single format. Poets may send books for review consideration. The editor says, "Editors favor authors who have studied other poets as well as their craft."

❀**SISTER VISION PRESS (IV-Ethnic, women)**, P.O. Box 217, Station E, Toronto, Ontario M6H 4E2 Canada, phone (416)533-9353, fax (416)533-9676, founded 1985, managing editor Makeda Silvera, publishes 6-8 paperbacks/year. They want **"poetry that reflects our lives as women of color; not restricted by form or length."** They have recently published poetry by Nikky Finney and Honor Ford-Smith. As a sample the editor selected these lines from "Crebo" in Espinet's book *Nuclear Seasons*:

> *My hands had wrinkles*
> *But rims grew around my eyes*
> *My skin became ebony and rose*
> *And my tongue grew long beyond words*

Submit a sample of work, to a maximum of 10 pages. Previously published poems and simultaneous submissions OK. Cover letter required. Replies to queries in 3 months, to mss (if invited) in 3-6 months. Pays 10% royalties and 10 author's copies. Write for samples. They say, "Know the publisher you are submitting mss to. This saves the poet and publisher time, money and energy."

SISTERS TODAY (II, IV-Spirituality/inspirational), The Liturgical Press, Collegeville MN 56321; phone (320)363-7065, e-mail mwagner@csbsju.edu, send submissions to: poetry editor Sister Mary Virginia Micka, C.S.J., 1884 Randolph, St. Paul MN 55105. *Sisters Today* has been published for about 60 years. Though it is a Roman Catholic magazine, **poetry may be on any topic, but "should clearly be *poems*, not simply *statements* or *prayers*." They want "short poems (not over 25 lines) using clean, fresh images that appeal to the reader's feelings in a compelling way."** They do not want poetry that depends "heavily on rhyme, verbal 'tricks' or excessive capitalization, manipulation of spacing, etc." *ST*, appearing 6 times/year, is 80 pgs., 6×9, saddle-stapled, professionally printed with matte card cover. They receive about 50 poems a month, accept 3-4. Press run is 4,000. Subscription: $22 US; $24 foreign. **Sample postpaid: $4.50 (Send to: Sister Mary Anthony Wagner, O.S.B., Editor, *Sisters Today*, St. Benedict's Monastery, St. Joseph MN 56374). Submit up to 5 poems at a time. No simultaneous submissions. Original poems much preferred. They require "each poem typed on a separate standard-size typing sheet, and each page must carry complete legal name, address and social security number typed in the upper right corner. Manuscripts without SASE will not be returned."** Time between acceptance and publication is 6-12 months. **Send SASE to Collegeville, MN address (above) for guidelines. Reports within 1-2 months. Pays $10/poem and 2 copies. Buys first rights.**

SITUATION (II), 10402 Ewell Ave., Kensington MD 20895, e-mail mdw@gwis2.circ.gwu.edu, founded 1991, contact Mark Wallace, appears 4 times/year and is interested in **"innovative work that explores how writing creates, dismantles, or restructures the possibility of identity. A poetry of situation. Works involving questions of race, class, gender or sexual preference are all encouraged." They want experimental or avant-garde poetry; "less likely to accept poetry in traditional forms."** They have published poetry by Charles Bernstein, Sterling Plumpp, Joan Retallack and Stephen-Paul Martin. As a sample we selected these lines from "Plaid Into Conquest" by Connie Deanovich:

> *the matador imagines*
> *that even an American woman*
> *in a plaid bikini*
> *who was basted with water*
> *from the River Nile*
> *would match the vivaciousness*
> *of his cape*
> *and would similarly use on him*
> *ancient movements of seduction*

Situation is 24 pgs., $7 \times 8\frac{1}{2}$, neatly printed on bond paper, saddle-stapled, no cover. They receive about 200 submissions a year, accept approximately 15%. Press run is 200 for 100 subscribers of which 5 are libraries. Subscription: $10. **Sample postpaid: $3. Make checks payable to Mark Wallace. Submit 7 poems at a time. No previously published poems; simultaneous submissions OK. Cover letter required.** "All submissions **must be accompanied by SASE."** Time between acceptance and publication is usually 6 months. **Seldom comments on rejections. Send SASE for guidelines or request via e-mail. Reports in 3 months. Sometimes sends prepublication galleys. Pays 2 copies. Acquires first rights.**

*****SIVULLINEN (V)**, Kaarelantie 86 B 28, 00420 Helsinki, Finland, founded 1985, editor Jouni Waarakangas, is a biannual publication of drawings, graphics, poems and short stories—**publishes all kinds of poetry. However, "due to enormous amount of poetry submissions received, I have enough poems for a few issues."** They have recently published poetry by Scott C. Holstad, Steven McDaris and William Kopecky. As a sample the editor selected these lines from "The Meaninglessness of Life" by Peter Stavropoulos:

> *The meaninglessness of life*
> *Assumes the absurd has some meaning.*

Am I correct?
Yes, if there is meaning in nothing.
No, if nothing has meaning.

The editor says *Sivullinen* is copied and varies between 28-56 pgs., A4 size and A5 size. They accept about 20% of poetry received. Press run is 500. **Sample postpaid: $2-4. When open to submissions, they accept 3-5 poems at a time. Previously published poems and simultaneous submissions OK.** Time between acceptance and publication is 6 months to 2 years. **Reports in 3-10 weeks. Pays 1 copy.**

‡*SIXTIES PRESS; POETRY NOW NEWSLETTER (III), 89 Connaught Rd., Sutton, Surrey SM1 3PJ England, founded 1995, contact Barry Tebb. Sixties Press aims to "gain acceptance at national/international levels for our poets." They publish **12 chapbooks/year. They want " 'high modernism' in the tradition of Pound and Eliot; lyrical poetry with a high intellectual content. No self-indulgent amateurism or rhyming verse."** They have recently published poetry by Brenda Williams. As a sample Mr. Tebb selected his poem "The Bridge Over the Aire":

And light through chandeliers glows
In a thousand shades, pale carousels
In mystic light begin to turn: we take
Our places for the ride and you are
Ten and I am twelve, your hair is blown
And blown again.

Chapbooks are usually 40 pgs., photocopied from typescript and saddle-stapled with glossy card cover. **Query first, with 6 poems and list of publication credits. Previously published poems and simultaneous submissions OK.** Time between acceptance and publication is 3-6 months. Replies to queries and mss in 1 month. **Pays 24 author's copies (out of a press run of 200). For sample chapbooks, send £4.50 or $10.** They also publish *Poetry Now Newsletter*, a monthly "review of new books of poetry and current poetry magazines; also publishes poems." Mr. Tebb says, "The poets we admire are (among the living) Charles Tomlinson, Lee Harwood and Geoffrey Hill. Intending contributors should aim to come near their standards of excellence!"

SKIPPING STONES: A MULTICULTURAL CHILDREN'S MAGAZINE (I, II, IV-Bilingual, children/ teen, ethnic/nationality, nature/ecology, social issues), P.O. Box 3939, Eugene OR 97403, phone (541)342-4956, founded 1988, editor Arun Toké, is a "nonprofit magazine published bimonthly during the school year (5 issues) that encourages cooperation, creativity and celebration of cultural and environmental richness." **They want poetry by youth under 18; 30 lines maximum on "nature, multicultural and social issues, family, freedom . . . uplifting." No work by adults.** As a sample we selected these lines from "The Sound and Rhythm of the Drum" by Alexander Harvey, age 10, from Washington, DC:

The rhythm is as natural as laying eggs is to a chicken
My great ancestors of the past, all heard the rhythm of the drum.
It's sounds are as beautiful
As a pack of wild horses running on the great plains.

Our ancestors have struggled to grow.
When our ancestors spirits are low and bum
It lifts us up far into the sun.
That's the rhythm and sound, of the drum.

SS is 8½×11, saddle-stitched, printed on recycled paper. They receive about 500-1,000 poems a year, accept approximately 10%. Press run is 3,000 for 1,700 subscribers. Subscription: $25. **Sample postpaid: $5. Submit up to 3 poems at a time. No previously published poems; simultaneous submissions OK. Cover letter preferred. "Include your cultural background, experiences and what was the inspiration behind your creation."** Time between acceptance and publication is 3-9 months. **Poems are circulated to a 3-member editorial board. "Generally a piece is chosen for publication when all the editorial staff feel good about it." Seldom comments on rejections. Publishes theme issues. Send SASE for guidelines and upcoming themes. Theme for October '97 is "How I'm Making A Difference." Reports in 2-4 months. Pays 1 copy, offers 25% discount on 4 or more. Acquires all rights. Returns rights after publication, but "we keep reprint rights."** Sponsors Annual Youth Honor Awards for 7-16 year olds. Deadline: June 20. Entry fee: $3, includes free issue containing the winners. *Skipping Stones* received a 1995 Golden Shoestring Award from Ed Press.

SKYLARK (I, II, IV-Themes), Purdue University Calumet, 2200 169th St., Hammond IN 46323, phone (219)989-2262, fax (219)989-2581, founded 1972, editor-in-chief Pamela Hunter, poetry editor Christine Shrader, is "a fine arts annual, **one section (about 25 pages) of which is devoted to a special theme.**" They are looking for **"fresh voices, original images, concise presentation and honesty; poems up to 25 lines; narrative poems to 75 lines. No horror, nothing extremely religious, no pornography." They are also interested in receiving more prose poems and more well-crafted surrealistic poems.** They have recently published poetry by Louis Bourgeois, Earl Coleman, Ray Greenblatt, Monika Lee and Francine Witte. As a sample the editor selected these lines from "Of Empires and Kazoos" by Brian Forry Wallace:

> *But all the armies*
> *of all the empires*
> *have no power compared to*
> *the grace*
> *of the smile*
> *of a boy with a kazoo.*

Skylark is 100 pgs., magazine-sized, professionally printed, perfect-bound, with matte card cover. Press run is 900-1,000 for 50 subscribers of which 12 are libraries. Single copy: $8. **Sample postpaid: $6. Submit 3-5 poems at a time. "Cover letter encouraged. No simultaneous submissions. Inquire (with SASE) as to annual theme for special section."** Fax submissions OK followed by SASE within 2 weeks. The theme for 1998 is "Old Age." Do not submit mss between June 1 and November 1. Reports in 4 months. Pays 1 copy. Acquires first rights. Editor may encourage rejected but promising writers. She says she would like to receive "poems with better editing, greater coordination of form and content, and sharper, more original imagery."

SLANT: A JOURNAL OF POETRY (II), Box 5063, University of Central Arkansas, 201 Donaghey Ave., Conway AR 72035-5000, phone (501)450-5107, founded 1987, editor James Fowler, is an annual using *only* poetry. They use **"traditional and 'modern' poetry, even experimental, moderate length, any subject on approval of Board of Readers; purpose is to publish a journal of fine poetry from all regions of the United States. No haiku, no translations."** They have recently published poetry by Gay Brewer, Twyla Hansen and John Sokol. As a sample the editor selected these lines from "The Bishop of Lincoln Visits Fecamp Abbey, Normandy, 1185" by Robert Cooperman:

> *When I beheld the arm bone*
> *of our blessed Magdalene—*
> *a lesson to all fallen women*
> *to rise above their oozing loins—*
> *I fell to my knees*
> *and kissed the relic;*
> *then I bit into the bone*
> *to carry back a sliver*
> *for my own cathedral.*

Slant is 125 pgs., professionally printed on quality stock, flat-spined, with matte card cover. They receive about 1,400 poems a year, accept approximately 70-80. Press run is 200 for 70-100 subscribers. **Sample postpaid: $10. Submit up to 5 poems of moderate length with SASE. "Put name, address and phone on the top of each page." No simultaneous submissions or previously published poems. Editor comments on rejections "on occasion."** Allow 3-4 months from November 15 deadline for response. **Pays 1 copy.** The editor says, "I would like to see more formal verse."

SLATE & STYLE (IV-Specialized: blind writers), Dept. PM, 2704 Beach Dr., Merrick NY 11566, phone (516)868-8718, fax (516)868-9076, editor Loraine Stayer, is a **quarterly for blind writers available on cassette, in large print and Braille,** "including articles of interest to blind writers, resources for blind writers. Membership/subscription is $10 per year, all formats. Division of the National Federation of the Blind." **Poems may be "5-36 lines. Prefer contributors to be blind writers, or at least writers by profession or inclination, but prefer poems *not* about blindness. No obscenities. Will consider all forms of poetry including haiku. Interested in new talent."** They have published poetry by Stephanie Pieck, Louise Hope Bristow, Janet Wolff and Ken Volonte. As a sample the editor selected these lines from "To Matthew" by M.J. Lord:

> *I feel your hand reach out to me.*
> *A velvety soft palm and tiny fingers*
> *reach through my skin,*
> *grab my hand with an amazing strength.*
> *Your father lies beside me,*
> *as he dreams of your premature birth.*

The print version is 28-32 pgs., magazine-sized, stapled, with a fiction and poetry section. Press run is 200 for 160 subscribers of which 4-5 are libraries. Subscription: $10/year. **Sample postpaid: $2.50. Submit 3 poems once or twice a year. No simultaneous submissions or previously published poems. Cover letter preferred.** "On occasion we receive poems in Braille. I prefer print, since Braille slows me down. Typed is best." **Fax submissions OK. Do not submit mss in July. Editor comments on rejections "if requested." Send SASE for guidelines. Reports in "two weeks if I like it." Pays 1 copy.** Reviews books of poetry. Open to unsolicited reviews. Poets may also send books for review consideration. They offer an annual poetry contest. Entry fee: $5/poem. Deadline: May 1. Write for details. Loraine Stayer says, "Poetry is one of the toughest ways to express oneself, yet ought to be the easiest to read. Anything that looks simple is the result of much work."

SLIPSTREAM (II, IV-Themes), Box 2071, New Market Station, Niagara Falls NY 14301-0071, phone (716)282-2616 (after 5PM, EST), founded 1980, poetry editors Dan Sicoli, Robert Borgatti and Livio Farallo. *Slipstream* is a "small press literary mag that is about 90% poetry and 10% fiction/prose, some artwork. The editors like **new work with contemporary urban flavor. Writing must have a cutting edge to get our atten-**

tion. We like to keep an open forum, any length, subject, style. Best to see a sample to get a feel. Like city stuff as opposed to country. Like poetry that springs from the gut, screams from dark alleys, inspired by experience." No "pastoral, religious, traditional, rhyming" poetry. They have published poetry by Gerald Locklin, Joan Jobe Smith, Charles Bukowski, Jim MiKoley, A.D. Winans, B.D. Love and E.R. Baxter III. As a sample the editors selected these lines from "Of Your Boyfriend's Attack and St. Vincent's Hospital" by Stephanie Dickinson:

> For days while oxygen fills your lung
> you watch television talk shows.
> On the air conditioning vent
> your chilled piss sits
> next to his long-stemmed roses.

Slipstream appears 1-2 times a year in a 7 × 8½ format, 80-100 pgs., professionally printed, perfect-bound, using b&w photos and graphics. It contains mostly free verse, some stanza patterns. They receive over 2,500 submissions of poetry a year, use less than 10%. Press run is 500 for 400 subscribers of which 10 are libraries. Subscription: $15/2 issues and 2 chapbooks. **Sample postpaid: $6. Editor sometimes comments on rejections. Publishes theme issues. Send SASE for guidelines and upcoming themes. Theme for 1997 is "Mens Room/ Ladies Room." Reports in 2-8 weeks, "if SASE included." Pays 1-3 copies.** Annual chapbook contest has December 1 deadline. Reading fee: $10. Submit up to 40 pgs. of poetry, any style, previously published work OK with acknowledgments. Winner receives $500 and 50 copies. All entrants receive copy of winning chapbook and an issue of the magazine. Past winners have included Gerald Locklin, Serena Fusek, Robert Cooperman, Kurt Nimmo, David Chorlton, Richard Amidon, Sherman Alexie, Kathatine Harer, and most recently, Matt Buys for his book *The Nietzche Itinerary*. Dan Sicoli advises, "Do not waste time submitting your work 'blindly.' Sample issues from the small press first to determine which ones would be most receptive to your work."

‡SLUGFEST, LTD. (I), P.O. Box 1238, Simpsonville SC 29681, founded 1991, contact M.T. Nowak, publishes **2 chapbooks/year. They want "any type of poetry, less than 3 pages or 300 lines. No pornographic or bad work."** They have recently published poetry by Conti, Semenovich, Nowak and Arnold. Chapbooks are usually about 60 pgs., 5½ × 8½. **Submit 3-5 poems at a time. Previously published poems and simultaneous submissions OK.** Time between acceptance and publication is 3-6 months. **Poems are circulated to an editorial board. Reports in 1-4 weeks. Always comments on rejections. Pays 1 copy. Send SASE for more details.**

SMALL POND MAGAZINE OF LITERATURE (II), P.O. Box 664, Stratford CT 06497, phone (203)378-4066, founded 1964, editor Napoleon St. Cyr, a literary triquarterly that features poetry . . . "and anything else the editor feels is original, important." Poetry can be **"any style, form, topic, except haiku, so long as it is deemed good, but limit of about 100 lines."** Napoleon St. Cyr wants **"nothing about cats, pets, flowers, butterflies, etc. Generally nothing under eight lines."** Although he calls it name-dropping, he "reluctantly" provided the names of Marvin Soloman, Marilyn Johnson, Richard Kostelanetz, Fritz Hamilton and Emilie Glen as poets published. The magazine is 40 pgs., digest-sized, offset from typescript on off-white paper, with matte card cover, saddle-stapled, artwork both on cover and inside. Circulation is 300, of which about a third go to libraries. Subscription: $9/3 issues. **Sample (including guidelines) postpaid: $2.50 for a random selection, $3.50 current. The editor says he doesn't want 60 pages of anything; "dozen pages of poems max." Name and address on each page. No previously published poems or simultaneous submissions. Brief cover letter preferred.** Time between acceptance and publication is within 3-18 months. **Reports in 10-45 days (longer in summer). Pays 2 copies. Acquires all rights. Returns rights with written request including stated use. "One-time use per request."** All styles and forms are welcome here. The editor usually responds quickly, often with comments to guide poets whose work interests him. He says, "I would like to receive more good surreal verse."

SMALL PRESS GENRE ASSOCIATION (SPGA); THE GENRE WRITER'S NEWS (IV-Membership, science fiction/fantasy, horror, mystery, westerns), P.O. Box 6301, Concord CA 94524, phone (510)254-7442 or 7053, editor Bobbi Sinha-Morey, assistant editor Joe Morey. The association publishes a quarterly digest with emphasis on aiding members, advice columns, short poetry, art, reviews and short fiction; provides a poetry commentary service for members only; and publishes a yearly anthology of members' work. **They don't want to see "religious, highly sentimental, pornographic, racial or political poetry."** They have recently published poetry by J.W. Donnelly and Nancy Bennett. As a sample they selected these lines from "Transcendence" by Brandon Totman:

> While the bluebird of death
> stitches her wounds with string-meat cherry,
> I move from cocoon to spider's web
> my buttered lips eager to decorate
> her soft eggs with dark magnolia kisses.

Send all poetry submissions to Bobbi Sinha-Morey, 30 Canyon View Dr., Orinda CA 94563. Staff reviews books of poetry in 200-500 words, single format. The Small Press Genre Association promotes "excellence in writing, illustration, calligraphy, editing, and publication of material related to the literary genres of fantasy, sword and sorcery, horror, western, mystery, weird, or science fiction." Membership is open to any writer, poet, artist, editor, publisher or calligrapher involved in the above genres. Dues are $25 for US members, $30 for members outside

US. For more information or to join, send SASE to *The Genre Writer's News* at the above Concord address.

THE SMITH; THE GENERALIST PAPERS (II), 69 Joralemon St., Brooklyn NY 11201-4003, founded 1964, editor Harry Smith, publishes 3 to 5 books yearly. They have published *Poems New & Selected 1962-1992* by Lloyd Van Brunt and *Matriarch* by Glenna Luschei. As a sample the editor selected these lines from "White" in David Rigsbee's *Your Heart Will Fly Away*:

> *No longer the nosy curator*
> *of my own dusty museum,*
> *I have become philosophical.*
> *Each reduction enriches me*
> *like a quarry into which*
> *the weather loves to come.*

"Send three to six poem sampling with query. No jingles, no standard academic verse. The decision process is relatively slow—about three months—as many mss are offered. Readers' reports are often passed along and the editor often comments." Always sends prepublication galleys. Pays 15% royalties, $500 advance, 10 copies. Send SASE for catalog or send $3 for a "slightly irregular" book ("with bumped corners or a little dust"). *The Generalist Papers*, appearing 6 times/year, consists of lively critical commentaries on contemporary writing—more candor than you will find in most reviews. Subscription: $12. **Sample postpaid: $2.** Harry Smith received a Poor Richard Award, a lifetime achievement award for distinguished contribution to small press publishing from the Small Press Center. He advises, "Revert to earlier models. *Avoid* university wordshops where there are standard recent models leading to standard mod verse. A close reading of *The Pearl Poet* will be more nourishing than all the asparagus of John Ashbery or Robert Bly."

GIBBS SMITH, PUBLISHER; PEREGRINE SMITH POETRY COMPETITION (III), P.O. Box 667, Layton UT 84041-0667, founded 1971, poetry series established 1988, poetry editor Gail Yngve. **They want "serious, contemporary poetry of merit."** They have recently published *Buying Breakfast for My Kamikaze Pilot* by Norman Stock, and *1-800-HOT-RIBS* and *Rock Farm* by Catherine Bowman. Books are selected for publication through competition for the Peregrine Smith Poetry Prize of $500 plus publication. **Entries are received in April only and require a $15 reading fee and SASE. Mss should be 48-64 typewritten pgs. "We publish only one unsolicited poetry ms per year—the winner of our annual Peregrine Smith Poetry Contest. For guidelines to the contest, interested poets should send a request with SASE through the mail."** The winner of the 1995 contest was H.L. Hix's *Perfect Hell*. The judge and general editor for the series is Christopher Merrill.

*SMITHS KNOLL (I, II), 49 Church Rd., Little Glemham, Woodbridge, Suffolk IP13 0BJ England, founded 1991, co-editors Roy Blackman and Michael Laskey, is a magazine appearing 3 times/year. They look for **poetry with honesty, depth of feeling, lucidity and craft.** As a sample the editors selected these lines from "At the End of the Killing Line" by Peter Wyton:

> *Places I seldom go, if I can help it: 1. Upstairs,*
> *where there are people in suits. 2. The opposite end*
> *of the killing line, where pigs are individually*
> *stampeded through a channel, underneath a rusted stile,*
> *where the man stands with the fag hanging from his lip,*
> *one eye closed, the long mallet arcing over and down.*

Smiths Knoll is 60 pgs., A5, offset-litho, perfect-bound, with 2-color card cover. They receive 8,000-10,000 poems a year, "accept about one in fifty." Press run is 450 for 300 subscribers. Single copy: £3.50; subscription: £10/3 issues (outside UK). **Submit up to 5 poems at a time. "We would consider poems previously published in magazines outside the U.K." No simultaneous submissions. Poems only. Doesn't commission work. "Cover letters should be brief: name, address, date, number of poems sent (or titles). We don't want life histories or complete publishing successes or what the poems are about. We do want sufficient IRCs for return of work. Constructive criticism of rejections where possible." Tries to report within 1 month (outside UK). Pays £5 plus 1 copy/poem.**

‡SNAKE NATION REVIEW; SNAKE NATION PRESS (II), 110 W. Force St., #2, Valdosta GA 31601, phone (912)249-8334, founded 1989, editor Roberta George, appears 4 times/year (2 contest issues, 2 noncontest issues). **"Any form, length of 60 lines or less."** They have published poetry by Hunt Hawkins, Penelope Schott

---

 AN ASTERISK before a listing indicates an overseas publisher, magazine, contest, conference or organization.

and David Kirby. The handsome magazine is 100 pgs., 6×9, flat-spined with matte card cover. Press run is 1,500 for 300 subscribers of which 25 are libraries. Subscription: $20. **Sample postpaid: $6. Sometimes comments on submissions. Send SASE for guidelines. Reports in 3 months. Pays $10 plus 2 copies. Deadlines: January 1 and June 1. Acquires first rights.** The review sponsors biannual contests with prizes of $100, $75 and $50 for the top three winners. Others published in contest issues receive $10. Entry fee: $1/poem. Deadlines: April 1 and September 1. Poets published in noncontest issues are eligible for the Editor's Choice Award. Prize of $100 is given to the top poem. Snake Nation Press publishes books of poetry. Submit 60-page ms with SASE. The press also sponsors the Violet Reed Haas Poetry Prize which awards $500, 50 copies and distribution to the winning book ms. For contest consideration, submit 75-page ms with $10 entry fee. Deadline: April 15, 1996.

SNAKE RIVER REFLECTIONS (II), 1863 Bitterroot Dr., Twin Falls ID 83301, phone (208)734-0746, e-mail william@micron.net, editor William White, appears 10 times/year using **short poems, up to 30 lines, any topic.** As a sample we selected these lines from "Christmas Past" by C. David Hay:

> The ghosts of cherished loved ones;
> They live and always will,
> For no one ever dies in
> The place where time stands still.
>
> The treasured scenes of yesteryear—
> Could prayer but make them last.
> Traditions of the heart live on
> In dreams of Christmas Past.

It is 8 pgs. (2 8½×11 sheets folded), printed on colored paper and saddle-stapled. Press run is 100-300. Subscription: $8.50/10 issues. **Sample postpaid: 30¢. Submit 5-10 poems at a time. No previously published poems or simultaneous submissions. Cover letter encouraged. Send SASE for guidelines. Pays 1 copy. Acquires first North American serial rights.** Reviews books of poetry. Send books for review consideration.

‡❀SNOWAPPLE PRESS (II), P.O. Box 66024, Heritage Postal Outlet, Edmonton, Alberta T6J 6T4 Canada, phone (403)437-0191, founded 1991, editor Vanna Tessier, is an "independent publisher dedicated to writers who wish to contribute to literature." They publish 4-5 paperbacks/year. **They want "contemporary, expansive, experimental and literary poetry."** They have recently published poetry by Gilberto Finzi, Peter Prest, Vanna Tessier and Paolo Valesio. As a sample the editor selected these lines from "Ice Fog" (poet unidentified):

> Snow braids Lodgepole pines, frost blooming lace flowers,
> Tires scrape ice raw, exhaust fumes
> The breath of a season etching ice fog, bleaching the sky
> Crystal rainbow, vision of sugar and plum.

Books are usually 120-160 pgs., offset printed with #10 colored card cover with "art/graphics suitable to theme." **Submit 5 poems at a time, 14-75 lines each. Previously published poems and simultaneous submissions OK. Cover letter preferred. Reads submissions September through March 31 only.** Time between acceptance and publication is 12-18 months. **Poems are circulated to an editorial board. Replies in 3-4 weeks. Pays 10% royalty, $100 honorarium and 25 author's copies (out of a press run of 500).** Sponsors an occasional anthology contest. The 1998 contest anthology is called *Undercurrents: An Anthology of International Poetry*. Submit up to 5 typed poems of 14-75 lines. Entry fee: $25. Deadline: November 30, 1997. Send SASE (or SAE and IRC) for guidelines and entry form.

SNOWY EGRET (II, IV-Nature), P.O. Box 9, Bowling Green IN 47833, founded 1922 by Humphrey A. Olsen, editor Philip Repp. **They want poetry that is "nature-oriented: poetry that celebrates the abundance and beauty of nature or explores the interconnections between nature and the human psyche."** As a sample they selected the opening lines of "In a Climax Forest" by Conrad Hilberry:

> The wooden past grows larger, I grow less
> and less convincing in this sullen air
> that wants a wind to stir its emptiness.

Snowy Egret appears twice a year in a 48-page, magazine-sized format, offset, saddle-stapled, with original graphics. They receive about 500 poems a year, accept approximately 20. Press run is 800 for 500 subscribers of which 50 are libraries. **Sample postpaid: $8. Send #10 SASE for writer's guidelines. Reports in 1 month. Always sends prepublication galleys. Pays $4/poem or $4/page plus 2 copies. Buys first North American or reprint rights.** Open to unsolicited reviews. Poets may also send books for review consideration.

‡SO YOUNG!; ANTI-AGING PRESS, INC. (I), P.O. Box 141489, Coral Gables FL 33114, phone (305)662-3928, fax (305)661-4123, e-mail julia@icanect.net, founded 1992 press, 1996 newsletter, editor Julia Busch. *So Young!* is a bimonthly newsletter publishing "anti-aging/holistic health/humorous/philosophical topics geared to a youthful body, attitude and spirit." **They want "short, upbeat, romantic, fresh, positive poetry. The newsletter is dedicated to a youthful body, face, mind and spirit. Work can be humorous, philosophical fillers. No off color, suggestive poems or anything relative to first night, or unrequited love affairs."** *So Young!* is 12 pgs., 8½×11 (11×17 sheets folded), unbound. They receive several hundred poems a year, use approximately

6-12. Press run is 700 for 500 subscribers. Subscription: $20. **Sample postpaid: $4. Submit up to 10 poems at a time. Previously published poems and simultaneous submissions OK. Cover letter preferred.** Time between acceptance and publication "depends on poem subject matter—usually 6-8 months." **Send SASE for guidelines. Reports in 2 months. Pays 10 copies. Acquires one-time rights.**

THE SOCIETY OF AMERICAN POETS (SOAP); IN HIS STEPS PUBLISHING COMPANY; THE POET'S PEN (I, II, IV-Religious), P.O. Box 750, Millen GA 30442, phone (912)982-1537, fax (912)982-1526, e-mail drrev@msn.com, website http://www.geocites.com/Athens/7283, founded 1984, editor Dr. Charles E. Cravey. *The Poet's Pen* is a literary quarterly of poetry and short stories. In His Steps publishes religious and other books and publishes music for the commercial record market. **"Open to all styles of poetry and prose—both religious and secular. No gross or 'X-rated' poetry without taste or character."** They have published poetry by James Pecquet, Claudette Clarke and Kelly Martin. As a sample the editor selected these lines from "Poetry Garden" by Najwa Salam Brax:

> *I step into your poetry garden*
> *with graceful pace; your emotions are spread*
> *as weird paintings sprouting up in Eden.*
> *I smell your luscious words as wine and bread.*

The Poet's Pen uses **poetry primarily by members and subscribers, but outside submissions are also welcomed.** (Membership: $25/year.) **Submit 3 poems at a time, include name and address on each page. "Submissions or inquiries will not be responded to without a SASE. We do stress originality and have each new poet and/or subscriber sign a waiver form verifying originality." Simultaneous submissions OK; previously published poems OK, if permission from previous publisher is included. E-mail submissions OK. Publishes seasonal/theme issues. Send SASE for upcoming themes or obtain via e-mail or website. Sometimes sends prepublication galleys. Query for book publication. 60/40 split of pay. Editor "most certainly" comments on rejections.** Sponsors several contests each quarter which total $250-500 in cash awards. Editor's Choice Awards each quarter, prizes $50, $25 and $15. President's Award for Superior Choice has a prize of $50; deadline is November 1. They also publish a quarterly anthology that has poetry competitions in several categories with prizes of $25-100. The editor says, "We're looking for poets who wish to unite in fellowship with our growing family of poets nationwide. We currently have over 850 poets and are one of the nation's largest societies, yet small enough and family operated to give each of our poets individual attention and pointers."

SOJOURNERS (IV-Religious, political), 2401 15th St. NW, Washington DC 20009, phone (202)328-8842, fax (202)328-8757, founded 1975, poetry editor Rose Berger, appears 6 times/year, "with approximately 40,000 subscribers. **We focus on faith, politics and culture from a radical Christian perspective. We publish one to three poems/month depending on length. All poems must be original and unpublished. We look for seasoned, well-crafted poetry that reflects the issues and perspectives covered in our magazine. We highly discourage simplistic, rhyming poetry. Poetry using non-inclusive language (any racist, sexist, homophobic poetry) will not be accepted."** The editor describes *Sojourners* as 52 pgs., offset printed. It appears bimonthly. They receive about 400 poems a year, accept approximately 6-8. Press run is 50,000 for 40,000 subscribers of which 500 are libraries, 2,000 shelf sales. Subscription: $30. **Sample postpaid: $3.95. Submit up to 3 poems at a time. Cover letter with brief bio required. Editor comments on submissions "sometimes." Publishes theme issues. Send SASE for guidelines and upcoming themes. Reports in 4-6 weeks. Pays $15-25/poem plus 5 copies. "We assume permission to grant reprints unless the author requests otherwise."** Staff reviews books of poetry in 600 words, single or multi-book format.

SOLO FLYER; SPARE CHANGE POETRY PRESS (III), 2115 Clearview NE, Massillon OH 44646-2003, e-mail mccoy@eznets.canton.oh.us, Spare Change Poetry Press founded 1979, editor David B. McCoy. *Solo Flyer* is a 4-page flyer appearing 2-5 times/year featuring the work of a single poet in each issue. They want **poetry using punctuation and capitalization. "Like to see poems with a common theme and more prose poems."** The flyers are folded 8½×11 sheets of colored paper. **Sample free with #10 SASE. Previously published material OK. Submissions and requests accepted via e-mail. Pays 20-25 copies.** The editor says, "Mail submissions without SASE are not read."

‡✤**SONO NIS PRESS (III)**, 1725 Blanshard St., Victoria, British Columbia V8W 2J8 Canada, phone (604)382-1024, founded 1968, contact the editor, publishes 2 paperbacks/year. "We publish contemporary poetry, usually 2 mss a year, and 6-8 nonfiction titles (predominantly history)." **They want "75 pages minimum; literature not limerick; connected or isolated poems acceptable. No rhyming ballads; haiku or religious verse."** They have recently published poetry by Robert Bringhurst, Christopher Wiseman and Charles Lillard. As a sample the editor selected these lines from "November" in *Dream Museum* by Liliane Welch:

> *Tucked into sleep's thick fur,*
> *The fetishes of summer recede.*
> *A lone car creeps home*
> *to quiet times*
> *over ice-patched, empty roads*

Books are usually 80-120 pgs., 6×9 with laminated color cover. **Previously published poems OK, "if magazine** publication only"; simultaneous submissions OK. Cover letter preferred. "Hard copy traditional submission only. No faxed submissions. Brief bio information and publication history helpful." Time between acceptance and publication is 14 months. **Replies to queries in 2 months; to mss in 3 months. Pays "10% of suggested list for all books sold at normal discounts, 10% of net if deep discount," plus 10 author's copies (out of a press run of 600). For sample books, order direct or check local library.** The editor says, "We are publishing only two poetry books a year—usually one established poet and one new poet. We almost never publish non-Canadians as the marketing is difficult. We are finding it harder and harder to publish limited market books. Promotion oriented authors can be a bonus."

SONORA REVIEW (II), Dept. of English, University of Arizona, Tucson AZ 85721, founded 1980, address all work to Poetry Editor, is a semiannual literary journal that publishes "non-genre" fiction and poetry. **The editors want "quality poetry, literary concerns. Translations welcome. No dull, well-crafted but passionless poetry. Experimental work welcome."** They have published poetry by James Tate, Thomas Lux and Alison Deming. As a sample, the editors chose the following lines by Kathleen McCarthy:

> . . . *You will emerge*
> *from your own intuition as a tablet dissolves in water:*
> *a solid blue dot drowning in the bottom of a glass*
>
> *and a white fog trailing where it leaves itself.*

Sonora Review is a handsome magazine, 130 pgs., 6×9, professionally printed on heavy off-white stock, flat-spined, with 2-color glossy card cover. Recent issues have tended to include lyric and narrative free verse, with some metered poetry, translations and sequences rounding out selections. Circulation is 1,000 for 350 subscribers of which 45 are libraries. Subscription: $12/year, $22/2 years. **Sample postpaid: $5. Submit typed copy. Simultaneous submissions OK. "Brief cover letter helpful but optional." Occasionally publishes theme issues. Reports in 3 months.** Time between acceptance and publication is 6 months. **Sometimes sends prepublication galleys. Pays 2 copies.** Send books for review consideration. The magazine also sponsors annual poetry awards. Send #10 SASE for deadlines and guidelines. In the past, contributors to *Sonora Review* have been listed in *Best of the West*, *Pushcart Prize*, *O. Henry* and *Best American Poetry* anthologies.

‡SOUNDINGS EAST (II), Salem State College, Salem MA 01970, phone (508)741-6000 ext. 2403 or 741-6270, founded 1978, "*SE* is published by the students of Salem State College. We accept short fiction and **contemporary poetry.** Purpose is to promote poetry and fiction in the college and beyond its environs. Although our standards are extremely high, **we publish both established and previously unpublished writers and artists. All forms of poetry welcome."** *SE* appears twice a year, 64 pgs., digest-sized, flat-spined, b&w drawings and photos, glossy card cover with b&w photo. They receive about 500 submissions a year, use approximately 40-50. Press run is 2,000 for 120 subscribers of which 35 are libraries. Subscription: $10/year. **Sample postpaid: $5. Submit 5 poems at a time. Simultaneous submissions OK with notification. Be prompt when notifying *SE* that the work(s) was accepted elsewhere. Reads submissions September 1 through April 20 only. Fall deadline: November 20; spring: April 20. Reports within 1-4 months. Pays 2 copies. Rights revert to author upon publication.** "We occasionally, when funding allows, publish an extra spring issue which features only poetry, fiction and artwork by Salem State College students."

‡THE SOUNDS OF POETRY; COFFEE CUP LIMITED EDITION; THE LATINO POETS ASSOCIATION (II, III), 2076 Vinewood, Detroit MI 48216-5506, founded 1983, publisher/editor Jacqueline Rae Sanchez. *The Sounds of Poetry* is published 3 times/year to "promote throughout the world an awareness (through poetry) that we are quite diverse, yet the same. We all love, hurt, laugh and suffer. **We are open to all types of poetry with substance, grit, feeling; prefer one column and/or shorter poetry. Always in need of fillers. Do not want to see fluff nor porn, although light erotica is acceptable."** They have recently published poetry by Trinidad Sanchez Jr., Duffy De France, Rene Cardenas and Bernard Hewitt. The publisher says *SOP* is 16-24 pgs., 8½×11, offset-printed, saddle-stitched, "covers are usually photographs." They receive several hundred poems a year, use approximately 50-98/issue. Press run is 200 for 60 subscribers of which 10 are libraries. Subscription: $8. **Sample postpaid: $2.50; $3.50 back issue. Submit 5 poems at a time. Previously published poems OK; prefer no simultaneous submissions. Cover letter preferred. "Please type poems, handwritten poems will be returned. If necessary use one 8½×11 sheet for several short poems instead of several smaller sheets. Name and current address on all pages submitted." Reads submissions January through October.** Time between acceptance and publication can be from several months to a couple years. **Seldom comments on rejections. Publishes theme issues. Send SASE for guidelines and upcoming themes. Reports in 1-6 months. Pays 1 copy to contributor, 2 to subscriber/contributor.** Staff will review books/chapbooks of 100 pages or less. "We do not review excerpts of books/chapbooks." Open to unsolicited reviews. Poets may also send books for review consideration; "mark 'Review Copy' and enclose cover letter." Also publishes *Coffee Cup Limited Edition*, which appears 3 times/year. *CCLE* is 24 pgs., digest-sized, desk-top published, saddle-stitched. Press run is 200. Subscription: $8. Ms. Sanchez, the publisher, is also director of The Latino Poets Association which meets the last Thursday of each month at the Bowen Branch Library, 3648 W. Vernor, Detroit MI 48216. Open to all poets. For more information call (313)297-9381, ask for Ken Miller. She says, "Write poetry using the knowledge you have, research and expand, add your own feelings, emotions then take that same poetry to your ultimate heights. Write and rewrite. Read new poets. Listen to other poets. Attend poetry readings. Participate in open-mike readings, get feedback from other older poets."

‡SOUR GRAPES: THE NEWSLETTER FOR REJECTED WRITERS AND OTHER TORMENTED SOULS (V, IV-Specialized), 26 Sheridan St., Woburn MA 01801-3542, e-mail sandyberns@aol.com, website http://members.aol.com/sgrapes/index.htm, founded 1995, co-editor/publisher Sandy Bernstein, published quarterly, is "dedicated to the discouraged, disgruntled, disillusioned and dejected writers of the universe." They have recently published poetry by Julianne Toomey, Mike Nowak and Paul Angelosanto. *Sour Grapes* is 16 pgs., 8½×5½, photocopied, saddle-stitched, with colored paper cover, interior art and exchange ads. Accept approximately 10% of the submissions they receive. Press run is 70-100; 10-20 distributed free to other publications and contributors. Subscription: $7.75. **Sample (including guidelines) postpaid: $1.95. Make checks payable to Sandy Bernstein. Query first. They are currently not accepting unsolicited mss. Backlog is large. "Only submissions that follow our guidelines are seriously considered by the two editors." Often comments on rejections. Send SASE for guidelines. Reports in 2 months. Pays 1 copy. Rights revert back to authors after publication.**

SOUTH ASH PRESS (I, II), 2311 E. Indian School Rd., Phoenix AZ 85016, founded 1991, publisher Chuck Hadd Jr., is a monthly poetry magazine sustained and distributed by community advertisers. **They want "well-crafted poems by beginning and established poets. 75 lines maximum."** They have published poetry by Denis Johnson. *South Ash Press* is 12 pgs., magazine-sized, saddle-stapled with card cover with b&w photo, numerous ads on same pages as poems. They receive about 1,500 poems a year, publish about 250. Each issue includes a number of poems by a "Featured Poet." Press run is 2,000, distributed free through advertisers. Subscription: $20/year. **Sample postpaid: $2. Submit up to 5 poems at a time. One poem to a page including name and address. No previously published poems; simultaneous submissions OK. "We do not provide critiques and/ or advice." Reports in 4-6 months. Pays 1 copy. Acquires first rights.**

SOUTH CAROLINA REVIEW (II), English Dept., 801 Strode Tower, Clemson University, Box 341503, Clemson SC 29634-1503, phone (803)656-5404 or 656-3457, fax (803)656-1345, founded 1968, managing editor Frank Day, is a biannual literary magazine "recognized by the *New York Quarterly* as one of the top 20 of this type." They will consider **"any kind of poetry as long as it's good. No stale metaphors, uncertain rhythms or lack of line integrity. Interested in seeing more traditional forms. Format should be according to new MLA Stylesheet."** They have published poetry by Pattiann Rogers, J.W. Rivers and Claire Bateman. It is 200 pgs., 6×9, professionally printed, flat-spined and uses about 8-10 pgs. of poetry in each issue. Reviews of recent issues back up editorial claims that all styles and forms are welcome; moreover, poems were accessible and well-executed. Circulation is 600, for 400 subscribers of which 250 are libraries. They receive about 1,000 submissions of poetry a year, use approximately 10, have a 2-year backlog. **Sample postpaid: $10. Submit 3-10 poems at a time in an "8×10 manila envelope so poems aren't creased." No previously published poems or simultaneous submissions. "Editor prefers a chatty, personal cover letter plus a list of publishing credits." Do not submit during June, July, August or December. Publishes theme issues. Reports in 6-9 months. Pays copies.** Staff reviews books of poetry.

SOUTH DAKOTA REVIEW (II, IV-Regional, themes), University of South Dakota, Vermillion SD 57069, phone (605)677-5229 or 677-5966, founded 1963, editor Brian Bedard, is a "literary quarterly publishing poetry, fiction, criticism, scholarly and personal essays. **When material warrants, an emphasis on the American West; writers from the West; Western places or subjects; frequent issues with no geographical emphasis; periodic special issues on one theme, or one place or one writer. Looking for originality, some kind of sophistication, significance, craft—i.e., professional work."** They use 10-15 poems/issue, "receive tons, it seems." Press run is 500-600 for 450 subscribers of which half are libraries. Subscription: $18/year, $30/2 years. **Sample postpaid: $4. Editor comments on submissions "occasionally." Reports in 6-8 weeks. Pays 2-3 copies and 1-year subscription. Acquires first and reprint rights.** They have a distinct bias against "stream-of-consciousness gibberish," confessional poems, and generally publish free verse with a strong sense of place, a strong voice and a universal theme. Read the magazine—it's attractive and well-edited—to get a feel for the type of poetry that succeeds here. The editor advises, "Find universal meaning in the regional. Avoid constant 'I' personal experiences that are not of interest to anyone else. Learn to be less self-centered and more inclusive of others."

THE SOUTHERN CALIFORNIA ANTHOLOGY (III, IV-Anthology); ANN STANFORD POETRY PRIZES (III), c/o Master of Professional Writing Program, WPH 404, University of Southern California, Los Angeles CA 90089-4034, phone (213)740-3252, founded 1983, is an "annual literary review of serious contemporary poetry and fiction. **Very open to all subject matters except pornography. Any form, style OK."** They have published poetry by Robert Bly, Donald Hall, Maxine Kumin, John Updike, Denise Levertov and Amiri Baraka. The anthology is 144 pgs., digest-sized, perfect-bound, with a semi-glossy color cover featuring one art piece. A fine selection of poems distinguish this journal, and it has an excellent reputation, well-deserved. The downside, if it has one, concerns limited space for newcomers. Circulation is 1,500, 50% going to subscribers of which 50% are libraries, 30% are for shelf sales. **Sample postpaid: $5.95. No simultaneous submissions or**

INSIDER REPORT

Poet finds voice in search-and-rescue work

Whether it concerns lost love, spirit, passion or any number of other intangibles poets across the ages have been searching for, the idea of the "lost" has long been used and abused as a poetical conceit. In the poetry of Taylor Graham, however, the word takes a more literal turn.

Taylor Graham

Drawing upon her experiences as a volunteer search-and-rescue dog handler for much of what she writes, Graham has created a powerful narrative voice for herself: the "search" poem. Missing children, wayward hikers, fallen climbers, runaways, victims of flood, fire and other natural disasters have found their way out of her life and her head and onto the written page. All in a vivid, unsentimental (yet not uncompassionate) way, evoking sobering, somber and often startling images—images that stay with the reader long after the poem has been read. "I don't really consider myself a poet of ideas—of trying to develop an idea," says Graham. "I more or less work with images and see where they take me."

And just what "took" Graham to this unique marriage of poetry and search-and-rescue work? As is the case with most would-be poets, Graham began writing in high school and continued to do so through college and graduate school. "What I wrote during that time, however, was just awful. I didn't keep any of it."

Then, just shy of completing her Ph.D. (she had already received undergraduate degrees in German and French and a master's degree in Comparative Literature), Graham dropped out of academia all together. "It just wasn't working out," she says. "Being in a position of constantly critiquing and analyzing text must have taken the creativity out of writing—at least for me.

"It was only when I gave up on my Ph.D., and I went out into the 'real' world that I started writing the poems I've kept. People who were older and knew better had told me 'Wait till you experience life a little before you expect to be a poet'—and they were right."

After taking a job as a reporter for a small paper, Graham met her husband, a forester and wildlife biologist. "Right after we were married he was transferred to Alaska. While we were up there, we got involved in search-and-rescue work using trained dogs. We had German shepherds we trained to find lost people. Eventually the searches got into the poems."

Despite the dearth of search-and-rescue workers publishing literary journals, Graham hasn't had a problem finding markets willing to consider her search poetry—acceptance is the tricky part, and she hasn't been doing too badly at that either. Today Graham's poems have appeared in a myriad of publications, including *New York Quarterly*, *Maryland Poetry Review*, *Willow Springs*, *The Christian Science Monitor* and *South Dakota*

INSIDER REPORT, *Graham*

"He Was Wearing a Yellow T-Shirt"

We search for childpaths in the woods.
Where would he go?

Cedars bunch gray and blind
with cobwebs.
Berries and honeysuckle
shoulder up higher
than a man. Not a boy. Birds
only sing from the tops and edges.
Warblers, orioles,
flicks of yellow
foliage trick the eye. Not
a boy.

We could be in Transylvania,
the Yucatan. Backwoods
of a suburb.

Where is he?
who walked out of his house
and down the civilized street
and out of the world?

He's finding the way roots
pull the red clay over,
and quilted creepers: every longbone
loosened from its muscle,
moving the way stones and twigs do,
the intricate small bones of fingers
easing out of their joints.
By fall
it will all be second nature
to him, how the blond hairs
scatter. When it rains
won't matter. Snow melts and runs away,
kid-stuff. And spring
shoves up a few yellow tatters,
flowers that never grew
on a stalk.

(first published in **Maryland Poetry Review**; also published in **Casualties**, by Taylor Graham, published by **Coal City Review**, 1995)

INSIDER REPORT, *continued*

Review. She is also on the editorial board of *The Acorn*, a regional literary journal focusing on the western Sierra. Graham has received nominations for the Pushcart Prize Series anthologies and has seen a collection of her search-and-rescue poems, *Casualties*, published by *Coal City Review*.

Other specialized poetry shouldn't have a problem either—as long as the author is patient and perseveres, and the poetry is strong and has a clear, fresh voice. Good poetry reaches out and draws a reader in—regardless of the subject matter. In fact, almost all of the poems in *Casualties* first appeared in journals. Of course many journals also have an area of specialization or specific issues dedicated to different subjects. This is why familiarity with a publication continues to be so important.

Graham, who now lives and works with her husband in California along the western slope of the Sierra Nevada, has been involved in search-and-rescue work for more than 20 years. Their search work has taken them from the wilds of pre-pipeline Alaska, to Mexico City following the devastating 1985 earthquake, to various forests, marshes and mountains across the country. It is these real-life experiences that have fed and continue to fuel much of her work.

"Every time I go on a search there's a chance a poem will come of it," Graham says. "I had been writing poetry a long time before I started doing search and rescue. But after I got involved, I felt there were so many things I needed to get into my poems about that work."

Perhaps the poems provide Graham a conclusion; perhaps a catharsis for work that too often allows neither. The sad truth is, in most of the searches ending up in Graham's poetry, the missing don't find their way home.

"The grim situations are the ones that stay with you. If somebody's found I pretty much stop thinking about the search. The most frustrating thing is to leave a search if the person hasn't been found. You wonder, did I miss him? What happened to this person? You just keep going through the time in your mind—for years sometimes. Or if it is a search that ends in tragedy, you think, what could I have done? What could anybody have done? How could we have fixed this?"

When writing about a tragedy, too many poets get mired in sentimentality to the point of mawkishness. This is not the case with Graham's poetry. It is compassionate without being puerile and powerful without being insensitive to the situation.

More than just grist for her poetry, Graham's search-and-rescue work has become intrinsically tied to her writing. Many of the same characteristics—such as meticulous attention to detail—serve her well both as a poet and as search-and-rescue worker. "In my poems, I'm always looking for the specific detail—it can be visual, auditory or whatever—that makes the experience real for the reader and helps tell a story. Just as clues on a search tell the story." This is what makes her voice so resonant: The work and the experience that informs the work are so inextricably bound together.

"I think the hardest thing is for a poet to find his voice. Sure, we can learn a lot by reading and even imitating other good poets. But, finally, we have to find our own voice because the best things we write nobody else could have written."

—*Patrick Souhan*

previously published poems. Submit 3-5 poems between September 1 and January 1 only. All decisions made by mid-February. Send SASE for guidelines. Reports in 4 months. Pays 3 copies. Acquires all rights. The Ann Stanford Poetry Prizes ($750, $250 and $100) have an April 15 deadline, $10 fee (5 poem limit), for unpublished poems. Include cover sheet with name, address and titles and SASE for contest results. All entries are considered for publication, and all entrants receive a copy of *SCA*.

SOUTHERN HUMANITIES REVIEW; THEODORE CHRISTIAN HOEPFNER AWARD (II), 9088 Haley Center, Auburn University, Auburn AL 36849-5202, co-editors Dan Latimer and Virginia M. Kouidis, founded 1967, is a literary quarterly **interested in poems of any length, subject, genre. Space is limited, and brief poems are more likely to be accepted. "Translations welcome, but also send written permission from the copyright holder."** This journal continues to gain influence and prestige in the literary world by publishing a wide variety of verse that displays careful attention to image, theme, craft and voice. They have published poetry by Eamon Grennan, Donald Hall, Brendan Galvin, Susan Ludvigson, Dave Smith, Dabney Stuart and Fred Chappell. *SHR* is 100 pgs., 6×9, circulation 700. Subscription: $15/year. **Sample: $5. "Send 3-5 poems in a business-sized envelope. Avoid sending faint computer printout."** No previously published poems or simultaneous submissions. Reports in 1-2 months, possibly longer in summer. Always sends prepublication galleys. Pays 2 copies. Copyright reverts to author upon publication. Reviews books of poetry in approximately 750-1,000 words. Send books for review consideration. Sponsors the Theodore Christian Hoepfner Award, a $50 award for the best poem published in a given volume of *SHR*. The editors advise, "For beginners we'd recommend study and wide reading in English and classical literature, and, of course, American literature—the old works, not just the new. We also recommend study of or exposure to a foreign language and a foreign culture. Poets need the reactions of others to their work: criticism, suggestions, discussion. A good creative writing teacher would be desirable here, and perhaps some course work too. And then submission of work, attendance at workshops. And again, the reading: history, biography, verse, essays—all of it. We want to see poems that have gone beyond the language of slippage and easy attitudes."

SOUTHERN POETRY REVIEW; GUY OWEN POETRY PRIZE (II), Advancement Studies, Central Piedmont Community College, Charlotte NC 28235, phone (704)330-6002, fax (704)330-6455, editor Ken McLaurin, founded 1958, a semiannual literary magazine "with emphasis on effective poetry. **There are no restrictions on form, style or content of poetry; length subject to limitations of space."** They have published work by Linda Pastan, Judith Ortiz Cofer, David Ray, Stephen Sandy, Betty Adcock and Walter McDonald. *Southern Poetry Review* is 78 pgs., 6×9, handsomely printed on buff stock, flat-spined with textured, one-color matte card cover. Circulation is 1,000. Subscription: $8/year. **Sample postpaid: $3. Queries answered with SASE. Submit up to 3-5 poems at a time. Reads submissions September 1 through May 31 only. Pays 1 copy. Acquires first-time rights.** Staff reviews books of poetry. Send books for review consideration. This is the type of literary magazine to settle back with in a chair and read, particularly during dry creative spells, to inspire one's muse. It is recommended as a market for that reason. It's a tough sell, though. Work is read closely and the magazine reports in a timely manner. There is a yearly contest, the Guy Owen Poetry Prize of $500, to which the entry fee is an $8 subscription; submission must be postmarked in April.

THE SOUTHERN REVIEW (II), 43 Allen Hall, Louisiana State University, Baton Rouge LA 70803, phone (504)388-5108, founded 1935 (original series), 1965 (new series), poetry editors James Olney and Dave Smith, "is a literary quarterly that publishes fiction, poetry, critical essays and book reviews, with emphasis on contemporary literature in the U.S. and abroad, and with special interest in southern culture and history. Selections are made with careful attention to craftsmanship and technique and to the seriousness of the subject matter." By general agreement this is one of the most distinguished of literary journals. Joyce Carol Oates, for instance, says, "Over the years I have continued to be impressed with the consistent high quality of *SR*'s publications and its general 'aura,' which bespeaks careful editing, adventuresome tastes and a sense of thematic unity. *SR* is characterized by a refreshing openness to new work, placed side by side with that of older, more established, and in many cases highly distinguished writers." The editors say, **"We are interested in any variety of poetry that is well crafted, though we cannot normally accommodate excessively long poems (say 10 pgs. and over)."** They have published poetry by Norman Dubie, Margaret Gibson, Seamus Heaney, Yusef Komunyakaa, Susan Ludvigson and Robert Penn Warren. The beautifully printed quarterly is massive: 6¾×10, 240 pgs., flat-spined, matte card cover. They receive about 6,000 submissions of poetry a year. All styles and forms seem welcome, although accessible lyric and narrative free verse appear most often in recent issues. Press run is 3,100 for 2,100 subscribers of which 70% are libraries. Subscription: $20. **Sample postpaid: $6. "We do not require a cover letter but we prefer one giving information about the author and previous publications."** Prefers submissions of up

● **A BULLET** introduces comments by the editors of *Poet's Market* indicating special information about the listing.

to 4 pgs. Send SASE for guidelines. Reports in 2 months. Pays $20/printed page plus 2 copies. Buys first North American serial rights. Staff reviews books of poetry in 3,000 words, multi-book format. Send books for review consideration. Work published in this review has been included in the 1995 and 1996 volumes of *The Best American Poetry*.

SOUTHWEST REVIEW; ELIZABETH MATCHETT STOVER MEMORIAL AWARD (II), 307 Fondren Library West, Box 374, Southern Methodist University, Dallas TX 75275, phone (214)768-1037, founded 1915, editor Willard Spiegelman. *Southwest Review* is a literary quarterly that publishes fiction, essays, poetry and interviews. "It is hard to describe our preference for poetry in a few words. We always suggest that potential contributors read several issues of the magazine to see for themselves what we like. But some things may be said: We demand **very high quality in our poems; we accept both traditional and experimental writing, but avoid unnecessary obscurity and private symbolism; we place no arbitrary limits on length but find shorter poems easier to fit into our format than longer ones. We have no specific limitations as to theme."** They have published poetry by Adrienne Rich, Amy Clampitt, Albert Goldbarth, Leonard Nathan, Molly Peacock and Charles Wright. The journal is 6×9, 144 pgs., perfect-bound, professionally printed, with matte text stock cover. They receive about 1,000 submissions of poetry a year, use approximately 32. Poems tend to be lyric and narrative free verse combining a strong voice with powerful topics or situations. Diction is accessible and content often conveys a strong sense of place. Circulation is 1,500 for 1,000 subscribers of which 600 are libraries. Subscription: $20. **Sample postpaid: $6. No simultaneous submissions or previously published work. Publishes theme issues. Send SASE for guidelines. Reports within a month. Always sends prepublication galleys. Pays cash plus copies.** The $150 Elizabeth Matchett Stover Memorial Prize is awarded annually for the best poem, chosen by editors, published in the preceding year. Poetry published in *Southwest Review* has been included in the 1993, 1994 and 1995 volumes of *The Best American Poetry*.

SOU'WESTER (II), Box 1438, Southern Illinois University, Edwardsville IL 62026, phone (618)692-3190, founded 1960, managing editor Fred W. Robbins, poetry editor Nancy Avdoian, appears twice a year. **"We like poetry with imagery and figurative language that has strong associations and don't care for abstract poetry. We have no particular preference for form or length."** They have published poetry by Marnie Bullock, Susan Swartwont and Bruce Guernsey. There are 30-40 pgs. of poetry in each 6×9, 100-page issue. The magazine is professionally printed, flat-spined, with textured matte card cover, circulation is 300 for 500 subscribers of which 50 are libraries. They receive 3,000 poems (from 600 poets) each year, use approximately 36-40, have a 4-month backlog. Subscription: $10/2 issues. **Sample postpaid: $5. Simultaneous submissions OK. Does not read during August. Rejections usually within 4 months. Pays 2 copies. Acquires all rights. Returns rights. Editor comments on rejections** "usually, in the case of those that we almost accept." He says, "Read poetry past and present. Have something to say and say it in your own voice. Poetry is a very personal thing for many editors. When all else fails, we may rely on gut reactions, so take whatever hints you're given to improve your poetry, and keep submitting."

THE SOW'S EAR POETRY REVIEW (II), 19535 Pleasant View Dr., Abingdon VA 24211-6827, phone (540)628-2651, founded 1988, managing editor Larry Richman, graphics editor Mary Calhoun, is a quarterly. **"We are open to many forms and styles, and have no limitations on length. We try to be interesting visually, and we use graphics to complement the poems. Though we publish some work from our local community of poets, we are interested in poems from all over. We publish a few by school-age and previously unpublished poets."** They have recently published poetry by Elton Glaser, Cappy Love Hanson, Charles Edward Mann and Susan Terris. As a sample the editors selected these lines from "Pig Lab" by Sarah Lindsay:

> It was scarcely moist when I turned its belly up
> and tied its four legs, strained apart, to the board with string.
> First, the oral cavity. My partner closed her eyes.
> They I felt brave. I parted its toothless mouth,
> showed its gray ribbed palate, slit my pig's lips
> to the ears and broke its jaw, to begin learning.

TSE is 32 pgs., 8½×11, saddle-stapled, with matte card cover, professionally printed. They receive about 2,000 poems a year, accept approximately 10. Press run is 800 for 700 subscribers of which 15 are libraries, 20-40 shelf sales. Subscription: $10. **Sample postpaid: $3.50. Submit up to 5 poems at a time. No previously published poems; simultaneous submissions OK if you tell them promptly when work is accepted elsewhere. Enclose brief bio. Reports in 3-6 months. Pays 1 copy. Buys first publication rights.** Most prose (reviews, interviews, features) is commissioned. They offer an annual contest for unpublished poems, with fee of $2/poem, prizes of $500, $100 and $50, and publication for 15-20 finalists. For contest, submit poems in September/October, with name and address on each poem. Submissions of 5 poems/$10 receive a subscription. Include SASE for notification. 1996 Judge: Betsy Sholl. They also sponsor a chapbook contest in March/April with $10 fee, $500 prize and publication; second and third prizes of $100. Send SASE for chapbook contest guidelines. The editor says, "Four criteria help us to judge the quality of submissions: Does the poem make the strange familiar or the familiar strange or both? Is the form of the poem vital to its meaning? Do the sounds of the poem make sense in relation to the theme? Does the little story of the poem open a window on the Big Story of the human situation?"

SPACE AND TIME (I, II, IV-Science fiction/fantasy, horror), 138 W. 70th St. (4B), New York NY 10023-4468, founded 1966, poetry editor Lawrence Greenberg, is a biannual that publishes "primarily science fiction/fantasy/horror; some related poetry and articles. **We do not want to see anything that doesn't fit science fiction/fantasy/weird genres.**" They have published poetry by Lyn Lif-shin, Susan Spilecki, Mark Kreighbaum and Cynthia Tedesco. As a sample we selected these lines from "Polarion" by Jessica Amanda Salmonson:

> *Fear, O Cruel Daughters,*
> *The return of Spring;*
> *Drink the salty waves*
> *That were dreamy towers of gleaming ice*
> *   between curtains of rainbows.*
> *Weep, O Cruel Daughters*
> *When Polarion melts into*
> *   diluvian madness.*

The issue of **Space and Time** we received was about 100 pgs., 5½×8½, perfect-bound. However, they are reformatting to 64 pgs., 8½×11, web press printed on 50 lb. stock and saddle-stitched with glossy card cover and interior b&w illustrations. They receive about 500 poems a year, accept approximately 5%. Press run is 2,000 for 200 subscribers of which 10 are libraries, 1,200 shelf sales. Single copy: $5; subscription: $10. **Sample postpaid: $6.25. Submit up to 4 poems at a time. No previously published poems or simultaneous submissions.** Time between acceptance and publication is 3-9 months. **Often comments on rejections. Poets may send SASE for guidelines "but they won't see more than what's here." Reports in 2-6 weeks, "longer if recommended." Pays 1¢/word ($5 minimum) plus 2 copies. Buys first North American serial rights.**

SPARROW: THE YEARBOOK OF THE SONNET (IV-Form), 103 Waldron St., West Lafayette IN 47906, founded 1954, editor/publisher Felix and Selma Stefanile, appears every October. **We are noted for our devotion to the publication of formal, contemporary sonnets. We occasionally publish other types of structured verse, but only rarely, and only when the poem seems to compel us to take it. No subject restrictions. We don't publish poems in poor taste.**" They have recently published poetry by Dana Gioia, Daniela Gioseffi, David Mason and Ronald Wallace. As a sample the editor selected these lines from "Dutiful" by David Berman:

> *"Make Mother proud of you—and Father too."*
> *Those good-boy chestnuts that I swallowed whole*
> *Upset my stomach; still I played the role*
> *Expected of me; doubting that they knew*
> *How long I worked to make their dream come true.*

Sparrow is about 100 pgs., 8½×11, attractively printed, perfect-bound with light card cover, using occasional graphics only by invitation. They receive about 2,000 mss a year, use less than 1%. Press run is 650 for about 400 subscribers of which about 50 are libraries, 200 shelf sales. Single copy: $6. **Sample back issue postpaid: $5. Submit 4-5 poems at a time, typed on 8½×11 bond paper. One poem to a page with name and address on each. "We consider previously published poems only now and then." No simultaneous submissions. No material returned without SASE. "We have a very cynical attitude toward long cover letters." Reads submissions January through September only. Seldom comments on rejections. "We are not in the business of offering criticism or advice." Send SASE with all queries. Reports in 6 weeks. Sometimes sends prepublication galleys. Pays $3 a sonnet plus 1 copy. Buys first and non-exclusive reprint rights. "We also offer a $25 prize for the best sonnet each issue."** Staff reviews books of poetry. Send books for review consideration. The editor says, "We are now essentially a 'new' magazine with a fine, old name. We pride ourselves on our liveliness and our currency. We also publish scores of musical settings for sonnets, by special arrangement with the composer. We are really not a market for beginners and the MFA degree does not impress us."

‡SPEAKING FROM THE BREAST . . . (II, IV-Specialized: motherhood), P.O. Box 854, Washington Crossing PA 18977-0854, founded 1996, editor K. Brittany Fedorev Vanderkleed, published quarterly, is a journal of literary expressions on motherhood. They want **"motherhood-related poems of up to 60 lines." They do not want "anything overtly cliché"** They have recently published poetry by Gayle Brandeis and Cindy Guenth-erman. As a sample the editor selected these lines from "In the City of Motherhood" by Ernest Slyman:

> *In the city of Motherhood, night falls on the clean*
> *   empty streets.*
> *The skies have hung their stars in the east.*
> *The children have gone to bed, and the mothers are*
> *   everywhere.*

SFTB is 40-48 pgs., 5½×8½, photocopied, saddle-stapled, with color cardstock cover. They receive about 500 poems a year, accept approximately 7%. Press run is 200 for 50 subscribers, 100 shelf sales. Single copy: $3; subscription: $10. **Sample postpaid: $2. Make checks payable to Scarlet Apple Enterprises, Inc. Submit 3-5 poems at a time. No previously published poems; simultaneous submissions OK. Cover letter preferred with a bio of 50 words of less.** Time between acceptance and publication is 1-2 months. **Editor evaluates submissions based on originality and literary merit. Seldom comments on rejections. Send SASE for guidelines. Reports in 1-2 months. Always sends prepublication galleys. Pays 1 copy. Acquires first North Ameri-**

can serial rights. Sponsors an Editor's Choice Award for the poem possessing the most originality and merit, awarding a certificate and $5. Send SASE for more information.

‡**SPELUNKER FLOPHOUSE (I, II)**, P.O. Box 617742, Chicago IL 60661, e-mail spelunkerf@aol.com, founded 1995, editors Chris Kubica and Wendy Morgan, is a quarterly literary magazine publishing "high quality poetry, fiction and artwork for an intelligent, imaginative readership." **We are extremely interested in poetry that shows a high consciousness of language, rhythm, and structure and attempts to deal with the minute, seemingly insignificant aspects/details of daily life. To quote the cliché, less is definitely more. However, we have little interest in poetry that deals directly with the larger aspects/summaries/absolutes of life, for instance obvious religious, political, or social commentary. Discussing emotions (telling without showing) without illustrations(s) of specific/vivid/tangible scenes, objects, situations, language, or people is not looked upon favorably by the editors."** The editors say *spelunker flophouse* is 96 pgs., 8½×7 (half legal), offset printed and perfect-bound with 4-color glossy card cover. "We publish fiction, poetry, b&w artwork, occasional reviews, quarterly thimble-fuls of editorial essay, and ads." They receive about 1,000 poems a year, accept approximately 50. Press run is 1,000. Subscription: $24.95/year. **Sample postpaid: $6.95. "Submit three to five poems at a time so that we may get a round survey of your work. Print name/address/phone on every first page, full name on subsequent pages. One poem per page, please. Submit on clean, white letter-sized paper. Electronic submissions are not accepted. However, electronic requests for guidelines and queries about submissions are accepted if brief. Please make every effort to include cover letters—tell us about the colorful, intense, perhaps quixotic hollow in which you live (include publication credits and a brief bio if you can). We favor submitters who clearly illustrate the fact that they've read our magazine."** No previously published poems; simultaneous submissions OK if notified. Often comments on rejections. Send SASE for guidelines or request via e-mail. Reports in approximately 4-10 weeks. Always sends prepublication galleys. Pays "copies and occasional small sums." Acquires first North American serial rights. "Cite us if published again elsewhere, we retain rights to anthologize work(s) with proper credit and notification given." Sponsors an annual contest. Guidelines available on request (with a SASE) and/or printed in the magazine itself. The editors say, "We offer the best poetry, fiction and artwork we can in an inventive, original format. We cooperate regularly with other literary magazines. Support this necessary forum for the arts by purchasing copies of literary magazines, reading them, and increasing local awareness of magazines/forums such as ours whenever possible. Study the market; then submit. And keep in touch! We love to hear from members/supporters of the literary community."

SPILLWAY; CALL AND RESPONSE POETRY CONTEST; SPILLWAY POETRY CONTEST (II), P.O. Box 6000-337, Huntington Beach CA 92646, founded 1991, editor Mifanwy Kaiser (all correspondence should be addressed to Ms. Kaiser), is a biannual journal "celebrating writing's diversity and power to affect our lives. **Open to all voices, schools and tendencies: Confessional, neo-narrative, deep image, new formalist, language, political, etc. We usually do not use writing which tells instead of shows, or writing which contains general, abstract lines not anchored in images."** They have published poetry by Richard Jones, Jack Grapes, Charles Bukowski, Stellasue Lee and James O'Hern. *Spillway* is about 100 pgs., digest-sized, attractively printed, perfect-bound, with 2-color card cover. Press run is 1,000. Subscription: $10. **Sample (including guidelines) postpaid: $6. Make checks payable to Spillway, Mifanwy Kaiser. Submit 3-6 poems at a time, 10 pages total. Previously published work ("say when and where") and simultaneous submissions ("say where also submitted") OK. Cover letter including brief bio required. "No cute bios—we need professional ones." Submission deadlines: March 27 for Spring/Summer issue, August 27 for Fall/Winter issue. Reports in 2 weeks to 6 months. Pays 1 copy. Acquires one-time rights.** Also sponsors Call and Response Poetry Contest, awarding $100 and publication in *Spillway*. Submissions may be entered in other contests. Submit up to 10 combined pages, up to 10 poems, of up to 400 lines by pairs of poets whose poems speak to each other. Send submissions to Robert Carroll at the above address. Entry fee: $10. Sponsors the *Spillway* Poetry Contest, awarding $50 and publication. Submissions must be unpublished and may be entered in other contests. Submit up to 3 poems of up to 6 pages to Mifanwy Kaiser at the above address. Entry fee: $5. Deadlines for contests: August 27 for fall/winter issue, March 27 for spring/summer issue. Reviews books of poetry in 250 words maximum. Open to unsolicited reviews. Poets may also send books for review consideration. The editors say, "We have no problem with simultaneous or previously published submissions. Poems are murky creatures—they shift and change in time and context. It's exciting to pick up a volume, read a poem in the context of all the other pieces and then find the same poem in another time and place. And, we don't think a poet should have to wait until death to see work in more than one volume. What joy to find out that more than one editor values one's work. Our responsibility as editors, collectively, is to promote the work of poets as much as possible—how can we do this if we say to a writer you may only have a piece published in one volume and only one time?"

‡*SPIN; POETRY ORBITAL WORKSHOPS (I)**, 7 Megan Ave., Pakuranga, Auckland 1706 New Zealand, phone 09 576 8577, founded 1986, contact PNW Donnelly, appears 3 times/year, March, July, November, and publishes poetry. **"We have no hard and fast rules but appreciate poetry that excels in its form and content. No stereotyped, imitative or boring work."** They have recently published poetry by George Gott, Catherine

Maur, John O'Connor and Joanna Weston. As a sample the editor selected these lines from "Like Florida" by David Gregory:

> No new ways of telling time,
> winking heart monitor digitals,
> cruel and precise.
> Autumn is made apocryphal;
> she extends herself south,
> ahead of the shadows.

SPIN is 72 pgs., A5, photocopied and saddle-stitched with light card cover. They receive about 600 poems a year, accept approximately 25%. Press run is 150 for 110 subscribers of which 6 are libraries. Single copy: NZ 6.50; subscription: NZ 18. **Sample postpaid: NZ 4.50. "We expect contributors to subscribe/purchase. We are unable to supply contributors copies." Submit approximately 6 poems at a time. No previously published poems or simultaneous submissions. Cover letter preferred. "All submissions returned at each publication."** Time between acceptance and publication is 1 month. **Sometimes comments on rejections. Publishes theme issues. Reports within 3 months.** Reviews books of poetry in 1-page (or more), or in multi 3-4 line notices. Open to unsolicited reviews. Poets may also send books for review consideration. Subscription covers (optional) membership in poetry orbital workshops. "Each workshop or 'orbit' comprises four or five poets who by post submit poems to each other for reading and comment." Send SASE (or SAE and IRC) for details.

SPINDRIFT (II), Shoreline Community College, 16101 Greenwood Ave., Seattle WA 98133, phone (206)546-5864, founded 1962, faculty advisor varies each year, currently Carol Orlock, is **open to all varieties of poetry except greeting card style.** They have published poetry by Lyn Lifshin, Mary Lou Sanelli, James Bertolino, Edward Harkness and Richard West. *Spindrift*, an annual, is 125 pgs., handsomely printed in an 8″ square, flat-spined. Circulation is 500. Single copy: $6.50. **Sample postpaid: $5. "Submit 2 copies of each poem, 6 maximum. Include cover letter with biographical information. We accept submissions until February 1— report back in April." Send SASE for guidelines. Pays 2 copies. All rights revert to author upon publication.** The editors advise, "Read what the major contemporary poets are writing. Read what local poets are writing. Be distinctive, love the language, avoid sentiment."

‡SPINNING JENNY (II), P.O. Box 1492, Cooper Station, New York NY 10276, founded 1994, first issue Fall 1995, editor C.E. Harrison, appears twice a year. **"We are especially devoted to the work of emerging writers, and welcome the opportunity to review poetry of all shapes, sizes, flavors, persuasions, and schools."** They have recently published poetry by Denise Duhamel and Matthew Lippman. *SJ* is 52 pgs., 5½×8½, perfect-bound with medium card cover. "We accept approximately 5% of unsolicited submissions." Press run is 2,000. Single copy: $4; subscription: $8/year. **Sample postpaid: $5. No previously published poems; simultaneous submissions OK. Seldom comments on rejections. Send SASE for guidelines. Reports within 1 month. Pays contributor copies. Authors retain rights.**

THE SPIRIT THAT MOVES US; THE SPIRIT THAT MOVES US PRESS (II); EDITOR'S CHOICE (IV-Anthology), P.O. Box 720820-PM, Jackson Heights, Queens NY 11372-0820, phone (718)426-8788, founded 1974, poetry editor Morty Sklar. *"The Spirit That Moves Us* will be continuing its *Editor's Choice* series and publishing regular issues only occasionally. *Editor's Choice* consists of selections from other literary magazines and small presses, where we choose from nominations by the editors of those magazines and presses." They have recently published poetry by Julia Alvarez, Rudy Kikel, Amiri Baraka, Crawdad Nelson and Gregory Corso. They offer *Patchwork of Dreams: Voices from the Heart of the New America*, an anthology, as a sample for $8 plus $1 postage (regularly $12 plus $1.50 postage) or their *15th Anniversary Anthology* for $6 and free shipping. **Publishes theme issues. Send SASE for upcoming themes and time frames.** The editor's advice: "Write what you would like to write, in a style (or styles) which is/are best for your own expression. Don't worry about acceptance, though you may be concerned about it. Don't just send work which you think editors would like to see, though take that into consideration. Think of the relationship between poem, poet and editor as personal. You may send good poems to editors who simply do not like them, whereas other editors might."

SPITBALL: THE LITERARY BASEBALL MAGAZINE; CASEY AWARD (IV-Sports/recreation), 5560 Fox Rd., Cincinnati OH 45239, phone (513)385-2268, founded 1981, poetry editor William J. McGill, is "a unique literary magazine devoted to poetry, fiction and book reviews *exclusively* about baseball. Newcomers are very welcome, but remember that you have to know the subject. We do and our readers do. Perhaps a good place to start for beginners is one's personal reactions to the game, *a* game, a player, etc. and take it from there." The 96-page, digest-sized biannual is computer typeset and perfect-bound. They receive about 1,000 submissions a year, use approximately 40. "Many times we are able to publish accepted work almost immediately." Circulation is 1,000 for 750 subscribers of which 25 are libraries. Subscription: $12. **Sample postpaid: $5. "We are not very concerned with the technical details of submitting, but we do prefer a cover letter with some bio info. We also like batches of poems and prefer to use several of same poet in an issue rather than a single poem." Pays 2 copies.** The editor says, "We encourage anyone interested to submit to *Spitball*. We are always looking for fresh talent. Those who have never written 'baseball poetry' before should read some first probably before submitting. Not necessarily ours. We sponsor the Casey Award (for best baseball book of the year) and hold the Casey Awards Banquet every January. Any chapbook of baseball poetry should be sent to us for consideration for the 'Casey' plaque that we award to the winner each year."

‡***SPLIZZ (I)**, 4 St. Marys Rise, Burry Port, Carms SA16 OSH Wales, e-mail ms9h5maj@swansea.ac.uk, founded 1993, editor Amanda Morgan, published quarterly, features poetry, prose, reviews of contemporary music, background to poets and art. **They want "any kind of poetry. We have no restrictions regarding style, length, subjects." They do not want "anything racist or homophobic."** They have recently published poetry by Colin Cross, Steve Andrews, Jake Webb and Doug Bateman. The editor says *Splizz* is 40-44 pgs., A5, saddle-stapled with art and ads. They receive about 100-200 poems a year, accept approximately 90%. Press run is 50 for 10 subscribers. Single copy: £1.30, £2 elsewhere; subscription: £5 UK, £8 elsewhere. **Sample postpaid: £1.20 UK, £1.50 elsewhere. Make checks payable to Amanda Morgan (British checks only). Submit 5 poems, typed submissions preferred. Previously published poems and simultaneous submissions OK. Cover letter required with short bio.** Time between acceptance and publication is 2-4 months. **Often comments on rejections. Charges criticism fee: "Just enclose SAE/IRC for response, and allow one to two months for delivery." Send SASE (or SAE and IRC) for guidelines. Reports in 1-2 months. Sometimes sends prepublication galleys.** Reviews books or chapbooks of poetry or other magazines in 50-300 words. Open to unsolicited reviews. Poets may also send books for review consideration. The editor says, "Beginners seeking to have their work published, send your work to *Splizz*, as we specialize in giving new poets a chance."

‡***SPOKES (II)**, 319a Hills Rd., Cambridge, Cambs CB22QT United Kingdom, founded 1982, contact Alistair Wisker, published biannually, contains "general poetry—international and national." They have recently published poetry by Les Murray and Peter Porter. The editor says *Spokes* is 50 pgs. with graphics. They receive about 1,000 poems a year, accept approximately 10%. Press run is 400 for 200 subscribers of which 20 are libraries; 20 distributed free. Subscription: £4.50. **Sample postpaid: £3. Although not required, the editor prefers contributors to purchase a copy. Submit up to 5 poems at a time. Previously published poems OK; no simultaneous submissions. Cover letter preferred.** Time between acceptance and publication is 3 months. **Poems are circulated to an editorial board of 2. Seldom comments on rejections. Send SASE (or SAE and IRC) for guidelines.** Staff reviews books or chapbooks of poetry or other magazines. Poets may also send books for review consideration. The editor says, "We prefer shorter poems. International submissions are encouraged."

THE SPOON RIVER POETRY REVIEW (III, IV-Regional, translations); EDITORS' PRIZE CONTEST (II), 4240/English Dept., Illinois State University, Normal IL 61790-4240, phone (309)438-7906, founded 1976, poetry editor Lucia Getsi, is a "poetry magazine that features newer and well-known poets from around the country and world." Also features **1 Illinois poet/issue** at length for the magazine's Illinois Poet Series. **"We want interesting and compelling poetry that operates beyond the ho-hum, so-what level, in any form or style about anything; language that is fresh, energetic, committed, filled with a strong voice that grabs the reader in the first line and never lets go."** They also use translations of poetry. They have published poetry by Frankie Paino, Marilyn Krysl, Kurt Leland, Tim Seibles, Dave Smith and Stuart Dybek. *SRPR* appears biannually, 128 pgs., digest-sized, laser set with card cover using photos, ads. They receive about 3,000 poems a month, accept approximately 1%. Press run is 1,500 for 700 subscribers of which 100 are libraries and shelf sales. Subscription: $14. **Sample: $9. "No simultaneous submissions unless we are notified immediately if a submission is accepted elsewhere. Include name and address on every poem." Do not submit mss May 1 through September 1. Editor comments on rejections "many times, if a poet is promising." Reports in 2 months. Pays a year's subscription. Acquires first North American serial rights only.** Staff reviews books of poetry. Send books for review consideration. Sponsors the Editor's Prize Contest for previously unpublished work. One poem will be awarded $500 and published in the fall issue of *SRPR*, and two finalists will receive $100 each and publication in the fall issue. Entry fee: $15, including 1-year subscription. Deadline: May 1. Write for details. Recent winners were Marilyn Krysl and Aleida Rodríguez. *The Spoon River Poetry Review* has received over 20 Illinois Arts Council Awards and is one of the best reads in the poetry-publishing world. Editor Lucia Cordell Getsi jampacks the journal with poems of varied styles and presents them in a handsome, perfect-bound product. You'll want to order a sample issue to get a feel for this fine publication. They are starting up two new imprints: TransGen(d)re—The Other Press and Thorngate Road Press. Write for information. Work published in this review has also been included in *The Best American Poetry 1993*.

SPOUT MAGAZINE (II), 28 W. Robie, St. Paul MN 55107, e-mail colb0018@gold.tc.umn.edu, founded 1989, editors John Colburn and Michelle Filkins, appears approximately 3 times/year providing "a paper community of unique expression." **They want "poetry of the imagination, poetry that surprises. We enjoy the surreal, the forceful, the political, the expression of confusion." No light verse, archaic forms or language.** They have recently published poetry by John M. Bennett, Emily Graves, Sean Brendan-Brown and Jeffrey Little. As a sample the editor selected these lines by Jennifer Willoughby:

> The dog knows it's hard to leave things lying on the ground.
> When he begins eating stones we think he'll die soon
> or collapse. But it is nothing, not a symptom
> but a package of his moving life,

the unexpected shape of warmth.

The editor says *Spout* is 40 pgs., 8½ × 11, saddle-stapled, card stock or glossy cover is a different color each issue. They receive about 400-450 poems a year, accept approximately 15%. Press run is 200-250 for 35-40 subscribers, 100-150 shelf sales. Single copy price: $3; subscription: $12. **Sample postpaid: $4. Submit up to 6 poems at a time. Previously published poems and simultaneous submissions OK. Cover letter preferred.** Time between acceptance and publication is 2-3 months. **Poems are circulated to an editorial board. "Poems are reviewed by two of three editors, those selected for final review are read again by all three."** Seldom comments on rejections. **Send SASE for guidelines. Reports in 2-4 months. Pays 1 copy.**

SPRING: THE JOURNAL OF THE E.E. CUMMINGS SOCIETY (IV-Specialized), 33-54 164th St., Flushing NY 11358-1442, phone (718)353-3631 or (718)461-9022, fax (718)353-4778, editor Norman Friedman, is an annual publication designed "to maintain and broaden the audience for Cummings and to explore various facets of his life and art." **They want poems in the spirit of Cummings, primarily poems of one page or less. Nothing "amateurish."** They have published poetry by John Tagliabue, Ruth Whitman, M.L. Rosenthal, William Jay Smith and Theodore Weiss. *Spring* is 100-120 pgs., 5½ × 8½, offset and perfect-bound with light card stock cover. Press run is 700 for 200 subscribers of which 15 are libraries, 450 shelf sales. Subscription or **sample postpaid: $15. No previously published poems or simultaneous submissions. Fax submissions OK. Cover letter required. Reads submissions January through March only.** Seldom comments on rejections. **Reports in 6 months. Pays 1 copy.** "Contributors are encouraged to subscribe."

‡**SPRING FANTASY; WOMEN IN THE ARTS (I)**, P.O. Box 2907, Decatur IL 62524, founded 1994, contact vice president. *Spring Fantasy* is "an annual collection of artwork, poetry, fiction, personal essays and photography on any theme." **They are open to all types of poetry ("except shaped"), up to 100 lines.** They have recently published poetry by Najwa Salam Brax, Linda Hutton, Kris Jagusch and Art Hullinger. As a sample they selected these lines from "Cardinal Attack" by Karen Olsen Murley:

> *When the sun rises over our glass-faced house*
> *during this February thaw, a staccato rhythm begins.*
> *A male cardinal defends territory by throwing his body repeatedly*
> *against his own image. I have pasted on the largest windows*
> *paper spread-eagle shapes creating an almost festive elementary-school*
> *facade in celebration of our own Bird-of-Prey Day*

Spring Fantasy is about 60 pgs., photocopied and spiral-comb bound. They receive 25-30 poems a year, accept approximately 50%. Press run is 100. **Sample postpaid: $6. Make checks payable to Women In The Arts. Submit 4 poems at a time. Previously published poems and simultaneous submissions OK. Do not submit mss in December.** Time between acceptance and publication is 3-4 months. **"A committee of Women In The Arts members chooses poems for publication."** Often comments on rejections. **Send SASE for guidelines. Reports in 1-2 months. Pays 1 copy plus 20% discount on additional copies. Acquires one-time rights.** Sponsors annual *Spring Fantasy* contest. See listing in Contests and Awards section. "Women In The Arts is a group of creative women (and men) who aim to encourage each other in all facets of creativity." They say, "Always send for guidelines before submitting."

‡**SPUYTEN DUYVIL (II)**, 1852 Cathedral Station, New York NY 10025, phone (212)978-3353, fax (212)727-8228, e-mail tunguska@tribeca.ios.com, founded 1982, publishes works of "quality content and form of perennial interest." Publishes 2 paperbacks, 2 hardbacks and **2 chapbooks/year. "Open to any formats of course, restrictions would be that to which not enough editing and testing of the waters has surfaced."** They have recently published poetry by Michael Stephens, Mark Rudman, Richard Pevear, Alice Rose George and Burt Kimmelman. Books or chapbooks are usually 60-100 pgs., 6 × 9, perfect-bound with color art covers. **"Only published poets need apply." Previously published poems OK; no simultaneous submissions. Cover letter required. "Send ms ideas, or e-mail ideas and/or the actual mogombo. We'll get to you as soon as possible with a yeh or nay." Prefers not to read submissions during the summer."** Poems are circulated to an editorial board and must be approved by all four editors. Replies to queries in 6 months. **Pays 100 author's copies (out of a press run of 1,000)** unless other arrangements have been made. For sample books or chapbooks, e-mail your address.

*****STAND MAGAZINE; NORTHERN HOUSE (I, II, IV-Translations)**, 179 Wingrove Rd., Newcastle on Tyne NE4 9DA England, phone/fax (0)191-273-3280, US editor: David Latané, Department of English, VCU, Richmond VA 23284-2005. *Stand*, founded by editor Jon Silkin in 1952, is a highly esteemed literary quarterly. Jon Silkin seeks more subscriptions from US readers and also hopes "that the magazine **would be seriously treated as an alternative platform to American literary journals."** He wants **"verse that tries to explore forms. No formulaic verse."** They have published poems by such poets as Peter Redgrove, Elizabeth Jennings and Michael Hamburger. *Library Journal* calls *Stand* "one of England's best, liveliest and truly imaginative little magazines." Among better-known American poets whose work has appeared here are Robert Bly, William Stafford, Michael Mott, Angela Ball and Naomi Wallace. Poet Donald Hall says of it, "among essential magazines, there is Jon Silkin's *Stand*, politically left, with reviews, poems and much translation from continental literature." In its current format it is 6 × 8, flat-spined, 84 pgs., professionally printed in 2 columns, small type, on thin stock with glossy cover, using ads. Circulation is 4,500 for 2,800 subscribers of which 600 are libraries. Subscription: $25. **Sample postpaid: $7. Cover letter required with submissions, "assuring us that work is not also being offered elsewhere." Publishes theme issues. Always sends prepublication galleys. Pays £25/ poem (unless under 6 lines) and 1 copy (⅓ off additional copies). Buys first world serial rights for 3 months after publication. If work(s) appear elsewhere** *Stand*/**Northern House must be credited.** Reviews books of poetry in 3,000-4,000 words, multi-book format. Open to unsolicited reviews. Poets may also send books for review consideration. Northern House (13 Queen's Terrace, Newcastle on Tyne NE2 2PJ England) "publishes mostly small collections of poetry by new or established poets. The pamphlets often contain a group of poems written to one theme. Occasionally larger volumes are published."

*STAPLE (II), Gilderoy East, Upperwood Rd., Matlock, Bath DE4 3PD United Kingdom, phone 0629-583867 and 0629-582764, founded 1982, co-editor Bob Windsor. This literary magazine appears 4 times/year including supplements. **"Nothing barred: Evidence of craft, but both traditional and modernist accepted."** They have recently published poetry by Alice Friman, Ulf Goebel, William Oxley, Roy Blackman and Christine McNeill. As a sample they selected these lines from "Tracking" by Stuart Henson:

> *And as we return, wrapped up in our scarves*
> *and hoods, like nursery creatures*
> *that lost and found themselves in the wood,*
> *we're amused by the prints of the story so far*
> *and the fields of the future closed*
> *like an uncut book.*

Staple is professionally printed, flat-spined, 90 pgs., with card cover. They receive about 10,000 poems a year, accept approximately 2%. Press run is 800 for 350 subscribers. Subscription: £14 (surface), £17.50 (air). **Sample postpaid: £3. Submit 6 poems at a time. No simultaneous submissions or previously published poems. Cover letter preferred. Editors sometimes comment on rejections. Submission deadlines are end of February, June and November. Reports in up to 3 months. Sometimes sends prepublication galleys. Pays overseas writers complimentary copies.** Send SASE (or SAE with IRC) for rules for their open biennial competitions (£1,200 in prizes) and for *Staple First Editions* monographs (sample postpaid: £8). Recently published monographs include *Preserving Lemons* by Gregory Warren Wilson. They also produce (to order) poetry postcards of poetry *published* in the magazine. The editor says, "In general, we don't go for haiku, performance pieces, concrete poetry, 'found' items."

‡STARBLADE MAGAZINE (I, IV-Science fiction/fantasy), P.O. Box 400672, Hesperia CA 92340, founded 1994, editor Stephanie O'Rourke, published quarterly, features "sword and sorcery, fantasy, science fiction—good writing that entertains." **They want "poetry of 25 lines or less, any style. Must be sword and sorcery or science fiction." They do not want "gooey romantic, blood and gore, political or garbled poems."** As a sample the editor selected these lines from her poem "At Mother's Knee":

> *The Court glitters; it shines like gold—*
> *and is just as chill and hard to hold.*
> *Nobles and courtiers are savage kin,*
> *kind without and killers within;*
> *they smile and flatter and charm*
> *all the while plotting harm.*

The editor says *Starblade* is 30 pgs., 8 × 11, laser-printed, perfect-bound, with "clear" cover and cover art. Press run is 50 for 3 subscribers. Single copy: $9; subscription: $20. **Sample postpaid: $4.50. Make checks payable to Stephanie O'Rourke. Submit 3 poems with name and address on left upper corner. No previously published poems; simultaneous submissions OK. Cover letter preferred; "age, experiences and previous credits OK, but not necessary. Be as wild as you like."** Time between acceptance and publication is 3-6 months. **Poems selected based on personal taste. Always comments on rejections. Send SASE for guidelines. Reports in 6-9 months. Pays 2 copies. Acquires one-time rights.** Reviews books or chapbooks of poetry or other magazines. Open to unsolicited reviews. Poets may also send books for review consideration.

‡STARK RAVING SANITY: AN ELECTRONIC LITERARY JOURNAL (I, II), 1835 Cedar River Dr., Jacksonville FL 32210-1301, e-mail mdubos@unf.edu or mdubose@mediaone.net, website http://www.unf.edu/

~mdubos/srs.htm, founded 1996, editor Mike S. DuBose. *SRS*'s frequency is "random and varied." It's purpose is "to provide to all interested the highest quality of poems, prose and theory. **We are open to any and all styles, although free verse is preferred.**" They have recently published poetry by Kimberly Frederick, Joe Flowers, Marc Awodey and CK Tower. As a sample the editor selected these lines from "The Power of Disappearing: The Religious Act of Taking Up Serpents" by Fred Dale:

> *This is religion:*
> *An Existence like holy sanguicolous shadows;*
> *A bouquet of poison to dance with;*
> *A chance to be saved by all untraceable*
> *A chance to be pierced*
> *with the agony of prayer*
> *in the river of your blood;*
> *A taste of his sleep.*

SRS is available for free via the Internet. **Submit 2-20 pages of poetry at a time. No previously published poems or simultaneous submissions. Cover letter and brief bio required. Submissions may be sent via e-mail, disk (DOS or Mac text only) or regular mail. "Please double space between works or note the distinction in brackets." Seldom comments on rejections. Obtain guidelines via website. Reports in 6 weeks, "longer if between school terms." Does not pay. "We are happy to provide any links or pointers toward the author's works in lieu of payment." Acquires first North American serial rights. "We do ask that reprints credit our journal with address."** Reviews books or chapbooks of poetry or other magazines. Open to unsolicited reviews of any length or type. Poets may also send books for review consideration. The editor says, "The literary scene is too caught up in trends and restrictions; overcome these by (a) submitting often and everywhere and (b) by supporting your local poetry outfits. For *SRS*, submissions are not only welcome, they are vital for our survival. However, works that do not follow our guidelines will be either sent back or left unanswered."

STATE STREET PRESS (II), P.O. Box 278, Brockport NY 14420, phone (716)637-0023, founded 1981, poetry editor Judith Kitchen, "publishes **chapbooks of poetry (20-24 pgs.) usually chosen in an anonymous competition**. State Street Press hopes to publish emerging writers with accomplished manuscripts and to offer a format for established writers who have a collection of poems that work together as a chapbook. We also occasionally publish full-length books including translations (query before sending). We want **serious traditional and free verse. We are not usually interested in the language school of poets. We ask only that the poems work as a collection, that the chapbook be more than an aggregate of poems—that they work together.**" They have recently published poetry by Debra Cummins, Sally Allen McNall, Jonathan Holden, Patricia Hooper, Jan Beatly, Pamela Stewart, Kath Anderson and Joe Survant. Chapbooks are beautifully designed and printed, 6×9, 30 pgs., with textured matte wrapper with art. **Send SASE for guidelines and chapbook contest rules. There is a $10 entry fee, for which you receive one of the chapbooks already published. Simultaneous submissions encouraged. Deadline: May 15. Always sends prepublication galleys. Pays copies and small honorarium. Authors buy additional copies at cost, sell at readings and keep the profits.** Judith Kitchen comments, "State Street Press believes that the magazines are doing a good job of publishing beginning poets and we hope to present published and unpublished work in a more permanent format, so we do reflect the current market and tastes. We expect our writers to have published individual poems and to be considering a larger body of work that in some way forms a 'book.' We have been cited as a press that prints poetry that is accessible to the general reader. We have become one of the most well-known chapbook series. Our authors have gone on to win many major national poetry awards as well as Whiting Foundation Fellowships and other honors. Our books receive national reviews."

‡STATE STREET REVIEW (I, II), FCCJ North, 4501 Capper Rd., Jacksonville FL 32218, phone (904)766-6697, fax (904)766-6654, e-mail hdenson@fccj.cc.fl.us, founded 1990, poetry and fiction editor Howard Denson, published biannually, strives "to publish the best prose and poetry that we can get our hands on." **They want "good, sharp poems. Generally no longer than 30 lines. No restrictions other than quality." They don't want "stuff that's been done before."** They have recently published poetry by Peter Meinke, Enid Shomer, Scott Ward and Jane Ellen Glasser. As a sample the editor selected these lines from "Piet Mondrian" by Louis Phillips:

> *Mondrian. Piet*
> *Did not sculpt the Piet*
> *a. Instead he settled on subjects less theatrical,*
> *But slightly more geometrical.*

The editor says *State Street Review* is 70-90 pgs., 5×8, offset printed, true binding with b&w photos and line art. They receive about 300-500 poems a year, accept approximately 40-60. Press run is 300-500 for 20 subscribers, 200-400 shelf sales, with 100 distributed free to libraries. Single copy: $5. **Sample postpaid: $3. Submit 5 poems at a time. No previously published poems, simultaneous sumbissions OK. Cover letter preferred with information for contributors' page. "For longer poems, we appreciate diskettes in WordPerfect, ASCII or RFT format."** Time between acceptance and publication is 1-6 months. **Poems are circulated to an editorial board. Always comments on rejections. Send SASE for guidelines or obtain via e-mail. Reports** in 1-6 months. **Always sends prepublication galleys. Pays 2 copies. Acquires first North American serial rights.** May review books or chapbooks of poetry in the future. Open to unsolicited reviews. Poets may also send books for review consideration. Also see their listing for Florida First Coast Writers' Festival in the Conferences section.

THE WALLACE STEVENS JOURNAL (II, IV-Specialized), Liberal Arts, Clarkson University, Box 5750, Potsdam NY 13699-5750, fax (315)268-3983, e-mail duemer@craft.camp.clarkson.edu, founded 1977, poetry editor Prof. Joseph Duemer, appears biannually using **"poems about or in the spirit of Wallace Stevens or having some relation to his work. No bad parodies of Stevens' anthology pieces."** They have recently published poetry by John Allman, Jacqueline Marcus, Charles Wright, X.J. Kennedy and Robert Creeley. As a sample the editor selected these lines from "A Holograph Draft" by Richard Epstein:

> Dear Sir:
> I have received your letter of
> the 26th. The offer it contains,
> that in exchange for ~~mermaids~~ a warranty deed
> to 1464 we drop our claim
> for 16,000 ~~blackbirds~~ dollars, will not do.
> Our client has decided to obtain
> ~~a pair of scarlet boots~~ a writ of execution to be served
> at his discretion. I remain, most truly,
> ~~the Rajah of Molucca blithely yours~~
> your obedient servant, Wallace Stevens

The editor describes it as 80-120 pgs., 6×9, typeset, flat-spined, with cover art on glossy stock. They receive 200-300 poems a year, accept approximately 15-20. Press run is 900 for 600 subscribers of which 200 are libraries. Subscription: $15. **Sample postpaid: $4. Submit 3-5 poems at a time. "We like to receive clean, readable copy. We generally do not publish previously published material, though we have made a few exceptions to this rule. No fax or e-mail submissions, though requests for information are fine." Reports in 4-10 weeks. Always sends prepublication galleys. Pays 2 copies. Acquires all rights. Returns rights with permission and acknowledgment.** Staff reviews books of poetry. Send books for review consideration "only if there is some clear connection to Stevens." *The Wallace Stevens Journal* is published by the Wallace Stevens Society. The editor says, "Brief cover letters are fine, even encouraged. Please don't submit to *WSJ* if you have not read Stevens. We like parodies, but they must *add* a new angle of perception. Most of the poems we publish are not parodies but meditations on themes related to Wallace Stevens and those poets he has influenced. Those wishing to contribute might wish especially to examine the Fall 1996 issue which has a large and rich selection of poetry."

STICKS; STICKS PRESS (III, IV-Form), P.O. Box 399, Maplesville AL 36750-0399, press founded 1989, journal 1991, editor/publisher Mary Veazey. *Sticks*, appearing irregularly, **publishes "the best short poems of experienced/established poets. All styles, subjects. Preferred length: 10 lines or less; width: 50 spaces per line."** She has published poetry by X.J. Kennedy and Richard Kostelanetz. As a sample the editor selected this poem, "Night" by Kyle Christopher:

> The night
> was cool, cricketed and inviting
> So I switched on the porchlight
> Went out to read poetry into it
> for hours unnoticing
> How meanwhile a snail
> saintly blazed a shiny
> trail before me.

The magazine is a 4¼×5½, saddle-stapled or saddle-sewn booklet, professionally printed on acid-free paper, 32 pgs. Press run is 500. Permanent mailing list in lieu of subscriptions. **Sample issue $3; sewn binding by request. Submit up to 3 poems at a time. "No guidelines, just be a master of the short poem." Does not comment on rejections. Reports in 3 months or less. Pays 2 copies.** The editor says, "*Sticks* is more mini-anthology than serial, since it often reveals a subtle thematic undercurrent and appears *only* when money for printing and a number of excellent small poems converge. *The Oxford Book of Short Poems* is the touchstone here; write the poem that will outlast us all; historically many such poems have been brief."

STILL WATERS PRESS (II, IV-Women), 459 S. Willow Ave., Galloway NJ 08201-4633, founded 1989, editor Shirley Warren, is a "small press publisher of poetry chapbooks and poet's handbooks (contemporary craft). Especially interested in **works by, for and about women. We prefer poetry firmly planted in the real world, but equally mindful of poetry as art. The transformation from pain to perseverance, from ordinary to extraordinary, from defeat to triumph, pleases us. But we reject Pollyanna poetry immediately. Nothing sexist, in either direction, nothing sexually erotic. No rhymed poetry unless you're a master of form who can meticulously avoid strange manipulations of syntax simply to achieve end-rhyme. No patriarchal religious verse. Preferred length: four lines to two pages per poem. Form: no restrictions—we expect**

content to dictate the form." They have published poetry by Linda Milstein and Susan Cavanaugh. The press publishes **4-8 chapbooks/year,** averaging 28 pgs. Sample chapbooks: $5; writer's guide booklets: $3. **Send SASE for guidelines, then query. Simultaneous submissions and previously published poems OK. Always sends prepublication galleys. Pays 10% of the press run. Royalties on second and subsequent press runs. Acquires first or reprint rights.** They hold 2 annual contests, each with $10 reading fee. Send SASE for detailed guidelines. The editor says, "Read other poets, contemporary and traditional. Attend workshops, establish rapport with your local peers, attend readings. Keep your best work in circulation. Someone out there is looking for you."

STONE SOUP, THE MAGAZINE BY YOUNG WRITERS AND ARTISTS; THE CHILDREN'S ART FOUNDATION (IV-Children), P.O. Box 83, Santa Cruz CA 95063, phone (408)426-5557, fax (408)426-1161, e-mail editor@stonesoup.com, website http://www.stonesoup.com, founded 1973, editor Ms. Gerry Mandel. *Stone Soup* publishes **writing and art by children through age 13; they want to see free verse poetry but no rhyming poetry, haiku or cinquain.** *Stone Soup*, published 5 times/year, is a handsome $6 \times 8\frac{3}{4}$ magazine, professionally printed on heavy stock with 4 full-color art reproductions inside and a full-color illustration on the coated cover, saddle-stapled. A membership in the Children's Art Foundation at $26/year includes a subscription to the magazine. The editor receives 5,000 poetry submissions a year, uses approximately 20. There are 4 pgs. of poetry in each issue. Circulation is 20,000 for 13,000 subscribers, 5,000 to bookstores, 2,000 other. **Sample postpaid: $4.50. Submissions can be any number of pages, any format, but not simultaneous. Criticism will be given when requested. "We prefer submissions by mail because we need an SASE in order to respond. Submissions that arrive via fax or e-mail will receive a response only if they are accepted." Send SASE for guidelines or obtain via e-mail or website. Reports in 1 month. Pays $10 and 2 copies plus discounts. Buys all rights. Returns rights upon request.** Open to reviews by children. Children through age 13 may also send books for review consideration. *Stone Soup* has received both Parents' Choice and Edpress Golden Lamp Honor Awards.

‡STONEFLOWER LITERARY JOURNAL; ENTRE NOUS (II), 1824 Nacogdoches, Suite 191, San Antonio TX 78209, e-mail stonflower@aol.com, founded 1995 (*Stoneflower*), 1997 (*Entre Nous*), editor Brenda Davidson-Shaddox. *Stoneflower Literary Journal*, published annually, and *Entre Nous*, published quarterly, strive to offer a forum for creative people who have daring for the new and respect for the traditional. *Stoneflower* **wants top-quality poetry of any style, any length, but prefers what will fit on one page;** *Entre Nous* **wants any subject, style or form up to 40 lines long.** *Stoneflower* **does not want sentimental, didactic or crude poetry;** *Entre Nous* **does not want pornographic poetry, didactic or religious.** They have recently published poetry by E'Lane Murray, Carolyn Hull and Linda Watanabe McFerrin. As a sample the editor selected these lines from "Come-alongs" by Scott Ward:

> *The pull of my father's arms*
> *survives in these fences, his legacy*
> *of order that marks*
> *the confines of hay barn,*
> *smoke house, the cattle's crowded*
> *shade, and open field.*

The editor says *Stoneflower* is 120 pgs., $4\frac{1}{4} \times 5\frac{1}{2}$, professionally offset printed on 50 lb. paper, perfect-bound with professional art and photos. The editor says *Entre Nous* is 60-75 pgs., $4\frac{1}{4} \times 5\frac{1}{2}$, 50 lb. paper, saddle-stapled with medium card cover, pen and ink drawings and b&w photos. *Stoneflowers* receives about 500-1,000 poems a year, *Entre Nous* receives about 100, they each accept approximately 10%. Press run for *Stoneflower* is 1,000 for 400 subscribers, 200 shelf sales; 25 distributed free to libraries and schools. Press run for *Entre Nous* is 300. For *Stoneflower*, single copy: $8. **Sample copy: $4 plus 6×9 envelope and $1.25 for postage.** For *Entre Nous*, single copy: $5; subscription: $12. **Sample copy: $2.50 plus 6×9 envelope and $1.24 postage. Make checks payable to Stoneflower Press. Submit 6 poems at a time. "Poems should appear on page as poet wants it printed with clean, clear type suitable for scanning. Include a short bio. E-mail submissions OK. Previously published poems and simultaneous submissions OK.** Time between acceptance and publication is up to 1 year. **Poems are circulated to an editorial board. Reading staff does first reading for general acceptability. Poetry editor makes final selections. Seldom comments on rejections.** *Entre Nous* **publishes theme issues. Send SASE for guidelines and upcoming themes. Reports within 3 months.** *Stoneflower* **pays $10/poem.** *Stoneflower* and *Entre Nous* **acquire one-time rights.** *Stoneflower* sponsors annual literary contest with $50 first prize and publication, $10 second place and copies to honorable mentions. Submit poems May through March in a scanable format, with name, address and phone in upper left corner of first page and number of lines in upper right. Send SASE for more information. The editor says, "Read our journal and others; go to readings. Follow guidelines exactly, otherwise the ms will not be read. A submission letter to an editor does nothing to improve your chances for publication. Your work will speak for itself."

STORMLINE PRESS, INC. (V), Box 593, Urbana IL 61801, phone (217)328-2665, founded 1985, publisher Raymond Bial, is an independent press publishing fiction, poetry and photography, **with emphasis upon the rural Midwest. They accept submissions "only by invitation. Do not send unsolicited manuscripts. Query in November and December only with SASE. We publish both established and new poets, but in the latter case prefer to publish those poets who have been working some years to master their craft."** The press publishes 1-2 books each year with an average page count of 48-64. They are 6×9, some flat-spined paperbacks and some hardcover.

STORY LINE PRESS (V); NICHOLAS ROERICH POETRY PRIZE FOR UNPUBLISHED FIRST BOOK OF POETRY (II), Three Oaks Farm, 27006 Gap Road, Brownsville OR 97327-9718, phone (541)466-5352, Story Line Press founded 1985, poetry editor Robert McDowell. Story Line Press publishes each year the winner of the Nicholas Roerich Poetry Prize for an Unpublished First Book of Poetry ($1,000 plus publication and a paid reading at the Roerich Museum in New York City; a runner-up receives a full Story Line Press Scholarship to the Wesleyan Writers Conference in Middletown, CT [see listing in Conferences and Workshops section]; $20 entry and handling fee). Deadline for submissions: October 15. Send SASE for complete guidelines. The press also publishes books about poetry and has published collections by such poets as Colette Inez, Rita Dove, Bruce Bawer, Louis Simpson, Frederick Morgan and George Keithley. **They consider unsolicited mss only for the Nicholas Roerich Poetry Prize competition. Always sends prepublication galleys.**

STRAIGHT; STANDARD PUBLISHING CO. (IV-Religious, teens), 8121 Hamilton Ave., Cincinnati OH 45231, phone (513)931-4050, editor Heather E. Wallace. Standard is a large religious publishing company. *Straight* is a weekly take-home publication (digest-sized, 12 pgs., color newsprint) **for teens. Poetry is *by* teenagers, any style, religious or inspirational in nature. No adult-written poetry**. As a sample the editor selected "Why Grace to Me" by Janice Dru:

> *This beat-up soul has*
> *Not much to give,*
> *Not much to say . . .*
> *Not much at all.*
> *Yet through it all,*
> *It is showered with Your grace.*

Teen author must include birthdate and social security number. Submit 1-5 poems at a time. Simultaneous submissions OK. Time between acceptance and publication is 9-12 months. **Publishes theme issues. Guidelines and upcoming themes available for SASE. Reports in 4-6 weeks. Pays $10/poem plus 5 copies. Buys first or reprint rights.** The editor says, "Many teenagers write poetry in their English classes at school. If you've written a poem on an inspirational topic, and your teacher's given you an 'A' on it, you've got a very good chance of having it published in *Straight*."

‡THE STRAIN (II), 1307 Diablo Dr., Crosby TX 77532-3004, poetry editor Michael Bond, editor Norman C. Stewart, Jr. *The Strain* is a monthly magazine using **"experimental or traditional poetry of very high quality."** They do not include sample lines of poetry here as they "prefer not to limit style of submissions." **Simultaneous submissions and previously published poems OK. Guidelines issue: $5 and 8 first-class stamps. Pays "no less than $5.** We would **prefer you submit before obtaining the guidelines issue which mostly explains upcoming collections and collaborations."** Send books for review consideration.

‡STREET BEAT QUARTERLY (I, IV-Specialized: homelessness/poverty), 301 Third Ave., Pittsburgh PA 15222, phone (412)765-3302, founded 1990, contact Patrick Reitz, their "emphasis is on publishing first-hand perspectives on homelessness and poverty. **We're pretty flexible on publishing works by those who've experienced homelessness/poverty . . . and ask others who submit work to stick to those themes only."** They have recently published poetry by Dennis Prutus, Adam Kirstenbaum and Paul Weinman. As a sample the editor selected these lines from "The Ow is Now" by Freddy Bosco:

> *I. Words*
> *There are so many who love having written.*
> *To me, the manuscripts can go*
> *headlong into the Hudson.*
> *No matter: the moving pen cuts like a surgeon*
> *through matter. To say what's in my heart*
> *is a fountain firecracker exploding light in all directions.*

SBQ is 32 pgs., saddle-stitched, newsprint with 2-color cover, illustrations and ads. They receive about 150 poems a year, accept approximately 40-50%. Press run is 2,500. Single copy: $2.50; subscription: $10. **Sample postpaid: $3. Make checks payable to Community Human Services. Submit up to 5 poems at a time. Previously published poems and simultaneous submissions OK. Cover letter preferred.** Time between acceptance and publication is 3-6 months. **Editor chooses poems. Seldom comments on rejections. Reports in 1-3 months. Pays $3/poem plus 1 copy. Acquires one-time rights.**

‡*STRIDE PUBLICATIONS (II), 11 Sylvan Rd., Exeter, Devon EX4 6EW England, e-mail rml@mubbear.demon.co.uk, website http://www.virtual-pl.com/targent/alt-exeter/stride, founded 1982, editor R.M. Loydell. Stride Publications publishes poetry, poetry sequences, prose and experimental novels, and an occasional arts magazine. **The editor wants to see any poetry that is "new, inventive, nothing self-oriented, emotional, no narrative or fantasy."** He has published work by Peter Redgrove, William Everson, Sheila E. Murphy and Charles Wright. Stride Publications publishes paperbacks 60-100 pgs. of poetry, plus a few novels and anthologies. **Unsolicited**

submissions for book publication are accepted. Authors should query first via e-mail or by sending sample poems with return postage or IRCs. Cover letter required with bio, summary and review quotes. Queries will be answered in 6 weeks and mss reported on in 3 months or more. Pays 30 author's copies. Magazine reviews books and tapes of poetry in 100-200 words, multi-book format. Send books etc. for review consideration.

STRUGGLE: A MAGAZINE OF PROLETARIAN REVOLUTIONARY LITERATURE (I, II, IV-Political, science fiction/fantasy, workers' social issues, women/feminism, anti-racism), P.O. Box 13261, Detroit MI 48213-0261, founded 1985, editor Tim Hall, is a "literary quarterly, content: the struggle of the working people and all oppressed against the rich. Issues such as: racism, poverty, aggressive wars, workers' struggle for jobs and job security, the overall struggle for a non-exploitative society, a genuine socialism." The **poetry and songs they use are "generally short, any style, subject matter must criticize or fight against the rule of the billionaires. We welcome experimentation devoted to furthering such content."** They have recently published poetry by Kimberly Sonnich, Bonnie Compton Hanson, Francesca J. Sidoti, Mike Catalano and Rowena Silver. As a sample we selected these lines from "To Whom It May Concern: Ref.: use of the word 'nigger' " by Carol Williams:

> Every time you use the word
> for yourself
> you are giving it
> as a gift
> to some uppity white
> who takes it and gratefully
> justifies using it
> himself.

Struggle is 36 pgs., digest-sized, photocopied with occasional photos of artwork, short stories and short plays as well as poetry and songs. Subscription: $10 for 4 issues. **Sample postpaid: $2.50. Submit 8 poems at a time. Make checks payable to "Tim Hall—Special Account." Accepted work usually appears in the next issue. Editor tries to provide criticism "with every submission." Tries to report in 3-4 months. Pays 2 copies.** Tim Hall says, "Show passion and fire. Formal experiments, traditional forms both welcome. Especially favor: works reflecting rebellion by the working people against the rich; works against racism, sexism, militarism, imperialism; works critical of our exploitative culture; works showing a desire for—or fantasy of—a non-exploitative society; works attacking the Republican New Stone Age and the Democrats' surrender to it."

STUDENT LEADERSHIP JOURNAL (IV-Students, religious), Dept. PM, P.O. Box 7895, Madison WI 53707-7895, phone (608)274-4823 ext. 425 or 413, editor Jeff Yourison, is a **"magazine for Christian student leaders on secular campuses. We accept a wide variety of poetry. Do not want to see trite poetry. Also, we accept little rhymed poetry; it must be very, very good."** *Student Leadership* is a quarterly, 32 pgs., magazine-sized, 2-color inside, 2-color covers, with no advertising, 70% editorial, 30% graphics/art. Press run is 8,000 going to college students in the US and Canada. Subscription: $16. **Sample postpaid: $3. No simultaneous submissions. Previously published poems OK.** "Would-be contributors should read us to be familiar with what we publish." Best time to submit mss is March through July ("We set our year's editorial plan"). Editor "occasionally" comments on rejections. Send SASE for guidelines. Reports in 2-3 months. Time between acceptance and publication is 1-24 months. **Pays $25-50/poem plus 2 copies. Buys first or reprint rights.** He says, "Try to express feelings through images and metaphor. Religious poetry should not be overly didactic, and it should never moralize!"

*STUDIO, A JOURNAL OF CHRISTIANS WRITING (II, IV-Religious, spirituality), 727 Peel St., Albury, New South Wales 2640 Australia, founded 1980, publisher Paul Grover, is a small press literary quarterly "with contents **focusing upon the Christian striving for excellence in poetry,** prose and occasional articles relating Christian views of literary ideas." **In poetry, the editors want "shorter pieces but with no specification as to form or length (necessarily less than three to four pages), subject matter, style or purpose. People who send material should be comfortable being published under this banner:** *Studio, A Journal of Christians Writing.*" They have published poetry by John Foulcher and other Australian poets. *Studio* is 36 pgs., digest-sized, professionally printed on high-quality recycled paper, saddle-stapled, matte card cover, with graphics and line drawings. Circulation is 300, all subscriptions. Subscription: $40 (Aud) for overseas members. **Sample available (airmail from US) for $8 (Aud). Submissions may be "double-spaced, typed copy or simultaneous." Name and address must appear on the reverse side of each page submitted. Cover letter required; include brief details of previous publishing history, if any. Reporting time is 2 months and time to publication is 9 months. Pays 1 copy. Acquires first Australian rights.** Reviews books of poetry in 250 words, single format. Open to unsolicited reviews. Poets may also send books for review consideration. The magazine conducts a biannual poetry and short story contest. The editor says, "Trend in Australia is for imagist poetry and poetry exploring the land and the self. Reading the magazine gives the best indication of style and standard, so send a few dollars for a sample copy before sending your poetry. Keep writing, and we look forward to hearing from you."

STUDIO ONE (II), Haehn Campus Center, College of St. Benedict, St. Joseph MN 56374, e-mail studio1@csbs ju.edu, founded 1976, editor changes yearly. *Studio One* is an annual literary and visual arts magazine designed as a forum for local, regional and national poets/writers. **They have no specifications regarding form, subject matter or style of poetry submitted. However, poetry no more than 2 pages stands a better chance of publication.** They have published poetry by Yuko Taniguchi and Larry Schug. As a sample the editor selected these lines from "Jewels for Waking" by Tiffaney Dawn Dressen:

> *Do not touch me*
> *when I sleep*
> *my bones are breaking*
> *into sapphires frozen*
> *deep arctic blue*

The editor says *Studio One* is 50-80 pgs., soft cover, typeset. It includes 1-3 short stories, 22-30 poems and 10-13 visual art representations. They receive 250-400 submissions a year. No subscriptions, but a **sample copy can be obtained by sending a SASE with no less than $2 postage. Previously published poems and simultaneous submissions OK. Deadline: February 16 for spring publication. Seldom comments on rejections. Send stamped, addressed postcard for confirmation of submissions received.** *Studio One* received the 1995 Medalist Award from The Columbia Scholastic Press Association, Columbia University.

‡**STYGIAN ARTICLES (I, IV-Horror, science fiction/fantasy)**, 3201 Sun Lake Dr., St. Charles MO 63301-3012, e-mail charon@i1.net, website http://www.i1.net/~charon, founded 1994, associate editor Natalie Smith, published quarterly, features works of horror, fantasy and science fiction. **They want "longer more sustained poems with concrete imagery, perhaps with a surrealistic flavor—shift perceptions." They do not want "short, rhyming, abstract poetry."** They have recently published poetry by John Grey and Kyle Christopher. As a sample the editor selected these lines from "Upper Berth" by Charlee Jacob:

> *This bit of veteran clitoris recognizes*
> *the terminal in your cracked marbles*
> *of eyes as the point of final convergence.*
> *And then there was the collision we both*
> *mistook for rapture, both screaming,*
> *until the car rolled and twisted.*

SA is 56 pgs., digest-sized, saddle-stapled, 300 dpi laser output, desktop-published, with colored medium card cover, illustrations and ads. They receive about 150-200 poems a year, accept approximately 10%. Press run is 200 for 50 subscribers; 25 distributed free to reviewers, ad swaps. Subscription: $18. **Sample postpaid: $5. Make checks payable to Jeremy E. Johnson. Submit 3 poems at a time. No previously published poems or simultaneous submissions. Cover letter required.** Time between acceptance and publication is 3-6 months. **"Poems are read by poetry editor and either rejected or sent on with recommendations to editor/publisher." Always comments on rejections. Send SASE for guidelines. Reports in 1 month or less. Pays 1 copy. Acquires first North American serial rights.** Reviews books or chapbooks of poetry or other magazines. Open to unsolicited reviews. Poets may also send books for review consideration.

‡**STYGIAN VORTEX PUBLICATIONS; IN DARKNESS ETERNAL; LORDS OF THE ABYSS: TALES OF HORROR; LORDS OF ETERNAL DARKNESS: TALES OF SUPERNATURAL HORROR; NEURONET; SHADOW SWORD: THE MAGAZINE OF FANTASY, FICTION, POETRY AND ART; SHAPE SHIFTER! (I, IV-Horror, science fiction/fantasy)**, 1085 NE 179 Terrace, North Miami Beach FL 33162-1256, phone (305)651-0187, e-mail stygian@mindspring.com, website http://www.mindspring.com/~stygian, founded 1992, editor-in-chief Glenda Woodrum. *In Darkness Eternal*, editor t'shaik, appears annually, is a "vampire-based publication." They receive about 100 poems a year, rate of acceptance varies. Press run is 200 for 150 subscribers. Single copy: $5.50; subscription: $8.50. **Sample postpaid: $5.25.** *Lords of the Abyss*, editor M. Barnette, and *Lords of Eternal Darkness*, editor t'shaik, are published annually, and strive "to promote the horror genre in fiction, poetry and art while providing a showcase for the work of our contributors." Single copy: $5.50. **Sample postpaid: $3.95.** *NeuroNet*, published annually, aims "to promote the cyberpunk science fiction." Press run is 100 for a varying number of subscribers. **Sample postpaid: $5.50.** *Shadow Sword* is published quarterly with an additional 2 special issues. Press run is 125 for 100 subscribers, with a varying number distributed free to reviewers and prisoners. Single copy: $5.25; subscription: $18/6 issues. **Sample postpaid: $3.95.** *Shape Shifter!*, editor Coyote Osborne, published annually, strives "to promote fiction, poetry and art about legendary creatures and beings able to change their outward form." Press run is 150 for 100 subscribers, with a varying number distributed free to reviewers. Single copy: $5.25. **Sample postpaid: $5.25.**

MARKET CATEGORIES: (I) Beginning; **(II)** General; **(III)** Limited;
(IV) Specialized; **(V)** Closed.

Make all checks payable to Stygian Vortex Publications. All the publications promote fiction, poetry and especially art while "creating a showcase for talented persons in the field/genre." **They want to see poetry within their genre and encourage obtaining their guidelines.** *Shadow Sword* **adds they can always use more good sword & sorcery poetry. They do not want to see romance-oriented, mainstream, inspirational, religious or media-related material (e.g., Dracula, Larry Talbot, Lestat, "Star Wars," "Star Trek," etc.).** All of the publications are between 56-80 pgs., 8½ × 11, printed by digital imaging to 20 lb. bond paper, saddle-stapled, with 67 lb. b&w (greyscale) bristol covers, a lot of art and ads. **Submit up to 5 poems at a time. Previously published poems OK "if more than two years have elapsed prior to publication." Simultaneous submissions OK. Cover letter required with "brief personal bio, not a list of publication credits. If you are a beginning writer with five or less acceptances, however, please note this in your cover letter. "Electronic disk submissions in ASCII format are fine. E-mail submissions must be followed by/preceeded by a SASE as we issue contracts." Address all submissions/correspondence to the title of the publication. Has backlog of 3-12 months.** Time between acceptance and publication is 1-24 months. **Poems are circulated to an editorial board. "The first reader is responsible for deciding which poems go on to the magazine editor. The editor of the respective magazine then submits them for approval to the editor-in-chief." Always comments on rejections. Publishes theme issues. Send SASE for guidelines and upcoming themes or obtain via e-mail or website. Reports in 1-16 weeks ("acceptances are slower than rejections"). Always sends prepublication galleys. Pays $1-3/poem plus 1 copy. Buys one-time or reprint rights.** Reviews books or chapbooks of poetry in *Shadow Sword* only. Open to unsolicited reviews, "but they must meet the genre requirement of *Shadow Sword* (sword & sorcery). Poets may also send books for review consideration to Michael Barnette, at the same address. Sponsors 'Best of *Shadow Sword*' Award for poetry. It is a reader's vote and a certificate is issued. The editor says, "Please familiarize yourself with our guidelines for the magazines you intend to submit to. Many poems are rejected because they did not meet our requirements."

♣**SUB-TERRAIN; ANVIL PRESS (II, IV-Social issues, political, form/style)**, P.O. Box 1575, Bentall Centre, Vancouver, British Columbia V6C 2P7 Canada, phone (604)876-8710, founded 1988, poetry editor Paul Pitre. Anvil Press is an "alternate small press publishing *Sub-Terrain*—a socially conscious literary quarterly whose aim is to produce a reading source that will stand in contrast to the trite and pandered—as well as broadsheets, chapbooks and the occasional monograph." They want **"work that has a point-of-view; work that has some passion behind it and is exploring issues that are of pressing importance (particularly that with an urban slant); work that challenges conventional notions of what poetry is or should be; work with a social conscience. No bland, flowery, uninventive poetry that says nothing in style or content."** As a sample the editor selected these lines from "Red and Black Chaos" by Sophia Kaszuba:

> *When the imagination has taken pictures*
> *and seen what is there*
> *at the back of the head,*
> *then she sometimes walks in.*
> *Once in a short pleated skirt of white linen,*
> *she now wears*
> *a heavy embroidered dress of black felt*
> *and on her head a hat, dark*
> *as puddles after it rains.*

Sub-Terrain is 40 pgs., 7½ × 10½, offset, with a press run of 3,000. Subscription: $18. **Sample postpaid: $5. Submit 4-6 poems at a time. Simultaneous submissions OK; no previously published poems. Reports in 8-10 weeks. Pays money only for solicited work; for other work, 4-issue subscription. Acquires one-time rights for magazine. "If chapbook contract, we retain right to publish subsequent printings unless we let a title lapse out-of-print for more than one year."** Staff occasionally reviews small press poetry chapbooks. Sponsors Last Poems Poetry Contest for "poetry that encapsulates North American experience at the close of the 20th Century"; information for SASE (or SAE and IRC). **For chapbook or book publication submit 4 sample poems and bio, no simultaneous submissions. "We are willing to consider mss. But I must stress that we are a co-op, depending on support from an interested audience. New titles will be undertaken with caution. We are not subsidized at this point and do not want to give authors false hopes—but if something is important and should be in print, we will do our best." Editor provides brief comment and more extensive comments for fees.** He says, "Poetry, in our opinion, should be a distillation of emotion and experience that is being given back to the world. Pretty words and fancy syntax are just that. Where are the modern day writers who are willing to risk it all, put it all on the line? Young, new writers: Show it all. The last thing the world needs is soppy, sentimental fluff that gives nothing and says nothing."

‡**SUFFUSION MAGAZINE (I)**, P.O. Box 57183, Lincoln NE 68505-7183, phone (402)465-5839, e-mail suffusion@aol.com, founded 1988, published quarterly, is an independent art and literary magazine. **"We accept free verse, avant-garde (experimental, traditional, haiku and occasionally humorous) poetry. There are no arbitrary limits on length, but we find shorter poems are easier to fit into our format."** They have recently published poetry by Simon Perchik. *Suffusion* is 27 pgs., 8½ × 11, professionally printed on 70 lb. paper, perfect-bound, with colored light card cover, art, graphics, photos, cartoons and ads. They receive about 150-200 poems a year, accept approximately 10%. Press run is 400 for 30 subscribers of which 4 are libraries, less than 5% shelf

sales; 75% distributed free through local stores and other public placements. Subscription: $11 ($11.72 for NE residents). **Sample postpaid: $4 ($4.26 for NE residents). Submit 2 poems at a time. Previously published poems and simultaneous submissions OK. Cover letter preferred. Reads submissions January 1 through April 1 only.** Time between acceptance and publication is 6-24 months. **Seldom comments on rejections. Send SASE for guidelines. Reports in 1-2 months. Sometimes sends prepublication galleys. Pays 1 copy. All rights retained by author.** Reviews single books of poetry in 25-50 words. Open to unsolicited reviews. Poets may also send books for review consideration.

SULPHUR RIVER LITERARY REVIEW (II), P.O. Box 19228, Austin TX 78760-9228, founded 1978, reestablished 1987, editor/publisher James Michael Robbins, is a semiannual of poetry, prose and artwork. **They have "no restrictions except quality." They do not want poetry that is "trite or religious or verse that does not incite thought."** They have published poetry by Duane Locke, B.Z. Niditch, Lyn Lifshin, Miles David Moore, Kyamil Tangaychev, Bernard Morris. As a sample the editor selected these lines from "Fission" by Hillary Lyon:

> there was no boundless towering forest first
> no vigorous talking river here
>
> we who lived together we who invented the city
> now confess our need
>
> bleed a fission of spirit
> as handshakes fail as foundations snap
>
> we scramble like dogs off the leash
> savage delicious with freedom

SRLR is digest-sized, perfect-bound, with glossy cover. They receive about 1,000 poems a year, accept approximately 5%. Press run is 400 for 200 subscribers, 100 shelf sales. Subscription: $12. **Sample postpaid: $7. No previously published poems or simultaneous submissions. Often comments on rejections. Reports in 1 month. Sometimes sends prepublication galleys. Pays 2 copies.** The editor says, "Poetry is, for me, the essential art, the ultimate art, and any effort to reach the effect of the successful poem deserves some comment other than 'sorry.' This is why I try to comment as much as possible on submissions, though by doing so I risk my own special absurdity. So be it. However, there can be no compromise of quality if the poem is to be successful or essential art."

SUMMER STREAM PRESS (II), P.O. Box 6056, Santa Barbara CA 93160-6056, phone (805)962-6540, founded 1978, poetry editor David D. Frost, publishes a series of books (Box Cars) in hardcover and softcover, each presenting 6 poets, averaging 70 text pgs. for each poet. "The mix of poets represents many parts of the country and many approaches to poetry. The poets previously selected have been published, but that is no requirement. We welcome traditional poets in the mix and thus offer them a chance for publication in this world of free-versers. **The six poets share a 15% royalty. We require rights for our editions worldwide and share 50-50 with authors for translation rights and for republication of our editions by another publisher. Otherwise all rights remain with the authors."** They have published poetry by Virginia E. Smith, Sandra Russell, Jennifer MacPherson, Nancy Berg, Lois Shapley Bassen and Nancy J. Wallace. To be considered for future volumes in this series, **query with about 12 sample poems, no cover letter. Replies to query in 6 months, to submission (if invited) in 1 year. Previously published poetry and simultaneous submissions OK. Editor usually comments on rejections. Always sends prepublication galleys. Pays 6 copies plus royalties.** He says, "We welcome both traditional poetry and free verse. However, we find we must reject almost all the traditional poetry received simply because the poets exhibit little or no knowledge of the structure and rules of traditional forms. Much of it is rhymed free verse."

‡A SUMMER'S READING (II), 804 Oakland Ave., Mt. Vernon IL 62864, phone (618)242-8364, fax (618)244-8047, founded 1996, contact Ted Morrissey and Barbara Hess, published annually, strives "to provide one more well edited, attractive outlet for new and emerging writers, poets and artists. **Willing to look at all kinds of poetry, prefer free verse or blank verse with clear images and ideas."** They do not want "sappy 'greeting card' stuff." They have recently published poetry by Fernand Roqueplan and Janisse Ray. As a sample the editor selected these lines from "Sabbatical" by Zarina Mullan Plath:

> In India I once listened to geckos
> falling from the ceiling, stretching
> my hands toward the spun threads
> of mosquito netting, a fairy-cloth
> holding me safe, I believed, from tigers
> and cobras.

The editor says *A Summer's Reading* is approximately 50 pgs., offset printed, with color cover, b&w artwork. Press run is 200-350 for 30 subscribers. Subscription: $5. **Sample postpaid: $5. Submit up to 10 poems with name, address, phone and line count on each. Previously published poems and simultaneous submissions**

OK if so noted. **Cover letter preferred with brief bio and publishing history.** Time between acceptance and publication is 3-12 months. **"Both editors read all submissions—may ask others for their opinions if needed." Often comments on rejections. Send SASE for guidelines. Reports in 3-12 weeks. Always sends prepublication galleys. Pays 2 copies. Acquires one-time rights plus request for acknowledgement if reprinted.** May include staff-written reviews of poetry books in the future. Poets may also send books for review consideration. The editor says, "Don't hesitate to submit—we will be respectful and fair to your work. We strive to publish newcomers with emerging and established artists. We would like to see more translations (include original text)."

THE SUN (II), 107 N. Roberson St., Chapel Hill NC 27516, phone (919)942-5282, founded 1974, editor Sy Safransky, is "a monthly magazine of ideas. Noted for honest, personal work that's not too obscure or academic. **We avoid traditional, rhyming poetry, as well as limericks, haiku and religious poetry. We're open to almost anything else: free verse, prose poems, short and long poems."** They have published poetry by Alison Luterman, Robert Hill Long, Sparrow, Kim Addonizio and Chris Bursk. As a sample the editor selected these lines from "Nudging a Poem" by Robert Bly:

> To nudge a poem along toward its beauty.
> Is that selfishness? Is it something silly?
>
> Do others love poems as I do? Longing
> To find you in a phrase, and be close
> There, kissing the walls and the door frame.
> Happy in the change of a single word.

The Sun is 40 pgs., magazine-sized, printed on 50 lb. offset, saddle-stapled, with b&w photos and graphics. Circulation is 29,000 for 26,000 subscriptions of which 50 are libraries. They receive 3,000 submissions of poetry a year, use approximately 36, have a 1- to 3-month backlog. Subscription: $32. **Sample postpaid: $3.50. Submit up to 6 poems at a time. Poems should be typed and accompanied by a cover letter. Previously published poems and simultaneous submissions OK, but should be noted. Send SASE for guidelines. Reports within 3 months. Pays $50-200 on publication plus copies and subscription. Buys first serial or one-time rights.** *The Sun* received an *Utne Reader* Award for General Excellence.

‡**THE SUNDAY SUITOR POETRY REVIEW (I)**, P.O. Box 252, Lathrop CA 95330, founded 1996, editor/publisher Elizabeth R. Fuller, published bimonthly, "encourages new writers as well as 'seasoned,' published artisans. Emphasis is on strong imagery, not amount of previous publication credits." **They want "creative work that reflects the mood of the review: love/life affirming presentations, natural wonder, and the beauty of the human spirit—pieces that uniquely touch the heart, mind and soul and woo the reader as if it were a 'suitor.' All forms/styles accepted. Length should not exceed 40 lines." They do not want "erotica, anything wildly experimental, vulgar or preachy."** They have recently published poetry by Douglas S. Johnson, Barbara Ann Porte, James F. O'Boyle and A.D. Winans. As a sample the editor selected these lines from "Scarce Times" by Johnny Mazzuca:

> Come scarce the wonder times . . .
> The marvel prism times
> That shine on dandelion
> Pressed against transparent walls . . .

TSSPR is 40-50 pgs., digest-sized, photocopied and saddle-stapled with heavy card cover and clip art. They receive about 500-700 poems a year, accept approximately 50%. Press run is 250 for 100 subscribers. Subscription: $15. **Sample postpaid: $4. There are no requirements for contributors, though subscribers "have the 'edge' on acceptance." Submit 5-7 poems at a time. Material must be typed, single spaced and name/address must appear in the upper corner. Do not send your only original copies. Material returned only upon request. Previously published poems and simultaneous submissions OK. Cover letter preferred.** Time between acceptance and publication is 1-5 months. **Editor selects material. Always comments on rejections. Publishes theme issues. Send SASE for guidelines. Reports "immediately (one to two weeks tops)." Sometimes sends prepublication galleys. Pays 1 copy. Acquires one-time rights.** Reviews books or chapbooks of poetry of any length from subscribers only. Open to unsolicited reviews. Poets may also send books for review consideration. Sponsors theme contests in each issue with $10 first prize, and one yearly prize of $50. Write for more information. The editor says, "We strive to encourage writers, not discourage by lengthy time waits, rejections and impersonal comments. We are a family-like publication, where each writer is treated with respect and recognition."

‡**THE SUNFLOWER DREAM; YOU CAN'T TAKE IT WITH YOU (I); THE SUNFLOWER ODYS-SEY; SUNFLOWER PRESS; SUNFLOWERS (V)**, 216 Riversview Dr., Carpentersville IL 60110-1743, phone (847)742-1864 (evenings), founded 1996, editor M.L. Moeller. *The Sunflower Dream*, published quarterly, has a general audience and focuses on family type and upbeat material. **They want "all styles and forms. All subject matter except for pornography and violence."** They have recently published poetry by Dolores Malaschak, Najwa Salam Brax, Harry T. Roman, Diana Kwiakowski Rubin and Michael Lizza. As a sample the editor selected these lines from "I Shall Return" by Kathryn Sibley Thomas:

> Should I not chance

to pass this way again,
hold tight to every shred
of beauty here,
hide them away to bring
to light some future year.

The editor says *The Sunflower Dream* is 100-150 pgs., comb-bound, with plastic cover, art, games and fillers. Press run is 200 for 100 subscribers. Subscription: $15. **Sample postpaid: $5. Make checks payable to M.L. Moeller.** *You Can't Take It With You*, a poetry newsletter published 6 times/year, focuses on offbeat, avant-garde or social commentary. It uses some material not appropriate for *The Sunflower Dream*. It is 6 pgs., 8½×14, corner-stapled with ads. Single copy: $2; subscription: $10. **Submit up to 10 poems at a time. Previously published poems and simultaneous submissions OK. Cover letter preferred. Disk submissions (IBM compatible) with hard copy OK; call first.** Time between acceptance and publication is 2-4 months. **"I select based on what I like and what I think readers will like." Seldom comments on rejections. Send SASE for guidelines. Reports within a month. Acquires one-time rights.** Reviews books or chapbooks of poetry. Poets may also send books for review consideration. *The Sunflower Odyssey*, published annually, features "entertaining poetry and short stories. Quality is a high priority." The editor says it is 100 pgs., combo-bound with plastic cover and artwork. They receive about 600 poems a year, accept approximately 300. Press run is 200. **Sample postpaid: $12. Work published is by invitation only.** Sunflower Press publishes family type material. They publish paperbacks and **chapbooks.** Books are usually flat-stapled, laser printed and comb-bound, card cover. **"I would need to see at least ten poems for a chapbook; for books I would like to see complete manuscript." Replies to queries in 1-2 months; to mss in 2 months.** Sponsors contests in *The Sunflower Dream*, with writing-related prizes and publication in their quarterly devoted to these winners: *Sunflowers*; send SASE for contest guidelines. Also publishes yearly poetry anthology, *The Sunflower Odyssey* (contributors by invitation only). The editor says, "The best advice is to write and submit. Write with the publication in mind as there are many different types of publications available. I do not confine my poetry or stories to one particular genre."

SUNSTONE (II), 343 N. 300 W., Salt Lake City UT 84103-1215, founded 1974, poetry editor Dixie Partridge, appears 8 times a year. *Sunstone* publishes "scholarly articles of interest to an open, Mormon audience; personal essays; fiction; and poetry." **They want "both lyric and narrative poetry that engages the reader with fresh, strong images, skillful use of language and a strong sense of voice and/or place. No didactic poetry, sing-song rhymes or in-process work."** They have published poetry by R.A. Christmas, Susan Howe, Anita Tanner, Robert Rees and Niranjan Mohanty. As a sample the editor selected these lines from "Sonora" by Georganne O'Connor:

. . . the wind's hot breath steals the air from your chest
and every bead of sweat from your skin.
From the canyon floor, I see hills
robbed of rain, studded with giant saguaro,
the sentinels. They have seen us coming.
In the accordian folds of their flesh,
elf owl rests, insulated from heat. . . .

Sunstone is 96 pgs., 8½×11, professionally printed and saddle-stapled with a semi-glossy paper cover. They receive more than 400 poems a year, accept 40-50. Press run is 10,000 for 8,000 subscribers of which 300 are libraries, 700 shelf sales. Subscription: $36/8 issues. **Sample postpaid: $4.95. No previously published poems or simultaneous submissions.** Time between acceptance and publication is a year or less. **Seldom comments on rejections. Send SASE for guidelines. Reports in 3 months. Pays 3 copies. Acquires first North American serial rights.** Reviews books of poetry. Open to unsolicited reviews. Poets may also send books for review consideration. The editor says, "Poetry does not have to be Mormon related at all. Most of it is not. We've published poems rooted strongly in place, narratives seeing life from another time or culture, poems on religious belief or doubt—a wide range of subject matter."

SURPRISE ME (I, IV-Spirituality, subscribers), P.O. Box 1762, Claremore OK 74018-1762, founded 1994, editor Lynda Nicolls. A biannual, *Surprise Me* only publishes work submitted by subscribers. **"*Surprise Me* is founded on the hope of providing a home for those souls who believe life's purpose is to serve Truth and Beauty. Our main interests are religion, mysticism, nature, art, literature, music, dance, relationships, love and peace. We are open on form, length and style to all kinds of poetry. Profanity, intolerance and pro-violence are not welcome."** They have recently published poetry by Kathy Bricker, Jo Lee Dilbert-Fitko, Ralph B. Johnson and David Salvaggio. As a sample the editor selected these lines from "Heaven" by Jeanette Raff:

This place called Heaven is a wondrous place to be
It is a quiet, still, magical place to me.
It's an inner place, magnificent and serene
Majestic sights and wondrous visions to be seen.
I have peace and contentment, no worries of any kind
For you see this place called Heaven is planted deep within my mind.

Surprise Me is 32 pgs., 8½×11, professionally printed by offset lithography on colored paper with b&w artwork and saddle-stapled. They receive about 1,000 poems a year, use approximately 10%. Press run is 60. Subscription:

$12 individual in US; $14 institution in US; $14 Canada and Mexico; $16 overseas. **Sample postpaid: $6. Submit up to 6 double-spaced pages at a time, name and address at the top of each page. Previously published poems and simultaneous submissions OK. Cover letter with brief bio required. "Submissions without cover letters (or at least a note) are too impersonal for me.** Submissions without SASE or IRCs will usually not receive a response." Time between acceptance and publication is about 2 years. **Seldom comments on rejections. Send SASE for guidelines. Reports ASAP. Pays 1 copy. Acquires one-time rights.** "We may review contributors' books and magazines in the future. Please query before sending books for review consideration." Open to unsolicited reviews. The editor says, "I don't like much of what is being currently published, because it lacks spirituality and often has shock value as its motive. I'm glad to see that rhyming poetry is making a comeback. I would advise beginners to read a lot—perhaps Yeats, Jeffers, Frost, Eliot, Whitman and Dickinson—and to remember that editorial comments (bad or good) are only one person's opinion. If one editor thinks your work is garbage, another editor may call it a treasure."

‡SWEET ANNIE & SWEET PEA REVIEW (I, II), 7750 Highway F-24 W, Baxter IA 50028, phone (515)792-3578, fax (515)792-1310, e-mail anniespl@netins.net, founded 1995, contact Beverly A. Clark, published quarterly, features short stories and poetry. **They want "poems of outdoors, plants, land, heritage, women, relationships, olden times—simpler times." They do not want "obscene, violent, explicit sexual material, obscure, long-winded materials, no overly-religious materials."** They have recently published poetry by Errol Miller, Margo Solod, Linda Goodman Robiner and CB Follett. As a sample the editor selected these lines from "Brooding the Heartlands" by M.L. Liebler:

> *There were those days*
> *Lonesome out on*
> *The Dakota Plains. Lonesome*
> *In my prairie rose daydreams—*
> *memories brooding across the heartland.*

SW&SPR is 56 pgs., 5¼ × 8½, offset, saddle-stapled, bond paper with onion skin page before title page, medium card cover, and cover art. They receive about 200 poems a year, accept approximately 25-33%. Press run is 100 for 30 subscribers of which 1 is a library, 20 shelf sales; 25-35 distributed free to contributors. Subscription: $24. **Sample postpaid: $7. Make checks payable to Sweet Annie Press. Submit 6-12 poems at a time. No previously published poems; simultaneous submissions OK. Cover letter preferred with personal comments about yourself and phone number.** Time between acceptance and publication is 6-9 months. **"We select for theme first, select for content second; narrow selections through editors." Often comments on rejections. Publishes theme issues. Send SASE for guidelines and upcoming themes. Reports in 6 months or sooner. Pays 1 copy. Acquires all rights. Returns rights with acknowledgment in future publications.** Will review chapbooks of poetry or other magazines of short length, reviews 500 words or less. Open to unsolicited reviews. Poets may also send books for review consideration.

SYCAMORE REVIEW (II), Dept. of English, Purdue University, West Lafayette IN 47907, phone (317)494-3783, fax (317)494-3780, e-mail sycamore@expert.cc.purdue.edu, website http://www.sla.purdue.edu/academic/engl/sycamore/, founded 1988 (first issue May, 1989), editor-in-chief Rob Davidson, poetry editor changes each year; submit to Poetry Editor. **"We accept personal essays, short fiction, drama, translations and quality poetry in any form. We aim to publish many diverse styles of poetry from formalist to prose poems, narrative and lyric."** They have recently published poetry by Sandra Gilbert, Paul Muldoon, Selima Hill, Roger Mitchell, Caroline Knox and Charles H. Webb. The magazine is semiannual in a digest-sized format, 160 pgs., flat-spined, professionally printed, with matte, color cover. Press run is 1,000 for 500 subscribers of which 50 are libraries. Subscription: $10; $12 outside US. **Sample postpaid: $7. Submit 3-6 poems at a time. Name and address on each page. No previously published poems except translations; simultaneous submissions OK, if notified immediately of acceptance elsewhere. No submissions accepted via fax or e-mail. Cover letters not required but invited; include phone number, short bio and previous publications, if any. "We read September 1 through May 1." Guidelines available for SASE. Reports in 4 months. Pays 2 copies.** Staff reviews books of poetry. Send books to editor-in-chief for review consideration. The editor says, "Poets who do not include SASE do not receive a response."

‡SYLVIA: A JOURNAL OF LITERATURE & ART (I), P.O. Box 654, Maple Shade NJ 08052, e-mail sylvia@marketavenue.com, website http://www.marketavenue.com/sylvia, founded 1996, editors Michelle Wittle and Susan Muaddi, published biannually, features "Poetry, short fiction, literary criticism, art and personal essays." **They want "crafted poetry with innovative imagery." They do not want "Hallmark-style, sentimental poetry."** As a sample the editor selected these lines from "Flower Pot Exile" by Tommy Wright, Jr.:

> *She holds out her hand*
> *and worlds implode*
> *the simplicity of horizons*
> *shimmer into pre-climactic intentions,*
> *while a revolution of words*
> *becomes the government of what i could not say.*

Sylvia is 52-80 pgs., 8½ × 5, photocopied, saddle-stapled with card cover, and b&w cover art. They receive about

100 poems a year, accept approximately 30-40%. Press run is 400 for 15 subscribers, 50 shelf sales. Single copy: $5; subscription: $8. **Sample postpaid: $4. Make checks payable to Susan Muaddi. Submit 4 poems at a time. No previously published poems or simultaneous submissions. Cover letter preferred.** Time between acceptance and publication is 6 months. **Seldom comments on rejections. Send SASE for guidelines. Reports in 6 months. Pays 1 copy. Acquires first North American serial rights.** The editor says, "Poets should study not only the great poets of the past, but also the poets publishing today. Only by reading others' poetry will you improve your own craft."

‡**SYNCOPATED CITY (I); SUN SPOT PRESS (V, IV-Regional)**, P.O. Box 2382, Providence RI 02906, e-mail litik@aol.com, founded 1996, editor Liti Kitiyakara. *Syncopated City*, published quarterly, strives "to provide an outlet for the expression of creativity—original voices excite us." **They want "poetry of any subject and style; generally 50 lines or less, but will consider longer poems if truly outstanding." They do not want greeting card verse or untitled work.** They have recently published poetry by John Grey, David Church, Allison Joseph and Milton Mannix. As a sample the editor selected these lines from "dolphins of diamonds & maidens of bronze" by Jerry Fogel:

> walk glide in peaceful fearsome face
> non-terran green skinned girl with
> broad toed land hug feet
> your non-walk glide in non earth home holds hope
> your heart beats boldly while your
> non-sun coldly glitters bot

Syncopated City is 60 pgs., 5½×8½, photocopied, saddle-stapled with cardstock cover, original b&w artwork and ads. They receive about 300-400 poems a year, accept approximately 25%. Press run is 150-200, all shelf sales; 20-25 distributed free to reviewers and contributors. Subscription: $12. **Sample postpaid: $3. Make checks payable to Sun Spot Press. Submit up to 5 poems at a time with full name on every page. Previously published poems and simultaneous submissions OK. Cover letter preferred.** Time between acceptance and publication is 3-6 months. **"Editors choose, but we often discuss choices with local poets who act as 'guest editors.' " Often comments on rejections. Send SASE for guidelines. Reports in 1-3 months. Pays 1 copy. Acquires one-time rights.** Sun Spot Press publishes books generally of artistic rather than academic writings, but open to all forms of expression. "At this point we rarely publish books by individual writers." Publishes 1 paperback and **1-3 chapbooks/year.** Books are usually 50-60 pgs., 5½×8½, saddle-stapled with cardstock cover. **"At this time we only publish chapbooks by local writers, so we are not open to inquiries."** The editor says, "Quality is important, but it is equally important to make us think, make us feel. Don't feel it's necessary to conform—originality is important. We lean toward poetry that is more art than craft. Surprise us."

*****TAK TAK TAK (V, IV-Themes)**, BCM Tak, London WC1N 3XX England, founded 1986, editors Andrew and Tim Brown, appears occasionally in print and on cassettes. **"No restrictions on form or style. However, we are currently not accepting poetry submissions. Each issue of the magazine is on a theme (e.g., 'Mother Country/Fatherland,' 'Postcards from Paradise'), and *all* contributions must be relevant. If a contribution is long it is going to be more difficult to fit in than something shorter. Write for details of subject(s), etc., of forthcoming issue(s)."** They have published poetry by Michael Horovitz, Karl Blake, Keith Jafrate, Ramona Fotiade and Paul Buck. The editors describe it as "100 pgs., A5, photolithographed, board cover, line drawings and photographs, plus cassette of spoken word, music, sounds." Press run is 1,000. **Sample postpaid to US: £7.06 airmail (without cassette), £8.11 airmail (with cassette).** The editors say, "Poetry is just one of the many creative forms our contributions take. We are equally interested in prose and in visual and sound media."

TALISMAN: A JOURNAL OF CONTEMPORARY POETRY AND POETICS; TALISMAN HOUSE PUBLISHERS (III), P.O. Box 3157, Jersey City NJ 07303-3157, phone (201)938-0698, founded 1988, editor Edward Foster, appears twice a year. "Each issue centers on the poetry and poetics of a *major* contemporary poet and includes a selection of new work by other important contemporary writers. **We are particularly interested in poetry in alternative (*not* academic) traditions. We don't want traditional poetry."** They have published poetry by William Bronk, Gerrit Lansing, Leslie Scalapino, Gustaf Sobin, Will Alexander and Susan Howe. *Talisman* is 268 pgs., digest-sized, flat-spined, photocopied from computer printed Baskerville type, with matte card cover. "We are inundated with submissions and lost track of the number long ago." Their press run is 1,000 with "substantial" subscriptions of which many are libraries. Subscription: $14 individual; $17 institution. **Sample postpaid: $7.50. Reporting time varies. Always sends prepublication galleys. Pays 1 copy. Acquires first**

USE THE GENERAL INDEX to find the page number of a specific publisher. Also, if a publisher from last year's edition is not included in this edition, the General Index will tell you why.

North American serial rights. Reviews books of poetry in 500-1,000 words, single format. Talisman House Publishers produces "distinguished" books of poetry, fiction and essays. Send SASE for more information.

‡**TALKING RIVER REVIEW (II)**, Lewis Clark State College, 500 Eighth Ave., Lewiston ID 83501, phone (208)799-2307, founded 1994, contact poetry editor, published biannually, considers itself a "high-quality literary magazine." **They want "any length, any style, any subject. We print one long poem each issue (up to 15 pages)." They do not want "sexist, racist or dumb poetry."** They have recently published poetry by Philip Dacey, Robert Wrigley and Marianne Boruch. As a sample the editor selected these lines from "Poverty" by Pattiann Rogers:

> *The lament wasn't in the stiff*
> *whips of willow or the ice-captures*
> *on pondweed and underwater tubers,*
> *as we expected. No moan rose*
> *from the frost-blackened spikelets*
> *of bluejoint or twisted cattail.*

The editor says *Talking River Review* is 150 pgs., perfect-bound with color cover and some art. They receive about 2,000 poems a year, accept approximately 5%. Press run is 500 for 175 subscribers of which 25 are libraries, 100 shelf sales; 200 distributed free to students/contributors. Single copy: $6; subscription: $10. **Sample postpaid: $4. Submit 5 poems at a time. No previously published poems; simultaneous submissions OK. Cover letter preferred. Reads submissions September 1 through March 1 only.** Time between acceptance and publication is 6 months. **"Faculty advisor picks poems for board to consider; majority rules." Often comments of rejections. Send SASE for guidelines. Reports in 1-3 months. Sometimes sends prepublication galleys. Pays 1-year subscription and 2 copies. Acquires first rights.**

‡**TALUS AND SCREE; THE FAR CRY (I)**, P.O. Box 851, Waldport OR 97394, phone (541)563-4159, e-mail talus@webjacks.com, website http://www.teleport.com/~cbs/TALUS, founded 1996, editors Carla Perry and Dave W. Mitchell, published semiannually, is "an international literary journal of poetry, fiction and graphics with a decisive slant toward quality writing and viewpoints intended to evoke lively discussion." **They want "controversial poems that are hard to place in normal channels because of content. Open to all work, even very long." They do not want rhymed verse or limericks.** They have recently published poetry by Andrés Berger-Kiss, Michael Estabrook and Barbara La Morticella. As a sample the editor selected these lines from "I Know What You Like" by Michael McNeilley:

> *I know what you like*
> *I know how the gleam*
> *on the black eye of midnight pulls you in*
> *I sway in the same breeze*
> *dive with the same fish*
> *camp on the same rock*
> *waiting out the hours before dawn . . .*

Talus and Scree is 176 pgs., 5½ × 8½, perfect-bound, text paper, desktop-published, with cover art and photos. They receive about 800 poems a year, accept approximately 40%. Press run is 1,000 for 250 subscribers of which 8 are libraries, 500 shelf sales; 100 distributed free to newspapers, libraries and reviewers. Single copy: $6; subscription: $14. **Sample postpaid: $8. Submit any number of poems. Previously published poems and simultaneous submissions OK. Cover letter preferred with short bio. E-mail submissions OK (include postal address).** Time between acceptance and publication is 1 month. **Poems are circulated to an editorial board. "Editors read everything and select those deemed acceptable or reworkable. A second review of the finalists determines inclusion." Seldom comments on rejections. "We comment if especially driven to comment or if cover letter requests comments and feedback." Send SASE for guidelines or request via e-mail. Reports in 1-4 months. Pays 2 copies plus discount on additional copies. Acquires first or one-time rights.** Open to unsolicited reviews. Poets may also send books for review consideration to Carla Perry, editor, at the above address. The editors advise, "consider submitting work deemed too risky for other publications."

TAMPA REVIEW (III), Dept. PM, University of Tampa, 401 W. Kennedy Blvd., Tampa FL 33606-1490, founded 1964 as *UT Poetry Review,* became *Tampa Review* in 1988, editor Richard Mathews, poetry editors Kathryn Van Spanckeren and Donald Morrill, is an elegant semiannual of fiction, nonfiction, poetry and art (not limited to US authors) wanting **"original and well-crafted poetry written with intelligence and spirit. We do accept translations, but no greeting card or inspirational verse."** They have published poetry by Vern Rutsala, Naomi Shihab Nye, Jim Daniels, Denise Levertov and Stephen Dunn. As a sample the editors selected these lines from "Arthritis in St. Petersburg" by Peter Meinke:

> *Heat in August flattens everyone*
> *brittles the potted ferns in three quick*
> *days if you forget to water*
> *Sun hammers the road and you*
> *drive toward a slick*
> *shimmer always a dream away*

TR is 78-96 pgs., 7½ × 10½ flat-spined, with a matte card color cover. They receive about 2,000 poems a year, accept approximately 50-60. Press run is 750 for 175 subscribers of which 20 are libraries. **Sample postpaid: $5. Submit 3-7 poems at a time. No previously published poems or simultaneous submissions. Unsolicited mss are read between September and December only. Reports by mid-February. Sometimes sends prepublication galleys. Pays $10/printed page plus 1 copy and 40% discount on additional copies. Buys first North American serial rights.** Poetry published in *Tampa Review* has been included in *The Best American Poetry 1995*.

TAPROOT LITERARY REVIEW (II), P.O. Box 204, Ambridge PA 15003, phone (412)266-8476, founded 1986, editor Tikvah Feinstein, is an annual contest publication, open to beginners. In addition to the contest, each year guest poets are selected; payment in copies. Writers published include Regina Wachtel, Florence McGinn, Rod Farmer, Elizabeth Howkins and B.Z. Niditch. As a sample the editor selected these lines from "The Daughter I Don't Have" by Lyn Lifshin:

> *hovers over the lilacs,*
> *a cloak over plum*
> *branches. She moves*
> *like a warm front*
> *east, is that*
> *buzz in the night,*
> *out of reach in*
> *blackness.*

The review is approximately 95 pgs., offset printed on white stock with one-color glossy cover, art and no ads. Circulation is 500, sold at bookstores, readings and through the mail. Single copy: $5.50. **Sample postpaid: $5. There is a $10 entry fee for up to 5 poems, "no longer than 30 lines each." Nothing previously published or pending publication will be accepted. Cover letter with general information required. "We cannot answer without a SASE." Submissions accepted between September 1 and December 31 only. Publishes theme issues. Send SASE for upcoming themes. Sometimes sends prepublication galleys. Pays 2 copies. All entrants receive a copy of *Taproot*; enclose $2 for p&h.** Send books for review consideration. The editor says, "We publish the best poetry we can in a variety of styles and subjects, so long as it's literary quality and speaks to us."

TAR RIVER POETRY (II), English Dept., East Carolina University, Greenville NC 27858-4353, phone (919)328-6046 or 328-6467, fax (919)328-4889, founded 1960, editor Peter Makuck, associate editor Luke Whisnant. **"We are not interested in sentimental, flat-statement poetry. What we would like to see is skillful use of figurative language."** They have recently published poetry by William Heyen, Samuel Hazo, Lee Evans, Deborah Cummins, Betty Adcock and Reg Saner. As a sample the editors selected this poem, "Scab" by Michael McFee:

> *This desert island's shrinking*
> *a little every day:*
> *whitecaps keep kissing*
> *its itchy shore*
>
> *until the crusted mountains*
> *collapse, leaving behind—*
> *just underwater—*
> *a shining scar.*

Tar River appears twice yearly and is 60 pgs., digest-sized, professionally printed on salmon stock, some decorative line drawings, matte card cover with photo. They receive 6,000-8,000 submissions a year, use approximately 150-200. Press run is 900 for 500 subscribers of which 125 are libraries. Subscription: $10. **Sample: $5.50. Submit 3-6 poems at a time. "We do not consider previously published poems or simultaneous submissions. Double or single-spaced OK. Name and address on each page. We do not consider mss during summer months." Reads submissions September 1 through April 15 only. Editors will comment "if slight revision will do the trick." Send SASE for guidelines. Reports in 4-6 weeks. Pays 2 copies. Acquires first rights.** Reviews books of poetry in 4,000 words maximum, single or multi-book format. This is an especially good market for intelligent, concisely written book reviews. Poets may also send books for review consideration. *Tar River* is an "all-poetry" magazine that accepts dozens of poems in each issue, providing the talented beginner and experienced writer with an excellent forum that features all styles and forms of verse. Frequently contributors' works are included in the *Anthology of Magazine Verse & Yearbook of American Poetry*. Poetry published in *Tar River* was also selected for inclusion in *The Best American Poetry 1994*. The editors advise, "Read, read, read. Saul Bellow says the writer is primarily a reader moved to emulation. Read the poetry column in *Writer's Digest*. Read the books recommended therein. Do your homework."

♣**"TEAK" ROUNDUP (I, IV-Subscribers)**, West Coast Paradise Publishing, #5-9060 Tronson Rd., Vernon, British Columbia V1T 6L7 Canada, phone (250)545-4186, fax (250)545-4194, editors Yvonne and Robert G. Anstey. *"Teak" Roundup* is an international quarterly **open to the work of subscribers only.** They publish work from authors and poets across North America and beyond. West Coast Paradise Publishing also publishes books and chapbooks. Send SASE for catalog. As a sample the editors selected these lines from Robert G. Anstey's poem "Song In The Trellises Of Love":

> I have long been entrenched in the facade
> of warm and friendly hands but they
> retreated as I blossomed in the sun
>
>
> now the slow echo of the summer reaches me
> and light in spears of colour sing
> a rhapsody in the trellises of love.

TR is A5, 52 pgs., offset, saddle-stapled, medium card cover with clip art, photos and ads. Subscription: $17 Canadian, $13 US, $24 overseas. **Sample: $5 Canadian, $3 US, $8 overseas. Accepts work from subscribers only. Submit 3-5 poems at a time. Fax submissions OK. SASE (or SAE with IRC) required for response. Send SASE for guidelines and upcoming themes. No payment. "It is our goal to become a paying market when circulation makes it feasible." Reports in one week.**

*TEARS IN THE FENCE (II), 38 Hodview, Stourpaine, Nr. Blandford Forum, Dorset DT11 8TN England, phone 01258-456803, founded 1984, general editor David Caddy, poetry editor Sarah Hopkins, is a "small press magazine of poetry, fiction, interviews, articles, reviews and graphics. **We are open to a wide variety of poetic styles. Work of a social, political, ecological and feminist awareness will be close to our purpose. However, we like to publish a balanced variety of work." The editors do not want to see "didactic rhyming poems."** They have recently published poetry by Fred Voss, Lee Harwood, Kim Taplin, John Freeman and Donna Hilbert. As a sample they selected these lines from "Homage To Nipper Nevins" by K.M. Dersley:

> Nipper Nevins, who ought to have had his own TV show
> Nipper Nevins with his charisma
> Nipper Nevins, the teachers were scared of him
> Nipper Nevins who went around with people who had air
>   rifles and jackdaws and cared neither for man nor God

Tears in the Fence appears 3 times/year. It is 84 pgs., A5, "docu-tech printed" on 110 gms. paper and perfect-bound with matte card cover and b&w art and graphics. It has a press run of 500, of which 302 go to subscribers. Subscription: $15/3 issues. **Sample: $5. Writers should submit 6 typed poems with IRCs. Cover letter with brief bio required. Publishes theme issues. Send SASE (or SAE and IRC) for upcoming themes. Reports in 3 months.** Time between acceptance and publication is 8-10 months "but can be much less." **Pays 1 copy.** Reviews books of poetry in 2,000-3,000 words, single or multi-book format. Open to unsolicited reviews. Poets may also send books for review consideration. The magazine is informally connected with the East Street Poets literary promotions, workshops and publications. They also sponsor an annual pamphlet competition open to poets from around the world. The editor says, "I think it helps to subscribe to several magazines in order to study the market and develop an understanding of what type of poetry is published. Use the review sections and send off to magazines that are new to you."

‡TEEN VOICES; SISTERWRITE (I, IV-Teen, women), P.O. Box 116, Boston MA 02123, phone (617)262-2434, fax (617)262-5937, e-mail womenexp@usa1.com, website http://www.usa1.com/womenexp, founded 1988, first published 1990, contact submissions director. *Teen Voices*, published quarterly, is a magazine by, for and about teenage girls and young adult women. As a sample the editor selected these lines from "Nakedness" by Elizabeth Circo:

> Wandering through the salmon pink room of
> her childhood
> She reminisces, smiling wistfully at the thought of
> herself
> at the innocent age of four
> a precocious free spirit—

The editor says *Teen Voices* is 34 pgs., with glossy cover, art and photos. "We accept 99% of the poems we receive, but can't afford to publish all of them timely." Press run is 10,000 for 4,000 subscribers of which 400 are libraries, 2,000 shelf sales. Single copy: $3; subscription: $20. **Sample postpaid: $5. Make checks payable to Teen Voices. Submit any number of poems with name, age and address on each. No previously published poems; simultaneous submissions OK. Cover letter preferred.** Time between acceptance and publication is 1 year. **Poems are circulated to an editorial board. Publishes theme issues. Send SASE for upcoming themes. Pays 3 copies.** Occasionally reviews books of poetry in 100 words. Open to unsolicited reviews.

‡TEENS IN MOTION NEWS; COSTA PUBLISHING (I, IV-Teen/young adult), P.O. Box 1264, Santa Clara CA 95052-1264, phone (408)244-3718, e-mail pkc@ix.netcom.com, founded 1995 (*Teens In Motion News*), 1994 (Costa Publishing), editor Pamela Costa. *Teens In Motion News*, published monthly (except December), features "young adult talents in poetry, short stories and artwork, information on drugs, gangs, careers, celebrities, humor and experiences." **They want "all/any type of poetry, maximum 30 lines."** They have recently published poetry by P.K. Costa and Pamela Daniels. As a sample the editor selected this poem by George Slavich:

> They walk the beach to hear the sound
> But miss the reasons which make it profound.
> To them, the water comes in and goes,
> To me, the sand yells at my toes.
> It says, what are you doing standing on me,
> Am I not what you want me to be?

The editor says **TIMN** is 20-24 pgs., 8½×5½, saddle-stitched with ads; the logo changes every year—created by a teen. They receive about 120 poems a year, accept approximately 80% ("eventually all are published"). Press run varies for 1,000 subscribers of which 15 are libraries; 10 distributed free to publishers. Subscription: $8.50. **Sample (including guidelines) postpaid: $1. Submit up to 2 poems at a time. Previously published poems and simultaneous submissions OK. Cover letter preferred with "brief description of new poet to print with poem—such as name and previous work published, projects and goals." E-mail submissions OK. Reads submissions first 2 weeks of each month.** Time between acceptance and publication is 2-5 months. **"Poems are published as is unless major grammatical errors." Seldom comments on rejections. Charges criticism fee. "If requested, critiques are provided, however, we do not like to critique poetry ($10/poem). Publishes theme issues. Send SASE for guidelines and upcoming themes or request via e-mail. Pays up to 5 copies. Acquires one-time rights.** "We will review books. There is a fee for review of books—price varies on length." Open to unsolicited reviews. Poets may also send books for review consideration. "Query first; no books will be accepted without prior authorization." Sponsors annual and monthly contests. Costa Publishing provides self-publishing assistance. Write for more information. The editor says, "young adults should never be discouraged from writing or submitting work. Don't write to please others—but do listen to what others think, if only to capture the perspective of another."

‡TEMPORARY VANDALISM RECORDINGS; FREEDOM ISN'T FREE; ESTHER—A DRIVING LITERARY MAGAZINE (I, II), P.O. Box 6184, Orange CA 92863-6184, founded 1991 (Temporary Vandalism Recordings), 1994 (*Freedom Isn't Free*), 1995 (*Esther*), editors Robert Roden and Barton M. Saunders. *Freedom Isn't Free*, is published biannually. **"Form, length, style and subject matter can vary. It's difficult to say what will appeal to our eclectic tastes." They do not want "strictly rants, overly didactic poetry."** They have recently published poetry by Mary Panza, Charles Ardinger, Feleciano E. Melgar and S.A. Griffin. As a sample the editor selected these lines from "sexual/sensual sexxx the three sexy S's" by Son B. Nguyen:

> so many positions, degrees, angles to try, experience
> so little time
> need a time schedule
> need a protractor
> need a ruler
> need a sharp pencil

FIF is 32 pgs., "4¼×5½, saddle-stapled, photocopied with colored card cover and some ads. They accept less than 25% of poems received. Press run is 300. Single copy free. **Sample postpaid: $1. Make checks payable to Robert Roden. Submit 5 neatly typed poems at a time. Previously published poems and simultaneous submissions OK. Cover letter preferred.** Time between acceptance and publication is 3 months. **"Two editors' votes required for inclusion." Seldom comments on rejections. Reports 3-6 months. Pays 2 copies. Acquires one-time rights.** Temporary Vandalism Recordings strives "to make the world safe for poetry (just kidding)." They publish **3 chapbooks/year.** Chapbooks are usually 40 pgs., photocopied, saddle-stapled, press run of 100 intially, with reprint option if needed. **Submit 10 sample poems, with SASE for response. "Publication in some magazines is important, but extensive publishing is not required." Replies in 3 months. Pays 50% royalty (after costs recouped) and 5 author's copies (out of a press run of 100).** For sample chapbooks send $5 to the above address. Mr. Roden says, "The magazine *Esther* is not sold or printed, it consists of poems displayed in the windows of my car and is a quarterly publication in that format. Hope to someday release a 'best of' anthology."

THE TENNESSEE REVIEW (II), Dept. of Literature and Language, Belmont University, 1900 Belmont Blvd., Nashville TN 37212-3757, phone (615)383-7001, founded 1994, co-editor Anthony Lombardy, appears 2 times/year (in the fall and spring). "*The Tennessee Review* publishes poems, short fiction, essays of general interest as well as of broad literary-critical and theoretical reach and translations." **They want poetry of "any form, subject or style, but we favor language highly marked whether by metrical form or rhetorical figure."** They have published poetry by Peter Russell, Emily Grosholz and Richard Moore and a translation by Dana Gioia. *The Tennessee Review* is 60-100 pgs., 6×9, professionally printed on quality stock and flat-spined with light matte card cover. They receive about 4,000-5,000 poems a year, accept approximately 50. Press run is 500 for 200 subscribers, 100 shelf sales. Subscription: $12/year. **Sample postpaid: $5. No previously published poems or simultaneous submissions. Reads submissions September 1 through June 15 only.** Time between acceptance and publication is 6 months. **Seldom comments on rejections. Reports usually within 1-2 months. Pays 2 copies. Acquires first North American serial rights.** Reviews books of poetry in up to 2,000 words. Open to unsolicited reviews. Poets may also send books for review consideration. Mr. Lombardy says,

"There is now more emphasis on publishing reviews of current poetry and fiction."

‡*TERRIBLE WORK; SPINELESS PRESS (III), 21 Overton Gardens, Mannamead, Plymouth, Devon PL3 5BX United Kingdom, founded 1993, contact Tim Allen. *Terrible Work*, published triannually, features "poetry/art/reviews illustrating the variety of non-mainstream work; new writers especially." **They want "post-modern, experimental, language, interesting, naive, warm, cold, speculative, minimal, expansionist, high-quality, computer, etc." They do not want "traditional formal, realist, well-crafted anecdotes, message/preaching, mystical, right-wing, bad poetry."** They have recently published poetry by Peter Redgrove, Bruce Andrews, Rosmarie Waldrop and Sheila E. Murphy. As a sample the editor selected these lines from "Investigations" by Steve Carll:

> *The arms encircle nothing;*
> *The eyes' radiance opens*
> *Only elsewhere, flickering*
> *Indifferent when I'm outside*
> *the glass*

> *Simple and regressive,*
> *I fall back on you,*
> *Each time breaking*
> *New little bones in*
> *Each of us.*

The editor says *Terrible Work* is 92 pgs., A5, perfect-bound, spined, laminated cover and graphics. They receive about 1,000 poems a year, accept approximately 10%. Press run is 300 for 200 subscribers of which 7 are libraries, 30 shelf sales; some distributed free as review copies. Single copy: $7.50 (£3.50 UK); subscription: $20 (£9 UK). **Sample postpaid: $4. Submit 5 poems at a time. No previously published poems or simultaneous submissions. Cover letter required with "a brief history of publications, etc."** Time between acceptance and publication is up to 4 months. **Often comments on rejections. Send SASE (or SAE and IRC) for guidelines. Reports in up to 4 months. Pays 1 copy.** Staff reviews books of poetry or other magazines "of critical and partisan reviewing." Poets may also send books for review consideration. Spineless Press publishes **5 chapbooks/year** of "experimental and more interesting quality poets—particularly those not well known." Chapbooks are usually under 60 pgs., A5, stapled, but good quality production and design. **"No submissions. By invitation only."** The editor says, "For submissions from USA/Canada for the magazine we are more interested in high-quality experimental work. We will trade copies of *TW* for interesting USA magazines/chapbooks."

‡UNIVERSITY OF TEXAS PRESS (V), P.O. Box 7819, Austin TX 78713-7819, website http://www.utexas.edu/utpress, founded 1950, is a "scholarly publisher; only poetry published is Latin American or Middle Eastern literature in translation." Publishes 1 paperback and 1 hardback/year. They have recently published poetry by Ramon Lopez Velarde and a collection of Latin American poetry edited by Stephen Tapscott. Book format varies. **They are not accepting unsolicited manuscripts.**

‡TEXAS REVIEW; TEXAS REVIEW PRESS (I, II); SOUTHERN AND SOUTHWESTERN BREAK-THROUGH COMPETITION IN POETRY (I, II, IV-Regional), Sam Houston State University, Dept. of English and Foreign Languages, Huntsville TX 77341-2146, phone (409)294-1992, fax (409)294-1414, founded 1976, contact Paul Ruffin. *The Texas Review*, published biannually, is a "scholarly journal publishing poetry, short fiction, essays and book reviews." They have recently published poetry by Donald Hall, X.J. Kennedy and Richard Eberhart. *The Texas Review* is 152 pgs., digest-sized, offset printed, perfect-bound, bond paper with 4-color cover and ads. Press run is 1,000 for 500 subscribers of which 250 are libraries. Single copy: $12; subscription: $24. **Sample postpaid: $5. Make checks payable to Friends of *Texas Review*. No previously published poems or simultaneous submissions. Cover letter preferred. Reads submissions September 1 through June 1 only.** Time between acceptance and publication is 6 months. **Poems are circulated to an editorial board. Seldom comments on rejections. Publishes theme issues. Send SASE for guidelines. Reports in a few months. Always sends prepublication galleys. Pays 1 year subscription and 1 copy (may request more). Acquires all rights. Returns rights "for publication in anthology."** Open to unsolicited reviews. Texas Review Press publishes 1,000 paperbacks and hardbacks/year, with 1 published as the result of the annual Breakthrough Competition for Southern and Southwestern Poets. Entrants must live and write in a Southern or Southwestern state. Write to the above address for guidelines. Books are usually 68 pgs., digest-sized, offset printed, perfect-bound, bond paper with 4-color cover. **Replies to queries "immediately"; to mss in "a few months." For sample books, write to the above address.** They are a recipient of the Townsend Award.

TEXAS TECH UNIVERSITY PRESS (V, IV-Series), P.O. Box 41037, Lubbock TX 79409-1037, phone (806)742-2982, founded 1971, editor Judith Keeling, publishes volumes of poetry in 2 categories only: **First-Book Poetry Series**: "Winning and finalist mss in an annual competition conducted by Poetry Editor Robert A.

Fink who surveys literary journals throughout the year and normally invites 12 poets to submit mss for consideration in the competition"; and **Invited Poets Series:** "Collections invited from established poets whose work continues to appear in distinguished journals." They have recently published *Stalking Joy* by Margaret Benbow and *An Animal of the Sixth Day* by Laura Fargas. **Does not read unsolicited manuscripts. Books published on royalty contracts.**

‡**TEXAS YOUNG WRITERS' NEWSLETTER (I, IV-Teen/young adult)**, P.O. Box 942, Adkins TX 78101, e-mail tywn1@aol.com, founded 1994, editor Susan Curne, published 9 times/year, is a "newsletter publishing information on the art and business of writing for young writers, as well as poetry and short stories **by young people ages 12-19.**" They want "**positive poetry, upbeat, no more than 30 lines—rhymed or unrhymed.**" They do not want "**depressing poetry, boring poetry, unoriginal poetry, 'roses-are-red-violets-are-blue' poetry.**" *TYWN* is 6-8 pgs., 8½ × 11, photocopied and stapled, desktop-published with clip art. They receive about 100 poems a year, accept approximately 25%. Press run is 150 for 50 subscribers of which 3 are libraries; 100 distributed free to supporters. Subscription: $10. **Sample postpaid: $1. Make checks payable to Susan Currie, *TYWN*. Contributors must be 12-19 years old. Submit 3-5 poems at a time. No previously published poems or simultaneous submissions. Cover letter preferred with author's age and bio. Submissions on disk OK in .wri or .txt formats. E-mail submissions OK.** Time between acceptance and publication is 8 months. **Often comments on rejections. Send SASE for guidelines or request via e-mail. Reports in 1 month. Sometimes sends prepublication galleys. Pays 2 copies. Acquires first rights.** The editor says, "We look for good writing. But we also look for potential in our submitters, and even if their work is returned, we work with them to improve. We're more than willing to help."

❧**TEXTSHOP (I)**, Dept. of English, University of Regina, Regina, Saskatchewan S4S 0A2 Canada, founded 1993, editors Andrew Stubbs, Judy Chapman and Richelle Leonard, is an annual "collaborative writing journal" that **seeks "experimental, postmodern poetry; one page in length, or sequences up to five pages. No thematic poetry.**" They have published poetry by Bruce Bond and Judith Miller. As a sample the editor selected these lines from "Connections" by Rienzi Crusz:

> Come summer
> and the family is back
> to its sun beginnings;
> suck the sweet rambuttan,
> let the mango juice run down your shirt

Textshop is 36 pgs., 7½ × 10, saddle-stapled with coated card cover and lots of shaded boxes used for graphic effects. They receive 400-500 poems a year, accept approximately 20%. Press run is 350 for 25 subscribers of which 15 are libraries, 200 shelf sales. Single copy: $4.50. **Sample free. Submit 5 poems at a time. Previously published poems OK; no simultaneous submissions. Cover letter with capsule bio required. Reads submissions January through April. Poems are circulated to an editorial board. Always comments on rejections. Reports in 2-3 months. Pays 2 copies** "plus 1 on request." At the end of each issue, in sections titled "Reflections," the editors also include written commentary regarding the work published in the issue.

❧**THALIA: STUDIES IN LITERARY HUMOR (I, IV-Subscribers, humor)**, Dept. of English, University of Ottawa, Ottawa, Ontario K1N 6N5 Canada, phone (613)230-9505, fax (613)565-5786, e-mail jtaverni@aixl.uot tawa.ca, editor Dr. J. Tavernier-Courbin, appears twice a year using "**humor (literary, mostly). Poems submitted must actually be literary parodies.**" The editor describes it as 7 × 8½, flat-spined, "with illustrated cover." Press run is 500 for 475 subscribers. Subscription: $22 for individuals, $25 for libraries. **Sample postpaid: $8 up to volume 11, $15 and $20 for volume 12-15 respectively (double issues). Contributors must subscribe. Simultaneous submissions OK but *Thalia* must have copyright. Will authorize reprints.** "Queries via phone, fax or e-mail OK. However, submissions must be in hard copy." **Editor comments on submissions. Reports in 3-4 months.** Reviews books of poetry. "Send queries to the editor concerning specific books."

THEMA (II, IV-Themes), Thema Literary Society, P.O. Box 74109, Metairie LA 70033-4109, founded 1988, editor Virginia Howard, is a triannual literary magazine **using poetry related to specific themes. "Each issue is based on an unusual premise. Please, please send SASE for guidelines before submitting poetry to find out the upcoming themes. Upcoming themes (and submission deadlines) include: 'An unexpected guest' (11-1-97), 'Don't call me Thelma!' (3-1-98) and 'Magnolias in my briefcase' (7-1-98). No scatologic language, alternate life-style, explicit love poetry.**" They have recently published poetry by Daniel Green, Sue Walker, Kaye Bache-Snyder and Nancy G. Westerfield. As a sample the editor selected these lines by Yvonne Patrick:

THE SUBJECT INDEX, located before the General Index, can help you select markets for your work. It lists those publishers whose poetry interests are specialized.

> *I sleuth the room for proof*
> *of your existence.*
> *But the house swallows*
> *me whole with its emptiness*

Thema is 200 pgs., digest-sized, professionally printed, with matte card cover. They receive about 400 poems a year, accept approximately 8%. Press run is 500 for 270 subscribers of which 30 are libraries. Subscription: $16. **Sample postpaid: $8. Submit up to 3 poems at a time. All submissions should be typewritten and on standard 8½ × 11 paper. Submissions are accepted all year, but evaluated after specified deadlines. Editor comments on submissions. Pays $10/poem plus 1 copy. Buys one-time rights.**

THIRD COAST (II), Dept. of English, Western Michigan University, Kalamazoo MI 49008-5092, phone (616)387-2675, website http://www.wmich.edu/thirdcoast, founded 1995, contact poetry editors, is a biannual national literary magazine of poetry, prose, creative nonfiction and translation. **They want "excellence of craft and originality of thought. Nothing trite."** They have published poetry by Dean Young, Alice B. Fogel, David Clewell and Alison Hawthorne Deming. As a sample we selected these lines from "Action at a Distance" by Alane Rollings:

> *Turn off the light; let's see how the sky affects us.*
> *With your cheekbone two inches from my forehead,*
> *tell me the mass and circumference of the universe*
> *and how at home you are in its basic emptiness. I can't do without*
> *these revelations, though they sound so disconsolate in your mouth.*

Third Coast is 140 pgs., 6 × 9, professionally printed and perfect-bound with a 4-color cover with art. They receive about 2,000 poems a year, accept 3-5%. Press run is 1,100 for 150 subscribers of which 20 are libraries, 350 shelf sales. Single copy: $6; subscription: $11/year, $20/2 years, $29/3 years. **Submit 3-5 poems at a time. No previously published poems; simultaneous submissions OK. Cover letter preferred. Reads submissions September 1 through May 1 only.** Poems are circulated to assistant poetry editors and poetry editors; poetry editors make final decisions. Seldom comments on rejections. Send SASE for guidelines. Reports in 1-2 months. Pays 2 copies and 1-year subscription. Acquires first rights.

*THE THIRD HALF LITERARY MAGAZINE; K.T. PUBLICATIONS (I, II), 16, Fane Close, Stamford, Lincolnshire PE9 1HG England, phone (01780)54193, founded 1987, editor Mr. Kevin Troop. *TTH* appears "as often as possible each year." K.T. Publications also publishes up to 6 other books, with a Minibooks Series, for use in the classroom. The editor wants **"meaningful, human and humane, funny poems up to 40 lines. Work which actually *says* something without being obscene."** They have published poetry by Lee Bridges (Holland), Ann Keith (Amsterdam), Toby Litt (Prague) and Edmund Harwood, Michael Newman, Louise Rogers and Steve Sneyd (Britain). *TTH* is up to 100 pgs., A5, perfect-bound, illustrated, printed on white paper with glossy cover. Press run is over 200. Individual booklets vary in length and use colored paper and card covers. **Submit 6 poems at a time. No simultaneous submissions. Cover letter and suitable SAE required. Reports ASAP. Pays 1 copy.** "Procedure for the publication of books is explained to each author; each case is different. *The Third Half* is priced at £4.95 each, £2.95 by post in UK, £8 overseas."

‡13TH HOUR BOOKS; WORLD OF HP LOVECRAFT FANZINE (I, IV-Horror, humor, fantasy), 5714 Fenwick Dr., Alexandria VA 22303, founded 1992, editor/publisher Les Thomas. 13th Hour Books publishes experimental works by young authors/poets. They publish **2-3 chapbooks/year. They want "dark fantasy or humorous horror poetry from short one stanzas to three to four pages in length." They do not want "love poems, seasonal."** As a sample the editor selected these lines from "Something Like a Dream" by Sutter Ceive:

> *Rivers of blood wrap around a blue world dangling from invisible cosmic strings in the black velvet*
> *of the night*
> *The man in the moon rapes the dark*
> *His lust shakes the heavens.*
> *His seed; the bright stars in the night sky*

Chapbooks are usually 5-30 pgs., offset printed with art. **Submit 2 poems at a time. Previously published poems OK; no simultaneous submissions. Cover letter required with name, address, phone number, poem's title, word count. Reads submissions March 1 through July 30 only.** Time between acceptance and publication is 6-12 months. **"Inhouse editor reads poems and decides if it fits our needs." Often comments on rejections. Replies in 2-4 weeks. Pays author's copies (out of a press run of 50-200). For sample chapbooks, send $5 to the above address.** The editor says, "Do not ever give up your dreams, but never let it get in the way of your day-to-day life."

13TH MOON (II, IV-Women), English Dept., University at Albany, 1400 Washington Ave., Albany NY 12222, phone (518)442-4181, founded 1973, editor Judith Johnson, is a feminist literary magazine appearing yearly (one double issue) in a 6 × 9, handsomely printed format with glossy card cover, using photographs and line art, ads at $200/page. Beyond a doubt, a real selection of forms and styles is featured here. For instance, free verse has appeared with formal work, concrete poems, long poems, stanza patterns, prose poems, a crown of sonnets and more. Press run is 2,000 for 690 subscribers of which 61 are libraries, 700 shelf sales.

Subscription: $10. **Sample postpaid: $10. Submit 3-5 poems at a time. No previously published poems or simultaneous submissions. Reads submissions September 1 through May 30 only. Publishes theme issues. Send SASE for guidelines and upcoming themes. Themes include "special issues on women's poetics, one focusing on poetry, one on narrative forms." Pays 2 copies. Acquires first North American serial rights.**

‡**THISTLE (I)**, P.O. Box 50094, Minneapolis MN 55405-0094, e-mail thistle@iceworld.org, founded 1993, editors Chelsea and Thaylor, published biannually, aims "to provide a small zine to the gothic community consisting of quality literature, art and information (not limited to 'goths')." **They want "poems with a dark bend to them: melancholia, romanticism, death, general oddities." They do not want "graphic violence or sex."** They have recently published poetry by Gary Jurecka, Robert Penick and John Sweet. As a sample the editor selected these lines from "a whisper among the screaming" by sasha i nyktos:

> i hear
> in between sobs
> a cricket nearby
> singing a lullaby for me

Thistle is 100 pgs., 4¼×5½, photocopied, saddle-stapled with light card cover, photography, cloth placemark and ads. Press run is 500 for 200-300 subscribers, 100-150 shelf sales; 100-150 distributed free "to goths and darkside record companies." Subscription: $5. **Sample postpaid: $1.50. Make checks payable to K. Holm. Submit up to 5 poems of works 21 lines or more and up to 10 poems of works 20 lines or less (send 2 copies of each poem). Previously published poems and simultaneous submissions OK. Cover letter preferred with SASE to return work. Accepts disk submissions (IBM format). E-mail submissions OK. "Thaylor and I read all submissions together and pick the ones we like best." Seldom comments on rejections. Send SASE for guidelines. Reports within 1 month. Pays 1 copy. Acquires one-time rights.** Rarely reviews books or chapbooks of poetry or other magazines, usually limited to about 30 words. Open to unsolicited reviews.

❧**THISTLEDOWN PRESS LTD. (IV-Regional)**, 633 Main St., Saskatoon, Saskatchewan S7H 0J8 Canada, founded 1975, editor-in-chief Patrick O'Rourke, is "a literary press that specializes in **quality books of contemporary poetry by Canadian authors. Only the best of contemporary poetry that amply demonstrates an understanding of craft with a distinctive use of voice and language. Only interested in full-length poetry mss with 53-71 pgs. minimum.**" They published *Wormwood Vermouth, Warpphistory* by Charles Noble and *Saved by the Telling* by Eva Tihanyi. **Do not submit unsolicited mss.** Canadian poets must **query first with letter, bio and publication credits. Submission guidelines available upon request. Replies to queries in 2-3 weeks, to submissions (if invited) in 3 months. No authors outside Canada. No simultaneous submissions. "Please submit quality laser-printed or photocopied material." Always sends prepublication galleys. Contract is for 10% royalty plus 10 copies.** They comment, "Poets submitting mss to Thistledown Press for possible publication should think in 'book' terms in every facet of the organization and presentation of the mss: Poets presenting mss that *read* like good books of poetry will have greatly enhanced their possibilities of being published. We strongly suggest that poets familiarize themselves with some of our poetry books before submitting a query letter."

‡**THORNY LOCUST (II)**, P.O. Box 32631, Kansas City MO 64171-5631, founded 1993, editor Silvia Kofler, published quarterly, is a "literary magazine that wants to be thought-provoking, witty and well-written." **They want "poetry with some 'bite' e.g., satire, epigrams, black humor and bleeding-heart cynicism." They do not want "polemics, gratuitous grotesques, sombre surrealism, weeping melancholy or hate-mongering."** They have recently published poetry by David Ray, Philip Miller, Simon Perchik and Lyn Lifshin. As a sample the editor selected these lines from "The Reflection" by Rod Farmer:

> Village India I romantically sought . . .
> Then feared . . .
> Dullness due to stunted brain growth
> That stamp of great malnutrition . . .
> A creature we are not free
> Not to know.

Thorny Locust is 28-32 pgs., 7×8½, desktop-published, saddle-stapled with medium cover stock, drawings and b&w photos. They receive about 300-350 poems a year, accept approximately 40%. Press run is 150-200 for 20 subscribers of which 5 are libraries; 60 distributed free to contributors and small presses. Single copy: $4; subscription: $15. **Sample postpaid: $3. Make checks payable to Silvia Kofler. Submit 3 poems at a time. No previously published poems; simultaneous submissions OK. Cover letter preferred.** Time between acceptance and publication is 1-2 months. **Seldom comments on rejections. Send SASE for guidelines. Reports in 2-3 months. Pays 1 copy. Acquires one-time rights.** The editor says, "Never perceive a rejection as a personal insult, keep on trying. Take advice."

THOUGHTS FOR ALL SEASONS: THE MAGAZINE OF EPIGRAMS (IV-Form, humor), % editor Prof. Em. Michel Paul Richard, 478 NE 56th St., Miami FL 33137-2621, founded 1976, "is an irregular serial: **designed to preserve the epigram as a literary form; satirical.** All issues are commemorative." **Rhyming**

poetry and nonsense verse with good imagery will be considered although most modern epigrams are prose. As a sample the editor selected this poem by Neil Megaw:

> Leonardo never had to be fretful
> Landing great ideas by the netful.
> If I hook one a week
> It's a poor little freak
> With a look in its eyes most regretful.

TFAS is 84 pgs., offset from typescript with full-page illustrations, card cover, saddle-stapled. The editor accepts about 20% of material submitted. Press run is 500-1,000. There are several library subscriptions but most distribution is through direct mail or local bookstores and newsstand sales. Single copy: $4.75 plus $1.50 postage. **Submit at least 1 full page of poems at a time, with SASE. Simultaneous submissions OK, but not previously published epigrams "unless a thought is appended which alters it." Editor comments on rejections. Publishes 1 section devoted to a theme. Send SASE for guidelines. Reports in 1 month. Pays 1 copy.**

‡*THREE (II)**, 18 Sunningdale Ave., Sale, Cheshire M33 2PM United Kingdom, founded 1993, editor Mr. M. Coleman, published annually, is "a forum for all aspects of modern writing, emphasis on originality, nonconformity and printing unpublished writers." **They want "anything with some originality not necessarily conforming to the rules of poetry and more submissions from women writers." They do not want "poetry that sticks rigidly to form and style. Overly-romanticised 'flowery' pieces or too lengthy items."** They have recently published poetry by Doug Bateman, Jon Summers, Colin Cross and Vincent DeSouza. As a sample the editor selected these lines from "The old woman's house at Moneyglass" by Gary Allen:

> I move through the residue
> of her presence
> the absence of ticking clocks
> unpolished wooden floor
> of connecting corridor
> dark of mizzled afternoon.

Three is 36 pgs., digest-sized, photocopied, saddle-stapled with colored paper cover, drawings and clip art. They receive about 300 poems a year, accept approximately 8-10%. Press run is 200, 150 shelf sales; 20-30 distributed free to contributors. **Sample postpaid: $3 and 3 IRCs. Make checks payable to M. Coleman. Submit 3-4 poems at a time. Previously published poems and simultaneous submissions OK. Cover letter preferred.** Time between acceptance and publication is up to 1 year. **"As editor I make all decisions on what's included for printing and what isn't." Seldom comments on rejections. Publishes theme issues. Send SASE (or SAE and IRC) for upcoming themes. Reports in 4-6 weeks. Sometimes sends prepublication galleys. Pays 1 copy.** Reviews books or chapbooks of poetry or other magazines. Open to unsolicited reviews. Poets may also send books for review consideration. The editor says, "*Three* is growing and improving all the time. To date, work from six different countries has appeared. It allows anyone with some original and new ideas to convey, a voice to do so. It breaks the rules of literature with style."

360 DEGREES (II), 980 Bush St., Suite 404, San Francisco CA 94109, founded 1993, managing editor Karen Kinnison, is a quarterly review, containing literature and artwork, "that is a mini-museum preserving the best from our times so readers in the future will seek us as a rare source." **They say they have "no real limits" on poetry, "only the limits of the submitter's imagination." However, they do not want to see "greeting card verse, simplified emotions or religious verse."** They have recently published poetry by Sean Brendan-Brown, Carrie Fitkin and Lyn Lifshin. As a sample the editor selected these lines from "it is a concept I don't understand" by Mark Sonnenfeld:

> walk away to wonderful wonderful volumes
> the beginning
> planets have gone this way
> do realize
> this isn't Kansas.

360 Degrees is 40 pgs., digest-sized, neatly printed and saddle-stapled with a 4-page full-color art insert. They receive about 500 poems a year, accept approximately 50. Press run is 500 for 100 subscribers. Subscription: $15. **Sample postpaid: $5. Submit 3 poems at a time. No previously published poems; simultaneous submissions OK. Cover letter preferred. Seldom comments on rejections. Send SASE for guidelines. Reports within 1 month. Pays $5/poem and 2 copies. Buys first North American rights.** The editor says, "Most of the poems we accept not only show mastery of words, but present new ideas. The mastery of language is something we expect from freelancers, but the content of the idea being expressed is the selling point."

THE THREEPENNY REVIEW (II), P.O. Box 9131, Berkeley CA 94709, phone (510)849-4545, founded 1980, poetry editor Wendy Lesser, "is a quarterly review of literature, performing and visual arts, and social articles aimed at the intelligent, well-read, but not necessarily academic reader. Nationwide circulation. **Want: formal, narrative, short poems (and others). Prefer under 50 lines but not necessary. No bias *against* formal poetry, in fact a slight bias in favor of it.**" They have published poetry by Thom Gunn, Frank Bidart, Seamus Heaney, Czeslaw Milosz and Louise Glück. There are about 9-10 poems in each 36-page tabloid issue. They receive about 4,500 submissions of poetry a year, use approximately 12. Press run is 10,000 for 8,000 subscribers of which 300 are libraries. Subscription: $16. **Sample: $6. Submit up to 5 poems at a time. Do not submit mss June-September. Send SASE for guidelines. Reports in 2-8 weeks. Pays $100/poem. Buys first serial rights.** Open to unsolicited reviews. "Send for review guidelines (SASE required)." Work published in this review has also been included in the 1993, 1994 and 1995 volumes of *The Best American Poetry*.

TIA CHUCHA PRESS (II), P.O. Box 476969, Chicago IL 60647-2304, phone (773)252-5321, fax (773)252-5388, e-mail guild@charlie.cns.iit.edu, website http://www.itt.edu/~guild, founded 1989, director Luis J. Rodriguez. They publish 2-4 paperbacks a year, **"multicultural, lyrical, engaging, passionate works informed by social, racial, class experience. Evocative. Poets should be knowledgeable of contemporary and traditional poetry, even if experimenting."** They have recently published poetry by Melvin Dixon, Carlos Champian and Elizabeth Alexander. As a sample the editor selected these lines from "Eating in Anger" in *Fallout* by Kyoko Mori:

> My friend lived with a man who ate
> peanut butter when they fought. She
> found the spoons in his pockets, sticky
> inverted mirrors in which her angry
> words blurred backwards. . . .

Submit complete ms of 48 pages or more with SASE ("unless you don't want the manuscript returned"). Simultaneous submissions OK, if notified. Only original, unpublished work in book form. "Although, we like to have poems that have been published in magazines and/or chapbooks." Deadline: June 30. Do not submit via fax. Reads submissions during the summer months. Pays 5 copies. They say, "We are known for publishing the best of what is usually spoken word or oral presentations of poetry. However, we like to publish poems that best work on the page. Yet, we are not limited to that. Our authors come from a diversity of ethnic, racial and gender backgrounds. Our main thrust is openness, in forms as well as content. We are cross-cultural, but we don't see this as a prison. The openness and inclusiveness is a foundation to include a broader democratic notion of what poetry should be in this country."

✤**TICKLED BY THUNDER: THE MAGAZINE THAT SET FICTION FREE (I, II, IV-Subscribers)**, 7385 129th St., Surrey, British Columbia V3W 7B8 Canada, e-mail larry_lindner@mindlink.bc.ca, website http://mindlink.bc.ca/larry_lindner.html, founded 1990, publisher/editor Larry Lindner, appears 4 times/year, using poems about **"fantasy particularly, about writing or whatever. Prefer original images and thoughts. Keep them short (up to 40 lines)—not interested in long, long poems. Nothing pornographic, childish, unimaginative. Welcome humor and inspirational verse."** They have published poetry by Laleh Dadpour Jackson and Helen Michiko Singh. It is 16-20 pgs., digest-sized, published on Macintosh. 5,000 distributed free in Vancouver. Subscription: $12/4 issues. **Sample postpaid: $2.50. Send SASE (or SAE and IRC) for guidelines. Include 3-5 samples of writing with queries. Cover letter required with submissions; include "a few facts about yourself and brief list of publishing credits." Reports in 2-3 months. Pays 5¢/line to $2 maximum. Buys first rights. Editor comments on rejections "99% of the time."** Reviews books of poetry in up to 300 words. Open to unsolicited reviews. Poets may also send books for review consideration. They also offer a poetry contest 4 times/year. Deadlines: the 15th of February, May, August and October. Entry fee: $5 for 1 poem; free for subscribers. Prize: cash, publication and subscription. They also offer a chapbook contest. Send SASE (or SAE and IRC) for details.

TIGHT; TIGHT PRESS (II), P.O. Box 1591, Guerneville CA 95446, founded 1990, editor Ann Erickson, appears 4 times/year. **"*tight* uses experimental poetry, post-LANGUAGE, surrealist, microchunks of experience."** They have published poetry by Cydney Chadwick, Susan Smith Nash, Ken Harris, Paul Weidenhoff, Darrel Pritchard, Jim McCrary, Pat Nolan, Nancy Ibsen, jake berry, Gregory Vincent St. Thomasino and John M. Bennet. As a sample the editor selected these lines from "The Blue Image" by Richard Paul Schmonsees:

> I lay on the bed as still as the night itself,
> as I watch a blue image speaking to me from the tin
> ceiling. It says,—Let me tell you a story son. Then I
> hear shot guns outside in the silent rain, and sirens,
> far off. Then it hovers for a moment, and freezes as if a
> holograph. Then there is the sound as if someone were
> placing a needle on the groove of a recording, and the blue
> image's message repeats. Let me tell you a story son. The
> gun shots. The sirens. This goes on all night long until dawn.

tight is 60 pgs., 8½ × 11, photocopied from typescript. **Sample postpaid: $5. Make checks payable to Ann Erickson. Reports in 2 months. Pays 1 copy. Acquires one-time rights.**

TIGHTROPE (II); SWAMP PRESS (V), 323 Pelham Rd., Amherst MA 01002-1654, founded 1977, chief editor Ed Rayher. Swamp Press is a small press publisher of poetry and graphic art in limited edition, letterpress chapbooks. *Tightrope*, appearing 1-2 times a year, is a literary magazine of varying format. Circulation is 300 for 150 subscribers of which 25 are libraries. Subscription: $10/2 issues. **Sample postpaid: $6. Submit 3-6 poems at a time. No simultaneous submissions.** Time between acceptance and publication is 6-12 months. **Sometimes comments on rejections. Send SASE for guidelines. Reports in 2 months. Pays "sometimes" and provides 2 copies. Acquires first rights.** Swamp Press has published books by Edward Kaplan, editor Ed Rayher, Alexis Rotella (miniature, 3×3, containing 6 haiku), Sandra Dutton (a 4 foot long poem), Frannie Lindsay (a 10×13 format containing 3 poems), Andrew Glaze, Tom Haxo, Carole Stone and Steven Ruhl. **The editor is not presently accepting unsolicited submissions for chapbook publication but when he publishes chapbooks he pays 5-10% of press run and, if there is grant money available, an honorarium (about $50).** Send SASE for catalog.

TIMBERLINE PRESS (V), 6281 Red Bud, Fulton MO 65251, phone (573)642-5035, founded 1975, poetry editor Clarence Wolfshohl. "We do limited letterpress editions with the goal of blending strong poetry with well-crafted and designed printing. **We lean toward natural history or strongly imagistic nature poetry but will look at any good work. Also, good humorous poetry. Currently, still not accepting submissions because we have a good backlog of mss to publish—enough for the next 2-3 years.**" They have recently published the book *Paris* by William Hart. As a sample the editor selected these lines from Walter Bargen's *The Vertical River*:

> Perhaps we too are hooked, inhaling
> scents that send us reeling, pausing
> as if planted firmly in the insubstantial,
> then exhaling the incensed fragility,
> its loosening definitions and dissolving
> edges. . . .

Sample copies may be obtained by sending $5, requesting sample copy, and noting you saw the listing in *Poet's Market*. **Reports in under 1 month. Pays "50-50 split with author after Timberline Press has recovered its expenses."**

‡♣**TIME FOR RHYME (I, IV-Form/style)**, P.O. Box 1055, Battleford, Saskatchewan S0M 0E0 Canada, phone (306)445-5172, founded 1995, editor Richard W. Unger, published quarterly, aims to "promote traditional rhyming poetry. Other than short editorial, contents page, review page, PoeMarkets (other markets taking rhyme), this magazine is all rhyming poetry." **They want "any rhyming poetry in any form up to about 32 lines on nearly any subject." They do not want "obscene (4-letter words), pornographic, profane, racist or sexist. No e.e. cummings' style either."** They have recently published poetry by Raymond Fenech, Sharon R. McMillan, J. Alvin Speers and Tony Cosier. *Time for Rhyme* is 32 pgs., 4×5½, photocopied, hand-bound with thread, hand press printed cover, with clip art, handmade rubber stamps, letterpress art and ads. They receive several hundred poems a year, accept approximately 25%. Subscription: $12. **Sample postpaid: $3.25.** "Preference given to **subscribers, however, no requirements." Previously published poems OK ("But must ensure poet retained rights on it. Prefer unpublished"). No simultaneous submissions. Cover letter preferred, list titles submitted and if first submission here give brief list of publications poet has been published in. No poems published yet? Send some general information." Often comments on rejections. Send SASE (or SAE and IRC) for guidelines. Reports ASAP. Pays 1 copy. Prefers to acquire first North American serial rights—will consider second serial rights.** Staff reviews books/magazines containing mostly or all rhyming poetry. Reviews vary in length but up to about 100 words. Poets may also send books for review consideration. The editor says, "though non-rhyming poetry can be excellent, *Time for Rhyme* was created to be a platform for poets who prefer rhyme and as a source for those who prefer to read it. Old-fashioned values popular here too. Might be best to read a back issue before submitting."

TIME OF SINGING, A MAGAZINE OF CHRISTIAN POETRY (I, IV-Religious, themes), P.O. Box 149, Conneaut Lake PA 16316, founded 1958-1965, revived 1980, editor Charles A. Waugaman, managing editor Lora Zill. "The viewpoint is **unblushingly Christian—but in its widest and most inclusive meaning.** Moreover, it is believed that the vital message of Christian poems, as well as inspiring the general reader, will give pastors, teachers, and devotional leaders rich current sources of inspiring material to aid them in their ministries. We tend to have a Fall/Christmas issue, a Lent/Easter one, and a Summer one. But **we do have themes quite often. We tend to value content, rather than form; prefer short poems for practical reasons.**" They have recently published poetry by Ralph Seager, Tony Cosier, John Grey, Edgar Hix, Mary Herbest, Frances P. Reid and Charles Waugaman. As a sample the editor selected these lines from "John the Baptist in Prison" by Nina Forsythe:

> This cell has rotted my voice to silence.

THE GEOGRAPHICAL INDEX, located before the Subject Index, can help you discover the publishers in your region. Publishers often favor poets (and work) from their own areas.

> *Now I must listen to my thoughts careen*
> *from wall to wall in this hoary prison*
> *of my mind. Suddenly nothing is clear*
> *as it was in the desert, where the sun*
> *and sand bleached bones and scoured wood clean.*

Time of Singing is 40 pgs., digest-sized, offset from typescript with decorative line drawings scattered throughout. Besides their 3 scheduled issues, they also publish 1-2 bonus issues a year. The bonus issues are *not* theme based. They receive over 500 submissions a year, use about 210. Circulation is 350 for 150 subscribers. Single copy: $6; subscription: $15 US, $18 Canada, $27 overseas. **Sample: $3. Submit up to 5 poems at a time, double-spaced. Simultaneous submissions and previously published poems OK.** Time between acceptance and publication is 6 months to 1 year. **Editor frequently comments with suggestions for improvement for publication. Send SASE for guidelines and upcoming themes. Reports in 1-2 months. Pays 1 copy plus 25¢/line ($1 minimum to $4 maximum/poem). Reserves right to reprint poems in other formats. "We tend to be traditional. We like poems that are aware of grammar. Collections of uneven lines, series of phrases, preachy statements, unstructured 'prayers,' and trite sing-song rhymes usually get returned. We look for poems that 'show' rather than 'tell.' "** They also publish chapbooks of poets of the editor's selection and offer contests, "generally one for each scheduled issue on a given subject related to our theme. Send SASE for rules."

‡TO TOPIO: AN ANNUAL ANTHOLOGY OF POETRY FOR THE INTERNATIONALLY MINDED (II, IV-Anthology), 712 NW 13th St., Corvallis OR 97330, phone (541)753-9955, founded 1996, editors Caan Zarosinski and Justin Taylor, founder Roger Weaver, is published annually. **"The landscape, site or locality that *To Topio* refers to is global, so we welcome quality poetry from all over the world and in any language, so long as it is accompanied by an English translation approved by the author and so indicated with the author's legible signature."** The editors say *To Topio* is 50-100 pgs., digest-sized, perfect-bound with card cover. Subscription: $4.50. **Submit up to 6 poems or pages with name and address on each page. No previously published poems; simultaneous submissions OK. Cover letter preferred. Reads submissions September 1 through June 30 only.** Time between acceptance and publication is 6 weeks. **Poems are circulated to an editorial board with two editors agreeing on the acceptances. Seldom comments on rejections. Send SASE for guidelines. Reports "immediately." Pays 1 copy. Acquires one-time rights.**

‡TOLEDO POETS CENTER PRESS; 11 BY 30; RADIO ROOM PRESS (IV-Regional), Toledo Poets Center, University of Toledo, Toledo OH 43606-3390, phone (419)530-2318, founded 1976, director Joel Lipman, specializes in "eclectic tastes; the area's edge." Publishes **1-6 chapbooks.** Chapbooks format varies with material or concept. **They accept no unsolicited manuscripts. Pays up to 60% royalties and author's copies (out of a press run of 200). For sample chapbooks, send $5 to publisher at the above address.** Toledo Poets Center provides, at different times and in various ways, poetry programming workshops, presenting and touring, and publication for the Toledo community.

TOMORROW MAGAZINE (II), P.O. Box 148486, Chicago IL 60614-8486, e-mail audrelv@tezcat.com, founded 1982, editor Tim W. Brown, is a biannual magazine appearing in January and July. "We focus roughly half on poets from Chicago, half from elsewhere. We prefer work that falls between the 'academic' and 'underground' extremes of the literary spectrum." **They want "free verse strong in image and emotion. No formalist and academic poetry, Hallmark verse, or religious poetry."** They have published poetry by Richard Kostelanetz, Lyn Lifshin, Hugh Fox and Antler. *TM* is 40 pgs., 8½×7, saddle-stitched, with card stock cover, b&w cover photo. They receive about 300 mss a year, accept approximately 10-12%. Press run is 300 for 200 shelf sales. **Sample postpaid: $5. Send 5-6 poems at a time. No previously published poems; simultaneous submissions OK. Cover letter with brief bio welcome. "Querying by e-mail is fine, but we prefer submissions on paper through the post."** Time between acceptance and publication is 6-9 months. **Seldom comments on rejections. Send SASE for guidelines. Reports in 3 weeks to 3 months. Pays 1 copy. Acquires first rights. Requests acknowledgment when reprinting in anthologies or collections.** The editor says, "There are too many tribes in poetry. At *Tomorrow* we like to think we have a pluralistic outlook."

‡TOTH PRESS (I), P.O. Box 640746, San Jose CA 95164-0746, e-mail bear@hooked.net, founded 1993, publisher David Bolduc, "seeks the strong modern voice of poets who might not otherwise be published." Publishes 1 paperback and **4 chapbooks/year.** Two books are selected through competitions. Winners receive $200 plus 10% of press run. Send ms marked as a contest entry and $10 entry fee. **They want "strong and unique voices." They do not want "sentimental, greeting card, light verse. Rhyme OK if uncompromising to poem."** They have recently published poetry by Nora-Maria Iancu. As a sample the editor selected these lines from "One Night, One Mountain, Three Poems" by Dancing Bear:

> *Now we are lost*
> *I imagine that he fears we will turn a corner*
> *and find the Ku Klux Klan still burns crosses*
> *along with Indians, homosexuals and free-thinking poets*
> *Damn, my engine is smoking again*

Books are usually 24-40 pgs., 6×9, printed or photocopied, saddle-stitched, with card stock cover and some

INSIDER REPORT

Christian poetry is more than preaching

For Charles Waugaman, a Baptist minister, poetry is as much a calling as the pulpit. "I don't see poetry as something I choose to do. It's something I have to do."

And Waugaman, who just retired as pastor of High Street Community Church in Conneaut Lake, Pennsylvania, makes no effort to separate his religious beliefs from his poetic practice. In fact, he says, they can't be separated. "I'm a Christian and that affects my point of view on everything. It comes out one way or another."

Apart from his own work, which has appeared in numerous journals and chapbook collections over the past four decades, Waugaman also edits poetry for the magazine *Time of Singing*. He has been associated with the Christian poetry magazine since its inception in 1958.

Charles Waugaman

Time of Singing was founded by Benjamin Browne, a Baptist writer, editor and educator, as an extension of an annual Christian writer's conference he directed. Browne felt there was a need for an outlet for Christian poets. Waugaman was associate editor and later editor until the magazine ceased publication in 1965.

In 1980, when Waugaman became minister of High Street Community Church, he asked church members if they would consider sponsoring a revived *Time of Singing*. "I knew from my own submissions the market [for Christian poetry] was shrinking drastically." The magazine now publishes three regular issues each year, plus smaller "intermezzo" issues. The Church of the First Born, also based in Conneaut Lake, co-sponsors the magazine.

Devoted to publishing poetry with Christian themes, *Time of Singing* is open to a wider category of work than many readers might think. "What is a Christian poet? That question has been debated for as long as I can remember and will be throughout eternity," says Waugaman. "And while I'm sure we have a Baptist point of view, we have published Catholics and Protestants. There's no limitation. We work with the poem; we don't determine what the poet believes."

And although the magazine publishes a diverse range of Christian poets, it does have certain preferences. "By Christian we don't mean theological or propaganda in any sense, but we're not ashamed to promote Christ or have a Biblical subject or even have a positive point of view on things." In fact, *Time of Singing*'s diversity is such that established poets like John Grey and Sheryl Nelms appear alongside beginners.

However, for Waugaman, this openness means all the poetry published in the magazine is not of equal quality. "I still like to encourage new or beginning poets and, if you remain that open, you can't stick to a completely high caliber of writing. You can't keep up with the really highbrow journals or compete with university presses."

INSIDER REPORT, *Waugaman*

Waugaman does see ***Time of Singing***'s niche in the poetry market as a small and shrinking one. Whereas denominational presses previously published religious poems in a variety of formats, those markets have "shrunk drastically." So, to help reach a more varied audience, ***Time of Singing*** reprints some of its poems in anthologies and special collections. "Some work deserves to go farther than one issue."

But despite the decreasing market for Christian poetry, Waugaman says his first loyalty as an editor is to the quality of the poetry he publishes. "I read the poetry in the religious publications that exist today and most of it I wouldn't publish. I'm afraid the religious market goes for sentiment rather than craftsmanship. A lot of the work I get I have to return, because the writers try to copy that sentiment-based style."

"Colors for Christmas"

Long had Christ robed in gold and amethyst,
Effulgent violet, celestial blue;
The radiance of rainbows often threw
A dazzle to the light with which he dressed
Yet drew from Him what glory it possessed.
He did not need the green of pine and yew;
And scarlet berries that the holly grew
Would scarcely have competed with the rest.

It was our earth tones that He came to wear;
The gray of weariness, the brown of work-
Stained fingers cultivating soil, the spare,
Dull ochre of his withered grass, tan, black,
And weathered-silver of a cattle shack.

Yes, every tone His proud disciples shirk.

(from Myrrh for my Birthday, 1986; reprinted by permission of the author)

And, according to Waugaman, Christian poets who only pay attention to the message aren't writing poetry; they're writing sermons. "I'm a minister. I preach all the time. A poem and sermon are different entirely. A lot of poems we get are written as propaganda or dogmatism. They're all addressed to you—you do this, you do that. If you draw from your experience—and it's a universal experience—it's going to speak. You don't have to add a moral."

These are the traits of Waugaman's own poetry. For instance, "Colors for Christmas," reprinted above, contrasts what he envisions as the glorious colors of heaven and the plain colors of earth. The poem's images and use of meter and rhyme establish the contrast effectively, without heavy-handed moralizing.

And, another problem Waugaman sees with many Christian poets, as with other poets, is they don't pay enough attention to the formal aspects of poetry, but only to the message. "Poetry is important because it can be remembered, which is why it was one of the first literary forms to come into being. That's how people passed it on. Rhyme and meter help you remember things."

Though he has self-published some of his work, Waugaman says 70 percent of the

INSIDER REPORT, *continued*

poems in his books appeared first in literary journals. However, he sees a tendency among young poets to try and publish books before they are ready. "This is very scary. With laptop publishing, anybody in the world can put out a chapbook—and they are. I'll get poets who are just beginning who have already put out a book. Whether they're working with a vanity press, a printer or their own laptop, most of them don't have an editor."

Waugaman advises young poets to seek out writers' groups for feedback on their work, and to concentrate on learning the basics of the poetic craft before seeking publication. "A beginning poet can't spend too much time crafting, and that begins with reading. All they want to do is see themselves in print. You have to read the poets of all ages and get the ideas in mind."

Currently, *Time of Singing* is undergoing a transition. With Waugaman's retirement from ministry and subsequent move to Vermont, Lora Zill, the magazine's managing editor, will oversee the day-to-day operations while Waugaman continues his involvement by producing illustrations for the magazine (he is a trained artist and handles *Time of Singing*'s layout and illustrations).

But even with this change of duties, Waugaman wouldn't change his deep involvement with poetry. "A poet is one who has a point of view on life. What you learn is the skill of expressing that point of view. Poetry is the way I find expression for my life."
—*Kevin Walzer*

---

graphics. **Submit complete chapbook ms of 24-40 pgs. with title sheet and $10 reading fee. Previously published poems and simultaneous submissions OK. Cover letter required with brief bio and publication credits.** Time between acceptance and publication is 6 months. **Poems are circulated to an editorial board. Seldom comments on rejections. Replies to queries in 1 month, to mss in 3-6 months. Pays 10% of press run plus discounted copies.**

TOUCHSTONE (I, II), Viterbo College, La Crosse WI 54601-4797, phone (608)796-3484, fax (608)796-3050, e-mail eng_ruppel@viterbo.edu, founded 1950, moderator Richard Ruppel, is a literary quarterly publishing poetry, short stories and artwork. As a sample the editor selected these lines from "The Choice" by Kerri Brostrom:

> Why did you come to me
> like a streak of scarlet,
> a swift red explosion
> landing in my passion?

The magazine is 48 pgs., digest-sized, saddle-stapled, with semi-glossy card cover. Press run is 1,200 for 100 subscribers of which 25 are libraries. Subscription: $15. **Sample postpaid: $7.50. Cover letter required; include "a note of origination" (i.e., that the work is original). "Poets may submit via fax, e-mail or snail-mail." Reads submissions August 1 through March 1 only. Send SASE for guidelines. Reports in 2 months. Pays 1 copy.**

TOUCHSTONE LITERARY JOURNAL; TOUCHSTONE PRESS (III, IV-Translations), P.O. Box 8308, Spring TX 77387-8308, founded 1975, poetry editor William Laufer, is an annual publishing **"experimental or well-crafted traditional form, including sonnets, and translations. No light verse or doggerel."** They have recently published poetry by Walter Griffin, Walter McDonald, Paul Ramsey and Janice Whittington. *Touchstone* is 100 pgs., digest-sized, flat-spined, professionally printed in small, dark type with glossy card cover. Subscription: $7.50. **Sample postpaid: $4. Submit 5 poems at a time. "Cover letter telling something about the poet piques our interest and makes the submission seem less like a mass mailing." Sometimes sends prepublication galleys. Pays 1 copy.** Reviews books of poetry. Open to unsolicited reviews. Poets may also send books for review consideration, to Review Editor. Touchstone Press also **publishes an occasional chapbook. Send SASE for chapbook submission guidelines.** "We previously published a book-length epic, *Kingdom of the Leopard: An Epic of Old Benin* by Nigerian poet chi chi layor. We are open to new projects. Query first, with SASE. Absolutely no mail is answered without SASE."

**WINTER EDITION 96-97
Vol. 45 No. 2**

Tower is published by the Tower Poetry Society, a nonprofit organization whose purpose is to promote poetry and encourage poets. The all-poetry publication is open to any style or subject matter, but poems may be no longer than 40 lines. "Submissions come from all over the world so our cover art must have a wide appeal—nature or rural scenes are often depicted," says Joanna Lawson, editor-in-chief of the Canadian biannual. "However, other than the seasons, illustrator Kim Davis has no way of knowing what poems were submitted or which were chosen, so her covers depict our world." Davis is a freelance illustrator who donates her own time to create covers for *Tower*. She receives much of her inspiration from her family—a husband, three kids and a dog.

✿**TOWER POETRY SOCIETY; TOWER (II)**, Dundas Public Library, 18 Ogilvie St., Dundas, Ontario L9H 2S2 Canada, phone (905)648-4878, founded 1951, editor-in-chief Joanna Lawson. "The Tower Poetry Society was started by a few members of McMaster University faculty to promote interest in poetry. We publish *Tower* twice a year. We want **rhymed or free verse, traditional or modern, but not prose chopped into short lines, maximum 40 lines in length, any subject, any comprehensible style.**" They have published poetry by Bill Moore and Helen Fitzgerald Dougher. As a sample the editor selected these lines by Joanna Lawson:

> *A poem is*
> *a slide under a microscope*
> *one thin slice*
> *of then,*
> *or now,*
> *or what might be,*
> *magnified for meaning*

Tower is 40 pgs., digest-sized. Circulation is 250 for 60 subscribers of which 8 are libraries. They receive about 400 poems a year, use approximately 70, no backlog. Subscription: $8 including postage; $9.50 abroad. **Sample postpaid: $3. Submit up to 4 poems at a time. Reads submissions during February or August. Reports in 2 months. Pays 1 copy.** The editor advises, "Read a lot of poetry before you try to write it."

‡***TRAFIKA (II)**, Veverkova 20, Prague 170 00 Czech Republic, phone/fax (422)382 654, e-mail trafika@interport.net, founded 1993, contact Jeffrey Young, published 3 times/year, features "current literature, introducing emerging writers from around the world." They have recently published poetry by Czeslaw Mitosz and Edoardo Albinati. As a sample the editor selected these lines from "Lacquer" by Tomaž Šalamun:

> *Destiny rolls over me. Sometimes like an egg. Sometimes*
> *with its paws, slamming me into the slope. I shout. I take*
> *my stand. I pledge all my juices.*

The editor says *Trafika* is 200 pgs., 24×16.5cm, professionally printed in Prague, with cover art and graphics. Press run is 6,000. Subscription: $35. **Sample postpaid: $10. Submit 5 or more poems at a time. No previously published poems; simultaneous submissions OK. Cover letter required, with "brief bio and all relevant contact info."** Time between acceptance and publication is 3 months. **Poems are circulated to an editorial board. "All considered poems are read by editors in New York and Prague." Seldom comments on rejections. Send SASE (or SAE and IRC) for guidelines. Reports in 1-3 months. Pays $15/published page and 2 copies. Buys first international publishing rights.** Poets may also send books for review consideration.

‡***TRANSNATIONAL PERSPECTIVES (III)**, CP161, 1211 Geneva 16 Switzerland, fax 334 50 047452, founded 1975, editor René Wadlow, is a "journal of world politics with some emphasis on culture that crosses frontiers." Uses 4-6 poems/issue, usually illustrated by drawing or photo. They want **"poems stressing harmony of nature, human potential, understanding of other cultures—relatively short. No humor, nationalistic themes, nothing 'overly' subjective."** They have published poetry by Verona Bratesch and Janet Pehr. *TP*

appears 3 times/year; it "is oriented toward making policy suggestions in international organizations, especially in the United Nations." It is 48 pgs., handsomely produced, magazine-sized, saddle-stapled with coated color paper cover. They receive about 100 poems a year, use approximately 16. Press run is 5,000 for 4,000 subscribers of which half are libraries. **Sample back issue free on request. No previously published poems; simultaneous submissions OK. Editor comments "rarely on quality, only why not for *TP*." Reports in 1 month. Pays 5 copies, more if desired.** René Wadlow says, "Poems in *TP* come from many countries, especially Eastern Europe, Scandinavia and India, often translated into English, usually 'upbeat' since most articles are on political and economic difficulties of the world."

TRESTLE CREEK REVIEW (II, IV-Regional), English Dept. North Idaho College, 1000 West Garden, Coeur d'Alene ID 83814, phone (208)769-3384, fax (208)769-3431, founded 1982-83, poetry editor Chad Klinger et al, is a "2-year college creative writing program production. Purposes: (1) expand the range of publishing/editing experience for our small band of writers; (2) expose them to editing experience; (3) create another outlet for serious, beginning writers. **We're fairly eclectic but prefer poetry on the Northwest region, particularly the innermountain West (Idaho, Montana, etc.). We favor poetry strong on image and sound, and country vs. city; spare us the romantic, rhymed clichés. We can't publish much if it's long (more than two pgs.)."** They have published poetry by Jesse Bier, Walter Griffin, Lance Olsen and Mary Winters. As a sample Chad Klinger selected these lines from "Trying to Pen What You Wish You Hadn't Said" by Daniel Mills:

> *What you said won't return to be fenced,*
> *a stallion of wild syllables your tongue tries roping back—*
> *but the words stumble, go lame,*
> *beg for you to shoot them.*

TCR is a 57-page annual, digest-sized, professionally printed on heavy buff stock, perfect-bound, matte cover with art. Circulation is 500 for 6 subscribers of which 4 are libraries. This publication is well-designed and features both free and formal verse by relative newcomers. The editors receive 100 submissions a year, use approximately 30. **Sample: $5. Submit before March 1 (for May publication), no more than 5 pgs. No previously published poems or simultaneous submissions. Reports by March 30. Pays 2 copies.** The editor advises, "Be neat; be precise; don't romanticize or cry in your beer; strike the surprising, universal note. Know the names of things."

TRIQUARTERLY MAGAZINE; TRIQUARTERLY BOOKS/NORTHWESTERN UNIVERSITY PRESS (II), 2020 Ridge Ave., Evanston IL 60208-4302, phone (847)491-7614, founded 1964, assistant editor Gwenan Wilbur, editors Reginald Gibbons and Susan Hahn. *TriQuarterly Magazine* is one of the most respected and visually appealing journals produced in the United States. Editors accept a wide range of verse forms and styles of verse (long poems, sequences, etc.) **with the emphasis solely on excellence,** and some issues are published as books on specific themes. They have published poetry by Tom Sleigh, Linda McCarriston, Alice Fulton, Campbell McGrath, Susan Stewart and Theodore Weiss. *TriQuarterly*'s three issues per year are 200 pgs., 6×9, professionally printed and flat-spined with b&w photography, graphics, glossy card cover. There are about 40 or more pgs. of poetry in each issue. They receive about 3,000 poems a year, use approximately 60, have about a year backlog. Press run is 5,000 for 2,000 subscribers of which 35% are libraries. Single copy: $11.95; subscription: $24; **Sample postpaid: $5. No simultaneous submissions. Reads submissions October 1 through March 31 only. Sometimes works with poets, inviting rewrites of interesting work. Reports in 3 months. Always sends prepublication galleys. Pays 2 copies, additional copies available at a 40% discount. Acquires first North American serial rights. "We *suggest* prospective contributors examine sample copy before submitting."** Reviews books of poetry "at times." Send books for review consideration. Work appearing in *TriQuarterly* has been included in *The Best American Poetry* (1993, 1994, 1995, 1996 and 1997) and the *Pushcart Prize* anthology. TriQuarterly Books (an imprint of Northwestern University Press) publishes 8-10 books/year of fiction, literary essays and poetry. They have recently published poetry by Bruce Weigl, Adrian C. Louis and Muriel Rukeyser. **Query with up to 10 sample pages of poetry with SASE, "but we cannot consider unsolicited manuscripts."** Send SASE for additional information.

‡TROUBADOUR; TOWERS AND RUSHING, LTD. (II, IV-Style), P.O. Box 691745, San Antonio TX 78269-1745, phone (210)696-1363, *Troubadour* founded 1997, Towers and Rushing Ltd. founded 1986, publisher/editor Dr. Ron Ribble. *Troubadour*, published biannually (February and September), intends "to bridge the gap between the general reader and the contemporary world of poetry." **They want "excellently-crafted, accessible poetry written in formal styles, but will accept any style that has the flavor of tradition and formality. Poems not to exceed 32 lines."** They do not want "forced rhyme or inversion, no epics, no self-pitying or self-indulgent verse, no useless profanity, mush or schlock." As a sample the editor selected these lines from "Shadow" by advisory editor Dan Kaderli:

> *. . . with unknown knowledge that the clock will spin;*
> *positioned over nine and over three,*
> *the slightly upturned hands create a grin.*
> *A moment granted is one burned away;*
> *the living darkness chases after day*

The editor says *Troubadour* is 48 pgs., 8½×5½, perfect-bound, with semi-gloss cover. Single copy: $6; subscription: $10. **Make checks payable to Towers and Rushing, Ltd. Submit up to 3 poems at a time. No previously published poems or simultaneous submissions. Cover letter preferred with "whether poet has been published before or not and a little bit about who the poet is—not how wonderful he or she may be."** Does not read submissions during December and August. Time between acceptance and publication is 2-5 months. **"Editor/publisher will make selections with selected input from advisory editor." Seldom comments on rejections. Send SASE for guidelines. Reports in 4-6 weeks. Pays honoraria to invitees and 2 copies to subscribers, 1 to non-subscribers. Acquires one-time rights.** Offers annual awards of $150, $75 and $50 for the best published poems during the previous year. Winner selected from published poems by an independent panel. The editor says, "During the past several years I have interviewed such poets as Rita Dove, Robert Pinsky, Maya Angelou, Gerald Stern and JD McClatchy. They would all agree that great poets are first great readers. Before submitting, be certain you have a grasp of what good poetry is. This is not a journal for the awkward neophyte."

TROUT CREEK PRESS (V), 5976 Billings Rd., Parkdale OR 97041-9610, phone (541)352-6494, e-mail lfh42@aol.com, founded 1981, poetry editor Laurence F. Hawkins, when accepting submissions, they prefer poetry **"with cerebral undertones or vice versa."** They have published poetry by Judson Crews, Gerald Locklin, Arthur Winfield Knight, Nathaniel Tarn and Sam Silva. **Trout Creek Press is not considering submissions in 1998, but when they resume, submit complete ms of up to 44 pgs. Replies to queries immediately, to submissions in 1-2 months. No simultaneous submissions. Editor sometimes comments on rejections. Always sends prepublication galleys for chapbooks. No payment until "material costs recovered. We also publish individual authors on cassette tape."** Send SASE for catalog to buy samples.

TUCUMCARI LITERARY REVIEW (II), 3108 W. Bellevue Ave., Los Angeles CA 90026, founded 1988, editor Troxey Kemper, assistant editor Neoma Reed, appears every other month. **"Prefer rhyming and established forms, 2-100 lines, but the primary goal is to publish good work. No talking animals. No haiku. No disjointed, fragmentary, rambling words or phrases typed in odd-shaped staggered lines trying to look like poetry. The quest here is for poetry that will be just as welcome many years later as it is now."** They have published poetry by Elizabeth Dabbs, Fontaine Falkoff, Marian Ford Park, Ruth Daniels, Wilma Elizabeth McDaniel, Andy Peterson, Harvey Stanbrough, Jim Dunlap and Dawn Zapletal. As a sample the editor selected these lines from "Plasticity" by John W. Crawford:

> Plastic flowers look so real
> They brighten up the room;
> Adding to the subterfuge,
> We squirt them with perfume.
> Plastic minds with plastic thoughts
> Perform in plastic space,
> Never separating false
> From natural truth and grace

The magazine is 48 pgs., digest-sized, saddle-stapled, photocopied from typescript, with card cover. Press run is 150-200. Subscription: $12, $20 for overseas. **Sample: $2, $4 for overseas. Submit up to 4 poems at a time. Simultaneous submissions and previously published poems OK. Send SASE for guidelines. Reports within 1 month. Pays 1 copy. Acquires one-time rights.** This magazine is inexpensively produced but contains some good formal poems. If you're looking to place a particular sonnet or villanelle, try Troxey Kemper's magazine. He reports quickly, by the way, and may comment on rejections. The editor says, "Writing is welcomed from amateurs, in-betweens and professors/scholars. Many college professors and writing teachers submit rhyming poems here. They say they're sick of non-rhyme junk. Oddly, some of the work by amateurs is more interesting than erudite, obscure allusions to Greek/Roman mythology personages and events—more honest, earnest and heart-felt. The main measure of acceptability is: It is interesting? Is it good? What counts is what it *says* not whether the work is handwritten on three-hole lined notebook paper or presented on expensive computer-generated equipment/paper which often is very difficult to read."

TUNDRA (I, IV-Form), (formerly *Woodnotes*), 248 Beach Park Blvd., Foster City CA 94404, phone (415)571-9428, e-mail welchm@aol.com, founded 1989, editor Michael Dylan Welch (who is also editor/publisher of Press Here). *Tundra*, published 3 times/year (February, June and October), **accepts short poetry in addition to haiku, senrya, tanka and related forms. Open to concrete poetry, but seldom accepts language poetry. "I want to see authentic and engaging short poetry rooted in the crystal image. I'm inclined toward objective and**

THE CHAPBOOK INDEX, located before the Geographical Index, lists those publishers who consider chapbook manuscripts. A chapbook, a small volume of work, is often a good middle step between magazine and book publication.

organic form, and value both lightness and depth." They have recently published work by Samuel Menashe, Dana Gioia, Ce Rosenow and Tom Clausen. As a sample the editor selected this piece by Lee Gurga:

> last bale of hay—
> we sit down on it
> and watch the moon

The editor says *Tundra* is 72-88 pgs., 5½ × 8½, offset printed and perfect-bound with cover photograph. They receive about 4,000 poems a year, accept approximately 10%. Press run is 500 for 350 subscribers of which 10 are libraries. Subscription: $18. **Sample postpaid: $7. Inquire about international rates. Make checks payable to Michael Welch. Preference given to poems 13 lines or less. No previously published poems or simultaneous submissions. Cover letter preferred. E-mail submissions OK if no payment is desired. Seldom comments on rejections. Reports usually in 1-4 weeks. Acquires first North American serial rights. Pays $1/poem (except e-mail submissions, which receive no pay).** Reviews books of short poetry (especially haiku, senryu, etc.) in anywhere from 50 to 1,000 words. Reviews are usually assigned or done by the editors, but they are open to unsolicited reviews. Poets may also send books for review consideration. The editor says, "For those wishing to submit haiku, please note that I see English haiku as a brief, one-breath form of poetry using objective words to convey heightened subjective feeling about nature and human nature. I recommend reading William J. Higginson's *Haiku Handbook* and Cor van den Heuvel's *The Haiku Anthology* for a good introduction to haiku and examples in English."

TURKEY PRESS (V), 6746 Sueno Rd., Isla Vista CA 93117-4904, founded 1974, poetry editor Harry Reese along with his wife, Sandra Reese, "is involved with publishing contemporary literature, producing traditional and experimental book art, one-of-a-kind commissioned projects and collaborations with various artists and writers. **We do not encourage solicitations of any kind to the press. We seek out and develop projects on our own."** They have published poetry by Thomas Merton, James Laughlin, Sam Hamill, Edwin Honig, Glenna Luschei, Tom Clark, Michael Hannon, Keith Waldrop, David Ossman, Peter Whigham, Jack Curtis, Kirk Robertson and Anne E. Edge.

TWILIGHT ENDING (I), 21 Ludlow Dr., Milford CT 06460-6822, phone (203)877-3473, founded 1995, editor/publisher Emma J. Blanch, appears 3 times/year publishing "poetry and short fiction of the highest caliber." They have featured the work of poets from the US, Canada, England, Japan, New Zealand and India. **They want "poems with originality in thought and style, reflecting the latest trend in writing, moving from the usual set-up to a vertical non-conformist approach, some following Kerouac's form, having none of the required punctuation. We prefer unrhymed poetry, however we accept rhymed verse if rhymes are perfect. We look for the unusual approach in content and style."** The editor says *TE* is 5½ × 8½, "elegantly printed on white linen with one poem per page (12-30 lines)." They receive about 1,500 poems a year, accept approximately 10%. Press run is 100 for 50 subscribers of which 25 are libraries. **Sample postpaid: $5 US, $6 Canada, $6.50 England, $7.50 India, Japan and New Zealand. Make checks payable to Emma J. Blanch. Submit 3-4 poems at a time. No previously published poems or simultaneous submissions ("including poems submitted to contests"). "When accepted, poems and fiction will not be returned so keep copies." Submission postmark deadlines: December 30 for Winter issue, April 30 for Spring/Summer issue, September 30 for Fall issue. No backlog, "all poems are destroyed after publication." Often comments on rejections. Send SASE for guidelines. Reports in 1 week. Pays nothing—not even a copy. Acquires first rights.** The editor says, "If editing is needed, suggestions will be made for the writer to rework and resubmit a corrected version. The author always decides; remember that you deal with experts."

TWISTED (IV-Horror, fantasy), P.O. Box 1249, Palmetto GA 30268-1249, phone (770)463-1458, founded 1985, editor/publisher Christine Hoard, uses **poetry of "horror/dark fantasy; humor OK. Form and style open. Not more than one page long."** They have published poetry by Gary William Crawford, Holly Day and Wayne Edwards. As a sample the editor selected these lines by Ann K. Schwader:

> black aftertaste
> rusted to blood on my tongue
> a smothered
> scream somewhere & me wondering
> if I'm not
> having my nightmare
> who is

Christine Hoard describes *Twisted* as "150 pgs., magazine-sized, offset, vellum bristol cover, much art, some ads, 60 lb. matte paper. I receive a lot of poetry submissions, use 30-50 per issue." Press run is 300 for single-copy sales. **Sample postpaid: $6. Make checks payable to Christine Hoard. "Don't submit more than four poems at a time. You should see a sample copy to get a 'feel' for what we publish."** No simultaneous submissions. Sometimes comments on rejections. **Send SASE for guidelines. Reports within 3 months. "We're not always an open market. We usually close when we're overstocked or preparing the next issue." Pays 1 copy.** She says, "Poets of science fiction, horror, fantasy will be pleased to know there are several markets in the small press and some organizations are available to offer support and market information."

2 AM MAGAZINE; 2 AM PUBLICATIONS (IV-Science fiction/fantasy, horror), P.O. Box 6754, Rockford IL 61125-1754, e-mail p.anderson2/@genie.geis.com, founded 1986, editor Gretta McCombs Anderson, is a quarterly that wants **"fantasy, science fiction, heroic fantasy, horror, weird; any form, any style; preferred length is one to two pgs. We want poetry that leaves an after-image in the mind of the reader."** They have published poetry by Mark Rich, G.N. Gabbard, Bruce Boston and Robert Frazier. The editor describes it as 68 pgs., magazine-sized, offset on 60 lb. stock, cover printed on glossy stock, illustrations "by leading fantasy artists" and ads. Circulation is 2,000 for 350 subscribers. Single copy: $4.95; subscription: $19/year. **Sample postpaid: $5.95. Submit up to 5 poems at a time. "Prefer original poems no more than two pages in length. Please type all manuscripts."** Time between acceptance and publication is 6-12 months. **Editor "sometimes" comments on rejections. Send SASE for guidelines. Reports in 2 months. Always sends prepublication galleys. Pays 5¢/line or $1 minimum plus 1 copy, 40% discount for more. Buys one-time rights.** Reviews books of poetry in 250 words, single format. Open to unsolicited reviews. Poets may also send books for review consideration, attn. Irwin Chapman. Gretta M. Anderson advises, "Read widely, be aware of what's already been done. Short poems stand a good chance with us. Looking for mood-generating poetry of a cosmic nature, poems with extended imagery that work on multiple levels. Not interested in self-indulgent poetry."

❦**TYRO PUBLISHING (I, II)**, 194 Carlbert St., Sault Ste. Marie, Ontario P6A 5E1 Canada, phone (705)253-6402, fax (705)942-3625, founded 1984, editor Stan Gordon. They only consider full-length mss for book publication. They have recently published *Night in the Exude* by David A. Groulx; *Beauty's Gentle Sadness* by Grace D. Hartley; and *Vision at Delphi* by Nancy Fisher. **Query first with at least 6 sample poems. Mss should be in standard format. Send SASE (or SAE and IRC) for guidelines and further information. Always sends prepublication galleys.**

‡**THE ULTIMATE UNKNOWN (I, IV-Science fiction, horror)**, P.O. Box 219, Streamwood IL 60107-0219, founded 1995, editor David D. Combs, published quarterly, is a "literary magazine of science fiction, horror and the future." **They want "science fiction, horror, future and politics of 20-30 lines, any style or meter."** They do not want "profanity of any kind or excessive violence." They have recently published poetry by John Grey. *The Ultimate Unknown* is 100 pgs., photocopied, saddle-stitched with color cover, art and ads. They receive about 50 poems a year, accept approximately 75%. Press run is 250 for 100 subscribers, 10 shelf sales; 50 distributed free to authors, advertisers and reviewers. Subscription: $14. **Sample postpaid: $4. Make checks payable to Combs Press. "I encourage the author to subscribe, but this is not required, and only done after the acceptance." Submit any number of poems, each on a separate piece of paper with name and address. Previously published poems and simultaneous submissions OK. Cover letter preferred.** Time between acceptance and publication is 3-6 months. **"All poems are judged on an individual basis and accepted for their own merits." Always comments on rejections. Publishes theme issues. Send SASE for guidelines and upcoming themes. Reports in 2-3 months. Pays 1 copy. Acquires first North American serial or one-time rights.** Staff reviews books or chapbooks of poetry or other magazines in 1-3 paragraphs. Poets may also send books for review consideration. The editor says, "We are very open to new poets. We give full credit to all poets."

ULTRAMARINE PUBLISHING CO., INC. (II), P.O. Box 303, Hastings-on-Hudson NY 10706-1817, phone (914)478-1339, fax (914)478-1365, founded 1974, editor C.P. Stephens, who says, "We mostly distribute books for authors who had a title dropped by a major publisher—the author is usually able to purchase copies very cheaply. We use existing copies purchased by the author from the publisher when the title is being dropped." Ultramarine's list includes 250 titles, 90% of them cloth bound, one-third of them science fiction and 10% poetry. **The press pays 10% royalties. "Distributor terms are on a book-by-book basis, but is a rough split." Authors should query before making submissions; queries will be answered in 1 week. No queries/submissions via fax. Simultaneous submissions OK, but no disks.**

‡*****UNDERSTANDING MAGAZINE; DIONYSIA PRESS LTD. (I)**, 20 A Montgomery St., Edinburgh, Lothion EH7 5JS Great Britain, phone (0131)4780727, fax (0131)4780089, founded 1989, contact Denise Smith. *Understanding Magazine*, published 1-2 times/year, features "poetry, short stories, parts of plays and reviews." **They want "original poetry."** They have recently published poetry by Susanne Roxman and Ron Butlin. As a sample we selected these lines from "Private Axis" by Thom Neirn:

> The circles grow relentlessly,
> His passage, inscrutably centrifugal
> On this terminal cycle to silence.

The editor says *Understanding* is A5 and perfect-bound. They receive about 2,000 poems a year. Press run is 1,000 for 500 subscribers. Single copy: £2.50; subscription: £5. **Sample postpaid: £2. Make checks payable to Dionysia Press. Submit 5 poems at a time. No previously published poems; simultaneous submissions OK.** Time between acceptance and publication is 6-10 months. **Poems are circulated to an editorial board. Often comments on rejections. Reports in 2-6 months. Always sends prepublication galleys. Pays 1 copy. Acquires all rights. Returns rights after publication.** Staff reviews books or chapbooks of poetry or other magazines. Poets may also send books for review consideration. Dionysia Press Ltd., publishes 2-7 paperbacks and **chapbooks of poetry/year.** "Sometimes we select from submissions or competitions." Books are usually

A5, perfect-bound, hard cover with art. **Query first, with a few sample poems and cover letter with brief bio and publication credits. Replies to queries in 2-6 months. Pays author's copies. "We usually get arts council grants or poets get grants for themselves." For sample books or chapbooks, write to the above address.** Sponsors poetry competitions with cash prizes. Write for guidelines.

❧UNDERWHICH EDITIONS (V), Box 262, Adelaide St. Station, Toronto, Ontario M5C 2J4 Canada, and, in western Canada, 920 Ninth Ave. N., Saskatoon, Saskatchewan S7K 2Z4 Canada, founded 1978, editors Karl Jirgens, Lucas Mulder, Jill Robinson, Susan Andrews Grace, Steven Ross Smith and Paul Dutton are "dedicated to presenting in diverse and appealing physical formats, new works by contemporary creators, **focusing on formal invention and encompassing the expanded frontiers of musical and literary endeavor"** in chapbooks, pamphlets, flat-spined paperbacks, posters, cassettes, records and anthologies. They have recently published poetry by Paul Dutton, Lucas Mulder and Gerry Gilbert. As a sample the editors selected these lines from "Aqueduct" by Gerry Shikatani:

> Tables, white so wrapped with light. Attention of work, and sun across
> touch the cup, coffee then. Oh, tables wrapped. Space beyond edges, far, here am I the heart's
>   movement, cased in light.

They are currently not accepting poetry submissions. "We have all the mss we can handle for the foreseeable future."

‡❧UNFINISHED MONUMENT PRESS; MEKLER & DEAHL, PUBLISHERS; HAMILTON HAIKU PRESS (IV-Form); THE ACORN-RUKEYSER CHAPBOOK CONTEST; THE SANDBURG LIVESAY ANTHOLOGY CONTEST (III), 237 Prospect St. S., Hamilton, Ontario L8M 2Z6 Canada, phone (905)312-1779, fax (905)312-8285, founded 1978 (Unfinished Monument Press), 1983 (Hamilton Haiku Press), managing partner James Deahl. Unfinished Monument Press and Hamilton Haiku Press, with their 2 imprints UnMon Northland (in Canada), UnMon America (in the USA), publish 3 paperbacks and **6 chapbooks/year** with 1 chapbook and 2 anthologies published as the result of contests. **They want "for Unfinished Monument Press: people's poetry; for Hamilton Haiku Press: haiku." They do not want "racist or sexist poetry."** They have recently published poetry by Jennifer Footman, Bernice Lever and Ted Plantos. As a sample the editor selected these lines from "The Hands" by Milton Acorn:

> Why man, those hands, dyed
> earth and tobacco brown, tough
> as an old alligator suitcase, fissured
> a dozen extra ways, have
> a grip all courtesy, a touch
> delicate and sure as a young woman's.

Books are usually 20-96 pgs., 6×9, offset-printed with art and/or graphics. **"Always query first with 5 sample poems." Previously published poems and simultaneous submissions OK. Cover letter required. "U.S. poets may use our Pittsburgh address: Unfinished Monument Press, P.O. Box 4279, Pittsburgh PA 15203." Has backlog of 1-2 years.** Time between acceptance and publication "varies greatly." **"I publish what I like. I also publish what I think will sell." Seldom comments on rejections.** Replies to queries in 6 months, to mss in 1 month. **Pays 10-12% royalties and 10-20 author's copies (out of a press run of 300-500). For sample books or chapbooks, write to the above address.** Sponsors The Acorn-Rukeyser Chapbook Contest, awarding 1 prize of $100 (Canadian), publication and 50 copies. Submissions may be entered in other contests. Submit a poetry ms of up to 30 pgs., poems must be within the People's Poetry tradition, as exemplified by the work of Milton Acorn and Muriel Rukeyser. Send SASE for guidelines. Entry fees: $10 (Canadian), $8 (U.S.). All entrants receive a copy of the winning chapbook. Postmark deadline: October 31. Winner will be notified in January. Also sponsors The Sandburg-Livesay Anthology Contest, awarding a $100 first prize and publication, and other prizes of publication. Submit up to 10 poems of up to 80 lines; poems must be within the People's Poetry tradition, as exemplified by the work of Carl Sandburg and Dorothy Livesay. Send SASE for guidelines. Entry fees: $10 (Canadian), $8 (U.S.). All entrants receive a copy of the anthology. Postmark deadline: October 31. Winners will be notified in January.

‡*UNICORN; SHELL PRESS (II, IV-Spirituality/inspirational, religious), 12 Milton Ave., Millbrook, Stalybridge, Cheshire SK15 3HB England, editor Alex Warner. *Unicorn* appears biannually and publishes "mainstream poetry from new poets and established poets with a section for Christian poets to share the Gospel of Jesus Christ." **They want "poetry of any length or genre." They do not want "dusty, dry academic stuff. No horror, either, please."** They have recently published poetry by George Gott. As a sample the editor selected these lines from an untitled poem by Alex Krysinski:

> We breathe a single breath
> holding it between us
> we are earth and fire
> human and magical
> we release the breath and each other
> back to our own realms
> I am swollen woman

the veins are thin now

The editor says *Unicorn* is 10 pgs., A4, photocopied and corner-stapled with a mix of graphics and artwork. They receive about 50 poems a year, accept approximately 25%. Press run varies. **Sample postpaid: £1.50. Make checks payable to Alex Warner. Submit 5 poems, camera-ready copy. No previously published poems; simultaneous submissions OK. Cover letter required with a brief bio.** Time between acceptance and publication varies. **"I read all contributions and decide what goes in the magazine. At the moment, no one else is involved!" Always comments on rejections. Send SASE (or SAE and IRC) for guidelines. Reports ASAP. Pays 1 copy. Acquires one-time rights.** Reviews books or chapbooks of poetry or other magazines in 150 words. Open to unsolicited reviews. Poets may also send books for review consideration. The editor says, "The U.K. 'small press' is a huge but fragmented series of markets. We hope to encourage new talent. It helps to have a clear vision of what you want to do."

UNITY MAGAZINE (IV-Religious), Unity School of Christianity, 1901 NW Blue Pkwy., Unity Village MO 64065, founded 1889. "Unity periodicals are devoted to spreading the truth of practical Christianity, the everyday use of Christ's principles. The material used in them is constructive, friendly, unbiased as regards creed or sect, and positive and inspirational in tone. We suggest prospective contributors study carefully the various publications before submitting material. **Sample copies are sent on request; please send 6×9 SASE. Complimentary copies are sent to writers on publication. We accept mss only with the understanding that they are original and previously unpublished. Mss should be typewritten in double space. Unity School pays on acceptance, buying first North American serial rights.** *Unity Magazine* is a monthly journal that publishes "articles and poems that give a clear message of Truth and provide practical, positive help in meeting human needs for healing, supply and harmony. Only one or two poems are published each month. We pay $50."**

♣UNMUZZLED OX (IV-Themes, bilingual/foreign language), 105 Hudson St., New York NY 10013, phone (212)226-7170, or Box 550, Kingston, Ontario K7L 4W5 Canada, founded 1971, poetry editor Michael Andre, is a tabloid literary biannual. **Each edition is built around a theme or specific project.** The editor says, "The chances of an unsolicited poem being accepted are slight since I always have specific ideas in mind." They have published poetry by Allen Ginsberg, Robert Creeley and Denise Levertov. As a sample the editor selected these lines from "CL" by Daniel Berrigan:

> *Let's be grandiose, it's a game*
> *Let's climb a balcony*
> *Let's issue a manifesto*

> *Why, we're turning things on their head*
> *we're making history*
> *we're—*

> *Harmless.*

Only unpublished work will be considered, but works may be in French as well as English." Subscription: $20.

‡UNO MAS MAGAZINE (II), P.O. Box 1832, Silver Spring MD 20915, fax (301)770-3250, e-mail unomasma g@aol.com, website http://www.unomas.com/, founded 1990, contact poetry editor, published quarterly, features "general culture, music, fiction, essays, photography, art." **They want "general poetry of short to medium length."** They have recently published poetry by Sparrow. As a sample the editor selected these lines from "Krishna Harry and His Voice" by Kristine Durden:

> *pulling me across a river bed*
> *baptism of sound*
> *floating on ripples*
> *riding each dip and wave*
> *like dream flying*

The editor says *UNo Mas* is 50 pgs., 8½×11, offset-printed with a glossy 2-color cover. They receive about 100-150 poems a year, accept approximately 20-25%. Press run is 3,000 for 40 subscribers and which 1 is a library, most are shelf sales; 100 distributed free to advertisers. Single copy: $2.50; subscription: $9. **Sample postpaid: $3. Make checks payable to Jim Saah. Submit up to 5 poems with name on each page. Previously published poems and simultaneous submissions OK. Cover letter preferred with SASE. Accepts faxed submissions. E-mail submissions OK.** Time between acceptance and publication is 3-6 months. **Poems are circulated to an editorial board, "if we like it, we publish it." Seldom comments on rejections. Send SASE for guidelines. Reports in 4-6 weeks. Sometimes sends prepublication galleys. Pays 3 copies. Acquires one-time rights.** Staff reviews books or chapbooks of poetry. Open to unsolicited reviews. Poets may also send books for review consideration.

THE URBANITE; URBAN LEGEND PRESS (II, IV-Horror, fantasy, themes), P.O. Box 4737, Davenport IA 52808-4737, founded 1991, editor Mark McLaughlin, appears 3 times a year "to promote literate, character-oriented and entertaining fiction and poetry in the genre of surrealism." **Each issue is based on a**

particular theme. Send SASE for details. They want contemporary fantasy/surrealism (maximum 2 pages/poem). No "slice-of-life, sentimental, gore, porn, Western, haiku or rambling rants against society." They have recently published poetry by Marni Griffin, Rhonda Eikamp and Brandon Totman. As a sample the editor selected the poem "Home Birth (twice a day)" by Joy Golisch:

> *Every poem is*
> *giving birth*
> *squatting in my chair*
> *groaning and screaming*
> *until happily*
> *I've turned myself inside out*
> *making something*
> *that grows apart from me*
>
> *I lay back on the rug*
> *panting*
> *white and black spotted child*
> *fluttering*
> *on my empty abdomen.*

The Urbanite is 64-92 pgs., 8½ × 11, saddle-stitched or perfect-bound with 2-color coated card cover. They receive about 500 poems a year, accept less than 10%. Press run is 1,000. Subscription: $13.50/3 issues. **Sample postpaid: $5. Submit only 3 poems at a time. No previously published poems or simultaneous submissions. Cover letter required. Sends checklist reply form, but sometimes comments on rejections. Send SASE for guidelines and upcoming themes. Reports within 1 month, sometimes longer. Pays $10/poem and 2 copies. Buys first North American serial rights and nonexclusive rights for public readings. ("We hold readings of the magazine at libraries and other venues.") Print rights revert to the writer after publication.** In addition to the magazine, Urban Legend Press **publishes 1 or more chapbooks a year. Interested poets should "submit to the magazine first, to establish a relationship with our readers."** A copy of Joy Golisch's chapbook, *Surfing with Monkeys and Other Diversions*, is available from the press for $4.

URBANUS MAGAZINE; URBANUS PRESS (III), P.O. Box 192921, San Francisco CA 94119-2921, founded 1987, editor Peter Drizhal, which appears 2-3 times/year, is a journal of fiction, poetry, features and art—with an urban emphasis. **"Seeks post-modernist, experimental and mainstream poetry—with a social slant."** They have recently published poetry by Yusef Komunyakaa, Kathleen de Azebedo, Adrian C. Louis, Alexander Theroux, Amy Scattergood, Chris Gilbert and Denise Duhamel. As a sample the editors selected these lines from "And What Do You Get" by Heather McHugh (which also appears in *The Best American Poetry 1995*):

> *Excise the er from exercise. Or from*
> *example, take the ex out: now it's bigger;*
> *to be lonely, take the amp out*
> *and replace it with an* i. *Take am or me*
> *away from name*
> *and suddenly there's not*
> *much left, the name's one of the many names*

The 64-page, digest-sized, perfect-bound magazine uses approximately 50 of the 5,000 submissions they receive annually. Circulation is 2,000. Subscription: $15.95 ($17 institutions). **Sample postpaid: $6.95. Submit 3-5 poems (under 40 lines each) at a time. No previously published poems or simultaneous submissions. Reports in 3-12 weeks.** Time between acceptance and publication is 6-12 months. **Pays $10-15/poem or $5/page, plus 5 copies.** Poetry published in *Urbanus* has been selected for inclusion in the 1994, 1995 and 1997 volumes of *The Best American Poetry*. The editor says, "*Urbanus Magazine* solicits much of its writing, and generally speaking, we are a very difficult market to break into; but talented newcomers are always welcome."

‡*URTHONA MAGAZINE (II, IV-Religious), 3 Coral Park, Henley Rd., Cambridge CB1 3EA United Kingdom, e-mail 100640,541@compuserve.com, founded 1992, contact the poetry editor, published biannually, explores the arts and western culture from a Buddhist perspective. **They want "poetry rousing the imagination." They do not want "undigested autobiography, political, or New-Agey poems."** They have recently published poetry by Peter Abbs and Peter Redgrove. As a sample the editor selected these lines from "The Shower" by Ananda:

SENDING TO A COUNTRY other than your own? Be sure to send International Reply Coupons (IRCs) instead of stamps for replies or return of your manuscript.

And somewhere there is gold,
and a song almost getting started
in the street we're leaving by:

something like tenderness, how
the spring light races and dies
over the washed squares

Urthona is 60 pgs., A4, offset, saddle-stapled with 4-color glossy cover, b&w photos, art and ads inside. They receive about 300 poems a year, accept approximately 40. Press run is 700 for 50 subscribers of which 4 are libraries, 500 shelf sales; 50 distributed free to Buddhist groups. Subscription: £6.50. **Sample (including guidelines) postpaid: £3. Submit 6 poems at a time. No previously published poems or simultaneous submissions. Cover letter preferred. Reads submissions January through July only.** Time between acceptance and publication is 6-8 months. **Poems are circulated to an editorial board and read and selected by poetry editor. Other editors have right of veto. Reports in 1-2 months. Pays 1 copy. Acquires one-time rights.** Reviews books or chapbooks of poetry or other magazines in 600 words. Open to unsolicited reviews. Poets may also send books for review consideration. Sponsors annual contest with £100 first prize, £40 second prize and 5 third prizes of a 2-year subscription. Submit any number of poems with a £1.50/poem entry fee. Poems must be no longer than 40 lines; 1 poem/page. Put name, address and phone on separate sheet only. Entries are not returned. Deadline: January 15.

‡URTHONA PRESS; BLACK SWAN PUBLICATIONS; WILLIAM BLAKE PRIZE COMPETITION (I), 34 Wall St., Suite 708, Asheville NC 28801, phone (704)254-2808, e-mail dhopes@unca.edu, founded 1995, editors David Hopes and Butch Lily. Urthona Press strives to "bring the best of poetry to an expanded audience." They publish 3 paperbacks/year. One book a year is selected through the William Blake Prize Competition. The winner also receives half of the profits after expenses. Entry fee: $10. Deadline: October 31. Write for more information. **They want "the best of the modern mode—like the mystical or explanatory." They do not want "workshop poems or APR clones."** They have recently published poetry by Ann Dunn and David Hopes. Books are usually 50-100 pgs., perfect-bound, "we are noted for our beautifully designed books." **Submit complete ms. Previously published poems and simultaneous submissions OK. Cover letter preferred.** Time between acceptance and publication is 1 year. **Poems are circulated to an editorial board. Often comments on rejections. Replies to queries "immediately," to mss in 6 months. Pays 50% of profits after expenses and 10 author's copies (out of a press run of 1,000). "We accept but do not require subsidation."** For sample books, call the above number.

US1 WORKSHEETS; US1 POETS' COOPERATIVE (II), % Postings, P.O. Box 1, Ringoes NJ 08551-0001, founded 1973, is a literary annual, circulation 500, which uses **high-quality poetry and fiction. "We use a rotating board of editors; it's wisest to query when we're next reading before submitting. A self-addressed, stamped postcard to the secretary will get our next reading period dates."** They have published poetry by Alicia Ostriker, Elizabeth Anne Socolow, Jean Hollander, Frederick Tibbetts, Lois Marie Harrod, James Haba, Charlotte Mandel and David Keller. *US1 Worksheets* is 28 pgs., 8½×11, offset, saddle-stapled, with b&w cover art. **"We read a lot but take very few. Prefer complex, well-written work." Sample: $5. Submit 5 poems at a time. Include name, address and phone number in upper right-hand corner. No simultaneous submissions; rarely accepts previously published poems. Requests for sample copies, subscriptions, queries, back issues, and all mss should be addressed to the secretary, % POSTINGS (address at beginning of listing). Sometimes sends prepublication galleys. Pays 1 copy.**

UTAH STATE UNIVERSITY PRESS (V), Logan UT 84322-7800, phone (801)797-1362, fax (801)797-0313, e-mail mspooner@press.usu.edu, website http://www.usu.edu/~usupress, founded 1972, poetry editor Michael Spooner, publishes poetry but is **not open for submissions.**

VEGETARIAN JOURNAL; THE VEGETARIAN RESOURCE GROUP (IV-Specialized, children/teens), P.O. Box 1463, Baltimore MD 21203, founded 1982. The Vegetarian Resource Group is a publisher of nonfiction. *VJ* is a bimonthly, 36 pgs., 8½×11, saddle-stapled and professionally printed with glossy card cover. Circulation is 20,000. **Sample: $3. "Please no submissions of poetry from adults; 18 and under only."** The Vegetarian Resource Group offers an annual contest for ages 18 and under, $50 savings bond in 3 age categories for the best contribution on any aspect of vegetarianism. "Most entries are essay, but we would accept poetry with enthusiasm." Deadline: May 1 postmark. Send SASE for details.

♣VEHICULE PRESS; SIGNAL EDITIONS (III, IV-Regional), P.O. Box 125 Station Place du Parc, Montreal, Quebec H2W 2M9 Canada, phone (514)844-6073, fax (514)844-7543, poetry editor Michael Harris, publisher Simon Dardick, is a "literary press with poetry series, Signal Editions, **publishing the work of Canadian poets only**." They publish flat-spined paperbacks and hardbacks. They have published poetry by Peter Dale Scott, Doug Beardsley, John Reibetanz, Rhea Tregébov, Susan Glickman and Jan Conn. As a sample they selected these lines by Carla Hartsfield:

Isn't it possible men

> *are jealous of women?*
> *How we root ourselves*
> *in autonomy. Like trees*
> *women can be both things:*
> *wound and tourniquet.*

They publish Canadian poetry which is **"first-rate, original, content-conscious." However, they are "booked until 1999."**

‡*VERANDAH (II)**, c/o Faculty of Arts, Deakin University, 221 Bwwood Hwy., Bwwood, Victoria, Australia 3125, founded 1986. *Verandah* is "a high-quality literary journal edited by professional writing students. **It aims to give voice to new and innovative writers and artists."** They have published poetry by Coral Hull, MTC Cornir and Peter Bakowski. As a sample the editor selected the poem "Perspective" by Jane Williams:

> *I do not care to know*
> *Your lover as you know her*
> *But I would care*
> *To crawl inside her*
> *And there inside her*
> *Be known to you.*

It is 100 pgs., flat-spined with full-color glossy card cover, professionally printed on glossy stock. **Sample postpaid: A$11.50. Annual deadline: May 31. Pays 2 copies plus cash as funds allow. Buys first Australian publishing rights.**

VERBAL EXPRESSION (I), 7 Pleasant St., Oxford MI 48371, founded 1995, appears quarterly and is **"open to all types of poetry."** As a sample the editor selected this poem, "Angel Tears," by Jon Camfield:

> *And the rain fell down here,*
> *Maybe not over the horizon,*
> *Maybe not a mile away,*
> *but it fell down here,*
> *here I am living,*
> *here it matters*
> *that the rain*
> *fell down.*

The editor says *VE* is 32 pgs., 5½×8½, photocopied and staple-bound with graphics, cover art and ads. They receive about 100 poems a year, accept approximately 30-40. Press run is 500 for 400 subscribers. Single copy: $3.50; subscription: $11. Make checks payable to Pleasant Publishing. **Submit up to 5 poems at a time, name and address on each page. Previously published poems and simultaneous submissions OK. Cover letter preferred.** Time between acceptance and publication is 3-9 months. **Reports in 1 month. Pays 1 copy. Acquires one-time rights.** Sponsors a yearly poetry contest with $1 entry fee. "Entry fee is waived if entry is enclosed with subscription."

VERSE (III), English Dept., College of William and Mary, P.O. Box 8795, Williamsburg VA 23187-8795, founded 1984, editors Nancy Schoenberger and Brian Henry, is "an international poetry journal which also publishes interviews with poets, articles about poetry and book reviews." They want **"no specific kind; we look for high-quality poetry. Our focus is not only on American poetry, but on all poetry written in English, as well as translations."** They have published poetry by Seamus Heaney, James Merrill, John Ashbery, Eavan Boland, Liz Lochhead, Charles Simic, Medbh McGuckian, Simon Armitage, A.R. Ammons, Iain Crichton Smith, Robert Pinsky and Carolyn Kizer. *Verse* is published 3 times/year. It is 128-256 pgs., digest-sized, professionally printed and perfect-bound with card cover. They receive about 5,000 poems a year, accept approximately 100. Press run is 1,000 for 600 subscribers of which 150 are libraries, 200 shelf sales. Subscription: $15 for individuals, $24 for institutions. **Sample postpaid: $5. Submit up to 5 poems at a time. No previously published poems; simultaneous submissions OK. Cover letter required.** Time between acceptance and publication is 3-9 months. **Reports in 2 months. Often comments on rejections. Publishes theme issues. Send SASE for upcoming themes. Usually sends prepublication galleys. Pays 2 copies.** Open to unsolicited reviews. Poets may also send books for review consideration. Poetry published in this journal has appeared in the 1992 and 1997 volumes of *The Best American Poetry*.

VERVE (II, IV-Themes), P.O. Box 3205, Simi Valley CA 93093-3205, e-mail vervemg@aol.com, founded 1989, editor/publisher Ron Reichick, editor Marilyn Hochheiser, associate editors Virginia Anderson and E.M. Mackey, is published twice a year and **"open to contemporary poetry of any form which fits the theme of the issue; we look for fresh metaphor, unique ideas and language and vivid imagery that informs."** They have recently published poetry by Philip Levine, Marge Piercy, Carol Muske, Denise Levertov, Alberto Rios and Quincy Troupe. *Verve* is approximately 40 pgs., digest-sized, saddle-stitched, using bios of each contributor. Press run is 750 for 100 subscribers of which 3 are libraries. **Sample postpaid: $3.50. Submit up to 5 poems, 2 pgs. maximum/poem; "36 lines or less has best chance."** Simultaneous submissions OK, if noted. No e-mail submissions or requests for info. **Publishes theme issues. Send SASE for guidelines and upcoming**

themes. **Sometimes sends prepublication galleys. Pays 1 copy. Acquires first rights.** Staff reviews books of poetry in 250 words, single format. Send books for review consideration. They also sponsor 2 annual contests, each having prizes of $100, $50 and $25. Entry fee: $2/poem. Deadlines: April 1 and October 1. The editor advises, "Read a copy of *Verve* before you submit. Read good contemporary poetry—then write. Listen to criticism, but follow your instinct *and* the poem. *Then*—keep submitting."

*VIGIL; VIGIL PUBLICATIONS (II), 12 Priory Mead, Bruton, Somerset BA10 ODZ England, founded 1979, poetry editor John Howard Greaves. *Vigil* appears 2 times/year. **They want "poetry with a high level of emotional force or intensity of observation. Poems should normally be no longer than 40 lines. Color, imagery and appeal to the senses should be important features. No whining self-indulgent, neurotic soul-baring poetry."** They have recently published poetry by Michael Newman, Claudette Bass, David Flynn, Sheila Murphy and Karen Rosenberg. As a sample we selected these lines from "A Language We Shared" by Mel C. Thompson:

> It feels lonely in our Orthodox Church
> where we proclaim our lack of racism
> in rooms full of colorless faces.
>
>
> "Gringo," a Guatemalan poet told me,
> "You could not even buy
> yourself a soul."

The digest-sized magazine is 40 pgs., saddle-stapled, professionally printed with colored matte card cover. They receive about 200 poems a year, accept approximately 60. Press run is 250 for 85 subscribers of which 6 are libraries. Subscription: £6. **Sample postpaid: £2.30. Submit up to 6 poems at a time. Send SASE (or SAE and IRC) for guidelines. Sometimes sends prepublication galleys. Pays 2 copies. Editor sometimes comments on rejections. Query regarding book publication by Vigil Publications.** The editor offers "appraisal" for £10 for a sample of a maximum of 6 poems.

VIKING PENGUIN, 375 Hudson St., New York NY 10014, president Peter Mayer. Prefers not to share information.

THE VILLAGER (II), Dept. PM, 135 Midland Ave., Bronxville NY 10708-1800, phone (914)337-3252, founded 1928, editor Carol Renner, poetry editor Josephine Colville, a publication of the Bronxville Women's Club for club members and families, professional people and advertisers, circulation 750, in 9 monthly issues, October through June. **Sample postpaid: $1.50. Submit 1 poem at a time, "unless it is very short."** They use 1 page or more of poetry/issue, prefer poems less than 20 lines, "in good taste only." Send seasonal (Thanksgiving, Christmas, Easter) 3 months in advance. SASE required. Pays 2 copies. They copyright material but will release it to author on request.

THE VINCENT BROTHERS REVIEW (II, IV-Themes), 4566 Northern Circle, Riverside OH 45424-5733, founded 1988, editor Kimberly A. Willardson, is a journal appearing 3 times/year. **"We look for well-crafted, thoughtful poems that shoot bolts of electricity into the reader's mind, stimulating a powerful response. We also welcome light verse and are thrilled by unusual, innovative subjects and styles. We do not accept previously published poems, simultaneous submissions or any type of bigoted propaganda. Sloppy mss containing typos and/or unintentional misspellings are automatically rejected.** *TVBR* publishes two theme issues/year—**poets should send us a SASE to receive details about our upcoming themes."** They have recently published poetry by Robert Miltner, Michael E. Waldeck, Paul Humphrey and Kerri Brostrom. As a sample the editor selected these lines from "The Great Paranoiac" by Todd Fry:

> I thrash about discomfited by all this flesh.
> A thought dislodged swims a bit, turns
> its brutish back, hides, surfaces again, demands
> consideration without a prayer of being soluble.
> She sleeps, she burrows into me, I must stay awake
> and try to protect her from plagued voices, human things.

TVBR is 96-120 pgs., digest-sized, perfect-bound, professionally printed with matte card cover. Press run is 350. They have 200 subscribers of which 10 are libraries. Subscription: $12. **Sample postpaid: $6.50. Back issue postpaid: $4.50. Submit up to 6 poems at a time, name and address on each page. Note in cover "where author read or heard about** *TVBR*. **We do not read in November or December."** Often comments on rejections. Publishes theme issues. Send SASE for guidelines and upcoming themes. **Theme for issue #25 is Dreams and Nightmares (deadline January 31, 1998). Reports in 3-4 months (after readings by editor and 2 associate editors). Always sends prepublication galleys. Pays 2 copies for poems printed. Pays $10 for poems printed on "Page Left" (the back page). "For 'Page Left,' we look for the unusual—concrete poems, wordplay, avant-garde pieces, etc." Acquires one-time rights.** Reviews books of poetry in 3,500 words maximum, single or multi-book format. Open to unsolicited reviews. Poets may also send books for review consideration. The editor advises, "*Don't* send your poetry to a magazine you haven't read. Subscribe to the little magazines you respect—they contain the work of your peers and competitors. Proofread your poetry carefully and read it aloud before sending it out."

‡**VIOLETTA BOOKS (V)**, P.O. Box 15191, Springfield MA 01115, founded 1983, editor Kathleen Gilbert. **They are currently not accepting unsolicited manuscripts.** The editor has published poetry by Teresa Burleson, Laurence F. O'Brien and Elaine Thomas. Anthologies are usually digest-sized, 35-40 pgs., offset from typescript, with matte card cover. **Sample postpaid: $3.50. (Make checks payable to Kathleen Gilbert.)** Kathleen Gilbert says, "I seek good, accessible work that offers the reader the benefits all good art offers its perceptors—hope, strength, renewal. My purpose in publishing poetry is to encourage poets of all ability levels to write accessible and yet individualistic poetry. I also offer how-to books on poetry marketing and independent publishing. Send SASE for details."

VIRGIN MEAT (IV-Horror), 2325 West Ave. K-15, Lancaster CA 93536, e-mail virginmeat@aol.com, website http://members.aol.com/VIRGINMEAT/MAGAZINE/Gothic.HTML, founded 1986. *VM* is a computerized, interactive magazine of gothic horror. Prints fiction, poetry, art, .SND Sound and .MooV Quick Time movies. **Obtain guidelines via e-mail or website. "Electronic submissions only." Simultaneous and previously published poems OK. Reports in 4 months. Pays 1 copy. Reviews anything with a cover price.**

THE VIRGINIA QUARTERLY REVIEW; EMILY CLARK BALCH PRIZE (III), 1 West Range, Charlottesville VA 22903, phone (804)924-3124, fax (804)924-1397, e-mail jco7e@virginia.edu, founded 1925, is one of the oldest and most distinguished literary journals in the country. **It uses about 15 pgs. of poetry in each issue, no length or subject restrictions.** Issues have largely included lyric and narrative free verse, most of which features a strong message or powerful voice. The review is 220 pgs., digest-sized, flat-spined, circulation 4,000. **Send SASE for submission details; do not request via e-mail or fax. Pays $1/line.** They also sponsor the Emily Clark Balch Prize, an annual prize of $500 given to the best poem published in the review during the year. Poetry published here has been included in *The Best American Poetry 1993*.

VIRTUE: THE CHRISTIAN MAGAZINE FOR WOMEN (IV-Religious, spiritual/inspirational), 4050 Lee Vance View, Colorado Springs CO 80918-7102, editor Laura J. Baker, associate editor Debbie Colclough, editor-at-large Nancie Carmichael, founded 1978, is a Christian magazine, appearing 6 times/year, to **"encourage and integrate biblical truth with daily living." As for poetry, they look for "rhythmic control and metric effects, whether free or patterned stanzas; use of simile and metaphor; sensory perceptions, aptly recorded; and implicit rather than explicit spiritual tone."** *Virtue* is 80 pgs., magazine-sized, perfect-bound, with full-color pages inside as well as on its paper cover. Press run is 115,000. Single copy: $3.95; subscription: $18.95. **Sample postpaid: $3. Submit up to 3 poems, each on separate sheet, typewritten; notify if simultaneous submission.** Time between acceptance and publication is 3-9 months. **Send SASE for guidelines. Reports in approximately 2 months. Pays $20-40/poem and 1 copy. Buys first rights.**

‡**VISTA PUBLISHING, INC. (IV-Specialized: nurses)**, 473 Broadway, Long Branch NJ 07740, phone (908)229-6500, fax (908)229-9647, founded 1991, contact Carolyn Zagury, provides "a forum for the creative and artistic side of our nursing colleagues." Publishes 10 paperback/year. **They want "poetry written by nurses, relating to nursing or healthcare."** They have recently published poetry by Craig Betson, Susan Farese, Sarah Kimberly Eiland and Carol Battaglia. Books are usually 100 pgs., 6×9, trade paper, perfect-bound with illustrations if appropriate and 4-color cover. **Submit complete ms. No previously published poems; simultaneous submissions OK. Cover letter preferred. Has backlog to Fall 2000.** Time between acceptance and publication is 2 years. **Often comments on rejections. Replies in 3 months. Pays "percentage of profits."**

VOICES INTERNATIONAL (II), 1115 Gillette Dr., Little Rock AR 72227, phone (501)225-0166, editor Clovita Rice, is a quarterly poetry journal. **"We look for poetry with a new focus, memorable detail and phrasing, and significant and haunting statement climax, all of which impel the reader to reread the poem and return to it for future pleasure and reference."** It is 32-40 pgs., 6×9, saddle-stapled, professionally printed with b&w matte card cover. Subscription: $10/year. **Sample postpaid (always a back issue): $2. Prefers free verse but accepts high-quality traditional. Limit submissions to batches of 5, double-spaced, 3-40 lines (will consider longer if good). No simultaneous submissions. Cover letter preferred; include personal data.** Time between acceptance and publication is an average of 18 months. **Send SASE for guidelines. Pays copies.** The editor says, "Too many poets submit poetry without studying a copy to become familiar with what we are publishing. Our guidelines help poets polish their poems before submission."

***VOICES ISRAEL (I, IV-Anthology); REUBEN ROSE POETRY COMPETITION (I); MONTHLY POET'S VOICE (IV-Members)**, P.O. Box 5780, 46157 Herzlia Israel, website http://members.tripod.com/~VoicesIsrael, founded 1972, *Voices Israel* editor Mark L. Levinson, with an editorial board of 7, is an annual anthology of poetry in English coming from all over the world. **You have to buy a copy to see your work in print. Submit all kinds of poetry (up to 4 poems), each no longer than 40 lines, in seven copies.** They have published poetry by Yehuda Amichai, Eugene Dubnov, Alan Sillitoe and Gad Yaacobi. As a sample the editor selected these lines from "Eating Fruit" by Dvora Kreda-Geller:

> *After treatment, in the parking lot behind*
> *the hospital, your father and I eat fruit.*
> *We watch the bay's three shades of green, blinding*
> *shards of light, floating net of foam, at noon.*
> *We promise: It's yours, if you are born alive—*
> *sun bolt; sea pulse; salt wave—if you arrive.*

The annual *Voices Israel* is 6½×9⅜, offset from laser output on ordinary paper, approximately 121 pgs., flat-spined with varying cover. Circulation 350. Subscription: $15. **Sample back copy postpaid: $10. Contributor's copy: $15 airmail. Previously published poems OK, "but please include details and assurance that copyright problems do not exist." No simultaneous submissions. Cover letter with brief biographical details required with submissions. Deadline: end of February each year. Reports in fall.** Sponsors the annual Reuben Rose Poetry Competition. Send poems of up to 40 lines each, plus $5/poem to P.O. Box 236, Kiriat Ata, Israel. Poet's name and address should be on a separate sheet with titles of poems. *The Monthly Poet's Voice*, a broadside edited by Ezra Ben-Meir, **is sent only to members of the Voices Group of Poets in English.** The *Voices Israel* editor advises, "We would like to see more humorous but well constructed poetry. We like to be surprised."

VOL. NO. MAGAZINE (II, IV-Themes), 24721 Newhall Ave., Newhall CA 91321, phone (805)254-0851, founded 1983, poetry editors Richard Weekley, Jerry Danielsen and Don McLeod. "*Vol. No.* publishes lively, concise, unafraid works. Vivid connections. **Each issue has a theme. Theme for August 1998 is "Overload." Send SASE for details. No trivial, clichéd or unthoughtout work. Work that penetrates the shadow within. One-page poems have the best chance.**" They have published poetry by Octavio Paz, Anne Marple, Jane Hirshfield and Julian Pulley. *Vol. No.* is a digest-sized, saddle-stapled, 32-page annual, circulation 300. They receive about 600 poems a year, use approximately 60, have a 6-month backlog. Subscription: $10/2 issues. **Sample postpaid: $5. Submit up to 6 poems at a time. Simultaneous submissions OK. Reports in 1-5 months. Pays 2 copies.**

‡VOLCANO QUARTERLY (IV-Specialized), 420 SE Evans Lane, Issaquah WA 98027, phone (425)392-7858, e-mail vqjantan@aol.com, website http://members.aol.com/vqjantan, founded 1992, editor Janet Tanaka, is an "interest" publication for professional and amateur volcanologists and volcano buffs. **They want "any kind of poetry as long as it is about volcanoes and/or the people who work on them." They do not want "over-emotive, flowery stuff or anything not directly pertaining to volcanoes."** They have recently published poetry by Dane Picard and C. Martinez. As a sample the editor selected these lines from "Farewell Observatory" by C. Scarpinati, translated from Italian by Claude Grandpey:

> *A coat of fire shrouded your shoulders*
> *and your sides, as tho' you were cold.*
> *Your masks, walls of iron*
> *didn't collapse.*

The editor says *Volcano Quarterly* is 26 pgs., 8½×11. They receive about 4-5 poems a year, accept approximately 100%. Subscription: $28 US, $30 Canada and Mexico, $34 overseas. **Submit any number of poems. E-mail and disk submissions (ASCII) OK. Previously published poems with permission of the original copyright holder and simultaneous submissions OK.** Time between acceptance and publication is 3-6 months. **Always comments on rejections. "I try not to outright reject, preferring to ask for a rewrite." Send SASE for guidelines. Reports in 1 month. Pays 3 copies. "Contributors may copyright in the usual fashion. But there is as yet no mechanism on the Internet to keep users honest."** Reviews books or chapbooks of poetry or other magazines by guest reviewers. Open to unsolicited reviews. Poets may also send books for review consideration if they are about volcanoes.

♣THE VOYANT; HOLLOW MAN PUBLISHING (II), Box 414, 20384 Fraser Highway, Langley, British Columbia V3A 4G1 Canada, founded 1994, editors Robert Ivins and Jamie Scott, appears annually. "*The Voyant* is an avant-garde arts mag with an emphasis on poetry and intermedia art. We publish poetry, music scores, drawings, photographs, essays, criticism and original art. Our journal is highly visual, covering intermedia and fringe arts. We publish some str8 lit. We are especially interested in computer technology and how it interfaces with the arts. Only the wildest, boldest artists need submit." As each issue will be in a different format, there are no subscription rates. **Query for cost of sample. Submit up to 10 poems at a time. Cover letter "appreciated." Previously published poems and simultaneous submissions OK. Comments on rejections "where time and merit allow." Send SASE (or SAE and IRC) for guidelines. Reports "as soon as humanly possible." Usually pays in copies. Acquires first North American serial or one-time rights.** Reviews books and chapbooks of poetry in 5,000 words or less. Open to unsolicited reviews. Poets may also send books for review consideration. Hollow Man Publishing may, in the future, publish chapbooks of outstanding material.

WAKE FOREST UNIVERSITY PRESS (IV-Bilingual/foreign language, ethnic/nationality), P.O. Box 7333, Winston-Salem NC 27109, phone (910)759-5448, fax (910)759-4691, e-mail wfupress@wfu.edu, founded 1976, director and poetry editor Dillon Johnston. **"We publish only poetry from Ireland and bilingual editions of French poetry in translation. I am able to consider only poetry written by Irish poets or translations of contemporary French poetry. I must return, unread, poetry from American poets."** They have published

Collected Poems by John Montague; *The Hudson Letter* by Derek Mahon; *The Brazen Serpent* by Eiléan Ní Chuilleanáin; and *Opera Et Cetera* by Ciaran Carson. As a sample the editor selected the poem "The White Garden" by Michael Longley from his book, *The Ghost Orchid*:

> *So white are the white flowers in the white garden that I*
> *Disappear in no time at all among lace and veils.*
> *For whom do I scribble the few words that come to me*
> *From beyond the arch of white roses as from nowhere,*
> *My memorandum to posterity? Listen. 'The saw*
> *Is under the garden bench and the gate is unlatched.'*

Query with 4-5 samples and cover letter. No simultaneous submissions. Replies to queries in 1-2 weeks, to submissions (if invited) in 2-3 months. Sometimes sends prepublication galleys. Publishes on 10% royalty contract with $500 advance, 6-8 author's copies. Buys North American or US rights. They say, "Because our press is so circumscribed, we get few direct submissions from Ireland. Our main problem, however, is receiving submissions from American poets, whom we do not publish because of our very limited focus here. I would advise American poets to read listings carefully so they do not misdirect to presses such as ours, work that they, and I, value."

‡THE WAR CRY (II, IV-Religious), 615 Slaters Lane, P.O. Box 269, Alexandria VA 22313, phone (703)684-5500, fax (703)684-5539, e-mail uswarcry@aol.com, founded 1880, editor-in-chief Lt. Colonel Marlene Chase, appearing biweekly, publishes "reports, commentary and testimonies that proclaim the gospel of Jesus Christ and His power to change lives today." **They want "Christian poetry, any style, 16 lines maximum."** As a sample the editor selected these lines from "Merciful Heavens!" by Ruth Glover:

> *Today my skies are clear;*
> *The night is gone,*
> *And all my midnight sighs*
> *And foolish fears*
> *Have faded with the dawn;*

The editor says *The War Cry* is 24 pgs., with photos and graphics. Press run is 300,000. **Sample postpaid: SASE. Submit any number of poems at a time. Previously published poems and simultaneous submissions OK. Cover letter preferred.** Time between acceptance and publication varies. **"Poems are screened by an editor who acts as a 'first reader,' then good ones are passed on to the editor-in-chief." Seldom comments on rejections. Publishes theme issues. Send SASE for guidelines and upcoming themes. Reports in up to 1 month. Pays 15-20¢/word. Buys one-time and reprint rights.**

WARTHOG PRESS (II), 29 South Valley Rd., West Orange NJ 07052, phone (201)731-9269, founded 1979, poetry editor Patricia Fillingham, publishes books of poetry **"that are understandable, poetic."** They have published *From the Other Side of Death* by Joe Lackey; *Wishing for the Worst* by Linda Portnay; and *Hanging On* by Joe Benevento. **Query with 5 samples, cover letter "saying what the author is looking for" and SASE. Simultaneous submissions OK. Ms should be "readable." Comments on rejections, "if asked for. People really don't want criticism." Pays copies, but "I would like to get my costs back."** Patricia Fillingham feels, "The best way to sell poetry still seems to be from poet to listener."

‡*WASAFIRI (II, IV-Ethnic/nationality), Dept. of English, Queen Mary and Westfield College, University of London, Mile End Rd., London E1 4NS United Kingdom, phone (0171)775 3120, fax (0181)980 6200, e-mail wasafiri@qmw.ac.uk, website http://www.qmw.ac.uk/~english/wasafiri.html, founded 1984, editor Sushiela Nasta, managing editor Tony Ilona, published biannually, "promotes new writing and debate on African, Asian, Caribbean and associated literatures." **They want "African, Asian, Caribbean, diaspora, post-colonial, innovative, high-quality poetry."** They have recently published poetry by Vikram Seth, Fred D'Aguiar, Marlene Nourbese Philip and Kamau Brathwaite. *Wasafiri* is 105 pgs., A4, professionally printed on coated stock, perfect-bound, with full color glossy cover, graphics, photos and ads. They receive about 350 poems a year, accept approximately 30%. Press run is 1,500 for 1,000 subscribers of which 450 are libraries, 300 shelf sales; 50 distributed free to arts council literature panel and education board. Single copy: $7.50; subscription: £12, £16 overseas. **Sample postpaid: £4, £5 overseas. Submit 3 poems at a time. Previously published poems OK; no simultaneous submissions. Cover letter required. Disk submissions (Word or WordPerfect) OK.** Time between acceptance and publication is 6-12 months. **Poems are circulated to an editorial board. "Poems are considered by the editor and editorial assistant. Where guest editors are involved, poetry is considered by**

MARKET CONDITIONS are constantly changing! If you're still using this book and it is 1999 or later, buy the newest edition of *Poet's Market* at your favorite bookstore or order directly from Writer's Digest Books.

them also. Associate editors with expertise are asked to participate also." Often comments on rejections. Publishes theme issues. Send SASE (or SAE and IRC) for guidelines and upcoming themes or obtain via e-mail or website. Reports in 6-12 months. Sometimes sends prepublication galleys. Pays 1 copy. Acquires all rights. Returns rights with editor's permission. Reviews books or chapbooks of poetry or other magazines. Open to unsolicited reviews. Poets may also send books for review consideration.

✤WASCANA REVIEW (II), Dept. of English, University of Regina, Regina, Saskatchewan S4S 0A2 Canada, phone (306)585-4302, fax (306)585-4827, e-mail kathleen.wall@uregina.ca, founded 1966, editor Kathleen Wall, appears twice a year publishing contemporary poetry and short fiction along with critical articles on modern and post-modern literature. "We look for high-quality literary poetry of all forms, including translations. No haiku or doggerel. No long poems. No concrete poetry." They have published poetry by Stephen Heighton, Robert Cooperman, Cornelia Hoogland and Eugene Dubnov. The editor says *WR* is a trade-sized paperback, 75-100 pgs., no art/graphics, no ads. They receive about 200-300 submissions a year, accept under 10%. Press run is 400 for 192 subscribers of which 134 are libraries, 100 shelf sales. Subscription: $10/year, $12 each Canada. Sample postpaid: $5. No previously published poems or simultaneous submissions. Cover letter required. SASE (or SAE and IRCs) necessary for return of mss. "Poems are read by at least two individuals who make comments and/or recommendations. Poetry editor chooses poems based on these comments. Poets may request information via e-mail. But no faxed or e-mailed submissions, please." Often comments on rejections. Reports within 6 months. Pays $10/page and 2 copies. Buys first North American serial rights. Reviews books of poetry in both single and multi-book format. The editor says, "*WR* will be featuring special issues from time to time. Poets should watch for news of these in upcoming editions."

WASHINGTON REVIEW; FRIENDS OF THE WASHINGTON REVIEW OF THE ARTS, INC. (II), P.O. Box 50132, Washington DC 20091-0132, phone (202)638-0515, founded 1974, literary editor Joe Ross, is a bimonthly journal of arts and literature published by the Friends of the Washington Review of the Arts, Inc., a nonprofit, tax-exempt educational organization. They publish local Washington metropolitan area poets as well as poets from across the US and abroad. "We have eclectic tastes but lean with more favor toward experimental work." *WR* is tabloid-sized, using 2 of the large pgs. each issue for poetry, saddle-stapled on high-quality newsprint. Circulation is 2,000 for 700 subscribers of which 10 are libraries. Sample postpaid: $2.50. Cover letter with brief bio required with submissions. Pays 5 copies. Reviews books of poetry in 1,000-1,500 words, single format—multi-book "on occasion." Open to unsolicited reviews. Poets may also send books for review consideration.

WASHINGTON WRITERS' PUBLISHING HOUSE (IV-Regional), P.O. Box 15271, Washington DC 20003, phone (202)543-1905, founded 1975. An editorial board is elected annually from the collective. "We are a poetry publishing collective that publishes outstanding poetry collections in flat-spined paperbacks by individual authors living in the greater Washington DC area (60-mile radius, excluding Baltimore) on the basis of competitions held once a year." They have published poetry by Laura Brylawski-Miller, Myra Sklarew, Ann Darr, Barbara Lefcowitz, Maxine Clair, Ann Knox, Nan Fry and Naomi Thiers. As a sample the editors selected these lines from "Bomb Document" in *Come Looking* by Dan Johnson:

> Some day, when you are the last to leave,
> the call came, the calm threat
> of a learned man with an accent
> who was once merely a strange boy
> without a name.

Send SASE for guidelines and a brochure of published poets. Pays copies. Poets become working members of the collective.

WATER MARK PRESS (V), 138 Duane St., New York NY 10013, founded 1978, editor Coco Gordon, proposes "to publish regardless of form in archival editions with handmade paper and hand-done elements in sewn, bound books, broadsides, chapbooks and artworks. I use only avant-garde material." Currently they do not accept any unsolicited poetry. They have published poetry by Carolyne Wright and Alison Knowles. The editor selected this sample from "After Eden" by Michael Blumenthal:

> Once again the invasion of purpose
> into gesture: the stem towards the vase,
> the hands towards the dreaded morning music
> of predictability, Indian paintbrush fades

That's from a collection of his poetry, *Sympathetic Magic*, 96 pgs., flat-spined, with art by Theo Fried, printed on archival, matte card cover with colored art, $9; hardbound $40. Note: Please do not confuse Water Mark Press with the imprint Watermark Press, used by other businesses.

WATERWAYS: POETRY IN THE MAINSTREAM (I, IV-Themes); TEN PENNY PLAYERS (IV-Children/teen/young adult); BARD PRESS (V), 393 St. Paul's Ave., Staten Island NY 10304-2127, phone (718)442-7429, fax (718)442-4978, e-mail 72713.3625@compuserve.com, founded 1977, poetry editors Barbara Fisher and Richard Spiegel, "publishes poetry by adult poets in a magazine that is published 11 times/year.

We do theme issues and are trying to increase an audience for poetry and the printed and performed word. The project produces performance readings in public spaces and is in residence year round at the New York public library with workshops and readings. We publish the magazine *Waterways*, anthologies and chapbooks. **We are not fond of haiku or rhyming poetry; never use material of an explicit sexual nature.** We are open to reading material from people we have never published, writing in traditional and experimental poetry forms. While we do 'themes,' sometimes an idea for a future magazine is inspired by a submission so we try to remain open to poets' inspirations. Poets should be guided however by the fact that we are children's and animal rights advocates and are a NYC press." They have published poetry by Ida Fasel, Kit Knight, Terry Thomas and Will Inman. *Waterways* is 40 pgs., 4¼×7, photocopied from various type styles, saddle-stapled, using b&w drawings, matte card cover. They use 60% of poems submitted. Circulation is 150 for 58 subscribers of which 12 are libraries. Subscription: $20. **Sample postpaid: $2.60. Submit less than 10 poems for first submission. Simultaneous submissions OK. Send SASE for guidelines for approaching themes.** "Since we've taken the time to be very specific in our response, writers should take seriously our comments and not waste their emotional energy and our time sending material that isn't within our area of interest. Sending for our theme sheet and for a sample issue and then objectively thinking about the writer's own work is practical and wise. Without meaning to sound 'precious' or unfriendly, the writer should understand that small press publishers doing limited editions and all production work inhouse are working from their personal artistic vision and know exactly what notes will harmonize, effectively counterpoint and meld. Many excellent poems are sent back to the writers by *Waterways* because they don't relate to what we are trying to create in a given month or months. Some poets get printed regularly in *Waterways*; others will probably never be published by us, not because the poet doesn't write well (although that too is sometimes the case) but only because we are artists with opinions and we exercise them in building each issue. Manuscripts that arrive without a return envelope are not sent back." **Editors sometimes comment on rejections. Reports in less than a month. Pays 1 copy. Acquires one-time publication rights.** They hold contests for children only. **Chapbooks published by Ten Penny Players are "by children and young adults only—and not by submission; they come through our workshops in the library and schools. Adult poets are published by us through our Bard Press imprint, by invitation only. Books evolve from the relationship we develop with writers who we publish in *Waterways* and whom we would like to give more exposure."** The editors advise, "We suggest that poets attend book fairs. It's a fast way to find out what we are all publishing."

‡WAY STATION MAGAZINE (I, II), 1319 S. Logan-MLK, Lansing MI 48910-1340, founded 1989, managing editor Randy Glumm, published quarterly, strives "to provide access and encourage beginning writers, while courting the established." **They want "emerging cultures, world view, humanity direction, relationships— try all. No rhyme unless truly terrific." They do not want "religious or openly militant gay or lesbian poetry. Use common sense and discretion."** They have recently published poetry by Diane Wakoski, Stuart Dybek, Ethridge Knight and Terri Jewell. *Way Station* is 52 pgs., 8½×11, offset, saddle-stitched with heavy card cover, b&w art, photos and ads. They receive about 300 poems a year, accept approximately 20-30%. Press run is 1,000 for 35 subscribers of which 2 are libraries, 200 shelf sales; 500 distributed free to potential advertisers, readers, libraries and universities. Subscription: $18. **Sample postpaid: $5. Submit 5 poems with name and address on each page and $5 processing fee (returned if work is rejected). Previously published poems and simultaneous submissions OK. Cover letter preferred.** Time between acceptance and publication is 1-2 months, sometimes longer. **"If not struck immediately, I then put it aside and re-read later 3-4 times. I might also circulate if through a panel of volunteer readers." Often comments on rejections. Send SASE for guidelines. Reports in 1-2 months. Pays 2 copies. Acquires one-time or first North American serial rights.** Reviews books or chapbooks of poetry or other magazines "if I have time." Open to unsolicited reviews. Poets may also send books for review consideration. The editor says, "It's best to check out your own work. Get advice from coaches, instructors prior to submitting. Also get sample copies of magazines you intend to submit to—this can only help you."

‡WєBER STUDIES: AN INTERDISCIPLINARY HUMANITIES JOURNAL (II), 1214 University Circle, Weber State University, Ogden UT 84408-1214, phone (801)626-6473, founded 1983, editor Neila C. Seshachari, appears 3 times/year and publishes fiction, poetry, criticism, personal essays, nonfiction and interviews. It is an interdisciplinary journal interested in relevant works covering a wide range of topics. **They want "125 lines maximum, including line spaces (stanza breaks). We will only publish 125 lines total of a poet per issue." They do not want "poems that are flippant, prurient, sing-song or preachy."** They have recently published poetry by Mark Strand, Janet Sylvester, Ingrid Wendt and Katharine Coles. As a sample the editor selected these lines from "Rhapsody for the Good Night" by David Lee:

> *nightbird*
> *and the hum of pickup tires*
> *on hardscrabble*
> *I listen*

> *behind the mockingbird behind the wind*
> *behind the sound a taproot makes*
> *working its way down to water*

INSIDER REPORT

Women poets must guard against critics—both internal and external

Susan Yuzna is an inspiration, an exemplar of how the dream of writing poetry—of being a poet—can be realized, even by those who have lived less-than-perfect lives. Indeed, it is the "hard-earned wisdoms" of one such life that characterizes Yuzna's work, that creates a poetry of "harrowing self-reckoning," a poetry that simultaneously illuminates and transforms.

Susan Yuzna

Yuzna began writing poetry in the Catholic high school she attended in her home state of Minnesota. Recognizing her talent, one of the nuns encouraged Yuzna to apply to the University of Iowa, which she felt to be the best writing school in the country.

"At Iowa, I was immediately intimidated, made suddenly aware of my total ignorance of contemporary poetry," says Yuzna. "I was surrounded by many talented and articulate young male poets. Naturally shy and insecure due to the cultural upbringing most girls endure, I found the competitive arena terrifying and fell back on what seemed easier—being a poet's girlfriend." By the time Yuzna earned her B.A., she'd stopped writing poetry and decided not to go on to graduate school. She was 25.

Over the next 15 years, Yuzna held a variety of jobs and moved from place to place until a family crisis summoned her back to Minnesota. It was during this time Yuzna's family confronted her with her drinking, a habit she'd begun in Iowa City, suggesting she enter a treatment center. Following treatment, Yuzna found work in the Minnesota Department of Administration where she met her husband. They had a child and Yuzna spent the next several years as a homemaker until, at the age of 40, she began to think about her life and about her dreams of becoming a writer. She also began reflecting on the daughter she'd been forced to give up for adoption years before when in high school.

Yuzna went on to earn her M.F.A. from the University of Montana in 1995, where she was a Richard Hugo Memorial Poetry Scholar. As a Bush Writing Fellow that same year, she began work on her memoir which explores the experience of giving a baby up for adoption, and her long and tumultuous relationship with writer Denis Johnson.

Yuzna attributes her success to perseverance and stubbornness. "Even though I was 40 before I was able to make the commitment to writing, once I did my will was unbendable. And, to my surprise, there was a relief to that. My thinking was that no matter how it turns out, success or failure, I *have* to do this before I die. I have to see if I can write one good book of poetry.

"I ran into a number of brick walls—relatives who thought I'd lost my mind, teachers who told me what I was writing wasn't poetry. But you have to be stubborn. You have to believe in your own vision and trust the validity of your life. Women especially. We are

INSIDER REPORT, *Yuzna*

so often dismissed in both subtle and not-so-subtle ways. You always have to be on guard for those voices that work against you—both the internalized voices and those from outside."

Yuzna has often been called courageous for addressing such risky topics as drugs, "kinky" sex and domestic abuse in her poetry. "It's not so much courage as it is a fascination with the idea of writing about what I hadn't seen much of in poetry. I thought, contemporary fiction is rife with drugs, sex, and disillusionment, so why does poetry shy away from the gritty stuff? Why must it be written from the perspective of privilege? I mean, what's the percentage of women English professors versus those women who have been raped, or hit, or consistently belittled until they have no self respect?"

"Crossing Texas by Bus"

I once heard a hospice nurse say that men, when dying,
recall their first time, while women speak of their children.

I had none then, crossing Texas by bus, with a man
who wanted none, it would ruin my figure, interfere

with his sex life. Possibly those endless rows of cotton,
all the white stuff erupting from pods, was what triggered

his imagination. He was like that, a poet, a collector
of experience: the time on a bus, the time on top of a ferry

crossing Puget Sound, mist in my face, tears in his eyes,
a memory like a jewel to carry with him into that violet sea.

O build your ship of death, for you will need it.
The driver, was he bored, too, piloting his forsaken bus,

going on Christmas, and if, distracted by what he saw
in his overhead mirror, he had crashed the bus, what pearls

would I be left with, fading into a bloody Texas highway, . . .

(from ***Her Slender Dress***, published by University of Akron Press, 1996)

Initially, Yuzna worried about the reception of her poems, about opening herself up to the possibility of ridicule. "They shocked people, as I knew they would. 'Pathetic' was how one fellow student in a poetry workshop described them. A dismissive word. And of course, I feared they would be beyond the pale of the publishing world. But once I'd broken through my own self-censorship, I became intrigued by the prospect of exploring these themes, and one poem led to another. I was energized, and so I kept going."

In spite of the often risky subject matter, Yuzna's poetry does not come across as diatribe; rather, it is compassionate, triumphant and transcendent. Elton Glaser, poet and director of the University of Akron Press, publisher of ***Her Slender Dress***, received hundreds of manuscripts during the annual Akron Series in Poetry competition, including those from poets who had already published two or three books. But Yuzna's work stood

INSIDER REPORT, *continued*

out. Charles Wright, final judge for the competition, noted, "There is no let-up in the linguistic intensity, imagistic intensity, or narrative intensity. The spirit of the word-warrior is in this writer." The poet David St. John called *Her Slender Dress* "a memorable debut" that "instantly places Susan Yuzna among the finest poets of her generation." Yuzna has also been honored as the 1997 recipient of the Norma Farber First Book Award from the Poetry Society of America.

"It's like a dream," says Yuzna. "Things have turned out better than I'd hoped. Of course, there's an element of luck involved. But to some degree you have to be a gambler, a risk taker. Part of this risk involves discovering your own method for writing, what works for you. Also, you have to trust in the logic of your own story, in the authenticity of your feelings and perceptions. Don't be so quick to crumble in the face of opposition. For women writers, this means you don't have to be nice; you don't have to be ladylike. Ask yourself: Are you going to define yourself or allow a hostile culture to tell you who you are?

"I've learned that Virginia Woolf was absolutely right. To be a woman writer, you need three things: a room of your own (with a door you can close), an independent income (so you're not emotionally dependent), and a release from the excessive demands of others (the last requirement is a thorny one for women, especially mothers, but also for daughters, daughters-in-law, and wives)."

Yuzna adds this advice: "You need to read and have a knowledge of contemporary poetry. Take classes, subscribe to literary magazines. Place less emphasis on getting published and more on getting good and the publication will follow. And, for me personally, I have to keep writing as my first priority. Whenever I've let it slip to a lower position, I stop writing. You just have to say to yourself, 'I *must* write, no matter what other people think I should be doing instead.' Forget the clean house."

—Michelle Moore

> past that I can hear them
> theygn hear me too
> if they want to

Weber Studies is 144-186 pgs., 6×9, offset printed on acid-free paper, perfect-bound, with 2-3 color cover, occasional color plates and exchange ads (with other journals). They receive about 150-200 poems a year, accept approximately 30-40. Press run is 800-1,000 for 600 subscribers of which 70-100 are libraries; 75 distributed free to on-campus faculty. Subscription: $10, $20 institutions. **Sample postpaid: $7-8. Submit 3 poems, 2 copies of each (one without name). No previously published poems; simultaneous submissions OK. Cover letter preferred.** Time between acceptance and publication is 12-15 months. **Poems are selected by an anonymous (blind) evaluation. Seldom comments on rejections. Publishes theme issues. Send SASE for guidelines and upcoming themes. Reports in 3-6 months. Always sends prepublication galleys. Pays $10-15/page; depend**ing on fluctuating grant monies. **Buys all rights. Copyright reverts to author after first printing.** Reviews books of poetry in 800-1,000 words. Cash award given every three years for poems published in **Weber Studies**. Only poetry published in **Weber Studies** during 3-year interval considered. Poetry published here has appeared in *The Best American Poetry 1996*. The editor advises, "This journal is referred by established poets—beginners not encouraged."

WESLEYAN UNIVERSITY PRESS (III), 110 Mt. Vernon, Middletown CT 06459, phone (860)685-2420, founded 1957, editor Suzanna Tamminen, is one of the major publishers of poetry in the nation. They publish 4-6 titles/year. They have published poetry by James Dickey, Joy Harjo, James Tate and Yusef Komunyakaa. **Send query and SASE. Considers simultaneous submissions. Send SASE for guidelines. Responds to queries in 6-8 weeks, to mss in 2-4 months. Pays royalties plus 10 copies.** Poetry publications from Wesleyan tend to get widely (and respectfully) reviewed.

WEST BRANCH (II), Bucknell Hall, Bucknell University, Lewisburg PA 17837, founded 1977, is a literary biannual, using **quality poetry.** Free verse is the dominant form—lyric, narrative and dramatic—occasionally longer than one page, much of it accessible with the emphasis on voice and/or powerful content. They have published poetry by D. Nurkse, Deborah Burnham, Jim Daniels, Anneliese Wagner, Betsy Sholl, David Citino, Barbara Crooker and David Brooks. It is 100-120 pgs., digest-sized, circulation 500. Subscription: $7, $11/4 issues. **Sample: $3. "We do not consider simultaneous submissions. Each poem is judged on its own merits, regardless of subject or form. We strive to publish the best work being written today." Reports in 6-8 weeks. Pays copies and subscription. Acquires first rights.** Reviews books and chapbooks of poetry but only those by writers who have been published in *West Branch.*

✿**WEST COAST LINE (II, IV-Regional)**, 2027 EAA, Simon Fraser University, Burnaby, British Columbia V5A 1S6 Canada, phone (604)291-4287, website http://www.sfu.ca/west-coast-line/WCL.html, founded 1990, editor Roy Miki. *West Coast Line* is published 3 times/year and **"favors work by both new and established Canadian writers, but it observes no borders in encouraging original creativity.** Our focus is on contemporary poetry, short fiction, criticism and reviews of books." They have published poetry by Rodrigo Toscano, Kyo Maclear and Pasquale Verdicchio. The magazine is handsomely printed on glossy paper, 6×9, flat-spined, 144 pgs. They receive about 500-600 poems a year, accept approximately 20. Approximately 26 pages of poetry/issue. Press run is 800 for 500 subscribers of which 350 are libraries, 150 shelf sales. Single copy: $10; subscription: $20. **No previously published poetry or simultaneous submissions.** Time between acceptance and publication is 2-8 months. **Publishes theme issues. Send SASE for guidelines or request via e-mail. Reports in 6-8 weeks. Pays approximately $8 (Canadian)/printed page plus a 1-year subscription and 2 copies. Mss returned only if accompanied by sufficient Canadian postage or IRC.** The editor says, "We have a special concern for contemporary writers who are experimenting with, or expanding the boundaries of, conventional forms of poetry, fiction and criticism. That is, poetry should be formally innovative."

WEST OF BOSTON (II), Box 2, Cochituate Station, Wayland MA 01778, phone (508)653-7241, press founded 1983, poetry editor Norman Andrew Kirk, wants to see **"poetry of power, compassion, originality and wit—and talent, too. Poetry that reveals the nature of life from the religious to the sensual, from personal exposures to universal truths. No subject is taboo so long as it is authentic and/or passionate."** They have published poetry by Mary K. Leen, R. Nikolas Macioci, Errol Miller, Lyn Lifshin and Barry Spacks. They are accepting submissions for a publication of previously unpublished poems, also called *West of Boston.* Depending on submissions, it will be an annual or semiannual, perfect-bound on high quality paper. **Submit up to 10 poems at a time. Include a brief bio and SASE with submission. All contributors will receive 1 copy.** Subscription available for $10/issue. **For book or chapbook submission, query with 5-10 sample poems, credits and bio. Simultaneous submissions and previously published poems OK. Editor "sometimes" comments on rejected mss. Sometimes sends prepublication galleys. Pays 10% of press run.**

WEST WIND WRITERS & ARTISTS PROJECT (II, IV-Anthology), English Dept., Southern Oregon State College, Ashland OR 97520, phone (541)552-6581, e-mail westwind@tao.sosc.osshe.edu, founded 1982, publishes an annual anthology each spring, editor and title of anthology change yearly. **They are "looking for sensitive but strong verse that celebrates all aspects of men's and women's experiences, both exalted and tragic. We are looking to print material that reflects ethnic and social diversity."** They have published poetry by Simon J. Ortiz and Lawson F. Inada. As a sample the editor selected these lines from "Terminus" by Patrick Bernard:

> *Loss: public and game show obvious.*
> *A timid, lurking hope in three parts,*
> *Twelve steps to peace*
> *(all of them reckless and expensive)*

The anthology is usually 224 pgs., digest-sized, handsomely printed and flat-spined. They receive about 1,200 submissions a year, publish 50-60 poems, 10 short stories and 16 pgs. of art. Press run is 600. **Sample "at current year's price. We take submissions—limit of 5 poems not exceeding 50 lines. Manuscripts should have poet's name and address on each page." No previously published poems; simultaneous submissions OK. Cover letter required; include brief bio and publication credits. No e-mail submissions. Deadline: December 1 for publication in late May or early June. Send SASE for guidelines or request via e-mail. Reports in 2-3 months after deadline. Pays 1 copy.** Offers $25 awards for each category.

‡✿**THE WESTCOAST FISHERMAN (IV-Specialized: commercial fishing)**, 1496 W. 72nd Ave., Vancouver, British Columbia V6P 3C8 Canada, phone (604)266-8611, fax (604)266-6437, e-mail fisherman@west-coast.com, website http://www.west-coast.com, founded 1986, managing editor Kevin MacDonell, published monthly, is "an apolitical, non-aligned publication serving the commercial fishing industry of Canada's west coast." **They want "brief pieces, related to commercial fishing, non-political, pieces by fisherman most welcome. Seasonal poems welcome, e.g., salmon in summer, herring in spring, etc."** They have recently published poetry by Tim Bowling. *TWF* is 56-64 pgs., 8½×11, professionally printed on 2-color newsprint, saddle-stapled, with full-color glossy cover, art, photos and ads. They receive about 20-40 poems a year, accept approximately 6. Press run is 7,000-8,000 for 1,600 subscribers; 1,550 distributed free. Subscription: $30 Cana-

dian plus $2.10 GST. **Sample postpaid: $3.95. Make checks payable to Westcoast Publishing Ltd. Submit any number of poems. Previously published poems and simultaneous submissions OK. Cover letter preferred with "previous publishing history of poems (i.e., to whom it's already been sold)."** Time between acceptance and publication could be as long as 1 year. **"Poems held on file until an appropriate time and space becomes available." Send SASE (or SAE and IRC) for guidelines. Reports in 2-3 months. Pays $25/ poem plus up to 10 copies. Buys one-time rights.** Reviews books or chapbooks of poetry in 700 words. Open to unsolicited reviews. Poets may also send books of poetry on commercial fishing for review consideration.

*WESTERLY; PATRICIA HACKETT PRIZE (II), Centre for Studies in Australian Literature, University of Western Australia, Nedlands 6907, Australia, phone (09)380-2101, fax (09)380-1030, e-mail westerly@uniwa.uwa.edu.au, founded 1956, editors Dennis Haskell, Delys Bird and Ron Shapiro. *Westerly* is a literary and cultural quarterly publishing quality short fiction, poetry, literary critical, socio-historical articles and book reviews with special attention given to Australia and the Indian Ocean region. **"No restrictions on creative material. Our only criterion [for poetry] is literary quality. We don't dictate to writers on rhyme, style, experimentation, or anything else. We are willing to publish short or long poems. We do assume a reasonably well-read, intelligent audience. Past issues of *Westerly* provide the best guides. Not consciously an academic magazine."** They have published work by Edwin Thumboo, Jean Kent, David Ray and Ouyang Yu. The quarterly magazine is 144 pgs., $5\frac{1}{2} \times 8\frac{1}{2}$, "electronically printed," with some photos and graphics. Press run is 1,200. Single copy: $8 (Aus.) plus overseas postage via surface mail; subscription: $38 (Aus.)/year or $10 by e-mail. **Sample: $8 (Aus.) surface mail, $12 (Aus.) airmail. Submit up to 6 poems at a time. Fax and e-mail submissions OK ("but replies may only be made for acceptances.") "Please do not send simultaneous submissions. Covering letters should be brief and nonconfessional."** Time between acceptance and publication is 3 months. **Publishes occasional theme issues. Theme for December 1997 is Literature and Painting. Reports in 2-3 months. Pays minimum of $30 plus 1 copy. Buys first publication rights; requests acknowledgment on reprints.** Reviews books of poetry in 500-1,000 words. Open to unsolicited reviews. Poets may also send books to Reviews Editor for review consideration. The Patricia Hackett Prize (value approx. $500) is awarded in March for the best contribution published in *Westerly* during the previous calendar year. The advice of the editors is: "Be sensible. Write what matters for you but think about the reader. Don't spell out the meanings of the poems and the attitudes to be taken to the subject matter—i.e., trust the reader. Don't be swayed by literary fashion. Read the magazine if possible before sending submissions."

WESTERN HUMANITIES REVIEW (II), Dept. of English, 3500 LNCO, University of Utah, Salt Lake City UT 84112, phone (801)581-6070, fax (801)585-5167, e-mail whr@lists.utah.edu, founded 1947, managing editor Tom Hawks, is a quarterly of poetry, fiction and a small selection of nonfiction. **They want "quality poetry of any form, including translations."** They have published poetry by Philip Levine, Bin Ramke, Lucie Brock-Broido, Timothy Liu and Rachel Wetzsteon. *WHR* is 96-125 pgs., 6×9, professionally printed on quality stock and perfect-bound with coated card cover. They receive about 900 submissions a year, accept less than 10%, publish approximately 60 poems. Press run is 1,100 for 1,000 subscribers of which 900 are libraries. Subscription: $20 to individuals in the US. **Sample postpaid: $6. "We do not publish writer's guidelines because we think the magazine itself conveys an accurate picture of our requirements." No previously published poems; simultaneous submissions OK. Reads submissions September 1 through May 31 only.** Time between acceptance and publication is 1-3 issues. **Managing editor Amanda Pecor makes an initial cut ("eliminating only a few submissions"), then the poetry editor makes the final selections. Seldom comments on rejections. Occasionally publishes special issues. Reports in 1-6 months. Pays $30/poem and 2 copies. Acquires first serial rights.** They also offer an annual spring contest for Utah poets. Prize is $250. Poetry published in this review has been selected for inclusion in the 1992, 1993 and 1995 volumes of *The Best American Poetry*.

♣WESTERN PRODUCER PUBLICATIONS; WESTERN PEOPLE (IV-Regional), P.O. Box 2500, Saskatoon, Saskatchewan S7K 2C4 Canada, phone (306)665-3500, fax (306)934-2401, e-mail people@producer. com, founded 1923, managing editor Michael Gillgannon. *Western People* is a magazine supplement to *The Western Producer*, a weekly newspaper, circulation 100,000, which uses **"poetry about the people, interests and environment of rural Western Canada."** The magazine-sized supplement is 16 pgs., newsprint, with color and b&w photography and graphics. They receive about 500 submissions of poetry a year, use 60-70. **Sample free for postage (2 oz.)—and ask for guidelines. Submit up to 3 poems at a time, 1 per page. Name, address and telephone number in upper-left corner of each page. Reports within 2 weeks. Pays $15-50/poem.** The editor comments, "It is difficult for someone from outside Western Canada to catch the flavor of this region; almost all the poems we purchase are written by Western Canadians."

WESTERN TALES (IV-Regional, cowboy), P.O. Box 33842, Granada Hills CA 91394, founded 1993, publisher Dorman Nelson, editor Mariann Kumke, is a quarterly publication of western genre fiction, poetry, pen and ink drawings, and event listings. **They want poetry of any length on nature, romance, animals, adventure; Native American and cowboy poetry, or any work pertaining to the "factual, mythical Wild West."** As a sample we selected this poem, "What a Cowboy's Got," by Carrie S. Walker:

> *Boots, tight jeans, a vest and a hat*
> *It doesn't get much better than that!*

> *Your country music, your horse and a rope*
> *You're a cowboy now, at least you hope.*
>
> *You've got your woman, you've got your beer,*
> *if that don't work, you've got your tears.*
> *But no matter what happens to that,*
> *you've always got:*
>   *Boots, tight jeans, a vest and a hat!*

Western Tales is 98 pgs., 8½×11, attractively printed and perfect-bound with full-color cover and b&w illustrations inside. They receive 400-500 poems a year, accept approximately 75. Press run is 6,000 for 1,500 subscribers. Single copy: $4.95; subscription: $16/year. **Sample postpaid: $6. Submit up to 3 poems at a time with SASE. Seldom accepts previously published poems; simultaneous submissions OK. Often comments on rejections. Send SASE for guidelines. Reports in 3 months. Pays $25 and 1 copy. Acquires first or one-time rights.**

WESTVIEW: A JOURNAL OF WESTERN OKLAHOMA (II), 100 Campus Dr., SOSU, Weatherford OK 73096, phone (405)774-3168, founded 1981, editor Fred Alsberg, is a quarterly that is **"particularly interested in writers from the Southwest; however, we are open to work of quality by poets from elsewhere. We publish free verse and formal poetry."** They have published poetry by Mark Sanders, Michael McKinney, Alicia Ostriker and James Whitehead. *Westview* is 44 pgs., magazine-sized, saddle-stapled, with glossy card cover in full-color. They receive about 500 poems a year, accept approximately 5%. Press run is 700 for 300 subscribers of which about 25 are libraries. Subscription: $10. **Sample postpaid: $4. Submit 5 poems at a time. Cover letter including biographical data for contributor's note required with submissions. "Poems on computer disk are welcome so long as they are accompanied by the hard copy and the SASE has the appropriate postage."** Editor comments on submissions **"when close. Mss are circulated to an editorial board; we usually respond within two to three months."** Pays 1 copy.

*WEYFARERS; GUILDFORD POETS PRESS (II), 1 Mountside, Guildford, Surrey GU2 5JD United Kingdom (for submissions), 9, White Rose Lane, Woking, GU22 7JA United Kingdom (for subscriptions), phone (01483)766918, founded 1972, administrative editor Martin Jones, poetry editors Margaret Pain, Martin Jones and Jeffery Wheatley. They say, "We publish *Weyfarers* magazine three times a year. All our editors are themselves poets and give their spare time free to help other poets." They describe their needs as **"all types of poetry, serious and humorous, free verse and rhymed/metered, but mostly 'mainstream' modern. Excellence is the main consideration. No hard porn, graphics, way-out experimental. Any subject publishable, from religious to satire. Not more than 40 lines."** They have recently published poetry by Kenneth Pobo and Richard Ball (US), Michael Henry and Susan Skinner. As a sample the editors selected these lines from "The Lonely Places" by R.L. Cook:

> *. . . Set in the rim of the globe, spots on the atlas,*
> *Stern, hard & desolate,*
> *Far from the bedlam towns, these lonely places,*
> *Have waited & will wait,*
>
> *Till they are left, one day, to the cold-eyed seabirds,*
> *Gannet, guillemot, gull,*
> *And the last croft, crumbling covered by the bracken,*
> *And the wild sheep's skull . . .*

The digest-sized, saddle-stapled format contains about 28 pgs. of poetry (of a total of 32 pgs.). They receive about 1,200-1,500 poems a year, accept approximately 125. The magazine has a circulation of "about 300," including about 200 subscribers of which 5 are libraries. **Sample (current issue) postpaid: $5 in cash US or £2 UK. Submit up to 6 poems, one poem/sheet. No previously published poems or simultaneous submissions. Closing dates for submissions are end of January, May and September. Sometimes comments briefly, if requested, on rejections. Pays 1 copy.** Staff reviews books of poetry briefly, in newsletter sent to subscribers. "We are associated with Surrey Poetry Center, which has an annual Open Poetry Competition. The prize-winners are published in *Weyfarers*." Their advice to poets is, "Always read a magazine before submitting. And read plenty of modern poetry."

WHETSTONE; WHETSTONE PRIZE (II), P.O. Box 1266, Barrington IL 60011-1266, phone (847)382-5626, fax (847)382-3685, editors Sandra Berris, Marsha Portnoy and Jean Tolle, is an annual. **"We emphasize quality more than category and favor the concrete over the abstract, the accessible over the obscure. We like poets who use words in ways that transform them and us."** They have recently published poetry by William Joliff, Louis Phillips, Helen Reed and Geri Rosenzweig. As a sample an editor selected these lines from "Dying Woman" by Sarah W. Bliumis:

> *Spread your feathered wings,*
> *Waterfalls of white,*
> *Orange feet like lilies*
> *Bright against the sheet.*

It is 96 pgs., digest-sized, professionally printed, perfect-bound with matte card cover. Press run is 700 for 200 subscribers of which 5 are libraries, 350 shelf sales. **Sample postpaid: $3. Reports in 1-4 months. Always sends prepublication galleys. Pays 2 copies plus a monetary amount that varies. Buys first North American serial rights.** Awards the Whetstone Prize of $500 for the best poetry or fiction in each issue, and additional prizes as well. *Whetstone* received two Illinois Arts Council 1995 Literary Awards and received an Honorable Mention for editorial content from the 1995 American Literary Magazine Awards.

WHISKEY ISLAND MAGAZINE (II), English Dept., Cleveland State University, Cleveland OH 44115, phone (216)687-2056, fax (216)687-6943, e-mail whiskeyisland@popmail.csuohio.edu, founded 1978, student editors change yearly, is a biannual magazine publishing poetry, fiction and an interview with a poet/writer each issue. **They want "advanced writing."** They have published poetry by Vivian Shipley, Kathleene West, Claudia Rankine, Patricia Smith and Dennis Saleh. As a sample the editor selected these lines from "Storm/Sewer" by Rita Grabowski:

> The Oyster-sky spits baroque ice-pearls larger than my fists over a big Dallas sky. Floods flash fast
> as a match-head lighting, I smell chlorine-scented skin, remembering you kissed me with your eyes
> opened, that you held the school record for the 400-meter butterfly,

> And I fear you may have jumped, there in Dallas, triathlon swimmer that you are, sucked into the
> rescue, trying the flood. A fast-forward of my nightmare, vortex pulling, bottomless blackness, cold
> and wet, slick brick tube, and black water, the falling . . .

Whiskey Island Magazine is 86-104 pgs., 6×9, professionally printed and perfect-bound with light card stock cover and b&w art. They receive 1,000-1,500 poetry mss a year, accept approximately 6%. Press run is 1,200 for 200 subscribers of which 20 are libraries, about 120 shelf sales. Subscription: $12. **Sample postpaid: $5. Submit up to 10 pgs. of poetry at a time. Include name, address and phone number on each page. No previously published poems. Include cover letter with brief bio. "Poets may fax inquiries and work that runs a few pages (longer submissions should be mailed). They may e-mail requests for submission and contest information." Poems are circulated to an editorial committee. Send SASE for guidelines. Reports within 3 months. Pays 2 copies.** From 1995 to 1997, they held a contest for both poetry and fiction. Query regarding contest for 1998. The editor says, "Send a full ten pages of poetry. We like to see a broad sample of your work. Include SASEs and your name, address and phone for reply."

WHITE EAGLE COFFEE STORE PRESS (II); FRESH GROUND (II, IV-Anthology), P.O. Box 383, Fox River Grove IL 60021-0383, phone (847)639-9200, e-mail wecspress@aol.com, founded 1992, is a small press publishing **5-6 chapbooks/year. "Alternate chapbooks are published by invitation and by competition. Author published by invitation becomes judge for next competition."** They are **"open to any kind of poetry. No censorship at this press. Literary values are the only standard. Generally not interested in sentimental or didactic writing."** They have published poetry by Annie Davidovicz, Timothy Russell, Martha M. Vertreace, Scott Lumbard, Leilani Wright and Jill Peláez Baumgaertner. **Sample postpaid: $5.95. Submit complete chapbook ms (20-24 pgs.) with a brief bio, 125-word statement that introduces your writing and $10 reading fee. Previously published poems and simultaneous submissions OK, with notice. No electronic submissions. Competition deadlines: March 30 for spring contest; September 30 for fall contest. Send SASE for guidelines.** "Each competition is judged by either the author of the most recent chapbook published by invitation or by previous competition winners." **Seldom comments on rejections. Reports 3 months after deadline. All entrants will receive a copy of the winning chapbook. Winner receives $200 and 25 copies.** *Fresh Ground* is an annual anthology that features "some of the best work of emerging poets. **We're looking for edgy, crafted poetry.** *Fresh Ground* is published in October. Poems for this annual are accepted during May through June." They say, "Poetry is about a passion for language. That's what we're about. We'd like to provide an opportunity for poets of any age who are fairly early in their careers to publish something substantial. We're excited by the enthusiasm shown for this new press and by the extraordinary quality of the writing we've received."

WHITE PINE PRESS (V); THE WHITE PINE PRESS POETRY PRIZE (II), 10 Village Square, Suite 28, Fredonia NY 14063, phone (716)672-5743, fax (716)672-4724, e-mail pine@net.bluemoon.net, website http://www.bluemoon.net/~pine/, founded 1973, editor Dennis Maloney, managing director Elaine LaMattina. White Pine Press publishes poetry, fiction, literature in translation, essays—perfect-bound paperbacks. **"At present we are accepting unsolicited mss only for our annual competition, The White Pine Poetry Prize. This competition awards $500 plus publication to a book-length collection of poems by a US author. Entry fee: $15. Deadline: October 15. Send SASE for details."** They have recently published poetry *Starry Night* by Marjorie

---

‡   **THE DOUBLE DAGGER** before a listing indicates that the listing is new in this edition. New markets are often the most receptive to submissions.

Agosin; *Treehouse* by William Kloefkorn; *Zoo & Cathedral* by Nancy Johnson (winner of the Poetry Prize); and *Certainty* by David Romtvedt. **Send for free catalog.**

‡**WHITE PLUME PRESS (III)**, 2442 NW Market St., Suite 370, Seattle WA 98107-4137, phone (206)768-9594, e-mail bd072@scn.org, founded 1989, publisher Gene Nelson, looks for poetry that "says something, or at least entertains, in an easy to read understandable manner." They publish 1-2 paperbacks/year. **They are "open to anything, except personal drivel that has not been critiqued."** They have recently published poetry by Kyle Kimberlin. Books are usually very simple, 64 pgs., 6×9, perfect-bound. **Submit up to 10 sample poems with a list of publication credits and bio. "Include a cover letter stating why this poetry is important and what the poet plans to do to help market it."** Previously published poems and simultaneous submissions OK. Submit poems "on paper—no computer disks." They have a 1-2 year backlog. "All poetry is reviewed by a select group of poets." Seldom comments on rejections. Replies to queries in 1 month. Pay is "open to negotiation." The publisher says, "Get yourself involved with a group—listen to the group—be open to suggestions and changes. Help critique others' works."

JAMES WHITE REVIEW: A GAY MEN'S LITERARY QUARTERLY; THE DAVID LINDAHL PRIZE FOR POETRY (IV-Gay), Box 3356, Butler Quarter Station, Minneapolis MN 55403, phone (612)339-8317, founded 1983, poetry editor Clif Mayhood, associate poetry editor William Reichard, **uses all kinds of poetry by gay men.** They have recently published poetry by Dean Kostos, Knox Gardner and Len Blanchard. They receive about 1,400 submissions a year, use approximately 100, have a 6-week backlog. Press run is 4,000 for 1,500 subscribers of which 50 are libraries. Subscription: $14/year (US). **Sample postpaid: $3. Submit up to 8 poems or 250 lines. A poem can exceed 250 lines, but it "better be very good." Reports in 4 months. Pays $10/poem and 2 copies.** Reviews books of poetry. Sponsors The David Lindahl Prize for Poetry which awards $500 to the best poem published in each calendar year.

❧**WHITE WALL REVIEW (I)**, 63 Gould St., Toronto, Ontario M5B 1E9 Canada, phone (416)977-9924, founded 1976, editors change every year, is an annual using **"interesting, preferably spare art. No style is unacceptable. Should poetry serve a purpose beyond being poetry and communicating a poet's idea? Nothing boring, self-satisfied, gratuitously sexual, violent or indulgent."** They have recently published poetry by R.L. Cook and Terry Watada. As a sample the editor selected these lines from "Lucifer to God" by B.A.H. Komori:

> *do You presume*
> *that I have need, as You do,*
> *for the comfort of companionship*
> *to stave off*
> *the bitter darkness of my*
> *nights?*

WWR is between 124-144 pgs., digest-sized, professionally printed and perfect-bound with glossy card cover, using b&w photos and illustrations. Press run is 500. Subscription: $9 in Canada, $9.50 in US and elsewhere. **Sample postpaid: $8. Submit up to 5 poems at a time with a $5 reading fee. "Please do not submit between January and August of a given year." Cover letter required; include short bio. Reports "as soon as we can (usually in April or May). We comment on all mss, accepted or not." Pays 1 copy.** They say, "Poets should send what they consider *their best work*, not everything they've got."

‡**TAHANA WHITECROW FOUNDATION; CIRCLE OF REFLECTIONS (IV-Ethnic)**, Box 18181, Salem OR 97305, phone (503)585-0564, e-mail tahana@open.org, website http://www.tahana.open.org, founded 1987, executive director Melanie Smith. The Whitecrow Foundation conducts **one spring/summer poetry contest on Native American themes in poems up to 30 lines in length. Deadline for submissions: May 31. No haiku, Seiku, erotic or porno poems. Fees are $2.75 for a single poem, $10 for 4.** Winners, honorable mentions and selected other entries are published in a periodic anthology, *Circle of Reflections*. Winners receive free copies and are encouraged to purchase others for $4.95 plus $1 handling in order to "help ensure the continuity of our contests." As a sample Melanie Smith selected these lines by David E. Sees:

> *Alas . .*
>   *I see*
>   *I hear . .*
> *my grandchild*
>   *move and speak . .*
> *the only thing native*
> *is the complexion*
> *of his skin . . his eyes and hair . .*
> *alas . . forgive*
>   *this lonely tear*

Obtain guidelines via e-mail. Reviews books of poetry for $10 reading fee (average 32 pages). Melanie Smith adds, "We seek unpublished Native writers. Poetic expressions of full-bloods, mixed bloods and empathetic non-Indians need to be heard. Future goals include chapbooks and native theme art. Advice to new writers: Keep writing, honing and sharpening your material; don't give up—keep submitting."

WHOLE NOTES; WHOLE NOTES PRESS (I, II, IV-Children, translations), P.O. Box 1374, Las Cruces NM 88004-1374, *WN* founded 1984, Whole Notes Press founded 1988, editor Nancy Peters Hastings. *WN* appears twice a year. Whole Notes Press publishes **1 chapbook/year** by a single poet. *WN* tends toward close observation of the natural world, the beauty of nature and a poetry which affirms the human spirit. "All forms will be considered." Under Whole Notes Press, they have published chapbooks by Dan Stryk (*A Sea Change*), Robert Dorsett (*Threshold*) and Roy Scheele (*To See How it Tallies*). As a sample the editor selected these lines from "Phases" by David Garrison:

> All the blue spaces and the possibilities of green.
> All the watery light in the afternoon, and the warm days.
> A dark evening near the crossroads, and easy wind.

WN is 32 pgs., digest-sized, "nicely printed," staple bound, with a "linen 'fine arts' cover." They receive about 800 poems a year, accept approximately 10%. Press run is 400 for 200 subscriptions of which 10 are libraries. Subscription: $6. **Sample postpaid: $3. Submit 4 poems at a time. Some previously published poems used; no simultaneous submissions. Reports in 2-3 weeks. Pays 2 copies. For 20-page chapbook consideration, submit 3-5 samples with bio and list of other publications. Pays 25 copies of chapbook. Editor sometimes comments on rejections.** The editor says, "In the fall of each even-numbered year I edit a special issue of *WN* that features writing by young people (under 21). Overall, we'd like to see more translations and more poems about rural experiences."

‡WICKED MYSTIC (IV-Horror), Dept. WD, 532 La Guardia Pl. #371, New York NY 10012, phone (718)638-1533, e-mail scheluchin@wickedmystic.com, website http://www.wickedmystic.com, founded 1990, editor Andre Scheluchin, is a quarterly of hardcore horror poetry and short stories. **They want "psychological horror, splatter-gore, erotic, death, gothic themes, etc. No safe, conventional, conservative poetry."** They have published poetry by Michael A. Arnzen, John Grey and James S. Dorr. *Wicked Mystic* is 100 pgs., magazine-sized, perfect-bound, with heavy stock colored cover and display ads. They receive about 1,000 poems a year, use approximately 5%. Press run is 10,000 for 4,500 subscribers of which 50 are libraries. Subscription: $23/4 issues. **Sample postpaid: $5.95. Submit typed poems, no longer than 30 lines. No previously published poems or simultaneous submissions. Cover letter required. Often comments on rejections. E-mail queries OK. Reports within 2-8 weeks. Pays 1 copy and $5/poem. Acquires first North American serial rights.**

‡THE W!DOW OF THE ORCH!D (I, IV-Specialized: dark, decadent, surreal), 2101 Hazel Ave., Virginia MN 55792-3730, phone (218)749-8645, founded 1994, contact Emella Loran, appears bimonthly and publishes work with "no happy endings . . . without a price. **I want to see dark poetry—any length or style or form is absolutely welcome—but the poetry must be of a dark and macabre nature. Surreal is a plus." They do not want "pretty, happy, mushy poetry. There are places for that sort of behavior."** They have recently published poetry by T.M. Jacobs, Gary Jurechka, Cinsearae Santiago, Walter Zimmerle, Timothy Hodor and Donna Taylor. As a sample Ms. Loran selected the following poem from her own work:

> Enter into my Mind;
>   into the dark desolation
>   and orchids frozen dead in bloom.
> Enter into my Soul;
>   shadows in the dark
>   and a cold ghost moon.
> Enter into my Heart
>   into dreams forgotten
>   and passions awry.
> Enter into my World;
>   there is freedom in the frozen shadows,
>   safety in death, and lost forevers . . .

WO is about 50 pgs., digest-sized, photocopied and saddle-stapled with colored card cover, b&w illustrations with occasional clip art if available, ads. They receive about 40 poems a year, accept approximately 60%. Press run is 100 for 70 subscribers, 30 shelf sales. Subscription: $11. **Sample postpaid: $5 for recent issue, $4 for back issue. Make checks payable to Raquel Bober. "Please invest in a copy if you're not sure about us. Then decide if we're the right zine for you." Must be 18 years or older to submit. Submit 6 poems at a time. Previously published poems OK; no simultaneous submissions. Cover letter preferred including bio "and I'd like the bio to be more then just a list of publications." Always comments on rejections. Publishes theme issues. Send SASE for guidelines and upcoming themes. Reports in 1 month or less. Pays 1 copy. Acquires first North American serial or one-time rights.** Reviews chapbooks, magazines or music (including books on tape). Open to unsolicited reviews. Poets may also send books for review consideration. Ms. Loran says, "Write what you want and definitely what you feel. No rules should bind your creativity. And if someone puts down your work, screw them. Enough said."

‡**WILD DUCK REVIEW (IV-Regional)**, 419 Spring St., Suite D, Nevada City CA 95959, phone (916)478-0134, founded 1994, editor Casey Walker, appears bimonthly and publishes reviews and features of Northern Californian literature. "We believe there is a direct link between the vitality of a community and its written and spoken word. Words which are shared act upon us by creating common memory and by spurring curiosity—the intelligence which places us in right relationship to land and each other. *Wild Duck Review* offers venues for local and regional prose and poetry." **They want poetry of Northern California life—cultural and natural.** They have recently published poetry by Philip Levine, Sandra McPherson and George Keithley. As a sample we selected these lines from "To the Ridge at the Edge" by Gary Snyder:

> *I was hitch-hiking to a gathering: down a freeway through desert*
> *mountain country. Decided to go for a walk in the hills. Intense pure*
> *air, clear sky-bright striated boulders, crisp pines, gleaming granite*
> *outcrops and long snaky ridges-forested valleys and gullies. Cool*
> *and sunny-just right.*

WDR is 24-28 pgs., 11×14 web offset on newsprint and unbound, folded to 7×11 for mailing and display; photos, pencil art and ads inside. They receive about 1,000 poems a year, use approximately 70. Press run is 10,000 for 200 subscribers, shelf sales 2,000; 8,000 distributed free to bookstores and cafes of Northern California. **Sample postpaid: $3. Must be a resident of Northern California. Submit 3-5 poems at a time. Previously published poems and simultaneous submissions OK. Cover letter required including bio and publication credits.** Time between acceptance and publication is 3-4 months. **Seldom comments on rejections. Send SASE for guidelines. Reports in 3-4 months. Pays 3-10 copies. Acquires anthology rights only.** Reviews books "very infrequently when solicited or when outstanding." They feature poetry readings through their reading series in Nevada City. Send SASE for details. The editor says, "Please only submit after reading several copies. We accept less than five percent of submissions which are unsolicited."

‡**WILD WORD; WILDER WORD (I)**, P.O. Box 2132, Idyllwild CA 92549, phone (909)659-2265, fax (909)659-4533, e-mail poemslady@aol.com, founded 1996, publisher Lorraine Lawhorne. *Wild Word* appears bimonthly "to give unknown poets a forum in which to be published and read." And, *Wilder Word* appears annually "to provide the more erotic/shocking the same chance." **They want all styles and formats of poetry; short stories and artwork are also considered.** They have recently published poetry by Robert Kensington and "Poet Wings." As a sample the editor selected this poem, "Love's Haiku" by Lori Jo Dickinson:

> *we fly in formation, wing tip to wing tip*
> *In perfect tandem*
> *together forever. mated.*

Wild Word is about 48 pgs., digest-sized, laser-printed and saddle-staple with 80 lb. cardstock cover with b&w illustration, b&w photos and illustrations inside, "ads are kept to the front page and in the rear pages so as not to interrupt the flow." Press run is 500 for 50 subscribers, about 400 shelf sales. Subscription: $17.50/year. **Sample postpaid: $3. Submit 3-5 pages of poetry at a time. No previously published poems; simultaneous submissions OK. Cover letter preferred.** Time between acceptance and publication is 2-4 months. **Seldom comments on rejections. Publishes theme issues. Send SASE for guidelines and upcoming themes. Reports in 2-4 months. Pays 1 copy.** The publisher says, "Poetry should have life, passion and a soul. The reader should be drawn in so that when they come to the end they have goose bumps and are only able to mutter 'Wow.' Rhyming? Don't stretch it!"

WILDWOOD JOURNAL (IV-Specialized: college affiliation); THE WILDWOOD PRIZE IN POETRY (II), T.H.S. Wallace, Arts 213, 1 HACC Dr., Harrisburg PA 17110-2999, phone (717)780-2487. *Wildwood Journal*, an annual, is **open only to students, alumni and faculty of Harrisburg Area Community College. Sample copy: $5.** The Wildwood Prize, however, is open to any poet, $500 annually, $5 reading fee made payable to HACC. Final selection for the prize is made by a distinguished poet (in 1997: DeAnna Spurlock) who usually remains anonymous until the winner is announced. Poems are accepted between October 15 and November 15. Rules available for SASE.

THE WILLIAM AND MARY REVIEW (II), Campus Center, College of William and Mary, P.O. Box 8795, Williamsburg VA 23187-8795, phone (757)221-3290, fax (757)221-3451, founded 1962, is a 120-page annual, **"dedicated to publishing new work by established poets as well as work by new and vital voices."** They have published poetry by Dana Gioia, Robert Morgan, Cornelius Eady, Amy Clampitt, Elizabeth Alexander, Robert Hershon, Diane Ackerman, Agha Shahid Ali, Bruce Weigl, Robert Bly and Phyllis Janowitz. As a sample the editor selected these lines from "The Broken-footed Angel" by Andrew Zawacki:

> *She crossed her legs, and the leaves outside*
> *Were composed. In between two movements, I asked her*
> *Which words really mattered anymore. "Poetry," she said,*
> *"is an arrangement of the space between us."*
> *I wasn't quite sure how to take this . . .*

They receive about 5,000 poems a year, accept approximately 15-20. Press run is 3,500. They have 250 library subscriptions, about 500 shelf sales. **Sample postpaid: $5.50. Submit 1 poem/page, batches of up to 6 poems addressed to Poetry Editors. Cover letter required; include address, phone number, past publishing history** and brief bio note. Reads submissions September 15 through February 15 only. Reports in approximately 4 months. Always sends prepublication galleys. Pays 5 copies.

WILLOW REVIEW; COLLEGE OF LAKE COUNTY READING SERIES (II), College of Lake County, 19351 W. Washington St., Grayslake IL 60030-1198, phone (847)223-6601, ext. 2956, fax (847)548-3383, founded 1969, editor Paulette Roeske. **"We are interested in poetry and fiction of high quality with no preferences as to form, style or subject."** They have published poetry by Lisel Mueller, Lucien Stryk, David Ray, Louis Rodriguez, John Dickson and Garrett Hongo and interviews with Gregory Orr, Diane Ackerman and Li-Young Lee. As a sample the editor selected this poem, "Daddy Long Legs" by Elaine Fowler Palencia:

> His mind trapped forever
> In a dream of shadows
> My son hunts bugs.
> All the day long
> Along the house foundations
> Mewling gently
> He pulls up grass
> Lets daylight under bricks
> To watch the bugs scurry.
> One day while I'm sunning
> He opens his palm to me
> And smiles.
> There sit five grey buttons
> Pulsing with surprise
> At the loss of their legs
>
> How like a god he is,
> My thoughtless child.

The editor says she selected this particular sample because "Palencia's powerful poem represents the simultaneous simplicity of language and complexity of idea I admire, along with a relentless credibility." The review is an 88- to 96-page, flat-spined annual, 6×9, professionally printed with a 4-color cover featuring work by an Illinois artist. In 1998, a double issue will celebrate the magazine's 30th year. Editors are open to all styles, free verse to form, as long as each poem stands on its own as art and communicates ideas. Circulation is 1,000, with distribution to bookstores nationwide. Subscription: $13 for 3 issues, $20 for 5 issues. **Sample back issue: $4. Submit up to 5 poems or short fiction/creative nonfiction up to 4,000 words. "We read year round but response is slower in the summer months." Sometimes sends prepublication galleys. Pays 2 copies. Acquires first North American serial rights. Prizes totaling $400 are awarded to the best poetry and short fiction/creative nonfiction in each issue.** The reading series, 4-7 readings/academic year, has included Angela Jackson, Thomas Lux, Charles Simic, Isabel Allende, Donald Justice, Gloria Naylor, David Mura, Galway Kinnell, Lisel Mueller, Amiri Baraka, Stephen Dobyns, Heather McHugh, Linda Pastan, Tobias Wolff, William Stafford and others. One reading is for contributors to *Willow Review*. Readings are usually held on Thursday evenings, for audiences of about 150 students and faculty of the College of Lake County and other area colleges and residents of local communities. They are widely publicized in Chicago and suburban newspapers.

WILLOW SPRINGS (II, IV-Translations), 526 Fifth St., MS-1, Eastern Washington University, Cheney WA 99004-2431, phone (509)623-4291, fax (509)623-4238, founded 1977. "We publish quality poetry and fiction that is imaginative, intelligent, and has a concern and care for language. **We are especially interested in translations from any language or period."** They have recently published poetry by James Grabill, Michael Heffernan, Robert Gregory and Paul Zimmer. *Willow Springs*, a semiannual, is one of the most visually appealing journals being published. It is 128 pgs., 6×9, professionally printed, flat-spined, with glossy 4-color card cover with art. They receive about 4,000 poems a year, accept approximately 1-2%. Editors seem to prefer free verse with varying degrees of accessibility (although an occasional formal poem does appear). Circulation is 1,500 for 700 subscribers of which 30% are libraries. Subscription: $10.50/year, $20/2 years. **Sample postpaid: $5.50. Submit September 15 through May 15 only. "We do not read in the summer months." Include name on every page, address on first page of each poem. Brief cover letter saying how many poems on how many pages preferred. No simultaneous submissions. Send SASE for guidelines. Reports in 1-3 months. Pays 2 copies plus a copy of the succeeding issue, others at half price, and cash when funds available. Acquires all rights. Returns rights on release.** Reviews books of poetry and short fiction in 200-500 words. Open to unsolicited reviews. Poets may also send books for review consideration. They have annual poetry and fiction awards ($100 and $250 respectively) for work published in the journal. The editor says, "We like poetry that is fresh, moving, intelligent and has no spare parts."

WIND PUBLICATIONS; WIND MAGAZINE (II), P.O. Box 24548, Lexington KY 40524, phone (606)885-5342, *Wind Magazine* founded in 1971, editor/publisher Charlie G. Hughes, poetry editor Leatha Kendrick. "Although we publish poets of national repute, we are friendly toward beginners who have something to say and do so effectively and interestingly. **No taboos, no preferred school, form, style, etc. Our interests are**

inclusive. Competition is keen; send only your best." *Wind* appears twice a year and is about 100 pgs., digest-sized, perfect-bound, containing approximately 40% poetry, also short fiction, essays and reviews ("Editor's Choice"). "We accept about 1% of submissions." Subscription: $10/year. **Sample postpaid: $4.50. Submit up to 5 poems at a time. No simultaneous submissions. "Cover letter optional; short bio desirable." Editor comments on submissions which are near misses. Reports in 6-8 weeks.** Time between acceptance and publication is within 1 year. Sometimes sends prepublication galleys. Pays 1 copy plus discount on extras. "Your submission is understood to guarantee Wind Publications first North American serial rights and anthology reprint rights only." Wind Publications sponsors a yearly poetry chapbook competition. Reading fee: $10. Send SASE for contest guidelines.

THE WINDLESS ORCHARD; THE WINDLESS ORCHARD CHAPBOOKS (II), English Dept., Indiana University, Fort Wayne IN 46805, phone (219)483-6845, founded 1970, poetry editor Robert Novak, is a "shoestring labor of love—chapbooks only from frequent contributors to magazine. Sometimes publish calendars." They want **"heuristic, excited, valid non-xian religious exercises. Our muse is interested only in the beautiful, the erotic and the sacred."** *The Windless Orchard* appears irregularly, 50 pgs., digest-sized, offset from typescript, saddle-stapled, with matte card cover with b&w photos. There are about 35 pgs. of poetry in each issue (**with a regular section of autobiographical poems on being age 17**). They receive about 3,000 poems a year, use approximately 200, have a 6-month backlog. Press run is 300 for 100 subscribers of which 25 are libraries. Subscription: $10. **Sample postpaid: $4. Submit only 3 poems or 10 haiku at a time. Considers simultaneous submissions. Reports in 1 day to 4 months. Pays 2 copies. Chapbook submissions by invitation only to contributors to the magazine. Poets pay costs for 300 copies, of which The Windless Orchard Chapbook Series receives 100 for its expenses. Sample: $4. Editors sometimes comment on rejections.** They advise, "Memorize a poem a day, do translations for the education."

THE WIND-MILL (IV-Specialized: genealogy, ethnic), P.O. Box 1727, El Cerrito CA 94530-1727, editor H.B. Harvey, is a semiannual publication featuring articles, poetry, reviews, art and photos relating to genealogy and family history. "The purpose of *Wind-Mill* is to provide a friendly, relaxed forum for sharing information about family history research and, in particular, information about Germanic/Dutch (Ostfriesen, East Frisian/North German) culture, history and ethnic traditions." Subscription: $14/year. **Sample postpaid: $7 plus SASE. Submit up to 3 poems, 30 lines maximum each. "Send SASE along with any material that you wish to be returned to you or if you want a response." Submission deadlines: March 1 for Spring/Summer issue; September 1 for Autumn/Winter issue. Pays 1 copy.** They are also interested in reviews of computerized genealogy software; beginning German or Plattdeutsch language instruction programs; reviews of books, tapes and other items related to genealogy research; Low German/Plattdeutsch writings, poems and teaching materials; German/Ostfriesen immigration patterns; amusing anecdotes about ancestors; and specific biographies of or details about individuals. Send SASE for details. The editor advises, "Please obtain and study a sample issue prior to submitting anything for publication."

✤**WINDSOR REVIEW (II)**, English Dept., University of Windsor, Windsor, Ontario N9B 3P4 Canada, phone (519)253-4232 ext. 2332, fax (519)973-7050, e-mail uwrevu@uwindsor.ca, founded 1966, poetry editor John Ditsky, appears twice a year. **"Open to all poetry but no epics."** They have published poetry by Ben Bennani, Walter McDonald, Larry Rubin and Lyn Lifshin. It is professionally printed, 100 pgs., digest-sized. They receive about 500 poems a year, accept approximately 15%. Press run is 400. Subscription: $19.95 (+7% GST) individuals, $29.95 (+7% GST) institutions (Canadian); $19.95 individuals, $29.95 institutions (US). **Sample postpaid: $7. Submit 5-10 poems at a time. Queries via e-mail OK. No e-mail submissions. Reports in 6 weeks.**

WISCONSIN ACADEMY REVIEW (IV-Regional), 1922 University Ave., Madison WI 53705, phone (608)263-1692, fax (608)265-3039, founded 1954, poetry editor Faith B. Miracle, "distributes information on scientific and cultural life of Wisconsin and provides a forum for **Wisconsin (or Wisconsin background) artists and authors."** They want **"good lyric poetry; traditional meters acceptable if content is fresh. No poem over 65 lines."** They have published poetry by Credo Enriquez, Jean Feraca, Felix Pollak, Ron Wallace, Sara Rath and Lorine Niedecker. *Wisconsin Academy Review* is a 52-page quarterly, magazine-sized, professionally printed on glossy stock, glossy card color cover. Press run is 1,800 for 1,500 subscribers of which 100 are libraries. They use 3-6 pgs. of poetry/issue. They receive about 150 submissions a year, accept approximately 24. They have a 6- to 12-month backlog. **Sample postpaid: $3. Submit 5 pgs. maximum, double-spaced, with SASE. Must include Wisconsin connection if not Wisconsin return address. Sometimes comments on rejections. Reports in 10-12 weeks. Always sends prepublication printouts. Pays 3 copies.** Staff reviews books of poetry with Wisconsin connection only. Send related books for review consideration. The editor says, "We would like to receive good traditional forms—not sentimental rhymes."

UNIVERSITY OF WISCONSIN PRESS; BRITTINGHAM PRIZE IN POETRY; FELIX POLLAK PRIZE IN POETRY (II), 114 N. Murray St., Madison WI 53715-1199, Brittingham Prize inaugurated in 1985, poetry editor Ronald Wallace. The University of Wisconsin Press publishes primarily scholarly works, but they offer the annual **Brittingham Prize and the Felix Pollak Prize, both $1,000 plus publication. These prizes are the only way in which this press publishes poetry. Send SASE for rules. For both prizes, submit between**

September 1 and October 1, unbound ms volume of 50-80 pgs., with name, address and telephone number on title page. No translations. Poems must be previously unpublished in book form. Poems published in journals, chapbooks and anthologies may be included but must be acknowledged. There is a non-refundable $20 reading fee which must accompany the ms. (Checks to University of Wisconsin Press.) Mss will *not* be returned. Enclose SASE for contest results. Qualified readers will screen all mss. Winners will be selected by "a distinguished poet who will remain anonymous until the winners are announced in mid-February." Past judges include Charles Wright, Gerald Stern, Mary Oliver, Donald Finkel, Donald Justice, Lisel Mueller, Henry Taylor, Carolyn Kizer, Philip Levine and Rita Dove. Winners include Stefanie Marlis, Judith Vollmer, Renée A. Ashley, Tony Hoagland, Stephanie Strickland, Lisa Lewis, David Clewell, Bob Hicok, Lynn Powell, Dennis Trudell and Juanita Brunk. The editor says, "Each submission is considered for both prizes (one entry fee only)."

WISCONSIN REVIEW; WISCONSIN REVIEW PRESS (II), Box 158, Radford Hall, University of Wisconsin-Oshkosh, Oshkosh WI 54901, phone (414)424-2267, founded 1966, is published 3 times/year. **"In poetry we publish mostly free verse with strong images and fresh approaches. We want new turns of phrase."** They have published poetry by Laurel Mills, Joseph Bruchac, Kenneth Frost, Paul Marion, Dionisio Martinez, Stephen Perry, Margaret Randall, David Steingass, Brian Swann and Peter Wild. As a sample the editor selected these lines from "The Man Who Invented Mirrors" by Laurie Blauner:

> He hadn't discovered the exact edges of his body
> except in the inconsistent kiss of water, until this moment.
> He pointed out the anomalous aspects of oranges
> to himself, his precise companion. No more variations
> on possible themes. The man who had lived in the clouds
> had become tethered to the earth by this remarkable piece of glass

The *Review* is 48-64 pgs., 6×9, elegantly printed on quality white stock, glossy card cover with color art, b&w art inside. They receive about 1,500 poetry submissions a year, use approximately 75. They use 30-40 pgs. of poetry in each issue. Press run is 2,000 for 40 subscribers of which 20 are libraries. Single copy: $3; subscription: $8. **Sample postpaid: $2. Submit mss September 15 through May 15. Offices checked bimonthly during summer. Submit up to 4 poems at a time, one poem/page, single-spaced with name and address of writer on each page. Simultaneous submissions OK, but previously unsubmitted works preferable. Cover letter also preferred;** include brief bio. Send SASE for guidelines. Reports within 2-8 months. Pays 2 copies.

‡WISH WOMEN (I, II, IV-Women), P.O. Box 25374, Colorado Springs CO 80936-5374, e-mail wishwomen @aol.com, website http://members.aol.com/wishwomen/home.htm, founded 1995, managing editor Jean M. Crocker, published bimonthly, "strives to offer encouragement to and a forum for women who are creative. *Wish Women* hopes to recreate the more useful elements of a writer's group or poetry reading on paper. Regular issues usually include 26-30 pages of poetry and feature a poem readers are invited to comment on; the following issue has a synopsis of reader comments. Reader comments on other poems are synopsized and sent directly to the poet." **They want "poetry with a positive attitude. We'll review any subject, any style, but don't want it tainted with anger or bitterness."** They have recently published poetry by Laurie Wagner Boxer, Sue Yonker and Sue Dekelver. As a sample the editor selected these lines from "Writing Biography" by Sharon Bailey:

> In cupped hands,
> I hold
> the threads of her experiences:
> red silk joy
> and
> white lace pain.

Wish Women is 24 pgs., digest-sized, offset, saddle-staped, with 2-color glossy cover. They receive about 150 poems a year, accept approximately 80%. Press run is 250 for 150 subscribers of which 15 are libraries, 12 shelf sales. Subscription: $15. **Sample postpaid: $2.50. Submit 3-5 poems at a time. Previously published poems and simultaneous submissions OK. Cover letter preferred.** Time between acceptance and publication is 6-12 months. **Poems are circulated to the managing editor and selected for quality and applicability to the editorial calendar. Seldom comments on rejections. Publishes theme issues. SASE for guidelines and upcoming themes. Reports in 1-2 months. Always sends prepublication galleys. Pays 3 copies. Acquires one-time rights.** Reviews books or chapbooks of poetry in 400-500 words, single format, usually by frequent contributors. Open to unsolicited reviews. Poets may also send books for review consideration. Each issue features a $10 Readers' Choice Award. Sponsors form contests twice a year. Write for more information.

THE WISHING WELL (IV-Membership, women/feminism, lesbian/bisexual), P.O. Box 713090, Santee CA 92072-3090, phone (619)443-4818, founded 1974, editor/publisher Laddie Hosler, is a "contact magazine for **women who love women** the world over; members' descriptions, photos, letters and poetry published with their permission only; resources, etc., listed. I publish writings only for and by members so membership is required." 1-2 pgs. in each issue are devoted to **poetry, "which can be up to 8″ long—depending upon acceptance by editor, 3″ width column."** It is 7×8½ offset press from typescript, with soft matte card cover. It appears bimonthly and goes to 800 members. **A sample is available for $5. Membership in *Wishing Well* is $35 for 3-5 months, $60 for 5-7 months, $120 for 15 months. Membership includes the right to publish**

poetry, a self description (exactly as you write it), to have responses forwarded to you, and other privileges. Personal classifieds section, 50¢/word for members and $1/word for nonmembers.

WITNESS (II, IV-Themes), Oakland Community College, Orchard Ridge Campus, 27055 Orchard Lake Rd., Farmington Hills MI 48334, phone (810)471-7740, founded 1987, editor Peter Stine, is a biannual journal of poetry, fiction and essays which often publishes special issues centered around themes. **They want "poetry that highlights the role of the writer as witness to his/her times. No real specifications, except nothing concrete or wildly experimental."** They have published poetry by John Balaban, Mary Oliver, Alicia Ostriker and Mark Doty. *Witness* is 192 pgs., 6×9, professionally printed and perfect-bound with coated card cover with full-color photo and b&w photos inside. They receive about 500 poems a year, accept approximately 5%. Press run is 2,800 for 400 subscribers of which 60 are libraries, 1,200 distributed to bookstores. Subscription: $12/year. **Sample postpaid: $7; upcoming special issues are announced inside. No previously published poems; simultaneous submissions OK. Cover letter required. Seldom comments on rejections. Reports in 2-3 months. Pays $10/page. Buys first serial rights.** Poetry published here has also been included in the 1992, 1994 and 1995 volumes of *The Best American Poetry*.

‡WOLF HEAD QUARTERLY (II), P.O. Box 3021, Duluth MN 55803, e-mail whmitch@aol.com, website http://www.cp.duluth.mn.us/~wolfhead, founded 1994, co-editor W.H. Mitchell, "endeavors to cultivate the senses of each reader by publishing quality prose and poetry by writers from across the country." **They want "a wide range of styles and subjects, no more than five pages." They do not want "overly political poems and foul language."** They have recently published poetry by Norman Leer, Diane Glancy, Lucille Lang Day and Mondecai Marcus. *Wolf Head* is 64 pgs., digest-sized, offset, saddle-stapled, with colored card cover, b&w cover and interior art and photos, and ads. They receive about 400-800 poems a year, accept approximately 4-5%. Press run is 200 for 100 subscribers of which 10 are libraries; 20-25 distributed free to advertisers and contributors. Single copy: $4; subscription: $14 plus $4 p&h. **Sample postpaid: $5. Submit 5 poems at a time. E-mail submissions OK "with an attached PC compatible document, or include the work in the e-mail itself." No previously published poems or simultaneous submissions. Cover letter preferred.** Time between acceptance and publication is 1-3 months. **"Poems are circulated to our three editors who read all submissions and decide as a group." Send SASE for guidelines. Reports in 1-3 months. Always sends prepublication galleys. Pays 1 copy. Acquires first North American serial rights.** The editor says, "Beginners should not feel discouraged. Magazines not only pick the best of the lot, but rather pick the best of the best they receive."

‡WOLFSONG PUBLICATIONS (III), 3123 S. Kennedy Dr., Sturtevant WI 53177, e-mail wolfsong@wi.net, founded 1974, editor/publisher Gary C. Busha, is "a small press with a well known, respected reputation for publishing talented, serious poets." They publish **1-3 chapbooks/year. They are open to all types of poetry, but have a bias toward nature/fishing.** They have recently published poetry by Chris Halla, Dave Eher, Russell King and Robert Schuler. As a sample the editor selected these lines from "April 10" in *Grace: A Book of Days* by Robert Schuler:

> Crocuses blossom
> lavendar out of snow and mud
> Canada geese honking
> circling the house
> in the soft evening rain.

Chapbooks are usually 30-36 pgs., 5½×8½, offset-printed or photocopied, saddle-stitched with line art on cover. **Query first. "Serious poets should send SASE for guidelines. Poets must have 5-10 publishing credits in respectable magazines and journals." Previously published poems and simultaneous submissions OK. Cover letter required.** They have a 6 month backlog. **Seldom comments on rejections. Replies to queries in 2 weeks. Pays 5 author's copies (out of a press run of 200-300).** The editor says, "Read extensively. Read literature, including all the classics. Read poetry and learn what poetry is, how it's written and apply those standards to your own work. You need to develop a critical eye and apply that eye to your own work. You need to know the elements of good writing and understand why something that is good stands the test of time, while the 95% of everything else is—thankfully—soon forgotten. You need to know the difference between writing for popular markets and literary markets."

♣WOLSAK AND WYNN PUBLISHERS LTD. (II), Box 316, Don Mills Post Office, Don Mills, Ontario M3C 2S7 Canada, phone (416)222-4690, fax (416)237-0291, founded 1982, poetry editor Maria Jacobs, publishes 5 flat-spined literary paperbacks/year (56-100 pgs.). They have published collections of poetry by Richard Har-

---

 THE MAPLE LEAF symbol before a listing indicates a Canadian publisher, magazine, conference, contest or organization.

rison and Polly Fleck. The books are handsomely printed. **Sample: $10 US or $12 Canadian. Send sample poems with query, bio, publications. No simultaneous submissions. Reports on queries in 4 months. Always sends prepublication galleys. Pays 10% royalties. Buys first rights.** Maria Jacobs says, "W&W prefers not to prescribe. We are open to *good* writing of any kind."

‡THE WOMEN'S REVIEW OF BOOKS (III), Wellesley College, Wellesley MA 02181, website http://www.wellersley.edu/WCW/CRW/WROB/welcome.html, founded 1983, contact Robin Becker, is a monthly review of works by and about women, in all fields, including some poetry reviews. **They want "good stuff. No junk."** They have recently published poetry by Alicia Ostriker, Maxine Kumin and Celia Gilbert. The editor says *TWRB* is 32 pgs., tabloid-sized (10×15), published on newsprint. They receive about 200 poems a year, accept approximately 5%. Press run is 14,000 for 10,000 subscribers of which 1,000 are libraries, 3,000 shelf sales. Single copy: $3; subscription: $23. **Sample copy is free. Submit 2 poems at a time. No previously published poems or simultaneous submissions. Cover letter required. Reads submissions in March and April only.** Time between acceptance and publication is up to 18 months. **Seldom comments on rejections. Reports in 2-3 months. Pays $75 plus unlimited copies. Buys first North American serial rights.** Staff reviews books or chapbooks of poetry in 500-2,000 words. Poets may also send books for review consideration.

WOMEN'S STUDIES QUARTERLY; THE FEMINIST PRESS AT CUNY (V, IV-Women/feminist, bilingual), Dept. PM, 311 E. 94th St., New York NY 10128, phone (212)360-5790. *Women's Studies Quarterly*, founded 1972, publisher Florence Howe, is a nonfiction quarterly publishing **"poetry that focuses on current issues of importance to women; emphasis on education or activism preferable."** They have published poetry by Mila Aguilar. The editor describes it as $5\frac{1}{2} \times 8\frac{1}{2}$, 150-200 pgs. Press run is 1,500. **Sample postpaid: $22. "Although poetry is included in each issue, the poems are chosen by the guest editor." Publishes theme issues. Send SASE for upcoming themes.** Theme for Spring 1999 is Teaching About Violence Against Women; deadline is January 1, 1998. **Pays 2 copies.** The Feminist Press publishes primarily both historical and contemporary fiction and nonfiction (12-15 titles/year), but it also publishes some poetry, such as the series, *The Defiant Muse,* bilingual volumes (Hispanic, French, Italian and German) of poetry by women from the Middle Ages to the present.

‡WOMEN'S WORK, THE SOUND ALTERNATIVE TO GOOD HOUSEKEEPING (II, IV-Women/feminism), 606 Avenue A, Snohomish WA 98290-2416, phone (360)568-5914, fax (360)568-1620, founded 1991, editor/publisher Andrea Damm, is a quarterly zine "dedicated to exploring the personal, professional, and creative work that we all do. *Women's Work* recognizes writers and artists of diverse cultural and economic backgrounds, and is committed to presenting empowering information and images." **They want "poetry of up to 100 lines maximum."** The editor says *WW* is 48 pgs., $8 \times 10\frac{1}{2}$, printed on bookstock paper and saddle-stitched with illustrations and photos. Subscription: $12/year, $20 foreign. **Sample postpaid: $4. Include name and address on each page. SASE required. "Please include a brief biography for inclusion upon publication."** Time between acceptance and publication is 1-3 issues" (3-9 months). **Publishes theme issues. Send SASE for guidelines and upcoming themes. Reports in 3-4 months. Pays 6-month subscription plus copies of issue in which work appears.**

WOMENWISE (III, IV-Women/feminism, health concerns), 38 S. Main St., Concord NH 03301-4817, founded 1978, run by an editorial committee, is "a quarterly newspaper that deals specifically with issues relating to women's health—research, education, and politics." They want **"poetry reflecting status of women in society, relating specifically to women's health issues." They do not want "poetry that doesn't include women or is written by men; poetry that degrades women or is anti-choice."** *WomenWise* is a tabloid newspaper, 12 pgs., printed on quality stock with b&w art and graphics. Press run is 3,000. Subscription: $10/year. **Sample: $2.95. Submissions should be typed double-spaced. Reads submissions March, June, September and December only. Publishes theme issues. Send SASE for upcoming themes. Reporting time and time to publication varies. Pays 5 copies. Acquires first North American serial rights.** Staff reviews books of poetry in "any word count," single format. They say they often receive mss with no SASE. "We throw them away. Please remember that we are a nonprofit organization with limited resources." The editor adds, "We receive a great deal of badly written free verse. We would appreciate receiving more poetry in traditional form, as well as more poetry in free verse written with skill and care."

WOODEN HEAD REVIEW; NON COMPOS MENTIS PRESS (II), 240 Thompson Ave., East Liverpool OH 43920, phone (330)386-4719, founded 1994, editor/publisher Mark Hartenbach. *Wooden Head Review* is a biannual journal containing poetry, b&w artwork and very short or "flash" fiction. **They want "street-level, honest, surreal, outsider, insane poems; also Dada/Beat, experimental and visual poetry. No academic or rhyming work."** They have published poetry by Charles Plymell, Gerald Locklin, Mark Weber, Steve Richmond and John M. Bennett. As a sample the editor selected these lines from "poem for the 21st century" by ron androla:

> *In early 90s we dissolve uranium, pack faster cigarettes, pity*
> *mass indiscriminate murderers, burn poets in hell-fire ignorance*
> *& declare art be moderately commercial & significant to billionaires*

> *thumbs of society pinch aids-infested pimples popping into citizens'*
> *wounds who petition the lord with public prayer*

WHR is 44 pgs., digest-sized, saddle-stapled with b&w art. They receive about 2,000 poems a year, accept approximately 10%. Press run is 300. Subscription: $7/year. **Sample postpaid: $4. Make checks payable to Mark Hartenbach. Submit 5-10 poems at a time. Previously published poems OK. No simultaneous submissions. Cover letter preferred. "We would like to know about writers, what motivates their art. No lengthy credits." Seldom comments on rejections. Reports in approximately 2-3 months. Pays 1 copy. Acquires first or one-time rights.** Non Compos Mentis Press publishes 6 chapbooks a year. They also publish poetry in broadsides and on postcards. Chapbooks are usually 20-30 pgs., digest-sized with card stock cover and b&w art. **"Chapbook submissions are generally selected from previous contributors, friendships with poets and collaborations." Replies to queries in 2 weeks, mss in 1-2 months. Pays 30 author's copies (out of a press run of 100). For sample chapbooks, send $2.**

WOODLEY MEMORIAL PRESS; THE ROBERT GROSS MEMORIAL PRIZE FOR POETRY (IV-Regional), English Dept., Washburn University, Topeka KS 66621, phone (913)234-1032, e-mail zzlaws@acc.w

uacc.edu, website http://www.wuacc.edu/reference/woodley-press/index.html, founded 1980, editor Robert Lawson, publishes 1-2 flat-spined paperbacks a year, **collections of poets from Kansas or with Kansas connections, "terms individually arranged with author on acceptance of ms."** They have published *Looking for the Pale Eagle* by Stephen Meats and *Killing Seasons* by Christopher Cokinos. As a sample the editor selected these lines from "Crows" in *Gathering Reunion* by David Tangeman:

> *A wintering of crows descended to roost*
> *in sheltering mulberries that, row by row,*
> *shield from north wind the clapboard house*
> *situated hard on the eastern section road.*
>
> *Their dark presence in the windbreak*
> *invaded the goosedown comforter and*
> *sent gloom into the sleeping floorboards*

Samples may be individually ordered from the press for $5. Replies to queries in 2 weeks, to mss in 2 months. Time between acceptance and publication is 1 year. Send SASE for guidelines for Robert Gross Memorial Poetry and Fiction Prize ($100 and publication).

WORCESTER REVIEW; WORCESTER COUNTY POETRY ASSOCIATION, INC. (II, IV-Regional), 6 Chatham St., Worcester MA 01609, phone (508)797-4770, founded 1973, managing editor Rodger

Martin. *WR* appears annually with emphasis on poetry. **New England writers are encouraged to submit, though work by other poets is used also. They want "work that is crafted, intuitively honest and empathetic, not work that shows the poet little respects his work or his readers."** They have published poetry by Kathleen Spivack, Bruce Weigl and Walter McDonald. *WR* is 160 pgs., 6×9, flat-spined, professionally printed in dark type on quality stock with glossy card cover. Press run is 1,000 for 300 subscribers of which 50 are libraries, 300 shelf sales. Subscription: $20 (includes membership in WCPA). **Sample postpaid: $5. Submit up to 5 poems at a time. "I recommend three or less for most favorable readings." Simultaneous submissions OK "if indicated." Previously published poems "only on special occasions." Editor comments on rejections "if ms warrants a response." Send SASE for guidelines. Reports in 4-6 months. Pays 2 copies. Buys first rights.** They have an annual contest for poets who live, work, or in some way (past/present) have a Worcester County connection or are a WCPA member. The editor advises, "Read some. Listen a lot."

‡WORD PROCESS (I), 623 N. Monterey St. #1, Alhambra CA 91801-1505, founded 1996, editor Don Craig

Campbell, is a biweekly that publishes one poem on a 5½×8½ postcard. "Our motto is 'cool poetry . . . for your refrigerator!' " **They want "quality poetry—35 lines maximum (including line breaks)." They do not want "poetry without images."** They have recently published poetry by Mike Carlin, Linda Gamboa, Charles Ardinger and Yvonne M. Estrada. As a sample the editor selected these lines from "Rapunzel" by Nancy Thomas:

> *"Let down your hair, girl!"*
> *And she did, every time,*
> *unbraided the silk,*
> *ribbons on the floor.*
> *White knuckles*
> *gripped the window frame*
> *as she cocked back her head,*
> *blood at the roots.*

They receive about 150 poems a year, accept approximately 26. Press run is 400 for 100 subscribers; 300 distributed free at poetry readings and workshops. Subscription: $10/year (26 cards plus free magnet). **Sample postpaid: $1. Make checks payable to Don Craig Campbell. Submit 3-5 poems at a time. Previously published poems and simultaneous submissions OK. "Please send brief biographical information (i.e., recent publications, reading notice, chapbook available, geographical, etc.)."** Time between acceptance and publication is 1-2 months. **Seldom comments on rejections. Reports in 1 month. Pays 20 copies and 1-year subscrip-**

tion. Sponsors annual contest with $100 first prize, $50 second and $25 third. Write for more information. The editor says, "We are seeking more quality submissions—would like to become a weekly publication."

THE WORD WORKS; THE WASHINGTON PRIZE (II), P.O. Box 42164, Washington DC 20015, phone (703)527-4568, fax (703)527-9384, website http://www.writer.org, founded 1974, poetry editors Karren Alenier, J.H. Beall, Hilary Tham, Robert Sargent and Miles David Moore, "is a nonprofit literary organization publishing contemporary poetry in single author editions usually in collaboration with a visual artist. We sponsor an ongoing poetry reading series, educational programs, the Capital Collection—publishing metropolitan Washington D.C. poets, and the Washington Prize—an award of $1,000 for a book-length manuscript by a living American poet." Previous winners include *Tipping Point* by Fred Marchant; *Stalking the Florida Panther* by Enid Shomer; *Farewell to the Body* by Barbara Moore; *The CutOff* by Jay Rogoff; and *Toward Desire* by Linda Lee Harper. Submission open to any American writer except those connected with Word Works. Send SASE for rules. Entries accepted between February 1 and March 1. Postmark deadline is March 1. They publish perfect-bound paperbacks and occasional anthologies and want **"well-crafted poetry, open to most forms and styles (though not political themes particularly). Experimentation welcomed."** As a sample the editors selected these lines from "Rembrandt's Head" by George Young:

> And this is the striking
> thing: the way his face changes with time like a wax head
> in a burning building, the way it softens, begins to
> sag and melt; yet
> as the features distintegrate, the eyes
>
> staring directly back
> at us, take on a new depth, a dark sorrow between the stars
> of some expanding inner universe, a look
> we might recognize from watching our own heads
> in the bathroom mirror each day.

"We want more than a collection of poetry. We care about the individual poems—the craft, the emotional content and the risks taken—but we want manuscripts where one poem leads to the next. We strongly recommend you read the books that have already won the Washington Prize. Buy them, if you can, or ask for your libraries to purchase them. (Not a prerequisite.) **Currently we are only reading unsolicited manuscripts for the Washington Prize."** Simultaneous submissions OK, if so stated. Always sends prepublication galleys. Payment is **15% of run (usually of 500). Send SASE for catalog to buy samples.** Occasionally comments on rejections. Their anthology, *The Stones Remember: Native Israeli Poetry*, was a recipient of the Witter Bynner Foundation Award and was selected as an "Outstanding Book" by *Choice* magazine. The editors advise, "Get community support for your work, know your audience and support contemporary literature by buying and reading the small press."

‡WORDPLAY (I), P.O. Box 2248, South Portland ME 04116-2248, phone (207)799-7041, fax (207)799-7488, e-mail wordplay@ime.net, founded 1994, editor-in-chief Helen Peppe, is a quarterly publication of "short stories, poetry, essays, artwork and photographs—a pretty even mix." **In regard to their poetry needs, they say, "accessibility is foremost, then content. No sexual poetry; rhymed love poems; excessively violent or excessively modern poems."** They have recently published poetry by Dennis Saleh, Robert M. Chute and Pat Ranzoni. As a sample the editor selected these lines from "Interlude" by Thomas Carper:

> At certain times of day, and every day,
> He stopped his work and, laying down his pen,
> Put all his prosy sentences away,
> Waiting for a music to begin.
> When he was very still, a single note
> Would come upon him suddenly while he sat,
> Hands folded as in prayer . . .

The editor says *Wordplay* is 28 pgs., 8½×11, printed on 60 lb. textpaper, saddle-stitched with card stock cover including artwork and photographs. They receive about 450 poems a year, use approximately 120. Press run is 500 for 125 subscribers of which 10 are libraries, 200 shelf sales. Single copy: $4; subscription: $14. **Sample postpaid: $4. Submit up to 10 poems at a time. Previously published poems and simultaneous submissions OK. Cover letter preferred.** Time between acceptance and publication is 8 months. **"All work submitted to WP is read by three to five people."** Send SASE for guidelines. Reports in 2-8 weeks. Always sends prepublication galleys. Pays 1 copy. Acquires one-time rights. The editor says, "Don't give up. Research the magazine—submit and submit again. Be cheerful, eventually the submission and *Wordplay* will match."

WORDSONG; BOYDS MILLS PRESS (IV-Children/teen/young adult), 815 Church St., Honesdale PA 18431, phone (800)490-5111, founded 1990, editor-in-chief Dr. Bernice E. Cullinan, is the imprint under which Boyds Mills Press (a *Highlights for Children* company) publishes books of poetry for children of all ages. **"Wordsong encourages quality poetry which reflects childhood fun, moral standards and multiculturalism. We are not interested in poetry for adults or that which includes violence or sexuality or promotes hatred."**

They have recently published *The Gooch Machine*, performance poems by Brod Bagert. As a sample the editor selected these lines from "Waterfall" in the book *Bicycle Riding*:

> Top to bottom see it fall,
> White and silver rushing,
> As if the world had tipped too far
> And spilled its river gushing
> Over rims of rock and stone
> To thunder in a pool,
> To glow and bubble in the sun,
> To hold and keep me cool.

"Wordsong prefers original work but will consider anthologies and previously published collections. We ask poets to send collections of 30-50 poems with a common theme; please send complete book manuscripts, not single poems. We buy all rights to collections and publish on an advance-and-royalty basis. Wordsong guarantees a response from editors within one month of our receiving submissions or the poet may call us toll free to inquire. Please direct submissions to Beth Troop, manuscript coordinator." Always sends prepublication galleys. Wordsong's *Inner Chimes* received the International Reading Association Teachers' Choice Award. Dr. Cullinan says, "Poetry lies at the heart of the elementary school literature and reading program. In fact, poetry lies right at the heart of children's language learning. Poetry speaks to the heart of a child. We are anxious to find poetry that deals with imagination, wonder, seeing the world in a new way, family relationships, friends, school, nature and growing up."

‡*WORKING TITLES (II)**, 5 Hillside, Clifton Wood, Bristol BS8 4TD England, founded 1990, contact Claire Williamson, is a publication with the purpose of "demonstrating the vacillations of life." **They want "no more than two A4 sides; any subject or length. No discriminating material (i.e., sexist, racist, etc.)."** As a sample we selected these lines from "Awaiting the News" by Chris Haslan:

> In this other hemisphere
> Flooded with December rains
> The waiting is diluted.
> A vapid lemon sun lies low,
> Brown rivers burst their heaving banks,
> Sandbags are saviours now.

Ms. Williamson says *WT* is 26 pgs., card cover, no graphics. They receive about 400 poems a year, accept approximately 5%. Press run is 300 for 200 subscribers, 100 shelf sales. Single copy: £1.50; subscription: £4.50/3 issues. **Make checks payable to Claire Williamson. Submit 6 poems at a time. Previously published poems and simultaneous submissions OK. Cover letter required, include short bio.** Time between acceptance and publication "depends; we publish sometime in March." **Often comments on rejections. Send SASE (or SAE and IRC) for guidelines. Reports in 1 month. Pays 1 copy.**

*WORKS MAGAZINE (IV-Science fiction)**, 12 Blakestones Rd., Slaithwaite, Huddersfield, Yorks HD7 5UQ United Kingdom, phone/fax 01484 842324, e-mail dwworks@aol.com, founded 1989, editor Dave W. Hughes, is a biannual using "speculative and imaginative fiction and poetry favoring science fiction." They want **"surreal/science fiction poetry. Nothing more than 50 lines. No romance or general work."** They have published poetry by Andy Darlington, Steve Sneyd, Paul Weinman and Brian Aldiss. *Works* is 40 pgs., A4, offset, on colored paper, saddle-stapled with b&w glossy cover and interior b&w art. They receive about 150 poems a year, use approximately 36. Press run is 400 for 200 subscribers of which 4 are libraries, 50 shelf sales. Single copy: £2 (£4.50 for US); subscription: £7.50/4 issues (£14 US). **No simultaneous submissions. Cover letter required. Disk submissions acceptable: IBM (3.5 inch) ASCII files only. Often comments on rejections. Send SASE (or SAE and IRC) for guidelines. Reports within a month. Pays 1 copy.** The editor says, "Study the market."

WORM FEAST!; TAPE WORM; VIDEO WORM; 8, DANCING WITH MR. D; KNIGHTMAYOR PRODUCTIONS (II)**, 809 W. Broad St. #221, Fallschurch VA 22046, *WoRM fEASt!*, an underground monthly, founded 1989, editor Llori Steinberg. *Tape WoRM* is an audio magazine with music, poetry, comedy and more. *Video WoRM* is a video endeavor with movies, visual art, animation, music videos, news events and more. Send SASE for details. *8, Dancing with Mr. D*, published 4-12 times/year, wants **"seriously sinister, doofy, weird, profound, erratic, manipulating poetry,"** For *Wf* they want **"as strange as humanoids can get; no traditional verse, no rhyme (unless it's way off the keister), no haiku, no love poems unless one-sided and morbid/dark and unusually sickening; and no Christian poetry."** They have published poetry by Gregory K.H. Bryant, Robert Howington, C.F. Roberts, Bill Shields and Vinnie Van Leer. The editor says *Wf* is usually 32 pgs., saddle-stitched, format size varies, with artwork and photos. "The digest is different every time." Press run is 1,500. The editor says *8DWMD* is 12-24 pgs., saddle-stapled, photocopied with photos and artwork. Press run is 800 for 800 subscribers. Subscription: $25 for *Tape WoRM;* $20 for *WoRM fEASt!,* when available; $24 for *8DWMD*. **Sample postpaid: $5 (make all checks and any other forms of payment to Llori Steinberg). Submit 3 poems at a time for *8DWMD*, for the others send 1 poem at a time. Previously published poems OK. Cover letter with SASE required; "don't have to be professional, just state the facts and why you're interested in** submitting." Publishes theme issues. Send SASE for guidelines and upcoming themes. "We report as quickly as we can." Sometimes sends prepublication galleys. Pays 1 copy of *WoRM fEASt!*, 1 copy of *Tape WoRM*, 1-2 copies of *8DWMD*; contact for submission guidelines. Reviews books of poetry. Open to unsolicited reviews. Send books to Llori Steinberg for review consideration. "We publish chapbooks for poets' personal use. They buy and they sell." Cost is $100 for 100 chapbooks of under 15 pgs. each. Sponsors contests. Send SASE for details. The editor says, "We want everything—*Video WoRM* and *Tape WoRM* especially—from serious to sick, profound to profane, from sane to insane, from graceful to gory—get it?"

THE WRITE WAY (I, IV-Writing); TAKING CARE OF YOURSELF (I, IV-Health concerns); ANN'S ENTERPRISES, P.O. Box 220102, Glenwood FL 32722, e-mail vegi@aol.com, founded 1988, editor Ann Larberg. *TWW* is a quarterly using **poems of up to 20 lines on the theme of writing.** As a sample the editor selected "Limerick Lamentation" by Donna Bickley:

> Composing a limerick's not easy
> Although my attempts make me queasy,
> I jot down a line, I stretch for a rhyme.
> Reaching as far as it pleases me.

TWW is an 6-page newsletter with articles on writing and ads. Single copy: $3; subscription: $6. **Sample free with SASE. Must include $1 reading fee and SASE with submissions (up to 5 poems). Do not submit in summer. Reads submissions January 1 through June 30 only. Publishes theme issues. Send SASE for upcoming themes. Reports in 6 weeks. Pays 1 copy.** Open to unsolicited reviews. Poets may also send books for review consideration. They hold contests quarterly and publish an annual holiday poetry edition with cash awards. Deadline for annual holiday issue is November 15. *Taking Care of Yourself*, a 4-page newsletter of well-being, is also published quarterly and **accepts 1-2 short poems/issue on the theme of health. Sample free with SASE. Pays copies.**

THE WRITER; POET TO POET (I, II), 120 Boylston St., Boston MA 02116-4615, founded 1887. This monthly magazine for writers has a quarterly instructional column, "Poet to Poet," to which poets may submit previously unpublished work for possible publication and comment. Subscription: $28 (introductory offer: 5 issues for $10). Single copy: $3.50 back issues; $2.50 newsstand. **Submit up to 3 poems, no longer than 30 lines each, not on onion skin or erasable bond, name and address on each page, 1 poem to a page. Send SASE for guidelines only; do not send SASE with submission. There is no pay and mss are not acknowledged or returned. Acquires first North American serial rights.**

‡THE WRITER'S BLOCK (I, II), P.O. Box 538, Whitewater WI 53190, e-mail editor-twb@cni-usa.com, founded 1996, editor Kellie Eggert, is a monthly literary magazine "providing a comfortable neighborhood atmosphere for writers of all ages and experience levels. We focus on poems and short stories, but also interview writers, discuss literary 'hot topics' and provide many opportunities for readers to get involved with us and with each other. We also have a kids' section, 'Building Blocks,' and a section on handling writer's block in each issue." Some people write for the sheer beauty of the sound of the words or of the images used; some write to evoke truth, to show something about our lives. **We feel that the best poetry encompasses both of these—that it is both a sensual and an intellectual experience. However, we recognize that our neighborhood is made up of people with varying tastes and we will look at any poetry which the poet feels is good enough to be reviewed. No overly didactic, blatantly political, occult or pornographic poetry."** They have recently published poetry by Laurel Yourke, Peg Sherry, Shawn Christenen and Roberta Fabiani. As a sample the editor selected this poem by Lynn Renor:

> Scarlet fire backlights a single silhouette
> as the form strides into the flickering distance
> away, into the curve of time . . .

TWB is 45 pgs., digest-sized, professionally printed and perfect-bound, card stock cover, contains graphics, photos and contributor's artwork. "As we are a new magazine, our estimates are that we will receive between 1,200-1,500 poems and use 20-25%. Press run is 100 for 40 subscribers of which 2 are libraries, 50 shelf sales. Subscription: $15.50/6 months, $28.50/year. **Sample postpaid: $2.95. Submit 5 poems at a time. Previously published poems OK; no simultaneous submissions. Cover letter required. "Cover letter should list the poems being submitted and should discuss (briefly) either the works themselves or writing in general (there is more detail in the guidelines). Cover letter must be signed by the author. All SASEs should be legal-sized."** Time between acceptance and publication is 2-3 months. **"I read each work then discuss it with my editorial assistant in depth before making a determination. We read each piece a minimum of two times, usually three to four. If we have questions, I contact the author. Whether the poem is accepted or rejected, I write back a personal letter offering a 'sickeningly large' amount of comments. I work individually with each poet to the extent of his/her interest and our mutual schedules." Publishes theme issues. Send SASE for guidelines and upcoming themes or request via e-mail. Reports in 1-2 months. Acquires first or one-time rights.** The editor says, "For beginners, remember that there are as many kinds of editors as there are poets. Learn from their comments, but don't be discouraged by them. Remember that your poems are that—yours. You are the artist; you have the vision. Think of looking for publications as similar to picking out a frame for a painting: one frame may not work, but that does not mean that either the frame or the painting is flawed, simply badly matched. Keep on looking—the right frame is out there! If I can help, let me know."

‡❧**WRITER'S BLOCK MAGAZINE; WRITER'S BLOCK CONTEST (I)**, P.O. Box 32, 9944-33 Ave., Edmonton, Alberta T6N 1E7 Canada, founded 1994, editor Shaun Donnelly. *Writer's Block Magazine* appears biannually and publishes assorted fiction, nonfiction and poetry. **They want poetry of any form, length or subject matter. The editor says** *WBM* is 48 pgs., digest-sized. They receive about 500 poems a year, accept approximately 12. Press run is 10,000 for 500 subscribers, 2,000 shelf sales; 7,500 distributed free to Edmonton neighborhoods. Single copy: 3.50; subscription: $12/2 years. **Sample postpaid: $5. Submit 3 poems at a time. Previously published poems and simultaneous submissions OK. Cover letter preferred.** Time between acceptance and publication is 6 months. **Always comments on rejections. Send SASE (or SAE and IRC) for guidelines. Reports in 6-8 weeks. Pays $25. Buys first North American serial rights.** Sponsors the biannual Writer's Block Contest for novice poets. Entry deadlines are March 1 and September 1. Awards $75 plus publication to the best poem.

WRITERS' CENTER PRESS; THE FLYING ISLAND; WRITERS' CENTER OF INDIANAPOLIS (II, IV-Regional), P.O. Box 88386, Indianapolis IN 46208, phone (317)955-6336, fax (317)955-6450, founded 1979, executive director Jim Powell. Writers' Center Press publishes *The Flying Island*, a biannual of fiction, poetry, reviews and literary commentary by those **living in or connected to Indiana. They want poetry of high literary quality; no stylistic or thematic restrictions.** They have published poetry by Jared Carter, Alice Friman, Yusef Komunyakaa and Roger Mitchell. *TFI*, a 24-page tabloid, includes artwork, graphics and photography. They receive about 1,000 poems a year, accept approximately 5%. Press run is 1,000 for 500 subscribers. **Submit 3 poems at a time. Previously published poems OK, but not encouraged. Simultaneous submissions OK, if so advised. Brief bio required. Often comments on rejections. Send SASE for guidelines. Reports in 3-6 months. Pays $5 minimum for previously unpublished work. Buys first North American serial rights.** Staff reviews books of poetry. Send books for review consideration. The center sponsors frequent contests for members through its quarterly newsletter and open readings. They advise, "Balance solitary writing time by getting involved in a writing community. We frequently recommend rejected writers join a poetry workshop."

‡**WRITER'S CRAMP (I)**, P.O. Box 84, Mukwonago WI 53149, founded 1996, editor Bonita Engen, a monthly, is focused on "making poetry accessible (and even fun) for the general public—to give all poets a place. **We welcome all styles of poetry and look for diversity in them.** *Writer's Cramp* **actually wants 'love poems,' nature poems, all poems. Our only specification is that the poems have life and feeling. They don't need to be 'way out' or wacky to catch our eye, but we do admire wit and fun with the language."** As a sample the editor selected this poem "The Sublet" by B.J. Bothner:

> I've sublet my brain
> and no one is renting
> inside it is vacant
> but the sign out says "sold"
> I wonder quite vaguely
> if it really matters
> by the time someone lives here
> I'll be much too old

WC is 20 pgs., 8½×11, side-stapled with colored paper cover containing art by local artists, graphics inside, no ads. Accepts over 95% of poems received. Subscription: $15.95. **Sample (including guidelines) postpaid: $2. Submit 5 poems at a time. Previously published poems and simultaneous submissions OK. Cover letter preferred.** "Submission should be typed as writer wishes them to appear (avoiding spelling errors, etc.) and double-spaced." Poems are reviewed by 3 editors, then voted on. **Seldom comments on rejections. Publishes seasonal theme issues. Reports in 2-3 weeks. Pays copies. Acquires first rights.** The editor says, "We would like to use *Writer's Cramp* to inspire other writers and offer an 'Inspiration Page' as well as a 'Kick Back' critic section. Need more submissions in these areas. We need writing inspirations and bad experiences in writing and how to avoid them—no more than 100 words. Our reason for existence is to provide poets with an alternative to 'swindler' publications that require huge subscription fees to see your work in print. We love poetry, want to see poets published. If you want to subscribe, we just happen to be inexpensive too."

WRITER'S DIGEST (IV-Writing, humor); WRITER'S DIGEST WRITING COMPETITION (II), 1507 Dana Ave., Cincinnati OH 45207, phone (513)531-2222, founded 1921, associate editor Amanda Boyd, is a monthly magazine for writers—fiction, nonfiction, poetry and drama. "All editorial copy is aimed at helping writers to write better and become more successful. **Poetry is included in 'The Writing Life' section of** *Writer's Digest* **only. Preference is given to short, light verse concerning 'the writing life'—the foibles, frenzies, delights and distractions inherent in being a writer. Serious verse is acceptable; however, no poetry unrelated to writing. Please avoid the trite or maudlin." Preferred length: 4-20 lines.** The magazine has published poetry by Charles Ghigna. They use a maximum of 2 short poems/issue, about 15/year of the 1,500 submitted. *Writer's Digest* has a circulation of 240,000. Subscription: $27. **Sample postpaid: $3.50. Do not submit to Michael Bugeja, poetry columnist for the magazine. Submit to Amanda Boyd, associate editor, each poem on a separate page, no more than 8/submission. Previously published poems and simultaneous submissions**

OK if acknowledged in cover letter. Editor comments on rejections "when we want to encourage or explain decision." Send SASE for guidelines and/or reply. Reports in 1-2 months. Always sends prepublication galleys. Pays $15-50/poem plus 1 copy. Poetry up to 32 lines on any theme is eligible for the annual Writer's Digest Writing Competition. Watch magazine for information, or send a SASE to Aimee Franklin, competition assistant, for a copy of the contest's rules. Deadline: May 31. (Also see Writer's Digest Books under Publications Useful to Poets.)

WRITER'S EXCHANGE; R.S.V.P. PRESS; NEW MARKETS; REMEMBRANCE (I), Box 394, Society Hill SC 29593-0394, phone (803)378-4556, e-mail eboone@aol.com, founded 1983, editor Gene Boone, is a quarterly newsletter of articles on any aspect of writing, poetry and artwork with a special emphasis on beginners. He wants **"poetry to 24 lines, any subject or style. I also consider short poems such as haiku, tanka, senryu and other fixed forms. I like writing that is upbeat, positive, enlightening or inspiring, especially humorous poetry. I will not consider material that is anti-religious, racist or obscene."** He has published poetry by Victor Chapman, Diane L. Krueger and Edd McWatters. As a sample he selected these lines by Sarah Jensen:

> *I am ancient wind.*
> *I am in the Garden of Eden;*
> *a place somewhere between*
> *the Tigris and Euphrates rivers.*

WE is 32 pgs., digest-sized, saddle-stitched, with a full-color cover. He accepts about half or more of the poetry received. Press run is 250. Subscription: $12. **Sample postpaid: $2. Submit 3-10 poems at a time. "I prefer typed mss, one poem per page, readable. Poets should always proofread mss before sending them out. Errors can cause rejection." Previously published poetry OK; no simultaneous submissions. Cover letter required; list "prior credits, if any, and other details of writing background."** Time between acceptance and publication is 4 months. **Send SASE for guidelines or request via e-mail. Reports in 2-4 weeks. Pays 1 copy. Acquires one-time rights.** Staff reviews books of poetry. Send books for review consideration. They offer cash awards for quarterly contests sponsored through the magazine. Send SASE for current rules. In 1995 they began publishing *New Markets*, a newsletter featuring information on small press and New Age markets. Send SASE for details. In 1996 they began publishing *Remembrance*, a biannual featuring poems and short nonfiction pieces about poets and loved ones who have passed away. **Sample: $4.95. Subscription: $8.95. Submit any number of poems with SASE. Cover letter including brief bio of poet (and if desired, the poems' subjects) preferred. Pays 1 copy.** The editor says he comments on rejections, "if I feel it will benefit the poet in the long run, never anything too harsh or overly discouraging." His advice to poets: "Support the small press publications you read and enjoy. Without your support these publications will cease to exist. The small press has given many poets their start. In essence, the small press is where poetry lives!"

WRITERS' FORUM (II, IV-Regional), Dept. PM, University of Colorado, Colorado Springs CO 80933-7150, founded 1974, poetry editor Victoria McCabe. *Writers' Forum*, an annual, publishes both beginning and well-known writers, giving **"some emphasis to contemporary Western literature**, that is, to representation of living experience west of the 100th meridian in relation to place and culture. We collaborate with authors in the process of revision, reconsider and frequently publish revised work. We are open to **solidly crafted imaginative work that is verbally interesting and reveals authentic voice. We would like to see more formal work, nicely executed."** They have published poems by William Stafford, David Ray, Kenneth Fields, Harold Witt and Judson Crews. The annual is 225 pgs., digest-sized, professionally printed with matte card cover, flat-spined, using 40-50 pgs. of poetry in each issue. They receive about 500 poems a year, accept approximately 25. Circulation is 800 for 100 subscribers of which 25 are libraries. **The list price is $8.95 but they offer it at $5.95 to readers of *Writer's Digest*. Submit 3-5 poems at a time with SASE. No previously published poems; simultaneous submissions OK, if acknowledged. Reads submissions September 1 through March 15 only. Reports in 3 months. Pays 1 copy. Acquires all rights, but returns them.**

*WRITERS FORUM; AND MAGAZINE (IV-Form), 89A Petherton Rd., London N5 2QT England, phone (0171)226-2657, founded 1963, editor Bob Cobbing, is a small press publisher of experimental work including sound and visual poetry in cards, leaflets, chapbooks, occasional paperbacks and a magazine. **"Explorations of 'the limits of poetry' including 'graphic' displays, notations for sound and performance, as well as semantic and syntactic developments, not to mention fun."** They have recently published poetry by Billy Mills, Betty Radin, Nicholas Johnson, Patrick Fetherston, Gilbert Adair and Bill Griffiths. As a sample the editor selected these lines by Patricia Farrell:

---

* AN ASTERISK before a listing indicates an overseas publisher, magazine, contest, conference or organization.

imperfections and anomalies of style—the
lifting and setting down of their feet—a
unique method—which replaces subjectivity
—justice is more like a sound—And a
desire that straightens up and moves forward
—sings and sings so well

The magazine is published "irregularly" and uses "very little unsolicited poetry; practically none." Press run "varies." **Submit 6 poems at a time. "We normally don't publish previously published work." Work should generally be submitted camera-ready. Pays 2 copies, additional copies at half price.** Under the imprint Writers Forum they publish 12-18 books a year averaging 28 pgs. **Samples and listing: £3. For book publication, query with 6 samples, bio, publications. Pays 12 copies, additional copies at half price.** The editor says, "We publish only that which surprises and excites us; poets who have a very individual voice and style."

‡**THE WRITER'S GAZETTE; PRESS-TIGE PUBLICATIONS INC. (I, II)**, HCRI, Box 309, IRA Vail Rd., Leeds NY 12451, phone (518)943-1440, fax (518)943-0702, founded 1993, editor-in-chief Martha Ivery, assistant editor Pamela Muzoleski. *The Writer's Gazette* is a monthly newsletter publishing "articles on writing, experiences, tips, classifieds, to help writers write and those that let them." The editors say *WG* is approximately 12 pgs., 8½×11, stapled with 4-color cover, includes graphics and ads. They receive about 500 poems a year, accept approximately 40%. Press run is 15,000 for 10,000 subscribers of which 300 are libraries, 1,000 shelf sales. Single copy: $6.99; subscription: $49. **Sample postpaid: $6. Make checks payable to Press-Tige Publications Inc. Submit 20 poems at a time. Previously published poems and simultaneous submissions OK. Cover letter preferred. "No handwritten poems."** Time between acceptance and publication is 6-12 months. **Poems are circulated to an editorial board. "We decide on accepted poems twice a month." Always comments on rejections. Publishes theme issues. Send SASE for guidelines and upcoming themes. Reports in 2 weeks. Pays at least $25 and 1 copy. Buys one-time rights.** Reviews books of poetry. Open to unsolicited reviews. Poets may also send books for review consideration to Martha Ivery, editor-in-chief, Press-Tige Publications, Dept. P-WD, 291, Main St., Catskill NY 12414. Press-Tige Publications' goals are "to publish new voices and to aim for success. We publish poetry, fiction, nonfiction, children's, young adult, most genres." They publish 300 paperbacks, 50 hardbooks and **15 chapbooks/year.** They also publish the semiannual anthology *Reflections*, containing love, inspirational and literary poems. Books are usually 135 pgs., 5½×8½, perfect-bound, 4-color cover, including art and graphics. **Submit a minimum of 15 poems, 50 lines maximum each. Include SASE for response. Requires poets to subscribe to the** *Writer's Gazette*. **Replies to queries in 3 weeks, to mss in 2 months. Pays 4-8% royalties plus $500 honorarium and 10 author's copies (out of a press run of 5,000). Contributors to the anthology must purchase a copy; no free contributor's copies are given.** Sponsors a Christmas Poetry Contest. Awards $500. The editor says, "Submit poems that will move the reader. Develop your craft by taking critiques seriously. If your poetry doesn't sound right, it probably isn't. Think positive and remember with God, all things are possible."

WRITER'S JOURNAL (I, II), P.O. Box 25376, St. Paul MN 55125, phone (612)730-4280, founded 1980, poetry editor Esther M. Leiper. *Writer's Journal* is a bimonthly magazine "for writers and poets that offers advice and guidance, motivation, inspiration, to the more serious and published writers and poets." Esther Leiper has 2 columns: "Esther Comments," which specifically critiques poems sent in by readers, and "Every Day with Poetry," which discusses a wide range of poetry topics, often—but not always—including readers' work. She says, **"I enjoy a variety of poetry: free verse, strict forms, concrete, Oriental. But we take nothing vulgar, preachy or sloppily written. Since we appeal to those of different skill levels, some poems are more sophisticated than others, but those accepted must move, intrigue or otherwise positively capture me.** 'Esther Comments' is never used as a negative force to put a poem or a poet down. Indeed, I focus on the best part of a given work and seek to suggest means of improvement on weaker aspects. **Short is best: 25-line limit, though** *very* **occasionally we use longer. Three to four poems at a time is just right."** They have published poetry by Lawrence Schug, Diana Sutliff and Eugene E. Grollmes. *Writer's Journal* is 64 pgs. (including paper cover), magazine-sized, professionally printed, using 4-5 pgs. of poetry in each issue, including columns. Circulation is 54,000. They receive about 400 submissions a year, use approximately 30-40 (including those used in Esther's columns). **Sample postpaid: $4. No query. Reports in 4-5 months. Pays 25¢/line.** The magazine also has quarterly poetry contests for previously unpublished poetry. Deadlines: February 28, April 15, August 15 and November 30. Reading fee for each contest: $2 first poem, $1 each poem thereafter.

♣**WRITER'S LIFELINE (I)**, P.O. Box 1641, Cornwall, Ontario K6H 5V6 Canada, phone (613)932-2135, fax (613)932-7735, e-mail sgull@glennet.ca, founded 1974, editor Stephen Gill, published 3 times a year, containing articles and information useful to writers, **poetry** and book reviews. **"We prefer poems on social concerns. We avoid sex."** *WL* is 36-40 pgs., digest-sized, saddle-stitched with 2-color paper cover, printed in small type, poems sometimes in bold or italics. Circulation is 1,500. Subscription: $18. **Sample postpaid: $3. Publishes theme issues. Send SASE (or SAE and IRC) for guidelines and upcoming themes. Responds in 1 month. Pays 3 copies. Acquires first North American serial rights.** Reviews books of poetry in 500-1,500 words. "We need book reviews." Query if interested.

‡WRITERS' ROUND TABLE (II, IV-Regional), P.O. Box 509, McHenry MD 21541, phone (301)387-9389, fax (301)387-9534, e-mail writers@miworld.net, founded 1997, publisher/editor Susan Haydel, published 10 times/year, is "a literary forum, calendar of events, and networking tool for writers in the mid-Atlantic states." **They want "poetry of any length. Prefer non-rhyming usually."** The editor says *WRT* is 12 pgs., tabloid-size newspaper with display and classified ads. Press run is 7,000. Subscription: $16 for home delivery. **Sample copy for 2 first-class stamps. Contributors must live in the mid-Atlantic region (MD, DC, VA, WV, NC, PA, DE, NJ). No previously published poems or simultaneous submissions. Cover letter required.** Time between acceptance and publication is 1-3 months. **Often comments on rejections. Send SASE for guidelines. Pays 2¢/word ($5 minimum) plus 1 copy. Buys first North American serial rights.** The editor says, "We have a column called 'Poetry in Motion' where a poem is published anonymously and readers write in critiques which are published two issues later. It's a workshop process. No pay for these, though. We also have a teen section, for ages 12-17, called 'The Teen Scene,' where we publish poetry and short fiction by teens."

WRITES OF PASSAGE (I, IV-Teens/young adult), 817 Broadway, 6th Floor, New York NY 10003, phone (212)473-7564, e-mail wpusa@aol.com, website http://www.writes.org, founded 1994, editor/publisher Laura Hoffman, is a biannual literary journal for teenagers across the country. **They only publish poems by teenagers (12-19). "We accept all topics and forms, but do not want poems longer than three pages."** As a sample the editor selected these lines from "We Were Bandits" by Megan McConnel:

> . . . And one of the saddest things
> about being able to drive these days
> is that you never really go anywhere—
> like across America,
> or all those places
> you only pretended to go in the car
> parked in the garage of your childhood.

Writes of Passage is 100 pgs., 5½×8½, professionally printed and perfect-bound with semiglossy color cover. They receive about 2,000 poems a year, accept approximately 100. Press run is 3,000 for 500 subscribers of which 100 are libraries, 1,500 shelf sales. Subscription: $12. **Sample postpaid: $6. Make checks payable to Writes of Passage USA, Inc. Submit up to 5 poems at a time. Previously published poems OK; no simultaneous submissions. Cover letter with brief bio (2-3 lines) preferred. Three editors review poems. Seldom comments on rejections. Send SASE for guidelines or request via e-mail. Reports in 6-8 weeks. Sometimes sends prepublication galleys. Pays 2 copies.** Writes of Passage USA is a nonprofit educational organization dedicated to providing teenagers with a forum for their creative writing. In addition to publishing the literary journal, they also occasionally conduct workshops and organize readings. The editor says, "We also accept tips and advice on writing poetry by authors and educators."

WRITING FOR OUR LIVES; RUNNING DEER PRESS (I, II, IV-Women), 647 N. Santa Cruz Ave., The Annex, Los Gatos CA 95030-4350, founded 1991, editor/publisher Janet McEwan, appears twice a year. "*Writing For Our Lives* serves as a vessel for poems, short fiction, stories, letters, autobiographies and journal excerpts from the life stories, experiences and spiritual journeys of women." They want **poetry that is "personal, women's real life, life-saving, autobiographical, serious—but don't forget humorous, silence-breaking, many styles, many voices. Women writers only, please."** They have recently published poetry by Melisa Cahnmann, Iris Fabiola Naguib, Jenny Potts, Mani Rao, Penina Ava Taesali and Le Thi Tham Van. As a sample the editor selected these lines from "Now We Are Here" by Stephanie Eleftheriou:

> We have dreamed of this
> for months, for years and years
> before we knew who we were
> and how many of us existed,
> before we knew how we would meet
> what we would say to each other

Writing For Our Lives is 80-92 pgs., 5¼×8¼, printed on recycled paper and perfect-bound with matte card cover. They receive about 400 poems a year, accept approximately 5%. Press run is 700. Subscription: $15.50 (CA residents add 7.75% sales tax). Back issues and overseas rates available, send SASE for info. **Sample postpaid: $8. Submit up to 5 typed poems with name and phone number on each page. Previously published poems ("sometimes") and simultaneous submissions OK. Include 2 self-addressed stamped envelopes; "at least one of them should be sufficient to return manuscripts if you want them returned." Closing dates are February 15 and August 15. Usually reports in 1-3 days, occasionally longer.** "As we are now shaping 2-4 issues in advance, we may ask to hold certain poems for later consideration over a period of 18 to 24 months." **Seldom comments on rejections. Send SASE for guidelines. Pays 2 copies, discount on additional copies and discount on 1-year subscription. Acquires first world-wide English language serial (or one-time reprint) rights.** The editor says, "Our contributors and circulation are international."

WYRD (IV-Psychic/occult), P.O. Box 624, Monroeville PA 15146-0624, e-mail easywind@juno.com, founded 1986, "editrix" Goldie Brown, is a quarterly. They want **poetry about magick, the occult, mystical experiences, nature or spirituality—no longer than 45 lines.** They have recently published poetry by Ken MacDonnell,

Patricia Ethelwyn Howell, Jay Bremyer and Elizabeth Kowols. As a sample the editor selected these lines from "Emerald Joy" by Phoenix:

> Dwelling within, seeing the unseen, my heart has turned to emerald green
> And, gleaming beams of Beltane dew, its rays extend from me to you.
> Emerald joy and May Eve bliss mingle sweetly in our kiss
> As diamonds in the sky above reflect the spectrum of our love.
> So as above then so below, the twinkling fires of passion glow
> In an ancient name, a jewel so fair, from water, fire, earth and air.

WYRD is 16 pgs., 8½×11, side stapled, with art and graphics. They receive about 200 poems a year, use approximately 40%. Press run is 150 for 100 subscribers. Subscription: $20. **Sample postpaid: $5. Submit 2 poems at a time. No previously published poems; simultaneous submissions OK. Cover letter required. Request guidelines via e-mail. Reports in 2 months. Pays 1 copy.** Reviews related books of poetry in 150-200 words, single format.

XANADU; POETIMES; LONG ISLAND POETRY COLLECTIVE (II)

XANADU; POETIMES; LONG ISLAND POETRY COLLECTIVE (II), % LIPC, P.O. Box 773, Huntington NY 11743, founded 1979, editors Lois V. Walker, Mildred Jeffrey, Sue Kain and Weslea Sidon, is an annual publishing "serious poems including prose poems, and an occasional adventuresome essay on contemporary poetry or critical theory." They want **"well-crafted quality poems. Nothing inspirational, obscene or from beginners."** They have recently published poetry by William Cannon, Lyn Stefenhagens, John J. Brugaletta, Rane Arryo and Anita H. Feng. As a sample the editors selected these lines from "Autumn" by EG Burrows:

> First cold slows flies
> though the spider weaves
> more brilliant mazes
> hung with grace notes.
> Webs ornament
> the double glass

Xanadu is 64 pgs., 5½×8½, perfect-bound with b&w CS1 cover stock cover. Press run is 300 for 100 subscribers of which 5 are libraries. **Sample postpaid: $7. No previously published poems; simultaneous submissions OK. Poems must be typed. Seldom comments on rejections. Send #10 SASE for guidelines. Reports in 2-20 weeks. Pays 1 copy. Acquires first North American serial rights.** The Long Island Poetry Collective also publishes *Poetimes*, a bimonthly newsletter edited by Binnie Pasquier that includes an extensive calendar of poetry events on Long Island, contests, market listings and poetry by its members. Subscription: $20/year, includes membership in LIPC and subscription to *Xanadu*. They say, "We would be glad to look at more quality postmodernist and formalist poetry."

‡**XAVIER REVIEW (II)**, Box 110C, Xavier University, New Orleans LA 70125, phone (504)486-7411, founded 1961, editor Thomas Bonner, Jr., is a biannual that publishes poetry, fiction, nonfiction and reviews (contemporary literature) for professional writers, libraries, colleges and universities. Press run is 500. **Submit 3-5 poems at a time with SASE.**

XIB; XIB PUBLICATIONS (V), P.O. Box 262112, San Diego CA 92126-2112, phone (619)298-4927, fax (619)278-5101, founded 1990, editor tolek, appears irregularly, usually annually, publishing poetry, short fiction and b&w artwork and photos. **They are currently not accepting unsolicited manuscripts. They publish poetry of any form, length, subject, style or purpose. "Prefer 'quirky' things, however."** They have published poetry by Christine C. Brown, Sheila E. Murphy and Judson Crews. *xib* is 60 pgs., 6½×8½, photocopied on heavy bond, saddle-stapled, 12 pt. gloss mimeo cover, 80% illustrated with art and photos, some ads. Press run is 500 for 50 subscribers of which a third are libraries, 350 shelf sales. Subscription: $10/2 issues and a chapbook. **Sample postpaid: $5, back issues $4; make checks payable to tolek.** xib publications **publishes 1-2 chapbooks/year, "irregularly and arbitrarily. Please do not query or submit with chapbook intent. Most chaps form out of friendly joint-efforts."** Press run for chapbooks is about 75-100. Authors receive half; the rest goes to subscribers, reviewers and trades.

XIQUAN PUBLISHING HOUSE; THE PARADOXIST LITERARY MOVEMENT JOURNAL; THE PARADOXIST MOVEMENT ASSOCIATION (IV-Form), 2456 S. Rose Peak Dr., Tucson AZ 85710-6122, founded 1990, editor Florentin Smarandache. *The Paradoxist Literary Movement Journal* is an annual journal of "avant-garde poetry, experiments, poems without verses, literature beyond the words, anti-language, non-literature and its literature, as well as the sense of the non-sense; revolutionary forms of poetry." They want **"avant-garde poetry, one to two pages, any subject, any style (lyrical experiments). No classical, fixed forms."** They have published poetry by Paul Georgelin, Titu Popescu, Ion Rotaru, Michéle de LaPlante and Claude LeRoy. The editor says *TPLM* is 52 pgs., digest-sized, offset, soft cover. Press run is 500. "It is distributed to its collaborators, U.S. and Canadian university libraries and the Library of Congress as well as European, Chinese, Indian and Japanese libraries." **No previously published poems or simultaneous submissions. Do not submit mss in the summer. "We do not return published or unpublished poems or notify the author of date of publication." Reports in 3-6 months. Pays 1-2 copies.** Xiquan Publishing House also publishes 2 paperbacks and **1-2 chapbooks/year, including translations. The poems must be unpublished and must meet**

the requirements of the Paradoxist Movement Association. Replies to queries in 1-2 months, to mss in 3-6 months. Pays 50 author's copies. Inquire about sample books. They say, "We mostly receive traditional or modern verse, but not avant-garde (very different from any previously published verse). We want anti-literature and its literature, style of the non-style, poems without poems, non-words and non-sentence poems, very upset free verse, intelligible unintelligible language, impersonal texts personalized, transformation of the abnormal to the normal. Make literature from everything; make literature from nothing!"

‡X-IT PRESS (V); THE BOBBY STAR NEWSLETTER; ZAP INC. MAGAZINE (II, IV-Form/style), P.O. Box 3756, Erie PA 16508, founded 1993, editor/publisher Bobby Star. *The Bobby Star Newsletter* appears 3 times/year and contains poetry, reviews, commentary and "lots of ads." **They want "beat/streetwise, working-class poetry. Gay. Real life. Open to haiku, sonnets, free verse, etc. Prefer 3-40 lines. No academic, bombastic or 'third person' work."** They have recently published poetry by Ana Christy, R.L. Nichols, Joe Rochette and Paul Weinman. As a sample the editor selected this poem, "Sylvia Plath" by Kevin Hibshman:

> little
> black
> frightened
> pigeon
> splattered under the chrome grill
> feathers
> blood
> oil

The editor says *BSN*'s format varies but, usually includes ads, art, photos and various graphics; side stapled. They receive hundreds of poems a year, accept approximately 10-60%. Press run is 300 for 4 subscribers. **Sample (including guidelines) postpaid: $1. Make checks payable to Robert L. Nichols.** They also publish *ZAP inc. magazine* which appears irregularly. Format varies. Press run is 120 for 3 subscribers. **Publishes theme issues. Send SASE for guidelines. For both publications, submit 5 poems at a time. Previously published poems and simultaneous submissions OK. Cover letter preferred. They prefer single-spaced, typed mss, but will consider handwritten. Reads submissions February through September only.** Time between acceptance and publication is 6-12 months. **Seldom comments on rejections. Reports in 1-17 weeks. Pays 1 copy. Acquires one-time rights.** X-it press is currently closed to submissions. The editor says, "Just be yourself and avoid typos."

YALE UNIVERSITY PRESS; THE YALE SERIES OF YOUNGER POETS COMPETITION (III), P.O. Box 209040, New Haven CT 06520-9040, founded 1919, poetry editor (Yale University Press) Richard Miller. The Yale Series of Younger Poets Competition is **open to poets under 40 who have not had a book previously published. Submit ms of 48-64 pgs. in February. Entry fee: $15. Send SASE for rules and guidelines.** Poets are not disqualified by previous publication of limited editions of no more than 300 copies or previously published poems in newspapers and periodicals, which may be used in the book ms if so identified. Previous winners include Richard Kenney, Carolyn Forché and Robert Hass.

THE YALOBUSHA REVIEW (II), P.O. Box 186, University MS 38677, e-mail yalobush@sunset.backbone.ol emiss.edu, website http://www.yalobush.olemiss.edu, founded 1995, contact poetry editor, is an annual literary magazine of the University of Mississippi. **They want "high-quality, professional material. No limericks, long prose poems or poems over ten pages."** As a sample the editor selected these lines from "The Weather of Escape" by David Powell:

> And leaving around the curve of Africa,
> you throw one wink in an arc edged
> with expense startlingly full and bare
> to return will last like moths.

The Yalobusha Review is about 100 pgs., 5½ × 8½, perfect-bound with matte card cover. They receive about 200 poems a year, accept approximately 10%. Press run is 500. **Sample postpaid: $6. Submit 6 poems at a time. No previously published poems; simultaneous submissions OK. Short cover letter preferred. Reads submissions October 1 through March 1. Poems are circulated to an editorial board. Seldom comments on rejections. Send SASE for guidelines. Reports in up to 6 months. Pays 2 copies.**

YANKEE MAGAZINE; YANKEE ANNUAL POETRY CONTEST (II), P.O. Box 520, Dublin NH 03444-0520, phone (603)563-8111, founded in 1935, poetry editor (since 1955) Jean Burden. Though it has a New England emphasis, the poetry is not necessarily about New England or by New Englanders, and it has a national distribution of more than 700,000 subscribers. They want to see **high-quality contemporary poems in either free verse or traditional form. Does not have to be regional in theme. Any subject acceptable, provided it is in good taste. We look for originality in thought, imagery, insight—as well as technical control." They do not want translations or poetry that is "cliché-ridden, banal verse."** They have published poetry by Maxine Kumin, Liz Rosenberg, Josephine Jacobsen, Nancy Willard, Linda Pastan, Paul Zimmer and Hayden Carruth. As a sample the editor selected these lines from "Planting the Impatiens on St. Norbert's Day" by Joan Vayo:

three Saturdays ago
the dogwood foamed

gone green now
I see white shells of it
in the impatiens
I rest around its roots

The monthly is 6×9, 144 pgs., professionally printed, saddle-stapled, using full-color and b&w ads and illustrations, with full-color glossy paper cover. They receive over 30,000 submissions a year, accept about 50-60 poems, use 4-5 poems/monthly issue. Subscription: $24. **Submit up to 6 poems at a time, up to 30 lines each, free verse or traditional. No previously published poems or simultaneous submissions. "Cover letters are interesting if they include previous publication information." Submissions without SASE "are tossed." Editor comments on rejections "only if poem has so many good qualities it only needs minor revisions." Reports in 2-3 weeks. Approximately 18-month backlog. Pays $50/poem, all rights; $35, first magazine rights.** Sponsors an annual poetry contest judged by a prominent New England poet and published in the February issue, with awards of $150, $100 and $50 for the best 3 poems in the preceding year. Jean Burden advises, "Study previous issues of *Yankee* to determine the kind of poetry we want. Get involved in poetry workshops at home. Read the best contemporary poetry you can find."

YARROW, A JOURNAL OF POETRY (II), English Dept., Lytle Hall, Kutztown State University, Kutztown PA 19530, founded 1981, editor Harry Humes, appears twice a year. They have published poetry by Gibbons Ruark, Jared Carter, William Pitt Root and Fleda Brown Jackson. It is 40 pgs., 6×9, offset. Press run is 350. Subscription: $5/2 years. **Reports in 1-2 months. Pays 2 copies plus 1-year subscription.** Poetry published in *Yarrow* was also selected for inclusion in a *Pushcart Prize* anthology.

YEFIEF (II), P.O. Box 8505, Santa Fe NM 87504-8505, phone (505)753-3648, fax (505)753-7049, e-mail arr@imagesformedia.com, founded 1993, editor Ann Racuya-Robbins, is an annual designed "to construct a narrative of culture at the end of the century." **They want "innovative visionary work of all kinds."** They have published poetry by Michael Palmer, Simon Perchik and Carla Harryman. *Yefief* is 176 pgs., 7½×10, offset and perfect-bound with color coated card cover and b&w photos, art and graphics inside. Press run is 1,000. Single copy: $10.95. **Submit 3-6 poems at a time. Previously published poems and simultaneous submissions OK. Reports in 6-8 weeks. Pays 2-3 copies.** Open to unsolicited reviews. Poets may also send books for review consideration.

‡*THE YELLOW CRANE (II), Flat 6, 23 Richmond Crescent, Roath, Cardiff CF2 3AH Wales United Kingdom, founded 1995, editor Jonathan Brookes, appears quarterly and publishes "interesting new poems from South Wales and beyond." **They want "intelligent, provoking, quirky poetry with modern feeling, short, fresh. No overlong, overacademic, over-literary, self-important work."** They have recently published poetry by Geoff Hattersley, Ian McMillan, Patrick Waites and Helen Kitson. As a sample the editor selected these lines from "10" by Sally Rooke:

Dying Jesus
on his cross
gives me his body
which I eat, but later
in the kandy kabin,
with lemon sherbert
on my tongue
he finds me out:
O where shall I hide
now he knows
I really prefer
Trebor's flying saucers?

YC is 20 pgs., A5, desktop-published and saddle-stitched with yellow card cover, no ads. Cover illustrations drawn by the editor. They receive about 500 poems a year, accept approximately 25%. Press run is 200 for 20 subscribers of which 6 are libraries, 50 shelf sales. Subscription: £7.50/year. **Sample postpaid: £1.50. Submit 3 poems at a time. Previously published poems OK. Cover letter preferred.** Time between acceptance and publication is 0-3 months. **Often comment on rejections. Reports within 1 week. Pays 2 copies.**

‡YEMASSEE; YEMASSEE AWARDS (II), Dept. of English, University of South Carolina, Columbia SC 29208, founded 1993, contact editor, appears semiannually and "publishes primarily fiction and poetry, but we are also interested in one-act plays, brief excerpts of novels, essays, reviews and interviews with literary figures. Our essential consideration for acceptance is the quality of the work; we are open to a variety of subjects and writing styles." They accept 10-25 poems/issue. **Prefer poems under 50 lines, but will consider poems of exceptional quality regardless of length. "No poems of such a highly personal nature that their primary relevance is to the author; bad Ginsberg."** They have recently published poetry by Robert Rehder, Robert

Parham and Susan Ludvigson. *Yemassee* is 60-80 pgs., 5½×8½, professionally printed and saddle-stitched, quality uncoated cover stock, one-color cover graphic, no ads. They receive about 400 poems a year, accept approximately 10%. Press run is 750 for 63 subscribers, 10 shelf sales; 275-300 distributed free to English department heads, creative writing chairs, agents and publishers. Subscription: $6 for students, $15 regular. **Sample postpaid: $4. Submit up to 5 poems at a time. No previously published poems; simultaneous submissions OK. Cover letter required. "Each issue's contents are determined on the basis of blind selections. Therefore we ask that all works be submitted in triplicate, without the author's name or address anywhere on the typescript. Include this information along with the title(s) of the work(s) in a cover letter. For longer submissions, please include an approximate word count." Reads submissions October 1 through November 15 and March 15 through April 30.** Time between acceptance and publication is 2-4 months. **"Staff reads and votes on 'blind' submissions." Seldom comments on rejections. Send SASE for guidelines. Reports in 8-10 weeks after submission deadline. Pays 2 copies with the option to purchase additional copies at a reduced rate. Acquires first rights.** Sponsors the *Yemassee* Awards when funding permits. Awards $400/issue, usually $200 each for poetry and fiction.

YESTERDAY'S MAGAZETTE (I, IV-Senior citizens), Independent Publishing Co., P.O. Box 18566, Sarasota FL 34276, editor and publisher Ned Burke, founded 1973. This bimonthly magazine is for **"all nostalgia lovers.** *YM* believes that everyone has a yesterday and everyone has a memory to share. Nothing fancy here . . . just 'plain folks' relating their individual life experiences. **We are always seeking new and innovative writers with imagination and promise, and we would like to see more '40s, '50s and '60s pieces."** *YM* is 36 pgs., magazine-sized, saddle-stapled, professionally printed on good stock with glossy color cover. Subscription: $15/year, $25/2 years. **Sample: $3. Submissions for "Quills, Quips, & Quotes" (their poetry page) should be "thoughtful, amusing, or just plain interesting for our 'plain folks' readers. Pays copies.** Sponsors contest. Send SASE for information.

‡*YORKSHIRE JOURNAL (IV-Regional), Illkey Rd., Otley, West Yorkshire LS2 3JP England, phone (01943)467958, fax (01943)850057, founded 1992, contact Rebecca Needham, a quarterly general interest magazine about Yorkshire. **They want poetry no longer than 25 lines with some relevance to Yorkshire.** They have recently published poetry by Vernon Scannell and Anna Adams. As a sample we selected these lines from "Magnum Opus In Memoriam Jacob Kramer 1892-1962" by Vernon Scannell:

> One night in The Victoria in Leeds
> Jacob said to me, "Before I die
> I'm going to paint a picture that will stun
> them all. They think I've lost
> whatever talent I once had,
> that drink and craziness have neutered me.
> I'll prove them wrong.
> It's going to be a northern landscape,
> forests, mountains, peaks, a pitiless sky—
> but non-specific, if you follow me—
> a landscape of the heart.
> It's haunted me for years.
> I'll show you . . . look . . ."

Ms. Needham says *YJ* is 120 pgs., highly illustrated. They receive about 500 poems a year, accept approximately 10%. Press run is 3,000 for 700 subscribers, 2,300 shelf sales. Subscription: £12. **Sample postpaid: £2.95. Make checks payable to SMITH Settle Ltd. Submit up to 6 poems at a time. Previously published poems and simultaneous submissions OK. Cover letter required including biographical information. Has a large backlog.** Time between acceptance and publication varies. **Often comments on rejections. Send SASE (or SAE and IRC) for guidelines. Reports within 1 month maximum. Pays 1 copy.** Staff reviews books of poetry in approximately 400 words, single format. Poets may also send books for review consideration.

YOUNG VOICES MAGAZINE; YOUNG VOICES (V, IV-Children), P.O. Box 2321, Olympia WA 98507, phone (360)357-4683, e-mail patcha@olywa.net, founded 1988, director Steve Charak, poetry editor Emma Russell, is "a magazine of **creative work of elementary through high school students. The age limit is rigid."** It appears every other month. Press run is 2,000 for 1,000 subscribers of which 100 are libraries. Membership/subscription: $20/year, $35/2 years. **Sample postpaid: $4. Query first. No longer accepting unsolicited poetry submissions.** The magazine is published by Young Voices, a nonprofit organization which also offers local workshops for children and publishes a newsletter on children's writing and creativity for parents and teachers. Send SASE for details. Steve Charak says, "Revise. Remember that in a poem, every word counts. Forget about the need to rhyme. Instead, put feeling into each word."

ZEPHYR PRESS (III, IV-Translations), 13 Robinson St., Somerville MA 02145-3698, founded 1980, editors Ed Hogan and Leora Zeitlin. **"We are now publishing very little poetry, and exclusively Russian and Eastern European poetry in translation."** An example publication is *In the Grip of Strange Thoughts: Russian Poetry in a New Era*, edited by J. Kates. **Query with 5 sample translations. Simultaneous submissions OK. "We**

will respond only if interested." Pays 10% of press run or by royalty, depending upon the particular project.

ZOLAND BOOKS INC. (III), 384 Huron Ave., Cambridge MA 02138, phone (617)864-6252, founded 1987, publisher Roland Pease, is a "literary press: fiction, poetry, photography, gift books, books of literary interest." **They want "high-quality" poetry, not sentimental.** They have published poetry by Joseph Torra, Alice B. Fogel, James Laughlin, William Corbett, Karen Fiser, Patricia Smith and Sam Cornish. They publish 8-10 books/ year, flat-spined, averaging 104 pgs. **Query with 5-10 sample poems, bio, publications and SASE. Sometimes sends prepublication galleys. Pays 5-10% royalties plus 5 copies. Buys all rights.**

ZUZU'S PETALS QUARTERLY ONLINE (II), P.O. Box 156, Whitehall PA 18052, phone (610)740-1645, e-mail: zuzu@lehigh.net, website http://www.lehigh.net/zuzu/, founded 1992, editor T. Dunn. "We publish high-quality fiction, essays, poetry and reviews on our award-winning website, which was The NCSA/Mosaic Pick of the Week and is featured in The Whole Internet Catalog Select. Becoming an Internet publication allows us to offer thousands of helpful resources and addresses for poets, writers, editors and researchers, as well as to greatly expand our readership. **Free verse, blank verse, experimental, visually sensual poetry, etc. are especially welcome here. We're looking for a freshness of language, new ideas and original expression. No 'June, moon and spoon' rhymed poetry. No light verse. I'm open to considering more feminist, ethnic, alternative poetry, as well as poetry of place."** They have recently published poetry by R. Nikolas Maciocii, Linda Batt, Timothy Russell and C.A. Conrad. As a sample the editor selected these lines from "San Francisco Earthquake" by Kathryn Young:

> *Padre Pablo, in the dream I could understand*
> *how the angels of death like wild birds*
> *can be entertained with kind gestures*
> *like strangers, how white their teeth,*
> *how warm and dark their skin*

ZPQO averages 70-100 pgs., using full-color artwork, and is an electronic publication available free of charge on the Internet. "Many libraries, colleges, and coffeehouses offer access to the Internet for those without home Internet accounts." They receive about 3,000 poems a year, accept approximately 10%. **A copy of *Zuzu's Petals Poetry Buffet*, a sample of writing from the past 4 years is available for $5. Submit up to 4 poems at a time. Previously published poems and simultaneous submissions OK. "Cover letters are not necessary. The work should speak for itself." Submissions via e-mail are welcome, as well as submissions in ASCII (DOS IBM) format on 3½ disks OK. Seldom comments on rejections. Send SASE for guidelines or request via e-mail. Reports in 2 weeks to 2 months. Acquires one-time electronic rights. Back issues are archived on their website.** Staff reviews books of poetry in approximately 200 words. Send books, galleys or proofs for review consideration. They also sponsor twice-yearly poetry contests. Entry fee: $2/poem, any style, length or subject. Deadlines are the first of March and September. 40% of proceeds goes to prize winners: 25% to first prize, 10% to second, 5% to third. Free critiques to honorable mentions. The remaining 60% of proceeds goes toward the publication and allows them to expand their writers' resources on the Internet. The editor says, "Read as much poetry as you can. Support the literary arts: Go to poetry readings, read chapbooks and collections of verse. Eat poetry for breakfast, cultivate a love of language, then write!"

Contests and Awards

The opportunities for poets to receive recognition and get work published are growing via the route of contests and awards. And while this section of *Poet's Market* is considerably smaller than Publishers of Poetry, it contains more than 40 new entries within its approximately 150 "markets."

Here you will find a wide range of competitions—everything from contests with modest prizes sponsored by state poetry societies, colleges or even cities to prestigious awards offered by private foundations. Among the various contests and awards included in this section are those that offer publication in addition to their monetary prizes. (To get an intimate look at a poetry book competition, see the interview with Richard Phillips, award director of the $1,000 Richard Phillips Poetry Prize, on page 490.) But even if publication is not included, the publicity generated upon winning some of these contests can make your name more familiar to editors.

SELECTING CONTESTS

Whether you're submitting one poem to a quarterly contest sponsored by a journal or an entire manuscript to an award offered by a book publisher, you should never submit to contests and awards blindly. Since many contests require entry fees, blind submissions will just waste your money. As in the Publishers of Poetry section, each listing here contains one or more Roman numerals in its heading. These "codes" will not only help you narrow the list of contests and awards, but they can also help you evaluate your chances of winning (and recouping your expenses).

The **I** code, for instance, is given to contests that are very open to beginners. While these contests may require small fees, or membership in the sponsoring organization, they typically are not exploitive of poets, beginning or otherwise. Keep in mind, however, that if a contest charges a $5 entry fee and offers $75 in prizes, the organizers only need 15 entries to cover the prizes. Even though fees may also go toward providing a small honorarium for the judge, 100 entries will surely net the organizers a tidy profit—at the expense of the participating poets. Be careful when deciding which of these contests are worth your money.

The **II** code follows the name of general literary contests, usually for poets with some experience. This code may also follow awards for recently-published collections, such as The Poets' Prize and The Poetry Center Book Award, or fellowships designed for poets of "demonstrated ability," such as the Guggenheims. And competitions like the Great Lakes Colleges Association New Writers Award, a first-book contest that accepts submissions from publishers only, are listed under this code. If you're just beginning, start building a reputation by having your work accepted by periodicals, they try your hand at these competitions.

Of all the codes, however, perhaps the most useful is **IV**, which designates specialized contests and awards. That is, you—or your poetry—must meet certain criteria to be eligible. Some contests are regional, so only poets from a certain area may enter. For example, the Pew Fellowship in the Arts (new to this edition) awards $50,000 every three years to a poet, 25 or older, residing in one of the Pennsylvania counties of Bucks, Chester, Delaware, Montgomery or Philadelphia for at least two years. Also, fellowships and grants offered by state and provincial arts councils are only open to residents of the particular state or province. Some of these programs are detailed here. For those not found, see the list of State and Provincial Grants following this section.

Other contests are limited to certain groups, such as women or students. For instance, the

Emerging Lesbian Writers Award offers a $10,000 prize to lesbian writers who have published at least one piece of writing, but not more than one book. And the "Giorgio La Pira" International Literary Prize is open only to poems written in Italian.

A few contests are for translations only. Still others are limited to poets writing in certain forms or on certain subjects. If you write sonnets, for example, consider the Salmon Arm Sonnet Contest. One award limited to a certain subject is the Boardman Tasker Award, which only considers work dealing with the mountain environment. Competitions that primarily consider themselves specialized are often open to both beginning and established poets.

While most of the contests and awards in this section are open to entries, there are a few to which you cannot apply. These are coded **V**, indicating the winners are chosen by nomination— often by an anonymous committee. See the listing for The Whiting Writers' Awards, for example. We include such awards because winning one is a very high honor and it is not only helpful to know these awards exist, but it is also important to know you should not attempt to apply for them.

In addition to the listings in this section, there are contests and awards (particularly those sponsored by journals) mentioned in listings in other sections of this book. For those, you should refer to the list of Additional Contests and Awards at the end of this section and consult the listings noted there for details.

Once you've narrowed the contests and awards you want to enter, treat the submission process just as you would if you were submitting to a magazine: Always send a SASE for more information. Many contests want you to submit work along with their specific entry form or application. Others offer guidelines detailing exactly how they want poetry submitted. Also, deadlines for entries are often subject to change and if your work arrives after the deadline date, it may automatically be disqualified. Finally, request a list of recent winning entries for any contest you are considering. This will give you a good idea of the kind of work the judges appreciate. However, this may not apply if the judges change each year.

DISCOVER OTHER RESOURCES

Besides this section of *Poet's Market*, there are other sources of information on competitions. In fact, some good places to locate contests are in your own city or town. Many bookstores and libraries post announcements for local contests on their bulletin boards. Calling a nearby college's English department may provide you with the scoop on regional competitions. And, many poetry groups publish newsletters containing information on competitions that are available to nonmembers. Finally, don't forget to check the classified ads of community arts/entertainment papers for those contests currently seeking entries.

For more information on the national level, *Poets & Writers Magazine* (see the listing in the Publications of Interest section) includes calls for entries for numerous contests and awards along the margins of its pages. In addition, the magazine also includes a Grants and Awards section listing recent winners of poetry and fiction prizes of $500 or more and prestigious nonmonetary awards in fiction and poetry. Reading the winners' work is a good way to determine the type of poetry these competitions are seeking.

Other publications containing information on contests and awards include *AWP Chronicle* published by Associated Writing Programs (see listing in Organizations Useful to Poets), *Grants and Awards Available to American Writers* (published by the PEN American Center, 568 Broadway, New York NY 10012-3225), *Writer's Digest* magazine and the annual directory *Writer's Market* (both published by Writer's Digest Books). Check local bookstores for these publications or order copies directly from the publisher.

For detailed information on selecting and submitting to contests, read Chapter Three: Entering Contests in Michael J. Bugeja's *Poet's Guide* (Story Line Press, 1995). The chapter also includes essays from some well-known poets on their experiences with and opinions on entering competitions.

OUR OWN EXPERIENCE

With the completion of the second *Poet's Market* Poetry Contest, we would like to thank all those who entered the competition. We would also like to thank our contest coordinator Sue Wesley for the wonderful job she did organizing the entries and keeping the contest together while we were busy working on this edition. We wouldn't be able to sponsor the contest without Sue's efforts.

For this year's contest we received 769 entries—141 more than last year—from every state in the U.S. except North Dakota, South Dakota and Alaska. (But I hope to receive some entries from those states next year. Hint, hint.) We also received entries from Australia, Bermuda, Canada, Romania, Sweden and Wales. And, as well as diverse locations, the publishing experience of the poets entering our contest ranged from those who were submitting their poetry for the first time to those with page-long lists of publishing credits.

When selecting the three winning poems from the more than 700 entries, we first read each poem for relevance to the topic, accessibility, craft and imagery. For each category the poems received a rating from zero to five with five being the highest. (By far, most poems with a "zero" rating received it in the "relevance to the topic" category.) After each poem was read and scored, the total score for each poem was determined. Then those poems with a total score of 17 or higher moved to the next round of the competition.

These poems were then judged on their creativity and originality. At this step in the competition, the poems went from being judged solely on their attributes to being judged in comparison with other poems. Many of the poems eliminated during this round were technically sound, but weren't unique in their treatment of the topic.

After narrowing the entries further, we spent a couple of days reading the remaining poems out loud to gain a different perspective. Since poetry originates from an oral tradition, we felt this was the truest test of a really good poem. Then, after reading and rereading the entries, we finally narrowed the field to the three poems we felt were the best of the 769 received.

Now, considering that any judge is subject to her own whims and personal taste, we are aware that our choices may not have been the same as other judges. So, if you entered this contest but did not win, don't be discouraged or think your work is not worthy of publication. It just may be that your poem did not connect with us at the time we read it. However, there is always a chance—and submitting your work is nothing if not a game of chance—that your work and the next judge will be a perfect match.

Speaking of "perfect matches," we would like to say congratulations to the winners of the *1998 Poet's Market* Poetry Contest. Following this page are the first-, second-, and third-place poems along with information about the winning poets.

FIRST PLACE
Jason Sibley

Why You Should Consider Poets Civil Servants

We descend through manholes in public places
> *to the private stench of your subconscious and*
> *don't emerge until we've fixed something.*
We sound the alarm to ourselves at 3:00 a.m. and
> *scramble, ink-hoses in hand, to put down the inferno within us.*
We thanklessly arrange letters each day to pile up
> *pleasantly in the mailbox of your mind, delivering you.*
We pull on the skins and feet of frogs, submerging
> *ourselves in a swamp of sleep to recover the*
> *rusting metaphors that fell from a mid-dream collision.*
We strap ourselves to the upper beams of half-built bridges
> *and struggle, wind-tossed, to rivet lives together.*
Midday, we open our lunchboxes to eat the emotions
> *left over from last week's heartbreak and blow cool air*
> *on searing spoonfuls of memory before re-tasting them.*
We provide the School Board with evidence that English can be taught,
> *like circus wires, violin strings, and these power lines*
> *we patch together to heat and illuminate you during storms.*
We defibrillate failing hearts and sometimes,
> *in the line of duty, stop healthy ones.*
We swallow the sewage of your cities and let it churn
> *in our gut until it's recycled as liquid, drinkable art.*
We pave your stress-pocked skull under steaming asphalt images
> *pressed smooth with simile to soothe you.*
You may not realize: we wear our words as brilliant orange and
> *reroute you with these pylon poems not just*
> *for your benefit, but because*
> > *it keeps us alive.*

SECOND PLACE
Julie Ritter

Mother Tongue

Dense, alive, changing
women align like planets
We women who align *the planets*
change 'world' to 'word'
Not a reducing, but a subtle art of quiet expansion.

Light,
born in a quiet home where women had words, but no tongues,
migrates, like stars make their way, through the histories of space,
reaching earth

We translate for old tongues—
those ritually excised, those masterfully muted
by an even quieter barbarism

The sun burns the ground with unpronounced wisdom
The stars shoot sparks of brittle agonies and volumes of desire

We set ourselves to the task of transcribing
We are archivists of fire, hut and reed
We are scriveners of kitchen and garret

If our story is long, it is because it has never been told
and it is long
If our story is angry, it is because it has never been told
and it is angry

Excavate. under mattress, in cupboard, behind the names of men
Extract. the distillation of women: it is truth
Circulate. because words were born to be itinerant
Preserve. so that when this silence is undone,
our science need not be redone.

How does a star that blazes with white extracted fury keep quiet?
How does an ancient bone lie, still, poised, even
with a marrow full of poisoned lead?

And how do we, bridled with this inheritance, call ourselves poet?

We are not poet, but archaeologist
We are not poet, but astronomer

Beverly L. Hamel

A Poet's Role

A poet not an Actor took to the center stage.

He stood in front of a quiet room, the people were still, seated in anticipation,
waiting.

He spoke, his first role that of a painter. The artistry of words that spewed
forth,
became a kaleidoscope of colors.

A musician now as each word turned to melody, altering pitch, cascading in
different
tunes and tones, playing upon ears.

Invisibly a baton waved and a Conductor he became, orchestrating conscious
thoughts,
twirling minds, hypnotizing,

A Magician, for the words like magic

transported to an unknown time and place, spellbound, chanting,

Tales,

Weaving as a Weaver, words, intertwining,

woven as a fine tapestry,

Meshing from line to line,

and Mind to Mind,

Where one leaves off the other begins.

As a Surgeon cutting through to the heart, grafting skin to skin, touching bone
to bone.

A Teacher of all, lastly, for ordinary words, once mundane when alone,

now become noble, scholarly and profound,

leaving something so extraordinary in us all.

JASON SIBLEY was inspired by the *Poet's Market* Poetry Contest to write his first-place poem. "The topic, 'the role of the poet,' stabbed me deeply; it being a challenge, essentially, to justify my existence. So many people see poets as eccentric intellectuals who spend their lives in ivory tower seclusion producing abstract creations for other eccentric intellectuals. I prefer to think of all artists as working-class people who labor to create things which cause each one of us to pause in wonder at, grievance for, and celebration of the world around us. In doing so, they provide a service that is both vital and revitalizing to society. However, what often motivates artists to sit down and work is not a tendency towards altruism but rather an addiction to creativity. To the reader, poetry is light. To the poet, it is food."

Sibley is a marine biologist, originally from Atlanta, who currently lives in San Diego and works for San Diego State University. And, having recently bought *Poet's Market* "on a whim," this is his first attempt at publication.

JULIE RITTER was inspired to write "Mother Tongue" during a women's writing workshop. "One night, Ursula K. Le Guin mentioned she writes while sitting in the dark at her computer. The image was fantastic. It struck me as very futuristic and I wondered about women's writing in both a historical and scientific context. I feel we women writers have a great deal of history to look back upon before we can look ahead."

Ritter is a singer/songwriter from Los Angeles, where she resides with her husband, and has had a lot of success with her music. In fact, her band, Mary's Danish, has appeared on both *Late Night with David Letterman* and *The Tonight Show*. Since the group's break-up, Ritter has released a solo album through Discovery Records and is currently working on music for a new sitcom airing on NBC. Until now, however, she has always been sidetracked from publishing her poetry. "After years of toiling in the world of spoken word, a friend and I have made a pact to get published. We meet every two months, we bring our copies of *Poet's Market* and all our work, and we encourage one another to submit our poems."

BEVERLY L. HAMEL, while killing time in her favorite bookstore, was drawn to a copy of the *1997 Poet's Market*. "Before I had finished the first few pages and saw the contest, my pen took off while my mind dictated. When I wrote 'A Poet's Role,' I envisioned how I am affected by great writers and how I wanted my poetry and words to be meaningful to other people."

Hamel, an independent consultant and freelance writer, had forgotten her dream of writing while moving up the corporate ladder and raising a family. But after being downsized and becoming a mother again at 40-something, Hamel needed to reevaluate her life and decide what she wanted. "I had to start writing again. My works-in-progress include two children's books, an historical novel, a cookbook, greeting cards and reams of poetry. I consider my poetry doodles of my mind because my thoughts invariably fly away into daydream bursts when they should be going in other directions." Hamel also publishes a newsletter for the 18th-century town, Bethania, North Carolina, where she resides with her husband and children.

AAA ANNUAL NATIONAL LITERARY CONTEST; ARIZONA LITERARY MAGAZINE (I), 3509 Shea Blvd., Suite 117-PM, Phoenix AZ 85028-3339, e-mail ggbenn@juno.com, established in 1981, sponsoring organization Arizona Authors' Association, award director Eileen Biven. 42 lines maximum, $5 entry fee, submit between January 1 and May 30. Prizes are $125, $75, $40 and 6 honorable mentions of $10 each. Include SASE with entry for contest results; no material will be returned. Winning entries are published in a special edition of *Arizona Literary Magazine*. Entries must be typed, double-spaced on 8½ × 11 paper. Send SASE for more information and entry rules. Must recent contest winners include Kristi Kajca, Tammy Rosen and Norla Chee (1996). Winners are announced and prizes awarded in October.

‡AKRON POETRY PRIZE (II), The University of Akron Press, 374B Bierce Library, Akron OH 44325-1703, phone (330)972-5342, fax (330)972-6383, e-mail press@uakron.edu, award director Elton Glaser, offers annual award of $500 plus publication. Submissions must be unpublished and may be entered in other contests (with notification of acceptance elsewhere). Submit 60-100 pages maximum, typed, double-spaced, postmarked between May 15 and June 30, with SASE for results. Mss will not be returned. Do not send mss bound or enclosed in covers. Send SASE for guidelines. Entry fee: $15. Deadline: entries are accepted May 15 through June 30 only. Judge for the 1997 prize was Alice Fulton. Winner will be announced in September. Copies of previous winning books may be obtained by contacting UAP or through your local bookstore. The University of Akron Press "is committed to publishing poetry that, as Robert Frost said, 'begins in delight and ends in wisdom.' Books accepted must exhibit three essential qualities: mastery of language, maturity of feeling, and complexity of thought."

‡THE AMY AWARD (IV-Women, form, regional), Guild Hall of East Hampton, 158 Main St., East Hampton NY 11937, phone (516)324-0806, fax (516)324-2722, website http://www.thehamptons.com/guild_hall, established in 1996, director of literary programs Robert Long, offers annual honorarium plus a reading with a well-known poet in the *Writers at Guild Hall* series. Submissions may be entered in other contests. Submit 3 lyric poems of no more than 50 lines each, with name, address and phone on each page. Enclose SASE and bio. Entrants must be women 30 years of age or under residing on Long Island or in the New York metropolitan region. Send SASE for guidelines. Postmark deadline: February 20. Most recent award winner was Alexandra Cordero (1997). Entrants will be notified of winner via their SASE approximately 2 months after contest deadline. Guild Hall is the East End of Long Island's leading cultural center. It hosts, besides major museum, theater, and musical events, the *Writers at Guild Hall* series. Recent readers: Tom Wolfe, Kurt Vonnegut, Joseph Brodsky, Maxine Kumin, Allen Ginsberg, Sharon Olds, John Ashbery, E.L. Doctorow, Eileen Myles and Linda Gregg.

*ANDREAS-GRYPHIUS-PREIS; NIKOLAUS-LENAU-PREIS (II, IV-Foreign Language), Die Künstlergilde e.V., Hafenmarkt 2, D-73728, Esslingen a.N., Germany, phone 0711/3969 01-0. "The prize is given annually to German-speaking authors who are dealing with the particular problems of the German culture in eastern Europe or to the best published literary works (which may be poems) that promote understanding between Germans and eastern Europeans." Prizes awarded: 1 Grand Prize of DM 25,000; 1 prize of DM 7,000. Submissions judged by a 7-member jury. They also sponsor the Nikolaus-Lenau-Preis for German-speaking poets. The prize is named in honor of Nikolaus Lenau, "a poet who facilitated understanding with the people of eastern Europe." The prize of DM 11,000 is awarded for unpublished poems. Write for details.

ARIZONA STATE POETRY SOCIETY ANNUAL CONTEST (I, II, IV), 317 Hackney Ave., Globe AZ 85501, phone (520)425-3639, established in 1967, director Audrey Opitz. Contest for various poetry forms and subjects. Prizes range from $10-75; first, second and third place winners are published in the winter edition of *The Sandcutters*, the group's quarterly publication, and names are listed for honorable mention winners. Contest information available for SASE. Fees vary. Deadline: August 31. "ASPS sponsors a variety of monthly contests for members. Membership is available to anyone anywhere."

ARKANSAS POETRY DAY CONTEST; POETS' ROUNDTABLE OF ARKANSAS (I), over 25 categories, many open to all poets. Brochure available in June; deadline in September; awards given in October. For copy send SASE to Verna Lee Hinegardner, 605 Higdon, Apt. 109, Hot Springs AR 71913.

ARTS RECOGNITION AND TALENT SEARCH (ARTS) (II, IV-Students), National Foundation for Advancement in the Arts, 800 Brickell Ave., Suite 500, Miami FL 33131, phone (305)377-1147, fax (305)377-1149, e-mail nfaa@nfaa.org, established in 1981, award director Laura Padrón. "ARTS is a national program designed to identify, recognize and encourage young people who demonstrate excellence in Dance, Music, Music/ Jazz, Music/Voice, Theater, Visual Arts, Photography and Writing." Offers annual awards of $3,000 (Level 1), $1,500 (Level 2), $1,000 (Level 3), $500 (Level 4) and $100 (Level 5). Submissions may be entered in other contests. Submit up to 6 poems in up to but not more than 10 pgs. Open to high school seniors and young people aged 17 or 18 by or on December 1 of the award year. Send SASE for entry form and guidelines. Entry fee: $25 (June 1 early application deadline), $35 (October 1 regular application deadline). Most recent award winners include Kirsten Noelle Anderson, Katherine Ruth Erb and Parker D. Everett (1997). Winners are announced by December 30 by mail.

*ARVON INTERNATIONAL POETRY COMPETITION (I, II), Kilnhurst, Kilnhurst Rd., Todmorden, Lancashire OL14 6AX England, phone 01706 816582, fax 01706 816359, established in 1980, award director David Pease, jointly sponsored by Duncan Lawrie Limited and *The Observer*. Poems (which may be of any length and previously unpublished) must be in English. First prize is £5,000 ($8,425), and other cash prizes. The competition is biennial. Send SASE for entry form and guidelines. Entry fee: $8. Most recent contest winner was Paul Farley (1995). Judges were Helen Dumore, Jackie Kay and Don Paterson. Though the contest (which raises funds by entry fees) may be better known internationally, the major function of the Arvon Foundation is to offer writing courses at three retreats: at Totleight Barton, Sheepwash, Beaworthy, Devon EX21 5NS, phone 01409 231338; at Lumb Bank, Heptonstall, Hebden Bridge, West Yorkshire HX7 6DF, phone (01422) 843714; and at Moniack Mhor, Teavarran, Kiltarlity, Beauly, Inverness-shire 1V4 7HT, phone (01463) 741675. These are residential programs at attractive country retreats, offered by established writers in subjects such as poetry, playwriting, short fiction, radio drama, and words and music. The tuition is £275 for, typically, 5 days, which includes tuition, food and accommodations, and there is scholarship available from the foundation for those who cannot otherwise afford to attend.

‡"AWKWARD POETRY" COMPETITION (I), Open Space Gallery, 913 Hamilton Blvd., Allentown PA 18101, is a $250 prize plus publication in an anthology for the best "Awkward" poem. "The concept of 'Awkwardology' is that human behavior has become 'Awkward.' Proof of this are such things as the argument of Ebonics (awkward speech in some quarters and the birth of a new language in other quarters), our high divorce rate (awkward relationships) and our rapidly developing technology, which has evolved past our physical facilities (awkward artifacts). 'Awkwardology' is defined as the accepted notion of diminished expectations, controls or originality becoming a new standard. It will offer a way for poets to express the awkwardness that is apparent in society at large (awkward ability or a new language). The idea is to capture a trend in non-comformist approaches to technique, where rawness is evident and manifested in either the language or the way it could be presented on a page. This is not the only criteria; if the poet can justify other ways to creating awkward poems, then, this will be acceptable." Entry fee: $3/poem, $5/set of 3 poems; any additional poems will be $1.50/poem. Deadline: January 15, 1998. Judge will be Julius Vitali, creator of "Awkwardology."

BARNARD NEW WOMEN POETS PRIZE; WOMEN POETS AT BARNARD; BARNARD NEW WOMEN POETS SERIES; BEACON PRESS (IV-Women), Barnard College, 3009 Broadway, New York NY 10027-6598, phone (212)854-3453, director Prof. Claudia Rankine. Women Poets at Barnard holds open competition and annual series. The winner receives an award of $1,000 and publication in the Barnard New Women Poets Series, Beacon Press. The competition is open to any woman poet with a book-length ms who has not yet published a book (exclusive of chapbooks). Deadline: October 15. Send SASE for guidelines.

*BAVARIAN ACADEMY OF FINE ARTS LITERATURE PRIZE (V), Max Joseph-Platz 3, 80539 Munich, Germany. An award of DM 30,000 given annually to an author in the German language, to honor a distinguished literary career—**by nomination only**.

BAY AREA BOOK REVIEWERS ASSOCIATION AWARDS (IV-Regional), 11A Commercial Blvd., Novato CA 94949, phone (415)883-2353, fax (415)883-4280, established in 1981, contact Jon Sharp, offers annual awards which recognize "the best of Northern California (from Fresno north) fiction, poetry, nonfiction, and children's literature." Submissions must be previously published. Submit 3 copies of each book entered. Open to Northern California residents. Send SASE for guidelines. Deadline: December 1. Most recent award winner was Adrienne Rich (1996). They also sponsor the Fred Cody Award, an annual award for lifetime achievement given to a writer who also serves the community, and give, on an irregular basis, awards for outstanding work in translation and publishing.

GEORGE BENNETT FELLOWSHIP (II), Phillips Exeter Academy, 20 Main St., Exeter NH 03833-2460, established in 1968, provides a $6,000 fellowship plus room and board to a writer with a ms in progress. The Fellow's only official duties are to be in residence while the academy is in session and to be available to students interested in writing. The committee favors writers who have not yet published a book-length work with a major publisher. Send SASE for application materials. Telephone calls strongly discouraged. Deadline: December 1. Most recent award winners include Brian Richards (1996-1997) and Richard Strand (1995-1996).

THE SUBJECT INDEX, located before the General Index, can help you select markets for your work. It lists those publishers whose poetry interests are specialized.

BEST OF OHIO WRITERS WRITING CONTEST (IV-Regional), Ohio Writer Magazine, P.O. Box 91801, Cleveland OH 44101, award director Linda Rome, offers annual contest for poetry, fiction, creative nonfiction, and children's fiction plus special categories for students grades 7-9 and 10-12. Prizes: $100 first prize, $50 second prize, $25 third prize, plus publication in a special edition of *Ohio Writer*. Submit up to 3 typed poems, no more than 2 pages each. Open to Ohio residents only. "Entries will be judged anonymously, so please do not put name or other identification on manuscript. Attach a 3×5 card with name, address, city, state, zip, and day and evening phone number. Manuscripts will not be returned." Entry fee: $5 for subscribers, $10 for nonsubscribers. (With $10 entry fee, you will receive subscription to *Ohio Writer*.) Deadline: June 30. Most recent contest winner was Nancy Bonnell-Kangas (1996). Judges were M.J. Abell, Robert Miltner, Linda Rome and Tricia Springstubb. Winners will be announced in the September/October issue of *Ohio Writer*. (See listing for *Ohio Writer* in Publications Useful to Poets.)

‡***BLUE NOSE POETRY POETS-OF-THE-YEAR COMPETITION (II)**, Blue Nose Poetry, 61 Athelstan House, Homerton Rd., Hackney, London E9 5PH United Kingdom, established in 1988, offers annual contest. £1,000 in prize money will be distributed at the discretion of the judges (none of the winners will receive less than £100) plus publication in an anthology. Submit up to 6 mss of 10 pages each of no more than 40 lines/page. Include SASE for winners list. Poems may have been previously published in a magazine or journal, but *not* in a collection or anthology. Pages should be consecutively numbered and stapled together in the top left-hand corner. Send SASE for entry form and guidelines. Entry fee: £6 sterling. Make checks payable to Blue Nose Poets. Postmark deadline: April 30. Most recent contest or award winner was Gordon Mason for *Stone Circle* (1995-1996). Judges were Martyn Crucefix, Sue Hubbard and Mario Petrucci. Winners will be announced in September.

‡**BLUESTEM PRESS AWARD (II)**, Bluestem Press, Emporia State University, English Dept., Box 4019, Emporia State University, Emporia KS 66801-5087, phone (316)341-5216, fax (316)341-5547, established in 1989, award director Jeff Thomson, offers annual award of $1,000 and publication for an original book-length collection of poems. Submissions must be unpublished and may be entered in other contests (with notification). Submit at least 48 pages on any subject in any form. Send SASE for guidelines. Entry fee: $15. Deadline: March 2, 1998. Most recent contest or award winner was Lesley Dauer (1996). Judge was Jonathan Holden. Winner will be announced by mail in July or August of 1998. Copies of previous winning poems or books may be obtained by contacting the Bluestem Press at the above number. Enter early to avoid entering after the deadline. Also, looking at the different winners from past years would help. Manuscripts will *not* be accepted after the deadline.

***THE BOARDMAN TASKER AWARD (IV-Specialized: mountain literature)**, The Boardman Tasker Memorial Trust, 14 Pine Lodge, Dairyground Rd., Bramhall, Stockport, Cheshire SK7 2HS United Kingdom, established in 1983, secretary Dorothy Boardman, offers prize of £2,000 to "the author or authors of the best literary work, whether fiction, nonfiction, drama or poetry, the central theme of which is concerned with the mountain environment. Entries for consideration may have been written by authors of any nationality but the work must be published or distributed in the United Kingdom between November 1, 1997 and October 31, 1998. (If not published in the U.K., please indicate name of distributor.) The work must be written or have been translated into the English language." Submit ms in book format. "In a collection of essays or articles by a single author, the inclusion of some material previously published but now in book form for the first time will be acceptable." Submissions accepted from the publisher only. Four copies of entry must be submitted with application. Deadline: August 1, 1998. Most recent winner was *Portrait of Leni Riefenstahl* by Audrey Salkeld, published by Jonathan Cape (1996).

BOLLINGEN PRIZE (V), Beinecke Rare Book and Manuscript Library, Yale University, P.O. Box 208240, New Haven CT 06520-8240, a biennial prize of $25,000 to an American poet for the best poetry collection published during the previous two years, or for a body of published poetry written over several years. **By nomination only.** "All books of poetry by American poets published during the two-year period are automatically considered." Judges change biennially. Prize awarded in January of odd-numbered years.

♣**BP NICHOL CHAPBOOK AWARD (IV-Regional)**, 316 Dupont St., Toronto, Ontario M5R 1V9 Canada, phone (416)964-7919, fax (416)964-6941, established in 1985, $1,000 (Canadian) prize for the best poetry chapbook (10-48 pgs.) in English published in Canada in the preceding year. Submit 3 copies (not returnable). Deadline: March 31.

BUCKNELL SEMINAR FOR YOUNGER POETS; STADLER SEMESTER FOR YOUNGER POETS; PHILIP ROTH RESIDENCE IN CREATIVE WRITING (IV-Students), Bucknell University, Lewisburg PA 17837, phone (717)524-1853, director Cynthia Hogue, includes the Stadler Semester for Younger Poets, the Seminar for Younger Poets and the Poet-in-Residence Series. The Stadler Semester is distinctive in allowing undergraduate poets almost four months of concentrated work centered in poetry. Guided by practicing poets, the apprentice will write and read poetry and will receive critical response. The two Fellows selected will work with Bucknell's writing faculty. The visiting Poet-in-Residence also will participate in the program. Fellows will earn a semester of academic credit by taking four units of study: a tutorial or individual project with a mentor poet, a poetry-writing workshop, a literature course, and an elective. Undergraduates from four-year colleges with at least one course in poetry writing are eligible to apply; most applicants will be second-semester juniors. Send a 10- to 12-page portfolio and a letter of presentation (a brief autobiography that expresses commitment to writing poetry, cites relevant courses and lists any publications). Also include a transcript, two recommendations (at least one from a poetry-writing instructor), and a letter from the academic dean granting permission for the student to attend Bucknell for a semester. Application deadline for the Stadler Semester is November 1. Students chosen for the fellowships will be notified by November 25. The Bucknell Seminar For Younger Poets is not a contest for poems but for 10 fellowships to the Bucknell Seminar, held for 4 weeks in June every year. Seniors and juniors from American colleges are eligible to compete for the 10 fellowships, which consist of tuition, room, board and spaces for writing. Application deadline for each year's seminar is March 1. Students chosen for fellowships will be notified by April 8. Please write for details. The Philip Roth Residence in Creative Writing, established in 1993, awards a residence in the Fall Semester for poets in even-numbered years and for fiction writers in odd-numbered years. Submit 15 pages of poetry on any subject, in any form. Open to residents of the US, over 21 years of age, not presently a student in a college or university. Some record of publication is expected. Send SASE for guidelines. Deadline: March 1 of even-numbered year. Most recent award winner was Joe Wenderoth (1996). Winner will be notified by letter April 15.

THE BUNTING FELLOWSHIP PROGRAM (IV-Women), Bunting Institute, Radcliffe College, 34 Concord Ave., Cambridge MA 02138, fax (617)495-8136, e-mail bunting_fellowships@radcliffe.harvard.edu, website http://www.radcliffe.edu/bunting, established in 1960, supports women of exceptional promise and demonstrated accomplishment who want to pursue independent study in the creative arts in a multidisciplinary setting. The stipend is $33,000 for a fellowship period, September 15 through August 15, and requires residence in the Boston area. Awards 6-10 fellowships. Applicants in creative arts should be at the equivalent stage in their careers as women who have received doctorates two years before applying. Send SASE for guidelines or obtain via e-mail or website. Deadline: October 15.

CALIFORNIA BOOK AWARDS OF THE COMMONWEALTH CLUB OF CALIFORNIA (IV-Regional), 595 Market St., San Francisco CA 94105, phone (415)597-6700, fax (415)597-6729, website http://www.sfgate.com/~common, established in 1931, award director Michael Brassington, annual awards "consisting of not more than two gold and eight silver medals" for books of "exceptional literary merit" in poetry, fiction and nonfiction (including work related to California and work for children), plus 2 "outstanding" categories. Submissions must be previously published. Submit at least 3 copies of each book entered with an official entry form. (Books may be submitted by author or publisher.) Open to books, published during the year prior to the contest, whose author "must have been a legal resident of California at the time the manuscript was submitted for publication." Send SASE for entry form and guidelines or obtain via website. Most recent award winners were August Kleinzahler and Thomas Centolella (1995).

CALIFORNIA WRITERS' ROUNDTABLE POETRY CONTEST (I), under the auspices of the Los Angeles Chapter, Women's National Book Association, 11684 Ventura Blvd., Suite 807, Studio City CA 91604-2613, phone (818)789-9175, chairman Lou Carter Keay. Annual contest with $50, $25 and $10 cash prizes for unpublished poems on any subject, in various forms, not more than 42 lines in length. Open to poets in any state or country. WNBA members may submit free; nonmembers pay $3/poem entry fee. Send SASE for guidelines. Deadline: September 30.

✤CANADIAN AUTHORS ASSOCIATION LITERARY AWARDS; THE AIR CANADA AWARD (V); CANADIAN AUTHORS ASSOCIATION (IV-Regional), Box 419, Campbellford, Ontario K0L 1L0 Canada, phone (705)653-0323, fax (705)653-0593, e-mail canauth@redden.on.ca. Canadian Authors Association Literary Awards provides $5,000 and a silver medal in each of 4 categories (fiction, poetry, nonfiction, drama) to Canadian writers, for a published book in the year of publication (or, in the case of drama, first produced), deadline December 15. Nominations may be made by authors, publishers, agents or others. The Air Canada Award is an annual award of two tickets to any Air Canada destination, to a Canadian author, published or unpublished, under 30 who shows the most promise. **Nominations are made before April 30 by Canadian Authors Association branches or other writers' organizations** and the award is given at the CAA banquet in June.

CAPRICORN POETRY AWARD (II); OPEN VOICE AWARDS (I, II); THE WRITER'S VOICE, Writer's Voice, 5 W. 63rd St., New York NY 10023, phone (212)875-4124, e-mail wtrsvoice@aol.com, website http://aol.users.com/wtrsvoice/files/WVintro.html. Capricorn Poetry Award, a cash prize of $1,000 and a reading at The Writer's Voice, limited to writers over 40. $15 entry fee. Deadline: December 31. Send SASE for application guidelines. Open Voice Awards, annual awards, $500 honorarium and a reading at The Writer's Voice, open to both published and unpublished poets who have not previously read at The Writer's Voice. $10 entry fee. Deadline: December 31. Send SASE for application form. "Write 'Genre' on the envelope." The Writer's Voice is a literary center sponsoring weekly readings, writing workshops, writing awards and other activities.

‡**CENTER FOR BOOK ARTS' ANNUAL POETRY CHAPBOOK COMPETITION (II)**, 626 Broadway, 5th Floor, New York NY 10012, phone (212)460-9768, e-mail bookarts@pipeline.com, established in 1995, award director Sharon Dolin, offers $500 cash prize, a $500 reading honorarium and publication of winning manuscript in a limited edition letterpress printed and handbound chapbook. Submissions may be entered in other contests. Submit no more than 500 lines on any subject, in any form. Mss must be typed on one side of 8½ × 11 paper. Send SASE for guidelines. Entry fee: $10/ms. Postmark deadline: December 31. Most recent contest winner was Andrew Kaufman (1996). Judges were Sharon Dolin and William Matthews. Judges for upcoming contest will be Sharon Dolin and Mark Doty. Winner will be contacted mid-April by telephone. Each contestant receives a letter announcing the winner. Copies of previous winning books may be obtained by sending $25. Reading fee is credited toward the purchase of the winning chapbook. "Center for Book Arts is a non-profit organization dedicated to the traditional crafts of bookmaking and contemporary interpretations of the book as an art object. Through the Center's Education, Exhibition and Workspace Programs we ensure that the ancient craft of the book remains a viable and vital part of our civilization."

CHICANO/LATINO LITERARY CONTEST (II), Dept. of Spanish & Portuguese, University of California-Irvine, Irvine CA 92697, established in 1974, contest director Prof. Alejandro Morales, is an annual contest focusing on 1 of 4 genres each year: drama (1998), novel (1999), short story (2000), poetry (2001). Prizes: First, $1,000, publication and transportation to Irvine to receive the award; second, $500; and third, $250. Work may be in English or Spanish. Only one entry/author. Open to US citizens or permanent residents of the US. Send SASE for guidelines. Deadline: April 30. Most recent contest winner was Mike Padilla. Judge was Axel Ramirez. Winners will be notified by letter by October 30. Prizes will be awarded during a ceremony in November.

CINTAS FELLOWSHIP PROGRAM (IV-Regional), Arts International, Institute of International Education, 809 United Nations Plaza, New York NY 10017, makes awards of $10,000 to professional visual artists of Cuban lineage living outside of Cuba. Call (212)984-5370, for applications and guidelines. Deadline for applications: May 15.

COLORADO BOOK AWARDS (IV-Regional), Colorado Center for The Book, 2123 Downing, Denver CO 80205, phone (303)839-8320, fax (303)839-8319, e-mail 103332.1376@compuserve.com, website http://www.aclin.org/~ccftb, award director Suzan Moore, offers annual award of $500 plus promotion for books published in November or December of the year prior to the award or published anytime during the year of the award. Submissions may be entered in other contests. Submit 6 copies of each book entered. Open to residents of Colorado. Send SASE for entry form and guidelines or obtain via e-mail or website. Entry fee: $30. Deadline: December 31. Winner will be announced at a ceremony/dinner in April. "We are a nonprofit organization affiliated with the Library of Congress Center for The Book. We promote books and reading. We annually sponsor the Rocky Mountain Book Festival which attracts 40,000 people. It's free and includes 300 authors from throughout the country. We are located in the home of Thomas Hornsby Ferril, Colorado's former poet laureate. This historic home is used as a literary center and a tribute to Ferril's life and work."

INA COOLBRITH CIRCLE ANNUAL POETRY CONTEST (IV-Regional), 2712 Oak Rd., #54, Walnut Creek CA 94596, treasurer Audrey Allison, has prizes of $10-50 in each of several categories for California residents and out-of-state members only. Three poems per contestant, but no more than 1 poem in any one category. Poems submitted in 2 copies, include name, address, phone number and member status on 1 copy only. Enclose a 3×5 card with name, address, phone number, category, title, first line of poem and status as member or nonmember. Members of the Ina Coolbrith Circle pay no fee; others pay $5 for 3 poems (limit 3). Send SASE for details. Deadline is August.

ABBIE M. COPPS POETRY COMPETITION; GARFIELD LAKE REVIEW (I, II), Dept. of Humanities, Olivet College, Olivet MI 49076, phone (616)749-7683, established in 1965, contest chairperson Linda Jo Scott. Annual contest awarding $150 prize and publication in the *Garfield Lake Review*. $2/poem entry fee for unpublished poem up to 100 lines. Submit unsigned, typed poem, entrance fee, and name, address and phone number in a sealed envelope with the first line of the poem on the outside. Deadline: February 1.

CREATIVE ARTIST GRANTS (IV-Regional), Cultural Arts Council of Houston/Harris County, 3201 Allen Parkway, Houston TX 77019, phone (713)527-9330. Offers awards to Houston visual artists, writers, choreographers and composers selected through an annual competition. The program also offers Artist Project and Visual Arts Travel grants. Write for deadline date, application forms and guidelines.

CREATIVE WRITING FELLOWSHIPS IN POETRY (II, IV-Regional), Arizona Commission on the Arts, 417 W. Roosevelt St., Phoenix AZ 85003, phone (602)255-5882, fax (602)256-0282, e-mail artscomm@primenet.com, website http://www.state.az.us/azarts, literature director Jill Bernstein, offers biennial prizes of $5,000-7,500. Poetry fellowships awarded in odd-numbered years. Submissions can be previously published or unpublished, and can be entered in other contests. Submit 10 pgs. maximum on any subject. Open to Arizona residents over 18 years old. Send SASE for entry form or request via e-mail. Entry deadline is in September of the year prior to the award.

CRUMB ELBOW PUBLISHING POETRY CONTESTS (I, IV-Themes), P.O. Box 294, Rhododendron OR 97049, phone (503)622-4798, established in 1996, award director Michael P. Jones, offers annual awards of publication and copies, "for both established poets and beginners to introduce their work to new audiences by having their work published in a collection of poetry." Crumb Elbow sponsors 7 contests all having different themes. They are the Scarecrow Poetry Harvest Contest (deadline August 1), Old Traditions & New Festivities: Winter Holiday Poetry Contest (deadline October 1), Natural Enchantment: Henry David Thoreau Poetry Contest (deadline February 1), Centuries of Journeys: History & Folk Traditions Poetry Contest (deadline April 1), Onward to the New Eden! Oregon Trail Poetry Contest (deadline January 1), Westward! Historic Trails Poetry Contest (deadline November 1), and Beyond the Shadows: Social Justice Poetry Contest (deadline June 1). Submissions may be entered in other contests. Submit at least 3 poems or verses. All submissions should be typed and accompanied by SASE. Send SASE for entry form and guidelines. Entry fees range from $2 for 3 poems to $15 for 22-30 poems. The award director says, "Have fun with your creativity. Explore with your words and don't be afraid of themes or to try something different." Crumb Elbow also publishes *The Final Edition* and *Wy'East Historical Journal*. Write for more information.

DALY CITY POETRY AND SHORT STORY CONTEST (I), Serramonte Library, 40 Wembley Dr., Daly City CA 94015, established in 1981. Contest held annually, awarding prizes of $40, $25, $20, $15 and $10 in various categories and $5 for honorable mention. All winners also receive certificates. Entry fee: $1/poem or $2/story. Stories must be unpublished. Send SASE for rules; attn: Ruth Hoppin, coordinator. Contest opens September 1. Postmark deadline: January 15.

‡DANA AWARD IN POETRY (I), 7207 Townsend Forest Ct., Browns Summit NC 27214, phone (910)656-7009, established in 1996, award director Mary Elizabeth Parker, offers annual award of $500 for the best group of 5 poems. Submissions must be unpublished and may be entered in other contests. Submit 5 poems on any subject, in any form; no light verse. Include SASE for winners list. No mss will be returned. Include a separate cover sheet with name, address, phone and title(s) of poem(s). Send SASE for guidelines. Entry fee: $10 for up to 5 poems. Postmark deadline: October 31. Most recent award winner was Tina Chang (1996). Judges were Christine Garren and Eve Shelnutt. Winner will be announced in January.

‡DANCING POETRY CONTEST (II), Artists Embassy International, 704 Brigham Ave., Santa Rosa CA 95404, established in 1993, award director Judy Hardin Cheung. Annual contest awarding three Grand prizes, five first prizes of $25, ten second prizes of $10, twenty third prizes of certificates. The 3 Grand prize winning poems will be danced, choreographed, costumed, premiered and videotaped at the annual Dancing Poetry Festival at Lincoln University, San Francisco (prize valued at more than $1,000). Submissions must be unpublished and may be entered in other contests. Submit 2 copies of any number of poems, 40 lines maximum (each), with name, address, phone on one copy only. Include SASE for winners list. Send SASE for entry form. Entry fee: $5/poem or $10/3 poems. Deadline: June 1. Judges for upcoming contest will be Natica Angelly's Poetic Dance Theater and various members of Artists Embassy International. Artist Embassy International has been a non-profit educational art organization since 1951, "Furthering intercultural understanding and peace through the universal language of the arts."

‡THE DOROTHY DANIELS ANNUAL HONORARY WRITING AWARD (I, II), The National League of American Pen Women, Inc.—Simi Valley Branch, P.O. Box 1485, Simi Valley CA 93062, established in 1980, award director Diane Reicheck. Annual award with first prize of $100 in each category: poetry, fiction, nonfiction. Submissions must be unpublished. Submit any number of poems on any subject in free verse or traditional. Manuscript must not include name and address. Include cover letter with name and address and poem titles. Poem must be titled and typed on 8½×11 white paper, single spaced and one poem per page. Send SASE for guidelines. Entry fee: $3/poem. Deadline: July 30. Most recent award winner was Donna Jean Tennis (1996). Judges were 3 poets from their Pen Women branch. Send SASE for winners list; announced by mail on or before November 1. The National League of American Pen Women, a non-profit organization headquartered in Washington, DC, was established in 1897 and has a membership of more than 6,000 professional writers, artists and composers. The Simi Valley Branch, of which noted novelists Dorothy Daniels and Elizabeth Forsythe Hailey are Honorary Members, was founded in 1977. "Request rules and follow them carefully—always include SASE."

BILLEE MURRAY DENNY POETRY AWARD (II), % Janet Overton, Lincoln College, 300 Keokuk St., Lincoln IL 62656, established in 1981. Annual award with prizes of $1,000, $500 and $250. Open to poets who have not previously published a book of poetry with a commercial or university press (except for chapbooks with a circulation of less than 250). Enter up to 3 poems, 100 lines/poem or less at $10/poem. (Make checks payable to Poetry Contest—Lincoln College.) Poems may be on any subject, using any style, but may not contain "any vulgar, obscene, suggestive or offensive word or phrase." Winning poems are published in *The Denny Poems*, a biennial anthology, available for $5 from Lincoln College. Send SASE for entry form. Postmark deadline: May 31. Most recent award winner was Molly Fink (1996).

MILTON DORFMAN NATIONAL POETRY PRIZE (II), % Rome Art & Community Center, 308 W. Bloomfield St., Rome NY 13440. Annual award for unpublished poetry. Prizes: $500, $200 and $100. Entry fee:

$3/poem (American funds only; $10 returned check penalty); make checks payable to: Rome Art & Community Center. Contest opens July 1. Deadline: November 1. Include name, address and phone number on each entry. Poems are printed in Center's Newsletter. Most recent winners for 1996 were: Mark Niakels, first place; Jay Rogoff second place; and Louise Kennelly, third place. Judge was Joellen Kwiatek. The judge for the upcoming award will be Sabra Loomis. Winners are notified by December 1. Send SASE for results.

‡*T.S. ELIOT PRIZE (V), The Poetry Book Society, Book House, 45 East Hill, London SW18 2Q2 United Kingdom, phone (0181)870 8403, fax (0181)877 1615, established in 1993, award director Clare Brown, offers annual award for the best poetry collection published in the UK/Republic of Ireland each year. Prize is £5000 (donated by Mrs. Valerie Eliot) and "winning book is bound in Moroccan leather." Submissions must be previously published. Book/ms must be submitted by publisher and have been published (or scheduled to be published) the year of the contest. Deadline: end of August. Send SASE for entry form and guidelines. Most recent contest winner was Les Murray (1996). Winners will be announced in January.

‡T.S. ELIOT PRIZE FOR POETRY; THOMAS JEFFERSON UNIVERSITY PRESS (II), MC111L 100 E. Normal, Kirksville MO 63501-4221, phone (816)785-7299, fax (816)785-4181, e-mail poetry@tjup.truman.edu, website http://www.truman.edu/tjup/, established in 1996, offers annual award of $1,500, publication and 10 copies first prize. All entrants will receive a copy of the winning book. Submit 64-96 pages, include 2 title pages, 1 with name, address, phone and ms title; the other with only the title. Individual poems may have been previously published in periodicals or anthologies, but the collection must not have been published as a book. Include SASE if you wish acknowledgement of receipt of your ms. Mss will not be returned. Send SASE for guidelines. Entry fee: $25. Deadline: October 31. Include an additional SASE to be notified the following January of the results. Thomas Jefferson University Press also publishes critical books about poetry or poets.

EMERGING LESBIAN WRITERS AWARD (IV-Lesbian), Astraea National Lesbian Action Foundation, 116 E. 16th St., New York NY 10003, phone (212)529-8021, fax (212)982-3321, e-mail anlaf@aol.com, website http://www.imageinc.com/astraea/, associate director Di Eckerle, offers an annual award of $10,000 to "support the work of emerging lesbian writers, and to acknowledge the contributions of established lesbian writers to our movement and culture." Submissions must be previously published and may be entered in other contests. Submit 10-15 pgs. of collated poetry. "You may only submit in one category (fiction or poetry) per year." Open to US residents who have published "at least one piece of writing (in any genre) in a newspaper, magazine, journal or anthology; but not more than one book." Submit 3 copies of ms with completed cover sheet and 1-paragraph bio. Send SASE for entry form and guidelines. Entry fee: $5. Deadline: March 8. Most recent award winners include Pamela Crow and Adrian Oktenberg. Applications are judged by a panel of lesbian writers who remain anonymous until after the competition. Applicants are notified by mail after June 30.

FLORIDA INDIVIDUAL ARTIST FELLOWSHIPS (II, IV-Regional), Florida Division of Cultural Affairs, Dept. of State, The Capitol, Tallahassee FL 32399-0250, phone (904)487-2980, annually offers an undetermined number of fellowships in the amount of $5,000 each. "The Individual Artist Fellowship Program is designed to recognize practicing professional creative artists residing in Florida through monetary fellowship awards. The program provides support for artists of exceptional talent and demonstrated ability to improve their artistic skills and enhance their careers. Fellowships may be awarded in the following discipline categories: dance, folk arts, interdisciplinary, literature, media arts, music, theatre and visual arts and crafts." Submissions can be previously published or unpublished. Submit 3-5 representative poems, single or double-spaced. "Reproductions of published work may not be submitted in published format. Open to Florida residents of at least 18 years of age who are not enrolled in undergraduate or graduate programs. Eight copies of the work sample must be included with 8 copies of the application form. Write for entry form and guidelines. Deadline: January 24.

‡FLORIDA INTERNATIONAL UNIVERSITY POETRY COMPETITION (II, V), Florida International University Library, Tamiami Trail At-136, Miami FL 33199, phone (305)348-2461, fax (305)348-3408, established in 1992, executive director of libraries Dr. Laurence Miller, offers annual contest with the winning journal and poet receiving $1,000. Submissions must be previously published and may be entered in other contests. North American poetry journals are to submit 1 poem published during 1997-1998 and 2 copies of the journal in which it appeared. Send SASE for guidelines. Postmark deadline: March 15. Most recent contest winners were Debora Gregor and *Gettysburg Review* (1995); Heather McHugh and *Jacaranda Review* (1995). Judges were Carolyn Forché and Les Standiford. Winner(s) will be announced at the Miami Book Fair International in November. See F.I.U.'s listing for *Gulf Stream Magazine* in the Publishers of Poetry section.

---

‡ **THE DOUBLE DAGGER** before a listing indicates that the listing is new in this edition. New markets are often the most receptive to submissions.

FOSTER CITY INTERNATIONAL WRITERS' CONTEST (II), Foster City Arts & Culture Committee, 650 Shell Blvd., Foster City CA 94404. Yearly competition for previously unpublished work. $10 entry fee. Awards $250 each first prize for rhymed and blank verse and $125 for each honorable mention. Send SASE for instructions. Deadline: November 1. Awards announced January 15.

*FRIENDS OF DOG WATCH OPEN POETRY COMPETITION (I), 267 Hillbury Rd., Warlingham, Surrey CR6 9TL England, phone 01883-622121, contact Michaela Edridge. Annual competition for poems up to 40 lines. Cash prizes. Entry fees: £2/poem. Contest information available for SASE (or SAE and IRCs). Deadline: November 1.

‡GARDEN STREET PRESS POETRY CONTEST (II), Garden Street Press, P.O. Box 1231, Truro MA 02666-1231, phone (508)349-1991, established in 1993, editor/publisher Naomi Chase, offers annual contest. awarding publication, royalties of 15% (after first 500 sales), or 100 copies out of a press run of 1,000. Submissions may be entered in other contests. Submit 48-68 pages, include acknowledgments of previously published poems, name, address and phone on separate page, author bio and SASE for return of ms. Entry fee: $15. Reads entries January through June 30 only.

‡GRANDMOTHER EARTH NATIONAL AWARD (II), Grandmother Earth Creations, 8463 Deerfield, Germantown TN 38138, phone (901)758-0804, fax (901)757-0506 (call first), established in 1994, award director Frances Cowden, offers annual award of $1,000 with varying distributions each year. (1997: $200 first, $100 second, $75 third, $50 fourth) with a minimum of seven $50 awards, plus publication in anthology. Submissions may be entered in other contests. Submit at least 3 poems, any subject, in any form. Include SASE for winners list. Send 2 copies with name and address on one copy and on a 3×5 card. Send SASE for guidelines. Entry fee: $10/3 poems, $2 each additional poem. Entry fee includes a copy of the anthology. Deadline: July 15. Most recent award winner was Pat Benjamin (1996). Judge was Andrea Hollander Budy. Winner will be announced on October 1 at the Mid-South Poetry Festival in Memphis. Copies of previous winning poems or books may be obtained by writing the above address. "Our contest anthology offers optional publication for non-winning entries. Each year the price of our publication goes down and quality goes up."

GREAT LAKES COLLEGES ASSOCIATION NEW WRITERS AWARD (II), GLCA, The Philadelphia Center, North American Bldg., 121 S. Broad St., 7th Floor, Philadelphia PA 19107-4577, phone (215)735-7300, fax (215)735-7373, director Mark Andrew Clark, Ph.D., offers annual award to "the best first book of poetry and the best first book of fiction among those **submitted by publishers**. The winning authors tour several of the Great Lakes Colleges reading, lecturing, visiting classes, doing workshops, and publicizing their books. Each writer receives an honorarium of at least $300 from each college visited, as well as travel expenses, hotel accommodations, and hospitality. Usually, one winner (fiction) tours in the fall, and the other winner (poetry) tours in the spring, following the competition." Submissions must be previously published. Submit 4 copies of galleys or the printed book plus a statement stating author's agreement to commit to the college tour. Send SASE for guidelines. Deadline: February 28. Most recent award winners were *Old & New Testaments* (poetry) by Lynn Powell (1996) (published by The University of Wisconsin Press) and *Dangerous Men* (fiction) by Geoffrey Becher (1996) (published by University of Pittsburgh Press).

GREEN RIVER WRITERS' CONTESTS (I, IV-Themes, forms), 1043 Thornfield Lane, Cincinnati OH 45224, established in 1991, contact contest chairman, offers 9 contests for poetry on various themes and in various forms. Entry fees range from $5-8 for nonmembers, prizes range from $5-150. Send SASE for rules. Deadline: October 31. Most recent contest winners include June Owens, Donna Jean Tennis and Martha Ralph.

GROLIER POETRY PRIZE; ELLEN LA FORGE MEMORIAL POETRY FOUNDATION, INC. (II), 6 Plympton St., Cambridge MA 02138, phone (617)547-4230, established in 1974, award director Louisa Solano. The Grolier Poetry Prize is open to all poets who have not published either a vanity, small press, trade or chapbook of poetry. Two poets receive an honorarium of $150 each. Up to 4 poems by each winner and 1-2 by each of 4 runners-up are chosen for publication in the *Grolier Poetry Prize Annual*. Opens January 15 of each year; deadline May 1. Submissions must be unpublished and may not be submitted in other contests. Submit up to 5 poems, not more than 10 double-spaced pages. Submit one ms in duplicate, without name of poet. On a separate sheet give name, address, phone number and titles of poems. Only 1 submission/contestant; mss are not returned. $6 entry fee includes copy of *Annual*, checks payable to the Ellen La Forge Memorial Poetry Foundation, Inc. Enclose self-addressed stamped postcard if acknowledgement of receipt is required. For update of rules, send SASE to Ellen La Forge Memorial Poetry Foundation before submitting mss. Most recent award winners include Jane Liv, Stephen Burt and Ann Keniston. The Ellen La Forge Memorial Poetry Foundation sponsors intercollegiate poetry readings and a reading series, generally 10/semester, held on the grounds of Harvard University. These are generally poets who have new collections of poetry available for sale at the Grolier Poetry Book Shop, Inc., which donates money toward costs (such as rental of the auditorium). They pay poets honoraria from $100-400 and occasionally provide overnight accommodations (but not transportation). Such poets as Mark Strand, Philip Levine, Robin Becker, Donald Hall and Brigit Pegeen Kelly have given readings under their auspices. The small foundation depends upon private gifts and support for its activities.

GUGGENHEIM FELLOWSHIPS (II), John Simon Guggenheim Memorial Foundation, 90 Park Ave., New York NY 10016, phone (212)687-4470, fax (212)697-3248, e-mail fellowships@gf.org, website http://www.gf.org. Approximately 158 Guggenheims are awarded each year to persons who have already demonstrated exceptional capacity for productive scholarship or exceptional creative ability in the arts. The amounts of the grants vary. The average grant is about $28,480. Most recent award winners were Agha Shahid Ali, Lucie Brock-Broido, David Ferry, Susan Howe, Mark Rudman and Robert Wrigley (1996). Application deadline: October 1.

HACKNEY LITERARY AWARDS; BIRMINGHAM-SOUTHERN COLLEGE WRITER'S CONFERENCE (II), Birmingham-Southern College, Box 549003, Birmingham AL 35254. This competition, sponsored by the Cecil Hackney family since 1969, offers $4,000 in prizes for novels, poetry and short stories as part of the annual Birmingham-Southern Writer's Conference. Novels postmarked by September 30. Poems and short stories must be postmarked by December 31. Send SASE for Hackney guidelines. Winners are announced at the conference, which is held in the spring. (Also see Writing Today in Conferences and Workshops.)

‡J.C. AND RUTH HALL FELLOWSHIP; THE DIANE MIDDLEBROOK FELLOWSHIP IN POETRY (IV-Specialized: MFA or equivalent degree in creative writing), Wisconsin Institute for Creative Writing, 7162 White Hall, 600 North Park St., Madison WI 53706, phone (608)263-3374, established in 1986, award director Jesse Lee Kercheval. Annual fellowships will pay $20,000 for one academic year. Applicants will teach one creative writing class per semester at U. of Wisconsin and give a public reading at the end of their stay. Submissions may be entered in other contests. Submit 10 poems maximum on any subject in any form. Applicants must have an MFA or equivalent degree in creative writing. Applicants cannot have published a book (chapbooks will not disqualify an applicant). Send SASE for guidelines. Deadline: last day of February. Most recent winner was Anne Caston (1996). Judges were faculty of creative writing program. Results will be sent to applicants by May 1. Winners announced in *Poets & Writers* and *AWP Chronicle*. "The Halls fellowships are administered by the Program in Creative Writing at the University of Wisconsin-Madison. Funding is provided by the Jay C. and Ruth Halls Writing Fund and the Carl Djerassi and Diane Middlebrook Fund through the University of Wisconsin Foundation."

THE HODDER FELLOWSHIP (II), The Council of the Humanities, 122 E. Pyne, Princeton University, Princeton NJ 08544, phone (609)258-4713, e-mail humcounc@princeton.edu, is awarded for the pursuit of independent work in the humanities. The recipient is usually a writer or scholar in the early stages of a career with one or two published books. Preference is given to applicants outside academia. "The Fellowship is designed specifically to identify and nurture extraordinary potential rather than to honor distinguished achievement." **Candidates for the Ph.D. are not eligible.** The Hodder Fellow spends an academic year in residence at Princeton working independently. Applicants must submit a résumé, sample of previous work (10 pgs. maximum, not returnable), a project proposal of 2 to 3 pgs., and SASE. Send SASE for guidelines or request via e-mail. The announcement of the Hodder Fellow is made in February by the President of Princeton University. Deadline: November 15.

HENRY HOYNS FELLOWSHIPS (II), Creative Writing Program, 219 Bryan Hall, University of Virginia, Charlottesville VA 22903, are fellowships in poetry and fiction of varying amounts for candidates for the M.F.A. in creative writing. Sample poems/prose required with application. Deadline: January 15.

‡*ILKLEY LITERATURE FESTIVAL POETRY COMPETITION (II), (formerly The Yorkshire Open Poetry Competition), Ilkley Literature Festival, The Manor House, Ilkley, W. Yorkshire LS29 9DT England, administrator D. Porter. Offers prizes of £250, £150, £75 and 10 prizes of £10 for any style of poetry. Fees are £2.50/poem, £6 for 3. "Please send SAE and IRCs for full details and conditions, before applying." Deadline: September 1.

IRISH AMERICAN CULTURAL INSTITUTE LITERARY AWARDS (IV-Ethnic, foreign language), 1 Lackawanna Place, Morristown NJ 07960, for Irish writers who write in Irish or English, **resident in Ireland,** with published work. A total of $10,000 in prizes awarded every year.

THE JAPAN FOUNDATION ARTIST FELLOWSHIP PROGRAM (IV-Specialized: US residents with Japanese affiliations), The Japan Foundation New York Office, 152 W. 57th St., 39th Floor, New York NY 10019, phone (212)489-0299, fax (212)489-0409, director general Mr. Natsuo Amemiya, offers annual fellowships of 2-6 months in Japan (during the Japanese fiscal year of April 1 through March 31) for "accredited professional writers, musicians, painters, sculptors, stage artists, movie directors, etc." Submissions may be entered in other contests. Open to citizens or permanent residents of the US. "Affiliation with a Japanese artist or institution is required. Three letters of reference, including one from the Japanese affiliate must accompany all applications." Deadline: December 1.

‡JMW PUBLISHING CO. POETRY PRIZE (I), JMW Publishing Co., P.O. Box 912, Blue Springs MO 64013, established in 1988, award director Jim Wyzard, offers annual award of $500 plus recognition in their annual publication, sent to public and private universities. Submissions may be entered in other contests. Submit up to 5 poems of no more than 32 lines in any form, typed, 1 poem/page, name and address on every page. The judge for upcoming award will be Jim Wyzard. Winner will be announced in January by mail. Send SASE for guidelines. Deadline: December 30.

*JOHANN-HEINRICH-VOSS PRIZE FOR TRANSLATION (V), German Academy for Language and Literature, Alexandraweg 23, 64287 Darmstadt, Germany, phone (06151)40920, fax (06151)409299, president Dr. Christian Meier, is an annual award of DM 20,000 for outstanding lifetime achievement for translating into German, **by nomination only**. Most recent award winner was Joachim Kalka (1996).

CHARLES JOHNSON AWARD FOR FICTION AND POETRY (IV-Ethnic, students), English Dept. 4503, Southern Illinois University at Carbondale, Carbondale IL 62901-4503, phone (618)453-5321, e-mail delacruz3@aol.com, award director Ricardo Cortez Cruz, offers annual award "intended to support increased artistic and intellectual growth, plus encourage excellence and diversity in creative writing." Prizes: $500 and a signed copy of a Johnson book will be awarded in each genre. Submissions must be unpublished and may be entered in other contests. Submit 3-5 poems on no more than 6 typed pages. Entries will not be returned. Open to ethnic or minority students in the US or to US students whose work "explores issues of minority/marginalized culture." Send SASE for guidelines or request via e-mail. Postmark deadline: January 28. Recent award winners were Sonia Gomez and Lisa Chen. The judges for upcoming contest will be prominent, nationally-known writers. All winners and finalists will be notified by letter in April. Results will also be announced in the September issue of *AWP Chronicle*. "When submitting, students need to be sure to include full address, phone number, and name of college or university they are attending."

THE CHESTER H. JONES FOUNDATION NATIONAL POETRY COMPETITION (II), P.O. Box 498, Chardon OH 44024, an annual competition for persons in the USA, Canadian and American citizens living abroad. Prizes: $1,000, $750, $500, $250, and $50 honorable mentions. Winning poems plus others called "commendations" are published in an anthology available for $3.50 from the foundation. Submissions must be unpublished. Submit no more than 10 entries, no more than 32 lines each. Send SASE for latest brochure. Entry fee $2 for the first poem, $1 each for others. Deadline: March 31. Distinguished poets serve as judges. 1997 judges were David Baker, John Koethe and Diane Wakoski.

KENTUCKY ARTISTS FELLOWSHIPS (II, IV-Regional), Kentucky Arts Council, 31 Fountain Place, Frankfort KY 40601, phone (502)564-3757, award director Irwin Pickett, offers biennial fellowships of $5,000 to "encourage excellence and assist Kentucky artists in the professional development of their various art forms and careers." Next fellowships awarded in 1998. Fellowship recipients will be selected by a panel of out-of-state professional artists in a "blind jurying" process. Submit 15 pgs. of poetry maximum, 1 poem/page. Open to Kentucky residents who have lived in the state 1 year immediately prior to the fellowship application deadline. Send SASE for entry form (available in July). Deadline: September 15.

"GIORGIO LA PIRA" INTERNATIONAL LITERARY PRIZE (IV-Foreign language), "G. Donati" Study Centre, Piazza S. Francesco, Pistoia 60-51100 Italy, phone (0573)367251, fax (0573)27140, contact Secretary, offers prizes of 1.500.000 lire (first prize), 1.000.000 lire (second prize) and 500.000 lire (third prize). Submit 6 copies each of 3 poems *in Italian*, not more than 40 lines each. Mss are not returned. Send SASE for guidelines. Entry fee: 25.00 lire. Deadline: May 31. Winners must collect prizes in person.

♣THE STEPHEN LEACOCK MEDAL FOR HUMOUR (IV-Humor, regional), Stephen Leacock Associates, P.O. Box 854, Orillia, Ontario L3V 3P4 Canada, phone (705)325-6546, award chairman Mrs. Jean Bradley Dickson, for a book of humor in prose, verse, drama or any book form—by a Canadian citizen. Submit 10 copies of book, 8×10 b&w photo, bio and $25 entry fee. Prize: Silver Leacock Medal for Humour and Laurentian Bank of Canada cash award of $5,000. Deadline: December 31. The 1996 winner was *Letters from the Country* by Marsha Boulton. The committee also publishes *The Newspacket* 3 times/year.

THE LEAGUE OF MINNESOTA POETS CONTEST (I, IV-Students), 1510 S. Seventh St., Brainerd MN 56401, contact Doris Stengel. Offers 20 different contests in a variety of categories and prizes of $5-100 for poems up to 55 lines, fees of $3 to enter all categories for members and $1/category for nonmembers. There is one category for students in grades 7 through 12 and one category for elementary students through grade 6. Send SASE for details. Deadline: July 31. Winners are not published.

‡MCKNIGHT INTERDISCIPLINARY FELLOWSHIP (IV-Regional), Interdmedia Arts, 2822 Lyndale Ave. S., Minneapolis MN 55408, (612)871-4444, fax (612)871-6927, e-mail allstaff@intermediaarts.org, website http://www.intermediaarts.org, established in 1990, award director Sandy Agustin, offers annual award of 5 fellowships of $12,000 and additional funds for an activity with Intermedia Arts. Submissions may be entered in other contests. Submit up to 10 poems on any subject and in any form. Must be Minnesota resident. Send SASE for entry form and guidelines. Deadline: generally in January. Winners will be announced by mail and news release in April. "This fellowship is for interdisciplinary artists, awarding excellence for past interdisciplinary work. Poets entering this should be incorporating their poetry with other disciplines, like visual, performing or media art."

‡**MARIN ARTS COUNCIL INDIVIDUAL ARTIST GRANTS (II, IV-Regional)**, 251 N. San Pedro Rd., San Rafael CA 94903, phone (415)499-8350, established in 1987, grants coordinator Bernadette Deamico, offers biennial grants ranging from $2,000-5,000 to residents of Marin County, CA only. Submissions must have been completed within last 3 years. Submit 10 pgs. on any subject in any form. Open to Marin County residents only—"must have lived in Marin County for one year prior to application, be 18 or over and not in an arts degree program." Send SASE for entry form and guidelines. Winners will be announced 3 months after deadline date. "The Marin Arts Council offers grants to individual artists (living in Marin County) in 13 different categories. Deadlines and categories change each year. Call for more information."

‡**MATURE WOMEN'S GRANTS (IV-Women)**, National League of American Pen Women, 1300 17th St., Washington DC 20036, (717)225-3023, established in 1976, award director Shirley Holden Helberg, offers biennial (even-numbered years) award of $1,000 each for the categories of arts, letters and music. Submit 3 poems. Include SASE for winners list. Open to women over the age of 35 during the calendar year of the award. "Women who enter may never have been a member of the Pen women." Include letter stating age, creative purpose and how you learned of the grant. Send SASE for guidelines during odd-numbered years. Entry fee: $8. Deadline: January 15th of the even-numbered year. Winner will be announced July 15.

MID-LIST PRESS FIRST SERIES AWARD FOR POETRY (I, II), Mid-List Press, 4324 12th Ave. S., Minneapolis MN 55407-3218, phone (612)822-3733, established in 1990, senior editor Lane Stiles. "The First Series Award for Poetry is an annual contest we sponsor for poets who have never published a book of poetry. The award includes publication and an advance against royalties." Individual poems within the book manuscript can be previously published and can be entered in other contests. Submit at least 60 single-spaced pages. "Other than length we have no restrictions, but poets are encouraged to read previous award winners we have published." Recent award winners include Dina Bencher, Neva Hacker, Jeff Worley, Neil Shepard, Douglas Gray, Stephen Behrendt, J.E. Sorrell and Mary Logue. Submissions are circulated to an editorial board. Send #10 SASE for guidelines. Entry fee: $15. Accepts submissions October 1 through February 1. "The First Series Award contest is highly competitive. We are looking for poets who have produced a significant body of work but have never published a book-length collection. (A chapbook is not considered a 'book' of poetry.)"

MILFORD FINE ARTS COUNCIL ANNUAL NATIONAL POETRY CONTEST (I, II), 40 Railroad Ave. S., Milford CT 06460, contact contest chairperson, awards 3 prizes of $50, $30 and $20. Submissions must be unpublished, have not received any other awards and not be submitted for publication. Poems must be typed (Pica or Elite only), single-space on white standard paper with name and address on middle back of page. Type only the words "unpublished original" above the poem, name and address should appear only on the back page in the middle. Each poem should be "10-30 lines plus title—rhymed or unrhymed—any style, any subject. There should be no more than 48 characters/line. Poetry will be judged on clarity, originality and universal appeal." Include SASE for contest results. Open to adults in the US. Send SASE for guidelines. "Observe rules, otherwise disqualified." Entry fee: $2 per entry, or $5 for 3 entries. Open to entries September 15 through January 31.

‡**VASSAR MILLER PRIZE IN POETRY (II)**, Old Dominion University, English Dept., Norfolk VA 23529, phone (804)683-4042, fax (804)683-5746, established in 1991, award director Scott Cairns, offers annual award of $500 and publication by the University of North Texas Press. Submit 50-80 pgs., include an additional title page without the name of the poet and SASE for winners list. Send SASE for guidelines. Entry fee: $16. Make checks payable to UNT Press. Entries are read September 1 through November 30 only. Most recent award winner was Mark Svenvold. Judge was Heather McHugh. Winner will be announced in May/June *Poets & Writers*.

MISSISSIPPI VALLEY POETRY CONTEST (I, II, IV), sponsored by North American Literary Escadrille, P.O. Box 3188, Rock Island IL 61204, director S. Katz, annually offers prizes of approximately $1,500 for unpublished poems in categories for students (elementary, junior and senior high), adults, Mississippi Valley, senior citizens, jazz, religious, humorous, rhyming, haiku, ethnic and history. Fee: $5 for up to 5 poems; 50 lines/poem limit. Fee for children: $3 for up to 5 poems. Professional readers read winning poems before a reception at an award evening in mid-October. Deadline: September 1.

‡**MODEST CONTEST FOR POETRY & FICTION (I); NEW STONE CIRCLE**, 1185 E. 1900 North Rd., White Heath IL 61884, established in 1996, award director Mary Hays, offers annual award of first prize $100 and publication, second prize $50 and publication, third prize $25 and publication. Submissions must be unpublished. Submit up to 5 poems on any subject in any form, legibly written or typed. Send SASE or stamped postcard for verification of receipt only. Manuscripts will not be returned. Send SASE for guidelines. Entry fee: $10. Deadline: October 1. Most recent contest winner was Judith Lyn Sutton (1996). Judge was Karen Singer. Each contestant will receive the Winter/Spring issue of *New Stone Circle* which will include the contest winners. Copies of previous winning poems may be obtained by sending $4.50 for a sample copy to *NSC*. "*New Stone*

Circle is an upstart poetry and fiction journal dedicated to publishing a wide range of work. Submit work and enter contests as often as you can. Even if you don't win, people are looking at your work. Send us your best and don't be afraid of rejection. We all get rejection letters."

‡**MONEY FOR WOMEN (IV-Women/feminism)**, Barbara Deming Memorial Fund, Inc., Box 40-1043, Brooklyn NY 11240-1043, fund administrator Pam McAllister, provides small grants to feminists in the arts. Send SASE for application form. Applicants must be citizens of US or Canada. Deadlines: December 31 and June 30.

MONTANA ARTS FOUNDATION POETRY CONTEST; MARY BRENNEN CLAPP MEMORIAL AWARD (IV-Regional), P.O. Box 1872, Bozeman MT 59771, annual contest. Open to Montana poets only, for 3 unpublished poems up to 100 lines total. Mary Brennen Clapp Memorial Award of $50 and prizes of $40, $30 and $20. Submit 3 poems and cover letter. Send SASE for guidelines.

JENNY MCKEAN MOORE FUND FOR WRITERS (II), Dept. of English, George Washington University, Washington DC 20052, provides for a visiting lecturer in creative writing about $40,000 for 2 semesters. Apply by November 15 with résumé and writing sample of 25 pgs. or less. Awarded to poets and fiction writers in alternating years.

SAMUEL FRENCH MORSE POETRY PRIZE (III), (formerly listed under Northeastern University Press in the Publishers of Poetry section), English Dept., 406 Holmes, Northeastern University, Boston MA 02115, editor Prof. Guy Rotella, for book publication (ms 50-70 pgs.) by Northeastern University Press and an award of $500. Entry fee: $10. Deadline of August 1 for inquiries, September 15 for single copy of ms. Ms will not be returned. Open to US poets who have published no more than 1 book of poetry.

NASHVILLE NEWSLETTER POETRY CONTEST (I), P.O. Box 60535, Nashville TN 37206-0535, editor/publisher Roger Dale Miller. Founded 1977. Reporting time 6-10 weeks. Published quarterly. Sample copy: $3. Awards prizes of $50, $25 and $10 plus possible publication in newsletter, and at least 50 Certificates of Merit. Any style or subject up to 40 lines. One unpublished poem to a page with name and address in upper left corner. Entry fee: $5 for up to 3 poems. Must be sent all at once. "All other nonwinning poems will be considered for possible publication in future issues." Recent contest winners include Jeanette Raff, Kenneth J. Bennet, Margaret Miller and Denny E. Marshall.

NATIONAL BOOK AWARD (II), National Book Foundation, 260 Fifth Ave., Room 904, New York NY 10001, phone (212)685-0261, award directors Neil Baldwin, Meg Kearney and Kevin LaFollette, offers annual grand prize of $10,000 plus 4 finalist awards of $1,000. Submissions must be previously published and **must be entered by the publisher**. Send SASE for entry form and guidelines. Entry fee: $100/title. Deadline: July 15.

NATIONAL ENDOWMENT FOR THE ARTS; FELLOWSHIPS FOR CREATIVE WRITERS; FEL-LOWSHIPS FOR TRANSLATORS (II), Attn: Literature Heritage & Preservation Division, Room 720, Nancy Hanks Center, 1100 Pennsylvania Ave. NW, Washington DC 20506, phone (202)682-5451. Fellowships for Creative Writers is a program of individual grants for American writers of poetry, fiction and creative nonfiction. Applications for prose and poetry are accepted in alternating years. Awards of $20,000 are made each year to published writers. Applications are reviewed and recommendations for funding are made by an advisory panel composed of experts from the literature field. In reviewing applications, advisory panelists consider solely the literary quality of the manuscripts submitted. To be eligible, a poet must have in publication a volume of at least 48 pages, or 20 or more poems or pages of poetry in five or more literary publications in the last 5 years. A limited number of $20,000 fellowship grants are awarded to published translators of creative literature for translation projects from other languages into English. Matching grants are also available to nonprofit organizations that have had programming for 4 years. Phone or write for guidelines and application.

NATIONAL POETRY SERIES ANNUAL OPEN COMPETITION (II), P.O. Box G, Hopewell NJ 08525, established in 1978, between January 1 and February 15 considers book-length mss (approximately 48-64 pgs.). Entry fee: $25. Manuscripts will not be returned. The 5 winners receive $1,000 each and are published by participating small press, university press and trade publishers. Send SASE for complete submissions procedures. Most recent award winners include Heather Allen, Marcus Cafagna and Daniel Hall (1995).

NATIONAL WRITERS UNION ANNUAL NATIONAL POETRY COMPETITION (II), P.O. Box 2409, Aptos CA 95001, e-mail monkerud@scruznet.com, website http://www.mbay.net/~NWU, chair Don Monkerud. See National Writers Union listing under Organizations Useful to Poets. The Santa Cruz/Monterey Local 7 chapter at this address sponsors an annual competition with entry fee: $3/poem; prizes of $200, $100 and $50 plus publication in newsletter, with prominent poets as judges. Send SASE for rules beginning in April. Deadline: September 30.

THE NATIONAL WRITTEN & ILLUSTRATED BY ... AWARDS CONTEST FOR STUDENTS; LANDMARK EDITIONS (IV-Students), P.O. Box 270169, Kansas City MO 64127, award director David

Melton, is an annual contest for unpublished work for a book written and illustrated by a student. Three books published, one from each of 3 age categories (6-9; 10-13; 14-19). Send #10 SAE with 2 first-class stamps for rules.

NATIONAL/INTERNATIONAL PENUMBRA POETRY COMPETITION (I, IV-Form), (formerly Penumbra Poetry Competition) Tallahassee Writers' Association, P.O. Box 15995, Tallahassee FL 32317-5995, editor Barbara Hogan, offers annual prizes plus publication in and one copy of a chapbook. Prizes: $100, $30 and $20 for poetry; $50, $20 and $10 for haiku. Submission must be unpublished. No simultaneous submissions. Two categories: (1) poetry of up to 50 lines (shorter poetry is of equal value) and (2) 3-line haiku. "Poems on 8½×11 paper; haiku on 3×5 cards. Please send two copies of each entry. On the back of one copy only, write author's name, full address, telephone number, and source of contest information." Send SASE for guidelines. Entry fee: $5/poem, $3/haiku. Deadline: June 30. Judges change every year and are always published, prize winning poets.

NEUSTADT INTERNATIONAL PRIZE FOR LITERATURE; WORLD LITERATURE TODAY (V), University of Oklahoma, 110 Monnet Hall, Norman OK 73019-0375. Award of $40,000 given every other year in recognition of life achievement or to a writer whose work is still in progress; **nominations from an international jury only**.

‡NEW ISSUES FIRST BOOK POETRY PRIZE (II), New Issues Press; New Issues Poetry Series, Dept. of English, Western Michigan University, Kalamazoo MI 49008-5092, phone (616)387-2592, fax (616)387-2562, website http://www.wmich.edu/english/fac/nipps, established in 1996, award director Herbert Scott, offers annual award of $1,000 and publication in paperback and hardback. "Manuscripts in addition to the winner will be considered for publication in the series." Submissions may be entered in other contests. Submit 48-64 pgs. on any subject in any form, single space, unbound with table of contents and SASE. Send SASE for guidelines. Entry fee: $12. Deadline: November 30. Most recent contest winner was Marsha de la O (1997). Judge was Chase Twichell. The judge for upcoming contest will be Philip Levine. Winner will be announced March 1998. Copies of previous winning poems may be obtained by writing to the above address. "Our belief is that there are more good poets writing than ever before. Our mission is to give some of the best of these a forum."

‡NEW YORK FOUNDATION FOR THE ARTS (IV-Regional), 155 Avenue of Americas, 14th Floor, New York NY 10013, phone (212)366-6900, ext. 217, e-mail nyfaafp@artswire.org, website http://www.artswire.org/Artswire/www/nyfa.html, established in 1984, offers fellowships of $7,000 every other year for poets who are at least 18 and have resided in New York State for 2 years prior to application. Submit up to 10 pages of poetry (at least 2 poems), 3 copies of a 1-page résumé, and an application form. Call for application form in June or request via e-mail. Deadline is October.

‡NEW YORK UNIVERSITY PRIZE FOR POETRY (I), New York University Press, 70 Washington Square S., New York NY 10012, phone (212)998-2575, fax (212)995-3833, e-mail nyupmark@elmer2.bobst.nyu.edu, website http://www.nyu.edu/pages/nyupress, established in 1990, offers annual award of a $1,000 honorarium, plus book publication. Submit 1 typewritten copy of a book length ms; a 1-page support letter on letterhead from a qualified reader (teacher, editor, agent, etc.); a cover sheet with name, address and daytime phone; a SASE postcard to acknowledge receipt. Send SASE for guidelines. Deadline: May 1, 1998. Most recent award winner was Anne Caston (1996). Winners will be notified in Fall, 1998. Copies of previous winning poems may be obtained by writing to the above address.

NEWBURYPORT ART ASSOCIATION ANNUAL SPRING POETRY CONTEST (II), 12 Charron Dr., Newburyport MA 01950, established in 1990, contest coordinator Rhina P. Espaillat, awards prizes of $100, First; $50, Second; and $25, Third; plus Honorable Mentions. Submit any number of unpublished poems; no restrictions as to length, style or theme. Open to anyone over 16 years old. Send 2 copies of each poem, one without identification, one bearing your name, address and telephone number, typed on 8½×11 paper with SASE for notification of contest results. Send SASE for guidelines. Entry fee: $3/poem. Make checks payable to Newburyport Art Association. Postmark deadline: March 14. Most recent contest winners include Len Krisak, Gary Whitehead and Barry G. Elms (1997). Judge was Joseph DeRoche. Prizes are awarded at a ceremony in May.

‡*NORDMANNS-FORBUNDET TRANSLATION GRANT (IV-Translation), NORLA, Bygdoy Allé 21, 0262 Oslo, Norway. In its desire to make Norwegian culture known abroad, the Nordmanns-Forbundet awards an annual grant (maximum 15,000 Norwegian crowns) to one or more publishing houses introducing Norwegian fiction or poetry in translation (preferably contemporary). Applications should be sent to NORLA (The Office for Norwegian Literature Abroad), and future decisions will be made by NORLA's Literary Advisory Board. Mark the application "Nordmanns-Forbundet's translation grant." Deadline: December 15.

‡FRANK O'HARA AWARD CHAPBOOK COMPETITION; THORNGATE ROAD PRESS (I, II, IV-Gay/lesbian/bisexual), Campus Box 4240, English Dept., Illinois State University, Normal IL 61790-4240,

INSIDER REPORT

Lack of venues and cause for tribute spawn poetry contest

For Richard Phillips, the love of poetry bloomed with the love of a girl. "I began writing poetry in the '60s as an expression of love for a girl in my high school class at Glide, Oregon. I would mentally compose poetry on the bus ride home while watching the beauty of the mountains and the North Umpqua River out my window. Sometimes I would take notes, but I never let anyone know what I was doing because, until recently, writing was a very private thing for me."

Richard Phillips

But in 1989, after over 20 years of writing poetry, Phillips decided it was time to share his work with the world and began marketing some of his poems. He soon realized, however, that publishing opportunities for new poets weren't good. "I was dismayed to discover there is almost no way for even the best of poets to make it, because most publishers are reluctant to take a chance on anyone who is not a household name."

Unfortunately, during this same period, Phillips learned his father, Richard Phillips, Sr., was dying. "I wanted to find some way to honor him while he was still alive. These two unrelated problems played tennis in my head for a few days until I realized I could attack them both."

The solution presented itself as The Richard Phillips Poetry Prize, an annual $1,000 award for a manuscript of poetry. By sponsoring this contest, Phillips offers new poets an outlet for getting their work into print while at the same time honoring his father. "Now, one of my favorite moments every year is the phone call I make to notify the winners. By talking with them on the phone, I get to feel some of their exhilaration."

Each year Phillips screens the initial entries and then passes the most promising to an outside judge—a new judge is selected for each competition. When selecting a judge, Phillips looks for someone whose work he respects and who has similar tastes in literature. "I'm interested in work addressing the important issues—the purpose of life, man's inhumanity to man, etc. I also respond well to clever metaphor if it's not so vague the buying public cannot get the message."

For the 1996 prize, Phillips was lucky enough to enlist Miller Williams as judge—who, at the time, was busy writing the poem for President Clinton's Inauguration. "His involvement has significantly increased the prestige of winning the prize," says Phillips.

When screening the entries, Phillips is open to both rhyme and free verse, but dislikes forced rhyme. "If it doesn't flow naturally, switch to free verse; and don't hesitate to rewrite. Many poets seem to feel a sense of sacrilege when they start to make changes in their work. That's the mark of an amateur. Don't be afraid to polish your poetry with numerous rewrites. It improves your chances of winning and the work invariably sells better to the general public."

The Richard Phillips Poetry Prize charges a $15 reading fee for a 40-page manuscript of previously-published or unpublished poems. The winner receives $1,000 and 100 contributor's copies of his or her published manuscript. And Phillips is currently negotiating with an international discount store to carry the winning collection on their bookshelves.

Along with worldwide distribution, Phillips is also looking into sponsoring additional contests in the near future. But in regard to his current competition Phillips says, "There are no anthologies to buy, no strings attached. Simply put, the poet who enters the best manuscript will win the prize."

—*Chantelle Bentley*

(309)438-7705, fax (309)438-5414, e-mail jmelled@ilstu.edu, established in 1996, award director Jim Elledge, offers annual award of $200, publication and 25 copies. All entrants receive copy of winning chapbook. Submissions may be a combination of previously published and unpublished work and may be entered in other contests. Submit 20 pages on any topic, in any form. Another 4 pages for front matter is permitted, making the maximum total of 24 pages. Poets must be gay, lesbian or bisexual (any race, age, background, etc.). One poem/page. Send SASE for guidelines. Entry fee: $10/submission. Deadline: February 1. Judge is a nationally-recognized gay, lesbian or bisexual poet. Judge remains anonymous until the winner has been announced. Winners will be announced by April 15 in various media—both lesbigay and "straight" in focus. Copies of previous winning poems or books may be obtained by sending $6 to the above address made out to Thorngate Road. "Thorngate Road publishes at least two chapbooks annually, and they are selected by one of two methods. The first is through the contest. The second, the Berdache Chapbook Series, is by invitation only. Although the contest is only open to gay, lesbian and bisexual authors, the content of submissions does not necessarily have to be gay, lesbian or bisexual."

‡OMMATION PRESS BOOK AWARD (I, II), Ommation Press, 5548 N. Sawyer, Chicago IL 60625, phone (312)539-5745, award director E. Mihopoulos, offers annual award of publication and 100 copies. Submissions may be entered in other contests. Submit up to 60 pgs. on any subject and any form. Send SASE for guidelines. Entry fee: $15 (includes free book—must include SASE with book rate postage). Deadline: December 31. Most recent judge was E. Mihopoulos. Ommation Press has published over 40 books in various formats including a Lamont selection from the Academy of American Poets (in New York) in 1985.

NATALIE ORNISH POETRY AWARD (IV-Regional); SOEURETTE DIEHL FRASER TRANSLA-TION AWARD (IV-Translations, regional); TEXAS INSTITUTE OF LETTERS, % James Hoggard, T.I.L., P.O. Box 9032, Wichita Falls TX 76308-9032, phone (817)689-4123, fax (817)761-1311, e-mail fhoggrd@nexus.mwsu.edu, established in 1947. The Texas Institute of Letters gives annual awards for books by Texas authors in 8 categories, including the Natalie Ornish Poetry Award, a $1,000 award for best volume of poetry. Books must have been first published in the year in question, and entries may be made by authors or by their publishers. Deadline is January 4 of the following year. One copy of each entry must be mailed to each of three judges, with "information showing an author's Texas association . . . if it is not otherwise obvious." Poets must have lived in Texas for at least two consecutive years at some time or their work must reflect a notable concern with matters associated with the state. Soeurette Diehl Fraser Translation Award ($1,000) is given for best translation of a book into English. Same rules as those for Natalie Ornish poetry award. Write during the fall for complete instructions. Most recent award winners include Betty Adcock, Jack Myers and Pattiann Rogers.

PACIFIC NORTHWEST WRITERS CONFERENCE ADULT LITERARY CONTEST (I), 2033 Sixth Ave., Suite 804, Seattle WA 98121-2546, phone (206)443-3807. For information, please request a contest brochure. Complete entry form must accompany entry.

PANHANDLE PROFESSIONAL WRITERS (I), P.O. Box 19303, Amarillo TX 79114, contact contest chairman, open to all poets, 2 categories (rhymed, unrhymed) any subject or form, 50 lines maximum, limit of 2 poems/category, awards of $20, $30 and $50, fee $7.50/poem. Send SASE for contest rules. Deadline: postmarked on or before June 10. Most recent winners include Patricia C. Wilson, Paul L. Goldman and Bernie Shwayden.

PAUMANOK POETRY AWARD COMPETITION; THE VISITING WRITERS PROGRAM (II), SUNY Farmingdale, Farmingdale NY 11735, website http://www.farmingdale.edu/Engdept/paward.html, established 1990, director Dr. Margery Brown. The Paumanok Poetry Award Competition offers a prize of $1,000 plus an all-expense-paid feature reading in their 1998-99 series. They will also award two runner-up prizes of $500 plus expenses for a reading in the series. Submit cover letter, 1-paragraph literary bio, up to 5 poems of up to 10 pgs. (published or unpublished), and $12 entry fee postmarked by September 15. Make checks payable to SUNY Farmingdale Visiting Writers Program (VWP). Send SASE for results. Results will be mailed by late December. Send SASE for guidelines or obtain via their website. Poets who have read in their series include Hayden Carruth, Allen Ginsberg, Linda Pastan, Marge Piercy, Joyce Carol Oates, Louis Simpson and David Ignatow. The series changes each year, so entries in the 1997 competition will be considered for the 1998-99 series, entries in 1998 for the 1999-2000 series, and so on.

JUDITH SIEGEL PEARSON AWARD (I, IV-Women), Wayne State University/Family of Judith Siegel Pearson, 51 W. Warren, Detroit MI 48202, phone (313)577-2450, offers an annual award of up to $250 for "the best creative or scholarly work on a subject concerning women." The type of work accepted rotates each year: plays and nonfictional prose, 1998; poetry, 1999; fiction, 2000. Submissions must be unpublished. Submit 4-10 poems on 20 pgs. maximum. Open to "all interested writers and scholars." Send SASE for guidelines. Deadline: March 1. Winner announced in April.

PEN CENTER USA WEST LITERARY AWARD IN POETRY (IV-Regional), PEN Center USA West, 672 S. Lafayette Park Place, #41, Los Angeles CA 90057, phone (213)365-8500, fax (213)365-9616, award director Sherrill W. Britton, offers annual $500 cash award to a book of poetry published during the previous calendar year. Open to writers living west of the Mississippi. Submit 4 copies of the entry. Send SASE for entry form and guidelines. Deadline: December 31. The 1995 award winner was Jack Gilbert. Judges were Holly Prado, Maurya Simon and Gary Soto. Winner will be announced in a spring press release and then honored at a ceremony in Los Angeles.

PENNSYLVANIA POETRY SOCIETY ANNUAL CONTEST; PEGASUS CONTEST FOR STUDENTS, 801 Spruce St., West Reading PA 19611-1448, phone (610)374-5848, newsletter editor and recording secretary Ann Gasser. The deadline for the society's annual contest, which has 12 categories open to nonmembers and 4 to members only, is January 15. Grand prize category awards 3 prizes of $100, $50, $25 and three poems may be entered at $2 each for members and nonmembers alike. All other categories award three prizes of $25, $15 and $10 and permit one poem in each category. Twelve categories are open to all poets; nonmembers pay $1.50 per category 2-12. PPS members pay $2.50 total for entries in categories 2-16. For information about the annual contest send a SASE to Lillian Tweedy, contest chairman, 2488 New Franklin Rd., Chambersburg, PA 17201. For information about the Pegasus Contest for Students, write to Anne Pierre Spangler, contest chairman, 1685 Christine Dr., R.D. #2, Lebanon PA 17042. Deadline for the Pegasus contest is March 1. The Carlisle Chapter of PPS sponsors the "Kids 'N Critters" contest which has a deadline of October 31. For information send SASE to Jessie Ruhl Miller, 670 West Louther St., Carlisle PA 17013. The Pennsylvania Poetry Society publishes a quarterly newsletter and an annual *Prize Poems* soft cover book, containing prize-winning and honorable mention award poems. Prize poems in the Pegasus contest are published in a booklet for the schools which enter. PPS membership dues are $15/year. Make check payable to PPS, Inc. and mail to Richard R. Gasser, Treasurer, at the above address.

‡PERSEPHONE BOOK PUBLICATION AWARD (V, IV-Regional), Persephone Press Endowment, 53 Pine Lake Dr., Whispering Pines NC 28327, phone (910)949-3993, established in 1987, award director Mary Belle Campbell, offers annual award of publication of poems in 32 pgs., letterpress, hand-sewn, hard and soft cover books. Paid in 250 copies, out of a press run of 280, to sell at readings and signings. Winner keeps all profits of what they sell. Submissions may be entered in other contests. Submit 24 pages with list of publications, enclose bio, introduction and signed nomination. Poets must be residents of North Carolina, with no more than 2 published books and **nominated by university poetry teachers or editors**. Send SASE for guidelines. Deadline: June 1998. The judge for upcoming award will be William Stafford, Robert Bly and Don Baker.

‡PEW FELLOWSHIP IN THE ARTS (IV-Regional), The University of the Arts, 250 S. Broad St., Suite 400, Philadelphia PA 19102, (215)875-2285, fax (215)875-2276, established in 1991, award director Melissa Franklin, offers every three years (1998, 2001, 2004) an award of $50,000 for poetry. Call or write for application and guidelines (available in mid-September). Must be a Pennsylvania resident of Bucks, Chester, Delaware, Montgomery or Philadelphia county for at least two years; must be 25 or older. Deadline: December of the preceding year. Most recent judge was a panel of artists and art professionals. Winner will be announced by letter. "The Pew Fellowships in the Arts provides financial support directly to artists so they may have the opportunity to dedicate themselves wholly to the development of their artwork for up to 2 years. Up to 12 fellowships (in 3 different categories) awarded each year."

THE RICHARD PHILLIPS POETRY PRIZE (II), The Phillips Publishing Co., P.O. Box 121, Watts OK 74964, founded 1993, award director Richard Phillips, Jr. Annual award of $1,000 open to all poets. Submit 40-

page ms, published or unpublished poems, any subject, any form. Include $15 reading fee/ms, payable to Richard Phillips Poetry Prize. Mss are not returned. Send SASE for guidelines. Postmark deadline: January 31. "Winner will be announced and check for $1,000 presented by March 31." Publication is the following September. Most recent prize winners were Deborah Vallet (1997) and Kathryn Presley (1996). "There are no anthologies to buy, no strings attached. The best manuscript will win the prize."

THE POETRY CENTER BOOK AWARD (II), 1600 Holloway Ave., San Francisco CA 94132, phone (415)338-3132, e-mail newlit@sfsu.edu, website http://www.sfsu.edu/~newlit/welcome.htm, established in 1980. Method for entering contest is to submit a published book and a $10 entry fee. "Please include cover sheet noting author's name, book title(s), name of person or publisher issuing check and check number." Book must be published and copyrighted during the year of the contest and submitted by December 31. "Beginners may enter but in the past winners have published several previous books." Translations and anthologies are not accepted. Books should be by an individual living writer and must be entirely poetry. Prize (only one) is $500 and an invitation to read for the Poetry Center. No entry form is required. Recent winners include Jane Hirshfield and Robert Wrigley. "The Poetry Center and American Poetry Archives at San Francisco State University was founded in 1954. Its archives is the largest circulating tape collection of writers reading their own work in the United States."

‡POETRY SOCIETY OF MICHIGAN ANNUAL CONTESTS; THE PSM PREMIER CONTEST; SCHNEIDER MEMORIAL NARRATIVE; MARGARET ELLIOTT CONTEST; VAN LEISHOUT-HEAFIELD YOUTH CONTEST; DOWN RIVER BALLAD, NARRATIVE OR CHARACTER CONTEST (I, IV-Children), P.O. Box 20114, Saginaw MI 48602-0114, contest coordinator Marion Frahm Ticknell. Sponsors 9 annual contests open to nonmembers: The PSM Premier Contest, any subject, form or length; Down River Ballad, Narrative, or Character Contest, any form or length; Margaret Elliott Contest, poetry for children, Van Leishout-Heafield Youth Contests, for poets age 10-14 and 15-18; Traditional, Classic or Lyric Contest; River Junction Poets Contemporary Contest; Humor Contest; Religious, Spiritual or Philosophical Contest. Various entry fees. Prizes range from $25-100, some include publication. Send SASE for guidelines on all contests and membership information. Deadline for all contests is April 30.

THE POETRY SOCIETY OF VIRGINIA ANNUAL CONTESTS (I, II, IV-Forms), 42 Twin Oaks, Rustburg VA 24588, contest chairperson Lisa Stinnett, offers 18 contests in various categories including: the Bess Gresham Memorial (garden or gardeners); Brodie Herndon Memorial (the sea); Judah, Sarah, Grace and Tom Memorial (inter-ethnic amity); Cenie H. Moon Prize (women); Karma Deane Ogden Memorial (PSV members only); Edgar Allen Poe Memorial and the Alice Sherry Memorial. (All of the previous contests are open to any form, have limits of 32-48 lines, and some have specific subjects as noted.) The following group of contests require specific forms: the J. Franklin Dew Award (series of 3-4 haiku), Carleton Drewry Memorial (lyric or sonnet about mountains), Handy Andy Prize (limerick), Emma Gray Trigg Memorial (lyric, 64-line limit, PSV members only), Nancy Byrd Turner Memorial (sonnet). The last group of contests are open to elementary, middle school and high school students only: Elementary School Prize (grades 1-5, any form or subject, 24-line limit), Middle School Prize (grades 6-8, any form or subject, 24-line limit), Musings/Northern VA Poets Prize—Grades 6-8 (sonnet, Shakespearean or Petrarchan, any subject), Shenandoah University Prize (grades 9-12, any form or subject, 32-line limit). All poems are open to nonmembers except those noted above. Cash prizes range from $10-100. Contest information available for SASE. Entry fees: Adults, $2/poem; $1/high school entry; no fee for elementary school entries. Send **all student entries** to Claudia Gary Annis, 217 Nottoway St. SE, Leesburg VA 22075, phone (703)771-9342. Deadline for all contests is January 19.

‡POETRY WORLD POETRY CONTEST (I, II), North Star Press/Chatfield Software Inc., P.O. Box 115, Hiram OH 44234-0115, phone (216)632-5447, e-mail chatsoft@world.std.com, offers annual prizes for individual poems and poetry chapbooks. For individual poems: first prize $100, publication, plus 5 copies of *North Star Three*; second prize $50, publication, plus 5 copies; 23 third prizes of publication and 3 copies. For poetry chapbooks: first prize publication of ms and 100 copies; second prize $50. Individual poems must be unpublished. Submit up to 3 poems for individual poems; submit ms of 32-40 pgs. for chapbook contest. Send SASE for guidelines. Entry fees: $5 for individual poems; $10 for chapbook (waived for owners of Chatfield software). Deadline: March 15, 1998. Winners will be announced by June 15, 1998. All entrants will receive a list of contest winners. No entries will be returned. *North Star Three*, to be published by North Star Press, will be an anthology of the 25 winning poems of the 1998 contest. North Star Press will also publish the winning chapbook.

POETS' CLUB OF CHICAGO INTERNATIONAL SHAKESPEAREAN/PETRARCHAN SONNET CONTEST; THE INTERNATIONAL NARRATIVE CONTEST (II, IV-Form), 130 Windsor Park Dr., C-323, Carol Stream IL 60188, chairman LaVone Holt. The International Shakespearean/Petrarchan Sonnet Contest is open to anyone **except** members of Poets' Club of Chicago. Submit only 1 entry of either a Shakespearean or a Petrarchan sonnet, which must be original and unpublished and must not have won a cash award in any contest sponsored previously by the Club. Write for rules, include SASE, no earlier than March. No entry fee. Prizes of $50, $35 and $15 plus 2 honorable mentions. Postmark deadline: September 1. Most recent contest winners include Susan Horowitz, Margaret Roemer and Nando Amabile. Winners will be notified by October

15. Send SASE with entry to receive winners' list. Also sponsors The International Narrative Contest, awarding annually a $75 first prize and a $25 second prize. Submissions must be unpublished. Submit 2 copies of 1 narrative poem, any form, any subject, of up to 40 lines to Robert Mills, Chairman, 2820 W. Birchwood Ave., Chicago IL 60645. Send SASE for guidelines. Entry must be typed on 8½×11 paper, single-spaced. Put name of contest and title of poem in the upper right-hand corner of both copies, and name and address in the upper left-hand corner on only one copy. No entry fee. Postmark deadline: September 1. Winners will be notified by October 15. The Poets' Club of Chicago meets monthly to critique original poetry, read at and man the Poetry Room in the Harold Washington Library, and read at open-mike coffeehouses. Members also conduct workshops at area high schools by invitation.

POETS' DINNER CONTEST (IV-Regional), 2214 Derby St., Berkeley CA 94705, phone (510)841-1217. Since 1926 there has been an annual awards banquet sponsored by the ad hoc Poets' Dinner Committee, usually at Spenger's Fish Grotto (a Berkeley Landmark). Three typed copies of original, unpublished poems in not more than 3 of the 8 categories are submitted anonymously without fee, and the winning poems (grand prize, first, second, third) are read at the banquet and honorable mentions awarded. **Contestant must be present to win.** Cash prizes awarded; honorable mention, books. The event is nonprofit. Send SASE for contest rules. Deadline: January 25.

THE POETS' PRIZE (II), The Poets' Prize Committee, % the Nicholas Roerich Museum, 319 W. 107th St., New York NY 10025, phone (212)864-7752, award directors Robert McDowell, Frederick Morgan and Louis Simpson. Annual cash award of $3,000 given for a book of verse by an American poet published in the previous year. The poet must be an American citizen. Poets making inquiries will receive an explanation of procedures. Books may be sent to the committee members. A list of the members and their addresses will be sent upon request with SASE.

PRESIDIO LA BAHIA AWARD; SUMMERFIELD G. ROBERTS AWARD (IV-Regional), Sons of the Republic of Texas, 1717 Eighth St., Bay City TX 77414, phone/fax (409)245-6644, contact Melinda Williams. Both may be awarded for poetry. The Presidio La Bahia Award is an annual award or awards (depending upon the number and quality of entries) for writing that promotes research into and preservation of the Spanish Colonial influence on Texas culture. $2,000 is available, with a minimum first prize of $1,200. Entries must be in quadruplicate and will not be returned. Deadline: September 30. The Summerfield G. Roberts Award, available to US citizens, is an annual award of $2,500 for a book or manuscript depicting or representing the Republic of Texas (1836-46), written or published during the calendar year for which the award is given. Entries must be submitted in quintuplicate and will not be returned. Deadline: January 15.

PULITZER PRIZE IN LETTERS (II), % The Pulitzer Prize Board, 702 Journalism, Columbia University, New York NY 10027, phone (212)854-3841, website http://www.pulitzer.org, offers 5 prizes of $5,000 each year, including 1 in poetry, for books published in the calendar year preceding the award. Submit 4 copies of published books (or galley proofs if book is being published after November), photo, bio, entry form and $50 entry fee. July 1 deadline for books published between January 1 and June 30; November 1 deadline for books published between July 1 and December 31. Most recent award winner was Jorie Graham for *The Dream of the Unified Field* (1996) (published by The Ecco Press).

❦QSPELL LITERARY AWARDS; FEWQ BEST FIRST BOOK AWARD; QUEBEC SOCIETY FOR THE PROMOTION OF ENGLISH LANGUAGE LITERATURE, (IV-Regional), 1200 Atwater Ave., Montreal, Quebec H3Z 1X4 Canada, phone/fax (514)933-0878, contact Award Director, offers annual awards of $2,000 each for poetry, fiction and nonfiction. Submissions must be previously published (except for the FEWQ Best First Book Award). Open to authors "who have lived in Quebec for 3 of the past 5 years." Submit a book published (or unpublished for the FEWQ First Book Award) between May 15 of the preceding year and May 15 of the current year. "Books should have at least 48 pgs." Write for entry form. Entry fee: $10/title. Deadline: May 31. Most recent award winner was Anne Carson (1996). Judges were Dianne Brand, Julie Bruck and Bob Holman. Winner will be announced in November. "QSPELL was formed in 1988 to honor and promote literature written in English by Quebec authors."

QUINCY WRITERS GUILD WRITING CONTEST (I), P.O. Box 433, Quincy IL 62306, established in 1990, offers annual award for original, unpublished poetry (serious poetry and light poetry), fiction and nonfiction. Cash prizes based on dollar amount of entries. 1st, 2nd and 3rd place will be awarded in all categories. Send

---

 THE MAPLE LEAF symbol before a listing indicates a Canadian publisher, magazine, conference, contest or organization.

SASE for guidelines. Entry fee: $2/poem; $4/nonfiction or fiction piece. Entries accepted from January 1 through April 15. Recent contest winners include "Nevada City to Squaw" and "Alternatively Abled" by Bob Austin and "Lee Remembers His Men" by Steven M. Thomas. The Quincy Writers Guild meets monthly and consists of Quincy-area writers working in various genres.

REDWOOD ACRES FAIR POETRY CONTEST (I), P.O. Box 6576, Eureka CA 95502, offers an annual contest with various categories for both juniors and seniors with entry fee of 50¢/poem for the junior contests and $1/poem for the senior contests. Deadline: June 2.

‡PHILLIP D. REED MEMORIAL AWARD FOR OUTSTANDING WRITING ON THE SOUTHERN ENVIRONMENT (IV-Nature/ecology), Southern Environmental Law Center, 201 W. Main St., Suite 14, Charlottesville VA 22902, phone (804)977-4090, fax (804)977-1483, e-mail selcva@mindspring.com, established in 1994, award director Cathryn McCue, offers annual award of $1,000. Submissions must be previously published and may be entered in other contests. Submit 10 poems maximum on southern environment. Send SASE for guidelines. Deadline: early to mid-March. Most recent award winner was Eric Bates (1996). Judges were William de Buys, Bill McKibben and Nikki Giovanni. Winners will be announced by press release in May. Southern Environmental Law Center is a nonprofit environmental advocacy group doing work in Alabama, Georgia, North and South Carolina, Virginia and Tennessee.

ROANOKE-CHOWAN POETRY AWARD (IV-Regional), North Carolina Literary and Historical Association, 109 E. Jones St., Raleigh NC 27501, phone (919)733-7442, contact Secretary, offers annual award for "an original volume of poetry published during the twelve months ending June 30 of the year for which the award is given." Open to "authors who have maintained legal or physical residence, or a combination of both, in North Carolina for the three years preceding the close of the contest period." Submit 3 copies of each entry. Most recent award winner was Robert Watson (1995). Winner will be announced during the annual meeting in November.

ANNA DAVIDSON ROSENBERG AWARD (IV-Ethnic), Judah L. Magnes Museum, 2911 Russell St., Berkeley CA 94705, website http://www.jfed.org/Magnes/Magnes, established in 1987, offers prizes of $100, $50 and $25, as well as honorable mentions, for up to 10 pgs. of 1-3 unpublished poems (in English) on the Jewish Experience. There is also a Youth Commendation for poets under 19, a Senior Award if 65 or over and a New/Emerging Poet Award. Do not send poems without entry form; write between April 1 and July 15 for form and guidelines (enclose SASE). Deadline: August 31. Most recent winners include Doren Robbins, Alice Friman, Florence Weinberger and Stuart Peterfreund (1987). The Magnes Museum is the third largest Jewish museum in the country and sponsors numerous programs in the arts and literature.

♣SALMON ARM SONNET CONTEST (IV-Form), Salmon Arm & Dist. Chamber of Commerce, Box 1270, Salmon Arm, British Columbia V1E 4P4 Canada. An annual contest for unpublished sonnets. Prizes: $100-500 and books. Entry fee: $6/poem. Limit 2 entries. New juvenile category for 18 and under, entry fee: $2/poem plus $6 to enter the main contest. Deadline: June 1. Copies of winning entries will be sent to all entrants.

‡THE CONSTANCE SALTONSTALL FOUNDATION FOR THE ARTS GRANTS (II, IV-Regional), 120 Brindley St., Ithaca NY 14850, phone/fax (607)277-4933, e-mail artsfound@clarityconnect.com, award director Kathy Durland Dewart, grants of $5,000 awarded to a limited number of individual painters, writers and photographers. Submit up to 30 pages. Must be 21 years or older and resident of New York State. Send SASE for entry form and guidelines. Deadline: January 15. Most recent judge was jury of distinguished writers. Winners will be announced April 15. The foundation was established according to the wishes of Connie Saltonstall, a painter and photographer, who asked that after her death her estate be used to benefit the arts. See the lising for The Saltonstall Arts Colony in the Writing Colonies section.

SAN FRANCISCO FOUNDATION; JOSEPH HENRY JACKSON AWARD; JAMES D. PHELAN AWARD (IV-Regional), % Intersection for the Arts, 446 Valencia St., San Francisco CA 94103, phone (415)626-2787, fax (415)626-1636, e-mail intrsect@thecity.sfsu.edu, website http://www.ecstatic.com/orgs/intersection. The Jackson Award ($2,000), established in 1955, will be made to the author of an unpublished work-in-progress in the form of fiction (novel or short stories), nonfictional prose, or poetry. Applicants must be residents of northern California or Nevada for three consecutive years immediately prior to the deadline date of January 31, and must be between the ages of 20 and 35 as of the deadline. The Phelan Award ($2,000), estblished in 1935, will be made to the author of an unpublished work-in-progress in the form of fiction (novel or short stories), nonfictional prose, poetry or drama. Applicants must be California-born (although they may now reside outside of the state), and must be between the ages of 20 and 35 as of the January 31 deadline. Mss for both awards must be accompanied by an application form, which may be obtained by sending a SASE to the above address or obtaining via e-mail or website. Entries accepted November 15 through January 31.

SAN MATEO COUNTY FAIR FINE ARTS COMPETITION (I), P.O. Box 1027, San Mateo CA 94403-0627, phone (415)574-3247, fax (415)574-3985, e-mail info@smexpo.xo.com, website http://www.ns.net/fairs/ca/sanmateo, established in 1939, for unpublished poetry. Adult and youth divisions. Write or call for entry form and additional information or request via e-mail. Adult Division awards of $100, $50, and $25; fee $10 for each poem. Youth Division awards of $50, $25 and $15; no fee. Limit 2 entries per division. June 27 deadline for poems.

CARL SANDBURG AWARDS (IV-Regional), sponsored by Friends of the Chicago Public Library, 400 S. State St., 10S-7, Chicago IL 60605, phone (312)747-4907, fax (312)747-4077, are given annually to native-born Chicago authors or present Chicago-area writers for new books in 4 categories, including poetry. Each author receives $1,000. Publisher or authors should submit 2 copies of books published between June 1 of one year and May 31 of the next. Deadline: August 1. Most recent award winner was Paulette Roeske.

*SCOTTISH INTERNATIONAL OPEN POETRY COMPETITION; THE AYRSHIRE WRITERS' & ARTISTS' SOCIETY (I, II), 42 Tollerton Dr., Irvine, Ayrshire, Scotland, established in 1972. Open to all poets. Inaugurated in 1972 it is the longest running poetry competition in the U.K. Entries are free, restricted to two per person and should be accompanied by SASE (or SAE and IRCs). December deadline. Special award ceremony March. First prize, U.K. Section, MacDiarmid Trophy and £100 sterling. First prize, International Section, The International Trophy. Scots Section, The Clement Wilson Cup. Diplomas are awarded to runners up. Competition opens September each year. Most recent winners include Anne Comerford (Ireland), Jim C. Wilson (Scotland), Andrew Kerr (Scotland) and Rosemarie Rawley (Ireland) (1996). "The Society, a charitable organisation, is dedicated to the promotion of poetry and poets of every calibre."

‡SKY BLUE WATERS POETRY CONTEST (I), Sky Blue Waters Poetry Society, 232 SE 12th Ave., Faribault MN 55021-6406, phone (507)332-2803, award director Marlene Meehl, semiannual award for first prize $50, second prize $40, third prize $30, fourth through tenth prizes $10. Submissions may be entered in other contests. Submit any number of poems on any subject; rhyme and meter preferred but not required. Guidelines available for SASE. Entry fee: $2 first poem, $1 each additional poem. Deadlines: March 31 and September 30. Most recent contest award winner was Nancy Gage (1995). Judge was Harland F. Hess. The judge for upcoming contest will be Marlene Meehl. Winner(s) will be announced by mail one month following deadline date. "The Sky Blue Waters Poetry Society is a group of Southern Minnesota poets who exist for the sheer 'love of writing.' Most members agree that writing is not just a love but a necessity. Keep writing. Keep submitting. Today's creation will be tomorrow's winner."

‡SLAPERING HOL PRESS CHAPBOOK COMPETITION (II), Hudson Valley Writer's Center, 300 Riverside Dr., Sleepyhollow NY 10591, phone (914)332-5953, established in 1990, co-editors Stephanie Strickland and Margo Stever, offers annual award of $200 plus 10 author's copies. Submissions must be from poets who have not previously published a book or chapbook. Submit 24 pages of poems with acknowledgements, any form or style, SASE and $10 reading fee. "Manuscript should be anonymous with second title page containing name, address and phone." Send SASE for guidelines. "See *Poets & Writers* for deadline, usually in the spring." Most recent contest winner was Lynn McGee (1996). Copies of previous winning poems or books may be obtained by requesting order form.

‡KAY SNOW WRITING AWARDS (I), Willamette Writers, 9045 SW Barbur Blvd., Suite 5A, Portland OR 97219-4027, phone (503)452-1592, fax (503)452-0372, e-mail wilwrite@teleport.com, established in 1986, award director Martha Miller, offers annual first prize of $200, second prize of $100, third prize of $50 and publication of excerpt only, in January issue of *The Willamette Writer*. Submissions must be unpublished. Submit 1-5 pages on any subject in any style or form, single spaced, one side of paper only. Send SASE for entry form and guidelines. Entry fee: $10 for members of Willamette Writers; $15 for nonmembers. Deadline: May 15. Most recent award winner was Sherron Norlen (1996). Winners will be announced July 31. Excerpts of winning entries are published in the Willamette Writer's newsletter, *The Willamette Writer*. "Write and send in your very best poem. Read it aloud. If it still sounds like the best poem you've ever heard, send it in."

‡THE SOUTHERN PRIZE (II), The Southern Anthology, 2851 Johnston St., #123, Layfayette LA 70503, established in 1995, award director Dr. R. Sebastian Bennett, offers annual Grand prize of $600, publication plus complementary copies. Also, top 3 finalists receive $50, publication and complimentary copies, remaining 3 finalists receive publication and complimentary copies. Submissions must be unpublished. Submit 3 poems on any subject in any format. Send SASE for guidelines. Entry fee $10/set of three poems. Deadline: May 30, 1998. Most recent contest award winner was David Ray (1996). Judged by an editorial panel. Winner will be announced in the Fall. "Literary Media and all entrants notified by mail." Copies of previous winning poems may be obtained by sending a request with $8/copy ordered, including p&h. "*The Southern Anthology* is published annually to promote outstanding poetry in fiction. *SA* encourages both traditional and avant-garde forms. Submissions need not address 'southern' themes. We are particularly interested in innovative and oppositional work."

SPARROWGRASS POETRY FORUM (I), Dept. PM, 609 Main St., Box 193, Sistersville WV 26175, phone (800)685-0848, established in 1987, offers 6 annual free contests, each of which has a minimum of $1,000 in prizes, including a $500 grand prize. Entrants are solicited to buy an anthology, but you do not have to buy the anthology to win. Send 1 original poem, no longer than 20 lines. Name and address at the top of the page. Any style, any subject. Contest deadlines are the last day of every other month.

SPRINGFEST AND WINTERFEST POETRY CONTESTS; MILE HIGH POETRY SOCIETY (I), P.O. Box 21116, Denver CO 80221, phone (303)657-8461, award director Jane C. Schaul. Each spring and fall they offer a contest with $300 1st prize, $100 2nd prize, and two 3rd prizes of $50 each for maximum 36-line poems. Entry fee $3/poem. Deadlines: June 30 and December 31. Send SASE for details. Most recent contest winners include Donald L. Ransom, Abelardo B. Delgado, Betty Copeland Morando and Marsha Mauchley (1996).

✿STARVING ROMANTICS POETRY COMPETITION (I, II), Starving Romantics, 93 Charnwood Place, Thornhill, Ontario L3T 5H2 Canada, phone (905)731-8055, established in 1996, award director I.J. Schecter, offers annual awards for poetry that "hearkens to the style of Romantic poetry." First place: $125 plus recitation at literary venues; Second place: $50 plus recitation; Third place: $25 plus recitation; Fourth through Tenth: recitation plus free entry for the following year. Submissions must be unpublished and may be entered in other contests. Submit up to 5 poems maximum. Include separate cover sheet with name and address and SASE for notification. Send SASE for guidelines. Entry fee: $3/poem. Deadline: July 31. Most recent award winners include William Dubnov, Martha Medford and John Fitzpatrick (1996). Winners notified by September 30. The director says, "Send me something that evokes the formidable beauty of Romantic Poetry and you've got a strong chance."

WALLACE E. STEGNER FELLOWSHIPS (II), Creative Writing Program, Stanford University, Stanford CA 94305, phone (415)725-1208, administrator Gay Pierce, 5 in poetry, $15,000 plus tuition of over $5,000, for promising writers who can benefit from 2 years instruction and criticism at the Writing Center. Previous publication not required, though it can strengthen one's application. Deadline: Postmarked by the first working day after December 1.

TOWSON STATE UNIVERSITY PRIZE FOR LITERATURE (II, IV-Regional), Towson State University, College of Liberal Arts, Towson MD 21252, phone (410)830-2128, award director Dean of the College of Liberal Arts, offers annual prize of $1,000 "for a single book or book-length manuscript of fiction, poetry, drama or imaginative nonfiction by a young Maryland writer. The prize is granted on the basis of literary and aesthetic excellence as determined by a panel of distinguished judges appointed by the university. The first award, made in the fall of 1980, went to novelist Anne Tyler." The work must have been published within the three years prior to the year of nomination or must be scheduled for publication within the year in which nominated. Open to Maryland residents under 40 years of age. Submit 5 copies of work in bound form or in typewritten, double-spaced ms form. Send SASE for entry form and guidelines. Deadline: May 15.

‡*THE TREWITHEN POETRY PRIZE (I, II, IV-Rural), Trewithen Poetry, Treskewes Cottage, Trewithen Moor, Stithians, Truro, Cornwall TR3 7DU England, established in 1995, award secretary D. Atkinson, offers annual award of first prize £200, second prize £100, third prize £50, plus 5 runner-up prizes of £10 each and publication in The Trewithen Chapbook. Submissions may be entered in other contests, "*but* must *not* previously have won another competition." Submit any number of poems on a rural theme in any form. Send SASE for entry form. Entry fee: £2.50 for the first poem and £1.50 for each additional poem. Deadline: October 31. Most recent award winner was Ann Drysdale (1996). Judge was a panel of 3-4 working poets who remain anonymous. Winners will be announced at the beginning of Decembr by results sheet and through poetry magazines and organizations. Winning poems published biennialy in March/April. Copies of previous winning poems may be obtained by using order form on entry form or by writing direct to the secretary enclosing a SAE with IRC. "We are seeking good writing with a contemporary approach, reflecting any aspect of nature or rural life in any country."

UTAH ORIGINAL WRITING COMPETITION (II, IV-Regional), Utah Arts Council Literary Program, 617 E. South Temple, Salt Lake City UT 84102-1177, phone (801)533-5895, fax (801)533-6196, e-mail glebeda@state.ut.us, website http://www.dced.state.ut.us/arts, established in 1958, award director Guy Lebeda, offers annual awards in 7 categories: novel, nonfiction book, book-length collection of poetry, juvenile book, poetry, short story and personal essay. Prizes range from $200-1,000 and a $5,000 publication prize is awarded to one of the book-length first place winners from the previous year's competition. Open to Utah residents only. "Submit work in standard publishing ms style." Write for entry form or request via e-mail. Deadline: mid-June.

‡LAURA BOWER VAN NUYS CREATIVE WRITING CONTEST (I, II), Black Hills Writers Group, P.O. Box 1539, established in 1968, Rapid City SD 57709-1539. **"We will be holding the contest in even-numbered years only."** Professional and nonprofessional categories in fiction, articles and poetry. Guidelines available after January 1 of contest year. Most recent contest winner (poetry) was Eric Lochridge (1996).

*THE VICTORIAN FELLOWSHIP OF AUSTRALIAN WRITERS; FAW AWARDS (IV-Regional), FAW (Vic) Inc., P.O. Box 528, Camberwell 3124, Australia, phone/fax (03)9349 3722, all awards for Australian authors. The FAW Anne Elder Poetry Award (prizes of $1,000 and $500) is for a first published book of poetry. The FAW Christopher Brennan Award is a bronze plaque to honor an Australian poet who has written work of sustained quality and distinction (entries not required; award by committee). The FAW John Shaw Neilson Poetry Award (prizes of $500 and $250) is for an unpublished poem of at least 14 lines. The FAW Fedora Anderson Young Writers' Poetry Award ($150 and $75) is for unpublished poems by Australian writers 15-20 years old. The FAW C.J. Dennis Young Writers' Poetry Award (prizes of $100 and $50) is for unpublished poems by Australian writers 10-14 years old.

THE W.D. WEATHERFORD AWARD (IV-Regional), Berea College, CPO 2336, Berea KY 40404, contact chairman, for the published work (including poetry) which "best illuminates the problems, personalities, and unique qualities of the Appalachian South." Work is nominated by its publisher, by a member of the award committee or by any reader. The award is for $500 and sometimes there are special awards of $200 each. Deadline: December 31 of the year work was published.

WESTERN HERITAGE AWARDS (IV-Specialized), National Cowboy Hall of Fame and Western Heritage Center, 1700 NE 63rd St., Oklahoma City OK 73111. Since 1960, this national museum has awarded excellence in western literature, music, television and film. Principal creators of winning entries in 15 categories receive the bronze "Wrangler," an original sculpture by artist John Free, during special awards ceremonies held at the museum each March. Entry forms are mailed annually in September for works published between January 1 and November 30 of that year. Deadline for entries: November 30. The 1995 award for poetry went to Jane Candia Coleman for her book *The Red Drum*, published by High Plains Press.

❦WFNB ANNUAL LITERARY CONTEST; THE ALFRED G. BAILEY AWARD; WRITERS' FEDERATION OF NEW BRUNSWICK (IV-Regional), P.O. Box 37, Station A, Fredericton, New Brunswick E3B 4Y2 Canada, phone (506)459-7228, established in 1985, offers prizes of $200, $100, $30, for unpublished poems of up to 100 lines (typed). Open to New Brunswick residents only. The Alfred G. Bailey Award is a $400 prize given annually for poetry mss of 48 pgs. or more. May include some individual poems that have been published. Entry fee: $10 for members, $15 for nonmembers. Send SASE for guidelines. Deadline: February 14. Most recent award winners include Steve McOrmond for the Bailey Award (1996) and Shari Andrews for the WFNB Contest (1996).

WHITING WRITERS' AWARDS; MRS. GILES WHITING FOUNDATION (V), 1133 Avenue of the Americas, 22nd Floor, New York NY 10036-6710, director Gerald Freund. The Foundation makes awards of $30,000 each to up to 10 writers of fiction, nonfiction, poetry and plays chosen by a selection committee drawn from a list of recognized writers, literary scholars and editors. Recipients of the award are selected from nominations made by writers, educators and editors from communities across the country whose experience and vocations bring them in contact with individuals of unusual talent. The nominators and selectors are appointed by the foundation and serve anonymously. **Direct applications and informal nominations are not accepted by the foundation.**

STAN AND TOM WICK POETRY PRIZE (I), Wick Poetry Program, Kent State University, P.O. Box 5190, Kent OH 44242-0001, phone (330)672-2676, e-mail wickpoet@kent.edu, established in 1994, award director Maggie Anderson, offers annual award of $1,000 and publication by The Kent State University Press. Submissions must be unpublished and may be entered in other contests. Submit 48-68 pages of poetry. Open to poets writing in English who have not yet published a full-length collection. Entries must include cover sheet with poet's name, address, telephone number and title of ms. Send SASE for guidelines or request via e-mail. Entry fee: $10. Deadline: May 1, 1997. Most recent contest winner was Rosemary Willey (1996). Judge was Yusef Komunyakaa. Judge for 1997 contest was Marilyn Hacker.

OSCAR WILLIAMS & GENE DERWOOD AWARD (V), New York Community Trust, 2 Park Ave., New York NY 10016, is an award given annually to nominees of the selection committee "to help needy or worthy artists or poets." **Selection Committee for the award does not accept nominations.** Amount varies from year to year.

WISCONSIN ARTS BOARD FELLOWSHIPS (II, IV-Regional), Wisconsin Arts Board, 101 E. Wilson St., 1st Floor, Madison WI 53702, phone (608)266-0190, award director Mark Fraire, offers fellowships to "recognize the significant contributions of professional artists." Open to Wisconsin residents who are *not* fulltime

FOR INFORMATION ON ENTERING the *1999 Poet's Market* Poetry Contest, see page 2.

students. Write for entry form and guidelines. Deadline: September ("call for exact date").

‡WOMEN IN THE ARTS SPRING FANTASY CONTEST (I), Women in The Arts, P.O. Box 2907, Decatur IL 62524, established in 1995, award director Linda Hutton, offers annual first prize of $30, second prize of $25, third prize of $15, honorable mention of $5. All winning poems are published in *Spring Fantasy*, an annual anthology. Submissions may be entered in other contests. Submit up to 5 poems of up to 32 lines on any topic in any form, no name or address on entry, include cover sheet. Send SASE for guidelines. Entry fee: $2/poem. Make checks payable to Women In The Arts. Deadline: November 15. Most recent contest winner was Art Hullinger (1996). Judge was WITA members committee. Winner will be announced by March 15 by mail. Copies of previous winning poems may be obtained by sending $6 postpaid to the above address. "WITA is a group of 60 women and 5 men who share and encourage creative ideas through art, literature, music, crafts, dance, photography, etc. Most of our members live in Illinois; those out-of-state send their work for critique by pen-palling. Follow the rules carefully; half the entries are disqualified for some infraction." (See *Spring Fantasy* listing in the Publishers of Poetry section.)

WORLD ORDER OF NARRATIVE AND FORMALIST POETS (II, IV-Subscription, form), P.O. Box 580174, Station A, Flushing NY 11358-0174, established in 1980, contest chairman Dr. Alfred Dorn. This organization sponsors contests in at least 15 categories of traditional and contemporary poetic forms, including the sonnet, blank verse, ballade, villanelle, free verse and new forms created by Alfred Dorn. Prizes total at least $5,000 and range from $20 to $300. Only subscribers to *The Formalist* will be eligible for the competition, as explained in the complete guidelines available from the contest chairman. "We look for originality of thought, phrase and image, combined with masterful craftsmanship. Trite, trivial or technically inept work stands no chance." Postmark deadline for entries: October 15, 1998. Most recent contest winners include Brian E. Drake, Rachel Hadras, Annie Finch and Len Krisak. (For more information on *The Formalist*, see their listing in the Publishers of Poetry section.)

WORLD'S WORST POETRY CONTEST (IV-Regional), Pismo Bob's True Value Hardware and Nursery, 930 Price St., Pismo Beach CA 93449, phone (805)773-NAIL, fax (805)773-6772, award director "Pismo Bob" Pringle. Contest for "bad (not necessarily conforming to normality)" poetry that mentions Pismo Beach. The contest is simple to enter. Just send a poem or poems to "Pismo Bob" Pringle, originator of the contest. The poems must include the word "Pismo," but aside from that there are no literary requirements. "In addition to the sheer pride of being the world's worst bard, the Chosen One will also win a free round trip to the wonderful shores of Pismo Beach, California." Send SASE for entry form and guidelines. Deadline: September 30. Winners will be announced in October.

WRITERS AT WORK FELLOWSHIP COMPETITION (II), Writers at Work, P.O. Box 1146, Centerville UT 84104, website http://www.ihi-env.com/watw.html, offers annual awards of $1,500 and $500 plus publication in *Quarterly West* (first place only). Submissions must be unpublished and can be entered in other contests, "but must be withdrawn if they win another contest." Submit 6 poems, 10 pgs. maximum, subject and form open. Entry must include 2 copies of ms, 2 #10 SASEs and cover letter stating name, address, phone number, genre and title of ms. "No names on mss." Mss will not be returned. Open to any writer who has not published a book-length volume of original work. Obtain guidelines via their website. Entry fee: $12/entry (make check payable to Writers at Work). Postmark deadline: March 15.

✤WRITERS' GUILD OF ALBERTA BOOK AWARD (IV-Regional), Writer's Guild, 11759 Groat Rd., 3rd Floor, Edmonton, Alberta T5M 3K6 Canada, phone (403)422-8174, awarded in six categories, including poetry. Eligible books will have been published anywhere in the world between January 1 and December 31. Their authors will have been a resident in Alberta for at least 12 of the 18 months prior to December 31. Contact the WGA head office for registry forms. Unpublished manuscripts are not eligible. Except in the drama category, anthologies are not eligible. Five copies of each book to be considered must be mailed to the WGA office no later than December 31. Submissions postmarked after this date will not be accepted. Exceptions will be made for any books published between the 15th and 31st of December. These may be submitted by January 15. Three copies will go to the three judges in that category; one will remain in the WGA library; and one will be placed in a WGA book display around the province. Works may be submitted by authors, publishers, or any interested parties.

Additional Contests and Awards

The following listings also contain information about contests and awards. See the General Index for page numbers, then read the listings and send SASEs (or SAEs and IRCs) for specific details about their offerings. Note: Double daggers (‡) preceding titles indicate listings new to this edition.

Abiko Quarterly With James Joyce FW Studies
Academy of American Poets, The
Acorn, The
Advocate
African Voices
‡Alabama State Poetry Society
Albatross
Alicejamesbooks
Amaranth
Amelia
America
American Poetry Review
American Tolkien Society
Amethyst Review, The
Analecta
Anamnesis Press
Anhinga Press
‡Anthology
‡Anthology of New England Writers, The
Antietam Review
Appalachia
Appalachian Heritage
Arc: Canada's National Poetry Magazine
‡Arizona Authors Association
Arkansas Press, The University of
Arkansas Writers' Conference
artisan, a journal of craft
Associated Writing Programs
Atlanta Review
Bay Area Poets Coalition (BAPC)
‡Beauty for Ashes
‡Behind Bars
Bellingham Review, The
Bell's Letters Poet
Beloit Poetry Journal, The
‡Bitter Oleander, The
Black Bear Publications
Black Warrior Review
Block's Magazine
Blue Light Press
Blue Penny Quarterly
Blue Unicorn, A Triquarterly of Poetry
BOOG Literature
‡BrickHouse Books, Inc.
‡Bright Hill Press
British Haiku Society
‡Burning Bush Publications
Byline Magazine
Calapooya Collage
Canada Council, The
Canadian Poetry Association
Canadian Writer's Journal
Candlelight Poetry Journal
CannedPhlegm
Cape Rock, The
Caribbean Writer, The
Carolina Quarterly, The
Carousel Magazine
Center Press
Chelsea

Chiron Review
Cleveland State University Poetry Center
Cló Iar-Chonnachta
Cochran's Corner
College of New Jersey Writers Conference, The
Colorado Review
‡Columbine State Poetry Society of Colorado
Comstock Review, The
Connecticut River Review
Conservative Review
‡Contemporary Verse 2
Country Woman
Cover Magazine
CQ (California State Poetry Quarterly)
Crab Creek Review
Craft of Writing
Cream City Review
Creative With Words Publications (C.W.W.)
‡Creativity Unlimited Press
Cricket
Crucible
Cumberland Poetry Review
Cutbank
Dancing Jester Press
Dead Metaphor Press
Defined Providence
Denver Quarterly
Devil's Millhopper Press, The
Dream Shop, The
Eagle's Flight
Echoes Magazine
1812
Eighth Mountain Press, The
‡Ekphrasis
ELF: Eclectic Literary Forum
Emerald Coast Review
Envoi
Epoch
Excursus Literary Arts Journal
Explorations
Explorer Magazine
Expressions
Fauquier Poetry Journal
Federation of British Columbia Writers
Feelings: America's Beautiful Poetry Magazine
Field
5th Gear
First Time
‡Fishtrap
Floating Bridge Press
‡Florida First Coast Writers' Festival
‡Fly by Night Magazine
Footwork: The Paterson Literary Review
Formalist, The
Fudge Cake, The
‡Garnet

Gaslight: Tales of the Unsane
‡Gathering of the Tribes, A
Gentle Survivalist, The
George & Mertie's Place: Rooms With A View
Georgetown Review
‡Georgia Poetry Society
Gerbil: A Queer Culture Zine
Golden Isis Magazine
‡Graffiti Rag
Grain
‡Great Midwestern Quarterly
‡Greater Cincinnati Writers' League
Greensboro Review, The
Haiku Headlines: A Monthly Newsletter of Haiku and Senryu
Half Tones to Jubilee
Harp-Strings Poetry Journal
Heartlands Today, The
Heaven Bone Magazine
Helicon Nine Editions
Hellas: A Journal of Poetry and the Humanities
Hippopotamus Press
Housewife-Writer's Forum
Hubbub
Hyacinth House Publications
I.E. Magazine, A Journal of Literature and the Arts
Imago: New Writing
‡Inc and the Arts
‡Indian Heritage Publishing
‡Indiana State Federation of Poetry Clubs
Intercultural Writer's Review, The
International Quarterly
‡Interpreter's House
Iowa Woman
Italian Americana
Joyful Noise: The Journal of Christian Poetry
Kalliope, a journal of women's art
Kansas Quarterly/Arkansas Review
‡Kentucky State Poetry Society, The
Kinesis
Lacunae Magazine
‡Lane Literary Guild, The
‡Laurels
League of Canadian Poets, The
Ledge, The
Lines n' Rhymes
Listening Eye, The
Literal Latté
‡Literary Focus Poetry Publications
‡Live Poets Society, Maine
Loft, The
‡Lone Stars Magazine
Long Island Quarterly
Lotus Press, Inc.
Louisiana Literature
Luz en Arte y Literatura
Lynx, A Journal for Linking Poets
Lyric, The
M.O.O.N. Magazine

MacGuffin, The
‡Mad Poets Review
Madison Review, The
Mail Call Journal
‡Malachite & Agate
Malahat Review, The
Malevolence Publications
‡Manchester Poets Press
Manitoba Writers' Guild Inc.
Many Mountains Moving
‡Marlboro Review, The
Maryland Poetry Review
Massachusetts Press, The University of
‡Massachusetts State Poetry Society, Inc.
Maverick Press, The
Medicinal Purposes Literary Review
Mid-American Review
Midwest Poetry Review
Midwest Writers' Conference
Minority Literary Expo
‡Mississippi Poetry Society, Inc.
Mississippi Review
Mississippi Valley Writers Conference
Missouri Review
Mockingbird
‡Mojo Risin' Magazine
‡MoonRabbit Review
Moose Bound Press
(m)öthêr TØñgué Press
‡Mount Olive College Press
Mudfish
Mystery Time
Nassau Review
Nation, The
National Federation of State Poetry Societies, Inc.
‡National Writers Association
Nebraska Review, The
Negative Capability
‡Nevada Poetry Society
‡New Delta Review
New England Poetry Club
New Era Magazine
New Frontiers of New Mexico
New Horizons Poetry Club
New Letters
‡New Millennium Writingss
New Press Literary Quarterly, The
New Renaissance, The
New Spirit Press
Nimrod: International Journal of Contemporary Poetry and Fiction
96 Inc Magazine
North Carolina Writers' Network
‡Northeast Corridor
Northwoods Press
Nostalgia: A Sentimental State of Mind
Oak, The
Oatmeal and Poetry
Ohio State University Press/The Journal Award in Poetry
Onionhead
Oracle Poetry
Orbis: An International Quarterly of Poetry and Prose
Oregon State Poetry Association, The
‡Our Journey
Outrider Press
Owl Creek Press

Oxford Poetry
Ozark Creative Writers Conference
Pacific Coast Journal
Painted Bride Quarterly
Palanquin/TDM
Paper Boat Magazine
Papyrus
Paris Review, The
Parnassus Literary Journal
Passager: A Journal of Remembrance and Discovery
Pavement Saw
‡Peace and Freedom
Pearl
‡Peer Poetry Magazine
PEN American Center
Peregrine: The Journal of Amherst Writers & Artists
Perivale Press
Permafrost: A Literary Journal
Phoebe
‡Phoenix
Piedmont Literary Review
Pig Iron
Pikeville Review
Pitt Poetry Series
Pittsburgh Quarterly, The
Plainsongs
Plowman, The
Poems & Plays
Poet Lore
Poet Magazine
Poetic Page
Poetic Realm
Poetry
Poetry Committee of the Greater Washington Area, The
‡Poetry Forum
‡Poetry Life Supplement
Poetry Miscellany, The
Poetry Northwest
Poetry Nottingham International
‡Poetry Review
‡Poetry Society of Tennessee
Poetry Society of America
‡Poetry Society of Texas, The
Poet's Attic Quarterly, The
Poet's Fantasy
Poet's Guild, The
‡Poet's Paradise
Poet's Review
Poets' Roundtable
Potato Eyes
‡Potomac Review
Potpourri
Prairie Schooner
Pudding House Publications
Purdue University Press
Pygmy Forest Press
Quarterly Review of Literature Poetry Book Series
Rambunctious Press
‡RB's Poets' Viewpoint
‡Ridge Runner Press
Rio Grande Press
River City
Riverstone, A Press for Poetry
Rockford Review, The
Rosebud
St. Davids Christian Writers Conference
Salmon Run Press
‡Salopian Poetry Society

‡Salt Hill Journal
‡San Diego Poet's Press
Santa Barbara Review
Santa Barbara Writers' Conference
Sarabande Books, Inc.
‡Satire
Scavenger's Newsletter
‡Sea Oats
Seasons of the Muse
Sewanee Review, The
Sheila-Na-Gig
Shenandoah
Silver Wings
Silverfish Review
Sinipee Writers Workshop
Skipping Stones: A Multicultural Children's Magazine
Slate & Style
Slipstream
Smith Publisher, Gibbs
‡Snake Nation Review
‡Snowapple Press
Society of American Poets, The
Songwriters and Poets Critique
Sonora Review
‡South Dakota State Poetry Society
Southern California Anthology, The
Southern Humanities Review
Southern Poetry Association
Southern Poetry Review
Southwest Florida Writers' Conference
Southwest Review
Sow's Ear Poetry Review, The
‡Spelunker Flophouse
Spillway
Spitball
Spoon River Poetry Review, The
‡Spring Fantasy
Staple
State of Maine Writers' Conference
State Street Press
Still Waters Press
‡Stoneflower Literary Journal
Story Line Press
Studio, A Journal of Christians Writing
‡Stygian Vortex Publications
Sub-Terrain
‡Sunday Suitor Poetry Review, The
‡Sunflower Dream, The
Taproot Literary Review
Tears in the Fence
‡Teens In Motion News
‡Texas Review
Texas Tech University Press
Tickled by Thunder: The Magazine That Set Fiction Free
Time of Singing, A Magazine of Christian Poetry
‡Toth Press
‡Troubadour
Tundra
‡Understanding Magazine
‡Unfinished Monument Press
University of Arizona Poetry Center
Unterberg Poetry Center of the 92nd Street Y, The
‡Urthona Magazine
‡Urthona Press
‡Utah State Poetry Society
Vegetarian Journal
Verbal Expression

State and Provincial Grants

Arts councils in the United States and Canada provide assistance to artists (including poets) in the form of fellowships or grants. These grants can be substantial and confer prestige upon recipients; however, **only state or province residents are eligible**. Because deadlines and available support vary annually, query first (with a SASE).

UNITED STATES ART AGENCIES

Alabama State Council on the Arts, *Becky Mullens, Literature Programs Manager, 201 Monroe St., Suite 110, Montgomery AL 36130; (334)242-4076*

Alaska State Council on the Arts, *Timothy Wilson, Executive Director, 411 W. Fourth Ave., Suite 1-E, Anchorage AK 99501-2343; (907)269-6610*

Arizona Commission on the Arts, *Tonda Gorton, Public Information Officer, 417 W. Roosevelt, Phoenix AZ 85003; (602)255-5882*

Arkansas Arts Council, *Sally Williams, Artists Program Coordinator, 1500 Tower Bldg., 323 Center St., Little Rock AR 72201; (501)324-9150*

California Arts Council, *Carol Shiffman, Individual Fellowships, 1300 I St., Suite 930, Sacramento CA 95814; (916)322-6555*

Colorado Council on the Arts and Humanities, *Daniel Salazar, Individual Artists Program Director, 750 Pennsylvania St., Denver CO 80203-3699; (303)894-2619*

Connecticut Commission on the Arts, *Linda Dente, Grants Information, 1 Financial Plaza, Lobby, 755 Main St., Hartford CT 06103; (860)566-7076*

Delaware State Arts Council, *Barbara King, Coordinator, Individual Artist Fellowships, Carvel State Office Building, 820 N. French St., Wilmington DE 19801; (302)577-8278*

District of Columbia Commission on the Arts and Humanities, *Carlos Arrien, Program Coordinator, Stables Art Center, 5th Floor, 410 Eighth St. NW, Washington DC 20004; (202)724-5613*

Florida Arts Council, *Valerie Ohlsson, Arts Consultant, Division of Cultural Affairs, Florida Dept. of State, The Capitol, Tallahassee FL 32399-0250; (904)487-2980*

Georgia Council for the Arts, *Ann Davis, Program Manager, Community Arts Development, 530 Means St. NW, Suite 115, Atlanta GA 30318-5793; (404)651-7920*

Hawaii State Foundation on Culture & Arts, *Hinano Campton, Artist Grant Coordinator, 44 Merchant St., Honolulu HI 96813; (808)586-0300*

Idaho Commission on the Arts, *Diane Josephy Peavey, Literature Director, P.O. Box 83720, Boise ID 83720-0008; (208)334-2119*

Illinois Arts Council, *Richard Gage, Communication Arts Director, 100 W. Randolph, Suite 10-500, Chicago IL 60601; (312)814-6750*

Indiana Arts Commission, *Joyce Ribble, Assistant Director for Programs, 402 W. Washington St., Room W072, Indianapolis IN 46204-2741; (317)232-1268*

Iowa Arts Council, *Julie Bailey, Grants Coordinator, Capitol Complex, 600 E. Locust, Des Moines IA 50319-0290; (515)281-4451*

Kansas Arts Commission, *Tom Klocke, Program Coordinator, Jay Hawk Tower, 700 Jackson, Suite 1004, Topeka KS 66603; (913)296-3335*

Kentucky Arts Council, *Irwin Pickett, Program Branch Manager, 31 Fountain Place, Frankfort KY 40601-1942; (502)564-3757*

Louisiana State Arts Council, *James Border, Program Director, P.O. Box 44247, Baton Rouge LA 70804; (504)342-8180*

Maine State Arts Commission, *Kathy Ann Jones, Associate for Contemporary Arts, State House, Station 25, 55 Capitol St., Augusta ME 04333-0025; (207)287-2750*

Maryland State Arts Council, *Charles Camp, Grants Officer, 601 N. Howard St., Baltimore MD 21201; (410)333-8232*

Massachusetts Cultural Council, *Lisa Sasier, Public Information, 120 Boylston St., 2nd Floor, Boston MA 02116; (617)727-3668*

Arts Foundation of Michigan, *Kim Adams, Executive Director, 645 Griswold, Suite 2164, Detroit MI 48226; (313)964-2244*

Minnesota State Arts Board, *Karen Mueller, Program Associate, Park Square Court, 400 Sibley St., Suite 200, St. Paul MN 55101; (612)215-1600*

Mississippi Arts Commission, *Kathleen Stept, Program Administrator, 239 N. Lamar St., Suite 207, Jackson MS 39201; (601)359-6030*

Missouri Arts Council, *Michael Hunt, Program Administrator, Wainwright State Office Complex, 111 N. Seventh St., Suite 105, St. Louis MO 63101; (314)340-6845*

Montana Arts Council, *Fran Morrow, Director of Art Services/Programs, 316 N. Park Ave., Suite 252, Helena MT 59620; (406)444-6430*

Nebraska Arts Council, *Suzanne Wise, Manager of Programs, 3838 Davenport St., Omaha NE 68131-2329; (402)595-2122*

Nevada State Council on the Arts, *Susan Bofkoff, Executive Director, 602 N. Curry, Carson City NV 89703; (702)687-6680*

New Hampshire State Council on the Arts, *Audrey Sylvester, Artists Services Coordinator, Phoenix Hall, 40 N. Main St., Concord NH 03301; (603)271-2789*

New Jersey State Council on the Arts, *Steve Runk, Grants Coordinator, CN 306, 3rd Floor, Roebling Bldg., 20 W. State St., Trenton NJ 08625; (609)292-6130*

New Mexico Arts Division, *Virginia Castellano, Operations Coordinator, 228 E. Palace Ave., Santa Fe NM 87501; (505)827-6490*

New York State Council on the Arts, *Kathleen Masterson, Director, Literature Program, 915 Broadway, New York NY 10010; (212)387-7022*

North Carolina Arts Council, *Deborah McGill, Literature Director, Department of Cultural Resources, 221 E. Lane St., Raleigh NC 27601-2807; (919)733-2111*

North Dakota Council on the Arts, *Patsy Thompson, Executive Director, 418 E. Broadway, Suite 70, Bismark ND 58501-4086; (701)328-3954*

Ohio Arts Council, *Bob Fox, Literature Coordinator, 727 E. Main St., Columbus OH 43205; (614)466-2613*

State Arts Council of Oklahoma, *Betty Price, Executive Director, P.O. Box 52001-2001, Oklahoma City OK 73152-2001; (405)521-2931*

Oregon Arts Commission, *Vincent Dunn, Assistant Director, 775 Summer St. NE, Salem OR 97310; (503)986-0086*

Pennsylvania Council on the Arts, *Jim Woland, Literature Program Director, Finance Bldg., Room 216, Harrisburg PA 17120; (717)787-6883*

Institute of Puerto Rican Culture, *P.O. Box 4184, San Juan PR 00902-4184; (787)724-0700*

Rhode Island State Council on the Arts, *Randall Rosenbaum, Executive Director, 95 Cedar St., Suite 103, Providence RI 02903; (401)277-3880*

South Carolina Arts Commission, *Sara June Goldstein, Literary Arts Director, 1800 Gervais St., Columbia SC 29201; (803)734-8696*

South Dakota Arts Council, *Dennis Holub, Director, 800 Governors Dr., Pierre SD 57501; (605)773-3131*

Tennessee Arts Commission, *Alice Swanson, Director of Literary Arts, 401 Charlotte Ave., Nashville TN 37243-0780; (615)741-1701*

Texas Commission on the Arts, *Laura Weigand, Program Director, Visual and Communication Arts, P.O. Box 13406, Austin TX 78711-3406; (512)463-5535*

Utah Arts Council, *Guy Lebeda, Literary Coordinator, 617 E. South Temple, Salt Lake City UT 84102-1177; (801)533-5895*

Vermont Council on the Arts, *Alexander Aldrich, Executive Director, 136 State St., Drawer 33, Montpelier VT 05633-6001; (802)828-3291*

Virgin Islands Council on the Arts, *Marie Daniel, Grants Officer, 41-42 Norre Gada, St. Thomas VI 00802; (809)774-5984*

Virginia Commission for the Arts, *Susan FitzPatrick, Program Coordinator, 223 Governor St., Richmond VA 23219; (804)225-3132*

Washington State Arts Commission, *Artist Fellowship, Karen Gose, Executive Director, 234 E. Eighth Ave., Olympia WA 98504-2675; (360)753-3860*

West Virginia Arts and Humanities Division, *Jill Ellis, Grants Coordinator, Cultural Center, 1900 Kanawha Blvd. E., Charleston WV 25305-0300; (304)558-0220*

Wisconsin Arts Board, *Mark Fraire, Individual Artists Program Director, 101 E. Wilson St., 1st Floor, Madison WI 53702; (608)264-8191*

Wyoming Council on the Arts, *Michael Shay, Literary Arts Coordinator, 2320 Capitol Ave., Cheyenne WY 82002; (307)777-7742*

CANADIAN PROVINCES ART AGENCIES

Alberta Arts and Cultural Industries Branch, *Clive Padfield, Director, 10405 Jasper Ave., 9th Floor, Edmonton, Alberta T5J 4R7; (403)427-6315*

British Columbia Arts Council, *Cultural Services Branch, Walter Quan, Coordinator of Individual Awards Program, 800 Johnson St., 5th Floor, Victoria, British Columbia V8V 1X4; (250)356-1728*

Manitoba Arts Council, *Pat Sanders, Writing/Publishing Officer, 525 - 93 Lombard Ave., Winnipeg, Manitoba R3B 3B1; (204)945-0422*

New Brunswick Department of Tourism, Recreation and Heritage, *Arts Branch, % Desmond Maillet, P.O. Box 6000, Fredericton, New Brunswick E3B 5H1; (506)453-2555*

Newfoundland & Labrador Arts Council, *Randy Follett, Executive Director, P.O. Box 98, St. John's, Newfoundland A1C 5H5; (709)726-2212*

Nova Scotia Arts Council, *Peter Kirby, Program Officer for Individual Artists, P.O. Box 666, Halifax Central, Halifax, Nova Scotia B3J 2T3; (902)422-1123*

The Canada Council, *General Information Officer, P.O. Box 1047, 350 Albert St., Ottawa, Ontario K1P 5V8; (613)566-4365*

Ontario Arts Council, *Lorraine Filyer, Literature Officer, 151 Bloor St. W., 6th Floor, Toronto, Ontario M5S 1T6; (416)961-1660*

Prince Edward Island Council of the Arts, *Judy McDonald, Executive Director, 115 Richmond, Charlottetown, Prince Edward Island C1A 1H7; (902)368-4410*

Saskatchewan Arts Board, *Gail Paul Armstrong, Literary & Multidisciplinary Arts Consultant, 3475 Albert St., Regina, Saskatchewan S4S 6X6; (306)787-4056*

Government of Yukon Arts Branch, *Laurel Parry, Arts Consultant, P.O. Box 2703, Whitehorse, Yukon Y1A 2C6; (403)667-5264*

Resources

Conferences and Workshops

Conferences and workshops are valuable resources for many poets, especially beginners. A conference or workshop serves as an opportunity to learn about specific aspects of the craft, connect with and gather feedback from other poets and writers, listen to submission tips from editors, and revel in a creative atmosphere that may stimulate one's muse.

In this section you'll find listings for 81 conferences and workshops—20 of which are new to this edition. All listings contain bold-faced information indicating to whom the event is open, its general purpose, and areas of concentration. Some, such as the Aran Islands International Poetry Festival (new to this edition), are specifically geared to poets. Most, however, are more general conferences with offerings for a variety of writers, including poets.

A "typical" conference may have a number of workshop sessions, keynote speakers and perhaps even a panel or two. Topics may include everything from writing fiction, poetry, and books for children to marketing one's work. Often a theme, which may change from year to year, will be the connecting factor.

Other conferences and workshops cover a number of topics but have a primary focus. For example, the Appalachian Writers Workshop offers daily sessions on poetry, but is geared toward writers and writing of the Appalachian region. There are also events especially for women writers, Christian writers and Jewish writers.

Despite different themes or focuses (indicated in bold), each listing in this section details the offerings available for poets. Each also includes information about other workshops, speakers and panels of interest. It is important to note, however, that conference and workshop directors were still in the organizing stages when contacted. Consequently, some listings include information from last year's events simply to provide an idea of what to expect this year. For more up-to-date details, including current costs, send a SASE to the conference and workshop directors a few months before the dates listed.

BENEFITING FROM CONFERENCES

Without a doubt, attending conferences and workshops is beneficial. First, these events provide opportunities to learn more about the poetic craft. Some even feature individual sessions with workshop leaders, allowing you to specifically discuss your work with others. If these one-on-one sessions include critiques (generally for an additional fee), we have included this information.

Besides learning from workshop leaders, you can also benefit from conversations with other attendees. Writers on all levels often enjoy talking to and sharing insights with others. A conversation over lunch can reveal a new market for your work, or a casual chat while waiting for a session to begin can acquaint you with a new resource.

Also, if a conference or workshop includes time for open readings and you choose to participate, you may gain feedback from workshop leaders and others. For some, however, just the

GET THE MOST FROM A CONFERENCE

Squeeze the most out of a conference by getting organized and staying involved. Follow these steps to ensure a worthwhile event.

Before You Go:

● **Become familiar with all the pre-conference literature**, particularly the agenda. Study the maps of the area, especially the locations of the rooms in which your meetings/events are scheduled.

● **Make a list of three to five objectives you'd like to obtain**, e.g., who you want to meet, what you want to learn more about, what you want to improve on, how many new markets you want to find.

At the Conference:

● **Budget your time**. Label a map so you know ahead of time where, when and how to get to each session. Note what you want to do most. Then, schedule time with editors for critique sessions.

● **Don't be afraid to explore new areas**. You are there to learn. Pick one or two sessions you wouldn't typically attend. This is an education; keep your mind open to new ideas and advice.

● **Allow time for mingling**. Some of the best information is given after the sessions. Find out "frank truths" and inside scoops. Asking people what they've learned at the conference will trigger a conversation that may branch into areas you want to know more about, but won't hear from the speakers.

● **Learn about editors and new markets**. Which are more open to new writers? Find a new contact in your area for future support.

● **Collect everything**: guidelines, sample issues, promotional fliers and especially business cards. Make notes about the personalities of the people you meet to later remind you who to contact and who to avoid.

● **Find inspiration for future projects**. While you're away from home, people-watch, take a walk, a bike ride or drive. You may even want to take pictures to enhance your memory.

After the Conference:

● **Evaluate**. Write down the answers to these questions: Would I attend again? What were the pluses and minuses, e.g., speakers, location, food, topics, cost, lodging? What do I want to remember for next year? What should I try to do next time? Who would I like to meet?

● **Write a thank-you letter** to an editor who has been particularly helpful. They'll remember you when you later submit.

relief from the solitude of writing can make a conference or workshop worthwhile.

Another reason conferences and workshops are valuable is the opportunity they provide to meet editors and publishers who often have tips about marketing work. The availability of these individuals, however, does not necessarily mean they will want to read your latest collection of poems (unless, of course, they are workshop leaders and you have separate meetings scheduled with them).

Although editors and publishers cannot give personal attention to everyone they meet, don't be afraid to approach them. If they weren't interested in speaking to writers, they wouldn't have agreed to attend the conference. However, if the editor or publisher's schedule is too full to allow discussion of your work, ask if you may follow up with a letter after the event. This will give you the benefit of his or her undivided attention and, perhaps, develop into a contact in the poetry field. For more tips on how to benefit from a conference, see the sidebar on page 507.

SELECTING A CONFERENCE OR WORKSHOP

When selecting a conference or workshop to attend, keep your goals in mind. If you want to learn how to improve your craft, for example, consider one of the events entirely devoted to poetry or locate a more general conference where one-on-one critique sessions are offered. If you're looking for more informal feedback, choose an event that includes open readings. If marketing your work seems like an ominous task, register for a conference that includes a session with editors. And if you also have an interest in other forms of writing, an event with a wide range of workshops is a good bet.

Of course, also take your resources into consideration. If both your time and funds are limited, search for a conference or workshop within your area. Many events are held during weekends and may be close enough for you to commute. On the other hand, if you want to combine your family vacation with time spent meeting other writers and working on your craft, consider workshops such as those sponsored by The Writers' Center at Chautauqua. In either case, it is important to at least consider the conference location and learn about other enjoyable activities in the area.

Still other factors may influence your decision. Events sponsoring contests, for instance, may allow you to gain recognition and recoup some of your expenses. Similarly, some conferences and workshops have financial assistance or scholarships available. Finally, many are associated with colleges or universities and offer continuing education credits. When available, these options are included in the listings. Again, send a SASE for more details.

For other conferences and workshops, see *The Guide to Writers Conferences* (ShawGuides, Inc., P.O. Box 1295, New York NY 10023, website http://www.shawguides.com); *Writers Conferences: An Annual Guide to Literary Conferences* (Poets & Writers, Inc., 72 Spring St., Suite 301, New York NY 10012-4019); or the May issue of *Writer's Digest* magazine (available on newsstands or directly from the publisher at 1507 Dana Ave., Cincinnati OH 45207). You may also want to check the bulletin boards at libraries and bookstores for local events.

AMERICAN CHRISTIAN WRITERS CONFERENCES, P.O. Box 110390, Nashville TN 37222, phone (800)21-WRITE, director Reg Forder. Annual 3-day events founded in 1981. Held throughout the year in cities including Houston, Dallas/Ft. Worth, Boston, Minneapolis, Chicago, St. Louis, Detroit, Orlando, Atlanta, Miami, Phoenix and Los Angeles. Usually located at a major hotel chain like Holiday Inn. Average attendance is 100. **Open to anyone. Conferences cover fiction, poetry, writing for children.** Cost is $199, participants are responsible for their own meals. Accommodations include special rates at host hotel. They also sponsor an annual Caribbean Christian Writers Conference Cruise each November. Send SASE for brochures and registration forms.

ANTIOCH WRITERS' WORKSHOP, P.O. Box 494, Yellow Springs OH 45387, phone (937)767-2077, director Gilah Rittenhouse. Annual 7-day event founded in 1986. Usually held in late July or early August at Antioch College in the village of Yellow Springs. "The campus is quiet, shady, relaxed. The village is unusual for its size: a hotbed of artists, writers and creative people." Average attendance is 70. **Open to everyone. "We create an intense community of writers and cover fiction, poetry and writing for children plus playwriting, screenwriting, mystery and nonfiction. Also talks by editors, agents, and others in the industry."** Offerings specifically available for poets include an introductory class in writing poetry, an intensive seminar, night sessions for participants to share poetry, and critiquing. Speakers for the 1997 conference included Herbert Woodward Martin and Colette Inez. Cost for 1997 conference was $475; scholarships and some work-study fellowships are available (including the Judson Jerome Scholarship sponsored by *Writer's Digest* magazine). Both graduate and undergraduate credit is available for an additional fee. Campus dining room meal ticket is $110 (for 20 meals); must be purchased in advance. Transportation from airport is provided. Information on overnight accommodations is available and includes housing in campus dorms. Individual critiques available. Submit work for critique in advance with $60 fee for poetry; $60 fee for story, book or script. Send SASE for brochures and registration forms.

APPALACHIAN WRITERS WORKSHOP, P.O. Box 844, Hindman KY 41822, phone (606)785-5475, e-mail tiss@eastky.com, director Mike Mullins. Annual 5-day event founded 1977. Usually held at the end of July or beginning of August. Location: Campus of Hindman Settlement School in Knott County, KY. "The campus is hilly and access for housing is limited for physically impaired, but workshop facilities are accessible." Average attendance is 60-70. **Open to "anyone regardless of sex, age or race." Conference is designed to promote writers and writing of the Appalachian region. It covers fiction, poetry, writing for children, dramatic work and nonfiction.** Offerings specifically available for poets include daily sessions on poetry, individual critique sessions and readings. Staff has included Lee Smith, Hal Crowther, George Ella Lyon, James Still and Barbara Smith. Cost for workshop is approximately $350 for room, board and tuition. Information on overnight accommodations is available for registrants. Accommodations may include special rates at area hotels "once our facilities are filled." Submit mss for individual critiques in advance. Send SASE for brochures and registration forms.

‡*ARAN ISLANDS INTERNATIONAL POETRY FESTIVAL, P.O. Box 1677, Kingston RI 02881-0488, phone (800)888-9724, fax (401)783-6398, e-mail marinertvl@aol.com, contact Marianne Kittridge. Annual weeklong event. 1997 dates were August 9-16 for the tour, with the Festival held August 12-14. Location: "Set in Galway, a thriving European university town still permeated by the ancient Celtic culture, and also in the rugged beauty of the Aran Islands. Enrollment is very limited and will be based on a first come, first served basis." **Open to anyone.** Offerings specifically available for poets included 15 performances by renowned poets and daily cultural/musical events. "Poets-teachers offer workshops and manuscript consultation for an additional charge." Speakers at last festival were U.S. Poet Laureate Robert Hass and Nobel Prize recipient Czeslaw Milosz; also poets Adrienne Rich, Eavan Boland, Eamon Grennan, Brenda Hillman and Brigit Pegeen Kelly. Other special features included bus tours of western Ireland and Dublin—"Coole Park, where many of Ireland's most famous writers signed the Autograph Tree; Thoor Ballylee, the tower home of W.B. Yeats; and the spectacular scenery of Connemura, the Burren, the Cliffs of Moher, and the Aran Islands." Cost for 1997 was $1,525 including round-trip airfare from Boston or New York; accommodations at Corrib Village in single- or double-occupancy apartment-style suites; and some meals (6 continental breakfasts, 4 lunches and 2 dinners). "Before, during and after the three-day Festival, participants will visit natural and historic landmarks with which the west of Ireland is particularly rich. Don't miss this experience, which U.S. Ambassador to Ireland Jean Kennedy Smith is calling 'an educational, cultural and travel opportunity without parallel.' "

ARKANSAS WRITERS' CONFERENCE, 6817 Gingerbread Lane, Little Rock AR 72204, phone (501)565-8889, director Peggy Vining. Annual 2-day event founded 1944. Always held the first weekend of June at the Holiday Inn West in Little Rock. Average attendance is 200. **Open to all writers. The conference is designed to "appeal both to beginning and already active writers with a varied program on improving their writing skills and marketing their work."** Offerings specifically available for poets include poetry contests and sessions with poetry editors. Guest speakers have included Leonard Bishop, author of *Dare to Be a Great Writer* (Writer's Digest Books); Andrea Hollander Budy, nationally known award-winning poet; Victor Fleming; Grif Stockley; and Gina Wilkins. Other special features have included an awards luncheon (door prizes such as *Writer's Market* and *Poet's Market*) and banquet, and the announcement of the person selected for Arkansas Writers' Hall of Fame. Cost for 1997 conference was $10 registration for 2 days, $5 for 1 day. Five-dollar fee to cover entry to 36 contests. Limousine service from airport to Holiday Inn West is provided. Accommodations include special rates at host hotel. Individual critiques are available. Thirty-six contests (4 require attendance and 8 are limited to Arkansas residents) are sponsored as part of the conference. Each contest has a chairman who will judge or secure a judge. Send SASE for brochures and registration forms after February 1 each year.

THE ASHEVILLE POETRY FESTIVAL, 20 Battery Park, Suite 505, Asheville NC 28801, phone (800)476-8172, fax (704)232-1045, e-mail festival@poetryalive.com, website http://www.poetryalive.com, director Allan Wolf. Annual 3-day event founded 1994. Usually held the second weekend in July at the campus of the University of North Carolina-Asheville. Average attendance is 600. **Open to "everyone and anyone. Our focus is poetry. Our mission is to bring together poets of different voices, styles, and backgrounds to celebrate the diversity of poetry and the spoken word."** Workshops for the 1997 festival included "Rewriting the Bible"; "Tapping Your Personal Mythology to Generate Poems"; "Fifty-four Tips for Writing Better Poetry and Getting it Published"; "Mastering Metaphor"; "Carl Sandburg Field Trip"; "Combining Natural History and Poetry"; "Breathing New Life into the Written Word." Speakers at 1997 festival included Joseph Bathanti, Katherine Stripling Byer, Richard Cambridge, Yusef Komunyakaa, Philip Levine, Jack Prelutsky and Marc Smith. Other special features included continual open mics, a poetry slam with cash prize, and readings by featured poets. Cost for the 1997 festival was $50 (weekend pass). Individual workshop prices vary from $5-35. "Participants are responsible for their own travel and lodging." Information on overnight accommodations is available for registrants. Accommodations include special rates at area hotels. Individual critiques are also available. Submit up to 10 poems on 10 pgs. maximum with $40 reading fee by June 1. Write or call for brochures and registration forms.

ASPEN WRITERS' CONFERENCE, P.O. Drawer 7726, Aspen CO 81612, phone (970)925-3122 or (800)925-2526, fax (970)920-5700, e-mail aspenwrite@aol.com, executive director Jeanne McGovern. Annual week-long event founded 1975. Usually held the second week of June. Location: The Aspen Institute, Aspen Meadows campus or other site in Aspen. Average attendance is 60. **Open to all writers. Conference includes intensive writing workshops in poetry, fiction, nonfiction and children's literature**. Offerings specifically available for poets included two poetry workshops, craft lectures and readings by faculty and participants. Speakers at last conference were Andrea Barrett and Rudolfo Anaya (keynote); Marcia Southwick and Gerald Stern (poetry); Ron Carlson and Valerie Miner (fiction); David Reiff (journalist); and Jan Greenberg (children's writer). Cost for 1997 conference was $495, does not include meals or lodging. Transportation to and from on-site lodging and event is available. Information on overnight accommodations is available for registrants. In 1997, cost of on-site accommodations was $60/person/day double occupancy or $85/person/day single occupancy. "We accept poetry in advance that will be discussed during workshop." Send SASE for brochures and registration forms or request via e-mail. Include mailing address with all e-mail requests for brochures/registration forms.

AUSTIN WRITERS' LEAGUE SPRING AND FALL WORKSHOPS, 1501 W. Fifth St., Suite E-2, Austin TX 78703, phone (512)499-8914, fax (512)499-0441, e-mail awl@eden.com, website http://www.eden.com/~awl, executive director Angela Smith. Biannual workshops founded 1982. "Workshops are usually 3- or 6-hour sessions." Usually held weekends in March, April, May and September, October, November. Location: Austin Writers' League Resource Center/Library. Registration limited. **Open to all writers, beginners and advanced. Workshops cover fiction, poetry, writing for children, nonfiction, screenwriting, book promotion and marketing, working with agents and publishers, journal writing, special interest writing, creativity, grantwriting, copyright law and taxes for writers.** Offerings specifically available for poets include at least 2 workshops during each series. Poetry presenters have included Ralph Angel, Rosellen Brown, Reginald Gibbons and Marion Winik. Past speakers have included Sandra Scofield, Sue Grafton, Peter Mehlman, Gregg Levoy, Lee Merrill Byrd and several New York agents and editors. "Occasionally, presenters agree to do private consults with participants. Also, workshops sometimes incorporate hands-on practice and critique." Cost is $35-75. Members get discount. Cost includes continental breakfast and refreshments for breaks. Meals not included. Arrangements can be made in advance for airport transportation. Information on overnight accommodations is available for registrants. Accommodations include special rates at area hotels. Requirements for critiques are posted in workshop brochure. Send SASE for brochures and registration forms or request via e-mail (include mailing address). The Austin Writers' League publishes *Poetography*, an anthology of poems selected by jury, and *The Austin Writer*, a monthly publication of prose and poetry selected from submissions each month. These poems are eligible for six $100 Word Is Art awards presented in January of each year. The League is also the umbrella for *Borderlands: Texas Poetry Review* (see listing in Publishers of Poetry section). Poetry guidelines for other publications, awards and grants programs, and market listings are available through the League library.

BREAD LOAF WRITERS' CONFERENCE, Middlebury College, Middlebury VT 05753, phone (802)388-3711 ext. 5286, fax (802)443-2087, e-mail blwc@mail.middleburg.edu, website http://www.middlebury.edu/blwc, administrative coordinator Carol Knauss. Annual 11-day event founded 1926. Usually held in mid-August. Average attendance is 230. **Conference is designed to promote dialogue among writers and provide professional critiques for students. Conference usually covers fiction, nonfiction and poetry.** Cost for 1997 conference was $1,670, including tuition, room and board. Fellowships and scholarships for the conference are available. "Candidates for fellowships must have a book published. Candidates for scholarships must have published in major literary periodicals or newspapers. A letter of recommendation, application and supporting materials due by April 1. Awards are announced in June for the conference in August." Taxis to and from the airport or bus station are available. Individual critiques are also available. Send for brochures and application forms or obtain via website.

BROCKPORT WRITERS FORUM SUMMER WORKSHOPS, 350 New Campus Dr., SUNY-Brockport, Brockport NY 14420-2968, phone (716)395-5713, fax (716)395-2391, e-mail srubin@acs.brockport.edu, director Dr. Stan Rubin. Annual 7-day event founded 1980. Usually held the second week in July. Average attendance is 60-75. **Open to all writers, "advanced beginners through published authors." Workshop usually covers fiction, poetry, creative nonfiction, journals/autobiography and fantasy/science fiction.** Panels for 1998 are on publishing, craft and on individual genre. Offerings specifically available for poets include poetry workshop with 2 nationally known leaders. Speakers for next conference are Stanley W. Linberg, Carol Houch Smith, Robert Blake and William Heyan. Other special features include individual conferences (critiques) for all participants, access to the Brockport Writers Forum videotape library and readings by faculty and participants. "Up to three college credits—graduate or undergraduate—can be earned." Cost for conference is approximately $450, lodging is extra. "We provide lunches and some dinners." Scholarship available. Transportation to and from the event is provided as required. Private and semiprivate, air-conditioned accommodations available in on-site conference center. Send SASE for brochures and registration forms. "We publish occasional broadsides and pamphlets of participant and faculty work."

‡CAPE COD WRITERS' CENTER SUMMER CONFERENCE; FALL STATE-OF-THE-GENRE SUNDAY SEMINARS, % Cape Cod Writers' Center, P.O. Box 186, Barnstable MA 02630, phone (508)375-0516, e-mail ccwc@capecod.net, website http://www.capecod.net/writers, contact Don Ellis or Nancy Richard. Annual week-long event founded in 1963. Usually held the third week of August at the Tabernacle, Craigville

Conference Center. Average attendance is 150. **Open to everyone. The conference covers poetry, fiction, mystery writing, young adult fiction, nonfiction, children's writing, screenwriting and writing humor**. Offerings include 9 courses (8 adult and 1 scholarship for youth, 12-16 years of age) plus one-evening Master Class. Faculty for the last conference included Sharon Dolin (poetry); Elizabeth Searle (fiction); Deborah Savage (young adult fiction); Margery Facklam and Mary Jane Auch (children's writing); Lois Ann Demko (screenwriting); David Bouchier (humor writing); Jeremiah Healy (mystery); Robert Finch (Master Class); and John Stewart (youth-in-writing scholarship class). Costs for 1997 conference: $60 registration fee for full time, $15 for one day; $85/course tuition for full time ($10 discount for each additional class taken), $30/course for one day; $15 fee for Master Class for full time, $30 for one day; scholarships available. Participants are responsible for their own meals. "It is recommended that participants stay at the Craigville Conference Center (early registration necessary)." Other housing information available from Bed & Breakfast Cape Cod. Manuscript evaluations ($60) and personal conferences ($30) are also available. For ms evaluation, submit a few poems, short story, article, or one book chapter by July 1st with $60 fee. Send SASE for brochures and registration forms or obtain via website. The Fall State-of-the-Genre Sunday Seminars are intensive workshops covering a single genre each Sunday. 1997 dates were October 5, 12, 19, 26. The genres covered for 1997 were mystery, creative nonfiction, screenwriting and children's books. Write or call for more details.

CHARLESTON WRITERS' CONFERENCE, Lightsey Conference Center, College of Charleston, Charleston SC 29424-0001, phone (803)953-5822, fax (803)953-1454, e-mail coned@cofc.edu, director Paul Allen. Annual 4-day event founded 1989. Usually held in March at the College of Charleston, founded 1770, in historic downtown Charleston, South Carolina, "a setting renowned for its beauty, history and intimacy." Average attendance is 150. **Open to everyone. Conference covers fiction, poetry and nonfiction.** Past offerings have included a panel discussion on issues in writing and workshops covering various genres. Speakers at last conference included Susan Ludvigson, Paul Allen, David Lee and Tom Paxton. Cost for 1997 conference was $125; participants are responsible for their own meals. Information on overnight accommodations is available for registrants. Accommodations include special rates at hotels within walking distance of conference. Individual critiques are also available. Submit up to 5 poems on 8 pgs. maximum in advance with $50 fee. Send SASE for brochures and registration forms or call Judy Sawyer at phone number above.

THE COLLEGE OF NEW JERSEY WRITERS CONFERENCE, (formerly Trenton State College Writers Conference), College of New Jersey, Hillwood Lakes CN 4700, Trenton NJ 08650-4700, phone (609)771-3254, director Jean Hollander. Annual 1-day event founded 1981. Usually held the beginning of April at the College of New Jersey campus. Average attendance is about 800. **Open to anyone. Conference covers all genres of writing. "We usually have a special presentation on breaking into print." 20 separate workshops as well as readings are offered.** Recent featured speaker was Alice Walker. Cost was $40 for day session; additional cost for workshops and evening session. Discounts available for students. Information on overnight accommodations is available for registrants. Poets and fiction writers may submit ms to be critiqued in writing by workshop leaders. Poetry and short story contest sponsored as part of conference. 1st prize: $100; 2nd prize: $50. Judges are workshop leaders and a special panel from the English Dept. Write or call for brochures and registration forms.

‡**COOS BAY WRITERS WORKSHOP**, P.O. Box 4022, Coos Bay OR 97420, phone (541)756-7906, director Mary Scheirman. Annual 5-day event founded 1987. Usually held in mid-August. Location: University of Oregon Biological Research Station at Charleston Harbor on the beach. Average attendance is 40. **Open to everyone. Workshop usually covers poetry and prose.** Special features include "a hike on the beach with practicing writers who lead exercises and discussions along the way." Cost for conference is $275 for tuition; participants responsible for their own meals. Information on overnight accommodations is available for registrants. Individual critiques are also available. "Submit ms with registration prior to the workshop." Send SASE for brochures and registration forms.

CRAFT OF WRITING, 4010 Midway Rd., Carrollton TX 75007, phone (972)768-5433, fax (972)818-2054, director of continuing education Janet Harris. Annual 2-day event founded 1983. 1998 dates: September 18 & 19. Location: Omni Richardson Hotel. Average attendance is 200. **Open to all writers. Conference covers the creative, technical and business aspects of writing.** Offerings specifically available for poets include workshops and critique sessions. Speakers at the 1997 conference included Donald Maass, Donald Maass Literary Agency; Deborah Adams, The Herman Literary Agency. Other special features include 28 workshops covering all facets of a writer's world, discussion sessions conducted by editors and agents, and tips for marketing yourself and your writing. Cost for 1997 conference was $228, includes 1 lunch and 1 banquet. Accommodations include special rates at the Omni Richardson where conference is held. Group critiques are available. Bring 3- to 8-page ms with you and sign up at registration desk. Contest sponsored as part of conference. You must be registered for the conference by July 18 to enter contest. Manuscript must be sent with registration. Write for brochures and registration forms.

DESERT WRITERS WORKSHOP, P.O. Box 68, Moab UT 84532, phone (801)259-7750, fax (801)259-2335, contact director of programs. Annual 3-day event founded 1985. Usually held the second weekend in November at Pack Creek Ranch in the foothills of the LaSal Mountains. Attendance is a maximum of 30. There is a limit of 10 for each session of the workshop. **Open to all. Workshop covers 3 categories—fiction, nonfiction and poetry.** Cost is $425, including meals, instruction and lodging. "All participants stay at Pack Creek." Individual critiques are also available. "Participants will be able to mail some samples to their instructor before the workshop for critique." Send SASE for brochures and registration forms.

EASTERN KENTUCKY UNIVERSITY CREATIVE WRITING CONFERENCE, Case Annex 467, Richmond KY 40475-3140, phone (606)622-5861, e-mail eng.brown@acs.eku.edu, director Harry Brown. Annual 5-day event founded 1964. Usually held Monday through Friday of the third week in June. Location: Eastern Kentucky University. Average attendance is 15. **Open to poetry, fiction and drama writers. The conference is designed to "help writers interested in increasing their skills in writing poetry, fiction and drama; and to offer networking."** A ms of 4-8 poems (8 pages maximum) must be submitted and accepted before enrollment in conference is allowed. Offerings specifically available for poets include workshop discussions and individual conferences. Speakers at last conference were Dorothy Sutton, Kristina McGrath, Joe Survant and Richard Hague. Cost for 1996 conference was $80 undergraduate and $115 graduate (in-state fees), $220 undergraduate and $319 graduate (out-of-state fees); participants are responsible for their own meals. "Conference attendees can eat at EKU grill or cafeteria or at nearby restaurants." In 1996, housing in on-site facilities cost $55/week single occupancy, $39/week double occupancy. Individual critiques are available. Submit ms in advance. Send SASE for brochures and registration forms or request via e-mail (include mailing address).

‡EASTERN WRITERS' CONFERENCE, Salem State College, Salem MA 01970, phone (508)741-6378, e-mail rkessler@mecn.mass.edu, director Rod Kessler. Annual 2-day event founded 1976. Usually held the last weekend in June. Average attendance is 60. **Open to anyone. Conference covers all genres. "We provide a venue for area writers to meet one another and to hear good speakers."** Offerings specifically available for poets include open reading, visiting poets and a manuscript and review. Speakers have included Gale Walden and Martha Ramsey. Cost was $65. Public transportation and area airport service available to and from event. Information on overnight accommodations is available for registrants. Housing in on-site facilities costs $35. Individual critiques are also available. Submit under 10 pgs. of poetry with $35 fee. Send SASE for brochures and registration forms.

FEMINIST WOMEN'S WRITING WORKSHOPS, INC., P.O. Box 6583, Ithaca NY 14851, co-directors Kit Wainer and Margo Gumosky. Annual 8-day event founded 1974. Usually held in early July. Location: Hobart and William Smith Colleges, Geneva, NY. Average attendance is 45. **Open to "feminist women writers." Workshop usually covers fiction, poetry, journal writing, playwriting, personal essay, autobiography, journalism and performance.** Offerings specifically available for poets include daily workshops, critiques and readings. Cost for 1997 workshop was $535, including tuition, room, board and all events. "We try to help arrange car pools." Participants are housed in a campus residence. Individual critiques while at the conference are optional. "We require a work sample for first-time attendees prior to acceptance." Submit "writing sample (nonreturnable) of up to 10 pgs. Type of sample is your choice. Work in progress, autobiographical writing, nonfiction prose or experimental writing are as welcome as fiction, poetry or drama." Send SASE for brochures and registration forms.

FESTIVAL OF POETRY, Robert Frost Place, Franconia NH 03580, phone (603)823-5510, executive director Donald Sheehan. Annual week-long event founded in 1978. Usually held first week of August at Robert Frost's mountain farm (house and barn), made into a center for poetry and the arts. Average attendance is 50-55. **Open to poets only.** Faculty has included Galway Kinnell, Grace Paley, Molly Peacock, Martin Espada, Dana Gioia and Ellen Bryant Voigt. Cost is $395-425 tuition, plus a $25 reading fee. "Room and board available locally; information sent upon acceptance to program." Application should be accompanied by 3 sample pages of your work. Send SASE for brochures and registration forms.

‡FISHTRAP, P.O. Box 38, Enterprise OR 97828, phone (541)426-3623, director Rich Wawdschneider. Holds 3 annual 3- to 4-day events. Founded 1988. 1998 dates: Winter Fishtrap—February 20-22; Summer Workshop—July 6-9; Summer Gathering—July 10-12. Location: "Winter site is a meeting room attached to a motel at Wallowa Lake, Chegum (off season); summer site is an old Methodist church camp." Average attendance is 50 for Winter Fishtrap ("always sold out"); 12/workshop for Summer Workshop; 90 for Summer Gathering. **Open to anyone. "Fishtrap's goal is to promote good writing and clear thinking about the West. Also to encourage and promote new writers. There are always craft workshops on fiction, poetry, nonfiction; sometimes in children's writing, playwriting, radio, etc."** Offerings specifically available for poets included a poetry workshop taught by Lucy Tapa Lanso. Theme for 1997 was "Circling Back" and featured Native American Writers. Speakers at last workshop included Janet Campbell Hale, Lucy Tapa Lanso, Sandy Osawa (filmmaker), Horace Axtell (Nez Perce elder and language teacher) and Kim Stafford. Cost for winter Fishtrap was $200-300 includes meals (higher price includes lodging); Summer Workshop was $220, Gathering was $175, meals and lodging available at $30/day at camp. Lodging also available at nearby motels. Awards 5 fellowships annually. Send SASE for brochures and registration forms. Each year the selected writings of workshop students and workshop instructors is published in an anthology.

THE FLIGHT OF THE MIND, WOMEN'S WRITING WORKSHOPS, 622 SE 29th Ave., Portland OR 97214, phone (503)236-9862, e-mail soapston@teleport.com, director Judith Barrington. Annual events founded 1983. Usually held at the end of June, beginning of July. Two workshops in summer for 7 days each at "a rustic retreat center (Dominican-owned) right on the wild McKenzie River in the foothills of the Oregon Cascades." Average attendance is 65 women/workshop in 5 different classes. **Open to women writers. Workshops cover fiction, poetry, essays, screenwriting, special-topic classes (e.g., "landscape and memory") with a feminist philosophy.** In 1996 workshop leaders included Ursula K. Le Guin, Naomi Shihab Nye and Charlotte Watson Sherman. Cost for workshop (including tuition, all meals and room) was $685 and up depending on accommodations chosen. Scholarships available. Transportation to and from the event is provided. Participants are selected on the basis of work submitted. Peer critique groups form at workshop. "Competition is discouraged." Send first-class stamp for brochures and registration forms.

‡FLORIDA CHRISTIAN WRITERS CONFERENCE, 2600 Park Ave., Titusville FL 32780, phone (407)269-6702 ext. 202, fax (407)383-1741, e-mail writer@digital.net, website http://www.kipertek.com/writer, director Billie Wilson. Annual 4-day event founded 1988. 1998 dates: January 29 through February 2. Location: retreat center setting—conferee housing at motel. Meals, workshops and all general sessions held at retreat center. Average attendance is 200. **Open to all writers. "The conference has an instructional and marketing thrust. All genres are usually covered—49 workshops. Publishers and editors from over 35 publishing houses attend. Writers may submit manuscripts to the editors and publishers for critique and sale."** Offerings specifically available for poets include 2 workshops plus marketing opportunities. Speakers at last conference were Clint Kelly (keynote), Christine Bolley (Honor Books), Lt. Col. Marlene Chase (The War Cry/The Young Salvationist), Jim Dahlman (Minister's Family), Bob Haslam (Light and Life Press), Linda Holland (Fleming H. Revell), Church Johnson (Focus on the Family) and Steve Laube (Bethany House). Other special features include "an extended continuing class (one hour each day) in a genre, i.e., fiction, poetry, etc." Cost is $285, includes meals and tuition. Discounts are available through early registration and scholarships. Transportation to and from the event is provided. "We provide shuttles from the Orlando International airport. Also, we provide transportation to and from the motel to the retreat center." Information on overnight accommodations is available for registrants. Individual critiques also available. "Each conferee may submit 4 manuscripts (5 poems constitutes 1 manuscript) for critique. No fee." Send SASE for brochures and registration forms.

‡FLORIDA FIRST COAST WRITERS' FESTIVAL, 101 W. State St., Box 289, Jacksonville FL 32202, phone (904)633-8243, fax (904)633-8435, e-mail hdenson@fccj.cc.fl.us or kclower@fccj.cc.fl.us, website http://www.jax.jaxnet.com/~media-pr/festival.html, coordinators Howard Denson and Kathy Clower. Annual 2-day event founded 1986. Usually held in early April. Location: Kent Campus of Florida Community College at Jacksonville (FCCJ). Average attendance is 150-200. **Open to anyone. Festival covers all areas of writing.** Speakers at last festival were Robert Bly and David Poyer. "On a first-come basis, participants may sign up for one-on-one sessions with the attending poets, novelists, freelancers, editors, agents." Cost was $75 for 2 days, $40 for 1 day; meals separate, banquet generally $25-30. Information on overnight accommodations is available for registrants. Contest sponsored as part of festival. The Douglas Freels Poetry Prize accepts original, unpublished poems of up to 30 lines. Entry fee: $5/poem. Deadline: October 1. Awards $220 for first, $150 for second and $110 for third. Send SASE for brochures and registration forms. FCCJ and the Writers' Festival, Inc. also publishes the biannual *State Street Review*, see it's listing in the Publishers of Poetry section.

FLORIDA SUNCOAST WRITERS' CONFERENCE, Dept. of English, University of South Florida, Tampa FL 33620, phone (813)974-1711, e-mail greenbau@chuma.cas.usf.edu, directors Steve Rubin and Edgar Hirshberg. Annual 3-day event founded 1970. 1998 dates: February 5-7. Location: University of South Florida, St. Petersburg campus. Average attendance is 350. **"Open to students, teachers, established and aspiring writers. Conference covers all areas—fiction, poetry, nonfiction, children's, mystery/detective, romance, etc."** Offerings specifically available for poets included seminars, workshops, poetry readings and ms evaluation. Speakers at past conferences included Gerald Stern, Sonia Sanchez, Nikki Giovanni, Yevgeny Yevtushenko, Maxine Kumin, Michael Dennis Brown, Toi Derricotte, Marge Piercy and Carolyn Forché. Cost for 1998 conference is $125; $110 for students and teachers. Information on overnight accommodations is available for registrants. Accommodations include special rates at area hotels. Manuscript evaluation available at extra cost. Write for brochures and registration forms. They also publish *Sunscripts*, an anthology of writing from Florida Suncoast Writers' Conference. All participants eligible to submit.

FLORIDA SUNCOAST WRITERS' WEEKEND WORKSHOP, Dept. of English, University of South Florida, Tampa FL 33620, phone (813)974-2403, directors Steve Rubin and Rita Ciresi. Annual 3½-day event founded 1995. Usually held in April at the University of South Florida, Tampa campus. Average attendance is 75-80. **"Open to all writers, beginning and advanced. Workshop covers poetry, fiction and nonfiction."** Offerings specifically available for poets include poetry workshop and readings. Speakers at past conferences included Tobias Wolff, Dannie Abse, Peter Meinke, Michael Dennis Browne and Dionisio Martínez. Other special features include intensive small-group seminars, guest speakers and a banquet. Cost for conference is approximately $200, additional fee for ms evaluation. Information on overnight accommodations is available for registrants. Accommodations include special rates at area hotels. Manuscript evaluation available for each participant. Write for brochures and registration forms. They also publish *Sunscripts*, an anthology of writing from Suncoast programs participants.

FOOTHILL WRITERS' CONFERENCE, 12345 El Monte Rd., Los Altos Hills CA 94022, phone (415)949-7316 or 949-7436, conference co-directors Kim Silveira Wolterbeek and Jim Whearty. Annual 6-day event founded 1975. Usually held the end of June/beginning of July. Location: Foothill College campus in Los Altos Hills. **Open to everyone. Conference includes panel discussions and manuscript workshops; poetry one-on-one sessions; and poetry and prose readings.** Past panels have included the List Poem, the state of the novel, nature and art, women's issues, and multicultural literature. Offerings specifically available for poets included a one-on-one manuscript workshop. Speakers at the last conference were Kim Addonizio, Alan Cheuse, Jim Houston, Jane Hirshfield and Roshi Rustomji-Kerns. Cost for conference was $75, included enrollment fees and admission to faculty afternoon and evening readings, intensive writing workshops, and lectures and panels by faculty (college credit available). Individual critiques available on a first come, first serve basis. "Sign up posted on the first day of conference." Send SASE for brochures and registration forms.

‡GREEN LAKE WRITERS CONFERENCE, Green Lake Conference Center, W2511 State Highway 23, Green Lake WI 54941-9300, phone (800)558-8898, fax (414)294-3848, e-mail glcc@worldnet.att.net, website http://www.abc-usa.org, vice president of program Jan DeWitt. Annual weeklong event founded in 1946. 1997 dates were July 5-12. "Attendees stay in a lovely Inn overlooking beautiful Green Lake located 30 miles southwest of Oshkosh. Large private bath, double occupancy rooms, with singles available, extra charge. After class enjoy boating on the lake, tennis courts, biking, exercise trails, a new indoor recreation center and a fully-equipped arts and crafts center. Site includes a 36-hole public golf course listed among the top 75 in the nation. It is located on 1,000 acres and is the national conference center for American Baptists. Alcoholic beverages are not permitted." Average attendance is 80-100. **Open to regional and national participants. Conference covers Writiting for Children, Exploring the Writer in You, Essay Writing, Poetry Writing, Article Writing for Fun and Profit, Fiction Writing and Devotional/Inspirational Writing.** Speakers at last conference were Jacqueline Mitchard, magazine and newspaper journalist, author of *The Deep End of the Ocean* and Emily Auerbach, Wisconsin Humanities Council. Cost for 1997 conference was $80, plus $262-434/person for double occupancy room with meals. Camping available. Shuttle service to and from the airport provided for an additional fee. Information on overnight accommodations is available for registrants. Individual critiques also available. Send SASE for brochures and registration forms. "A past participant wrote, 'I would recommend this conference to anyone committed to writing and sharing their work in a spiritual atmosphere. What I found to be most incredible was the fact that everyone was friendly, willing to talk, and incredibly generous with their time.' "

HARVARD SUMMER WRITING PROGRAM, 51 Brattle St., Dept 5810, Cambridge MA 02138, phone (617)495-4024, fax (617)495-9176, e-mail summer@hudce.harvard.edu, website http://summer.dce.harvard.edu. Annual 8-week event. 1998 dates: June 22 through August 14. Location: Harvard University. Average attendance is 700. **Open to all levels, from beginner to published author. Course offerings include creative, expository and professional writing.** Offerings specifically available for poets included beginning poetry, intermediate poetry and graduate level poetry courses. Other special features included small classes, undergraduate and graduate credit, individual conferences, access to the Writing Center at Harvard, visiting writers, a reading series and a literary magazine. Instructors are writers, editors, and faculty members from Harvard as well as other universities. Cost for 1997 conference was $1,500/course (2 courses is considered full-time), plus $2,500 for room and board (dormitory housing). Phone (617)495-0519 or write for brochures or request via e-mail (include mailing address). Their catalog is also available on their website.

HAYSTACK WRITING PROGRAM, School of Extended Studies, Portland State University, P.O. Box 1491, Portland OR 97207, phone (800)547-8887 ext. 4027, fax (503)725-4840, e-mail herringtonm@ses.pdx.edu, website http://www.extended.portals.pdx.edu.haystack.htm, contact Maggie Herrington. Annual summer program founded 1968. One-week courses over the six weeks of the program. 1997 dates: July 7 through August 8. Classes are held in the local school of this small coastal community; some evening lectures and other activities. Average attendance is 10-15/class; 350 total. **Open to all writers. One-week workshops cover fiction, poetry, mystery, radio essay and nonfiction.** Cost for workshops is $110-375; participants pay for their own lodging and meals. Accommodation options range from camping to luxury hotels. Write for brochures and registration forms (no SASE necessary).

‡HEARTLAND WRITERS CONFERENCE, P.O. Box 5, Cape Girardeau MO 63701, contact registrar. Biannual 3-day event founded 1989. 1998 dates: June 4-6. Location: Coach House Inn, Sikeston MO. Average attendance is 150. **Open to all writers of popular fiction, nonfiction and poetry.** Offerings specifically available for poets include critique sessions. Speakers for next conference are 10 agents and editors from prominent New York-based publishing houses/agencies, as well as 12 published authors from the Midwest. Cost for 1996 conference was $175, including meals. Information on overnight accommodations is available for registrants. Accommodations include special rates at area hotels. Contest sponsored as part of conference. Judges are industry professionals. Send SASE for brochures and registration forms.

THE HEIGHTS WRITER'S CONFERENCE, Writer's World Press, P.O. Box 24684, Cleveland OH 44124, phone (216)481-1974, fax (216)481-2057, e-mail writersworld@juno.com, conference director Lavern Hall. Annual 1-day event founded 1992. Held the first Saturday in May. "The conference is held at the Marriott hotel in Beachwood, OH. Conference rooms are centrally located and handicapped accessible. Lunch is served in the ballroom." Average attendance is 125. **"Open to all writers who are interested in learning about the craft and business of writing and networking with professionals. We cover a variety of genres including poetry, fiction, science fiction, romance, mystery, travel, etc.** We don't have themes; however, each year two intensive hands-on workshops will vary. In 1997, the workshops were in short story writing and writing for children. These intensive workshops are limited to 25 students who must pre-register and are taken on a first come, first serve basis." Guest speaker for the last conference was Dr. Sherri Szeman, who spoke on "Dare to Be A Writer." They say, "Our format is unique. We have four major sessions (two in the morning and two in the afternoon) with three concurrent one-hour seminars. In addition, we offer two 2½-hour intensive workshops, one in the morning, the other in the afternoon. The genre teaching workshops vary each year." Cost for 1997 conference was $75 preregistration; $85 late registration. "All activities are included: continental breakfast, seminars/workshops, lunch with guest speaker program, networking reception and author autographing at conclusion of day. In addition there are many free handouts and The Writer's Book Shop℠ offers a selection of writing-related books. We provide accommodation information upon request for those arriving the day before." Critiques are handled through speakers directly. Send SASE for brochure, map and area hotels or request via fax or e-mail. "Conference brochures can be faxed but we don't want to e-mail brochures. Information on local poetry readings and poetry publishers soliciting work available."

HIGHLAND SUMMER WORKSHOP, P.O. Box 7014, Radford University, Radford VA 24142, phone (703)831-5366, fax (540)831-5970, e-mail gedwards@ruacad.ac.runet.edu, director Grace Toney Edwards. Annual 2-week event founded 1977. Usually held the last 2 weeks in June. Location: Radford University campus. Average attendance is 20-25. **Open to everyone. "The conference, a lecture-seminar-workshop combination, is conducted by well-known guest writers and offers the opportunity to study and practice creative and expository writing within the context of regional culture." Topics covered vary from year to year. Poetry, fiction and essays (prose) are generally covered each year.** In 1997, the first week of the workshop was led by poet, playwright and teacher George Ella Lyon, author of *A Regular Rolling Noah*, *Come a Tide* and *Borrowed Children*. The second week was led by poet, editor and teacher Peter Stillman, author of *Writing Your Way*, *Families Writing* and *Gilead: Notes on a Catskill Hamlet*. Cost for the conference ranged from $406-925 plus $15/day for meals. Individual meals may also be purchased. On-site housing costs range from $16-26/night. On-site accommodations are available at Norwood Hall. Accommodations are also available at local motels. Send SASE for brochures and registration forms.

HOFSTRA UNIVERSITY SUMMER WRITERS' CONFERENCE, Hofstra University, U.C.C.E., Hempstead NY 11550-1090, phone (516)463-5997, fax (516)463-4833, e-mail dcelcs@hofstra.edu, director Lewis Shena. Annual 10-day event founded 1972. Usually starts the Monday after July 4th. Location: Hofstra University. Average attendance is 50-60. **Open to all writers. Conference covers fiction, nonfiction, poetry, children's writing, stage/screenwriting and, on occasion, one other area (science fiction, mystery, etc.).** Guest speakers (other than the workshop leaders) "usually come from the world of publishing." There are also "readings galore and various special presentations." Cost for 1996 conference was $300/workshop. Additional fee of $450 for air-conditioned dorm room, one dinner and coffee/tea on a daily basis. For those seeking credit, other fees apply. Individual critiques are also available. "Each writer receives a half hour one-on-one with each workshop leader." They do not sponsor a contest, but "we submit exceptional work to various progams sponsored by Writers Conferences and Festivals." Write for brochures and registration forms (available as of April).

‡IMAGINATION, Cleveland State University, English Dept., Euclid at 24th, Cleveland OH 44115, phone (216)687-4522, fax (216)687-6943, e-mail imagination@popmail.csuohio.edu, director (Creative Writing Program) Neal Chandler. Annual 5½-day event founded 1991. 1997 dates were July 8-13. "The conference is held in Mather Mansion, which is located on the campus of Cleveland State University. There are several large conference rooms and a number of smaller workshop rooms." Average attendance is 90. **Open to "all writers, in any genre, who have submitted a writing sample to the director and who have been accepted on the basis of that writing sample.** *Imagination* is a writing conference about strong, imaginative writing from minimalism to magical realism; from mainstream to science fiction; from poetry to the novel. It includes classes and workshops without genre bias or boundaries. Courses are about distinctive creative writing, period."** Speakers at the last conference were Toi Derricotte (poetry); Karen Joy Fowler (fiction); James Patrick Kelly (science fiction); David Jauss (fiction); David Mura (poetry); Sheila Schwartz (fiction); Alberta Turner (poetry); and Leigh Allison Wilson (fiction). "Each year the Poets League of Greater Cleveland stages a performance called 'Mirror of the Arts' to which conference participants are invited to submit their poetry or short short fiction." Cost for 1997 conference was $420; participants are responsible for their own meals. A limited number of scholarships is available. Information on overnight accommodations is available for registrants. "Limited housing is available on campus through the university. Campus housing is one block from conference site. Participants are responsible for their own transportation to and from the conference." Housing in on-site facilities costs approximately $35/night. Individual critiques also available. "Every participant has her/his work critiqued twice—once in a workshop, once in an individual conference with another faculty member." Submit 8-10 pgs. to Dr. Neal Chandler with $10 fee. Send a first-class stamp for brochure and registration form. Cleveland State University's Poetry Center publishes 2-6 books of poetry per year, including the winners of its national poetry prize competition. (See listing in the Publishers of Poetry section.)

‡**INC AND THE ARTS**, P.O. Box 1754, Post Falls ID 83854, phone (208)667-9730, fax (208)667-9730, e-mail inc.arts@ior.com, director Sheri Stone. Annual 4-day event founded 1988. Usually held the fourth week of May at the Coéur d'Alene Resort Hotel, on Lake Coéur d'Alene, Idaho. Average attendance is 300. **A Christian conference open to writers, entertainers and artists. Covers all areas in writing and entertainment and areas in the visual arts.** Offerings specifically available for poets include workshops, manuscript evaluation by editors, manuscript editing and critique. Speaker at last conference was Frank Peretti. Cost for 1998 conference is $275, some meals are included. Discounts are available for early registration. Information on overnight accommodations is available for registrants. Accommodations include special rates at area hotels. Individial critiques also available. Submit 5 poems with a limit of 1/page. Contest sponsored as part of conference. Send SASE for details. Judges are editors and keynote speakers. Send SASE for brochures and registration forms.

INDIANA UNIVERSITY WRITERS' CONFERENCE, Ballantine Hall 464, Indiana University, Bloomington IN 47405, phone (812)855-1877, website http://www.indiana.edu/~engweb/special/conf.html, director Maura Stanton. Annual week-long event founded 1940. Usually held the last week in June at the university student union. Average attendance is 100. **Open to all. Conference covers fiction and poetry.** Offerings specifically available for poets included workshops and classes. Speakers at last conference included Gerald Stern (poetry) and Frances Sherwood (fiction). Cost for 1997 conference was $200 for conference and classes, $300 for conference, classes and workshop; plus $25 application fee. Information on overnight accommodations is available for registrants. "Rooms available in the student union or in a dorm." Individual critiques are also available. Submit 10 pgs. of poetry in advance. "All manuscripts are considered for scholarships." Send SASE for brochures and registration forms.

IOWA SUMMER WRITING FESTIVAL, University of Iowa, 116 International Center, Iowa City IA 52242-1802, phone (319)335-2534, fax (319)335-2740, e-mail amy-margolis@uiowa.edu, website http://www.uiowa.edu/~iswfest, coordinators Amy Margolis and Peggy Houston. Annual event founded in 1987. Held each summer in June and July for six weeks, includes one-week and weekend workshops at the University of Iowa campus. Average attendance is 125/week. **Open to "all adults who have a desire to write." Conference offers courses in nearly all writing forms. In 1997, offerings available for poets included 21 poetry classes for all levels.** Speakers were Marvin Bell, Michael Dennis Browne, Christopher Davis, Jim Heynen, Timothy Liu, James McKean and Jane Mead. Cost for 1997 conference was $150 for a weekend course and $375-400 for a one-week course. Participants are responsible for their own meals. Accommodations available at the Iowa House and the Holiday Inn. Housing in residence hall costs about $27/night. Participants in week-long workshops will have private conference/critique with workshop leader. Send for brochures and registration forms. "Requests for info are accepted via phone, fax or e-mail. However, we typically send info by post."

THE IWWG SUMMER CONFERENCE, The International Women's Writing Guild, P.O. Box 810, Gracie Station, New York NY 10028, phone (212)737-7536, fax (212)737-9469, e-mail iwwg@iwwg.com, executive director Hannelore Hahn. Annual week-long event founded 1978. Usually begins on the second Friday in August and runs through following Friday. Location: Skidmore College in Saratoga Springs, NY. Average attendance is 450. **Open to all women. Sixty-five workshops offered. "At least four poetry workshops offered for full week."** Cost is $700 for conference program and room and board. "Critiquing available throughout the week." Send SASE for brochures and registration forms or request via e-mail (include mailing address for response). The International Women's Writing Guild's bimonthly newsletter publishes and features hundreds of outlets for poets. See listing in Organizations Useful to Poets.

LIGONIER VALLEY WRITERS CONFERENCE, P.O. Box B, Ligonier PA 15658, phone (412)238-5749, fax (412)238-5190, president John Dougherty. Annual 3-day event founded 1986. Usually held in July. "This is a relaxing, educational, inspirational conference in a scenic, small town." Average attendance is 80. **Open to anyone interested in writing. Conference covers fiction, creative nonfiction, poetry and writing for children.** Poetry workshops each day. 1997 workshops conducted by Len Roberts. Cost for conference is approximately $200. Participants are responsible for their own dinner and lodging. Information on overnight accommodations is available for registrants. Individual critiques are also available. Must send samples in advance. Send SASE for brochures and registration forms. "We also publish *The Loyalhanna Review*, a literary journal, which is open to participants."

THE LITERARY FESTIVAL AT ST. MARY'S, (formerly Festival of Poets and Poetry at St. Mary's), St. Mary's College of Maryland, St. Mary's City MD 20686, phone (301)862-0239. An annual event held during the last two weekends in May. Approximately 18 guest poets and artists participate in and lead workshops, seminars and readings. Concurrent with the festival, St. Mary's College offers 2-week intensive writing workshops in poetry and fiction and a 10-day writer's community retreat. **The poetry workshop engages the participants**

in structured poetry writing experiences. **Intended for anyone with a serious interest in writing poetry**, it offers four college credits or may be taken as a non-credit course. **The retreat, designed for the serious writer, offers individual plans for writing alone or in conjunction with other participants.** Three 90-minute workshop sessions are organized for participants. There is also a 12-day fiction writing workshop offered during the festival. For applications or more information on these workshops or the festival, please write to Michael S. Glaser at the above address.

‡**MANHATTANVILLE'S WRITERS' WEEK**, Manhattanville College, 2900 Purchase St., Purchase NY 10577, phone (914)694-3425, fax (914)694-3488, e-mail rdowd@mville:edu, dean—adult and special programs Ruth Dowd, RSCJ. Annual 5-day event founded 1983. Usually held the last week in June at the Manhattanville College campus—"suburban surroundings 45 minutes from downtown Manhattan." Average attendance is 90. **Open to "published writers, would-be writers and teachers of creative writing. The conference offers workshops in five genres: fiction, short story, creative non-fiction, poetry, children's/young adult literature. There is also a special workshop in The Writers' Craft for beginners."** Offerings specifically available for poets include a poetry workshop. "We have had such distinguished poet/workshop leaders as Mark Doty, Stephanie Strickland and Honor Moore. We generally feature a lecture by a distinguished writer. In 1997 Susannah Lessard, author of the highly acclaimed *Architect of Desire* spoke on 'The Creative Process.' " Cost for conference is $560. Participants are responsible for their own meals. Information on overnight accommodations is available. "Rooms in the residence halls are available or students may choose to stay at area hotels. Housing in on-site facilities costs $25/night."

♣**MARITIME WRITERS' WORKSHOP**, UNB Dept. of Extension, Box 4400, Fredericton, New Brunswick E3B 5A3 Canada, phone (506)454-9153, fax (506)453-3572, coordinator Glenda Turner. Annual 1-week event founded 1976. Usually held the first week in July. Location: University of New Brunswick campus. Average attendance is 50. **Open to all writers. Workshop covers fiction, nonfiction, poetry and writing for children.** Offerings specifically available for poets included a daily workshop group for poets, limited to 10 participants, and individual conferences arranged with instructors. Instructors at last conference were Stephen Henighan and Robyn Sarah (fiction); Nadine McInnis (poetry); David Folster (nonfiction); Barbara Greenwood (writing for children). Other special features included readings. Cost for 1997 conference was $300 plus $270 for room and board. Scholarships are available. "All participants must submit a manuscript which is then 'workshopped' during the week." Phone, fax or write for brochures and registration forms.

MIDLAND WRITERS CONFERENCE, Grace A. Dow Memorial Library, 1710 W. St. Andrews, Midland MI 48640, phone (517)835-7151, fax (517)835-9791, e-mail kred@vlc.lib.mi.us, conference coordinator Katherine Redwine. Annual 1-day event founded 1979. 1997 date: May 31. Location: Grace A. Dow Memorial Library in Midland, MI. Average attendance is 100. **Open to any writer, published or unpublished. Conference includes sessions that vary in content.** In 1996, children's poet Patricia Hooper conducted a 2-hour poetry workshop, and the keynote speaker was Pat Conroy. "We always have a well-known keynoter. In the past we have had Judith Viorst, Kurt Vonnegut, Mary Higgins Clark, David McCullough, P.J. O'Rourke, Dave Barry." Cost for 1997 conference was $50 until 2 weeks prior to the event ($60 after that). For students, senior citizens and handicapped participants, cost was $40 until 2 weeks prior to the event ($50 after that). Information on overnight accommodations is available for registrants. Send for brochures and registration forms or request via e-mail (include mailing address for response).

MIDWEST WRITERS' CONFERENCE, 6000 Frank Ave. NW, Canton OH 44720-7599, phone (330)499-9600, fax (330)494-6121, e-mail druhe@stark.kent.edu, assistant director of continuing studies Debbie Ruhe. Annual 2-day event founded 1968. 1998 dates: October 2-3. Location: Kent State University Stark Campus in Canton, Ohio. Average attendance is 350. **Open to aspiring writers in any category, but the writing contest is directed toward fiction, nonfiction, juvenile literature and poetry. "The conference provides an atmosphere in which aspiring writers can meet with and learn from experienced, established writers through lectures, workshops, competitive contests, personal interviews and informal group discussions."** Offerings specifically available for poets include a lecture session in the poetry area and a contest. Past panelists have included Joyce Carol Oates, Edward Albee, Kurt Vonnegut and John Updike. One special feature of the conference is an all day book fair which includes several Ohio small presses. Cost for 1998 conference is $65, including conference registration, workshops, keynote address, lunch and ms entry fee. Contest entry fee exclusively: $40 for two mss and $10 for each additional ms. Participants are responsible for other meals. Information on overnight accommodations is available for registrants. Special conference rates are available through the Sheraton Inn.

Individual critiques are also available in the areas of poetry, fiction, nonfiction and juvenile literature. Submit one individual poem up to 200 lines. Contest sponsored as part of conference. "Work must be original, unpublished and not a winner in any contest at the time of entry." Judging is performed by local professionals in their appropriate categories. Send SASE for brochures and registration forms. Co-sponsor of the Midwest Writers' Conference is the Greater Canton Writers' Guild, 919 Clinton Ave. SW, Canton OH 44706-5196.

MISSISSIPPI VALLEY WRITERS CONFERENCE, 3403 - 45th St., Moline IL 61265, phone (309)762-8985, founder/director David R. Collins. Annual week-long event founded in 1973. Usually held the second week in June at the Liberal Arts College of Augustana College. Average attendance is 80. **Open to all writers, "beginning beginners to polished professionals." Conference provides a general professional writing focus on many genres of writing. Offers week-long workshop in poetry.** Evening programs as well as daily workshops are included. Cost for conference was $25 registration, $40 one workshop, $70 two workshops, $30 each additional workshop. Conferees may stay on campus or off. Board and room accommodations are available at Westerlin Hall on Augustana campus, 15 meals and 6 nights lodging approximately $200. Individual critiques are also available. Submit up to 10 poems. Awards presented by workshop leaders. Send SASE for brochures and registration forms.

MOUNT HERMON CHRISTIAN WRITERS CONFERENCE, P.O. Box 413, Mount Hermon CA 95041, phone (408)335-4466, fax (408)335-9218, director of specialized programs David R. Talbott. Annual 5-day event founded 1970. Always held Friday through Tuesday over Palm Sunday weekend. 1998 dates: April 3-7. Location: Full hotel-service-style conference center in the heart of the California redwoods. Average attendance is 150-200. **Open to "anyone interested in the Christian writing market." Conference is very broad-based. Always covers poetry, fiction, article writing, writing for children, plus an advanced track for published authors.** In 1995, offerings specifically available for poets included a 4-day, 8-hour track on "Writing the Published Poem," plus individual one-hour workshops on poetry. "We usually have 35-40 teaching faculty. Faculty is made up of publishing reps of leading Christian book and magazine publishers, plus selected freelancers." Other special features included an advance critique service (no extra fee); residential conference, with meals taken family-style with faculty; private appointments with faculty; and an autograph party. "High spiritual impact." Cost for 1997 conference was $670 deluxe; $560 standard; $480 economy; including 13 meals, snacks, on-site housing and $285 tuition fee. No-housing fee: $450. $15 airport, Greyhound or Amtrack shuttle from San Jose, CA. Send SASE for brochures and registration forms.

‡MOUNTAIN WRITERS SERIES, 3624 SE Milwaukee Ave., Portland OR 97202, phone (503)236-4854, fax (503)232-4517, e-mail pdxmus@aol.com, director Sandra Williams. Founded in 1976, workshops, readings and craft talks are held seasonally; length varies. Events are held at the Mountain Writers Center or at Mt. Hood Community College. The 1997 season included poets Marvin Bell, Kim Addonizio, David Mura, Agha Shahid Ali, David James Duncan, Knute Skinner, Linda Gregg, Clemens Starck and Patricia Goedicke. Average attendance is 15-25, "depending on the session." **Open to everyone. The series' purpose is "to broaden the community's sense of literary knowledge."** Offerings specifically available for poets include readings, "craft talks" and workshops. Cost varies. Discounts are available. "Center members receive a varied, by session discount." Individual critiques also available. Submit up to 3 pages of poems with fee; amount varies depending on session. Send SASE for brochures and registration forms.

NAPA VALLEY WRITERS' CONFERENCE, Napa Valley College, 1088 College Ave., St. Helena CA 94574, phone (707)967-2900, fax (707)967-2912, managing director Anne Evans. Annual week-long event founded 1981. Usually held the last week in July or first week in August at Napa Valley College's new facility in the historic town of St. Helena, 30 minutes north of Napa in the heart of the valley's wine growing community. Average attendance is 48 in poetry and 48 in fiction. **"The conference has maintained its emphases on process and craft, featuring a faculty as renowned for the quality of their teaching as for their work. It has also remained small and personal, fostering an unusual rapport between faculty writers and conference participants. The poetry session provides the opportunity to work both on generating new poems and on revising previously written ones. Participants spend time with each of the staff poets in daily workshops that emphasize writing new poems—taking risks with new material and forms, pushing boundaries in the poetic process."** The 1997 poetry staff was Jane Hirshfield, Edward Hirsch, Jack Gilbert and Carol Snow. "Participants register for either the poetry or the fiction workshops, but panels and craft talks are open to all writers attending. Evenings feature readings by the faculty that are open to the public and hosted by Napa Valley wineries." Cost is $475, not including meals or housing. There are some limited partial scholarships, depending on donations. A list of valley accommodations is mailed to applicants on acceptance and includes at least one reduced-rate package. "Through the generosity of Napa residents, limited accommodations in local homes are available on a first-come, first-served basis." All applicants are asked to submit a qualifying ms with their registration (no more than 5 pgs. of poetry or 10-15 pgs. of fiction) as well as a brief description of their background as a writer. Application deadline: June 1. Send SASE for brochures and registration forms.

‡NEW ENGLAND WRITERS' WORKSHOP, Simmons College, 300 The Fenway, Boston MA 02115, phone (617)521-2220, fax (617)521-3199, conference administrator Cynthia Grady. Annual 5-day event founded in 1977. Usually held the first week of June. "Simmons College is located in the Fenway area in Boston near the Museum of Fine Arts, Symphony Hall and Fenway Park." Average attendance is 45. **Open to intermediate and advanced writers. Workshop covers fiction and poetry.** Offerings specifically available for poets include poetry workshops in the morning and discussion and speakers in the afternoon. Speakers at last workshop included David Godine, Steven Cramer, Elizabeth Cox, Jill McCorkle, Elizabeth Benedict, C. Michael Curtis and Christopher Keane. Cost for 1997 workshop was $550; participants are responsible for their own meals. Information on overnight accommodations is available. On-site accommodations are available. Cost: $150 for the week, single or $105 double occupancy. Linens included. Individual critiques also available. Submit 15 pgs. of poetry for 20-minute critique consultation. Send SASE or call for brochures and registration forms.

OAKLAND UNIVERSITY WRITERS' CONFERENCE, Division of Continuing Education, 265 SFH, Oakland University, Rochester MI 48309-4401, phone (810)370-2140, fax (810)370-4280, e-mail gjboddy@oakland. edu, director Gloria J. Boddy. Annual 1½-day event founded 1961. 1997 dates: October 17-18. "The Oakland University Writers' Conference is conducted in the university student center, in meeting rooms and large dining/ meeting areas, plus adjoining classroom buildings with lecture halls." Average attendance is 400-500. **Open to beginning through professional adult writers. "No restrictions as to geographic area." The conference is designed to "help writers develop their skills, to provide information (and contact) for getting published; to provide a current picture of publishing markets; to furnish a venue for networking. All genres of writing are covered."** The conference offers "critiques, both one-on-one and group, as well as auditing, on Friday. On Saturday, 36 concurrent sessions dealing with all aspects of writing in a variety of genres are available in four time slots. A well-known professional writer speaks at lunch. A panel of the major speakers answers questions in the concluding session." Cost for 1997 conference was $28-38 for Friday critiques; $65 for Saturday conference plus $8 for lunch. "Discounts are not offered." Information on overnight accommodations is available for registrants. Work must be submitted, in advance, for individual critiques. Brochures and registration forms available each September 1 prior to the October conference.

OZARK CREATIVE WRITERS CONFERENCE, 6817 Gingerbread Lane, Little Rock AR 72204-4738, phone (501)565-8889, fax (501)565-7220, conference counselor Peggy Vining, founded 1968. Annual 3-day event. Held in October at the Inn of the Ozarks in Eureka Springs, Arkansas. 1997 dates: October 9-11. **Open to all writers.** Registration fee is $40 prior to September 1. Various writing contests sponsored as part of conference. Awards of $25, $15 and $10 ("many higher") for all types of writing. Send #10 SASE for brochure after April 1.

‡PIMA WRITERS' WORKSHOP, Pima College, 2202 W. Anklam Rd., Tucson AZ 85709, phone (520)884-6974, fax (520)884-6020, e-mail mfiles@pimacc.pima.edu, director Meg Files. Annual 3-day event founded 1987. 1998 dates: May 29-31. Location: Pima College's Center for the Arts, "a complex that includes a proscenium theater, a black box theater, a recital hall, and conference rooms, as well as a courtyard with amphitheater." Average attendance is 200. **Open to all writers, beginning and experienced. "The workshop includes sessions on all genres (nonfiction, fiction, poetry, writing for children and juveniles, screenwriting) and on editing and publishing, as well as manuscript critiques and writing exercises."** In the past, featured poets have included Linda McCarriston, Lawrence Lieberman, Frank Gaspar and Maurya Simon. Other past speakers have included Larry McMurtry, Barbara Kingsolver, Ron Carlson and Antonya Nelson. Other special features include "the workshop's accessible to writers, agents and editors; and the workshop's atmosphere—friendly and supportive, practical and inspirational." Cost for 1997 workshop was $65; participants are responsible for their own meals. Information on overnight accommodations is available. Individual critiques also available. Submit 3 poems in advance to Meg Files.

PORT TOWNSEND WRITERS' CONFERENCE, c/o Centrum, P.O. Box 1158, Port Townsend WA 98368, phone (360)385-3102, fax (360)385-2470, director Carol Jane Bangs. Annual 10-day event founded 1974. Usually held the second week in July at a 400-acre state park at the entrance to Puget Sound. Average attendance is 160. **Open to "all serious writers who pass our preliminary manuscript screening." Conference usually covers fiction (no genre fiction), poetry, creative nonfiction, and writing for children.** Offerings specifically available for poets include "three limited-enrollment workshops, private manuscript conference, open-mike readings, faculty readings and technique classes." Speakers at the last conference were Mark Doty, Billy Collins, Linda Bierds, Marilyn Chin, Valerie Miner, Bret Lott, John Keeble, Robin Hemley, Jane Yolen and Stanley Crawford. Cost for the conference was $425 tuition including workshop, ms conference, classes, readings, lectures; $300 tuition without workshop or ms conference; plus $330 optional for dormitory housing and 3 meals per day. Information on overnight accommodations is available for registrants. Individual critiques are also available at no extra charge, however "you must be enrolled in a manuscript workshop." Send SASE for brochures and registration forms. "Also, in 1998, a 3-day literary event is being organized in celebration of the 25th year of this writers' conference. The literary festival, tentatively called 'A celebration for writers and readers,' will take place on the three days immediately preceding the 1998 writers' conference. Conference participants will receive a reduction on the festival fee."

♣SAGE HILL WRITING FALL POETRY COLLOQUIUM, P.O. Box 1731, Saskatoon, Saskatchewan S7K 3S1 Canada, phone/fax (306)652-7395, executive director Steven Ross Smith. Annual 21-day event founded

1995. Usually held the first three weeks in October at "the peaceful milieu of St. Peter's College, adjoining St. Peter's Abbey, in Muenster, 150 kilometers east of Saskatoon." **Open to poets, 19 years of age and older, who are working in English. The colloquium offers "an intensive three-week workshop/retreat designed to assist poets with manuscripts-in-progress. Each writer will have a significant publishing record and will wish to develop his/her craft and tune a manuscript. There will be ample time for writing, one-on-one critiques, and group meetings to discuss recent thinking in poetics. Eight writers will be selected. Writers in and outside Saskatchewan are eligible."** Cost for 1997 is $775, including tuition, accommodations and meals. "A university registration fee of $25 will be added if taking this course for credit." Transportation from Saskatoon can be arranged as needed. On-site accommodations included in cost. Send SASE for brochures and registration forms.

✤**SAGE HILL WRITING SUMMER EXPERIENCE**, P.O. Box 1731, Saskatoon, Saskatchewan S7K 3S1 Canada, phone/fax (306)652-7395, executive director Steven Ross Smith. Annual 7-day and 10-day events founded in 1990. Usually held the end of July through the beginning of August. The Summer Experience is located at St. Michael's Retreat, "a tranquil facility in the beautiful Qu'Appelle Valley just outside the town of Lumsden, 25 kilometers north of Regina." Average attendance is 54. **Open to writers, 19 years of age and older, who are working in English. No geographic restrictions. The retreat/workshops are designed to "offer a special working and learning opportunity to writers at different stages of development. Top quality instruction, a low instructor-writer ratio, and the rural Saskatchewan setting offers conditions ideal for the pursuit of excellence in the arts of fiction, poetry, playwriting, and creative nonfiction."** Offerings specifically available for poets include a poetry workshop and poetry colloquium. In 1996, the faculty included Rosemary Nixon, William Robertson, Janice Kulyk Keefer, Di Brandt and Patrick Lane. Cost for 1996 conference ranged from $425-495, included instruction, accommodations and meals. Limited local transportation to the conference is available. "Van transportation from Regina airport and a downtown hotel, to Lumsden will be arranged for out-of-province travellers." On-site accommodations offer individual rooms with a writing desk and washroom. Individual critiques offered as part of workshop and colloquium. Writing sample required with application. Application deadline: May 1. Send SASE for brochures and registration forms.

ST. DAVIDS CHRISTIAN WRITERS CONFERENCE, 87 Pines Rd. East, Hadley PA 16130, phone (717)394-6758, registrar Audrey Stallsmith. Annual 5-day event founded 1957. Usually held in June at the campus of Geneva College in Beaver Falls, PA. Average attendance is 100-120. **Open to "anyone interested in writing." Conference is designed to "train and develop skills of writers for Christian and secular markets."** Offerings include a series of advanced classes that require prior acceptance to attend. Cost for conference is $400-500, including classes, room and board. Price varies according to choice of study packages. Housing in on-site facilities costs $200-230. Individual critiques are also available. "Must have a body of work to submit." Contest sponsored as part of conference. "Must be a conference attendee. Faculty members judge contest." Send SASE for brochures and registration forms.

SANTA BARBARA WRITERS' CONFERENCE, P.O. Box 304, Carpinteria CA 93014, phone (805)684-2250, fax (805)684-7003, conference director Barnaby Conrad. Annual week-long event founded in 1973. Held the last Friday to Friday in June at the Miramar Hotel on the beach in Montecito. Average attendance is 350 people. **Open to everyone. Covers all genres of writing.** Workshops in poetry offered. Past speakers have included Ray Bradbury, Phillip Levine, Sol Stein, Dorothy Wall, Gore Vidal and Willian Styron. Cost for 1997 conference, including all workshops and lectures, 2 al fresco dinners and room (no board), was $1,065 single, $792 double occupancy, $360 day students. Individual critiques are also available. Submit 1 ms of no more than 3,000 words in advance with SASE. Competitions with awards sponsored as part of conference. Send SASE for brochures and registration forms.

SEWANEE WRITERS' CONFERENCE, 310 St. Luke's Hall, Sewanee TN 37383-1000, phone (615)598-1141, fax (615)598-1145, conference administrator Cheri B. Peters. Annual 12-day event founded 1990. Usually held the last 2 weeks in July at The University of the South ("dormitories for housing, Women's Center for public events, classrooms for workshops, Sewanee Inn for dining, etc."). Attendance is about 105. **Open to poets, fiction writers and playwrights who submit their work for review in a competitive admissions process. "Genre, rather than thematic, workshops are offered in each of the three areas."** In 1997, faculty members included fiction writers Alice McDermott, Russell Banks, Ernest Gaines, Margot Livesay, Jill McCorkle, Brent Spencer and Francine Prose; poets John Hollander, Charles Martin, Chase Twichell and Donald Justice; playwright Laura Maria Censabella. Other speakers included editors, agents and additional writers. Cost for 1997 conference was $1,200, including room and board. Each year scholarships and fellowships based on merit are available on a competitive basis. "We provide bus transportation from the Nashville airport on the opening day of the conference and back to the airport on the closing day at no additional cost." Individual critiques are also available. "All writers admitted to the conference will have an individual session with a member of the faculty." A ms should be sent in advance after admission to the conference. Write for brochure and application forms. No SASE necessary.

SINIPEE WRITERS WORKSHOP, P.O. Box 902, Dubuque IA 52004-0902, phone (319)556-0366, director Linda Crossitt. Annual 1-day event founded 1986. Usually held the 3rd or 4th Saturday in April on the campus of Loras College, Dubuque, Iowa. Average attendance is 50-100. **Open to anyone, "professional or neophyte," who is interested in writing. Conference covers fiction, poetry and nonfiction.** Cost for 1997 workshop was $60 pre-registration, $65 at the door. Scholarships covering half of the cost are traditionally available to senior citizens and to full-time students, both college and high school. Cost includes handouts, coffee and donut break, lunch, snacks in afternoon and book fair with authors in attendance available to autograph their books. Information on overnight accommodations is available for out-of-town registrants. Annual contest for nonfiction, fiction and poetry sponsored as part of workshop. There is a $5 reading fee for each entry (article/essay of 1,500 words, short story of 1,500 words or poetry of 40 lines). First prize in each category is $100 plus publication, second prize $50 and third prize $25. Entrants in the contest may also ask for a written critique by a professional writer. The cost for critique is an additional $15/entry. Send SASE for brochures and registration forms.

SOCIETY OF THE MUSE OF THE SOUTHWEST (SOMOS), P.O. Box 3225, Taos NM 87571, phone/fax (505)758-0081. Founded 1983. "We offer workshops at different times during the year, many during the summer." Length of workshops vary. Held at various sites in Taos. Average attendance is 10-50. **Open to anyone. "We offer workshops in various genres—fiction, poetry, nature writing, etc."** In 1997 workshop speakers included Denise Chavez, Naomi Shihab Nye, Alfred Depew, Marjorie Agosin, Peggy Shumaker and Pierre Delattre. Other special features include writing in nature/nature walks and beautiful surroundings in a historic writer's region. Cost for workshops range from $50-175, excluding room and board. Information on overnight accommodations is available. Individual critiques are also available. Send SASE for brochures and registration forms. "Taos has a wonderful community of dedicated and talented writers who make SOMOS workshops rigorous, supportive and exciting."

‡**SOFER, JEWISH WRITERS WORKSHOP**, 555 Skokie Blvd., Suite 225, Northbrook IL 60062, phone (847)509-0990, fax (847)509-0970, e-mail dunnfried@aol.com, assistant director Deanne Dunn Friedman. Annual 4-day event founded 1996. 1997 dates were August 21-24. Location: Olin-Sang-Ruby Union Institute Camp and Conference Center in Oconomowoc, WI. Average attendance: 25-50. **Open to all people interested in writing, poetry, playwriting, etc. with a Jewish theme.** Speakers at last conference were Gerald Stern, Howard Schwartz, Dina Elenbuger, Don T. Maseng and Steve Stern. Cost for 1997 conference was $350, including meals. Housing in on-site facilities is included in the cost. Individual critiques are also available. Write or call for brochures and registration forms.

‡**SOUTHERN CALIFORNIA WRITERS' CONFERENCE*SAN DIEGO**, 3735 India St., San Diego CA 92103, phone (619)291-6805, e-mail scwcsd@aol.com, website http://members.aol.com/cdbourbon/scwcsd.htm, executive director Michael Gregory. Annual 4-day event founded 1986. 1998 dates: March 13-16. Usually held at the Ramada Inn Conference Center in San Diego. Average attendance: 300. **Open to all aspiring and accomplished writers of fiction, nonfiction, screen and poetry. Conference offers 55 read and critique sessions as well as Q&A workshops.** Cost for conferences is $250; participants are responsible for their own meals. Information on overnight accommodations is available for registrants. Accommodations include special rates at area hotels. Housing in on-site facilities costs $515 for single room (including cost of conference) and $405 shared double room (including cost of conference). Individual critiques are also available. Submit poetry in advance to Leroy Quintana at the above address. Contest sponsored as part of conference. Send SASE for brochures and registration forms.

‡**SOUTHWEST CHRISTIAN WRITERS SEMINAR**, P.O. Box 1008, Flora Vista NM 87415, phone (505)334-0617 or 334-2258, president Kathy Cordell. Annual 1-day event founded 1980. Usually held the third Saturday in September at the Hesperus Baptist Camp in Hesperus, Colorado, near the foot of the La Plata Mountains. Average attendance is 30. **Open to all writers. Conference is designed to "help authors learn more about their craft. In the past, we have covered writing poetry, short stories, fact or fiction; some marketing tips and query letter."** Cost for 1997 seminar was $47, plus $5.50 for meals; discounts available "if you are a member of SCWA or to anyone who registers before September 1. There will be rooms to rent for the night at the camp. It is a short walk to conference room from cabins." Call or write for more information.

SOUTHWEST FLORIDA WRITERS' CONFERENCE, P.O. Box 60210, Ft. Myers FL 33906-6210, phone (941)489-9226, fax (941)489-9051, director Joanne Hartke. Annual event founded 1980. Held in late January, 2 days, on or near the campus of Edison Community College. Average attendance is 150-200. **Open to anyone interested in writing, including full-time high school and college students. "We cover many areas; in 1997 our offerings included poetry and writing for children. Sessions are usually varied to provide something for both beginning and published writers."** The 1997 poetry session was with Dr. Jack Crocker. Cost for the 1997 conference sessions was $135; Saturday only was $65, including a continental breakfast and lunch. Limited scholarships are usually available and full-time students can attend the full conference for only $50. Information on overnight accommodations available for registrants. An annual contest (including poetry) is sponsored as part of the conference. Judges are published authors and writers in the Ft. Myers community. Send SASE for brochures and registration forms.

SQUAW VALLEY COMMUNITY OF WRITERS POETRY WORKSHOP, P.O. Box 2352, Olympic Valley CA 96146, phone (916)274-8551 or 583-5200, e-mail svcw@oro.net, executive director Brett Hall Jones.

Annual 7-day event founded 1969. 1997 dates: July 19-26. The workshop is held in The Squaw Valley Ski Corporation's Olympic House Lodge. Squaw Valley is located in the Sierra Nevada near Lake Tahoe. "The workshop takes place in the off-season of the ski area. Participants can find time to enjoy the Squaw Valley landscape; hiking, swimming, river rafting and tennis are available." Average attendance is 64. **Open to high quality talented writers of diverse ethnic backgrounds and a wide range of ages. "The Poetry Program differs in concept from other workshops in poetry. Our project is to help our participants to break through old habits and write something daring and difficult. Workshops are intended to provide a supportive atmosphere in which no one will be embarrassed, and at the same time to challenge the participants to go beyond what they have done before. Admissions are based on quality of the submitted manuscripts."** Offerings include regular morning workshops, craft lectures and staff readings. "The participants gather in daily workshops to discuss the work they wrote in the previous 24 hours." Speakers at the 1997 conference were Yusef Komunyakaa, Sharon Olds, Galway Kinnell, Deborah Digges, Robert Hass and Cleopatra Matthis. Cost was $555, included regular morning workshops, craft lectures, staff readings and dinners. Scholarships are available. "Requests for financial aid must accompany submission/application, and will be granted on the perceived quality of manuscript submitted and financial need of applicant." Transportation to workshop is available. "We will pick poets up at the Reno International Airport if arranged in advance. Also, we arrange housing for participants in local houses and condominiums on the valley. Participants can choose from a single room for $320/week or a double room for $220/week within these shared houses. We do offer inexpensive bunk bed accommodations on a first come, first serve basis." Individual conferences are also available. "Only work-in-progress will be discussed." Send SASE for brochures and registration forms or request via e-mail (include mailing address for response). "We also publish an annual newsletter."

STATE OF MAINE WRITERS' CONFERENCE, P.O. Box 7146, Ocean Park ME 04063, phone (207)934-9806 (May/June through September), phone (413)596-6734 (September through May), e-mail rburns0@kraken.m vnet.wnec.edu (winter only), director Dick Burns. Annual August event founded 1941. Runs from Tuesday afternoon to Friday noon. 1998 dates: August 25-28. Average attendance is 50-75. **Open to any interested person. Conference is "very eclectic, covers writing to publishing for both poetry and prose."** Every year there is a poetry tournament including a poetry booklet, Poems to be Put on Trees Contest and Beach Inspiration Poetry. "In 1995, there was a Haiku Workshop. Something similar is expected to be continued annually." In 1997 cost was $85. Those 21 and under may attend at half price. Information on overnight accommodations is available for registrants. "Local accommodations are reasonable." There are many contests, 15-20/year. Contest announcement is available in advance to registrants. Send SASE for brochure and registration forms.

TENNESSEE MOUNTAIN WRITERS CONFERENCE, P.O. Box 4895, Oak Ridge TN 37831-4895, phone/fax (423)482-6567, e-mail tmwq@compuserve.com, executive director Patricia Hope. Annual 3½-day event founded 1989. 1998 dates: April 15-18. Location: Garden Plaza Hotel in Oak Ridge. Average attendance is 150-200. **Open to "all aspiring writers, including students." Conference covers fiction, poetry, nonfiction and writing for children, plus special classes on romance, mystery, business, etc.** Speakers at last conference included Sydney Lea, Brett Lott, Cheryl Ware, Gay Martin, Wesley Brown, Bill Brown, Sharyn McCrumb and Michael Seidman. Other special features included a contest in conjunction with conference offering prizes to adults/students and a book fair featuring participants' books. Cost for 1997 conference was $165 for full participants, $120 for day-only participants, $35 for students. Information on overnight accommodations is available for registrants. Host hotel provides discount to participants. Cost for 1997 was $62/night. Individual critiques are also available. Submit up to 10 pgs. prior to conference. Send SASE for brochures and registration forms. Tennessee Mountain Writers also sponsor the Tennessee Literary Awards which is separate from the conference.

***TŶ NEWYDD WRITERS' CENTRE**, Taliesin Trust, Llanystumdwy, Cricieth, Gwynedd LL52 0LW Wales, Great Britain, phone 01766 522811, fax 01766 523095, director Sally Baker, founded 1990. 4½-day courses held throughout the year. Courses run Monday evening through Saturday morning at Tŷ Newydd, "a house of historical and architectural interest situated near the village of Llanystumdwy. It was the last home of Lloyd George, the former British prime minister. It stands in landscaped gardens and has fine views over Cardigan Bay towards the mountains of Meirionnydd." Average attendance is 12/course. **Open to anyone over 16 years of age. Courses are designed to "promote the writing and understanding of literature by providing creative writing courses at all levels for all ages.** Courses at Tŷ Newydd provide the opportunity of working intimately and informally with 2 professional writers." Courses specifically for poets, of all levels of experience and ability, are offered throughout the year. Cost for a 4½-day course is £275 (inclusive), some weekend courses available, cost is £100

✳ AN ASTERISK before a listing indicates an overseas publisher, magazine, contest, conference or organization.

(inclusive). Transportation to and from Centre is available if arranged at least a week in advance. Participants stay at Tŷ Newydd House in shared bedrooms; single bedrooms available on a limited basis and for an additional fee. "Vegetarians and people with special dietary needs are catered for but please let us know in advance. Course participants help themselves to breakfast and lunch and help to prepare one evening meal as part of a team. Participants should bring towels and their own writing materials. Some typewriters and word processors are available." Send SASE for brochures and registration froms.

UNIVERSITY OF WISCONSIN-MADISON'S SCHOOL OF THE ARTS AT RHINELANDER, 726 Lowell Hall, 610 Langdon St., Madison WI 53703-1195, administrative coordinator Kathy Berigan. Annual 5-day event founded 1964. Usually held the third or fourth week in July. Held at a local junior high school. Average attendance is 300. **Open to all levels and ages.** Offerings specifically available for poets include poetry workshops. Guest speaker at last workshop was Larry Watson. Cost for 1997 workshop ranged from $150-300. Information on overnight accommodations is available for registrants. Write for brochures and registration forms.

‡❀**VICTORIA SCHOOL OF WRITING**, 607 Linden Ave., Victoria, British Columbia V8V 4G6 Canada, phone (250)385-8982, fax (250)995-9391, e-mail writeawy@islandnet.com, website http://www.islandnet.com/~writeawy, director Margaret Dyment. Annual 4-day event founded 1996. 1998 dates: July 14-17. Location: "Heritage school, spacious classrooms, facing onto Beacon Hill Park with 154 acres of exotic plant life, peacocks, ocean cliff." Average attendance is 100. **"A 3- to 10-page manuscript is required as part of the registration process, which is open to all. The general purpose of the workshop is to give hands-on assistance with better writing, working closely with established writers/instructors. We have workshops in fiction, poetry and work-in-progress; plus two other workshops which vary."** Offerings specifically available for poets include 2 intensive 4-day workshops (12 hours of instruction and one-on-one consultation). One workshop will be co-led by Patricia and Terence Young; the other by Linda Rogers. Cost for 1997 workshop was $395 Canadian; participants are responsible for their own meals. "For people who register with payment in full before May 1, the cost is $350 Canadian." Information on overnight accommodations is available. Accommodations include special rates at area hotels and "a few tent sites and billets for low-income participants." Send SASE for brochures and registration forms. "We are affiliated with 'Write Away!' a company which offers courses in creative writing in Victoria and publishes a chapbook of poetry 3 times/year."

WESLEYAN WRITERS CONFERENCE, Wesleyan University, Middletown CT 06457, phone (860)685-3604, fax (860)347-3996, e-mail agreene@wesleyan.edu, director Anne Greene. Annual 5-day event founded 1956. Usually held the last week in June on the campus of Wesleyan University. The campus is located "in the hills overlooking the Connecticut River, a brief drive from the Connecticut shore. Wesleyan's outstanding library, poetry reading room, and other university facilities are open to participants." Average attendance is 100. **"Open to both experienced and new writers. The participants are an international group. The conference covers the novel, short story, fiction techniques, fiction-and-film, poetry, literary journalism and memoir."** Special sessions in 1997 included "Reading of New Fiction," "The Writers Life," "Writing Memoirs," and "Publishing." Offerings specifically for poets included manuscript consultations and daily seminars with Pulitzer Prize-winner Henry Taylor, and panel discussions with Robert Phillips and Kate Rushin. Other faculty included Dorothy Allison, Amy Bloom, Robert Stone, Tom Drury, Lis Harris and James Lardner. Cost in 1997, including meals, was $655 (day rate); $765 (boarding rate). "Wesleyan has scholarships for journalists, fiction writers, nonfiction writers and poets. Request brochure for application information." Information on overnight accommodations is available. "Conference participants may stay in university dormitories or off campus in local hotels." Individual critiques are also available. Registration for critiques must be made before the conference. Send SASE for brochures and registration forms.

WESTERN RESERVE WRITERS AND FREELANCE CONFERENCE, 34200 Ridge Rd., #110, Willoughby OH 44094, phone (216)943-3047 or (800)653-4261, e-mail fa837@cleveland.freenet.edu, coordinator Lea Leever Oldham. Annual 1-day event founded 1983. Usually held the second Saturday in September. Average attendance is 150. **Open to "writers, published and aspiring."** Conference usually covers fiction, nonfiction, poetry, articles, books, sometimes photography and other freelance subjects, copyright, writing for children, etc. "We always include a presentation specifically for poetry." Cost for conference is about $49, plus lunch. Participants can make arrangements one-on-one for possible time with guest speakers. Send SASE for brochures and registration forms.

WESTERN RESERVE WRITERS MINI CONFERENCE, 34200 Ridge Rd., #110, Willoughby OH 44094, phone (216)943-3047 or (800)653-4261, e-mail fa837@cleveland.freenet.edu, coordinator Lea Leever Oldham. Annual ½-day conference founded 1991. Usually held the last Saturday in March. Average attendance is 100. **Open to "published and aspiring writers."** Conference usually covers fiction, nonfiction, poetry, writing for children, articles and romance writing. "We always have a session with a published poet." Cost for conference is $29, including morning refreshments. Attendees can make their own arrangements with presenters for possible critiques. Send SASE for brochures and registration forms.

WILDACRES WRITERS WORKSHOP, 233 S. Elm St., Greensboro NC 27401, phone/fax (910)273-4044, director Judith Hill. Annual week-long event founded 1983. Usually held the second week in July at "a beautiful retreat facility in the Blue Ridge Mountains of North Carolina." Average attendance is 100. **Open to all "serious adult writers." Conference covers fiction, poetry, screen and play writing, and nonfiction. "We have two poetry workshops with a limit of twelve to a class.** In total, we have eleven writers on staff who read and give programs. Plus we have an agent in residence." Cost is approximately $410, including a double room, all meals and ms critique. Van transportation to and from the Asheville Airport is provided. Send SASE for brochures and registration forms. Some years they also publish *The Wildacres Review*.

‡WINTER POETRY & PROSE GETAWAY IN CAPE MAY, 18 North Richards Ave., Ventnor NJ 08406, phone (609)823-5076, e-mail pembroke9@aol.com, founder/director Peter E. Murphy. Annual 4-day event founded 1994. 1998 dates: January 16-19. "The Conference is held at the Grand Hotel on the Oceanfront in Historic Cape May, New Jersey. Participants stay in comfortable rooms with an ocean view, perfect for thawing out the muse. Hotel facilities include a pool, sauna, and whirlpool, as well as a lounge and disco for late evening dancing for night people." Average attendance is 75. **Open to all writers, beginners and experienced, over the age of 18. "The poetry workshop meets for an hour or so each morning before sending you off with an assignment that will encourage and inspire you to produce exciting new work. After lunch, we gather together to read new drafts in feedback sessions led by experienced poet-teachers who help identify the poem's virtues and offer suggestions to strengthen its weaknesses. The groups are small and you receive positive attention to help your poem mature. In late afternoon, you can continue writing or schedule a personal tutorial session with one of the poets on staff."** 1997 staff included Renee Ashley, Robert Carnevale, Cat Doty, Paul Drexel, Stephen Dunn, Kathleen Rockwell Lawrence, Charles Lynch, Peter Murphy and Robbie Clipper Sethi. There are usually 10 participants in each poetry workshop and 5 in each of the prose workshops. Other special features include extra-supportive sessions for beginners. Cost for 1997 conference was $310, includes breakfast and lunch for 3 days, all sessions as well as a double room; participants are responsible for dinner only. Discounts are available. "Early Bard Discount: Deduct $25 if paid in full by November 16, 1997." Single-occupancy rooms are available at additional cost. Individual critiques also available. "Each poet may have a 20-minute tutorial with one of the poets on staff." Write for brochures and registration forms. "The Winter Getaway is known for its challenging, yet supportive atmosphere that encourages imaginative risk-taking and promotes freedom and transformation in the participants' writing."

WISCONSIN REGIONAL WRITERS' ASSOCIATION, 912 Cass St., Portage WI 53901, phone (608)742-2410, president Elayne Clipper Hanson. Biannual conferences. Founded in 1948. Usually held first Saturday in May and last weekend in September at various hotel-conference centers around the state. Average attendance is 100-130. **Open to all writers, "aspiring, amateur or professional." All forms of writing/marketing rotated between conferences. "The purpose is to keep writers informed and prepared to express and market their writing in a proper format." Poetry covered once a year.** A book fair is held at both conferences where members can sell their published works. A banquet is held at the fall conference where the Jade Ring writing contest winners receive awards. Writing contest winners receive awards at the spring conference as well. Spring conference is approximately $30-35, fall conference approximately $35-40. Conferences includes coffee and sweet rolls, lunch and hors d'oeuvres at book fair. Fall conference also includes dinner and entertainment. Information about overnight accommodations is available for registrants. "Our organization 'blocks' rooms at a reduced rate." Sponsors 3 writing contests/year. Membership and small fee are required. Send SASE for brochures and registration forms. "We are affiliated with the Wisconsin Fellowship of Poets and the Council of Wisconsin Writers. We also publish a newsletter four times a year for members."

THE WRITERS' CENTER AT CHAUTAUQUA, Box 408, Chautauqua NY 14722, phone (814)796-4196, registrar Charlene Stull. Annual event founded 1988. Usually held 9 weeks in summer from late June to late August. Participants may attend for one week or more. "We are an independent, cooperative association of writers located on the grounds of Chautauqua Institution." Average attendance is 38 for readings and speeches, 12 for workshops. **Readings and speeches are open to anyone; workshops are open to writers (or auditors). The purpose is "to make creative writing one of the serious arts in progress at Chautauqua; to provide a vacation opportunity for skilled artists and their guests (one each); and to help learning writers improve their skills and vision."** Workshops are available all 9 weeks. Poetry Works meets 2 hours each day offering 1 hour of class for every hour of workshop. In 1997, leaders included Emily Grosholz, Liz Rosenberg, Stephen Corey and Margaret Gibson. Prose Works offers 2 hours a day in fiction and nonfiction, writing for children and Young Writers' Workshops. Poets are welcome to explore other fields. Other special features include 2 speeches a week and 1 reading, usually done by the Writers-In-Residence. Cost is $70/week. Participants are responsible for gate fees, housing and meals and "may bring family; sports, concerts, activities for all ages. A week's gate ticket to Chautauqua is $180/adult (less if ordered early); housing cost varies widely, but is not cheap; meals vary widely depending on accommodations—from fine restaurants to cooking in a shared kitchen." Access is best by car or plane to Jamestown, NY, where a limousine service is available for the 14 miles to Chautauqua ($18). Phone number for Accommodations Directory Service is available for registrants. Individual critiques are also usually available. Information published in spring mailing. Send SASE for brochures and registration forms.

WRITERS' FORUM, Community Education Dept., Pasadena City College, 1570 E. Colorado, Pasadena CA 91106-2003, phone (818)445-0704, fax (818)585-7910, contact Meredith Brucker. Annual 1-day event founded

1954. Usually held all day Saturday in early March at Pasadena City College. Average attendance is 150. **Open to all. Conference covers a wide variety of topics and always includes one poet.** Speakers have included poet Ron Koertge, *ONTHEBUS* editor Jack Grapes, Philomene Long speaking on "Poetry for Non-poets," and Dennis Phillips of Littoral Books. Cost for the 1997 conference was $85, including lunch. Write for brochures and registration forms. No SASE necessary.

WRITING TODAY, Birmingham-Southern College, Box 549003, Birmingham AL 35254, phone (205)226-4921, fax (205)226-3072, director of special events Martha Andrews. Annual 2-day event founded 1978. 1997 dates were March 14-15. Location: Birmingham-Southern College campus. Average attendance is 400-500. **Open to "everyone interested in writing—beginners, professionals and students. Conference topics vary year to year depending on who is part of the faculty."** In 1997, Joyce Carol Oates, was the major speaker and Grand Master Award recipient. Other speakers at the last conference were Joy Harjo, Clifton Taulbert and Gay Talese. Cost for 1997 conference was $90 before deadline ($95 after deadline), including lunches and reception. Cost for a single day's events was $50, including luncheon. Either day's luncheon was only $20. $10 cancellation fee. Information on overnight accommodations is available for registrants. Accommodations include special rates at area hotels. Individual critiques are also available. In addition, the Hackney Literary Awards competition is sponsored as part of the conference. The competition, open to writers nationwide, offers $2,000 in prizes for poetry and short stories and a $2,000 award for the novel category. Send SASE for conference information and see the listing for the Hackney Literary Awards in Contests and Awards.

YELLOW BAY WRITERS' WORKSHOP, Center for Continuing Education & Summer Programs, The University of Montana, Missoula MT 59812, phone (406)243-4470, fax (406)243-2047, program manager Shauna Miller. Annual week-long event founded 1987. 1997 dates: August 17-23. Location: University of Montana's biological research station located on beautiful Flathead Lake. The facility includes informal educational facilities, and rustic cabin or dorm living. Maximum attendance is 60. **Open to all writers. Conference offers two workshops in fiction, one in nonfiction and one in poetry.** In 1997, workshop faculty included Kevin Canty, David James Duncan, Jane Hirshfield and Jayne Anne Phillips. "Special guests usually include editors/publishers/agents who engage in a forum of discussion and information dissemination." Cost for 1997 workshop was $495, commuter fee; $825, tuition and single-occupancy lodging/meals; $800, tuition and double-occupancy lodging/meals. Round-trip shuttle from Missoula to Yellow Bay (85 miles) is available for $40 and airfare packages are offered. Applicants must send a writing sample. Full and partial scholarships are available. Deadline for scholarship applications is June 10. Call or write for brochures and registration forms.

Writing Colonies

Writing colonies are places for writers (including poets) to find solitude and spend concentrated time focusing on their work. While a residency at a writing colony may offer participation in seminars, critiques or readings, the atmosphere of a colony or retreat is much more relaxed than that of a conference or workshop. Also, a writer's stay at a colony is typically anywhere from one to twelve weeks (sometimes longer), while time spent at a conference may only run from one to fourteen days.

Like conferences and workshops, however, writing colonies and retreats span a wide range. Yaddo, perhaps the most well-known colony, limits its residencies to writers "who have already achieved some recognition in their field and have new work under way." The Saltonstall Arts Colony (new to this edition) restricts its colony to residents of New York State. The N.A.L.L. Art Association, on the other hand, limits its residencies to writers who are members of the association. And, in addition to listings for colonies across the United States, this section contains listings for residencies in the Dominican Republic, France, Scotland and Spain.

Despite different focuses and locations, all writing colonies and retreats have one thing in common: They are places where you may work undisturbed, usually in very nature-oriented, secluded settings. A colony serves as a place for rejuvenation, a place where you may find new ideas for poems, rework old ones, or put the finishing touches to a collection.

SELECTING A WRITING COLONY

When selecting a colony or retreat, the primary consideration for many writers is cost, and you'll discover that arrangements vary greatly. The Blue Mountain Center (new to this edition) and The Millay Colony for the Arts, Inc., for instance, don't have fees. Other colonies provide residencies as well as stipends for personal expenses. Some suggest donations of a certain amount. Still others offer residencies for substantial sums but have financial assistance available.

When investigating the various options, consider meal and housing arrangements and your family obligations. Some colonies provide meals for residents, while others require residents to pay for meals. Some colonies house writers in one main building; others provide separate cottages. (In both cases, you are given private work space, although you must usually bring along your own reference materials and typewriter or personal computer.) A few writing colonies have provisions for spouses and families. Others prohibit families altogether.

Overall, residencies at writing colonies and retreats are competitive. Since only a handful of spots are available at each place, you often must apply months in advance for the time period you desire. A number of locations are open year-round, and you may find planning to go during the "off-season" lessens your competition. Other colonies, however, are only available during certain months. In any case, be prepared to include a sample of your best work with your application. Also, know what project you'll work on while in residence and have alternative projects in mind in case the first one doesn't work out once you're there.

Each listing in this section details fee requirements, meal and housing arrangements, and space and time availability, as well as the retreat's surroundings, facilities and special activities. Of course, before making a final decision, send a SASE to the colonies or retreats that interest you to receive their most up-to-date details. Costs, application requirements and deadlines are particularly subject to change.

For other listings of writing colonies, see *The Guide to Writers Conferences* (available from ShawGuides, Inc., P.O. Box 1295, New York NY 10023, website http://www.shawguides.com), which not only provides information about conferences, workshops and seminars but also residencies, retreats and organizations. Another resource is *Havens for Creatives*, available from ACTS Institute, Inc. (% Charlotte Plotsky, P.O. Box 30854, Palm Beach Gardens FL 33420-0854). Also check the Publications of Interest section in this book for newsletters and other periodicals providing this information.

‡**ACADIA NATIONAL PARK ARTIST-IN-RESIDENCE**, P.O. Box 177, Bar Harbor ME 04609, phone (207)288-3338, e-mail shirley_beccue@nps.gov, website http://www.nps.gov/acad/anp.html/, assistant chief interpreter Shirley Beccue, founded 1993. Offers 2-week residencies from May through early June and September through November for visual and performing artists, writers and poets at Acadia National Park. Accommodates 1 resident at one time in a 1 or 2 bedroom apartment with access to park library. Activities include park orientation. Participants are responsible for their own meals. Each artist is responsible for own transportation. A private vehicle is highly recommended to access the park. Send SASE for application forms and guidelines. When sending application, include 6 copies of the following items: 1- to 2-page résumé, summary of creative works, poems, statement about what one hopes to achieve from the residency, type of public presentation one will present, and 2 references. Application deadline: January 10.

THE EDWARD F. ALBEE FOUNDATION, INC.; THE WILLIAM FLANAGAN MEMORIAL CREATIVE PERSONS CENTER ("THE BARN"), 14 Harrison St., New York NY 10013, phone (212)226-2020, for information and application forms. The Albee Foundation maintains the center (better known as "The Barn") in Montauk, on Long Island, offering 1-month residencies for writers, painters, sculptors and composers, open June 1 through October 1, accommodating 5 persons at a time. Write or call for application. Applications accepted at the above address by regular mail only January 1 through April 1. Fellowship announcements by May 15. "Located approximately 2 miles from the center of Montauk and the Atlantic Ocean, 'The Barn' rests in a secluded knoll that offers privacy and a peaceful atmosphere. The foundation expects all those accepted for residence to work seriously and to conduct themselves in such a manner as to aid fellow residents in their endeavors. The environment is simple and communal. Residents are expected to do their share in maintaining the condition of 'The Barn' as well as its peaceful environment."

***ALTOS DE CHAVÓN**, % Parsons School of Design, 2 W. 13th St., Room 707, New York NY 10011, New York coordinator Carmen Lorente, arts/education director Stephen D. Kaplan. Offers 3½-month residencies to artists working in various fields: painting, sculpture, dance, music, crafts, writing, etc. "The village of Altos de Chavón is located on the southeast coast of the Dominican Republic, an 1½-hour drive from the bustling capital city of Santo Domingo." Accommodates 15 international artists during the year in "comfortable" apartments with small balconies and kitchenettes; basic furniture and some housewares provided. Individual studio space available near apartments. "Many artists agree to teach an occasional workshop in their area of expertise." Cost for residencies is $300/month and a $100 nonrefundable registration fee; participants are responsible for airfare, meals and daily living expenses. To be considered, submit a letter of interest, sample of work and résumé. Artist couples may apply. "A panel meets in New York in July to select the participants for the following year." Write for more information.

ATLANTIC CENTER FOR THE ARTS, 1414 Art Center Ave., New Smyrna Beach FL 32168, phone (904)427-6975, program director Nicholas Conroy, program assistant Jim Frost. The center was founded in 1977 by sculptor and painter Doris Leeper, who secured a seed grant from The Rockefeller Foundation. That same year the center was chartered by the state of Florida and building began on a 10-acre site. The facility now covers 67 acres. The center was officially opened in 1982. Since 1982, 70 Master Artists-in-Residence sessions have been held. At each of the 3-week sessions, internationally known artists from different disciplines conduct interdisciplinary workshops and lectures and critique works in progress. They also give readings and recitals, exhibit their work and develop projects with their "associates"—mid-career artists who come from all over the US to work with them. The center is run by an advisory council which chooses Master Artists for residencies, helps set policies and guides the center in its growth. The process of becoming an associate is different for each Master Artist. Recent poets in residence at the center include Rachel Hadas (January 1995), Sonia Sanchez (May 1995), Ntozake Shange (May 1996), Carolyn Kizer (January 1997) and Poet David Lehman (May 1997).

‡**BLUE MOUNTAIN CENTER**, P.O. Box 109, Blue Mt. Lake NY 12812, phone (518)352-7391, director Harriet Barlow, founded 1982. Offers 1-month residencies from mid June through October to poets, fiction and nonfiction writers, playwrights, visual artists, composers and "burned-out" activists at "an old rustic Adirondack lodge on a lake in the woods (two hours from Albany airport or a five hour drive from New York City or

Boston)." Accommodates 14 residents at one time in single rooms, some with private baths; desks, chairs and a "pretty good" library available. "The Center exists to provide a peaceful and comfortable environment in which guests are able to work, free from the distractions and demands of normal daily life." Other than transportation, the residency is free. Transportation to and from the center is provided. "We will meet trains and planes at Albany, NY. Residents are chosen by an Admissions Committee of nationally-known authors and artists. The committee is particularly interested in fine work which evinces social and ecological concern and is aimed at a general audience." Send SASE for application forms and guidelines. Application deadline: February 1.

BYRDCLIFFE ARTIST COLONY, The Woodstock Guild, 34 Tinker St., Woodstock NY 12498, phone (914)679-2079, fax (914)679-4529, executive director Caroline Harris, founded 1901. Offers 1-month residencies from June through September to visual artists, crafts people, writers, musicians and theater artists at a historic 600-acre colony in the Catskill Mountains, 1½ miles from the Woodstock village center and 90 miles north of New York City. Accommodates 10 residents in Villetta Inn, "a spacious turn-of-the-century mountain lodge," in single and double rooms with shared bathrooms and kitchen; separate individual studio space also available. Activities include hiking, concerts, theater, art exhibitions and literary events. Cost for residency is $500. Send SASE for application forms and guidelines. Work sample, project description, résumé, reviews, contact information for 2 references and $10 fee, must accompany application. Application deadline: April 1.

CENTRUM, Residency Program, P.O. Box 1158, Port Townsend WA 98368, fax (360)385-2470, offers 1-month residencies, September through May, for writers, composers, choreographers and printmakers. Centrum provides individual cabins, a stipend of $75/week and solitude. Families welcome. Located in Fort Worden State Park on the Strait of Juan de Fuca. Request application via mail or fax. Also sponsors the Port Townsend Writers' Conference (See Conferences and Workshops) and other seminars. Contact Marlene Bennett, for more information on these programs.

*CHATEAU DE LESVAULT, 58370 Onlay, France, phone 33-03-86-84-32-91, fax 33-03-86-84-35-78, director Bibbi Lee. This French country residence is located in the national park "Le Morvan" of western Burgundy, halfway between Nevers and Autun and is surrounded by green hills and forests. The chateau accommodates 5 residents at a time in 5 large rooms with private baths, fully furnished and equipped for working. The facilities of the chateau are at the disposal of residents, including the salon, library and grounds. Requests for residencies from October through April should be made at least 3 months in advance. The cost is 4,500 FF per month for room, board and utilities.

THE CLEARING, Box 65, Ellison Bay WI 54210, fax (414)854-4088, e-mail buchholz@mail.wisnet.net, resident managers Donald and Louise Buchholz, "is first a school, then a place of self-discovery," founded in 1935. It is made up of cabins and lodges in a rustic setting overlooking Green Bay, it offers a variety of courses, including courses in writing and poetry, May through October. Fees include tuition, room (dormitory or twin-bedded room) and board.

‡CLEAVELAND HOUSE, MARTHA'S VINEYARD, P.O. Box 3041, West Tisbury MA 02575, phone (508)693-9352, e-mail criggs@vineyard.net, manager Cynthia Riggs, founded late 1800s and reopened in 1988. Bed & breakfast open year-round, open to poets and writers and those who wish to be around lots of books and papers and creative energy. The House was built around 1750; modernized 1860; on main road; on about 12 acres. Doors don't have locks; no TV; no phones in rooms, floors creak. Accommodations are 2 double rooms (large corner rooms), 1 single room and shared baths; desks and tables, reference books. Activities include Wednesday afternoon poetry workshop for Island poets and guests (critique, reading). Cost for residency is $75-125 daily, $350-625 weekly, including breakfast. Guest will need their own car or bicycle. Send SASE for information.

DOBIE-PAISANO PROJECT, Attn: Audrey N. Slate, Main Building 101, The University of Texas, Austin TX 78712. Offers two annual fellowships of $7,200 and 6-month residency at Frank Dobie's ranch, Paisano, for native Texans, those who have resided in the state at least 2 years, or writers with published works about Texas. Write for application and guidelines. Application deadline: January 23, 1998.

DORLAND MOUNTAIN ARTS COLONY, P.O. Box 6, Temecula CA 92593, e-mail dorland@ez2.net, website http://www.ez2.net/dorland/, established 1979. A 300-acre nature preserve which offers 1-month residences for writers, visual artists and composers in a rustic environment with no elecricity, propane appliances

---

 THE DOUBLE DAGGER before a listing indicates that the listing is new in this edition. New markets are often the most receptive to submissions.

(refrigerator, water heater, cooking stove, some lights) and oil lamps. Residents provide their own meals. A donation of $300/month is requested. Send SASE for application form and guidelines. Deadlines are the first of September and March.

DORSET COLONY HOUSE RESIDENCIES; AMERICAN THEATRE WORKS, INC., P.O. Box 519, Dorset VT 05251, managing director Mr. Gene Sirotof. Residencies available to writers fall and spring for periods of 1 week to 2 months for intensive work. Requested fee of $95/week, but ability to pay is essential in awarding residencies.

FINE ARTS WORK CENTER IN PROVINCETOWN, 24 Pearl St., Provincetown MA 02657, provides monthly stipends of $375 and studio/living quarters for 7 uninterrupted months for 20 young artists and writers (fiction writers, playwrights and poets) who have completed their formal training and are capable of working independently. The center arranges readings and slide presentations and visits from other distinguished writers and artists. Sessions run from October 1 through May 1. Applications, accompanied by a $35 processing fee, must be received by February 1. To receive an application and program brochure, send a SASE to Writing Fellowship. Unlike the winter residency, the Summer Program offers open-enrollment workshops with "an outstanding faculty in the visual arts and writing." The 10-week program consists of 40 one-week workshops in poetry, fiction, nonfiction, painting, sculpture, installation, printmaking and photography. Write for catalog of course descriptions and registration materials.

*FUNDACIÓN VALPARAÍSO, Apt. 836, 04638 Mojácar Playa, Almerío Spain, phone/fax (34)50-47 23 80, founded 1992. Offers 1-month residencies (except in March, August and between Christmas and New Year) to writers, painters, sculptors, musicians, etc., from all countries at a converted olive oil mill in Andalucía, Spain. Accommodates 8 residents at one time in single rooms with private baths and shared kitchen facilities; one computer and a small library also available. Residents *do not* pay for accommodations and meals. However, "traveling costs and insurance are not paid." To be considered, submit publication with application for the Board to evaluate. Write for application form. Application deadline: May, September and December.

GELL WRITERS CENTER OF THE FINGER LAKES, % Writers & Books, 740 University Ave., Rochester NY 14607, phone (716)473-2590, fax (716)729-0982, director Joseph Flaherty. Offers 1-week to 1-month residencies on a year-round basis for writers and readers who "seek a quiet and restorative time away from their usual routine. The center is located at the southern end of Canandaigua Lake, in the center of New York State's famous Finger Lakes region. Rich in natural diversity, the area contains one of the world's great grape-growing regions, as well as many fine cultural and recreational attractions such as hiking trails. Visitors stay in The Gell House, a completely furnished hillside home surrounded by a beautifully landscaped yard and 23 acres of woodlands." Accommodates 2 writers at a time in single rooms with private baths and shared kitchen facilities; private desks and an extensive library available. Activities include workshops, lectures and readings at a nearby literary center. Cost is $25/day for members of Writers & Books; $35/day for nonmembers. Memberships are available. Participants are responsible for own meals. Send SASE for application forms, guidelines and membership information for Writers & Books. A 5- to 10-page work sample must accompany application.

GUEST HOUSE AT NEW LIGHT STUDIOS, 1890 Turtle Town Hall Rd., Beloit WI 53511, phone (608)362-8055 or 365-7907, fax (608)362-1417, partner Sharon Blakeley, founded 1992. Offers 3-day to 1-month residencies throughout the year to writers/artists working in any field at New Light Studios, located between Chicago and Madison in the Wisconsin countryside. "The guest house is simple, self-contained and quiet. Two of the three artist-partners reside in nearby farmhouses." Accommodates up to 4 residents at one time in a 2-bedroom house with bath and fully equipped kitchen. "Since we emphasize privacy, we accept dual residencies for artists previously unknown to each other only by special arrangement with those concerned." Desks and a small library of reference books available. Residents may bring their own computers and typewriters. "We host poetry readings on a regular basis. Residents are invited to read their own work. Participation is encouraged but not mandatory. Residents may attend cultural events at nearby Beloit College. We can provide transportation." Residencies are free "to deserving artists who desire solitude for their work." Residents are responsible for their own meals. Hourly bus service from Chicago's O'Hare Airport to Beloit available. "We can provide transportation from the bus to New Light. Having your own car will help maintain visiting artists' autonomy." Send SASE for application materials and more details. "We want to provide quiet inspiration and encouragement for artists, especially poets. We encourage artists at all stages of their careers to apply. (The partners in New Light Studios are artists themselves. We have received encouragement from others, and want to return the favor.)" Application deadline is 30-60 days prior to desired date of residency.

*THE TYRONE GUTHRIE CENTRE, Annaghmakerrig, Newbliss, Co. Monaghan, Ireland, phone (353)47-54003, fax (353)47-54380, e-mail thetgc@indigo.ie, resident director Bernard Loughlin. Offers residencies, normally 3 weeks to 3 months, for artists, including poets. "Each resident has a private room with attached bathroom within the house . . . and all the centrally heated central on an Irish Big House can afford. It is set on a wooded estate of 650 acres and overlooks a large lake. The house is surrounded by gardens and a working farm. Five newly built, self-contained farmyard cottages are also available for individuals and couples for longer stays. To qualify for residence it is necessary to show evidence of a significant level of achievement in the relevant field. Once accepted, Irish artists are asked to contribute what they can afford toward the cost of their stay. Overseas artists are expected to pay the whole cost of a residency."

HAMBIDGE CENTER FOR CREATIVE ARTS AND SCIENCES, P.O. Box 339, Rabun Gap GA 30568, phone (706)746-5718. The Center is located on 600 acres of unspoiled wooded slopes, mountain meadows and streams, near Dillard, Georgia. It is listed on the National Register of Historic Places. Resident Fellowships of 2 weeks to 2 months are awarded to individuals engaged in all artistic disciplines for the purpose of solitude and the pursuit of creative excellence. Accommodates 90 Fellows each year. Those accepted are given a private cottage equipped with a bath, kitchen, living and studio/work space. Center is open from March through December. "The average cost to maintain a Resident Fellow at the Center is $600/week. Residents are asked to contribute a minimum of $125/week toward the total cost." For more information and application forms send SASE. A $20 processing fee must accompany application. Application deadline: November 1 for residencies taking place March through August, May 1 for residencies taking place September through December.

HAWK, I'M YOUR SISTER; WOMEN'S WILDERNESS CANOE TRIPS; WRITING RETREATS, Beverly Antaeus, P.O. Box 9109, Santa Fe NM 87504-9109, phone (505)984-2268, founded 1985. This organization offers wilderness retreats for women, many of them with writing themes, including A Writing Retreat with Sharon Olds in New Mexico and A Writing Retreat with Deena Metzger also in New Mexico. The canoe trips are held all over North America plus Russia and Peru, and typically last 8 days to 2 weeks with fees of $1,000-2,500. Write for annual listing of specific trips, a few offered for women and men.

***HAWTHORNDEN CASTLE INTERNATIONAL RETREAT FOR WRITERS**, Hawthornden Castle, Lasswade, Midlothian EH18 1EG Scotland, phone (0131)440-2180, contact administrator, founded 1982. Offers four-week sessions from February through July and September through December for dramatists, novelists, poets or other creative writers who have published one piece of work. Located in a "remotely situated castle amid wild romantic scenery, a 30-minute bus ride to Edinburgh." Accommodates 5 writers at a time in study bedrooms with communal breakfasts and evening meals; desks, typewriters for hire, and limited reference materials available. Board and lodging are free. Write for application forms and guidelines. Application deadline is the end of September for upcoming year.

‡HEADLANDS CENTER FOR THE ARTS, 944 Fort Barry, Sausalito CA 94965, phone (415)331-2787, fax (415)331-3857, residency manager Holly Blake, founded 1982. Offers 1- to 3-month live-in residencies for artists from California, Ohio and North Carolina, and 11-month residencies for artists from the Bay Area, from February through November at a former army fort built in 1907, set in a 13,000 acre national park ten minutes north of San Francisco. Accommodates 10 live-in residents at one time in private rooms with shared baths and kitchen facilities; desks, 1 older Macintosh, some access to Center's computers and laser printers and 1 older typewriter available. Activities include workshops, lectures and readings. North Carolina and Ohio artists receive $500 monthly stipend, dinner 5 nights a week and roundtrip travel. California live-in artists receive $500 monthly stipend and dinner 5 nights a week. 11-month California live-out artists receive a total stipend of $2,500 and dinner 2 nights a week. Send SASE for application forms and guidelines in the spring. When sending application, include writing sample as specified in guidelines, résumé, letter of interest. There is no application fee. Application deadline: first Friday in June each year.

HEDGEBROOK, 2197 E. Millman Rd., Langley WA 98260, phone (360)321-4786, founded 1988. Offers 1-week to 2-month individual residencies from early January through May and mid-June through early December for "women writers of all ages and from all cultural backgrounds. The Hedgebrook community, on 30 acres of farmland and woods located on Whidbey Island in Washington State, seeks to balance human needs with those of the earth while providing a nurturing environment in which creativity can thrive." Accommodates 6 writers at a time. "Each writer has her own cottage with writing space, living room, sleeping loft, small kitchen, bathroom, electricity and a woodstove. Writers gather for dinner in the farmhouse every evening and may read in the living room/library afterwards. A bathhouse serves all six cottages." Public libraries with excellent interlibrary loan located within 2-6 miles. Computers available for rent. Activities include occasional cultural celebrations and field trips. Free room and board. Limited, need-based travel scholarships are available. Send #10 SASE for application forms and guidelines. When sending application, include writing sample and $15 application fee. Application deadlines: April 1 for residencies from mid-June to mid-December; September 30 for mid-January through May.

KALANI HONUA OCEANSIDE ECO-RESORT, RR2, Box 4500, Pahoa HI 96778-9724, phone (808)965-7828 or (800)800-6886, fax (808)965-9613, e-mail kh@ilhhawaii.net, website http://www.randm.com/kh.html, director Richard Koob, founded 1980. Offers 2-week to 2-month residencies on a year-round basis for visual, literary, folk and performing artists. "Kalani Honua is situated near Kalapana on the big island of Hawaii on 113 acres of secluded forest and dramatic coastline, 45 minutes from the city of Hilo and one hour from Hawaii Volcanoes National Park. Visitors stay in 4 two-story wooden lodges and 8 private cottage units that provide comfortable accommodations." Accommodates 100 (generally about 5 artists-in-residence) at a time in private rooms with full meal service plus optional kitchen facilities and shared or private baths; private desks and access to computers, typewriters and reference material available. Activities include a variety of dance, drawing, fitness and mind/body classes; also available are an olympic pool, sauna, volleyball, tennis, basketball and fitness room. Cost for residency ranges from $45/night (multiple occupancy) to $85/night (private cottage); plus $25/day for meals. Stipends are most available in the periods of May through July and September through December. Stipends provide for 50% of lodging costs; balance is responsibility of the artist (stipends may *not* be applied toward dorm lodging or camping, or reduction in food or transportation costs). Send SASE for application forms and guidelines or obtain via e-mail or website. When sending application, include $10 fee.

THE MACDOWELL COLONY, 100 High St., Peterborough NH 03458, phone (603)924-3886, founded 1907, "to provide creative artists with uninterrupted time and seclusion to work and enjoy the experience of living in a community of gifted artists." Residents receive room, board and exclusive use of a studio. Average residency is 6 weeks. Ability to pay for residency is not a factor. Application deadlines: January 15 for summer (May through August); April 15 for fall/winter (September through December); September 15 for winter/spring (January through April). Please write or call for application and guidelines.

‡THE MAINE RETREAT, P.O. Box 76, Troy ME 04987, phone (207)948-3427, fax (207)947-5088, e-mail potatoeyes@uninet.net, co-editor Carolyn Page, founded 1993. Offers 1- to 4-week residencies from June through October at a cabin in the Maine woods, 23 miles from Belfast and the sea. Accommodates 1 resident at one time in a one-room cabin with screened porch, or alternate accommodations in guest room of main house with 11 rooms; electricity, deck, typewriter and reference library available. Activities include workshops. Cost for 1998 residency is $250/week including meals. Residents may choose to perform work study for a half scholarship ($125 reduction). Work can include farm work, organic gardening, weeding or wood lot care. Send SASE for application forms and guidelines.

THE MILLAY COLONY FOR THE ARTS, INC., East Hill Rd., P.O. Box 3, Austerlitz NY 12017-0003, e-mail application@millaycolony.org, founded in 1973, assistant director Gail Giles. Provides work space, meals and sleeping accommodations at no cost for a period of 1 month. Send SASE for brochure and application forms or request via e-mail. Apply with samples of your work before February 1 for June through September; before May 1 for October through January; before September 1 for February through May.

MONTALVO CENTER FOR THE ARTS; MONTALVO BIENNIAL POETRY COMPETITION (IV-Regional), Box 158, Saratoga CA 95071, phone (408)961-5818, presents theatre, musical events and other artistic activities. They have an Artist Residency program, director Judy Moran, which has 5 apartments available for artists (including poets) for maximum 3-month periods. (No children or pets.) Limited financial assistance available. Deadlines: March 1 (fall and winter) and September 1 (spring and summer) of every year. They offer a biennial poetry competition in odd-numbered years (1999, 2001, etc.). Open to residents of Oregon, Nevada, Washington and California, with a prominent judge, with a first prize of $1,000 (and artist residency), other prizes of $500, $300 and 8 honorable mentions. Submit 3 poems in duplicate with $5 entry fee. Deadline: October 2. Send SASE for rules.

‡MONTANA ARTISTS REFUGE, Box 8, Basin MT 59631, phone (406)225-3525, fax (406)225-9225, residency co-ordinator M.J. Williams, founded 1993. Offers residencies of 3 months up to a year for artists of all disciplines at a large two-story former bank building/masonic lodge. Downstairs has combination living space with adjoining all-purpose studio. Upstairs has a combination painting studio (large open room) with adjoining living space. Small one study former retail space; small studio with kitchen and bath. Accommodates 3-5 residents at one time. All three spaces have private baths and fully equipped kitchens. "Residents are free to participate in any way. We have a varied program offered by residents and other community members including readings, art shows, music performances." Cost for residency is $200-400 monthly, depending on the location, plus heat; participants are responsible for their own meals. Transportation to and from the colony is available. "We can assist up to 50% of residency cost. We have an application process that looks at quality of the work and degree of commitment." Send SASE for application forms and guidelines. Submit a sample of work and specific financial request. "We do as much as we can to make residencies possible within our limited ability."

MY RETREAT, P.O. Box 1077, South Fallsburg NY 12779, phone (914)436-7455 or (800)484-1255 ext 2485, owner Cora T. Schwartz, founded 1993. Offers "a room of one's own" for a weekend, week or month on a year-round basis for writers, poets and "artists of life." Located in the foothills of the Catskill Mountains, My Retreat is approximately 90 miles northwest of New York City. An unpretentious, peaceful setting consisting of a main house and cottages. The modest 1950-style cottages (open May through October) have 7 furnished bedrooms, 3 kitchens and 4 bathrooms. Accommodates 5-12 guests depending on season. Cottages also have private accommodations with own kitchen/porch/bathroom and single or double bedrooms. The main house, with 5 bedrooms, is available year-round. There are screened and open porches, and a library of mostly vintage books for lending or for sale. Activities include ongoing workshops. Nearby activities include a park with a lake for row boating and a pool, horseback riding, downhill skiing, art galleries, gift shop, classes at nearby famous ashram and a local museum. Cost for residency per person starts at $110 for the weekend and $225 for 1 week, including continental-style breakfast. There is a 2 night minimum. Residents are responsible for the remainder of their meals. Special rates available on longer stays of 1 week or more. Send SASE for information.

*N.A.L.L. ART ASSOCIATION, 232, Blvd. de Lattre, Vence 06140 France, phone (33)493 58 1326, fax (33)493 58 0900, founded 1993. Once an artist becomes a member of N.A.L.L. (annual donation of 500 French francs required), houses are available on a monthly basis throughout the year. Open to all artists. The N.A.L.L. (Nature, Art and Life League) is located between Vence and Saint-Paul, fifteen minutes from the Mediterranean Sea and Nice-Cote d'Azur Airport, and "consists of independent houses or cabins, complete with equipped kitchens and baths and each is quietly situated on a wooded hillside connected by rustic terraced trails." Accommodates up to 12 residents at one time. Large studios are available, but "each artist must have his own supplies." Activities include exhibitions, lectures and workshops. Cost ranges from 1,500-5,000 francs. To be considered, send work sample, an outline of education and accomplishments, and brief description of future projects. Write for further details.

NAUTILUS FOUNDATION, P.O. Box 368, Lloyd FL 32337, phone (904)997-1778, fax (904)997-0440, president Francois Bucher, founded 1987. Offers 3-week residencies from February through October to published poets and writers at the Foundation's grounds in Lloyd, "an unspoiled 400-acre wooded area blessed with wildlife, brooks and ponds." Accommodates 2 residents at one time in single rooms with private baths and kitchen facilities; a large library with reference materials available. No cost, however, residents are required to pay utilities. Some meals provided. Participants responsible for transportation to and from retreat. To be considered, send résumé. Send SASE for more details.

THE NEW YORK MILLS ARTS RETREAT, 24 N. Main Ave., Box 246, New York Mills MN 56567, phone (218)385-3339, fax (218)385-3366, e-mail nymills@uslink.net, founded 1990, coordinator Kent Scheer. Offers 2- to 4-week residencies on a year-round basis for emerging artists and writers of demonstrated quality and commitment. "While the vast majority of the artists' time is his/her own, eight hours per week are designated specifically for community impact such as working in the local schools." Accommodates one writer/artist at a time. Housing is provided in the local B&B, and studio space is a large room in the community's art's center. "All residencies in our program are supported by the Jerome Foundation. In this way we can provide stipends for 5 to 7 visiting artists annually. Beyond this, we will do all the necessary coordination for any artists interested in funding themselves for a personal retreat within our community. Artists and writers selected for our program receive up to $1,500 as a stipend. The criteria are artistic excellence as demonstrated by work samples, commitment to the arts as demonstrated by the résumé and a creative proposal for interaction with the community of New York Mills." Send SASE for application forms and guidelines. When sending application, include a résumé, artist's statement and a retreat proposal. Application deadlines: April 1 and October 1.

THE NORTHWOOD UNIVERSITY ALDEN B. DOW CREATIVITY CENTER, 3225 Cook Rd., Midland MI 48640-2398, phone (517)837-4478, fax (517)837-4468, founded 1979. Offers fellowships for 2-month summer residencies at the Northwood University Campus. Travel, room and board plus $750 stipend for personal expenses and/or project materials. No families/pets. Applicants can be undergraduates, graduates, or those without any academic or institutional affiliation, including citizens of other countries (if they can communicate in written and spoken English). Projects may be in any field, but must be new and innovative. Write for application. Annual deadline is December 31 for the following summer.

PENDLE HILL, 338 Plush Mill Rd., Wallingford PA 19086-6099, phone (800)742-3150 or (610)566-4507, fax (610)566-3679, e-mail pendlehill@aol.com, website http://www.quaker.org/pendle-hill, outreach associate Bobbi Kelly, founded 1930. Sojourns from 1 day to 1 month offered year round. Three 10-week residential study courses offered from October through June. Open to "all who seek a peaceful, spirit-centered setting." Pendle Hill's facilities include 16 buildings which house informal classrooms and meeting rooms, a library, bookstore, crafts studio and housing for students and staff. The buildings are "set on 23 acres of beautiful woods and gardens." Accommodates 60 residents at one time in single rooms with shared baths; communal dining. Twenty-four-hour library and typewriters available. "Classes in the resident program are open to sojourners. Weekend conferences also available. Guests may organize interest groups for writing support or readings." Cost for resident study is $3,970/term, $11,570/year, including room and board. Nightly rates available for sojourns. Limousine ride from airport available for $17. "Some financial aid available for Resident Program. Requires some work in exchange." Write for application forms and guidelines. "No application necessary to sojourn."

PUDDING HOUSE PUBLICATIONS, 60 N. Main St., Johnstown OH 43031. See listing in Publishers of Poetry section.

RAGDALE FOUNDATION; FRANCES SHAW FELLOWSHIP, 1260 N. Green Bay Rd., Lake Forest IL 60045, phone (847)234-1063, fax (847)234-1075, founded 1976, provides a peaceful place and uninterrupted time for 12 writers, composers and artists. Meals, linen and laundry facilities are provided. Each resident is assigned private work space and sleeping accommodations. Couples are accepted if each qualifies independently. Residents may come for 2 weeks to 2 months. Cost for residency is $105/week. Some full and partial fee waivers available. The foundation also sponsors poetry readings, concerts, workshops and seminars in writing. Ragdale is open year-round except for the month of May and 2 weeks at Christmas. Send SAE for application. Apply by January 15 for residencies in June through December and June 1 for January through May. Application fee: $20. Sponsors annual Frances Shaw Fellowship, awarding a 2-month residency at Ragdale. Submissions may be entered in other contests. Submit 12 typed poems on any subject in any form, include a letter stating why you need a 2-month residency at Ragdale. Send SASE for entry form and guidelines. Deadline: February 1. Most recent award winner was Joan Southgate (1996). Winner notified by personal phone call, and announced in *Poets & Writers* by March.

‡**THE SALTONSTALL ARTS COLONY**, 120 Brindley St., Ithaca NY 14850, phone/fax (607)277-4933, e-mail artsfound@clarityconnect.com, director Kathy Durland Dewart, founded 1994. Offers 1-month residencies during June, July and August for artists, photographers and writers, 21 or older and a resident of New York State. Situated in the hills of western New York State, the colony is 5 miles from Ithaca. Two buildings, the Carriage House and the Center, house the residents. There are miles of marked trails in the woods and fields, ideal for hiking and bird watching. Accommodates 2 writers, 2 painters and 1 photographer at one time in single rooms with private bath, private deck/patio and shared kitchen and dining room. Participants are responsible for preparing their own meals (kitchen is stocked for residents); however, dinners on weeknights are provided. Send SASE for application forms and guidelines. When sending application include short professional résumé, statement of purpose and up to 15 pages writing sample. Deadline: January 15. Recipients are notified by April 15. See the listing for The Constance Saltonstall Foundation for the Arts Grants in the Contests and Awards section.

SPLIT ROCK ARTS PROGRAM, University of Minnesota, 306 Wesbrook Hall, 77 Pleasant St. SE, Minneapolis MN 55455, phone (612)624-6800, fax (612)625-2568, e-mail srap@mail.cee.umn.edu. The program is a summer series of week-long workshops in the visual and literary arts and in the nature and applications of creativity, on the Duluth campus of UM "in the green hills overlooking Lake Superior." Tuition is $385-410 with an additional charge for graduate credit. Housing ranges from $150-504, depending on type of accommodation. Most students choose single or double rooms in 2-bedroom apartments on campus. Other housing options also available. Meals are in UMD's cafeteria, cooked by participants in their apartments, or in Duluth restaurants. Write or call for complete catalog in March.

UCROSS FOUNDATION RESIDENCY PROGRAM, 2836 US Hwy. 14-16, Clearmont WY 82835, phone (307)737-2291, fax (307)737-2232, executive director Sharon Dynak. There are 8 concurrent positions open in various disciplines, including poetry, each extending from 2 weeks to 2 months. No charge for room, board or studio space, and they do not expect services or products from guests. However, there is a $20 application fee required, plus $50 refundable deposit if accepted. Send SASE for information and application guidelines. Residents are selected from a rotating panel of professionals in the arts and humanities. Semiannual application postmark deadlines are March 1 (fall session) and October 1 (spring session).

VERMONT STUDIO CENTER; VISUAL ARTISTS AND WRITERS RESIDENCIES, P.O. Box 613NW, Johnson VT 05656, phone (802)635-2727, founded 1984. Offers a month-long independent writing residency featuring 2 prominent writers per month on a year-round basis. Includes craft talks, individual conferences and readings. 1998 faculty will include C.K. Williams, Charles Baxter, Michael Ryan, Michael Harper, Cornelius Eady, David Bradley and Carol Maso. Room, working studio and meals are included in all programs. Numerous work-exchange Fellowships are available. Write or call for more information and application.

VIRGINIA CENTER FOR THE CREATIVE ARTS, Mt. San Angelo, Sweet Briar VA 24595, phone (804)946-7236, fax (804)946-7239. Provides residencies for 12 writers (and 9 visual artists and 3 composers) for 2 weeks to 2 months at the 450-acre Mt. San Angelo estate. All accommodations provided. Cost for residency is normally $30/day. Financial assistance is available. Call or fax for more information.

THE HELENE WURLITZER FOUNDATION OF NEW MEXICO, Box 545, Taos NM 87571, fax (505)758-2559. Offers residencies to creative, *not* interpretive, artists in all media, for varying periods of time, usually 3 months, from April 1 through September 30, annually. Rent free and utilities free. Residents are responsible for their own meals. No families. No deadlines on application. However, all residencies are assigned into 2000. Send SASE or fax request for application.

YADDO, Box 395, Saratoga Springs NY 12866-0395, phone (518)584-0746, fax (518)584-1312, founded 1900, offers residencies to writers, visual artists, composers, choreographers, film/video artists and performance artists who have already achieved some recognition in their field and have new work under way. During the summer 35 guests can be accommodated at a time, 14 during the winter, approximately 200/year. The hours 9-4 are a quiet period reserved for work. Send SASE for applications to: Admissions, Yaddo, address above. Application deadlines are January 15 and August 1. A $20 application fee is required.

Organizations Useful to Poets

The organizations listed in this section offer encouragement and support to poets and other writers through a wide variety of services. They may sponsor contests and awards, hold regular workshops or open-mike readings, or release publications with details about new opportunities and area events. Many of these groups provide a combination of these services to both members and nonmembers.

The PEN American Center, for instance, holds public events, sponsors literary awards, and offers grants and loans to writers in need. Poets seeking financial assistance should also refer to the listing for the Authors League Fund or contact the arts council in their state or province (see State and Provincial Grants on pages 503-505).

Many organizations provide opportunities to meet and discuss work with others. Those with access to computers and modems can connect with poets around the world through computer online services like the CompuServe Information Service (also read Trends in the Field beginning on page 7 for more Internet news). The National Federation of State Poetry Societies, Inc., the National Writers Association (new to this edition) and the Canadian Poetry Association are all national organizations with smaller affiliated groups which may meet in your state or province. And for those seeking gatherings more local or regional in focus, there are organizations such as the Live Poets Society, Maine (new to this edition), Ozark Poets and Writers Collective, and Writers of Kern.

In addition to local and regional associations, there are also organizations that focus on helping certain groups of writers. For instance, the International Women's Writing Guild supports women writers through various national and regional events and services.

For organizations close to home, check for information at a library or bookstore, or contact the English department at a nearby college. Your local branch of the YMCA is also a good source for information on writing groups and programs. In fact, The National Writer's Voice Project sponsors both open-mike readings and readings by nationally-known writers in approximately 15 YMCAs throughout the country. For more information, contact your local YMCA or the New York-based offices of the National Writer's Voice Project at (212)875-4123.

If you are unable to find a local writer's group, however, start one by placing an ad in your community newspaper or posting a notice on a library or bookstore bulletin board. There are sure to be others in your area who would welcome the support, and the library or bookstore might even have space for your group to meet on a regular basis.

To locate some of the larger organizations (or representative samples of smaller groups), read through the listings that follow. Then send a SASE to those groups that interest you to receive more details about their services and membership fees. Also refer to the list of Additional Organizations Useful to Poets at the end of this section, as well as the Publications Useful to Poets section on pages 551-555.

THE ACADEMY OF AMERICAN POETS; FELLOWSHIP OF THE ACADEMY OF AMERICAN POETS; WALT WHITMAN AWARD; THE JAMES LAUGHLIN AWARD; HAROLD MORTON LANDON TRANSLATION AWARD; THE LENORE MARSHALL POETRY PRIZE; THE ERIC MATHIEU KING FUND; THE RAIZISS/DEPALCHI TRANSLATION AWARD; THE TANNING PRIZE, 584 Broadway, Suite 1208, New York NY 10012-3250, phone (212)274-0343, founded 1934, executive director William Wadsworth. Robert Penn Warren wrote in *Introduction to Fifty Years of American Poetry*, an anthology published in 1984 containing one poem from each of the 126 Chancellors, Fellows and Award Winners of the Academy: "What does the Academy do? According to its certificate of incorporation, its purpose is 'To encourage, stimulate and foster the production of American poetry. . . .' The responsibility for its activities lies with the Board of Directors and the Board of 12 Chancellors, which has included, over the years, such figures as Louise Bogan, W.H. Auden, Witter Bynner, Randall Jarrell, Robert Lowell, Robinson Jeffers, Marianne Moore, James Merrill, Robert Fitzgerald, F.O. Matthiessen and Archibald MacLeish—certainly not members of the same poetic church." They award fellowships, currently of $20,000 each, to distinguished American poets (no applications taken)—61 to date—and other annual awards. The Walt Whitman Award pays $5,000 plus publication of a poet's first book by a major publisher. Mss of 50-100 pgs. must be submitted between September 15 and November 15 with a $20 entry fee. Entry form required. Send SASE. The James Laughlin Award, for a poet's second book, is also a prize of $5,000. Submissions must be made by a publisher, in ms form, prior to publication. The Academy distributes 4,000 copies to its members. Poets entering either contest must be American citizens. The Harold Morton Landon Translation Award is for translation of a book-length poem, a collection of poems or a verse-drama translated into English from any language. One award of $1,000 each year to a US citizen. Only publishers may submit the book. Write for guidelines. Most recent award winner was Guy Davenport (1996). The Lenore Marshall Poetry Prize is a $10,000 award for the most outstanding book of poems published in the US in the preceding year. The contest is open to books by living American poets published in a standard edition (40 pgs. or more in length with 500 or more copies). Self-published books are not eligible. Publishers may enter as many books as they wish. Deadline: June 1. Most recent award winner was Charles Wright (1996). Write for guidelines. The Eric Mathieu King Fund assists noncommercial publishers of poetry. Send SASE for guidelines. The Raiziss/dePalchi Translation Award is for outstanding translations of modern Italian poetry into English. A $5,000 book prize and a $20,000 fellowship are given in alternate years. No applications accepted for the book prize. Submissions for the fellowship are accepted in odd-numbered years from September 1 through November 1. Most recent award winner was Anthony Molino (1996). The Tanning Prize, of $100,000, is given annually for proven mastery in the art of poetry. No applications are accepted. *American Poet* is an informative periodical sent to those who contribute $25 or more/year or who are members. Membership: $45/year. The Academy inaugurated the first Annual National Poetry Month in April 1996. It also sponsors a national series of poetry readings and panel discussions and offers for sale select audio tapes from its archive of poetry readings.

ADIRONDACK LAKES CENTER FOR THE ARTS, P.O. Box 205, Rte. 28, Blue Mountain Lake NY 12812, phone (518)352-7715, fax (518)352-7333, e-mail alca@netheaven.com, director Robert C. Lilly. An independent, private, nonprofit educational organization founded in 1967 to promote "visual and performing arts through programs and services, to serve established professional and aspiring artists and the region through educational programs and activities of general interest." Open to everyone. Currently has 1,300 members. Levels of membership available are individual, family and business. Offerings available for poets include workshops for adults and children, reading performances, discussions and lectures. Offers a "comfortable, cozy performance space—coffeehouse setting with tables, candles, etc." Computers available for members and artists. Publishes a triannual newsletter/schedule that contains news, articles, photos and a schedule of events. "All members are automatically sent the schedule and others may request a copy." Sponsors a few readings each year. "These are usually given by the instructor of our writing workshops. There is no set fee for membership, a gift of any size makes you a member." Members meet each July. Send SASE for additional information.

‡ALABAMA STATE POETRY SOCIETY; THE SAMPLER; THE MUSE MESSENGER, P.O. Box 230787, Montgomery AL 36123-0787, (334)244-8920, e-mail poettennis@the-link.net, editor and membership chair Donna Jean Tennis. Founded in 1968 to promote "poetry as a vital cultural medium, improve our skills, share opportunities and support one another, and join with others who enjoy the written and spoken word to delight in good poetry of every form and persuasion." State-wide organization open to anyone engaged in writing poetry, or in furthering the cause of poetry. Currently has 225 total members. Levels of membership available are Regular Membership open to anyone engaged in writing poetry or furthering the cause of poetry. Student Membership available to any person enrolled full-time in a college or university. Affiliated with the National Federation of State Poetry Societies, and payment of dues to Alabama State Poetry Society includes membership with all its privileges into NFSPS. Sponsors conferences, workshops, contests and awards, semi-annual luncheons featuring speakers/workshops and members' poetry. ASPS sponsors spring and fall poetry contests, the fall contest open to non-members. Also sponsors an annual student contest for grades one through five. "Each year we publish *The Sampler*, an annual anthology of members' poems, now in it's 29th year." Publishes *The Muse Messenger*, a quarterly newsletter designed to be a teaching tool, featuring poetry forms, techniques, and terms, as well as publishing poetry by a wide range of poets including members. Members or nationally-known writers give readings that are open to the public. Sponsors open-mike readings. Membership dues are $10 per year for Regular and Associate members and $5 for Student members. Members meet quarterly. Send SASE for additional information. "The Alabama State Poetry Society meets the needs of poets around the country. Our fall contests are open to non-members as well as members, and guidelines are available with an SASE."

‡THE AMERICAN POETS' CORNER, THE CATHEDRAL CHURCH OF ST. JOHN THE DIVINE, (formerly Poets' Corner, The Cathedral Church of St. John the Divine), Cathedral Heights, 1047 Amsterdam Ave. at 112 St., New York NY 10025, phone (212)316-7500, website http://www.stjohndivine.org/Cathedral, initiated in 1984 with memorials for Emily Dickinson, Walt Whitman and Washington Irving. It is similar in concept to the British Poets' Corner in Westminster Abbey, and was established and dedicated to memorialize this country's greatest writers. A Board of Electors comprised of thirteen eminent poets and writers chooses two deceased authors each year for inclusion in The Poets' Corner. The Cathedral is also home to the Muriel Rukeyser

Poetry Wall, a public space for posting poems, which was dedicated in 1976 by Ms. Rukeyser and the Cathedral's Dean, The Very Reverend James Parks Morton. Send poems for the Poetry Wall to the above address.

‡ARIZONA AUTHORS ASSOCIATION; ARIZONA LITERARY MAGAZINE; ARIZONA AUTHORS NEWSLETTER, 3509 E. Shea Blvd., #117, Phoenix AZ 85028, (602)942-9602, e-mail ggbenn@juno. com, president Gerry Benninger. Founded in 1978 to provide education and referral for writers and others in publishing. State-wide organization. Currently has 250 total members. Levels of memberships available are Professional (published in commercial medium); Associate (seeking publication); Affiliate (printers, agents, publishers, etc.); Student. Sponsors conferences, workshops, contests, awards. Sponsors annual literary contest with 3 categories: poetry, short story and essay. Awards publication in *Arizona Literary Magazine* and $125 first prize, $75 second prize, $40 third prize and $10 for honorable mention (6 awarded) for poetry. Submissions must be unpublished and may be entered in other contests, "but not preferred." Submit any number of poems on any subject of up to 42 lines. Submissions must be typed on 8½×11 paper, single-spaced stanzas and double-spaced between. Include a 3×5 index card for each poem with name, address, phone and title of poem (or first line). Do not put name on submissions. Include SASE for winners list. Send SASE for entry form and guidelines. Entry fee: $5/poem. Submission period: January 1 through July 29. Judges are Arizona authors. Winners will be announced by November 15. Publishes *Arizona Literary Magazine*. Also publishes *Arizona Authors Newsletter*, available to nonmembers for $25/year. Members or nationally-known writers give readings that are open to the public. Membership dues are $40. Members meet monthly. Send SASE for additional information.

ASSOCIATED WRITING PROGRAMS; AWP CHRONICLE; THE AWP AWARD SERIES, Tallwood House, MS 1E3, George Mason University, Fairfax VA 22030, phone (703)993-4301, e-mail awp@gmu.e du, website http://www.web.gmu.edu/departments/awp, founded 1967. Offers a variety of services to the writing community, including information, job placement assistance, publishing opportunities, literary arts advocacy and forums. Annual individual membership is $55; placement service extra. For $20 you can subscribe to the *AWP Chronicle* (published 6 times/year), containing information about grants and awards, publishing opportunities, fellowships, and writing programs. They have a directory, *The Official Guide to Writing Programs*, of over 250 college and university writing programs for $25.95 (includes shipping). The AWP Award Series selects a volume of poetry (48 pg. minimum) each year ($10 entry fee for members; $15 for nonmembers) with an award of $2,000 and publication. Deadline: February 28. Send SASE for submission guidelines. Query after November. Their placement service helps writers find jobs in teaching, editing and other related fields.

THE AUTHORS GUILD, INC., 330 W. 42nd St., New York NY 10036, phone (212)563-5904, fax (212)563-8363, e-mail staff@authorsguild.org, executive director Paul Aiken. Founded in 1919, it "is the largest association of published writers in the United States. The Guild focuses its efforts on the legal and business concerns of published authors in the areas of publishing contract terms, copyright, taxation and freedom of expression. Writers must be published by a recognized book publisher or periodical of general circulation to be eligible for membership. We do not work in the area of marketing mss to publishers nor do we sponsor or participate in awards or prize selections." Write, call or e-mail for information on membership.

AUTHORS LEAGUE FUND, 330 W. 42nd St., New York NY 10036. Makes interest-free loans to published authors and professional playwrights in need of temporary help because of illness or an emergency. No grants.

THE BEATLICKS, 1016 Kipling Dr., Nashville TN 37217, phone (615)366-9012, e-mail in%"hirstp@harpo.tn state.edu or in%"speerj@harpo.tnstate.edu, editors Joe Speer and Pamela Hirst. Founded in 1988 to "promote literature and create a place where writers can share their work." International organization open to "anyone interested in literature." Currently has 200 members. "There is no official distinction between members, but there is a core group that does the work, writes reviews, organizes readings, etc." Offerings available for poets include publication of work (they have published poets from Australia, Egypt, India and Holland), reviews of books and venues, readings for local and touring poets and a poetry hotline. "We have also hosted an open mic reading in Nashville since 1988. We have read in bars, bookstores, churches, libraries, festivals, TV and radio. We produce an hour show every Friday on public access TV. Poets submit audio and video tapes from all over. We interview poets about their work and where they are from." Publishes two newsletters: *Speer Presents* (monthly) and *Beatlicks' Newsletter* (bimonthly). The *Beatlicks' Newsletter* is a networking tool, designed to inform poets of local events and to bring awareness of the national scene. "We include poems, short fiction, art, photos, and articles about poets and venues." Submit short pieces, no vulgar language. "We try to elevate the creative spirit. We publish new voices plus well-established talents." Subscription: $10/year. Members meet twice a month. Send SASE for additional information or request via e-mail. "We promote all the arts."

BERGEN POETS, 180-G1 Summit Ave., Summit NJ 07901, phone (908)277-6245, fax (908)277-2171, president Ms. Roberta L. Greening, founded in 1969 to "bring together poets and friends of poetry in our area, help the individual in writing and appreciation of poetry, and add to the cultural life of the community." Open to anyone in the community interested in poetry. "Our base is in Bergen County, New Jersey. However, our members extend from New York to Florida." Currently has 50 members. Offerings available to poets include workshops on craft and readings at area facilities. "Our meetings are held at various public libraries and local bookstores."

Publishes a quarterly newsletter at an annual cost of $5 to new members. Sponsors open-mike readings following featured members' readings. Membership dues are $5 to receive newsletter and meeting announcements. Members meet a minimum of 4 times/year. Send SASE for additional information. "Bergen Poets is one of the oldest poetry organizations in the state of New Jersey."

BEYOND BAROQUE LITERARY/ARTS CENTER, 681 Venice Blvd., Venice CA 90291, phone (310)822-3006. A nonprofit arts center established in 1968 that has been funded by the NEA, state and city arts councils, corporate donations and individual donors. Members get a calendar of events, discounts on regularly-scheduled programs and discounts in the bookstore. Beyond Baroque contains a bookstore, has a Friday night literary reading series, an archive of chapbooks and rare works, and features open readings and poetry and fiction workshops.

✤**BLACK CULTURAL CENTRE FOR NOVA SCOTIA**, 1149 Main St., Dartmouth, Nova Scotia B2Z 1A8 Canada, phone (902)434-6223, or (800)465-0767, fax (902)434-2306. Founded in 1983 "to create among members of the black communities an awareness of their past, their heritage and their identity; to provide programs and activities for the general public to explore, learn about, understand and appreciate black history, black achievements and black experiences in the broad context of Canadian life. The centre houses a museum, reference library, small auditorium and workshops."

✤**BURNABY WRITERS' SOCIETY**, 6584 Deer Lake Ave., Burnaby, British Columbia V5G 3T7 Canada, contact person Eileen Kernaghan. Founded in 1967, corresponding membership in the society, including a newsletter subscription, is open to anyone, anywhere. Yearly dues are $25. Sample newsletter in return for SASE with Canadian stamp. The society holds monthly meetings at The Burnaby Arts Centre (located at 6450 Deer Lake Ave.), with a business meeting at 7:30 followed by a writing workshop or speaker. Members of the society stage regular public readings of their own work.

THE WITTER BYNNER FOUNDATION FOR POETRY, INC., P.O. Box 10169, Santa Fe NM 87504, phone (505)988-3251, fax (505)986-8222. The foundation awards grants, ranging from $1,000 to $20,000, exclusively to nonprofit organizations for the support of poetry-related projects in the area of: 1) support of individual poets through existing nonprofit institutions; 2) developing the poetry audience; 3) poetry translation and the process of poetry translation; and 4) uses of poetry. The foundation "may consider the support of other creative and innovative projects in poetry." Grant applications are accepted annually from January 1 through February 1; requests for application forms should be submitted to Steven Schwartz, executive director, at the address above.

✤**THE CANADA COUNCIL; GOVERNOR GENERAL'S LITERARY AWARDS; CANADA-JAPAN BOOK AWARD**, P.O. Box 1047, 350 Albert St., Ottawa, Ontario K1P 5V8 Canada, phone (613)566-4414, fax (613)566-4416. Established by Parliament in 1957, the Canada Council "provides a wide range of grants and services to professional Canadian artists and art organizations in dance, media arts, music, theatre, writing, publishing and the visual arts." The Governor General's Literary Awards, valued at $10,000 (Canadian) each, are given annually for the best English-language and best French-language work in each of seven categories, including poetry. Books must be first-edition trade books written, translated or illustrated by Canadian citizens or permanent residents of Canada and published in Canada or abroad during the previous year (September 1 through the following September 30). Collections of poetry must be at least 48 pgs. long and at least half the book must contain work not published previously in book form. In the case of translation, the original work must also be a Canadian-authored title. Books must be submitted by publishers with a Publisher's Submission Form, which is available from the Writing and Publishing Section. All entries must be received at the Canada Council by August 15. The Canada Council administers the Canada-Japan Book Award worth $10,000 (Canadian). Awarded for a book by a Canadian citizen or permanent resident of Japanese descent, on the subject of Japan, or a translation (into English or French) by a Canadian citizen or permanent resident of a book written by a Japanese citizen. Book must be first-edition trade book published in Canada or abroad during the previous year. The deadline is March 31. Books must be submitted by publishers. Winners are selected by peer assessment committees.

✤**CANADIAN CONFERENCE OF THE ARTS (CCA)**, 189 Laurier Ave. E., Ottawa, Ontario K1N 6P1 Canada, phone (613)238-3561, fax (613)238-4849, is a national, nongovernmental, not-for-profit arts service organization dedicated to the growth and vitality of the arts and cultural industries in Canada. The CCA represents

 THE MAPLE LEAF symbol before a listing indicates a Canadian publisher, magazine, conference, contest or organization.

all Canadian artists, cultural workers and arts supporters, and works with all levels of government, the corporate sector and voluntary organizations to enhance appreciation for the role of culture in Canadian life. Each year, the CCA presents awards for contribution to the arts. Regular meetings held across the country ensure members' views on urgent and ongoing issues are heard and considered in organizing advocacy efforts and forming Board policies. Members stay informed and up-to-date through *Blizzart*, a newsletter, which is published 5 times a year, and receive discounts on conference fees and on all other publications. Membership is $30 (plus GST) for Canadian individual members, $35 for US members and $45 for international members.

✤CANADIAN POETRY ASSOCIATION; POEMATA; THE SHAUNT BASMAJIAN CHAPBOOK AWARD; THE HERB BARRETT AWARD, 237 Prospect St. S., Hamilton, Ontario L8M 2Z6 Canada, phone (905)312-1779, fax (905)312-8285, e-mail ad507@freenet.hamilton.on.ca or cpa@wwdc.com, national coordinator Wayne Ray. Founded in 1985, it is a broad based umbrella organization that aims to promote the reading, writing, publishing, purchasing and preservation of poetry in Canada through the individual and combined efforts of its members; to promote and encourage all forms and styles of poetry; to promote communication among poets, publishers and the general public; to promote the establishment and maintenance of poetry libraries and archives in educational institutions across Canada; and to develop an international connection for Canadian poets through *Poemata*, its bimonthly magazine, and events organized by independent, locally-run chapters. Through its 6 autonomous local chapters, CPA organizes poetry readings, literary and social events. Membership is open to anyone with an interest in poetry, including other literary organizations, for $25/year. Also sponsors The Shaunt Basmajian Chapbook Award, awarding $100 (Canadian) and publication, plus 10 copies. Submissions may be entered in other contests. Submit up to 24 pages of poetry, in any style or tradition. Mss must be typed, with title on each page. A separate sheet should give the title and the author's name and address. Send SASE for guidelines. Entry fee: $10 (Canadian). All entrants receive a copy of the winning chapbook. Postmark deadline: November 30. Sponsors The Herb Barrett Award, with 3 prizes of $75, $50 and $25 (Canadian), and publication in anthology. Submit haiku no more than 4 lines long. Mss must be typed or printed, 1 poem/page, on letter-size paper with no identifying marks. Name, address and phone, with titles or first lines, should be on a separate sheet of paper. Submissions will not be returned. Send SASE for guidelines. Entry fees: $10 (Canadian)/1-2 poems $15 (Canadian)/3 or more poems. Each entrant will receive a copy of the anthology. Deadline: November 30. *Poemata* publishes articles, book reviews and essays related to writing. Sample newsletter: $3. Request information via e-mail.

✤CANADIAN SOCIETY OF CHILDREN'S AUTHORS, ILLUSTRATORS & PERFORMERS, 35 Spadina Rd., Toronto, Ontario M5R 2S9 Canada, phone (416)515-1559, fax (416)515-7022, e-mail canscaip@interlog.com, website http://www.interlog.com/~canscaip, is a "society of professionals in the field of children's culture. Puts people into contact with publishers, offers advice to beginners, and generally provides a visible profile for members; 365 professional members and over 1,000 associates who are termed 'friends.' An annual conference in Toronto the last week of October provides workshops to people interested in writing, illustrating, and performing for children." Membership is $60 for professional members (and a free copy of the Membership Directory); $25 for associates/year. Both include a subscription to the quarterly *CANSCAIP News*.

‡COLUMBINE STATE POETRY SOCIETY OF COLORADO, 10751 Routt St., Broomfield CO 80021, phone (303)465-0883, e-mail wagil@aol.com, secretary/treasurer Anita Gilbert. Founded in 1978 to promote the writing and appreciation of poetry throughout Colorado. State-wide organization open to anyone interested in poetry. Currently has 84 total members. Levels of membership available are Members at Large who do not participate in either of our 2 local chapters, but who belong to the National Federation and the State level; members who belong to the national, state and local chapter, either in Denver or in Evergreen, Colorado. Offerings for poets include weekly workshops and monthly critiques. Sponsors contests, awards. Sponsors the Annual Poets Fest in Golden, CO, where members or nationally-known writers give readings and workshops that are open to the public. Membership dues are $8 state and national, $20 local, state and national. Members meet weekly. Send SASE for additional information.

COMPUSERVE INFORMATION SERVICE, 5000 Arlington Centre Blvd., P.O. Box 20212, Columbus OH 43220, phone (800)848-8199 from outside Ohio or (614)457-8600 from within Ohio or outside the US, fax (614)538-1780. An international online information service available via modem from any computer. On CIS are many forums on specialized topics of interests, including Litforum. This is basically a bulletin board where various members post and respond to public messages (though you may communicate with them privately, too, either through the CompuServe Mail system or by leaving private messages in Litforum). A CompuServe membership is $9.95/month for 5 hours of online time; each additional hour is $2.95. The CompuServe Information Manager software is free and available in a Windows, Mac or OS/2 platform. There are many services available through CIS (in addition to electronic mail), but most of the action is in the forums. In Litforum sometimes the talk is quite funny, often bawdy, and far-ranging, though there is a lot of practical, professional communication, too, and many people make contact via Litforum with agents, editors, other writers, researchers, and so on, that prove quite useful. You join Litforum (anyone can join; a number of the regulars are not even writers—just people interested in literature, writing, publication, chitchat), read the messages posted in some or all of the 17 sections (on such things as poetry and lyrics, fiction, nonfiction, speculative fiction, and so on), respond to any that you wish to, or just lurk. (CompuServe members interested in Litforum use go:books.) Each section has a library where you can post material you have written or download material by others, and comment if you wish. There is also a workshop for which you can request admission (and you're in automatically) where each writer has a turn to have material criticized by the other workshop members.

COUNCIL OF LITERARY MAGAZINES AND PRESSES, 154 Christopher St., Suite 3-C, New York NY 10014-2839, phone (212)741-9110. Compiles an annual directory useful to writers: The *Directory of Literary Magazines*, which has detailed descriptions of over 600 literary magazines, including type of work published, payment to contributors and submission requirements. The directory is $15 postage paid and may be ordered by sending a check to CLMP.

COWBOY POETRY GATHERING; WESTERN FOLKLIFE ROUNDUP; WESTERN FOLKLIFE CENTER, 501 Railroad St., Elko NV 89801. Both of these gatherings are sponsored by Western Folklife Center, Box 1570, Elko NV 89803, phone (702)738-7508, fax (702)738-2900, e-mail wfc@wfc.isat.com, website http://www.westfolk.org. There is an annual 6-day January gathering of cowboy poets in Elko. The Western Folklife Roundup is held annually the last weekend in August. The Western Folklife Center publishes and distributes books and tapes of cowboy poetry and songs as well as other cowboy memorabilia. The well-established tradition of cowboy poetry is enjoying a renaissance, and thousands of cowboy poets participate in these activities. For further information and details, contact the Center, or visit their website.

❦FEDERATION OF BRITISH COLUMBIA WRITERS, M.P.O. Box 2206, Vancouver, British Columbia V6B 3W2 Canada, executive director Corey Van't Haaff. The federation "is a nonprofit organization of professional and emerging writers of all genres." They publish a journal of markets, awards and literary news/events; act as "a network centre for various other provincial writer's organizations; host, promote and organize workshops, readings, literary competitions and social activities; distribute directories which are distributed to schools, businesses, and organizations which may request the services of writers; and represent writers' interests to other professionally related organizations."

‡GEORGIA POETRY SOCIETY; BYRON HERBERT REECE CONTEST; EDWARD DAVIN VICKERS CONTEST; CHARLES B. DICKSON CHAPBOOK CONTEST; GEORGIA POETRY SOCIETY NEWSLETTER, 6426 Woodstone Terrace, Morrow GA 30260, phone (770)961-5653, president Emily B. Vail. Founded in 1979 to further the purposes of the National Federation of State Poetry Societies, Inc. in securing fuller public recognition of the art of poetry; to stimulate a finer and more intelligent appreciation of poetry; and to provide opportunity for study of and incentive for practice in the writing and reading of poetry. State-wide organization open to any person who is in accord with the objectives listed above. There are no restrictions as to age, race, religion, color, national origin or physical or mental abilities. Currently has 190 total members. Levels of membership available are Active, fully eligible for all aspects of membership; Student, same as Active except they pay lower dues, and do not vote or hold office, they must be full-time enrolled students through college level; Lifetime, same as Active but pay a one-time membership fee the equivalent of approximately 12 years dues, they receive free anthologies each year and pay no contest entry fees. Offerings available for poets include affiliation with NFSPS. At least one workshop is held annually, contests are throughout the year, some for members only and some for general submissions. Workshops deal with specific areas of poetry writing, publishing, etc. Contests include the Byron Herbert Reece Contest, Edward Davin Vickers Contest, Charles B. Dickson Chapbook Contest (members only) and many ongoing or one-time contests, with awards ranging from $250 downwards. Entry fee: $15 first poem, $1 each additional. Deadline: January 31 for Reece Awards; November 20 for Vickers Awards. Send SASE for guidelines. Publishes *Georgia Poetry Society Newsletter*, a quarterly. Also available to nonmembers for free. Readings are held annually to celebrate National Poetry Day (October) and National Poetry Month (April) in public forums such as libraries; some are with specified poets reading their own poetry or works of famous poets, and some are open-mike readings. At each quarterly meeting (open to the public) members have an opportunity to read their own poems. Membership dues are Active: $20; Family: $35; Student: $10; Lifetime: $300. Members meet quarterly. "Our bylaws require rotation in office. We sponsor an active and popular Poetry in the Schools project, conducting workshops or readings in schools throughout the state by invitation. We also sponsor the annual Marel Brown Youth Awards contest in all Georgia schools and winning poems are submitted to the Manningham Youth Awards contest of NFSPS. Our membership ranges from 9 to 93 years of age."

‡GREATER CINCINNATI WRITERS' LEAGUE, 3805 St. Lawrence, Cincinnati OH 45205, (513)471-0487, fax (513)221-0825, e-mail cmrs@one.net, president Caren Theuring. Founded in 1930s "to promote and support poetry and those who write poetry in the Cincinnati area and the attainment of excellence in poetry as an art and a craft. We believe in education and discipline, as well as creative freedom, as important components in the development of our own poetry and open, constructive critique as a learning tool." Regional organization open to anyone interested in and actively writing. Currently has 35 total members. Offerings available for poets include a monthly meeting/workshop or critique. Critics are published poets, usually faculty members from local universities, who critique poems submitted by members. The group also joins in the critique. Sponsors conferences, workshops, contests, awards with monetary awards, and an anthology published every 2 years. Members give readings that are open to the public or sponsor open-mike readings at Joseph-Beth Bookstores and other locations. Membership dues are $10. Members meet monthly. Send SASE for additional information.

‡INDIANA STATE FEDERATION OF POETRY CLUBS; THE POETS RENDEZVOUS CONTEST; THE POETS SUMMER STANZAS CONTEST; THE POETS WINTERS FORUM CONTEST; INDIANA POET, 11659 S. US 35, Selma IN 47383, phone (317)774-4728, president Esther Towns. Founded in 1941 to unite poetry clubs in the state; to educate the public concerning poetry; and to encourage poet members. State-wide organization open to anyone interested in poetry. Currently has 151 total members. Offerings available for poets include 2 conventions each year, and membership in NFSPS. Sponsors conferences, workshops. Sponsors The Poets Rendezvous Contest. Offers $1,000 in prizes for poems in 25 categories. Entry fee: $5. Deadline: August 15. Sponsors the Poets Winters Forum and The Poets Summer Stanzas contests, with prizes of $25, $15 and $10 with 3 honorable mentions. Entry fee: $1/poem. Deadlines: January 15 and June 15 (respectively). Send SASE for details. Publishes *Indiana Poet*, a bimonthly newsletter. Members or nationally known writers give readings that are open to the public. Sponsors open-mike readings. Membership dues are $10/year (includes national membership). Members meet monthly. Send SASE for additional information.

INTERNATIONAL WOMEN'S WRITING GUILD, P.O. Box 810, Gracie Station, New York NY 10028, phone (212)737-7536, website Hanelore@http://www.iwwg.com, founded 1976, "a network for the personal and professional empowerment of women through writing." The Guild publishes a bimonthly 32-page newsletter which includes members' needs, achievements, contests, and publishing information. A manuscript referral service introduces members to literary agents. Other activities and benefits are annual national and regional events, including a summer conference at Skidmore College (see listing under Conferences and Workshops); "regional clusters" (independent regional groups); round robin manuscript exchanges; and group health insurance. Membership in the nonprofit Guild costs $35/year in the US and $45/year foreign.

JUST BUFFALO LITERARY CENTER, 2495 Main St., Suite 436, Buffalo NY 14214, phone (716)832-5400, fax (716)832-5710, founded 1975, executive director Debora Ott, coordinator of marketing and membership Jennifer Palisano. It offers readings, workshops, master classes, an annual competition for Western New York writers, Spoken Arts Radio broadcasts on National Public Radio affiliate WBFO, and Writers-in-Education programs for school-age populations. Just Buffalo acts as a clearinghouse for literary events in the Greater Buffalo area and offers diverse services to writers and to the WNY region. "Although we are not accepting submissions for publication at this time, we will review works for possible readings."

‡THE KENTUCKY STATE POETRY SOCIETY; PEGASUS; KSPS NEWSLETTER, 3289 Hunting Hills Dr., Lexington KY 40515, contact Miriam Woolfolk. Founded in 1966 to promote interest in writing poetry, improve skills in writing poetry, assist those who desire to become critics and judges of poetry, present poetry readings, have poetry workshops, and assist in publishing poetry. Regional organization open to everyone. Currently has 250 members. Levels of membership available are Life, Patron, Benefactor, Sponsor, Regular, Student, and Senior Adult. They are affiliated with The National Federation of State Poetry Societies. Offerings available for poets include association with other poets; and a yearly state and national convention. Sponsors workshops, contests, awards. "We have a recognized small press publication, *Pegasus*, published three times a year, open to all poets." Publishes the bimonthly *KSPS Newsletter*. Also available to nonmembers for $6 a year. Members or nationally-known writers give readings that are open to the public. Sponsors open-mike readings at annual convention and at all state meetings. Membership dues are students $5; adults $15. Members meet monthly. Send SASE for additional information.

‡THE LANE LITERARY GUILD, Lane Arts Council, 164 W. Broadway, Eugene OR 97401-3004. The guild is "a volunteer organization dedicated to encouraging and supporting poets and writers in Lane County, Oregon. We hold monthly readings featuring new and established poets and writers. Our readers are drawn from talent locally as well as from other cities and parts of the country. We also hold workshops, symposia and literary contests. Our funding comes from membership fees, donations at readings and from grant support by the Cultural Services Division of the City of Eugene and by the Lane Arts Council. We are interested in hearing from poets and writers from around the country who will be in our neighborhood and might be interested in being one of our readers."

❧THE LEAGUE OF CANADIAN POETS; POETS IN THE CLASSROOM; WHO'S WHO IN THE LEAGUE OF CANADIAN POETS; POETRY MARKETS FOR CANADIANS; LIVING ARCHIVES SERIES; NATIONAL POETRY CONTEST; GERALD LAMPERT MEMORIAL AWARD; PAT LOWTHER MEMORIAL AWARD, 54 Wolseley, 3rd Floor, Toronto, Ontario M5T 1A5 Canada, phone (416)504-1657, fax (416)703-0059, e-mail league@io.org, website http://www.swiftly.com/lc, founded 1966, contact Edita Petrauskaite. The league's aims are the advancement of poetry in Canada and promotion of the interests of professional, Canadian poets. Information on full, associate student and supporting membership can be obtained via e-mail, website or by sending a SASE for the brochure, League of Canadian Poets: Services and Membership. The league publishes a biannual *Museletter* (30 pgs., magazine-sized) plus six newsletters; *Poets in the Classroom*, on teaching poetry to children; a directory called *Who's Who in The League of Canadian*

GET YOUR WORK INTO THE RIGHT BUYERS' HANDS!

You work hard... and your hard work deserves to be seen by the right buyers. But with the constant changes in the industry, it's not always easy to know who those buyers are. That's why you'll want to keep up-to-date and on top with the most current edition of this indispensable market guide.

Keep ahead of the changes by ordering *1999 Poet's Market* today. You'll save the frustration of getting poems returned in the mail, stamped MOVED: ADDRESS UNKNOWN. And of NOT submitting your work to new listings because you don't know they exist. All you have to do to order the upcoming 1999 edition is complete the attached order card and return it with your payment or credit card information. Order now and you'll get the 1999 edition at the 1998 price—just $22.99—no matter how much the regular price may increase! *1999 Poet's Market* will be published and ready for shipment in September 1998.

Keep on top of the fast-changing industry and get a jump on selling your work with help from the *1999 Poet's Market*. Order today! You deserve it!

Turn over for more books to help you get your poems published →

☐ **Yes!** I want the most current edition of *Poet's Market*. Please send me the 1999 edition at the 1998 price – $22.99.* (NOTE: *1999 Poet's Market* will be ready for shipment in September 1998.) #10558

I also want:

Book # _____ Price $_____

Book # _____ Price $_____

Book # _____ Price $_____

Book # _____ Price $_____

Subtotal $_____

*Add $3.50 postage and handling for one book; $1.50 for each additional book.

Postage and handling $_____

Payment must accompany order. Ohioans add 6% sales tax. Canadians add 7% GST.

Total $_____

☐ **FREE CATALOG.** Ask your bookstore about other fine Writer's Digest Books, or mail this card today for a complete catalog.

VISA/MasterCard orders call
TOLL-FREE 1-800-289-0963

☐ Payment enclosed $_____ (or)

Charge my: ☐ Visa ☐ MasterCard Exp._____

Account #_____

Signature _____

Name _____

Address_____

City_____ State/Prov. _____ Zip/P.C. _____

Phone Number _____
(will be used only if we must contact you regarding this order.)

**30-Day Money Back Guarantee
on every book you buy!**

 Mail to:

Writer's Digest Books
1507 Dana Avenue
Cincinnati, OH 45207

6333

More Great Books to Help You Write and Sell Your Poetry!

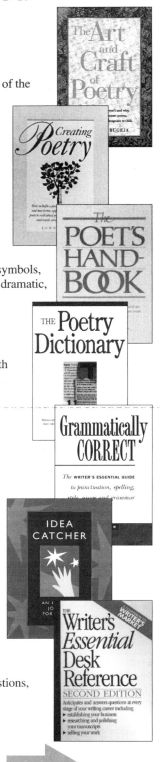

The Art & Craft of Poetry
by Michael J. Bugeja

Nurture your poetry-writing skills with inspiration and insight from the masters of the past and present. From idea generation to methods of expression, you'll find everything you need to create well-crafted poetry!
#10392/$19.99/352 pages

Creating Poetry
by John Drury

Definitions, examples, and hands-on exercises show you how to use language text, subject matter, free and measured verse, imagery, and metaphor to create your own wonderful works!
#10209/$18.99/224 pages

The Poet's Handbook
by Judson Jerome

With expert instruction, you'll unlock the secrets of using figurative language, symbols, and concrete images. Plus, you'll discover the requirements for lyric, narrative, dramatic, didactic, and satirical poetry!
#01836/$14.99/224 pages/paperback

The Poetry Dictionary
by John Drury

This comprehensive book unravels the rich and complex language of poetry with clear, working definitions. Several different poems are used to demonstrate the evolution of the form, making *The Poetry Dictionary* a unique anthology. It's a guide to the poetry of today and yesterday, with intriguing hints as to what tomorrow holds.
#48007/$18.99/352 pages

New!
Grammatically Correct
by Anne Stilman

Let editor/instructor Anne Stilman guide you through the nuts-and-bolts basics of punctuation, spelling, style, usage and grammar. The expert tips, techniques, exercises and examples will help you create more professional—and salable—writing.
#10529/$19.99/352 pages

Idea Catcher

This spirited journal will help you open your eyes to the creative possibilities in your everyday world. You'll find something on every page of this journal to stimulate your senses and spark your imagination.
#48011/$14.99/160 pages

Writer's Essential Desk Reference, 2nd Edition

Find quick, complete, accurate answers to your important writing-business questions, including information on the World Wide Web.
#10485/$24.99/384 pages

Order these helpful references today from your local bookstore, or use the handy order card on the reverse.

Poets that contains 1 page of information, including a picture, bio, publications and "what critics say" about each of the members; Living Archives Series, chapbooks of feminist studies in Canada; and *Poetry Markets for Canadians* which covers contracts, markets, agents and more. The league's members go on reading tours, and the league encourages them to speak on any facet of Canadian literature at schools and universities, libraries or organizations. The league has arranged "thousands of readings in every part of Canada"; they are now arranging exchange visits featuring the leading poets of such countries as Great Britain, Germany and the US. The league sponsors a National Poetry Contest with prizes of $1,000, $750 and $500; the best 50 poems published in a book. Deadline: January 31. Entry fee: $6/poem. Poems should be unpublished, under 75 lines and typed. Names and addresses should *not* appear on poems but on a separate covering sheet. Please send SASE for complete rules, info on judges, etc. Open to Canadian citizens or landed immigrants only. The Gerald Lampert Memorial Award of $1,000 is for a first book of poetry written by a Canadian, published professionally. The Pat Lowther Memorial Award of $1,000 is for a book of poetry written by a Canadian woman and published professionally. Write for entry forms. The league also sponsors a Canadian chapbook manuscript competition with prizes of $1,000, $750 and $500. Submit 15-24 pg. ms with $12 entry fee. Deadline: March 1.

‡**LIVE POETS SOCIETY, MAINE; OFF THE COAST**, 117 Fitch Rd., Washington ME 04574, phone/fax (207)845-2476, executive director George V. Van Deventer. Founded in 1989 to establish and maintain a venue for poetry in mid-coast Maine. State-wide organization. Currently has 135 total members. "We visit 25-30 schools a year, K-12. We judge poetry in schools and have an annual 'Festival of Children and Poetry.' We sponsor a national contest with a financial award and publication in our annual anthology. Also the opportunity to spend three days in Maine, accommodation supplied but not travel." Publishes *Off The Coast* monthly journal. Also available to nonmembers for $3. Members or nationally known writers give readings that are open to the public. Sponsors open-mike readings. Membership dues are Minstrel $10; Bard $25; Laureate $50. Members meet monthly. Send SASE for additional information.

THE LOFT; THE NATIONAL PRIZE IN POETRY AND FICTION, Pratt Community Center, 66 Malcolm Ave. SE, Minneapolis MN 55414, phone (612)379-8999, fax (612)951-4423, website http://www.loft.org, founded 1974, executive director Linda Myers. The Loft was started by a group of poets looking for a place to give readings and conduct workshops and has evolved into "the most comprehensive literary center in the country," offering opportunities for writers in all genres and at all levels of development, managed by a 21-member board of directors and staff of 12. Membership: 2,400. In addition to membership dues, financial support came from tuition for creative writing classes, fees from benefit performances, and contributions from individuals, corporations and foundations. The Loft offers over 100 courses each year in addition to 40 workshops and panels. Its reading series presents established and emerging writers throughout Minnesota and the Mentor Series and Creative Nonfiction Program feature nationally-known writers. The Loft publishes *A View from the Loft*, a monthly magazine on craft. The Mentor Series, Creative Nonfiction Program, and Inroads Programs provide opportunities for area writers to study intensively with local and national writers. The National Prize in Poetry and Fiction awards $1,000 annually to a poet and fiction writer, plus publication.

MAINE WRITERS & PUBLISHERS ALLIANCE, 12 Pleasant St., Brunswick ME 04011-2201, phone (207)729-6333, fax (207)725-1014, founded 1975, program director Jill Shutz. This organization is "a nonprofit organization dedicated to promoting the value of literature and the art of writing by building a community of writers, readers, and publishers within Maine. Our membership currently includes over 1,500 writers, publishers, librarians, teachers, booksellers and readers from across Maine and the nation." For an individual contribution of $30 per year members receive discounts on MWPA programs, books, and *Maine in Print*, a monthly compilation of calendar events, updated markets, book annotations, interviews with Maine authors and publishers, articles about writing and more. The alliance distributes selected books about Maine and by Maine authors and publishers, and it maintains a bookstore and reference library at its office in Brunswick. "We also have extensive writing and publishing workshops and offer an annual fall writing retreat."

❦**MANITOBA WRITERS' GUILD INC.**, 206-100 Arthur St., Winnipeg, Manitoba R3B 1H3 Canada, phone (204)942-6134, fax (204)942-5754. Founded in 1981 to "promote and advance the art of writing, in all its forms, throughout the province of Manitoba." Regional organization open to "any individual with an interest in the art of writing." Currently has 430-500 members. Levels of membership are Regular and Student/Senior/Fixed income. Programs and services include: the Manitoba Workshop Series, intensive one-day sessions conducted by professional writers; Open Workshops, monthly evening sessions held in the fall and winter; an Annual Spring Conference, a one-day event which includes panel discussions, readings, performances and special events; the Mentor Program, a limited number of promising writers selected to work one-on-one with experienced mentors; the Manitoba Literary Awards which include the McNally Robinson Book of the Year Award and the John Hirsch Award for Most Promising Manitoba Writer, all awards are to "recognize and celebrate excellence in Manitoba writing and publishing"; the Café Reading Series, a weekly series showcasing emerging and established local writers; the Writers' Resource Centre, containing information about writing, publishing, markets, as well as Canadian periodicals and books by Manitoba authors; and a studio offering writers comfortable, private work space. Published 7 times/year, their newsletter, *WordWrap*, includes feature articles, regular columns, information on current markets and competitions, and profiles of Manitoba writers. They also publish *The Writers' Handbook*, the Guild's "comprehensive resource manual on the business of writing." Membership fees are $40 Regular, $20 Student/Senior/Fixed Income. Send SASE for additional information.

‡MASSACHUSETTS STATE POETRY SOCIETY, INC.; BAY STATE ECHO; THE NATIONAL POETRY DAY CONTEST; THE GERTRUDE DOLE MEMORIAL CONTEST, 64 Harrison Ave., Lynn MA 01905, phone (617)599-1349, president Jeanette C. Maes. Founded in 1959, dedicated to the writing and appreciation of poetry and promoting the art form. State-wide organization open to anyone with an interest in poetry. Currently has 200 total members. Offerings available for poets include critique groups. Sponsors workshops, contests. Sponsors The National Poetry Day Contest, with prizes of $25, $15 and $10 (or higher) for each of 25 categories. Entry fee: $5. Deadline: August 1. Also sponsors The Gertrude Dole Memorial Contest, with prizes of $25, $15 and $10. Entry fee: $2. Deadline: March 1. Send SASE for guidelines. Publishes a yearly anthology of poetry and a yearly publication of student poetry contest winners. Publishes *Bay State Echo*, a newsletter, 5 times/year. Members or nationally-known writers give readings that are open to the public. Sponsors open-mike readings. Membership dues are $10/year. Members meet 5 times/year. Send SASE for additional information.

‡MISSISSIPPI POETRY SOCIETY, INC., 110 Winchester Dr., Ocean Springs MS 39564, phone (601)872-0732, state president Monita McLemore ("This changes annually when new officers are installed"). Founded in 1932 "to foster interest in the writing of poetry through a study of poetry and poetic form; to provide an opportunity for, and give recognition to, individual creative efforts relating to poetry; and to create an audience for poetry; and suggest or otherwise make known markets and contests for poetry to its members." Statewide organization, affiliated with the National Federation of State Poetry Societies, consisting of three branches open to "anyone who writes poetry or is interested in fostering the interests of poetry." Currently has 108 total members. Offerings available for poets include monthly meetings, annual contests and an annual awards banquet. "The state also holds a Mini-Festival in the fall and an annual Spring Festival each spring. The Mini-Festival is a one-day event (plus Night-Owl readings at a get-together the night before); and the Spring Festival is two days, plus the Night-Owl event the night before. We also have noted speakers and sponsor contests at these events." The state publishes the newsletter *Magnolia Muse* on a quarterly basis while the branches publish a newsletter of the same name on a monthly basis. "The state organization also publishes journals of all winning poems each year, and often of other special contests. There are occasionally 'featured poets,' and two or three of their poems are featured in an issue of *Magnolia Muse*." Members or nationally-known writers give readings that are open to the public. Membership dues are $17. Members meet monthly at branches, semiannually at the state level. Send SASE for additional information.

NATIONAL FEDERATION OF STATE POETRY SOCIETIES, INC.; STEVEN'S MANUSCRIPT COMPETITION, Membership Chairperson: Sy Swann, 2712 Scott Ave., Ft. Worth TX 76103, phone (817)535-7304, contest chairperson Claire Van Breeman Downes, 1206 13th Ave. SE, St. Cloud MN 56304. Founded in 1959, "NFSPS is a nonprofit organization exclusively educational and literary. Its purpose is to recognize the importance of poetry with respect to national cultural heritage. It is dedicated solely to the furtherance of poetry on the national level and serves to unite poets in the bonds of fellowship and understanding." Any poetry group located in a state not already affiliated but interested in affiliating with NFSPS may contact the membership chairperson. Canadian groups may also apply. "In a state where no valid group exists, help may also be obtained by individuals interested in organizing a poetry group for affiliation." Most reputable state poetry societies are members of the National Federation and advertise their various poetry contests through the quarterly bulletin, *Strophes*, available for SASE and $1, editor Linda Banks, 2912 Falls Church Lane, Mesquite, TX 75149. Beware of organizations calling themselves state poetry societies (however named) that are not members of NFSPS, as such labels are sometimes used by vanity schemes trying to sound respectable. Others, such as the Oregon State Poetry Association, are quite reputable, but they don't belong to NFSPS. NFSPS holds an annual meeting in a different city each year with a large awards banquet, addressed by an honorary chairperson. They sponsor 50 national contests in various categories each year, including the NFSPS Prize of $1,500 for first place; $500, second; $250, third; with entry fees ($3 for the entire contest for members, $5 for NFSPS Award; $1/poem for nonmembers and $5 for NFSPS Award, up to 4 poems/entry). All poems winning over $10 are published in an anthology. Rules for all contests are given in a brochure available from Linda Banks at *Strophes* or Claire Van Breeman Downes at the address above; you can also write for the address of your state poetry society. They also sponsor the annual Steven's Manuscript Competition with a first place prize of $1,000 and publication, second place prize $500; October 1 deadline; contact Amy Zook, 3520 St. Rd. 56, Mechanicsburg OH 43044. Scholarship information is available from Pj Doyle, 4242 Stevens Ave., Minneapolis MN 55409.

THE NATIONAL POETRY FOUNDATION; SAGETRIEB; PAIDEUMA, University of Maine, 5752 Neville Hall, Room 302, Orono ME 04469-5752, phone (207)581-3813, e-mail sapiel@maine.maine.edu, website http://www.ume.maine.edu/~npf/, publications coordinator Jill Randall. "The NPF is a nonprofit organization concerned with publishing scholarship on the work of 20th century poets, particularly Ezra Pound and those in the Imagist/Objectivist tradition. We publish *Paideuma*, a journal devoted to Ezra Pound scholarship, and *Sagetrieb*, a journal devoted to poets in the imagist/objectivist tradition, as well as books on and of poetry. NPF occasionally conducts a summer conference." Sample copies: $8.95 for *Paideuma* or *Sagetrieb*. Send SASE for information or obtain via e-mail or website.

‡**NATIONAL WRITERS ASSOCIATION; AUTHORSHIP**, 1450 S. Havana, Suite 424, Aurora CO 80012, phone (303)751-7844, fax (303)751-8593, executive director Sandy Whelchel. Founded in 1937. National organization with regional affiliations open to writers. Currently has 3,000 total members. Levels of membership available are Published Writers and Other Writers. They have an annual Summer Conference where workshops/panels etc. are available to all attendees, including poets. Also offer a yearly poetry writing contest with cash awards of $100, $50 and $25. Entry fee: $10/poem. Deadline: October 1. Send SASE for judging sheet copies. Publishes *Authorship*, an annual magazine. Also available to nonmembers for $18. Memberships dues are Professional $60; others $50. Members meet monthly. Send SASE for additional information.

NATIONAL WRITERS UNION, 113 University Place, 6th Floor, New York NY 10003, phone (212)254-0279, e-mail nwu@nwu.org, website http://www.nwu.org/nwu/. Offers members such services as a grievance committee, contract guidelines, health insurance, press credentials, car rental discounts, and caucuses and trade groups for exchange of information about special markets. Members receive *The American Writer*, the organization's newsletter. Membership is $80 for those earning less than $5,000/year; $132 for those earning $5,000-25,000; and $180 for those earning more than $25,000.

‡**NEVADA POETRY SOCIETY; NEVADA NATIONAL POETRY CONTEST; NEWSLETTER**, P.O. Box 7014, Reno NV 89510, (702)322-3619, president Sam Wood. Founded in 1976 to encourage the writing and critiquing of poetry. State-wide organization. Currently has 30 total members. Levels of membership available are Active and Emeritus. Offerings available for poets include membership in the National Federation of State Poetry Societies, including their publication *Strophes*; monthly challenges followed by critiquing of all new poems; distribution of contest fliers; lessons on types of poetry. Sponsors contests, awards. "We sponsor an annual Nevada National Poetry Contest with more than $500 in prizes." Publishes *Newsletter* occasionally. Also available to nonmembers for free. Members of the society are occasionally called upon to read to organizations or in public meetings. Membership dues are $6 (this includes membership in NFSPS). Members meet monthly. "We advise poets to enter their poems in contests before thinking about publication."

NEW ENGLAND POETRY CLUB, 2 Farrar St., Cambridge MA 02138, president Diana Der-Hovanessian, founded in 1915 by Amy Lowell, Robert Frost and Conrad Aiken to "bring the best poets to the area and foster fellowship among writers." National organization open to beginning poets, professional poets and teachers of poetry. Currently has 500 members. Offerings available for poets include a newsletter with poetry information, free admission to readings and contests and free participation in workshops. Nationally known writers regularly give readings that are open to the public. Sponsors open-mike readings for members only. Membership dues are $20. Readings and workshops are held monthly. Of the 12 contests they sponsor, 9 are open to nonmembers for an entry fee of $3/poem. Entries must be original, unpublished poems in English. Most recent winners include David Ray and Frank Bidart (1996). Send SASE for details or membership information to Victor Howes, 137 West Newton St., Boston MA 02118.

NEW HAMPSHIRE WRITERS & PUBLISHERS PROJECT, P.O. Box 2693, Concord NH 03302-2693, phone (603)226-6649, fax (603)226-0035, e-mail nhwpp@aol.com, executive director Patricia Scholz-Cohen. Founded in 1988 "to foster the literary arts community in New Hampshire, to serve as a resource for and about New Hampshire writers, to support the development of individual writers, and to encourage an audience for literature in New Hampshire." State-wide organization open to anyone. Currently has 750 members. Offerings specifically available for poets include workshops, seminars and information about poetry readings and slams held throughout northern New England. Sponsors a day-long workshop and 4- to 6-week intensive courses. Also sponsors a biennial award. Publishes *Ex Libris*, a bimonthly newsletter for members only. Members and nationally known writers give readings that are open to the public. Also sponsors open-mike readings. Membership dues are $35/year; $20/year for Seniors and students. Members meet annually. Send SASE for additional information or obtain via e-mail.

THE NORTH CAROLINA POETRY SOCIETY; BROCKMAN/CAMPBELL BOOK AWARD CONTEST, 518 West Main St., Mt. Olive NC 28365, phone (919)658-2511, president Cecil Cahoon. Founded in 1932 to "foster the writing of poetry; to bring together in meetings of mutual interest and fellowship the poets of North Carolina; to encourage the study, writing, and publication of poetry; and to develop a public taste for the reading and appreciation of poetry." Regional organization open to "all interested persons." Levels of membership available are Regular ($20/year) and Student ($5/year). NCPS conducts 3 general meetings and numerous statewide workshops each year, sponsors annual poetry contests with categories for adults and students (open to anyone, with small fee for nonmembers; December/January deadline; cash prizes), publishes the contest-winning poems in the annual book *Award Winning Poems*; publishes a newsletter and supports other poetry activities. They also sponsor the annual Brockman/Campbell Book Award Contest for a book of poetry (over 20 pgs.) by a North Carolina poet (native-born or current resident for 3 years). $100 cash prize and a Revere-style bowl is awarded. $5 entry fee for nonmembers. Deadline: May 1. For details, send SASE to Sharon A. Sharp,

P.O. Box 3345, Boone NC 28607. For membership information, send SASE to address at beginning of listing.

NORTH CAROLINA WRITERS' NETWORK; THE NETWORK NEWS; NORTH CAROLINA'S LITERARY RESOURCE GUIDE; RANDALL JARRELL POETRY PRIZE, P.O. Box 954, Carrboro NC 27510, phone (919)967-9540, fax (919)929-0535, e-mail nc_writers@unc.edu. founded in 1985. Supports the work of writers, writers' organizations, independent bookstores, little magazines and small presses, and literary programming statewide. $35 membership dues annually brings members *The Network News*, a 28-page bimonthly newsletter containing organizational news, national market information and other literary material of interest to writers, and access to the Resource Center, other writers, workshops, conferences, readings and competitions, and a critiquing service. 1,700 members nationwide. They also publish the *North Carolina's Literary Resource Guide*, an annual including information about retreats, fellowships, markets, writers groups, conferences, agents and literary organizations. Available to members for $5 postpaid and to nonmembers for $6.50 postpaid. Annual fall conference features nationally-known writers, publishers and editors. It is held in a different North Carolina location each year in November. Sponsors competitions in short fiction, nonfiction essays and chapbooks of poetry for North Carolinians and members. Also sponsors three international competitions: Randall Jarrell Poetry Prize, Thomas Wolfe Fiction Prize and Paul Green Playwrights Prize. The Randall Jarrell Poetry Prize annually awards $500, reading and reception in Greensboro, NC, and publication in *Parnassus: Poetry in Review*. Submissions must be unpublished. Entry fee: $7. Deadline: November 1. Most recent award winner was Lisa Parker (1996). Judge was Marvin Bell. Winner will be announced in February. Send SASE for guidelines.

THE OREGON STATE POETRY ASSOCIATION, % President David Hedges, 20750 S. Sweetbriar Rd., West Linn OR 97068, phone (503)655-1274; website http://www.peak.org/~ospa, treasurer Mang Petersen, 3284 SW Knollbrook, Corvallis OR 97333, phone (541)753-6310. Founded in 1936 for "the promotion and creation of poetry," the association has over 200 members, $18 dues, publishes a quarterly *OSPA Newsletter*, and sponsors contests twice yearly, October and April, with total cash prizes of $300 each (no entry fee to members, $3/poem for nonmembers; out-of-state entries welcome). Themes and categories vary. For details write to OSPA, contest chair Joan Henson, 6071 SW Prosperity Park Rd., Tualatin OR 97062, phone (503)638-7488 after August 1 and February 15 each year. The association sponsors workshops, readings and seminars around the state.

OZARK POETS AND WRITERS COLLECTIVE, P.O. Box 3717, Fayetteville AR 72702, phone (501)443-7575 or 521-0119, e-mail poemedy@aol.com or bjmoossy@aol.com, website http://www.ipa.net/~sloan, co-chairpersons Lisa Martinovic and Brenda J. Moossy. Founded reading series in 1993, incorporated in 1995, "to support and promote community involvement in Ozark literary arts; to encourage an appreciation of local writers by providing access to their work through readings, publications, workshops and other events; to ensure that the experience of writing and reading remain a vital part of life in the Ozarks." Regional organization open to any interested poets and writers. "Most participants come from the Ozarks, which encompasses parts of Arkansas, Missouri and Oklahoma." Offerings available for poets include slams with cash prizes and informal poetry workshops. "OPWC also runs a weekly column in the *Northwest Arkansas Times* with space to showcase local and not so local poets, provide information about upcoming readers and events, and invite comment about the feast of poetry and all its flavors. *The Fayetteville Free Weekly* runs a monthly column showcasing the monthly featured reader." Nationally and locally known writers give readings that are open to the public. The readings are held on the last Wednesday of each month and are immediately followed by an open-mike session. "Poets on Tour, the performing arm of the OPWC, is available for performances nationwide. They were recently added to the Arts on Tour Roster of the Arkansas Arts Council, becoming the first performance poetry troupe to do so." Board members meet the second Wednesday of every month; interested poets and writers may attend the meetings. Send SASE for additional information or request via e-mail.

PEN AMERICAN CENTER; PEN WRITERS FUND; PEN TRANSLATION PRIZE; GRANTS AND AWARDS, 568 Broadway, New York NY 10012, phone (212)334-1660, "is the largest of more than 100 centers which comprise International PEN, founded in London in 1921 by John Galsworthy to foster understanding among men and women of letters in all countries. Members of PEN work for freedom of expression wherever it has been endangered, and International PEN is the only worldwide organization of writers and the chief voice of the literary community." Its total membership on all continents is approximately 10,000. The 2,700 members of the American Center include poets, playwrights, essayists, editors, novelists (for the original letters in the acronym PEN), as well as translators and those editors and agents who have made a substantial contribution to the literary community. Membership in American PEN includes reciprocal privileges in foreign centers for those traveling abroad. Branch offices are located in Cambridge, Chicago, Portland/Seattle, Baton Rouge and San Francisco. Among PEN's various activities are public events and symposia, literary awards, assistance to writers in prison and to American writers in need (grants and loans up to $1,000 from PEN Writers Fund). Medical insurance for writers is available to members. The quarterly *PEN Newsletter* is sent to all members and is available to nonmembers by subscription. The PEN Translation Prize is sponsored by the Book-of-the-Month Club, 1 prize each year of $3,000 for works published in the current calendar year. They publish *Grants and Awards* biennially, containing guidelines, deadlines, eligibility requirements and other information about hundreds of grants, awards and competitions for poets and other writers: $13 postpaid. Send SASE for booklet describing their activities and listing their publications, some of them available free.

‡**PHILADELPHIA WRITERS ORGANIZATION**, P.O. Box 42497, Philadelphia PA 19101, phone (610)630-8670, president Bill Wartman. Founded in 1982 to promote "educational and social programs for writers." Regional organization open to all writers. Currently has 200 members. Levels of membership available are full (published writers) and associate (unpublished writers). Offerings available for poets include monthly meetings with speakers, social events, a monthly newsletter, job bank and group health insurance. Membership dues are $50/year. Members meet monthly. Send SASE for additional information.

PITTSBURGH POETRY EXCHANGE, P.O. Box 4279, Pittsburgh PA 15203, phone (412)481-POEM. Founded in 1974 as a community-based organization for local poets, it functions as a service organization and information exchange, conducting ongoing workshops, readings, forums and other special events. No dues or fees. "Any monetary contributions are voluntary, often from outside sources. We've managed not to let our reach exceed our grasp." Their reading programs are primarily committed to local and area poets, with honorariums of $25-75. They sponsor a minimum of three major events each year in addition to a monthly workshop. Some of these have been reading programs in conjunction with community arts festivals, such as the October South Side Poetry Smorgasbord—a series of readings throughout the evening at different shops (galleries, bookstores). Poets from out of town may contact the exchange for assistance in setting up readings at bookstores to help sell their books. Contact Michael Wurster at the above address or phone number.

THE POETRY COMMITTEE OF THE GREATER WASHINGTON AREA, ℅ Washington Independent Writers, 220 Woodward Bldg., 733 15th St. NW, Washington DC 20005, An independent, nonprofit group, the membership (by invitation) consists of about 60 people who represent poetry organizations in the metropolitan area. Annual sponsors of Celebration of Washington Poetry, a reading and book sale highlighting area poets and presses, the Columbia Book Award for best book of poetry by Washington area poet within the past calendar year and the Columbia Merit Award for service to area poetry.

THE POETRY PROJECT AT ST. MARK'S CHURCH-IN-THE-BOWERY, 131 E. 10th St., New York NY 10003, phone (212)674-0910, fax (212)529-2318, website http://www.poetryproject.com, was established in 1966 by the US Dept. of H.E.W. in an effort to help wayward youths in the East Village. It is now funded by a variety of government and private sources. Artistic Director: Ed Friedman. Program Coordinator: JoAnn Wasserman. From October through May the project offers workshops, talks, staged readings, performance poetry, lectures, an annual 4-day symposium, literary magazines and a series of featured writers who bring their books to sell at the readings. If the reading is a publication party, the publisher handles the sales.

POETRY SOCIETY OF AMERICA; POETRY SOCIETY OF AMERICA AWARDS, 15 Gramercy Park, New York NY 10003, phone (212)254-9628, fax (212)673-2352, e-mail poetsocy@panix.com, website http://www.poetrysociety.org, founded in 1910, is a nonprofit cultural organization in support of poetry and poets, member and nonmember, young and established, which sponsors readings, lectures and workshops both in New York City and around the country. Their Peer Group Workshop is open to all members and meets on a weekly basis. They publish a newsletter of their activities and sponsor a wide range of contests. The following are open to members only: Alice Fay Di Castagnola Award ($1,000); *Writer Magazine*/Emily Dickinson Award ($100); Cecil Hemley Memorial Award ($300); Lucille Medwick Memorial Award ($500); Lyric Poetry Award ($500). Nonmembers may enter as many of the following contests as they wish, no more than 1 entry for each, for a $5 fee: Louise Louis/Emily S. Bourne Student Poetry Award, $100 for students in grades 9-12; George Bogin Memorial Award, $500 for a selection of 4 to 5 poems which take a stand against oppression; Robert H. Winner Memorial Award, $2,500 for a poem written by a poet over 40, still unpublished or with one book. (All have a deadline of December 22; awards are made at a ceremony and banquet in late spring.) The Society also has 2 book contests open to works submitted by publishers only. They must obtain an entry form, and there is a $10 fee for each book entered. Book awards are: Norma Farber Award, $500 for a first book; William Carlos Williams Award, a purchase prize of $500-1,000 for a book of poetry published by a small, nonprofit or university press, by a permanent resident of the US—translations not eligible. The Shelley Memorial Award of $2,000-6,000 and The Frost Medal are by nomination only. For necessary rules and guidelines for their various contests send #10 SASE between October 1 and December 22 or request via e-mail. Rules and awards are subject to change. Membership: $40.

‡**POETRY SOCIETY OF TENNESSEE; TENNESSEE VOICES**, 8463 Deerfield Lane, Germantown TN 38138, corresponding secretary Frances Cowden. Founded in 1953 to promote the reading and writing of fine poetry. State-wide organization open to residents of Tennessee. Currently has 125 total members. Levels of membership available are Regular, Student (grades 1-12), Associate (non-TN residents). Sponsors monthly contests for members, 2 student contests each year and 2 annual contests open to everyone. Publishes an annual volume of prize winning poems available to nonmembers for $10. Publishes *Tennessee Voices*, a newsletter published bimonthly. Members or nationally-known writers give readings that are open to the public. Memberships dues are $20/year. Members meet monthly September through May. Send SASE for additional information.

‡**THE POETRY SOCIETY OF TEXAS; THE BULLETIN**, 3005 Stanford, Plano TX 75075, membership chairman Alan Birkelbach. Founded in 1921 to secure fuller public recognition of the art of poetry and to

encourage the writing of poetry by its members. State-wide organization. Currently has 600 total members. Levels of membership available are active, associate, participating, sustaining, supporting, benefactors, patrons and student. Offerings available for poets include membership with the National Federation of State Poetry Societies, an annual state conference and NFSPS Convention. Sponsors conferences, workshops, contests, awards. Award-winning poems are published annually in A Book of the Year, with $5,000 in prizes. Publishes **The Bulletin** a monthly newsletter. Members or nationally-known writers give readings that are open to the public. Chapters participate in many reading activities. Membership dues are $20 for Active and Associates. Members meet monthly December through June, and October. Send SASE for additional information.

POETS & WRITERS, INC. See listing under Publications Useful to Poets.

POETS HOUSE: THE REED FOUNDATION LIBRARY; THE POETRY PUBLICATION SHOWCASE; DIRECTORY OF AMERICAN POETRY BOOKS; POETRY IN THE BRANCHES; NYC POETRY TEACHER OF THE YEAR, 72 Spring St., New York NY 10012, phone (212)431-7920, founded 1985, executive director Lee Ellen Briccetti. Poets House is a 30,000-volume (noncirculating) poetry library of books, tapes and literary journals, with reading and writing space available. This comfortably furnished literary center is open to the public year-round. Over 30 annual public events include 1) poetic programs of cross-cultural and interdisciplinary exchange, 2) readings in which distinguished poets discuss and share the work of other poets, 3) workshops and seminars on various topics led by visiting poets, and 4) an annual $1,000 award for the designated NYC Poetry Teacher of the Year. In addition, Poets House continues a 3-year pilot collaboration with The New York Public Library, Poetry in The Branches, aimed at bringing poetry into NYC neighborhoods—through collection-building, public programs, seminars for librarians, and poetry workshops for young adults—in three branch libraries around the City (information available upon request). Finally, each fall Poets House hosts the Poetry Publication Showcase—a comprehensive exhibit of the year's new poetry releases from commercial, university, independent, and micro presses across the country. Related Showcase events include receptions, panel discussions, and a contributor's poetry reading, which is open to the public and of special interest to poets, publishers, booksellers, distributers and reviewers. (Note: Poets House is not a publisher.) Following each Showcase, copies of new titles are added to the library collection and an updated edition of the **Directory of American Poetry Books**—edited by Poets House and available by mail is compiled. "Poets House depends, in part, on tax-deductible contributions of its nationwide members." Membership levels begin at $40/year, and along with other graduated benefits each new or renewing member receives a free copy of the most current directory.

POETS-IN-THE-SCHOOLS. Most states have PITS programs that send published poets into classrooms to teach students poetry writing. If you have published poetry widely and have a proven commitment to children, contact your state arts council, Arts-in-Education Dept., or other writing programs in your area to see whether you qualify. Three of the biggest programs are Teachers & Writers Collaborative, Inc., 5 Union Square W., Seventh Floor, New York NY 10003, phone (212)691-6590, which requires poets in its program have some prior teaching experience; California Poets-in-the-Schools, 870 Market St., Suite 1148, San Francisco CA 94102, phone (415)399-1565; and Writers & Artists in the Schools, COMPAS, 304 Landmark Center, 75 W. Fifth St., St. Paul MN 55102, phone (612)292-3254, which includes both Minnesota-based writers and artists in their program.

‡*SALOPIAN POETRY SOCIETY; SALOPEOT, 54 Coronation Dr., Donnington, Telford, Shropshire TF2 8HY United Kingdom, secretary Lilian Parker. Founded in 1976 to promote modern poetry by modern poets, also to encourage and advise the novice. International organization with regional affiliations open to anyone 15 years or older. Currently has 111 members. Offerings available for poets include contests. Sponsors annual poetry competition awarding £100 first prize, £50 second prize, £30 prize and publication in *Salopeot*. Submissions must be unpublished. Submit any number of typed poems of up to 36 lines, without identification. Send SASE for entry form and guidelines. Entry fee: £2/poem. Deadline: August 16. Publishes **Salopeot** occasionally and tapes called "Newspapers for the Blind." Also publishes *Snippets*, a quarterly loose-leafed magazine that contains information about the society and happenings in the poetry field. Also available to nonmembers for $5. Members or nationally-known writers give readings that are open to the public. Sponsors open-mike readings and charity events. Membership dues are £10/year ($10 US). Members meet quarterly. Send SASE (or SAE and IRC) for additional information.

*SCOTTISH POETRY LIBRARY; SCHOOL OF POETS; CRITICAL SERVICE, Tweeddale Court, 14 High St., Edinburgh EH1 1TE Scotland, phone (031)557-2876, director Tessa Ransford, librarian Penny Duce. It is a reference information source and free lending library, also lending by post and has a travelling van service lending at schools, prisons and community centres. The library has a computerized catalogue allowing subject-based searches and indexes of poetry and poetry magazines. The collection comprises over 15,000 items of Scottish and international poetry. The School of Poets is open to anyone; "at meetings members divide into small groups in which each participant reads a poem which is then analyzed and discussed." Meetings normally take place at 7:30 p.m. on the first Tuesday of each month at the library. They also offer a Critical Service in which groups of up to 6 poems, not exceeding 200 lines in all, are given critical comment by members of the School: £15 for each critique (with SAE).

SONGWRITERS AND POETS CRITIQUE, 11599 Coontz Rd., Orient OH 43146, phone (614)877-1727, founded in 1985 by Ellis Cordle. A nonprofit association whose purpose is to serve songwriters, poets and musicians in their area. The president of the organization says, "We have over 200 members from over 16 states at several levels of ability from novice to advanced, and try to help and support each other with the craft and the business of poetry and songs. We have published writers and recorded artists. We share information about how to pitch, send and package a demo and who to send it to. We also have a songwriting contest for member writers." Annual dues are $25.

‡SOUTH DAKOTA STATE POETRY SOCIETY; PASQUE PETALS; SERENDIPITY, Box 398, Lennox SD 57039, (605)647-2447, membership chair Verlyss V. Jacobson. Founded in 1926 to provide a place for members to publish their poetry. Regional organization open to anyone. Currently has 200-225 total members. Levels of membership available are Regular, Patron, Foreign, Student. Sponsors conferences, workshops and 2 annual contests, one for adults and one for students, with 12 categories. Deadlines: August 31 for adults, February 1 for students. Publishes the magazine *Pasque Petals* 8-10 times/year. Also publishes *Serendipity* a quarterly newsletter. Membership dues are $20 regular, $30 patron, $5 students. Members meet biannually. Send SASE for additional information.

SOUTHERN POETRY ASSOCIATION; THE POET'S VOICE, P.O. Box 524, Pass Christian MS 39571, founded 1986, poetry editor Mildred Klyce. SPA offers networking, publishing, free critique service for members through Round Robin Groups and assistance in publishing chapbooks. $12 annual membership fee includes *The Poet's Voice* quarterly newsletter. The association sponsors a number of contests, including Voices of the South, Yarn Spinner, Poetry in Motion, Special People; some are for members only; some, such as the Voices of the South-Contest, are open to all. High-scoring poems are published in an anthology (which the poet is not required to purchase). Send #10 SAE with 64¢ postage for details. *The Poet's Voice* contains poetry book reviews, articles on great poets of the past, current activities, input from SPA members and contest winning poems. "We have been nominated to receive the 1996 Mississippi State Governor's Award for Excellence in the Arts for our work with senior citizens, students and prison inmates. This is the fourth year SPA has been nominated."

THE THURBER HOUSE; JAMES THURBER WRITER-IN-RESIDENCE, 77 Jefferson Ave., Columbus OH 43215, phone (614)464-1032, officially opened in 1984. Listed on the National Register of Historic Places, The Thurber House is a literary center, bookstore and museum of Thurber materials. Programs include writing classes for children, author readings, Thurber celebrations and an art gallery. The Thurber House sponsors a writer-in-residence program that brings 2 journalists, a playwright, a poet or a fiction writer to spend a season living and writing in The Thurber House while teaching a course at The Ohio State University. Each writer will receive a stipend and housing in the third-floor apartment of Thurber's boyhood home. Please send a letter of interest and a curriculum vitae to Michael J. Rosen, literary director before December 15, 1977. Please note that The Thurber House is *not* a publishing house and does not accept unsolicited material.

UNIVERSITY OF ARIZONA POETRY CENTER, 1216 N. Cherry Ave., Tucson AZ 85719, phone (520)321-7760, fax (520)621-5566, website http://www.coh.arizona.edu/poetry/, director Alison Deming. Founded in 1960 "to maintain and cherish the spirit of poetry." Open to the public. The Center is located in two historic adobe houses near the main campus and contains a nationally acclaimed poetry collection that includes over 27,000 items. Programs and services include: a library with a noncirculating poetry collection and space for small classes, poetry-related meetings and activities; facilities, research support, and referral information about poetry and poets for local and national communities; the Free Public Reading Series, a series of 12 to 18 readings each year featuring poets, fiction writers, and writers of literary nonfiction; a guest house for residencies of visiting writers and for use by other University departments and community literary activities; a one-month summer residency at the Center's guest house offered each year to an emerging writer selected by jury; and poetry awards, readings, and special events for undergraduate and graduate students. Publishes a biannual newsletter. Send SASE for additional information. "We do not have members, though one can become a 'Friend' through a contribution to our Friends of the Poetry Center account."

THE UNTERBERG POETRY CENTER OF THE 92ND STREET Y; "DISCOVERY"/THE NATION POETRY CONTEST, 1395 Lexington Ave., New York NY 10128, phone (212)415-5760. Founded in 1939. Offers annual series of readings by major literary figures (weekly readings October through May), writing workshops, master classes in fiction and poetry, and lectures and literary seminars. Also co-sponsors the "Discovery"/*The Nation* Poetry Contest. Deadline January 31. Send SASE for information. "No phone queries, please."

‡UTAH STATE POETRY SOCIETY; POET TREE, Utah Arts Council & NEA, 7685 Dell Rd., Salt Lake City UT 84121-5221, phone (801)943-4211, treasurer Rosalyn Ostler. Founded in 1950 to secure a wider appreciation of the poetry arts and to promote excellence in writing poetry. State-wide organization. Membership is open to all citizens of the State of Utah, without consideration of age, race, regional, religious, educational or other backgrounds. It is also accorded to interested people from any other state in the union, and to all former Utahns, wherever they may reside. Currently has 243 total members. Levels of membership available are regular and student. Sponsors conferences, workshops, contests, awards. USPS publishes, biannually, work of members.

Publishes *Poet Tree*, a biannual newsletter. Members or nationally-known writers give readings that are open to the public. Individual chapters meet once a month and conduct open readings. Open readings are also encouraged at the annual Award Festival. Membership dues are $20/year ($15 for students). Members meet monthly. Send SASE for additional information. "We welcome all potential members."

*WELFARE STATE INTERNATIONAL, The Ellers, Ulverston, Cumbria LA12 0AA England, phone 01229-581127, fax 01229 581232, founded 1968, artistic director John Fox, is a "celebratory arts company of national and international status creating functional poetry both visual and verbal, for ceremonial occasions. They have published *The Dead Good Funerals Book: a guide to new and alternative funeral ceremonies*. Commissions range from small-scale domestic celebrations to city-scale spectaculars." They publish poster poems in limited editions, dramatic songs and interludes for performance works, and poetic masques.

WALT WHITMAN CULTURAL ARTS CENTER, Second and Cooper St., Camden NJ 08102, executive director René L. Huggins, program coordinator J. Daniel Johnson, phone (609)964-8300. A writers' center, founded 1975, it offers a variety of programs such as Notable Poets and Writers Series, Walt Whitman Poetry Series, school programs, adult and children's theater, musical presentations and Fine Art Exhibitions. Their regular season runs September through June. During the summer months they provide a children's theater series entitled "10 Fridays of Fun."

‡WISCONSIN FELLOWSHIP OF POETS; MUSELETTER, N. 66 Pine Place, Merrillan WI 54754, phone (715)333-2422, e-mail mardifries@aol.com, website http://www.execpc.com/~jon, president Mardi Fries. Founded in 1950 to secure fuller recognition of poetry as one of the important forces making for a higher civilization and to create a finer appreciation of poetry by the public at large. State wide organization open to current and past residents of Wisconsin who write poetry acceptable to the Credentials Chairperson. Currently has 320 total members. Levels of memberships available are Associate, Active, Student and Life. Sponsors conferences, workshops, contests, awards. Publishes "Wisconsin Poets' Calendar" poems of Wisconsin (resident) poets. Also publishes *Museletter* a quarterly newsletter. Members or nationally-known writers give readings that are open to the public. Sponsors open-mike readings. Membership dues are Active $15, Associate $10, Student $1, Life $100. Members meet biannually. Send SASE for additional information to WFOP Vice President Josephine Zell, 1109 Linda Vista Rd., Madison WI 53716.

‡WOMEN WHO WRITE; WRITER'S NOTES, P.O. Box 652, Madison NJ 07940, phone (201)731-2841, secretary Alice Johansen. Founded in 1990 to assist woman writers, beginners and pros alike, with every phase of the writing process, through writing groups, classes, workshops, lectures and panel discussions. To bring the work of women writers into the community through readings, publications and performances. To provide information, encouragement, assistance and a sense of community to women writers who might otherwise write alone or not at all. Statewide organization open to all women interested in writing. Currently has 140 total members. Offerings available for poets include critique groups (mixed genre as well as poets only), courses through local adult schools (reduced tuition to members). Sponsors 3-5 workshops per year, and offer 3-4 courses through adult schools. Publishes *Writer's Notes*, a quarterly newsletter. They also publish a literary journal annually, with work submitted by members, selected by a group of editors. Also available to nonmembers for $1.50/issue or $5/year. Members or nationally-known writers give readings that are open to the public. Sponsors open-mike readings. Membership dues are $30/year. Members meet twice a month. Send SASE for additional information.

WOODLAND PATTERN, P.O. Box 92081, 720 E. Locust St., Milwaukee WI 53212, phone (414)263-5001. Executive director Anne Kingsbury calls it "a semi-glamorous literary and arts center." Kingsbury regards the center as a neighborhood organization; it includes a bookstore that concentrates on contemporary literature, much of it small press, much of it poetry, and also on multicultural children's literature. It also incorporates a multipurpose gallery/performance/reading space, where exhibitions, readings, a lecture series, musical programs and a reading and study group are held. The *Woodland Pattern Newsletter*, mailed free to 2,800 people, contains an annotated calendar and pieces about visiting writers.

WORDS—THE ARKANSAS LITERARY SOCIETY, P.O. Box 174, Little Rock AR 72203, phone (501)821-2447, e-mail beggsm@holly.hsu.edu, president Marck L. Beggs. Founded in 1984 to "help support literature and literary activities in the state of Arkansas. WORDS is a statewide group of people who love the language and encourage its use and celebration by Arkansans. Some of us are writers; some of us are readers. All hope, together, to accomplish good things for our state." Currently has over 200 members. Offerings available for poets include an annual contest and workshops, periodic readings and a quarterly newsletter. The annual literary contest awards a $250 prize in four categories: poetry, fiction, nonfiction and screenplays. Deadline: early June. They also support the Porter Fund Award, an annual state award for literary excellence. The quarterly newsletter, *Words from WORDS*, includes information on contests, readings, events, submission information, reviews, workshops, in-state conferences and other items of interest for members. It is not generally distributed to nonmembers. WORDS helps support different literary readings—some by members and some by nationally known writers. Some of the readings offer open-mike time. Membership dues are $20/year for an individual or family, $10/year for students and senior citizens. Board meetings are held quarterly and are open to anyone. Send

SASE for additional information. "WORDS always welcomes suggestions, ideas, and volunteers to help support and nurture the literary community in Arkansas."

WORLD-WIDE WRITERS SERVICE, INC.; WRITERS INK; WRITERS INK PRESS; WRITERS UNLIMITED AGENCY, INC., P.O. Box 698, Centereach NY 11720-0698, phone (516)821-2945, fax (516)821-2945, e-mail axelrod@sunysuffolk.edu, founded in 1976, Writers Ink Press founded 1978, director Dr. David B. Axelrod. "World-wide Writers Service is a literary and speakers' booking agency. With its not-for-profit affiliate, Writers Unlimited Agency, Inc., it presents literary workshops and performances, conferences and other literary services, and publishes through Writers Ink Press, chapbooks and small flat-spined books as well as arts editions. **We publish only by our specific invitation at this time.**" *Writers Ink* is "a sometimely newsletter of events on Long Island, now including programs of our conferences. We welcome news of other presses and poets' activities. Review books of poetry. We fund raise for nonprofit projects and are associates of Long Island Writers Festival and Jeanne Voege Poetry Awards as well as the Key West Poetry Writing, January Workshops and Writing Therapy Trainings throughout the year in various locations. Arts Editions are profit productions employing hand-made papers, bindings, etc. We have editorial services available at small fees ($50 minimum), but only after inquiry and if appropriate. We are currently concentrating on works in translation, particularly Chinese."

THE WRITER'S CENTER; WRITER'S CAROUSEL; POET LORE, 4508 Walsh St., Bethesda MD 20815, phone (301)654-8664, fax (301)654-8667, e-mail poet@erols.com. website http://www.writer.org, founder and artistic director Allan Lefcowitz, executive director Jane Fox. Founded in 1976. This is an outstanding resource for writers not only in Washington DC but in the wider area ranging from southern Pennsylvania to North Carolina and West Virginia. The Center offers 200 multi-meeting workshops each year in writing, word processing, and graphic arts. It is open 7 days a week, 10 hours a day. Some 2,300 members support the center with $30 annual donations, which allows for 5 paid staff members. There is a book gallery at which publications of small presses are displayed and sold. The center's publication, *Writer's Carousel*, is a 24-page magazine that comes out 6 times a year. They also sponsor 80 annual performance events, which include presentations in poetry, fiction and theater. The Center is publisher of *Poet Lore*—100 years old in 1989 (see listing in the Publishers of Poetry section). Their website has news and information about the Washington metropolitan literary community.

WRITERS OF KERN, P.O. Box 6694, Bakersfield CA 93386-6694, phone (805)871-5834, president Barbara Gabel, founded 1993. Writers of Kern is the Bakersfield Branch of the California Writers' Club and is open to "published writers and any person interested in writing." Currently has 100 members. Levels of membership available are professional, writers with published work; writers working toward publication; and students. Membership benefits include "meetings on the third Saturday of every month, except in September which is our conference month, with speakers who are authors, agents, etc., on topics pertaining to writing; several critique groups including fiction genres, nonfiction and poetry; a monthly newsletter with marketing tips; access to club library; and discount to annual conference." The conference is held on the third Saturday in September. They also sponsor an annual writing contest. Winners are announced at the conference. Membership dues are $35/year. Send SASE for additional information.

THE WRITERS ROOM, 10 Astor Place, 6th Floor, New York NY 10003, phone (212)254-6995, fax (212)533-6059. Founded in 1978 to provide a "home away from home" for any writer who needs a place to work. It is open 24 hours a day, 7 days a week, offering desk space, storage and comraderie at the rate of $175/quarter. It is supported by the New York State Council on the Arts, the New York City Department of Cultural Affairs and private sector funding. The Writers Room also offers monthly readings and workshops for its residents. Call for application.

‡❧THE WRITERS' UNION OF CANADA, 24 Ryerson Ave., Toronto, Ontario M5T 2P3 Canada, phone (416)703-8982, fax (416)703-0826, e-mail twuc@the-wire.com, website http://www.swifty.com/twuc. Founded in 1973 and dedicated to advancing the status of Canadian writers. The Union is devoted to protecting the rights of published authors, defending the freedom to write and publish, and serving its members. National organization. Open to poets who have had a trade book published by a commercial or university press; must be a Canadian citizen or landed immigrant. Currently has 1050 total members. Offerings available for poets include contact with peers, contract advice/negotiation, grievance support, electronic communication, random royalty audit, ms evaluation service. Sponsors conferences, workshops. Sponsors Annual General Meeting, usually held in May, where members debate and determine Union policy, elect representatives, attend workshops, socialize, and renew friendships with their colleagues from across the country. Publishes *The Writers' Union of Canada Newsletter* 9 times/year. Membership dues are $180/year. Regional reps meet with members when possible. Send SASE (or SAE and IRC) for additional information. For writers not eligible for membership, the Union offers, for a fee: publications on publishing, grants, contracts, awards, and more; a Manuscript Evaluation Service for any level writer; Contract Services, including a Self-Help Package, a Contract Evaluation Service, and a Contract Negotiation Service; and Workshops for Developing Writers.

WYOMING WRITERS, INC., 5312 Westedt Rd., Cheyenne WY 82009. Founded in 1974 to "encourage writers." Regional organization open to "writers, poets, and those interested in the writing profession." Wyoming

Writers sponsors an annual conference each June and an annual writing competition. The annual conference features authors/presenters plus a variety of panels on different writing-related subjects. For information about the conference, contact co-chair Larry K. Brown, 209 E. Iowa, Cheyenne WY 82009-8929, phone (307)637-5248, e-mail hogranch@msn.com. Also publishes the *Wyo-Writer*, a newsletter published 10 times a year that provides information on writing, marketing, contests and organizations. Membership dues are $25/year. Send SASE for additional information.

Additional Organizations Useful to Poets

The following listings also contain information about organizations useful to poets. See the General Index for page numbers. Note: Double daggers (‡) preceding titles indicate listings new to this edition.

Publications Useful to Poets

The publications in this section are designed to help poets with all aspects of writing and publishing poetry. While few are actual markets, many detail new publishing opportunities in addition to providing information on craft, advice on marketing, or interviews with poets and writers.

Poets & Writers Magazine, in fact, is one of the most useful resources for both poets and fiction writers. In addition to informative articles and interviews, it includes calls for submissions and contests and awards. *Writer's Digest*, on the other hand, covers the entire field of writing and features market listings as well as a monthly poetry column by Michael J. Bugeja, author of *The Art and Craft of Poetry* (Writer's Digest Books, 1994) and *Poet's Guide: How to Publish and Perform Your Work* (Story Line Press, 1995).

Other publications, such as *Taproot Reviews* (new to this edition), *Small Press Review* (see Dustbooks) and *Literary Magazine Review*, include reviews of poetry books and chapbooks or reviews of small press magazines. These reviews provide further insight into the different markets.

For poets seeking resources more regional in focus, several of the listings in this section are publications that include, among other items, markets, news and events for specific areas of the United States and Canada. For example, *First Draft* publishes information of interest to Alabama writers, *Next . . . Magazine* provides information on happenings in Southern California, and *Word: The Literary Calendar* focuses on literary events in Ontario, Canada. In addition to these publications, *Slam* is a magazine with information on poetry slams held in various locations around the world.

Finally, for those interested in various publishing opportunities, this section also includes information about other market directories as well as materials on self-publishing. And, in addition to the listings that follow, you will find other useful publications, such as *Canadian Author* and *New Writer's Magazine*, noted in Additional Publications Useful to Poets at the end of this section.

To determine which of these publications may be most useful to you, read sample issues. Many of these books and periodicals may be found in your local library or located on newsstands or in bookstores. If you are unable to locate a certain magazine, order a copy directly from the publisher. For books, send a SASE with a request for the publisher's current catalog or order information.

✸**CANADIAN POETRY**, English Dept., University of Western Ontario, London, Ontario N6A 3K7 Canada, phone (519)661-3403, founded 1977, editor Prof. D.M.R. Bentley. A biannual journal of critical articles, reviews and historical documents (such as interviews). It is a professionally printed, scholarly edited, flat-spined, 150-page journal which pays contributors in copies. Subscription: $15. **Sample: $7.50. Note that they publish no poetry except as quotations in articles.**

DUSTBOOKS; INTERNATIONAL DIRECTORY OF LITTLE MAGAZINES AND SMALL PRESSES; DIRECTORY OF POETRY PUBLISHERS; SMALL PRESS REVIEW; SMALL MAGAZINE REVIEW, P.O. Box 100, Paradise CA 95967. Dustbooks publishes a number of books useful to writers. Send SASE for catalog. Among their regular publications, *International Directory* is an annual directory of small presses and literary magazines, over 6,000 entries, a third being magazines, half being book publishers, and the rest being both. There is very detailed information about what these presses and magazines report to be their policies in regard to payment, copyright, format and publishing schedules. *Directory of Poetry Publishers* has similar information for over 2,000 publishers of poetry. *Small Press Review* is a monthly magazine, newsprint, carrying current updating of listings in *ID*, small press needs, news, announcements and reviews—a valuable way to stay abreast of the literary marketplace. *Small Magazine Review*, which began publication in June, 1993, is included within *Small Press Review* and covers small press magazines in a similar fashion.

FIRST DRAFT: THE JOURNAL OF THE ALABAMA WRITERS' FORUM, The Alabama Writers' Forum, Alabama State Council on the Arts, 201 Monroe St., Montgomery AL 36130-1800, phone (334)242-4076 ext 233, fax (334)240-3269, e-mail jeanie@arts.al.us, website http://www.auburn.edu/~cahawf, editor Jeanie Thompson, founded 1992, appears 3 times a year, publishing news, features, book reviews, and interviews relating to Alabama writers. "We do not publish original poetry or fiction." It is 28 pgs., 8½×11, professionally printed on coated paper and saddle-stitched with b&w photos inside and on the cover. Lists markets for poetry, contests/awards and workshops. Sponsored by the Alabama Writers' Forum, "the official literary arts advocacy organization for the state of Alabama." Reviews books of poetry by "Alabama poets or from Alabama presses." Subscription: $25/year. Sample postpaid: $3.

LAUGHING BEAR NEWSLETTER; LAUGHING BEAR PRESS, P.O. Box 6133, Dallas TX 75261-3322, phone (817)283-6303, e-mail laughingbr@aol.com, website http://members.aol.com/laughingbr/lbp.htm, founded 1976, editor Tom Person. *LBN* is a monthly publication of small press information for writers and publishers containing articles, news and reviews. Cost: $12/year. Send SASE for sample copy or request via e-mail. *LBN* is interested in short (200- to 300-word) articles on self-publishing and small press. Pays copies.

THE LETTER EXCHANGE, published by The Readers' League, P.O. Box 6218, Albany CA 94706-0218, founded 1982, editor/publisher Stephen Sikora. Published 3 times a year, *The Letter Exchange* is a digest-sized magazine, 36 pgs., that publishes 4 types of listings: regular (which are rather like personal classifieds); ghost letters, which contain lines like "Send news of the Entwives!"; amateur magazines, which publicizes readers' own publishing ventures; and sketch ads, in which readers who would rather draw than write can communicate in their chosen mode. All ads are coded, and readers respond through the code numbers. Subscription to *The Letter Exchange* is $22/year, and sample copies are $9 postpaid for current issue. Poets who are so inclined often exchange poems and criticism with each other through this medium.

‡*LIGHT'S LIST**, 29 Longfield Rd., Tring, Herts HP23 4DG England, editor John Light, founded 1986, is an annual publication "listing some thousand small press magazines publishing poetry, prose, market information, articles and artwork with address and brief note of interests. All magazines publish work in English. Listings are from the United Kingdom, Europe, United States, Canada, Australia, New Zealand, South Africa and India." It is 32 pgs., A5, photocopied and saddle-stitched with paper cover. Lists markets for poetry. Single copy: $4 (air $5).

LITERARY MAGAZINE REVIEW, Dept. of English Language and Literature, The University of Northern Iowa, Cedar Falls IA 50614-0502, phone (319)273-2821, fax (319)273-5807, e-mail grant.tracey@uni.edu, founded 1981, editor Grant Tracey. A quarterly magazine (digest-sized, saddle-stitched, about 48-64 pgs.) that publishes critiques, 2-5 pgs. long, of various literary magazines, plus shorter "reviews" (about ½ page) of new journals during a particular year. Single copies: $5; subscriptions: $13.50/year. Request copies via e-mail.

MINNESOTA LITERATURE, One Nord Circle, St. Paul MN 55127, phone (612)483-3904, editor Mary Bround Smith, founded 1975. *ML* appears 10 times a year (September through June), providing news and announcements for Minnesota writers. Regularly features "Minnesota literary events such as readings, lectures, workshops, conferences and classes; news of publications written by Minnesotans or published in Minnesota; and opportunities for writers, such as grants, awards and want-ads." It is 8½×11, 8 pgs. (two 11×17 sheets folded), unbound. Subscription: $10 for 10 issues.

NEXT . . . MAGAZINE, Orange Ocean Press, P.O. Box 13019, Long Beach CA 90803, phone/fax (310)930-0587, e-mail nextmag@aol.com, editor G. Murray Thomas, founded 1994, is a monthly publication providing a calendar of southern California poetry events, news and reviews. It is 12-24 pgs., newsprint, with photos and cartoons, accepts ads. Reviews books, chapbooks, tapes, CDs, videos and performances of poetry in 100-500 words. Poets may send books for review consideration to Attn: Reviews. Single copy: $1.50; subscription: $15/year. "*Next . . . Magazine* covers the rapidly growing performance poetry scene in southern California with a monthly calendar, news, reviews, commentary and lots of humor. We are an essential resource for poets in southern California." Request copies via e-mail.

OHIO WRITER, P.O. Box 91801, Cleveland OH 44101, editor Ron Antonucci, is a bimonthly newsletter for Ohio writers or those connected with Ohio. It is 16 pgs., professionally printed in colored ink on off-white stock, containing news and reviews of Ohio writing events, publications and regional opportunities to publish. Subscription: $12/year, $18 for institutions. It also sponsors an annual contest for Ohio writers. See the Best of Ohio Writers Writing Contest listing in the Contests and Awards section.

OPEN HORIZONS, P.O. Box 205, Fairfield IA 52556-0205, phone (515)472-6130, fax (515)472-1560; e-mail John Kremer@bookmarket.com, website http://www.bookmarket.com, founded 1982, publisher John Kremer, publishes how-to books about book publishing and self-publishing, such as *1001 Ways to Market Your Books*, *Book Marketing Update*, *Directory of Book Printers*, and *Book Publishing Resource Guide* (also available on IBM PC or Macintosh disk as a database). Send SASE for catalog.

OXFORD UNIVERSITY PRESS, 198 Madison Ave., New York NY 10016, phone (212)726-6000, founded 1478, literature editor T. Susan Chang (NY), is a large university press publishing academic, trade and college books in a wide variety of fields. **Not accepting poetry mss.** "Our list includes editions of English and American poets for classroom use, thematically-oriented anthologies and critical studies of poets and their work for general readers. Unfortunately, we do not publish new poetry by contemporary writers."

PARA PUBLISHING, Box 8206-880, Santa Barbara CA 93118-8206, phone (805)968-7277, orders (800)727-2782, fax (805)968-1379, e-mail danpoynter@parapublishing.com, website http://www.parapublishing.com. Author/publisher Dan Poynter publishes how-to books on book publishing and self-publishing. *Is There a Book Inside You?* shows you how to get your book out. *The Self-Publishing Manual, How to Write, Print and Sell Your Own Book* is all about book promotion. *Publishing Short-Run Books* shows you how to typeset and lay out your own book. Poynter also publishes *Publishing Contracts on Disk, Book Fairs* and 19 Special Reports on various aspects of book production, promotion, marketing and distribution. *Free* book publishing information kit. Available through Para Publishing is a 24-hour fax service called Fax-On-Demand. This service enables you to obtain free documents on book writing and publishing; and lists of workshops and presentations offered by Dan Poynter. Call (805)968-8947 from your fax machine handset, then follow the voice prompts to hear a list of documents and to order. The fax machine will retrieve the documents and print them instantly. This is a good way to sample Para Publishing's offerings.

PERSONAL POEMS, % Jean Hesse, Villa B-7, 16591 Perdido Key Dr., Pensacola FL 32507, phone (904)492-7909. Jean Hesse started a business in 1980 writing poems for individuals for a fee (for greetings, special occasions, etc.). Others started similar businesses, after she began instructing them in the process, especially through a cassette tape training program and other training materials. Send SASE for free brochure or $25 plus $4.50 p&h (make checks payable to F. Jean Hesse) for training manual, *How to Make Your Poems Pay*.

*POETRY BOOK SOCIETY, Book House, 45 East Hill, London SW18 2QZ England, founded in 1953. A book club with an annual subscription rate of £40, which covers 4 books of new poetry, the *PBS Bulletin*, and a premium offer (for new members). The selectors also recommend other books of special merit, which are obtainable at a discount of 25%. The Poetry Book Society is subsidized by the Arts Council of England. Please write (Attn: Clare Brown) for details or phone 0181-877-1615 (24-hour fax/answer service).

POETRY CALENDAR, 611 Broadway #905, New York NY 10012, phone (212)260-7097, fax (212)475-7110, publisher Martin Paddio, editor Molly McQuade, founded 1975. "*Poetry Calendar* is a monthly magazine that combines reviews, interviews, excerpts, and essays along with one of the most comprehensive literary listings in New York City. Eleven-thousand copies are distributed each month providing a comprehensive schedule of poetry and fiction readings, performances, lectures, exhibits, workshops and related activities." It is 24-32 pgs., 8½×11, newsprint, saddle-stitched. Subscription: $20. Sample available for free.

THE POETRY CONNECTION, 13455 SW 16 Court #F-405-PM, Pembroke Pines FL 33027, phone (954)431-3016, editor/publisher Sylvia Shichman. *The Poetry Connection*, a monthly newsletter, provides information in flyer format. Poets, writers and songwriters receive information on how to sell their poetry/books, poetry and musical publications and contests, and obtain assistance in getting poetry published. *TPC* has information on writing for greeting card companies, poetry and songwriting publications, and greeting card directories. Sample issue: $7. Also sponsors The Magic Circle, a poetry reading/musical network service. Send SASE for more information.

POETRY FLASH, 1450 Fourth St. #4, Berkeley CA 94710, phone (510)525-5476, fax (510)525-6752, editor Joyce Jenkins, founded 1972, appears 6 times a year including double issues. "*Poetry Flash*, a Poetry Review & Literary Calendar for the West, publishes reviews, interviews, essays and information for writers. Poems, as well as announcements about submitting to other publications, appear in each issue." *PF* focuses on poetry, but its literary calendar also includes events celebrating all forms of creative writing in areas across the nation. It is about 44 pgs., printed on newsprint. Lists markets for poetry, contests/awards and workshops. *Poetry Flash* also sponsors a weekly poetry reading series at Cody's Books in Berkeley and sponsors the Bay Area Book Reviewers Association. (Also see listing in Contests and Awards.) Reviews books and chapbooks of poetry. Poets may send books for review consideration. Subscription $16/year. Sample postpaid: $2. "We publish one to three poems per issue—sometimes more in a special feature." Even though *Poetry Flash* publishes a limited amount of poetry, work published here has also been selected for inclusion in *The Best American Poetry 1996*.

POETS & WRITERS, INC.; A DIRECTORY OF AMERICAN POETS AND FICTION WRITERS; LITERARY AGENTS; LITERARY BOOKSTORES; POETS & WRITERS MAGAZINE, 72 Spring St., New York NY 10012, phone (212)226-3586 or (800)666-2268 (California only), website http://www.pw.org, is a major support organization. Its many helpful publications include *Poets & Writers Magazine*, which appears 6 times a year ($19.95 or $3.95 for a single copy), 88 pgs., magazine-sized, offset, has been called *The Wall Street Journal* of our profession, and it is there that one most readily finds out about resources, current needs of magazines and presses, contests, awards, jobs and retreats for writers, and discussions of business, legal and other issues affecting writers. *Poets & Writers Magazine* does not accept advertising from vanity/subsidy presses. P&W also publishes a number of valuable directories such as its biennial *A Directory of American Poets and Fiction Writers* ($27.95 paperback), which editors, publishers, agents and sponsors of readings and workshops use to locate over 7,000 active writers in the country. (You may qualify for a listing if you have a number of publications.) They also publish *Literary Agents* (available for $10); and "Into Print: Guides to the Writing Life," a comprehensive, updated and revised collection of the best articles from *Poets & Writers Magazine*, that includes *Out of the Slush Pile and Into Print*; *Contracts and Royalties: Negotiating Your Own*; *On Cloud Nine: Writers' Colonies, Retreats, Ranches, Residencies, and Sanctuaries*; and *Helping Writers Help Themselves: A National Guide to Writers' Resources* (available for $12.95). The chapbooks and resource lists are available from P&W for $12.95.

BERN PORTER INTERNATIONAL, 1436 Lombard St., #1R, Philadelphia PA 19146, co-editor Sheila Holtz, founded in 1911, is a monthly literary newspaper. *BPI* specializes in "the bizarre, the strange, the conceptual: poetry and prose which stretches the envelope." They review books of poetry and publish poetry and prose. Send SASE for guidelines. Sample copy: $1.

PUSHCART PRESS, P.O. Box 380, Wainscott NY 11975. Publishes a number of books useful to writers, including the Pushcart Prize Series—annual anthologies representing the best small press publications, according to the judges; The Editors' Book Award Series, "to encourage the writing of distinguished books of uncertain financial value"; *The Original Publish-It-Yourself Handbook*; and the Literary Companion Series. Send SASE for catalog.

SLAM, 24 Arlington St., Medford MA 02155, (617)488-3636, fax (617)488-3228, e-mail bosslam@cybercom.net, website http://www.slamnews.com, editor Michael R. Brown, founded 1992, is a quarterly publication containing international news and events on poetry slams. "*Slam* is the official publication of the poetry slam." It is 4 pgs., 8½×11, offset. Subscription: $6/year, add $4 for first-class mail. Sample copy available for free, request via phone, fax, mail, e-mail or website.

‡TAPROOT REVIEWS; BURNING PRESS INC., P.O. Box 585, Lakewood OH 44107, phone (216)221-8940, e-mail au462@cleveland.freenet.edu, website http://wings.buffalo.edu/epc/ezines/, editor luigibob drake, founded 1980, is an quarterly publication "providing reviews of experimental and alternative poetry, fiction, visual-literature, spoken-word recordings, hypertext, intermedia, etc. We intend to expand readers access to a wide variety of literatures; each issue reviews 200-300 publications. We do not accept submissions of poetry." Devotes 80% of its pages to reviews of poetry publication. *Taproot Reviews* is 40 pgs., A5, tabloid-sized, offset-printed on newsprint and folded. Lists markets for poetry. Reviews books or chapbooks of poetry. Poets may send books for review consideration. Subscription: $10/year. Sample postpaid: $5. The editor says, "We accept review submissions, however, potential reviews must be familiar with our format (i.e., read us before submitting). Strong emphasis on independent publishers and non-mainstream writing. We do not read poetry manuscripts."

THE WASHINGTON INTERNATIONAL ARTS LETTER, P.O. Box 12010, Des Moines IA 50312-9401, phone (319)358-6777, fax (319)358-6786, e-mail washletter@aol.com, contact Nancy Fandel. Appears 4 times a year, 6- to 8-page newsletter on grants and other forms of assistance for the arts and humanities—mostly lists various programs of support to artists, including many for poets. Reviews books of poetry. Subscription: $124 full rate; $55 for individuals; $82 for institutions. Send all orders and requests for information to the address above.

WHERE POETS SPEAK, 1516 South 16th Ave., Birmingham AL 35205, phone (205)933-6012, editor Gene Crutcher, founded 1991, is a monthly publication providing "listings of other publications that consider poetry for publication, listings of coffeehouses, bookstores or other places that schedule poetry readings, especially 'Open Mike' nights. Also publish reviews of other publications I receive from time to time, and fill up blank space with poems I have found recently that I like." Devoted entirely to poetry. *WPS* is 4 pgs., 5×7 (8½×11 sheet folded). "Occasionally 6 pages and once or twice I have had an 8-page issue." Reviews books and chapbooks of poetry. Poets may send books for review consideration. Subscription: $10/year. Sample copy available for "a poem or a buck or nothing. I don't do this to make money but to encourage youngsters to write. I am *not* a poet, but I am a pretty good oral interpreter. I will often start reading something at a reading if I sense that the people there are too timid to begin. Once the ice is broken, they often reveal some fine works."

♣WORD: THE LITERARY CALENDAR, 378 Delaware Ave., Toronto, Ontario M6H 2T8 Canada, phone (416)536-4308, fax (416)588-4198, publisher Mike O'Connor, founded 1995, a monthly publication providing an "all inclusive calendar of literary events, book launches, readings, slams and workshops in Ontario (also lists contests and calls for submissions)." It is 8 pgs., 8½×11, offset printed, unbound, with ads. Subscription: $10/year. Make checks payable to Insomniac Press. "All listings are free. An excellent resource for poets in Ontario."

♣WORDWRIGHTS CANADA, P.O. Box 456 Station O, Toronto, Ontario M4A 2P1 Canada, e-mail susioan@ican.net, website http://www.home.ican.net/~susioan, director Susan Ioannou, publishes "books on poetics in layman's, not academic terms, such as *Writing Reader-friendly Poems: Over 50 Rules of Thumb for Clearer Communication*; *The Crafted Poem: A Step-by-Step Guide to Writing and Appreciation* (rev. ed.); and *The Canadian Writers' Contest Calendar*." They consider manuscripts of such books for publication, paying $50 advance, 10% royalties and 5% of press run. They also conduct "Manuscript Reading and Editing Services, as well as The Poetry Tutorial correspondence course for writers." Request order form via mail or e-mail to buy samples.

WRITER'S DIGEST BOOKS; WRITER'S DIGEST, 1507 Dana Ave., Cincinnati OH 45207, phone (800)289-0963 or (513)531-2690. Writer's Digest Books publishes a remarkable array of books useful to all types of writers. In addition to *Poet's Market*, books for poets include *The Poet's Handbook* by Judson Jerome, *Creating Poetry* and *The Poetry Dictionary* by John Drury, and *The Art and Craft of Poetry* by Michael J. Bugeja. Call or write for a complete catalog. *Writer's Digest* is a monthly magazine about writing with frequent articles and market news about poetry, in addition to a monthly poetry column. See the listing in the Publishers of Poetry section.

Additional Publications Useful to Poets

The following listings also contain information about publications useful to poets. See the General Index for page numbers. Note: Double daggers (‡) preceding titles indicate listings new to this edition.

Academy of American Poets, The
Acumen Magazine
‡Alabama State Poetry Society
American Poetry Review
‡Anarchist Angel—Youth Poetry Magazine
‡Arizona Authors Association
Associated Writing Programs
Beatlicks, The
Best of Ohio Writers Writing Contest
Black Bear Publications
Black Buzzard Press
Borealis Press
Byline Magazine
Canadian Author
Canadian Conference of the Arts
Canadian Poetry Association
Canadian Society of Children's Authors, Illustrators & Performers
Canadian Writer's Journal
Candlelight Poetry Journal
Council of Literary Magazines and Presses
‡Dandelion Arts Magazine
Domino
Emerald Coast Review
Federation of British Columbia Writers
‡Georgia Poetry Society
Harp-Strings Poetry Journal
International Women's Writing Guild
IWWG Summer Conference, The

Laureate Letter, The
Leacock Medal for Humour, The Stephen
League of Canadian Poets, The
Ligonier Valley Writers Conference
Loft, The
Maine Writers & Publishers Alliance
Manitoba Writers' Guild Inc.
‡Misc. Proj.: A Poetry Newsletter
National Federation of State Poetry Societies, Inc.
National Poetry Foundation, The
National Writers Union
New Hampshire Writers & Publishers Project
New Horizons Poetry Club
New Writer's Magazine
North Carolina Writers' Network
Northwoods Press
Oak, The
Papyrus
Parnassus: Poetry in Review
PEN American Center
‡Pen & Keyboard Magazine
Pequod: A Journal of Contemporary Literature and Literary Criticism
Piedmont Literary Review
‡Pigasus Press
Poetic Realm
Poetic Space: Poetry & Fiction
Poets House: The Reed Foundation Library
Poets' Roundtable

Prosetry: Newsletter For, By and About Writers
Rio Grande Press
‡Rose Alley Press
‡Salopian Poetry Society
Scavenger's Newsletter
‡Sixties Press
Small Press Genre Association
Smith, The
Southern Poetry Association
Squaw Valley Community of Writers Poetry Workshop
‡Time For Rhyme
Verse
‡Violetta Books
Wildacres Writers Workshop
Wisconsin Regional Writers' Association
Words—The Arkansas Literary Society
World-wide Writers Service, Inc.
Write Way, The
Writer, The
Writer's Digest
Writer's Exchange
Writer's Journal
Writer's Lifeline
Writers of Kern
‡Writers' Round Table
Wyoming Writers, Inc.
Xanadu

Websites of Interest to Poets

BY TARA A. HORTON

The Internet can be a useful tool for crafting and publishing poetry (see Trends in the Field: Internet Opportunities for Poets on pages 7-10). Doing searches for specific forms of poetry will bring up many sites catering to your forms of choice. The following list can be used as a starting point for investigating pertinent websites for poets. We have broken them into four categories: The Business, The Organizations, The Search, and The Craft.

THE BUSINESS

IRS: http://www.irs.ustreas.gov/basic/cover.html
  Information, forms and publications, plus comments and help.
U.S. Copyright Office: http://www.loc.gov/copyright
  General information and forms you can print.

THE ORGANIZATIONS

  The following websites contain information about the organization, list poetry awards and contests, and provide links to other literary resources, conferences and workshops.
The Academy of American Poets: http://www.poets.org
The International Organization of Performing Poets: http://www.slamnews.com/iopp.htm
Poets & Writers: http://www.pw.org
Poetry Society of America: http://www.bookwire.com/psa/psa.html
Teachers & Writers Collaborative: http://www.twc.org
Zuzu's Petals Organizations of Interest to Poets and Writers: http://www.lehigh.net/zuzu/wrt-org.htm
  This site provides links to different organizations.

THE SEARCH

  The following are search directories providing literary links.
Electronic Poetry Center: http://wings.buffalo.edu/epc/
Factsheet Five—Electric 'Zines!: http://www.well.com/conf/f5/f5index2.html
John Labovitz's e-zine-list: http://www.meer.net/~johnl/e-zine-list
The Poetry Forum World Wide Registry: http://www.poetryforum.org/registry.htm
Writer's Resources: http://www.arcana.com/shannon/writing.html
Writers Write™—The Write Resource™: http://www.writerswrite.com/

THE CRAFT

  These sites can serve as a source of inspiration when creating your poetry.
Alan Cooper's Homonym List: http://www.cooper.com/alan/homonym.html
  List of words that are pronounced the same, but are spelled differently and have different meanings like "see" and "sea."
The Albany Poetry Workshop: http://www.sonic.net/poetry/albany/
  Online workshop where poets read and comment on each others' works-in-progress.
JavaScript Vocabulary Stretchers: http://www.netnet/users/jgales/game1.html
  Two vocabulary-building games to play.

Richard Lederer's Verbivore Page: http://pw1.netcom.com/~rlederer/index.htm

Contains excerpts from his articles along with language-related organizations, publications and literary links.

Rhetorical Figures: http://www.uky.edu/ArtsSciences/Classics/rhetoric.html

Glossary of rhetorical terms like anaphora, simile and hyperbole.

Rhyming Dictionary: http://www.cs.cmu.edu/~dougb/rhyme.html

Provides a list of words that rhyme with the word you enter, each linked to its definition and thesaurus entry.

A Word a Day: http://www.wordsmith.org/awad/index.html

Website for the list that mails a vocabulary word and its definition to subscribers daily.

The Word Wizard: http://wordwizard.com/

Club with free membership offering new words, quotations and competitions.

PUBLICATIONS ACCEPTING E-MAIL SUBMISSIONS

The following publications accept e-mail submissions. See the General Index for their page numbers. As submission guidelines are subject to change, we recommend sending for their guidelines and verifying they still accept e-mail submissions.

@Evolute.org
A.L.I. (The Avon Literary Intelligencer)
A Small Garlic Press
Aethlon
Aha Books
American Tanka
Anaconda Press
Appalachian Heritage
The Argotist
Arnazella
Asspants
Backspace
Beauty for Ashes
Black Bear Publications
Blue Penny Quarterly
(the) Brave New Tick
Broken Boulder Press
The Brownstone Review
The Café Review
Chaff
Cherry Street Grill
Context South
Copper Moon Publishing
Costa Publishing
Coteau Books
Curriculum Vitae Literary Supplement
Depth Charge
James Dickey Newsletter
Distant Frontier Press
1812
Entre Nous
Etcetera
Evernight
Expressions
The Far Cry
Filling Station
Fly By Night Press
The Fractal
Free Thought Conceptions
Fuck Decency
Fuel
Full-Time Dads
Garnet
A Gathering of the Tribes

Gerbil: A Queer Culture Zine
Gestalten
Gotta Write Network Litmag
The Hawk
Healthy Body-Healthy Minds
Heliotrope
In Darkness Eternal
In His Steps Publishing Company
Irving St. Press, Inc.
The Journal
Journal of Experimental Fiction
Kimera
Kuumba
Lacunae Magazine
The Lamp-Post
The Laureate Letter
Laurels
Linq
Literal Latte
Lockert Library of Poetry in Translation
Lords of Eternal Darkness
Lords of the Abyss
The Lost Library of Alexandria Magazine
Lungfull! Magazine
Lynx
Mail Call Journal
Many Mountains Moving
Maren Publications
Medicinal Purposes
Medusa's Hairdo
The Midwest Quarterly
Mind Matters Review
Mind Purge
Negative Capability
Neon Quarterly
Neuronet
Northwest Literary Forum
Nova Express
Office Number One
Olympia Review
Our Journey
Paperplates
Papyrus
Paramour Magazine

The Peking Duck
Penny Dreadful Press
The Penny Dreadful Review
Peoplenet Disability Datenet
The Plaza
Poet to Poet, Inc.
The Poetic Soul
Poetry & Prose Annual
Poetry Forum
Poetry in Motion
The Poet's Attic Quarterly
The Poet's Pen
Portlandia Review of Books
Prairie Dog
Princeton University Press
Prism International
Queen's Quarterly
Red Dancefloor
Rocket Press
Shadow Sword
Shadowfire Press
Shape Shifter
Silhouette Magazine
Simpson Publications
Spuyten Duyvil
Stark Raving Sanity
Stoneflower Literary Journal
Stride Publications
Stygian Vortex Publications
Talus and Scree
Teens In Motion News
Texas Young Writers' Newsletter
Thistle
Thunder Creek Publishing Co-Op
Tomorrow Magazine
Touchstone
TPE Press
Uno Mas Magazine
Virgin Meat
Volcano Quarterly
Wolf Head Quarterly
Woman Magazine
Wood Mountain Series
Writers Gazette
Zero City
Zuzu's Petals Quarterly Online

Glossary of Poetic Forms and Styles

Abstract poem: uses sound, rhythm and rhyme to convey emotion. The words' meanings are secondary to their sound.

Acrostic: the first or last letter in a line, read downward, form a word, phrase or sentence.

Alphabet poem: uses letters of the alphabet as points of departure for lines or whole poems.

Ballad: stories commonly about fatal relationships. Stanzas are quatrains with four beats in lines 1 and 3; and three beats in lines 2 and 4, which also rhyme.

Ballade: three stanzas rhyming *ababbcbC* (capital "C" meaning a refrain) and an envoie (half the number of lines of a stanza) rhyming *bcbC*.

Beat poetry: an anti-academic school of poetry born in the '50s in San Francisco. It is fast-paced free verse resembling jazz. The language is irreverent and slangy.

Blank verse: unrhymed, usually with iambic pentameter.

Calligram: poems whose words on the page form a shape or object related to the poem.

Cento: poem made up of pieces from poems by other authors.

Chant: poem where one or more line is repeated over and over.

Cinquain: five-line stanza; or poem of five lines with 2, 4, 6, 8 and 2 syllables, respectively.

Concrete poem: the words dramatize their meaning by where they appear on the page; make use of space and sound.

Dada: movement based on deliberate irrationality and rejection of traditional artistic values.

Epigram: short, witty, satirical poem or saying written to be easily remembered. Like a punchline.

Free verse: no regular beat or rhyme.

Ghazal: usually five to fifteen lines of long-lined couplets, customarily expressing mystical thoughts. The couplets are not connected, but separate units.

Haibun: a Japanese form where prose is mixed with verse, specifically haiku, often in diary or travel journal form.

Haiku: poem about how nature is linked to human nature. Only three short lines containing 17 syllables, generally arranged 5-7-5. Uses simple words and expression, almost no adjectives.

Language poetry: attempts to detach words from their traditional meanings so something new arises. The poetry tries to break away from what we already know about poetry to experiment.

Limerick: five lines rhyming *aabba*, with a bawdy or scatalogical theme. The stresses in the lines are 3-3-2-2-3.

Lune: three-line poem of 13 syllables (5-3-5).

Lyric: intimate poem where poet speaks in own voice or a monologue, expressing emotion.

Nonsense verse: doesn't make sense, but it's not gibberish. Poem is consistent, but wacky.

Pantoum: poem of any length in four-line stanzas. Lines 2 and 4 are repeated as lines 1 and 3 of the next stanza, and so on. Doesn't have to rhyme. Ideally, in the last stanza, lines 2 and 4 repeat the opening stanza's lines 1 and 3.

Prose poem: looks like prose, but reads like poetry. No rhyme or set rhythm. It's unlike regular prose because of its intense and condensed language.

Quatrain: a four-line stanza.

Renga: long, image-filled in alternating stanzas of three and two lines, customarily created by a big group of poets taking turns.

Rondeau: the repeating lines and rhyme give the poem the quality of a round. It's usually 15 lines that rhyme *aabba aabR aabbaR* ("R" is the refrain).

Senryu: like haiku, but about human nature, often humorous, using direct language.

Sequence: a series of poems, often numbered. The poems must be connected in some way e.g., by theme, subject, stanza form, or ongoing narrative.

Sestina: six unrhymed stanzas of six lines each. The words at the end of the first stanza's lines repeat at ends of other lines. Each subsequent stanza rearranges the previous stanza's end-words as 6, 1, 5, 2, 4, 3. Ends with a three-line stanza using all six end-words, two to a line.

Sijo: a Korean form of poetry, 44 to 46 syllables, usually on three lines.

Skeltonic verse: short lines whose rhymes continue as long as they work, then changes to another rhyme.

Sonnet: often written about love and/or philosophy. It's a 14-line poem in two parts: octave (eight lines) and a sestet (six lines). There are three types: the Petrarchan (or Italian) rhymes *abbaabba* and varies the last six lines (*cdcdcd* or *cdecde* or *cdedce* or *ccdccd* or *cddcdd* or *cddcee*); the Shakespearean rhymes *abab cdcd efef gg*; the Spenserian rhymes *ababbcbccdcdee*.

Surrealism: literary and artistic movement stressing the importance of dreams, the unconscious, irrational thought, free associations and disturbing imagery.

Tanka: frequently about love, seasons, sadness, with strong images and poetic devices haiku avoids. Five lines, with lines 1 and 3 being shorter. Syllables per line are 5-7-5-7-7.

Triolet: eight lines, with two rhymes and two repeating lines. The first line is repeated as lines 4 and 7. Lines 2 and 8 are the same: *ABaAabAB* (capitals indicate repeated lines or refrains).

Villanelle: six stanzas. The first five are three lines long, the sixth is four lines long. The first and last lines of the first stanza repeat as the final line of the next four stanzas and are also the last two lines of the poem. Rhyme scheme of *aba* for first five stanzas.

Visual: a combination of text and graphics usually only reproduced photographically.

Glossary of Listing Terms

A3, A4, A5. Metric equivalents of 11¾ × 16½, 8¼ × 11¾ and 5⅞ × 8¼ respectively.

Anthology. A collection of selected writings by various authors.

Bio. A short biographical paragraph often requested with a submission; it is commonly called a "bio." In your bio, publishers may ask you to note your most recent and noteworthy publication credits.

Chapbook. A small book of approximately 20-25 pages of poetry. Such a book is less expensive to produce than a full-length book collection, though it is seldom noted by reviewers.

Contributor's copy. Copy of an issue of a magazine or published book sent to an author whose work is included.

Cover letter. Letter accompanying a submission; it usually lists titles of poems and gives a brief account of publishing credits and biographical information. (See sample on page 15.)

Digest-sized. Approximately 5½ × 8½, the size of a folded sheet of conventional typing paper.

Electronic magazine. Publication circulated solely via the Internet or e-mail.

E-mail. Mail that has been sent electronically using a computer and modem.

Flat-spined. What many publishers call "perfect-bound," glued with a flat edge (usually permitting readable type on the spine).

Galleys. Typeset copies of your poem(s). You should proofread and correct any mistakes and return galleys to editors within 48 hours of receipt.

Honorarium. A small, token payment for published work.

IRC. International Reply Coupon, postage for return of submissions from another country. One IRC is sufficient for one ounce by *surface mail*. If you want an airmail return, you need one IRC for each half-ounce. Do not send checks or cash for postage to other countries: The exchange rates are so high it is not worth the inconvenience it causes editors. (Exception: Many Canadian editors do not object to U.S. dollars; use IRCs the first time and inquire.)

Magazine-sized. Approximately 8½ × 11, the size of conventional typing paper unfolded.

ms, mss. Manuscript, manuscripts.

Multi-book review. Also known as an omnibus or essay review. A review of several books by the same author or by several authors, such as a review of four or five political poetry books.

Multiple submission. Submission of more than one poem at a time; most poetry publishers *prefer* multiple submissions and specify how many poems should be in a packet. Some say a multiple submission means the poet has sent another manuscript to the same publication before receiving word on the first submission. This type of multiple submission is generally discouraged (see Simultaneous submission).

p. Abbreviation for pence.

pg., pgs. Page, pages.

Perfect-bound. See Flat-spined.

Query letter. Letter written to a publisher to elicit interest in a manuscript or to determine if submissions are acceptable.

Rights. First North American serial rights means the publisher is acquiring the right to publish your poem first in a U.S. or Canadian periodical. All rights means the publisher is buying the poem outright. Selling all rights usually requires that you obtain permission to reprint your work, even in a book-length collection.

Royalties. A percentage of the retail price paid to an author for each copy of the book that is sold.

Saddle-stapled. What many publishers call "saddle-stitched," folded and stapled along the fold.

SAE. Self-addressed envelope.

SASE. Self-addressed, stamped envelope. *Every* publisher requires, with any submission, query or request for information, a self-addressed, stamped envelope. This requirement is so basic it is repeated in bold type at the bottom of a number of pages throughout this book. The return envelope (usually folded for inclusion) should be large enough to hold the material submitted or requested, and the postage provided—stamps if the submission is within your own country, IRCs if it is to another country—should be sufficient for its return.

Simultaneous submission. Submission of the same manuscript to more than one publisher at a time. Most magazine editors *refuse to accept* simultaneous submissions. Some book and chapbook publishers do not object to simultaneous submissions. In all cases, notify them that the manuscript is being simultaneously submitted if that is what you are doing.

Slush pile. The stack of unsolicited manuscripts received by an editor or publisher.

Status. The current situation concerning a particular manuscript: 1) The manuscript was never received. 2) We received the manuscript but cannot locate it. 3) We received and rejected said manuscript. 4) We are still considering it. 5) We are in the process of accepting your manuscript.

Subsidy press. See Vanity press.

Tabloid-sized. 11 × 15 or larger, the size of an ordinary newspaper folded and turned sideways.

Unsolicited manuscript. A manuscript an editor did not specifically ask to see.

Vanity press. A slang term for a publisher that requires the writer to pay publishing costs, especially one that flatters an author to generate business. These presses often use the term "subsidy" to describe themselves. Some presses, however, derive subsidies from other sources, such as government grants, and do not require author payment. These are not considered vanity presses.

Indexes

Chapbook Publishers

A chapbook is a slim volume of a poet's work, usually 20-25 pages (although page requirements vary greatly). Given the high cost of printing, a publisher is more apt to accept a chapbook than an entire book from an unproven poet.

Some chapbooks are published as inserts in magazines. (The winner of The Tennessee Chapbook Prize, for instance, is published as an insert in *Poems & Plays*.) Others are separate volumes. A physical description (binding, method of printing, cover, etc.) is usually included in the listings, but whenever possible, request submission guidelines and samples to determine the quality of the product.

You'll find many presses, particularly those that sponsor chapbook contests, charge reading fees. Avoid any over $10. (Some folks go as high as $15 for book-length manuscripts, but chapbooks are easier to process.)

If your chapbook is published, by the way, you may still participate in "first-book" competitions. For more information about both chapbook and book publishing, read Charting Your Path to Poetry Publication, beginning on page 11.

Following are publishers who consider chapbook manuscripts. See the General Index for the page numbers of their market listings. Note: Double daggers (‡) preceding titles indicate listings new to this edition.

i.e. Magazine, A Journal of Literature
  and the Arts
Implosion Press
Insects Are People Two
Intercultural Writer's Review, The
Inverted-A, Inc.
Juniper Press
Lake Shore Publishing
‡LaSpina, Vincent
Ledge, The
Lilliput Review
Limited Editions Press
Lone Willow Press
‡Longhouse
Lucidity
Luna Bisonte Prods
Mad River Press
Malevolence Publications
Maverick Press, The
Merrimack Books
Mid-American Review
Minority Literary Expo
(m)öthêr TØñgué Press
‡Mount Olive College Press
Negative Capability
Nerve Cowboy
New Earth Publications
New Hope International
New Orleans Poetry Journal Press
New Spirit Press
Oasis Books
Ohio Review, The
Onionhead
ONTHEBUS
Outrider Press
Owl Creek Press
Pacific Coast Journal
Palanquin/TDM
Paper Boat Magazine
Parting Gifts
Pavement Saw
Pearl

‡Pecan Grove Press
Peking Duck, The
Pennywhistle Press
Peregrine: The Journal of Amherst
  Writers & Artists
Perivale Press
Permafrost: A Literary Journal
Philomel Books
‡Phoenix
Pine Press
Pirate Writings
Plowman, The
Poems & Plays
Poetic Space: Poetry & Fiction
Poetical Histories
‡Poetry Forum
Poetry Harbor
Poetry in Motion
Poetry Miscellany, The
Poets at Work
Poets' Roundtable
Potato Eyes
Prairie Journal, The
Press Here
Pudding House Publications
PYX Press
‡Queen of Swords Press
Rag Mag
‡Raw Nervz Haiku
Red Candle Press, The
Red Dancefloor Press
‡Red Dragon Press
Red Herring Poets
‡Red Moon Press
‡Ridge Runner Press
Riverstone, A Press for Poetry
Runaway Spoon Press, The
Rustic Rub
St. Andrew Press
Score Magazine
Serpent & Eagle Press
‡Shadowfire Press
Shamal Books
Sheila-Na-Gig

Ship of Fools
‡Sixties Press
Slipstream
‡Slugfest, Ltd.
Sow's Ear Poetry Review, The
‡Spuyten Duyvil
Stand Magazine
State Street Press
Still Waters Press
Sub-Terrain
‡Sunflower Dream, The
‡Syncopated City
"Teak" Roundup
‡Temporary Vandalism Recordings
‡Terrible Work
Third Half Literary Magazine, The
‡13th Hour Books
Tightrope
Time of Singing, A Magazine of
  Christian Poetry
‡Toledo Poets Center Press
‡Toth Press
Touchstone Literary Journal
Trout Creek Press
‡Understanding Magazine
Underwhich Editions
‡Unfinished Monument Press
Urbanite, The
Voyant, The
Waterways: Poetry in the Mainstream
West of Boston
White Eagle Coffee Store Press
Whole Notes
Wind Publications
Windless Orchard, The
‡Wolfsong Publications
Wooden Head Review
WoRM fEASt!
Writers Forum (England)
‡Writer's Gazette, The
xib
Xiquan Publishing House

Geographical Index

Use this index to locate poetry-related publishers and events in your region. Much of the poetry published today reflects regional interests. In addition, publishers often favor poets (and work) from their own areas. For the first time, we have included conferences, workshops and writing colonies in this index to help you easily find local happenings. Also, keep your neighboring areas in mind for other opportunities.

Here you will find the names of U.S. publishers, conferences, workshops and writing colonies arranged alphabetically within their state or territory. Following them are lists of publishers in Canada, the United Kingdom, Australia, Japan, France and other countries. See the General Index for the page numbers of their corresponding listings. Note: Double daggers (‡) preceding titles indicate listings new to this edition.

Conferences and Workshops

Writing Colonies

COLORADO

Publishers of Poetry

Conferences and Workshops
Aspen Writers' Conference

CONNECTICUT
Publishers of Poetry
Amaranth
‡Black Roses
Broken Streets
Chicory Blue Press
Connecticut Poetry Review, The
‡Connecticut Review
Connecticut River Review
‡Creative Juices
‡Dirigible
‡Etcetera
‡IBIS review
Papyrus
Singular Speech Press
Small Pond Magazine of Literature
Twilight Ending
Wesleyan University Press
Yale University Press

Conferences and Workshops
Wesleyan Writers Conference

DISTRICT OF COLUMBIA
Publishers of Poetry
Aerial
American Scholar, The
Conscience
Middle East Report
New Republic, The
‡Reflections of You® Journal
Sojourners
Washington Review
Washington Writers' Publishing House
Word Works, The

FLORIDA
Publishers of Poetry
Albatross
Anhinga Press
Apalachee Quarterly
Candlelight Poetry Journal
Central Florida Contemporary Poetry Series, University of
Chaff
Ediciones Universal
Emerald Coast Review
Florida Review, The
Gulf Stream Magazine
Half Tones to Jubilee

Harp-Strings Poetry Journal
Home Times
Human Quest, The
International Quarterly
Kalliope, a journal of women's art
‡Kings Estate Press
‡Mangrove
National Enquirer
New CollAge Magazine
New Writer's Magazine
Nuthouse
‡Oasis
Onionhead
Poetry Digest
Poetry of the People
Runaway Spoon Press, The
‡Sea Oats
‡Shadowfire Press
Silver Web: A Magazine of the Surreal, The
Siren, The
‡So Young!
‡Stark Raving Sanity
‡State Street Review
‡Stygian Vortex Publications
Tampa Review
Thoughts for All Seasons: The Magazine of Epigrams
Write Way, The
Yesterday's Magazette

Conferences and Workshops
‡Florida Christian Writers Conference
‡Florida First Coast Writers' Festival
Florida Suncoast Writers' Conference
Florida Suncoast Writers' Weekend Workshop
Southwest Florida Writers' Conference

Writing Colonies
Atlantic Center for the Arts
Nautilus Foundation

GEORGIA
Publishers of Poetry
Atlanta Review
babysue
‡Blood and Fire Review
Chants
Chattahoochee Review, The
Classical Outlook, The
Dickey Newsletter, James
Georgia Journal
Georgia Press, University of

Georgia Review, The
Habersham Review
‡L'ouverture: A Literary Call to Action
Midwest Poetry Review
‡Misc. Proj.: A Poetry Newsletter
Old Red Kimono, The
Parnassus Literary Journal
Poet's Review
Press of the Nightowl, The
‡Snake Nation Review
Society of American Poets, The
Twisted

Writing Colonies
Hambidge Center for Creative Arts and Sciences

HAWAII
Publishers of Poetry
Aloha, The Magazine of Hawaii and the Pacific
Chaminade Literary Review
Hawaii Pacific Review
‡Kaimana: Literary Arts Hawaii
Manoa: A Pacific Journal of International Writing

Writing Colonies
Kalani Honua Oceanside Eco-Resort

IDAHO
Publishers of Poetry
Ahsahta Press
American Cowboy Poet Magazine, The
‡Confluence Press
Emshock Letter, The
Fugue
Rocky Mountain Review of Language and Literature
Snake River Reflections
‡Talking River Review
Trestle Creek Review

Conferences and Workshops
‡Inc and the Arts

ILLINOIS
Publishers of Poetry
‡A Small Garlic Press
ACM (Another Chicago Magazine)
Aim Magazine
Anaconda Press
artisan, a journal of craft
Brilliant Star

Southern Review, The
Thema
‡Xavier Review

MAINE
Publishers of Poetry
Alicejamesbooks
Beloit Poetry Journal, The
Café Review, The
Full-Time Dads
Northeast Arts Magazine
Northwoods Press
‡Peninsula Review, The
Potato Eyes
Puckerbrush Press, The
‡Wordplay

Conferences and Workshops
State of Maine Writers'
    Conference

Writing Colonies
‡Acadia National Park Artist-in-
    Residence
‡Maine Retreat, The

MARYLAND
Publishers of Poetry
Abbey
Antietam Review
‡Black Moon: Poetry of
    Imagination
‡BrickHouse Books, Inc.
Cochran's Corner
Dancing Shadow Press
Dolphin-Moon Press
Feminist Studies
‡Free Thought Conceptions
Gut Punch Press
Jewish Vegetarians Newsletter
Johns Hopkins University
    Press, The
Maryland Poetry Review
Maryland Review
Nightsun
Oracle Poetry
Passager: A Journal of
    Remembrance and
    Discovery
Pegasus Review, The
Plastic Tower, The
Poet Lore
‡Potomac Review
Samsara
‡Satire
Scop Publications, Inc.
Shattered Wig Review
Situation
‡Uno Mas Magazine

Vegetarian Journal
‡Writers' Round Table

Conferences and Workshops
Literary Festival at St. Mary's,
    The

MASSACHUSETTS
Publishers of Poetry
Adastra Press
Agni
Amherst Review, The
Appalachia
Ark, The
Arts End Books
Atlantic, The
The Aurorean: A Poetic
    Quarterly
Backspace
Bay Windows
Boston Review
Brave New Tick (the)
Button Magazine
Christian Science Monitor, The
College English
Djinni
‡doublebunny press
‡Dreams of Decadence:
    Vampire Poetry and Fiction
Eidos Magazine: Sexual
    Freedom & Erotic
    Entertainment for Women,
    Men & Couples
Faber and Faber, Inc.
‡Fledgling
Freezer Burn Magazine
Godine, Publisher, David R.
Harvard Advocate, The
Houghton Mifflin Co.
Little River Press
Loom Press
Mad River Press
Massachusetts Press, The
    University of
Massachusetts Review, The
Muse Portfolio
‡Neologisms
New Renaissance, The
96 Inc Magazine
Old Crow Review
Osiris, An International Poetry
    Journal/Une Revue
    Internationale
Paramour Magazine
Partisan Review
Pearl, The
Peregrine: The Journal of
    Amherst Writers & Artists

Ploughshares
Point Judith Light
Provincetown Arts
Radcliffe Quarterly
‡Soundings East
‡Sour Grapes
‡Teen Voices
Tightrope
‡Violetta Books
West of Boston
‡Women's Review of Books,
    The
Worcester Review
Writer, The
Zephyr Press
Zoland Books Inc.

Conferences and Workshops
‡Cape Cod Writers' Center
    Summer Conference
‡Eastern Writers' Conference
Harvard Summer Writing
    Program
‡New England Writers'
    Workshop
‡Cleaveland House, Martha's
    Vineyard
Fine Arts Work Center in
    Provincetown

MICHIGAN
Publishers of Poetry
Above the Bridge Magazine
American Tolkien Society
Angelflesh Press
Bennett & Kitchel
‡Bridge: A Journal of Fiction
    and Poetry, The
Centennial Review, The
Clubhouse
‡Ethereal Green
Expedition Press
Gazelle Publications
‡Graffiti Rag
Howling Dog
‡Java Snob Review
Lotus Press, Inc.
MacGuffin, The
Michigan Quarterly Review
Möbius
Nada Press
Passages North
‡Perspectives
Poetic Page
Rarach Press
Red Cedar Review
Riverrun
‡Sounds of Poetry, The

Lactuca
Lincoln Springs Press
‡Lips
Literary Review: An
   International Journal of
   Contemporary Writing, The
Long Shot
‡Lucid Moon
Mail Call Journal
Naturally: Nude Recreation for
   All Ages
Overview Ltd. Poetry
‡Phati'tude
Princeton University Press
Quarterly Review of Literature
   Poetry Book Series
‡Raised Ink
Raritan Quarterly
St. Joseph Messenger and
   Advocate of the Blind
Saturday Press, Inc.
Sensations Magazine
Still Waters Press
‡Sylvia: A Journal of Literature
   & Art
Talisman: A Journal of
   Contemporary Poetry and
   Poetics
US1 Worksheets
‡Vista Publishing, Inc.
Warthog Press

Conferences and Workshops
College of New Jersey Writers
   Conference, The
‡Winter Poetry & Prose
   Getaway in Cape May

NEW MEXICO
Pubishers of Poetry
‡Asher Publishing, Sherman
Atom Mind
Blue Mesa Review
Herb Network, The
Katydid Books
New Frontiers of New Mexico
Pennywhistle Press
Puerto Del Sol
‡RB's Poets' Viewpoint
Whole Notes
Yefief

Conferences and Workshops
Society of the Muse of the
   Southwest (SOMOS)
‡Southwest Christian Writers
   Seminar

Writing Colonies
Hawk, I'm Your Sister
Wurlitzer Foundation of New
   Mexico, The Helene

NEW YORK
Publishers of Poetry
Adrift
Advocate
African Voices
Alms House Press
America
Amicus Journal, The
Antipodes
Aphrodite Gone Berserk: A
   Journal of Erotic Art
‡Arachne, Inc.
Ararat
Art Times: A Literary Journal
   and Resource for All the
   Arts
Asian Pacific American Journal
Bantam Doubleday Dell
   Publishing Group
‡Barbaric Yawp
Belhue Press
‡Birch Brook Press
‡Bitter Oleander, The
‡Black Thistle Press
Blind Beggar Press
‡Blue Ink Press
Blueline
Boa Editions, Ltd.
Bomb Magazine
BOOG Literature
Bookpress: The Newspaper of
   the Literary Arts, The
‡Bright Hill Press
Brooklyn Review
‡Brouhaha
Brownstone Review, The
Buffalo Spree Magazine
‡Cafe Eighties Magazine
Camellia
‡CC Motorcycle News
   Magazine
Chelsea
Commonweal
Comstock Review, The
Confrontation Magazine
Conjunctions
Cover Magazine
Cross-Cultural
   Communications
Dial Books for Young Readers
Dolphin Log
‡Down Under Manhattan
   Bridge

Earth's Daughters: A Feminist
   Arts Periodical
1812
ELF: Eclectic Literary Forum
Epoch
Excursus Literary Arts Journal
Farrar, Straus & Giroux/
   Books for Young Readers
Firebrand Books
Fish Drum
Free Focus
‡Gathering of the Tribes, A
Gerbil: A Queer Culture Zine
Golden Isis Magazine
Grand Street
Grove Atlantic
Hanging Loose Press
Heaven Bone Magazine
Helikon Press
Holiday House, Inc.
Holt & Company, Henry
Hudson Review, The
Iconoclast, The
Italica Press
Jewish Currents
Jewish Women's Literary
   Annual
Journal of Poetry Therapy
Kiosk
Kitchen Table: Women of
   Color Press
Knopf, Alfred A.
Lacunae Magazine
Lang Publishing, Inc., Peter
‡LaSpina, Vincent
Ledge, The
Lilith Magazine
Lintel
Literal Latté
Lodestar Books
Long Island Quarterly
Long Islander
Lothrop, Lee & Shepard Books
Low-Tech Press
‡LUNGFULL! Magazine
Macmillan Publishing Co.
‡Malachite & Agate
Manhattan Review, The
Medicinal Purposes Literary
   Review
Mellen Poetry
‡Midmarch Arts Press
Midstream: A Monthly Jewish
   Review
Modern Bride
Morrow and Co., William
Ms. Magazine
Mudfish

Poets at Work
Raw Dog Press
Riverstone, A Press for Poetry
‡Scranton Press, University of
‡Singing Horse Press
‡Speaking from the Breast . . .
‡Street Beat Quarterly
Taproot Literary Review
Time of Singing, A Magazine of
    Christian Poetry
West Branch
Wildwood Journal
Wordsong
Wyrd
‡X-it Press
Yarrow, A Journal of Poetry
Zuzu's Petals Quarterly Online

**Conferences and
Workshops**
Ligonier Valley Writers
    Conference
St. Davids Christian Writers
    Conference

Writing Colonies
Pendle Hill

RHODE ISLAND
Publishers of Poetry
Copper Beech Press
Defined Providence
Haunts
Hunted News, The
Italian Americana
Merlyn's Pen: The National
    Magazine of Student
    Writing, Grades 6-12
Nedge
‡Poetic Soul, The
‡Syncopated City
Devil's Millhopper Press, The

SOUTH CAROLINA
Publishers of Poetry
Emrys Journal
Ninety-Six Press
Nostalgia: A Sentimental State
    of Mind
Palanquin/TDM
‡Slugfest, Ltd.
South Carolina Review
Writer's Exchange
‡Yemassee

**Conferences and
Workshops**
Charleston Writers'
    Conference

SOUTH DAKOTA
Publishers of Poetry
Hen's Teeth
Longneck, The
Prairie Winds
South Dakota Review

TENNESSEE
Publishers of Poetry
Aethlon: The Journal of Sport
    Literature
Alive Now
Cumberland Poetry Review
‡Ideals Magazine
‡Indian Heritage Publishing
Mature Years
‡New Millennium Writings
Now and Then
Penny Dreadful Press
Poems & Plays
‡Poet House, The
Poetry Miscellany, The
‡RFD: A Country Journal For
    Gay Men Everywhere
River City
Romantist, The
Rural Heritage
Sewanee Review, The
Tennessee Review, The

**Conferences and
Workshops**
American Christian Writers
    Conferences
Sewanee Writers' Conference
Tennessee Mountain Writers
    Conference

TEXAS
Publishers of Poetry
American Atheist Press
American Literary Review
‡American Tanka
Analecta
Black Tie Press
Blue Violin
Borderlands: Texas Poetry
    Review
‡Chachalaca Poetry Review
Concho River Review
Context South
Dagger of the Mind
Dancing Jester Press
Descant: Fort Worth's Journal
    of Poetry and Fiction
‡Didactic, The
Encodings: A Feminist Literary
    Journal
Gulf Coast: A Journal of

Literature and Fine Art
i.e. Magazine, A Journal of
    Literature and the Arts
Illya's Honey
Inverted-A, Inc.
‡Lime Green Bulldozers
‡Literary Focus Poetry
    Publications
‡Lone Stars Magazine
Maverick Press, The
Mind Purge
Mississippi Mud
Nerve Cowboy
‡Nova Express
‡O!!Zone
Office Number One
Palo Alto Review
‡Patchwork Poems
‡Pecan Grove Press
Peking Duck, The
Prose Poem Press
RE:AL—The Journal of Liberal
    Arts
Red Rampan' Press
‡Rio Grande Review
Riverside Quarterly
Salt Lick
Southwest Review
‡Stoneflower Literary Journal
‡Strain, The
Sulphur River Literary Review
‡Texas Press, University of
‡Texas Review
Texas Tech University Press
‡Texas Young Writers'
    Newsletter
Touchstone Literary Journal
‡Troubadour

**Conferences and
Workshops**
Austin Writers' League Spring
    and Fall Workshops
Craft of Writing

Writing Colonies
Dobie-Paisano Project

UTAH
Publishers of Poetry
Ellipsis Magazine
Gentle Survivalist, The
Literature and Belief
New Era Magazine
‡Of Unicorns and Space
    Stations
Paper Salad Online Poetry
    Journal, The
Quarterly West
Smith Publisher, Gibbs

Sunstone
Utah State University Press
‡Wēber Studies
Western Humanities Review

Conferences and Workshops
Desert Writers Workshop

VERMONT
Publishers of Poetry
‡Anthology of New England Writers, The
Green Mountains Review
‡Longhouse
‡Marlboro Review, The
New England Review

Conferences and Workshops
Bread Loaf Writers' Conference

Writing Colonies
Dorset Colony House Residencies
Vermont Studio Center

VIRGINIA
Publishers of Poetry
Black Buzzard Press
Blue Penny Quarterly
Bogg Publications
Brunswick Publishing Corporation
Callaloo
Chronicle of the Horse, The
Chrysalis Reader
Conservative Review
Dominion Review, The
Fauquier Poetry Journal
5th Gear
‡Fractal, The
‡Garnet
Hollins Critic, The
‡Iris: A Journal About Women
Lingo: a language art journal
Lyric, The
Masonia Roundup
‡New Virginia Review
Orchises Press
Phoebe
Piedmont Literary Review
Pocahontas Press, Inc.
Ranger Rick Magazine
‡Red Dragon Press
Red Moon Press
Reflect
‡Roanoke Review
St. Andrew Press

Shenandoah
Sow's Ear Poetry Review, The
‡13th Hour Books
Verse
Virginia Quarterly Review, The
‡War Cry, The
William and Mary Review, The
Worm Feast!

Conferences and Workshops
Highland Summer Workshop

Writing Colonies
Virginia Center for the Creative Arts

WASHINGTON
Publishers of Poetry
Ag-Pilot International Magazine
Arnazella
Bellingham Review, The
Bellowing Ark
Brooding Heron Press
Cleaning Business Magazine
Copper Canyon Press
Crab Creek Review
Fine Madness
Floating Bridge Press
Frontiers: A Journal of Women Studies
George & Mertie's Place: Rooms With A View
‡Heliotrope
‡Jack Mackerel Magazine
‡Kimera: A Journal of Fine Writing
Murderous Intent
Muse of Fire
Olympia Review
‡Open Bone, The
Open Hand Publishing Inc.
Owl Creek Press
Paper Boat Magazine
‡Pemmican
‡Poem & The World, The
Poetry Northwest
‡Poison Ivy
‡Rose Alley Press
Score Magazine
Seattle Review
Spindrift
‡Volcano Quarterly
‡White Plume Press
Willow Springs
‡Women's Work, The Sound Alternative to Good Housekeeping
Young Voices Magazine

Conferences and Workshops
Port Townsend Writers' Conference
Centrum
Hedgebrook

WEST VIRGINIA
Publishers of Poetry
Aegina Press, Inc.
Bohemian Bridge
‡Laurels

WISCONSIN
Publishers of Poetry
Abraxas Magazine
Acorn Whistle
Blank Gun Silencer
Block's Magazine
Caxton Ltd., Wm
Country Woman
Cream City Review
‡First Class
Glass Cherry Press, The
‡Hodge Podge Poetry
Juniper Press
‡Laughing Boy Review
M.O.O.N. Magazine
Madison Review, The
Magazine of Speculative Poetry, The
Modern Haiku
‡Neovictorian/Cochlea, The
‡Nerve Bundle Review
Poet's Fantasy
‡Porcupine Literary Arts Magazine
Rosebud
Seems
Student Leadership Journal
Touchstone
Wisconsin Academy Review
Wisconsin Press, University of
Wisconsin Review
‡Wolfsong Publications
‡Writer's Block, The
‡Writer's Cramp

Conferences and Workshops
‡Green Lake Writers Conference
‡Sofer, Jewish Writers Workshop
University of Wisconsin-Madison's School of the Arts at Rhinelander
Wisconsin Regional Writers' Association

‡Apostrophe
Aquarius
ARC Publications
‡Argotist, The
‡Bats and Red Velvet
　　Magazine
‡Beyond The Boundaries
‡Blade Magazine
‡Breakfast All Day
British Haiku Society
‡Cadmium Blue Literary
　　Journal
Calder Publications Ltd.
Carn
‡Christian Poetry Review
Cló Iar-Chonnachta
Crescent Moon Publishing
‡Crooked Stare
‡Dandelion Arts Magazine
‡Dark Horizons
‡Dialogos: Hellenic Studies
　　Review
‡Diehard
‡Dissident Editions
Enitharmon Press
Envoi
European Judaism
‡Feather Books
‡Fenice Broadsheets
‡Firewater Press Inc.
First Time
‡Flambard
‡Flaming Arrows
‡Fortnight Magazine
Frogmore Papers
Gairm
Global Tapestry Journal
‡Handshake
Hangman Books
Hilltop Press
Hippopotamus Press
HQ: The Haiku Quarterly
Hrafnhoh
HU
‡Interpreter's House
Iota
‡Journal of Contemporary
　　Anglo-Scandinavian Poetry
Kawabata Press
Krax
Lines Review
London Magazine
‡Making Waves
‡Manchester Poets Press

‡Maypole Editions
‡Modern Poetry In Translation
New Hope International
New Welsh Review
Oasis Books
Orbis: An International
　　Quarterly of Poetry and
　　Prose
‡Other Press
Outreach: For the
　　Housebound, Elderly and
　　Disabled
‡Oversteps Books
Oxford Poetry
‡Peace and Freedom
‡Peer Poetry Magazine
‡Pen & Keyboard Magazine
Pennine Ink
Pennine Platform
Perceptions: Women's Poetry
　　for a Change
Peterloo Poets
‡Pigasus Press
Planet: The Welsh
　　Internationalist
Plantagenet Productions
‡Poetic Hours
Poetical Histories
‡Poetry Life Supplement
Poetry Nottingham
　　International
‡Poetry Review
Poetry Wales
‡Polygon
‡Presence
Psychopoetica
‡Pulsar Poetry Magazine
‡Purge
‡Purple Patch
‡Pussy Poetry
Reality Street Editions
Red Candle Press, The
‡Rustic Rub
‡S.W.A.G., The Magazine of
　　Swansea's Writers and
　　Artists
‡Scottish Cultural Press
Second Aeon Publications
‡Sixties Press
Smiths Knoll
‡Splizz
‡Spokes
Stand Magazine
Staple
‡Stride Publications
Tak Tak Tak

Tears in the Fence
‡Terrible Work
Third Half Literary Magazine,
　　The
‡Three
‡Understanding Magazine
‡Unicorn
‡Urthona Magazine
Vigil
‡Wasafiri
Weyfarers
‡Working Titles
Works Magazine
Writers Forum (England)
‡Yellow Crane, The
‡Yorkshire Journal

Writing Colonies
Hawthornden Castle
　　International Retreat for
　　Writers

OTHER COUNTRIES
Publishers of Poetry
‡Cyphers (Republic of Ireland)
‡Horizon (Belgium)
‡Jewish Affairs (South Africa)
Landfall: New Zealand Arts and
　　Letters
‡Mandrake Poetry Review
　　(Poland)
Prakalpana Literature (India)
Renditions: A Chinese-English
　　Translation Magazine
　　(Hong Kong)
Sivullinen (Finland)
‡Spin (New Zealand)
‡Trafika (Czeck Republic)
‡Transnational Perspectives
　　(Switzerland)
Voices Israel

**Conferences and
Workshops**
‡Aran Islands International
　　Poetry Festival (Galway,
　　Ireland)

Writing Colonies
Altos de Chavón (Dominican
　　Republic)
Fundación Valparaíso (Spain)
Guthrie Centre, The Tyrone
　　(Republic of Ireland)

Subject Index

Use this index to save time in your search for the best markets for your poetry. The categories are listed alphabetically and contain the magazines, publishers, contests and awards that buy or accept poetry dealing with specific subjects. Most of these markets are coded **IV** in their listings.

Check through the index first to see what subjects are represented. Then look at the listings in the categories you're interested in. For example, if you're seeking a magazine or contest for your poem about "life on the farm," look at the titles under **Nature/Rural/Ecology**. After you've selected a possible market, refer to the General Index for the page number. Then read the listing *carefully* for details on submission requirements.

We've also expanded the category **Sports** in this edition to **Sports/Recreation**. Now, poets who write about juggling or mountain climbing can find markets under this category as well as those writing about a specific sport.

Under **Themes**, you will find those book and magazine publishers that regularly publish anthologies or issues on announced themes (if interested, send a SASE to these publishers for details on upcoming topics). **Regional** includes those outlets which publish poetry about or by poets from a certain geographic area; and the category **Form/Style** contains those magazines and presses that seek particular poetic forms or styles, such as haiku or sonnets or experimental work. Finally, those publishers listed under **Specialized** are very narrow in their interests—too narrow, in fact, to be listed in one of our other categories.

We do not recommend you use this index exclusively in your search for markets. Most magazines, publishers and contests listed in *Poet's Market* have wide-ranging poetry preferences and don't choose to be listed by category. Also, many of those who specialize in one subject are often open to others as well. Reading *all* the listings is still your best marketing strategy. Note: Double daggers (‡) preceding titles indicate listings new to this edition.

Animal: Cat Fancy; Chronicle of the Horse, The; Just About Horses; New Methods: The Journal of Animal Health Technology

Anthology: Anthology of Magazine Verse & Yearbook of American Poetry; Ashland Poetry Press, The; Asian Pacific American Journal; Blind Beggar Press; Catamount Press; Coteau Books; Crescent Moon Publishing; Cross-Cultural Communications; Helicon Nine Editions; Hen's Teeth; Illinois Press, University of; Intercultural Writer's Review, The; Kawabata Press; Kitchen Table: Women of Color Press; Lake Shore Publishing; ‡Literary Focus Poetry Publications; Meadowbrook Press; Moose Bound Press; Nada Press; New Horizons Poetry Club; Night Roses; Northwoods Press; Outrider Press; Passeggiata Press; ‡Peace and Freedom; Perivale Press; Plowman, The; ‡Poem & The World, The; Prairie Journal, The; Pudding House Publications; ‡Queen of Swords Press; ‡Red Moon Press; ‡Ridge Runner Press; Science Fiction Poetry Association; Seven Buffaloes Press; Shamal Books; Society of American Poets, The; Southern California Anthology, The; Spirit That Moves Us, The; ‡To Topio; ‡Unfinished Monument Press; ‡Violetta Books; Voices Israel; Waterways: Poetry in the Mainstream; West Wind Writers & Artists Project; White Eagle Coffee Store Press; Wind Publications; Word Works, The; Writer's Gazette, The

Bilingual/Foreign Language: Andreas-Gryphius-Preis (German); Bilingual Review Press (Spanish); ‡Bueno; Carn (Celtic); Cló Iar-Chonnachta (Irish); Cross-Cultural Communications; Doc(k)s (French); Ediciones Universal (Spanish); Ellipse (French); Footwork: The Paterson Literary Review (Spanish); Gairm (Scottish Gaelic); Irish American Cultural Institute Literary Awards; Italica Press (Italian); La Pira" International Literary Prize, "Giorgio (Italian); ‡Luz en Arte y Literatura (Spanish); M.I.P. Company (Russian); New Renaissance, The; Osiris, An International Poetry Journal/Une Revue Internationale (Danish, French, German, Italian, Polish); Plaza, The (Japanese); ‡Polygon (Gaelic); Prakalpana Literature (Bengali); Princeton University Press; RE:AL—The Journal of Liberal Arts; Sachem Press (Spanish); Skipping Stones: A Multicultural Children's Magazine; Unmuzzled Ox (French); Wake Forest University Press (French); Women's Studies Quarterly (French, German, Italian, Spanish)

Children/Teen/Young Adult: Alive Now; Benjamin Franklin Literary and Medical Society, Inc.; Blind Beggar Press; Brilliant Star; Chickadee Magazine; Clubhouse; Communications Publishing Group; Coteau Books;

Creative With Words Publications (C.W.W.); Cricket; Dial Books for Young Readers; Dolphin Log; Farrar, Straus & Giroux/Books for Young Readers; Fudge Cake, The; Gospel Publishing House; Hanging Loose Press; Herald Press; Highlights for Children; Holiday House, Inc.; Hopscotch: The Magazine For Girls; ‡Kids' World; Lodestar Books; Louisville Review, The; Meadowbrook Press; Merlyn's Pen: The National Magazine of Student Writing, Grades 6-12; New Era Magazine; Night Roses; Oak, The; Pelican Publishing Company; Place in the Woods, The; ‡Poetry Society of Michigan Annual Contests; Ranger Rick Magazine; Salmon Arm Sonnet Contest; Shofar; Skipping Stones: A Multicultural Children's Magazine; Stone Soup, The Magazine by Young Writers and Artists; Straight; Teen Voices; ‡Teens In Motion News; ‡Texas Young Writers' Newsletter; Vegetarian Journal; Waterways: Poetry in the Mainstream; Whole Notes; Wordsong; Writes of Passage; Young Voices Magazine

Cowboy: American Cowboy Poet Magazine, The; Western Tales

Ethnic/Nationality: Adrift (Irish, Irish-American); Africa World Press (African, African-American, Caribbean, Latin American); African American Review; African Voices; Afro-Hispanic Review; Aim Magazine; Alicejamesbooks; American Indian Studies Center; Ararat (Armenian); Asian Pacific American Journal; Bilingual Review Press (Spanish); Black Scholar, The; Blind Beggar Press; Callaloo (North, South, Central and Latin American; African; Caribbean; European); Carn (Celtic); Carolina Wren Press (minorities); Communications Publishing Group (African-American, Asian-American, Hispanic, Native American); Ediciones Universal (Cuban); European Judaism; Firebrand Books; Gairm (Scottish Gaelic); Gentle Survivalist, The (Native American); Guernica Editions Inc. (Italian, Italian-Canadian, Italian-American); Hrafnhoh (African, African diaspora); India Currents; Indian Heritage Publishing; Irish American Cultural Institute Literary Awards; Italian Americana; Jewish Affairs; Jewish Women's Literary Annual; Johnson Award for Fiction and Poetry, Charles (minorities); ‡Journal of Contemporary Anglo-Scandinavian Poetry (Scandinavian); Kitchen Table: Women of Color Press; Kuumba (African-American); Lilith Magazine (Jewish women); Lotus Press, Inc. (African-American); Melting Trees Review; Middle East Report; Midstream: A Monthly Jewish Review; Minority Literary Expo; ‡MoonRabbit Review (Asian-American); New Welsh Review; Oracle Poetry (African); ‡Other Press (British women); Papyrus (African-American); Passeggiata Press (African, Asian/Pacific, Caribbean, Middle East); Path Press, Inc. (African-American, Third World); Poetry Wales (Welsh, Anglo-Welsh); Rarach Press (Czech); Response (Jewish); Review: Latin American Literature and Arts; Revista/Review Interamericana (Caribbean, Hispanic, Puerto Rican); Rosenberg Award, Anna Davidson (Jewish); ‡Scottish Cultural Press; Shamal Books (African-American, Caribbean); Shofar (Jewish); Sister Vision Press (women of color); Skipping Stones: A Multicultural Children's Magazine; Wake Forest University Press (Ireland); ‡Wasafiri (African, Asian, Caribbean, diaspora); ‡Whitecrow Foundation, Tahana (Native American); Wind-Mill, The (German, Dutch)

Form/Style: Alpha Beat Soup (Beat); Amelia (all forms); ‡American Tanka; American Writing: A Magazine (experimental); ‡Amy Award, The; ‡Anthology of New England Writers, The (free verse); Bennett & Kitchel; black bough (haibun, haiku, senryu, sequences, tanka); Blue Violin (free verse); Bouillabaisse; British Haiku Society (haiku, senryu, tanka); Canadian Writer's Journal (haiku, renga, senryu, sequences, sijo, tanka); Champion Books, Inc. (neo-Beat); Formalist, The (metrical); Found Street Press (visual); Free Focus; ‡frisson: disconcerting verse; Generator (concrete, language, visual); ‡gestalten [experimental poetry]; Green River Writers' Contests; Haiku Headlines: A Monthly Newsletter of Haiku and Senryu; Hellas: A Journal of Poetry and the Humanities; ‡Heron Quarterly of Haiku and Zen Poetry; High/Coo Press; Hippopotamus Press; Hrafnhoh (metrical Christian); Juniper Press; Lamp-Post, The (formal Christian); Lilliput Review (no longer than 10 lines); Lingo: a language art journal (language, experimental); Luna Bisonte Prods (collaborations, experimental, surrealistic, visual); Lynx, A Journal for Linking Poets (renga); Lyric, The (rhymed verse); Malahat Review, The (long poems); Mississippi Valley Poetry Contest (haiku, rhyming); Modern Haiku; Nada Press (objectivist-based, short); National/International Penumbra Poetry Competition (haiku); Northwest Literary Forum; ‡Of Unicorns and Space Stations; Office Number One (haiku, limericks, rhymed/metered quatrains); Orbis: An International Quarterly of Poetry and Prose; Penny Dreadful Press; Piedmont Literary Review; Poetry Society of Virginia Annual Contests, The (haiku, limerick, lyric, sonnet); Poets' Club of Chicago International Shakespearean/Petrarchan Sonnet Contest; Point Judith Light (haiku, senryu); Prakalpana Literature (avant-garde, experimental); ‡Presence (haiku); Press Here (haiku, senryu, tanka); Press of the Third Mind, The (Dada, surrealistic); Prose Poem Press; ‡Raw Nervz Haiku; Red Candle Press, The; ‡Red Moon Press; Reflect (spiral); Runaway Spoon Press, The (textual, visual); Salmon Arm Sonnet Contest; Score Magazine (concrete, experimental, visual); ‡Sea Oats (American genre 'shofo,' haiku, senryu, Korean, sijo, tanka); Singular Speech Press (formal); Sparrow: The Yearbook of the Sonnet; Sticks (10 lines or less); Sub-Terrain; Thoughts for All Seasons: The Magazine of Epigrams; ‡Time For Rhyme; ‡Troubadour; Tundra (short poetry); ‡Unfinished Monument Press; World Order of Narrative and Formalist Poets; Writers Forum (England) (experimental, sound, visual); Xiquan Publishing House (avant-garde); ‡X-it Press

Gay/Lesbian/Bisexual: Backspace; Bay Windows; Belhue Press; Brave New Tick (the); ‡BrickHouse Books, Inc.; Calyx, A Journal of Art & Literature by Women; Carolina Wren Press; Church-Wellesley Review, The; Crescent Moon Publishing; Dwan; Emerging Lesbian Writers Award; Evergreen Chronicles, The; Firebrand Books; Gerbil: A Queer Culture Zine; GLB Publishers; ‡Great Lawn, The; Kitchen Table: Women of Color Press; Kuumba; Libido: The Journal of Sex and Sexuality; ‡Malachite & Agate; Modern Words; ‡O'Hara Award Chapbook Competition, Frank; Outrider Press; ‡RFD: A Country Journal For Gay Men Everywhere; ‡Salome; Sinister Wisdom; White Review: A Gay Men's Literary Quarterly, James; Wishing Well, The

Footwork: The Paterson Literary Review (Passaic County, NJ); Georgia Journal; Goose Lane Editions (Canada); Guernica Editions Inc. (Italy, Canada, US); Habersham Review; Harbour Publishing (West Coast); Heartlands Today, The (Midwest); High Plains Press (WY, US West); House of Anansi Press (Canada); HU (Honest Ulsterman) (Northern Ireland); Imago: New Writing (Queensland, Australia); India Currents; ‡Interpreter's House; Journal of New Jersey Poets; ‡Kaimana: Literary Arts Hawaii; Kansas Quarterly/Arkansas Review; Kelsey Review (Mercer County, NJ); Kentucky Artists Fellowships; Landfall: New Zealand Arts and Letters; Leacock Medal for Humour, The Stephen (Canada); Lines Review (Scotland); Long Island Quarterly; Loonfeather (MN); Louisiana Literature; ‡McKnight Interdisciplinary Fellowship (MN); ‡Marin Arts Council Individual Artist Grants (Marin County, CA); Maverick Press, The (TX); Middle East Report; Midwest Villages & Voices; Mississippi Valley Poetry Contest; Montana Arts Foundation Poetry Contest; (m)öthêr TØñgué Press (Canada); New Rivers Press (IA, MN, ND, SD, WI); ‡New York Foundation for the Arts; 96 Inc Magazine (New England); Ninety-Six Press (South Carolina); ‡Northeast Corridor (Northeastern US); Now and Then; On Spec: The Canadian Magazine of Speculative Writing; Oregon East; Ornish Poetry Award, Natalie (TX); "Over The Back Fence" Magazine (southern Ohio); Pelican Publishing Company; PEN Center USA West Literary Award in Poetry; Permafrost: A Literary Journal (AK); ‡Persephone Book Publication Award (NC); ‡Pew Fellowship In The Arts (PA); ‡Poem & The World, The (Seattle, WA; Seattle's sister cities); Poetry Harbor (upper Midwest); Poets' Dinner Contest; ‡Potomac Review (MD); Prairie Journal, The (Canada); Prescott Street Press (Northwestern US); Presidio La Bahia Award (TX); Puckerbrush Press, The (ME); Pueblo Poetry Project; Puerto Del Sol (Southwestern US); QSPELL Literary Awards (Quebec, Canada); Queen's Quarterly: A Canadian Review; Rambunctious Press; Review: Latin American Literature and Arts; Revista/Review Interamericana (Caribbean, Puerto Rico); ‡Ridge Runner Press (Ozark Plateau); Riverwind (Appalachia); Roanoke-Chowan Poetry Award (NC); Ronsdale Press (Canada); ‡Rubyshadow (AL, OH); San Francisco Foundation; Sandburg Awards, Carl (Chicago, IL); Scop Publications, Inc. (MD); ‡Scranton Press, University of (northeastern PA); Seven Buffaloes Press (CA, US West, southern Appalachia); South Dakota Review; Spoon River Poetry Review (IL), The; ‡Syncopated City (RI); Thistledown Press Ltd. (Canada); ‡Toledo Poets Center Press; Towson State University Prize for Literature (MD); Trestle Creek Review (innermountain West); Utah Original Writing Competition; Vehicule Press (Canada); Victorian Fellowship of Australian Writers, The; Washington Writers' Publishing House (DC); Weatherford Award, The W.D. (southern Appalachia); West Coast Line (Canada); Western Producer Publications (western Canada); Western Tales (US West); WFNB Annual Literary Contest (New Brunswick, Canada); ‡Wild Duck Review (northern CA); Wisconsin Academy Review; Wisconsin Arts Board Fellowships; Woodley Memorial Press (KS); Worcester Review (New England); World's Worst Poetry Contest (Pismo Beach, CA); Writers' Center Press (IN); Writers' Forum (CO) (US West); Writers' Guild of Alberta Book Award (Canada); ‡Writers' Round Table (mid-Atlantic); ‡Yorkshire Journal

Religious: Alive Now; ‡Bible Advocate; Brilliant Star; Broken Streets; ‡Burning Light: A Journal of Christian Literature; Capper's; Christian Century, The; ‡Christian Poetry Review; Christianity and the Arts; Commonweal; Cornerstone; Covenant Companion, The; Crescent Moon Publishing; European Judaism; ‡Evangel; Expedition Press; Feather Books; Fellowship in Prayer; Gospel Publishing House; Herald Press; Hrafnhoh; ‡Image: A Journal of Arts & Religion; Jewish Spectator; Jewish Vegetarians Newsletter; Joyful Noise: The Journal of Christian Poetry; Lamp-Post, The; Literature and Belief; Manna; Manna Forty, Inc.; Mature Years; Miraculous Medal, The; Mississippi Valley Poetry Contest; New Era Magazine; Oblates; Other Side Magazine, The; Our Family; Outreach: For the Housebound, Elderly and Disabled; ‡Penwood Review, The; ‡Perspectives; ‡Prayerworks; Presbyterian Record, The; Queen of All Hearts; St. Andrew Press; St. Anthony Messenger; St. Joseph Messenger and Advocate of the Blind; Shofar; Silver Wings; Society of American Poets, The; Sojourners; Straight; Student Leadership Journal; Studio, A Journal of Christians Writing; Time of Singing, A Magazine of Christian Poetry; ‡Unicorn; Unity Magazine; ‡Urthona Magazine; Virtue: The Christian Magazine for Women; ‡War Cry, The

Science Fiction/Fantasy: BadLands Press; ‡Beyond The Boundaries; Companion in Zeor, A; Dagger of the Mind; ‡Dark Horizons; Dreams and Nightmares; ‡Dreams of Decadence: Vampire Poetry and Fiction; ‡Fractal, The; Freezer Burn Magazine; ‡Fuck Decency; Gaslight: Tales of the Unsane; Gotta Write Network Litmag; ‡Handshake; Haunts; Hilltop Press; Magazine of Speculative Poetry, The; ‡Mentor, The; Mkashef Enterprises; Night Roses; Oak, The; ‡Of Unicorns and Space Stations; On Spec: The Canadian Magazine of Speculative Writing; Once Upon A World; Pablo Lennis; Pirate Writings; Poetry of the People; Poet's Fantasy; PYX Press; Riverside Quarterly; Romantist, The; Scavenger's Newsletter; Science Fiction Poetry Association; ‡Shadowfire Press; Silver Web: A Magazine of the Surreal, The; Small Press Genre Association; Space and Time; ‡Starblade Magazine; Struggle: A Magazine of Proletarian Revolutionary Literature; ‡Stygian Articles; ‡Stygian Vortex Publications; ‡13th Hour Books; Twisted; 2 AM Magazine; ‡Ultimate Unknown, The; Urbanite, The; Works Magazine

Senior Citizen: Chicory Blue Press; Creative With Words Publications (C.W.W.); Mature Years; Mississippi Valley Poetry Contest; Oak, The; Outreach: For the Housebound, Elderly and Disabled; Passager: A Journal of Remembrance and Discovery; Yesterday's Magazette

Social Issues: Afterthoughts; Aguilar Expression, The; Aim Magazine; Black Bear Publications; Carolina Wren Press; Christian Century, The; Collages & Bricolages, The Journal of International Writing; Haight Ashbury Literary Journal; Implosion Press; Left Curve; Other Side Magazine, The; Pudding House Publications; San Fernando Poetry Journal; Skipping Stones: A Multicultural Children's Magazine; Struggle: A Magazine of Proletarian Revolutionary Literature; Sub-Terrain

Specialized: Ag-Pilot International Magazine; American Atheist Press; American Tolkien Society; Bishop Publishing Co. (folklore); Blue Mountain Arts, Inc. (greeting cards); Boardman Tasker Award, The (mountain literatuare); ‡Brilliant Corners: A Journal of Jazz & Literature (jazz-related literature); Carnegie Mellon Magazine (university affiliation); Classical Outlook, The; Cleaning Business Magazine; Communities: Journal of Cooperative Living; ‡Dissident Editions (non-anecdotal, dissident, metaphysical verse); Dream International Quarterly; ‡Dreams of Decadence: Vampire Poetry and Fiction; ‡Dry Bones Press (nursing); ‡Ekphrasis (ekkphrastic verse); ‡Equilibrium[10]; Exit 13 (geography/travel); ‡Free Spirit (traveling on two-wheeled motor vehicles); Friends Journal (Quakerism); Full-Time Dads; ‡Halls Fellowship, J.C. and Ruth (creative writing degree); Harvard Advocate, The (university affiliation); ‡Healing Woman, The (women survivors of childhood sexual abuse); Herb Network, The; ‡Inner Voice (prisoners); Insects Are People Two; Japan Foundation Artist Fellowship Program, The (US residents with Japanese affiliations); Jewish Vegetarians Newsletter; ‡Journal of African Travel-Writing; Kaleidoscope: International Magazine of Literature, Fine Arts, and Disability; The Lonsdale: The International Quarterly of the Romantic Six; Mail Call Journal (American Civil War); Midwifery Today (childbirth); ‡Mock Frog Publishing (regional history); Musing Place, The (poets with a history of mental illness); Naturally: Nude Recreation for All Ages; ‡O!!Zone (visual poetry, photography, collage); ‡Our Journey (recovery issues); Outreach: For the Housebound, Elderly and Disabled; Peoplenet Disability Datenet (disabled people, love/romance); Pep Publishing ("ethical multiple relationships"); Pipe Smoker's Ephemeris, The; ‡Poison Ivy (men); Psychopoetica (psychologically-based); Radcliffe Quarterly (alumnae); Ragged Edge Magazine, The (disabled community); Samsara (suffering/healing); Slate & Style (blind writers); ‡Speaking from the Breast . . . (motherhood); Spring: The Journal of the e.e. cummings Society; Stevens Journal, The Wallace; ‡Street Beat Quarterly (homelessness/poverty); Vegetarian Journal; ‡Vista Publishing, Inc. (nurses); ‡Volcano Quarterly; ‡Westcoast Fisherman, The (commercial fishing); Western Heritage Awards; ‡W!dow of the Orch!d, The (dark, decadent, surreal); Wildwood Journal (college affiliation); Wind-Mill, The (geneology)

Spirituality/Inspirational: ‡Acropolis Books, Inc.; Alive Now; ‡Avocet; Capper's; Chrysalis Reader; Color Wheel; Crescent Moon Publishing; Explorer Magazine; Gentle Survivalist, The; Heaven Bone Magazine; Intercultural Writer's Review, The; New Earth Publications; New Thought Journal; Oak, The; Oblates; Presbyterian Record, The; ‡Science of Mind; Sharing the Victory; Silver Wings; Sisters Today; Studio, A Journal of Christians Writing; Surprise Me; ‡Unicorn; Virtue: The Christian Magazine for Women

Sports/Recreation: Aethlon: The Journal of Sport Literature; ‡CC Motorcycle News Magazine; Climbing Art, The; Journal of Asian Martial Arts; Juggler's World; Sharing the Victory; Spitball

Students: Allegheny Review; Analecta; Arts Recognition and Talent Search; Bucknell Seminar for Younger Poets; Dream Shop, The; Fiddlehead, The; Hanging Loose Press; Johnson Award for Fiction and Poetry, Charles; League of Minnesota Poets Contest, The; Merlyn's Pen: The National Magazine of Student Writing, Grades 6-12; Mississippi Valley Poetry Contest; Modern Haiku; National Written & Illustrated By . . . Awards Contest for Students, The; Night Roses; Offerings; Pennsylvania Poetry Society Annual Contest; Response; ‡Rubyshadow; Student Leadership Journal

Themes: Alive Now; American Tolkien Society; Apalachee Quarterly; Ashland Poetry Press, The; Black Mountain Review; Blue Mesa Review; Chrysalis Reader; Collages & Bricolages, The Journal of International Writing; Colorado Review; Communications Publishing Group; Cosmic Trend; Crab Creek Review; Creative With Words Publications (C.W.W.); Crumb Elbow Publishing Poetry Contests; Dolphin Log; Earth's Daughters: A Feminist Arts Periodical; Event; Green River Writers' Contests; Haight Ashbury Literary Journal; Heartlands Today, The; Jewish Currents; Journal of the American Medical Association (JAMA); Kaleidoscope: International Magazine of Literature, Fine Arts, and Disability; Kalliope, a journal of women's art; ‡Lime Green Bulldozers; Maverick Press, The; Middle East Report; Musicworks; Now and Then; Palo Alto Review; Partisan Review; Passager: A Journal of Remembrance and Discovery; Pegasus Review, The; Pig Iron; Poetic Realm; Poetry New York: A Journal of Poetry and Translation; Poetry of the People; Prairie Journal, The; ‡Rio Grande Press; Rosebud; Sensations Magazine; Skylark; Slipstream; South Dakota Review; Tak Tak Tak; Thema; Time of Singing, A Magazine of Christian Poetry; Unmuzzled Ox; Urbanite, The; Verve; Vincent Brothers Review, The; Vol. No. Magazine; Waterways: Poetry in the Mainstream; Witness

Translations: Abiko Quarterly With James Joyce FW Studies; Artful Dodge; Birmingham Poetry Review; Black Buzzard Press; Black River Review; Blue Unicorn, A Triquarterly of Poetry; British Haiku Society; Chants; Chelsea; Chicago Review; Classical Outlook, The; Collages & Bricolages, The Journal of International Writing; Colorado Review; Cross-Cultural Communications; Cumberland Poetry Review; Dwan; Eagle's Flight; Ellipse; Field; Formalist, The; Guernica Editions Inc.; Hrafnhoh; International Poetry Review; International Quarterly; Intertext; ‡Iris: A Journal About Women; Johann-Heinrich-Voss Prize for Translation; ‡Journal of Contemporary Anglo-Scandinavian Poetry; Kalliope, a journal of women's art; Lactuca; Lang Publishing, Inc., Peter; Lines Review; ‡Luz en Arte y Literatura; ‡Making Waves; ‡Mandrake Poetry Review; Manhattan Review, The; Mid-American Review; ‡Modern Poetry In Translation; New Earth Publications; New Native Press; New Renaissance, The; New Rivers Press; New Yorker, The; Nordmanns-Forbundet Translation Grant; Ornish Poetry Award, Natalie; Osiris, An International Poetry Journal/Une Revue Internationale; Panjandrum Books; Partisan Review; Passeggiata Press; Perivale Press; Poetic Space: Poetry & Fiction; Poetry New York: A Journal of Poetry and Translation; ‡Polyphonies; Princeton University Press; Puerto Del Sol; Quarterly Review of Literature Poetry Book Series; RE:AL—The Journal of Liberal Arts; Renditions: A Chinese-English Translation Magazine; Review: Latin American Literature and Arts; Rocky Mountain Review of Language and Literature;

Sachem Press; Seneca Review; Sonora Review; Spoon River Poetry Review, The; Stand Magazine; Tampa Review; Touchstone Literary Journal; Wascana Review; Whole Notes; Willow Springs; Zephyr Press

Women/Feminism: Alicejamesbooks; ‡Amy Award, The; Atlantis: A Women's Studies Journal; Barnard New Women Poets Prize; Bunting Fellowship Program, The; Calyx, A Journal of Art & Literature by Women; Carolina Wren Press; Chicory Blue Press; Collages & Bricolages, The Journal of International Writing; ‡Copper Moon Publishing; Country Woman; Crescent Moon Publishing; Earth's Daughters: A Feminist Arts Periodical; Eidos Magazine: Sexual Freedom & Erotic Entertainment for Women, Men & Couples; Eighth Mountain Press, The; Encodings: A Feminist Literary Journal; Feminist Studies; Firebrand Books; Free Focus; Frontiers: A Journal of Women Studies; Housewife-Writer's Forum; Implosion Press; Iowa Woman; ‡Iris: A Journal About Women; Jewish Women's Literary Annual; Kalliope, a journal of women's art; Kitchen Table: Women of Color Press; Lilith Magazine; ‡Mature Women's Grants; ‡Midmarch Arts Press; ‡Mock Frog Publishing; ‡Money For Women; ‡Musk Gland Sally; Night Roses; ‡Other Press; Outrider Press; Pearson Award, Judith Siegel; Perceptions: Women's Poetry for a Change; ‡Poison Ivy; Primavera; ‡Pussy Poetry; Radiance: The Magazine for Large Women; Sing Heavenly Muse!; Sinister Wisdom; Sister Vision Press; Still Waters Press; Struggle: A Magazine of Proletarian Revolutionary Literature; ‡Teen Voices; 13th Moon; ‡Wish Women; Wishing Well, The; Women's Studies Quarterly; ‡Women's Work, The Sound Alternative to Good Housekeeping; Womenwise; Writing For Our Lives

Writing: Byline Magazine; Canadian Writer's Journal; New Writer's Magazine; PYX Press; Scavenger's Newsletter; Write Way, The; Writer's Digest

General Index

As you use this index to locate specific markets and resources, you'll notice double daggers (‡) preceding hundreds of entries. This symbol denotes those listings which are new to this edition.

Also in this index, we list the names of those markets and resources that appeared in the *1997 Poet's Market* but do not appear in this edition. Instead of page numbers beside these titles, you will find two-letter codes in parentheses explaining why these entries no longer appear.

The codes are: **(ED)—Editorial Decision; (NR)—No (or late) Response** to Requests for Updated Information; **(NS)—Not Accepting Submissions** (which include publishers who are overstocked as well as those who no longer publish poetry); **(OB)—Out of Business** (or, in the case of contests, cancelled); **(RR)—Removed by Request** (no reason given); and **(UF)— Uncertain Future** (which includes publishers who have suspended publication or are reorganizing their operation).

More Great Books for Poets!

1998 Writer's Market: 4,000 Places to Sell What You Write—Get your work into the right buyers' hands and save yourself the frustration of getting manuscripts returned in the mail. You'll find 4,000 listings loaded with submission information, as well as real life interviews on scriptwriting, networking, freelancing and more! *#10512/$27.99/1088 pages/paperback*

Now Available on CD-ROM!

1998 Writer's Market Electronic Edition—Customize your marketing research and speed to the listings that fit your needs using this compact, searchable CD-ROM! #10517/$39.99

1998 Writer's Market Combination Package—For maximum usability, order both the book and CD-ROM in one convenient package! #10537/$49.99/paperback

The Poetry Dictionary—This comprehensive book unravels the rich and complex language of poetry with clear, working definitions. John Drury's discussions of poetic forms, elements, tools and traditions result in a volume that is the definitive source for today's poet. In many cases, several different poems are used to illustrate the many ways poets have put theories to work, making *The Poetry Dictionary* a unique anthology. *#48007/$18.99/336 pages*

Creating Poetry—Designed to encourage budding poets to explore and practice poetry writing skills, John Drury's nuts-and-bolts instruction addresses all elements of creating poetry. Each chapter offers an overview of each element discussed, a definition of terms, poetry examples, plus hands-on exercises. *#10209/$18.99/224 pages*

The Poet's Handbook—Here's expert instruction on how to use figurative language, symbols and concrete images; how to tune the ear to sound relationships; the requirements for lyric, narrative, dramatic, didactic and satirical poetry and more. *#01836/$14.99/224 pages/paperback*

The Art and Craft of Poetry—Find help from the masters of the past and present in fostering your own poetry-writing skills, from generating ideas to constructing the poem. Through exercises, you'll first learn how to develop observation and discovery skills; then focus on the craft itself: voice, line, stanza, meter and rhyme; and finish up with the modes and methods of expression—from narrative, lyric and dramatic verse to fixed, free and sequence styles. *#10392/$19.99/352 pages*

Idea Catcher—Open your eyes to the creative possibilities in your everyday world. You'll find something on every page of this journal to stimulate your senses and spark your imagination. *Idea Catcher* will teach you to use rich, surprising sources of inspiration through several writing "prompts." Plus, you'll find insightful quotes from well-known writers and short anecdotes about how authors "caught" the ideas that became great works of literature. *#48011/$14.99/160 pages*